ARBITRATION IN THE NETHERLANDS, IN PARTICULAR NAI ARBITRATION

SERIE ONDERNEMING EN RECHT

Onder redactie van

deel 158

ARBITRATION IN THE NETHERLANDS, IN PARTICULAR NAI ARBITRATION

ONDER REDACTIE VAN

PROF. DR. C.J.M. KLAASSEN
PROF. DR. G.J. MEIJER
T. DE BOER
C.L. SCHLEIJPEN

Serie Onderneming en Recht
deel 158

WOLTERS KLUWER – 2025

Published by:
Kluwer Law International B.V.
PO Box 316
2400 AH Alphen aan den Rijn
The Netherlands
E-mail: lrs-sales@wolterskluwer.com
Website: www.wolterskluwer.com/en/solutions/kluwerlawinternational

Sold and distributed by:
Wolters Kluwer Legal & Regulatory U.S.
920 Links Avenue
Landisville, PA 17538
United States of America
E-mail: customer.service@wolterskluwer.com

ISBN 978-94-035-2849-6

e-Book: ISBN 978-94-035-2859-5
web-PDF: ISBN 978-94-035-2869-4

PREFACE

In the spring of 2019 the Radboud Business Law Institute ("OO&R") published, in collaboration with the Netherlands Arbitration Institute ("NAI"), the volume "Going Dutch: ADR in Nederland, in het bijzonder bij het NAI".[1] That volume marked the 70th anniversary of the NAI and fitted in beautifully with the tradition of both the practice of the NAI and the research of the OO&R. The current, English language volume "Arbitration in the Netherlands, in particular NAI Arbitration" builds on this.

The NAI is (and has been for more than 75 years) a leading institute in the field of "ADR": Alternative Dispute Resolution. In this context, ADR means arbitration, binding advice and (corporate) mediation. The OO&R has been devoting attention to the foundations and practical implications of these forms of ADR from an academic perspective for many years. In 2012, Pauline Ernste, currently a professor in Nijmegen, obtained her doctorate degree with her dissertation *Bindend advies*.[2] Shortly before this (in 2011), the volume *Onderneming en ADR* was published in the Series *Onderneming en Recht*.[3] In that volume, the opportunities and limitations of ADR for the resolution of business-law disputes were examined from various points of view. The volume *Verzekering en ADR* was published in the same series several years later, in 2014.[4] That volume builds on the previous volumes in a sense and focuses on the insurer. "Work in progress" are two soon expected dissertations in the OO&R Series, one written by Carmen

1 C.J.M. Klaassen, G.J. Meijer & C.L. Schleijpen (eds), *Going Dutch: ADR in Nederland, in het bijzonder bij het NAI* (Series Onderneming en Recht, part 113), Deventer: Wolters Kluwer 2019.

2 P.E. Ernste, *Bindend advies* (Series Onderneming en Recht, part 74), Deventer: Wolters Kluwer 2012.

3 C.J.M. Klaassen, G. van Solinge, H.M. de Mol van Otterloo & P.E. Ernste (eds), *Onderneming en ADR* (Series Onderneming en Recht, part 66), Deventer: Wolters Kluwer 2011.

4 C.J.M. Klaassen, N. van Tiggele-van der Velde, P.E. Ernste & A.Ch.H. Franken (eds), *Verzekering en ADR* (Series Onderneming en Recht, part 83), Deventer: Wolters Kluwer 2014.

Schleijpen, concerning civil liability of arbitrators, and one written by Jim van Mourik, on the applicability and legal aspects of mediation during bankruptcy.

In 2019, the volume "Going Dutch: ADR in Nederland, in het bijzonder bij het NAI" was published. This volume has found its way to both academia and legal practice. Various voices arose requesting an English language version of the volume. The present volume more or less responds to this call. "More or less", because it is in fact more than a translation of the aforementioned volume. The focus of this volume is on arbitration, more so than in the volume published in 2019. More importantly, the focus of the present volume is on recent developments, including in particular the NAI Arbitration Rules as amended in 2024.

With this volume, the editors (once again) aim to contribute to the legal development of ADR. But more specifically they wish to contribute to making Dutch arbitration law and more specifically arbitration at the NAI – the NAI is, after all, the most general Dutch arbitration institute – accessible for foreign interested parties with this English language publication.

Creating a volume such as this one takes great effort from all involved: from the editors – C.J.M. Klaassen, G.J. Meijer, C.L. Schleijpen and T. de Boer – and from all of the authors. This volume was once again prepared for publication with great dedication by Marianne Koopman. Willemijn Wortelboer, a student from the research master's programme Business and Law, provided excellent assistance in preparing the volume for publication. We, as editors of the OO&R Series, are deeply grateful to all who contributed to the creation of this volume for their efforts.

Nijmegen, January 2025

S.C.J.J. Kortmann
N.E.D. Faber
C.J.H. Jansen
B.A. Schuijling

TABLE OF CONTENTS

Preface V

List of abbreviations XXIII

Chapter 1 Arbitration in the Netherlands, in particular NAI arbitration; an introduction 1
Carla Klaassen & Gerard Meijer

I - WHICH (TYPES OF) DISPUTES LEND THEMSELVES TO (NAI) ARBITRATION? 7

Chapter 2 Settlement of art-related disputes: the significance of the Court of Arbitration for Art 9
Karin Verduyn

2.1 Introduction 9
2.2 The Court of Arbitration for Art 10
2.2.1 Foundation and scope 10
2.2.2 CAfA Rules and Proceedings 11
2.2.3 Arbitrator Pool 13
2.2.4 Evidence: Expert Pool and Technical Process Advisor 14
2.2.5 The arbitral award; remedies and publication 15
2.3 Art-related disputes and arbitrability 16
2.3.1 Categorization 16
2.3.2 Ownership: cultural heritage and looted art 17
2.3.3 Copyright 21
2.3.4 Contracts; authenticity of art and other art-related issues 22
2.4 Advantages of CAfA arbitration 24
2.4.1 Art-specific expertise 24
2.4.2 Confidentiality 25
2.4.3 Impartiality 25
2.4.4 Costs 26
2.4.5 Enforceability 26
2.5 Conclusion 26

Chapter 3 The Hague Court of Arbitration for Aviation 29
Jan K. Schäfer & Rüdiger Morbach
3.1 Aviation disputes 29
3.2 The Hague CAA 37
3.3 The Hague CAA Rules 38
3.4 Summary 44

Chapter 4 Arbitration in intellectual property disputes 47
Anne Marie Verschuur
4.1 Introduction 47
4.2 Jurisdiction 49
4.2.1 Jurisdictional rules in DCCP and IP laws 49
4.2.2 Case law 50
4.2.2.1 Infringement 50
4.2.2.2 Granting and entitlement 51
4.2.2.3 Interim conclusion 52
4.2.2.4 Analysis 53
4.2.3 Foreign literature and case law 58
4.2.4 Some specific IP arbitration regimes 59
4.2.4.1 WIPO Arbitration and Mediation Center 60
4.2.4.2 UPC Patent Mediation and Arbitration Centre 61
4.2.4.3 .nl domain names 62
4.2.5 Conclusion 63
4.3 Benefits of arbitration and (Dutch) court proceedings 64
4.3.1 Why arbitration? 64
4.3.2 Why the court? 67
4.3.3 When arbitration and when court litigation? 69
4.3.4 The choice 69
4.4 Conclusion 70

Chapter 5 IT disputes and arbitration 73
Dorine ten Brink
5.1 Introduction 73
5.2 IT disputes 78
5.3 IT dispute resolution through arbitration 80
5.3.1 Introduction 80
5.3.2 IT arbitration specifics 81
5.3.3 Differences between the NAI and the SGOA 84
5.3.4 Indications for and against arbitration in an IT dispute 86
5.4 IT terms 87
5.4.1 Introduction 87
5.4.2 Suppliers in the IT sector 87

5.4.2.1 NLdigital 87
5.4.2.2 Compulsory mediation 89
5.4.2.3 Large IT companies in the Netherlands 91
5.4.3 Clients in the IT sector 93
5.4.3.1 Introduction 93
5.4.3.2 Central government 93
5.4.3.3 Municipal authorities 94
5.4.3.4 Private and (semi) private sector 95
5.4.4 Why which choice? 96
5.5 Conclusions and recommendations 98

Chapter 6 Building on with the NAI: internationalisation of (construction) arbitration in the Netherlands 101
Shawn Conway & Céline Goedhart
6.1 Introduction 101
6.2 Already implemented arbitration practices 101
6.3 Practices increasingly being implemented 104
6.3.1 Cost orders 104
6.3.2 Ways of gathering evidence 105
6.3.3 Dispute Resolution Boards 111
6.4 Practices yet to be implemented 113
6.4.1 Introduction 113
6.4.2 Building up delay and disruption claims 114
6.4.3 Delay analysis methods 117
6.4.3.1 Time impact (window) analysis 117
6.4.3.2 As-planned vs. as-built method 118
6.4.3.4 Reconstructed final planning method (collapsed as-built) 119
6.4.3.5 Adjusted base planning (impacted-as-planned) 120
6.4.4 Disturbance analysis methods 121
6.4.4.1 Introduction 121
6.4.4.2 Project-specific studies 122
6.4.4.2.1 The Measured Mile Analysis 122
6.4.4.2.2 Earned Value Analysis 123
6.4.4.2.3 Schedule analysis 123
6.4.4.2.4 Work sampling 124
6.4.4.2.5 System dynamics modelling 124
6.4.4.3 Project-comparative studies 125
6.4.4.4 Industry studies 125
6.4.5 The future of analysis methods for the Dutch market 126
6.5 In conclusion 126

Chapter 7 Arbitration in Dutch corporate disputes 129
Bastiaan Kemp & Romy Menasalvas Garrones
7.1 Introduction 129
7.2 What are corporate disputes? 131
7.3 Characteristics of corporate disputes and challenges to resolving such disputes through arbitration 132
7.3.1 The relevance of litigation to the development of corporate law 132
7.3.2 The role of parties in corporate litigation 134
7.3.3 The potential challenges when resolving corporate disputes through arbitration 136
7.3.4 Arbitration of corporate disputes should be further facilitated 144
7.4 Instruments to mitigate the challenges around resolving corporate disputes through arbitration 146
7.5 Towards a more dynamic corporate disputes arbitration approach 160

Chapter 8 Arbitration in insurance disputes 163
Natalie Vloemans
8.1 Introduction 163
8.2 Procedural perils 164
8.2.1 The arbitration agreement 164
8.2.2 Third parties in the proceedings 167
8.2.3 Arbitration and consumers 169
8.2.4 The 'action directe' 170
8.3 Practical advantages and practical objections 171
8.3.1 Availability of arbitrators 172
8.3.2 Costs 173
8.4 Insurance arbitration abroad 174
8.5 Conclusion 177

Chapter 9 Arbitration v. Judicial Adjudication of mass claims: an assessment of dispute resolution in the global market 179
Ianika Tzankova & Lilian Meinen
9.1 Introduction 179
9.2 Taxonomy of Global Disputes 180
9.3 (Individual) arbitration and (collective) actions before Dutch courts: a comparison 184
9.3.1 Collective action v. collective arbitration? 184
9.3.2 Party autonomy 186

9.3.3 Length of proceedings and time for resolution of the dispute 189
9.3.4 Confidentiality 191
9.3.5 Costs 193
9.3.6 Conclusion 196
9.4 The adjudication of consumer disputes 197
9.4.1 The European and Dutch approaches 198
9.4.2 Approaches in other jurisdictions 202
9.5 The adjudication of financial securities disputes 204
9.5.1 Example: Petrobras 206
9.6 The adjudication of competition disputes 209
9.6.1 Example: CDC Hydrogen Peroxide (follow on claim) 210
9.6.2 Example: Apple/eBizcuss (abuse of dominance position) 213
9.6.3 Implications 214
9.7 Observations and conclusion 215

Chapter 10 Arbitration meets ESG: an introduction 217
Guillaume Croisant & Piotr Wiliński
10.1 ESG – from soft law and voluntary standards to hard law and mandatory regulations 218
10.2 Key ESG developments and associated dispute risks 222
10.2.1 Fight against climate change and environmental protection 222
10.2.2 Sustainability disclosure obligations 225
10.2.3 Greenwashing 227
10.2.4 Value chain environmental and human rights due diligence 229
10.2.5 Directors' and officers' fiduciary duties and general duty of care 234
10.2.6 Backlash 236
10.3 Relevance for arbitration 238
10.3.1 Commercial arbitration 239
10.3.2 Investor-State arbitration 245
10.4 Impact on the arbitration's actors and process 248
10.5 Conclusion 251

Chapter 11 Arbitration in the Dutch Caribbean 253
Sebastiaan Barten
11.1 Introduction 253
11.2 The use of arbitration in the Dutch Caribbean 254

11.3 The implementation of the Model Law in the Dutch Caribbean 257
11.4 Scope of application of the Model Law in the Dutch Caribbean 258
11.5 Issues that have not been addressed in the Model Law 259
11.6 The arbitration agreement 261
11.7 Arbitrability 263
11.8 Appointment of the arbitral tribunal 263
11.9 (Exemption of) arbitrator's liability 266
11.10 Assistance by courts in deadlock situations and other court-ordered interim measures 268
11.11 Interim relief by the arbitral tribunal 269
11.12 Setting aside of the arbitral award 270
11.13 Recognition and enforcement of arbitral awards in the Dutch Caribbean 272
11.13.1 Procedure and grounds for refusal 272
11.13.2 Separate exequaturs required for the Dutch Caribbean 274
11.13.2.1 Does an exequatur granted by a court in the European Netherlands have effect in the other countries of the Kingdom of the Netherlands? And does it make any difference whether the exequatur in question was granted under an enforcement treaty, such as the New York Convention? 274
11.13.2.2 Does an exequatur granted by the Dutch court also have effect in the BES islands (Caribbean Netherlands)? 276
11.13.2.3 Does an exequatur granted by a court from a Dutch Caribbean territory have effect in the other Dutch Caribbean territories? 277
11.14 Investment arbitration 277
11.15 Conclusion 279

Chapter 12 Corporate Mediation: The Dutch approach to mediation vs. Anglo-American practices and the enforceability of mediation clauses 281
Peter Kamminga & Bart Fleuren
12.1 Introduction 281
12.2 Part I: Characteristics and dynamics of corporate mediation 282
12.2.1 Corporate mediation 282
12.2.2 What makes corporate mediation unique 283
12.2.2.1 Complexity of corporate disputes 283
12.2.2.2 Specialized expertise 284
12.2.2.3 Confidentiality 284

12.2.2.4 Outcome-oriented focus 284
12.2.2.5 Preservation of long-term business relationships 284
12.2.2.6 Time sensitivity 285
12.2.3 Corporate mediation: a comparative analysis of the US, the UK, and the Netherlands 285
12.2.3.1 Legal framework 285
12.2.3.2 The role of mediators 287
12.2.3.3 Confidentiality and enforceability of settlement agreements 288
12.2.4 Mediation styles in corporate disputes 290
12.2.4.1 Facilitative mediation 290
12.2.4.2 Evaluative mediation 291
12.2.4.3 Which style is best for corporate mediation? 292
12.2.5 The current state of corporate mediation in the Netherlands 293
12.2.5.1 The growing call for proactive mediators 294
12.2.5.2 Speed and cost-effectiveness: A key advantage 295
12.2.5.3 The preservation of long-term business relationships 295
12.2.5.4 The rise of hybrid models: med-arb and Its growing popularity 296
12.2.6 The role of the Netherlands Arbitration Institute (NAI) in mediation 297
12.3 Part II: The enforceability of a mediation clause 298
12.3.1 Introduction 298
12.3.2 The advantages and disadvantages of an enforceable mediation clause 300
12.3.2.1 Voluntary mediation versus pacta sunt servanda 301
12.3.2.2 To what extent would parties be bound to a mediation clause? 305
12.3.3 Enforceability in different jurisdictions 306
12.3.4 A new Dutch regime in favour of enforceability 310
12.3.4.1 The 2006 judgment of the Supreme Court 310
12.3.4.2 Discussions among authors contrast with a uniform approach in case law of the lower courts following the 2006 judgment 312
12.3.4.3 The Supreme Court accepts enforceable mediation clauses in the lotamblau judgment 315
12.3.5 What is next for the now-enforceable mediation clause in the Netherlands? 319

12.3.5.1 Drafting of mediation clauses after the Lotamblau Judgment 319
12.3.5.2 Potential amendment of procedural rules of court and arbitral institutions 322
12.3.5.3 The next step for the legislator? 324
12.4 Conclusion 325

Chapter 13 NAI and NCC(A): competitors or peers in resolving international commercial disputes? 327
Rieme-Jan Tjittes
13.1 Introduction 327
13.2 Amicable settlement of commercial disputes 328
13.3 Arbitration 329
13.3.1 The perceived advantages of arbitration 329
13.3.2 The perceived disadvantages of arbitration 330
13.3.3 The preferred arbitral institutions and seats 331
13.4 The Netherlands Commercial Court (of Appeal) 332
13.4.1 Introduction 332
13.4.2 The reasons for the Dutch legislator to initiate the NCC(A) 334
13.4.3 Tailormade proceedings at the NCC(A) 336
13.4.4 Requirements for jurisdiction of the NCC(A) 339
13.4.5 The NCC(A) jurisdiction clause and other procedural agreements between the parties to be considered 343
13.5 The preferred choice of international companies: arbitration or NCC(A)? 344
13.6 Some brief concluding remarks 348

II - SOME PARTICULAR ASPECTS OF THE ARBITRAL TRIBUNAL & THE ARBITRAL PROCEEDINGS 349

Chapter 14 The tribunal secretary revisited 351
Martijn Scheltema
14.1 Introduction 351
14.2 The position of the tribunal secretary 352
14.3 Assessing contractual relationships 354
14.3.1 Multi-party relationship 354
14.3.2 The arbitrator(s) choose(s) the tribunal secretary 355
14.3.3 The parties appoint the tribunal secretary 356
14.3.4 The administering institution appoints the tribunal secretary 357

14.4 Procedural rules in national law and in institutional arbitration rules 358
14.4.1 Introduction 358
14.4.2 The Netherlands 358
14.4.3 Foreign institutions and rules 359
14.5 Addressing excess of the role of the tribunal secretary 361
14.5.1 Introduction 361
14.5.2 Excess of mandate 362
14.5.3 Challenge of the tribunal secretary 366
14.5.4 Composition of the tribunal 367
14.5.5 Liability of the tribunal secretary 367
14.6 Conclusion 371

Chapter 15 The NAI challenge regime 373
Martine Honée & Camilla Perera-de Wit
15.1 Introduction 373
15.2 The legal framework 373
15.3 The challenge procedure under the 2024 NAI Arbitration Rules 375
15.4 Data on NAI Challenges 378
15.5 Method of assessment of a challenge request 378
15.5.1 Presumption of impartiality and independence 378
15.5.2 IBA Guidelines on Conflicts of Interest in International Arbitration 380
15.5.3 Assessment of challenge – influence of state court case law 382
15.6 Some final observations 382
15.7 Conclusion 384

Chapter 16 Arbitrator's (limitation of) liability 387
Daniella Strik
16.1 Introduction 387
16.2 No special statutory regime concerning arbitrators' liability and exoneration 388
16.3 Arbitrator's liability in the Netherlands: state of case law 390
16.4 Contractual exoneration clauses 403
16.4.1 Introduction 403
16.4.2 Elements of exoneration clauses in arbitration rules 404
16.4.2.1 The group of persons whom the provision is intended to protect 405
16.4.2.2 Legal basis of the exoneration 406

16.4.2.3 Subject matter to which the exclusion relates 407
16.4.2.4 Scope of the exoneration 408
16.4.3 Admissibility of exoneration clauses 410
16.5 Closing 413

Chapter 17 Emergency and expedited arbitral proceedings at the Netherlands Arbitration Institute 415
Rogier Schellaars & Fleur Potter
17.1 Introduction 415
17.2 Emergency Arbitration (formerly: summary arbitral proceedings) 419
17.2.1 Emergency Arbitration at the NAI 421
17.2.1.1 Emergency Arbitration need not be connected to proceedings on the merits 421
17.2.1.2 Requirements – details 423
17.2.1.3 Jurisdiction 424
17.2.1.4 Constitution of the Arbitral Tribunal 424
17.2.1.5 Conduct of the proceedings 425
17.2.1.6 Award 426
17.2.2 How do the NAI's Emergency Arbitration relate to the Dutch Arbitration Act – further remarks 427
17.2.3 The relationship between Emergency Arbitral proceedings and the jurisdiction of the Dutch state courts 428
17.3 Expedited arbitration 432
17.3.1 Expedited proceedings on the merits are internationally widely accepted 432
17.3.1.1 Gatekeeper function 434
17.3.1.2 Monetary value of claims 435
17.3.1.3 Sole arbitrator 436
17.3.1.4 Concentrating and accelerating the debate 437
17.3.1.5 Limited possibility of providing evidence 437
17.3.1.6 Short (and hard) deadline for issuing an award 438
17.3.2 How does the expedited proceedings relate to the Dutch Arbitration Act? 439
17.3.3 Expedited Proceedings: further remarks on the structure 441
17.3.3.1 Assurance of the quality of arbitral awards: introduction of 'scrutiny light' 442
17.3.3.2 Appeal: show the parties the way, but don't impose it 443
17.3.4 Emergency Arbitration 444
17.4 Concluding Remarks 444

Chapter 18 Arbitration and confidentiality: existence and ramifications of a principle 445
Filip De Ly
18.1 Introduction 445
18.2 Assumption of confidentiality in arbitration and its foundations 445
18.3 Australian and Swedish unrest 447
18.4 Attention for confidentiality: legislation and Arbitration Rules 448
18.5 The Netherlands and confidentiality 450
18.6 Ramifications of the principle of confidentiality 452
18.6.1 Definition of the principle of confidentiality 452
18.6.2 Confidentiality principle and party autonomy 457
18.6.3 Object of the principle of confidentiality 458
18.6.4 Persons subject to confidentiality 461
18.6.5 Exceptions to confidentiality 463
18.6.6 Procedural aspects 465
18.7 Conclusion 467

III - THE ARBITRAL AWARD 469

Chapter 19 The award on costs in arbitration: suggestions to promote predictability, transparency and uniformity 471
Mirjam van de Hel-Koedoot & Pieter Fritschy
19.1 Introduction 471
19.2 Costs in the current NAI Rules: general principles 473
19.3 Costs in the current NAI Rules: the viewpoints of the new Article 59(4) 475
19.4 The tension between discretion and the values of predictability, transparency and uniformity 477
19.5 Possibility of brief party debate regarding costs and the award on costs 478
19.6 Arbitral tribunal's obligation to provide reasons 480
19.7 Conclusion 483

Chapter 20 The oral arbitral award 485
Toon van Mierlo
20.1 Introduction 485
20.2 Ruling by the court 486
20.2.1 Main rule: in writing 486

20.2.2 Oral ruling; Article 30p DCCP (old) as predecessor of Article 29a DCCP 489
20.2.3 No exclusivity Article 30p DCCP; Supreme Court 20 April 2018 491
20.2.4 Five further rules applicable to oral rulings 494
20.3 Article 29a DCCP instead of Article 30p DCCP (old) 498
20.4 Arbitral awards 499
20.4.1 The adoption of the judgment; majority decision-making 499
20.4.2 The arbitral award shall be in writing 501
20.4.3 The oral arbitral award 504
20.4.4 Daily practice? 506
20.5 Closing remarks 508

Chapter 21 From settlement to award: challenges and opportunities of consent awards 511
Pietro Ortolani
21.1 Introduction 511
21.2 Why go from settlement to award? 512
21.3 Settlement reached after the commencement of arbitration 514
21.4 Settlement reached after mediation and recorded in an arbitral award 519
21.5 Challenges at the setting aside and recognition and enforcement stages 522
21.6 Relationship between the consent award and the United Nations Convention on International Settlement Agreements Resulting from Mediation 530
21.7 Conclusions 532

Chapter 22 Time limits for correction and supplementation, as well as recommendations to avoid clerical errors and failures to decide 533
Isabelle van den Nieuwendijk
22.1 Introduction 533
22.2 Time limit for request for correction and/or supplementation 535
22.2.1 General 535
22.2.2 Starting point is the agreed time limit 537
22.2.2.1 General 537
22.2.2.2 Arbitration Rules 539

22.2.3 No agreed time limit: within three months after the day the arbitral award was sent 540
22.2.4 No agreed time limit but deposit: three months from the day of deposit of the arbitral award 541
22.3 Length of procedure and decision period 541
22.4 Time limit has expired; alternatives? 545
22.4.1 General 545
22.4.2 Time limit has expired for request for correction 546
22.4.3 Time limit has expired for request for supplementation 548
22.5 Time limit for application for setting aside after request for correction and/or supplementation 549
22.6 Recommendations 551
22.6.1 General 551
22.6.2 Checklist for the arbitral award 551
22.6.3 Checklist for correction and supplementation 552
22.6.4 Request for additional administration fees 553
22.6.5 A 'scrutiny' provision 554
22.7 In conclusion 556

Appendix 1 Chapter 22 NAI award checklist (2024) 559
Appendix 2 NAI checklist on correction and supplementation (2024) 563

Chapter 23 Setting aside of arbitral awards: lessons for (NAI) arbitrators? 567
Pauline Ernste & Carmen Schleijpen
23.1 Introduction 567
23.2 Grounds for setting aside 569
23.2.1 In general 569
23.2.2 Absence of a valid arbitration agreement (Article 1065(1)(a) DCCP) 571
23.2.3 Composition of the arbitral tribunal (Article 1065(1)(b) DCCP) 582
23.2.4 Breach of mandate (Article 1065(1)(c) DCCP) 585
23.2.4.1 In general 585
23.2.4.2 Essential defences 586
23.2.4.3 The arbitral tribunal failed to decide on one or more claims 590
23.2.4.4 Supplementation of facts 594
23.2.4.5 Addition to the grounds 596

23.2.4.6 To grant more or something other than claimed 597
23.2.4.7 Wrong decision-making standard 599
23.2.4.8 Breach of the formal side of the mandate 600
23.2.5 Defects in the signing of the arbitral award (Article 1065(1)(d) DCCP) 603
23.2.6 Failure to state reasons (Article 1065(1)(d) DCCP) 608
23.2.7 Breach of public policy (Article 1065(1)(e) DCCP) 614
23.2.7.1 In general 614
23.2.7.2 Breach of mandatory (EU) law of a fundamental nature 614
23.2.7.3 Fraud and corruption 615
23.2.7.4 Breach of the equal right to heard 619
23.2.7.5 Evidence 624
23.2.7.6 Breach of the principle of impartiality and independence 627
23.3 Remission (Article 1065a DCCP) 631
23.4 Conclusion 635

IV - CLOSING REMARKS 639

Chapter 24 Arbitration in the Netherlands, in particular NAI arbitration 641
Conclusion and closing remarks 641
Carla Klaassen & Gerard Meijer
24.1 Introduction 641
24.2 What (types of) disputes lend themselves to (NAI) arbitration? 642
24.2.1 Specialised arbitration institutes under the auspices of the NAI 642
24.2.2 The various types of disputes and the (potential) role of NAI arbitration 643
24.2.3 Arbitration in the Dutch Caribbean 647
24.2.4 Corporate mediation 648
24.2.5 The NAI alongside the NCC 649
24.3 Some particular topics regarding the arbitral tribunal & the arbitral proceedings 650
24.3.1 The position of the arbitral secretary 650
24.3.2 Challenges 651
24.3.3 Liability risks 652
24.3.4 Emergency and expedited arbitration 652
24.3.5 Confidentiality 653

24.4 The arbitral award 655
24.4.1 Costs 655
24.4.2 The possibility of an oral award 656
24.4.3 Consent awards 657
24.4.4 Flawed awards 658
24.5 Other topics 661
24.5.1 Quality assurance 661
24.5.2 Diversity and inclusion 662
24.5.3 E-arbitration and sustainability 663
24.6 Conclusion 663

APPENDIX 665

NAI RULES (31 December 2024) 665

LIST OF ABBREVIATIONS

AA	Ars Aequi
AAA	American Arbitration Association
ADR	alternative dispute resolution
Arb. Int.	Arbitration International
ARO	Actuele Rechtspraak Ondernemingspraktijk
AV&S	Aansprakelijkheid, Verzekering en Schade
B.V.	besloten vennootschap
Bb	Bedrijfsjuridische berichten
BIE	Berichten industriële eigendom
BIT	Bilateral investment treaty
BR	Tijdschrift Bouwrecht
B2C	business-to-consumer
c.s.	cum suis
CAfA	Court of Arbitration for Art
cf.	confer (compare)
CJB	Caribisch Juristenblad
CJEC	Court of Justice of the European Communities
CJEU	Court of Justice of the European Union
DCCP	Dutch Code of Civil Procedure
DCC	Dutch Civil Code
DIS	Deutschen Institution für Schiedsgerichtsbarkeit (German Arbitration Institute)
diss.	dissertation
dr	doctor
e.g.	exampli gratia
EB	Tijdschrift voor scheidingsrecht
EC	European Community
ECHR	European Convention on Human Rights
ECRM	European Commission of Human Rights
ECT	Energy Charter Treaty
ECtHR	European Court of Human Rights
ed	editor

eds	editors
EPC	European Patent Convention
ESG	Environment, Social and Governance
et al	et alii
etc.	etcetera
et seq.	et sequentes
EU	European Union
EUR	euro
EWCA	Court of Appeal of England and Wales
EWHC	High Court of Justice of England and Wales
GDP	gross domestic product
GTC	general terms and conditions
HKIAC	Hong Kong International Arbitration Centre
i.a.	inter alia
i.e.	id est
IBA	International Bar Association
ICAO	International Civil Aviation Organization
ICC	International Chamber of Commerce
ICCA	International Council for Commercial Arbitration
ICDR	International Centre for Dispute Resolution
ICSID	International Centre for Settlement of Investment Disputes
ICT	Information and communication technology
IER	Intellectuele Eigendom en Reclamerecht
IT	Information technology
JAR	Jurisprudentie Arbeidsrecht
JBPr	Jurisprudentie Burgerlijk Procesrecht
JOR	Jurisprudentie Onderneming & Recht
LCIA	London Court of International Arbitration
LG	Landgericht
LJN	Landelijk Jurisprudentie Nummer
LLC	Limited Liability Company
LLM	Master of Laws
LLP	Limited Liability Partnership
KEI	Kwaliteit en Innovatie
KG	Kort Geding
KNVB	Koninklijke Nederlandse Voetbalbond
M&A	mergers and acquisitions
MoA	Memorandum of Answer
MvA	Memorie van Antwoord (Memorandum of Answer)
MvO	Maandblad voor Ondernemingsrecht

MvV	Maandblad voor Vermogensrecht
N.V.	naamloze vennootschap
NAFTA	North American Free Trade Agreement
NAI	Netherlands Arbitration Institute
NCC	Netherlands Commercial Court
NCCA	Netherlands Commercial Court of Appeal
NGO	non-governmental organisation
NIPR	Nederlands Internationaal Privaatrecht
NJ	Nederlandse Jurisprudentie
NJB	Nederlands Juristenblad
NJF	NJ Feitenrechtspraak
NJK	NJ Kort
no	number
NOFOTA	Netherlands Oils, Fats and Oilseeds Trade Association
NOvA	Nederlandse orde van advocaten
NTBR	Nederlands Tijdschrift voor Burgerlijk Recht
NTHR	Nederlands Tijdschrift voor Handelsrecht
O&A	Overheid en Aansprakelijkheid
O&F	Onderneming en Financiering
OECD	Organisation for Economic Co-operation and Development
OJ	Official Journal
OLG	Oberlandesgericht
OO&R	Onderzoekcentrum Onderneming & Recht (Radboud Business Law Institute)
p	page
para	paragraph
paras	paragraphs
PCA	Permanent Court of Arbitration
P-G	procureur-generaal
Prg.	Praktijkgids
Rev. Arb.	Revue de l'arbitrage
RMThemis	Rechtsgeleerd Magazijn Themis
(Wet) RO	Judicial (Organisation) Act
RvA	Raad van Arbitrage in bouwgeschillen
RvdW	Rechtspraak van de Week
SCC	Stockholm Chamber of Commerce
SGOA	Stichting Geschillenoplossing Automatisering
SIAC	Singapore International Arbitration Centre
SMEs	small and medium-sized enterprises
Stb.	Staatsblad (Bulletin of Acts and Decrees)

TAMARA	Stichting Transport and Maritime Arbitration Rotterdam-Amsterdam
TBR	Tijdschrift voor Bouwrecht
TC	Tijdschrift Conflicthantering
TCR	Tijdschrift voor Civiele Rechtspleging
TDM	Transnational Dispute Management
TFEU	Treaty on the Functioning of the European Union
TMD	Tijdschrift voor mediation
Trb.	Tractatenblad (Treaty Series)
TvA	Tijdschrift voor Arbitrage
TvC	Tijdschrift voor Consumentenrecht & handelspraktijken
TvPP	Tijdschrift voor de Procespraktijk
UAV-GC	Uniforme Administratieve Voorwaarden voor Geïntegreerde Contractvormen
UK	United Kingdom
UKSC	United Kingdom Supreme Court
UN	United Nations
UNCITRAL	United Nations Commission on International Trade Law
UNESCO	United Nations Educational, Scientific and Cultural Organization
US	United States
USD	United States Dollar
v	versus
VA	Verzekerings-archief
VAT	Value Added Tax
Vol.	Volume
VU	Vrije Universiteit (Amsterdam)
WAMR	World Arbitration & Mediation Review
WODC	Wetenschappelijk Onderzoek- en Datacentrum
WPNR	Weekblad voor Privaatrecht, Notariaat en Registratie
WRRA	Wet rechtspositie rechterlijke ambtenaren

CHAPTER 1

ARBITRATION IN THE NETHERLANDS, IN PARTICULAR NAI ARBITRATION; AN INTRODUCTION

Carla Klaassen & Gerard Meijer[1]

This volume is the result of a continued collaboration between the Radboud Business Law Institute affiliated to the Faculty of Law of the Radboud University Nijmegen ("OO&R") and the Netherlands Arbitration Institute ("NAI"). Already as a result of this collaboration,[2] the Dutch-language volume "Going Dutch: ADR in Nederland, in het bijzonder bij het NAI" was published five years ago, back in 2019. This volume was created and released in order to mark the 70th anniversary of the NAI. From that moment in time, various voices arose – including foreign associates working at Dutch branches of firms active within the (international) arbitration practice, OO&R partners as well as fellow arbitration institutes abroad – requesting that an English translation of this volume be made available. With the release of this volume, we have decided to forego a one-to-one translation. Instead, we opted for a follow-up volume, partly based on the aforementioned Dutch-language volume, and partly based on a new approach. After all, a lot has happened since 2019. The NAI is now 75 years old, for starters, but more important is that, as of 1 March 2024, the NAI's new ruleset has come into force. These Rules subsequently underwent a

1 Professor Dr C.J.M. (Carla) Klaassen is Professor of Civil Law and Civil Procedure at Radboud University Nijmegen (Radboud Business Law Institute (*OO&R*)), Professor of Private Law at the University of Curacao and Vice-Chair of the Board of the Netherlands Arbitration Institute, Professor Dr G.J. (Gerard) Meijer is a partner at Linklaters LLP in Amsterdam, Professor of Arbitration & Dispute Resolution at the Erasmus School of Law, Erasmus University Rotterdam, and Chair of the Board of the NAI. The authors would like to thank C.L. (Carmen) Schleijpen and T. (Thomas) de Boer for their support in writing this introduction and for their efforts as co-editors of this volume. Carmen Schleijpen (LLM), is a lecturer at Radboud University Nijmegen and a PhD Candidate at the Radboud Business Law Institute of Radboud University Nijmegen. Her doctoral research concerns the civil liability of arbitrators. Thomas de Boer (LLM), is an associate at Linklaters LLP in Amsterdam.

2 This cooperation also involves the Nijmegen CPO, which is responsible for implementing the training courses offered and made compulsory by the NAI for quality assurance purposes.

clerical brush-up on 31 December 2024. Developments in the field of arbitration have not stood still, either. These developments occurred through new case law, for example, but through other aspects as well. We refer, for example, to the increased digitalisation of arbitral proceedings – partly in light of environmental concerns – as well as the focus on diversity.

Although much has happened and is still happening in the fields of the other forms of Alternative Dispute Resolution ("ADR"), which featured more prominently in the previous volume, a more limited focus has been chosen this time with arbitration taking centre stage. Binding advice is thus only discussed indirectly and mediation is the focus of only one contribution;[3] but this contribution immediately touches on a key issue: the increased interest in corporate mediation and the relationship between this method of dispute resolution and arbitration.

On the other hand, in some ways the scope has also been broadened this time compared to the previous "Going Dutch: ADR in the Netherlands, in particular at the NAI". After all, not only in the "European Netherlands" does arbitration present a viable method of dispute resolution to consider when faced with a certain dispute. This applies equally to disputes that (also) occur in the overseas or Caribbean parts of the Kingdom of the Netherlands: Aruba, Curaçao, Sint Maarten, Bonaire, Sint Eustatius and Saba.[4]

Also in this volume, it is assumed that the arbitration is conducted under the rules of the NAI. This is not without reason: after all, the NAI is not only the largest Dutch arbitration institute, it is also the (only) general arbitration institute. The NAI focuses on commercial disputes, regardless of their nature. The various other arbitration institutes in the Netherlands have a more specific focus, which, as a rule, is often already apparent from their names. We refer to the *Raad van Arbitrage in bouwgeschillen* ("RvA"; Arbitration Institute for the Construction Industry), for example.[5]

A few words on the background and development of the 75-year-old NAI.[6]

---

3 That is: Y.P. Kamminga & B.M.H. Fleuren, 'Corporate Mediation: The Dutch Approach to Mediation vs. Anglo-American Practices and the Enforceability of Mediation Clauses', chapter 12.

4 On this topic: S.H. Barten, 'Arbitration in the Dutch Caribbean', chapter 11.

5 Cf. also Asser Procesrecht/Sanders, Meijer & Ernste *8* 2023/21.

6 Retrieved from C.J.M. Klaassen, G.J. Meijer & C.L. Schleijpen, 'ADR en 70 jaar NAI', in: C.J.M. Klaassen et al (eds), *Going Dutch: ADR in Nederland, in het bijzonder bij het NAI,* Deventer: Wolters Kluwer 2019, p 2-4.

The NAI was founded in 1949 on the initiative of Rudolph Cleveringa and Piet Sanders.[7] In doing so, Sanders was inspired by the American Arbitration Association ("AAA").[8] In the early days of the NAI, the initial focus was therefore on Dutch-American commercial arbitration. This shifted fairly quickly, however, to a more general focus on international, commercial arbitration.[9] Sanders found it desirable that the Netherlands also possessed its own general arbitration institute. An institute that not only focused on specific areas – such as the Arbitration Council for the Metal Industry or the Dutch Southern Fruits Association – but instead provided for an option to settle all conceivable, concrete disputes suitable for arbitration. A strong motive for the establishment of a general arbitration institute was the existing preference of commercial parties for dispute resolution through arbitration, rather than state court adjudication.[10] This coincided with a need from practitioners for a well-regulated, easily accessible mechanism for this form of dispute resolution, facilitated via a set of arbitration rules.[11] This gap has been filled by the NAI ever since. While the NAI still played a modest role in the early years following its establishment[12] 75 years ago, the NAI has since grown into an indispensable player in the field of alternative dispute resolution.

As mentioned, the NAI is the only institute in the Netherlands which focuses on (commercial) disputes in a general sense, without limiting itself to one or more specific areas of law or practice. As is also evident from the contributions included in this volume (see Part I in particular), the NAI therefore plays a significant role in a wide range of fields. While the Institute has traditionally held an important position in both international and national arbitration, its role is not limited thereto. Indeed, binding advice proceedings (currently under the 2015 NAI Binding Advice Rules) and – since 1995[13] – mediation (currently under the 2017 NAI Mediation Rules)

7 P. Sanders, *Herinneringen*, Amsterdam: SUN Publishers (now Boom Publishers) 2009, p 55.

8 P. Sanders, 'TvA/NAI 50 jaar', in: NAI (ed), *NAI 50 jaar. Arbitrage: in wiens handen?*, Deventer: Kluwer 2000, p 9; P. Sanders, 'Het NAI veertig jaar!', *TvA* 1989, p 143.

9 A. Marsman, *International Arbitration in the Netherlands. With a Commentary on the NAI and PCA Arbitration Rules*, Alphen aan den Rijn: Kluwer Law International 2021, p 555; Sanders 1989, p 143.

10 R.P. Cleveringa, 'Het Nederlands Arbitrage Instituut', *Arbitrale Rechtspraak* 1950, no 357, p 259.

11 Sanders 1989, p 143.

12 Sanders 2000, p 10.

13 H.J. Snijders, 'Arbitrage bij het Nederlands Arbitrage Instituut', in: H.J. Snijders & G.J. Meijer (eds), *Vademecum Burgerlijk Procesrecht*, Deventer: Gouda Quint 2002, p 75. Initially, this mediation bore the name 'minitrage'.

can also be conducted at the NAI. While the NAI originally focused on the resolution of disputes "in the field of commerce in the broadest sense"[14] by way of arbitrations surrounded by proper safeguards, its goals have now increased in scope. The NAI aims to promote all the aforementioned forms of alternative dispute resolution by providing a well-regulated arbitration, binding advice and mediation procedure. By providing (in no uncertain terms) for arbitration, binding advice or mediation at the NAI via an agreement, parties (in principle) also opt for a procedure according to the relevant NAI Rules, which guarantees a correct, careful and independent resolution of their dispute.

In its 75 years of existence, the NAI has remained anything but static. During these years, the Institute went through two major legislative changes (in 1986 and in 2015)[15] and amended its rulesets several times.[16] The Arbitration Rules were amended most recently in 2024.[17]

Looking back, it is safe to say that the establishment of the NAI in 1949 has turned out to be an unqualified success, much to the credit of Piet Sander's undeniable foresight in this regard. After all, the NAI has played a very prominent role as a general ADR institute in the Netherlands, and over the years has had the privilege of administering an extraordinarily large number of (national and international) arbitrations, binding advice proceedings and mediations.

After this brief overview of the NAI's history, it is time to turn to both the present and the future. The reasons for the NAI's existence are as relevant today as when it was founded: even today, the commercial market has a great need for adequate, effective mechanisms for institutional ADR, both on a national and international level. We are convinced that the NAI will

---

14 Expanded purpose of the Institute, adopted 23 December 1949, see Sanders 1989, p 143; Cleveringa 1950, p 259.

15 *Stb.* 1986, 372 and *Stb.* 2014, 200. On these legislative changes: H.J. Snijders, *Nederlands arbitragerecht*, Deventer: Wolters Kluwer 2018, para 1.2; G.J. Meijer, in: *T&C Rv*, commentary on book 4 DCCP.

16 On the 2015 amendments, following the aforementioned legislative changes: G.J. Meijer & H.J. van der Baan, 'NAI Arbitragereglement 2015', *TvA* 2015/37, p 59.

17 On the 2024 amendments: M. Hetterscheidt, 'NAI Arbitragereglement 2024. Op weg naar efficiëntere en snellere beslechting van (internationale) handelsgeschillen', *TCR* 2024, p 31-40; P.E. Ernste, 'Het NAI Arbitragereglement 2024. De waarborgen voor de onafhankelijkheid en onpartijdigheid van de arbiters en de kwaliteit van de arbitrage', *WPNR* 2024, issue 7470, p 469-471; G.J. Meijer & C.M.L. Perera-de Wit, 'Het NAI Arbitragereglement 2024. De hoofdlijnen en belangrijkste wijzigingen', *TvA* 2024/76.

continue to play its part in this regard. First, it will do so by keeping an eye on new developments and market needs in relation to the use of arbitration and other forms of ADR. We refer, by way of example, to the efforts to further develop corporate mediation (see Chapter 12). Second, the NAI will be able to maintain its strong position, and possibly even expand it, by remaining responsive to developments and needs in and outside the Netherlands, specifically in relation to the regulation and contents of the different forms of ADR. In this context, one example is the facilitation of digital litigation by the NAI. What is certainly necessary, however, is the continued offering and (where possible) improvement of the high quality dispute resolution that the NAI's users attribute to the institute. And with that, we return to the contents of this volume, which is the fourth that the NAI has produced.[18]

The authors of this volume are all (or have been) involved in one way or another with the NAI and/or are all (experienced) experts in the field of ADR – particularly arbitration. They have been asked by us to shed light on various aspects of arbitration, as well as corporate mediation in relation to arbitration, with an emphasis on bringing forward the current (untapped) opportunities for institutional dispute resolution, in particular at the NAI.

The book opens with an overview of the various areas in which arbitration (at the NAI) plays, or could play a (more) significant role. Following that, various issues that (may) arise at the start, during and after the arbitral proceedings take centre stage. The aim is to provide insight into the practical course of proceedings, but also into possible bottlenecks within the framework of arbitration (at the NAI) and thus to indicate where there may be room for improvement. In addition, the authors (and editors) seek to identify opportunities for arbitration and corporate mediation (at the NAI), in order to remain responsive to the continued developments in the (international) field of dispute resolution, and the needs of the market and everchanging society. The volume ends with a reflection, looking back at the various contributions and, in particular, at the opportunities and pos-

18 Previously published: NAI (ed), *NAI 50 jaar. Arbitrage: in wiens handen?*, Deventer: Kluwer 2000 and C.J.M. Klaassen, G.J. Meijer & C.L. Schleijpen, 'ADR en 70 jaar NAI', in: C.J.M. Klaassen et al (eds), *Going Dutch: ADR in the Netherlands, in het bijzonder bij het NAI*, Deventer: Wolters Kluwer 2019, p 1-6. See further: P. Sanders, 'Het Nederlands Arbitrage Instituut', *Arbitrale Rechtspraak* 1959, no 460, p 97-100, Sanders 1989, p 143-144 and, in a more indirect sense about the NAI, the Piet Sanders Special in *TvA* 2012, issue 4.

sibilities for arbitration and corporate mediation in the Netherlands and at the NAI in particular, as argued by various authors. It also touches on some other current themes concerning dispute resolution (at the NAI).

This is a volume by and for the OO&R and the NAI, but also by and for the arbitration practice as a whole. It aims to offer a "bird's eye view" of arbitration in the Netherlands. The editors hope it will provide sufficient information to non-Dutch parties interested in arbitration in the Netherlands, and the NAI in particular. In addition, with this work the editors aim to contribute to the debate on (the position of) arbitration in the Netherlands and, again, at the NAI in particular. For a broader picture of NAI Arbitration, we would like to refer to the comprehensive overview of the 2024 NAI Arbitration Rules and the corresponding Explanatory Notes, to be found in the Appendix. They also cover topics that are otherwise not separately discussed in this volume.

The editors thank all those who contributed in any way to the production of this volume, specifically its authors.

All that remains is for us to express our sincere hope that you will enjoy reading this book!

I – WHICH (TYPES OF) DISPUTES LEND THEMSELVES TO (NAI) ARBITRATION?

CHAPTER 2

SETTLEMENT OF ART-RELATED DISPUTES: THE SIGNIFICANCE OF THE COURT OF ARBITRATION FOR ART

Karin Verduyn[1]

2.1 Introduction

This contribution aims to draw attention to the opportunities that the Court of Arbitration for Art (hereinafter: CAfA) provides for resolving disputes regarding works of art.

Some art-related disputes may never be solved, when a convenient court is lacking, and the parties are (or at least one of them is) not prepared to submit the dispute to alternative dispute resolution. Other disputes on art will find their way to state courts; in general, these disputes concern merely legal issues. Still there remains a category of disputes concerning art, of which the resolution by state courts will be considered not or less suitable by one or more of the parties. In case the parties are of different nationality, the national court of one party will often not be considered impartial by the other party. Other reasons for not taking art-related disputes to state courts may be that these courts lack technical or art-specific expertise, and that their decisions are public. A specialized court of arbitration, like CAfA, can provide relief. In commercial transactions regarding art, like the sale of artworks by galleries or through auctioneers, the underlying contracts or applicable general conditions not seldom comprise an arbitration clause. If a dispute has already risen, a condition for submitting it to arbitration is, opposite to litigation before state courts, that parties have to agree on this. That might not be an impediment if the advantages of arbitration for settling art-related disputes, depending on the type of dispute, are taken into consideration.

In this contribution, firstly, the rationale of the founding of CAfA will be outlined and some of het CAfA Arbitration Rules will be highlighted. Sub-

1 C.J. (Karin) Verduyn (LLM) is a senior judge in the Court of Appeal in The Hague. She has a bachelor's degree in art history.

sequently, it will be examined which categories of disputes regarding art are suitable to arbitration. Further, the advantages of arbitration by CAfA as a means of resolving art-related disputes will be lined up. The conclusion will be that CAfA offers opportunities that so far have been overlooked.

2.2 The Court of Arbitration for Art

2.2.1 Foundation and scope

CAfA was founded in 2018 under the auspices of the foundation Authentication in Art (hereinafter: AiA) in The Hague and the Netherlands Arbitration Institute (hereinafter: NAI) in Rotterdam. AiA's goal centers on establishing a means by which the art market can address questions of authenticity of paintings in a more orderly, reliable and legally effective manner. According to its mission statement, AiA comprises a group of prominent art world professionals who joined together to create a forum that can act to catalyze and promote best practices in art authentication.[2] In the art market, the authentication of art is not seldom the subject of a dispute and AiA came up with the idea to establish a specialized court for deciding authentication disputes.[3] For this purpose, it found a natural partner in the NAI, which is experienced in administering arbitrations, both national and international, and features a well-equipped secretariat. Their cooperation resulted in the foundation of CAfA, which offers a means for the resolution of all art-related disputes through mediation and arbitration. Thus, its scope is much broader than disputes on authentication. Neither CAfA,

---

2 https://authenticationinart.org/about-us/.

3 Other specialized bodies for dispute resolution concerning art by arbitration are scarce. The Venice Chamber of Arbitration has established a department dedicated to the resolution of national and international disputes related to art. http://www.camera-arbitrale-venezia.com/?IdPagina=536.
The World Intellectual Property Office (WIPO) established in 1994 the Alternative Dispute Resolution for Art and Cultural Heritage Service. According to the website, the WIPO Mediation, (Expedited) Arbitration and Expert Determination Rules are well suited for art and cultural heritage disputes. https://www.wipo.int/amc/en/center/specific-sectors/art/.
However, WIPO does not exclusively deal with art disputes. It mainly deals with galleries, producers of artistic performances, museums, artists and indigenous communities. S. Bhutoria, S. Ghaffari & A. Motamedi, 'Art Disputes and the Court of Arbitration for Art: Evolution of Revolution?', *The American Review of International Arbitration Blog*, 21 January 2021.

nor its arbitration rules, provide(s) for a definition of art. Given the origin of CAfA, art should apparently be read as (only) visual art.[4]

2.2.2 CAfA Rules and Proceedings

CAfA has its own arbitration rules, consisting of the Arbitration Rules of the NAI (hereinafter: the NAI Rules), supplemented and modified to meet the wishes of the international art community: the CAfA Arbitration Rules (hereinafter: the CAfA Rules), in force as of March 1, 2019. Article 2 of the CAfA Rules determines that a reference to arbitration according to the CAfA Rules shall constitute a reference to the most recent version of the NAI Rules as well. Thus, CAfA arbitrations that are commenced as from March 1, 2024 will also be governed by the new 2024 NAI Rules.[5] The CAfA Rules generally correspond to the NAI Rules. They will be explained below, primarily to the extent that they derogate from the NAI Rules. It is noted that where the NAI Rules comprise provisions that are lacking in the CAfA Rules – e.g. about another method of composition of the arbitral tribunal (Article 18 NAI Rules) or a midstream conference (Article 30 NAI Rules) – these provisions can be considered as additionally applicable in CAfA Arbitrations.

As a rule, CAfA arbitral proceedings are conducted in English, but parties may agree to another language (Article 5(1)). The administration of CAfA arbitrations is taken care of by the Secretariat of the NAI. The place of arbitration is not at the discretion of parties: in all cases, The Hague is the place of arbitration, although the arbitral tribunal may hold hearings, deliberate and hear witnesses and experts at any place (Article 21(7) and 21(8) CAfA Rules).[6] Regarding the governing law, Article 42(2) CAfA Rules determines that if a choice of law has been made by the parties, the arbitral tribunal shall decide in accordance with those rules of law. If the parties have not agreed to a governing law, the arbitral tribunal is to

---

4 Art is a comprehensive notion and includes both visual (fine art and applied art) and performing arts (music, dance, theatre). The website of AiA only mentions *art objects*. In this contribution it is assumed that, in terms of the CAfA Rules, art means fine and applied art, therefore objects. Consequently, it must be understood that CAfA does not deal with digital artworks such as non-fungible tokens (NFTs).

5 'NAI Rules' refer to the 2024 NAI Arbitration Rules.

6 The Explanatory Notes (para 6.1) mention that the parties may agree upon another place of arbitration, although elsewhere (para 10.2) they remark that 'Since the place of arbitration is in the Netherlands (...)'. Unclear is whether deviation from Article 21(7) is allowed. Such deviation cannot be extracted from the text: 'The place of arbitration shall be The Hague'.

determine the appropriate applicable law. An appropriate choice of law for the arbitral tribunal may be the law of the principal location of the seller, if known at the time of the transaction. In matters other than a sale, an appropriate choice is the law of the principal location of the current (purported) owner of the art object in question at the time of the commencement of the arbitration. The arbitral tribunal is to base its decisions on the rules of law, while respecting any applicable (art) industry trade usages (Article 42(4) CAfA Rules). Should the parties prefer instead that the arbitral tribunal not be bound by such law, so as to decide equitably as *amiable compositeur*, the parties must so authorize the arbitral tribunal (Article 42(3) CAfA Rules). It is not uncommon in the area of art disputes for a party to attempt to bring claims many years or even decades after they have arisen, particularly in the context of restitution claims. Article 42(5) of the CAfA Rules determines that the arbitral tribunal will, subject to the provisions in Article 42(1)-(4), respect applicable periods of limitation, prescription and repose, as well as similar time-bar principles, when claims or defenses have not been acted on within a reasonable time according to the governing law. According to the Explanatory Notes (para 9.3), this provision confirms that prescriptive periods and similar time-bar principles are intended to be respected where the party raising a claim or defense has no justification for its failure to timely advance its case. It is outlined that the purpose of this provision is to protect the other party from 'stale' claims or defenses which were not pursued with reasonable diligence and other situations of undue prejudice, such as where evidence has been lost due to the long passage of time. This suggests that in case of a justification for not filing the claim in a timely manner, such prescriptive periods and time-bar principles may not be strictly employed.

An interesting provision is Article 21(6) CAfA Rules: each party may appear in the proceedings in person, or be represented by a practicing lawyer of by a representative expressly authorized in writing for this purpose. A similar provision can be found in Article 28 NAI Rules. Thus, in CAfA arbitrations legal representation is not mandatory. In state court proceeding in the Netherlands, claims with a monetary interest of more than € 25,000 must be brought before the District Court, where legal representation is mandatory.[7] The absence of mandatory legal representation in CAfA (and NAI) arbitrations enables parties to conduct the arbitral proceedings in

7 Cases regarding a financial interest up to € 25,000 must be brought before the Cantonal Judge, who in addition has exclusive jurisdiction to decide cases regarding some specific subjects, of which the most important are labor and rental agreements.

person, without having to hire a lawyer, which may be suitable in cases that are not legally complicated. This will be discussed later on.

The CAfA Rules include rules for provisional relief (Articles 35 CAfA Rules) and arbitral summary proceedings (Articles 36 CAfA Rules).

2.2.3 *Arbitrator Pool*

CAfA features an Arbitrator Pool. Paragraph 2.1 of the Explanatory Notes states that the Arbitrator Pool is composed of international lawyers with demonstrated experience in litigating or counseling clients in art law disputes and/or international arbitration. According to the selection criteria, the arbitrators in the pool are (formerly) admitted private practice lawyers, judges and law professors who have at least five years of significant experience in one or more of the relevant fields. These fields comprise, but are not limited to, chain of title of art or cultural property (including heritage/patrimony/restitution), purchase and sale of art works through private sale and/or auction, copyright in the field of art, insurance of fine art or cultural property, museum exhibition and loan agreements, UNESCO, and international arbitration.[8] Arbitrators must be appointed from among the Arbitrator Pool (Article 11(6) CAfA Rules). Only in the event of compelling reasons and after hearing all parties, can the NAI administrator – this is initially the director of the NAI (Article 1(a) CAfA Rules) – in consultation with the CAfA Board, decide to authorize a deviation from the Arbitrator Pool (Article 13(4) CAfA Rules). Such reasons can be the desirability of an arbitrator with a very specific background and the absence of such an arbitrator in the Arbitrator Pool. As a rule, the arbitral tribunal consists of three arbitrators. If the parties have agreed to appoint just one arbitrator or the dispute is about objects of art with a value of less than € 1,500,000, a sole arbitrator will be appointed. The arbitrators are appointed either by (or after nomination by[9]) parties – if a tribunal consists of three arbitrators, the two party-appointed arbitrators jointly appoint the Chair – or via the List Procedure (Articles 13(2), 13(3), and 14(1) CAfA Rules). The Chair of every arbitral tribunal must have a university legal background; it is assumed

8 Selection criteria for CAfA arbitrators. https://www.cafa.world/arbitration/arbitrators/.

9 Article 16(2) of the NAI Rules of 2024 differ from Article 13 CAfA Rules (as well as from Article 13 of the NAI Rules of 2019) in this respect that the parties must nominate a prospective arbitrator, while the appointment takes place by the NAI Case Management Committee. Since the most recent version of the NAI Rules is likewise applicable to CAfA arbitrations, Article 13 CAfA Rules should be read that parties nominate, and the NAI Case Management Committee appoints an arbitrator.

that the same is true for the sole arbitrator. In the case that a sole arbitrator is to be appointed, the parties have to do their best efforts to jointly select one from the Arbitrator Pool (Article 13(1) CAfA Rules). If the parties are unable to agree, the arbitrator will be appointed by the NAI administrator pursuant to the List Procedure (Article 14 CAfA Rules).

2.2.4 *Evidence: Expert Pool and Technical Process Advisor*

As a unique feature, CAfA comes with an Expert Pool, composed of carefully selected and renowned experts in the field of forensic science, material analysis or provenance of art objects, in particular for authentication purposes.[10] The authenticity of art is evaluated according to standards of connoisseurship, provenance research and forensic science.[11] Article 28(7) CAfA Rules provides that on issues of forensic science or the provenance of an art object, the only admissible expert evidence is from an expert appointed by the arbitral tribunal under Article 29. Such an expert will normally be chosen from the Expert Pool. These renowned experts in the field of provenance research and forensic science are capable of a general analysis regarding the authenticity of art objects. When a particular artist or type of art object is subject to authentication, relevant connoisseurs or scholars can be approached on a case-by-case basis. The Arbitral Tribunal may only appoint an expert after consultation with the parties (Article 29(1) CAfA Rules). While the parties may retain their own consulting experts, the tribunal-appointed expert from the Expert Pool provides the exclusive analysis as far as forensic science or provenance is concerned.[12]

10 The selection criteria for these experts are presented on CAfA's website: https://www.cafa.world/arbitration/provenance_and_forensic_experts/.

11 To explain these terms: 'connoisseurship' is a form of stylistic, or *subjective* authentication. It relies on the eye and intuition of art experts, which will develop as they analyze and evaluate hundreds, or even thousands, of works over the course of their career. Art experts will focus on the artist's style, carefully observing brush stroke, composition, color, iconography, among other details. 'Provenance' is a documented ownership history of an object from when its creation to its most recent sale. Forms of provenance include sale receipts between owners and galleries, auction and dealer catalogues, museum records, and catalogue raisonnés. 'Forensics' is a form of scientific, or *objective* authentication. Scientific testing consists of methods such as radiocarbon dating, X-ray imaging, and infrared analysis. Methods like these, date the materials existent in both the external and internal structure of the works. https://itsartlaw.org/2024/06/19/the-cost-of-fakes-the-aesthetic-legal-and-economic-implications-of-forgeries/#post-65417-footnote-ref-17.

12 Explanatory Notes, paras 2.2, 7.1 and 7.3 under B. A party may object to the appointment of an expert on the ground of lack of impartiality or independence. Explanatory Notes, para 7.3 under C.

For all other matters, evidence from party-appointed experts is admissible (Article 28(1) CAfA Rules).

In cases concerning highly complex or technical issues, such as concerning an art object's authenticity, the arbitral tribunal may appoint a technical process advisor, where appropriate, from the Expert Pool (Article 29(7) CAfA Rules). The role of the technical process advisor is a fairly unique aspect of the CAfA Rules. Such an advisor is intended to assist the arbitral tribunal and to help identifying and facilitate the gathering of relevant evidence in an efficient and cost-effective manner. Primarily, he or she is to advise the arbitral tribunal with respect to pre-hearing evidence gathering and evidence exchange processes. The technical process advisor is not an extension of the arbitral tribunal and does not attend the hearing on the merits, or participate in the arbitral tribunal's deliberations. The arbitral tribunal may, however, at the request of a party or on its own initiative, invite the technical process advisor to be present at the hearing in order to answer specific questions.[13] A technical process advisor can only be appointed with the parties' consent following an arbitral tribunal engagement proposal spelling out the contemplated role, scope of authority, advisory mandate, and other matters concerning the appointment.

With respect to evidence, the CAfA Rules contain an additional provision as compared to the NAI Rules: Article 26(3) CAfA Rules states that the arbitral tribunal may seek guidance from the IBA Rules on the Taking of Evidence in International Arbitration on all matters addressed therein.

2.2.5 *The arbitral award; remedies and publication*

Paragraph V of the CAfA Rules deals with the arbitral award. Attention is paid, very briefly, to a few provisions.

If the arbitral award contains a manifest computing, clerical or other error, a party can request the rectification within two months after the date of the award. The correction of an error or omission in the award regarding certain particulars may be requested as well. The request must be submitted to the administrator. The arbitral tribunal can, within two months after the date of the award, also proceed such correction of its own motion. A rectification of the award is possible only after the parties have had the opportunity to comment on the matter (Article 47(1), (2), (3), (4) and (5) CAfA Rules). The CAfA

13 Explanatory Notes, paras 8.1 and 8.3.

Rules do not provide for (the option of) arbitral appeal against an arbitral award. The sole remedy available is the setting aside of the arbitral award by a state court. Since the place of arbitration always is The Hague, setting aside proceedings will be governed by the relevant articles of the Dutch Code of Civil Procedure (hereinafter: DCCP). The competent court is the Court of Appeal in The Hague (Article 1064a(1) DCCP). If it finds a ground for setting aside the arbitral award, it may instead enable the arbitral tribunal to reverse the ground for setting aside by remission. In that case, the arbitral tribunal's mandate revives for this purpose. The arbitral tribunal can reopen the arbitral proceedings or take any other measure it considers appropriate (Article 49 CAfA Rules).

In disputes about authenticity, confidentiality is considered paramount. At the same time, NAI is authorized to publish an anonymized – i.e. with omission of all information that might reveal the parties' identities – arbitral award, unless a party objects within two months of the date of the award. It is noted that AiA is authorized to publish the award in the same way *and* to reveal the name or identity of the art object (Article 51 CAfA Rules). The question rises whether publication 'in the same way' by AiA includes the right of a party to object. The rationale behind publishing the name or identity of the art object is that fake pieces or forgeries should be prevented from recirculating in the art market. Hence, it must be understood that parties cannot object to the publication of an (anonymized) award that identifies the art object within a limited circle, being the authentication community. Evidently, this exception to the rule of confidentiality and party autonomy applies only in cases regarding authentication.

2.3 Art-related disputes and arbitrability

2.3.1 Categorization

As set out in the introduction, disputes regarding art occur in many varieties. Although CAfA has a broad scope, not all those disputes are suitable to resolution by CAfA arbitration: the disputes should concern art-specific issues. It being noted that 'art-specific' is not limited to disputes on authenticity or provenance of art, the fields in which experts from CAfA's Expert Pool are specialized. After all, the Arbitrator Pool features arbitrators with knowledge and experience in several relevant fields of law, such as chain of title of art or cultural property, copyright law and contract law (sale, loan, insurance). The suitability of CAfA arbitration will generally depend on various factors – apart from the availability of art-specific expertise:

the (different) nationality of the parties, the importance of confidentiality, the costs etc. – and, in each specific case, on the weight to be assigned to the advantages over state court proceedings, which will be discussed later. Meanwhile, in conflicts regarding authenticity of art, the suitability of CAfA arbitration is evident, if only because the specific experience and expertise in these fields (by the arbitrators and, especially, the experts from the Pools) are not available in state courts. It is observed that authenticity may be the subject of different kinds of disputes, both in contractual relations (misrepresentation, error, breach of contract) and non-contractual relations (ownership, wrongful acts). The latter category, including claims or requests for restitution of looted art and cultural heritage, will concentrate on provenance. Besides the abovementioned fields of law, other issues of (contract) law may be involved, while sometimes aspects of (private) international law have to be added.

The following categories of art-related disputes will be elaborated on: (i) ownership: cultural heritage and looted art, (ii) copyright to works of (applied) art and (iii) contracts related to artworks. It is noted that some disputes may be assigned to more than one category. Within the different categories, multiple legal issues may apply. Where appropriate, some specific legal issues will be addressed.

2.3.2 *Ownership: cultural heritage and looted art*

Disputes regarding cultural heritage and looted art form a specific category.

When conflicts arise about objects that are considered cultural heritage, generally one or both parties are states and, thus, national interests are concerned. Think of the everlasting and still unresolved dispute between Greece and the British Museum about the ownership of the Parthenon Marbles. Conflicts about ownership of cultural heritage involve issues of (public) international law, human rights and politics, rather than property law.[14] It mostly concerns cultural objects that were appropriated by former colonial powers from their colonies or, as once was usual, plundered by the victors of war from conquered territories.[15] These cultural objects are

14 On standards of justice and the legal classification of claims regarding the restitution of cultural heritage and colonial loot, see: E. Campfens, 'Restitutie van betwiste kunst vanuit een juridisch perspectief', *MvV* 2023, p 282-288.

15 S. Verhoeven, 'The Art of War: Protecting Art in War', in: B. Demarsin et al (eds), *Art & Law*, Oxford: Hart Publishing 2008, p 378-380.

often (still) exhibited in museums or in the public domain of the other state.[16] The president of CAfA, Professor Bert Demarsin, does not believe conflicts regarding cultural heritage will ever be adjudicated at CAfA. He observes: 'Private institutions most likely are not going to be entrusted with the resolution of this type of conflicts. Should CAfA become the ultimate authority in art-related matters and develop a flawless reputation and credibility, these cases might one day come before CAfA. However, I remain skeptical about this prospect.'[17]

Another important category of looted art is art that was confiscated from, or sold under duress by, individual owners before or during World War II. Almost 80 years after World War II, the restitution of art objects that were involuntarily lost during the Nazi regime is by no means a closed chapter. The Washington Conference Principles on Nazi-Confiscated Art (hereinafter: the Washington Principles), endorsed by 44 countries in 1998, serve as an important foundation for restitution policies in several countries.[18] Principle 11 determines that nations are encouraged to develop national processes to implement these Principles, particularly as they relate to alternative dispute resolution mechanisms for resolving ownership issues. The Netherlands have implemented the Washington Principles by adopting a restitution policy and establishing the Advisory Committee on the Assessment of Restitution Applications for Items of Cultural Value and the Second World War, abbreviated as the Restitutions Committee. Under the current Dutch restitution policy, cultural property that is highly likely or certain to have been stolen, confiscated or forcibly sold between 1933 and 1945 can be returned to the pre-war owners or their heirs. A request for restitution of a cultural good in possession by the Dutch state can be sub-

16 In contrast to ideals that were accepted for centuries, the actual concept stands that cultural treasures should not be considered legitimate spoils of conquest and many initiatives have emerged to outlaw the confiscation of cultural property. In 2017, the French president Emmanuel Macron called for the return of African heritage to the continent. Since then, France has (only) repatriated 28 African objects, mainly to Benin. Following the report of the Commission Colonial Collections of May 12, 2023, the Netherlands announced to grant the request of Indonesia and Sri Lanka for the return of 478 cultural objects, amongst which the 'Lombok Schat' (to Indonesia).

17 Bert Demarsin was interviewed by Federica Violi and Antonio Cappuccio, assisted by Hannah Driesens, in September 2023. The interview was published in *Law Art. Journal of Law, Art and History* 2023, issue 4, p 323-330. https://www.lawart.it/Article/Archive/index_html?ida=72&idn=4&idi=-1&idu=-1#_ftnref1.

18 Cultural Heritage Agency, *Newsletter Cultural goods World War II* (8) 2024, p 1. Eleven principles were established. These are the most important principles imposed to date, yet they are non-binding, since the signatory nations are not obligated to implement them within their respective legal systems, serving solely as guidelines.

mitted to the Restitutions Committee. The Restitutions Committee makes a recommendation to the State Secretary of Culture and Media (OCW), who will finally decide on the request.[19] In respect of cultural objects not in possession of the state, claims for restitution have to be litigated in court, although the parties concerned may agree to submit the dispute to the Restitution Committee that will decide by way of binding opinion ('bindend advies').[20] By no means all countries enable pre-war owners of art and their heirs to bring their claims before a restitutions committee. So far, only five of the 44 countries that endorsed the Washington Principles have created such a committee.[21] In other countries, claims for the return of Nazi-looted art have to be submitted to a (national) court. This is not a very attractive option; state courts lack expertise, while claimants from abroad might have little confidence in the impartiality of such courts. Art works in possession of a state are often exhibited in national museums that might not be happy if they are forced to relinquish these artworks. In such cases, CAfA arbitration may be a suitable alternative. However, the states or national museums concerned must be prepared to conclude a submission agreement. Bert Demarsin indicates that he can imagine that in states where restitutions committees are missing, authorities might consider submitting these kinds of disputes to CAfA, depending on the situation and the legal framework of each jurisdiction.[22] It is observed that statutes of limitations regarding claims for restitution of stolen property differ materially per jurisdiction. In general, in civil law jurisdictions like the Netherlands, limitation periods for revindication of stolen objects are short and will have expired as far as Nazi-era looted objects are concerned, while in common law jurisdictions, claims for revindication of stolen objects do not expire.[23] While this used to mean that claims for the return of Nazi-looted art were inadmissible in civil law countries, presently such claims will not

19 https://english.cultureelerfgoed.nl/topics/cultural-goods-ww2-1933-1945/requests-for-restitution/procedure-restitution-goods-in-possession-of-the-state.

20 Article 2.2 of the Rules of Procedure of the Restitution Committee 2021: https://www.restitutiecommissie.nl/wp-content/uploads/2020/12/RC-Reglement-miv15072021_0.pdf.

21 Austria, France, Germany, the Netherlands, and the United Kingdom. Best Practices for the Washington Principles, 5 March 2024, sub I. https://www.state.gov/best-practices-for-the-washington-conference-principles-on-nazi-confiscated-art/.

22 See footnote 16. Attorney Margot Span mentions CAfA as an institution capable of dealing with claims for restitution of looted art. M. Span, 'Bemiddelen bij conflicten over restitutie van kunst', *TC* 2023/68.

23 E.J.H. Schrage, 'Het belang van het Court of Arbitration for Art', in: C.J.M. Klaassen, G.J. Meijer & C.L. Schleijpen (eds), *Going Dutch: ADR in Nederland, in het bijzonder bij het NAI (Onderneming en recht no 113)*, Deventer: Wolters Kluwer 2019, para 4.3; Campfens 2023, p 285-286 (para 5).

be barred by limitation periods, at least when brought against governments or public bodies, like national museums. They will, in accordance with adopted regulations or restitution policies, refrain from recourse to a statute of limitation.[24] Under French law, all subsequent sales of goods sold under duress or looted under German occupation are considered null and void.[25]

In this context, it is worthwhile to examine a famous dispute on Nazi-looted art between an individual claimant and a national museum that was submitted to arbitration. It concerns the claim of Maria Altman, citizen of the United States, against the Republic of Austria for the surrender of five paintings by Gustav Klimt. These paintings, amongst which the *Woman in Gold* – a portrait of Mrs. Altman's aunt Adele Bloch-Bauer, also referred to as the Austrian *Mona Lisa* – were in the possession of the Austrian state and kept in the Belvedere Museum in Vienna. Mrs. Altman contended that the paintings were stolen from her relatives – in fact, tax evasion proceedings had been used as an excuse to confiscate the property that her uncle, who was forced to flee Austria, had left behind – by the Nazis in Vienna just prior to World War II. After her request to the Art Restitution Board in Austria was denied, Mrs. Altman wanted to bring the case before an Austrian court. However, the costs of court proceedings were proportional to the amount in controversy and, due to the enormous (estimated) value of the paintings, Mrs. Altman could not afford to pay the filing fee. Instead, she brought the case to the American court. The US Supreme Court ruled that Austria was not immune from litigation for acts that first arose from criminal conduct during World War II and remanded the case for trial in the Los Angeles district court. The parties then signed a submission agreement for arbitration in Austria and, subsequently, an (ad hoc) arbitral tribunal was composed. By arbitral award of January 15, 2006, the arbitral tribunal ruled that the conditions of the applicable Federal Act Regarding the Restitution of Artworks from Austrian Federal Museums and Collections

---

24 The Washington Principles stipulate that in establishing that a work of art had been confiscated by the Nazis and not subsequently restituted, consideration should be given to unavoidable gaps or ambiguities in the provenance in light of the passage of time and the circumstances of the Holocaust era (Principle 4). According to Best Practices, countries should consider making exceptions to barriers such as, among others, statutes of limitations, good faith acquisition. Best Practices for the Washington Principles, 5 March 2024, sub K. https://www.state.gov/best-practices-for-the-washington-conference-principles-on-nazi-confiscated-art/.

25 The Art Newspaper of February 1, 2023. https://www.theartnewspaper.com/2023/02/01/french-court-orders-christies-to-restitute-a-nazi-looted-painting-sold-in-london.

were fulfilled and that the five paintings must be returned to the heirs of Ferdinand Bloch-Bauer.[26]

The conclusion is that CAfA arbitration may well provide a feasible option for settling disputes regarding cultural heritage and looted art in particular cases.[27]

2.3.3 *Copyright*

According to WIPO (World Intellectual Property Organization) it is now broadly accepted that disputes relating to intellectual property rights (such as copyright) are arbitrable and arbitration is increasingly being used to resolve such disputes, especially when involving parties from different jurisdictions.[28]

Disputes regarding copyright on works of (applied) art are common. Most often, they concern the infringement of copyright. In general, as far as works of (applied) art are concerned, there are no contractual relations between artists and infringers of their copyright. Artists who seek a remedy to end the infringement of their copyright, have an urgent interest to obtain an injunction and will turn to a state court. Thus, even though CAfA provides for summary proceedings and provisional measures, in the absence of an arbitration agreement this is not a feasible option. Resale rights entitle artists, as copyright holders, to a percentage of the sale price – a resale royalty – when their (original) work of art is resold by an art market professional. The collection and distribution of resale rights is taken care of by designated organizations like, in the Netherlands, the non-profit foundation Pictoright. Legislation on resale rights within the European Union results from the im-

26 Altmann v. Republic of Austria (*ad hoc*, January 15, 2006). http://bslaw.com/altmann/Klimt/award.pdf. (German language); https://jusmundi.com/en/document/decision/en-maria-v-altmann-francis-gutmann-trevor-mantle-and-george-bentley-and-dr-nelly-auersperg-v-the-republic-of-austria-award-sunday-15th-january-2006 (translation in English). The case is discussed more extensively in Schrage 2019, para 4.3.5.

27 A useful overview of the discussed categories of looted art and developments in restitution policies, including the establishment of the Washington Principles and subsequent regulations, is to be found in: A. Buonaiuto, 'From Stolen Heritage to Restitution: The Story behind Looted Art', Center for art law, 6 May 2024, https://itsartlaw.org/2024/05/06/from-stolen-heritage-to-restitution-the-story-behind-looted-art/.

28 https://www.wipo.int/AMCON/en/arbitration/why-is-arb.html. For Dutch law: J.H. Spoor, D.W.F. Verkade & D.J.G. Visser, *Auteursrecht (Recht en Praktijk no IE2)* 2019, para 11.42. Dutch copyright law provides for the resolution of conflicts regarding copyright licenses (e.g. assessment of an equitable remuneration) by an arbitration committee ('Geschillencommissie Auteurscontractenrecht').

plementation of European Directive 2001/84/EC on the resale right for the benefit of the author of an original work of art. Disputes about the interpretation of the law and the Directive must be considered not arbitrable, being the exclusive domain of the national courts and, of last resort, the Court of Justice of the European Union.

Hence, most probably there will not be much room left for CAfA arbitration when art-related disputes concern copyright.

2.3.4 *Contracts; authenticity of art and other art-related issues*

Examples of contracts regarding works of (applied) art are, e.g., purchase, loan, donation, transport, storage and insurance agreements. These contracts are concluded between various parties, e.g. the purchase agreement between a collector of art and an art gallery or an auctioneer, the loan agreement between two museums or a museum and an art collector, the insurance agreement between a museum or an art collector and an insurance company, to name a few. The fact that these contracts involve works of art, does not necessarily mean that disputes over such contracts differ from disputes over similar contracts regarding objects other than art, in the sense that art-specific expertise is required. However, it may happen that in order to decide on issues like default (non-conformity), error, fraud and, when appropriate, (the estimation of) damages to be compensated, knowledge of the law is insufficient to make a well-considered judgment. This occurs when the authenticity of the artwork is in dispute: it is contended that the artwork is fake or that its attribution is not correct.[29] This is particularly significant in respect of purchase agreements. For instance, the purchaser has acquired a painting that is attributed to a famous master and reproaches the seller for the reason that it has, instead, been painted by a studio assistant or, worse, that it is a forgery. The same may occur when the purchase concerns applied art; think of designer objects. The estimation of damages in case of the loss (theft) of or damage to a work of art is also relevant in respect of loan and insurance agreements.

29 Disputes about authenticity of art frequently involve experts and art authentication committees themselves. Several significant lawsuits have been brought against them for rejecting the attribution to a certain artist (such as Alexander Calder, Andy Warhol, Keith Haring, Jean-Michel Basquiat). Many committees' contracts include clauses prohibiting the collector from suing them. S. Schlackman, 'How to Authenticate Art and Spot Remarkable Forgeries', *Art Journal*, 9 January 2024. https://journal.atp.art/authenticating-art/. C. Danziger & T. Danziger, 'On the Case: Exploring Real World Art Law Issues', *Artnet*, 23 April 2014. https://news.artnet.com/market/on-the-case-exploring-real-world-art-law-issues-11677.

In case of litigation in a state court, parties will usually come up with expert opinions in order to convince the court of the validity of their claim and the court itself may appoint an independent expert for obtaining subject-specific information. The problem remains that state court judges are not familiar with the art market. The decision that an artwork cannot be attributed to a certain reputed artist, or that it is a forgery, has a disastrous effect on its market value. State court decisions are public, and will therefore not go unnoticed in the art world. Even if such a decision is overturned in appeal and the work is, after all, attributed to the artist concerned, doubts as to its authenticity will remain: the work is 'burnt'. As a result, the artwork becomes unsellable altogether or is at least devalued. CAfA arbitration offers a suitable alternative; due to the availability of specific expertise in the Expert Pool, the risk of incorrect attributions will be neglectable. Further, if a state court has to value an artwork in order to assess damages, it lacks the necessary expertise. The value of, for instance, a painting by a certain artist will depend on various relevant factors: the period in which it was made, the quality of the work, its subject, its size and the material of which it was made. State court judges need to appoint experts but are not or less able to select the right experts and evaluate the expert opinions. CAfA features arbitrators who are specialized in dealing with such cases and, moreover, experts in the field of authentication of art. It seems clear that disputes on the afore-mentioned subjects are very well suited for resolution by CAfA arbitration. Even if the resolution of a dispute about art does not involve art-specific questions, CAfA arbitration may be recommended for other reasons. Some art collectors prefer that their possession of certain very valuable art does not become public. CAfA arbitration will protect their anonymity.

When parties conclude a contract about art and wish, in case a dispute arises, to submit it to arbitration, it is advisable that they include an arbitration clause, preferably referring to CAfA arbitration.[30] Professional parties may incorporate an arbitration clause in their general or sales conditions. It is noted that if the other party is a non-professional private person, for instance an art collector who purchases an artwork, this party will generally be considered as a consumer. An arbitration clause may form an impediment for the fundamental right of access to a court, as determined in Article 6(1) European Convention on Human Rights. Many law systems provide for consumer protection regulations in order to guarantee this right. According to Article 6:236, preamble and under n, of the Dutch Civil

30 The CAfA Rules contain a recommended CAfA arbitration clause.

Code (DCC), an arbitration clause, contained in general conditions that are applicable to a contract between a consumer and the user of such conditions, is deemed to be unreasonably burdensome for the consumer unless it still allows him or her to choose for a settlement of the dispute by a state court. An arbitration clause in general conditions without this option can be annulled by the consumer. Even after the arbitral proceedings have taken place and an arbitral award was rendered, this provision can throw a spanner in the works. The Supreme Court of the Netherlands ruled that if in such case leave for enforcement of an arbitral award is requested, the (in that matter competent) provisional judge is required to examine, of its own motion, whether (i) the arbitration clause, or (ii) a stipulation that was ground for rendering an arbitral award against a consumer, is unfair as determined in European Directive 1993/13 and whether (iii) the arbitration clause allowed the consumer a period of at least one month to opt for settlement by a state court and (iv) the consumer was actually granted such period.[31] If the competent provisional judge considers the arbitration clause or the stipulation unfair or assesses that a period for opting out was not allowed or granted, he is required to deny the request. If those conditions are not fulfilled, this may also constitute grounds for setting aside the arbitral award. Contracting parties dealing with consumers are advised to take this into consideration when drafting their general conditions. It is recommendable to add the following sentence to the model CAfA arbitration clause, in accordance with Article 6:236, preamble and under n, DCC: 'If the counterparty is a natural person who did not act in the course of his or her professional practice or business when (s)he entered into the contract, (s)he is allowed to choose for a settlement of the dispute by the court with jurisdiction pursuant to law and this choice can be made within a period of at least one month after [name of the user] has invoked the stipulation in writing.'

2.4 Advantages of CAfA arbitration

2.4.1 Art-specific expertise

The most significant advantage of CAfA arbitration over litigation in a state court is that the CAfA arbitrators are qualified and experienced in several art-specific fields and can engage experts from the Expert Pool. This is particularly relevant when authenticity of an artwork is at issue. Disputes

31 Supreme Court 11 November 2019, ECLI:NL:HR:2019:1731.

on authentication were the main reason for founding CAfA. As an important side effect, arbitral awards rendered under the CAfA Rules will be more authoritative than court rulings and, therefore, better accepted in het art market.[32] Further, as set out before, the CAfA Arbitrator Pool and the Expert Pool also feature arbitrators and experts equipped with art-related qualifications and expertise outside the field of authentication. Depending on the particulars of the conflict, said qualifications and expertise may be a good reason to opt for CAfA arbitration instead of court litigation.

2.4.2 *Confidentiality*

An important reason to opt for the resolution of art-related disputes by arbitration is that both the arbitral proceedings and the arbitral award are not public as opposed to state court proceedings and judgements. Confidentiality is highly prized in art transactions between private buyers and sellers, and even art sales and purchases at public auction are often conducted via intermediaries to preserve the anonymity of the ultimate buyer and seller. Especially when the monetary value of the artwork is (extremely) high, private collectors often wish to stay anonymous.[33] As set out above (para 2.2.5), CAfA awards may be published within a limited circle, provided that parties do not object and all information that might reveal the parties' identities are omitted.

2.4.3 *Impartiality*

Requests for restitution of cultural heritage or looted art often involve national interests of states and (national) museums. Contracts regarding art are frequently concluded between parties of different nationality. In such cases, claimants might have less confidence in the impartiality of state courts, especially when they are foreigners.[34] CAfA arbitrators and experts are more likely to be perceived as impartial. Moreover, parties have control over the selection of arbitrators. If parties agree to the appointment of arbitrators according to the list procedure and they do not have the same nationality, Article 14(4) CAfA Rules provides that each of the parties may require that a sole arbitrator or the Chair of an arbitral tribunal consisting of three arbitrators, does not have the same nationality as any of the parties.

---

32 The art market has often even chosen to ignore courts' rulings on the authenticity of artworks. T. Braulotte, 'Art Law Dispute Resolution and the Court of Arbitration for Art', *b-Arbitra* 2022/2, p 223-224 (paras 8-11).

33 Braulotte 2022, p 235 (para 53).

34 Braulotte 2022, p 224-225 (paras 12-14) and p 233-234 (paras 47-49).

2.4.4 Costs

In general, arbitration is more expensive than litigation in a state court. The costs of CAfA arbitration, governed by paragraph VI of the CAfA Rules, obviously depend on the particulars of the case. The administration costs of CAfA arbitration are calculated on basis of the total monetary interest of the claim, using a scale from € 500 (interest of less than € 25,000) to a maximum of € 50,000 (interest of more than € 250,000,000). The administration costs must be advanced by the claimant. The administrator notifies the claimant of the amount due and sees to the collection of the administration costs. If a counterclaim is submitted, the respondent shall also be charged administration costs, in the same way (Article 53(1), (2), (3) and (5) CAfA Rules). To be added up are the arbitrator fees and disbursements. The total amount of the arbitrator fees evidently relates to the number of arbitrators; even if the monetary value of the relief sought is more than € 1,500,000, the parties can opt for the appointment of a sole arbitrator. In addition to the fees and disbursements of the arbitrator, the costs of legal assistance (not mandatory) and costs of experts and witnesses are due. The unsuccessful party has to pay the costs of the arbitration and may be ordered to pay the reasonable compensation for the successful party's legal assistance (Articles 56 and 57(2) CAfA Rules). It should be noted that Dutch courts award costs according to standard amounts that are, as a rule, not cost covering. The exception to the rule that arbitration is more expensive than litigation in a state court is confirmed by the arbitration *Altman v. Austria*, discussed above. Another aspect that may influence the price tag of arbitration positively is the absence of mandatory legal representation, meaning that it is not necessary to hire a counsel. In cases that are not legally complicated, this may bring about a significant reduction of costs.

2.4.5 Enforceability

In the event that the parties to a conflict are of different nationality, a further reason for submitting an art-related dispute to CAfA arbitration may be that arbitral awards in general are widely enforceable under the New York Convention.

2.5 Conclusion

It follows that CAfA arbitration is a suitable means of resolving various kinds of art-related disputes. This is particularly true for disputes about cultural heritage and looted art as well as contracts where the authentication of art is at issue. In other art-related disputes, the suitability depends on various relevant factors that have to be taken into consideration on a case-specific base. Thus far, these disputes have not found their way to CAfA arbitration yet. It is therefore worthwhile drawing attention to the opportunities that CAfA arbitration has to offer.

CHAPTER 3

THE HAGUE COURT OF ARBITRATION FOR AVIATION

Jan K. Schäfer & Rüdiger Morbach[1]

The Hague Court of Arbitration for Aviation ("Hague CAA") is a promising new arbitral institution under the auspices of the NAI. It is targeted at the particularly attractive global aviation market, where high amounts are in dispute and a particular need for speedy and efficient proceedings prevail. After an overview of the market for aviation disputes (1), the authors take a comparative look at the organization and rules of the Hague CAA (2) so as to explain in a short summary (3) how the Hague CAA makes the Netherlands an even more attractive venue for arbitration.

3.1 Aviation disputes

a) Industry overview

Aviation is a trillion-dollar business that is said to contribute up to 5% to global gross domestic product.[2] It is also a very diverse industry. Its stakeholders include aircraft production companies (airframe, aircraft engine and aircraft equipment manufacturers), aircraft operating companies (air carriers and their suppliers such as aircraft lessors and insurers, maintenance shops, jet brokers and travel agents), and infrastructure providers (airports, air traffic control, regulatory authorities) including all of their suppliers.

At the same time, the aviation industry is less litigation-prone than other industries (with EU passenger rights claims being a notable exception).[3]

1 Jan K. Schäfer (LLM) (Singapore) is a Partner at King & Spalding LLP in Frankfurt, Germany. He is a member of the Rules Standing Committee of the Hague CAA. Dr. Rüdiger Morbach, Maître en droit (Aix-Marseille III) is an Associate at King & Spalding LLP in Frankfurt, Germany, and a licensed pilot.

2 ICAO, World Aviation and the World Economy, https://www.icao.int/sustainability/pages/facts-figures_worldeconomydata.aspx (last accessed 18 December 2024).

3 In some EU countries, passenger rights claims on the basis of Regulation (EC) no 261/2004 are known to massively overload the local courts competent for the respective departure/arrival airport.

This is due to the fact that its stakeholders depend more on each other than in other industries. While a manufacturer will usually be able to switch suppliers if they run into trouble with a supplied part, switching suppliers is more complex for aviation companies whenever products need to be certified, as the new supplier needs to obtain certification. Therefore, an aircraft manufacturer will think twice before suing the only available supplier of a certain product, such as the manufacturer of the only aircraft engine or APU[4] certified for its aircraft.

For the same reason, the (currently) only two manufacturers of long-haul airliners have an immense bargaining power vis-à-vis their customers, as the quarrel between Qatar Airways and Airbus over paint cracks on delivered A350 aircraft illustrates.[5] While Qatar Airways initially sued Airbus at the High Court of London for damages in the amount of USD 2 billion,[6] the case was amicably settled, which might have had to do with Airbus cancelling an order of Qatar Airways for 50 A321neo aircraft.[7] With the Boeing 737 MAX 10 as the only possible competing product not being certified either at that point in time or even today, Qatar Airways apparently did not have many other options than to settle the dispute.

However, there is a strategic place for lawsuits in the aviation industry. As the Qatar Airways case seems to demonstrate, lawsuits apply pressure on the opposing party so as to improve a party's position in ensuing (settlement) negotiations. Lawsuits are also initiated to obtain interim measures with the aim of mitigating the consequences of the opposing party's breach of contract, for example through emergency arbitration. Lastly, lawsuits are initiated to resolve the dispute whenever the parties cannot reach a commercial solution.

Given the complexity and the highly regulated legal environment, disputes may arise in many different forms. As an example from the airframe manufacturer's perspective, provided by Airbus' Karl Hennessee (Head of Litigation, Investigations & Regulatory Affairs) at a Hague CAA event

4 Auxiliary Power Unit.

5 G. Mifsud, 'Qatar Airways v. Airbus', *Air & Space Law* 2022, p 519-522.

6 T. Hepher, 'Airbus and Qatar Airways settle bitter A350 jet row', *Reuters*, 2 February 2023, https://www.reuters.com/business/aerospace-defense/airbus-qatar-aim-settle-a350-row-early-today-sources-2023-02-01/ (last accessed 18 December 2024).

7 J. Flottau, 'Airbus, Qatar Airways Conflict Escalates With A321neo Order Termination', *Aviation Week*, 21 January 2022, https://aviationweek.com/air-transport/aircraft-propulsion/airbus-qatar-airways-conflict-escalates-a321neo-order-termination (last accessed 18 December 2024).

during Paris Arbitration Week 2024,[8] the following phases can be distinguished in the lifecycle of an aircraft:

Conception and initial design phase:
The aircraft is conceptualized based on market demand, technological advancements, and regulatory requirements, which requires collaboration between the aircraft manufacturer, suppliers, and potential customers to define specifications and features. Research and development are conducted to explore innovative technologies and design elements. Regulatory bodies may provide initial guidance, and governments and financial institutions provide development support. Disputes may arise, for example, from joint venture and consultancy contracts.

Development and testing:
Detailed engineering design of aircraft components and systems takes place. Prototypes and test aircraft are manufactured, and rigorous testing, including flight tests, ground tests, and simulations, takes place to ensure safety, performance, and compliance with regulations. Certification authorities work closely with the aircraft manufacturer to obtain airworthiness certification. Already at this stage, serious delays may occur, as Boeing currently experiences with its 737 MAX 10 aircraft.[9]

Manufacturing and production:
Production facilities are constructed or expanded. Suppliers for components, materials, and subsystems are selected. Aircraft components are assembled, systems are integrated, and final assembly takes place, quality control and assurance processes are implemented. Government involvement may include incentives, subsidies, or export support. The 17-year long trade dispute between Airbus and Boeing shows the great potential for disputes arising from government involvement in this phase.[10]

Entry into service:
The first aircraft is delivered to the launch customer. Training programs are conducted for pilots, maintenance crews, and ground staff. Maintenance and support infrastructure, including spare parts distribution networks, is established. Initial commercial flights and operational testing in real-world conditions take place. Marketing and promotion efforts are made to attract additional customers and orders. Problems occurring in this phase of the life cycle will affect opera-

8 Paris, 29 March 2024. Both authors were present.
9 G. Joshi, 'Will The Boeing 737 MAX 10 Be Certified This Year?', *Simple Flying*, 13 March 2024, https://simpleflying.com/boeing-737-max-10-certification-update-march-2024/ (last accessed 18 December 2024).
10 S. Amaro & L. Josephs, U.S. and EU resolve 17-year Boeing-Airbus trade dispute, CNBC,15June2021,https://www.cnbc.com/2021/06/15/us-and-eu-truce-boeing-airbus-dispute.html (last accessed 18 December 2024).

tions later, as can be seen from the failure of the Sukhoi Superjet outside of Russia (partly) due to problems with spare parts management.[11]

Commercialization and operation:
Full-scale production and delivery of aircraft to various customers worldwide. Airlines operate the aircraft within their fleets, generating revenue through passenger transport or cargo services. Continuous support and maintenance services are provided by the manufacturer and third-party service providers. Governments may offer financial incentives or support for airlines adopting environmentally friendly technologies. Continuous technical improvement and updates are made according to airworthiness requirements. Maintenance contracts are particularly critical (and therefore prone to disputes) as airlines lose money with every minute an aircraft cannot fly (so-called aircraft-on-ground, AOG events).

End of program and exit from service:
Demand for an aircraft can change due to market shifts, technological obsolescence, or regulatory challenges. Aircraft models are phased out from production lines, and older aircraft are retired from airline fleets, either being replaced by newer models or disposed due to economic factors. Retired airframes and components are recycled, overseen by certification authorities to ensure compliance. This includes the conversion of passenger aircraft to freighter aircraft (P2F). Owners, financial institutions, and investors assess the residual value of the aircraft and its parts. Suppliers and risk-sharing partners assess contractual exposure from the end of the program, for example long-term spare parts management.

Each and any of these steps may give rise to a dispute. And these are only the issues that aircraft manufacturers deal with. Aviation stakeholders are also responsible for some of the biggest infrastructure projects worldwide, such as the construction of new airports. In such constructions and the above steps in the lifecycle of an aircraft alike, many time-sensitive issues may surface. Thus, having a dispute resolution strategy at hand when confronted with a time-sensitive issue is vital. As part of such a dispute resolution strategy, aviation stakeholders often choose to insert an arbitration clause into their contracts. There are a number of good reasons for this.

b) Aviation Arbitration

Firstly, aviation disputes tend to be cross-border disputes, as manufacturers and suppliers, lessors and lessees, and insurers and insurants are scattered all over the world. As an example, Airbus Canada's approved suppliers for the A220 program (former Bombardier C-Series) in 2024 in-

11 'Last European operator gives up on Sukhoi Superjet 100?', *Aerotime*, 18 February 2019, https://www.aerotime.aero/articles/22377-last-european-operator-gives-up-on-sukhoi-superjet-100 (last accessed 18 December 2024).

cluded suppliers from 40 countries and 6 continents.[12] Choosing arbitration allows the parties to benefit from easier enforcement through the New York Convention, which 172 out of 193 UN Member States have signed (among them all approved A220 supplier states).[13] This is a major advantage compared to state court litigation, especially when more than two parties are involved.

Secondly, arbitration allows for quicker proceedings when compared to the different instances available at most state courts. Even with a well operating state court system, such as in the Netherlands, litigation takes time, especially in high-value disputes.[14] The involvement of court-appointed experts in civil law state court proceedings can also be protracted and time-consuming. Arbitration can be significantly quicker, with particularly pressing matters being handled by emergency arbitration instead of state court interim relief (which has its benefits too, which is why it should not be excluded in the arbitration agreement). However, arbitration is not always quicker. If highly in demand arbitrators are chosen, arbitration can even be substantially slower than first-instance state court proceedings. If the parties chose arbitration but need state court support in the proceedings (for example for the appointment of arbitrators, for challenging arbitrators, or for annulment proceedings after the award is rendered), the proceedings can be significantly slower.

Thirdly, arbitration allows for confidentiality. This plays a particular role in aircraft manufacturing, where any upcoming issue may be perceived by the public as a safety threat and therefore lead to reputational damage. An example of this is the public scrutiny Boeing is receiving at the moment of writing.[15] Incidents unrelated to Boeing's quality problems in manufacturing, such as a nose gear up landing of a 10-year-old freighter aircraft, receive worldwide coverage.[16] In this climate, any news of a conflict with a

---

12 Airbus Canada, Approved Suppliers List revised 21 February 2024, https://www.airbus.com/sites/g/files/jlcbta136/files/2024-02/A220-Program-Approved-Supplier-List.pdf (last accessed 18 December 2024).

13 New York Convention Contracting States, https://www.newyorkconvention.org/contracting-states (last accessed 18 December 2024).

14 D. Pistora, F. Van Dijk & R. Verkerk, 'Time Taken for Disposition of Commercial Disputes in the Netherlands', *Utrecht Law Review* 2024, p 44-63.

15 A. Fleck, 'Trust in Boeing Plummets After Safety Incidents', *Statista*, 18 March 2024, https://www.statista.com/chart/31928/net-trust-among-us-familiar-with-boeing-brand/ (last accessed 18 December 2024).

16 N. Turak, 'Boeing cargo plane lands without front nose gear in Istanbul; investigation launched', *CNBC*, 9 May 2024, https://www.cnbc.com/2024/05/09/boeing-

supplier would make the headlines. Confidential arbitration may prevent just that.

Fourthly, arbitration allows the parties to choose arbitrators who know the aviation business. This may make it easier for the parties to plead their case, especially when the case contains complicated technical details, which happens regularly in aviation cases. While state court judges and arbitrators alike rely on experts for these details, not having to explain every element in an aircraft engine is a significant upside of arbitrating aviation disputes.

Lastly, arbitration might even allow for lower legal fees. Aviation disputes tend to be high-stakes disputes, as every item to be purchased and every service to be paid is more expensive if it is labelled "aviation". From bolts and nuts that are five times the price, just because they are installed in an aircraft and not in a car, to simple maintenance tasks that require more paperwork than other work, nothing comes cheap in aviation. If the court fees are determined by the amount in dispute, these might be substantial even though the case is not complicated at all. If the arbitrators are paid by the hour, arbitration might even come cheaper than state-court litigation. In any event, the winning party may usually recover its attorney fees in full, and not only the statutory attorney fees as would often be the case in state court litigation (e.g., in Germany).

For these reasons and others, aviation stakeholders chose arbitration.
The number of arbitration cases in the public domain testify to this. Aircraft purchasers have taken aircraft manufacturers to arbitration,[17] lessees have sued lessors[18] and maintenance shops have sued airlines.[19] While the

---

cargo-plane-lands-without-front-nose-gear-in-istanbul-investigation-launched-.html (last accessed 18 December 2024).

17 Oceltip Aviation v. Gulfstream, ICDR Case No. 01-14-0001-3711, Final Award, 15 April 2016, https://jusmundi.com/fr/document/decision/en-oceltip-aviation-1-pty-ltd-v-gulfstream-aerospace-corporation-final-award-friday-15th-april-2016#decision_11320, (last accessed 18 December 2024).

18 Gryphon and FK Aviation v. Alpha Sierra Aviation *et al.*, JAMS Case No. 1100074613, Amended Final Award, 15 August 2014, https://jusmundi.com/fr/document/decision/en-gryphon-holdings-llc-and-fk-aviation-v-alpha-sierra-aviation-inc-sna-aircraft-sales-ltd-l-c-yacht-sales-charter-inc-aircraft-sales-ltd-jet-stream-escrow-and-title-service-inc-and-michael-k-stevens-plus-other-entities-amended-final-award-friday-15th-august-2014#decision_17049 (last accessed 18 December 2024).

19 GA Telesis v. Transaero Airlines, LCIA Case No. 153171, Final Award, 28 January 2016, https://jusmundi.com/fr/document/decision/en-ga-telesis-llc-v-ojsc-transaero-airlines-final-award-thursday-28th-january-2016 (last accessed 18 December 2024).

mentioned cases were commercial arbitrations, there are also a number of investor-state cases, mainly airlines[20] or airport developers[21] suing states.

c) Current and future disputes

A current source of disputes is the fallout of the Pratt & Whitney PW1000G crisis.[22] Teething problems of the newly developed geared turbofan engine have left and will leave hundreds of aircraft grounded for need of (replacement) engines[23] which may lead to billion-dollar damage claims and has led to at least one arbitration already.[24] Another arbitration concerns Pratt & Whitney's older and smaller PW600 series.[25] Pratt & Whitney's competitor Rolls-Royce is plagued by engine issues as well, concerning the new

20 Teinver v. Argentina, ICSID Case No. ARB/09/1, Award, 21 July 2017, https://jusmundi.com/en/document/decision/en-teinver-s-a-transportes-de-cercanias-s-a-and-autobuses-urbanos-del-sur-s-a-v-argentine-republic-award-friday-21st-july-2017#decision_334 (last accessed 18 December 2024); Air Canada v. Bolivarian Republic of Venezuela, ICSID Case No. ARB(AF)/17/1, Award, 13 September 2021, https://jusmundi.com/en/document/decision/en-air-canada-v-bolivarian-republic-of-venezuela-award-monday-13th-september-2021#decision_17731 (last accessed 18 December 2024).

21 Malicorp Limited v. Arab Republic of Egypt, ICSID Case No. ARB/08/18, Award, 7 February 2011, https://jusmundi.com/fr/document/decision/en-malicorp-limited-v-arab-republic-of-egypt-award-monday-7th-february-2011 (last accessed 18 December 2024).

22 D. Martinez Gabuno, "The Global Impact Of The Pratt & Whitney Engine Issues", *Simple Flying*, 17 November 2023, https://simpleflying.com/global-impact-pratt-whitney-engine-issues/ (last accessed 18 December 2024).

23 V. Insinna & A. Ganapavaram, 'RTX engine issue will ground 350 planes per year through 2026', *Reuters*, 12 September 2023, https://www.reuters.com/business/aerospace-defense/rtx-expects-3-bln-hit-q3-pratt-whitney-gtf-engine-issues-2023-09-11/ (last accessed 18 December 2024).

24 Go Airlines v. International Aero Engines, SIAC Case No. ABR077/23/RHM (C-ARB078/23/RHM, ARB079/23/RHM, ARB80/23/RHM), Award on the Claimant's Application for Emergency Interim Relief (No. 045 of 2023), 30 March 2023, https://jusmundi.com/fr/document/decision/en-go-airlines-india-limited-v-international-aero-engines-llc-award-on-the-claimants-application-for-emergency-interim-relief-thursday-30th-march-2023#decision_49539 (last accessed 18 December 2024).

25 Canada Superior Court of Quebec, 25 June 2024, 500-17-130087-243, Globe Air/Pratt & Whitney, Decision on Application for Referral to Arbitration and Interim Measures, 2024 QCCS 2451, https://www.canlii.org/en/ca/fct/doc/2004/2004fc38/2004fc38.html (last accessed 18 December 2024).

Trent XWB-97 engines[26] and the older GE90 engines.[27] The ongoing Boeing crises in which the delivery of the Boeing 777X has been severely delayed and is not likely to enter service before 2026[28] will likely result in aviation disputes as well.

Another source of disputes is Russia's invasion of Ukraine and ensuing international sanctions, which have left aircraft belonging to Western lessors and operated by Russian airlines stranded in Russia. Some of these aircraft were later re-registered in Russia and therefore effectively stolen.[29] While Russia has bought some of these planes from the respective lessors so as to avoid them from being attached by the lessors when flown on international routes,[30] this is not the case for all of them.

A potential area of future aviation disputes is the transition to eco-sustainable operations, which is particularly difficult in the aviation sector. Since battery or hydrogen powered airplanes will not become available for commercial air transport before the mid-2030s (and might never be an option for long-haul air transportation), airlines have to procure large amounts of Sustainable Aviation Fuel (SAF) and/or carbon credits, which are both a scarce resource and might come with quality problems. A number of airlines recently got a glimpse of this future when they were accused of greenwashing because their carbon offset schemes did not keep the promises they had made to their customers.[31]

26 L. Barrington, 'Cathay Pacific Airbus A350 engine part failure: What you need to know', *Reuters*, 3 September 2024, https://www.reuters.com/business/aerospace-defense/what-is-issue-with-cathay-pacifics-a350-rolls-royce-engines-2024-09-03/ (last accessed 18 December 2024).

27 M. Russel, 'Boeing 777 Engine Defect: FAA Proposes GE90 Airworthiness Directive The Global Impact Of The Pratt & Whitney Engine Issues', *Simple Flying*, 3 September 2023, https://simpleflying.com/faa-proposes-boeing-777-ge90-airworthiness-directive (last accessed 18 December 2024).

28 A. Chua, G. Dunn & L. Harpe, 'Emirates and Lufthansa chiefs reiterate concerns over 777X delivery dates', *FlightGlobal*, 4 June 2024, https://www.flightglobal.com/fleets/emirates-and-lufthansa-chiefs-reiterate-concerns-over-777x-delivery-dates/158608.article (last accessed 18 December 2024).

29 J. Ballantyne, 'LCIA hears claims over aircraft stranded in Russia', *Global Arbitration Review*, 1 June 2023, https://globalarbitrationreview.com/article/lcia-hears-claims-over-aircraft-stranded-in-russia (last accessed 18 December 2024).

30 'Russia completes buyouts of 92 foreign-owned planes', *Reuters*, 22 December 2023, https://www.reuters.com/business/aerospace-defense/russia-completes-buyouts-92-foreign-owned-planes-2023-12-22/ (last accessed 18 December 2024).

31 T. Sterling & J. Plucinska, 'Dutch court finds KLM ads were misleading in 'greenwashing' case', *Reuters*, 21 March 2024, https://www.reuters.com/business/aerospace-defense/dutch-court-rule-klm-greenwashing-case-2024-03-20/ (last accessed 18 December 2024); P. Georgiadis & K. Bryan, 'EU investigates 'Greenwashing'

3.2 The Hague CAA

Aviation disputes need a forum. If the parties choose arbitration in a contract, they usually also choose an arbitral institution according to whose rules the arbitration will be administered. Until recently, there was no dedicated body to turn to specifically for an aviation dispute, with the exception of the Shanghai International Aviation Court of Arbitration, a platform founded by the Shanghai International Arbitration Center (SHIAC) in 2014, and, limited to a panel of selected arbitrators, the International Centre for Dispute Resolution of the American Arbitration Association (AAA-ICDR), Panel for Aerospace, Aviation and National Security Disputes.

At the Farnborough International Airshow 2022, the Netherlands Arbitration Institute (NAI) launched The Hague Court of Arbitration for Aviation (Hague CAA), as a dedicated dispute resolution forum under its auspices and brain-child of its president, Gerard Meijer. From the aviation business side, the Hague CAA's founder Paul P. Jebely recruited a large international team of attorneys with an aviation and arbitration background who volunteered for supporting roles, such as sitting on the Advisory Board, the Technical Standing Committee, the Rules Standing Committee, and the Mediation Standing Committee or the Governance Support Team. Together, they aim to provide aviation stakeholders with a dedicated platform for aviation disputes that caters to the needs of speedy and cost-efficient proceedings with arbitrators that know the industry well.

The Hague CAA is not an own arbitral institution. Rather, proceedings under the Hague CAA rules are administered by the NAI, which has the necessary resources as well as 75 years of experience with arbitration matters. The administration fees and the hourly rates of arbitrators and tribunal secretaries are the same as in any NAI proceedings, which means that the aviation competence of the Hague CAA comes at no additional costs for the parties.

The Hague CAA adds significant value for aviation disputes. It curated a list of arbitrators with a background in aviation, which helps the parties to quickly identify a suitable candidate for the role of sole or presiding arbitrator. The Hague CAA Arbitration Rules are particularly adapted to the needs

at 20 airlines', *Financial Times*, 30 April 2024, https://www.ft.com/content/adec5d6d-24ed-4723-942a-d94d0aa53b8a (last accessed 18 December 2024).

of the aviation community (see below). The Hague CAA is more than a service provider for aviation disputes, though. It holds conferences throughout the world which particularly attract members of the aviation industry. Thereby, the Hague CAA also serves as a network of enthusiasts that promote aviation-specific dispute resolution, arbitration, and the rule of law.

The strong ties between the Hague CAA and the NAI are mutually beneficial. While the Hague CAA can count on the administrative support and the experience of the NAI, the Hague CAA connects the NAI to arbitration practitioners all over the world, which will bring in additional cases for the NAI to administer. Furthermore, the Hague CAA helps positioning the NAI as a truly international arbitral institution. Just recently, the Hague CAA signed a memorandum of understanding with the Singapore Mediation Center (SIMC) to help establish mediation as means of dispute resolution for aviation disputes in Asia.[32]

3.3 The Hague CAA Rules

The Hague CAA Rules, implemented in 2022 and updated in 2023,[33] do not differ greatly from the NAI Rules. Frequent users of the NAI Rules will feel at home when working with the Hague CAA rules, as the Hague CAA Rules were crafted on the basis of the 2015 NAI Rules.

a) Compared to the 2015 NAI Rules

The structure of the 2023 Hague CAA Rules follows the 2015 NAI Rules, with many provisions having been adopted almost verbatim. However, a number of new elements have been included in the Hague CAA Rules.

The most important novelty concerns the speed of the arbitration proceedings. The Hague CAA Rules oblige the arbitrators to render the final arbitral award within six months after the case management conference (Article 40 Hague CAA Rules), which (in conjunction with Article 23 Hague

32 'Asia's first specialized alternative dispute resolution mechanism for mediation in the aviation industry set to take off', *SIMC press release*, 21 February 2024, https://simc.com.sg/news/asias-first-specialized-alternative-dispute-resolution-mechanism-mediation-aviation-industry (last accessed 18 December 2024).

33 For an overview over the changes between both versions of the Hague CAA Rules see J. Schäfer & R. Morbach, 'Engine Overhaul: The Hague Court of Arbitration (Hague CAA) Updates its Rules', 22 June 2023, https://www.kslaw.com/news-and-insights/engine-overhaul-the-hague-court-of-arbitration-hague-caa-updates-its-rules (last accessed 18 December 2024).

CAA Rules) equals six months and ten days after the constitution of the arbitral tribunal. This is a novelty of the 2023 update of the Hague CAA Rules and represents a tectonic shift towards speedier proceedings. What had been expedited proceedings under the 2022 Hague CAA Rules, is now the default procedure. This follows frequent calls from members of the aviation community for more time-efficient proceedings, which are vital in aviation disputes. The time limit in Article 40 Hague CAA Rules is a significant deviation from the 2015 NAI Rules, which merely state that the arbitral tribunal "*shall decide expeditiously*" (Article 40 (1) 2015 NAI Rules) and do not set a time limit, not even for a decision in summary proceedings for provisional relief pursuant to Article 36 2015 NAI Rules.

The default expedited proceedings under the Hague CAA Rules are complemented by the possibility for the parties or the NAI case administrators to extend the contained time limits, which provides the necessary flexibility if a case cannot be handled in the ambitious timeline of the default proceedings. Furthermore, the arbitral tribunal (by its own motion or upon request of the parties) may conduct the proceedings as an "*extended arbitration*" without a time limit to render an award and with more generous deadlines for other procedural steps, if it determines that the matter is not suitable for the default, speedy approach (Article 22 (11) Hague CAA Rules). This is of particular relevance where the dispute proves to be more complex than anticipated and has to be established by different types of experts, for example in corrosion cases.[34]

Another new instrument is the early determination mechanism (Article 39 Hague CAA Rules), pursuant to which the parties may ask the arbitral tribunal to rule, in the form of a reasoned order or award, that individual factual or legal points are manifestly outside of the arbitral tribunal's jurisdiction, manifestly inadmissible, or manifestly without legal merit. It may help to delimit the dispute early on in the proceedings, which is of particular importance when one of the parties tries to blow the dispute out of proportion by making the dispute appear more complex than it actually is, which is a popular delaying tactic. Once the arbitral tribunal decides to make an early determination, it has to issue an order or an award making the early determination within 30 days.

34 See, for example, the case of Aloha Airlines Flight 243: National Transportation Safety Board (NTSB), Report of 28 April 1988, https://www.ntsb.gov/investigations/AccidentReports/Reports/AAR8903.pdf (last accessed 18 December 2024).

Further new provisions address multi-contract arbitrations (Article 10 Hague CAA Rules), diversity and environmental impact of the arbitration proceedings (Article 59 Hague CAA Rules), and personal data (Article 60 Hague CAA Rules). Under the Hague CAA Rules, the Parties have to disclose third-party funding (Article 7 (2) (j), Article 8 (2) (f) Hague CAA Rules), which will play a significant role in the high-stakes proceedings that the aviation industry is known for.

Other rules have been significantly modified. The Hague CAA Rules contain a far more comprehensive provision on confidentiality (Article 6 Hague CAA Rules) than the 2015 NAI Rules, which helps to protect the reputation of aviation stakeholders in cases that appear, at least *prima facie*, to be safety-related.

The paragraph on interim measures has been fully rewritten and now includes emergency arbitration (Artt. 35, 36 Hague CAA Rules), which is particularly helpful in an AOG event, where airport fees and lost profits quickly add up and may even threaten the existence of the aircraft operator.[35]

Furthermore, the Hague CAA Rules provide for more detailed rules on the case management conference (Article 23 Hague CAA Rules), on joinders (Article 37 Hague CAA Rules), and on consolidation (Article 38 Hague CAA Rules). Smaller changes include the requirement for the Chair of the arbitral tribunal or the sole arbitrator to be qualified to practice law (Article 12 (6) Hague CAA Rules), a default appointment method for sole arbitrators (direct appointment by the NAI case administrators, Article 14 (1) Hague CAA Rules), and the rule that the hearing is to take place electronically by default (Article 26 (2) Hague CAA Rules). Given that aviation disputes will often involve parties, witnesses, and experts from the four corners of the world, this might significantly reduce the costs of the dispute.

Conversely, some provisions of the 2015 NAI Rules have not been adopted by the Hague CAA Rules, for example Article 31 2015 NAI Rules on the

35 Go Airlines v. International Aero Engines, SIAC Case no ABR077/23/RHM (C-ARB078/23/RHM, ARB079/23/RHM, ARB80/23/RHM), Award on the Claimant's Application for Emergency Interim Relief (no 045 of 2023), 30 March 2023, https://jusmundi.com/fr/document/decision/en-go-airlines-india-limited-v-international-aero-engines-llc-award-on-the-claimants-application-for-emergency-interim-relief-thursday-30th-march-2023#decision_49539 (last accessed 18 December 2024).

personal appearance of the parties. The same applies to Article 49 2015 NAI Rules on the procedure following a state court's remission of the case to the arbitral tribunal in setting aside proceedings and Article 59 2015 NAI Rules on the jurisdiction of the provision relief judge if the arbitration is seated in the Netherlands. These provisions were, apparently, not deemed to be relevant in aviation disputes.

b) Compared to the 2024 NAI Rules

While the Hague CAA Rules were conceived on the basis of the 2015 NAI Rules, their successor, the 2024 NAI Rules, appear, in turn, to have been inspired by the Hague CAA Rules. However, the influence of the Hague CAA Rules on the 2024 NAI Rules appears to be significantly lower than the influence of the 2015 NAI Rules on the Hague CAA Rules.

Most importantly, the 2024 NAI Rules follow the Hague CAA Rules' push for faster arbitral proceedings, although not to the same degree. While the 2015 NAI Rules merely provided for expedited summary proceedings for provisional relief with a very narrow scope (Article 36 2015 NAI Rules) and no time limit to render the arbitral award, Article 46 2024 NAI Rules require the arbitrators to render an award within eight weeks after the last hearing, Article 41 and Appendix C 2024 NAI Rules provide for emergency arbitration, Article 42 and Appendix D 2024 NAI Rules for expedited proceedings (which are, however, not the default mode, other than in the Hague CAA). In this respect, the current version of the Hague CAA Rules serves the parties of an aviation dispute better, unless it is not time-critical.

The 2024 NAI Rules also contain provisions on diversity (Article 15 (5) 2024 NAI Rules), sustainability (Article 25 (5) 2024 NAI Rules) and personal data (Article 63 2024 NAI Rules). The Hague CAA Rules' obligation to disclose third-party funding has been adopted (Article 8 (2) (k), Article 9 (2) (f) 2024 NAI Rules). In addition to that, they also feature an early determination mechanism (Article 45 2024 NAI Rules), with the same time limit of 30 days as in the Hague CAA Rules, and a rule on multi-contract arbitrations (Article 11 2024 NAI Rules). Both are more elaborate than in the Hague CAA Rules, but not significantly different.

Overall, the 2024 NAI Rules provide a greater level of detail for most aspects of the arbitration proceedings, be it electronic communications (Article 4 2024 NAI Rules), the constitution of the arbitral tribunal (Article 13-19 2024 NAI Rules) or interim measures (Article 40 2024 NAI Rules). They also contain six appendices with details on case management, the challenge procedure, emergency and expedited arbitration, consolidation and the costs of the arbitration.

Several instruments that the 2015 NAI Rules already provided for but which the Hague CAA Rules did not adopt can be found in the 2024 NAI Rules, for example the third-party intervention or the impleader (Article 37/38 2015 NAI Rules, now Article 43 2024 NAI Rules). They are unlikely to appear in future versions of the Hague CAA Rules.

The 2024 NAI Rules also include an entirely new and innovative element, the mandatory midstream conference (Article 30 2024 NAI Rules), which has been said to have the potential of greatly improving the efficiency of arbitration proceedings.[36] This might not necessarily be true for aviation disputes. Given the short time limits in Hague CAA proceedings, having to organize a midstream conference might just overburden the tight timeline the parties and the arbitral tribunal are confronted with. Even if a suitable date can be found, the celerity of the proceedings might overtake the plans to hold a mandatory midstream conference. Flexibility is key in time-critical proceedings, which is why the mandatory midstream conference is probably not the right fit for aviation disputes.

From an administrative point of view, the 2024 NAI Rules introduce the NAI arbitration platform, a digital platform to electronically exchange documents which most arbitral institutions have implemented in recent years. This is particularly helpful in time-critical proceedings in which large numbers of emails are exchanged and can get lost in the rush of inbound mail. Furthermore, Article 27 (1) 2024 NAI Rules sets the default seat of the arbitration proceedings to Amsterdam, which is helpful when the parties have not determined the seat. The Hague CAA does not contain such a provision.

Given the influence the 2015 NAI Rules had on the Hague CAA Rules, it appears likely that future versions of the Hague CAA Rules will be inspired by the updated 2024 NAI Rules, if only for significant updates vis-à-vis the Hague CAA Rules such as the NAI arbitration platform and the midstream conference.

36 K. Sachs, 'Do We Deliver: How to Make International Arbitration More Efficient', in: N. Kaplan et al (eds), *International Arbitration: When East Meets West – Liber Amicorum Michael Moser*, Deventer: Wolters Kluwer 2020, p 224-227.

c) Compared to other institutional rules

When compared to other institutions for aviation disputes, the Hague CAA Rules are one of a kind.

The AAA-ICDR only provide for a dedicated panel of arbitrators for aviation disputes (which the Hague CAA also does), not for specific rules for such disputes. The 2024 SHIAC Aviation Arbitration Rules merely contain a few amendments and modifications to the default 2024 SHIAC Rules, while the Hague CAA Rules are an independent set of rules that do not make reference to the NAI Rules. This adds to the Hague CAA's character of a self-standing institution for aviation disputes but comes at the price of having to update the Hague CAA Rules independently from the NAI Rules, which requires consent between Hague CAA and NAI executives (Article 62 (2) Hague CAA Rules).

When compared to other institutional rules, the Hague CAA Rules are on a par with the rules of other arbitration institutions. While they were crafted from the 2015 NAI Rules which appear somewhat outdated today, the Hague CAA Rules modernized in the most relevant areas, for example by using expedited proceedings as a default and by implementing emergency arbitration. Of course, innovations of the 2024 NAI Rules, such as the midstream conference (Article 30 2024 NAI Rules), have yet to be implemented into the Hague CAA Rules.

Regarding the costs of the arbitration proceedings, the Hague CAA Rules follow the approach of the NAI to charge a certain administration fee depending on the amount in dispute (between € 660 and € 75,000) and to calculate the arbitrator fees by the hours spent and the amount in dispute, ranging between € 175 and € 575 per hour. Most arbitration institutions (e.g., the ICC) do not apply hourly arbitrator fees, but rather use a certain percentage of the amount in dispute which they can then adapt according to the time and efforts the arbitrator had to apply. In this respect, the Hague CAA Rules follow the Rules of the London Court of International Arbitration (LCIA).[37] Like the LCIA Rules, the Hague CAA Rules also provide for hourly fees for the tribunal's secretary.

Other than the 2021 ICC Rules, the Hague CAA Rules do not provide for a formal scrutiny mechanism. The ICC scrutiny mechanism is often said

37 LCIA Schedule of Arbitration Costs (2023).

to improve the quality of arbitral awards,[38] but it also requires significant resources at the arbitral institution. The 2024 NAI Rules now provide for a limited scrutiny of arbitral awards, which excludes, however, the reasoning of the award (Article 50 2024 NAI Rules). Implementing at least this limited scrutiny mechanism into the Hague CAA Rules would certainly be beneficial for the quality of arbitral awards rendered under the Hague CAA Rules.

3.4 Summary

The Hague CAA is the first dedicated forum for aviation disputes in the world which not only provides arbitrators with the relevant expertise and a capable and experienced arbitral institution in the background (the NAI), but also a comprehensive set of rules that were developed from the 2015 NAI Rules specifically for aviation disputes. This combination sets it apart from other aviation arbitration fora like the SHIAC's Shanghai International Aviation Court of Arbitration, and the AAA-ICDR's Panel for Aerospace, Aviation and National Security Disputes.

The Hague CAA Rules provide a balance between a proven set of rules, the 2015 NAI Rules, and a number of innovations, some of which made their way into the 2024 NAI Rules. Further innovations in the 2024 NAI Rules that make sense for aviation disputes have yet to be implemented into the Hague CAA Rules, which might happen rather sooner than later, given the Hague CAA's pledge to keep their rules updated and the first significant update of the Hague CAA Rules coming one year after their launch in 2023.

All these elements make the Hague CAA a good choice for any aviation dispute, whether it concerns aircraft or aircraft engine construction, maintenance, leasing, insurance or any other aviation dispute. Time will tell whether the industry prefers the Hague CAA over other fora. Given that aviation contracts are often one sided (for example a dispute between an aircraft manufacturer and a small equipment supplier), with the dispute resolution mechanism depending on what the dominant party provides for in its general terms, it will come down to convincing the big players

38 S. Greenberg, 'Arbitral Award Scrutiny under Scrutiny – An Assessment', in: P. Habegger et al (eds), *Arbitral Institutions Under Scrutiny – ASA Special Series No. 40*, 2013, p 104.

of the aviation industry that the Hague CAA is the place to resolve their disputes. If they go ahead, the rest will follow.

In any event, the Hague CAA is a great addition to the already strong arbitration market in the Netherlands. Aviation stakeholders from all over the world will consider having their disputes administered by the NAI, with probably many of them also opting for a Dutch seat of the arbitration. This will bring more arbitration business to the Netherlands, including to Dutch state courts in ancillary proceedings. These developments, brought about by the Hague CAA, will help spread the word that it is a good idea to arbitrate in the Netherlands.

CHAPTER 4

ARBITRATION IN INTELLECTUAL PROPERTY DISPUTES

Anne Marie Verschuur[1]

4.1 Introduction

According to the World Intellectual Property Organisation ("WIPO"),[2] arbitration is well suited for intellectual property ("IP") cases:

> "Intellectual property rights are as strong as the means to enforce them. In that context, arbitration, as a private and confidential procedure, is increasingly being used to resolve disputes involving intellectual property rights, especially when involving parties from different jurisdictions. Intellectual property disputes have a number of particular characteristics that may be better addressed by arbitration than by court litigation."[3]

Does the field of IP indeed lend itself so well to arbitration?[4] This question can be divided into two key questions: (i) is arbitration allowed from a jurisdictional point of view (see para 4.2 below), and (ii) is arbitration a suitable medium for resolving IP cases (see para 4.3 below)? The present article addresses both questions, focusing in particular on the Dutch perspective: I will therefore mostly look at Dutch law and NAI arbitration. I will also briefly discuss the WIPO Arbitration and Mediation Center as well as the (potential) role of the Patent Mediation and Arbitration Centre, which is part of the Unified Patent Court system (a new European court for patent cases, currently in force in 18 EU member states[5]).

---

1 A.M.E. (Anne Marie) Verschuur (LLM) is a lawyer (*advocaat*) at De Brauw Blackstone Westbroek N.V. in Amsterdam, the Netherlands.

2 In existence since 1967, WIPO describes itself as "the United Nations agency that serves the world's innovators and creators, ensuring that their ideas travel safely to the market and improve lives everywhere" (see www.wipo.int/about-wipo/en/).

3 www.wipo.int/amc/en/arbitration/why-is-arb.html.

4 In this article, I do not discuss other modes of alternative dispute resolution, such as mediation.

5 See for more information https://www.unified-patent-court.org/en.

Before I turn to the actual topic of this article, I will first, however, for those readers who do not specialise in IP law, make some introductory remarks on the variety of IP disputes that can arise, as well as on some specific procedural IP rules.

IP-related disputes often concern an alleged infringement of an IP right. One party then argues that the other party is infringing this right (e.g., a trade mark or patent) and the other defends itself against this by arguing that this is not the case; e.g., because one does not perform the alleged act and, moreover, the right invoked is not valid. Also often invoked, under Article 6:162 Dutch Civil Code ("DCC"), is unfair competition: more particularly the unnecessary causing of a likelihood of confusion (also called "slavish imitation"). Furthermore, a revocation action (i.e. an action aimed at invalidating an IP right) can be filed. Another type of dispute that regularly occurs is an (alleged) breach of: an IP licence agreement, a non-disclosure agreement ("NDA"), or a research & development ("R&D") agreement. Trade secrets are also increasingly in dispute, likely influenced by the implementation of the Trade Secrets Directive.[6]

If such disputes escalate, the most customary route in the Netherlands is to start preliminary injunction proceedings or proceedings on the merits; this will come as no surprise to practitioners. Importantly, there are various IP-specific rules mainly laid down in Article 1019 ff of the Dutch Code of Civil Procedure ("DCCP"). For instance, pursuant to Article 1019e DCCP, there is the possibility of requesting an "*ex parte*" injunction in urgent infringement cases, particularly if delay would cause irreparable harm; this can be done without the alleged infringer having been heard and such an injunction can be obtained as quickly as an attachment order. Furthermore, for patent cases, the District Court of The Hague has created accelerated proceedings on the merits, known as the "*Versneld Regime Octrooizaken*" ("VRO").[7] It is also relevant to mention that both the District Court of The Hague and the Court of Appeal of The Hague have

6 Directive (EU) 2016/943 of the European Parliament and of the Council of 8 June 2016 on the protection of undisclosed know-how and business information (trade secrets) from unauthorised acquisition, use and disclosure, OJ 2016, L 157/1.

7 For more on this, see https://www.rechtspraak.nl/Organisatie-en-contact/Organisatie/Rechtbanken/Rechtbank-Den-Haag/Over-de-rechtbank/Rechtsgebieden-en-teams/Paginas/Procesreglement-voor-versnelde-bodemprocedure-in-octrooizaken.aspx.

special expertise in IP cases. This is no coincidence, as they have exclusive jurisdiction in most patent, EU trade mark and Community design cases.[8]

After this brief introduction, one may wonder whether it is really necessary to devote attention to the subject outlined at the beginning of this article. After all, IP is a very specialised subject, there are specific procedural rules and there are specialised judges. In my view, however, a conclusion along those lines is a bit too hasty. While all true, arbitration also has advantages: think, for instance, of automatic confidentiality (a hearing "behind closed doors" is an option in Dutch courts, but not a given) and the cross-examination of witnesses and experts. I will discuss this, and more, below.

4.2 Jurisdiction

An important question to be answered, as also indicated above, is of course whether a choice of arbitration can in fact be made in IP disputes. Does the court not have exclusive jurisdiction, at least in certain disputes? Below, I will first mention the most relevant legal provisions and will then turn to the (limited) available case law, as well as an analysis of both. This is followed by a small foray abroad, a brief introduction to three existing specific IP arbitration regimes, and, lastly, a conclusion.

4.2.1 Jurisdictional rules in DCCP and IP laws

Article 1020(1) DCCP provides that parties may by agreement submit disputes to arbitration. This may involve both disputes resulting from a legal relationship arising from an agreement and other disputes. Yet, it is clear from Article 1020(3) DCCP that the parties do not enjoy absolute freedom in this respect: namely, the arbitration agreement may not serve to determine legal consequences that may not be freely determined by the parties.

Various IP laws contain specific rules regarding jurisdiction. Article 80 of the Dutch Patent Act 1995 ("DPA"), for instance, provides that the court of The Hague has exclusive jurisdiction over all kinds of patent disputes: including infringement, nullification, entitlement and compulsory licences. There is a similar provision for plant variety cases: Article 78 Dutch Plant

8 For an overview of IP procedural law, see, for example, A.M.E. Verschuur, 'Chapter XII. Handhaving', in: P.G.F.A. Geerts & A.M.E. Verschuur (eds), *Kort Begrip van het Intellectuele Eigendomsrecht*, Deventer: Wolters Kluwer 2024, p 789-826.

Variety Act 2005. The District Court of The Hague has also been designated as an EU Trade Mark and Community Design Court (Article 3 Community Trade Mark Regulation Implementation Act ("CTMR Implementation Act") in conjunction with Article 123 EU Trade Mark Regulation and Article 3 EC Community Designs Regulation Implementation Act in conjunction with Article 81 Community Designs Regulation).[9] Furthermore, the Dutch Copyright Act, for example, designates the District Court of The Hague as the court with exclusive jurisdiction in several articles (see Article 15e and Article 16g Dutch Copyright Act). However, such an arrangement does not exist in relation to all IP rights, albeit that the special expertise of the courts of The Hague does have the effect of attracting relevant cases: if a choice can be made between different Dutch IP courts, the court of choice is often The Hague.

4.2.2 *Case law*

An important question, given the special jurisdiction rules mentioned above, is of course whether these rules preclude certain disputes being resolved through arbitration. There is some case law on this point (both arbitral awards and court judgments) and I will thus discuss this. A handicap here, it should be noted, is the confidentiality of arbitral awards, so it is quite possible that there are relevant awards that I am unaware of.

4.2.2.1 Infringement

A 1997 judgment by the District Court of Amsterdam[10] indicates that patent infringement had been ruled on in an arbitration some years earlier. The arbitrator had ruled that a certain product fell within the scope of protection of a patent and that the parties concerned both had to pay damages. Both parties then requested that the arbitral awards be set aside, but

9 As an aside, in reply to a question raised by the Supreme Court regarding the possible jurisdiction of other courts in relation to provisional and protective measures, the CJEU ruled: "Article 90(1) of Council Regulation (EC) no 6/2002 of 12 December 2001 on Community designs must be interpreted as meaning that the courts and tribunals of the Member States with jurisdiction to order provisional measures, including protective measures, in respect of a national design also have jurisdiction to order such measures in respect of a Community design" (CJEU 21 November 2019, case C-678, ECLI:EU:C:2019:998). This means, for the Netherlands, that also courts outside The Hague have jurisdiction for such measures.

10 Amsterdam District Court 19 March 1997, *TvA* 1998, p 72, annotated by W.D.H. Asser & G.J. Meijer (*Woudsma/Woodcap en Woodcap/Woudsma*).

did not address the question of whether the dispute could, in view of Article 80 DPA, be submitted to arbitration.

In another case, *Est/Ipco*,[11] the District Court of The Hague held that it had jurisdiction despite an arbitration clause. The claim in question concerned an action to stop infringement of a Community trade mark and defendant Ipco argued, among other things, that the court did not have jurisdiction in view of an arbitration clause in a distribution agreement. However, the court ruled that reliance on the arbitration clause could not succeed already on the basis of the exclusive jurisdiction of the District Court of The Hague laid down in Article 92 Community Trade Mark Regulation in conjunction with Article 3 of its implementation act.

4.2.2.2 Granting and entitlement

In 1944, the Dutch Patent Office held in a decision[12] that the parties to the dispute could not, by way of an arbitration clause, exclude the Patent Office from deciding their dispute. The dispute concerned the issue to whom a patent should be granted in whole, in part or in co-ownership. The applicant had argued that under an agreement entered into by the parties, all disputes between them were to be decided by arbitration. But the Patent Office did not go along with this argument, stating, among other things, that the law exclusively entrusts the granting of patents to the Patent Office, and that it was inconsistent with such a system (in which the Patent Office is the entity that decides) to accept that proceedings to be conducted before the Patent Office could be replaced by proceedings before arbitrators through agreement by the parties.

In a ruling by the Foundation Council for Arbitration for the Metal Industry and Trade, the arbitrator ruled that, in view of Article 54 of the Dutch Patent Act 1910 (similar to the current Article 80 DPA), he did not have jurisdiction over the filed patent entitlement claim and the claim for compensation.[13]

11 The Hague District Court 7 November 2006, ECLI:NL:RBSGR:2006:BB2077, *BIE* 2007/107 (*Est/Ipco*).

12 Dutch Patent Office, Appellate Division, 7 December 1944, *BIE* 1945/26 (*aanvrager/Penners*).

13 Foundation Council for Arbitration for the Metal Industry and Trade (in Dutch: "Stichting Raad van Arbitrage voor de Metaalnijverheid en -Handel") 15 May 2000, *TvA* 2002/32 (*P and Z/S*).

In 2012, in the *Ruma/Swellfix* case, the District Court of The Hague declared that it lacked jurisdiction because of an arbitration clause.[14] In this case, Ruma claimed a number of patents and patent applications. Such an entitlement claim falls within the scope of Article 80 DPA, which would mean that the court had jurisdiction. However, Swellfix took the position that the NAI arbitrator appointed in a cooperation agreement concluded between the parties had exclusive jurisdiction. Ruma disputed this and, citing various sources,[15] argued that the case could not be subject to arbitration pursuant to Article 1020(3) DCCP. This article (further discussed below) states that the arbitration agreement shall not serve to determine legal consequences that may not be freely determined by the parties.

However, the court rejected the reliance on Article 1020(3) DCCP and ruled that Article 80 DPA is aimed at concentrating entitlement claims in one court to promote specialisation, but does not exclude arbitration. According to the court, the question of who is entitled to apply for patents for certain inventions is not a question the answer to which leads to the determination of legal consequences that may not be freely determined by the parties.

The court further examined whether the arbitration clause was compatible with higher regulations. Since it also concerned applications for a European patent, the court held that the Protocol on Jurisdiction and the Recognition of Decisions in respect of the Right to the Grant of a European Patent should also be considered. However, the Protocol contains no provision on arbitration and the court saw no reason to assume that the Protocol precludes arbitration.

4.2.2.3 Interim conclusion

As the above shows, the amount of case law is limited. Nevertheless, to some extent a common denominator can be discerned. In the two infringement cases, the question of jurisdiction arose only once, and the court's ruling was that there was no room for arbitration. In the cases about enti-

14 The Hague District Court 2 May 2012, ECLI:NL:RBSGR:2012:BW7047, *IER* 2012/61, annotated by F. Eijsvogels (*Ruma/Swellfix*).

15 These sources are: H.J. Snijders, *Nederlands Arbitragerecht*, Deventer: Kluwer 2007, note 5(d) at Article 1020 DCCP; G.J. Meijer, *Overeenkomst tot arbitrage*, Deventer: Kluwer 2011, p 832-833; P. Sanders, *Het Nederlandse arbitragerecht*, Deventer: Kluwer 2001, p 36-37; Supreme Court 10 November 2006, ECLI:NL:HR:2006:AY4033, *NJ* 2007/561, annotated by H.J. Snijders (*Groenselect/Van den Boogaard*).

tlement, the opinion in the two older cases discussed above was negative, but the District Court of The Hague ruled in a more recent case that there is room for arbitration.

I further note that the above decisions all concern cases in which there is a specific statutory provision designating a competent court. Whether similar issues arise in cases where this is not the case, for example, is in any case not apparent from this case law. Furthermore, the case law discussed looks at the more classic IP disputes such as entitlement and infringement of IP rights and therefore does not, for example, cover disputes on the amount of the fee to be paid under an IP licence, nor does it cover related areas such as trade secrets or slavish imitation (unfair competition).

4.2.2.4 Analysis

As mentioned, the amount of case law on the question of jurisdiction is scarce; moreover, it all concerns decisions by lower authorities. Nevertheless, especially the fairly recent *Ruma/Swellfix* judgment by the specialised court in The Hague, discussed above, does indicate a line of thought; namely, that: (i) the existence of a specific designation of a court does not exclude arbitration; and (ii) the key question to be answered (in line with Article 1020(3) DCCP) is whether the question at issue leads to the determination of *"legal consequences that may not be freely determined by the parties"*.

The logical follow-up question then becomes: in what circumstances are there *"legal consequences that may not be freely determined by the parties"*? This is not elaborated in statutes, but according to the literature, it concerns *"matters that are of public policy because they have effect against everyone"*, citing as an example the grant or nullification of a patent.[16]

An important decision in this respect is the *Groenselect* judgment.[17] In it, the Supreme Court ruled that the annulment of a decision of a legal entity may not be freely determined by the parties; the decisive factor in this respect was that such an annulment often has far-reaching legal consequences,

16 *Parliamentary Papers II* 2012/13, 33 611, no 3, p 4; see also G.J. Meijer et al, *Parlementaire geschiedenis Arbitragewet*, Deventer: Kluwer 2015, p 20 and G.J. Meijer, *T&C Burgerlijke Rechtsvordering*, Article 1020 DCCP, note 6(a) (online, last updated 1 January 2024).

17 Supreme Court 10 November 2006, ECLI:NL:HR:2006:AY4033, *NJ* 2007/561, annotated by H.J. Snijders (*Groenselect/Van den Boogaard*).

including for third parties. And the court order nullifying such decision or declaring it null and void (both when it has internal effect and when it also has external effect!) by its nature has an effect in relation to everyone – not only in relation to the person who requested the annulment.

When may legal consequences not be freely determined by the parties? In other words when are they a matter of public policy? According to Meijer, this must be assessed on a case-by-case basis, but indications as to whether a case is of public policy include the following:

- legal provisions prescribing exclusive jurisdiction for a specific, named, court. However, Meijer also notes that the intention of such provisions is often only to declare a court to have exclusive jurisdiction vis-à-vis other courts, so the exclusive jurisdiction need not apply vis-à-vis arbitration;
- whether far-reaching legal consequences are involved and whether legal certainty is at stake; and
- whether, by its nature, the judgment sought has effect in relation to any person and not just the litigants involved.[18]

Applying this to IP cases, on the first point, as already explained above, there are several legal provisions in which the District Court of The Hague has been afforded exclusive jurisdiction. However, the reasons for this mainly seem to be specialisation, uniformity of case law[19] and (specifically for trade marks and designs) a wish to delimit the powers of the Benelux Office for Intellectual Property[20] (see also *Ruma/Swellfix*, discussed above).[21]

18 G.J. Meijer, in: *T&C Rv*, Article 1020 DCCP, note 6 (online, last updated 1 January 2024), with reference to Supreme Court 10 November 2006, ECLI:NL:HR:2006:AY4033, *NJ* 2007/561, annotated by H.J. Snijders (*Groenselect/Van den Boogaard*).

19 See the Explanatory Memorandum to the law with which the Dutch Patent Act 1910 was implemented (Schuurman & Jordens, *Rijksoctrooiwet*, Zwolle: W.E.J. Tjeenk Willink 1992).

20 Previously named the Benelux Trade Marks Office.

21 See also Sanders, who writes that in his view, a reference to a court in a legal provision does not automatically mean that only that court has jurisdiction; see P. Sanders, *Het nieuwe arbitragerecht*, Deventer: Kluwer 1996, p 26. He, however, continues by writing that the provisions regarding Benelux trade marks and patents exclude arbitration in those areas (Sanders 1996, p 29-30; see also Sanders 2001, p 36-38); see thus (re Benelux trade marks) also A. Komen & D.W.F. Verkade, *Het nieuwe merkenrecht*, Deventer: Kluwer 1970, p 122; A.J. van den Berg, R. van Delden & H.J. Snijders, *Arbitragerecht*, Zwolle: W.E.J. Tjeenk Willink 1992, p 39; A. Tsoutsanis, 'Artikel 14D BMW en 92 GMV: .nl-domeinnaamarbitrage onwettig', *BIE* 2003, p 153-157. However, the majority of the literature seems of the view that infringement claims *can* be submitted to arbitration; see e.g. W.L. Haardt, 'Procesrechtelijke

The second point, in particular legal certainty, may play a role in IP cases. For example, this can be the case in infringement cases in which the scope of protection of a patent is at issue and the patentee relies on, for example, the description of the patent (and thus not only the literal text of the claims). According to the Protocol on the Interpretation of Article 69 EPC, the interpretation of a patent must provide both a fair protection for the patent proprietor and a reasonable degree of legal certainty for third parties. Although in principle a decision on infringement only directly concerns the parties to the case, it may be relevant for the interpretation of the patent in other similar cases.

According to Van der Burg, an arbitral tribunal can rule on the scope of protection of a patent and the infringement thereof.[22] Eijsvogels also holds this view; he writes that he believes that the parties are free to agree with each other that an arbitral tribunal is competent to rule on the scope of protection and infringement of a patent, including on any invalidity defence. He adds that the arbitral award will only have effect *inter partes*.[23] Several other writers also believe that infringement cases can be submitted to arbitration.[24]

However, I think this is still open to debate, especially if a nullity defence is also raised; compare the *Groenselect* case mentioned above[25] in which the annulment of a decision with *internal* effect was also held not to be arbitrable. Does a successful nullity defence, as a result of which an IP right in fact does not apply between the parties, not amount to *de facto* holding the right invalid in the internal relationship of the parties? And also externally, the success or failure of such a defence may influence other, comparable

---

aspecten van de Benelux-Merkenwet', *BIE* 1970, p 305 and the more recent sources mentioned in footnote 24.

22 M.W.D. van der Burg, 'De arbitrabiliteit van inbreuk en nietigheid in octrooizaken', *TvA* 2003, p 8.

23 The Hague District Court 2 May 2012, ECLI:NL:RBSGR:2012:BW7047, *IER* 2012/61, annotated by F. Eijsvogels (*Ruma/Swellfix*). See also F.W.E. Eijsvogels, 'Alternatieve geschillenbeslechting', in: F.W. Grosheide (ed), *Handhaving van intellectuele Eigendom*, Amsterdam: deLex 2016, p 371.

24 See T. Cohen Jehoram, C.J.J.C. van Nispen & J.L.R.A. Huydecoper, *Industriële Eigendom. No 2. Merkenrecht*, Deventer: Kluwer 2008, p 381-382 and p 573; C.J.J.C. van Nispen, J.L.R.A. Huydecoper & T. Cohen Jehoram, *Industriële Eigendom. No 3. Vormen, namen en reclame*, Deventer: Kluwer 2012, p 278; Eijsvogels 2016, p 371; H.J. Snijders, in: *GS Burgerlijke Rechtsvordering*, Article 1020 DCCP, note 4.5 (online, last updated 1 May 2018); D.W.F. Verkade, *Bescherming van het uiterlijk van producten*, Deventer: Kluwer 1985, p 105.

25 Supreme Court 10 November 2006, ECLI:NL:HR:2006:AY4033, *NJ* 2007/561, annotated by H.J. Snijders (*Groenselect/Van den Boogaard*).

situations. Parties may, for instance, decide to market a product falling within the scope of protection of an IP right if a nullity defence succeeds (after all, the risk does not seem so great then). Or a patentee may start summoning parties, reinforced by the failure of such a defence. And yet another example: a patentee may decide to limit its patent if a nullity defence succeeds. What all of these examples have in common is that they have been influenced by a more informed assessment of possible chances of litigation, albeit with no certainty about those. A counter-argument might be that this may be more about the consequence of the public nature of the administration of justice than legal certainty – but does this not touch on public policy, or is this not otherwise a principle to be respected?

The third issue, namely whether, by its nature, the judgment sought has effect in relation to any person and not only in relation to the litigants involved, in any event arises in cases where the annulment, nullity or lapse of an IP right is sought.[26] After all, if an IP right is annulled or declared lapsed, it no longer exists, both vis-à-vis the litigants and vis-à-vis third parties. This means, for example, that it can no longer be invoked against third parties. The decision may also be relevant to, for example, licences and rights of pledge.

Van den Burg writes that nullifying a patent also interferes with competition and is, therefore, also related to public policy. Incidentally, he also describes some possibilities to circumvent the "nullity objections by entering into legally creative agreements".[27] Here, however, I think caution is appropriate because this is not in line with the spirit of Article 1020(3) DCCP. Furthermore, as Eijsvogels also notes, the question is whether certain "creative" agreements cannot still lead to the setting aside of an arbitral award under Article 1065(1)(e) DCCP.[28]

In any case, De Witt Wijnen is not convinced; he disagrees with the competition law line of thinking (which I do not further discuss here – no doubt a separate article can be written about this) and further states that he has

26 See also Van der Burg 2003, p 6-7. See also H.W. Wefers Bettink, 'Arbitrage van Merkengeschillen', *TvA* 2004/2, p 6-7; he also writes, after having established that arbitrators cannot issue a decision *erga omnes* and it is thus not logical that they would be able to declare an IP right invalid or lapsed, that arbitrators can issue a decision binding the parties (p 70).

27 Van der Burg 2003, p 7 et seq.

28 Eijsvogels 2016, p 369-370.

never seen a (proper) definition of the *"erga omnes effect"*. He adds that there are many arbitral decisions with *erga omnes* effect.[29]

Whatever may be said of the latter, a decision on, for example, the nullity of a patent does, in my view, have effect "vis-à-vis everyone", as now also follows from the legislative history mentioned above. This means that claims for nullification, invalidity or lapse of an IP right cannot be subjected to arbitration.[30] A parallel with the *Groenselect case*[31] mentioned above also arises: there too, nullity/nullification, albeit of a decision of a legal person, was held not arbitrable.

Also an entitlement claim can have legal effect towards third parties; for example, as Eijsvogels notes in his case comment to the *Ruma/Swellfix* judgment, a final decision on an entitlement claim is entered in the patent register (Article 78(8) DPA) and an award of such a claim can also have legal effect against third parties, such as licensees and pledgees.[32]

It is also relevant to note that various arguments are often made in IP disputes. In an infringement case, for example, a nullity defence, and often a corresponding counterclaim, are fairly standard. Furthermore, in many disputes, different rights are invoked: a claim based on, for example, trade mark infringement, copyright infringement and slavish imitation is certainly not unusual. And cross-border claims are also quite often brought. All this can complicate the assessment of the arbitrability of a claim.

---

29 O.L.O. de Witt Wijnen, 'De herziening en het ABC', *TvA* 2005/28, p 11-13. Also of the view that invalidity claims are, or can be, arbitrable: H.J. Snijders, in: *GS Burgerlijke Rechtsvordering*, Article 1020 DCCP, note 4.5 (online, last updated 1 May 2018).

30 Also of the view that invalidity/lapse cannot be claimed in arbitration: Ch. Gielen & L. Wichers Hoeth, *Merkenrecht*, Zwolle: W.E.J. Tjeenk Willink 1992, p 536; 14; P.A. Stein et al, *Compendium Burgerlijk Procesrecht*, Deventer: Wolters Kluwer (online), 14.1.4; Cohen Jehoram, Van Nispen & Huydecoper 2008, p 573; L.C.M. Berger & E.H. Janssen, 'De voor- en nadelen van arbitrage', *Bb* 2017/10, p 31; Verkade 1985, p 105. And see also Meijer, albeit that he does note: "Is it really undesirable that this kind of cases only ends up at the common courts?" (G.J. Meijer, 'Arbitrage in het ondernemingsrecht; inleiding en enkele aanvullende beschouwingen', *Ondernemingsrecht* 2010/2, sub 2.7).

31 Supreme Court 10 November 2006, ECLI:NL:HR:2006:AY4033, *NJ* 2007/561, annotated by H.J. Snijders (*Groenselect/Van den Boogaard*).

32 The Hague District Court 2 May 2012, ECLI:NL:RBSGR:2012:BW7047, *IER* 2012/61, annotated by F. Eijsvogels (*Ruma/Swellfix*).

4.2.3 *Foreign literature and case law*

Although a comparative law analysis of the subject of this contribution is beyond the character of this article – and I certainly did not do any in-depth research of the foreign literature and jurisprudence – I will briefly touch upon some points that caught my attention.

It is relevant to mention, first of all, that also abroad there seems to be a reluctance to consider invalidity proceedings arbitrable. For example, in *Scherk Enterprises/SGM*, the parties had a dispute about a trade mark licence agreement under Swiss law that contained an arbitration clause that chose Zurich as the seat of arbitration. Scherk claimed that SGM was using the trade marks in question in Italy without paying a licence fee and sought "*cancellation*" of the agreement in arbitration. Among other things, SGM asked the Italian court to declare the trade marks in question invalid. The Italian Supreme Court ruled that the arbitration could proceed insofar as it concerned contractual rights relating to the trade marks, but that the Italian court had exclusive jurisdiction over the invalidity claim, which was therefore not arbitrable.[33]

Along the same lines, Grantham concludes, after having conducted comparative law research in quite a few countries:[34]

> "It is clear (...) that in a substantial number of jurisdictions a bald assertion by an arbitral tribunal that a patent or trademark is invalid will create a risk of non-enforcement of the award."[35]

And Adamo concludes:

> "Generally, patent infringement and licensing issues are arbitrable in most countries, but invalidity/validity challenges are not. To the extent that invalidity/validity challenges are arbitrable, the resulting arbitration decision/award has a binding (or any) effect usually only as between the particular parties to the proceeding."[36]

---

33 *Corte di Cassazione (Sez. Un.)*, 12 May 1977, no 3989 (*Scherk Enterprises/SGM*), known from A.J. van den Berg, *The New York Arbitration Convention of 1958*, Deventer: Kluwer 1981, p 370.

34 Argentina, Belgium, China, France, Germany, Italy, Japan, Switzerland, United Kingdom, United States of America, Brazil, Canada, Finland, Israel, the Netherlands, Spain, and Sweden.

35 W. Grantham, 'The Arbitrability of Intellectual Property Disputes', *Berkeley J. Int'l Law.* (14) 1996, p 220.

36 K.R. Adamo, 'Overview of International Arbitration in the Intellectual Property Context', *Global Bus. L. Rev.* (2) 2011, p 17.

At the same time, as also Van den Burg writes, there are increasing calls for also ruling invalidity issues arbitrable. He even refers to a 1989 interlocutory arbitral award[37] in which an arbitral tribunal considered itself competent under the ICC rules to rule on the invalidity of a patent, arguing that the decision bound only the parties in the arbitration.[38]

Wu is illustrative of advocates for invalidity claims being arbitrable; he argues fervently in favour of the arbitrability of validity/invalidity disputes relating to patents. Among other things, he argues that the parties have the right to ask a neutral arbitrator to settle their dispute and that the enforcement of an arbitral award against the parties does not mean that the award also has effect against third parties. Among other things, he writes:

> "(...) The sovereign-grant arguments forget the fact that the arbitral award only exists inter partes; the international tendency is to accept the arbitrability of patent validity. However, it is clearly not popular if the arbitration could affect third parties as to a patent's validity. (...) Patent disputes are special because they usually concern foreign elements and high-level technology. Hence, international commercial arbitration has become an important consideration for replacing cross-border patent litigation. In fact, there are several advantages (...) including time-savings, cost-savings, confidentiality, predictability, harmony, flexibility, and expertise, among others. (...) Due to the high value of patents, handling a patent dispute has become an enduring war in which numerous financial resources, human capital, and precious time will be invested. The result may be a life or death matter for an enterprise. Unless a party has confidence in gaining more through litigation, arbitration can reduce the risks involved and bring more certainty to patent disputes."[39]

4.2.4 *Some specific IP arbitration regimes*

If arbitration is the chosen, and possible, way forward, one should bear in mind that there are different arbitration institutes that may be chosen. The readers of this book will already be well acquainted with, for example, NAI and ICC arbitration, but this may be different for the following institutes, which come to mind from a Dutch IP perspective.

37 Interlocutory award in case 6097 (1989), *ICC Ct. Arb. Bull.* October 1993, 76; *non vidi.*

38 Van der Burg 2003, p 11.

39 W. Wu, 'International Arbitration of Patent Disputes', *J. Marshall Rev. Intell. Prop. L.* 2011, p 408-409.

4.2.4.1 WIPO Arbitration and Mediation Center

The first specific IP arbitration institute I would like to mention briefly is the *WIPO Arbitration and Mediation Center*, which itself states:

> "The WIPO Center is international and specialized in IP and technology disputes."[40]

On its website, the Center acknowledges the discussion on arbitrability on certain IP disputes:

> "Traditionally, arbitrability, the question of whether the subject matter of a dispute may be resolved through arbitration, arose in relation to arbitration of certain IP disputes. As IP rights, such as patents, are granted by national authorities, it was argued that disputes regarding such rights should be resolved by a public body within the national system."[41]

However, it goes on to state that as long as the dispute is one that parties could settle, arbitration is also possible:

> "(...) it is now broadly accepted that disputes relating to IP rights are arbitrable, like disputes relating to any other type of privately held rights. Any right of which a party can dispose by way of settlement should, in principle, also be capable of being the subject of an arbitration since, like a settlement, arbitration is based on party agreement. As a consequence of the consensual nature of arbitration, any award rendered will be binding only on the parties involved and will not as such affect third parties."[42]

Importantly though, in my view this does not mean that there will always be jurisdiction. Parties may be free to settle a dispute which for instance includes a dispute over the (in)validity of an IP right, but this does not mean that because of that an arbitral tribunal automatically has jurisdiction to rule over (in)validity of that same IP right.

Interestingly, the number of disputes referred to the WIPO Arbitration and Mediation Center has risen significantly in recent years. While the years from 2014 to 2020 saw a slow but steady increase (from 71 to 182 disputes referred annually), in 2021 this number jumped to 263 and then 548 in 2022

40 https://www.wipo.int/amc/en/.
41 https://www.wipo.int/amc/en/arbitration/why-is-arb.html.
42 https://www.wipo.int/amc/en/arbitration/why-is-arb.html;seefurtherexamples of WIPO arbitration cases at www.wipo.int/amc/en/arbitration/case-example.html.

and even 679 in 2023. In terms of IP areas, 50% of the cases (all time) concerned copyright & digital content, 21% trade marks and 15% patents.[43]

4.2.4.2 UPC Patent Mediation and Arbitration Centre

A development that also merits mentioning is the Patent Mediation and Arbitration Centre ("PMAC") established pursuant to Article 35(1) UPC Agreement. It is not known yet though when the PMAC will be fully operational but recently a director was appointed, who started early September 2024.

As to the disputes that can be handled by the PMAC, Article 35(2) UPC Agreement provides: "*The Centre shall provide facilities for mediation and arbitration of patent disputes falling within the scope of this Agreement. (…).*" According to the UPC website, this Centre thus aims to offer "*support in the settlement of disputes relating to 'classic' European patents and Unitary Patents*".[44] Article 35(2) UPC Agreement sets some boundaries though: it explicitly states that a patent may not be revoked or limited in mediation or arbitration proceedings.

How popular and relevant this new Centre will be remains to be seen. Furthermore, in literature, a number of questions have been raised that will have to be resolved. For example, Hooft queries whether PMAC will *only* accept disputes that concern unitary patents and not 'mixed disputes' that also concern foreign (e.g. US) patents.[45] And, importantly, questions regarding the enforcement of an arbitral award have been raised. In particular, there are concerns that because the PMAC may not request the CJEU for a preliminary ruling and Article 20 UPCA prescribes the application of EU law and its primacy, there may be a risk that enforcement of an

43 https://www.wipo.int/amc/en/center/caseload.html. Additionally, as can be seen on this same webpage, the WIPO Arbitration and Mediation Center also administers cases under the Uniform Domain Name Dispute Resolution Policy (UDRP, which e.g. applies to international domains such as .com, .net, .org) and related policies; in recent years, these have risen to about 5,000-6,000 cases annually (e.g. 6,192 in 2023).

44 https://www.unified-patent-court.org/en/court/patent-mediation-and-arbitration-centre.

45 A. van Hooft, 'Arbitration and Intellectual Property', in: D. De Meulemeester et al (eds), *Liber Amicorum CEPANI (1969-2019): 50 Years of Solutions*, Deventer: Wolters Kluwer 2019, para 27.

arbitral award could be refused for reasons of public policy (Article V.2(b) New York Convention).[46]

4.2.4.3 .nl domain names

It cannot go unmentioned that one specific area where "arbitration" has been used for a long time is domain names. It is generally accepted that domain names are not *sui generis* IP rights,[47] but they do constitute a playing field in which IP rights are frequently invoked. The claim is then, for example, that the use and/or registration of a domain name infringes an older IP right.

According to the Dispute Resolution Regulations for .nl Domain Names,[48] all domain name registrants are subject to these regulations if a third party files a complaint against them pursuant to these regulations challenging ownership. By submitting a complaint against a registrant, third parties submit themselves to these regulations and are bound by them. However, Article 21 states:

> "Participation in proceedings covered by these regulations (including the mediation process) does not prevent either the respondent or the complainant from submitting the dispute to an independent court of competent jurisdiction."

What is generally called ".nl domain name arbitration" is, however, in fact a somewhat hybrid figure, for which the more neutral official name "dispute resolution" might be a better choice.

Some writers believe that .nl domain name arbitration is not "lawful" in light of the specific jurisdiction provisions in various IP laws designating the (The Hague) court. Others, however, disagree. For example, Cohen Jehoram et al, citing Article 1020(1) and (3) DCCP, write that the provisions on jurisdiction concerning Benelux and EU trademarks do not prevent domain name arbitration: any prohibition imposed, or a decision that a do-

46 D. Ruggero di Bella, 'Fixing Enforceability issues of the Patent Mediation and Arbitration Centre', *Kluwer Patent Blog* 19 February 2024 (https://patentblog.kluweriplaw.com/), with reference to CJEU 6 March 2018, C-284/16, ECLI:EU:C:2018:158. See also Van Hooft 2019.

47 A domain name is as such not more than an internet address (see e.g. J.M. Boelens, 'Chapter VII. Handelsnaamrecht', in: P.G.F.A. Geerts & A.M.E. Verschuur (eds), *Kort begrip van het intellectuele eigendomsrecht*, Deventer: Wolters Kluwer 2024, p 486; Cohen Jehoram, Van Nispen & Huydecoper 2012, p 263.

48 Available at www.sidn.nl.

main name should be transferred, is something different than invalidating or revoking a trademark. The latter may not be freely determined by the parties; the former may be.[49]

4.2.5 Conclusion

Where does all this take us? Bearing the above in mind, I think definitive conclusions are somewhat premature, but the following can perhaps be taken as initial guidelines, always assuming that the parties have agreed to submit the dispute to arbitration:

- in disputes in which only the annulment, invalidity or lapse of an IP right is invoked, the court has exclusive jurisdiction and there is no place for arbitration;
- in disputes in which among other things the annulment, invalidity or expiry of an IP right is invoked, the court has exclusive jurisdiction over that part of the dispute; there is therefore no place for arbitration, unless, perhaps, it is possible to for instance stay the arbitration until the case before the court has been concluded. If the argument in question is raised only as a defence though (and thus not as a counterclaim), this may be different;
- with regard to infringement claims, there are arguments for and against; and it will also depend on the circumstances of the case what the arguments for and against arbitration are;
- whether an entitlement claim can be submitted to arbitration is not entirely clear;
- disputes in adjacent areas, such as trade secrets or slavish imitation, can be submitted to arbitration;
- disputes about agreements with IP components (including licence agreements and research & development agreements) can be submitted to arbitration, with the same caveat as mentioned above under the second bullet.

49 Cohen Jehoram, Van Nispen & Huydecoper 2008, p 381-382; see also Cohen Jehoram, Van Nispen & Huydecoper 2012, p 278. See also K. Gilhuis & H.W. Wefers Bettink, 'Artikel 14D BMW en artikel 91 j° 92 Gemeenschapsmerkenverordening vormen geen beletsel voor .nl-domeinnaamarbitrage (reactie op A. Tsoutsanis, *BIE* 2003, p. 3/10)', *BIE* 2003, p 307-309. See about the discussion also A.P. Meijboom, 'Ontwikkeling van domein- naambescherming in Nederland', *Computerrecht* 2007/41.

4.3 Benefits of arbitration and (Dutch) court proceedings

If a dispute can be submitted to arbitration, the question remains, of course, whether this is desirable. That there are advantages and disadvantages to arbitration is no secret,[50] but nevertheless, I think it is good to look at this more closely specifically from an IP perspective; think, for example, of trade secret disputes, where the confidentiality of arbitration is attractive by definition. I note that my comments below focus on NAI arbitration in particular, as this is the type of arbitration I have had the most exposure to and, moreover, it is perhaps also the most logical form of arbitration for Dutch law disputes. I will first discuss the main advantages of (NAI) arbitration, and then of (Dutch) court proceedings.

4.3.1 *Why arbitration?*

A first important advantage of arbitration in IP cases is, as I already mentioned, its confidentiality. Article 7(1) NAI Arbitration Rules (2024) states, for example:

> "An arbitration is confidential and all persons involved either directly or indirectly in an arbitration are bound to secrecy, except and insofar as disclosure ensues from the law or the parties' agreement."

This means that the hearing automatically takes place behind closed doors and the award is, in principle,[51] not published, not even in anonymised form.

Although there are also safeguards in court proceedings, these must always be specifically requested and may be refused; it is thus not a given that a request for a hearing without access for the public ("behind closed doors"), for example, or for keeping certain data confidential, is granted. The most obvious example of cases where this comes into play are those involving trade secrets. However, the desirability of confidentiality is not limited to these cases. For example, trade mark cases often involve the disclosure of information on sales, the amounts invested in advertising and other information that is business confidential. And often companies find

---

50 See e.g. Berger & Janssen 2017, p 30-33.

51 But Article 7(3) NAI Arbitration Rules (2024) provides: "The NAI may publish, or have published, an award, order or a decision on a challenge, omitting the names of the parties and leaving out all other information that might reveal the parties' identities, except where a party objects to such publication with the NAI Secretariat within two months of the date of the award, order or decision on a challenge."

it more generally undesirable if disputes are fought out in public, with the accompanying (negative) publicity. It should be noted, however, that confidentiality may still be compromised if setting aside of an arbitral award or revocation is sought in court (pursuant to Article 1065 and Article 1068 DCCP, respectively), which does happen regularly. After all, those proceedings are, in principle, public.

A second advantage of arbitration may be found in the longer oral hearing. In more straightforward cases, this is not so much an issue: the Dutch system, with its relatively short hearing, will generally work well. However, in more complex cases from a factual, technical and/or legal point of view, the length of a Dutch oral hearing is sometimes perceived as (too) short. A one-day hearing is usually the maximum in an IP case; and parties often have to make do with less. My experience in arbitrations is that the hearings are (often) much longer, and both parties are given as much time as necessary. There is thus much more time to examine the underlying facts in detail and to allow the experts, e.g. technical experts, to speak, and to question them (I discuss this in more detail below). That said, this does not alter the fact that I generally find the Dutch system to be very reliable, good and efficient; this will be discussed below in para 4.3.2. Especially in more complex patent cases, however, I have sometimes felt that the hearing time was too short.

Also the written phase of arbitration is extensive; several rounds of written submissions mean that discussions are also intensive in writing.

A fourth point that I find valuable in arbitrations is that, in general, the core figures playing a role actually get to speak and can be examined and cross-examined. In the context of establishing the truth and getting to the bottom of things, this has obvious advantages. After all, the opposing party and arbitrator(s) can put critical questions to witnesses and experts. Specifically with regard to technical experts, arbitrators can also ask technical questions; this can be very helpful also because other than the parties, they do not have technical "helplines" in the form of experts or patent attorneys. At the same time, this possibility should not be overestimated either: witnesses have often prepared their testimony well and may be focused on telling their own story. The same applies to experts. And, also, witnesses or experts are sometimes interrogated in such a way by skilful lawyers that a bad impression is wrongly left behind; some persons simply come across as more self-assured and look better "on the stand" than others, without this necessarily meaning that their testimony is inherently more reliable. Sometimes even the opposite is true. Incidentally, witness hearings are of course also possible in court proceedings and judges may also appoint experts.[52] My experience is, though, that this does not happen very often in Dutch IP court proceedings, probably because of the delay and costs, and because it is simply less of a standard integral part of the proceedings.

A further advantage of arbitration is that, in principle, the case is decided in one round: appeals, Supreme Court appeal, etc. are normally not part of the process and thus the case has a more predictable length than court proceedings. Of course, this is different if the parties have agreed on an arbitral appeal (Article 1061a DCCP et seq). And it is also possible to claim setting aside (Article 1065 DCCP) or revocation (Article 1068 DCCP).

A sixth advantage lies in the fact that arbitration often takes place in English, while the language used in court is generally Dutch. It should be noted, though, that Dutch courts also accept documents in English (and, in principle, French and German as well),[53] judges often put questions to parties in English and, if asked, normally give permission for simultaneous translation during hearings. In addition, the English-language Netherlands Commercial Court[54] (which will not have jurisdiction in all IP-related cases, but will have jurisdiction in some) was launched in 2019; and on 1 June 2023 the Unified Patent Court (UPC)[55] opened its doors, which means that there is now a patent court where English can be, and often is, the working language.

A seventh advantage can be concentrating the dispute with one body, namely the arbitrator or arbitral panel in question. The nature of IP disputes is often cross-border and this can mean that actions would normally

52 Article 194 DCCP et seq.

53 Supreme Court 15 January 2016, ECLI:NL:HR:2016:65, *IER* 2016/30, annotated by R.W. de Vrey.

54 https://www.rechtspraak.nl/English/NCC/Pages/default.aspx.

55 As stated on its website (https://www.unified-patent-court.org/en/court/presentation), "The Unified Patent Court is a court common to currently eighteen EU Member States, in which the Agreement on a Unified Patent Court (UPCA) is in force. The UPCA can be ratified by any of the other six EU Member States which have signed it at any time. Furthermore, any of the remaining EU Member States could still accede to it anytime. The UPC offers a uniform, specialised, and efficient framework for patent litigation at a European level. It hears both infringement and revocation actions." Notably, the Court has exclusive jurisdiction in respect of "classic" European patents as well as European patents with unitary effect (Unitary Patents), however during the current transitional period (of seven years), actions concerning "classic" European patents can also still be started at national level. Also, "classic" European patents can be opted out of the system.

have to be started at different courts, applying different national laws. Arbitration may then be much more efficient.

Another advantage of arbitration is the broad international enforceability of arbitral awards. If there is no agreement on enforcement regarding "regular" judgments (which is often the case outside the EU), arbitration can be an attractive alternative. After all, many countries are party to the New York Convention.[56]

Lastly, arbitration may also be advantageous if the (otherwise) competent court lacks IP and/or technical expertise, or if there is otherwise some hesitation about the quality of the administration of justice. It must be said, however, that the Dutch IP courts are of a high standard, so this argument hardly comes into play if at all if the Dutch court is the competent court (see also para 4.3.2 below). At most, this may be different if the parties desire a very specific expertise in, say, a certain technical field and believe that there are arbitrators with the desired profile.

4.3.2 *Why the court?*

At the beginning of this article, I already mentioned some of the advantages of regular (Dutch) court proceedings over arbitration. I explain these in more detail below and will mention a few more.

To begin with, there are excellent, specialised judges at the District Court of The Hague, the Court of Appeal of The Hague and also the Supreme Court. In arbitration, one does not automatically find the same level of IP expertise, i.e. experience with IP cases and also with the applicable law. In an arbitral panel of three arbitrators, for example, it can easily occur that not all of them have IP experience; or have IP experience but not in relation to Dutch/EU (or other relevant) IP laws; or have only limited IP experience. More generally, the Dutch legal system, also internationally, has an excellent reputation.[57]

A second advantage is that, in my experience, Dutch court proceedings often work very well and efficiently, with the now (partly EU-inspired) special procedural rules for IP cases in addition to the good quality of the courts. A Dutch case in court is "*front-loaded*", with an emphasis on the

56 United Nations Convention on the Recognition and Enforcement of Foreign Arbitral Awards (New York, 10 June 1958).
57 See www.rechtspraak.nl/English/NCC/Pages/key-features-NCC.aspx.

exchange of written documents. The oral hearing is admittedly relatively short, but the other side of this is that this makes it relatively compact and efficient. Moreover, the quality of the judgments is such that the Dutch IP courts have an excellent international reputation.

The latter brings me to a third advantage, which is that the costs may be lower than, for example, in countries with *discovery* such as England, but also lower than the costs of an arbitration, e.g. because the oral hearing of court proceedings is much shorter and because the court fee is lower than the cost of arbitration payable to the arbitration institute (which cost, incidentally, is generally lower at the NAI than at the ICC[58]). At the same time, though, the cost argument may be different if, in court proceedings, an appeal is lodged and this is followed by a trip to the Supreme Court and perhaps even the CJEU (but at least then the costs are spread over a much longer period). In terms of reimbursement of costs, the systems do not have to differ much, by the way. Under Article 1019h DCCP, the prevailing party in an IP case that concerns infringement or is related to infringement can claim the actual costs incurred, provided they are reasonable; and also in an arbitration, the successful party can claim the costs (Article 59(3) NAI Arbitration Rules (2024)). However, it must be said that the court can (substantially) limit the award of costs (and often does so, awarding costs in line with a court-set table with standard amounts) and that there is no place for a full award of costs in cases that, for example, deal only with invalidity, or that are based on adjacent areas such as trade secrets or slavish imitation.

A fourth advantage relates to the fact that arbitration is often decided in one round, as described above. This may have advantages, but also disadvantages. After all, a case may only really develop on appeal, for instance as a result of the exchange of arguments in first instance which leads to further discussion on those on appeal, insights that progressed over time, documents that only emerged at a late stage, etc. In the Dutch courts, parties have the right to file a (de novo) appeal. Nor should it go unmentioned that in IP cases, questions are relatively often referred to the CJEU, which are necessary to clarify ambiguities in the law.

Yet another advantage is the counterpart of confidentiality, namely publicity. Indeed, publication of a judgment is often a claim in IP cases, also to deter other infringers. And by extension, later cases often refer to earlier

58 https://nai.nl/arbitration/, para 2.2.

case law to make it clear to a new infringer that a positive judgment was already obtained in a similar case. Thus, confidentiality is by no means always desired in IP cases.

4.3.3 *When arbitration and when court litigation?*

As the above shows, litigation in the Dutch courts and arbitration both offer advantages; as well as, often on the flip side of the coin, disadvantages.

All things considered, I think arbitration is particularly appropriate for (i) complex technical disputes, (ii) disputes in which confidentiality, for whatever reason, is of great importance, and (iii) disputes in which a significant budget is available and in which the parties want clarity on the matter in one instance, in a (relatively) manageable period of time. This is all the more true if enforcement difficulties are expected if arbitration is not chosen. In that case it is very important, though, that the list of arbitrators contains a sufficient number of IP specialists, and this can be quite a challenge. Another consideration is whether the case contains undecided points of law; if so, especially if it is a case of principle, arbitration is less suitable. And if publicity is desired, going to court is appropriate. Notably, if a choice of arbitration is made, a second choice still remains to be made, namely which arbitration institute is most suitable. This choice will need to be made on a case-by-case basis, e.g. taking specific expertise required and costs into account; generally though, the NAI is a good option for the reasons discussed above.

When does going to the "regular court" make sense? Well, obviously at least when it comes to legal consequences that may not be freely determined by the parties – after all, then there is no choice. Furthermore, the court is also the most logical choice for disputes that are more straightforward (arbitration may be relatively costly then), that are expected to require more "time" (instances), that involve questions of principle or in which publicity is desired. And the court also remains a good option for complex cases, although as already mentioned, the procedure is structured differently than arbitration.

4.3.4 *The choice*

It should be borne in mind, as also pointed out above, that there is not always a choice: this may be because the arbitrators do not have jurisdiction pursuant to Article 1020(3) DCCP; or because they, on the contrary, do have jurisdiction in view of a contractual agreement already made between the parties; or because the parties do not agree on arbitration (so that the ordinary court has jurisdiction).

It is therefore important that parties are at least aware of the moments when there *is* a choice, and that at such moment they make a conscious and informed choice. Essentially, there are two such moments:

(i) the moment parties enter into an agreement, at a stage where they do not yet have a conflict (e.g. a licence agreement or R&D agreement); and

(ii) the moment parties have a conflict.

At the first moment, the parties are often (fortunately) mainly concerned with building a commercial relationship as constructively as possible, and in a way that is commercially advantageous for both parties. Still, it is then important for them to think carefully about the most appropriate method of dispute resolution, should it come to that. And further, it is important to then phrase the clause agreed on in question in such a way that it is neither too narrow nor too broad.

At the second moment, the parties are often not on such speaking terms that they are willing to agree on anything, including on the method of dispute resolution. What does happen regularly, however, is that a party invokes the lack of jurisdiction of the court or tribunal before which the other party filed proceedings. Nevertheless, in a matter that involves trade secrets (as referred to above), for example, it may be worth trying to agree on arbitration anyway.

4.4 Conclusion

This article began with the question whether the field of intellectual property lends itself to arbitration. The answer to that question is, as so often is the case in legal matters, that it depends.

After all, arbitrators do not have jurisdiction if the question before them serves "*to determine legal consequences that may not be freely determined by the parties*". What matters here is whether the cases regard public policy in that they have effect vis-à-vis everyone. Indications for this may be: (i) the existence of legal provisions in which a specific court is given exclusive jurisdiction, (ii) the issue of far-reaching legal consequences or legal certainty, and (iii) whether the decision sought is by its nature valid vis-à-vis everyone. In IP cases this can be problematic, especially if the invalidity of an IP right is invoked. Also, the curtain obviously falls if the parties have not agreed on arbitration.

If these hurdles are overcome, the question that remains is determining the type of IP cases for which arbitration is suitable. In my view, the answer to this question is that arbitration is particularly appropriate for: (i) complex technical disputes, (ii) disputes in which confidentiality, for whatever reason, is of great importance, (iii) disputes in which sufficient budget is available and parties want clarity on the matter in a single instance, in a relatively manageable period of time, and (iv) disputes in which enforcement issues are expected if arbitration is not chosen.

CHAPTER 5

IT DISPUTES AND ARBITRATION[1]

Dorine ten Brink[2]

5.1 Introduction

This contribution deals with the resolution of IT disputes through arbitration.[3] While also a very interesting topic, this contribution is not about the role IT can have in dispute resolution.[4]

The field of IT law is relatively new and, moreover, still developing. The broad advance of the computer[5] and the use of increasingly complex IT systems began in the late 1980s. The term IT originated around the same time, when the internet as we know it today was invented in the United States. With the growing importance of the IT sector, the field of IT law also developed during those years.[6] In the past five years, IT has only grown in importance in our society. Artificial intelligence (AI) is undergo-

1 This article is an adaptation of a contribution previously published under the same title in C.J.M. Klaassen, G.J. Meijer & C.L. Schleijpen (eds), *Going Dutch: ADR in Nederland, in het bijzonder bij het NAI (Onderneming en recht no 113)*, Deventer: Wolters Kluwer 2019, on the occasion of the 70th anniversary of the NAI.

2 T.P. (Dorine) ten Brink (LLM) is a lawyer/partner at Ploum | Rotterdam Law Firm and editorial secretary of *Tijdschrift voor Arbitrage*. She also acts as an arbitrator in arbitrations on IT disputes, which take place under the auspices of the NAI and the SGOA.

3 I have chosen to refer to 'IT' rather than 'ICT' in this contribution. IT usually refers to the entire domain encompassing hardware, software, peripherals and networks. ICT refers to digital equipment or services aimed at communication (e.g. computers, telephony, printers, etc.). IT is an umbrella term, with ICT being a part of IT.

4 See in this context, among others, H.J. Snijders, 'Arbitrage en AI. Van arbitrage naar robotrage en van menselijke arbiter naar robotarbiter?', *TvA* 2019/1, p 1-8. Compare also the recent commotion about the verdict of the Gelderland District Court (cantonal team) of 7 June 2024, ECLI:NL:RBGEL:2024:3636, in which a district judge, using ChatGPT, estimated the average lifespan of solar panels from 2009 at 25 to 30 years, after which the lifespan was set by the court at 27.5 years.

5 IBM introduced the first personal computer in 1981.

6 The first Grotius Informatics Law course, for example, was held in 1996; I was one of the participants. The VIRA (Vereniging voor Informaticarecht Advocaten), a specialisation association recognised by the NOvA, was founded on 24 February 1995.

ing stormy development, but as a technology it is partly still in its infancy.[7] From Europe, there are numerous legislative initiatives, largely aimed at protecting consumers from unfair commercial practices and citizens from illegal content and misinformation, and thus at the same time limiting the power of the tech giants, such as Google, Facebook, Apple, Amazon and Microsoft. In this context, consider, for example, the Digital Services Act, the Digital Markets Act, the eIDAS regulation, the General Data Protection Regulation, the Data Governance Act, the NIS2 directive and – last but not least – the AI Act. Knowledge of IT law in general and the resolution of IT disputes in particular therefore certainly fills a need. I see opportunities for the NAI to play a significant role in this.

Moreover, to say that things still sometimes go wrong in IT projects is an understatement. Based on long-term research, Dutch IT gurus Hans Mulder and Theo Mulder concluded a bit more than a decade ago (in 2013) that things actually rarely go right.[8] They noted then that only 7% of all IT projects are successfully completed. Until a few years ago, the renowned Standish Group published a report every two years, analysing 50,000 technology projects worldwide. According to the "CHAOS 2020" report, 66% of those technology projects end in partial or complete failure.[9] This includes projects that are stopped prematurely or still reach the finish line with a major delay and budget overrun. Even the smallest software projects fail one in 10 times. Large projects are successful less than 10% of the time. The Standish Group also found that 31% of IT projects in the US were cancelled completely and 53% had performance "so worrisome that it was challenged". McKinsey's 2020 study found that 17% of large IT projects perform so poorly that the survival of the client company is threatened. Boston Consulting Group estimated in 2020 that 70% of digital transformation efforts fail to meet targets.[10]

---

7 Reason for the Personal Data Authority to call for vigilance, as control of AI risks is not keeping pace with the deployment of the technology. See https://www.autoriteitpersoonsgegevens.nl/actueel/ap-onstuimige-opkomst-ai-vraagt-om-waakzaamheid-van-iedereen.

8 H. Mulder & T. Mulder, 'Waarom grote IT-projecten vaak mislukken', *Information*, May 2013.

9 This is reportedly the latest CHAOS report issued by Standish Group.

10 F. Faeth, 'IT Project Failure Rates: Facts and Reasons'. https://faethcoaching.com/it-project-failure-rates-facts-and-reasons/#:~:text=Here%20are%20some%20updated%20facts%3A&text=Standish%20also%20found%20that%2031,very%20existence%20of%20the%20company.

In short, dramatic figures worldwide. In the Netherlands, things have not improved in recent years, it seems. Particularly, appealing billion-dollar government projects have been in the news in recent years. The debacle surrounding the digitisation of the judiciary, which should enable digital litigation by 2018, dates back only a few years.[11] In 2018 the digitisation project "was reset" as the principal itself called it.[12] More recent examples of incidents around the central government's IT services and infrastructure include the problems at the national and regional health services (known in the Netherlands under the name of "GGD") that arose during the corona pandemic in 2021. More specifically this involved the corona test policy: the security of the website coronatest.nl, the government website for test appointments and results, was failing and, as a result, the data of millions of people who got tested for the coronavirus at the GGD were not sufficiently secured. Another example is the Tax Administration's inability to adapt its own IT systems to comply with legislation passed by parliament. For instance, the government wanted to abolish the jubilee tax credit (donation of € 100.000 to children to buy a house) and reduce VAT on fruit and vegetables, but these adjustments proved impossible within the current IT system. The new IT system that all municipalities have to work with for the new Environment Act has also been delayed.[13]

Some of these IT disputes involving the government have led to case law. The aforementioned safety issues at the GGD surrounding corona testing has led to a mass claim, in which the Amsterdam court ruled on 17 July 2024. A foundation called "ICAM" filed a mass claim against the state, various health organisations (GGDs), security regions and municipalities following a data breach during the corona pandemic. During corona time, 6.5 million people entrusted personal data to a GGD when they got tested or vaccinated, or during a source and contact investigation. GGD employ-

11 The major digitisation operation of the judiciary started in 2012. The project was focused on quality and innovation of the judiciary (in the Netherlands the project was known under the name of "KEI", short for "Kwaliteit En Innovatie"). The costs ran to over € 200 million with no prospect of successful completion, after which the project was discontinued in 2018. Partly as a result of the experience gained during the corona pandemic, digital litigation is now possible in a variety of cases.

12 See the letter of 10 April 2018 from the then Chair of the Council for the Judiciary Frits Bakker to the Minister for Legal Protection, retrievable at https://www.rechtspraak.nl/SiteCollectionDocuments/2018-brief-reset-digitalisering.pdf. On the debacle of KEI, see also D.C. Theunis, 'KEI, alt, delete', *TvPP* 2018, p 69-71.

13 F. Hulshoff Pol, 'Rijksoverheid leert nog steeds niet van mislukte IT-projecten', see: https://www.techzine.nl/blogs/privacy-compliance/477714/rijksoverheid-leert-nog-steeds-niet-van-mislukte-ict-projecten/.

ees had access to that personal data, and police investigations revealed that there were instances when that data was made available to others. The foundation demanded payment of compensation, not only to those whose personal data has been established to have been made available to third parties, but also to anyone who should fear that their personal data had fallen into the wrong hands. According to ICAM, this applies to anyone who provided data to a GGD. The claim meant that those 6.5 million people should receive € 500 for immaterial damages and € 50 for material damages. The total stake of the case was thus over € 3.5 billion. ICAM's claim for compensation for all 6.5 million people who had entrusted their personal data to a GGD during the corona pandemic was not granted.[14]

Another example, which has frequently hit the media, is the ransomware attack at the municipality of Court of Twente in December 2020, in which the municipality's network and backup systems were encrypted and rendered inaccessible and many virtual servers were deleted. The municipality held the IT service provider liable for the damages suffered, including on the grounds of breach of its duties of care. The claimed damages reached an amount of millions of euros. The court rejected the claims, however, and concluded that the municipality itself was responsible for the damage.[15]

A further example is the dispute between the organisation that regulates the enforcement of custodial sentences and measures on behalf of the Ministry of Justice and Security. (*Dienst Justitiële Inrichtingen, DJI*) and Unisys Netherlands over the delivery of a software application contracted by DJI to ensure automated support for certain primary processes of DJI, such as detention and reintegration of persons subject to judicial sentences.[16] The IT project went badly wrong, leading to the court ruling that DJI was allowed to dissolve the agreement and Unisys had to repay over seven million euros. However, the claimed damages and contractual penalty were rejected.[17]

14 See Amsterdam District Court 17 July 2024, ECLI:NL:RBAMS:2024:4264.

15 See Overijssel District Court 10 May 2023, ECLI:NL:RBOVE:2023:1731. The court dismissed the municipality's claims, as there was no evidence that the IT service provider breached contractual obligations or acted negligently, so that there could be no unlawful conduct. The municipality appealed. The state of affairs at the time of publication of this publication is not known to the author.

16 This could include an overview of available cells, who is in which cell, with what restrictions, when a person is eligible for leave and release, and what goods this person was carrying on admission.

17 See The Hague District Court 31 January 2024, ECLI:NL:RBDHA:2024:762, *Computer Law* 2024/100, annotated by W.F.R. Rinzema.

Not only governmental IT projects fail. In the private sector, things are not much better. A telling example is the failed introduction of an electronic health record at the Jeroen Bosch Hospital in Den Bosch and the Tweesteden Hospital in Tilburg and Waalwijk by supplier Alert. For years, both issues were litigated in government courts.[18]

IT projects seem – partly because of these high-profile cases – to be a *"lawyers' paradise"*. If things go wrong so often, while the financial stakes are high, the expectation is that there will be a lot of disputes. This does not necessarily appear to be the case: the number of proceedings over IT disputes in the public courts and in arbitration is limited.[19] Perhaps the reverse is true: precisely because (failed) IT projects are a legal minefield, with many uncertainties and thus litigation risks on both sides, there is an incentive for parties to resolve their matters out of court. IT projects may be *"too complex to litigate."*[20]

In this contribution, which looks at IT disputes in both the public and private sectors, I will explore the advantages and disadvantages of IT dispute resolution through arbitration. In doing so, I will successively discuss the specific features of IT arbitration and examine which forms of IT dispute resolution suppliers and customers opt for. I will close with some conclusions and recommendations.

18 The Jeroen Bosch Hospital/Alert case has been litigated up to and including the Supreme Court: see Supreme Court 23 March 2018, ECLI:NL:HR:2018:426, followed by a referral back to the Arnhem-Leeuwarden Court of Appeal; see Arnhem-Leeuwarden Court of Appeal 24 September 2019, ECLI:NL:GHARL:2019:7734, in which the court ruled that the Jeroen Bosch Hospital was entitled to some € 1.2 million for amounts already paid (plus interest from 15 October 2011) and a sum of € 1.5 million in damages. The Tweesteden Ziekenhuis/Alert case was litigated up to and including the Court of Appeal of 's-Hertogenbosch, where the court – after no less than three interlocutory judgements had been delivered (in connection with the appointment of experts) – delivered its final judgment on 17 December 2019. In the final judgment, the court found, unlike the East Brabant court, that the hospital validly terminated the agreement with the software company in 2011. Alert had to repay the Tweesteden Ziekenhuis an amount of over € 4,5 million, which had been paid to the company for services to be provided (with interest and (litigation) costs). The additional compensation sought was rejected. See 's-Hertogenbosch Court of Appeal 17 December 2019, ECLI:NL:GHSHE:2019:4535.

19 Enquiries with the NAI reveal that around 25 IT/technology cases are involved in the 2019-2023 period. Enquiries to the SGOA reveal that, on an annual basis, it will be a few dozen cases (mainly mediation and, to a lesser extent, arbitration, summary arbitral proceedings and binding advice).

20 E.J. van der Pas, 'Oplossen van Tech-geschillen: welke opties zijn er en welke is het meest geschikt?', see https://www.dirkzwager.nl/expertises/ie-en-innovatie.

5.2 IT disputes

An IT project can be defined as a temporary organisation that aims to deliver one or more IT systems required to realise a product or service for the business. Designing, building and implementing IT systems, delivering documentation, creating or modifying management processes, training administrators and educating end users, are part of such an IT project.[21]

An IT project is successful when, in the eyes of those involved (client, user, customer, architect, project team), there is a measurable net improvement compared to the situation before. This applies not only at the time of project delivery, but also about a year afterwards. Only then can it be determined whether an IT system is manageable and whether the delivered result is still desired.[22] To achieve this, on average, the IT project needs to be delivered on time, within budget and in accordance with all pre-specified properties. Things regularly go wrong on one or more of these three points. The annual report Bedrijfsvoering Rijk 2023, for example, shows that more than half of all IT activities experience a delay. In about a third of cases, this involves a delay of more than a year, making the average lead time slightly longer than 5 years. Some 45 percent of IT activities were completed within, or earlier, than the initially estimated lead time.[23]

IT projects are characterised by a high degree of complexity, a long lead time and a significant investment in people and resources. Partly as a result thereof, many IT projects deal with more or less serious problems. A significant part of these can be traced back to specification problems.[24] In addition, organisational problems occur, there is a lack of good internal cooperation or there is a lack of user involvement in the project, because they did not ask for a new IT system and do not see the added value of it.

---

21 B.E. Dado & R.G.M. Dahmen, *Kaleidoscope voor succesvolle ICT-projecten, De belangrijkste kenmerken van succesvolle ICT-projecten in de financiële sector en mogelijke interventies om de kans op succes te vergroten,* 2013, p 15.

22 Dado and Dahmen 2013, p 15.

23 See Figure 44 on page 75 of the annual report; see https://www.rijksoverheid.nl/documenten/jaarverslagen/2024/05/15/jaarrapportage-bedrijfsvoering-rijk-2023.

24 For example: Customer and supplier thought they understood each other well at the start, but on delivery certain functionality turns out to be missing. Or: the customer's expanding number of additional functional specifications, which leads to annoyance with the supplier.

The complexity of IT projects means that disputes arising from such a project are also complex. For the purposes of this contribution, I understand an IT dispute to mean any legal dispute arising from an IT project. Matters that arise concern, for instance, the interpretation of IT agreements, often with regard to the nature of the (care) obligations under the agreement and about the failure to fulfil agreements, or to do so on time. In many cases, it is not clear whether the requested functionality was actually offered or whether the functionality the client intended to buy was actually requested by him. Suppliers and customers turn out to have very different expectations of what should be delivered during the project. For example, due to changes in personnel (successive project managers on the part of the supplier or shifts with unclear division of responsibilities at the client) a confused situation arises, as a result of which a project gets out of hand and complaints follow, in which it is not always clear whether they qualify as proper notices of default. The client threatens to pull the plug on the project. After proper discussion, a restart of the project follows, without it being clear what the legal consequences of such a restart are. For example, what is the status of a newly agreed delivery date: is it a (new) deadline or does the supplier only have a best-efforts obligation and is, in principle, a notice of default required if the delivery date is not met? Getting answers to these questions may again involve interpretation of the agreement. What did the parties mean by the first and then the second (third, fourth) deadline? If new setbacks follow after a go-around, the client no longer has any confidence in it and the contract is terminated, after which the client claims damages. Also, the client wants to appoint a new supplier, who does get to use things that have already been delivered. Discussions about intellectual property rights are the possible result. And is the original supplier obliged to cooperate with the new supplier? In the absence of proper exit arrangements, this can lead to a lot of discussion and uncertainty. Sometimes the termination by the client is too premature, causing the supplier to suffer damages because it cannot finish the project. In addition, questions are often raised about the authority to proceed with suspension or settlement, privacy aspects, soundness of software specifications, additional work, liability of experts, soundness of advice provided, standards relating to escrow, security and competition law questions can also play a role.[25]

25 For a more detailed description of the legal problems arising in failing IT projects, see P.G. van der Putt, 'De gevolgen van niet-nakoming bij IT-projecten', *Computerrecht* 2011/33, P.G. van der Putt, 'De afdwingbaarheid van contracten bij falende IT-projecten', *Computerrecht* 2016/44 and P.G. van der Putt, 'Update Nederlandse IT-wanprestatiejurisprudentie', *Computerrecht* 2019/214, P.G. van der Putt & J.J.H.

Incidentally, IT disputes should not only consider the supplier-customer relationship,[26] but may also involve disputes between producers of software and their dealers/distributors. These cases often involve a difference of interpretation of marketing obligations arising from the distribution contract in question. Understanding market relations and the complex technical aspects of the product then play a major role in resolving or settling the dispute.

Outside the definition of the term "IT disputes" are corporate law disputes between (groups of) shareholders, shareholders and regulators, shareholders and directors, etc. I therefore leave aside the whole soap opera surrounding IT company Centric (a major supplier of software for digital services to Dutch municipalities) and its founder Gerard Sanderink in this contribution.[27]

5.3 IT dispute resolution through arbitration

5.3.1 *Introduction*

The previous paragraph shows that IT projects often involve a host of issues that are more or less escalated and in any cases require time and attention from those involved and, partly as a result, are often costly if they become the subject of a dispute.

There are several options for settling IT disputes. If the parties' intention is to arrive at a judgment that has the force of law, the choice – as with

Vos, 'Ontwikkelingen rechtspraak IT-wanprestatie – papier versus praktijk', *Computerrecht* 2023/211.

26 In other words: contractor – client.

27 See, inter alia, Amsterdam Court of Appeal (Enterprise Chamber) 3 November 2022, ECLI:NL:GHAMS:2022:3139 (suspension of Sanderink as a director of Centric); Amsterdam Court of Appeal (Enterprise Chamber) 27 January 2023, ECLI:NL:GHAMS:2023:149 (granting request by Advocate General to order an investigation at Centric); Amsterdam Court of Appeal (Enterprise Chamber) 18 January 2024, ECLI:NL:GHAMS:2024:118 (rejecting Sanderink's request for additional immediate provisions on the payment of dividends and the conditions for a possible sale of the company); Amsterdam Court of Appeal 24 April 2024, ECLI:NL:RBAMS:2024:2251 (Sanderink has to pay Centric € 80 million with interest and costs in connection with a money loan); Amsterdam Court of Appeal (Enterprise Chamber) 17 September 2024, ECLI:NL:GHAMS:2024:2660 (Centric Holding may proceed with the sale of its shares to Gouda Group), not to mention the many rulings in the conflict between Sanderink and his ex-girlfriend Brigitte van Egten, in which Sanderink also lost time and again, by the way.

any other dispute – is between IT court litigation and arbitration. In both cases, a formal procedure is followed, with all the documents that go with it, after which judges or arbitrators reach a decision that is binding on the parties.

If there is a need for a less formal procedure, there are several options for resolving IT disputes outside court litigation and arbitration. In that case, binding advice is an alternative. In this case, no judgment is rendered. Instead, a settlement agreement is drawn up to conclude the dispute. If compliance with the settlement agreement has to be enforced, an enforceable title will still have to be obtained and proceedings will (still) be inevitable. Mediation as a non-litigious variant should also be mentioned in this list. If mediation leads to a solution, this too will be recorded in a settlement agreement. Responding to practical needs, new forms of alternative dispute resolution are also being developed, such as "med-arb" clauses (this usually means a procedure whereby a mediator can become an arbitrator if the mediation process does not lead to a solution).[28]

In this contribution, I will only indirectly discuss IT dispute resolution through the public courts, binding advice, mediation or med-arb, as this goes beyond the scope of this volume. In the following, I will concentrate instead on IT dispute resolution through arbitration.

5.3.2 IT arbitration specifics

The two main arbitration institutes in the Netherlands for resolving disputes specific to the IT industry are the Netherlands Arbitration Institute (NAI) and the Foundation for the Settlement of Automation Disputes (in Dutch: "Stichting Geschillenoplossing Automatisering", or – in short – SGOA). While the NAI is the largest, general arbitration institute in the Netherlands, the SGOA focuses specifically on resolving IT disputes.

In this paragraph, I will discuss the main features of IT arbitration, including its advantages. These features apply to both an arbitration at the NAI and an arbitration at the SGOA. In the next paragraph (paragraph 5.3.3), I will discuss some salient differences between IT arbitration at the NAI and at the SGOA.

28 See B. van Zelst, 'Van expert determination tot *Med-Arb*: nieuwe markten voor het NAI? – een verkenning', in: C.J.M. Klaassen, G.J. Meijer & C.L. Schleijpen (eds), *Going Dutch: ADR in the Netherlands, in particular at the NAI (Onderneming en recht no 113)*, Deventer: Wolters Kluwer 2019.

One of the major advantages of arbitration is confidentiality. Unlike in state courts, neither the hearings nor the awards are public in arbitration. In cases submitted to the NAI and the SGOA, there are often big interests at stake. It is therefore quite understandable that parties are keen that no information should be made public about their dispute and the manner of its settlement. This also avoids a public defeat. It is highly unpleasant when a court rules that a website builder did not deliver a properly functioning web shop and that it *"can be blamed for having started building without having sufficient information about this specific coupling of [the plaintiff], as well as having insufficient general knowledge about MD AX couplings. Given the quotation, in which [website builder] profiled itself as an expert in listing, specifying and developing complex interfaces, [claimant] should not have had to expect this."*[29] Not only the customer, but also competitors and potential new customers can take note of the public judgment, especially since not all court judgments are fully anonymised. The arbitration rules of the NAI and the SGOA guarantee the confidential nature of arbitrations.[30] It should be noted, however, that the NAI did add a refinement to this in the latest version of its Arbitration Rules, to the effect that the NAI may publish, or have published, an award, order or a decision on a challenge, omitting the names of the parties and leaving out all other information that might reveal the parties' identities, except where a party objects to such publication with the NAI Secretariat within two months of the date of the award, order or decision on a challenge.[31]

Another major advantage of arbitration compared to court litigation is that arbitrators can be chosen by the parties for their specific expertise. The arbitrators' practical knowledge of and experience with IT projects and with IT contracts are often necessary to reach a sound verdict in the often complex IT disputes. Both the NAI and the SGOA allow arbitral tribunals to comprise legal experts and IT experts. This offers major advantages over state courts, where IT dispute resolution is exclusively conducted by legal experts. If the state court needs specific expertise, it will have to appoint an IT expert. In practice, this often leads to delays in handling the case. Moreover, the question is whether the judge always fully understands the IT expert. When legal experts and IT experts are on one and the same panel,

29 See the judgment of the Oost-Brabant District Court of 13 December 2023, ECLI:NL:RBOBR:2023:5782 on a failed delivery of multiple e-commerce platforms (web shops).

30 See Article 7 of NAI Arbitration Rules 2024 and Article 6 of SGOA Arbitration Rules 2022, respectively.

31 See Article 7.3 of the NAI Arbitration Rules 2024.

the IT knowledge is incorporated and legal experts and IT experts can consult and ensure that they "understand" each other.

Besides confidentiality and expertise, speed is a key asset of arbitration. Both the NAI and the SGOA are known for the speed with which arbitrations can be conducted. Both arbitration institutes maintain short deadlines. The average turnaround time of arbitral proceedings on the merits at the NAI is less than 9 months.[32] Similar lead times apply to the SGOA to my knowledge. When an IT expert has to be appointed in proceedings before the state court, it is inconceivable that a judicial (final) decision will be obtained within 9 months after the summons is issued. In urgent cases, both the NAI and the SGOA allow a hearing in summary arbitral proceedings to take place within a few days of the case being brought.[33] This also applies to disputes in which interim measures must be obtained, such as the issuance of a bank guarantee. The request for interim measures occurs quite often in IT projects, for instance if there is a discussion between the parties about a change request. A provision can be a quick solution, especially when the IT project should otherwise continue as usual. These cases are usually dealt with by means of arbitral summary proceedings.

Finally, as an important advantage of arbitration in IT disputes, I would mention that, in principle, no appeal is possible; an arbitral award is normally final and arbitration thus leads to a final decision that is binding on the parties.[34] If the parties want appeal to be possible, they will have to explicitly agree as much. In any event, the NAI and SGOA arbitration rules, which – when referred to in the arbitration clause – form part of the arbitration agreement, do not provide for appeal. The advantage is that both parties have relatively quick clarity on the outcome of their dispute. With an average turnaround time of nine months, the parties know where they stand. Especially as the arbitrators have great and, above all, specific expertise, it is easy to live with the fact that only one instance (arbitral) award is given.[35]

---

32 See information on the NAI website (based on 2021 figures), https://nai.nl/nl/arbitrage/#:~:text=De%20doorlooptijd%20van%20een%20NAI,zijn%20in%20plaats%20van%20maanden.

33 For example, in the case where the release of source codes is required; see SGOA No 26, https://sgoa.eu/informatie/vonnissen/vonnis-26-arbitraal-vonnis-in-kort-geing/.

34 See Article 1061b DCCP.

35 Of course, this does not affect the nullification of the appeal on the grounds mentioned in para 1065(1) DCCP. The basic principle is that the government court may not be a disguised Court of Appeal: see established case law of the Supreme Court deployed with *Benetton/Eco Swiss* (Supreme Court 25 February 2000, ECLI:NL:HR:2000:AA4947).

5.3.3 *Differences between the NAI and the SGOA*

In the previous paragraph, I mentioned some features or advantages that apply generally to IT arbitration, i.e. both the NAI and the SGOA. In this paragraph, I will discuss some of the differences between the NAI and the SGOA.

The differences start with the fact that the NAI is a general arbitration institute and focuses on settling a wide variety of disputes, both national and international. The NAI, founded by Professor P. Sanders, has been in existence since 1949, making it the oldest arbitration institute in the Netherlands. The combination of the two means that the NAI has an extraordinary amount of experience in arbitration. This leads, among other things, to a highly professional office (the NAI Case Management Committee and the NAI Secretariat) which currently employs – besides the secretary-general/general manager and the administrator – eight people. The administration of arbitrations is very routinised and there is a lot of knowledge when it comes to checking arbitral awards for a number of formal requirements (so-called "*scrutiny light*")[36] (and this, of course, also applies to the other forms of alternative dispute resolution offered by the NAI). The NAI also has a highly competent and reputable Board (consisting of five people). This Board and the NAI's Advisory Board consists of the crème de la crème of the Dutch arbitration community.

The SGOA focuses on settling IT, privacy and security-related disputes, which includes not only disputes between suppliers and customers, but also disputes between manufacturers and dealers/distributors. The SGOA was founded in 1989 by, among others, Professor H. Franken. The SGOA also has a great deal of knowledge. Besides the board (consisting of one IT expert and three very experienced IT lawyers), there is a list of independent legal experts and IT experts who can be appointed arbitrators, mediators or binding advisers. The institute is (by its nature) of more limited size than the NAI and the office also has less capacity, but (as is the case with the NAI) provides professional case administration, including a "*scrutiny light*" of arbitral awards.

Another difference between the two institutes concerns the composition of the arbitral tribunal. At the SGOA, the arbitral tribunals are always multidisciplinary. This means that the arbitral tribunals are composed of, on the one hand, legal experts with extensive experience in (arbitration) procedural law

36 In "*scrutinising*" arbitral awards, essential quality aspects are assessed, including with a view to preventing the arbitral award from being exposed to annulment.

and IT disputes and, on the other hand, leading IT experts with long-standing experience in information technology. In case of arbitration, three persons are appointed: two legal experts and an IT expert or two IT experts and one legal expert (depending on the choice of the parties). The chair of an arbitral panel is always a legal expert with long-standing practical experience in procedural law, either as a judge or as a lawyer. The SGOA uses the so-called list procedure and sends the parties an identical list of names of persons who can, in principle, be appointed as arbitrators. This list is as similar as possible to the list of persons associated with the SGOA as arbitrators.[37]

That possibility of multidisciplinary arbitral panels also exists at the NAI, but it is not standard and it is primarily up to the parties to express their wishes in this regard. A factor here is that since the introduction of the NAI Arbitration Rules on 1 January 2015, the so-called list procedure is no longer the "*default option*"; the party-appointed arbitrator has served as the starting point since then. Thus, parties may each appoint their own arbitrator; the two co-arbitrators together appoint a third party, who acts as Chair. If parties are unsure who to appoint as arbitrator, there is the possibility of still asking the NAI to pass on a list of names.[38] In those scenarios, only lawyers and IT experts who have a lot of relevant experience and are considered an authority in their field will be on the list. In the case of arbitrations on IT disputes, these could be the same people who are on the list at the SGOA.

A third difference is that arbitral tribunals appointed under the NAI Arbitration Rules 2024 in principle make awards according to the rules of law,[39] while arbitrators in a SGOA arbitration in principle make awards as good persons in equity.[40] There has been much debate in the past about what exactly is the difference between the measure of decision "according to the rules of law" and "as good persons in equity".[41] The conclu-

37 See https://sgoa.eu/deskundigen/. The SGOA's lawyers are all on the VIRA (Information Lawyers Association) membership list and all have years of experience.

38 Practice showed, at least in the first years after the implementation of the system change, that many parties still like to use the list of names; see F.D. von Hombracht-Brinkman, 'Drie jaar NAI Arbitragereglement 2015', *TvA* 2018/46. It is not known to me how in demand the list of names is anno 2024.

39 See Article 48(1) NAI Arbitration Rules 2024. The parties may agree that a different standard of decision shall be applied and that the arbitral tribunal shall make award as good persons in equity; see Article 48(3) NAI Arbitration Rules 2024.

40 Unless the parties have expressly agreed that the arbitrators should make award according to the rules of law; see Article 29.1 SGOA Arbitration Rules 2021.

41 See, among others, G.J. Meijer & H.A.M. van Roesel, 'Enige beschouwingen over goede mannen naar billijkheid', *TvA* 2010/12, p 35-45 (part I) and *TvA* 2010/28, p 75-82 (part II).

sion is that there are hardly any identifiable differences; at most, they are nuances.[42] That does not alter the fact that it is obviously of the utmost importance that the arbitral award does state the correct measure of decision.[43] In both NAI arbitrations and SGOA arbitrations, the arbitral tribunal takes into account applicable commercial customs in all cases.[44] In the case of a multidisciplinary arbitral tribunal, emphases in assessing the IT dispute may be slightly different to an arbitral tribunal composed of only lawyers, especially if the multidisciplinary arbitral tribunal has to decide as "good persons in equity".[45] Whether that is an advantage or a disadvantage cannot be said in general terms. That will depend (among other things) on the role of the parties in the IT project and the circumstances of the case.

5.3.4 *Indications for and against arbitration in an IT dispute*

Based on the characteristics of (IT) arbitration, the following aspects can be considered, when deciding whether to opt for arbitration as a form of dispute resolution.[46]

As considerations in favour of arbitration can be mentioned:

- The parties wish to resolve their dispute confidentially.
- Handling the dispute requires (technical) knowledge of the industry and trade customs.

42 See Supreme Court 27 March 2009, ECLI:NL:HR:2009:BG4003, *NJ* 2010/169 (*Hendrix Poultry/Burshan*), annotated by H.J. Snijders.

43 The fact that there are hardly any identifiable differences between the two measures does not mean that the distinction is of no importance. How important it is for the arbitral tribunal to apply the correct measure was shown, for example, in Amsterdam Court of Appeal 27 November 2018 (ECLI:NL:2018:GHAMS:4323), in which an arbitral award rendered on appeal under the applicability of the 2015 Arbitration Rules of the Arbitration Council for the Construction Industry was referred back by the Court of Appeal of Amsterdam to overturn the ground for setting aside (applying incorrect measure for decision-making).

44 See Article 48.4 NAI Arbitration Rules 2024 and Article 29.2 SGOA Arbitration Rules 2021 respectively; P.F. Salome, J. Turner & J.A. Kruit, 'Handelsgebruiken & arbitrage: het Nederlandse en het Engelse perspectief', *TvA* 2024/21; B. van Zelst & I.C. van Dam, 'De procesrechtelijke aspecten van handelsgebruiken in Nederlandse arbitrage', *TvA* 2024/22.

45 A similar situation occurs in construction arbitrations administered by the Construction Arbitration Council, where engineers (both ir. and ing.) act as arbitrators in addition to lawyers.

46 Where appropriate, a new consideration can be made after an IT dispute has arisen. If the parties initially opted for the government court, the parties can still choose to submit their IT dispute to arbitrators by way of a deed of compromise.

- Parties do not have time or patience for proceedings on the merits in court (speed of handling in arbitration and finality).

As considerations against arbitration can be mentioned:
- Parties want a public decision by a court judge, for example in connection with precedent or in connection with desired transparency and/or the wish or the need for full accountability for spending public money on resolving disputes.
- The parties want to be able to appeal (which, as said, can only be done in arbitration if expressly agreed beforehand, moreover the NAI and the SGOA arbitration rules do not provide for this in any case).
- Parties do not want formal proceedings (which means that they then perhaps prefer binding advice or mediation or med-arb).

5.4 IT terms

5.4.1 Introduction

In the previous chapter, I discussed the specifics of IT arbitration. Arbitration offers some telling advantages over government litigation. The question is whether the market also sees and appreciates this. In this paragraph, I will look at the dispute resolution clauses included in the various standard terms and conditions or standard contracts used by suppliers in the IT sector. I have also looked at the procurement terms and conditions used by some large clients. This produces a diverse picture.

5.4.2 Suppliers in the IT sector

5.4.2.1 NLdigital

The IT industry has long used its own terms and conditions. NLdigital is the trade association for IT companies, which has some 2,000 members, and is the author of the NLdigital Terms and Conditions. The NLdigital Terms and Conditions were introduced in 2020 as a successor to the Netherlands ICT Terms and Conditions.[47]

47 The Nederland ICT conditions were in turn preceded by the ICT-Office conditions, which in turn were the successor to the Fenit conditions (from 2003 and earlier from 1994) and which in turn were an amalgamation of the Cosso conditions and the Vifka conditions. The Fenit conditions are still regularly referred to; they are also declared applicable in relatively young ICT contracts.

According to NLdigital, a major advantage of the NLdigital Terms and Conditions is that they can count on a broad support base within the IT sector, including among customers, because they cover so many important topics and because they are up-to-date with laws and regulations and changed services in IT. In the legal literature, there is also considerable criticism of the NLdigital Terms and Conditions, which are (still) labelled as (very) supplier-friendly and therefore unfavourable to customers.[48]

The NLdigital Terms and Conditions consist of several chapters. The first chapter contains a general part that in principle applies to all deliveries; the subsequent chapters contain additional, specific provisions depending on the nature of the services to be provided and the goods to be delivered respectively (provision of services, Software-as-a-Service, etc.).

In the general part of Chapter 1, Article 22 contains a provision on applicable law and disputes. The Article on disputes reads:

> "22.2 Disputes arising as a result of the agreement concluded between the parties and/or as a result of further agreements resulting therefrom shall be settled by arbitration in accordance with the Arbitration Regulations of the Foundation for the Settlement of Automation Disputes (Stichting Geschillenoplossing Automatisering) (www.sgoa.eu), all this without prejudice to the right of either party to request a provision in (arbitral) summary proceedings and without prejudice to the right of either party to take precautionary remedies. The place of arbitration shall be Amsterdam, or such other place as mentioned in the Arbitration Rules."

In the case of small claims – in deviation from the provisions of Article 22.2 – a party may decide not to submit the case to arbitrators but to the (sub)district court:

> "22.3 If a dispute arising from the agreement concluded between the parties or further agreements resulting therefrom falls within the jurisdiction of the Dutch subdistrict court, each of the parties shall be entitled, notwithstanding the provisions of article 22.2, to bring the case as a subdistrict case before the legally competent

48 See, among others, the blog by M. Jansen, '10 artikelen uit NLdigital in normaal Nederlands en waarom u die niet moet willen', available at https://www.dirkzwager.nl/kennis/artikelen/tien-bepalingen-uit-nldigital-in-normaal-nederlands-en-waarom-u-die-voorwaarden-niet-moet-willen; see also the blog by B. de Vos, 'De opvolger van de Nederland ICT Voorwaarden is beschikbaar, maar is nog even klantonvriendelijk', available at https://www.ictrecht.nl/blog/de-opvolger-van-de-nederland-ict-voorwaarden-is-beschikbaar-maar-is-helaas-nog-even-klantonvriendelijk; as well as the blog by W. Dammers, 'Nieuwe ICT-branchevoorwaarden NLdigital gepubliceerd', available at https://lawfox.nl/blog/nieuwe-ict-branchevoorwaarden-nldigital-gepubliceerd/.

> court in the Netherlands. The parties shall only have the aforementioned authority if no arbitration proceedings have already been instituted in respect of that dispute in accordance with the provisions of Article 22.2. If, with due observance of the provisions of this Article 22.3, the case has been brought before the legally competent court for hearing and decision by one or more of the parties, the subdistrict court judge of that court shall have jurisdiction to hear and decide the case."

There is also the option of opting for mediation:

> "22.4 Each of the parties is in respect of a dispute arising from the agreement concluded between the parties or further agreements resulting therefrom, in all cases entitled to commence an ICT-mediation procedure in accordance with the ICT-Mediation Regulations of the Foundation for the Settlement of Automation Disputes. The counterparty is obliged to actively participate in a pending ICT-mediation, which legally enforceable obligation includes in any case attending at least one joint meeting of mediators and parties, in order to give this extrajudicial form of dispute resolution a chance. Each of the parties is free to terminate the ICT-mediation procedure at any time after a first joint meeting of mediators and parties. The provisions of this paragraph do not preclude a party who deems it necessary from requesting a provision for (arbitral) summary proceedings or taking precautionary measures."

5.4.2.2 Compulsory mediation

NLdigital's choice of mandatory mediation (at least mandatory for the other party), which is also legally enforceable, is a remarkable one. Until recently, literature and case law assumed that mediation is always based on voluntariness and that a mediation clause is precisely not enforceable as a matter of law.[49]

On 12 July 2024, the Supreme Court delivered its judgment on the interpretation of a mediation clause.[50] In doing so, the Supreme Court answered the question whether parties are obliged under a mediation clause to try mediation before bringing proceedings. In brief, the Supreme Court's opinion boils down to the fact that the content of the mediation clause must be determined by interpretation (according to the Haviltex standard), whereby

---

49 See E.J.M. van Beukering-Rosmuller, 'De juridische afdwingbaarheid van een mediationclausule. Een bespreking van de procesrechtelijke invalshoek, aan de hand van recente wetgevingsontwikkelingen', *TvA* 2017/2.

50 See Supreme Court 12 July 2024, ECLI:NL:HR:2024:1078, *TvA* 2024/56. The recent Supreme Court judgment on mediation is also discussed in detail by Kamminga and Fleuren in their contribution in this volume, see Chapter 12. See E.J.M. van Beukering-Rosmuller, 'Hoge Raad 12 juli 2024, ECLI:NL:HR:2024:1078 *(CSW/PPSB)*, De afdwingbaarheid van de mediationclausule anno 2024', *TvA* 2024/77.

a mediation clause can have a mandatory or a non-compulsory character. The nature of mediation does not prevent a mediation clause from being mandatory in a specific case. The circumstances that a mediation clause has been agreed between professional parties and that the agreement and the resulting dispute have a business character may play a role in the interpretation of the clause, the Supreme Court said.[51] If a mediation clause imposes an obligation to try mediation, the scope of that obligation and thus the question of when a party who so wishes may terminate its cooperation in the mediation process is also a matter of interpretation of the mediation clause. The Supreme Court also answered the follow-up question, namely whether a judge (or arbitrator) – if the other party so requests – must declare the party that brought the proceedings (or arbitration) inadmissible on the grounds that the (mandatory) mediation process was not followed. On this point, the Supreme Court ruled that if a mediation clause provides that parties are obliged to try mediation before commencing legal (or arbitration) proceedings and a party commences proceedings without having fulfilled that obligation, the court (or arbitrator) may, at the other party's request, stay proceedings to give the parties the opportunity to still fulfil their obligations under the mediation clause. However, he is not obliged to do so. The court may decide not to stay the proceedings, for example because the case is too urgent to do so or because there is no point in trying mediation.[52] The recent Supreme Court judgment is thus a very welcome clarification of the Supreme Court's previous case law, in particular its judgment of 20 January 2006.[53]

Following the recent Supreme Court judgment on the interpretation of mediation clauses, we therefore know that a mediation clause can be binding in certain circumstances and that the (voluntary) nature of the mediation does not prevent that. My conclusion is that the mediation clause in Article 22.4 of the NLdigital Terms and Conditions is mandatory in nature, at least for the other party. The decision to start a mediation now lies with one of the two parties and the other party must then go along with it, whether it wants to or not, even though each of the parties may call it quits after the first round. Especially in a dispute where there are claims back and forth, it can therefore be of great strategic importance who takes the first step. An interesting question is the following: in the context of a counterclaim by the other party, can the party that has initiated a SGOA arbitration without opting for a mediation process beforehand still be forced by that other

51 See para 3.2.2.
52 See para 3.2.3.
53 See Supreme Court 20 January 2006, ECLI:NL:HR:2006:AU3724, *NJ* 2006/75.

party to cooperate in a mediation process, and what does that mean for the arbitration that is underway in the meantime? I do not have the answer to that question and this will remain to be seen.

5.4.2.3 Large IT companies in the Netherlands

Practice shows that IT suppliers by no means always declare the NLdigital Terms and Conditions to be applicable to their contracts. In this paragraph, I will elaborate on this.

Of the top 10 Dutch IT companies,[54] only a few use the NLdigital Terms and Conditions. or a precursor to them. The majority of the largest IT companies in the Netherlands use their own general terms and conditions, which they declare applicable to their IT contracts. Those general conditions always include a provision on dispute resolution. It is striking that a large number of these conditions opt for the public courts. A sample of the general terms and conditions of major Dutch IT companies provides the following picture:[55]

- ASML: ICC arbitration.[56]
- Afas Software: district court Midden-Nederland, location Utrecht.[57]
- Adyen: ICC arbitration.[58]
- KPN: competent court in Amsterdam.[59]
- NXP Semiconductors: competent court in Amsterdam.[60]

---

54 Various lists circulate on the internet. Computable, which focuses on IT professionals and IT managers working in the Netherlands with (news) reports, backgrounds and opinion articles on IT, published the following list of the top 10 most popular Dutch IT companies on 10 January 2024: (1) ASML, (2) Afas Software, (3) Adyen, (4) KPN, (5) NXP Semiconductors, (6) Surf (o.a. Surfnet), (7) ilionx, (8) Topdesk, (9) Conclusion and (10) Nedap; see https://www.computable.nl/2024/01/10/wie-komt-er-na-neerlands-trots-asml/.

55 I always checked the general conditions of sale and/or delivery, with the exception of ASML, where I could only access the terms of purchase through public sources.

56 See https://edge.sitecorecloud.io/asmlnetherlaaea-asmlcom-prd-5369/media/project/asmlcom/asmlcom/asml/files/legal/general-terms-and-conditions.pdf.

57 See https://klant.afas.nl/file/download/default/6487C22C1BEE42D08C4FD7A8D1674470/AFAS%20Algemene%20Voorwaarden%20en%20Service%20overeenkomst%20-%20NL.pdf.

58 See https://www.adyen.com/legal/adyen-terms-and-conditions.

59 See https://www.kpn.com/algemeen/algemene-voorwaarden/zakelijk/ict.htm. It is remarkable that KPN chooses the competent court in Amsterdam, given that the Rotterdam court has exclusive jurisdiction in the field of telecommunications law and that KPN's head office is also located in Rotterdam (actually opposite the Rotterdam court).

60 See https://www.nxp.com/docs/en/supporting-information/GEN-CONDITIONS-OF-SALE-US-TX.pdf.

- Surf: competent court in Amsterdam.[61]
- Ilionx: mediation through the SGOA, possibly followed by District Court Central Netherlands in Utrecht.[62]
- Topdesk: competent court in The Hague.[63]
- Conclusion: competent court in Utrecht.[64]
- Nedap: arbitration through the SGOA, whether or not preceded by mediation.[65]

Seven out of 10 IT companies opt for government courts, while two opt for ICC arbitration. None of these top 10 Dutch IT companies opt for the NAI. Nedap – in this case via the (outdated) ICT~Office Conditions route – opts for arbitration through the SGOA, possibly preceded by mediation. Ilionx seems to be the only party in the list of the largest Dutch IT companies to wholeheartedly opt for mediation with the following provision in Article 12.4 of the General Terms and Conditions: "*Because disputes are better resolved than settled, Parties will first try to resolve a dispute, which they have not resolved themselves, by means of mediation. The mediation will take place at the Foundation for the Settlement of Automation Disputes (SGOA). The ICT Mediation Regulations of the SGOA shall apply. If Parties do not find a solution mutually or through mediation, the dispute will be settled by the District Court of Midden Nederland in Utrecht.*" If mediation does not lead to a solution, Ilionx therefore does not opt for arbitration at the SGOA, but for the government court.

I will try to explain below (in paragraph 5.4.4) why there is a preference among suppliers in the IT sector for the government courts, but first (in paragraph 5.4.3) I would like to look at the perspective of clients in the IT sector.

---

61 See https://www.surf.nl/files/2021-10/algemene-voorwaarden-surf_v-1.3.pdf.

62 See https://www.ilionx.com/media/yfhphsuw/algemene-voorwaarden-ilionx-nl-2023.pdf.

63 See https://library.topdesk.com/share/368B9652-84BE-4001-8EE034FE3ABC12D9/?mediaId=0871786C-AEA7-4C7A-96DDC0BDAE69081F.

64 https://yellowtail.nl/app/uploads/2024/07/1613040787-algemenevoorwaardenconclusionb-v.pdf.

65 Nedap uses the ICT~Office Conditions, one of the precursors to the NLdigital Terms and Conditions; see https://nedap.com/wp-content/uploads/2020/04/ICTOffice-Voorwaarden-Module-Algemeen-NL.pdf.

5.4.3 *Clients in the IT sector*

5.4.3.1 Introduction

As I briefly touched upon above in paragraph 5.4.2.1, the NLdigital Terms and Conditions are seen as very supplier-friendly, and thus customer-unfriendly. Jansen, in his blog mentioned in footnote 49 of this contribution, lists 10 reasons why customers should not want the NLdigital Terms and Conditions: (1) the customer always has to pay, (2) budgets say nothing, (3) the supplier does not have to listen to the customer, (4) the schedule says nothing, (5) fatal deadlines are not fatal after all, (6) specifications can change and support law change is not guaranteed, (7) the supplier only has to try to fix *bugs*, (8) no money is ever refunded, (9) the supplier is allowed to mutilate and destroy data or allow it to leak, and (10) the supplier is hardly liable. For buyers with purchasing power or buyers otherwise in a position to negotiate, there is every reason to reject applicability of the NLdigital Terms and Conditions.

5.4.3.2 Central government

The government is one of the largest clients in the field of IT projects. The government has also long used its own standard contracts and/or standard terms and conditions when procuring goods and services. Special conditions apply to the procurement of IT goods and services. The General Government Conditions for IT Agreements 2022 ("ARBIT-2022") have been adopted and entered into force as of 10 September 2022.[66]

According to the explanatory notes to the ARBIT-2022, these are mainly intended for modal IT procurement (i.e. small, medium-sized IT purchases and procurement of standard products/services whether through category management tenders or not).[67] For large and special IT projects, customised contracts are mostly used, tailored to the complexity and size of the contract in question.[68] That said, even in those cases the ARBIT-2022 can serve as a starting point for establishing a more specific contractual relationship with the IT market. Because of the flexibility of the associated

66 Earlier versions date from 2014, 2015, 2016, 2017 and 2018. The precursor to the ARBIT terms and conditions were the BiZa contracts (where BiZa stood for "Home Affairs" as the client).

67 See https://www.pianoo.nl/sites/default/files/media/documents/2022-09/toelichting_gebruik_arbit-2022_sept2022.pdf.

68 See, for example, https://www.rijksoverheid.nl/ministeries/ministerie-van-defensie/contact/zakendoen-met-defensie/voorwaarden.

model agreement, the ARBIT-2022 can usually also be used when deploying specific IT products and services, such as web hosting or SaaS (software as a service).[69]

Article 37.1 of the ARBIT 2022 designates the competent court in The Hague, but expressly leaves open the possibility of alternative dispute resolution through arbitration or mediation.

Worth reading is the note to Article 37.1 of the ARBIT:

> "Increasingly, forms of justice other than court-based justice are being used to resolve disputes. This may include arbitration and mediation. In principle, the ARBIT still assumes jurisdiction by the courts but does explicitly leave open the possibility for parties to agree on another method of dispute resolution. To this end, the Model Agreement includes an optional provision. If they choose to do so, parties can, for example, turn to organisations specialised in dispute resolution such as the Stichting Geschillenoplossing Automatisering (SGOA) and the Netherlands Arbitration Institute. The agreement not to submit a dispute to the ordinary courts can also be made at a later date.
>
> Especially when adjudicating IT disputes, there will often be a need for the substantive opinion of an IT expert. This can be obtained by engaging an expert in ordinary proceedings but also, for example, by opting for arbitration as a form of dispute resolution. Mediation, unlike ordinary court proceedings and arbitration, focuses mainly on clarifying personal motives of the parties and less on a legal and technical assessment of the dispute. Incidentally, the ordinary court may also advise parties, in cases which in its opinion give rise to it, to engage a mediator."[70]

5.4.3.3 Municipal authorities

For the quality of their services and execution, municipalities are increasingly dependent on purchased IT products and services from almost two hundred different suppliers. The Municipal Procurement Conditions for IT (in the Netherlands known under the abbreviation of "GIBIT") help municipalities ensure that they are supplied with a product or service that meets their procurement needs. The umbrella association of Netherlands municipalities (operating under the name "VNG Realisatie") therefore ad-

69 See https://www.pianoo.nl/nl/regelgeving/voorwaarden/rijksoverheid/algemene-rijksinkoopvoorwaarden-bij-it-overeenkomsten-arbit.

70 Notes to the General Conditions of Government IT Agreements 2022 (ARBIT-2022), p 25-26, see https://www.pianoo.nl/sites/default/files/media/documents/2022-09/toelichting_gebruik_arbit-2022_sept2022.pdf.

vises municipalities and municipal partnerships to include the GIBIT in their procurement policy and to use them when procuring IT.

The GIBIT were adopted by the Association Board of VNG on 5 December 2023. The creation of the GIBIT is part of the Digital Agenda 2020 programme, which has as one of its spearheads to professionalise IT commissioning at municipalities.

The GIBIT designate the competent court of the client's district (see Article 27.3 GIBIT). Unlike the ARBIT-2022, the possibility of arbitration or mediation is not kept open here. The explanatory notes to Article 27 of the GIBIT show that a deliberate choice was made to use the public courts rather than arbitration:

> "Considerations here include costs and the publicity of the hearing. It is important for government bodies to publicly account for the spending of taxpayers' money. In that context, it is not appropriate to settle disputes by means of (in principle) secret and often costly arbitration procedures."[71]

5.4.3.4 Private and (semi) private sector

Several major parties in the private and (semi)private sector also seem to have a preference for the state courts. A random sample yields the following:
- NS: competent court in Utrecht.[72]
- UWV: the competent court in Amsterdam, unless the parties choose the SGOA.[73]
- ABN-AMRO: competent court in Amsterdam.[74]
- ING Group: the competent court in Amsterdam.[75]
- Heineken: the competent court in the Netherlands.[76]
- Wolters Kluwer: the competent court of The Hague.[77]

71 See page 42 of the explanatory statement which can be accessed at https://vng.nl/sites/default/files/2023-12/vng_gibit_2023_toelichting.pdf.
72 General purchasing conditions IT goods and services 2013, see https://www.nsprocurement.nl/prod_diensten_nederlands.pdf.
73 See algemene-inkoopvoorwaarden-ict_tcm94-459453.pdf.
74 See https://assets.ctfassets.net/1u811bvgvthc/5wCLKPVAfblH0v45ZNOKaN/844c941b79e2c414094b549608bec2bd/ABN_AMRO_Algemene_inkoopvoorwaarden_2020.pdf.
75 See https://www.ing.com/About-us/ING-Purchase-Conditions.htm.
76 See https://www.heinekennederland.nl/sites/theheineken-netherland/files/supplier-portal/Inkoopvoorwaarden-hn-2014-engels.pdf.
77 See https://www.legalintelligence.com/files/ALV_LI_WKNL_2022.pdf.

- Eneco, Stedin and Joulz: competent court in Rotterdam (the general purchase conditions IT, however, leave open the possibility for parties to still choose the NAI; see Article 29.3 GTC Stedin).[78]
- Airbus: arbitration at the ICC.[79]
- Universal Music Group: competent court in Amsterdam.[80]

5.4.4 *Why which choice?*

With the NLdigital Terms and Conditions being regarded as very supplier-friendly, it is remarkable, to say the least, that the top 10 Dutch IT companies choose en masse not to apply the NLdigital Terms and Conditions, but their own general conditions to their IT contracts. What is also striking in this respect is that instead apply – with one exception – these IT companies do not choose to have disputes with customers settled by arbitration, either through the NAI or through the SGOA. What is behind this?

I have not been able to do any (empirical) research on this, but I do not exclude the possibility that one of the reasons that prevents the big Dutch IT companies from declaring the NLdigital Terms and Conditions applicable is the mediation clause of Article 22.4 and in particular its mandatory nature for the other party: if the customer is dissatisfied and starts a mediation, the IT supplier *has to* go along with it. IT suppliers may have no appetite for that.

Another reason for IT suppliers to avoid the NLdigital Terms and Conditions and the SGOA may be (but maybe that is negative thinking of me) that some suppliers do not wish IT experts looking into their kitchen and giving an opinion on how the supplier has (under)performed. Some suppliers may feel that they stand a better chance before the state courts because their legal defences have more chance with court judges than with arbitrators, especially of one or two arbitrators in a panel of three are IT experts rather than legal experts. Leaving aside the question of whether such a premise would be correct, this (potential) advantage seems to be negated if the court judge still appoints an IT expert in the proceedings,

78 See https://www.eneco.nl/-/media/eneco-com/files/algemene-inkoopvoorwaarden-eneco.pdf?rev=91303955b5794b50845ad4b3facf0614&sc_lang=en, https://www.stedin.net/over-stedin/inkoop-en-aanbestedingandhttps://joulz.nl/nl/algemene-voorwaarden/algemene-inkoopvoorwaarden.

79 See https://www.airbusdefenceandspacenetherlands.nl/dsstuff/uploads/2019/10/Algemene_Inkoopvoorwaarden.pdf.

80 See https://universalmusic.nl/wp-content/uploads/2019/04/AVLV-NL-2019.pdf.

on whom he will rely for his final judgment. Moreover, there is then a significant risk that the judgment will become public, which could result in unpleasant publicity and reputational damage.

By extension, another possible factor is that arbitration is perceived by users as less predictable. Arbitral awards are – as mentioned above – confidential. NAI awards are not published on the NAI website. Relevant parts thereof may be published in the Dutch Journal for Arbitration (in Dutch: *Tijdschrift voor Arbitrage*) completely anonymously, unless the parties object against such (anonymised) publication. This means that readers will not easily be able to take note of arbitral awards in IT disputes settled under the auspices of the NAI. SGOA awards are published on the SGOA website, completely anonymously, but here the special feature is that the names of arbitrators are not mentioned, making it difficult for the reader to determine which line of thought a particular arbitrator adheres to.

In addition, it is conceivable that there is a preconception that arbitration is costly, and more costly than court litigation. That remains to be seen. It is undeniably true that arbitrators – unlike court judges – have to be paid by the parties and that, depending on the circumstances, there is a hefty price tag attached. I would counter that if proceedings before the public courts require the involvement of an expert, the cost of this can also be considerable and can easily reach € 25,000 or more.[81] Those costs can be saved in arbitration if a multidisciplinary panel is chosen. Moreover, arbitration avoids the costs of any appeal (unless the parties have expressly agreed otherwise, of course, but then the associated costs are apparently also factored in). The circumstance that from the list of most popular Dutch IT companies, two companies opt for ICC arbitration seem to point in a different direction, which is that money (or costs) does not play a role in that decision.

Be that as it may, a limited research seems to show that both large Dutch IT companies and customers do not yet massively embrace arbitration as a dispute resolution mechanism for settling IT disputes. In many cases,

81 By way of comparison, in the case of Tweesteden Hospital v Alert, those costs were set at € 44.610 including VAT per expert (two experts had been appointed, so a total of € 88.320 including VAT was involved) (see para 12.8 of the judgment of the 's-Hertogenbosch Court of Appeal of 22 August 2017, ECLI:NL:GHSHE:2017:3660) and in the case of Jeroen Bosch Ziekenhuis v Alert, the expert costs were € 53.884,33 (see para 19 of the judgment of the 's-Hertogenbosch Court of Appeal of 17 December 2019, ECLI:NL:2019:4535).

both the supplier side and the buyer side prefer the traditional government courts. In the public sector, transparency and spending of public funds play a role, but these arguments do not apply to the private and semi-public sector. It is anyone's guess what the motives are for them to avoid arbitration. In my view, suppliers as well as buyers should consider the benefits of arbitration and – if they have become convinced of those benefits – include an arbitration clause in their contract or general terms and conditions.

5.5 Conclusions and recommendations

IT projects tend to go wrong quite often. A large percentage of IT projects fail: based on various studies, it is safe to assume that more than 50% of IT projects do not make it to the finish line, or only with a considerable delay and with a substantial budget overrun. And then it remains to be seen whether the software does what it should do. In many cases, the software does not possess the specifications the customer had hoped for, resulting in more or less severe limitations in its operation. The complexity of IT projects means that the resulting disputes are also complex. This makes the question of which form of dispute resolution is best suited to solve and/or bring these problems to an end of relevance. When parties want formal proceedings resulting in a judgment (enforceable title), they can choose between proceedings in the public courts or arbitration. If the parties choose arbitration, the most obvious choice is either the NAI (as the largest general arbitration institute) or the SGOA (as an arbitration institute specifically focused on IT disputes). The NLdigital Terms and Conditions, the industry's standard terms and conditions for IT companies, refer to the SGOA. However, by no means all standard terms and conditions or agreements used in the IT industry refer to the NAI or the SGOA. Many of the top 10 Dutch IT companies apply their own general terms and conditions, which (with a few exceptions) do not refer to the SGOA, opting instead for public courts. Moreover, of those top 10 Dutch IT companies, not one refers to the NAI. Customers, inside and outside the government, also choose the state courts in many cases. This is remarkable, because IT arbitration offers considerable advantages. In addition to confidentiality and speed, one can especially think of specific expertise among arbitrators of IT law and the IT industry. Unlike in court proceedings, it is possible in arbitration to opt for multidisciplinary arbitral tribunals consisting of renowned legal experts and IT experts. IT suppliers and IT buyers do not yet seem to sufficiently recognise these advantages. The reasons for that are conjectural. Possibly the mandatory mediation in the NLdigital Terms and Conditions scares off suppliers. It is also conceivable that parties are apprehensive about the costs of arbitration. Or that they are reluctant to give up the possibility of an appeal. Regarding the latter two objections, I would suggest to suppliers and customers that costs can be saved if no separate expert needs to be engaged and if no appeal is possible. Those costs will normally certainly outweigh the costs associated with the arbitrators' fees. If the arbitral tribunal is multidisciplinary or consists of three renowned IT lawyers, this should give sufficient confidence in a fair final award in the form of a party-binding decision. In case something were to go fundamentally wrong, there is always the option of asking the state court to set aside the arbitral award.[82] There is therefore still a world to win for the NAI. With arbitration-loving Netherlands, it should continue to work with relentless energy to ensure that suppliers and buyers know how to find the way to the NAI (even better).

82 Whereby, of course, the possibilities of setting aside an arbitral award are very limited. I refer in this regard to the standard case law of the Supreme Court, including Supreme Court 25 February 2000, ECLI:NL:HR:2000:AA4947, *NJ* 2000/508 (*Benetton/Eco Swiss*); Supreme Court 17 January 2003, ECLI:NL:HR:2003:AE9395; Supreme Court 9 January 2004, ECLI:NL:HR:2004:AK8380, *NJ* 2005/190, annotated by H.J. Snijders (*Nannini/SFT*); Supreme Court 22 December 2006, ECLI:NL:HR:2006:AZ1593, *NJ* 2008/4 (*Kers/Rijpma*) and – more recently – Supreme Court 16 July 2021, ECLI:NL:HR:2021:1171 (*Wells/Bariven*).

CHAPTER 6

BUILDING ON WITH THE NAI: INTERNATIONALISATION OF (CONSTRUCTION) ARBITRATION IN THE NETHERLANDS

Shawn Conway & Céline Goedhart[1]

6.1 Introduction

The Netherlands Arbitration Institute ("NAI") is the leading arbitration institute in the Netherlands that administers national and international disputes arising from numerous market segments. Among other things, the NAI Arbitration Rules are readily applicable to construction law disputes. The Rules are also sufficiently flexible to keep up with developments in arbitral proceedings, whether arising from the adoption of certain customs from specific industries or from international arbitration practice. Where necessary to modernise, the NAI has also amended the Arbitration Rules repeatedly over the years to respond to developments. Over the years, more and more customs in arbitral proceedings have come over from international practice and from specific industries. That process is expected to continue. In line with that, the most recent amended version of the NAI Arbitration Rules entered into force on 31 December 2024, being the clerical brush-up of the new 1 March 2024 NAI Arbitration Rules. This article takes stock of various developments in the international arbitration practice and construction practice which have already been implemented in the NAI's arbitral proceedings (para 10.2), certain practices which are gradually being implemented (para 10.3) and those which are yet to be implemented (para 10.4).

6.2 Already implemented arbitration practices

A key custom deriving from international arbitration practice is the possibility for parties to choose the person of the arbitrator. Over the years,

1 S.C. (Shawn) Conway (LLM) is an attorney at Conway Arbitration law firm in Rotterdam and C. (Céline) Goedhart (LLM) is an attorney at Kneppelhout law firm in Rotterdam.

several studies have shown that litigants find it important to nominate their own arbitrator.[2] When revising the arbitration rules in 2015, the NAI amended the provisions regarding the appointment of arbitrators to accommodate this wish of the parties.

The starting point for appointing arbitrators used to be that the NAI compiled a list of prospective arbitrators.[3] Parties then had to make their preferences and objections known through a ranking of the listed candidates.[4] That default approach, known as the list procedure, has given way to party nomination of arbitrators with the introduction of the 2015 NAI Arbitration Rules. Although parties can under the current 2024 NAI Arbitration Rules still opt for the list procedure, in principle, parties are now required to jointly appoint an arbitrator of their own choosing to arbitral tribunals consisting of one person. In the case of arbitral tribunals consisting of three persons, each party should in principle nominate a party-selected arbitrator separately. In the latter case, the third arbitrator, who will also serve as Chair, will be nominated by the two arbitrators nominated by the parties.[5] This custom of party appointments has long been practiced in international arbitration.[6] The list procedure is still employed by the NAI, but only if parties opt for it or if a joint choice is not made known in time.[7]

For construction law practitioners, the greater direct influence on the choice of arbitrator is a godsend. The parties themselves largely control the composition of the arbitral tribunal, including the arbitrators' background, expertise, and experience. With this, the parties can seek an optimal balance between legal and technical expertise.

2 See Queen Mary studies on international arbitration: *International Arbitration: Corporate Attitudes and Practices* (2006), p 5; *International Arbitration Survey: Choices in International Arbitration* (2010), p 3; *International Arbitration Survey: Current and Preferred Practices in the Arbitral Process* (2012), p 2; *International Arbitration Survey: Improvements and Innovations in International Arbitration* (2015), p 6.

3 Depending on the number of arbitrators to be appointed, a list of at least three candidates (in case of a single arbitrator tribunal) or at least nine candidates (in case of a three-arbitrator tribunal).

4 Article 14 NAI Arbitration Rules 2010.

5 Article 13 NAI Arbitration Rules 2015 and Article 16(2) NAI Arbitration Rules 2024.

6 Especially in arbitral tribunals consisting of three persons, it has long been customary for parties to appoint an arbitrator. See, for example, Article 12 of the ICC Rules 2017/Article 8 of the ICC Rules 1998, Article 17 of the SCC Rules 2017/Article 13 of the SCC Rules 2007 and Articles 7 and 8 of the HKIAC Rules 2018/Articles 7 and 8 of the HKIAC Regulations 2008.

7 Articles 15 and 17 NAI Arbitration Rules 2024.

In regular "extra work" claims concerning whether a particular part of the work performed is within the agreed scope/specifications and whether or not a contractor is therefore entitled to additional compensation, the dispute can probably be well adjudicated by an arbitral tribunal composed exclusively of lawyers. However, if the claim concerns the question of conformity of a (particular portion of a) technical installation, it may be desirable to have an arbitrator on the arbitral tribunal with a technical background. Especially when a conformity dispute concerns a fairly uncommon (part of a) work, parties may be better equipped than the NAI to appoint a suitable arbitrator with the appropriate technical background. After all, parties will have more knowledge about the specific issue at hand and the required technical knowledge to assess such dispute. The NAI's arbitrator pool does, however, contain a number of highly qualified arbitrators with technical backgrounds.

If both parties to a three-member arbitral tribunal appoint non-lawyers, then it may be desirable for the non-lawyers to jointly appoint a lawyer as Chair. If they do not do so, the administrator of the NAI may suggest to arbitrators that they would do well to engage a lawyer as secretary to the arbitral tribunal.[8] With the addition of a second paragraph to Article 24 of the NAI Arbitration Rules 2024, the NAI clarified the role of the arbitral secretary: the work of a secretary is performed for, on behalf of, and under the supervision of the arbitral tribunal. The arbitral secretary does not have any decision-making power. Although the secretary never had such power to begin with, the role of the secretary has regularly been a point of discussion within the international arbitration practice, which even led to several settings-aside proceedings for arbitral awards.[9] With the delineation of the specific role of the arbitral secretary in the NAI Arbitration Rules, the NAI created more clarity (also for the less experienced arbitrator without a legal background).

8 Article 24 NAI Arbitration Rules 2024.

9 One of the first setting-aside proceedings in this regard was *Compagnie Honeywell Bull S.A. v. Computacion Bull de Venezuela C.A.*, Paris Court of Appeal, 21 June 1990, 1991(1) Rev. Arb. 96. Another well-known case in which this issue played a role was *Yukos Universal Limited (Isle of Man) v. Russia*, United Nations Commission on International Trade Law (UNCITRAL), PCA Case no AA 227.

6.3 Practices increasingly being implemented

In addition to customs and practices that already fully drifted over from international arbitration practice into NAI procedures, there are several customs and practices that are not yet in widespread use, but are used with increasing frequency in NAI arbitrations. Examples of such customs include the award of actual arbitration costs, the ways of gathering evidence, and, specifically in relation to construction arbitrations, the use of dispute boards.

6.3.1 *Cost orders*

In international arbitration practice, it is common for the unsuccessful party to be ordered to pay the prevailing party's costs of the arbitration based on the *"costs follow the event"* principle.[10] That principle is also laid down in the NAI Arbitration Rules with regard to both legal fees and other arbitration costs.[11] In international practice, it is also common for an award of costs to cover the actual costs incurred for legal assistance and not a fixed rate.

Refusal to grant an award of a party's actually incurred legal assistance costs may be justified if the degree of success of the prevailing party is relatively low (e.g. liability is established, but only half of the damages claimed are awarded), the costs incurred are unreasonable (in relation to the amount in dispute or other circumstances, such as the complexity of the legal grounds or technical issues in dispute), or if the conduct of the parties justifies it.

Article 59 of the NAI Arbitration Rules 2024 authorizes a tribunal to award to the prevailing party its actual costs incurred for legal assistance. The Rules refer to a 'reasonable compensation' for legal assistance of the successful party. This provides the arbitral tribunal with the discretionary power to determine what they deem to be reasonable in the circumstances at hand.

The cost orders for legal assistance in national court proceedings in the Netherlands are based on ensuring adequate access to justice. There are concerns that cost orders based on costs actually incurred for legal assistance create too high of a threshold for access to the domestic courts and

10 ICC Commission Report, 'Decisions on Costs in International Arbitration', *ICC Dispute Resolution Bulletin* 2015, issue 2, p 4, para 13.

11 Article 59 NAI Arbitration Rules 2024.

could result in frontier justice.[12] Cost orders in national court proceedings in the Netherlands are based on standard fixed rates, which are calculated by means of a point system (awarding points for each separate step in the court proceedings). However, the costs actually incurred for legal assistance are in reality usually much higher than the fixed rates, meaning parties will almost inevitably lose substantial sums of money for being involved in proceedings, even if they win the case. It is therefore debatable whether this fixed rate system indeed ensures adequate access to justice, as it can sometimes be a reason for parties not to commence court proceedings because of the associated costs that cannot be recovered.

In arbitration, the desire to ensure adequate access to (private) justice plays much less of a role.[13] Arbitration is consensual. By agreeing to arbitration, parties themselves choose to waive the right of access to public courts.

Incidentally, cost awards based on actual legal assistance costs incurred can also yield a significant advantage over national court or other arbitration institutions (where lump-sum legal assistance costs are awarded). Indeed, parties may choose NAI arbitration because of the likelihood to recover all of their arbitration costs. It also seems fair in arbitration, which often involves commercial disputes, to award actual costs for legal assistance as a starting point. After all, if a (fully) successful party only receives a small portion of its arbitration costs, it is not fully put in the position it would have been in had arbitration not been necessary.

A cost award based on the actual costs incurred for legal assistance also provides an incentive to project owners, contractors, and advisers not to pursue (overly broadly formulated) claims that have a limited chance of success if this results in additional costs. It also provides an incentive to honour (settle) genuine claims at an early stage so that an arbitration is unnecessary or can be resolved promptly.

6.3.2 *Ways of gathering evidence*

There are basically two ways in which the procedure to obtain evidence in an arbitration seated in the Netherlands can take place. The first way is

12 See, for example, C. Boot & J. Quist, (title translated from Dutch) 'Litigation cost award: not all or nothing', *Advocatenblad* 2011, issue 8, p 27, paragraph on Litigation policy.

13 For a further assessment on cost awards in (NAI) arbitrations, we refer to the contribution in this volume (chapter 19) by Van de Hel-Koedoot & Fritschy.

based on the methods used in litigation before national courts, the second way is derived from international arbitration practice.[14]

The first way is based on the premise that when parties submit written memorials prior to a hearing, they also submit all available documents with these first written submissions. If a party wishes to support its position with further evidence, it should make a (sufficiently specific) offer of evidence, preferably in a written statement. The party may indicate in which form it wishes to provide evidence, namely by submitting further documents or by hearing witnesses. If a party wishes to rely on documents that it does not have at its disposal, it may seek them through an order of the tribunal[15] or in separate (interlocutory) proceedings before the national courts under Article 843a of the Dutch Code of Civil Proceedings ("DCCP"). These so-called '843a-proceedings' before the Dutch courts can be a powerful tool to obtain evidence that may be in the possession of the counterparty or a third party, but would be helpful to support a party's argument in a particular case. These requests before the Dutch courts should be distinguished from common law discovery proceedings, as these Dutch proceedings specifically want to avoid so-called 'fishing expeditions'. Therefore, a request to obtain evidence from another party should be well substantiated, giving reasons as to why it has a legitimate interest in obtaining certain documents concerning a legal relationship to which it is a party, while there should also be an indication that such evidence is indeed in the other party's possession.

The second mode of proceedings is based on the principle that the gathering of evidence takes place at a single stage in the arbitration (*frontloading* of evidence). When submitting written memorials, parties should not just submit all available written documents, they should also submit written witness statements (or at least inform the arbitral tribunal that witnesses should be heard at a hearing) and/or expert reports.[16] If a party wishes to provide evidence by means of documents that it does not have at its disposal, an opportunity to request documents from the other party is usually given after the initial round of written submissions. The full exercise of

---

14 For an elaborate assessment on evidence in international arbitration, reference is made to the book written by N. O'Malley, *Rules of Evidence in International Arbitration*, Abingdon, Oxfordshire: Informa 2019.

15 The request for production of documents can be ruled upon either through a procedural order or in the form of interlocutory award, which will often be rendered without a hearing.

16 See for example: G.J. Meijer et al, *Parliamentary history of arbitration law*, Deventer: Wolters Kluwer 2015, p 452 (Proposals Van den Berg 2006).

gathering evidence is brought forward so that when a hearing takes place, all the evidence (of each party's case-in-chief) has already been submitted. The hearing can then be centered around an oral explanation of the parties' positions and the further submitted documents, and by witness and/or expert examinations.

Arbitral tribunals can determine the mode of proceedings tailored to the circumstances of the case. There are advantages and disadvantages to both modes of proceedings. The first mode of proceedings has the advantage that it can be cost-efficient, but only if an arbitral tribunal considers further gathering of evidence unnecessary. If the arbitral tribunal deems further evidence necessary, then the proceedings are delayed and costs increase. The first mode of proceedings with regard to the gathering of evidence seems better suited to proceedings before the public courts than proceedings in arbitration. This method is also more often used by arbitrators with a background in the judiciary, or at least usually not applied by arbitrators with a background in international arbitration proceedings.

The second mode of litigation has the advantage of being time-efficient because all the evidence gathering takes place at a single stage. There is a disadvantage to that method in that it may be cost-inefficient to gather all the evidence at an early stage that may not be entirely relevant for the assessment of the dispute. On detailed assessment, the advantages of the first method of litigation seem illusory and the disadvantages of the second mode of proceedings limited. Both modes of proceedings with regard to evidence gathering are applied in NAI arbitrations.[17]

Matters are less formal in arbitration practice. The parties need not wait for the arbitral tribunal to accept an offer of evidence before evidence can be gathered.[18] Arbitral tribunals can also on their own initiative order parties to provide evidence through, for example, witnesses.[19] It is not unusual that at the start of an arbitration when determining the procedural order (with input from the parties) that it is discussed, *inter alia*, that if witness evidence is required, in principle witness statements should be submitted at the same time as the written initial round of submissions.

17 For a further assessment of evidence in Dutch arbitrations, reference is made to the contribution in this book (chapter 22) by A. Hammerstein.
18 Meijer et al 2015, p 451.
19 Article 1041(1) Dutch Code of Civil Procedure ("DCCP").

Furthermore, in arbitration, a request to submit evidence should in principle not be rejected lightly. This starting point seems appropriate because, as a rule, the handling of the dispute takes place in only one factual instance. The parliamentary history of the Dutch Arbitration Act offers various points of departure to conclude that in any case witness hearings should be conducted if (timely) requested. The explanatory memorandum to the 1986 Arbitration Act contains the following consideration:

> "(...) In general, the arbitral tribunal will also comply with such a request [to have witnesses heard]. However, there may be circumstances under which the arbitral tribunal should be able to refuse (...)."[20]

Even if there is a recalcitrant witness, according to the parliamentary history, the starting point should be that a hearing of the witness in question be held. The same explanatory memorandum contains the following consideration:

> "(...) Not lightly will the arbitral tribunal reject such a request [for the state court to hear a recalcitrant witness] (...)."[21]

However, the right to produce evidence is not unlimited and there is a large degree of discretion for arbitrators. The Dutch Supreme Court has ruled with regard to disregarding an offer of evidence in arbitration that:

> "(...) it is in principle left to the discretion of the arbitral tribunal whether and to what extent it will allow the parties to present evidence of their contentions, in which it is not bound by the [national court] rules of civil procedure, and that the freedom of the arbitral tribunal to reject an offer of evidence finds its limit only where it would contravene the requirements of due process or other fundamental principles of procedural law (...)."[22]

The considerations of the Dutch legislator and the Supreme Court are in line with each other. The parliamentary history shows that there is no absolute right to provide evidence, while the Supreme Court points out some limitations to the (too cursory) disregarding of an offer of evidence. If these views are read together, the conclusion seems to be that a timely

---

20 Meijer et al 2015, p 676, with regard to Article 1039(3) (old) DCCP, now amended to Article 1041(1) DCCP.

21 Meijer et al 2015, p 682, with regard to Article 1041(2) (old) DCCP, now amended to Article 1041a(1) DCCP.

22 Supreme Court 24 April 2009, ECLI:NL:HR:2009:BH3137, para 4.3.3, *TvA* 2010/4 (*IMS/Modsaf*).

offer of evidence should, in principle, be honoured because ignoring it constitutes a violation of fundamental principles of procedural law that may result in the setting aside of an arbitral award pursuant to Article 1065 DCCP.[23] An arbitral tribunal will, however, be entitled to disregard an offer of evidence if the offer is untimely, not relevant to the decision, or not sufficiently concrete or serious.[24]

The "admissibility in almost all instances of arbitral witness and expert evidence [...]"[25] of parties may substantially delay proceedings when applying the first mode of proceedings in gathering evidence because arbitration quickly requires an additional phase.[26] The situation is different when applying the second mode of evidence-gathering proceedings.

The parties can influence how the proceedings are conducted, for example, by including provisions on the conduct of the proceedings and the taking of evidence in the arbitration agreement or by making joint or unilateral proposals to the arbitral tribunal. An arbitral tribunal will, as a rule, respect agreed procedural rules and joint proposals contained in the arbitration agreement, if only because failure to act accordingly may constitute a breach of the tribunal's mandate which may lead to the setting aside of the arbitral award. In any event, if the parties desire a time-efficient procedure, they would do well to communicate that desire to the arbitral tribunal in good time.

The construction industry in particular may benefit from the speedy resolution of disputes and a fixed opportunity to request the production of documents from their opposing party, also due to the risk of loss or deterioration of evidence by the passage of time, as further explained below. A more consistent adoption of such a form of proceedings in construction law disputes therefore seems desirable and fitting. The NAI Arbitration Rules provide a suitable basis for this.

---

23 H.J. Snijders, in: *GS Burgerlijke Rechtsvordering*, Article 1041 DCCP, note 2 (online, updated May 2018).

24 H.J. Snijders, in: *GS Burgerlijke Rechtsvordering*, Article 1041 DCCP, note 2 (online, updated May 2018) signals the need for an adequate (relevant, concrete and serious) offer of evidence. The principle of due process requires that an offer of evidence also be made in a timely manner. What is timely depends on the circumstances of the case.

25 H.J. Snijders, in: *GS Burgerlijke Rechtsvordering*, Article 1041 DCCP, note 2 (online, updated May 2018).

26 A speedy settlement of a dispute with a better quality of truth finding can be more easily pursued if (arbitral) appeals are omitted and if proceedings on the merits take place where the starting point is that all evidence is gathered in a single phase.

The new NAI Arbitration Rules 2024 are more aimed at a dialogue between the parties and the arbitral tribunal on the manner of proceedings. In Articles 26 and 30 of the NAI Arbitration Rules 2024, the procedural conferences or hearings are introduced, in which *inter alia* the rules of evidence and the taking of evidence are discussed. During these moments in the arbitral procedure the arbitral tribunal (in consultation with the parties) can instruct the parties on the required evidence and the manner in which this evidence should be provided. Article 30 NAI Arbitration Rules 2024 even goes so far as to obligate the holding of a so-called mid-stream conference after the submission of the statement of defence.

After the first exchange of written submissions, it will be clearer for an arbitral tribunal what the issues exactly are and which allegations it deems not yet sufficiently proven or substantiated at that point. The arbitral tribunal will then be able to provide specific instructions related to evidence, without the parties feeling the need to throw as much evidence as possible in the mix. The mid-stream conference may be an outcome for the construction industry, as it avoids the arbitral tribunal being buried in evidence that is not relevant for a proper assessment of the dispute.

Speedy resolution of disputes is desirable in construction cases because there is a risk that evidence may be lost or its quality may deteriorate if it is not secured in a timely manner. In particular, the quality of witness evidence deteriorates with the passage of time.[27] After a construction project is completed, digital project documentation is often not preserved and witnesses such as project and contract managers may be employed on new projects or change employers.

Based on the foregoing, it seems advisable to embrace arbitral dispute resolution through *frontloading* of evidence in construction projects. Furthermore, the new NAI Arbitration Rules 2024 provide the opportunity to review the status of the proceedings after the first exchange of written submissions at which point it can be assessed what else may be required in terms of the taking of evidence. While the mandatory mid-stream conference may not always be desired for other fields of industry, this may be beneficial for the resolution of complex construction disputes.

27 A. Kapardis, *Psychology and Law: A Critical Introduction*, Cambridge: Cambridge University Press 2010, chapter 2.5, p 41ff (Event Characteristics).

6.3.3 Dispute Resolution Boards

Dispute Resolution Boards ("DRBs") have been widely used abroad for decades. DRBs, also called *Dispute [Review/Avoidance/Adjudication] Boards* or Advisory Boards, serve to avoid construction disputes, or at least settle them at the earliest possible stage. The use of DRBs stems from a need in the construction industry to settle disputes more quickly as well as more efficiently, *inter alia*, to minimize costly project delays. DRBs (often consisting of one or three members) are established upon the execution of the project contract(s) and typically serve as an additional step in an escalation ladder of dispute resolution. Depending on what the parties have agreed, the DRB can either be appointed at the outset of a project for its duration or only after a dispute arises (on an *ad hoc* basis). The DRB can further issue binding or non-binding opinions depending on the parties' agreement. Soon after a dispute arises that parties cannot resolve by themselves, the DRB may be involved in its resolution during execution of the project. Recommendations or decisions may follow on how issues in dispute will be settled while the project can proceed accordingly. Often the decision is "binding, unless", i.e. it becomes binding only if a party does not timely object to it. If an objection is made, the DRB's decision should be honoured until a decision to the contrary is made in arbitration or the public courts.

The modus operandi of a DRB depends on the assignment it agrees to with the parties. DRBs appointed for the duration of a project "tag along" and have a more proactive role than *ad hoc* DRBs. They are periodically updated by the parties about the (progress of the) project, as well as the parties' respective performance. They usually, even if they are not specifically requested to do so, offer advice on their own initiative if they identify issues that could potentially lead to a dispute. In construction projects, DRBs that do not operate on an *ad hoc* basis are expected to visit the work with some regularity. DRBs, whether appointed on an *ad hoc* basis or for the entire duration of a project, are expected to be able to advise quickly and decisively on the (most likely) outcome of a dispute so that formal settlement of points of dispute does not affect the progress of a project and its completion.

A shortcoming of a DRB is that they increase project costs. If it concerns a construction project, it is usually the contractors who budget for the costs of a DRB, but only if the principal proposes or allows it. Contractors otherwise run the risk of the work being awarded to another party who does not budget for DRB costs.

However, an investment in costs for an expert DRB can lead to a reduction in final project costs. Indeed, research has shown that construction disputes in which DRBs are appointed are almost all resolved without further court proceedings being necessary: only a small portion of around 1% of the disputes are subsequently settled in further legal proceedings.[28] For all those disputes that are settled without further proceedings, the significant costs of further legal proceedings are saved while the costs of a DRB are significantly lower than the costs of proceedings in either courts or arbitration.

The additional costs for DRBs are limited, especially if opting for a board consisting of one person and if that person is engaged only on an *ad hoc* basis.[29] For those who fear a DRB will give rise to "double" costs, it should be noted that these costs may be recoverable from the non-prevailing party as (1) reasonable costs to establish damages and liability, or at least to obtain satisfaction out of court, or as (2) procedural costs.[30]

DRBs have been applied to Dutch projects for about 25 years. Although there has been some development in this department, this development has been limited.[31] The reason for the limited application in the Dutch market may lie in a greater reluctance among contractors to tender for large integrated projects[32] which are precisely the projects that most lend themselves to the application of expert DRBs. Furthermore, clients may be insufficiently familiar with this mechanism, unconvinced of its benefits or simply unwilling to bear the costs. These circumstances, possibly perceived as disadvantages, can be overcome.

For internationally operating project owners and contractors, DRBs are not an unknown phenomenon. The International Federation of Consulting Engineers ("FIDIC") and the International Chamber of Commerce ("ICC")

---

28 R. Sluijter, (Title translated from Dutch): 'The Board of Experts of the Construction Arbitration Council. In national and international perspective', *TBR* 2016/184, para 2.1.

29 It is often necessary, and in other cases preferable, to agree the rules of procedure for the board when the main contract is concluded as well as to already appoint the person of the expert.

30 The procedural costs to be awarded may be limited to a fixed rate depending on the type of further legal proceedings, as discussed above.

31 Compare older articles by, among others, V. Molenaar, (title translated from Dutch): 'Experiences with a dispute review board', *TMD* 1999, p 31 et seq and J. Rozemond, 'The Board of Specialists/Experts', *BR* 2000, p 208 et seq with the more recent contribution by Sluijter 2016, para 2.1.

32 R. Bleeker, (title translated from Dutch): 'End of integral contracts or settlement of major setbacks', *Cobouw* 20 December 2018 (online).

have had *dispute board* regulations in place for quite some time.[33] However, DRBs are not yet commonplace in the Netherlands. Some DRB rules have also been drawn up specifically for the Dutch market. The model DRB rules of CROW, published in 2004, and the model regulations of the Council of Arbitration for the Construction Industry, first published in 2013, were intended to contribute to the acceptance of DRBs in the Netherlands. However, such rules are not applied as a default in standard agreements in the Dutch market, but only offered as an option.[34]

The market's relative unfamiliarity with DRBs can be overcome if more alternative dispute resolution providers such as the NAI offer this method to its users. These institutions can also (better) educate the market about the advantages over other methods of dispute resolution. In particular, the focus should be on educating more owners of large projects, such as the central government and energy companies, as they often have the decision-making power to prescribe their use.

Alternative dispute resolution providers who offer this method may eventually see a shift in their work towards DRB procedures for the large-project construction industry. This while providers who do not offer the method may see a possible follow-up procedure (such as an arbitration) pass them by because users are more likely to have all the (institutionalized) steps in the dispute resolution method go through a single provider. The NAI could contribute to (further) awareness and education about DRBs as an alternative dispute resolution method by drafting its own DRB rules. In this way, it could also better engage users.

6.4 Practices yet to be implemented

6.4.1 Introduction

There are many other practices arising both from international arbitration practice and international construction law practice, which are not yet applied in the Netherlands, or at least to a very limited extent, in both national

33 FIDIC applies as a default provision since its 2017 standard contracts suite (the red, yellow and silver book, reprinted in 2022) a dispute board appointed at the outset of projects under general terms and conditions. The International Chamber of Commerce ICC also issued separate rules for dispute boards in 2015 (accessible via the Dispute Resolution Services section of the ICC website: www.iccwbo.org).

34 The Model Basic Agreement belonging to the UAV-GC 2005 contains the option to adopt a DRB. These UAV-GC 2005 are currently being updated.

and international arbitrations.[35] Not every practice is suitable for application to the Dutch arbitration market. For example, common law practices such as the submission of skeleton arguments prior to a hearing and *adjudication* do not lend themselves for application to the Dutch market.

Skeleton arguments are commonly used in Commonwealth jurisdictions and serve to further educate arbitral tribunals prior to a hearing on exactly what issues are and are not in dispute. *Adjudication* is a form of alternative dispute resolution used mainly in the UK and Ireland, which finds it basis in the law.[36] Such customs have a more regional international character and are (still) so little used in the international arbitration market that application to the Dutch market is (currently) not appropriate. However, we can learn something from other international practices used in international construction law practice and arbitration, such as various different methodologies used to analyse delay and disruption claims, which will be discussed below.

6.4.2 *Building up delay and disruption claims*

Another practice, which would indeed lend itself to application to the Dutch construction arbitration market, is the methodology used to analyse delay and disruption claims. In construction disputes, the disputes most commonly evolve around either extra (out-of-scope) work being required (and the discussion on the costs associated therewith), or delays or disruptions that occur which lead to problems with the initial planning of a project. Deviating from the initial planning usually results in extra costs, especially in complex projects where a lot of subcontractors are involved. A survey shows that methods to structure and assess such delay and disruption claims is underdeveloped in the Dutch market, especially compared to the international arbitration practice. It may be helpful to apply guidelines to substantiate and assess such claims. Such guidelines can be used alongside contractual terms and need not prejudice the applicable legal framework, such as a requirement to demonstrate a causal link. In line with this specific need, in 2022 the *Guidelines on Delay and Disruption*

35 One example could be the simultaneous hearing of witnesses or experts on a particular subject. This practice is known as "witness conferencing" and "hot-tubbing" of experts.

36 Under the Construction Act 1996 (UK), construction law disputes can be submitted in *adjudication*. Through *adjudication*, construction law disputes are referred to an *adjudicator* in the first instance. The adjudicator must render a decision within 28 days. The decision can then be appealed in arbitration or before the state court (much the same as some DRB decisions).

(avoid, solve and settle) were published by the Dutch Arbitration Association and the Institute for Construction Law.[37] This publication attracted a lot of attention within the field of construction law in the Netherlands. Upon consultation of parties within the industry, we can confirm that these guidelines are effectively used by parties in the field of construction, as well as for the settlement of construction disputes.

Delay claims can sometimes be detected quite easily and analysed by simply counting the days on which work could not start on time or was effectively stopped altogether. The additional costs of these delays can subsequently be calculated.

Disruption claims and the combination of delay and disruption claims tend to be more complex in nature. Once delays and disruptions are less detectable (work is regularly not completely stopped), it is complicated to make sense of them. In particular, disruption claims quickly become very complex due to the combination of reduced progress and loss of efficiency. Assessing a causal link between the decreased efficiency (and hence the damage suffered) and its cause can prove to be challenging. Various forensic analysis methods can then be helpful in establishing the links.

Several of these methods have been developed in international construction arbitrations. The methods were mainly accepted because they are applicable to complex factual conditions where it is complicated to measure delay and/or disruption and causes are difficult to retrace precisely. These types of analytical methods are already used in many countries.

In the UK, for example, a (first edition of a) *Delay and Disruption Protocol* was published by the *Society of Construction Law,* also known as the SCL Protocol.[38] The guidelines contained therein have been further developed and supplemented over the years, leading to the second edition of the SCL Protocol in 2017. This protocol was later translated into French. Other organisations, such as the *Association for Advancement of Cost Engineering International* ("AACEI"), have published similar guidelines. The AACEI has issued the *AACEI Recommended Practice no 29R-03 for Forensic Schedule Analysis.*[39] These guidelines rely on scheduling methods dating back to

37 In Dutch: Leidraad Vertraging en Verstoring (voorkomen, oplossen, beslechten).
38 Society of Construction Law, *Delay and Disruption Protocol*, Leicestershire: SCL 2002.
39 This document has undergone many revisions, see revisions dated 25 June 2007, 23 June 2009 and 25 April 2011.

the 1950s. These methods include DuPont's critical-path analysis and the US Navy's project evaluation and assessment technique.[40]

While critical path analysis and forensic analysis to determine cause, effect, and liability[41] are, for example, applied in national construction disputes in the Netherlands,[42] more advanced methods applied to delay and disruption claims in international practice, are not commonly used yet. However, the most advanced developed methods discussed below have not yet gained a serious foothold in Dutch construction law practice. In our opinion, the Netherlands is ready for their wider application.

However, it should be kept in mind that the methods should only be applied in those situations where it is necessary. For example, if there is a well-developed critical-path schedule (a so-called 'baseline schedule') which includes a detailed description of items such as labour and other requirements per work activity,[43] then the consequence of a cause leading to delay may be quite clear. In cases where the delay is simultaneously documented and the counterparty has also received written notification in the process, it may be unnecessary to apply the methods of analysis to be detailed below. This may lead to cost savings, especially since forensic analysis is often done by an external expert assisting to establish liability. However, the reality is more complex as there is often no access to the necessary tools to identify the cause, consequence and liable party of a delay and/or disruption in a relatively simple manner, such as agreed schedules, adequate project documentation and correspondence.

40 J. Lifschitz, E.M. Barba & A.M. Lockshin, 'A Critical Review of the AACEI Recommended Practice for Forensic Schedule Analysis', *The Construction Lawyer* 2009, p 15.

41 Critical path analysis is a widely used method for planning projects. It identifies the longest sequence of dependent activities in order to measure the time required to complete a project from head to tail. It is particularly useful for complex projects that require a number of different activities, such as research, development, design, procurement, construction, component supply, manufacturing and testing. In addition, the critical path method is used to track the impact of changed execution, to plot progress against schedule and to identify where and why a project has gone off track. The latter is normally achieved by combining the critical path with a forensic analysis of the schedule to investigate causal links as well.

42 See, for example, RvA (arbitration board for the building industry) 20 February 2018, no 36.043 (*A/B*).

43 Such "resource-loaded" planning indicates not only the time, but also the manhours and cost of tools, equipment, facilities, and materials for each activity. This makes it easier to measure the amount of additional costs.

We focus below on the more realistic situations where forensic analysis methods are helpful and when not all necessary tools as explained above are available.

We first consider different delay analysis methods below, after which we also consider disruption analysis methods. Whether a particular method is applicable and which of the available methods is most appropriate for a particular project depends on many circumstances. Circumstances that are relevant here include the terms of the agreement, the applicable law, the facts of the case and the availability of documentation.[44] For each method, we list the requirements for applying the various delay analysis methods.

If it follows from the application of a particular delay and/or disruption analysis method that delay and/or disruption has occurred that is not attributable to the contractor, the contractor will usually claim construction time extension and compensation of (acceleration) costs. Such claims are also discussed below (albeit briefly).

6.4.3 *Delay analysis methods*[45]

6.4.3.1 Time impact (window) analysis

A time impact analysis can be made if a (adequately detailed) baseline schedule is in place, an *as-built* schedule[46] has been maintained each time during project implementation, and the events that caused delays have been identified.

The analysis is performed by first breaking down the final *as-built* schedule into time segments. These time segments are also referred to as *windows*. A *window* will be shorter (for more relevant conditions) or longer (for less relevant conditions) depending on the extent of the relevant developments.

---

44 See, for example, Association for Advancement of Cost Engineering International, *AACEI Recommended Practice* (25 April 2011), p 9.

45 D'Onofrio and Meager break down the four general categories of delay analysis into 14 subcategories. See R.M. D'Onofrio & A. Meagher, 'What Is a Schedule Good For? A Study of Issues Posed By Schedules on Complex Projects', *Construction Lawyer* (33) 2013, issue 6.

46 An as-build schedule retrospective after-the-fact analysis on how progress and activities actually occurred on a project as opposed to how they were planned to occur at the outset of the project.

After performing this first step, it is clear how individual components of the project have actually developed through time. The time actually spent on a particular component can then be compared with the time agreed, or at least included, in the basic planning. In this comparison, the delay-causing circumstances are then taken into account to identify the liable party.

Comparisons by *window* may show that a particular component has been, or several components have been, delayed. However, if the overall delay is significant, this analysis may also show that certain parts have been executed faster than agreed. From this, acceleration measures taken can be traced.

Applying this method will provide insight in changes from the original schedule in a chronological manner. This method can be applied most reliably if the schedules are available and if the delay-causing circumstances are actually evident from the project documentation.

6.4.3.2 As-planned vs. as-built method

This method is a simplified version of the time impact method mentioned above. In principle, the application of this method therefore also requires basic planning, final *as-built* planning and information regarding delay-causing circumstances.

When using this method, the final situation (*as built*) is also compared with the originally intended situation (*as planned*). This method is simplified because, as a starting point, it does not break up the chronological course of a project into separate time elements. A final *as built* planning is compared with the original *as planned* planning. This involves identifying exactly where deviations have occurred from the original planning and the critical path (included therein). On the basis of these deviations, the cause and the party responsible for them can be identified.

As this method involves a more general approach compared to the time impact method, it is less precise. It is therefore recommended, for instance in the SCL Protocol, that in case of doubts about the reliability of the basic planning, a time impact analysis should be used based on the updated planning at the time of execution of the work. Using this time impact methodology, the critical path can then become clearer, making it easier to identify the liable party for a delay. This additional step is sometimes referred to as a "common sense and practical analysis of the available facts".[47]

With this more generic method, there remains room for differences of opinion to some extent. Whenever possible, it is therefore preferable to carry out a time impact analysis in line with those starting points. However, the application of the as-planned/as-built method has the advantage that it often reveals delays better than project documentation, such as project reports.

However, the method is somewhat limited because it incorporates subjective elements, especially if reconstructed *as-built* planning is used. The extent of a particular delay-causing event and its impact on the critical path is more reliable with a more detailed analysis. This must then be able to be made, which is not always possible.

6.4.3.4 Reconstructed final planning method (*collapsed as-built*)

This method is suitable for projects where not all desired project documentation is available. Having a basic schedule and a final *as-built* schedule available is not necessary.

Through this method, a detailed *as-built* schedule is reconstructed in which the critical path is also identified. The available project documentation is used for this purpose. Once the final *as-built* schedule is reconstructed, the delay-causing events are eliminated from that schedule. Thus, a basic schedule is reconstructed. On the basis of this reconstruction, it can then be assessed whether, without the delay-causing event(s), the basic schedule (if available) would have been achieved or whether the work would have been completed within the original construction time.

This method offers a solution to analyse delay-causing events without (all) the ideally desired documentation being available. Applying this method is more time-consuming than applying the methods described above. A disadvantage that this method entails is that the result may be tainted by subjective judgements of the analyst about "what might have happened if

47 Association for Advancement of Cost Engineering International, *AACEI Recommended Practice* (25 April 2011), p 36.

no delay-causing event had occurred".[48] That disadvantage need not be an impediment, however, not to use this method.

6.4.3.5 Adjusted base planning (*impacted-as-planned*)

Both the *AACEI Recommended Practice* and the SCL Protocol have incorporated the *impacted-as-planned* method. As the name suggests, this method takes basic planning as its starting point. If basic planning does not exist, or if it is not realistic[49] or does not incorporate a logical critical path, it is not appropriate to apply this method.

When applying this method, the individual delay-causing circumstances with their impact are focused on separately. Once these are brought in focus, the original delivery date can be adjusted with the impact of the delay-causing circumstances. This is often done by using software designed for this purpose.

In essence, this method involves the mirror image of the Reconstructed Final Planning Method. Instead of reconstructing the basic planning using the *as-built* planning and removing the delay-causing events, one starts with the basic planning and the individual delay-causing events are added to it, as it were.

Although this method is the simplest, it does not (purely) include the actual progress achieved or changes in the work. Partly for this reason, (US) courts[50] have rejected this method. As this method leaves out many events of interest, it does not seem very appropriate to apply and embrace this method in Dutch construction arbitrations (if other methods can be applied).

48 Association for Advancement of Cost Engineering International, *AACEI Recommended Practice* (25 April 2011), p 37.

49 Projects are sometimes based on unrealistic planning. For example, in times of an economic industry crisis, it may be interesting to bid on projects with an unrealistic schedule in order to obtain the award of a project. The additional cost of incurring delays on one's own account may be justified because, for instance, if the project is not awarded, a round of employee redundancies may follow.

50 *Titan Pacific Construction Corporation v. United States*, 17 Ct. Cl. 630 (1989).

6.4.4 Disturbance analysis methods

6.4.4.1 Introduction

Proving the impact of a disruption-causing event is usually more complex than for a delay claim. The nature of disruption implies that the construction process does not come to a complete halt but that progress is hindered. The consequence is productivity loss. Achieving the same level of progress as in the situation where there is no disruption can take many times more effort. With disruption, lost days or man-hours cannot simply be added up.

Several methods have been developed to understand the impact of disruption. The productivity loss that has occurred due to a circumstance not attributable to the contractor is central to this.

The methods that we believe are most appropriate to apply measure relative productivity. Productivity analysis methods can be divided into three categories: (1) project-specific studies, (2) project-comparative studies, and (3) industry studies.[51] Methods that have also been developed, but are less appropriate because of limited reliability, compare the difference between planned and actual costs incurred.[52] This latter category is not considered in this contribution.

When applying each of these methods, one analyses to some extent the labour and activeness at work and other items affected by the disruption. However, it may also be justified to also pass on indirect (overhead) costs if they have also increased due to disruption. However, those indirect costs are not central to application of the developed methods.

51 We only discuss the described methods here because, in our opinion, other methods do not lend themselves to application on the Dutch market. Those methods only compare planned with actual costs in the absence of the possible application of other more reliable methods to measure productivity loss. These methods fail to establish a causal link between the disruption events and are based on the assumption that the planned costs were realistic and correct. They also fail to take into account the extent to which increased costs are attributable to the contractor.

52 Each category and subcategory is discussed in decreasing degrees of strength and acceptance.

6.4.4.2 Project-specific studies

There are several types of widely accepted project-specific studies. Each of these types is related to a specific project. For that reason, application of these types yields the most reliable result with respect to production losses. These types concentrate on the individual disruption-causing events attributable to the client. This approach avoids discussions about the originally planned productivity and to what extent the productivity loss is attributable to the contractor itself.

6.4.4.2.1 The Measured Mile Analysis

Using this method, the situation is compared between comparable activities in one period in which disturbance occurred and another period in which no disturbance occurred. The productivity in the period in which disruption occurred is lower. The difference between the productivity with and without disturbance is used as a basis for a disturbance claim.

This method is the most widely accepted method for understanding the degree of disruption and the impact on productivity. However, this method does not lend itself to all works because it must be borne in mind that truly comparable situations must be compared. If the disturbance occurs in a non-comparable situation, for example, because a part of the execution of a work is unique and has not been performed several times during the work, a reliable comparison cannot be made.

As an example, we refer to the construction of a pipeline. When laying a pipeline, disruption may occur, for instance, on a certain part of the route because the connection between pieces of pipeline cannot be closed. That impossibility may lie in the project owner's failure to make equipment or parts available on time, or in the project owner's providing only limited access to the work site. If the same work could have taken place undisturbed at an earlier or later time, a proper comparison can be made.

In this way, insight can be gained on basic productivity achieved without disruption. Productivity as it would follow from a baseline planning need not be included in this assessment. Determining the basic productivity in this way is considered more reliable than deriving it from a basic planning, because a basic planning can always be questioned as to whether it was initially drawn up realistically. Inefficiencies attributable to the contractor itself are usually filtered out when this method is applied. In our opinion, this method does not necessarily require the use of an external expert, although it is advisable within the framework of the more objective convincing power of analysis.

6.4.4.2.2 Earned Value Analysis

This method focuses on the execution of individually separable portions of a work. The application of this method requires an original basic planning that includes an accrual of man-hours and other cost elements for each individual component of the work. Such planning is also referred to as *resource-loaded planning*.[53] It also requires the actual man hours spent per activity to be recorded.

For each portion of the work, the actual number of man-hours spent should be compared with the amount of man-hours as included in the basic planning. When a part is completed, it is assumed that the budgeted man-hours (and associated costs) in the schedule have been "earned", meaning they have been efficiently spent, are accounted for and should be paid for. If more man-hours were actually spent on a disrupted part of the work, these extra hours are classified as inefficiencies.

This method can be reliable, depending on the realistic value of the basic planning. That should therefore preferably be demonstrated (or at least approved by the project owner at the outset). Moreover, disruptive events attributable to the contractor should be taken into account separately.

6.4.4.2.3 Schedule analysis

A planning analysis also applies a *resource-loaded* schedule, but one that is reconstructed after the project is completed by using software that allocates the man-hours and costs of tools, equipment, provisions, and materials for each portion of a work over the course of the project.

Based on this method, one then compares the actual number of man-hours spent and costs with the reconstructed basic schedule in a similar way to the method described above.

This method assumes reconstruction of a basic planning and budget. For this reason, this method is more subjective than the methods described

53 See also note 43.

above. However, it can provide a solution in those situations where none of the methods described above can be used due to the lack of work activities of a similar nature to the disturbed work or of sufficiently detailed basic planning.

6.4.4.2.4 Work sampling

When this method is used, productivity is investigated by conducting field surveys and taking samples from workers. These usually take place on a limited part of the work. On the basis of those surveys and samples, a baseline productivity for a particular activity can be established. Once that has taken place, that baseline productivity can be compared with the productivity actually achieved.

Based on the results of the surveys and tests, workers' time use is divided into three categories:
(1) full-production (e.g. laying bricks, pulling cables or welding);
(2) semi-productive (e.g. delivering materials to colleagues and taking instructions); and
(3) unproductive (breaks, waiting for tool repairs).

Using this data, full-productive vs. semi-productive vs. non-productive time can be expressed as a baseline productivity. This baseline productivity should then be compared with the disrupted productivity.[54]

Applying this method requires securing adequate data during project implementation. The reliability of this method is limited because basic productivity is only measured indirectly. Again, in certain situations, this method can still offer a solution.

6.4.4.2.5 System dynamics modelling

This method is based on a comparison performed by software. Therefore, this method of calculating productivity loss is more abstract than the methods described above. To make the comparison, it is necessary to input a great deal of project documentation. Based on the input of that data, various connections are drawn that affect labour productivity at different stages of the execution of a work.

---

54 See, for example, S.P. Dozzi & S.M. Abourizk, *Productivity in Construction* (online, accessed at web.mit.edu/parmstr/Public/NRCan/nrcc37001.pdf).

The software first reproduces the actual construction progress. This includes changes to the work and the like. Then the project is simulated again but without the disturbance being included. The disturbance-causing conditions are thus filtered out.

This method is applicable if not all the necessary documentation is available at the time a work is performed. The reliability of this method is limited because the outcome is influenced to a relatively significant extent by the judgment of the analyst entering the data, making subjective choices before the analysis is performed.

6.4.4.3 Project-comparative studies

If the project documentation is insufficient to conduct a proper investigation of disruptions and productivity, a comparison study may provide an outcome.

When applying this method, one should compare the productivity on a given work with the productivity achieved on a similar work within the same industry where no disruption has occurred. To maximise reliability, the work being compared should preferably have been carried out by the same contractor as well as preferably with the same workers. However, this will not always be feasible.

If the work performed, or at least its relevant parts, and the work being compared to are not virtually identical, there is a danger of being accused of comparing "apples to oranges".

If the objection described above can be addressed, then this approach can be convincing to measure the impact of disturbance-causing events. Furthermore, the comparison can then also serve to verify the reliability of baseline planning.

6.4.4.4 Industry studies

In situations where documentation of a work is limited or deficient, parties are still sometimes seen resorting to comparisons that are not based on data from the work performed. In such situations, reference is then made to studies conducted with respect to an entire industry. Such studies then use the average productivity of a legion of works as a benchmark, which benchmark is then compared with the productivity achieved in the specific work.

This method is general in nature and therefore less reliable than the methods discussed above. This method does not easily lend itself to individual application. However, it can be well applied as a complementary comparative study to support another analysis.

6.4.5 *The future of analysis methods for the Dutch market*

The methods for understanding delay and disruption are helpful in drafting and assessing claims in which construction time extensions and/or additional cost compensation are claimed. Application of the methods does not always lead (directly) to being able to assume a causal link between a delay and/ordisruption-causing circumstance and the occurrence of damage consisting, for example, of more or longer deployment of personnel and incurring higher costs. Applying such methods does lead to a better understanding of the extent of damage.

More widespread application of these methods of analysis and more detailed analyses of delay and disruption claims may lead judges and arbitrators to become more convinced that in certain cases, an estimation of the extent of damages is necessary and can be achieved if it is established that some damage has occurred and a causal link can be assumed in a general sense.

6.5 In conclusion

The NAI has already contributed a great deal to the application in Dutch arbitration practice of internationally accepted practices arising from the sphere of international arbitration. However, the law does not stand still. National and international practice as well as specific industries continue to evolve. The Dutch market in general and the NAI in particular should remain aware that parties seeking justice may have an interest in the application of practices developed abroad or in specific sectors and in greater predictability.

This contribution has addressed several current practices and existing opportunities for further development. In particular, the opportunity exists for the NAI to position itself (even) better in the market by addressing the *fear of the unknown nature* of various practices. Addressing this can lead to a greater appeal resulting in more disputants choosing NAI arbitration.

The mere possibility of appointing an arbitrator according to one's own preference may provide a reason for choosing arbitration at the NAI in particular. This possibility is indeed helpful for the construction industry, where parties may be better suited to pick an arbitrator with the required knowledge for a complex construction dispute than an arbitral institution may be. Although the Rules have had this possibility for some time now, this possibility is not yet used to its full potential. One reason may be that (especially) inexperienced users are not (sufficiently) familiar with the possibility of nominating an arbitrator themselves or together with the opposing party, or do not realize the advantages thereof. The NAI can play a role in increasing awareness of this use and its advantages and disadvantages by educating users about it. If users deliberately decide to have a preference for the list procedure, this should of course be respected. However, it is the authors' view that the list procedure is quite often used because of insufficient awareness of the possibility for parties to appoint an arbitrator of their liking and its advantages.

There is also a certain degree of unfamiliarity, or at least lack of clarity, with the procedural method with regard to the gathering of evidence. Although parties can design the proceedings in the manner they consider most convenient, parties are often guided by the proposals of arbitrators. Arbitrators with a background in the judiciary and with a more Dutch domestically oriented arbitration practice tend to establish a summary procedural order in which no or limited attention is paid to the exact manner of conducting the proceedings and gathering evidence. However, gathering evidence in a timely manner is important in the construction practice, as the passage of time often leads to loss or deterioration of evidence, especially when the persons involved with a dispute start working on new projects and the dispute as well as the relevant facts are no longer 'top of mind'. Arbitrators with a more internationally oriented background generally pay more attention to an agreed procedure and evidence gathering in procedural orders. The NAI could seize an opportunity by educating arbitrators and users more about how arbitral proceedings differ from national court practice and that there is a lot of freedom for parties and arbitrators to determine the procedure and gathering of evidence in a manner best suited to a particular dispute. This freedom exists partly because, in short, books I to III of the Dutch Code of Civil Procedure do not apply. For the predictability of proceedings, it is advisable to pay more attention to this at the start of an arbitration. Users and arbitrators will only pay sufficient attention to this if they are sufficiently aware of the need to fill in the method of proceedings and gathering of evidence. This is currently not always the case. The NAI can play an important role in increasing knowledge on this point.

New and innovative forms of alternative dispute resolution are regularly used in the construction industry, with several steps in an escalation pathway before finally reaching arbitration or state court. One such form involves expert DRBs. In the Netherlands, this intermediate step in an escalation ladder is not yet widely used. The NAI can play a role in making the market more familiar with this form of dispute resolution. It can do so by drawing up a rulebook that can be applied in conjunction with the NAI Arbitration Rules. The drafting of such regulations by a distinguished institute may result in a greater degree of market acceptance.

In construction, various claims, such as extra work, construction time extensions, penalty payments, and compensation for delay and disruption of works, occur regularly. In the resolution of delay and disruption claims, for example, there is still a way to go in the level of detail of how such claims are analyzed in the Dutch market. The NAI can better position itself in the construction market if it cooperates with initiatives as it has that attempt to set frameworks for such analyses.

In short, plenty of opportunities exist for the NAI to position itself with increased foundation in the international construction law market in particular. *The future is looking bright.*

CHAPTER 7

ARBITRATION IN DUTCH CORPORATE DISPUTES

Bastiaan Kemp & Romy Menasalvas Garrones[1]

> "Considering that irrespective of the distinct juridical identity of each of its members, a group of companies constitutes one and the same economic reality (une realité économique unique) of which the arbitral tribunal should take account when it rules on its own jurisdiction subject to Article 13 (1955 version) or Article 8 (1975 version) of the ICC Rules."[2]

7.1 Introduction

The Netherlands Arbitration Institute (NAI) celebrated its 75th birthday in 2024, and publishes this book – in cooperation with Radboud Business Law Institute ('OO&R') – in honour of that milestone. We have been requested to write a contribution on the role of arbitration in Dutch corporate (law) disputes. This is an apt subject, as the Netherlands has traditionally been a jurisdiction with both progressive company and arbitration laws.[3] Further, due to the strong investment climate as well as the well-developed tax regime, many companies – and joint ventures between companies – are incorporated in the Netherlands.[4] This naturally leads to an increasing

1 B. (Bastiaan) Kemp is a professor of Corporate Governance and Corporate Regulation at Maastricht University and a lawyer and partner at Loyens & Loeff. R.R. (Romy) Menasalvas Garrones (LLM) is a lawyer at Loyens & Loeff at London.

2 *Dow Chemical France et al v. Isover Saint Gobain*, ICC Interim Award in case no 4131 of 23 September 1982, excerpt in IX Yearbook Commercial Arbitration (1984). The arbitral tribunal consisted of none other than NAI-founder Pieter Sanders as its chair, and Berthold Goldman and Michel Vassuer as co-chairs. This award will be discussed in para 7.4 under B below.

3 In the debate on regulatory competition on corporate law between Member States, the Netherlands has been referred to as the "Delaware of Europe", with the Netherlands – as Delaware – proactively making its corporate law attractive to (foreign) investors and companies in order to attract businesses. See for more detail: G. van Solinge et al, *Nederland, het Delaware van Europa? Voordrachten en discussieverslag van het gelijknamige congres van het Van der Heijden Instituut op 20 en 21 november 2015 (Serie Van der Heijden Instituut no 135)*, Deventer: Wolters Kluwer 2016.

4 As for instance confirmed in the U.S. Department of State's Investment Climate Statement: *"The Netherlands is among the largest recipients and sources of foreign direct investment (FDI) in the world and one of the largest historical recipients of direct invest-*

number of corporate disputes and – especially given the international context – arbitrations. It is therefore not surprising that resolving corporate disputes through arbitration has long been a much-discussed subject in Dutch scholarly research.[5] The main focus of this literature has been on arbitrability and whether specialised corporate law proceedings, such as the Dutch inquiry proceedings (*de enquêteprocedure*), could be replicated in arbitral proceedings. While these are important questions, we will in this contribution instead focus on the multi-party nature of corporate disputes, the challenges this brings to resolving such disputes through arbitration and what can be done to mitigate these challenges. We will suggest that both the legislator and arbitral institutions could do more to mitigate the challenges by either binding corporate actors to arbitration agreements or providing such actors with the option to become a party to an arbitration agreement or pending arbitration proceedings. We will also – cautiously –

---

ment from the United States. This can be attributed to the Netherlands' competitive economy, historically business-friendly tax climate, and many investment treaties containing investor protections." See: https://www.trade.gov/country-commercial-guides/netherlands-investment-climate-statement.

5 See amongst others: H.J.M.N. Honée, 'Arbitrage in het vennootschapsrecht', in: P. van Schilfgaarde et al, *Rechtspleging in het ondernemingsrecht (Instituut voor Ondernemingsrecht no 26)*, Deventer: Kluwer 1997, p 27-42; O.L.O. de Witt Wijnen, 'Ondernemingsrecht en arbitrage', in: J.M.M. Maeijer et al (eds), *Conflicten rondom de rechtspersoon*, Deventer: Kluwer 2000, p 103-134; P. Wakkie, 'Spoedarbitrage bij ondernemingsgeschillen', in: G. van Solinge et al (eds), *Geschriften vanwege de Vereniging Corporate Litigation 2001-2002*, Deventer: Kluwer 2002, p 203-212; M.J. Kroeze, 'Arbitrage in het vennootschapsrecht', *WPNR* 2007, issue 6702, p 215-216; P. van Schilfgaarde, 'De Hoge Raad en de arbitrabiliteit van een vordering tot vaststelling van de nietigheid of vernietiging van een besluit', *TvA* 2008/2; J.M. Blanco Fernandez, 'Arbitrabiliteit van besluiten van rechtspersonen', *TvA* 2010/46; F. Grapperhaus, 'Arbitrage in het Ondernemingsrecht', *Ondernemingsrecht* 2010/1; G.J. Meijer, 'Arbitrage in het ondernemingsrecht; inleiding en enkele aanvullende beschouwingen', *Ondernemingsrecht* 2010/2; H.M. de Mol van Otterloo, 'Arbitrabiliteit van vennootschapsrechtelijke geschillen; het Groenselect-arrest', *Ondernemingsrecht* 2010/3; C.J.M. Klaassen et al (eds), *Onderneming en ADR (Onderneming en recht no 66)*, Deventer: Kluwer 2011; E.R. Meerdink & S. Vermeulen, 'Arbitrage over besluiten van organen van de vennootschap: hoog tijd voor wetgeving', *TvA* 2012/59; R.J. Pleiter, 'Het enquêterecht een toetsing van besluiten in arbitrage', *O&F* 2014, issue 2, p 24-37; K.A.M. van Vught, 'Arbitrage van besluiten in rechtspersonen. Fremdkörper of geheimtip?', *Ondernemingsrecht* 2016/101, p 494-502; H.J. Snijders, *Nederlands arbitragerecht*, Deventer: Wolters Kluwer 2018, para 2.1.4; O. Oost, 'Arbitrage en de intrekking van rechtspersonenrechtelijke besluiten', *Ondernemingsrecht* 2019/143, p 802-807 and K.A.M. van Vught, *Het besluit van de rechtspersoon (diss. Nijmegen; Serie Van der Heijden Instituut no 162)*, Deventer: Wolters Kluwer 2020; D.A.M.H.W. Strik, 'Enquêterecht en arbitrage', in: C.D.J. Bulten et al (eds), *Handboek Enquêterecht (Serie Van der Heijden Instituut no 175)*, Deventer: Wolters Kluwer 2022, p 1185-1210.

suggest to broaden the applicability of arbitration clauses by giving more weight to the economic reality and will argue for more restraint by the Enterprise Chamber in inquiry proceedings.

The purpose of this contribution is to provide a broad overview on how to improve the possibilities to resolve corporate disputes through arbitration. As a result, and given the limitations to the length of this contribution, certain elements are only briefly discussed, even if they ultimately deserve a more detailed analysis. These may be explored further in future contributions by the authors or others.

7.2 What are corporate disputes?

When writing about corporate disputes, it is important to clarify the terminology. Corporate disputes can refer to general disputes involving companies, including on investment and transactional agreements (such as share purchase agreements). Corporate disputes can also be understood more narrowly, as referring only to disputes concerning the validity of resolutions by a corporate body. This approach seems to be taken in the German DIS-rules, where under the DIS Supplementary Rules for Corporate Law Disputes, corporate disputes are understood, in short, as disputes requiring a single decision, in particular those regarding the validity of corporate resolutions.[6] For the purposes of this contribution, however, the term corporate disputes refers to disputes involving matters traditionally viewed as issues belonging to the field of corporate law,[7] including disputes about the division of power between and behaviour of corporate bodies of the company and minority shareholder protection. These disputes have as common elements that they (a) involve corporate law and (b) are centred around the rights, obligations and behaviour of shareholders, managing

6 DIS Supplementary Rules for Corporate Law Disputes, and in particular the comment at para 2 ("In disputes requiring a single decision binding all shareholders, in particular those regarding the validity, voidability or invalidity of shareholder resolutions as well as resolutions by the advisory board, supervisory board (Aufsichtsrat) or other boards [...]"). See for the narrow definition of corporate disputes under these rules also: C. Borris, 'Arbitrability of Corporate Law Disputes in Germany', in: C.J.M. Klaassen et al (eds), *Onderneming en ADR (Onderneming en recht no 66)*, Deventer: Kluwer 2011, p 55. See in more detail on these rules para 7.4 under A below.

7 See on what corporate law means: R.C. Clark, *Corporate law*, Boston: Little, Brown and Company 1986, p 30.

and supervisory directors involved with the company and its governance.[8] This understanding is similar to how corporate disputes are understood under the Supplemental Swiss Rules for Corporate Law Disputes.[9]

7.3 Characteristics of corporate disputes and challenges to resolving such disputes through arbitration

7.3.1 *The relevance of litigation to the development of corporate law*

It is broadly recognised that it is essential for the success of the company that the actors involved in the company – such as shareholders, managing and supervisory directors – cooperate with each other.[10] Corporate law has traditionally been focused on the (capital) structure of the company and the division of powers within the company,[11] and does not specifically regulate how the company, its corporate bodies and their members should act vis-à-vis each other. Corporate law stipulates to whom certain powers are allocated to determine particular subjects, who can represent and legally bind the company, how to issue, repurchase and cancel shares, etc. As to norms specifying the behaviour of the actors, corporate law is predominantly limited to broadly formulated standards, or very specific provisions tailored to limited circumstances. Examples of these broadly

8 We thereby use a narrow scope when referring to what corporate actors are relevant. Recently, there has been a strong movement to not only consider the rights, duties and interests of traditional corporate law actors such as those we mention in the main text, but also the rights, duties and interests of other stakeholders (see for overviews of this development: Lucian A. Bebchuk & R. Tallarita, 'The Illusory Promise of Stakeholder Governance', *Cornell Law Review* (106) 2020, p 91-178; J.E. Fisch & S.D. Solomon, 'Should Corporations Have a Purpose?', *Texas Law Review* (99) 2021, p 1309; B. Kemp, 'The Role of the General Meeting in Corporate Governance', in: H.S. Birkmose, M. Neville & K.E. Sørensen (eds), *Instruments of EU Corporate Governance: Effecting Changes in the Management of Companies in a Changing World*, Alphen aan den Rijn: Kluwer Law International 2023, p 215-238). While in some jurisdictions there has long been an interest in the corporate law rights, duties and interests of creditors and employees, more recently the recognition of other actors such as local communities, the environment, etc., has become more prominent. In this contribution, for practical purposes we will largely ignore this important debate.

9 Supplemental Swiss Rules for Corporate Law Disputes, as issued by the Swiss Arbitration Centre per 1 January 2023.

10 B. Kemp, 'Gedragsnormen en rechtsvorming in het ondernemingsrecht', *MvO* 2024, issue 3-4, p 73.

11 See: H.J. de Kluiver, 'Goede trouw en rechtspersonenrecht', in: J.B. Huizink et al, *A-T-D, Opstellen aangeboden aan prof. mr. P. van Schilfgaarde*, Deventer: Kluwer 2000, p 233.

formulated standards – under Dutch law – are the duty for managing and supervisory directors to act in the interest of the company[12] and the duty for all involved with the company to act reasonably and fairly towards the company and each other.[13] These open standards provide only limited guidance to parties on how to act in specific situations. As a result, it is largely up to state courts and arbitral tribunals to set the standards for the actors in specific cases and – where helpful – develop new substandards.[14] An example of such a substandard, (further) developed in case law, are the rules on conflicts of interest[15] of managing and supervisory directors, a *species* of the more general standard that directors have a duty to act solely in the interest of the company.[16]

The above demonstrates that it is up to state courts and arbitral tribunals to determine the behaviour of the actors under specific circumstances and

12 Articles 2:129(5)/2:239(5) DCC.

13 Article 2:8 DCC.

14 L. Timmerman, 'Structuur en gedragsnorm in de ondernemingsrechtspraak van de Hoge Raad', *WPNR* 2013, issue 6969, p 245-248; B.F. Assink & J.M. de Jongh, 'Gedragsnormen, enquêterecht en aandeelhouder', in: B.F. Assink et al (eds), *De toekomst van het ondernemingsrecht (Instituut voor Ondernemingsrecht no 99)*, Deventer: Wolters Kluwer 2015, p 2 and Kemp 2024a, p 77-82.

15 Articles 2:129(6)/2:140(5) DCC and Articles 2:239(6)/2:250(5) DCC; Enterprise Chamber of the Amsterdam Court of Appeal 22 July 2014, ECLI:NL:GHAMS:2014:4666, *JOR* 2015/98, annotated by M. Holtzer (*Xeikon I*); Enterprise Chamber of the Amsterdam Court of Appeal 31 August 2017, ECLI:NL:GHAMS:2017:3532, *JOR* 2018/41, annotated by A.F.J.A. Leijten (*Staphorst Ontwikkeling*); Enterprise Chamber of the Amsterdam Court of Appeal 22 December 2017, ECLI:NL:GHAMS:2017:5354, *JOR* 2018/210, annotated by C.D.J. Bulten (*Intergamma*); Enterprise Chamber of the Amsterdam Court of Appeal 6 February 2018, ECLI:NL:GHAMS:2018:377, *JOR* 2018/94, annotated by M.W. Josephus Jitta (*Xeikon II*); Enterprise Chamber of the Amsterdam Court of Appeal 28 April 2022, ECLI:NL:GHAMS:2022:1287, *JOR* 2022/176, annotated by A.F.J.A. Leijten (*Flevo Berry*); Enterprise Chamber of the Amsterdam Court of Appeal 8 June 2022, ECLI:NL:GHAMS:2022:1734, *JOR* 2022/175, annotated by A.F.J.A. Leijten (*Omines Services*); Enterprise Chamber of the Amsterdam Court of Appeal 6 April 2023, ECLI:NL:GHAMS:2023:844, *JOR* 2023/182, annotated by A.F.J.A. Leijten (*i3*) and Enterprise Chamber of the Amsterdam Court of Appeal 6 April 2023, ECLI:NL:GHAMS:2023:846, *JOR* 2023/183, annotated by A.F.J.A. Leijten (*Ergo Buildings*).

16 Other recent examples include to whom the right to determine the 'strategy' of the company is allocated (see: Garcia Nelen (S.B. Garcia Nelen, *De beursvennootschap, corporate governance en strategie (Instituut voor Ondernemingsrecht no 120)*, Deventer: Wolters Kluwer 2020) and Terstegge (J.A. Terstegge, *Beperking van de bestuursbevoegdheid bij de naamloze en besloten vennootschap (Instituut voor Ondernemingsrecht no 127)*, Deventer: Wolters Kluwer 2022)) and the information rights of (minority) shareholders in private companies (see: P.L. Hezer, *Informatierechten van aandeelhouders (Instituut voor Ondernemingsrecht no 134)*, Deventer: Wolters Kluwer 2024).

develop new substandards.[17] This is especially relevant, as companies often exist for a long time and operate under dynamic conditions, making it even harder to predict future desired behaviour of the actors involved with the company.[18] Another challenge – that is central to this contribution – is that corporate disputes in many instances involve multiple parties. Because the company is essentially a legal instrument for individual actors to cooperate with each other, corporate disputes in many cases not only affect the claimant and defendant in the proceedings, but also impact the interests, rights and obligations of others involved in the company. For instance, when a shareholder disagrees with a resolution passed by the management board, it would formally need to identify the company as the defendant, as under Dutch law a resolution of a corporate body of the company is considered a legal act of the company itself.[19] However, challenging such a resolution will likely also require challenging the (voting) behaviour of the individual managing directors and potentially the role of the supervisory directors for supervising this behaviour. The resolution itself might be supported by other shareholders. As a result, as set out in more detail below, when litigated, it is more likely that third parties will (want to) intervene in the dispute brought by the primary parties.

7.3.2 The role of parties in corporate litigation

Civil procedural law applied in litigation before state courts provides for tools to cater for these multi-party disputes. In 'ordinary' civil procedures before the state court, parties can join and/or intervene in the proceedings, subject to court approval.[20] The same applies for impleading a third party in proceedings.[21] In the Netherlands, it is also possible to bring corporate disputes before the Enterprise Chamber.[22] This is a spe-

17 G.C. Makkink, 'Toetsing door de Ondernemingskamer, opmerkingen in de marge', in: H.J. de Kluiver (ed), *De rol van de rechter in het ondernemingsrecht*, Zutphen: Uitgeverij Paris 2020, p 58-59.

18 Kemp 2024a, p 77.

19 Asser/Kroeze 2-*I* 2021/290.

20 Article 217 DCCP et seq. See: E. Gras, R.G. Hendrikse & A.W. Jongbloed, *Compendium van het Burgerlijk procesrecht*, Deventer: Wolters Kluwer 2024, para 8.6.1; G. Snijders, 'Voeging en tussenkomst', in: P. Vlas & T.F.E. Tjong Tjin Tai (eds), *GS Burgerlijke Rechtsvordering*, Deventer: Wolters Kluwer 2024; Asser Procesrecht/Van Schaick 2 2022/45-47.

21 Article 210 DCCP. See also: M.O.J. de Folter, *Vrijwaring & Interventie (Burgerlijk Proces & Praktijk no 11)*, Deventer: Kluwer 2009, p 26-27.

22 See on inquiry proceedings: M.J. Kroeze, 'The Companies and Business Court as a specialized court', *Ondernemingsrecht* 2007/29; M. Muller, *Corporate Law in the Netherlands*, Deventer: Wolters Kluwer 2013, para 10.

cialised business court, that is part of the Amsterdam Court of Appeal, and always sits with three professional judges and two layman judges with business knowledge. In the Netherlands, many corporate disputes are brought before the Enterprise Chamber.[23] Inquiry proceedings at the Enterprise Chamber can only be initiated by persons to whom such right is granted, so-called *'enquêtegerechtigden'*, and the formal defendant is always the company itself. Who qualifies as such is specified in statutory law, and includes shareholders whose shareholdings meet a certain threshold, holders of depositary receipts (*certificaten*) if they meet the same thresholds, the company itself, the bankruptcy trustee, employee unions and the attorney general of the Amsterdam Court of Appeal.[24] The Supreme Court has over time expanded this qualification slightly to include – in short – parties that are economically equal to the providers of risk bearing capital to the company.[25] Similarly, the Supreme Court has also created the possibility to not only initiate inquiry proceedings against the company in which the petitioner has a direct stake, but also at the same time against a subsidiary if the subsidiary is part of the group and the parent has determined the policy of affairs of the subsidiary.[26] In its judgment, the Supreme Court also explicitly mentioned the economic reality as ground for this reasoning.[27] Once inquiry proceedings are initiated, any interested party is allowed to intervene in the proceedings and submit its own statements and claim immediate relief, as long as the

23 In the period 2008-2019, the annual average number of inquiry requests was 46,4. See: J.B.S. Hijink & L.A. van de Sandt, 'Een empirisch onderzoek van het enquêterecht over de periode 2008-2020', in: C.D.J. Bulten et al (eds), *Handboek Enquêterecht* (Serie Van der Heijden Instituut no 175), Deventer: Wolters Kluwer 2022, para 4.4.1.

24 Articles 2:344/2:345 DCC.

25 Supreme Court 6 June 2003, ECLI:NL:HR:2003:AF2161, *JOR* 2003/61, annotated by M.W. Josephus Jitta (*Scheipar*); Supreme Court 8 April 2011, ECLI:NL:HR:2011:BP4943, *JOR* 2011/178, annotated by A. Doorman (*TESN*); Enterprise Chamber of the Amsterdam Court of Appeal 7 February 2012, ECLI:NL:GHAMS:2012:BV7329, *JOR* 2012/143, annotated by A. Doorman (*Chinese Workers*); Supreme Court 11 April 2014, ECLI:NL:HR:2014:905, *NJ* 2014/296, annotated by P. van Schilfgaarde (*Slotervaart*); Enterprise Chamber of the Amsterdam Court of Appeal 19 July 2016, ECLI:NL:GHAMS:2016:3002, *JOR* 2016/272, annotated by K. Spruitenburg (*FEIST*); See in more detail: D.J.F.F.M. Duynstee, 'De enquêtebevoegdheid van kapitaalverschaffers bij de NV en de BV', in: C.D.J. Bulten et al (eds), *Handboek Enquêterecht (Serie Van der Heijden Instituut no 175)*, Deventer: Wolters Kluwer 2022, para 6.3.

26 Supreme Court 3 April 2020, ECLI:NL:HR:2020:478, *NJ* 2021/103, annotated by M.A. Verbrugh (*SNS*).

27 See for more detail: B. Kemp & M. Olaerts, 'De concernenquête', in: C.D.J. Bulten et al (eds), *Handboek Enquêterecht (Serie Van der Heijden Instituut no 175)*, Deventer: Wolters Kluwer 2022, para 7.3.

requests by the intervening party are related to the claim of the party that initiated the inquiry proceedings.[28] The 'test' for whether a party qualifies as an interested party is broad and relatively easily met.[29] Empirical research shows that such intervention takes place regularly. Over the years 2008-2020, in 509 of the 585 inquiry proceedings initiated during that time (87%), one or more interested parties intervened in pending inquiry proceedings.[30] This data confirms that in corporate disputes there is a high likelihood of parties involved with the company formally engaging in these corporate disputes.

7.3.3 *The potential challenges when resolving corporate disputes through arbitration*

Unsurprisingly, multi-party conflicts and the potential involvement of a range of third parties pose several challenges to resolving corporate disputes in arbitration.[31] These challenges can in our view be divided into three categories, namely: (i) certain issues relevant to corporate disputes

28 Article 282(4) DCCP.

29 Supreme Court 6 June 2003, ECLI:NL:HR:2003:AF2161, *JOR* 2003/61, annotated by M.W. Josephus Jitta (*Scheipar*): "(...) dat in art. 282 lid 1 niet in het algemeen is aangegeven wie tot de belanghebbenden in de zin van deze bepaling zijn te rekenen, en dat dit uit de aard van de procedure en de daarmee verband houdende wetsbepalingen moet worden afgeleid (HR 25 oktober 1991, NJ 1992, 149). Bij de beantwoording van de vraag of iemand belanghebbende is, zal een rol spelen in hoeverre deze door de uitkomst van de desbetreffende procedure zodanig in een eigen belang kan worden getroffen dat deze daarin behoort te mogen opkomen ter bescherming van dat belang of in hoeverre deze anderszins zo nauw betrokken is of is geweest bij het onderwerp dat in de procedure wordt behandeld, dat daarin een belang is gelegen om in de procedure te verschijnen". The legal entity where the investigation is requested is always considered an interested party by the Enterprise Chamber. In addition thereto, the shareholders, depositary receipt holders, (former) managing and supervisory directors, the Enterprise Chamber appointed managing and supervisory directors and trustee of shares, and, if applicable, the bankruptcy trustee, are considered interested parties. Also, the works council and, in the case of healthcare institutions, the clients council have been designated interested parties by the Enterprise Chamber. The same is the case for the members of a cooperative, mutual insurance association or association. Also, (members of) other statutory bodies may qualify as interested parties. For other parties, the Enterprise Chamber determines on a case-by-case basis whether that party should be regarded as an interested party. See also: B.J. Blok & G.C. Makkink, 'Belanghebbendenbegrip', in: C.D.J. Bulten et al (eds), *Handboek Enquêterecht (Serie Van der Heijden Instituut no 175)*, Deventer: Wolters Kluwer 2022, para 16.2.2.

30 Hijink & Van de Sandt 2022, para 4.4.2.6.

31 See on the general challenges of multiparty arbitration: N. Blackaby, C. Partasides & A. Redfern, *Redfern and Hunter on International Arbitration*, Oxford: Oxford University Press 2022, paras 2.234 et seq; B. Hanotiau, *Complex Arbitrations: Multiparty, Multicontract, Multi-issue and Class Actions*, Alphen aan den Rijn: Kluwer Law In-

cannot be arbitrated, (ii) parties cannot, at least not easily, be involved in arbitral proceedings if they are not a party to the arbitration agreement, and (iii) parties can relatively easily 'circumvent' an arbitration clause by bringing certain claims, including certain interested parties and/or going to certain courts, in particular the Enterprise Chamber.

(i) Certain issues relevant to corporate disputes cannot be arbitrated
Whether parties can submit a particular dispute to arbitration is governed by Article 1020(3) DCCP, which states that the arbitration agreement may not lead to the determination of legal consequences that are not at the free disposal of the parties. This is only assumed to be the case if the full dispute is of public policy.[32] The arbitral tribunal will not be allowed to rule contrary to public policy, since the arbitral award will then be subject to refusal of leave for enforcement and setting aside.[33] Already before the 2006 landmark ruling of the Supreme Court in the *Groenselect*-case, it was generally accepted in academic literature that corporate resolutions could only be annulled by a state court, because such an annulment would impact the 'state of the company'.[34] In 2006, the Supreme Court confirmed this view in the Curacao-case *Groenselect* and ruled that disputes regarding resolutions by a corporate body based on Articles 2:14-16 DCC cannot be arbitrated.[35] According to the Supreme Court, determining the validity of resolutions by a corporate body is not at the free disposal of parties, due to, in short, the often far-reaching legal consequences of a resolution of a corporate body, both for the company and for third parties, and in connection with legal certainty. In addition, the court decision should, by its nature, be valid with regard to all affected parties and not only with regard to the claiming party that is a formal party to the proceedings. The Supreme Court stated that this *erga omnes* effect requires the intervention of the state courts.[36]

ternational 2005 and Commission on International Arbitration, Final Report on Multiparty Arbitrations, Paris, June 1994, published in *ICC Bulletin* (6) 1995.

32 Meijer 2010. See also: H.J. Snijders, in: *GS Burgerlijke Rechtsvordering,* Article 1020 DCCP, note 4.1.2.

33 Article 1063(1) DCCP and Article 1065(1)(e) DCCP.

34 E.J.J. van der Heijden, W.C.L. van der Grinten & H.J.M.N. Honée, *Handboek voor de naamloze en de besloten vennootschap,* Zwolle: W.E.J. Tjeenk Willink 1992, no 89; Honée 1997, p 27-42. See for a more nuanced view: De Witt Wijnen 2000, p 129.

35 Supreme Court 10 November 2006, ECLI:NL:HR:2006:AY4033, *JOR* 2007/5, annotated by P. Sanders (*Spee c.s. en Groenselect/Van den Boogaard*).

36 Supreme Court 10 November 2006, ECLI:NL:HR:2006:AY4033, para 3.5, *JOR* 2007/5, annotated by P. Sanders (*Spee c.s. en Groenselect/Van den Boogaard*).

While confirmed again in 2010 by the Supreme Court in the Dutch-case *Silver Lining*-case,[37] this judgment is strongly criticised in legal literature.[38] Critics note, amongst others, that non-arbitrability also applies to resolutions with only internal effect, whereas in such a situation there is no *erga omnes* effect, or at least the protection of third parties is not at issue.[39] Others note that arbitrability should also be possible for resolutions with external effect if certain conditions are met, such as the company being a party to the arbitral proceedings and third parties having the chance to intervene in the proceedings or to challenge the arbitral award afterwards.[40] Setting the merits of this debate aside, it is important to recognise that while a significant part of the academic literature on Dutch corporate law and arbitration focuses on these cases and their consequences, for a corporate litigator the limitations that arise out of *Groenselect* and *Silver Lining* are of limited consequence. The reason for this is twofold. Firstly, the effects of these judgments are generally interpreted narrowly. While a corporate resolution cannot be nullified in arbitration, the effects of such a resolution can be challenged.[41] It is therefore possible to claim damages that a party sustained because of the resolution, to claim interim relief prohibiting any party from implementing the resolution, etc. in arbitration. As a result thereof, attempts to nullify or declare a corporate resolution null and void are relatively uncommon in any proceedings.[42] Secondly, the prevailing view in academic literature seems to be that claims that relate

---

37 Supreme Court 26 November 2010, ECLI:NL:HR:2010:BN8533, *JOR* 2011/7, annotated by R.G.J. de Haan (*Silver Lining*).

38 See amongst others: De Mol van Otterloo 2010; Blanco Fernandez 2010; Van Schilfgaarde 2008 and W. van Baren, 'De enquêteprocedure en arbitrage: privatisering van de dienstmaagd?', in: C.J.M. Klaassen et al (eds), *Onderneming en ADR (Onderneming en recht no 66)*, Deventer: Kluwer 2011, p 190.

39 Van Schilfgaarde 2008, paras 10 et seq; Blanco Fernandez 2010, para 2; De Mol van Otterloo 2010, para 15 and Van Vught 2020, paras 2.2-2.3.

40 See H.M. de Mol van Otterloo, 'Vennootschapsrechtelijke geschillen arbitrabel?', in: C.J.M. Klaassen et al (eds), *Onderneming en ADR (Onderneming en recht no 66)*, Deventer: Kluwer 2011, p 13 and Van Vught 2020, paras 2.2-2.3 et seq.

41 See for example: Supreme Court 3 June 2016, ECLI:NL:HR:2016:1061, *JOR* 2016/233, annotated by K.A.M. van Vught (*IMG*). See on this: A.F. Verdam, 'Strijd met redelijkheid en billijkheid of onrechtmatige daad als rechtsmiddel in relatie tot besluiten van de rechtspersoon', *AA* 2017, p 283-290 and O. Oost, 'De toetsing van (bestuurs)besluiten in arbitrage', in: J.M. de Jongh et al (eds), *Bestuursbesluiten (Instituut voor Ondernemingsrecht no 123)*, Deventer: Wolters Kluwer 2021, p 225-234.

42 See on the limited added value of such claims: J.M. de Jongh, 'De reikwijdte van art. 2:14-16 BW', in: J.M. de Jongh et al (eds), *Bestuursbesluiten (Instituut voor Ondernemingsrecht no 123)*, Deventer: Wolters Kluwer 2021, p 25-40 and B. Kemp, 'Het besluit als rechtshandeling: de verhouding tussen het Nederlandse rechtspersonen- en vermogensrecht', in: J.M. de Jongh et al (eds), *Bestuursbesluiten (Instituut voor Ondernemingsrecht no 123)*, Deventer: Wolters Kluwer 2021, p 49-66.

directly to the resolution can be resolved through arbitration, such as a claim to revoke the resolution, a claim to order a party to vote in a certain manner, etc.[43] This combined with the fact that in most cases parties will not be looking to 'just' nullify a corporate resolution, but also (or even only) want relief that is aimed at challenging the effects of the resolution – which is considered arbitrable, means that the limitations of *Groenselect* and *Silver Lining* are of limited practical relevance.

(ii) Parties cannot, at least not easily, be involved in arbitral proceedings if they are not a party to the arbitration agreement

In accordance with Articles 1020(1) and 1059(1) DCCP, the arbitral award only binds the parties in the arbitration and not third parties, and the arbitral proceedings only involve parties that have committed themselves to arbitration vis-à-vis each other. This means that the *erga omnes* effect of an arbitral award is excluded and the arbitral award only has *inter partes* effect. Moreover, one of the fundamental principles of arbitration is that parties cannot be forced to arbitrate without having (explicitly) agreed thereto.[44] These characteristics create difficulties when resolving corporate disputes because, as set out above, in many such disputes multiple actors are involved, and these actors frequently are not all a party to the arbitration agreement. By way of example, consider that a minority shareholder disagrees with a resolution taken by the management board and approved by the supervisory board. While the minority shareholder, other shareholders and the company itself might be a party to a shareholders' agreement that includes an arbitration agreement, the individual managing and supervisory directors in most cases are not. And while their involvement as a party in the arbitration might not always be strictly legally necessary to obtain an effective award, because resolutions of a corporate body of the company are considered legal acts of the company itself,[45] and can be challenged by arbitrating against the company, not having the possibility to (also) bring actions in arbitration against the managing and supervisory directors can create challenges. For instance, document production tools can in most instances not be used, at least not directly, vis-à-vis these persons.

Such challenges are even more prominent in case the company itself is also not a party to the arbitration agreement. If a minority shareholder wants to act against both the majority shareholder and the company, but the share-

43 Oost 2019, p 804 and Van Schilfgaarde 2008.
44 Blackaby, Partasides & Redfern 2022, paras 1.20 and 2.01.
45 Asser/Kroeze *2-II* 2021/290.

holders' agreement is only between the shareholders, the minority shareholder might have to initiate proceedings before the state court (for the company) and in arbitration (for the majority shareholder) to achieve the desired legal effect.[46] Not only is this more burdensome, and a potential source of complex questions on jurisdiction and concurrence of arbitral and state court proceedings, but it also deprives the minority shareholder of the benefits of arbitration when litigating against the company. The same applies the other way around. If the company believes it should be involved in the arbitration on the matter that the minority shareholder is arbitrating against the majority shareholder, it will want to intervene in or join the arbitral proceedings. It can, however, in principle only do so with consent of the parties already involved in the arbitration.[47] If the minority shareholder believes it is not in its interest for the company to join or intervene in the arbitral proceedings (as the company will likely support the majority shareholder), it can withhold its consent.

Another element to this challenge is that when not all relevant parties are involved in the arbitration, the arbitrators could feel less informed because third parties have not had the opportunity to present their position on the matter in the way they could have done in state court proceedings with their more expansive opportunities for intervention and joinder. While the arbitral award only has *inter partes* effect, and the decision therefore only binds the parties to the arbitration and not third parties, arbitrators might still feel they should rule only narrowly or even dismiss a claim because of a lack of information on the facts or on the position taken by the third parties. By way of example, assume that there is a dispute about a resolution taken by the former managing directors of a joint venture. The shareholders and company are party to the arbitration agreement, but the former managing directors are not. One of the shareholders initiates arbitral proceedings, effectively challenging the effects of the resolution, and argues that the former managing directors had a personal conflict of interest when taking the resolution. While challenging the effects of the resolution is arbitrable and such proceedings can be initiated against the company, because corporate resolutions are considered legal acts of the company, the arbitrators are effectively forced to rule on the personal interests of the

46 See on this challenge in a general multiparty context: L.J.E. Timmer, 'Derdenwerking van arbitrageovereenkomsten in commerciële contracten', *NTHR* 2020, p 167-176.

47 Article 1045(1) DCC. See for confirmation that all parties have to agree to the rejoinder or intervention: *Parliamentary Papers II* 1985/86, 18464, no 6, p 23; *Parl. Gesch. Arbitragewet* 2015, p 695-696, and Asser/Sanders, Meijer & Ernste *8* 2023/225-226.

former managing directors and whether that affected the resolution taken. While this is legally possible, and it happens in practice that arbitrators determine facts that principally involve or impact third parties,[48] an arbitrator might prefer to receive information and pleadings directly from the former managing directors when ruling firmly on this matter. Moreover, if certain parties in the arbitration or especially those unable or willing to participate in the arbitration have (also) brought the matter before the state court, this might further incline the arbitrators to not rule in full on the matter. This could especially be the case when legal proceedings are pending before the Enterprise Chamber, as this is a specialised business court with far reaching powers and – for now[49] – a clear track record of stating that it is not in any way limited by an arbitration agreement between the parties. Under such circumstances, arbitrators might prefer to await the judgment of the Enterprise Chamber or decline to get involved in matters that are also within the remit of the Enterprise Chamber.

(iii) Parties can relatively easily circumvent an arbitration clause by bringing certain claims, including certain interested parties and/or going to certain courts

In line with the challenges described in (ii) above, parties can 'steer' a corporate dispute away from arbitration by (a) bringing certain claims that are non-arbitrable, (b) involving parties that are not a party to the arbitration agreement in the proceedings and/or (c) initiating legal proceedings before the Enterprise Chamber. The first (a) can be achieved by requesting a state court to declare a resolution null and void or to nullify the resolution. As discussed above, pursuant to Supreme Court case law, such a claim cannot be resolved through arbitration and must be brought before a state court.[50] There is conflicting case law from lower courts on whether the claimant is also able to bring auxiliary claims in these state court proceedings, even though such claims should have been brought in arbitration when considered stand-alone.[51] While – as discussed under

48 S. Brekoulakis, 'The effect of an arbitral award and third parties in international arbitration: res judicata revisited', *The American Review of International Arbitration* (16) 2006, issue 1, p 16.

49 See para 7.4 under C below.

50 See para 7.3.3 under (i) above.

51 See in favour: Rotterdam District Court 9 November 2016, ECLI:NL:RBROT:2016:8659, para 4.6, *TvA* 2017/17; Roermond District Court 25 July 2012, ECLI:NL:RBROE:2012:6123, paras 2.9-2.11, *TvA* 2014/19; Utrecht District Court 25 May 2011, ECLI:NL:RBUTR:2011:BQ7177, paras 2.1-2.3, *TvA* 2012/46; and Rotterdam District Court 22 September 2010, ECLI:NL:RBROT:2010:BO1691, paras 4.3-4.4, *TvA* 2011/50. See against: Rotterdam District Court 30 September 2020, ECLI:NL:RBROT:2020:8558, para 5.5.1, *TvA* 2021/27; Oost-Nederland District

(i) – corporate litigation provides for various ways to challenge certain behaviour, this has the flip side that the claimant can choose to structure his claim in such a way that he can avoid or aim for the matter to be resolved through arbitration. The second (b) essentially entails the same "trick" as the first, but then with the parties instead of the claims. A claimant can in certain cases structure the litigation in such way that it is comprised solely of parties that are not a party to the relevant arbitration agreement.[52] In corporate disputes these possibilities might be more influential than 'ordinary' contractual disputes, because of the large variety of actors involved in the company and the possibility to litigate against individual managing and supervisory directors based on a breach of fiduciary duties. The third (c) is very specific to Dutch company law, as it – as set out above – provides for the possibility for certain parties – including shareholders and the company itself – to initiate inquiry proceedings before the Enterprise Chamber of the Amsterdam Court of Appeal.[53] The Enterprise Chamber has ruled that these proceedings belong to the exclusive domain of the state courts, and parties cannot be kept away from these proceedings because they have agreed on arbitration.[54] In other words, even if the shareholders and company have agreed to arbitration, they in principle still have the possibility to request the Enterprise Chamber to intervene in the

Court 16 January 2013, ECLI:NL:RBONE:2013:BZ0464, para 14, *TvA* 2013/53; and Rotterdam District Court 19 May 2010, ECLI:NL:RBROT:2010:BN1358, para 4. See also: A. Marsman, *International Arbitration in the Netherlands, With a Commentary on the NAI and PCA Arbitration Rules,* Alphen aan den Rijn: Kluwer Law International 2021, para 7-044.

52 This was one of the points raised by Advocate General Timmerman in his advisory opinion rendered prior to the *Groenselect*-case, where he believed the Court of Appeal allowed the binding of the company to the arbitration agreement, while a non-signatory to that agreement, because otherwise it would have been easy for the claimants to circumvent the arbitration clause (see on this: Advocate-General Timmerman, advisory opinion rendered prior to Supreme Court 10 November 2006, ECLI:NL:HR:2006:AY4033, *JOR* 2007/5, annotated by P. Sanders (*Spee c.s. en Groenselect/Van den Boogaard*), para 2.12.

53 See para 7.3.2 above.

54 Enterprise Chamber of the Amsterdam Court of Appeal 18 October 2012, ECLI:NL:GHAMS:2012:BY5614, para 3.2, *JOR* 2013/8, annotated by H.M. de Mol van Otterloo (*Harbour Antibodies*); Enterprise Chamber of the Amsterdam Court of Appeal 24 October 2013, ECLI:NL:GHAMS:2013:4637, para 3.2, *JOR* 2014/159, annotated by W.H. van Baren; Enterprise Chamber of the Amsterdam Court of Appeal 4 September 2014, ECLI:NL:GHAMS:2014:3738, para 3.2, *ARO* 2014/181 (*Café Kobalt*); Enterprise Chamber of the Amsterdam Court of Appeal 22 December 2017, ECLI:NL:GHAMS:2017:5493, para 3.5, *ARO* 2018/54 (*Prosolar*); and Enterprise Chamber of the Amsterdam Court of Appeal 1 February 2018, ECLI:NL:GHAMS:2018:361, *JOR* 2018/93, annotated by F. Eikelboom (*Europa Leasing*).

matter and order far-reaching interim measures to (temporarily[55]) affect the governance of the company. While the broad way in which the Enterprise Chamber has set aside arbitration clauses is not without criticism,[56] this case law has been in place for over a decade and has not met heavy resistance.[57] As a result, summarising, shareholders and the company can also avoid arbitration by simply starting inquiry proceedings, even while an arbitration is ongoing.

Potential ineffectiveness of an arbitration clause in the articles of association

One point that further reinforces these challenges is the debate on the relative ineffectiveness of including an arbitration clause in the articles of association of the company. Although it is possible to include an arbitration clause in the articles of association,[58] and a shareholder that voted in favour of the arbitration clause will be bound by it, many other elements of the arbitration clause remain unclear. For instance, will a person who became a shareholder after the arbitration agreement was included in the articles of association become a party to the arbitration agreement? There is no case law that directly answers this question, and the academic literature is divided.[59] Another question is whether a shareholder that voted against the inclusion of the arbitration clause in the articles of association can be bound by such a clause. A majority in Dutch academic literature seems to reason that such shareholders cannot be bound by the arbitration clause, because they did not agree to it.[60] Moreover, in line with the above, it is at the least unclear whether managing and supervisory directors could be bound by the arbitration clause included in the articles of association, unless they explicitly agreed to be bound. This uncertainty and the narrow interpretation of when a shareholder, managing or supervisory director is

55 Immediate measures may be granted and remain in effect until the earlier of the end of the inquiry proceedings or a set date so determined by the Enterprise Chamber at its sole discretion.

56 See for instance: Enterprise Chamber of the Amsterdam Court of Appeal 18 October 2012, ECLI:NL:GHAMS:2012:BY5614, *AA* 2013, p 932-937, annotated by M. J.G.C. Raaijmakers (*Harbour Antibodies*) and Strik 2022, para 45.3.1.

57 The Supreme Court has not yet had the opportunity to rule on this matter.

58 Article 104(5) DCCP.

59 See: M. Meinema, *Dwingend recht voor de besloten vennootschap: een beschouwing van de contractsvrijheid van aandeelhouders in rechtsvergelijkend perspectief* (diss. Maastricht), Deventer: Kluwer 2003, p 60-61; O. Oost, 'De statutaire arbitrageclausule in het licht van artikel 2:81 en 2:192 BW', *Ondernemingsrecht* 2017/72 and Kroeze 2007. See also: The Hague Court of Appeal 29 June 2010, ECLI:NL:GHSGR:2010:BM9599, *JOR* 2011/35. The Hague Court of Appeal held that an exoneration clause in the articles of association was also binding on new members of an association.

60 See: Wakkie 2002; Oost 2017 and Kroeze 2007. Otherwise: De Witt Wijnen 2000, p 133.

bound to the arbitration clause in the articles of association, if he did not explicitly agree to it, means that such a clause is arguable currently not a very effective tool to help resolve corporate disputes. We believe a more pragmatic view on this would be both defensible and helpful. Defensible, because an arbitration clause in the articles of association would not be a very effective tool if any individual resisting (or not explicitly accepting) shareholder could frustrate the applicability of such clause, thereby strongly limiting the effect of article 1020 (5) DCCP. Moreover, the European Court of Justice has held on forum clauses in articles of association that these bind shareholders if they are and stay a shareholder in the company, which – although it is a slightly different question – could provide inspiration on how to consider arbitration clauses.[61] Helpful, because it would create the possibility to – as is the case under Swiss law – bind all relevant actors to the arbitration clause.

7.3.4 *Arbitration of corporate disputes should be further facilitated*

The above shows various challenges that make arbitration less effective as a means to resolve corporate disputes. Is this however a problem and does it deserve to be – to the extent possible – resolved? We would argue that the answer to that question is unequivocally 'yes'. Arbitration is recognised as an important instrument to resolve disputes in a commercial setting, where aspects such as picking your own arbitrators, confidentiality and adverse costs orders are material incentives for parties to agree to arbitration,[62] especially in joint ventures. One point to zoom in on is choosing the decision-makers. Dutch state court judges are generally considered to be of a high quality, reliable and fast.[63] However, at the same time most judges – as in many continental systems – are career judges, with no or only limited experience in advocacy, let alone international commercial/ corporate advocacy. Dutch courts are also not structured in such a way that a judge (or judges) with ample experience in international corporate disputes always presides over the legal proceedings. As a result, parties 'risk' having a judge allocated to the case that has little or no experience

61 HvJ EG 10 March 1992 (*Powell Duffryn/Petereit*), *NJ* 1996, 279. See for more detail specifically on arbitration clauses: Meijer 2008; Meijer 2010.

62 Another incentive is generally the relatively uncomplicated enforcement of arbitral awards. This will, however, in many cases be less important with respect to corporate disputes, as the enforcement will often be against a company domiciled in the Netherlands, which would not be more complicated when having obtained a Dutch state court judgment.

63 The Netherlands is ranked 5th in the WJP Open Government Index rankings. See: https://worldjusticeproject.org/open-government-around-world.

in international corporate disputes. This 'risk' can be avoided by agreeing to arbitration and choosing your own arbitrators, which can also provide parties with more comfort in the capabilities of the persons resolving the dispute. This is, however, only possible if such an agreement is effective in keeping parties away from state courts and in arbitration.

More in general, Dutch civil (procedural) law recognises the advantages of arbitration and has a tradition of being arbitration friendly.[64] This was again reiterated by the legislator when the Dutch arbitration law was updated in 2015.[65] As in other countries, a Dutch state court must declare itself incompetent in case parties have agreed to arbitration.[66] Contrary to the UNCITRAL Model Law on International Commercial Arbitration[67] and the national arbitration laws of most countries with a modern arbitration law,[68] this is even the case when parties request preliminary relief.[69] Dutch arbitration law determines that if the relief can be requested and timely granted in arbitration, which according to the Dutch state courts is the case under the ICC- and NAI-rules,[70] a preliminary relief judge is in principle not competent to rule on the requested relief.[71] There is conflicting case law from lower courts whether this is even the case if parties agreed, either explicitly in their arbitration agreement or through the relevant rules of the arbitral institutions, that they have the possibility to request emergency relief before state courts.[72] Also, specifically in corporate disputes, the legislator has promoted the use of arbitration as a means of resolving disputes.

64 See: Marsman 2021, p 5 et seq.
65 *Parliamentary Papers II* 2012/13, 33611, no 3, p 1.
66 Article 1022 DCCP.
67 Article 17J of the 2006 Revision to the UNCITRAL Model Law.
68 G.B. Born, *International Commercial Arbitration. Volume II: International Arbitral Proceedings*, Alphen aan den Rijn: Kluwer Law International 2021, p 2729-2733, which gives an incomplete description of the laws of the Netherlands.
69 See for more detail on emergency relief in Dutch arbitration law: Marsman 2021, p 301 and Snijders 2018, p 354 et seq.
70 See for a relatively recent overview: N. Peters, 'De vraag naar de uitvoerbaarheid van arbitrale voorlopige voorzieningen in het Koninkrijk mede bezien in het licht van art. 1022c Rv en art. 1074d Rv', *TvA* 2022/2, and references included there. See specifically on the LCIA: R. Schellaars, 'A Tale of Two Cities – aangepaste reglementen van de LCIA en de ICC', *TvA* 2021/2, p 7-15.
71 Articles 1022a and 1022c DCCP.
72 See: Preliminary relief judge of the The Hague District Court 12 June 2015, ECLI:NL:RBDHA:2015:6959, *TvA* 2016/15 (*Can-Pack*); Preliminary relief judge of the Amsterdam District Court 12 January 2017, ECLI:NL:RBAMS:2017:282 (*Cygne/Cofco*); Preliminary relief judge of the Rotterdam District Court 24 August 2020, ECLI:NL:RBROT:2020:7383, *TvA* 2020/74 (*Essilorluxottica/Grandvision*) and Amsterdam Court of Appeal 6 April 2021, ECLI:NL:GHAMS:2021:941, *TvA* 2021/62 (*Essilorluxottica/Grandvision*). See on this case law: Peters 2022, p 7-13.

Under Dutch law, there is the possibility for shareholders, holding at least one third of the shares in a company, to initiate so-called statutory shareholder dispute resolution proceedings, by which a claiming shareholder can either aim to be bought out or force another shareholder to transfer his shares.[73] As part of these proceedings, the parties to the proceedings can also bring auxiliary claims and request interim measures required to resolve the exit.[74] Dutch company law explicitly states that parties can agree to bring these proceedings, and if they do so, parties should (only) bring these proceedings, in arbitration.[75] With the recent legislative update of these proceedings, this provision will be upheld.[76]

Given the above, we would argue that Dutch law, and therefore also the Dutch courts, should strive to facilitate that corporate disputes can be resolved through arbitration where possible. In our view, more could be done to achieve this, by the legislator, the Enterprise Chamber and arbitral institutions, such as the NAI. Below we will discuss various options, in part based on experiences and developments in other jurisdictions.

7.4 Instruments to mitigate the challenges around resolving corporate disputes through arbitration

To mitigate the aforementioned challenges and seek the effective resolution of corporate disputes through arbitration, when the actors in the company agree to arbitration, various instruments can be considered. Below, three such instruments are discussed, being (a) more effectively facilitating the intervention or joinder of third parties to the arbitration or those third parties being bound to the outcome of the arbitration, (b) the broader application of the so-called groups of companies doctrine binding related parties to an existing arbitration agreement and (c) a more restrained approach of the Enterprise Chamber to its own jurisdiction when a petitioning party has agreed to arbitration and the dispute could be timely resolved in arbitration. For instruments (a) and (b), inspiration will also be taken from the German DIS Supplementary Rules for Corporate Law Disputes, the Supplemental Swiss Rules for Corporate Law

73 Book 2 DCC, Title 8, Chapter 1.
74 Articles 2:336(5) and 2:343(2) DCC and Article 223 DCCP.
75 Article 2:337(2) DCC.
76 Bill amending the statutory shareholder dispute resolution proceedings and clarification of the admissibility criteria for Dutch corporate inquiry proceedings (Wet aanpassing geschillenregeling en verduidelijking ontvankelijkheidseisen enquêteprocedure (*Stb.* 2024, 174)).

Disputes of the Swiss Arbitration Institute and the largely French case law on the groups of companies doctrine.

A. More effectively facilitate the intervention of third parties in an arbitration and/or being bound by the outcome of that arbitration

As set out above, it is difficult for third parties to willingly join or intervene in arbitral proceedings without already being a party to the arbitration agreement or obtaining consent from all other parties to the proceedings, as intervention or joinder require being a party or such consent.[77] The rules of the most relevant arbitral institutions in a Dutch context, such as the NAI and the Arbitration Board for the Building Industry (RvA), mirror this requirement. Article 43 NAI Rules (2024) states that the arbitral tribunal may allow a party to join or intervene, provided that the same arbitration agreement as between the original parties applies or enters into force between the original parties to the arbitration and the third party. Article 15 RvA Rules similarly states that the request to join by a third party can only be considered by the arbitral tribunal if sufficient evidence is provided that an arbitration agreement has been concluded between the third party and one of the parties in the arbitral proceedings. This is similar to the provisions included in major international institutional rules, such as Article 7 of the ICC Rules and Article 22.1(x) of the LCIA Rules. Moreover, parties cannot be forced to arbitrate against their will, as a key principle of arbitration is that parties have to willingly – and explicitly – agree to arbitration. The requirement of consent is also relatively strictly upheld in the Netherlands.[78]

There are, however, also institutional rules that, specifically in the context of corporate disputes, provide a set of rules that help to more effectively resolve those disputes in arbitration. As most arbitrations, especially in a corporate setting, are conducted under the rules of arbitral institutions,[79] these can be an effective tool to supplement arbitration agreements and applicable arbitration laws when resolving corporate disputes. In this contribution, the focus will be on the German DIS Supplementary Rules for Corporate Law Disputes (2009) and the Swiss Supplemental Swiss Rules for Corporate Law Disputes (2023). For Germany, brief reference will also be made to the recently introduced Supplementary Rules for Third Party Notices, as these are an important contribution to effectively deal with the position of third parties in arbitral proceedings.

77 Article 1045 DCCP.
78 See para 7.4 under B below.
79 Snijders 2018, para 2.1.8.1.

DIS Supplementary Rules for Corporate Law Disputes 2009

In 2009, the German Arbitration Institute (DIS) introduced rules specifically designed to enable parties to resolve the annulment of corporate resolutions through arbitration'.[80] This development followed a landmark judgment by the *Bundesgerichtshof* of that same year, in which that court ruled – contrary to previous case law[81] – that the validity of a shareholders' resolution in a limited liability company (GmbH)[82] can, under certain minimum conditions, be resolved through arbitration.[83] These minimum conditions are, in short, (i) consent to arbitration by all shareholders, (ii) the opportunity to participate in the arbitral proceedings by all shareholders, (iii) the opportunity to participate in the constitution of the arbitral tribunal by all shareholders and (iv) concentration of jurisdiction.[84] These conditions address the *erga omnes* effect of a judgment as provided for in Article 246 II(1) of the Aktiengesetz (as also deemed applicable to the GmbH), which provides that a judgment on the validity of a shareholders' resolution should have effect towards all affected parties if the company has been involved in the proceedings.

The DIS designed a model arbitration clause and developed supplementary rules for arbitrating corporate law disputes to meet these minimum conditions, the DIS Supplementary Rules for Corporate Law Disputes.[85] It did that by including in the annex rules that are focused on the inclusion of so-called "concerned others", being shareholders who need to necessarily be bound to the outcome of the arbitration.[86] These concerned others are invited to join the arbitral proceedings as a party or compulsory intervener.[87] One of the main features of the DIS Supplementary Rules is that it determines that even if the concerned others opt to not join the arbitral

80 See on this: Borris 2011 and Berow, 'Arbitrating Shareholder Resolutions Disputes in Germany: The new DIS-Supplementary Rules for Corporate Law Disputes (DIS-SRCoLD)', in: *SAD ARBITRAZOWY PRZY KRAJOWEJ IZBIE GOSPODARCZEJ* (Wydawca ed, 2010).

81 Bundesgerichtshof 29 March 1996, II ZR 124/95 (*Arbitrability I*), 1996 NJW 1753.

82 This has later been expanded by that same court to also apply to limited partnerships: Bundesgerichtshof 6 April 2017, I ZR 23/16.

83 Bundesgerichtshof 6 April 2009, II ZR 255/08 (*Arbitrability II*), 2009 NJW 1962.

84 Borris 2011, p 62-64.

85 The 2009 DIS Supplementary Rules for Corporate Law Disputes can be found here: https://www.disarb.org/en/tools-for-dis-proceedings/dis-rules.

86 The DIS Supplementary Rules also include various provisions on the amendment and withdrawal of claims, the participation in the constitution of the arbitral tribunal, the concentration of jurisdiction in parallel cases, extension of effects of the arbitral awards and time limits and costs.

87 See para 69 German Procedural Rules. Such a position in legal proceedings differs on certain key points from being a formal party.

proceedings, they will still be bound by the outcome. For the DIS Supplementary Rules to be applicable, parties need to explicitly refer to these rules in the arbitration agreement.[88] The model arbitration clause provided by the DIS shows what such a reference could look like, and for completeness sake also restates that an award rendered in accordance with the DIS Supplementary Rules extends to "others concerned" even if these persons decided not to participate in the arbitral proceedings.[89] The DIS Supplementary Rules exclusively cover corporate law disputes, which are, pursuant to the DIS Supplementary Rules, deemed disputes requiring a single decision binding the company and all shareholders, in particular those regarding the validity, voidability or invalidity of shareholder resolutions, as well as resolutions by an advisory board, a supervisory board or other boards. As a result, the DIS Supplementary Rules take a more narrow view on what constitutes a corporate dispute than we do in this contribution.

A related development worth mentioning is that on 15 March 2024 the DIS Supplementary Rules for Third-Party Notices (DIS-TPNR) were introduced. These rules, that have to be agreed upon by the parties to the initial arbitration and in the contract between the parties to the subsequent dispute,[90] grant the parties to the initial arbitration the right to join a third party. The third party is then allowed to participate in the initial arbitration[91] and – in turn – agrees to be bound by the award rendered in the initial arbitration. This binding effect extends to the determination and legal assessment of the facts. By providing for this option, the DIS aims to provide for rules that prevent the same factual or legal issues being re-litigated and assessed differently in any subsequent proceedings against a third party.

Supplemental Swiss Rules for Corporate Law Disputes 2023
More recently, in 2023, the Swiss Arbitration Centre also introduced an arbitration clause and developed supplementary rules for arbitrating corporate law disputes, the Supplemental Swiss Rules for Corporate Law Disputes.[92] These rules were introduced in response to changes in the Swiss Code of Obligations that entered into force 1 January 2023, which introduced the possibility for Swiss companies to include an arbitration

88 Article 1.1 of the DIS Supplementary Rules for Corporate Law Disputes.
89 Para 2 of the Model Arbitration Clause.
90 Article 1.1 of the DIS-TPNR.
91 Article 6.2 of the DIS-TPNR.
92 The 2023 Supplemental Swiss Rules for Corporate Law Disputes can be found here: https://www.swissarbitration.org/centre/arbitration/arbitration-rules/.

clause in the articles of association and thereby bind not only the company to the arbitration agreement, but also the managing and supervisory directors and shareholders.[93] In response to these statutory changes, the Swiss Arbitration Centre issued the Supplemental Swiss Rules and provided a so-called Model Statutory Arbitration Clause.[94] The Supplemental Swiss Rules should either be included in an arbitration clause included in the articles of association or in a contractual arbitration clause, provided that the clause explicitly refers to the applicability of the Supplemental Swiss Rules.[95] In essence, the aim of the Supplemental Swiss Rules is to enable "affected persons" to be involved in the arbitral proceedings, either through becoming a party to the proceedings or by becoming a "non-party intervener" that may upon request of the arbitral tribunal comment on certain acts in the arbitration. To this end, the Supplemental Swiss Rules provide, amongst other things, that persons who may be directly affected by the legal effects of the arbitral award, *i.e.*, 'affected persons', shall be informed of the commencement and termination of arbitral proceedings.[96] Affected persons may submit comments on the appointment of the arbitral tribunal.[97] Third persons may under certain circumstances participate in the arbitral proceedings and the tribunal shall ensure that affected persons are properly able to exercise their rights.[98] The secretariat may, upon request, inform affected persons of the names of the arbitrators and the arbitral tribunal may grant affected persons access to certain information concerning the arbitral proceedings.[99] This way, it is safeguarded that

93 Article 697n(1) of the Swiss Code of Obligations: "The articles of association may provide that disputes arising under company law are to be decided by an arbitration tribunal in Switzerland. Unless otherwise provided in the articles of association, the company, its organs, the members of the organs and the shareholders are bound by the arbitration clause." It will not bind other third parties, such as creditors (BGE 136 III 107 E. 2.5.).

94 This model clause reads as follows: "(1) Any corporate law dispute, excluding matters subject to summary proceedings pursuant to Article 250(c) of the Swiss Civil Procedure Code [and excluding actions for cancellation of outstanding equity shares according to the Federal Act on Financial Market Infrastructures and Market Conduct in Securities and Derivatives Trading], shall be resolved by arbitration in accordance with the Swiss Rules of International Arbitration of the Swiss Arbitration Centre in force on the date on which the Notice of Arbitration is submitted in accordance with those Rules. (2) The seat of the arbitration shall be [insert name of the company seat/other city in Switzerland]. (3) The arbitration proceedings shall be conducted in [insert desired language)."

95 Article 1 of the Supplemental Swiss Rules.

96 Article 2 of the Supplemental Swiss Rules.

97 Article 3 of the Supplemental Swiss Rules.

98 Article 4 of the Supplemental Swiss Rules.

99 Article 5 of the Supplemental Swiss Rules.

those bound to the outcome of an arbitration have the opportunity to participate in the arbitration.

The scope of the Supplemental Swiss Rules is also broader than the DIS Supplementary Rules. While the DIS Supplementary Rules are in practice only applicable with respect to corporate law disputes on the validity of resolutions of corporate bodies, the Supplemental Swiss Rules are applicable to a broad range of corporate disputes including liability actions against members of the corporate bodies of the company, actions regarding unduly paid dividend to shareholders and actions on the liquidation and dissolution of the company.[100] The Supplemental Swiss Rules, with reference to Article 697n of the Swiss Code of Obligations, provide that 'corporate law disputes' are to be settled by an arbitral tribunal seated in Switzerland.

Rules of arbitral institutions and model arbitration agreements

As seen above, in various jurisdictions, the rules of arbitral institutions aim to make arbitration a more effective tool for resolving corporate disputes. This is mainly achieved by providing for a model arbitration clause in combination with supplemental rules specifically tailored for corporate disputes by (a) other parties to the arbitration agreement being informed of the arbitral proceedings and (b) allowing these parties to join the arbitral proceedings in some capacity. In Switzerland, this is combined with an explicit statutory provision stating that if an arbitration clause is included in the articles of association, this will in principle be binding on the other actors in the company, including managing and supervisory directors and shareholders.[101] The introduction of this statutory provision makes this

100 Explanatory Note to the Supplemental Swiss Rules (p. 2): "(...) disputes said to fall within the scope of corporate law disputes (...) include (i) challenges against resolutions of the general meeting (Articles 706, 691(3) and 689f(2) read in conjunction with Article 691(3) CO; Article 106 Swiss Merger Act); (ii) declaratory actions regarding the nullity of resolutions of the general meeting and the board of directors (Articles 706b and 714 CO); (iii) liability actions against members of the governing bodies of the Company (Articles 752 et seqq. CO; Article 108 Swiss Merger Act); (iv) actions for the return of benefits (Article 678 CO; these actions are covered at least insofar as they are directed against shareholders, members of the board of directors, and persons involved in the management of the Company and members of the advisory board;3 (v) actions for the dissolution of the Company (Article 736(1) CO); (vi) actions for an appropriate compensation payment following a restructuring (Article 105 Swiss Merger Act); (vii) further actions, including actions of the Company against a shareholder for the performance of the obligation to pay the share capital and actions in connection with transfer restrictions."

101 Unless the articles of association themselves provide otherwise: Article 697n(1) of the Swiss Code of Obligations.

arrangement particularly effective, because it binds the various relevant actors in the company to the arbitration clause. Introducing such a system in the Netherlands would help mitigate many of the issues associated with challenges (ii) and (iii) above.

However, it should be noted that, even without a statutory provision, parties may already partially adopt the Swiss approach allowing other corporate actors to become parties to the arbitration clause or pending arbitral proceedings. This could be done both contractually and in the articles of association. Parties could for instance draft an 'open' arbitration agreement, which in essence determines that (i) any party initiating arbitration under this agreement will inform the (other) managing and supervisory directors and shareholders in the company of the pending arbitration and (ii) that all parties to the arbitration will consent to the joinder or intervention of any managing or supervisory director or shareholder in the arbitral proceedings. Such clauses are, however, uncommon in practice for obvious reasons, amongst others, because it would lead to very extensive arbitration clauses. Arbitral institutions could facilitate such an 'open' arbitration agreement for corporate disputes by providing for a model clause in combination with supplementary rules that include more detailed arrangements for the provision. We will expand on this suggestion below in paragraph 7.5.

B. The broader application of the group of companies doctrine to bind parties to an arbitration clause

Another instrument to mitigate issues arising out of the challenges mentioned above would be to bind certain non-signatory corporate actors to an arbitration agreement because of their affiliation with the (direct) parties to the arbitration agreement. In the context of corporate law, the most well-known example of such a mechanism is the 'group of companies' doctrine.[102] As the name suggests, this doctrine is applied in the context of company groups. Although recognising the separate legal personality, including rights and obligations, of individual legal entities is the starting point under all corporate laws in modern jurisdictions, there are many

102 See for general descriptions and references to further literature on this subject: Born 2021-II, p 1558, and the extensive references included there; J.F. Poudret & S. Besson, *Comparative Law of International Arbitration*, London: Sweet & Maxwell 2007, p 210 et seq; E. Gaillard & J. Savage, *Fouchard Gaillard Goldman on International Commercial Arbitration*, The Hague: Kluwer Law International 1999, paras 500 et seq and B. Hanotiau, 'Groups of Companies in International Arbitration', in: L.A. Mistelis & J.D.M. Lew (eds), *Pervasive problems in international arbitration*, Alphen aan den Rijn: Kluwer Law International 2006, p 279-290.

exceptions where obligations are also attributed to other legal entities in the group.[103] This is mainly the case when enterprises abuse the separate legal personality in order to have certain entities in the group avoid being bound to legal obligations. Enterprises can abuse individual legal entities in the context of an arbitration agreement, for instance when an entity that was closely involved in drafting the contract at dispute is not a party to the arbitration agreement. To create the possibility to still involve that legal entity in the arbitration, the 'groups of companies' doctrine was developed.

Under this doctrine, non-signatories may be deemed a party to the arbitration agreement if (a) it can be demonstrated that the intention of all the parties involved was to consider the whole of the group as the contracting party without giving specific importance to which company would conclude the contract and (b) the non-signatories actively participated in the negotiations, performance and/or termination of the agreement, even if they did not sign it.[104] The core question therefore is whether the parties intended certain non-signatory affiliate entities to be bound to the arbitration agreement.[105] The 'group of companies' doctrine has only been accepted in a limited number of jurisdictions,[106] with France as its most prominent defender. In France, the 'group of companies' doctrine originated with the *Dow Chemical* award,[107] in which the undivided economic reality *'une réalité économique unique'* was the key for the arbitral tribunal to bind non-signatory group companies to the arbitration agreement. In this case, amongst others, the reasoning for this outcome was found in the absolute control of one of the group companies over the subsidiaries, the role of the group companies in the conclusion, perfor-

103 See more detailed on this development, also in its historic context: J.E. Antunes, *Liability of Corporate Groups: Autonomy and Control in Parent-Subsidiary Relationships in U.S., German and EEC Law: An International and Comparative Perspective*, Deventer: Kluwer Law and Taxation Publishers 1994, p 13; B. Kemp, 'Developments in European Company Group Law, from Formalism Towards the Economic Reality', in: B. Kemp & M. Olaerts, *Twenty Years European Company Law*, Deventer: Wolters Kluwer 2024, p 269-281 and R.M. Manóvil (ed), *Groups of Companies: A Comparative Law Overview*, Cham: Springer 2020.

104 P. Ferrario, 'The Group of Companies Doctrine in International Commercial Arbitration: Is There Any Reason For This Doctrine to Exist?', *Journal of International Arbitration* (26) 2009, p 647-648.

105 See the case law referenced in: G.B. Born, *International Commercial Arbitration. Volume I: International Arbitration Agreements*, Alphen aan den Rijn: Kluwer Law International 2021, p 1564, footnote 249. See also: Gaillard & Savage 1999, para 500.

106 G. Wegen & S. Wilske (eds), *Getting the deal through: Arbitration in 55 Jurisdictions Worldwide*, London: Law Business Research Ltd 2013.

107 *Dow Chemical France et al v. Isover Saint Gobain*, ICC Interim Award in case no 4131 of 23 September 1982, excerpt in IX Yearbook Commercial Arbitration (1984), p 131 et seq.

mance, or termination of the relevant agreements and the mutual intentions of the parties with regard to the transaction and the agreements in question. The *Dow Chemical* arbitral award was confirmed by the Paris Court of Appeal.[108] French courts have since also confirmed awards based on the 'group of companies' doctrine.[109] In certain other jurisdictions, the group of companies doctrine has been expressly rejected, such as in England.[110] In essence, the argumentation there seems to follow a more strict legal approach and sees less room than the French courts for the application of the economic reality.

Dutch arbitration (case) law seems an arid soil for applying the groups of companies doctrine, as to date the Netherlands has adopted a strict approach in accepting non-signatories as parties to the arbitration agreement.[111] By way of illustration, in Dutch setting aside proceedings, the Amsterdam Court of Appeal in 2022 set aside an arbitral award rendered under the arbitration rules of the NAI because one of the parties was held not to be party to the arbitration agreement.[112] The relevant party co-signed the agreement containing the arbitration clause as 'acknowledged and agreed' but this circumstance was deemed insufficient by the Amsterdam Court of Appeal. The Court of Appeal stated that circumstances are indeed conceivable where a third party must reasonably allow a contractual term against it, but only if there is sufficient justification for this in the nature of the matter at hand.[113] It concluded that there were no facts and circumstances that could support the opinion that it must reasonably be assumed that the relevant party had to assert the arbitration clause against itself. Also, there was insufficient basis to consider giving third-party effect to the arbitration clause. The Court of Appeal held that with respect to the arbitration clause, it could at most be found that the relevant party had 'agreed' that disputes between the other parties would be settled by means of NAI arbitration.[114] Specifically in the sphere of corporate law, there are

---

108 Paris Court of Appeal 23 October 1983, Rev. arb. (1984), p 98 et seq.

109 Born 2021-I, p 1560; Poudret & Besson 2007, p 217 et seq and Gaillard & Savage 1999, p 286 et seq.

110 See for more detail: Born 2021-I, p 1558 et seq.

111 G.J. Meijer, *Overeenkomst tot arbitrage. Bezien in het licht van het bewijsvoorschrift van artikel 1021 Rv (diss. Rotterdam; Burgerlijk Proces & Praktijk no 13)*, Deventer: Kluwer 2011, para 9.3.3.1 and V. Lazic, 'Using the 'Group of Companies' Doctrine to Extend Arbitration Agreements to 'Third-Parties'', *NTHR* 2013, p 332-341.

112 Amsterdam Court of Appeal 30 August 2022, ECLI:NL:GHAMS:2022:2493, *TvA* 2022/93.

113 With reference to: Supreme Court 20 June 1986, ECLI:NL:HR:1986:AD5694, *NJ* 1987/35, annotated by W.C.L. van der Grinten (*Khaly/Freezer*).

114 Amsterdam Court of Appeal 30 August 2022, ECLI:NL:GHAMS:2022:2493, para 4.32, *TvA* 2022/93.

also examples that demonstrate a reluctance to bind non-signatories. The Almelo District Court ruled that the fact that two legal entities have the same director and shareholder is insufficient to bind the non-signatory entity.[115] Similarly, the Supreme Court upheld a judgment of the The Hague Court of Appeal in which an arbitral award was set aside because the tribunal ruled that the Dutch subsidiary of a German parent was party to an arbitration agreement on the basis that the director of the Dutch subsidiary was one of the board members of the German parent and it had requested the counterparty to send all invoices to the Dutch subsidiary (in copy to the German parent).[116]

Compared to Dutch arbitration law, Dutch corporate law seems to generally take a more pragmatic and flexible approach.[117] Under Dutch corporate law, there has been a strong development towards recognising the 'economic reality' in recent years.[118] Such recognition can be found in statutory provisions, such as Article 2:24b DCC, which gives a definition of the company group and in that respect refers to the 'economic unit', as well as various judgments by the Supreme Court in which the Supreme Court expands the right to initiate inquiry proceedings to certain parties not explicitly mentioned in the statutory provisions based on the economic reality.[119] And specifically in company groups, the Supreme Court has re-

115 Almelo District Court 19 September 2012, ECLI:NL:RBALM:2012:BX9241, *TvA* 2013/13.

116 Supreme Court 20 January 2006, ECLI:NL:HR:2006:AU4523, *TvA 2007/7* (ASB Grünland en ASB Greenworld/Sagro). See on this case Lazic, who notes that the group of companies doctrine was not explicitly mentioned in the case and it therefore difficult to say that the courts expressly rejected the doctrine: Lazic 2013, p 332-341.

117 In principle, the fact that arbitration takes a more formalistic approach compared to company law can also reasonably be explained. Assuming that a party is bound to an arbitration agreement means that the specific party can – in principle – no longer petition the state courts. It is widely accepted that such courts and tribunals should be cautious and exercise restraint when accepting that a non-signatory is bound to an arbitration agreement. In contrast, in company law there is more need for a flexible approach, because it is difficult to foresee future behaviour of parties and issues that come up, and companies can be active for a long period of time, during which the company itself, the market in which it operates and society itself might change significantly. See on the dynamics of company law: Kemp 2024a.

118 See on this subject amongst others: B.F. Assink, 'De 'economische werkelijkheid' in het Nederlandse Ondernemingsrecht', *WPNR* 2014, issue 7037, p 1026-1029; C.D.J. Bulten, 'De vennootschap en de geconstrueerde werkelijkheid', *Ondernemingsrecht* 2014/94 and B.F. Assink & L. Timmerman, 'Is de economische werkelijkheid een uitgangspunt voor het gehele ondernemingsrecht?', *Ondernemingsrecht* 2023/101, p 715-716.

119 See the case law included in footnote 25 above.

cently reconfirmed the importance of the economic reality.[120] Under Dutch law, shareholders of a company have the responsibility to act reasonable and fair towards the company, other shareholders and other "institutional stakeholders".[121] The question before the Supreme Court was whether indirect shareholders under certain circumstances have the same responsibility. The Supreme Court answered this question in the affirmative and pointed out that even though Article 2:8 DCC, the Dutch statutory provision on corporate reasonableness and fairness, is formulated in such a way that it focuses on the single legal entity, this provision also applies, under specific circumstances, to the relationship between companies and their institutional stakeholders in an organisational group.[122] In other words, the Supreme Court was willing to expand the applicability of statutory rights and obligations to persons that do not directly have that right according to the relevant legal provisions, on the basis of the economic reality.

The question could be raised whether this more pragmatic approach could 'spill over' into Dutch arbitration law, when answering the question whether non-signatory companies could be bound to an arbitration agreement. While this should – as is the case for the groups of companies-doctrine as a whole[123] – be the exception to the rule, we believe there is an argument to be made for allowing more room for the economic reality in corporate disputes when deeming a non-signatory bound to an arbitration agreement. We see this view confirmed by professor and former Advocate General Timmerman, a strong supporter of recognising the economic reality in corporate law. In his advisory opinion rendered prior to the *Groenselect*-case, he argued that Groenselect should be bound by the arbitration clause between its shareholders and another party on the grounds of identification. His reasoning was in short, that (i) the substantive and procedural position of Groenselect and those of its shareholders were highly

120 Supreme Court 22 September 2023, ECLI:NL:HR:2023:1283, *JOR* 2024/1, annotated by E.C.H.J. Lokin (*Funda*). See in more detail on the economic reality in company groups amongst others: Kemp 2024b.

121 The term "*institutional stakeholders*" is used for persons that fall under the scope of Article 2:8 DCC and therefore have the obligation to act reasonably and fairly towards each other and the company. See in more detail on this term: J.B. Huizink, in: *GS Rechtspersonen*, Article 2:8 DCC, note 6.

122 Supreme Court 22 September 2023, ECLI:NL:HR:2023:1283, *JOR* 2024/1, annotated by E.C.H.J. Lokin (*Funda*): "The circumstances of the case may therefore mean that, in addition to the persons mentioned above in the first sentence of this recital, the scope of section 2:8(1) of the Dutch Civil Code also includes the legal entity organisationally related to the legal entity mentioned in that first sentence and those who are involved in the organisation of the latter legal entity by virtue of the law and the articles of association."

123 Born 2021-I, p 1562.

intertwined, and (ii) it followed the spirit of the arbitration clause, from which the intention of the shareholders in Groenselect to submit all disputes arising from their joint existing and future corporate interests to arbitration followed.[124] The Supreme Court ultimately did not address this point in its judgment, because it considered corporate resolutions non-arbitrable. In legal literature, the suggestion of binding the company to the arbitration agreement in this case was criticised mainly by arbitration lawyers. Snijders, for instance, noted that to argue that the company is bound to an arbitration agreement because a significant majority of shareholders are a party to it, should be considered a bridge too far.[125] Meijer is mainly critical of whether the Court of Appeal provided sufficient motivation for binding the company as non-signatory to the arbitration agreement.[126] While we understand this criticism and there should indeed be a sufficient motivation in the case at hand, we feel that there is some merit to assuming a doctrine based on economic reality in corporate disputes when considering the position of non-signatory corporate actors.

While case law on the group of companies doctrine primarily relates to binding other affiliate companies that were involved in the negotiations and drafting of the contract, it could also be considered to extend this doctrine to managing and supervisory directors under extraordinary circumstances. By way of illustration, if the managing and supervisory directors were closely involved with the drafting of the shareholders' agreement on behalf of the company and specific obligations for those directors are included therein, it could be argued that binding the managing and supervisory directors to the arbitration agreement included in the shareholders' agreement is considered reasonable. The same could be achieved by taking a more pragmatic view on the corporate actors bound to an arbitration clause in the articles of association.[127] If it would be accepted that shareholders, as well as managing and supervisory directors are in principle bound to an arbitration clause when introduced into the articles of association, this would make such a clause considerably more effective. It would also in part effectively achieve what was proposed above under A. It would, however,

124 See Advocate-General Timmerman, advisory opinion rendered prior to Supreme Court 10 November 2006, ECLI:NL:HR:2006:AY4033 (*Spee c.s. en Groenselect/Van den Boogaard*), para 2.11 et seq and note H.J. Snijders in *NJ* 2007/561.

125 See note H.J. Snijders to Supreme Court 10 November 2006, ECLI:NL:HR:2006:AY4033, *NJ* 2007/561 (*Spee c.s. en Groenselect/Van den Boogaard*) and Meijer 2010.

126 G.J. Meijer, *Overeenkomst tot Arbitrage*, Deventer: Kluwer 2008, para 9.3.3.3. See also: Meijer 2010.

127 See para 7.3.3 under (iii) above.

be (much) better if the arbitration laws and/or rules of arbitral institutions provide for effective instruments on this point, as basing such a doctrine solely on case law has its own difficulties.

C. Advocating for more restraint by the Enterprise Chamber when parties agreed to arbitration

As set out above, the starting point under Dutch civil procedural law is that a state court should decline jurisdiction if a party invokes the existence of an arbitration agreement before all defences, unless the agreement is held to be invalid.[128] However, the Enterprise Chamber has effectively ruled that this provision is not applicable when parties initiate inquiry proceedings before that court. In consistent case law since 2012, the Enterprise Chamber has confirmed that inquiry proceedings are the exclusive domain of state courts and parties cannot be denied access to that court on the basis of an arbitration agreement.[129] From a legalistic perspective, the position taken by the Enterprise Chamber is understandable, as inquiry proceedings are specifically tailored towards whether an inquiry (investigation) should take place into the policy and affairs of the company. If such an inquiry is ordered, the court-appointed investigator has certain powers to force the relevant actors to cooperate with the investigator to ensure that a full investigation can take place.[130] However, in practice, very few inquiry proceedings are initiated with the main purpose to obtain an investigation. Instead, most parties initiating inquiry proceedings are mainly focused on convincing the Enterprise Chamber to order immediate relief measures.[131] These relief measures, even measures with a similar effect to those ordered by the Enterprise Chamber, can however also be obtained in provisional relief proceedings before the

128 Article 1022 DCCP.

129 Enterprise Chamber of the Amsterdam Court of Appeal 18 October 2012, ECLI:NL:GHAMS:2012:BY5614, para 3.2, *JOR* 2013/8, annotated by H.M. de Mol van Otterloo (*Harbour Antibodies*); Enterprise Chamber of the Amsterdam Court of Appeal 24 October 2013, ECLI:NL:GHAMS:2013:4637, para 3.2, *JOR* 2014/159, annotated by W.H. van Baren (*Staat Creative Agency*); Enterprise Chamber of the Amsterdam Court of Appeal 4 September 2014, ECLI:NL:GHAMS:2014:3738, para 3.2, *ARO* 2014/181 (*Café Kobalt*) and Enterprise Chamber of the Amsterdam Court of Appeal 22 December 2017, ECLI:NL:GHAMS:2017:5493, para 3.5, *ARO* 2018/54 (*Prosolar*).

130 See: J.M. Blanco Fernandez, 'Het onderzoek', in: C.D.J. Bulten et al (eds), *Handboek Enquêterecht (Serie Van der Heijden Instituut no 175)*, Deventer: Wolters Kluwer 2022, para 21.

131 In the period 2008-2020, in 89% of the inquiry proceedings one or more immediate relief measures were requested. See: Hijink & Van de Sandt 2022, para 4.4.2.3. See also on this trend: J.H.M. Willems, 'Van kern naar randverschijnsel: Gucci en wat volgde', in: G.C. Makkink, M.P. Nieuwe Weme & A.J. van Wees (eds), *Ik ben niet overtuigd (Prinsengrachtreeks)*, Nijmegen: Ars Aequi Libri 2015, p 557-563.

state court[132] or – in many cases – in emergency arbitral proceedings.[133] The peculiar result of the position taken by the Enterprise Chamber is that if such relief is requested by a party before a district court in provisional relief proceedings, the judge would have to decline jurisdiction if the relief can be obtained timely in emergency arbitration,[134] while in inquiry proceedings the Enterprise Chamber feels that it is not held to the same rule. The justification that the Enterprise Chamber itself gives for its 'immunity' to arbitration agreements is that Articles 2:344-359 DCC provide for an extraordinary procedure and that this procedure can lead to direct intervention in the state of the company, both by ordering immediate relief and by final relief, and the broad possibilities for third parties to intervene.[135] Only in extraordinary cases, such as where the arbitral proceedings are already pending, and the Enterprise Chamber is requested to rule on matters that are a point of dispute in that arbitration, has the Enterprise Chamber decided to not order an inquiry on the basis of a balancing of the interests involved and the fact that there were insufficient grounds for ordering an inquiry.[136] We believe that this approach and the reasons given for it are insufficient to justify the position taken by Enterprise Chamber.[137] The Enterprise Chamber should, in our view, solely accept jurisdiction if it is clear that requesting an inquiry is at the core of the request or if the requested relief cannot be timely obtained in emergency arbitration.[138] If the primary purpose of the inquiry seems to

132 See on the concurring jurisdiction of the Enterprise Chamber and the provisional relief judge: B. Kemp, 'De voorzieningenrechter en Ondernemingskamer als 'bedrijvendoktoren': over houdgrepen en wurggrepen, vlieggewichten en zwaargewichten', in: B. Bier et al (eds), *Geschriften vanwege de Vereniging Corporate Litigation 2018-2019 (Serie Van der Heijden Instituut no 157)*, Deventer: Wolters Kluwer 2019, para II.1.2. See also the Enterprise Chamber itself in Enterprise Chamber of the Amsterdam Court of Appeal 7 March 2023, ECLI:NL:GHAMS:2023:583, *JOR* 2023/181, annotated by S.C.M. van Thiel, where it held that the Enterprise Chamber has concurring jurisdiction next to the provisional relief judge.

133 See on the ability to request interim relief in emergency arbitration similar to the measures ordered by the Enterprise Chamber: Strik 2022, para 45.3.5 and Kemp 2019, para II.1.3.2.

134 Article 1022c DCCP.

135 See Enterprise Chamber of the Amsterdam Court of Appeal 18 October 2012, ECLI:NL:GHAMS:2012:BY5614, *JOR* 2013/8, annotated by H.M. de Mol van Otterloo.

136 See for a description of relevant case law: F. De Ly, 'Parallele Procedures: Raakvlakken tussen Ondernemings- en Arbitragerecht', in: M.A. Verbrugh et al (eds), *Eindeloos getob. Liber Amicorum Kid Schwarz (Instituut voor Ondernemingsrecht no 125)*, Deventer: Wolters Kluwer 2022, p 581-593.

137 See also critical, at least of the reasons given by the Enterprise Chamber: Strik 2022, para 45.3.1.

138 Although we recognize that this is not always easy for the Enterprise Chamber to do. However, the Enterprise Chamber does have experience in reviewing the intention of the parties as part of the proceedings, as part of the admissibility is a balancing of the interests of the parties to the proceedings (see: M.H.C.

be obtaining immediate relief that could also be obtained timely in (emergency) arbitration, the Enterprise Chamber should deny jurisdiction.

If the Enterprise Chamber were to take on this alternative position, the consequence would be that parties are forced to adhere to what they agreed on with the other parties and – in principle – to turn to arbitration in order to obtain immediate relief and settle corporate disputes. In our view, this is more in line with the intentions of the legislator on the position of arbitration in our civil (procedural) law, including corporate law.[139] It would also further incentivise parties, practitioners and arbitral institutions to develop arbitration clauses and – if necessary – push for legislative changes to further support resolution of corporate disputes through arbitration and tackle the aforementioned challenges.

7.5 Towards a more dynamic corporate disputes arbitration approach

What does the above lead to? There are clearly challenges to litigating corporate disputes in arbitration. Currently, these challenges are in part avoided by parties resolving corporate disputes not through arbitration but instead opting for inquiry proceedings before the Enterprise Chamber. This, however, deprives parties of the advantages of arbitration in an international commercial setting. Moreover, it is against the intentions of the legislator, who wants to facilitate resolving commercial disputes, including corporate disputes, through arbitration. We believe an alternative more dynamic approach is also possible, through which the challenges are tackled in such a way that arbitration can be an effective tool to resolve corporate disputes. We do not believe it to be necessary to – as part of this – revoke the Supreme Court case law on arbitrability of corporate resolutions. What could be done instead is the following:

1. The legislator and arbitral institutions could consider ways to improve the position of non-signatories in corporate disputes. There are various ways to achieve this. One more far-reaching option is to determine in statutory law that certain corporate actors, such as managing and

Sinninghe Damsté & P.L. Hezer, 'Afwijzing van het enquêteverzoek', in: C.D.J. Bulten et al (eds), *Handboek Enquêterecht (Serie Van der Heijden Instituut no 175)*, Deventer: Wolters Kluwer 2022, para 19.3.2.1), and the Enterprise Chamber itself has by way of its presidents acknowledged that parties regularly petition the Enterprise Chamber primarily to obtain relief (C.D.J. Bulten et al, 'Een kwartet OK-voorzitters aan het woord', in: C.D.J. Bulten et al (eds), *Handboek Enquêterecht (Serie Van der Heijden Instituut no 175)*, Deventer: Wolters Kluwer 2022, para 3.3).

139 See para 7.3.4 above.

supervisory directors and shareholders, are bound to a statutory arbitration agreement or even – under specific circumstances – a contractual arbitration agreement. The Swiss have in essence embraced such a system, although it is too early to determine what the experiences are there. The German rules seem to serve as less of an inspiration, because of the lack of relevance of annulling corporate resolutions in Dutch corporate disputes. Introducing a statutory provision similar to the Swiss Article 697n(1) Code of Obligations would in our view be both ambitious and helpful. A less far reaching – and in the short term maybe more realistic – option would be not to *force* corporate actors into becoming a party to the arbitration agreement or pending arbitration, but for those actors to get the *opportunity* do so. This would mean that the (original) parties to the arbitration agreement would at the time of concluding the arbitration agreement provide other corporate actors with this possibility, as a result of which the signatories cannot block such actors from being involved once a dispute arises or is pending in arbitral proceedings. For this option, no legislative changes are necessary. Parties can already agree to this and the NAI could – as a neutral party – facilitate this further by providing for a model arbitration clause. It would be helpful to combine this with an annex to the NAI Arbitration Rules, in which certain procedural arrangements are set out in more detail.[140] That way, the technical complexities of the arbitration clause can be outsourced to separate arbitration rules and the arbitration clause itself can remain relatively short, as is customary in most instances.[141] Moreover, the annex can be changed relatively easily to further improve it, without the need to amend individual arbitration agreements. Such rules could also include the distinction made under the Swiss rules between 'parties to the arbitration' and 'non-party interveners'.

2. Arbitrators, and state courts in setting aside proceedings, could consider taking small steps towards a more flexible approach to bind non-signatories to an arbitration agreement based on the importance of the economic reality in corporate law. Of course, this power should be exercised with caution, and only when the facts demonstrate that it was the intention of the parties that the specific actor/third party should be a party to the arbitration agreement. In our view, this could potentially also be the case when a managing director was closely involved in the negotiations on a sharehold-

140 As has also been done in Switzerland and Germany, see para 7.4 under A above.

141 See for this argument specifically in relation to the DIS Supplementary Rules: Borris 2011, p 65.

ers' agreement and that agreement includes provisions with explicit obligations for that managing director. Similarly, a more pragmatic approach could be taken on when corporate actors are bound to an arbitration clause in the articles of association.[142] This would make it possible, in certain situations, to ensure that the relevant parties can properly be involved in the arbitration.

3. The Enterprise Chamber could take a more critical stance on its own jurisdiction when parties have entered into an arbitration agreement. Under those circumstances, in our view, the Enterprise Chamber could review whether (a) parties are actually interested in and helped by an inquiry, and (b) the requested immediate relief – if any – could also be timely obtained in (emergency) arbitration. If parties do not require intervention by the Enterprise Chamber but can also resolve their dispute through arbitration, the Enterprise Chamber should decline jurisdiction and refer parties to the agreed upon arbitration agreement. To the extent the Enterprise Chamber feels that the possibility for third parties to intervene is a justification to ignore arbitration clauses, this argument would become weaker if the actions under 1. and 2. above are put into practice.

If these steps could be taken, it would be a significant step to solving the challenges that may be encountered when resolving corporate disputes through arbitration. We believe the Netherlands as a progressive arbitration and corporate law jurisdiction, and the NAI as the perfectly placed arbitral institution, could help push the cart towards these steps and make it happen, so that at the next lustrum of the NAI it can be concluded that the Netherlands is a leading jurisdiction when it comes to resolving corporate disputes through arbitration. And who knows, it might even provide sufficient comfort to the Supreme Court to take a different view when again confronted with the question whether the challenging of resolutions can be resolved through arbitration if certain conditions are met.[143]

142 Such as is the case in Switzerland, where a shareholder voting against the inclusion of an arbitration clause in the articles of association is still considered bound to the arbitration agreement: BGE 24 II 552 E. 8 (p. 564). See also: T. Ritter, *Einheitliche Entscheidung gesellschaftsrechtlicher Beschlussanfechtungsklagen vor Schiedsgerichten* (diss. Zürich), Zürich: Schulthess Verlag 2015, para 644; and V. Meier, *Schiedsklauseln in Statuten schweizerischer Aktiengesellschaften* (diss. Zürich) Zürich: Schulthess Verlag 2017, paras 172 et seq and 191.

143 See for a similar conclusion on addressing the *erga omnes* effect by facilitating the involvement of third parties: De Mol van Otterloo 2011, p 28-29.

CHAPTER 8

ARBITRATION IN INSURANCE DISPUTES

Natalie Vloemans[1]

8.1 Introduction

The Netherlands Arbitration Institute (NAI) turns seventy-five in 2024, which is a great opportunity to consider whether institutional dispute resolution, particularly at the Netherlands Arbitration Institute, lends itself to application to different areas of law. In this contribution, the focus is on insurance disputes.

The short and somewhat simplified answer to the question whether insurance disputes lend themselves to settlement by national or international arbitration is: yes. Yet the number of insurance disputes that have been resolved in arbitrations administered by the NAI (or any other Dutch arbitration institute) is limited. There are several reasons for this. In this contribution, I discuss the possible procedural hurdles and the possible practical objections. I then turn to answering the question whether arbitration at an arbitration institute, and in particular the NAI, is suitable for the resolution of insurance disputes.

For the purposes of this contribution, I take the resolution of coverage disputes under an insurance contract as my starting point. Such coverage disputes arise in very different areas. In terms of the nature of the case, the capacity of the parties and the financial importance of the case, there is a substantial difference between, say, a dispute over a claim under a disability insurance policy and a dispute on coverage under a Construction All Risks policy. This does not make it easy to give a straightforward answer to the question whether insurance disputes lend themselves to arbitration.

Moreover, insurance law practice is broader. In legal practice, 'insurance law' often includes disputes between the insured and a third party (e.g. the claimant: the party that incurred losses), which are handled under the

1 N. (Natalie) Vloemans (LLM) is an attorney and partner at Ploum Rotterdam Law firm and a member of the Advisory Board of the Netherlands Arbitration Institute.

direction and at the expense of the insurer. This type of disputes cannot be separated from coverage disputes: when a liability insurer denies coverage, it may affect the dispute between the insured and the third party claiming damages. This is because the coverage dismissal puts the insured in a position where its own assets for recovery will be called upon by the third party. The insured's own asset position may be problematic in this regard, giving the third party an interest in establishing that, different to what the insurer argues, the liable party is entitled to compensation under its liability insurance policy. Moreover, if personal injury is involved, the issue of '*action directe*' laid down in Article 7:954 of the Dutch Civil Code may play a role. I will try to touch upon the various issues in this contribution.

Insurance disputes may also involve regulatory issues, such as whether a company that provides a broad guarantee when selling its products may be offering insurance, or mediating the conclusion of an insurance policy, but it goes beyond the scope of this contribution to examine whether these too can be settled by arbitrators. I also leave aside disputes between insurers themselves (recourse cases or issues between insurer and reinsurer). As regards disputes between insurers it can, however, generally be said that they lend themselves ideally to arbitration, as the confidentiality of the arbitral proceedings may be an important aspect that the insurers involved value. In particular, reinsurance disputes are mainly settled by arbitration in the countries where the major reinsurers are based (the UK, Germany and Switzerland).[2] Reinsurance disputes are only occasionally litigated in the Netherlands and exploring whether the settlement of these disputes could be facilitated by the NAI, for example, would therefore become a rather theoretical exercise.

8.2 Procedural perils

8.2.1 The arbitration agreement

In an earlier publication, my colleague Dorine ten Brink and I wrote that in Dutch insurance practice, arbitration is not often conducted on the ba-

2 K. Noussia, *Reinsurance Arbitrations*, Berlin Heidelberg: Springer-Verlag 2013, p 15 et seq.

sis of an arbitration agreement concluded in advance.[3] Exceptions include in particular reinsurance contracts and Construction All Risks (CAR) insurance, in which an arbitration clause is included with some regularity (but is certainly not standard). Meijer also mentions directors' liability insurance as an exception,[4] but in my experience the arbitration clause in that type of insurance is mainly seen in contracts with foreign insurers in cases where a significantly higher than average risk (with correspondingly higher sum insured) is insured. These are often the excess policies (the policies that are triggered only after cover under the underlying primary insurance has been exhausted). In my experience, the smaller, more standard directors' liability insurance policies still mainly refer to the state court as the competent court. This can lead to problems: in my practice, I have come across cases where the primary directors' liability policy between a Dutch policyholder and a Dutch insurer refers to the state court, while the excess policies with (often in co-insurance) one or more foreign insurers have an arbitration clause. Because the insurance terms and conditions of the primary policy and the excess insurance are usually (largely) the same and the parties aim for the terms and conditions therein to also be interpreted the same,[5] the settlement of disputes through different means of dispute resolution is unsatisfactory.

We have cited several reasons for the fact that arbitration is not often conducted on the basis of a pre-arbitration agreement in insurance practice, and one of them is the awkward position of third parties playing a role besides the insured and its insurer. It is common for a 'third party' to be involved: brokers, agents, co-insureds, beneficiaries under the insurance contract, injured parties and other third parties may play a role in the dispute. If the dispute leads to litigation, it is generally preferable that all possible contractual and noncontractual disputes are adjudicated by the same court and the same type of procedure (arbitral proceedings *versus* court proceedings). However, the inclusion of all interested or relevant third

3 See paras 10.2 and 10.3 of D. ten Brink & N. Vloemans, 'Het gebruik van arbitrage en bindend advies in de verzekeringspraktijk vanuit het perspectief van partijen', in: C.J.M. Klaassen et al (eds), *Verzekering en ADR (Onderneming en recht no 83)*, Deventer: Kluwer 2014, p 175-210.

4 G.J. Meijer, 'Overeenkomst tot arbitrage in het verzekeringsrecht: op welke wijze(n) raken verzekeraars, verzekeringnemers en verzekerden daaraan zoal gebonden?', in: C.J.M. Klaassen et al (eds), *Verzekering en ADR (Onderneming en recht no 83)*, Deventer: Kluwer 2014, p 231-250.

5 Many excess policies have a so-called *Follow Form clause*, meaning that the excess insurance is done on the terms of the primary policy. The purpose of this clause is to ensure *back-to-back* coverage of the excess insurance against the primary policy.

parties in arbitral proceedings is almost impossible to define in advance in an agreement. After all, an arbitration agreement is in principle only valid between the contracting parties, who have waived their (constitutional) right of access to the state courts.

The inclusion of a third party as a co-insured third party under the policy is considered a third-party clause. In the aforementioned publication, we pointed out that a co-insured third party may not always be aware of its designation as an insured under the insurance contract or may not even be aware of the insurance at all. We conclude that a co-insured third party is not bound by an arbitration clause contained in the insurance contract unless it expressly accepts such a clause.[6]

Kalff and Van Zelst have suggested the inclusion of an 'open arbitration agreement' as a possible model on the basis of which it could be achieved that the various parties involved in an insurance dispute could submit their issue in one arbitration.[7] In fact, their proposal does not involve an arbitration agreement, but an open offer to arbitrate that could be included in the insurance contract. I do not immediately see the advantage of this, except in cases involving co-insurance and several *layers* (layers of insurance; i.e. a primary policy and one or more excess policies) with several insurers involved. In that case, the insurers involved are bound by the arbitration offer they make in the policy (assuming that the primary policy and the excedent policies contain an identical and cross-referenced open arbitration clause). If only one insurer is involved in the policy, the 'open arbitration agreement' is not much different from the situation where the parties involved in a dispute, including the third parties involved, decide to enter into an arbitration agreement with each other after the dispute arises. In other words, if an insurer prefers arbitration, it will be willing to enter into an arbitration agreement even after a dispute arises. If the insurer is wary of arbitration proceedings, it will be reluctant to include an open arbitration clause in the policy in advance. Moreover, insured parties are usually reluctant to allow third parties like the injured party to inspect the terms and clauses of their insurance contract. Thus, third parties will

---

6 The same conclusion is reached by G.J. Meijer, who makes an interesting comparison with the European Court of Justice's ruling that the co-insured third party must have explicitly accepted a forum clause in the (insurance) contract, CJEC 14 July 1983, C-201/82, ECLI:EU:C:1983:217, *NJ* 1984/716, annotated by J.C. Schultz (*Gerling v Administrazione del Tesoro Dello Stato*) (see Meijer 2014).

7 M.L.S. Kalff & B. van Zelst, 'Arbitrage in de verzekeringspraktijk', in: C.J.M. Klaassen et al (eds), *Verzekering en ADR (Onderneming en recht no 83)*, Deventer: Kluwer 2014, p 27-42.

also be unaware of the open arbitration clause in the insurance terms and conditions and may not accept the offer to arbitrate unless the existence of the open arbitration clause is expressly communicated to them. That situation is hardly different from the situation in which the parties concerned conclude an arbitration agreement after the dispute occurs and the proceedings are then also settled along the lines of joinder or intervention (see below).

What would be possible, however, is the inclusion of an "option clause" for alternative dispute resolution in the policy conditions. I came across an example in a US directors' liability insurance policy:

> "**ADR Options:** All disputes or differences which may arise under or in connection with this Coverage Section, whether arising before or after termination of this policy, including any determination of the amount of Loss, shall be submitted to an alternative dispute resolution (ADR) process as provided in this Clause. The Named Entity may elect the type of ADR process discussed below; provided, however, that absent a timely election, the Insurer may elect the type of ADR. In that case, the Named Entity shall have the right to reject the Insurer's choice of the type of ADR process at any time prior to its commencement, after which, the Insured's choice of ADR shall control."

The advantage of this "option clause" is that it encourages parties to consider a form of alternative dispute resolution (which could also be mediation or binding advice) without being bound in advance to a particular institution, number of arbitrators or form of dispute resolution. The parties cannot reach an impasse either: the policyholder may choose but if he does not, the insurer determines the method of dispute resolution.

8.2.2 Third parties in the proceedings

Besides the issue that a third party (co-insured, injured party etc.) cannot be legally bound to an arbitration agreement in the terms of insurance, Ten Brink and I discussed the procedural possibilities and impossibilities for third parties to join pending proceedings in our aforementioned contribution.

In terms of procedural options, Dutch arbitration law has the same options as procedural law before the state courts. Article 1045 of the Dutch Code of Civil Procedure (DCCP), for instance, provides for legal concepts such as joinder, intervention and indemnification (third party proceedings). The NAI Arbitration Rules 2024 provide for the same in Article 43. A third party may request the arbitral tribunal in pending proceedings (in writing) to be allowed to join one of the parties or to intervene between the two parties.[8] For joinder or intervention, it is required that the third party has joined the arbitration agreement by written agreement with the parties.[9] If the arbitral tribunal grants the request, the third party becomes a party to the pending proceedings.[10] However, the arbitral tribunal takes its decision only after giving the parties an opportunity to express their views. The third party may also be given the opportunity to express its opinion, but the arbitral tribunal is not obliged to do so.[11]

Under Article 1045a DCCP and under Article 43(4) NAI Arbitration Rules 2024, a party may also involve a third party in indemnification proceedings.[12] Also in this case, involvement of a third party can only be admitted by the arbitral tribunal if the third party has joined the arbitration agreement by written agreement with the parties. Since 1 January 2015[13], the arbitral tribunal is obliged to hear the parties as well as the third party (orally or in writing) before deciding on the request. The arbitral tribunal will not allow indemnification if it considers it implausible in advance that the third party will be obliged to bear the adverse consequences of any judgment against the interested party, or if it considers that unreasonable or unnecessary delay can be expected as a result of indemnification proceedings.[14] The rationale behind this is to ensure the effectiveness of the arbitral proceedings; the arbitral tribunal has to consider the issue based on rulings in case law of the state courts.[15]

Conversely, it is conceivable that proceedings are pending before the state court and that one of the parties decides to call a third party in those proceedings on indemnification, while an arbitration agreement has been con-

8 See Article 1045(1) DCCP/Article 43(1) NAI Arbitration Rules 2024.
9 See Article 1045(4) DCCP/Article 43(1) NAI Arbitration Rules 2024.
10 See Article 104594) DCCP/Article 43(1) NAI Arbitration Rules 2024. See further on the legal concepts of joinder and intervention Ten Brink & Vloemans 2014.
11 See Article 1045(3) DCCP/Article 43(5) NAI Arbitration Rules 2024.
12 See Article 1045a(1) DCCP/Article 43(4) NAI Arbitration Rules 2024. Previously, indemnification was regulated in Article 1045 DCCP, together with joinder and intervention. This changed following the entry into force of the Arbitration Law Modernisation Act on 1 January 2015 (Act of 2 June 2014 amending Book 3, Book 6 and Book 10 of the Civil Code and the Fourth Book of the Code of Civil Procedure in connection with the modernisation of arbitration law, *Parliamentary Papers II* 2013/14, 33611).
13 See footnote 12.
14 See Article 1045a(4) DCCP/Article 43(5) NAI Arbitration Rules 2024.
15 Explanatory Memorandum to Article 1045a DCCP of the Arbitration Law Modernisation Act, *Parliamentary Papers II* 2012/13, 33611, no 3.

cluded between the calling party and the third party. In our contribution to the book Insurance and ADR, we discussed several examples of cases in which, under those circumstances, an arbitration agreement was set aside by the court by relying on Article 6:248(2) of the Dutch Civil Code.[16]

The third procedural possibility leading to multiparty proceedings is consolidation. Aggregation of arbitral proceedings (*consolidation*) before the same dispute resolution body is regulated in Article 1046 DCCP and Article 44 NAI Arbitration Rules 2024, respectively. If the arbitral proceedings are conducted under the rules of arbitration law in the DCCP, a request for consolidation may be submitted to a third party designated by the parties. If they have not designated a third party, they may apply to the preliminary relief judge of the District Court of Amsterdam. If the parties have agreed to arbitration under the NAI Rules (2024) and do not jointly appoint a third party, the third party is appointed by the responsible member of the NAI Case Management Committee.[17] For joinder, it is sufficient that the two proceedings to be joined are pending. The arbitral tribunal does not yet have to be composed in both cases. The requested third party or the interim relief judge may grant or refuse the request after giving all parties and – if appointed – the arbitrators the opportunity to express their views (orally or in writing).[18] Considerations in this regard are whether consolidation does not unreasonably delay the pending proceedings, and whether there is such a close connection between the arbitral proceedings that the proper administration of justice requires that they be heard and adjudicated simultaneously in order to avoid irreconcilable decisions being rendered in separate proceedings.[19]

8.2.3 Arbitration and consumers

Consumers occupy a special position in procedural law and the same is certainly true in arbitration law. It remains a tricky issue that an arbitration clause deprives a party of access to the state courts. It is therefore not surprising that, with the entry into force of the Modernisation of Arbitration Law Act on 1 January 2015, the arbitration clause included in general terms

16 See Ten Brink & Vloemans 2014, p 194 et seq.
17 Appendix E (2) NAI Arbitration Rules 2024.
18 See Article 1046(3) DCCP/Appendix E (4) NAI Arbitration Rules 2024.
19 See Article 1046(2) DCCP/Article 44(2)(a) & (b) NAI Arbitration Rules 2024. See further on the legal concept of consolidation Ten Brink & Vloemans 2014, p 196 et seq. See also J.W. Bitter, 'Samenvoeging van arbitrale gedingen in Nederland volgens art. 1046 Rv, nut en noodzaak; *opting in* or *opting out*', *TvA* 2012/55.

and conditions has been added to the black list of unreasonably onerous clauses in consumer contracts (Article 6:236(n) of the Dutch Civil Code). This means that an arbitration clause in a user's general terms and conditions in a contract with a consumer is unreasonably onerous and therefore voidable, unless the general terms and conditions give the consumer a period of at least one month to choose the state court to settle the dispute.

As a result, an arbitration clause included in the general terms and conditions of a consumer's insurance is equally unreasonably onerous and therefore voidable. An arbitration clause will not be considered a core clause, unlike what applies to several other general insurance conditions, such as provisions on the premium, description of coverage and coverage exclusions.[20]

8.2.4 The 'action directe'

An interesting position is held by the injured party with personal injury, who has the right under Article 7:954 of the Dutch Civil Code to exercise the claim of the liable party against his insurer. This right is often referred to as *'action directe'* but that qualification is not entirely accurate. At least, it follows from the Parliamentary Explanation to the provision that it is not, as it is in Belgian or French law, a direct right of its own to sue the insurer of the liable party.[21] The Dutch right of the injured party is a derivative right of action: the injured party may in fact exercise the right of the liable party itself, i.e. its right to compensation under the liability contract.[22] In that case, is the injured party bound by an arbitration clause in the contract between the liable party and its insurer?

---

20 The Supreme Court has considered in its judgment of 19 September 1997 that the term 'core clause' should be construed in a limited way (Supreme Court 19 September 1997, ECLI:NL:HR:1997:ZC2435, *NJ* 1998/6 (*Lottospel*)), but that clauses defining and framing the coverage belong to the core clauses is generally accepted. See on this, for example, M.L. Hendrikse in Chapter 30 of B. Wessels & R.H.C. Jongeneel, *Algemene voorwaarden* (Recht en Praktijk, deel CA1), Deventer: Wolters Kluwer 2017 and Asser/Wansink, Van Tiggele & Salomons *7-IX* 2012/179.

21 *Parliamentary Papers II* 1999/2000, 19529, no 5, p 36 et seq. See also N. Frenk & F.R. Salomons, 'Het nieuwe verzekeringsrecht bijgewerkt', *VA* 2001/1, p 22.

22 The scope of this right of action has recently been stretched. In Supreme Court 1 February 2019, ECLI:NL:HR:2019:150, the Supreme Court considered that an employee suffering personal injury as a result of an accident at work may claim against his employer's insurer under Article 7:954 of the Dutch Civil Code, even after the employer has gone bankrupt before reporting the injury to the insurer. This constitutes an exception to the rule that the liable party must have reported to its insurer as the insured party for the personal injury victim to be able to sue the insurer directly.

Meijer thinks so, because it is not an injured party's own right.[23] That seems correct as such but it has something unsatisfactory, because the intention of Article 7:954 of the Dutch Civil Code is to protect the victim, especially in the event of insolvency of the liable insured. It seems contrary to this that the victim – always a private party – can be forced to give up his right of access to the state courts in order to get his 'protection'. This stings all the more as a co-insured third party, which itself becomes a party to the insurance contract when it accepts its designation as a co-insured, is required to explicitly accept the arbitration clause, while the personal injury victim does not become a party to the insurance contract when exercising the right under Article 7:954 of the Dutch Civil Code.

In light of this, it is interesting that legal authors argue that the injured party's right is indeed a subjective right, contrary to what is stated in the Parliamentary History on this subject.[24] In my opinion, if this view is followed, it also has implications for whether an injured party can be bound by an arbitration clause in the insurance contract between the liable party and its insurer. I would argue that binding the injured party to an arbitration clause in an insurance contract can then only be at issue after expressly accepting it, as in the case of a co-insured third party.

8.3 Practical advantages and practical objections

The book Insurance and ADR lists the advantages and disadvantages of arbitration in insurance practice in several places.[25] I am not going to repeat those points here, but – given the nature of this book – limit myself to two points of interest when conducting arbitral proceedings at the NAI if the dispute concerns an insurance matter.

23 Meijer 2014.

24 See, with convincing arguments, A.Ch.H. Franken, 'De directe actie: een (onnodig) complexe regeling', *AV&S* 2011/13, p 121 et seq and F.M.J. Verstijlen, 'De directe actie in het vermogensrecht', *NJB* 2009/1258, p 1630 et seq.

25 See, for example, Kalff & Van Zelst 2014 as well as J.H. Wansink, 'Arbitrale mijmeringen bij de "wilde" arbitrage in verzekeringsland', in: C.J.M. Klaassen et al (eds), *Verzekering en ADR (Onderneming en recht no 83)*, Deventer: Kluwer 2014, p 165-174, Ten Brink & Vloemans 2014 and Chr. Harris & T. van Nouhuys, 'English ADR processes, in particular arbitration, with emphasis on the insurance context', in: C.J.M. Klaassen et al (eds), *Verzekering en ADR (Onderneming en recht no 83)*, Deventer: Kluwer 2014, p 379-410.

8.3.1 *Availability of arbitrators*

Let me just immediately touch on a thorny issue: there is only a limited number of available arbitrators with expertise in Dutch insurance law. It may be that the NAI has a larger list of names than the 'usual suspects' that are known to the parties' counsel as potential arbitrators. However, I do not know the NAI's list of available arbitrators (as this is not a published list)[26] and it is fairly likely that also the NAI list contains only a limited number of insurance law experts.

Kalff and Van Zelst suggested that this problem could be overcome by including experts in liability law as possible arbitrators. This is indeed what people tend to do in practice, but this removes an important theoretical advantage of arbitration over state jurisdiction. Even state judges are generally well versed in liability law. And while I would not venture to say that insurance law is so complex that a dispute could not be assessed by an expert in a related field, a liability expert will still have to read up on issues such as coverage disputes or interpretation of policy terms before he is up to speed.

Nevertheless, 'a limited number of available arbitrators' does not mean that arbitrators with the necessary expertise and availability can rarely be found. Surely, I estimate that our country has several dozen experts in insurance law, and it would go far to claim that they – or their offices – are all, always, involved in every case. It is up to the NAI to ensure that it knows, better than the parties themselves, which experts are available and have the expertiseto act as arbitrators. In that context, it is useful for the NAI to identify which experts are working in which subareas. For example, many construction lawyers will have the necessary knowledge about CAR insurance, but an expert on credit insurance could perhaps be found in banking law practice. Private liability insurance experts might also be personal injury lawyers, while transport insurance has traditionally been a particular expertise of maritime law lawyers.

Incidentally, the NAI offers an attractive solution for parties who do not want to litigate at the NAI but get stuck in appointing arbitrators. The NAI has special rules for this purpose, the '*NAI Rules for the Appointment of Arbitrators in Ad Hoc Arbitration*'. These Rules provide for the NAI to appoint arbitrators provided the parties have entered into an arbitration

---

26 The list is not published because in principle it is up to the parties to appoint the arbitrators. See infra in this paragraph.

agreement. The parties themselves may determine the number of arbitrators. If they do not, the NAI decides on the number. Appointment is then made through the list procedure: the NAI places several names of suitable arbitrators on a list and submits this list to the parties. The parties can indicate whether they object to a particular arbitrator and may place the remaining names in order of their preference. The NAI then appoints arbitrators based on the lists returned by the parties. If appointment based on the returned lists is not possible (e.g. because too many names have been crossed out), the NAI will appoint the arbitrators directly. As is customary, the NAI takes the wishes of the parties into account as much as possible and these wishes can be indicated by them in advance.

A similar arrangement can be found in the '*NAI Rules for the Appointment of a Binding Advisor in Ad Hoc Proceedings*'. Again, this can be a solution in cases where the parties want to be completely free to set up binding advice proceedings, but do not (together) agree on the appointment of the binding advisor.

The existence of these special rules raises the question as to why parties would not want to resolve their dispute at the NAI. The NAI Arbitration Rules (2024), one would think, offer enough flexibility for a tailor-made procedure. It is true that the NAI charges administrative costs, but this is offset by an often more limited hourly rate for the arbitrators than if the parties arrange an ad hoc arbitration. The NAI also safeguards some other important things: it keeps an eye on arbitrators' costs and monitors deadlines. These are aspects the importance of which should not be underestimated, as has already been pointed out by several writers in the book Insurance and ADR.[27]

8.3.2 *Costs*

Another concern is that the cost of arbitration can be quite high, especially compared to court proceedings. This is partly due to the obligation to pay arbitrators' fees. Incidentally, the hourly fee for arbitrators seems to be generally lower if the arbitration is conducted at the NAI than at various arbitral institutions across the border or in case of ad hoc arbitrations, especially if the rates are compared with the average hourly rates of lawyers specialising in insurance law. Another possible cost not charged by the

27 See, for example, Wansink 2014, Ten Brink & Vloemans 2014 and Harris & Van Nouhuys 2014.

state court is the rent of courtrooms and sometimes travel expenses, as well as the cost of a tribunal secretary.

In low-interest insurance disputes, often involving a private insured, the cost of court proceedings is quite often a stumbling block. For this reason, private individuals often seek a binding or non-binding opinion from the Financial Services Complaints Institute (*KiFiD*) rather than arbitration. Proceedings at the KiFiD are free of charge for the claimant if the claimant is a private insured, subject to any legal costs. The owners of small business entities have to pay a small fee.[28] Another reason for addressing the KiFiD is the fact that this institution is included as an obligatory form of alternative dispute resolution in many insurance policy conditions.

The NAI offers an interesting alternative for those cases where the insurance dispute involves a minor interest. Provided parties live or are domiciled in the Netherlands and have concluded an arbitration agreement, they can go through the Small Claims Track (SCT). This track provides for an arbitration procedure with a single arbitrator appointed by the NAI. The procedure is simpler and faster than standard arbitral proceedings and the costs are limited: € 750 in administration costs for the NAI and a maximum of € 4,500 in fees for the arbitrator, assuming that there is only a claim in convention. By comparison, court fees payable when starting subdistrict court proceedings are lower than the NAI's administration costs; court fees for court proceedings are higher. But in proceedings before state courts, a party does not have to pay an arbitrator's fee.

8.4 Insurance arbitration abroad

Abroad, settling insurance disputes via arbitration seems to be preferred to litigation in the state courts. In Europe, this is particularly true for the countries where the insurance industry is largest and where the main reinsurers are based, such as the UK, Germany and Switzerland.

28 On the Financial Services Ombudsman and the KiFiD, see contributions by M. Gonçalves Ribeiro Sousa Pereira, 'De Ombudsman Financiële Dienstverlening', N. van Tiggele-van der Velde, 'Afdoening van een geschil door de burgerlijke rechter of door de geschillencommissie financiële dienstverlening. Hetzelfde recht?', and D.P.C.M. Hellegers, 'Enkele knelpunten bij het procederen bij de commissie van beroep van het Kifid nader belicht', in: C.J.M. Klaassen et al (eds), *Verzekering en ADR (Onderneming en recht no 83)*, Deventer: Kluwer 2014, p 123-144 and p 145-162.

In the UK, a society specifically focused on the insurance industry was established in 1991, the Insurance and Reinsurance Arbitration Society: ARIAS.[29] ARIAS is one of the UK national branches of AIDA (the global Association Internationale de Droit des Assurances). The other UK national division is AIDA UK. The two divisions should be properly distinguished: AIDA is an insurance law association; ARIAS is a society specifically focusing on dispute resolution through arbitration. ARIAS UK once started as an initiative of a few insurance companies and law firms, but many companies and firms have since joined ARIAS and it has a list of around 120 arbitrators[30] with a clear expertise in insurance law. ARIAS requires parties to become members of the organisation before they can access details of the list of names of potential arbitrators.[31] The list includes not only English arbitrators but also some individuals from, for example, the United States and Germany.

In 1994, an ARIAS division was also established in the United States.[32] ARIAS US is also a national branch of AIDA. ARIAS US provides access to a list of around 170 names of potential arbitrators and mediators, mainly from the US. Incidentally, several more generic arbitral institutions in the US (such as The American Arbitration Association (AAA), JAMS and The Center for Public Resources (CPR)) also have insurance law experts on their arbitration lists, but with these institutions, parties have less to choose from, as these institutions are "*self-selecting*".

Later, ARIAS departments were also established in several other countries, including Germany,[33] France,[34] Hong Kong[35] and most recently, in 2021, Ireland.[36] The focus of these departments is on arbitrations between insurers and, albeit to a lesser extent, arbitrations relating to disputes over directors' liability insurance.[37]

29 https://arias.org.uk/.
30 The website mentions that there are more than 100 arbitrators on the list; I was informed of the number 'around 120' by a former board member of ARIAS UK.
31 The list of names is published on AIDA's website, but further details are only available to members.
32 https://arias.org.uk/.
33 https://www.arias-deutschland.de/.
34 www.cefarea-arias.fr. This organisation has combined its strengths in know-how and arbitration lists with CMAP, the Centre for mediation and arbitration of Paris (www.cmap.fr).
35 https://arias-asia.org/.
36 https://aidainsurance.org/arias-societies/arias-ireland.
37 Incidentally, on the basis of the information available to me, I cannot properly assess the scale on which the national divisions of ARIAS mentioned here operate.

Switzerland, the third European country (besides the UK and Germany) where large reinsurers are based and relatively many reinsurance disputes are fought, has no specialised arbitral institution for insurance disputes. Arbitrations are generally settled *on an ad hoc basis*, including disputes between reinsurers. Policy disputes between the insurer and the policyholder are mostly brought before state courts.

The national branch of AIDA in the Netherlands is the Association for Insurance Science (Vereniging voor Verzekeringswetenschap, "VvVW"). The question arises whether there would also be room in the Netherlands for a separate society focusing on dispute resolution, alongside the VvVW, similar to ARIAS UK and ARIAS US. My assessment is that there is little appetite for this. In addition, in the countries where ARIAS has a branch, significantly more insurance arbitrations take place than in the Netherlands. Without question, the number of insurance arbitrations in the Netherlands remains more limited than abroad, mainly because the Netherlands does not have large reinsurers. Moreover, as indicated earlier, there is not a very large number of potential Dutch arbitrators with insurance expertise here. If an insurance institution such as the NAI could ensure that most of the potential arbitrators are known to it and/or are on its arbitration list, insurance arbitration could also be facilitated just fine by the NAI. To the extent that a foreign arbitrator is sought, one of the foreign institutions can be contacted.

Moreover, critical voices can also be observed towards organisations like ARIAS. Because these institutions grew out of initiatives from the insurance industry and the law firms that assist them, there is still a certain suspicion among companies/policyholders that have a dispute with their insurer. That suspicion is focused on the arbitrators who are largely drawn from the same pond as the initiators,[38] and who may even have a (self-)in-

I suspect that these departments administer significantly fewer arbitrations than those in the United States and England. The departments in Germany and Hong Kong seem to be strongly driven by a few law firms that are particularly active in the reinsurance industry.

38 To qualify for inclusion on the arbitration list, a prospective arbitrator must have demonstrable experience in the insurance industry. At ARIAS US, a certain number of years of insurance litigation experience on the side of a policy holder is being considered as an alternative prerequisite. That suspicion can even lead to litigation is evidenced by *National Union Fire Ins. Co. of Pittsburgh, PA v. Beelman Truck Co*, no 17-CV-2946 (VEC), 2017 U.S. Dist. LEXIS 111136 (S.D.N.Y. Jul. 17, 2017), in which a court had to rule on a policyholder's refusal to agree to an arbitrator proposed by insurers and listed by AIDA US. The court incidentally held that the fact that an arbitrator was on the AIDA US list was not evidence of his bias.

terest in maintaining a certain popularity with the insurance industry and their lawyers, which could lead to several future arbitrator appointments. ARIAS US and ARIAS UK, which for the most part administer arbitration disputes between insurers, are therefore trying to expand their arbitrator lists to include names of individuals who have been active on the policyholders' side. This suspicion is not felt (or at least less so) at a less specialised arbitral institution such as the NAI.

That a special institution dedicated to insurance disputes does not seem to be on the wish list in the Netherlands may also be demonstrated by the more or less dormant existence of the Gordiass Foundation. Gordiass was established in 2011 as an independent institution for settling disputes between insurance companies through binding advice, but does not seem to have administered a significant number of disputes.[39]

In light of this, an alternative could also be the system used by the Arbitration Institute of the Stockholm Chamber of Commerce: no separate institution, but special arbitration rules for insurance disputes.[40] These rules are based on a consolidation of the rules of the Stockholm Chamber of Commerce (SCC) and the *Rules for Expedited Arbitrations*. The latter rules are similar to the NAI's Small Claims rules and in principle apply to an insurance dispute unless the complexity of the case, the importance and other circumstances require that the SCC Rules apply. In the latter case, the SCC determines whether to appoint one or three arbitrators.[41]

8.5 Conclusion

By itself, arbitration seems an appropriate method of dispute resolution in case of disputes between insurers or between insurer and policyholder. If all parties want to arbitrate, it should not be an issue that it is a requirement that all parties need to be party to an arbitration agreement.

It does not seem necessary in the Netherlands to have an arbitral institution dedicated to insurance disputes. Larger reinsurance disputes are generally not fought with or between Dutch (re)insurance companies, so the

39 The foundation's website is also no longer findable on the internet.

40 *Insurance Arbitration Rules of the Arbitration Institute of the Stockholm Chamber of Commerce*, entered into force on 1 April 1999 (www.intracen.org).

41 Of course, the applicability of these arbitration rules also requires that the parties have entered into an arbitration agreement.

amount of work done in this area in countries like the United States or the United Kingdom, where this provides fertile ground for an independent insurance arbitral institution, is not present in the Netherlands.

However, it is advisable to have an arbitration administered by a professional organisation rather than *ad hoc*. Control by an arbitral institution over the appointment of arbitrators, speed of proceedings and costs constitutes, in my view, a major advantage of institutional arbitration over *ad hoc* arbitration. In this respect, the NAI may meet a need, provided the NAI makes sure that it can offer a sufficiently wide choice of specialised arbitrators. That the NAI should also offer special insurance arbitration rules, as the Stockholm Chamber of Commerce does, is less obvious as far as I am concerned. The Swedish SCC administers less complex insurance disputes by applying simplified arbitration rules. For simpler disputes in the Netherlands, in cases where a limited financial interest is at stake, the parties involved are likely to turn to the KiFiD rather than the NAI's Small Claims procedure.

CHAPTER 9

ARBITRATION V. JUDICIAL ADJUDICATION OF MASS CLAIMS: AN ASSESSMENT OF DISPUTE RESOLUTION IN THE GLOBAL MARKET

Ianika Tzankova & Lilian Meinen[1]

9.1 Introduction

In a 2021 publication, Tzankova[2] introduced the metaphor of the Global Village as a useful concept to explain the phenomenon and dynamics of global dispute resolution. The narrative is, in short, that the Global Village is populated by a vast number of repeat players and that in a globalised world, there are different ways to deal with the 'Global Disputes' between them.[3] Absent global corporate or private courts, the domestic courts and arbitral tribunals are two categories of adjudicators with jurisdiction in Global Disputes. While in the early days of the existence of the Global Village these two adjudicators were seen as complementary to each other, the scope of their competences seemed clear cut and there was 'peaceful co-existence', with the passage of time and as multinationals expanded their activities, the situation has changed and is continuing to change. The area of mass claims is an example of the latter.

This contribution uses primarily Global Disputes that have some link with the Netherlands as a case study to illustrate how the emergence of mass claims has encouraged multinationals to use arbitration to avoid adjudication via class and/or collective litigation. As we will demonstrate, the

1 Professor I.N. (Ianika) Tzankova is an attorney at Rubicon Impact & Litigation in Amsterdam and Professor of Global Dispute Resolution and Mass Disputes at Tilburg University. She is a board member of Stichting Petrobras Compensation Foundation and a supervisory board member of Stichting Massaschade & Consument; L. (Lilian) Meinen (LLM) is an attorney at Birkway in Amsterdam.

2 I.N. Tzankova, 'Anti-specialisation Trends in Dispute Resolution or a Shift Towards a New Paradigm? An Initial Exploratory Analysis of Dispute Resolution in the Global Village', in: X.E. Kramer et al (eds), *New Pathways to Civil Justice in Europe: Challenges of Access to Justice*, Cham: Springer 2021, p 277-297.

3 There are different types of global disputes as we will explain further below, but for now it suffices to state that they have 'high impact' on (numerous) parties domiciled in different jurisdictions.

success of this approach varies, depending on the nature of the Global Dispute and the applicable national law. We will examine this through the lens of mass claims in the consumer, securities and competition areas, and as adjudicated primarily before the Dutch courts. In these cases, defendants have invoked an arbitration clause to refer the case to arbitration. Whenever appropriate in view of the limited scope of this contribution, we will draw parallels and/or distinctions with the judicial approaches applied in the context of mass claims in the same substantive law areas (consumer, securities and competition) by other domestic courts (for example in the US, the UK, Canada, France and Germany) and the CJEU.

We will proceed as follows. Firstly, in paragraph 9.2, we will define Global Disputes and provide clarification on the focus and the scope of this contribution. In paragraph 9.3, we will outline the advantages and disadvantages of the two main forms of adjudication of Global Disputes: (individual) arbitration versus (class and/or collective) litigation. While our analysis is focused on the Netherlands as a forum, we believe our analyses can be relevant also for the assessment of similar cases in other jurisdictions. In paragraph 9.4, we will evaluate the interplay between arbitration and court adjudication with respect to consumer claims. As we will demonstrate, the interaction between arbitration and court adjudication differs significantly in the Dutch context compared to other legal areas, such as securities and competition. In paragraph 9.5, we will illustrate, using the *Petrobras*[4] matter as a case study, how arbitration and court adjudication 'compete' with each other in the context of securities litigation and are used by the parties as strategic tools in the resolution of their Global Disputes. In paragraph 9.6, we will explore the interplay between arbitration and court adjudication in two competition cases in the European context (the *Hydrogen Peroxide*[5]- and the *eBizcuss*[6]-case), regarding follow on and abuse of dominance position claims. We will conclude with some observations and a conclusion in paragraph 9.7.

9.2 Taxonomy of Global Disputes

Global Disputes and mass claims are key terms in this contribution and deserve special attention since there are different ways to define both.[7]

4 Rotterdam District Court 19 September 2018, ECLI:NL:RBROT:2018:7852 (*Petrobras*).
5 CJEU 21 May 2015, C-352/13, ECLI:EU:C:2015:335 (*CDC Hydrogen Peroxide*).
6 CJEU 24 October 2018, C-595/17, ECLI:EU:C:2018:854 (*Apple Sales International et al/ EBizcuss.com*).
7 For an extensive discussion of the taxonomy of global disputes we refer to Tzankova 2021, p 286-289.

With respect to the definition of Global Disputes, Michaels, Hensler and Tzankova have come to different interpretations depending on respectively the nature of the issue in dispute (Michaels), the nature of the interaction with other related disputes (Hensler) and the nature of the parties involved (Tzankova). In sum, Michaels[8] distinguishes three categories of global problems, hence Global Disputes. Firstly, problems that are global by nature, for example the problems created by global markets, such as fraud on financial markets or cartels. Secondly, the problems that are global by design: the global character of the problem is a consequence of its design, as is the case with legal issues arising from the internet, privacy-related infringements and data breaches. Thirdly, there are problems that are global by definition, i.e. because that is how we choose to frame them, for example human rights abuses, including environmental damage, climate change and pandemics.

Another way to classify Global Disputes, according to Hensler[9], is to look at their interaction and functional connection with other disputes. This approach goes beyond the conventional thinking about transnational or cross-border litigation that typically is seen as a single lawsuit that happened to involved parties, domiciled in different jurisdictions. The classic challenges presented by this type of problem include where to file a claim; how to achieve service of documents; how to gather evidence; what law prevails and how to ensure enforcement of an award.[10] According to Hensler, nowadays the term transnational or global litigation and dispute resolution increasingly conjures up images of a 'family' of related lawsuits pending in parallel in multiple jurisdictions and before various tribunals. Applying a line of thinking that goes beyond the conventional approach, she distinguishes a different, more procedure-oriented typology of Global Disputes. First, there are the 'families of related disputes', where multinationals use the available dispute resolution mechanisms and the differences between national civil procedures pro-actively and strategically

8 See for a proposed typology of global problems based on the nature they aim to address: R. Michaels, 'Global Problems in Domestic Courts', in: S. Muller et al (eds), *The Law of the Future and The Future of Law*, Oslo: Torkel Opsahl Academic EPublisher 2021, p 167-176. Although one may wonder whether the typology by Michaels is the most adequate one, there could be little doubt that the various examples he refers to are 'global' and impact our modern society.

9 This typology that we attribute to Hensler is based on her co-teaching with Tzankova (2012-2024).

10 S.P. Baumgartner, 'Transnational Litigation in the United States: he Emergence of a New Field of Law', *The American Journal of Comparative Law* (55) 2007, p 793-808 reviewing G.B. Born & P.B. Rutledge, *International Civil Litigation in the United States*, Philadelphia: Wolters Kluwer 2007.

to advance their interests or optimise their market position. This type of dispute generally involves parties that are all more or less repeat players and it assumes that there is more or less a level playing field between them from the start. The second category of 'families of related disputes' consists of multi-party actions (mass claims) resulting from globally marketed products or services (e.g. financial services, consumer goods, medical devices or global cartels). Such cases involve a large number of claimants, often natural persons dispersed in different jurisdictions, suffering losses attributed to the same corporate or State entity or individuals typically based or domiciled in another jurisdiction. Typically, the claimants and defendants in this type of case are not equal in terms of financial predisposition and there is also information asymmetry.

Finally, a third way to distinguish Global Disputes suggested by Tzankova is to do so based on the capacity or nature of the parties involved. On this basis, once again three types of Global Disputes can be identified. Firstly, there are so-called business-to-State (or B2S) disputes.[11] Secondly, there are the business-to-business (or B2B) disputes and finally, there are the consumer-to-business disputes and/or business-to-consumer (or B2C) disputes.

Is one of these three definitions preferrable or can they be combined and does one suffice? In our view, neither is the case here. The study and practice of global law form a new territory for both practitioners and academic researchers. When studying a new phenomenon, it is crucial to keep an open mind to different theoretical angles and approaches. Depending on the goal and subject of the study, in a certain context one definition may be more appropriate and helpful than the other to observe and interpret socio-legal phenomena or to explain developments. Different typologies can provide, in different ways, a helpful structure to test assumptions and conclusions, to detect patterns and sharpen analyses.

Keeping in mind the three taxonomies of Global Disputes discussed above, we define the (limited) scope of this contribution as follows. We do not include the investor-State type of disputes and will limit our analyses to business-to-business and consumer-to-business matters,[12] the reason for which is not merely pragmatic. Here, we focus on the families of related disputes that consist of multi-party actions (mass claims).[13] These

11 Investor-State disputes is another way to describe these.
12 According to Tzankova's definition.
13 According to Hensler's definition.

are less prevalent in the State-investor context.[14] Furthermore, we limit our research to mass claims resulting from globally marketed products or services.[15]

The use of Hensler's taxonomy warrants a further definition of mass claims dispute resolution: it is often used as an umbrella term for a wide range of procedural devices facilitating the aggregation of individual claims.[16]

In the Netherlands, there are various forms of mass claims dispute resolution in the domestic courts with differing formal requirements and legal effects. For instance, multiple claimants may submit their claims collectively in a single procedure, or alternatively, a form of legal representation may be employed. In terms of legal representation, there are two main scenarios: (i) the claimant is the formal but not the substantive party to the proceedings (this could be the case with a power of attorney (Article 3:60 DCC[17]) or a mandate (Article 7:414 DCC)) and (ii) the claimant is both the formal and the substantive party to the proceedings. The latter is the case with assignment of claims (Article 3:84 DCC) and the collective action filed by an interest group acting as representative on an opt out or opt in basis (Article 3:305a DCC). While the power of attorney, the mandate and the assignment are in fact bundled individual disputes, the collective action within the meaning of Article 3:305a DCC is quite different. In such cases, the claimant interest organisation is bringing the action *on behalf of* others.[18] It abstracts from the individual interests of the constituency represented by the interest group. Instead, only the common questions of fact and law are assessed by the court.[19] Modelling the action via opt out (see para 9.3) is the most effective use of resources, representing the cutting edge of collective interest litigation. In this contribution, collective action refers to the action brought by interest organisations within the meaning of Article 3:305a DCC.

14 Although examples perhaps could be found in nationalisations of financial institutions with a diverse international shareholder base.

15 According to Michaels' definition.

16 N. Touw & I.N. Tzankova, 'Parallel actions in cross-border mass claims in the EU: A (comparative) lawyer's paradise?', *NIPR* 2023/9, p 9-30, in relation to the interaction with the rules of private international law.

17 Dutch Civil Code. The Dutch Code of Civil Procedure is referred to as DCCP.

18 T.M.C. Arons, 'Vaststelling van de internationale bevoegdheid en het toepasselijk recht in collectieve geschilbeslechting. In het bijzonder de ipr-aspecten van de Richtlijn representatieve vorderingen', *NIPR* 2021/172, p 21-22.

19 Arons 2021, p 23.

Before we discuss, in the following paragraphs, how arbitration and judicial adjudication interact with each other before the Dutch courts in the areas of consumer law, financial (securities) and competition in the context of mass disputes, it is instructive to understand the advantages and disadvantages of each of these two methods of dispute resolution for claimants and defendants.

9.3 (Individual) arbitration and (collective) actions before Dutch courts: a comparison

9.3.1 Collective action v. collective arbitration?

The collective action was introduced in the Netherlands in 1994, and in 2016 a bill was enacted to improve the settlement of mass damages in a collective action (Wet afwikkeling massaschade in collectieve actie or Dutch Act on Settlement of Mass Damage in Collective Action, hereinafter: the WAMCA).[20] The WAMCA came into force in 2020 and was subsequently amended in June 2023 in line with the Representative Actions Directive[21], which introduced a few specific requirements for consumer collective actions only. The WAMCA differs from the old collective action regime in that it allows claimants to seek monetary damages. Under the old regime, the primary objective of a collective action was to obtain a declaratory judgment on the liability of the defendant. Individual claimants would be required to conduct their own proceedings to recover their damages. Furthermore, the WAMCA requires the interest organisation to publish the summons in a dedicated register for collective actions (under penalty of inadmissibility), as the legislator considered it important for the constituency to be able to take cognisance of the action brought. Furthermore, the admissibility requirements for interest organisations have also been tightened. The court will also assess whether the interest organisation has the necessary resources to undertake the action and whether it has sufficient control over the proceedings. This addition refers to the scenario where there is third-party funding is involved. It stipulates that the court will conduct an ex officio examination of the extent of influence a funder

20 *Parliamentary Papers II* 2016/17, 34608, no 3. The final bill is included in *Parliamentary Papers I* 2018/19, 34608, A.

21 Directive (EU) 2020/1828 of the European Parliament and of the Council of 25 November 2020 on representative actions for the protection of the collective interests of consumers and repealing Directive 2009/22/EC (OJ L 409/1).

has over the proceedings in accordance with the funding agreement.[22] Additionally, the WAMCA requires that the interest organisation must have a supervisory body and sufficient experience in initiating and conducting litigation.

The WAMCA divides the collective action into two phases. The court will only consider the merits of the claim if the interest organisation has satisfied the requirements for admissibility set out in Article 3:305a DCC and has demonstrated that pursuing the collective claim is more efficient and effective than pursuing an individual claim, and the claim is not summarily unfounded (Article 1018c(5) DCCP). This is designed to prevent a lengthy and costly debate on the merits of the claim in cases that clearly cannot result in a decision.[23] This extensive admissibility stage is similar to the 'certification' process used in more experienced jurisdictions for the handling of mass claims.

In addition to the public judicial system described above, the Netherlands also has private methods of dispute resolution, including arbitration. Dutch arbitration law has been part of the Code of Civil Procedure since 1838 and was most recently modernised in 2015 in the light of national and international developments.[24] While arbitration law has long been part of the legal landscape, collective settlement of (damages) claims through arbitration plays, to our knowledge, no role in the Netherlands.[25] Consequently, the comparison between the two modes of dispute resolution in the rest of this paragraph will be between individual arbitration and collective actions. Furthermore, at the end of each subparagraph we will identify the extent to which a feature or characteristic of individual arbitration is more favourable to the claimant or the defendant than a collective action.

This comparative choice may appear somewhat artificial, as though 'comparing apples with pears'. We believe there are two key benefits in apply-

22 *Parliamentary Papers II* 2017/18, 34608, no 9, p 2 and no 10.

23 *Parliamentary Papers II* 2016/17, 34608, no 3, p 39-40.

24 *Parliamentary Papers II* 2012/13, 33611, no 3. We refer hereinafter to the arbitration law amended in 2015 as the Dutch Arbitration Act.

25 This is consistent with the general observation that examples of mass arbitration in global disputes are scarce. The *Abaclat*, *Ambiente* and *Alemanni* cases, which were all brought on the basis of the Argentina-Italy BIT, are some of these rare examples. See: *Abaclat and Others v. Argentine Republic*, ICSID Case no ARB/07/5; *Ambiente Ufficio S.p.A. and others v. Argentine Republic*, ICSID Case no ARB/08/9; *Giovanni Alemanni and Others v. Argentine Republic*, ICSID Case no ARB/07/8.

ing it in a systematic way. First and foremost, in the absence of collective or class arbitration, individual arbitration is typically the norm when dealing with global mass claims. Secondly, arbitration and mass claim dispute resolution are two separate and distinct fields. Professionals and scholars active in the respective fields of dispute resolution may be less familiar with developments outside their own area of expertise. An analysis of the potential advantages of arbitration in comparison to collective action can contribute to a better understanding of the dynamics of dispute resolution of global mass claims.

To conclude this paragraph, it should be noted that although the aggregation of multiple individual claims has advantages for both claimants and defendants, collective actions are typically considered to be more favourable for claimants than for defendants, particularly if they are modelled as an opt out action. The latter is also the case in class actions in the US, Canada and Australia.[26]

9.3.2 *Party autonomy*

There are multiple facets to party autonomy, which manifests in various forms. It is a fundamental feature of arbitration. This is inherent to the very nature of arbitration: the arbitrator's authority to decide a case is derived from the arbitration agreement and the subsequent contract for the provisions of services between the parties and the arbitrator. These agreements set out the scope of the arbitrator's authority to make decisions. The principle of party autonomy is evident at various stages of the process, including the selection of arbitration, the commencement and scope of the proceedings, and the conduct of the proceedings.[27] In arbitration, the parties have significant influence over the composition of the arbitral tribunal. It is sometimes asserted that the quality of an arbitration is contingent upon the individuals serving as arbitrators.[28] The law sets out a number of guidelines regarding the composition of the arbitral tribunal, for example Article 1023 DCCP on nationality and Articles 1026-1027 DCCP on the number of arbitrators and their appointment. In practice, the agreed rules on the composition of the arbitral tribunal are typically included in the arbitration rules of the relevant arbitration institute that the parties have declared applicable. While there are no legal requirements regarding

26 D.R. Hensler et al, *The Globalization of Mass Civil Litigation. Lessons from the Volkswagen "Clean Diesel" Case*, RAND Research Report 2021.
27 Asser Procesrecht/Sanders, Meijer & Ernste *8* 2023/65.
28 Asser Procesrecht/Sanders, Meijer & Ernste *8* 2023/147.

the quality of arbitrators, many arbitration rules set out specific standards. In certain instances, the Chair of the arbitral tribunal is required to be a judge.[29] A good arbitrator must possess the necessary experience in resolving disputes and demonstrate expertise in the relevant field of law. This should take into account the nature and/or content of the dispute. This is why arbitration is widely used in certain industries, such as construction and energy. It is also crucial that the arbitrator is independent and impartial and has sufficient time. Those requirements are essential not only for resolving the substantive dispute, but also for determining the procedural order.[30] Overall, as a fundamental right, party autonomy is viewed as an advantage of (individual) arbitration for both claimants and defendants. In practice, one could state that the more powerful and wealthier party benefits more from it than its counterpart.

In collective actions, party autonomy is less prevalent, particularly in those that are modelled as opt out actions. This is because the courts have a fiduciary duty to actively monitor whether the interests of the class and the absent class members are well taken care of and sufficiently safeguarded. Furthermore, while claimants may occasionally have the option of selecting the district court in which they can file their action, they do not have the ability to choose the judges who will preside over their case. Moreover, even in complicated matters such as the one under the WAMCA, the court may at its own discretion decide that a single judge will determine the dispute rather than a panel of judges.[31] Dutch law does not set out explicit quality requirements for domestic judges, other than that a judge must be independent and impartial. The original intention of the WAMCA bill was to concentrate collective actions in a specialised court (the Amsterdam District Court) in order to build up expertise in this area, for example with regard to the appointment of the Exclusive Representative (Article 1018e DCCP).[32] However, concentrating cases in a specific court was deemed unnecessary to achieve the objective of developing specific expertise in this area, given that expertise is also required in the subject matter of the collective claim (such as State liability or maritime matters).[33] It was also

29 Asser Procesrecht/Sanders, Meijer & Ernste *8* 2023/149.

30 Asser Procesrecht/Sanders, Meijer & Ernste *8* 2023/149.

31 Amsterdam District Court 17 July 2024, ECLI:NL:RBAMS:2024:4264 (*Stichting ICAM/Staat*). It is unclear to what extent this is going to become a standing practice or should be considered as an exception to the rule of a panel of three judges. The collective action brought by Stichting ICAM was not a collective action in summary proceedings.

32 *Parliamentary Papers II* 2016/17, 34608, no 3, p 35.

33 *Parliamentary Papers II* 2017/18, 34608, no 6, p 20.

assumed that the number of cases would be limited and would not necessitate the involvement of judges with specific expertise, as they would mainly concern general issues of liability in tort or breach of contract.[34]

Following the removal of the concentration provision in the final bill, a number of additional practical avenues for enhancing expertise in mass tort litigation were put forth. For instance, judges with the requisite expertise could be assigned to collective actions pending before another court. This could be achieved by having each judge in the court also serve as a substitute for this particular subject matter, with at least one of the judges in the pool sitting in each collective action.[35] This is consistent with standard arbitration practice, which does not require that each arbitrator on the tribunal has specific expertise in the substantive dispute. It is crucial that the best composition of the arbitral tribunal – or the best combination of arbitrators – is realised to resolve the dispute in question. While it is not clear to what extent the judiciary has followed these legislative suggestions, we are aware that at least some measures in line with the proposals have been taken. For example, judges experienced in court-approved collective settlements in the Amsterdam Court of Appeal serve on judicial panels adjudicating collective actions in the Rotterdam District Court. Additionally, there is an informal expertise centre within the Dutch court system for the exchange of case management practices under the WAMCA. At the European level, a similar initiative exists, although its scope is broader, encompassing designated legal entities and legislators.[36]

In conclusion, the principle of party autonomy is of great importance to the civil justice system, both in the context of arbitration and court adjudication. While arbitration allows for greater flexibility in selecting adjudicators and making procedural arrangements, it is crucial to assess whether that benefits both parties. Typically, the more powerful and wealthier side, which is often the defendant, stands to gain the most from this flexibility. In the context of collective actions on opt out basis, the principle of party autonomy is subject to more restrictions. This is paradoxically done to safeguard the interests of absent parties and enhance the rule of law.

---

34 *Parliamentary Papers II* 2016/17, 34608, no 3, annex Opinion Council for the Judiciary, p 2 and 13.
35 *Parliamentary Papers II* 2017/18, 34 608, no 7, p 5.
36 EC React: https://representative-actions-collaboration.ec.europa.eu/ (visited on 9 August 2024).

9.3.3 *Length of proceedings and time for resolution of the dispute*

Another potential advantage of arbitration over collective actions is the speed with which the process can be completed. In general, arbitral proceedings are conducted in a single instance. Arbitral appeal is only possible if the parties have so agreed (Article 1061a and 1061b DCCP). In practice, the parties can agree to this in the arbitration rules referenced in their arbitration agreement (Article 1020(6) DCCP). While some arbitral institutions have included it in their rules,[37] this remains exceptional. The majority of national and international arbitral institutions (explicitly) exclude the possibility of appeals.[38] Arbitral appeal is possible in a situation in which the arbitral tribunal declares itself incompetent for a reason other than the absence of a valid arbitration agreement (Article 1061f(1) in conjunction with Article 1052(5) DCCP). Moreover, arbitral proceedings are typically not divided into a jurisdictional phase and a substantive phase. In many cases, this option is only available when one of the parties invokes the lack of jurisdiction of the arbitral tribunal.[39]

While we do not advocate that collective actions should be dealt with in a single instance and that appeals should only be allowed if the parties have explicitly agreed to it, it should be noted that collective actions currently have a rather long processing time. Of the collective actions currently listed in the register of collective actions, only one action for damages has resulted in a final judgment on the merits.[40] This is due to a combination of factors, including the procedural framework established by law and the manner in which it is operationalised in practice. Firstly, the proceedings are automatically suspended as soon as the summons is filed and entered in the register (Article 1018c(3) DCCP). The suspension period lasts for a minimum of three months, with the possibility of an additional three-month extension. No procedural acts are carried out during the period of suspension. The rationale behind this provision is to enable other interest organisations to initiate a collective action for the same event on similar factual and legal grounds, provided that they declare these within the three-month period.[41] Should the three-month period prove insuffi-

---

37 The arbitration rules of the Council of Arbitration in construction disputes, NOFOTA and the Royal Committee for Grain Holders.

38 Asser Procesrecht/Sanders, Meijer & Ernste *8* 2023/447.

39 G.J. Meijer & P.B. Fritschy, '"Dynamic Bifurcation"', *TVA* 2022/48, p 100.

40 The register can be accessed at https://www.rechtspraak.nl/Registers/centraal-register-voor-collectieve-vorderingen. Amsterdam District Court 9 October 2024, ECLI:NL:RBAMS:2024:6118 (*Stichting Nuon-Claim/Vattenfall*).

41 *Parliamentary Papers II* 2017/18, 34608, no 3, p 38.

cient for the interest organisation in question, an extension of up to three months may be granted (Article 1018d(2) DCCP).[42] The law stipulates that the defendant must file a statement of defence six weeks after the expiry of the three-month or six-month period (Article 1018c(4) DCCP). In practice, however, this period is considerably prolonged due to the parties (or the court) proposing a procedural order in which the admissibility phase is again divided into several stages. In some cases, a pre-trial hearing may be held for this purpose, although the court may also regulate this in writing. For instance, the defendants may initially be given the chance to comment on the jurisdiction of the Dutch court. This would then be followed by an oral hearing and an interim judgment. In the second stage, the interest organisations could be invited to comment on the appointment of the Exclusive Representative and the defendants could be given the opportunity to comment on the admissibility of the interest organisations, the applicable law and the appointment of the Exclusive Representative, again followed by an oral hearing and interim judgment. Due to the aforementioned division, it is not uncommon for the defendant to take up to nine months to a year to file its first procedural submission. Following the appointment of the Exclusive Representative (Article 1018e DCCP), claimants are given the option to submit an opt out declaration (or an opt in declaration if they are not domiciled or resident in the Netherlands; Article 1018f DCCP) and a brief interlude is observed. The purpose of this interim period is to allow the parties to reach an agreement and to enable the interest organisation (then: Exclusive Representative) to supplement the grounds of the claim, for instance in response to grounds raised by other non-designated interest organisations in their summons. Furthermore, the defendant may supplement its defence at this stage if it has limited its defence to the admissibility of the interest organisation(s) in the first instance (Article 1018g DCCP). The case then proceeds to the substantive hearing.

The legal framework governing arbitration makes it a faster process than collective actions. However, the speed of arbitration is inextricably linked to the flexibility that characterises it. One of the first steps taken by an arbitral tribunal upon appointment is to convene a case management conference. This conference allows the tribunal to discuss and determine the course of the proceedings, including the timetable, in consultation with the parties.[43] This approach could also be adopted by the courts in collective actions, and indeed, recent developments have seen courts implement

42 *Parliamentary Papers II* 2017/18, 34608, no 3, p 41.

43 See, for example, currently Articles 26 and 30 of the NAI Arbitration Rules 2024 and currently Article 24 ICC Arbitration Rules.

similar measures. It is typically more straightforward to arrange a meeting between the parties' representatives via digital means. Furthermore, the court's timetable does not have to take into account the availability of a room large enough for all parties' attorneys. Dividing the procedure into phases and immediately setting dates for the parties to file submissions and for the oral hearing to take place would also improve the speed of the procedure. This would allow parties to communicate their unavailability dates for a certain period before the case management conference or pre-trial hearing.

To conclude, it can be stated that arbitration currently has advantages over collective actions in terms of the length of the process and the time within which the dispute is (to be) resolved for the party that is benefited with an expedient process. This is typically the claimant. However, procedural and practical improvements to the case management of collective actions are underway, with some already gradually being implemented.

9.3.4 *Confidentiality*

The confidential nature of arbitration is traditionally seen as an advantage, although it is not provided for in the Dutch Arbitration Act. This can be beneficial when there are significant interests at stake that the parties prefer not to disclose publicly, when commercially sensitive information is involved, or when there is a need to prevent a party's share price from fluctuating during the proceedings.[44] In any case, confidentiality is regarded as a fundamental aspect and principle of unwritten Dutch arbitration law.[45] The extent to which confidentiality applies, is not always clear. One argument is that all elements relating to the arbitration are confidential, unless the parties have agreed otherwise (e.g. by declaring a particular arbitration rule applicable).[46] This may include the fact that proceedings are pending, the identity of the arbitrators, the subject matter of the dispute, the (contents of the) procedural documents, the fact that an award has been made and the contents of that award.

In contrast, proceedings before domestic courts are subject to the principle of publicity,[47] which encompasses the publicity of both the case and the

44 H.J. Snijders, *Nederlands arbitragerecht*, Deventer: Wolters Kluwer 2018, para 5.1.5.1.
45 Snijders 2018, para 5.1.5.1, and authors cited there.
46 Asser Procesrecht/Sanders, Meijer & Ernste *8* 2023/62; Snijders 2018, para 5.1.5.3.
47 See Article 6 ECHR, Article 121 Constitution, Articles 4 and 5 Judicial Organisation Act and Articles 27 and 28 DCCP.

judgment. The purpose is to allow public scrutiny, to protect against arbitrary and partial decisions by the judge, and generally to ensure a 'fair trial'.[48] Publicity is a means of achieving this goal: a fair trial.[49] Additionally, the publicity of the judiciary (through the media) provides information to the general public and is necessary to promote the unity of the judiciary and the development of the law. This requires that the courts provide sound reasoning for their decisions.[50]

It is of particular importance to the parties that these objectives are guaranteed in arbitration. The arbitrator is required to act independently and impartially, and to provide reasons for the award. In the event that he fails to do so, the award may be set aside by the domestic court. Article 1065(1) DCCP provides five exhaustive grounds for doing so. However, there is a conflict between the importance of informing the public at large and the confidential nature of arbitral proceedings. In particular, this transparency is vital in the context of collective actions. As previously stated in paragraph 9.3.1, the WAMCA has introduced more rigorous criteria for the admissibility of interest organisations. The detailed requirements aim to ensure that interest organisations prioritise the interests of the aggrieved parties. An interest organisation must demonstrate sufficient representation in terms of constituency and the range of interests it represents. This prevents an interest organisation from pursuing claims without the necessary constituency support. In this context, there are also a number of transparency requirements that an interest organisation must meet in order to ensure that the interests of aggrieved parties are adequately safeguarded. It is a requirement for interest organisations to set up a website that is accessible to the general public. This website must contain certain essential information (Article 3:305a(2)(d) DCCP). This information allows an aggrieved party to make an informed decision as to whether or not to join a particular interest organisation and to be kept informed of the progress of the proceedings.[51] This is particularly crucial in cases where multiple interest organisations have submitted claims pertaining to the same event, with one being designated as the Exclusive Representative. It is also important to provide information to aggrieved parties, given that they are bound by the outcome of the proceedings. A collective action judgment is binding on all members of the class. This significant binding obligation

48 Asser Procesrecht/Giesen *1* 2015/339.
49 P. Smits, *Artikel 6 EVRM en de civiele procedure (Burgerlijk Proces & Praktijk no 10)*, Deventer: Kluwer 2008, para 4.1.3.
50 Asser Procesrecht/Giesen *1* 2015/339.
51 *Parliamentary Papers II* 2016/17, 34608, no 3, p 20.

necessitates that aggrieved parties be afforded the opportunity to indicate their desire not to be bound by the outcome. The law has established this moment after the appointment of the Exclusive Representative (Article 1018f DCCP). At this juncture, individuals must consider whether to join the collective action or to pursue an individual course of action with the expectation of a superior outcome.[52] It should be noted that there is some limited scope for applying the principle of confidentiality also under the WAMCA. In the *Vattenfall* case, part of the oral hearing on the merits took place behind closed doors at the request of the defendant to protect its trade secrets. In addition, claimant organisations often do not need to share the litigation funding agreement with the defendants at all, or at most a redacted version.

In conclusion, the confidentiality of arbitration may be seen as a disadvantage for claimants in comparison to collective actions. The situation is different for defendants. Collective actions are typically initiated against (large) companies or the State. Given the high stakes involved, it may be preferable for them that the public is unaware of the existence of a dispute and the facts surrounding it.

9.3.5 Costs

One disadvantage of arbitration that has become apparent in recent years is the cost of the adjudicator's and related fees, which are higher than those associated with ordinary (individual) litigation. The costs associated with arbitration are typically high, frequently exceeding the expenses incurred in pursuing litigation in a domestic court.[53] While domestic courts are primarily funded by the State, the parties are responsible for paying the fees and disbursements of the arbitral tribunal, the administrative costs of the arbitral institution and their own legal fees. The total cost can add up significantly. In a 2022 study, law firm Allen & Overy analysed over one hundred investor-State arbitrations to determine, among other things, the costs of arbitration. The study revealed, among other things, that claimants' costs are considerably higher than those of respondents ($ 6.4 million versus $ 4.7 million). This can be at-

52 *Parliamentary Papers II* 2016/17, 34608, no 3, p 46-47.

53 M. van de Hel-Koedoot & P.B. Fritschy, 'De kostenveroordeling in arbitrage: suggesties ter bevordering van voorspelbaarheid, transparantie en uniformiteit', in: C.J.M. Klaassen, G.J. Meijer & C.L. Schleijpen (eds), *Going Dutch: ADR in Nederland, in het bijzonder bij het NAI (Onderneming en recht no 113)*, Deventer: Wolters Kluwer 2019, para 24.1.

tributed to the fact that claimants bear the burden of proof and often face higher expenses in gathering evidence and formulating their claims.[54] In contrast, the costs of the arbitral tribunals surveyed were relatively comparable ($ 741,000 at ICSID and $ 685,000 at UNCITRAL).[55] In arbitration, the general rule is that the losing party is required to reimburse the winning party for the costs it has actually incurred. There is some variation in the way that arbitration rules deal with the award of costs. The UNCITRAL Arbitration Rules provide in Article 42 that the costs of the arbitration shall in principle be borne by the losing party. The 2024 NAI Arbitration Rules are more detailed, providing in Article 59 that the losing party shall be ordered to pay the costs of the arbitration, except in special cases. The losing party may be ordered to pay reasonable compensation for legal assistance to the successful party if and to the extent that such costs were necessary in the opinion of the arbitral tribunal. In determining the allocation of costs, the tribunal may consider the conduct of the parties throughout the proceedings and the extent to which each party has contributed to the expeditious and efficient conduct of the proceedings. The ICC Arbitration Rules do not expressly state that the losing party shall bear the costs; rather, Article 38 states that the arbitral tribunal shall decide which party shall bear the costs or how they shall be divided between the parties. The conduct of the arbitral proceedings may be taken into account by the arbitral tribunal, which may consider such circumstances as it deems relevant, including whether the proceedings were conducted in an expeditious and cost-effective manner. Furthermore, the potential for substantial costs to be incurred may also encourage parties to settle the matter at an earlier stage.[56]

In civil proceedings before the domestic courts, Article 237 DCCP provides that the party against whom a judgment is rendered shall be directed to pay the costs. The court determines the costs, which may also include any unnecessary costs incurred by the party that has incurred them. If both parties are partly unsuccessful, costs are often shared, with each party paying its own costs. If costs are awarded, the attorney's salary is estimated according to the liquidation rate, which can amount to several thousand euros. This means that the parties usually bear most of the costs of their legal representation themselves.

---

54 M. Hodgson, L. Raimanová & D. Hrčka, *2022 Empirical Study: Costs, Damages and Duration in Investor-State Arbitration in the CEE Region*, Allen & Overy 2022, p 9.

55 Hodgson, Raimanová & Hrčka 2022, p 4.

56 M.R. Ruygvoorn, *Contracten in de praktijk. Handleiding opstellen en beoordelen van commerciële contracten*, Deventer: Wolters Kluwer 2023, para 4.4.2.7.

The objective is to ascertain the costs regime under the WAMCA and to gain an understanding of how this compares to the costs of (individual) arbitration, as discussed above. A study commissioned by the Ministry of Justice on the utility, necessity and viability of a class actions proceedings fund in the Netherlands mentions figures of multiple millions that are needed for collective damages actions under the WAMCA.[57] It would appear that, to the extent there is a gap between the two, this is becoming less substantial than in the past.

Furthermore, in Article 1018l DCCP, the WAMCA deviates from the normal rule of Article 237 DCCP. In the event that the interest organisation's claim is summarily found to be unfounded, the defendant's attorney's remuneration may be increased up to fivefold (Article 1018l(1) DCCP). This is the result of an amendment to the law, as otherwise judges would not have the ability to take appropriate measures against litigation funders and interest organisations that submit 'frivolous claims', which impede careful advocacy.[58] In addition, the judge may issue an order for costs that differs from the liquidation rate (Article 1018l(2) DCCP) and require that the actual costs of the dispute be reimbursed to the claimant. This is only applicable in the event that the court issues a judgment establishing a collective settlement or a collective damages award, that is to say, a (partially) awarded claim. In the event that only a declaratory judgment is issued or the claim is dismissed, the standard rules of Article 237 et seq DCCP apply. The objective of the legislator was to slightly reduce the financial burden on the interest organisation appointed as Exclusive Representative,[59] i.e. the costs actually incurred, including the costs of the litigation funder.[60] It is not yet clear whether the contingency fee of a litigation funder can be included in that award.[61] As no collective actions have yet concluded with a judgment on the merits awarding damages, so that Article 1018l DCCP has not yet been applied by the courts.

It would appear that the award of costs under Dutch law is not significantly different from that in arbitration, with the losing party being required to

57 X.E. Kramer et al, *Utility, necessity, design and costs of a (revolving) litigation fund for collective actions*, Report for the Research and Documentation Centre (WODC), 25 June 2023.

58 *Parliamentary Papers II* 2018/19, 34608, no 22, p 2.

59 *Parliamentary Papers II* 2016/17, 34608, no 3, p 54.

60 *Parliamentary Papers II* 2017/18, 34608, no 9, p 5.

61 B.V. Rozema, 'Financiering van collectieve acties: wie draait op voor de succesvergoeding van de financier? Over de verhaalbaarheid van de succesvergoeding van procesfinanciers', *NTBR* 2023/25, p 242.

pay the costs. However, the most significant cost saving factor in collective actions compared to individual arbitration is the significantly lower cost of domestic court proceedings for the parties (compared to the amounts of around $ 700,000 under ICSID and UNCITRAL). Furthermore, the costs of the arbitral tribunal (especially if there are three arbitrators instead of one) and the administrative costs of the arbitral institution are saved. Finally, since the enforcement of arbitral awards is generally viewed as less problematic[62] (and therefore less costly) than the enforcement of court judgments, a proper comparison between the two should also include the enforcement costs, which can be substantial.

9.3.6 Conclusion

In the preceding paragraphs, we conducted a comparative analysis of individual arbitration and collective actions in the Dutch context, applying several parameters that are widely regarded as defining characteristics of arbitration. These include party autonomy, length of process and time to resolution, confidentiality and costs, including enforceability. The comparison demonstrates that the discrepancies on a few parameters are more nuanced. For example, party autonomy and confidentiality are typically advantageous for the respondents or the defendants. While the level of costs in absolute terms may appear to be the same, it is relatively lower in collective actions because it is borne by the collective. Collective actions, especially those modelled as an opt out action, are often the only viable mechanism for claimants, and particularly consumers, in global mass claims to obtain redress. Absent the availability of that procedural mechanism, there is little actual advantage and benefit in party autonomy or in an (unaffordable) expedient arbitration process.[63]

62 In this context, we are referring to the New York Convention (New York Convention on the Recognition and Enforcement of Foreign Arbitral Awards (1958), 330 UNTS 38; 21 UST 2517; 7 ILM 1046 (1968) Cmnd 6419), to which many States are parties. As a result, an arbitral award can be enforced in many countries.

63 L.G. Barnes, 'How Mandatory Arbitration Agreements and Class Action Waivers Undermine Consumer Rights and Why We Need Congress to Act', *Harvard Law & Policy Review* (9) 2015, p 329-354, arrived at the same conclusion for the US context. See also E. Lundy, 'The New Yellow Dog Contract: Mandatory Arbitration Agreements and Collective Action Waivers in the Aftermath of Epic Systems', *Nevada Law Journal Forum* (8) 2024, p 1-28 for a different angle and perspective, but with the same outcome.

9.4 The adjudication of consumer disputes

In some jurisdictions, consumer protection laws and regulations are (also) designed to address potential abuse of the arbitration process by businesses. Multinationals operating in global markets should be aware that their goods and/or services may be subject to different levels of consumer protection in different jurisdictions, reflecting a varying balance between arbitration and consumer rights protection.[64] The most striking contrast can be observed between the European and the American approaches, which we will examine in more detail later.[65]

At the European and Dutch levels, companies are not permitted to use arbitration as a means of circumventing class actions with regard to consumer matters. A number of legislative and regulatory measures have been introduced with the objective of safeguarding the interests of consumers. It is important to note that the consumer's right of access to the domestic courts cannot be unduly restricted. This is in line with the Unfair Terms Directive.[66] We will provide an overview of how this has been transposed into national law by the Dutch legislator. The legal position of consumers has been further strengthened since the Representative Actions Directive came into force. The objective of this Directive is to guarantee that each Member State provides an efficient and effective mechanism for consumers to pursue representative actions. In other words, it should be possible for a group of consumers in each Member State to seek injunctions or damages. This should boost consumer confidence in the internal market, improve access to justice for consumers and enhance consumer protection.[67] The Representative Actions Directive has been declared applicable on a long list of European statutory instruments in various substantive fields of law, for example in the area of competition law and prospectus liability.[68]

---

64 M. Benard, *Navigating arbitration with consumers – insights from recent cases*, Clifford Chance 2023, p 1. See also L.S. Mullenix, 'Class Action Waivers in Arbitration Agreements: The Twenty-First Century Arbitration Battleground and Implications for the EU Countries', *Emory International Law Review* (38) 2024, issue 4, p 785-818.

65 With the American approach we mean the United States of America and not North America, since we are aware that Canada follows the European approach as we will explain later. See also M.E. Steiner, 'When American Exceptionalism Isn't Exceptional: Consumer Arbitration in the United States', *Journal of the University of Latvia* (10) 2017, 5-28.

66 Council Directive 93/13/EEC of 5 April 1993 on unfair terms in consumer contracts (OJ 1993, L 95/29).

67 *Parliamentary Papers II* 2021/22, 36034, no 3, p 2.

68 Directive (EU) 2020/1828 of the European Parliament and of the Council of 25 November 2020 on representative actions for the protection of the collective interests

Given that consumers have already been able to pursue damages collectively since the WAMCA came into force in 2020, the Dutch legislator saw no need to create a whole new collective redress regime to implement the Representative Actions Directive in 2023. The WAMCA has been amended in a few select areas. The most significant amendments are that foreign organisations can apply for cross-border representation in the Netherlands and, conversely, Dutch interest organisations can also represent consumer interests in another Member State (of the EU). This is only possible if the organisation has been designed as such in advance. In addition, the litigation funder must not be a competitor of or dependent on the defendant, and the required information about the action, to be provided on the website of interest organisations, will be expanded. In contrast, in the United States, where class action waivers and consumer arbitration have become the norm, consumer class actions for damages are a rare occurrence.[69]

9.4.1 *The European and Dutch approaches*

In the European directives, which are primarily designed to protect consumers, the term 'consumer' is defined in a similar manner.[70] The Unfair Terms Directive defines a consumer as "any natural person who, in contracts covered by this Directive, is acting for purposes which are outside his trade, business or profession".[71] In accordance with the Directive, a term in a contract which has not been individually negotiated is unfair if, contrary to good faith, it significantly distorts the balance of the parties' rights and obligations arising under the contract, to the detriment of the consumer.

In the context of arbitration, the Directive stipulates that a term which has the object or effect of preventing or hindering a consumer from bringing an action or obtaining a remedy, in particular by requiring the consumer to refer exclusively to an arbitration tribunal not governed by law, shall be regarded as an unfair term.[72] An unfair term is not legally binding on the

---

of consumers and repealing Directive 2009/22/EC (OJ L 409/1), Annex I. We note that based on that list there is no right to collective redress under the Directive for representations to consumers in the so called 'secondary market'.

69 W. Vandenbussche, 'Moeten ook wij beducht zijn voor '*class action waivers*' in de overeenkomsten die wij aangaan?', *NTBR* 2021/25, p 195. J. Downing, 'An Important Time for the Future of Class Action Waivers and the Power Struggle between Businesses and Consumers', *Missouri Law Review* (81) 2016, issue 4, p 1151-1171 and Barnes 2015.

70 Asser/Hartkamp *3-I* 2023/163.

71 Article 2(b) Unfair Terms Directive.

72 Article 3(3) in conjunction with Annex under (1)(q) Unfair Terms Directive.

consumer in accordance with the conditions set forth in domestic law.[73] In the *Mostazo Claro* case, the Court of Justice of the European Union ruled on an arbitration agreement contained in a Spanish consumer contract. Following the initiation of arbitration proceedings by her telephone operator against Ms Mostazo Claro, she was granted ten days to refuse the arbitration, subject to the right to bring her case to the domestic courts. Ms Mostazo Claro did not oppose the arbitral proceedings nor did she challenge the arbitration agreement in the proceedings. Ms Mostazo Claro only sought to have the arbitration agreement annulled before the Spanish court after the arbitral tribunal ruled against her. In response to a request for a preliminary ruling from the Spanish court, the Court of Justice ruled that Article 6 of the Unfair Terms Directive must be interpreted as meaning that the court is required to set aside an arbitral award if the arbitration agreement is null and void, even if the nullity is raised for the first time in the setting aside proceedings and not during the arbitral proceedings.[74] Furthermore, the Court ruled that the domestic court is obliged to do so ex officio. The Court considered ex officio review to be an appropriate means both of preventing an individual consumer from being bound by an unfair term and of reinforcing the deterrent effect which helps to prevent the use of unfair terms in consumer contracts.[75] This approach ensures effective consumer protection, particularly in light of the risk, which should not be underestimated, that consumers may be unaware of their rights or may encounter difficulties in exercising them.[76] In the *Pannon* case, the Court of Justice confirmed that domestic courts must examine of their own motion whether a term is unfair, as soon as the court has before it the legal and factual elements necessary for that purpose. If the court determines that the term is unfair, it must disapply it unless the consumer objects.[77]

In accordance with Dutch law, Article 6:233 DCC stipulates the circumstances under which a clause in general terms and conditions is deemed voidable. In particular, this is the case if the clause is unreasonably onerous. In the case of a contract between a business and a consumer, a clause that is included on the black list of Article 6:236 DCC is regarded as unreasonably onerous. Additionally, a clause that is on the grey list of Article 6:237 DCC is deemed to be unreasonably onerous.

73 Article 6 Unfair Terms Directive.
74 CJEU 26 October 2006, C-168/05, ECLI:EU:C:2006:675, para 39 (*Mostazo Claro*).
75 CJEU 26 October 2006, C-168/05, ECLI:EU:C:2006:675, para 27 (*Mostazo Claro*).
76 CJEU 26 October 2006, C-168/05, ECLI:EU:C:2006:675, para 28 (*Mostazo Claro*).
77 CJEU 4 June 2009, C-243/08, ECLI:EU:C:2009:350, para 35 (*Pannon*).

Under the old Dutch Arbitration Act, the arbitration agreement was not included in the black and grey lists of Articles 6:236 and 6:237 DCC. This resulted in the Supreme Court overturning the ruling of the Leeuwarden Court of Appeal in the *Van Marrum/Wolff* case.[78] The contested judgment of the Court of Appeal was deemed to be based on an inadequate assessment of the specific circumstances of the case, and as such, the arbitration agreement was incorrectly placed on the black list of Article 6:236 DCC.[79] The Supreme Court held that the fact that the arbitration agreement appears in the annex to the Unfair Terms Directive will be taken into account by the court in its interpretation of Article 6:233 DCC. However, the court is not obliged to assume that the clause is unreasonably onerous.[80]

One of the key objectives of the amendments made to the Dutch Arbitration Act in 2015, was to boost consumer confidence in arbitration.[81] The arbitration agreement is now on the black list of unreasonably onerous clauses, which means that a dispute between a consumer and a professional cannot be settled by arbitration without further consent. In light of this, the arbitration agreement in general terms and conditions thus becomes unreasonably onerous and therefore voidable.[82] In the event that the general terms and conditions include an arbitration agreement invoked by the trader, the consumer is entitled to a minimum one-month cooling-off period during which they may elect to have the dispute resolved by the domestic courts.[83] This therefore allows for consumer disputes to be settled by an arbitral tribunal while ensuring that consumers retain their right of access to the domestic courts (Article 17 of the Dutch Constitution). It is the responsibility of the arbitral tribunal to assess ex officio whether the arbitration agreement is unreasonably onerous, as has been ruled by the Court of Justice.[84] In light of the Supreme Court's judgment in the *Van Marrum/Wolff* case, the legislator deemed it appropriate to include the arbitration agreement on the black list, thereby making it clear

78 In this case, the consumer client sued the construction company before the domestic court for damages for defective work. The General Conditions for Construction Contracts (AVA 1992) had been declared applicable to the contract by the construction company, and these conditions contained an arbitration clause for arbitration before the Construction Arbitration Council.

79 Supreme Court 21 September 2012, ECLI:NL:HR:2012:BW6135, para 3.4 (*Van Marrum/Wolff*).

80 Supreme Court 21 September 2012, ECLI:NL:HR:2012:BW6135, para 3.3 (*Van Marrum/Wolff*).

81 *Parliamentary Papers II* 2012/13, 33611, no 3, p 5.

82 *Parliamentary Papers II* 2012/13, 33611, no 3, p 7.

83 *Parliamentary Papers II* 2012/13, 33611, no 3, p 5.

84 *Parliamentary Papers II* 2012/13, 33611, no 3, p 7.

that certain arbitral clauses are inadmissible as general terms and conditions in all circumstances. This approach is consistent with the Unfair Terms Directive, which is based on minimum harmonisation.[85] National legislation can provide more consumer protection.

Once arbitration proceedings against a consumer have concluded, consumers may still prevent an arbitral award from being enforced against them. In the Netherlands, an arbitral award may be enforced following the granting of leave by the provisional relief judge at the request of one of the parties (Article 1062(1) DCCP). The provisional relief judge may only refuse leave if, following a summary examination, it appears likely that the award will be set aside (Article 1063(1) in conjunction with Article 1065(1) and Article 1068(1) DCCP). It is therefore a marginal review. In light of the case law of the Supreme Court (in answer to preliminary questions), it can be concluded that when assessing an application for leave to enforce an arbitral award, the court in provisional relief proceedings is obliged to assess ex officio whether (i) it is plausible that the arbitration agreement is unfair within the meaning of the Unfair Terms Directive; and (ii) it is plausible that a contractual term which forms the basis of the claim set out in the arbitral award is unfair within the meaning of the Unfair Terms Directive.[86] In light of the robust consumer protection measures in place, the provisional relief judge is not in a position to accept a mere marginal assessment. Furthermore, the judge is not at liberty to rely solely on the arbitral award. In the event that the provisional relief judge determines that the clause is unfair, it is probable that the clause will be declared void,[87] and the provisional relief judge will be obliged to refuse permission. In the event that the issue of unfairness pertains to the arbitration agreement, the refusal will be based on Article 1063(1) in conjunction with Article 1065(1)(a) DCCP (the ground for setting aside that no valid arbitration agreement exists). In the event that the issue of unfairness pertains to a contractual term that forms the basis of the claim set out in the arbitral award, the requirements set forth by the EU principle of equivalence dictate that the refusal is based on the analogous interpretation of Article 1063(1) in conjunction with Article 1065(1)(e) DCCP (the ground for setting aside that the arbitral award or the manner in which it was made is contrary to pub-

85 *Parliamentary Papers II* 2012/13, 33611, no 3, p 7.

86 Supreme Court 8 November 2019, ECLI:NL:HR:2019:1731, para 2.5.5 (*Stichting Intermaris/X*).

87 Supreme Court 13 September 2013, ECLI:NL:HR:2013:691, para 3.7.3.

lic policy).[88] If the consumer objects to the refusal of permission, the provisional relief judge will not refuse the leave.[89] Finally, the Supreme Court has ruled that in the case of an arbitration agreement that forms part of general terms and conditions, the regime of the Unfair Terms Directive and that of Article 6:236 DCC will always apply concurrently. This approach can then be followed, which will enhance the clarity of the relevant rules.[90]

In continental Europe, consumer protection legislation, as exemplified by the Netherlands, frequently precludes businesses from utilising arbitration as a means of circumventing collective litigation. In the absence of a valid arbitration agreement, consumers retain the right to pursue their claims in domestic courts, both individually and collectively.

9.4.2 *Approaches in other jurisdictions*

The majority of other (common) law jurisdictions adhere to a similar approach to that taken in continental Europe. The United Kingdom is a case in point. The consumer rights legislation in the UK is largely based on EU law and no substantial modifications have been made post-Brexit. The Unfair Terms Directive was transposed into UK law through the Consumer Rights Act 2015 (CRA 2015). In addition, paras 89-91 of the English Arbitration Act 1996 (AA 1996) and the Unfair Arbitration Agreements (Specified Amount) Order 1999 extend the application of the relevant provisions of the CRA 2015 to arbitration. In summary, under UK law[91]: (i) arbitration agreements entered into by consumers in relation to claims of £ 5,000 or less are automatically unfair under para 91(1) of the AA 1996, and are therefore unenforceable against the consumer; (ii) arbitration clauses in consumer contracts relating to claims exceeding £ 5,000 may also be deemed unfair to be under the CRA 2015; and (iii) an arbitration clause in a consumer contract is likely to be deemed unfair if it excludes or hinders the consumer's right to take legal action before the courts, if the arbitrator's fees are relatively high compared to the amount of the claim, and if the impact of the arbitration clause would not have been apparent to a layperson.[92]

88 Supreme Court 8 November 2019, ECLI:NL:HR:2019:1731, para 2.5.5 (*Stichting Intermaris/X*).
89 CJEU 30 May 2023, C-488/11, ECLI:EU:C:2013:341, para 49 (*Asbeek Brusse en de Man Garabito*); Supreme Court 13 September 2013, ECLI:NL:HR:2013:691, para 3.8.
90 Supreme Court 8 November 2019, ECLI:NL:HR:2019:1731, para 2.8.4 (*Stichting Intermaris/X*).
91 G. Lazarev & J. Trevellick, 'Consumer class arbitration in the UK: where we are and what next?', *Practical Law Arbitration Blog* 9 October 2017.
92 *Mylcrist Builders Limited v Mrs G Buck. Mylcrist Builders Limited v Mrs. G Buck* [2008] EWHC 2172 TCC.

Historically, these protections have rarely been invoked and have featured in virtually no cases in the last two decades. However, this is now changing.[93] One potential explanation is the globalisation of the markets for goods and services. US-based multinationals and service providers, including those active in the crypto business such as exchanges, have frequently required users to accept user agreements mandating arbitration or other forms of alternative dispute resolution, such as online dispute resolution, of any disputes. This is common practice in the US, where consumer arbitration is widespread, and without making any distinction for where the users are based. As explained above, this is problematic in the European context, as illustrated by the case law of the English courts.[94]

The situation in Canada is broadly similar. Canadian courts have ruled that provincial consumer protection laws indicate a legislative intent to permit consumer class proceedings despite the presence of mandatory arbitration provisions. The Canadian Supreme Court's decision in *TELUS Communications Inc. v. Wellman*[95] clearly limits this principle to the consumer context and reaffirms the enforceability of such arbitration provisions in the commercial context. The cases *TELUS Communications Inc. v. Wellman* and *Seidel v. TELUS Communications Inc.*[96] confirm that the mandatory arbitration clauses in consumer agreements are not enforceable in accordance with the relevant provincial consumer protection act.

In contrast to the aforementioned approaches, the US methodology diverges considerably. A recent study,[97] that examined the use of arbitration agreements in connection with consumer transactions by the top 100 largest domestic US companies, as ranked by Fortune Magazine in 2018, reached some noteworthy conclusions. The researcher identified these companies as the most successful and powerful in the US, with combined revenues totalling over $ 12.8 trillion, profits of $ 1.0 trillion, a market value of $ 21.6 trillion, and a contribution to the US GDP of over two-thirds. It goes without saying that they all operate on a global scale. As the author explains in greater detail in the study, due to their market power and capacity to impose arbitration agreements on consumers, these leading com-

93 Benard 2023, p 1.

94 *Payward Inc v Chechetkin* [2023] EWHC 1780; *Amir Soleymani v Nifty Gateway LLC* [2022] EWCA Civ 1297.

95 *TELUS Communications Inc. v. Wellman*, 2019 SCC 19.

96 *Seidel v. TELUS Communications Inc.*, 2011 SCC 15.

97 I.S. Szalai, 'The Prevalence of Consumer Arbitration Agreements by America's Top Companies', *US Davies Law Review Online* (52) 2019, p 233-259.

panies are able to circumvent the traditional judicial system for disputes involving consumers. The study concentrated on two main issues: (i) how many of these top companies have used arbitration agreements in connection with customer transactions since 2010; and (ii) of those companies, how many use arbitration agreements containing a 'class waiver' requiring customers to waive their right to proceed collectively or as part of a class. The study's principal findings are as follows: (i) a total of eighty-one companies in the Fortune 100, including subsidiaries or related affiliates, have utilised arbitration agreements in conjunction with consumer transactions; (ii) of the eighty-one companies in the Fortune 100 with consumer arbitration agreements, seventy-eight companies include class waivers in their arbitration agreements; (iii) it is estimated that at least a majority of US households (and possibly almost two-thirds) are covered by broad consumer arbitration agreements; (iv) over sixty percent of US retail e-commerce sales are covered by broad consumer arbitration agreements; and (v) in 2018, at least 826,537,000 consumer arbitration agreements were in force, based on estimates from just a few companies for which information was readily available. The author suggests that the actual number of consumer arbitration agreements in the US is likely to be higher. For context, the US population is approximately 328 million.

9.5 The adjudication of financial securities disputes

In the context of securities litigation in a globalised market, we are observing a growing trend among listed companies to include arbitration clauses in their shareholders agreements with the aim of avoiding adjudication via class and/or collective litigation. The globalisation of financial markets has resulted in a proliferation of companies listed on multiple exchanges worldwide. Their investors are dispersed across the globe. As a consequence, in the event of a shareholders dispute, there are a number of places where the dispute could be resolved.

In the EU, in accordance with the Brussels Recast Regulation[98] (which has its equivalents in the DCCP), a defendant may be sued in the courts of their domicile. In the case of legal persons, this refers to the statutory seat, central administration or principal place of business. In addition, there are specific grounds for jurisdiction. In cases where there are multiple defend-

98 Regulation (EU) No 1215/2012 of the European Parliament and of the Council of 12 December 2012 on jurisdiction and the recognition and enforcement of judgments in civil and commercial matters (recast) (OJ L 351/1).

ants who are not all domiciled in the Netherlands, domestic courts may assume jurisdiction, provided there is an anchor defendant. In order for the court to assume jurisdiction under this ground, there must be a close connection between the claims in question. This connection must be such that it is expedient for the court to hear and determine them together, in order to avoid the risk of irreconcilable judgments resulting from separate proceedings. Furthermore, the courts in the place where the harmful event occurred or may occur have jurisdiction. This jurisdiction is applicable at both the place where the damage occurred (*Erfolgsort*) and the place of the event causing the damage (*Handlungsort*). In the event of investor damage, the courts of the jurisdiction in which a listed company has fulfilled its statutory disclosure obligations for the purpose of its listing have jurisdiction, on the basis of the damage occurring in that jurisdiction.[99] In the case of claims based on prospectus liability, the Court of Justice ruled that the courts in the applicant's domicile also have jurisdiction by virtue of the damage occurring. This is particularly the case where alleged damage occurs directly to a bank account held by the applicant with a bank established in the jurisdiction of those courts.[100]

The number of potential dispute resolution venues for global securities disputes in the US has been reduced following the Supreme Court's decision in *Morrison v. National Australia Bank.*[101] Prior to this, as the prevailing anti-fraud measure regulating secondary markets[102] did not address its territorial application,[103] lower federal judges frequently treated it as a matter of subject matter jurisdiction. This meant that US courts could potentially have jurisdiction over claims with extraterritorial elements if the claim was based on conduct taking place in the US, or if the effects of the conduct were felt within the US.[104] This approach was broadly consistent with European norms and practices.

In the case of *Morrison v. National Australia Bank*, foreign investors initiated legal proceedings against a foreign defendant, namely an Australian

99 CJEU 12 May 2021, C-709/19, ECLI:EU:C:2021:377, para 35 (*VEB/BP*).

100 CJEU 12 September 2018, C-304/17, ECLI:EU:C:2018:701, para 28 (*Löber*).

101 *Morrison v. National Australia Bank*, 561 US 247 (2010).

102 Para 10(b) of the Securities and Exchange Act of 1934.

103 N.M. Geevarghese, 'A Shocking Loss of Investor Protection: The Implications of Morrison v. National Australia Bank', *Brooklyn Journal of Corporate, Financial & Commercial Law* (6) 2011, issue 1, p 236.

104 H.L. Buxbaum, 'Multinational Class Actions Under Federal Securities Law: Managing Jurisdictional Conflict', *Columbia Journal of Transnational Law* (46) 2007, issue 14, p 18-20.

bank that had traded its ordinary shares (equivalent to common stock) on Australian and other foreign exchanges, but not on any US exchange. The claimants were purchasers of those ordinary shares. They alleged that statements made by bank officials had artificially inflated the share price, and that these statements had derived from misleading accounting used by one of the bank's subsidiaries in the US. The lower courts ruled that the case should be dismissed on the grounds that the alleged harm was limited to foreign investors and that the purported fraudulent conduct was not sufficiently connected to the asserted injury. The Supreme Court upheld the dismissal of the action, but on grounds that differed from those previously considered. It introduced a test that focused solely on the location where securities are purchased and sold. Therefore, fraud involving securities traded exclusively on foreign markets or platforms is not subject to US antifraud protection, even if the investors submitting orders reside in the US.

The consequence of this ruling is that whereas in the past global investor disputes often could concentrated in the US, post *Morrison*, that is no longer the case. As evidenced by the *Petrobras* case study below, the US court ruled that it did not have jurisdiction over claims by investors who had purchased shares on the Brazilian stock market. Consequently, they were excluded from the US class and restored to arbitration. Businesses operating on a global scale, such as Petrobras, seek to limit the potential for dispersed litigation in different jurisdictions by including arbitration clauses in their shareholder agreements, aiming to divert the proceedings before a single adjudicator: an arbitral tribunal.

9.5.1 Example: Petrobras

The *Petrobras* case,[105] which we use as an example of a global investor dispute in this contribution, demonstrates how arbitration and court adjudication can be used as strategic tools by parties in securities litigation, competing with each other as a means of resolving global disputes.

A 2014 investigation into a small car wash for money laundering in Brazil revealed a significant corruption scheme within the Brazilian federal government, particularly within State-owned companies, including the listed

105 Rotterdam District Court 19 September 2018, ECLI:NL:RBROT:2018:7852 (*Petrobras*). The final judgment on the merits in this case rendered after the submission of this contribution and is therefore not included in our analysis. See Rotterdam District Court 30 October 2024, ECLI:NL:RBROT:2024:10725 (*Petrobras*).

oil company Petrobras. This resulted in a landmark anti-corruption investigation, also known as *Operation Car Wash.*[106] One consequence was that Petrobras entered into agreements with the US and Brazilian authorities, agreeing to pay a combined total of $ 853.2 million in penalties. The penalties were agreed as a resolution to the US governments' investigations into violations of the Foreign Corrupt Practices Act (FCPA) in connection with Petrobras's role in facilitating payments to Brazilian politicians and political parties, as well as a related Brazilian investigation.[107] Investors in Petrobras subsequently filed a class action lawsuit in the US, which was eventually settled for $ 3 billion.[108]

In summary, Petrobras asserted in the US class action that investors who purchased Petrobras securities in the US (American Depository Receipts or ADRs) and also purchased Petrobras common or preferred shares on the Brazilian stock exchange, were subject to mandatory arbitration in São Paolo in accordance with the company's bylaws. The judge ruled that the arbitration clause was not binding on investors who had acquired Petrobras ADRs on US securities markets. However, he denied competence for claimants who had purchased shares on the Brazilian stock exchange, given that he recognised the binding force of the arbitration clause in that regard.[109] A significant number of investors in Petrobras shares initiated individual arbitration proceedings in Brazil, based on similar facts and grounds to those alleged in the US securities fraud class action.

Some of the investors elected to pursue an alternative strategy, initiating a class action in the Netherlands (on the basis of Article 3:305a (old) DCC), where a number of Petrobras subsidiaries were incorporated.[110] The defendants argued before the domestic court that it should decline jurisdiction to hear the interest organisation's claims insofar as they were brought on behalf of shareholders in Petrobras. The interest organisation argued that the English-language version of the arbitration clause in Petrobras' articles of association was insufficiently clear and specific. It did not desig-

106 Rotterdam District Court 19 September 2018, ECLI:NL:RBROT:2018:7852, para 2.7 (*Petrobras*).

107 'Petróleo Brasileiro S.A. – Petrobras Agrees to Pay More Than $ 850 Million for FCPA Violations', *US Department of Justice Office of Public Affairs* 27 September 2018.

108 Rotterdam District Court 19 September 2018, ECLI:NL:RBROT:2018:7852, para 2.10 (*Petrobras*).

109 Rotterdam District Court 19 September 2018, ECLI:NL:RBROT:2018:7852, para 2.9 (*Petrobras*).

110 Ianika Tzankova is a board member of the interest organisation (Stichting Petrobras Compensation Foundation), which initiated this class action.

nate a forum to adjudicate disputes covered by the clause. As the majority of shareholders are based internationally and are mostly not fluent in Portuguese, they have had to rely on the English text.[111]

The Rotterdam District Court ruled that, in light of the international scope of the text in question, the English-language version of the arbitration clause was the only text relevant to the court's question of jurisdiction. In accordance with both Brazilian and Dutch law, the court ruled that the arbitration clause was not valid. The text did not clearly and unambiguously state that the dispute should be submitted to arbitrators, which is a prerequisite for waiving the fundamental right of access to the state courts.[112] In contrast with the US court's opinion, the Rotterdam District Court ruled that it also had jurisdiction to consider the claims brought by the interest organisation on behalf of investors who had purchased their shares on the Brazilian stock exchange. However, this ruling did not extend to investors who had initiated arbitration proceedings or proceedings before the Brazilian domestic courts.[113] The court ruled that the interest organisation was admissible.[114]

While businesses have an interest in limiting forum shopping on the claimant side and settling securities disputes in arbitration, the *Petrobras* case demonstrates that this strategy is not always successful. In particular, it does not always lead to the desired result for the company, which is a concentration of disputes in one jurisdiction and making it more difficult for investors to procedurally organise themselves in mass tort cases to achieve economies of scale. The judges' approach in the US and the Netherlands was not uniform, and the arbitration clause included in Petrobras' articles of association was ineffective in preventing a collective action in the Dutch courts. For wealthy institutional investors who are (or can be) externally funded, it could be argued that arbitration proceedings are a less onerous option. However, this does not provide a solution for smaller (retail) investors, often natural persons or 'consumers'. The only means of recourse for these (retail) investors is to join a collective action with large institutional investors. At present, this is only feasible through an opt out collective ac-

111 Rotterdam District Court 19 September 2018, ECLI:NL:RBROT:2018:7852, paras 5.30-5.31 (*Petrobras*).

112 Rotterdam District Court 19 September 2018, ECLI:NL:RBROT:2018:7852, paras 5.37-5.39 (*Petrobras*).

113 Rotterdam District Court 26 May 2021, ECLI:NL:RBROT:2021:4668, para 2.9 (*Petrobras*).

114 Rotterdam District Court 26 May 2021, ECLI:NL:RBROT:2021:4668, para 2.10 (*Petrobras*).

tion before the domestic courts, as there is no analogous mechanism in arbitration.

9.6 The adjudication of competition disputes

Competition law is an area of substantive law that regulates the legal order in the Global Market by, essentially, establishing fair play rules between companies operating in that space. These rules impact the relationship between companies in at least two ways. Firstly, they make sure that competition is possible in the first place and that no single entity dominates the (Global) Market. Secondly, they guarantee that competition between the companies operating in the relevant (geographical) region is fair. The underlaying rationale is that (fair) competition fuels innovation and benefits consumers and society as a whole, leading to better products, services and reasonable prices. Competition law also regulates the relationship between the companies and their customers, namely the purchasers of products and/or services. The latter (the customers) can be other companies, but are frequently consumers.

Conflicts can arise in all these vertical or horizontal legal relationships, leading to disputes between companies (B2B) and/or between companies and consumers (B2C), and sometimes both. This is due to the fact that marketing and distribution processes in the Global Market often involve multiple participants and long distribution chains. In the context of competition law, the term 'direct' and 'indirect' purchasers is frequently used in the context of disputes arising from supply and distribution chains and/or in the vertical legal relationships. The latter group, often consumers, are the last ones of a (long) distribution chain of products or services. The direct purchasers are, in most cases, (other) companies that are the business partner of the multinational, but not always. It goes without saying that infringements of competition law affect a significant number of businesses and consumers, leading to mass claims.

In the event of an abuse of a dominant position or price fixing by cartels, resulting in damages, compensation must be provided. The result of an abuse of a dominant position is that the competitors of the dominant company and numerous clients suffer damages. Equally, in the event of a price-fixing cartel, the purchasers of the cartel members' goods and services have paid an inflated price, which would not have been the case in a healthy competitive market. Sometimes, the cartels have an 'umbrella' effect, impacting even the prices of goods or services offered by competitors who were not participating in the cartel. When the action for damages follows a regulatory finding of an infringement by a regulatory authority, this is referred to as a 'follow on'-claim. In the absence of a prior finding by a regulatory authority of unlawful conduct, one speaks of 'standalone'-cases. In the European context, both direct and indirect purchasers are in principle entitled to damages in the event of a price fixing cartel.[115] In the US, it has long been accepted that only direct purchasers can ever claim damages of price fixing, although nowadays more than half of the states acknowledge that indirect purchasers also have that right.[116]

In any case, these disputes need to be adjudicated, again, via arbitration and/or court proceedings, depending on the nature of the parties involved and the (valid) contractual arrangements between them. As previously discussed in paragraph 9.4, the implications of arbitration clauses in consumer contracts must be considered. The aforementioned observations are also relevant in follow on or standalone actions on behalf of consumers (either as direct or indirect purchasers). This paragraph will focus mainly on competition claims on behalf of companies that have been the victims of anticompetitive behaviour. It is common practice for companies to include a commercial arbitration clause in their agreements, which frequently gives rise to questions regarding the validity of jurisdiction clauses. The case study discussed below illustrates that the two main mechanisms for addressing competition disputes are intertwined and can lead to complex discussions and different resolution pathways, depending not only on the nature of the parties involved. It is also relevant which domestic court is dealing with the issue, which law applies to the interpretation of the arbitration clause, and whether the underlying cause of action is an abuse of a dominant position or price-fixing.

9.6.1 *Example: CDC Hydrogen Peroxide (follow on claim)*

On 3 May 2006 the European Commission announced that a significant number of companies, including Akzo Nobel NV, EKA Chemicals AB and Kemira Oyj, had infringed the European cartel prohibition by participating

115 Supreme Court 8 July 2016, ECLI:NL:HR:2016:1483 (*TenneT/ABB*).

116 P. Garofalo & L. Hepner, 'Reforming Antitrust Policy to Challenge Corporate Power: A Guide for State Lawmakers', *American Economic Liberties Project* 2022, p 14-16; F. Cengiz, 'Antitrust damages actions: Lessons from American indirect purchasers' litigation', *The International and Comparative Law Quarterly (59) 2010, issue* 1, p 39-63.

in a single and continuous infringement regarding the hydrogen peroxide market, covering the whole EEA between 1994 and 2000. The members of the hydrogen peroxide cartel fixed and monitored target prices, allocated market shares and customers, exchanged commercially important and confidential information, and limited production. On 16 March 2009, CDC, a commercial company specialising in the purchase and private enforcement of competition claims, filed the claims purchased from 32 companies in the paper and pulp industry against some of the cartel members, including Akzo Nobel NV, before the Regional Court of Dortmund, Germany. The companies were purchasers of hydrogen peroxide with a total of 94 production sites located in 13 European countries. CDC filed the suit seeking damages of at least € 254 million. The damages were calculated based on the purchase agreements between the various cartel members and the 32 companies. It is customary for such contractual agreements to include jurisdiction clauses, and sometime cases, commercial arbitration is agreed.

The Regional Court of Dortmund decided to request a preliminary ruling from the European Court of Justice in relation to certain aspects of its jurisdiction. One of the questions put forward before the Court was whether standard jurisdiction clauses included in supply agreements also cover claims for damages resulting from secret cartels. In 2015, the Court delivered a judgment[117] finding that broadly worded jurisdiction clauses do not extend to competition-related tortious damages claims. The Court concluded that, under the Brussels Regulation,[118] a jurisdiction clause in favour of an EU Member State cannot be interpreted as including cartel damages claims unless the agreement is explicit and specific. Given the unpredictable and unforeseeable nature of cartel damages claims, "a clause which abstractly refers to all disputes arising from a contractual relationship" cannot be interpreted as "extending to a dispute relating to the tortious liability that one party allegedly incurred as a result of the other's participation in an unlawful cartel. Given that the undertaking which suffered the loss could not reasonably foresee such litigation at the time that it agreed to the jurisdiction clause and that that undertaking had no knowledge of the unlawful cartel at that time, such litigation cannot be regarded

117 CJEU 21 May 2015, C-352/13, ECLI:EU:C:2015:335 (*CDC Hydrogen Peroxide*).

118 Council Regulation (EC) No 44/2001 of 22 December 2000 on jurisdiction and the recognition and enforcement of judgments in civil and commercial matters (OJ L 012 *16/01/2001 P. 0001 – 0023*).

as stemming from a contractual relationship. Such a clause would not therefore have validly derogated from the referring court's jurisdiction".[119]

The Court's decision on this point was based on the application of autonomous EU law on jurisdiction clauses in favour of EU Member States. As a result, its decision was not legally directly relevant to the interpretation of arbitration clauses. The latter would be, generally speaking, determined by the national law which falls to be applied to the clause before the relevant tribunal or court. Despite the Court not addressing arbitration clauses, it was expected that a spill over into that area might take place. It is worth noting that, both prior to and after the Court's judgment, courts in Member States have been dealing with the issue of the scope of broad arbitration clauses. The resulting decisions have been conflicting, as illustrated below.

The first national courts to consider this issue – the Amsterdam Court of Appeal regarding a sodium chloride cartel[120] and the Rotterdam District Court regarding an elevator cartel[121] – reached the same conclusion as the European Court in respect of the arbitration clauses before them. By contrast, the English High Court held in *Microsoft Mobile OY (Ltd) v. Sony Europe Limited & Ors*[122] that an arbitration clause (to which English law applied) covered a private cartel damages action (based on the interpretation of the clause in the context of the supply contract in question). In refusing to hear a cartel damages action brought before it in relation to a rail cartel, the Regional Court of Dortmund reached the same end result as the English High Court did in the *Sony* case.[123] The contracts between the claimant and one of the cartel members contained arbitration clauses (in respect of which German law fell to be applied by the Regional Court) referring to arbitration "all disputes out of this contract" and "all disputes out of and in connection with this contract". Accordingly, the defendant relied on the arbitration clauses and requested the court to dismiss the action. The claimant, however, maintained that the arbitration clauses did not cover cartel damages claims and explicitly referred to the Court of Justice's decision in *CDC Hydrogen Peroxide*. The Regional Court of Dortmund

119 CJEU 21 May 2015, C-352/13, ECLI:EU:C:2015:335, paras 69-70 (*CDC Hydrogen Peroxide*).

120 Amsterdam Court of Appeal 21 July 2015, ECLI:NL:GHAMS:2015:3006 (*Kemira/CDC*).

121 Rotterdam District Court 25 May 2016, ECLI:NL:RBROT:2016:4164 (*Stichting De Glazen Lift/Kone et al*).

122 *Microsoft Mobile OY (Ltd) v. Sony Europe Limited & Ors* [2017] EWHC 374 (Ch).

123 Landgericht Dortmund 13 September 2017, 8 O 30/16 [Kart].

disagreed with the claimant and held that the action fell within the arbitration clauses. The Dortmund court emphasised that an arbitration-friendly stance must be taken when interpreting arbitration clauses under German law. This generally results in a broad interpretation, whereby arbitration agreements concluded with a view to contractual claims are generally considered to also cover concurring tortious claims. Since cartel damages actions are categorised as tortious claims under German law, they are subject to an arbitration clause (when German law applies) if they arise from a set of facts that also gives rise to a concurrent contractual claim. The German court took a rather independent position by establishing that none of the factors that have relevance under EU law are relevant for its evaluation of the arbitration clause under German law.[124]

9.6.2 *Example: Apple/eBizcuss (abuse of dominance position)*

In a case that was not about price fixing, but about abuse of a dominant position, the European Court took a different view on the applicability of jurisdiction clauses than the one in the *CDC Hydrogen Peroxide*-matter. eBizcuss was a former authorised distributor of Apple products in France. In 2012, eBizcuss filed a damages claim before the Paris Commercial Court against Apple. The claim alleged that Apple's discriminatory practices had caused eBizcuss to incur significant financial damage and that these practices constituted abuse within the meaning of Article 102 TFEU. The distribution contract between Apple and eBizcuss included a jurisdiction clause, which stipulated that the Irish courts would have jurisdiction in the event of any dispute arising out of the contract. In light of this clause, the Paris Commercial Court declined jurisdiction. On appeal, the Paris Court of Appeal upheld the Paris Commercial Court's rejection of the case, on the basis that the French courts lacked jurisdiction. However, the Court of Cassation and the Versailles Court of Appeal reached a different conclusion and referred the case back to the Paris Commercial Court. Following further appeal by Apple to the Court of Cassation, the latter stayed proceedings and asked the

124 For example, it did not matter when the cartel infringement took place (prior to or after entering into the agreement), nor its nature or seriousness of the fault. Furthermore, it has no bearing on the interpretation that private enforcement also serves public interests since the same holds true for other tortious claims. With the same argument, the court decided against applying the foreseeability test stipulated by the CJEU in *CDC Hydrogen Peroxide* regarding jurisdiction clauses. According to the court, such test is not convincing and there is no principle that the same standards must be applied regarding jurisdiction clauses in favour of EU Member States (governed by the Brussels Regulation) and arbitration clauses to which German law applies.

European Court for clarification of Article 23 Brussels Regulation. The Court held that Article 23 Brussels Regulation does not exclude the invocation of a jurisdiction clause in an action for damages based on Article 102 TFEU, provided that the clause does not expressly refer to disputes relating to liability resulting from an infringement of competition law.[125] The CJEU's ruling in *eBizcuss* therefore stands in contrast to the position taken in *CDC Hydrogen Peroxide* in the context of a follow-on cartel damages action based on Article 101 TFEU. In support of its contrasting position, the Court held that "while the anti-competitive conduct covered by Article 101 TFEU, namely an unlawful cartel, is in principle not directly linked to the contractual relationship between a member of that cartel and a third party affected by the cartel, the anticompetitive conduct covered by Article 102 TFEU, namely the abuse of a dominant position, can materialise in contractual relations that an undertaking in a dominant position establishes and by means of contractual terms". Not surprisingly, the Court considers that actions based on Article 102 TFEU are more likely to be directly linked to such a contractual relationship than damages actions for breach of Article 101 TFEU.

9.6.3 *Implications*

The case law of the CJEU and various domestic courts discussed above demonstrates that the key challenges in resolving mass claims in competition law in B2B-disputes are 'fragmentation' and 'legal uncertainty'.

The Dutch courts' decisions in cartel damages claims appears to facilitate the consolidation of mass claims before a single adjudicator, namely the domestic court with jurisdiction over the tort under the Brussels Recast Regulation. The decision of the Regional Court of Dortmund, on the other hand, implicates that in cases where a relevant arbitration clause is subject to German law, a claimant in a cartel damages case may encounter a fragmentation of proceedings when pursuing legal action against several cartelists and agreed on arbitration with some of them. It is unclear how potential claimants can address a potential issue at the drafting stage. For defendants, invoking an arbitration agreement carries certain risks. It would most likely result in the dispute between themselves and the claimant being resolved in arbitration involving only themselves and the claimant. This would prevent the defendant from securing a contribution claim from other cartelists by means of third-party notices and interventions in

125 CJEU 24 October 2018, C-595/17, ECLI:EU:C:2018:854 (*Apple Sales International et al/ EBizcuss.com*).

that forum. In the long run, a court's dismissal of a cartel damages claim in favour of arbitration may have a boomerang effect.

In the case of claims based on abuse of dominance position, the situation is slightly different but still unfavourable for the claimant that is a business. If there is a valid jurisdiction clause, then that is 'simply' applicable. With its judgment in the *eBizcuss* case, the Court added another piece to the puzzle in clarifying how Article 23(1) of the Brussels Regulation (now Article 25 Brussels Recast Regulation) must be interpreted in the context of the applicability of jurisdiction clauses in competition law damages actions based on Article 102 TFEU (in the case of abuse of a dominant position).

One outstanding issue is whether arbitration (as opposed to jurisdiction) clauses should be considered binding in relation to damages claims based on Articles 101 and 102 TFEU. The Court missed the opportunity to address that issue at the time of the *CDC Hydrogen Peroxide* judgment in 2015. By contrast, the Advocate General in *CDC Hydrogen Peroxide* opined that an arbitration clause is not in itself inapplicable in the context of a competition law damages action. However, in the case of a clandestine cartel, claimants would likely have had insufficient knowledge of an infringing agreement and its unlawful nature to give consent to an arbitration clause covering claims arising from an illicit agreement. Therefore, in such circumstances, the invocation of an arbitration clause should be precluded. In our view, the Court's approach to this discussion is not inherently pro or against arbitration. The issue is one of ensuring access to justice in the context of mass claims. The analyses in paragraph 9.3 indicate that the context of mass claims arbitration is disadvantageous for claimants.

9.7 Observations and conclusion

This contribution examines the topic of mass claim dispute resolution in the Global Village. It is a multi-facetted and multi-layered phenomenon where disputes are resolved mainly via arbitration and court adjudication. After defining Global Disputes and examining the advantages and disadvantages of both, we concluded that, currently, and in the context of mass claims, court adjudication is more advantageous for claimants and for access to justice than arbitration. This is largely because of the absence of class and collective actions in arbitration. We then examined three different areas of law: consumer law, financial law and competition law – how multinationals utilise jurisdiction and arbitration clauses to create (what is perceived to be) a strategic advantage for defendants. To that end, we have used the Netherlands and/or actual cases with a link to the Netherlands as examples. Indeed, in the context of mass claims, it is the defendants who typically invoke jurisdiction clauses, including arbitration clauses, rather than the claimants. The success of this varies depending on the following factors. Firstly, the nature of the parties. In some instances, consumers are not precluded from opting for court adjudication or arbitration. This is particularly prevalent in the European and Canadian contexts, while the US, with its case law regarding class action waivers, represents the opposite end of this spectrum. Secondly, the nature of the dispute itself can also impact the arbitration process. For instance, consumers may have more protection than retail investors in securities cases, despite both groups being natural persons. Thirdly, the applicable national law on the arbitration clause and/or the dispute: Dutch courts appear to adopt a more rigorous approach to the interpretation of the validity of arbitration clauses in securities and competition law than English, US and German courts, for example. Lastly, the cause of action. In EU competition cases, it seems to be relevant whether the infringement concerns price fixing or abuse of a dominant position, even though the Court has only explicitly addressed jurisdiction (and not arbitration) clauses in these judgments. This has different implications for the different parties involved in Global Disputes. For example, for multinationals it will be relevant what their geographical market is and whether they are dealing with (European) consumers. For (small) companies that are doing business with powerful counterparties the situation is probably most disadvantageous as they would not be in the position to negotiate contractual terms that grant them access to the courts. Ironically, when it comes to mass claims arbitration has evolved into a strategic tool, a dispute resolution mechanism that no longer facilitates, but 'hampers' the access to justice. That is a somewhat disappointing conclusion that does not do justice to the potential that arbitration could have for the resolution of mass claims.

CHAPTER 10

ARBITRATION MEETS ESG: AN INTRODUCTION

Guillaume Croisant[1] *& Piotr Wiliński*[2]

Companies, and their directors and officers, are subject to an increasing pressure from stakeholders (including legislators, regulators, investors, employees, the civil society and customers) to conduct their businesses in a sustainable manner, taking into consideration Environment, Social and Governance ("**ESG**") factors. This "ESG megatrend" has entailed a wave of new regulations and landmark court cases, as well as associated new litigation and liability risks.

These developments will lead to, or play an important role in, a material number of claims, including many claims that will be subject to arbitration. The seller of a company will overpraise its transition plan or downplay its supply chain risks. A company will terminate its relationship with a supplier on the ground that it did not abide by emission reduction objectives or was involved in forced labour. Minority shareholders will challenge the sustainability strategy (or lack thereof) of the board and/or the controlling shareholder. Investors will claim that the investee company's disclosures were misleading. A company will offer arbitration as a voluntary grievance mechanism to stakeholders affected by its activities. An investor will claim that ESG requirements adopted by the host State is a breach of an investment treaty. A host State will introduce a counterclaim alleging violations of environmental obligations by the investor. Arbitration parties will request the environmental impacts of the proceedings to be calculated, mitigated and borne by the defeated party. And those are just a few examples.

1 G. (Guillaume) Croisant lectures on ESG at the Université libre de Bruxelles and is a Counsel at Linklaters LLP in Brussels. The opinions expressed in this contribution are the authors' only. Some paragraphs of this contribution are an update (as of 1 September 2024) of R. Barrett & G. Croisant, 'The ESG Megatrend', in: D. De Meulemeester (ed), *ESG and international arbitration. Beyond the acronyms*, Deventer: Wolters Kluwer 2023, p 187-222.

2 P. (Piotr) Wiliński is an Assistant Professor at the Erasmus University and Managing Associate (Knowledge) at Linklaters LLP in Amsterdam.

While acknowledging that many issues only touched upon here would deserve dedicated contributions, this contribution aims to provides NAI users with a general introduction and "panorama" of the consequences of the ESG megatrend relevant to their practice, and to arbitration in general. It starts with a brief overview of the emergence of this megatrend and the key drivers associated with the shift from what has historically been mostly soft law standards to ever-increasing mandatory obligations (para 10.1). It then sets out the main legal developments in the key areas tackled by ESG regulations and case law (para 10.2), before presenting their relevance to commercial arbitration (para 10.3.1), investment arbitration (para 10.3.2), as well as the arbitration's process and actors themselves (para 10.3.3). We conclude that, despite the growing "backlash" against the extent of the ESG megatrend (para 10.2.6), there is no doubt that ESG considerations will be key for many disputes in the years and decades to come and brings challenges, but also major opportunities, to arbitration institutions, such as the NAI, and arbitration practitioners (para 10.4).

10.1 ESG – from soft law and voluntary standards to hard law and mandatory regulations

As the acronym implies, the concept of ESG – which has progressively replaced "corporate social responsibility" (or CSR) as the most prevalent buzzword used to describe recent trends in sustainable business – focusses on a range of environmental, social and governance factors, allowing for a multifaceted understanding of a business's sustainability risks and impacts. In line with its origin in sustainable finance, it aims to permit a readily quantifiable assessment of sustainability risks and impacts given its granularity. ESG strategies typically include a range of ESG performance metrics and targets, through which businesses set measurable goals against which they can measure and disclose progress. It is also increasingly associated with mandatory regulations and standards and the migration of soft law into hard law.

To name some of the most relevant soft law instruments for the next paragraphs of this contribution, long-lasting efforts of the United Nations (UN) to establish a corporate code of conduct for multinational companies[3] led to the adoption of the **UN Guiding Principles on Business and Human**

3 Such as the UN Commission on Transnational Corporations, established in 1973, or the UN Working Group on Transnational Corporations, established in 1998.

Rights (UNGP), a set of guidelines for States and companies to prevent, address and remedy human rights abuses committed in business operations. They were endorsed by the UN Human Rights Council in June 2011. In the same resolution, the UN Human Rights Council established the UN Working Group on Business & Human Rights.

The UNGP benefited from the prior work on the **OECD Guidelines for Multinational Enterprises on Responsible Business Conduct**, adopted as early as 1976 and regularly updated since then (most recently in June 2023). The OECD Guidelines are recommendations addressed by governments to multinational enterprises aiming to encourage positive contributions enterprises can make to economic, environmental and social progress, and to minimise adverse impacts on matters covered by the Guidelines that may be associated with an enterprise's operations, products and services. The Guidelines cover all key areas of business responsibility, including human rights, labour rights, environment, bribery, consumer interests, disclosure, science and technology, competition, and taxation.

The concept of "Responsible Business Conduct (RBC)" is at the crux of the Guidelines. It sets out an expectation that all businesses – regardless of their legal status, size, ownership or sector – avoid and address negative impacts of their operations, while contributing to sustainable development in the countries where they operate.

The Guidelines also establishes National Contact Points for RBC (NCPs) by Governments, to promote the OECD Guidelines and to handle, as non-judicial grievance mechanisms, cases against companies when they are not observed.

The sustainability agenda has known key developments in 2015, with the adoption of the Sustainable Development Goals and the Paris Climate Agreement.

The **Sustainable Development Goals (SDGs)**, formulated by the UN General Assembly in its resolution "Transforming our world: the 2030 Agenda for Sustainable Development"[4], are a set of 17 interlinked ob-

4 UN General Assembly, 25 September 2015, 'Transforming our world: the 2030 Agenda for Sustainable Development', A/RES/70/1, available at: https://documents-dds-ny.un.org/doc/UNDOC/GEN/N15/291/89/PDF/N1529189.pdf?OpenElement. This resolution was completed by another one in 2017, that identifies specific targets for each goal and provides indicators to measure progress (UN

jectives[5] designed to serve as a *"shared blueprint for peace and prosperity for people and the planet, now and into the future"*[6]. The goal was for these objectives to be achieved by 2030, although some have no end date. This framework has been used by many corporations to showcase their sustainability efforts, as well as by investors in the context of responsible investment (a trend usually described as "SDG driven investment").

The impact of the adoption of the **Paris Climate Agreement**, on the "E" of ESG in particular, cannot be emphasised enough. As we will see throughout this contribution, it has been the cornerstone of a number of key developments of these recent years, including in case law. It has been adopted by the EU and 194 States[7] at the 2015 COP21, under the aegis of the United Nations Framework Convention on Climate Change (UNFCCC). It entered into force on 4 November 2016. As per its Article 2, the agreement's overarching goal is to hold *"the increase in the global average temperature to well below 2°C above pre-industrial levels"* and pursue efforts *"to limit the temperature increase to 1.5°C above pre-industrial levels"*. Interestingly, the link with sustainable finance is also blatant as the objective of *"making finance flows consistent with a pathway towards low greenhouse gas emissions and climate-resilient development"* is also included. The agreement is legally binding, but a number of its provisions do not imply specific and detailed obligations, or are there to facilitate international collaboration. The party States determine their plans (the so-called "nationally determined contributions" (NDCs), set every five years) to achieve the treaty's objectives themselves.

In the context of the COP21 (still in 2015), the **Taskforce on Climate-related Financial Disclosures (TCFD)** has also been established by the G20

General Assembly, 6 July 2017, 'Work of the Statistical Commission pertaining to the 2030 Agenda for Sustainable Development', A/RES/71/313, available at: https://documents-dds-ny.un.org/doc/UNDOC/GEN/N17/207/63/PDF/N1720763.pdf?OpenElement.

5 Namely: "no poverty; zero hunger; good health and well-being; quality education; gender equality; clean water and sanitation; affordable and clean energy; decent work and economic growth; industry, innovation and infrastructure; reduced inequalities; sustainable cities and communities; responsible consumption and production; climate action; life below water; life on land; peace, justice, and strong institutions; and partnerships for the goals".

6 See the dedicated website set up by the UN Department of Economic and Social Affairs: https://sdgs.un.org/goals.

7 The United States withdrew from the agreement in 2020, but rejoined in 2021. Iran, Libya and Yemen are the three states that have not ratified the agreement, representing around 2% of the worldwide emissions.

and the Financial Stability Board in an effort to further consider climate in the global financial system and to address the perceived lack of transparency and international standards by which countries demonstrate or disclose that they are meeting their commitments under the Paris Agreement. The TCFD publishes recommendations designed to standardise worldwide climate-related disclosures that could *"promote more informed investment (...) and in turn, enable stakeholders to understand better concentrations of carbon-related assets in the financial sectors"*. These recommendations allow companies to use a standardised way to report their climate-related financial risks, consisting of physical, liability and transition risks, to stakeholders.

The 2021 COP26 provided for the setting up of the **International Sustainability Standards Board (ISSB)**, with the role of creating a global baseline for sustainability reporting. The ISSB is a standard-setting board of the International Financial Reporting Standards (IFRS) Foundation, a not-for-profit organisation that sets global, corporate reporting standards, through the International Accounting Standards Board (IASB). ISSB published its first 2 new standards on 26 June 2023.[8] They incorporate the recommendations of the TCFD, and the IFRS Foundation has taken over the monitoring of the progress on companies' climate-related disclosures from the TCFD.

As summarised in the next paragraphs, these soft law instruments, recommendations and guidelines to businesses (UNGP, OECD Guidelines, TCFD recommendations, etc.) have increasingly been sources of inspiration[9] for mandatory requirements that have been fuelled by a number of drivers, including geopolitical and societal developments (the climate emergency of course, but also various human and environmental disasters involving multinational companies, the COVID-19 pandemic, the Black Lives Matter movement, etc.), the increased support of stakeholders, the perceived limitations of voluntary engagements and landmark case law developments.

8 IFRS S1: General Requirements for Disclosure of Sustainability-related Financial Information and IFRS S2: Climate-related Disclosures. See https://www.ifrs.org/groups/international-sustainability-standards-board/.

9 And, in some cases, have been incorporated into hard law. This is particularly the case for the OECD Guidelines and the UNGPs, that are relevant to assess the companies' duty of care under Dutch law according to the *Shell* case discussed below. As another example, the Taxonomy Regulation requires economic activities to be carried out in alignment with these instruments to qualify as "environmentally sustainable".

10.2 Key ESG developments and associated dispute risks

10.2.1 Fight against climate change and environmental protection

The European Climate Law[10] makes reaching the EU's climate goal of reducing EU emissions by at least 55% by 2030 (compared to 1990 levels), and climate neutrality by 2050, a legal obligation for the EU and its Member States. To achieve this environmental target, the EU has developed a broad legislative agenda, in particular the "European Green Deal" and the "fit for 55" package, a set of proposals to revise and update EU legislation and to put in place new initiatives with the aim of ensuring that the policies of the EU and its Member States are in line with the EU's climate goal.[11]

While express statutory requirements for companies to adopt climate change transition plans have now been introduced at EU level, the pressure to adapt business models to mitigate climate risks has initially come from investors and through strategic litigation by activist stakeholders. The first litigation successes were obtained against States, for which an obligation to tackle climate change is easier to conceive, especially after the adoption of the Paris Agreement.[12]

A growing number of activist non-profit organisations, and other types of claimants, are also seeing the potential for litigation to drive an increase in *corporate* climate change mitigation activity, across a range of claim types. As further discussed in the next paragraphs, these can include claims of

---

10 Regulation (EU) 2021/1119 of the European Parliament and of the Council of 30 June 2021 establishing the framework for achieving climate neutrality and amending Regulations (EC) No 401/2009 and (EU) 2018/1999 ('European Climate Law'), *O.J.* L 243, 9 July 2021, p 1-17.

11 See the Council of the EU dedicated webpage, https://www.consilium.europa.eu/en/policies/green-deal/fit-for-55-the-eu-plan-for-a-green-transition/.

12 The leading case was the *Urgenda* decision in the Netherlands, where the Hague District Court ordered in 2015 the Dutch State to reduce Dutch greenhouse gas emissions by 25% by the end of 2020 (compared to 1990 levels). See Supreme Court 20 December 2019, ECLI:NL:HR:2019:2007 (*The Netherlands vs Urgenda Foundation*). Its decision was confirmed by The Hague Court of Appeal in 2018 and the Supreme Court in 2019. The courts based their decisions on the Paris Agreement and Articles 2 (right to life) and 8 (right to private and family life) of the European Convention on Human Rights ("**ECHR**"). A wave of "public" cases against states, governments and public institutions followed suit, throughout Europe and globally. On 9 April 2024, in *Verein Klimaseniorinnen Schweiz v. Switzerland* (Application no 53600/20), the Grand Chamber of the European Court of Human Rights ("**ECtHR**") ruled that States' inaction or insufficient action with respect to climate change may be considered as violating human rights.

"greenwashing" in relation to environmental claims of companies that are allegedly misleading or unsubstantiated or claims against parent companies for the ESG related harms caused by a subsidiary, but arguably the most ground-breaking ones are probably those made regarding the impact of the company's (and its value chain's) activities on the climate and the environment.

As is well-known, in the landmark *Shell* case a Dutch court has found that the unwritten duty (or standard) of care imposes on companies to go above and beyond respecting applicable legislation to fight climate change.[13] The Shell group was found to be in breach of the general standard of care under Dutch law and was ordered to reduce its CO_2 emissions by 45% by 2023. The Court ruled that Shell had an obligation of result to reduce CO_2 emissions from the activities of the Shell group (scope 1 and 2 emissions), but also a significant best efforts obligation to reduce the emissions of its end users (scope 3 emissions).[14] In a key statement (para 4.4.13), the Court considered that:

> "The responsibility of business enterprises to respect human rights, as formulated in the UNGP [UN Guiding Principles on Business and Human Rights], is a global standard of expected conduct for all business enterprises wherever they operate. It exists independently of States' abilities and/or willingness to fulfil their own human rights obligations and does not diminish those obligations. And it exists over and above compliance with national laws and regulations protecting human rights. Therefore, it is not enough for companies to monitor developments and follow the measures states take; they have an individual responsibility. It can be deduced from the UNGP and other soft law instruments that it is universally endorsed that companies must respect human rights."

Following this decision, appealed by Shell in August 2021, Milieudefensie (the plaintiff NGO) sent a letter to the CEOs of a number of large companies, stating that *"a healthy company has a climate plan. In Milieudefensie/Friends of the Earth Netherlands' view, the ruling in the case against Royal Dutch Shell implies that every large emitter has a de minimis obligation to reduce its emissions in line with the global imperative resulting from the Paris Climate*

13 The Hague District Court 26 May 2021, ECLI:NL:RBDHA:2021:5339 (*Milieudefensie et al. v Royal Dutch Shell*).

14 The Greenhouse Gas Protocol Corporate Standard classifies a company's greenhouse gas emissions into three 'scopes'. Scope 1 emissions are direct emissions from owned or controlled sources. Scope 2 emissions are indirect emissions from the generation of purchased energy. Scope 3 emissions are all indirect emissions (not included in scope 2) that occur in the value chain of the reporting company, including both upstream and downstream emissions.

Agreement. And this is what we ask of you." The NGO announced that it would review such transition plans and implied that it could start litigation against the *"straggler"*.[15]

Investors are also subject to increased scrutiny, in particular those investing in carbon intensive businesses. End of 2022, NGOs have started legal proceedings in France – on the basis of the French Vigilance Duty Act (see below, para 10.2.4) – against BNP Paribas, in a case described by these NGOs as the *"first in the world to target a commercial bank for its high-risk activities in the oil and gas sector"*.[16] In January 2024, Milieudefensie announced that it intended to start legal proceedings in the Netherlands against ING, with respect to the bank's transition plan and to "ensure that it is not linked to adverse climate impacts of large business clients".[17]

The EU Corporate Sustainability Due Diligence Directive ("**CSDDD**"),[18] finally adopted in June 2024 after a roller-coaster legislative process started in February 2022, constitutes a game changer in this respect. It imposes on in-scope companies (large EU-incorporated companies and groups, but also non-EU ones having substantial business activities in the EU) to adopt and put into effect[19] a transition plan for climate change mitigation. The plan must aim to ensure, through best efforts, that the business model and strategy of the company are compatible with the transition to a sustainable economy and with limiting global warming to 1.5°C. The CSDDD will be applicable as from 26 July 2027, 2028 or 2029 depending on the in-scope companies concerned. The directive's due diligence limb, and enforcement mechanisms, are discussed below, in paragraph 10.2.4.

These legislative developments are likely to be invoked on both sides of climate change disputes, by claimants considering that they would merely

15 The letter is available at: https://milieudefensie.nl/actueel/foe-letter-to-ceos-13-january-2022-1.pdf.

16 See Oxfam's press release of 26 October 2022, "Climate NGOs take unprecedented legal action against number one European financier of fossil fuel expansion, BNP Paribas", available at: https://www.oxfam.org/en/press-releases/climate-ngos-take-unprecedented-legal-action-against-number-one-european-financier.

17 See Milieudefensie's press release: https://en.milieudefensie.nl/climate-case-ing/our-climate-case-against-ing.

18 Directive (EU) 2024/1760 of the European Parliament and of the Council of 13 June 2024 on corporate sustainability due diligence and amending Directive (EU) 2019/1937 and Regulation (EU) 2023/2859, *O.J.* L 2024/1760, 5 July 2024.

19 And not only to disclose information on their transition plan, if they have one, as imposed by the CSRD (see next paragraph).

reflect the already existing unwritten corporate duties of care in relation to climate change and by defendants contenting, conversely, that their express inclusion would be justified by the fact that they are not yet positive law.

10.2.2 Sustainability disclosure obligations

Measures aiming at channelling private capital towards greener activities to help finance the sizeable funding gap are key for the success of the EU target of climate neutrality by 2050.[20] One of the key measures is to offer investors reliable, consistent and comparable information and data for their investment decisions, on climate change but also on a much wider range of sustainability issues.

The EU regime rests on three key instruments.

First, the EU Corporate Sustainability Reporting Directive ("**CSRD**"),[21] which revises and extends the rules introduced by the Non-Financial Reporting Directive ("**NFRD**")[22], was published in the Official Journal on 16 December 2022. Under the CSRD, applicable in four stages between 2024-2028 depending on the types of undertakings, in-scope companies (defined more broadly than under the NFRD)[23] have to report information on the full range of ESG issues relevant to their business, in accordance with *mandatory* EU sustainability reporting standards that include very detailed ESG-related reporting requirements. The process for determining material sustainability matters that must be reported (based on so-called "double

20 See Th. Tilquin (ed), *Les instruments de droit des sociétés et de droit financier de l'économie durable*, Brussels: Larcier 2021.

21 Directive (EU) 2022/2464 of the European Parliament and of the Council of 14 December 2022 amending Regulation (EU) No 537/2014, Directive 2004/109/EC, Directive 2006/43/EC and Directive 2013/34/EU, as regards corporate sustainability reporting, *O.J.* L 322, 16 December 2022, p 15-80.

22 Directive 2014/95/EU of the European Parliament and of the Council of 22 October 2014 amending Directive 2013/34/EU as regards disclosure of non-financial and diversity information by certain large undertakings and groups, *O.J.* L 330, 15 November 2014, p 1-9.

23 CSRD will apply to all large EU companies, that is, EU companies (including EU subsidiaries of non-EU parent companies) exceeding at least two of the following criteria: (i) more than 250 employees; (ii) a turnover of more than € 40 million; or (iii) total assets of € 20 million. CSRD will also apply to companies with securities listed on an EU-regulated market, irrespective of whether the issuer is established in the EU or a non-EU country. This includes listed SMEs, except for certain listed micro-enterprises.

materiality"[24]), and information that is reported, is subject to limited assurance (and may evolve to reasonable assurance). The European Sustainability Reporting Standards ("**ESRS**") setting out the detailed disclosure requirements under the CSRD were adopted on 31 July 2023.

Second, the **Sustainable Finance Disclosure Regulation** ("**SFDR**"),[25] the main substantive provisions of which having been appliable since 10 March 2021, lays down harmonised rules for financial market participants and financial advisers on transparency with regard to the integration of sustainability risks and the consideration of adverse sustainability impacts in their processes and the provision of sustainability-related information with respect to financial products.[26] Under the SFDR, asset managers, pension funds and financial advisers are required to consider sustainability when making investor decisions and report on a wide range of sustainability issues in respect of all the financial products they market as "sustainable". This has a knock-on effect on the companies in which they invest, in particular where those investments are branded as "sustainable".

Third, the **Taxonomy Regulation**[27] requires companies and financial institutions covered by the NFRD/CSRD to report on how (and to what extent) their activities are aligned with the so-called "EU taxonomy", a classification system which establishes per economic activity technical sustainability criteria which must be met by the relevant economic activity in order for it to qualify as "sustainable" under one of the six environmental objectives.

As is clear from these legislative developments, the ability to produce and to stand behind reliable data and appropriate internal governance pro-

24 Under this concept of "double-materiality", it is not only sustainability-related impacts on the company that can be material (as is the case under the other non-financial information reporting regimes), but also the impact of the company's activities on sustainability.

25 Regulation (EU) 2019/2088 of the European Parliament and of the Council of 27 November 2019 on sustainability-related disclosures in the financial services sector, *O.J.* L 317, 9 December 2019, p 1-16.

26 Delegated Regulation 2021/1256 also provides specific rules imposing the integration of sustainability risks in the governance of insurance and reinsurance undertakings. It will, among others, extend to sustainability risks the prudent person principle laid down in Article 132 of Directive 2009/138/EC (Solvency II), which requires that insurance and reinsurance undertakings only invest in assets the risks of which they can identify, measure, monitor, manage, control and *report* properly.

27 Regulation (EU) 2020/852 of the European Parliament and of the Council of 18 June 2020 on the establishment of a framework to facilitate sustainable investment, and amending Regulation (EU) 2019/2088, *O.J.* L 198, 22 June 2020, p 13-43.

cesses to produce these, as well as to explain how ESG factors may impact a business (and therefore an investor's decision) has gained in importance and has come under increased scrutiny. Despite the current legislative efforts to ensure the disclosure of reliable, consistent and comparable information, the new reporting obligations of companies are likely to lead to many difficulties, especially for global multinationals that face a number of different disclosure regimes.[28]

As ESG becomes increasingly material to investor decision-making, failure to properly disclose material risks and impacts may give rise to liability under contractual liability, tort law and/or specific liability regimes (e.g. prospectus liability), in addition to the penalties provided for in case of breach of the relevant instruments.[29]

10.2.3 Greenwashing

Given the speed at which efforts are being made to use the market economy to drive environmental progress, and as companies race to secure market share among increasingly eco-conscious consumers, allegations of "greenwashing" have also skyrocketed in the corporate world. The same is true, to a lesser extent, with respect to "bluewashing", i.e. marketing claims that overstates a company's commitment to responsible social practices and human rights.

Two recent EU legislative initiatives aim at tackling greenwashing out of the financial sector.

The new **EU Directive on Empowering Consumers for the Green Transition** aims to promote sustainable consumption by (i) tackling unfair commercial business practices such as greenwashing that prevent consumers from making sustainable consumption choices (by amending the Unfair Commercial Practices Directive (UCPD)) and (ii) improving pre contractual information on the durability and reparability of products (by way of amendments to the Consumer Rights Directive (CRD) amongst other

28 Although the European Commission and the UK Government highlighted that the sustainability disclosure requirements were based on the global standards drawn up by the ISSB, they present a number of divergences entailing serious difficulties for companies having to report under various regimes.

29 See e.g., with respect to the G of ESG in particular, ING's press release of 7 February 2024, 'ING receives summons from investors', available at: https://www.ing.com/Newsroom/News/Press-releases/ING-receives-summons-from-investors.htm.

things). While a number of greenwashing behaviours are already caught by the prohibition of unfair commercial practices under the current version of the UCPD, these modifications should increase focus on such behaviours.

On 22 March 2023, the European Commission published a proposal for a directive on the substantiation and communication of environmental claims (**Green Claims Directive**).[30] The purpose of the proposal is to complement the EU Directive on Empowering Consumers for the Green Transition by setting minimum criteria that companies making claims to consumers in the EU about the environmental benefits and performance of their products or services need to meet, as well as minimum criteria for environmental labelling schemes. The text is currently discussed among the EU legislative bodies in the so-called "trilogues".

Regulators, be it consumer protection, financial or advertising regulators, have not waited for these legislative initiatives to take action. In the Netherlands, for instance, the Dutch Consumer and Market Authority (ACM) began action against six clothing companies which it found had made significantly misleading claims about sustainability[31], while the Dutch Advertising Code Committee ruled that an ad campaign that promoted carbon-dioxide emission credits was misleading and must be withdrawn.[32] In June 2024, the European Supervisory Authorities (ESAs)[33] have published greenwashing reports calling for enhanced supervision and improved market practice on sustainability-related claims.[34]

---

30 Proposal for a Directive of the European Parliament and of the Council on substantiation and communication of explicit environmental claims (Green Claims Directive), 22 March 2023, COM(2023) 166 final, available at: https://eur-lex.europa.eu/legal-content/EN/TXT/?uri=COM%3A2023%3A166%3AFIN&qid=1679566917246.

31 ACM, press release of 4 November 2021, 'ACM continues its campaign against misleading sustainability claims in the clothing sector', available at: https://www.acm.nl/en/publications/acm-continues-its-campaign-against-misleading-sustainability-claims-clothing-sector.

32 College van Beroep, Reclame Code Commissie, 20 October 2022, case no 2022/00100-CVB, available at: https://www.reclamecode.nl/uitspraken/resultaten/vervoer-2022-00100-cvb/365319/.

33 Composed of the European Securities and Markets Authority (ESMA), the European Banking Authority (EBA) and the European Insurance and Occupational Pensions Authority (EIOPA).

34 ESAs, press release of 4 June 2024, 'ESAs call for enhanced supervision and improved market practice on sustainability-related claims', available at: https://www.esma.europa.eu/press-news/esma-news/esas-call-enhanced-supervision-and-improved-market-practice-sustainability.

Court cases have also been launched by consumer associations and other organisations in many jurisdictions. In the Netherlands, in one striking example, the district court of Amsterdam ruled on 20 March 2024 that KLM breached the Dutch implementation of the UCPD by making misleading statements suggesting that flying can be or become sustainable, and that the purchase of or contribution to a "compensation" product actually reduces, absorbs, or compensates for part of the climate effect of flying.[35]

10.2.4 Value chain environmental and human rights due diligence

The focus of EU and national legislative initiatives has increasingly shifted from mere reporting obligations to the imposition on in-scope companies to conduct environmental and human rights risk assessment and due diligence throughout their value chain (for their worldwide activities, including non-EU or non-domestic activities), often subject to specific liability provisions. These due diligence duties have initially been specific to certain sectors or issues (modern slavery/child labour, conflict minerals, deforestation, batteries, etc.), but general legislations have been imposed at national level and, following the adoption of the CSDDD, at EU level. Even without the support of specific legislation, there have been court claims targeting companies for the harmful impact of their supply chain.

Historically, business efforts to address human rights and environment supply chain risks have been guided by **soft law standards** and voluntary industry initiatives, including those discussed above such as the UN Guiding Principles on Business and Human Rights (UNGPs) or the OECD Guidelines for Multinational Enterprises. Gradually, their concepts have found their way into legislation, and have sometimes been incorporated in the judicial interpretation of the corporate duty of care (see in particular the *Shell* case discussed in para 10.2.1).

France went one step further with the so-called **Vigilance Duty Act** of 2017 (formally *loi n° 2017-399 du 27 mars 2017 relative au devoir de vigilance des sociétés mères et des entreprises donneuses d'ordre*). This legislation imposes on large companies operating in France to adopt and implement so-called "vigilance plans" that must establish effective measures to identify risks and prevent severe impacts on human rights and the environment resulting from the company's own activities, and the activities of its value chain (subsidiaries and established business partners). The enforcement regime

35 Amsterdam District Court 20 March 2024, ECLI:NL:RBAMS:2024:1512.

is first and foremost based on private enforcement, i.e. the possibility for interested parties (including NGOs) to resort to courts to obtain orders imposing the adoption of compliant vigilance plan and (for victims) to seek compensation. Although the legislation has initially not led to a wave of court cases, this has evolved and around 20 cases have now been started, on topics ranging from industrial projects affecting local projects, carbon emission and the financing of fossil fuel companies,[36] worker rights, deforestation, plastic pollution, sex discrimination, etc.[37]

Germany followed suit in 2021, by adopting the Supply Chain Due Diligence Act (***Lieferkettensorgfaltspflichtengesetz***) which entered into force on 1 January 2023. The Act applies to companies having their head office, principal place of business, administrative headquarters or registered office in Germany and employing a minimum of 3,000 employees (reduced to 1,000 employees as of 2024). The supply chain is understood to extend to the entire supply chain of a company, which means it comprises all activities inside and outside of Germany that are required to manufacture goods or provide services. In-scope companies are obliged to (i) assess whether violations of certain defined human and environmental rights occur in their supply chains, (ii) take respective prevention and mitigation measures, (iii) adopt a policy statement on human rights protection in their supply chains, (iv) implement grievance procedures to allow for the reporting of human rights violations and ensure appropriate follow-up measures and (v) document their compliance with the due diligence obligations. As opposed to the French regime, the German legislation favours public enforcement. the Federal Office for Economic Affairs and Export Control (*Bundesamt für Wirtschaft und Ausfuhrkontrolle*, BAFA) has the power to take action, ex officio or following complaints, to monitor compliance with the Act. The BAFA may also take action upon request if the person making the complaint has a substantiated claim that protected legal positions have been violated or such violation is imminent.

Finally, at **EU** level, the **CSDDD** (mentioned at para 10.2.1 above in the context of transition plans), imposes on in-scope companies far-reaching human rights and environmental due diligence obligations with respect to their own activities, those of their subsidiaries and of their upstream and

36 On whether "due diligence can act as a catalyst to directly compel multinationals to reduce their greenhouse gas emissions", see P. Mougeolle, 'La diligence raisonnable en matière des droits de l'homme, un catalyseur de la responsabilité climatique des multinationales?', *J.D.E.H.* 2022, issue 2, p 117.

37 See the list available at: https://plan-vigilance.org/les-affaires-en-cours/.

downstream chain of activities (as specifically defined in the directive, and excluding the sale of goods and provision of most services as part of the downstream activities, meaning that financial services are carved out).

The due diligence obligations encompass the following six steps (in line, though not fully aligned, with existing international soft law standards, in particular the UNGPs and the OECD Guidelines): (i) integrate due diligence into companies' policies, (ii) identify actual and potential adverse human rights and environmental impacts, (iii) prevent, cease or minimise actual and potential adverse impacts (including by seeking contractual assurances from direct business partners that they will ensure compliance with the company's code of conduct and prevention action plan), (iv) assess the effectiveness of these measures, (v) communicate on these measures[38] and (vi) remediate the potential adverse impacts, i.e. drawing up a corrective action plan and neutralise the adverse impacts or, if impossible, minimise their extent (including by the payment of damages to the affected persons and by financial compensation to the affected communities).[39]

The CSDDD's implementation shall be ensured by both public and private enforcement mechanisms. For public enforcement,[40] EU Member States are required to designate one or more authorities to supervise compliance with the Directive's obligations (with respect to both due diligence obligations and the transition plans). They will have the power to request information and carry out investigations, on their own motion or as a result of substantiated concerns submitted to them by any natural or legal person who has reasons to believe a company is not complying. They will also have the power to order the cessation of infringements, impose administrative fines (with a maximum of no less than 5% of the net worldwide turnover of the company in the financial year preceding the fining decision), and adopt interim measures in case of imminent risk of severe and irreparable harm. Decisions of the supervisory authority shall be published and a judicial remedy against these decisions shall also be provided for under national law. The supervisory authorities will cooperate in the context of a newly established European Network of Supervisory Authorities to ensure the coordination and alignment of regulatory, investigative,

38 In order to avoid duplicating reporting obligations, the CSDDD does not introduce any new reporting obligations in addition to those under the CSRD. In-scope companies that do not fall under the proposed CSRD should publish on their website an annual statement in respect of their activities.

39 CSDDD, Article 5(1), with reference to Articles 7 to 16.

40 CSDDD, Articles 24 to 28.

sanctioning and supervisory practices of the supervisory authorities and, as appropriate, sharing of information among them.

With respect to private enforcement,[41] in-scope companies may be held liable for damages caused to a natural or legal person provided that (i) the company intentionally or negligently failed to comply with their obligations to prevent, mitigate, end or minimise adverse impacts, when the protected right, prohibition or obligation is aimed to protect the person; and (ii) the failure caused damage to the person's legal interest protected under national law. A company will not be liable for damages caused only by its business partner. A number of further procedural aspects are also tackled by the CSDDD, as Member States will, inter alia, have to ensure that: the limitation period is at least five years and, in any case, not lower than the limitation period laid down under general national regimes; the cost of proceedings are not prohibitively expensive for claimants to seek justice; claimants may seek injunctive measures (including through provisional relief proceedings); an alleged injured party may reasonably authorise trade unions or human rights or environmental non-governmental organisations to bring the injured party's claim; courts may require appropriate disclosure of additional evidence that lies in the control of the company and is not accessible to the claimant (with appropriate protective measures); and the provisions of national law transposing the CSDDD's requirements on civil liability (i.e. the lex fori of the EU courts seized of the case) are of overriding mandatory application in cases where the applicable law is not the Member State's law.

Even in the absence of specific legislation creating statutory liability for parent companies for damages occurring in their group or supply chain, in certain jurisdictions, such as the UK and the Netherlands, courts have been increasingly open to holding parent companies to account in relation to harms caused by other entities within their group under a general duty of care (so-called "**parent company litigation**"). This also appears in the context of criminal law for environmental and health and safety offences where enforcement action can sometimes be taken against a shareholder if they have involved themselves in subsidiary operations, for example.

In *Vedanta*[42] and *Okpabi*,[43] the UK leading decisions on the topic, the UK Supreme Court has ruled that whether a parent company has a duty of

41 CSDDD, Article 29.

42 *Vedanta Resources PLC v Lungowe*, 10 April 2019, [2019] UKSC 20.

43 *Okpabi v Royal Dutch Shell Plc*, 12 February 2021, [2021] UKSC 3.

care (e.g. for local communities affected by alleged environmental damage caused by a subsidiary) *"depends on the extent to which, and the way in which, the parent availed itself of the opportunity to take over, intervene in, control, supervise or advise the management of the relevant operations (including land use) of the subsidiary"* (Vedanta, para 49). In *Okpabi*, the England and Wales Court of Appeal ruled that none of the evidence put forward by the claimants went beyond showing the existence of centralised, group level standards as opposed to any specific degree of control by the parent over the subsidiary. The Court therefore held that the case was unarguable. The UK Supreme Court overturned this decision, ruling that there were real issues to be tried in relation to the degree to which the parent may have taken over the management of the subsidiary. The outcomes of such cases will thus depend on the facts and corporate structure before the court, but in certain cases there appears to be a real prospect for parent companies to be held liable.

Dutch courts have applied these principles in a case brought against Shell by Nigerian farmers following oil spills in Nigeria.[44] Applying Nigerian common law (and thus the principles identified by the UK Supreme Court[45]), the Hague Court of Appeal held that the local subsidiary (Shell Nigeria) was responsible for two oil spills in the Niger Delta, and liable to pay compensation. It further ruled that the parent company, Royal Dutch Shell, owed a duty of care to the villagers affected by the oil spill and was liable (together with Shell Nigeria) for any failure to prevent future oil spills and was ordered to install leak detection equipment in its pipelines.

As indicated, in the above-mentioned other *Shell* case,[46] the Hague District Court ordered, this time on the basis of the general duty of care under Dutch law (itself interpreted through the lenses of the UNGP), Shell's parent company to reduce the emission of its entire group as well as use significant best efforts to reduce its value chain emissions, considering that (para 4.4.17):

> "The UNGP are based on the rationale that companies may contribute to the adverse human rights impacts through their activities as well as through their busi-

44 The Hague Court of Appeal 29 January 2021, ECLI:NL:GHDHA:2021:132 (*Oguru et al. v Shell*), available at: https://uitspraken.rechtspraak.nl/#!/details?id=ECLI:NL:GHDHA:2021:132.

45 The Hague Court of Appeal 29 January 2021, ECLI:NL:GHDHA:2021:132, paras 3.27-3.28 (*Oguru et al. v Shell*).

46 The Hague District Court 26 May 2021, ECLI:NL:RBDHA:2021:5339 (*Milieudefensie et al. v Royal Dutch Shell*), available at: https://uitspraken.rechtspraak.nl/#!/details?id=ECLI:NL:RBDHA:2021:5339.

> ness relationships with other parties. (...) "Business relationships" are understood to include relationships with business partners, entities in its value chain, and any other non-state or state entity directly linked to its business operations, products or services. The responsibility to respect human rights encompasses the company's entire value chain. Value chain is understood to mean: 'the activities that convert input into output by adding value. It includes entities with which it has a direct or indirect business relationship and which either (a) supply products or services that contribute to the enterprise's own products or services, or (b) receive products and services from the enterprise.'"

Where adverse ESG impacts may lead to criminal offences, the veil of separate corporate personality may also be lifted in case the parent company and/or its directors and officers were involved in, or aware of (including "willingly blind"), an offence. The case law of French courts, in particular, is worth highlighting.

With respect to the supply chain, as early as 2012, in the *Erika* case, the French Supreme Court (*Cour de cassation*) held Total, charterer of the boat, criminally and civilly responsible for the oil spill, considering that Total made a reckless fault (including by failing to inspect the boat, although it had the contractual rights to do so) and was severally liable with other parties involved (the shipowner, the classification society and the ship management company).[47] In the same decision, the Court recognised the existence of a "purely ecological damage" head of damage in French tort law.

More recently, in a landmark decision of 16 June 2021, the French Supreme Court (*Cour de cassation*) ruled that employees of a foreign subsidiary may be, in certain circumstances (in the case at hand, in view of the internal organisation of the group and the strong hierarchical links within business groups and geographical zones), considered as representatives of the parent company and that their actions may thus be imputable to the same.[48]

10.2.5 Directors' and officers' fiduciary duties and general duty of care

There is, currently, no EU legislation imposing specific and express duties to directors with respect to ESG or sustainability. The attempt to introduce

47 Cass. crim., 25 September 2012, case no 10-82.938, available at: https://www.legifrance.gouv.fr/juri/id/JURITEXT000026430035/.

48 Cass. crim., 16 June 2021, case no 20-83.098, ECLI:FR:CCASS:2021:CR00768, available at: https://www.legifrance.gouv.fr/juri/id/JURITEXT000043684156?page=1&pageSize=10&query=20-83098&searchField=ALL&searchType=ALL&sortValue=DATE_DESC&tab_selection=juri&typePagination=DEFAULT.

such duties in the CSDDD has been pushed back by EU Member States at the Council level. Accordingly, in most cases, ESG should be assessed through the prism of the directors' general fiduciary duties, which vary from one (EU Member) State to another.

ESG-related claims against individual directors have – at least at this stage – remained limited. In virtually all jurisdictions, it has not (yet) been found that directors would have a duty to act in favour of ESG, beyond ensuring that the companies of which they are a director abide by the ESG-related obligations imposed by specific legislation. In addition, the applicable enforcement framework often renders claims against directors challenging since, in a number of jurisdictions, directors' liability can in most cases only be triggered by the company itself or its (minority) shareholders.

However, with the increased focus on ESG, what is expected of directors under their general duty of care has been evolving and direct legislative intervention introducing specific and express ESG duties for directors may be at the horizon. Accordingly, more claims are likely in the future, from a variety of stakeholders (including from investors and (minority/activist) shareholders) on the grounds that directors have not sufficiently taken ESG risks and opportunities into consideration or that directors have an individual duty to take positive action to mitigate the impact of climate change. Conversely, investors may argue that directors have given too much weight to sustainability, to the detriment of financial returns (on the "ESG backlash", see the next paragraph).

A notable recent example of a case against directors is the shareholder claim (derivative action on behalf of the company) started by NGO ClientEarth against Shell's directors in the UK,[49] which is one of the few jurisdictions where directors' statutory fiduciary duties expressly include sustainability criteria. ClientEarth's claim was dismissed by the English High Court on 12 May 2023.[50] The court accepted that "*Shell faces material and foreseeable risks as a result of climate change which have or could have a material effect on it.*" However, it considered that Shell's directors should be granted broad discretion to decide how to best promote the success of the company.

49 See ClientEarth's press release of 15 March 2022 "We're taking legal action against Shell's Board for mismanaging climate risk", https://www.clientearth.org/latest/latest-updates/news/we-re-taking-legal-action-against-shell-s-board-for-mismanaging-climate-risk.

50 ClientEarth v Shell Plc & Ors. [2023] EWHC 1137 (Ch), available at: https://caselaw.nationalarchives.gov.uk/ewhc/ch/2023/1137.

As indicated, where adverse ESG impacts may lead to criminal offences (including environment and social criminal law), directors and officers may also face individual criminal liability risks, including if they remained "wilfully blind" regarding the offences committed by their company (see e.g. the cases mentioned in the previous paragraph).

10.2.6 Backlash

The change of paradigm that these ESG developments requires has of course led to heated debates and a number of criticisms and pushback, even litigation risks.

As with many important legal developments, which are often the result of a number of compromises, it has been argued that the ESG megatrend goes too far too quickly or, conversely, is not sufficiently ambitious and fast. As one striking example, French President Macron, who famously rebuked U.S. President Trump's decision to leave the Paris Agreement with the motto "Make Our Planet Great Again" in June 2017, has called in May 2023 for a "pause" of EU environment regulation to safeguard European companies to compete against less environmentally friendly countries.[51] Same-level playing field is a key area of concern (though the EU attempts to mitigate this by imposing key obligations on companies operating in the EU, regardless of their place of incorporation), and so is the fear that the obligations imposed on businesses are too heavy, unrealistic in practice or not always adapted to the challenges that they aim to address and to the ambition to re-industrialise the EU.[52]

Geopolitical developments, such as the Russian invasion of the Ukraine and the ensuing energy and inflation crisis, have influenced this debate and given arguments to both sides. In support of ESG critics, this crisis shed light on the importance of the military industry (which comes rarely on top of the ESG ratings)[53] and the necessity to be able to count on pol-

---

51 Le Monde, 12 May 2023, 'Macron's call for 'pause' of EU environmental regulation causes controversy', available at: https://www.lemonde.fr/en/politics/article/2023/05/12/macron-calls-for-pause-of-european-environmental-regulation-confusion-ensues_6026448_5.html.

52 With respect to the Deforestation Regulation, see e.g. Bloomberg, 9 August 2023, 'World's Top Food Producers Push Back on Deforestation Rules', available at: https://www.bloomberg.com/news/articles/2023-08-09/world-s-top-food-producers-push-back-on-eu-deforestation-rules?srnd=null.

53 'Ukraine war prompts investor rethink of ESG and the defence sector', *Financial Times*, 9 March 2022, available at: https://www.ft.com/content/c4dafe6a-2c95-4352-ab88-c4e3cdb60bba.

luting energy, such as coal, in times of necessity. Conversely, this crisis highlighted Europe's geopolitical exposure towards Russia, that could accelerate European countries investing in alternative energy sources and focus on energy efficiency and insulation.

It is also clear that ESG considerations have a strong political component, and are not limited to technical debates in the finance industry. It is probably nowhere as clear as in the U.S., where conservative politicians and lawmakers have argued that responsible investment imposes unnecessary constraints on corporations and undermine financial returns and that companies do not have to take stance on societal questions, such as abortion or same sex marriage.

These debates have now reached the courtrooms. As a few examples, in April 2023, Disney started legal proceedings against the governor of Florida, containing that he retaliated against the company for its opposition to a state law which broadly prohibits classroom instruction of sexual orientation or gender identity.[54] In August 2024, X filed a claim before Texas courts against the Global Alliance for Responsible Media (GARM) and individual companies, arguing that the defendants breached competition law by coordinating with brands to dissuade them from continuing to advertise on the social network following its change of moderation policies after its acquisition by Elon Musk.[55]

A number of cases have also been started by corporates to curtail activist actions. For example, in March 2024, the Judicial Court of Paris dismissed TotalEnergies' claims against a NGOs, based on the fact that they would disseminate misleading information (regarding the major's carbon emissions) in relation to a publicly traded company, within the meaning of the French Monetary and Financial Code.[56] As another example, in June 2024, a Texas District Court dismissed a lawsuit ExxonMobil filed against a shareholder activist group after it agreed not to pursue future proxy filings regarding the company's greenhouse gas emissions at its annual general meetings.[57] In

54 'Disney-DeSantis Fight Tests Boundaries of Corporate ESG Push', *Bloomberg*, 28 April 2023, available at: https://news.bloomberglaw.com/esg/disneys-battle-with-desantis-tests-corporate-governance-freedom.

55 X's complaint is available at: https://www.documentcloud.org/documents/25033227-x-v-garm.

56 Tribunal judiciaire de Paris, 28 March 2024, case no 23/06215, available at: https://www.courdecassation.fr/decision/6605c3b485819597271e5b52.

57 U.S. District Court for the Northern District of Texas (Fort Worth Division), 17 June 2024, case no 4:24-cv-00069-P, available at: https://mcusercontent.com/

this context, and without comments on the merits of the above-mentioned cases, it is worth flagging the adoption by the EU of the so-called "strategic lawsuits against public participation directive" or "SLAPPs Directive", to be transposed by Member States by 7 May 2026.[58] It provides safeguards against manifestly unfounded claims or abusive court proceedings brought against natural and legal persons due to their involvement in public participation. This includes journalists, publishers, media organisations, whistleblowers and human rights defenders, as well as civil society organisations, NGOs, trade unions, artists, researchers and academics.

Another point that has been debated is the role assumed by courts, especially in the civil law jurisdictions where Montesquieu's vision of the judge *"no more than the mouth that pronounces the words of the law, mere passive beings, incapable of moderating either its force or rigour"*[59] remains strong.

This debate will progressively become less relevant in view of the broad legislative agenda in the EU and in the UK, imposing the adoption of transition plans, the liability of parent companies for ESG harms that occurred throughout their value chain, potentially the explicit mention of sustainability criteria in the directors' fiduciary duties, etc. However, the role of the courts, and indeed arbitrators (in the circumstances discussed in the next paragraph), will remain of paramount importance for the enforcement of these new obligations, many of which principle-based (and thus offering a broad margin of appreciation to courts). This will bring a number of challenges. As one striking example, the thorough review of the adequateness of the transition plans of multinational companies entails complex and controversial technical assessment.

10.3 Relevance for arbitration

As is clear from the above paragraphs, many "ESG disputes" will not be subject to arbitration. First, a number of new ESG instruments set up so-

d7ed26dfe659b48d9b7d9a37d/files/88b34244-f0d0-48cb-921e-bec65e-bf63c2/EX240717_dismissal_on_mootness.01.pdf?mc_cid=66466e0e18&mc_eid=e6e9bcc8d8.

58 Directive (EU) 2024/1069 of the European Parliament and of the Council of 11 April 2024 on protecting persons who engage in public participation from manifestly unfounded claims or abusive court proceedings ('Strategic lawsuits against public participation'), *O.J.* L 2024/1069, 16 April 2024.

59 Montesquieu, *L'Esprit des lois*, 1748, book XI, chapter 6 (translation of *Les juges ne sont que la bouche qui prononce les paroles de la loi ; des êtres inanimés qui ne peuvent en modérer ni la force ni la vigueur*).

called "public enforcement" mechanisms, i.e. grant supervisory and sanction powers to public regulators. Second, in many cases the agreement to arbitrate will be missing. Activist plaintiffs, in particular, will usually seek publicity for their case, and will thus usually not consider arbitration (often confidential in nature) for ESG disputes.

At the same time, an increasing number of disputes subject to arbitration will include the ESG dimension. This is particularly true for certain contractual disputes between or within businesses, as well as disputes between victims of adverse ESG impacts and the companies having set up voluntary grievance mechanisms (para 10.3.2). The same applies to disputes between investors and states (para 10.3.2). Certainly arbitration (so as any other service) industry is also not alien to comply with the new ESG guidelines (para 10.4). In these different contexts, it will be key for NAI practitioners to have a general understanding of the ESG "megatrend" presented in the previous paragraphs.

10.3.1 Commercial arbitration

It would be a mistake to assume that the consensual and contractual nature of arbitration would mean that ESG disputes would be alien to arbitration. ESG commitments are increasingly becoming key contractual provisions, including as warranties, due diligence, or compliance clauses.[60] These contract provisions will allow for contractual remedies in case of breach.[61] Consequently, a significant number of future disputes will likely be resolved through arbitration, given the common use of arbitration agreements in international contracts whether they are supply-chain, M&A, or corporate agreements mentioned earlier.[62]

---

60 See *i.a.* https://chancerylaneproject.org/, also https://www.americanbar.org/groups/human_rights/business-human-rights-initiative/contractual-clauses-project/, IBA Arbitration Committee Report on use of ESG contractual obligations and related disputes, p 10-18, available at: https://www.ibanet.org/document?id=report-on-use-of-ESG-contractual-obligations.

61 See IBA Arbitration Committee Report on use of ESG contractual obligations and related disputes, p 15-17, available at: https://www.ibanet.org/document?id=report-on-use-of-ESG-contractual-obligations.

62 A. Welsh KC, 'Navigating the ESG Labyrinth – What Role Will Arbitration and ADR Play?', *ICC Dispute Resolution Bulletin* 2024, issue 1, p 124 ("(…) what the IBA survey tells us is that in-house counsel consider that arbitration and ADR do have a role to play in resolving ESG disputes, and that confidentiality is one of the key considerations.").

The recently published IBA Arbitration Committee Report on the use of ESG contractual obligations and related disputes (the "**IBA ESG Report**") offers useful insights into the current landscape of ESG disputes. It includes a survey (the "**IBA Survey**") which reveals that a staggering 42% of respondents (in-house counsel and compliance staff at large multinationals) had already resolved ESG disputes through contractual mechanisms and 37% of respondents through external grievance mechanisms.[63]

Respondents of the IBA Survey were asked to rank the importance of factors for choosing a specific ESG dispute resolution forum in two scenarios: (i) business to business disputes and (ii) third-party ESG claims against them.

Confidentiality emerged as the most crucial factor for respondents in both types of disputes,[64] indicating that "reputation management is a key driver in the resolution of these disputes".[65] This highlights the role arbitration can play, given its typically confidential nature, in the ESG dispute resolution framework.[66] Significantly, transparency was ranked as the second most important factor in business-to-business disputes.[67] This discrepancy

63 See IBA Arbitration Committee Report on use of ESG contractual obligations and related disputes, p 33, available at: https://www.ibanet.org/document?id=report-on-use-of-ESG-contractual-obligations. See also Welsh KC 2024, p 124.

64 IBA Arbitration Committee Report on use of ESG contractual obligations and related disputes, p.33, available at: https://www.ibanet.org/document?id=report-on-use-of-ESG-contractual-obligations.

65 Welsh KC 2024, p 124.

66 See for example, *ICC Arbitration Commission Report on Resolving Climate Change Related Disputes Through Arbitration and ADR* (2019), available at: https://iccwbo.org/wp-content/uploads/sites/3/2019/11/icc-arbitration-adr-commission-report-on-resolving-climate-change-related-disputes-english-version.pdf, also J.P. Gaffney, 'In Praise and Criticism of Arbitration as a Means of Resolving ESG Disputes', *Kluwer Arbitration Blog*, 18 April 2023, available at: https://arbitrationblog.kluwerarbitration.com/2023/04/18/in-praise-and-criticism-of-arbitration-as-a-means-of-resolving-esg-disputes/. Not everyone agrees, however, see the European Law Institute Report on Business and Human Rights: Access to Justice and Effective Remedies (2022), available at: https://www.europeanlawinstitute.eu/fileadmin/user_upload/p_eli/Publications/ELI_Report_on_Business_and_Human_Rights.pdf ("Human rights breaches are so fundamental that any consensual system of dispute resolution such as mediation or arbitration is open to capture by the stronger party unless effectively and externally controlled. This is not to dismiss these options but merely to indicate that in a report dealing with access to effective remedy for human rights breaches by corporates, we felt the emphasis should be on stronger public facing options with the necessary coercive powers.").

67 IBA Arbitration Committee Report on use of ESG contractual obligations and related disputes, p 33, available at: https://www.ibanet.org/document?id=report-on-use-of-ESG-contractual-obligations.

between the top two factors may be due to competing interest: on the one hand, the private interest of companies involved, on the other hand, the public interest inherent in ESG disputes.[68]

The high score of transparency underscores that embracing it is viewed as essential for maintaining the legitimacy of arbitration in the ESG context.[69] Arbitral institutions, such as NAI, have a great role to play in this process. Facilitating access to the information related to the ESG-related disputes allows for a better understanding of the ESG challenges.

ESG considerations will naturally be critical in disputes pertaining to **projects designed to mitigate greenhouse gas emissions or adapt to climate change**, where contractual agreements, particularly in an international setting, often include arbitration clauses. As noted in the 2019 ICC report "Resolving Climate Change Related Disputes through Arbitration and ADR" (paras 4.1 and 4.2):

> "Arbitration has already been used to determine climate change related disputes arising under the UNFCCC's Green Climate Fund and the Kyoto Protocol. A broad range of climate change related initiatives concerning renewable energy, climate change adaptation and mitigation, with diverse funding from international, domestic and business sources, will need to consider dispute resolution procedures.
>
> Moreover, commercial disputes with a climate change related genesis are increasingly likely to be brought by businesses as they adjust to increasing regulation of emissions following the entry into force of the Paris Agreement. Disputes in the context of asset divestment, new renewable energy investments, carbon trading and pricing, and increasingly stringent environmental representations and warranties are some of the issues that are emerging."[70]

68 C. Deves & P. Wiliński, 'Transparency in international arbitration as a catalyst to combat climate change: is it time to embrace democratised access to data in climate change related disputes?', in: S. Ali et al (eds), *Diversity in International Arbitration: Why it Matters and How to Sustain It.*, Edward Elgar Publishing 2022, p 258-275.

69 Deves & Wiliński 2022, p 258-275; also Gaffney 2023.

70 ICC Arbitration Commission Report on Resolving Climate Change Related Disputes Through Arbitration and ADR (2019), available at: https://iccwbo.org/wp-content/uploads/sites/3/2019/11/icc-arbitration-adr-commission-report-on-resolving-climate-change-related-disputes-english-version.pdf. Same confirmed by the IBA ESG Report, see IBA Arbitration Committee Report on use of ESG contractual obligations and related disputes, p 33, available at: https://www.ibanet.org/document?id=report-on-use-of-ESG-contractual-obligations.

Likewise, ESG factors are increasingly considered in supply chain **contractual relationships**, which often include ESG clauses (see para 10.2.4 above, on the contractual assurances in the context of the CSDDD and soft law standards, as well as the IBA ESG Report which identifies various types of typical ESG clauses[71]). Companies and financial institutions subject to ESG reporting and due diligence obligations impose various types of **ESG covenants** on their counterparties, such as the obligation to report on environmental metrics, to reduce the carbon footprint of industrial projects or ensuring products are free from deforestation or forced labour. These clauses constitute a fertile ground for disputes on questions such as termination rights (where the alleged breach of ESG clauses may constitute an "excuse" found by a party to escape a contractual relationship it wants to end), renegotiation of contracts (to adapt them to evolving ESG statutory obligations and determining who will have to bear the new compliance costs), or warranty mechanisms (e.g. in case an EU company faces a regulatory fine because of an issue occurring at the level of one of its suppliers and seek compensation from the latter).

To align with their ESG goals, companies seeking to rectify the ESG harms they have potentially caused might also choose arbitration as a **voluntary grievance mechanism** offered to affected parties.[72] The IBA ESG Report highlights that 37% of respondents from the IBA Survey had experience with external grievance mechanisms, whereas 58% reported having standing grievance mechanism in place.[73] As we discuss below at paragraph 10.4, the recourse to arbitration to handle business and human rights disputes raises a number of challenges with respect to costs, transparency, etc.

---

71 See IBA Arbitration Committee Report on use of ESG contractual obligations and related disputes, p 10-18, available at: https://www.ibanet.org/document?id=report-on-use-of-ESG-contractual-obligations.

72 Access to effective remedy is a core component of the UNGPs. They envisage the setting up by companies of so called "*grievance mechanisms*" (which refer to the options that affected persons or stakeholders can use to lodge complaints or disputes against organisations), including "*non-state-based grievance mechanisms*", and the necessity for companies to remedy the harm caused (remedy being understood as "*apologies, restitution, rehabilitation, financial or non-financial compensation and punitive sanctions (whether criminal or administrative, such as fines)*"). See the dedicated webpage on "access to remedy" of the website of the UN Working Group on Business and Human Rights, available at: https://www.ohchr.org/en/special-procedures/wg-business/access-remedy.

73 See IBA Arbitration Committee Report on use of ESG contractual obligations and related disputes, p 33, available at: https://www.ibanet.org/document?id=report-on-use-of-ESG-contractual-obligations. See for example https://www.adidas-group.com/en/sustainability/social-impacts/human-rights.

In relation to increasing significance for investors and business decisions, ESG considerations have become crucial in mergers and acquisitions (**M&A**) and **shareholder disputes**, whether between shareholders and the company (and/or their directors) or among shareholders themselves.

ESG factors have gained importance during due diligence processes, with acquirers focusing on ESG criteria both during target selection and eventual in-depth evaluations. ESG representations and warranties have also begun appearing in share purchase agreements (SPAs). With the rise in ESG statutory obligations, these factors are also relevant for "catch-all" representations such as compliance with applicable laws and accuracy of annual accounts.

Given the frequent inclusion of arbitration clauses in SPAs, post-acquisition claims regarding ESG issues including misleading disclosure by the target (in line with legislation like the CSRD) and the accuracy of sellers' representations are likely to surface. ESG considerations may also play a significant role in pricing disputes, where valuations are based on contractual formulas typically tied to the target's financial results or share price.[74]

Berkeley Research Group's Mid-Year M&A Disputes Report 2023 revealed that 64% of respondents agreed that increased regulatory scrutiny of ESG metrics and commitments would be the most common cause for ESG related M&A litigation.[75] A 2023 KPMG survey found that over half of respondents reported cancelling deals due to significant findings during ESG due diligence.[76]

To illustrate potential issues in post-M&A disputes, we can reference publicly known cases where breaches of environmental warranties were contested.[77]

74 See e.g. M. Sato et al, *Impacts of climate litigation on firm value*, 2023, available at: https://www.lse.ac.uk/granthaminstitute/publication/impacts-of-climate-litigation-on-firm-value/, where authors find empirical evidence that climate litigation has on the company's value.

75 'Regulation and Market Volatility Are Driving M&A Disputes in Digital Assets and ESG', *Berkely Research Group*, 5 July 2023, available at:https://www.thinkbrg.com/insights/publications/mid-year-ma-disputes-report-2023/ https://www.thinkbrg.com/insights/publications/mid-year-ma-disputes-report-2023/.

76 'New diligence: the rise of ESG in deals', *KPMG*, 3 August 2023, available at: https://kpmg.com/uk/en/blogs/home/posts/2023/07/new-diligence-the-rise-of-esg-in-deals.html.

77 These cases were also mentioned in the IBA Arbitration Committee Report on use of ESG contractual obligations and related disputes, p 15-17, available

First, in *DW Holdings Limited v. Norvill & Ors*, the England and Wales High Court had to decide a dispute concerning the sale of G.D. Environmental Services Limited (GDE) from the Norvills to MDW Holdings Limited. MDW acquired the entire share capital of GDE for £ 3,584,224. MDW claimed that GDE had systematically breached environmental laws and evaded compliance costs, thereby inflating its profits and leading MDW to overpay for the shares. MDW sought damages for breach of environmental warranty,[78] misrepresentation, and deceit. It was found that the Norvills had breached the warranties under the SPA, which assured compliance with all applicable laws and regulations.[79] Consequently. the court awarded MDW £ 382,600 in damages, accounting for the reduction in GDE's value due to the defendants' failures in environmental compliance and fraudulent practices during the sale negotiations.

Second, in *Solvay Specialty Polymers Italy v. Edison S.p.A.*, an ICC tribunal examined whether Solvay was misled during the acquisition of the Bussi and Spinetta sites because of deliberate manipulation and omission of critical data by Edison in the characterization plans, which understated the extent of historical pollution. The Arbitral Tribunal found a breach of warranty stipulated in the SPA which required the company and its subsidiaries to substantially comply with all health, safety, and environmental laws regarding their operations and conduct at respective properties and sites.[80] The tribunal concluded that Edison, through its negotiators and Ausimont employees, failed to provide complete and accurate information about the environmental condition of the Bussi and Spinetta Sites as mandated by the applicable regulations and the SPA.[81]

Arbitration clauses are also common in companies' articles of incorporation and shareholders' agreements. Increased ESG shareholder activism might lead arbitrators to adjudicate ESG disputes within the context of these agreements, particularly concerning the duty of care owed by companies and their directors.

---

at: https://www.ibanet.org/document?id=report-on-use-of-ESG-contractual-obligations.

78 See reproduced at *MDW Holdings Limited v. Norvill*, [2021] EWHC 1135 (Ch); [2022] EWCA Civ 883, para 197.

79 *MDW Holdings Limited v. Norvill*, [2021] EWHC 1135 (Ch); [2022] EWCA Civ 883, para 249.

80 *Solvay Specialty Polymers Italy v. Edison S.p.A.*, ICC Case no 18666/FM/MHM/GFG, Partial Award, 22 June 2021, para 908.

81 *Solvay Specialty Polymers Italy v. Edison S.p.A.*, ICC Case no 18666/FM/MHM/GFG, Partial Award, 22 June 2021, paras 591 et seq.

10.3.2 *Investor-State arbitration*

ESG considerations are becoming more significant in investor-State arbitration. In numerous instances, which are more accessible due to the enhanced transparency of investment arbitration compared to commercial arbitration, especially regarding the energy transition, investors have argued that **"ESG" legislation has impaired their investments** and are seeking compensation from States (e.g., the phase-out of coal in the Netherlands, nuclear energy in Germany, the end of renewable energy subsidies in Spain and Italy, etc.).[82] Inevitably, new ESG-related arguments will be tested soon. For instance, in *Koch v. Canada,* an investor probed a novel argument, while challenging the cancellation of an emissions trading programme. The ICSID tribunal ultimately decided that emissions trading allowances do not qualify as NAFTA-protected investments, because the allowances lacked "exclusive control" under Ontario law and thus they could not be regarded as property.[83] Nevertheless, the ICSID tribunal acknowledged that the issue was a "close call"[84] potentially encouraging similarly natured claims.

The most recent investment treaties (and investment contracts, especially in the energy, mining and infrastructure sectors) generally stress the broad regulatory autonomy retained by States particularly concerting their energy policy.[85] For example, the Dutch Model BIT (2019) provides that:

> "The provisions of this Agreement shall not affect the right of the Contracting Parties to regulate within their territories necessary to achieve legitimate policy

---

82 For a useful overview, see L. Barber, *Zeph Investments v Australia: The Latest in Investor-State Climate Change-Related Claims*, 2023, available at: https://arbitrationblog.kluwerarbitration.com/2023/08/24/zeph-investments-v-australia-the-latest-in-investor-state-climate-change-related-claims/. Notably, the 2022 study by the Climate Change Counsel reviewed nearly all publicly accessible ECT cases. It concluded that climate change was not a primary topic of discussion in the ECT arbitration proceedings. See A. Magnusson, 'Energy Charter Treaty and the Paris Agreement – Friends or Foes? – 7th EFILA Lecture (28 October 2021)', *European Investment Law and Arbitration Review* (7) 2022, p 175-187; P. Wiliński & M. Brown, *Is the Energy Charter Treaty Fit for the Energy Transition? The analysis of the Climate Change Counsel Report*, available at: https://blog.jusmundi.com/is-the-energy-charter-treaty-fit-for-the-energy-transition-the-analysis-of-the-climate-change-counsel-report/.

83 *Koch Industries, Inc. and Koch Supply & Trading, LP v. Canada*, ICSID Case no ARB/20/52.

84 *Koch Industries, Inc. and Koch Supply & Trading, LP v. Canada*, ICSID Case no ARB/20/52, paras 316 and 426.

85 See for example Articles 13(2) and 23(1) of the Morocco-Nigeria BIT.

> objectives such as the protection of public health, safety, environment, public morals, labor rights, animal welfare, social or consumer protection or for prudential financial reasons. The mere fact that a Contracting Party regulates, including through a modification to its laws, in a manner which negatively affects an investment or interferes with an investor's expectations, including its expectation of profits, is not a breach of an obligation under this Agreement."[86]

Furthermore, the Dutch Model BIT explicitly addresses sustainable development. Article 6 of the Model Dutch BIT stipulates:

> "1. The Contracting Parties are committed to promote the development of international investment in such a way as to contribute to the objective of sustainable development.
>
> 2. Each Contracting Party shall ensure that its investment laws and policies provide for and encourage high levels of environmental and labor protection and shall strive to continue to improve those laws and policies and their underlying levels of protection. (…)"[87]

Beyond reform of bilateral treaties there are also imminent changes in the multilateral policy space. In particular, the Energy Charter Treaty ("**ECT**")[88] has faced increased scrutiny due to concerns over its adequacy to support measures necessary to effectively combat climate change. ECT Contracting Parties, led by the EU and the UK have been advocating for modernisation to address these issues. In June 2022, an agreement in principle was reached on the ECT's modernisation,[89] incorporating a "flexibility mechanism" that would allow contracting parties to exclude investment protection for fossil fuels in their territories. This measure would have impacted existing investments after ten years from the relevant provisions' entry into force and new investments made after 15 August 2023.

However, as these reform efforts drew to a close in late 2022, some EU Member States expressed dissatisfaction with the agreed revisions, finding them insufficient to effectively tackle climate change. A cascade of

86 Article 2(2) of the Dutch Model BIT (2019).

87 Article 6 of the Dutch Model BIT (2019). Notably, neither of the Dutch BIT has been signed based on this Model. See https://investmentpolicy.unctad.org/international-investment-agreements/countries/148/netherlands.

88 The ECT has emerged as the most prolific basis for investment treaty claims against European states, by providing investors in the energy sector specific protections, including against expropriation without appropriate compensation, discrimination and violation of a fair and equitable treatment standard.

89 https://policy.trade.ec.europa.eu/news/agreement-principle-reached-modernised-energy-charter-treaty-2022-06-24_en.

EU Member States – starting with Poland, Spain and the Netherlands, then followed by France, Belgium, Germany, Slovenia, Luxembourg and Austria – announced their intention to withdraw from the ECT. Italy had already withdrawn from the ECT in 2016. This led the European Commission on 7 July 2023 to propose a coordinated EU withdrawal.[90] On 27 June 2024, the European Union formally notified its withdrawal from the Energy Charter Treaty in line with the so-called "Belgium roadmap". The proposal prepared by the Belgium presidency allows to unlock a potential to modernize the ECT for non-EU, ECT Contracting Parties, even when the EU exits the ECT.[91] It is reported, that the modernisation of the ECT will be discussed at the Energy Charter Conference scheduled for the end of 2024.[92]

Both individual States, and the EU further their ESG policies by integrating **ESG provisions into their investment treaties to support sustainability objectives**. For example, on 1 September 2024 the EU-Angola Sustainable Investment Facilitation Agreement entered into force ("the EU-Angola SIFA").[93] This groundbreaking agreement underscores the commitments of the States' to uphold high standards of environmental and labour protection (which should not be compromised to attract investment)[94] and includes explicit provisions mandating urgent climate action,[95] promotion of sustainable and biodiversity-friendly investments,[96] encouragement of corporate social responsibility and responsible business conduct,[97] and enhancement of gender equality in investment policies.[98] It remains to

90 European Commission's press release of 7 July 2023, "European Commission proposes a coordinated EU withdrawal from the Energy Charter Treaty", available at: https://energy.ec.europa.eu/news/european-commission-proposes-coordinated-eu-withdrawal-energy-charter-treaty-2023-07-07_en.

91 https://www.consilium.europa.eu/en/press/press-releases/2024/05/30/energy-charter-treaty-council-gives-final-green-light-to-eu-s-withdrawal/.

92 L. Bohmer, *Parties reach agreement in principle on modernizing Energy Charter Treaty, including carve-outs for fossil fuels and intra-EU disputes, stricter definitions and standards of protection, and application of 2014 UNCITRAL Rules on transparency*, 2022, available at: https://www.iareporter.com/articles/breaking-parties-reach-agreement-in-principle-on-modernizing-energy-charter-treaty-including-carve-outs-for-fossil-fuels-and-intra-eu-disputes-stricter-definitions-and-standards-of-protection-and/.

93 See https://ec.europa.eu/commission/presscorner/detail/en/ip_24_4462; see also https://circabc.europa.eu/ui/group/09242a36-a438-40fd-a7af-fe32e36cbd0e/library/a17ccfe1-ce36-428f-bc7f-76bcb902c36a/details?download=true.

94 See Article 29 of the EU-Angola SIFA.

95 See Article 32 of the EU-Angola SIFA.

96 See Article 33 of the EU-Angola SIFA.

97 See Article 34 of the EU-Angola SIFA.

98 See Article 35 of the EU-Angola SIFA.

be seen how this treaty will interact with the existing investment treaty framework.[99]

The inclusion of ESG obligations may also lead to emergence of **ESG counterclaims** in investor-State arbitration.[100] While investment arbitration has mainly dealt with investor claims against States for treaty violations, there is increasing support for the possibility for States to start counterclaims against investors in case of breach of ESG standards. Consequently, States may start presenting counterclaims related to investors' failure to meet ESG obligations. These counterclaims could potentially harmonize public interest with investment protection, promoting responsible and sustainable investment behaviours.

Investor-State arbitration continues to be a vital mechanism for resolving ESG-related disputes. Despite changes influenced by international agreements like the Paris Agreement and 2050 climate goals, investor-State arbitration is likely to remain an effective means of safeguarding investors' interests.[101]

10.4 Impact on the arbitration's actors and process

Disputes with material ESG limb(s) will often require specialised expertise from counsel, arbitrators and experts – be it for the legal rules introduced by ESG instruments and contractual clauses and/or technical and sectorial issues (such as carbon emissions, transition planning, supply chain organ-

99 See Article 2(3) of the EU-Angola SIFA: "This Agreement does not create or modify commitments relating to the liberalisation of investments, nor does it create or modify rules on the protection of established investors in the territories of the Parties, or of their investments, or on investor-state dispute settlement."

100 See e.g. Y. Lahlou, *The Rise of Environmental Counterclaims in Mining Arbitration*, 2019 available at: https://www.lexology.com/library/detail.aspx?g=bbc29b22-4e33-4d55-810f-296765e218d2.

101 See C. de Stefano, 'Giving "Teeth" to Climate Change Related Obligations Through International Investment Law', in: S. Maljean-Dubois & J. Peel (eds), *Climate Change and the Testing of International Law/Le droit international au défi des changements climatiques*, Boston: Brill 2023, p 251-288, ("Having regard to the prong of effectiveness, international investment law and arbitration may importantly give to the ICCR those "teeth" that are lacking under both the Paris Agreement and the UNFCCC, thus tempering their admitted compliance and enforcement gaps. Indeed, the prescriptions relating to climate change that are established in investment awards may be successfully recognized and enforced under the ICSID Convention and the New York Convention in accordance with the requirements set forth therein."). Critically: *UN A/78/168*, D.R. Boyd, *Paying polluters: the catastrophic consequences of investor-State dispute settlement for climate and environment action and human rights*, 2023.

isation, etc.). Similar to other specialist areas – such as construction, sports, post-M&A, etc. – an "ESG arbitration ecosystem" of recurring actors with specialised expertise is likely to emerge.

More fundamentally, key features of the arbitration process itself will have to be reconsidered for certain types of disputes. Arbitration, for example under the NAI rules, offers several benefits in business and human rights as well as supply chain disputes, such as increased flexibility, the involvement of independent and expert adjudicators (which is crucial for technically complex or challenging issues), and the ease of global enforcement of arbitral awards. However, it also faces various challenges. The first one is costs of course, where the victims are not in a position to disburse important amounts to have their case heard. In addition, if some businesses may consider the confidentiality of the proceedings an advantage, a number of business and human rights disputes may require publicity to constitute an acceptable and effective remedy. In view of its consensual nature, the centralisation of disputes in a single forum where there are many parties and/or contracts at stake will also often be problematic.[102]

In this context, the Center for International Legal Cooperation (CILC) introduced The Hague Rules on Business and Human Rights Arbitration on 12 December 2019 to address these topics, describing the project as follows:

> "International arbitration holds great promise as a method to be used to resolve human rights disputes involving business. These disputes often occur in regions where national courts are dysfunctional, corrupt, politically influenced and/or simply unqualified. Parties to such disputes, generally multinational business enterprises (MNEs) and the victims of human rights abuse linked to MNEs, are in need of a private system that can function in these regions. Arbitration also has certain unique attributes that could serve the parties well even where fair and competent courts are available. In addition, arbitration can serve a useful tool to assist MNEs to prevent abuse from occurring in their supply chains and development projects.
>
> The rules in use today for international arbitration were written without a focus on the special requirements of human rights disputes. Hence, changes were needed to ensure that, among other things, there is greater transparency of pro-

102 Supply chains usually involve many actors and contracts and providing for the same dispute resolution mechanism in all of them requires great care and organisation. In addition, certain disputes will involve third parties which are not party to the contractual relationships (victims, public institutions, other companies, etc.), and leading them to accept the arbitration mechanism will be challenging in many cases.

> ceedings and awards, that numerous victims are able to aggregate their claims and that the arbitrators chosen are prominent experts in business and human rights matters."[103]

With respect to environmental disputes, it is also worth flagging a 2001 initiative led by the Permanent Court of Arbitration in the Hague, which introduced Optional Rules for Arbitration of Disputes Relating to the Environment and/or Natural Resources ("**The PCA Environmental Rules**"). According to the PCA Statement:

> "The PCA's Environmental Rules are referred to in a treaties and contracts, such as the 2003 Protocol on Civil Liability and Compensation for Damage Caused by the Transboundary Effects of Industrial Accidents on Transboundary Waters and the Model Emissions Reduction Purchase Agreements developed by the International Emissions Trading Association."[104]

The arbitration process is not only impacted by the idiosyncrasies of ESG disputes, but also by the obligations that ESG instruments and expectations presented in the paragraph 10.2 above impose on the actors of the arbitration process, including the NAI, arbitrators, counsel for the parties, and experts.

Although many counsels would like to see it otherwise, external lawyers are part of companies' supply chains and subject to procurement requirements like any other supplier. The parties (or "users"), many of which subject to reporting and due diligence obligations, increasingly request from their counsel information and undertakings on how they operate, in particular with respect to carbon emission reduction, but also with respect to the "S" of ESG, including diversity and inclusion criteria.

In addition, a sizeable number of large law firms will meet the EU turnover thresholds of instruments such as the CSRD and CSDDD (see para 10.2 above), meaning that they will also have to report on ESG criteria (including their carbon emissions), implement transition plans and conduct due diligence on their value chains. Under other ESG instruments, they will also have to avoid greenwashing claims, report on pay transparency, etc.

---

103 See CILC's website, https://www.cilc.nl/project/the-hague-rules-on-business-and-human-rights-arbitration/#:~:text=The%20Hague%20Rules%20on%20Business%20and%20Human%20Rights%20Arbitration%20Project,UN%20Guiding%20Principles%20on%20Business.

104 See: https://pca-cpa.org/en/services/arbitration-services/environmental-dispute-resolution/.

In turn, this will have a knock-on effect on the work of counsel and arbitrators that are part of these firms (and, indirectly, on actors from smaller structures and/or without activities in the EU).

These drivers will lead to the need to calculate the carbon emission of arbitrations (and potentially the carbon costs to be included in the arbitration costs), increased pressure on the decrease of such impact (regarding travel of course, but also the impact of printing, potentially the use of AI, etc.), further push for greater diversity in the arbitrator, expert and counsel teams, etc.

These issues are not new and a number of well-known initiatives are already well established to tackle them, including the Campaign for Greener Arbitration (CGA; currently working on a methodology to calculate the environmental impact of an arbitration as well as on identifying the key ESG obligations relevant to the arbitration community) for the "E",[105] as well as the Equal Representation in Arbitration (ERA) Pledge,[106] the Equal Representation in Expert (ERE) Witnesses Pledge,[107] and changes of arbitration rules to include diversity and inclusion criteria in the selection process of arbitrators for the "S".[108]

10.5 Conclusion

The time where a focus on sustainability was seen as mostly voluntary, and based on soft law standards, is over. Companies, and their directors and officers, face a wave of ESG legislation, regulations, court decisions and expectations from their stakeholders. The shift has been swift, in line with the realisation of the urgency of, and the change of paradigm entailed by, the climate crisis (and broader considerations on companies' sustainability duties). The backlash against the increased ESG obligations is unlikely to change this direction of travel.

105 See: https://www.greenerarbitrations.com/.
106 See: https://www.arbitrationpledge.com/.
107 See: https://www.expertwitnesspledge.com/take-the-pledge.
108 See e.g. 'CEPANI makes diversity a rule', *Global Arbitration Review*, 27 January 2023, available at: https://globalarbitrationreview.com/article/cepani-makes-diversity-rule LCIA press release of 31 May 2024, 'LCIA Unveils New Equality, Diversity, and Inclusion Initiative', available at: https://www.lcia.org/News/lcia-unveils-new-equality-diversity-and-inclusion-initiative.aspx.

Such rapid change necessarily brings with it many uncertainties and risks, especially in view of the emergence of new far-reaching and untested standards and obligations (be it fully new ones, or new interpretations given to existing general duties). In turn, this creates a fertile ground for (contractual and treaty) disputes, a material number of which will be adjudicated through arbitration. Arbitration practitioners mastering these new developments are likely to be sought after in the years to come.

ESG requirements, however, do not only matter for the substance of the disputes subject to arbitration. The arbitration community, including the NAI and its users, has never been in a vacuum; it will have to continue adapting its rules and practices to the idiosyncrasies of ESG disputes as well as to embrace the consequences brought by the ESG shift on the expectations of the parties and the obligations imposed on the actors of the arbitration process.

CHAPTER 11

ARBITRATION IN THE DUTCH CARIBBEAN

Sebastiaan Barten[1]

11.1 Introduction

Since the constitutional reform in 2010, the Kingdom of the Netherlands (hereinafter also: the "Kingdom") has consisted of four constituent countries: The Netherlands, Aruba, Curaçao and Sint Maarten.[2] In addition, the Caribbean islands of Bonaire, Sint Eustatius and Saba (the "BES islands") have special status as public entities (*openbare lichamen*) forming part of the Netherlands. Hereinafter, the Caribbean part of the Kingdom is also referred to as the 'Dutch Caribbean' and the European part as the "European Netherlands"). Only the European Netherlands is a Member State of the European Union (EU). The Dutch Caribbean jurisdictions have the status of Overseas Countries and Territories in the European Union.[3]

Each of these four constituent countries and the BES islands has its distinct civil law system. In total, there are thus five territories within the Kingdom with their own legal systems, creating a complex 'inter-regional private law' with jurisdictional and conflict of laws rules between these parts of the Kingdom.[4]

The five legal systems are closely related.[5] Under the 'principle of concordance' enshrined in Article 39 of the Charter of the Kingdom of the Netherlands (the "Charter"), civil law should be interpreted in the same way

1 S.H. Barten (LLM) is an attorney-at-law in Willemstad, Curaçao and a guest lecturer at the University of Curaçao.
2 Previously, the Kingdom of the Netherlands consisted of three countries: The Netherlands, The Netherlands Antilles and Aruba (since 1986). The Netherlands Antilles ceased to exist on 10 October 2010.
3 This means that EU law does not, in principle, apply in the Dutch Caribbean. See H.E. Bröring, 'UPG als wenkend perspectief en juridische werkelijkheid', *WPNR* 2011, issue 6898, p 686.
4 G.C.C. Lewin, *Interregionaal privaatrecht*, The Hague: Boom 2024, para 1-2.
5 Lewin 2024, para 1.

as far as possible.[6] The Supreme Court of the Netherlands, as the highest court in civil cases in both the European Netherlands and the Dutch Caribbean countries, also has a role in maintaining this consistency between the civil law systems (also referred to as 'concordance of case-law').[7]

Procedurally, the four Dutch Caribbean territories (Aruba, Curacao, Sint Maarten and the BES islands) together form a single area for the purpose of application of the respective codes of civil procedure of the jurisdiction.[8] Jurisdiction in the Dutch Caribbean is administered by the Courts of First Instance, after which parties may appeal to the Joint Court of Justice of Aruba, Curaçao, Sint Maarten and of Bonaire, Sint Eustatius and Saba (the "Joint Court of Justice").

Even though the procedural laws of the Dutch Caribbean are also closely related to Dutch law, there are important differences, for example, in relation to the manner in which proceedings are instituted, and the manner in which the appellate court may determine the scope of the appeal. Arbitration is an area in which also major differences have emerged between Dutch and Dutch Caribbean laws. This contribution will explore several aspects of arbitration law in the Caribbean parts of the Kingdom, highlighting any notable differences from Dutch law.

11.2 The use of arbitration in the Dutch Caribbean

On paper, the Dutch Caribbean is well-positioned for development as a hub for international dispute resolution. The islands benefit from a well-established legal system based on Dutch procedural law, and the judiciary in these territories enjoys a strong reputation for impartiality and

6 Article 39(1) of the Charter reads: "Civil and commercial law, civil procedure, criminal law, criminal procedure, copyright, industrial property, the office of notary, as well as provisions concerning weights and measures shall be regulated in the Netherlands, Aruba, Curaçao and Sint Maarten as much as possible in a corresponding manner." [*machine translation*].

7 Article 23 Charter. See Asser/Vonken *10-I* 2023/660 and the legal literature referred therein.

8 Article A of the Codes of Civil Procedure of Curacao, Sint Maarten and the BES islands and Article B of the Aruban Code of Civil Procedure. See R.F. van den Heuvel, 'Bij een honderdste verjaardag: over rechtsmacht van de burgerlijke rechter in de Cariben op grond van de regel 'distributie is attributie'', *CJB* 2016, issue 3, p 180.

independence.[9] The judiciary comprises both judges with a predominantly Caribbean background and those who have relocated there temporarily or permanently, a diversity also reflected in the legal profession.[10] Additionally, the availability of cassation (appeal) to the Supreme Court in The Hague may instill further confidence in the judicial process. The islands' geographical location between South and North America, combined with good flight connections to the Netherlands, the United States, other Caribbean countries, and various South American destinations, further enhances their potential as an international dispute resolution center.

In addition, with prior permission from the courts, foreign counsel may, in circumstances, represent their clients together with local counsel during oral pleadings before the Dutch Caribbean courts, *for example,* if specific expertise is required.[11] English has been designated as one of the official working languages of the Joint Court of Justice.[12] Even so, procedural documents in the Caribbean territories are drafted in Dutch and interpreters are often used at hearings. The law also explicitly prescribes that court judgments must be issued in the Dutch language.[13] Exhibits can be submitted in English, Papiamentu (a language spoken predominantly on Aruba, Bonaire and Curaçao) or Spanish, without requiring a Dutch translation in each case.[14]

While the Dutch Caribbean has considerable potential for arbitration, there is still room for growth in this area. Arbitration remains relatively rare on these islands.[15] International arbitration in the Dutch Caribbean could be encouraged by explicitly making it possible to conduct enforce-

9 C.J.M. Klaassen, 'Caraïbisch Nederland, (inmiddels) 'the place to be for arbitration?'', in: P. Koerts & E.F. Verheul (ed), *Toonaangevend,* Deventer: Wolters Kluwer 2024, p 34.

10 According to a local newspaper article, 25 of the 60 judges with the local courts would have a local background. See ''Caribisering' Hof uitdaging', *Antilliaans Dagblad* 22 April 2024.

11 Para 28b Rules of procedure for civil cases at first instance and on appeal from the Joint Court of Justice (version 2023) (Procesreglement voor civiele zaken in eerste aanleg en in hoger beroep van het Gemeenschappelijk Hof van Justitie).

12 Article 9 of the Kingdom Act of 7 July 2010, on the tasks and powers of the Joint Court of Justice of Aruba, Curaçao, Sint Maarten and of Bonaire, Sint Eustatius and Saba (Kingdom Act on the Joint Court of Justice; Rijkswet Gemeenschappelijk Hof van Justitie).

13 Article 9 Kingdom Act on the Joint Court of Justice.

14 Joint Court of Justice 19 January 2016, ECLI:NL:OGHACMB:2016:4, *CJB* 2018, issue 2, p 148, annotated by P. Klik. It is nevertheless advisable to attach an (automatic) translation.

15 Klaassen 2024, p 38.

ment and setting aside proceedings in English, similar to the Netherlands Commercial Court.[16]

Currently, there is no local arbitration institute active in the Dutch Caribbean islands.[17] However, the Netherlands Arbitration Institute (NAI) offers to administer arbitrations in the Dutch Caribbean jurisdictions[18] The NAI does not (yet) have a (permanent) physical presence in the Dutch Caribbean territories, but with modern communication technologies, this should not cause too many problems. The recently introduced 2024 NAI Arbitration Rules take into account the possibility that the procedural law of another legal system may apply to arbitral proceedings administered by the NAI, by stating in several places that the provisions apply "without prejudice to any provision of mandatory arbitration law".[19] In addition, the NAI may also act as appointing authority under Article 6 of the Arbitration Rules of the United Nations Commission on International Trade Law (UNCITRAL), if the arbitration is conducted under these rules, or the NAI may appoint arbitrators pursuant to the 2015 NAI Rules for the Appointment of an Arbitral Tribunal in Ad Hoc Arbitration, if the parties agree on appointment of arbitrators by the NAI without having referred to the NAI Arbitration Rules.[20]

16 See https://www.rechtspraak.nl/English/NCC/ (website accessed 28 September 2024). Pursuant to Article 1064a of the Dutch Code of Civil Procedure the place of arbitration must be Amsterdam for the Netherlands Commercial Court to have jurisdiction in setting aside proceedings. For this reason, in Article 27 of the 2024 NAI Arbitration Rules, Amsterdam is designated as the place of arbitration, if the Parties have not specified the place of arbitration by agreement. See on the NCC also the contribution written by R.P.J.L. Tjittes, chapter 13 of this book.

17 To my knowledge, the Arbitration Institute of the Netherlands Antilles and Aruba (renamed to the Caribbean Arbitration Institute) is no longer active.

18 See https://nai.nl/nl/arbitrage/ (website accessed 28 September 2024).

19 Articles 2(4), 25(1), 40(3), 42(4), Article 44(3) and Article B3(7) of the NAI Arbitration Rules 2024.

20 The appointing authority designated in accordance with Article 6 of the UNCITRAL Arbitration Rules has the power to appoint arbitrators in the event parties cannot agree or do not timely appoint arbitrators. If this concerns a sole arbitrator or presiding arbitrators, the appointing authority will, in principle, appoint in accordance with the list procedure laid down in Article 8 of the UNCITRAL Arbitration Rules, unless the parties have agreed otherwise. If the NAI Rules for the Appointment of an Arbitral Tribunal in Ad Hoc Arbitration apply, in principle, the NAI will follow the list procedure laid down in Article 13 thereof, unless the Parties have agreed otherwise.

11.3 The implementation of the Model Law in the Dutch Caribbean

The Caribbean islands of the Dutch Kingdom chose to fully implement the latest adopted version of the UNCITRAL Model Law on International Commercial Arbitration (the "Model Law"), hoping that this would make the jurisdictions more attractive for international arbitration.[21] In contrast, the European Netherlands has not fully implemented the Model Law, which means that there are two different legal regimes for arbitration within the Kingdom. According to Van Mierlo, this disparity is undesirable.[22] The Caribbean legislator's choice to adopt the Model Law cannot be directly explained by social, cultural and economic differences, but seems to have been an experiment.[23] The Dutch Caribbean legislator merely noted that the choice of implementing an international instrument could inspire confidence among foreigners.[24]

The legislature of the islands only introduced two provisions in their Code of Civil Procedure ("CCP"): Articles 1020 and 1021 CCP. Article 1020(1) CCP provides that 'arbitration' is governed by the Model Law.[25] Paragraph 1020(2) CCP designates the Courts of First Instance of the various islands as the courts as referred to in Article 6 of the Model Law. Article 1021 CCP provides that arbitrators may instruct parties to refer their dispute to a mediator.

By declaring the most recently adopted version of the Model Law applicable, the Caribbean legislation remains in line with international standards without requiring enactment of new legislation. However, this method of implementation is unconventional and is not to be recommended.[26] Van Mierlo previously qualified the implementation of the Model Law by mere

---

21 *Explanatory Memorandum*, National Ordinance establishing a new Code of Civil Procedure, Staten van de Nederlandse Antillen, 2002-2003, p 80: "Maybe the applicability of an internationally accepted legal instrument like the UNCITRAL Model Law is suitable to instill confidence in foreigners." [machine translation].

22 A.I.M. van Mierlo, *Aruba, the place to be for arbitration? Studiereeks Nederlands-Antilliaans en Arubaans recht*, The Hague: Boom legal 2005, p 9.

23 See J. de Boer, 'Het NBW in de West', *NJB* 2001, p 289-294 for examples of differences that can be explained by social, cultural or economic reasons.

24 *Explanatory Memorandum*, National Ordinance establishing a new Code of Civil Procedure, Staten van de Nederlandse Antillen, 2002-2003, p 80.

25 Article 1020(i) CCP reads "An arbitration shall be governed by the UNCITRAL Model Law on International Commercial Arbitration (…) as most recently adopted by the United Nations Commission on International Trade Law, and in the English text thereof." [machine translation].

26 Van Mierlo 2005, p 41; Klaassen 2024, p 37.

reference to the latest version as "rather unique".[27] Van Mierlo pointed out that several ambiguities could arise under the previous version of the Model Law and the manner of implementation in the Dutch Caribbean territories, including: (i) when does the Model law apply and which version of the Model Law applies (see under para 11.10.4 below); (ii) how to deal with aspects not regulated by the Model Law (see para 5 below); and (iii) what requirements apply to the arbitration agreement (see under para 10.6 below).[28]

Van Mierlo raised these concerns in 2005. Unfortunately, none of the Dutch Caribbean islands have since supplemented its legislation to address these ambiguities.[29] However, as to Van Mierlo's objections, no serious "procedural accidents" have (yet) resulted in practice to my knowledge.[30] This may partly be due to the limited use of arbitration in the Dutch Caribbean, as rightly pointed out by Klaassen.[31] Another explanation may be that certain of the problems identified by Van Mierlo are ultimately solvable through party agreements or by reference to Dutch law. Moreover, certain issues, such as those related to interim measures by arbitral tribunals, have been addressed in the 2006 version of the Model Law.

11.4 Scope of application of the Model Law in the Dutch Caribbean

The private international law of the Dutch Caribbean territories is largely uncodified. The same applies to the law applicable to arbitration.[32] However, also in the Dutch Caribbean territories, it is beyond doubt that the law of the place of arbitration constitutes the applicable (procedural) law to the arbitration and triggers the applicability of several provisions of the

27 Van Mierlo 2005, p 19. At the time, Van Mierlo mentioned Singapore as an example of a jurisdiction that also declared the Model Law applicable by a reference. This is no longer (entirely) the case. The current version of the Singapore International Arbitration Act does declare (a specific version of) the Model Law applicable, but only to the extent that it is not derogated from in the Singapore International Arbitration Act, and excludes, inter alia, Chapter VIII (*Recognition and Enforcement*). See https://sso.agc.gov.sg/Act/AA2001 (accessed on 5 September 2024).

28 Van Mierlo 2005, p 41. See for a list of subjects that (intentionally) have not been included in the 2006 version of the Model Law: M. Holtzmann et al., *A Guide to the 2006 Amendments to the UNCITRAL Model Law on International Commercial Arbitration: Legislative History and Commentary*, Alphen aan de Rijn: Kluwer Law International 2015, p 671-679.

29 Klaassen 2024, p 37 and p 42.

30 Van Mierlo 2005, p 50.

31 Klaassen 2024, p 37.

32 Van Mierlo 2005, p 42.

Model Law.[33] Article 20 of the Model Law provides that parties may designate the place of arbitration and if they have not done so, that the arbitral tribunal has the power to determine the place of arbitration, as is also the case in the European Netherlands (Article 1037(1) of the Dutch Code of Civil Procedure).

According to Articles 1(1) and 1(2) of the Model Law, the scope of application of the Model Law is limited to *'international commercial arbitration'* and cases where "the place of arbitration is in the territory of this State". Article 1(3) of the Model Law further defines when an arbitration qualifies as 'international'. The CCP of the Dutch Caribbean territories declares the Model Law applicable to 'arbitration' and does not distinguish between 'international commercial arbitration' and other types of arbitration.[34] Even though the legislator has not made this abundantly clear, it must be assumed that the Model Law applies to all arbitrations where the place of arbitration is in the Dutch Caribbean and to recognition and enforcement proceedings in the event that the New York Convention does not apply, regardless of the subject matter of the arbitration.

Unfortunately, the Dutch Caribbean legislatures have failed to introduce transitional law clarifying the temporal scope of application of subsequent versions of the Model Law. It remains unclear which version of the Model Law applies in relation to arbitration agreements made when only a previous version of the Model Law was available to the parties.[35] Lacking any transitional rules it must, in my opinion, be assumed that the new version of the Model law immediately applies to any subsequently initiated arbitrations, but if this leads to unjust or unpractical outcomes, arbitral tribunals and courts may decide differently.

11.5 Issues that have not been addressed in the Model Law

The Model Law does not cover all issues relevant to arbitration in the Dutch Caribbean. Consequently, if the legal place of arbitration is located on one of the islands, parties may find themselves with limited statutory regulation to rely upon in the absence of specific agreements. To address this, parties should consider agreeing on additional procedural rules, such as established arbitration rules like the 2024 NAI Arbitration Rules.

33 Van Mierlo 2005, p 42.
34 Van Mierlo 2005, p 44-46.
35 Van Mierlo 2005, p 46.

Under the principle of concordance, as laid out in the Charter of the Kingdom of the Netherlands, the civil laws of the countries within the Kingdom are generally interpreted uniformly when there are similar legislative provisions. This principle may also guide the resolution of 'legislative gaps'.[36] Van Mierlo suggested that issues not covered by the Model Law could potentially be resolved by applying Dutch arbitration law, following the principle of concordance within the Kingdom.[37]

However, it may not always be appropriate for courts in the Caribbean territories to apply Dutch law. First, the Caribbean legislator made a conscious decision not to adopt the arbitration provisions from the Dutch Code of Civil Procedure. Therefore, courts in the Caribbean territories are not bound to align their case law with Dutch law, whether regarding the interpretation of the Model Law or in addressing areas not covered by it.[38] While the courts may use Dutch law provisions as a source of inspiration, they are not obliged to do so.[39]

Second, the Model Law itself is grounded in international harmonization. Article 2A of the Model Law states:

> "(1) In the interpretation of this Law, regard is to be had to its international origin and to the need to promote uniformity in its application and the observance of good faith.
>
> (2) Questions concerning matters governed by this Law which are not expressly settled in it are to be settled in conformity with the general principles on which this Law is based."

This provision, which is also found in other UNCITRAL Model Laws and the 1980 Convention on Contracts for the International Sale of Goods (CISG), aims to ensure the Model Law's uniform interpretation.[40] Specifically, Article 2A(1) requires courts to consider the Model Law's drafting history (*travaux préparatoires*), case law from other jurisdictions that have

36 H.J. van Kooten, 'Over de rol van concordantie van rechtspraak bij de invulling van leemtes in de wet', *WPNR* 2015, issue 7045, p 27-32; G.C.C. Lewin, 'Over de rol van leemtes in de wet bij de ontwikkeling van concordante rechtspraak', *CJB* 2015, issue 2, p 75. Lewin defined a 'legislative gap' as "a missing written rule of law, which should have been there" (translated).

37 Van Mierlo 2005, p 39.

38 See Lewin 2015, p 75 on when courts are bound by the principle of concordance.

39 Lewin 2015, p 82.

40 J.F. Sanchez, 'Applying the Model Law's Standard for Interim Measures in International Arbitration', *Journal of International Arbitration* (37) 2020, p 57.

adopted the Model Law, and prevailing opinions in international legal literature on the Model Law and the New York Convention.

If and to the extent that aspects of Dutch arbitration law would at any time be in conflict with the general principles underlying the Model Law, the courts in the Caribbean territories must, pursuant to Article 2A (2) Model Law, give priority to the fundamental principles of the Model Law. These include party autonomy, empowerment of the tribunal, equal treatment, arbitrator impartiality, finality of awards and limiting court intervention.[41]

In summary, while the principle of concordance applicable within the Kingdom may suggest alignment with Dutch law in some instances, the Model Law should always be interpreted in line with its international origins and fundamental principles.

11.6 The arbitration agreement

Article 7 of the Model Law gives the implementing legislature two choices to regulate the requirements for arbitration agreements. Option A requires that an arbitration agreement be in writing, while Option B imposes no specific requirement regarding the form or evidence of the agreement.

In the legislation of the Caribbean territories, no choice was made between option A and option B of Article 7 of the Model Law. When introducing the Model Law, it appears that the Caribbean legislatures did not anticipate that future versions of the Model Law would include such an option.[42] It could be argued that the intention of the legislature in the Dutch Caribbean when implementing the Model Law and even future versions (without reviewing the contents thereof) was to be an arbitration-friendly jurisdiction and that Option B of Article 7 Model Law should therefore be applied in the Dutch Caribbean.

As in the European Netherlands, certain clauses in general contractual conditions between businesses and consumers in the Dutch Caribbean may be rendered invalid if they are deemed 'unreasonably onerous' to the

41 M. Campbell, *The Model Law Approach to International Arbitration*, Cheltenham: Edward Elgar Publishing 2024, p 14; Holtzmann et al. 2015, p 25.

42 So it soon became clear that the legislative technique that was used was inadequate.

consumer.[43] When implementing Directive 13/93/EEC on unfair terms in consumer contracts, the Dutch legislator introduced Article 6:236(n) DCC, which states that arbitration clauses in business-to-consumer contracts are, by definition, unreasonably onerous if they do not allow the consumer to opt out of arbitration within one month after the business invokes the arbitration clause.[44] According to Dutch case law, courts and arbitral tribunals are required to assess, of their own motion, whether an arbitration clause is unreasonably onerous within the meaning of Article 6:236(n) DCC.[45]

In contrast, the civil codes of the Dutch Caribbean do not automatically designate arbitration clauses which do not contain the one-month opt-out option as unreasonably onerous.[46] However, also in the Dutch Caribbean arbitration clauses may be considered unreasonably onerous under the general rule of Article 6:233 of the Civil Codes in the Dutch Caribbean, which would require an assessment of all relevant circumstances.[47] In addition, it has been argued that courts in the Dutch Caribbean should take into account the protection the Dutch implementation of Directive 13/93/EEC offers to consumers when applying Dutch Caribbean consumer protection laws, even though said EU legislation was not implemented in the Dutch Caribbean.[48] Businesses in the Dutch Caribbean may for this reason prefer to align with Dutch practices by including in their general conditions a one-month opt-out period in arbitration clauses.

Under the Model Law, only the non-arbitrability of the subject-matter and violations of public policy are considered to be grounds for setting

43 Article 6:233 of the Dutch Civil Code and of the Dutch Caribbean Civil Codes.

44 Article 6:236(n) of the Dutch Civil Code.

45 Supreme Court 8 November 2019, ECLI:NL:HR:2019:1731, *NJ* 2020/305, annotated by H.J. Snijders; P.E. Ernste & C.L. Schleijpen, 'De vernietiging van arbitrale vonnissen: lessen voor (NAI-)arbiters?', in: C.J.M. Klaassen, G.E. Meijer & C.L. Schleijpen (ed), *Going Dutch: ADR in Nederland, in het bijzonder bij het NAI*, Deventer: Wolters Kluwer 2019, para 27.2.2, p 651-700.

46 This follows from Article 6:236(n) of the Dutch Caribbean Civil Codes, which has the same wording as the Dutch legislation prior to the amendments made by the Dutch legislator effective 1 January 2015.

47 See C.J.M. Klaassen, 'Het Fundamentele recht op toegang tot de rechter alsook het recht en overwegingen om daarvan af te zien, in het bijzonder op Curaçao', in: O.E. Kostrzewski & L.J.J. Rogier (ed), *Fundamentele rechten in Curaçao*, The Hague: Boom legal 2019, para 2, p 77-91.

48 M.V.R. Snel, 'De 'europeanisering' van de algemene voorwaardenregeling in het Nederlands BW. Consequenties voor de Caribische landen?', *TvC* 2021, issue 2, p 82-92. Snel did not specifically address the subject of arbitration clauses.

aside the courts may consider of its own initiative.[49] Therefore, courts in the Dutch Caribbean, in exequatur and setting-aside proceedings, may not necessarily of their own motion assess whether an arbitration clause in business-to-consumer contracts is invalid because it is unreasonably onerous, even though according to the Supreme Court, this concerns the fundamental nature of the consumer's right to court access.[50]

11.7 Arbitrability

The Model Law contains no provision on the arbitrability of disputes (in contrast with Article 1020(1), (2) and (3) Dutch Code of Civil Procedure). Nevertheless, also under the law of the Caribbean territories, disputes arising from a particular legal relationship may be submitted to arbitration and arbitration may not lead to the determination of legal consequences which are not within the autonomy of the parties to agree. Differences may arise between the European Netherlands and the Dutch Caribbean regarding which disputes are considered arbitrable due to variations in their substantive laws.

11.8 Appointment of the arbitral tribunal

Under the law of the Caribbean islands, the appointment agreement between arbitrators and parties is not subject to any formal requirements.[51] Pursuant to Article 10(1) of the Model Law, the parties are free to choose the number of arbitrators. In the absence of an agreement on the number of arbitrators, the default number of arbitrators is three (Article 10(2) of the Model Law). It is possible, for example, to conclude an arbitration agreement and agree that there will be two arbitrators with an arrangement for

49 Explanatory Note by the UNCITRAL secretariat on the 1985 Model Law on International Commercial Arbitration as amended in 2006, para 46.

50 Pursuant to Dutch case law, a Dutch court must assess compliance with Article 6:236(n) of the Dutch Civil Code of its own initiative. Supreme Court 26 September 2014, ECLI:NL:HR:2014:2837, annotated by H.J. Snijders; Supreme Court 8 November 2019, ECLI:NL:HR:2019:1731, *NJ* 2020/305, annotated by H.J. Snijders. In Joint Court of Justice 21 February 2012, ECLI:NL:OGHACMB:2012:BW0535, *TvA* 2012/39, the Joint Court of Justice ruled that a party was prevented to rely on the potential invalidity of an arbitration clause pursuant to Article 6:233 of the (presumably) Dutch Civil Code, because it had not raised such defence in the arbitration. This judgment was rendered prior to the Supreme Court case law on the application of EU consumer law in respect of arbitration clauses.

51 Van Mierlo 2005, p 27.

the appointment of an 'umpire' in case of 'deadlock' situations.[52] This differs from Dutch arbitration law, where the mandatory provision in Article 1026(1) of the Dutch Code of Civil Procedure requires an arbitral tribunal to consist of an odd number of arbitrators, a restriction that does not apply in the Dutch Caribbean.

Parties may further agree under Art 11(1) of the Model Law to exclude arbitrators on the basis of an arbitrator's nationality (similar to Article 1023 Dutch Code of Civil Procedure). This can be desirable to ensure the independence and impartiality of arbitrators, at least in the eyes of the parties, and such exclusions also appear in arbitration rules.[53] Since the Caribbean territories are not part of the European Union, the question of whether such agreements may conflict with anti-discrimination principles of Union law does not arise.[54]

Article 11(2) of the Model Law provides that the parties determine the appointment procedure, for example by declaring the 2024 NAI Arbitration Rules applicable, which contain default rules for the appointment of arbitrators of arbitral tribunals and fail-safe options for the appointment of arbitrators in the event parties or co-arbitrators do not timely nominate arbitrators.[55] Therefore, if the 2024 NAI Arbitration Rules apply, it is not to be expected that court intervention will be necessary.

52 See for an example Supreme Court 11 January 1985, ECLI:NL:HR:1985:AG4938, *NJ* 1985/421, annotated by W.H. Heemskerk.

53 Asser Procesrecht/Sanders, Meijer & Ernste *8* 2023/150.

54 See F.J.M. De Ly, 'Overeenkomst tot arbitrage en Europees discriminatierecht', *TvA* 2012/62 and Asser Procesrecht/Sanders, Meijer & Ernste *8* 2023/150.

55 Article 16 of the 2024 NAI Arbitration Rules contains the default rules for the appointment of arbitrators. A sole arbitrator is, in principle, appointed by a joint nomination by the parties within two weeks after the transmission of the short answer and otherwise the responsible member of the NAI Case Management Committee will appoint the arbitrator (Article 16(1) of the 2024 NAI Arbitration Rules). If there are three arbitrators, each of the Parties nominate a co-arbitrator for appointment (in the request for arbitration and the short answer). If the request for arbitration or the short answer does not contain a nomination for the appointment of an arbitrator, the responsible member of the NAI Case Management Committee will directly appoint the arbitrator. The two appointed co-arbitrators will then appoint a chair of the arbitral tribunal. The parties may agree on different procedures for the appointment of the arbitrators, such as the list procedure in accordance with Article 17 of the 2024 NAI Arbitration Rules. If the rules on expedited arbitration apply (Article 42 and Appendix D of the 2024 NAI Arbitration Rules), in principle, the appointment of the sole arbitrator will take place in accordance with a list-procedure included in Article D4(2) of the 2024 NAI Arbitration Rules.

In the absence of such agreement, the procedure in Article 11(3) Model Law applies, which differs from the default rule under Dutch law (Article 1027 of the Dutch Code of Civil Procedure). If the arbitration involves three arbitrators, each party appoints an arbitrator, after which the two arbitrators appointed by the parties appoint a third arbitrator. If a party does not appoint an arbitrator within 30 days of receiving a request to do so, or if the two arbitrators appointed by the parties do not appoint a third arbitrator within 30 days, the parties may apply to the Court of First Instance to make the missing appointments. If the parties cannot reach an agreement on appointment of a sole arbitrator, they may also apply to the Court of First Instance to appoint the arbitrator (Article 11(3)(b) of the Model Law). This process can be initiated through an injunction in preliminary relief proceedings, even though this is not explicitly provided in the Model Law or the Codes of Civil Procedure of the Dutch Caribbean territories ("CCP").

Pursuant to Article 11(5) of the Model Law, decisions made by the Courts of First Instance on the basis of Article 11(3) Model Law are not subject to appeal. The Dutch Arbitration Act contains an identical rule in Article 1070 Dutch Code of Civil Procedure. Despite this, the Dutch Supreme Court has ruled that a decision in which a Dutch preliminary relief judge denied a request to appoint an arbitrator is nevertheless subject to appeal.[56] The Dutch Supreme Court reasoned that the intention behind the rule was to expedite the arbitral proceedings and thus, the provision barring appeals should not apply in cases where the application for appointment of arbitrators was denied.[57] In addition, under Dutch procedural law an appeal can also be lodged if the court has wrongly applied the provision of the law pursuant to which the judge made a decision or has disregarded fundamental aspects of due process.[58]

56 Supreme Court 21 October 2011, ECLI:NL:HR:2011:BQ8777, *NJ* 2013/23, annotated by H.J. Snijders (*Hasfeld/Cohen*).

57 Supreme Court 21 October 2011, ECLI:NL:HR:2011:BQ8777, *NJ* 2013/23, annotated by H.J. Snijders (*Hasfeld/Cohen*).

58 J.W. Bitter, in: *Sdu Commentaar Burgerlijk procesrecht*, Article 1070 of the Dutch Code of Civil Procedure, note 4. It is standard case law under Dutch law that such decisions are always subject to appeal. See Supreme Court 18 December 2015, ECLI:NL:HR:2015:3633 (*X/Stichting Jeugdbeschermig Rotterdam*), Supreme Court 18 April 2014, ECLI:NL:HR:2014:943 (*Verzoeksters/verweerder*) and Supreme Court 26 October 2007, ECLI:NL:HR:2007:BA7626 (*X/Hoogheemraadschap Delfland e.a.*).

Article 11(5) of the Model has a similar background and was also introduced to expedite arbitration.[59] Even though this has not yet been addressed in case law, a refusal to grant an injunction to appoint one or more arbitrators pursuant to Article 11(3) of the Model Law rendered by the Court of First Instance of a Dutch Caribbean territory might thus be subject to appeal for the same reason. Some Model Law jurisdictions have held that Article 11(5) does not apply if the appeal does not directly concern the appointment procedure or appointment of the arbitrators.[60] In my view, it would be in line with such an approach to allow an appeal where the decision to refuse to grant an injunction for the appointment of arbitrators is based on the evident absence of a valid arbitration agreement.[61]

11.9 (Exemption of) arbitrator's liability

Both the Netherlands and the Caribbean islands lack statutory provisions defining the conditions for liability of arbitrators. In the Netherlands, this issue has been addressed in case law of the Supreme Court.[62] Under the Dutch case law, arbitrators can only be held personally liable, with regard to both substantive and procedural errors, if they acted intentionally or knowingly recklessly or with manifest gross disregard for what constitutes proper performance of duties.[63] Liability based on intent and deliberate recklessness cannot be contractually excluded.[64]

59 See Explanatory Note by the UNCITRAL secretariat on the 1985 Model Law on International Commercial Arbitration as amended in 2006, para 24: "Where under any procedure, agreed upon by the parties or based upon the suppletive rules of the Model Law, difficulties arise in the process of appointment, challenge or termination of the mandate of an arbitrator, articles 11, 13 and 14 provide for assistance by courts or other competent authorities designated by the enacting State. In view of the urgency of matters relating to the composition of the arbitral tribunal or its ability to function, and in order to reduce the risk and effect of any dilatory tactics, short time-periods are set and decisions rendered by courts or other authorities on such matters are not appealable."

60 UNCITRAL 2012 Digest of Case Law on the Model Law on International Commercial Arbitration, p 63.

61 As was the case in Supreme Court 21 October 2011, ECLI:NL:HR:2011:BQ8777, *NJ* 2013/23, annotated by H.J. Snijders.

62 Asser Procesrecht/Sanders, Meijer & Ernste *8* 2023/200. The Model Law is silent on the issue of liability of arbitrators. See on this topic chapter 16 of this book, written by D.A.M.H.W. Strik.

63 Supreme Court 4 December 2009, ECLI:NL:HR:2009:BJ7834, *NJ* 2010/131, annotated by J.B.M. Vranken (*Greenworld/Arbiters*).

64 Asser Procesrecht/Sanders, Meijer & Ernste *8* 2023/213.

A lighter standard applies to 'business errors' unrelated to the judicial task.[65] These are errors that cannot lead to the setting aside of the arbitral award and are otherwise insufficiently related to the arbitral function (which involves taking substantive and procedural decisions leading to an award). Examples include losing documents or leaving files containing confidential information on the train.[66]

There are divergent views in Dutch literature on whether an arbitrator can only be held liable in relation to arbitral awards that are capable of being set aside.[67] According to some authors, it is recommended that the standard for (exclusion of) arbitrators' liability be laid down in statute to take away any ambiguities.[68]

The Dutch Supreme Court developed its standard for liability of arbitrators i.a. based on the similarities between the roles of state courts and arbitrators. There is no compelling reason to assume that a different standard should apply in the Dutch Caribbean territories because of the (spirit of the) Model Law, especially given the diverging approaches to this issue across jurisdictions.[69]

If the parties have declared the 2024 NAI Arbitration Rules applicable, the Dutch law doctrine for arbitrators' liability will clearly apply. Article 65 of the 2024 NAI Arbitration Rules declares Dutch law applicable to the agreement between arbitrators and the parties and Article 64 of the NAI Arbitration Rules 2024 excludes liability to the extent permitted under Dutch law.

---

65 Supreme Court 30 September 2016, ECLI:NL:HR:2016:2215, *NJ* 2017/141, annotated by J.B.M. Vranken (*Qnow*).

66 Asser Procesrecht/Sanders, Meijer & Ernste *8* 2023/213.

67 Asser Procesrecht/Sanders, Meijer & Ernste *8* 2023/205; N. Peters & J.J. Bakker, 'Aansprakelijkheid van arbiters. Enkele gedachten over maatstaf, vernietiging, grondslag, ipr en exoneratie', *MvV* 2020, issue 10, p 364-371; D.A.M.H.W. Strik, 'Aansprakelijkheid(sbeperking) van de arbiter', in: C.J.M. Klaassen, G.J. Meijer & C.L. Schleijpen (ed), *Going Dutch: ADR in Nederland, in het bijzonder bij het NAI*, Deventer: Wolters Kluwer 2019, p 383-384; H.J. Snijders, in: *GS Burgerlijke Rechtsvordering*, Article 1029 DCCP, note 1.4.3.

68 Asser Procesrecht/Sanders, Meijer & Ernste *8* 2023/200; E. Dekker & W. van Boom, 'Arbiters en aansprakelijkheid: Drie aandachtspunten bij herziening arbitragerecht', *NJB* 2013/1543, para 6; Strik 2019, p 383-384.

69 Holtzmann et al. 2015, p 674.

11.10 Assistance by courts in deadlock situations and other court-ordered interim measures

As mentioned above, Article 1020(2) CCP designates the Courts of First Instance of the islands as the competent courts referred to in Article 6 of the Model Law. This empowers state courts in the Dutch Caribbean to resolve various 'deadlock' situations, such as when parties cannot agree on the appointment of arbitrators and have not agreed on other mechanisms for the appointment, such as included in the 2024 NAI Arbitration Rules.

In addition, parties seeking interim relief are in principle free to reserve the right to choose between the state courts and the arbitral tribunal for all types of interim measures. Summary proceedings before courts in the Caribbean territories are relatively expedited and can be completed within a few weeks or even days. Under Article 9 of the Model Law, the state courts retain jurisdiction to grant interim relief in the context of a dispute subject to an arbitration clause. When a court exercises its jurisdiction to grant interim measures under Article 17J Model Law, the court must consider the "specific features of international arbitration", but otherwise there are no restrictions on the state court's jurisdiction concerning interim measures.[70]

In contrast, a Dutch preliminary relief judge will only declare that it has jurisdiction under Articles 1022c and 1074d of the Dutch Code of Civil Procedure if the requested remedy cannot be obtained in arbitration or cannot be obtained in time in arbitration. In some judgments, the Dutch preliminary relief judge has declined jurisdiction on the ground that the same remedy could be obtained in arbitration in a timely fashion, even though the parties had reserved the right to apply to the state court for interim relief.[71] This limitation on the jurisdiction of the preliminary relief judge, as established by the Dutch Arbitration Act, has been criticized for creating

---

70 The Dutch Caribbean courts have regularly exercised jurisdiction pursuant to Article 17J Model Law. See for example: Joint Court of Justice 10 March 2023, ECLI:NL:OGHACMB:2023:33 and Joint Court of Justice 18 May 2021, ECLI:NL:OGHACMB:2021:275.

71 N. Peters, 'De (on)mogelijkheid van erkenning en tenuitvoerlegging van arbitrale voorlopige voorzieningen op grond van het Verdrag van New York en artikel 1076 Rv', *TvA* 2023/85, para 2; provisional relief judge District Court The Hague 12 June 2015, ECLI:NL:RBDHA:2015:6959, *TvA* 2016/15 (*Can-Pack*) and provisional relief judge District Court Amsterdam 12 January 2017, ECLI:NL:RBAMS:2017:282 (*Cygne/Cofco*).

uncertainty about the parties' litigation options and for conflicting with the principle of voluntary arbitration.[72]

An interim measure granted by a Dutch Caribbean court can be directly executed throughout the Kingdom under Article 40 of the Charter. In this context, the The Hague Court of Appeal refused to issue an exequatur in relation to an arbitral award rendered in Curaçao that contained an interim-measure prohibiting the enforcement of an interim injunction granted by the Curaçao Court of First Instance.[73] According to the The Hague Court of Appeal recognition and enforcement of the interim measure issued by the arbitral tribunal would violate public policy, because this would create an additional procedural remedy against a court decision that is not available pursuant to Curaçao procedural law and is a non-arbitrable matter.[74]

11.11 Interim relief by the arbitral tribunal

The 2006 version of the Model Law also contains a framework for interim measures that the arbitral tribunal may award, which applies unless the parties have agreed otherwise. According to Article 17A(1)(a) of the Model Law, one of the conditions for granting an interim measure in arbitral proceedings is that there must be a risk of "irreparable harm" if the interim measure is not granted ("harm not adequately reparable by an award of damages"). Paragraph 17(2) Model Law provides an exhaustive list of interim measures that an arbitral tribunal may grant. The arbitral tribunal may, by interim measure, order a party to: (a) maintain or restore the status quo pending determination of the dispute; (b) take action that would prevent, or refrain from taking action that is likely to cause, current or imminent harm or prejudice to the arbitral process itself; (c) provide a means of preserving assets out of which a subsequent award may be satisfied and (d) preserve evidence that may be relevant and material to the resolution of the dispute. If no other arrangements have been made between the Parties, the requirement of 'irreparable harm' in the Model Law may make it

72 J.K. van Hezewijk, '"Een gulden regel, waard, dat er voor zijn naleving angstvallig wordt gewaakt"', *TvA* 2024/47; Peters 2023.

73 The Court of First Instance had ordered the defendant to pay an advance payment to the claimant by way of interim relief; See The Hague Court of Appeal 14 September 2021, ECLI:NL:GHDHA:2021:1636, para 3.3, *JBPr* 2022/56, annotated by P.E. Ernste.

74 The Hague Court of Appeal 14 September 2021, ECLI:NL:GHDHA:2021:1636, *JBPr* 2022/56, annotated by P.E. Ernste; See also G.J. Meijer, in: *T&C Rv*, Article 1075 of the Dutch Code of Civil Procedur, note 1.

more appealing for a plaintiff to seek interim relief from the state courts. In state courts throughout the Kingdom, including those in the Caribbean territories, it is generally sufficient to show that the plaintiff has an urgent interest in the injunction and that a balancing of interests favors the plaintiff.

In practice, the provisions of the Model Law on interim measures may be of limited importance to an arbitral tribunal, because the arbitration agreement may confer broad powers on the arbitral tribunal to issue interim measures.[75] In many sets of arbitration rules, including the 2024 NAI Arbitration Rules, arbitral tribunals have a broad discretion regarding the way the arbitral proceedings are conducted and to grant interim measures.[76]

In accordance with Article 17H of the Model Law, in the Dutch Caribbean, interim measures ordered by an arbitral tribunal shall be recognized as binding and, unless otherwise provided by the arbitral tribunal enforced upon application to the Courts of First Instance. The Model Law has adopted a 'substance over form' approach.[77] For the enforceability of interim measures in the Dutch Caribbean, it is thus not material whether the arbitral tribunal has laid down the interim measure in an arbitral award or order.

11.12 Setting aside of the arbitral award

Under Article 34 of the Model Law, setting aside is the only remedy available against an arbitral award originating from the Caribbean territories.[78] Unlike the Dutch arbitration law, the laws of the Dutch Caribbean territories do not explicitly provide for the possibility of revoking an arbitral award on the grounds of fraud, false documents or withholding docu-

75 J.E. Castello, 'Generalizing About the Virtues of Specificity: The Surprising Evolution of the Longest Article in the UNCITRAL Model Law', *WAMR* (6) 2012, issue 1, p 19.

76 For example, the 2024 NAI Arbitration Rules do not specify the types of interim measures available under those rules. See in relation to the UNCITRAL Arbitration Rules and the ICC Rules: Castello 2012, p 19.

77 J.E. Castello & R. Chahine, 'Enforcement of Interim Measures', in: J.W. Rowley & B. Siino (ed), *Challenging and Enforcing Arbitration Awards Guide*, Global Arbitration Review 2023, p 141; P.E. Ernste in her note to The Hague Court of Appeal 14 September 2021, ECLI:NL:GHDHA:2021:1636, *JBPr* 2022/56, para 8.

78 For an overview of the grounds for setting aside of arbitral awards pursuant to Dutch law: Ernste & Schleijpen 2019, p 651-700. See also chapter 23 of this book, written by Ernste & Schleijpen.

ments. Those cases will therefore have to be subsumed under a ground for setting aside the award listed in Article 34 of the Model Law.

Under Article 34(3) of the Model Law, an action to set aside an arbitral award must be brought within three months of receipt of the arbitral award, or at least within three months after an application to correct an arbitral award as referred to in Article 33 of the Model Law has been rejected. This should be done by filing an application with the Court of First Instance, pursuant to Article 1020(2) CCP. There is a presumption of receipt of the arbitral award under Article 3 of the Model Law if the arbitral award is delivered to the addressee personally or if it is delivered at addressee's place of business, habitual residence or mailing address. Unlike under Dutch law (Article 1064a (2) Dutch Code of Civil Procedure), under the Model Law no second opportunity to file setting aside proceedings is available from the service of the arbitral award on the award debtor.

The grounds for setting aside an arbitral award are set out in Article 34(2) of the Model Law and are substantively the same as the grounds for refusal of enforcement under Article V of the New York Convention.[79] Article 34(2) of the Model Law does not explicitly provide for setting aside of an award due to the omission of the signature of the arbitrator (s) as prescribed by Article 31(1) of the Model Law.[80] If such a situation arises in the Caribbean territories, the ground for setting aside would likely need to be argued as a violation of public policy.[81]

Van Mierlo has pointed out that the Model Law does not specify the consequences of setting aside an arbitral award.[82] Van Mierlo considers anal-

79 As these are listed in the Explanatory Note by the UNCITRAL secretariat on the 1985 Model Law on International Commercial Arbitration as amended in 2006, para 46: lack of capacity of the parties to conclude an arbitration agreement; lack of a valid arbitration agreement; lack of notice of appointment of an arbitrator or of the arbitral proceedings or inability of a party to present its case; the award deals with matters not covered by the submission to arbitration; the composition of the arbitral tribunal or the conduct of arbitral proceedings are contrary to the effective agreement of the parties or, failing such agreement, to the Model Law. Grounds that a court may consider of its own initiative are as follows: non-arbitrability of the subject-matter of the dispute or violation of public policy (which is to be understood as serious departures from fundamental notions of procedural justice).

80 Pursuant to Article 1065(1)(d) of the Dutch Code of Civil Procedure, this is an express ground for setting aside of the arbitral award under Dutch law.

81 Asser Procesrecht/Sanders, Meijer & Ernste *8* 2023/513.

82 Van Mierlo 2005, p 39.

ogous application of the Dutch rules appropriate on the basis of the principle of concordance as laid down in the Charter.[83]

Under Article 1076 of the Dutch Code of Civil Procedure, the jurisdiction of the state court is only revived after setting aside an arbitral award if the setting aside is based on the absence of a valid arbitration agreement. If the arbitral award is set aside on any other ground, the arbitration agreement remains in force unless the parties have agreed otherwise.[84] It has been argued in the past that the current Article 1076 of the Dutch Code of Civil Procedure aligns with international standards and the rationale behind the New York Convention.[85] In my view, therefore, Article 2A(2) of the Model Law does not preclude applying a rule similar to Article 1076 of the Dutch Code of Civil Procedure in the Dutch Caribbean territories. This approach would ensure consistency with international arbitration standards and maintain the integrity of the arbitration agreement unless its invalidity is the basis for setting aside the award.

11.13 Recognition and enforcement of arbitral awards in the Dutch Caribbean

11.13.1 Procedure and grounds for refusal

The Kingdom of the Netherlands is a party to the New York Convention across all four countries within the Kingdom. The New York Convention takes precedence over the Model Law (see also Article 1(1) of the Model Law). Therefore, the recognition and enforcement of arbitral awards in the Dutch Caribbean is governed by Article V of the New York Convention, when it concerns an arbitral award from a Contracting State (other than countries within the Kingdom). For all other arbitral awards (including awards originating from countries within the Kingdom), the Dutch Caribbean courts should apply Articles 35 and 36 Model Law (which match Article V and VI of the New York Convention).[86]

83 Van Mierlo 2005, p 39.
84 On the history of this and preceding statutory provisions in the Dutch Code of Civil Procedure, see J. van Hezewijk & J. Drok, 'Het geheim van artikel 1067 Rv: hoe de uitzondering de hoofdregel werd zonder dat iemand het merkte', *TvA* 2015/23.
85 Van Hezewijk & Drok 2015.
86 Lewin 2024, para 157.

There is no specific provision in the CCPs of the Dutch Caribbean governing jurisdiction for legal proceedings to recognize and enforce arbitral awards. The Courts of First Instance are designated as the competent courts as referred to in Article 6 of the Model Law, but this provision of the Model Law does not cover proceedings to enforce arbitral awards under the New York Convention or the Model Law.[87] However, in practice, this does not cause any problems. The Courts of First Instance have regularly accepted jurisdiction.

The Caribbean procedure for recognition and enforcement of arbitral awards differs in some respects from the Dutch regime. Unlike in the Netherlands, Caribbean legislation for recognition and enforcement does not distinguish between arbitral awards rendered on the islands themselves and arbitral awards rendered in foreign states or other parts of the Kingdom. The procedure for obtaining an exequatur for both domestic and foreign arbitral awards is an adversarial procedure that begins at the Courts of First Instance. In all cases, there is also the possibility of appeal to the Joint Court of Justice, followed by cassation to the Supreme Court of the Netherlands. Unlike under Dutch law, the right to lodge an appeal is not restricted in the event permission for enforcement is granted, as is the case in the European Netherlands under Article 1062(3) of the Dutch Code of Civil Procedure. As a general rule, however, the order rendered in first instance is declared 'provisionally enforceable', ensuring that any appeal or cassation usually does not suspend the enforcement.

Consequently, the baseline is that foreign arbitral awards are enforceable in the Caribbean parts of the Kingdom. Under Article 17H of the Model Law, interim measures issued by an arbitral tribunal are also eligible for recognition and enforcement in the Dutch Caribbean.[88]

The Dutch Caribbean courts will need to exercise a similar restraint to Dutch courts in applying the grounds for refusal in Articles 35 and 36 of the Model Law. Under Dutch law, however, in respect of the grounds for refusal for the absence of a valid arbitration agreement and due process violations the arbitral award should be reviewed in full.[89] This exception to the doctrine of restraint arguably does not apply to the other grounds for

87 Van Mierlo 2005, p 48-49.

88 See for the potential enforcement of arbitral awards or orders with interim measures under the New York Convention: Peters 2023.

89 Opinion of P-G P. Vlas, ECLI:NL:PHR:2024:659 (*Telem/MER*) with reference to Asser Procesrecht/Sanders, Meijer & Ernste *8* 2023/399.

refusal in Article 36 of the Model Law because these grounds are aligned with those of the New York Convention.[90]

11.13.2 Separate exequaturs required for the Dutch Caribbean

Pursuant to Article 40 of the Charter of the Kingdom of the Netherlands, judicial decisions from one of the countries of the Kingdom are directly enforceable in the other countries of the Kingdom. A similar rule is applicable in respect of the relationship between the European part of the Netherlands and the BES islands.[91]

This has led to the following questions:

11.13.2.1 Does an exequatur granted by a court in the European Netherlands have effect in the other countries of the Kingdom of the Netherlands? And does it make any difference whether the exequatur in question was granted under an enforcement treaty, such as the New York Convention?

An exequatur granted by a court in the European Netherlands does not have legal effect in the other countries of the Kingdom (Aruba, Curaçao, and Sint Maarten) if it was granted under an enforcement treaty such as the New York Convention. According to the *Sonera/Cukurova* judgment of the Dutch Supreme Court an exequatur for the enforcement of arbitral awards originating from a Contracting State does not fall within the scope of Article 40 of the Charter.[92]

According to the Supreme Court's reasoning, the countries within the Dutch Kingdom maintained their full autonomy regarding recognition

90 Opinion of P-G P. Vlas, ECLI:NL:PHR:2024:659 (*Telem/MER*) with reference to Asser Procesrecht/Sanders, Meijer & Ernste *8* 2023/399.

91 Article 5 of the Public Entities of Bonaire, St. Eustatius and Saba Implementation Act (*Invoeringswet Openbare Lichamen Bonaire, St. Eustatius and Saba*) (BES Implementation Act).

92 Supreme Court 8 December 2017, ECLI:NL:HR:2017:3104, *NJ* 2018/7 (*Sonera v Cukurova*). See for a discussion on this case law: Klaassen 2024, p 40; G.J. Meijer, in: *T&C Rv*, Article 1075 of the Dutch Code of Civil Procedure, note 1; Asser Procesrecht/Sanders, Meijer & Ernste *8* 2023/428; Asser/Vonken *10-I* 2023/660; J. Israel, 'Het verlof tot tenuitvoerlegging (het exequatur) in interregionaal verband. Annotatie bij Hoge Raad 8 december 2017, ECLI:NL:HR:2017:3104 (Sonera/Çukurova)', *CJB* 2018, issue 4, p 318; Lewin 2024, para 157; N. Peters, 'De vraag naar de uitvoerbaarheid van arbitrale voorlopige voorzieningen in het Koninkrijk mede bezien in het licht van Article 1022c Rv en Article 1074d Rv', *TvA* 2022/2, para 6.

and enforcement of foreign court and arbitral tribunal judgments.[93] All countries in the Kingdom can decide independently whether they wish to become parties to a recognition and enforcement treaty, such as the New York Convention. The Supreme Court then ruled that it is incompatible with this system that a country would be obliged, under Article 40 of the Charter, to allow enforcement of the foreign judgment on the ground that an exequatur has been granted in another country of the Dutch Kingdom.[94] It is irrelevant whether the exequatur was granted on the basis of a treaty to which all countries in the Kingdom are parties, such as the New York Convention.

Even though the European Netherlands and the other parts of the Dutch Kingdom may apply the same rules for the recognition and enforcement of a foreign arbitral award, e.g. the New York Convention, it is in theory possible that recognition and enforcement of a foreign arbitral award will be allowed in the Netherlands, while it might be refused overseas in the Caribbean territories. This is particularly possible where the public policy ground for refusal is involved, for example if it concerns violations of European Union law (as the Caribbean parts of the Kingdom are not part of the European Union).[95]

The prevailing doctrine is that the New York Convention does not apply between the countries within the Kingdom.[96] Therefore, the question has been raised whether an exequatur issued for an arbitral award originating from one of the countries of the Kingdom should be treated differently from an exequatur that was granted in relation to an arbitral award originating from a Contracting State.[97] However, it is generally assumed that Article 40 of the Charter does not apply to an exequatur issued in respect of arbitral awards from the Kingdom either.[98] Arguments to that effect are that

93 Supreme Court 8 December 2017, ECLI:NL:HR:2017:3104, *NJ* 2018/7 (*Sonera v Cukurova*).

94 Supreme Court 8 December 2017, ECLI:NL:HR:2017:3104, para 3.4.3, *NJ* 2018/7 (*Sonera v Cukurova*).

95 Lewin 2024, para 61.

96 Opinion of P-G P. Vlas, ECLI:NL:PHR:2017:1082 to Supreme Court 8 December 2017, ECLI:NL:HR:2017:3104, *JOR* 2018/87, annotated by C.G. van der Plas; Joint Court of Justice 21 February 2012, ECLI:NL:OGHACMB:2012:BW0535, para 2.6; Lewin 2024, para 157; Peters 2022, para 6; Differently: Israel 2018, p 325.

97 Klaassen 2024.

98 See Asser/Vonken *10-I* 2023/660 and the legal literature referred to therein. Klaassen seems to have argued that arbitral awards made within the Kingdom should be treated differently from arbitral awards made outside of the Kingdom, because the New York Convention does not apply. See: Klaassen 2024, p 41.

(i) Article 40 of the Charter does not apply to arbitration and therefore also does not apply to a grant of leave to enforce arbitral awards and that (ii) an exequatur is a means of enforcement and by its nature does not extend beyond the jurisdiction of the court.[99]

11.13.2.2 Does an exequatur granted by the Dutch court also have effect in the BES islands (Caribbean Netherlands)?

Article 40 of the Charter refers only to the enforcement of judgments between the countries of the Kingdom. The BES islands are part of the European Netherlands and do not constitute an independent country within the Kingdom. For this reason, the provision in the Charter does not apply to the BES islands. However, similar wording is included in separate Dutch legislation, pursuant to which judgments of European Dutch courts are enforceable, directly and without exequatur, in the BES islands.[100]

According to Steneker, an arbitral award with a Dutch exequatur can indeed be enforced in the BES islands due to the special status as 'public entities' forming part of the European Netherlands.[101] However, in my opinion, this is not obvious. First, it could be argued that paragraph 11.5 of the BES Implementation Act does not apply to arbitration, due to the wording similar to Article 40 of the Charter in relation to which the same can be argued.[102] Second, there are in my view no indications that the Dutch legislator intended to extend the territorial jurisdiction of the European Netherlands courts with regard to exequaturs to the BES islands when the Netherlands Antilles were dissolved in 2010. To the contrary, the Dutch legislator maintained the regime for recognition and enforcement applicable in the BES islands based on the Model Law and local procedural law.[103] As a consequence, a court in one of the BES islands will only grant an exequatur for the Caribbean territories (and not for enforcement in the

99 Opinion P. Vlas, ECLI:NL:PHR:2017:1082 to Supreme Court 8 December 2017, ECLI:NL:HR:2017:3104, *JOR* 2018/87, annotated by C.G. van der Plas; Lewin 2024, para 157.

100 Article 5 BES Implementation Act. See Lewin 2024, para 157.

101 Asser Procesrecht/Steneker 5 2023/577.

102 Opinion P. Vlas, ECLI:NL:PHR:2017:1082 to Supreme Court 8 December 2017, ECLI:NL:HR:2017:3104, *JOR* 2018/87, annotated by C.G. Van der Plas; Lewin 2024, para 157.

103 It is not clear why the legislator would choose to maintain two (potentially) conflicting regimes for the recognition and enforcement of arbitral awards in the BES islands and in the European Netherlands, if the courts of the European Netherlands would have jurisdiction to grant exequaturs for recognition and enforcement of arbitral awards in the BES islands.

Netherlands).[104] One can ask the question whether a Dutch court should then have the power to issue a leave for enforcement covering the BES islands. Third, given the potential differences in the assessment of the public policy ground for refusal between the European Netherlands and the BES islands, an exequatur granted by a Dutch court should arguably be limited to the territory of the European Netherlands.

11.13.2.3 Does an exequatur granted by a court from a Dutch Caribbean territory have effect in the other Dutch Caribbean territories?

Finally, the question has been raised by other authors whether an exequatur issued by one of the Caribbean courts of first instance has effect in the other Caribbean territories.[105] According to Israel – and I agree – that must have been the intention of the Dutch Caribbean legislator.[106] As mentioned, the starting point in the Codes of Civil Procedure is that the complete Caribbean part of the Kingdom forms a single area for the purposes of procedural law.[107] In practice, the Dutch Caribbean Courts have indeed issued exequaturs in relation to arbitral awards for all of the Dutch Caribbean jurisdictions.

11.14 Investment arbitration

The Kingdom of the Netherlands has a relatively extensive network of bilateral investment treaties (BITs), many of which contain Investor-State Dispute Settlement (ISDS) provisions.[108] Previously, the Netherlands had also concluded a number of intra-EU BITs. However, following the EU Agreement for the Termination of Intra-EU Bilateral Investment Treaties of May 2020, all intra-EU BITs have been terminated.[109] This treaty was made in response of the Achmea judgment of the Court of Justice of the European Union, which found that ISDS provisions in the intra-EU BITs

104 This follows from the single procedural area these territories form for the application of the Code of Civil Procedure. See Israel 2018, p 323-324.
105 Israel 2018, p 324.
106 Israel 2018, p 324.
107 Van den Heuvel 2016, p 180.
108 For an overview of the Dutch BITs, see A. Marsman et al., 'Investment Treaty Arbitration: Netherlands' available on the website of GAR: https://globalarbitrationreview.com/insight/know-how/investment-treaty-arbitration/report/netherlands (accessed on 10 September 2024).
109 CJEU 6 March 2018, case C-284/16, ECLI:EU:C:2018:158, *NJ* 2019/353, annotated by H.J. Snijders (*Achmea*).

were in violation of Article 267 and 344 of the Treaty on the Functioning of the European Union (TFEU).[110]

Even though the Caribbean territories are not part of the EU, the Kingdom of the Netherlands also terminated these intra-EU BITs in relation to the Dutch Caribbean territories. Although the Kingdom government had apparently sought to exclude the operation of the May 2020 Treaty for the Caribbean parts of the Kingdom, this was not accepted by the other EU countries.[111] In a statement accompanying the termination treaty, the Kingdom stressed that the Achmea judgment does not prevent the conclusion of investment treaties between the Dutch Kingdom and other EU countries as far as the Dutch Caribbean countries and territories are concerned.[112]

Additionally, all countries of the Kingdom are parties to the Washington Convention on the Settlement of Investment Disputes between States and Nationals of Other States (ICSID Convention).[113] This means that ICSID awards are in principle enforceable in the Caribbean parts of the Kingdom with only limited review of the arbitral award in accordance with Article 54 of the ICSID Convention. Local legislation designates the Courts of First Instance as the competent court under Article 54 ICSID.[114]

---

110 CJEU 6 March 2018, case C-284/16, ECLI:EU:C:2018:158, *NJ* 2019/353, annotated by H.J. Snijders (*Achmea*).

111 Letter from the Minister of Foreign Affairs to the Dutch Lower House, *Parliamentary Papers I/II*, 35649 (R2150), no 1, para 1.6. Apparently, these states took the position that they would have the right to unilaterally terminate the relevant BIT in respect of the Caribbean countries of the Kingdom, which right was expressly included in certain of the intra-EU BITs.

112 The statement can be found on https://verdragenbank.overheid.nl/en/Treaty/Details/013636_b.html (accessed on 10 September 2024). The statement reads: "The Kingdom of the Netherlands notes that bilateral investment treaties have been concluded by the Kingdom for one or more of its constituent parts. The Kingdom of the Netherlands takes the view that the judgment of the CJEU in Achmea only applies to bilateral investment treaties between the Member States of the European Union in respect of the European part of the Kingdom, and that this judgment does not apply to these bilateral investment treaties in respect of the Caribbean parts of the Kingdom, the latter parts being Overseas Countries and Territories. The present Agreement terminates the (bilateral) investment Treaties in respect of all parts of the Kingdom of the Netherlands. The Kingdom of the Netherlands wishes to stress that the CJEU's judgment in Achmea did not oblige the Kingdom of the Netherlands to terminate the bilateral investment treaties for its Overseas Countries and Territories and the decision to do so was taken irrespective of the CJEU's judgment in Achmea."

113 Convention on the settlement of investment disputes between States and nationals of other States, Washington, 18 March 1965 (*Trb*. 1966, 152).

114 National Ordinance of 18 April 1980 designating a court on the basis of Article 54 of the Washington Convention of 18 March 1965 on the settlement of investment

The Dutch law interpretation of Article 54 of the ICSID Convention is that the court should grant a request pursuant to Article 54 ICSID Convention as soon as it has verified that it has received an authentic copy of the ICSID arbitral award signed by the Secretary-General of ICSID.[115] Dutch law does not stipulate this explicitly, but the The Hague District Court handles these requests on an *ex parte* because of this limited review. Although not stated in so many words in its statutes either, in the Dutch Caribbean territories the court should also handle such request on an *ex parte* basis.

11.15 Conclusion

Even though there are several areas where statutory fallback options could have provided greater legal certainty, many of these issues can, in my view, be effectively resolved through party agreements. Moreover, it is likely that courts in the Dutch Caribbean will draw inspiration from Dutch legal concepts and, in any event, should not issue rulings that run counter to the fundamental principles underlying the Model Law. With their well-established legal systems and reliable judiciaries, the Dutch Caribbean jurisdictions still have a significant opportunity to attract more international arbitration. The ability for parties to rely on the experience of the NAI for international arbitration in Curaçao should also have a positive impact on the development of international arbitration in the Dutch Caribbean.

Parties should nevertheless consider carefully whether they wish to designate a Dutch Caribbean territory as the place of arbitration. Another option for parties doing business in the Dutch Caribbean would be to designate Amsterdam as the place of arbitration.[116] This does of course not prevent oral pleadings to take place within the Dutch Caribbean nor does it prevent the arbitral tribunal to apply the laws of the Caribbean

disputes between States and nationals of other States (Landsverordening van de 18de april 1980 tot aanwijzing van een rechter op grond van artikel 54 van het Verdrag van Washington van 18 maart 1965, inzake de beslechting van geschillen met betrekking tot investeringen tussen Staten en onderdanen van andere Staten) (*Trb.* 1966, 152).

115 M. van Leyenhorst, 'Beschouwingen naar aanleiding van het Achmea-arrest van het Hof van Justitie EU', *TvA* 2019/65, para 19; A. Marsman, *International Arbitration in the Netherlands: With a Commentary on the NAI and PCA Arbitration Rules*, Alphen aan de Rijn: Kluwer Law International 2021, p 435-436.

116 As suggested by Van Mierlo 2005, p 50; Klaassen 2024, p 42.

territories.[117] A potential advantage may be that setting aside proceedings may be conducted in English before the Netherlands Commercial Court and that any setting aside proceedings will be limited to two court instances. In addition, Dutch courts issue exequaturs on an *ex parte* basis in respect of arbitral awards rendered in the Netherlands potentially expediting the enforcement process if enforcement is expected in the European Netherlands.

117 Klaassen 2024, p 42.

CHAPTER 12

CORPORATE MEDIATION: THE DUTCH APPROACH TO MEDIATION VS. ANGLO-AMERICAN PRACTICES AND THE ENFORCEABILITY OF MEDIATION CLAUSES

Peter Kamminga & Bart Fleuren[1]

12.1 Introduction

Corporate disputes are an inevitable aspect of business operations. Mediation has increasingly become a key method for resolving conflicts across different jurisdictions. However, the practice of corporate mediation and views of enforcement of mediation clauses vary across countries. This chapter explores these differences, with a particular focus on the Netherlands.

It is structured into two parts. Part I examines the distinctive characteristics of corporate mediation in the Netherlands, drawing comparisons with Anglo-American approaches. It highlights the legal frameworks, cultural influences, and practical application of mediation in corporate settings. The role of proactive mediators and the Netherlands Arbitration Institute (NAI) in providing mediation services is also discussed. Part II addresses the enforceability of mediation clauses in the Dutch legal system, referencing recent judicial developments, including the Lotamblau Judgment of the Netherlands Supreme Court (the "**Lotamblau Judgment**"),[2] and analyzing its impact on the enforceability of mediation clauses.

---

1 Dr. Y.P. (Peter) Kamminga (LLM) is an international arbitrator and mediator at JAMS, a Fellow at Harvard Program On Negotiation, and an Associate Professor of Law at the law faculty of the VU Amsterdam.
B.M.H. (Bart) Fleuren (LLM) is a lawyer admitted to the Netherlands Supreme Court Bar (*Advocaat bij de Hoge Raad*) and counsel at Linklaters LLP in Amsterdam. He acted on behalf of Lotamblau in the case that led up to the Supreme Court's decision in this matter (Supreme Court 12 July 2024, ECLI:NL:HR:2024:1078 (*Lotamblau Investments (CSW)/PPSB)*). This article is written on a personal title only and does not reflect a party position. The authors thank T. (Thomas) de Boer (LLM) for his assistance in writing this article.

2 Supreme Court 12 July 2024, ECLI:NL:HR:2024:1078 (*Lotamblau*).

This chapter analyzes these aspects and provides legal professionals with key insights into corporate mediation's growing relevance in the Dutch business landscape and practical tools to leverage mediation for efficient dispute resolution.

12.2 Part I: Characteristics and dynamics of corporate mediation

12.2.1 Corporate mediation

Corporate mediation is a term that covers the mediation of a variety of business-related disputes between two or more organizations. In the Netherlands it is also often more generally referred to as business mediation ("*zakelijke mediation*") or commercial mediation. It generally includes disputes between companies, their departments, or disputes with external professional parties, including shareholders.[3] Corporate mediation offers a structured method for resolving disputes, involving an impartial third-party mediator who facilitates communication between the parties. This process aims to resolve disputes while maintaining confidentiality, preserving business relationships, and ensuring cost-effectiveness.

The disputes handled through corporate mediation can involve management, employees, shareholders, external stakeholders, or business partners. The complexity of the issues often demands mediators with specific expertise in legal and financial matters. The well-known advantages include:

a) Confidentiality: corporate mediation ensures that sensitive information, such as trade secrets and intellectual property, is protected from public exposure;
b) Cost-Effectiveness: mediation is generally faster and less expensive than litigation, especially when time-sensitive business operations are at stake;
c) Preservation of Relationships: mediation promotes a non-adversarial process that helps parties to either dissolve or maintain business relationships after resolving conflicts.

3 See for a variety of definitions of corporate mediation for instance: M. Brink, 'Corporate mediation in the Netherlands', European Company Law (14) 2017, p 91-97; E. Schutte, 'Mediation in ondernemings(rechtelijke) geschillen', in: C.J.M. Klaassen, G.J. Meijer & C.L. Schleijpen (eds), Going Dutch. ADR in Nederland, in het bijzonder bij het NAI (Onderneming en recht no 113), Deventer: Wolters Kluwer 2019, p 324.

Common types of disputes handled through corporate mediation include contractual disagreements, shareholder disputes, insurance coverage disputes, mergers and acquisitions conflicts, and intellectual property issues.

Corporate mediation is also characterized by its ability to offer tailored solutions. Unlike court-imposed rulings, which are often rigid and based on legal precedent, mediation allows for more creative resolutions that can meet the unique needs of the parties involved. Mediators facilitate a dialogue that helps parties reach mutually beneficial outcomes, often addressing not only the legal aspects of a dispute but also operational and relational concerns. This flexibility is particularly valuable in complex, multi-faceted corporate disputes, where the issues at stake extend beyond purely legal arguments to encompass broader business interests, such as future partnerships, reputational concerns, and market positioning.

Moreover, the voluntary nature of corporate mediation contributes to its effectiveness. Parties who engage in mediation do so with the intent to find a solution outside of the courtroom, fostering a cooperative environment. This willingness to collaborate often leads to faster, more amicable settlements, which is crucial for businesses that prioritize swift resolutions to maintain continuity in their operations. The voluntary aspect also empowers parties to have greater control over the process, as they can dictate the pace of negotiations and agree on the terms without the constraints of formal litigation.

12.2.2 *What makes corporate mediation unique*

Corporate mediation differs significantly from other forms of mediation due to the complexity of the disputes that are mediated, the need for specialized expertise, and its emphasis on confidentiality and long-term business relationships. These characteristics distinguish corporate mediation from, for instance, personal or community-based mediations, where emotional resolution is often one of the primary goals.

12.2.2.1 Complexity of corporate disputes

Corporate disputes often involve multiple parties, intricate contracts, and detailed regulatory frameworks. Mediators in this context must have a robust understanding of both legal intricacies and the operational realities of business. For example, in a shareholder dispute, the mediator must navigate complex corporate governance laws, different classes of shares, and minority shareholder rights. Such disputes require mediators who are adept in both legal and financial matters.

12.2.2.2 Specialized expertise

Corporate mediation often demands mediators with deep legal and industry-specific knowledge. Unlike mediations in personal disputes, where emotional intelligence is crucial, corporate mediation requires technical expertise to guide parties toward practical, enforceable resolutions. For instance, in merger disputes, mediators with experience in M&A law and valuation techniques are essential to helping the parties reach a settlement that addresses both legal and financial complexities.

12.2.2.3 Confidentiality

Confidentiality is critical in corporate mediation, particularly when sensitive business information is involved. Disclosing trade secrets or other confidential information could cause significant reputational and financial harm to a business. For example, in an intellectual property dispute, the protection of sensitive details concerning patents and proprietary technology is crucial. Mediators must ensure that all discussions remain private to prevent external exposure.

12.2.2.4 Outcome-oriented focus

Corporate mediation tends to be highly outcome-oriented, seeking practical, swift solutions that allow businesses to continue operations with minimal disruption. Unlike in family mediation, where emotional reconciliation may be prioritized, the focus in corporate mediation is on delivering results that safeguard the business. For instance, in disputes over contracts, the goal is often to resolve the matter as quickly as possible to avoid disruptions to business operations.

12.2.2.5 Preservation of long-term business relationships

The non-adversarial nature of mediation helps parties maintain business relationships after resolving a dispute, which is crucial in ongoing partnerships. For example, a supply chain dispute between a manufacturer and a key supplier may be settled in a way that preserves the business relationship, ensuring future cooperation.

12.2.2.6 Time sensitivity

Corporate mediation typically requires fast resolutions to avoid significant financial losses or missed business opportunities. Mediators must work efficiently to resolve disputes before they cause lasting harm to the business. For example, in a time-sensitive dispute, such as a breach of contract affecting a major project, mediation can prevent project delays and financial losses.

12.2.3 Corporate mediation: a comparative analysis of the US, the UK, and the Netherlands

While corporate mediation shares common goals across jurisdictions, the practices vary significantly between the United States, the United Kingdom, and the Netherlands. These differences stem from distinct legal frameworks, business cultures, and mediators' roles in the process.[4] For legal professionals and businesses engaged in cross-border disputes, understanding these nuances is crucial to effectively navigating international mediation.[5] What follows is a detailed comparison of corporate mediation in these three countries, focusing on the legal framework, the role of mediators, and the confidentiality and enforceability of settlement agreements.

12.2.3.1 Legal framework

In the United States, mediation is firmly embedded in the legal system as part of the broader Alternative Dispute Resolution (ADR) movement.[6] Mediation is often mandated by courts as a pre-trial step in civil and commercial cases, with the primary aim of reducing litigation costs and alleviating the burden on an already congested judicial system.[7] In many jurisdictions, judges encourage or even require parties to engage in mediation before proceeding to litigation, particularly in corporate disputes. The US approach to mediation is typically evaluative – mediators are expected to

4 C. Menkel-Meadow, 'Variations in the uptake of and resistance to mediation outside of the United States', in: W. Rovine (ed), *Contemporary issues in international arbitration and mediation: The Fordham papers 2014*, Leiden: Brill Nijhoff 2015, p 189-221.

5 Y.P. Kamminga, '6 key factors for successful cross-border dispute mediation', *Law360* 2022.

6 J. Folberg, 'A mediation overview: History and dimensions of practice', *Mediation Quarterly* 2015, p 3.

7 M. Galanter, '... A settlement judge, not a trial judge: Judicial mediation in the United States', *Journal of Law & Society* (12) 1985, p 1-18.

assess the legal merits of each party's position and provide informed guidance on the likely outcome should the dispute proceed to court.[8] For example, in a contract dispute between two corporations, a mediator might evaluate the enforceability of the contract and offer an opinion on what damages could be awarded by a judge, guiding the parties toward settlement by highlighting potential litigation risks. This evaluative approach is especially useful in cases where legal clarity and efficiency are paramount, helping the parties reach a resolution based on the mediator's legal insight and experience.

In contrast, mediation in the United Kingdom is generally voluntary, though strongly encouraged as a cost-effective and efficient alternative to litigation.[9] The Civil Procedure Rules in the UK promote the use of mediation, particularly following the Woolf Reforms, which were introduced to modernize and streamline the legal process.[10] However, mediation is not mandatory in most cases. The UK favors a facilitative approach to mediation, where the mediator's role is to guide the parties toward a solution without offering legal opinions or specific recommendations.[11] Mediators are focused on creating an environment conducive to open dialogue, helping the parties understand each other's positions and negotiate a mutually beneficial outcome. For example, in a merger dispute between two companies, the mediator might facilitate discussions to explore areas of agreement without providing detailed legal advice on how a court might interpret the terms of the merger. This facilitative model reflects the UK's broader business culture, which values negotiation and compromise.

In the Netherlands, mediation operates within a civil law framework and remains largely voluntary. While Dutch courts may suggest mediation as an option for resolving disputes, it is not typically mandated. The Dutch approach to mediation emphasizes neutral facilitation, with mediators focusing on helping parties communicate effectively and work toward a

---

8 S.B. Goldberg et al, *Dispute resolution: Negotiation, mediation, arbitration, and other processes*, Boston: Aspen Publishing 2020.

9 A. de Roo & R. Jagtenberg, 'Mediation en modernisering van de rechtspraak in Engeland', *Nederlands-Vlaams tijdschrift voor mediation en conflictmanagement* 2024, issue 1, p 33-56.

10 L.H. Woolf, 'Civil justice in the United Kingdom', *The American Journal of Comparative Law* (45) 1997, p 709-736.

11 P. Brooker & A. Lavers, 'Mediation outcomes: Lawyers' experience with commercial and construction mediation in the United Kingdom', *Pepperdine Dispute Resolution Law Journal* (5) 2005, p 161-213; J. Player, 'Mediation of corporate disputes in UK', *European Company Law* (14) 2017, p 104-107.

consensus without imposing legal judgments or offering specific opinions on the merits of the case. Mediators in the Netherlands are seen as facilitators of dialogue, rather than evaluators of legal positions. For example, in a shareholder dispute, a Dutch mediator would encourage open communication, ensuring that both parties' interests are addressed, and that the conversation remains constructive. The mediator would avoid steering the parties toward a particular outcome or offering a legal analysis, in keeping with the Dutch emphasis on collaboration and consensus-building.

12.2.3.2 The role of mediators

The role of mediators varies significantly across jurisdictions, shaped by the legal traditions and business cultures of each country.

In the United States, mediators frequently take an evaluative role, particularly in corporate and commercial disputes. This means that they actively assess the strengths and weaknesses of each party's legal position and provide opinions on the likely outcome should the case proceed to litigation. Mediators in the US, many of whom come from legal backgrounds, such as judges or senior attorneys, are often seen as quasi-advisors who help guide the parties toward settlement by offering realistic assessments of the potential risks and benefits of continuing with formal litigation. Their expertise allows them to offer more directive feedback, helping parties make informed decisions about whether to settle or litigate. This evaluative model is particularly suited to disputes where legal clarity and expediency are critical, such as high-stakes commercial contract cases.

In the United Kingdom, mediators generally adopt a facilitative approach.[12] Their primary role is to help parties reach their own solutions through interest-based negotiations, without providing legal opinions or specific recommendations. UK mediators focus on fostering open communication and creating an environment in which the parties can explore their interests, discuss their needs, and work together to craft a mutually acceptable resolution. However, in more complex or high-value commercial disputes, there is a growing trend toward evaluative mediation, where mediators may offer limited guidance or suggest potential settlement terms based

12 M. Schonewille & J. Lack, 'Mediation in the European Union and abroad: 60 states divided by a common word?', in: M. Schonewille & F. Schonewille (eds), *The variegated landscape of mediation,* The Hague: Eleven International Publishing 2014, p 19; N. Andrews, *Mediation in England. The Three paths of justice: Court proceedings, arbitration, and mediation in England,* New York: Springer 2018, p 265-288, p 13.

on their understanding of the case. Nonetheless, UK mediators typically avoid being as directive as their US counterparts, instead aiming to maintain the autonomy of the parties throughout the negotiation process.

In the Netherlands, mediators continue to adhere to a neutral and facilitative model, reflecting the country's broader cultural preference for consensus-building. Dutch mediators are trained to ensure that both parties are given equal opportunity to express their positions and interests, guiding the conversation without imposing judgments or recommendations. Their role is to maintain a balanced and neutral environment in which parties can collaboratively work toward a resolution that suits their mutual interests. This neutral facilitation is particularly important in a corporate context, where ongoing business relationships may be at stake, and the parties are often seeking to resolve disputes in a way that allows for future collaboration. By refraining from offering legal opinions, Dutch mediators help the parties retain control over the outcome, ensuring that the resolution is one they are both fully invested in.

12.2.3.3 Confidentiality and enforceability of settlement agreements

Confidentiality and enforceability are two fundamental aspects of corporate mediation, particularly when sensitive business information, trade secrets, or intellectual property is involved. The manner in which these elements are treated varies significantly between jurisdictions, requiring legal professionals to have a comprehensive understanding of the applicable rules and their implications for dispute resolution. This section provides an overview of how confidentiality and enforceability are addressed in the United States, the United Kingdom, and the Netherlands.

In the United States, confidentiality in mediation is governed by state law, resulting in significant variation across jurisdictions. Some states, such as California, have stringent laws that protect the confidentiality of mediation sessions, ensuring that nothing said during mediation can be used as evidence in subsequent court proceedings. Other states have less clearly defined rules, which may leave confidentiality protections open to interpretation. Additionally, while most states enforce confidentiality through statutes or case law, there is no uniform federal standard governing mediation confidentiality. This lack of consistency can pose challenges for legal practitioners, particularly in cross-state or cross-border disputes.

Settlement agreements in the US are generally enforceable as contracts, provided they meet the requirements of contract law in the relevant jurisdiction. However, the enforceability of these agreements can differ depending on the specific state's laws. In some cases, parties may seek to have their settlement agreements formalized through a consent decree or incorporated into a court judgment to ensure easier enforcement. For legal professionals, it is crucial to understand the nuances of state law and ensure that settlement agreements are drafted in a way that maximizes their enforceability.

In the United Kingdom, confidentiality is strongly protected by the "Without Prejudice" rule, which ensures that any communications or disclosures made during mediation cannot be used as evidence if the dispute proceeds to litigation.[13] This rule provides businesses with the assurance that they can negotiate openly during mediation without fear that their statements will be used against them in court. The robust confidentiality protections in the UK are a key factor in the widespread use of mediation in corporate disputes, allowing parties to engage in candid discussions that are essential for resolving complex business conflicts.

Settlement agreements in the UK are enforceable as contracts and can be made legally binding through consent orders. This means that, once a settlement is reached, the parties can ask the court to formalize the agreement, making it enforceable as a court order. This provides an additional layer of security, as failure to comply with the terms of a consent order can result in sanctions or enforcement actions. For legal practitioners, advising clients on the benefits of formalizing settlement agreements through consent orders is essential for ensuring that the settlement can be upheld if any issues arise post-mediation.

In the Netherlands, confidentiality is a cornerstone of the mediation process. Dutch law provides strong protections for the privacy of mediation sessions, ensuring that sensitive business information remains confidential. Mediation participants are generally bound by confidentiality agreements, and mediators are required to maintain the confidentiality of all communications made during the mediation process. This focus on confidentiality is particularly important in the Netherlands' corporate mediation landscape, where the protection of trade secrets, proprietary technologies, and internal business strategies is often a critical concern.

13 Andrews 2018, p 13.

Settlement agreements in the Netherlands are enforceable under Dutch contract law, which recognizes these agreements as binding contracts between the parties. If necessary, parties can seek to have their settlement agreements formalized through a court order, giving them the same legal standing as other contractual obligations. In cross-border disputes, Dutch settlement agreements can also be converted into arbitral awards, ensuring easier enforcement across jurisdictions. This flexibility makes mediation a particularly attractive option for resolving complex corporate disputes in the Netherlands, especially in cases involving international parties.

While confidentiality and enforceability are integral to corporate mediation across all three jurisdictions, the approach taken in each country reflects their respective legal traditions. In the US, state-specific rules necessitate careful drafting to ensure enforceability, while in the UK, the Without Prejudice rule and the use of consent orders provide strong protections and enforcement mechanisms. In the Netherlands, the emphasis on confidentiality and the ability to formalize settlements agreements through court orders or arbitral awards ensures both privacy and legal security. Legal practitioners must navigate these differences carefully to provide effective guidance to clients engaging in corporate mediation, particularly in cross-border disputes. In the second part of this chapter, we will go in much more detail on enforceability of mediation clauses.

12.2.4 Mediation styles in corporate disputes

In corporate mediation, two primary approaches are commonly employed: facilitative mediation and evaluative mediation.[14] Each style serves distinct purposes and is suited to different types of disputes, depending on the nature of the conflict and the desired outcome.[15] Legal professionals advising clients on mediation strategies must understand the nuances of each approach to guide them effectively.

12.2.4.1 Facilitative mediation

Facilitative mediation centers on fostering open communication and encouraging the parties to explore their underlying interests.[16] The media-

14 See for an overview of styles per country: Schonewille & Lack 2014.

15 J.J. Alfini, 'Evaluative versus facilitative mediation: A discussion', *Florida State University Law Review* (24) 1997, p 919-935.

16 C.J. Brown, 'Facilitative mediation: the classic approach retains its appeal', *Pepperdine Dispute Resolution Law Journal* (4) 2004, p 279-296.

tor's role in this approach is to facilitate discussions without offering legal advice or steering the parties toward a specific outcome. Instead, the mediator helps the parties themselves generate potential solutions through negotiation and dialogue.

This approach is particularly valuable when preserving long-term relationships is a priority, such as in partnerships or supplier agreements. The mediator encourages both parties to focus on their shared interests and mutual goals, rather than their differences. Facilitative mediation is also highly effective in multi-party disputes, where differing interests need to be balanced but the parties remain motivated to work collaboratively.

For example, consider a dispute between a manufacturing company and several of its key suppliers over delayed deliveries. In such a case, facilitative mediation might focus on uncovering the root causes of the delays while ensuring that the parties work together to maintain the supply chain. Rather than imposing a solution, the mediator would guide the parties toward a resolution that meets the needs of both sides, allowing the business relationship to continue without further disruption. This collaborative problem-solving approach helps the parties reach a creative, interest-based solution that goes beyond traditional legal remedies and is tailored to their specific needs.

12.2.4.2 Evaluative mediation

On the other hand, evaluative mediation involves a more active role for the mediator, who provides opinions on the legal merits of each party's case and may predict likely court outcomes. This approach is typically more directive – the mediator assesses the strengths and weaknesses of the parties' positions and may suggest potential settlement options based on these assessments.[17]

Evaluative mediation is often chosen for high-stakes disputes, where the parties seek a clear, legally grounded resolution. It is particularly suited for disputes involving contract breaches, financial disagreements, or intellectual property issues, where legal clarity and time sensitivity are crucial. In these scenarios, the mediator's guidance can expedite the settlement

17 See for a breakdown of the process e.g. Y.P. Kamminga, 'Ex parte mediation: voor de pragmatische partij die het zonder al te veel drama opgelost wil hebben', *Tijdschrift Conflicthantering* 2019, issue 4, p 34-39.

process by helping the parties understand the legal risks associated with continuing litigation.

For example, in a high-value contract dispute between two financial institutions, evaluative mediation allows the mediator to weigh in on the interpretation of the contract and assess whether a breach has occurred. By offering a realistic forecast of how a court might rule, the mediator helps both parties to make informed decisions about whether to settle or proceed to court. This evaluative input accelerates the process, leading to a faster resolution while still considering the legal complexities of the case.

12.2.4.3 Which style is best for corporate mediation?

There are strong proponents and critics of both facilitative and evaluative mediation approaches. The appropriate choice between facilitative and evaluative mediation largely depends on preference and the specific circumstances of the dispute.[18] Facilitative mediation is ideal when the goal is to preserve ongoing business relationships and explore innovative, interest-based solutions. This approach works particularly well in industries where future cooperation is crucial, and the parties are motivated to reach a solution that will allow them to continue working together after the dispute is resolved.

In contrast, evaluative mediation is better suited for cases where a legally focused and swift resolution is required, especially in high-stakes disputes. Here, the parties are more interested in obtaining a legally sound outcome and may benefit from the mediator's legal expertise and insight into likely court outcomes. This approach tends to be more effective when the parties prioritize legal clarity over relationship preservation, such as in complex contract disputes or matters involving significant financial implications.

In the United States the evaluative style is the most common approach in corporate disputes. In the Netherlands, corporate mediation has historically favored the facilitative approach,[19] in line with the country's preference for consensus-driven and collaborative solutions. Dutch business culture places a high value on maintaining long-term relationships, and facilitative mediation aligns well with this focus on building sustainable outcomes. However, as corporate disputes become more complex, particularly in sec-

18 D.J. Della Noce, 'Evaluative mediation: In search of practice competencies', *Conflict Resolution Quarterly* (27) 2009, p 193-214.

19 P. Boshouwers, 'Stijlverschillen', *Adv.bl.* 2015, issue 9, p 56.

tors like finance and technology, there is a growing call for and acceptance of evaluative mediation.[20] This shift reflects the need for timely resolutions and legal certainty, particularly in cross-border disputes or cases involving substantial financial risk.

For example, in a cross-border corporate merger dispute involving a Dutch company and a UK-based partner, the facilitative approach could help the parties explore their underlying concerns without getting bogged down in legal technicalities. However, if the dispute involves complex financial and regulatory issues, an evaluative approach may be more appropriate. In this case, the mediator could provide legal assessments to help the parties understand the risks and benefits of potential settlement options, guiding them toward a resolution that reflects both legal realities and business priorities.

12.2.5 The current state of corporate mediation in the Netherlands

Mediation is currently used in a relatively small percentage of corporate disputes, yet it is a common topic of conversation when disputes arise, and its use seems to be on the rise.[21] The views on corporate mediation in the Netherlands have experienced notable evolution over the past decade, driven by a growing call for faster, more pragmatic dispute resolution methods. Research suggests that Dutch businesses increasingly view mediation as an effective tool for resolving corporate disputes, with a clear shift in expectations regarding the role of mediators and the overall mediation process.[22] This shift is supported by data from both a 2018 survey

20 Two surveys of the views on and experiences with business mediation were conducted over the past years. The 2018 and 2024 surveys both seem to indicate that users and attorneys prefer a more pro-active and directive mediator: M. Simon Thomas et al, *ZAM/ACB Onderzoek naar kansen en belemmeringen voor zakelijke mediation*, Utrecht: Montaigne Centrum voor Rechtsspraak en Rechtspleging 2018 (last visited on September 17, 2024), available at: www.uu.nl/nieuws/onderzoeksrapport-naar-zakelijke-mediation-in-nederland (hereafter: ZAM/ACB-onderzoek 2018); S. Thomas et al, *PBM Vervolgonderzoek naar kansen en belemmeringen voor zakelijke mediation: onder advocaten en bedrijven in Nederland* (last visited on September 17, 2024), available at: https://platformbusinessmediation.nl/rapport-vervolgonderzoek-naar-kansen-en-belemmeringen-voor-zakelijke-mediation-in-nederland/ (hereafter: PBM Vervolgonderzoek 2024).

21 See on obstacles for the use of mediation in complex corporate disputes, for instance, Y.P. Kamminga, 'Using mediation in multi-party disputes, or Why complex matters still go to litigation', in: P. Cecchi Dimeglio & B. Brenneur (eds), *Interdisciplinary handbook of dispute resolution*, Brussels: Larcier 2015.

22 M. Schonewille & M.S. Thomas, 'Veel potentie voor zakelijke mediation', *Nederlands Vlaams Tijdschrift voor Mediation, en conflictmanagement* 2019, issue 1, p 6-12;

among users of mediation, attorneys and Judges, and an updated 2024 report, which provide valuable insights into the changing landscape of corporate mediation.[23] Both were follow-ups of earlier studies into mediation experiences and expectations.[24]

12.2.5.1 The growing call for proactive mediators

According to the 2018 survey, Dutch businesses expressed a clear preference for proactive mediators who take an active role in guiding discussions and offering solutions.[25] The traditional facilitative model, where mediators primarily facilitate dialogue without providing specific advice, was seen as less effective in the face of complex corporate disputes. Businesses favored mediators who could leverage their legal and industry expertise to not only facilitate conversations but also provide structured guidance that helped the parties understand the legal ramifications of their positions.[26] This reflects the complexity of corporate disputes in the Netherlands, where parties often need more than just facilitation to reach a resolution.

The updated 2024 report further reinforces this trend, showing that both businesses and legal professionals now expect mediators to have deep knowledge of legal frameworks and industry practices.[27] The report suggests that mediators are no longer seen as mere facilitators of communication but are expected to act as strategic partners who help shape the resolution process. This shift has been particularly noticeable in high-stakes disputes involving multi-party contracts, cross-border mergers, and complex regulatory issues, where proactive mediation helps parties navigate legal intricacies while maintaining a cooperative atmosphere. The proactive approach aligns well with the needs of businesses seeking not just a resolution but one that considers the long-term implications for ongoing business relationships and compliance with regulatory requirements.

E. Schutte & J. Spierdijk, 'Wat kunnen (Zakelijk) mediators leren van de markt?', *Tijdschrift Conflicthantering* 2024, issue 2, p 63-65.

23 ZAM/ACB-onderzoek 2018.

24 Global Pound Conferences 2016-2017. Local voting results, Amsterdam 2017 (hereafter: GPC 2017); M. Schonewille, *Winst maken bij het oplossen van geschillen: conflictmanagement en mediation in Nederlandse ondernemingen*, The Hague: ACB Mediation 2004, http://toolkitcompany.com/data/files/Resource%20center/Research%20and%20surveys/ marktonderzoek_rapport%20ACB%202004.pdf (last visited September 17, 2024).

25 ZAM/ACB-onderzoek 2018.

26 Schonewille & Thomas 2019.

27 PBM Vervolgonderzoek 2024.

For instance, in disputes related to mergers and acquisitions, it is of great benefit if mediators have expertise in M&A law, financial structuring, and post-merger integration. These mediators assist parties in understanding not only the immediate terms of the settlement, but also the broader impacts on corporate governance, shareholder rights, and financial health, guiding them toward a resolution that is both legally sound and strategically aligned with their business goals.

12.2.5.2 Speed and cost-effectiveness: A key advantage

Both the 2018 survey and the 2024 report highlight the value Dutch businesses and their attorneys place on the speed and cost-effectiveness of mediation as compared to litigation. The ability to resolve disputes quickly without incurring the heavy costs associated with court proceedings is a major reason why corporate mediation is starting to gain traction in the Netherlands. The 2024 report underscores that time-sensitive industries, such as technology, logistics, and financial services, particularly benefit from the use of mediation to avoid the delays and resource drain that can result from protracted litigation.

12.2.5.3 The preservation of long-term business relationships

A central benefit of corporate mediation that users identify, as confirmed by both the 2018 survey and the 2024 report, is its ability to preserve long-term business relationships. Dutch users, particularly those with complex supply chains or joint ventures, value the ability to resolve disputes without permanently damaging professional relationships. Mediation's collaborative nature encourages parties to work together to find mutually beneficial solutions, focusing on common interests rather than entrenching adversarial positions.

The reports indicate that companies and their attorneys appreciate the way mediation fosters goodwill between parties, even in the face of serious disagreements. This emphasis on preserving relationships is particularly important in industries where partnerships and long-term contracts play a crucial role in business continuity. By resolving disputes through mediation, businesses can avoid the lasting harm that often accompanies contentious litigation. Also the role of mediators reflecting on emotions and the interaction between parties are indicated as important factors, even in business settings.[28]

28 Schonewille & Thomas 2019; Schutte & Spierdijk 2024.

12.2.5.4 The rise of hybrid models: med-arb and Its growing popularity

One other trend identified in the 2024 report is the rising popularity of hybrid dispute resolution models among users, particularly med-arb (mediation-arbitration).[29] The report highlights that med-arb has become an attractive option for Dutch businesses seeking the benefits of both mediation and arbitration.[30] In a med-arb process, the parties first attempt to resolve their dispute through mediation.[31] If mediation is unsuccessful, the mediator can transition into the role of an arbitrator, or a separate arbitrator can be appointed, to take a binding decision on any unresolved issues.

This model is gaining traction because it combines the flexibility and collaboration of mediation with the finality and enforceability of arbitration. Any settlement reached during med-arb can later be formalized as a final award by the tribunal, allowing it to benefit from the enforcement provisions of the New York Convention.[32] Businesses are increasingly drawn to med-arb because it offers a structured pathway to resolution while ensuring that the matter will be conclusively settled even if consensus cannot be reached during the mediation phase.

Corporate mediation in the Netherlands is evolving, with businesses favoring proactive mediators, seeking greater speed and cost-effectiveness. Yet, it is still far from the default route in resolving corporate disputes. As the corporate mediation landscape continues to shift, legal professionals must stay informed of these developments to advise clients effectively and ensure that mediation is leveraged to its fullest potential.

---

29 Schutte & Spierdijk 2024.

30 The interest in these models is also reflected the outcomes of the Global Pound Conference in Amsterdam 2017. Among the highest ranked answers given in response to a question about how to improve future commercial dispute resolution was combining adjudicative (i.e. arbitration) and non-adjudicative (i.e. mediation) processes, GPC 2017.

31 See about this model and its potential in the Dutch setting for instance Y.P. Kamminga, 'Quickscan van efficiente ADR vormen', *Tijdschrift Conflicthantering* 2019, issue 4, p 27-29.

32 Potential issues that may arise if a party challenges the process over concerns about impartiality or fairness can be reduced by procedural safeguards, see on med-arb and enforceability also B. van Zelst, 'European perspectives on enforcement of med-arb clauses and med-arb awards', *Corporate Mediation Journal* 2018, p 12.

12.2.6 *The role of the Netherlands Arbitration Institute (NAI) in mediation*

A number of providers and institutions offer mediation services in the Netherlands. The Netherlands Arbitration Institute (NAI), renowned for its arbitration services, also offers mediation as a flexible, confidential, and effective method for resolving corporate disputes. The NAI's mediation services are designed to offer a structured but adaptable process tailored to the particular needs of commercial disputes.[33] The flexibility inherent in the mediation process allows for innovative solutions, ensuring that all parties have the opportunity to address their concerns fully, while the mediator helps facilitate dialogue and resolution.

Mediation at the NAI is entirely voluntary, reflecting the Dutch legal culture that values choice and flexibility in dispute resolution. This voluntary nature ensures that parties enter the process willingly and in good faith, making it more likely that they will reach an agreement. Legal counsel and businesses may opt for mediation as a standalone process, or they can use it as a precursor to more formal arbitration or litigation, depending on the evolving needs of the dispute.

If the mediation process successfully results in an agreement, the parties can formalize their settlement, which can be legally binding and enforceable under Dutch contract law. Additionally, the flexibility of NAI mediation allows parties to convert their settlement into an arbitral award, which facilitates cross-border enforcement. This combination of mediation and arbitration strengthens the overall dispute resolution process by providing parties with multiple avenues for finality and legal enforceability.

The NAI regularly updates its mediation rules to ensure that the process remains transparent and fair.[34] These rules are designed to provide clear guidelines, minimizing potential disputes about procedure and ensuring that both parties are aware of their rights and responsibilities throughout the process.

One of the key aspects of NAI mediation is the list procedure used when parties cannot agree on a mediator. In such cases, the NAI proposes a list of qualified mediators, from which the parties can rank or veto potential

33 See https://nai.nl/mediation/.

34 See https://nai.nl/nai-mediation-rules and F. Von Hombracht, 'Wijziging NAI-reglement per 1 januari 2017', *Nederlands Vlaams Tijdschrift voor Mediation, en conflictmanagement* 2017, issue 1, p 53-54.

candidates. This process ensures that the appointed mediator is acceptable to both sides, thereby reducing the risk of bias or dissatisfaction with the mediator's neutrality.

The NAI's approach to mediation primarily follows the facilitative model, focusing on helping parties understand each other's perspectives and work collaboratively toward a solution. This style of mediation aligns with the Dutch emphasis on consensus-building and cooperation, ensuring that the process remains flexible and open-ended, with the mediator encouraging negotiation but refraining from providing legal opinions or making evaluative judgments, unless explicitly requested by the parties.

Transparency is a cornerstone of the NAI's approach to mediation, and mediator fees are typically based on hourly rates, with the NAI ensuring that these rates are clearly communicated to all parties from the outset. This approach to affordability has made mediation an attractive alternative for many Dutch businesses, who seek to resolve their disputes without the financial burden and time constraints often associated with more formal dispute resolution methods.

Having explored the intricate dynamics and characteristics of corporate mediation in the Netherlands, contrasting it with mediation in other leading countries, we now turn our attention to a critical aspect that underpins the practical application of mediation clauses: their enforceability. While Part I detailed the tailored approaches and the flexibility that mediation offers in corporate disputes, Part II delves into the legal frameworks that govern these practices. The enforceability of mediation clauses, as tested in recent judicial decisions, in particular the Lotamblau Judgment, plays a pivotal role in shaping the landscape of dispute resolution. This section will examine how these legal principles interact with the practicalities of mediation, thus influencing the willingness of parties to engage in and adhere to mediation clauses, ultimately affecting the overall efficacy of mediation in the corporate sector.

12.3 Part II: The enforceability of a mediation clause

12.3.1 Introduction

Mediation clauses are part of contracts in all shapes and sizes. By a mediation clause, we mean an agreement or part of an agreement, by which the parties agree to attempt to settle disputes through mediation.[35] Parties often choose a so-called multi-tier dispute resolution clause, which requires that parties attempt to try to resolve disputes through mediation before they can initiate court or arbitral proceedings. What then if a party decides to skip this step and go straight to court or an arbitral tribunal without having attempted mediation?

Contrary to (for example) arbitration, the Netherlands does not have any specific legislation governing mediation.[36] Over the past decade, four different initiatives have arisen (and failed). Two of these are most relevant for this contribution.[37] First, in 2013 a Member of Parliament[38] submitted three bills[39] that provided for extensive regulation of the field of mediation. Importantly, one proposed provision entailed that a court would have been compelled to stay proceedings in case the parties had bypassed a mediation clause agreed on prior to initiation of the court proceedings. Only after the parties informed the court that mediation failed, would proceedings continue.[40] Second, after the 2013 Bills were revoked,[41] the Dutch government presented a draft bill in 2016[42] which, while still providing legislation on mediation clauses, did not attach as much effect to them. Specifically, whereas the 2013 Bills would have subjected the courts to a straightforward rule (i.e., to stay proceedings in case a mediation clause had not been effectuated),

35 A mediation clause should be sharply distinguished from a mediation agreement (i.e. the contract between the parties and mediator, by which the mediator is appointed). A mediation clause may oblige a party to enter into a mediation agreement or only to attend an introductory meeting with a mediator, which may or may not lead to the conclusion of a mediation agreement.

36 See Opinion of Advocate General De Bock rendered prior to Supreme Court 12 July 2024, ECLI:NL:PHR:2024:103, para 9, wherein these attempts are described in detail. The discussion of the (draft) bills below is primarily based on De Bock's work.

37 The other two initiatives did not contemplate the effects of (enforceable) mediation clauses.

38 G.A. (Ard) van der Steur.

39 Hereafter referred to as the '2013 Bills'.

40 The proposed provision (Article 22a(2) DCCP) reads (translated): "If the parties have agreed in advance to apply mediation in the event of a dispute regarding a legal relationship between them, the judge before whom a dispute is brought that is subject to the relevant clause, shall stay the proceedings if it appears that the parties have not effectuated the clause. The proceedings will be continued after the parties have informed the judge that the mediation, after its commencement, has ended without agreement."; see *Parliamentary Papers II* 2013/14, 33723, 33722 and 33727, no 4, p 36.

41 Van der Steur left parliament to become Minister of Security and Justice (*Veiligheid en Justitie*), a position he would hold between 2015 and 2017. No other members of parliament took over the 2013 Bills.

42 Hereafter referred to as the '2016 Draft Bill'.

the 2016 Draft Bill allowed them more discretion. In the event a mediation clause had not been adhered to, a court would have had to assess (through discussion with the parties) if an amicable settlement through mediation was possible, and refer parties to mediation if this was the case.[43] In the end, however, the 2016 Draft Bill was never enacted.[44]

Absent legislation, development of the legal framework on mediation has been left to the Dutch judiciary. Historically, Dutch courts attached no consequences to bypassed mediation clauses. They did so on the basis of a Supreme Court judgment that was commonly held to provide as much. A majority of Dutch authors fiercely disagreed, however, and argued that mediation clauses were, in fact, binding upon the parties. These authors have been proven right. In its Lotamblau Judgment, the Supreme Court clarified that mediation clauses can be binding and/or enforceable if the mediation clause stipulates that parties are required to attempt mediation prior to starting proceedings. In its Lotamblau Judgment, the Supreme Court took a stance in a longstanding debate between proponents of 'voluntary' mediation on the one hand, and proponents of the principle of *pacta sunt servanda* (i.e., enforceable mediation clauses) on the other.

Below, we will first discuss the advantages and disadvantages of making mediation clauses enforceable. Subsequently, we will assess the approach other jurisdictions have taken in relation to enforceable mediation clauses. Finally, we address the Lotamblau Judgment and further questions it has given rise to.

12.3.2 *The advantages and disadvantages of an enforceable mediation clause*

One of the main principles of mediation is that the parties involved take part in the process on a voluntary basis. This voluntary nature of mediation can be construed in many different ways, however. This is particularly true if parties have previously added a mediation clause to their contracts.

43 The proposed draft provision (Article 22a(2) DCCP) reads (translated): "In matters that are at the discretion of the parties, and where the parties have agreed to apply mediation in the event of a dispute concerning a legal relationship between them, the judge investigates whether an amicable resolution with the help of mediation is possible." (accessed via https://www.internetconsultatie.nl/wetmediation/details).

44 See Opinion of Advocate General De Bock rendered prior to Supreme Court 12 July 2024, ECLI:NL:PHR:2024:103, paras 9.30-9.31. The reason for this was a lack of support due to the manner in which the draft bill sought to legislate the profession of mediator. See also *Parliamentary Papers II*, 29528, no 13, p 3-4.

Generally speaking, the discussion on the desirability of an enforceable mediation clause can be broken down into two questions. First, the question is whether it is desirable that parties are bound to their (enforceable) mediation clause in the first place. Assuming this question must be answered in the affirmative, the subsequent question is *to what extent* parties must be bound to the mediation clause. These matters are addressed below.

12.3.2.1 Voluntary mediation versus pacta sunt servanda

The first question – whether it is desirable to be able to enforce mediation clauses – is more difficult to answer, and authors have offered differing views. The reason for this divergence is that formulating an answer necessarily requires a normative assessment of the balance between the aforementioned voluntary nature of mediation (or the principle of party autonomy) along with the right to access to the courts on the one hand, and the principle of *pacta sunt servanda* on the other hand.[45]

In principle, mediation is voluntary in nature. As such, forcing a party to mediate could be considered pointless or even counterproductive. The rationale behind mediation is that the parties that voluntarily undergo mediation actually want to amicably settle their dispute, whilst it could be said that parties that are coerced to attend the mediation process do not.[46] Subsequently, one could argue that a party forced to attend against their will means that the mediation is essentially doomed from the start. In such a scenario, mediation would only serve to add time and costs, and would damage the effectiveness of mediation as a whole.[47] This position has also found support in the Netherlands.[48]

---

45 E.J.M. van Beukering-Rosmuller, *Mediation in juridisch perspectief (Burgerlijk Proces & Praktijk no 7)*, Deventer: Wolters Kluwer 2024, para 88.

46 Cf. J. Holas, 'Development and Forms of Systems of Approach to Mediation in the EU', in: L. Holá et al (eds), *Mediation in the Reflection of Law and Society. European Perspectives*, Alphen aan den Rijn: Kluwer Law International 2021, p 118; see also A. Broekhuijsen-Molenaar, 'Mediation. Vrijwillig of afdwingbaar?', *NJB* 2019/1200, paras 4-5.

47 See e.g. *Halsey v Milton Keynes General NHS Trust* [2004] EWCA Civ 576, at [10]; C. Titi, 'Between Utopia and Realism. Mediation and the Settlement of International Investment Disputes', in: C. Titi & K. Fach Gómez (eds), *Mediation in International Commercial and Investment Disputes*, Oxford: Oxford University Press 2019, p 34.

48 See A. de Roo, 'Tien jaar moderne mediation in de Nederlandse rechtspraak', *Nederlands-Vlaams tijdschrift voor mediation en conflictmanagement* 2007, issue 1, p 79-80; L. Coenraad & P. Ingelse, 'Afscheid van de klassieke civiele procedure?', in: *Afscheid van de klassieke procedure?* (Preadvies voor de Nederlandse Juristen Vereniging 2017), Deventer: Wolters Kluwer 2017, p 84; E.J.M. van Beukering-Rosmuller,

Moreover, one could also wonder how an enforceable or binding mediation clause relates to the right of access to the courts as enshrined in (*inter alia*) Article 6 ECHR. When discussing this topic, the comparison between a mediation clause and an arbitration clause also comes to mind. After all, both are agreements aimed at settling a dispute outside the state court system. Lord Justice Dyson of the English Court of Appeal stated:

> "We heard argument on the question whether the court has power to order parties to submit their disputes to mediation against their will. It is one thing to encourage the parties to agree to mediation, even to encourage them in the strongest terms. It is another to order them to do so. It seems to us that to oblige truly unwilling parties to refer their disputes to mediation would be to impose an unacceptable obstruction on their right of access to the court. The court in Strasbourg has said in relation to article 6 of the European Convention on Human Rights that the right of access to a court may be waived, for example by means of an arbitration agreement, but such waiver should be subjected to "particularly careful review" to ensure that the claimant is not subject to "constraint": (...). If that is the approach of the ECtHR to an agreement to arbitrate, it seems to us likely that compulsion of ADR would be regarded as an unacceptable constraint on the right of access to the court and, therefore, a violation of article 6. (...)."[49]

This line of thinking essentially entails the view that, by agreeing to mediate, parties are *waiving* their right of access to the courts. This view has also been espoused in Dutch scholarly literature on the topic.[50] Not all will agree with this assessment, however. Advocate General De Bock, in an opinion (non-binding) to the Supreme Court,[51] advised that a mediation clause does *not* exclude a path to the state court. After all, the mediation clause at issue only entailed the obligation to *first* attempt mediation before initiating court proceedings. This differs from an arbitration agreement, whereby the parties fully exclude the state court from adjudicating the dispute.[52] Those defending this position, thus, argue that a mediation clause does not exclude access to the courts, but rather that it forms a preliminary hurdle.[53] In the *Alassini* and *Menini* judgments, the CJEU ac-

---

'Alternatieve beslechting van consumentengeschillen in het licht van het Menini-arrest', *TvA* 2018/70, p 129.

49 *Halsey v Milton Keynes General NHS Trust* [2004] EWCA Civ 576, at [9], as also cited in N. Alexander, *International and Comparative Mediation. Global Trends in Dispute Resolution (Volume 4)*, Alphen aan den Rijn: Kluwer Law International 2009, p 185.

50 See e.g. Asser Procesrecht/Giesen *1* 2015/212.

51 To be discussed in more detail below in para 12.3.4.3.

52 Opinion of Advocate General De Bock rendered prior to Supreme Court 12 July 2024, ECLI:NL:PHR:2024:103, paras 13.1-13.4.

53 A.F.M. Brenninkmeijer et al, *Juridische aspecten van mediation*, The Hague: Sdu Uitgevers 2005, p 126-127, as referred to by A.H. Santing-Wubs, *Mediation in juridisch*

cepted, in principle, that mechanisms that compelled mediation prior to commencing court proceedings did not violate Article 6 ECHR, so long as the parties' right of access to the judicial system is maintained.[54]

On the other side, it is obvious that once parties agree to something, they are expected to follow through on the corresponding commitment (*pacta sunt servanda*). In other words, the parties have made a promise and they are expected to keep that promise under all circumstances.[55] Consequently, parties that have included a mediation clause in their contract should be, in principle, held to that clause.[56] Parties should not be able to unilaterally dismiss their obligations under an agreement because they decided that they do not agree with those obligations anymore.[57] A prior agreement to try mediation in case of a dispute would otherwise be rendered meaningless.[58] This appears to us as an undesirable situation, especially given the potential benefits of mediation.[59]

As also indicated above, some authors find it difficult to reconcile the voluntary nature of mediation and an ability to compel parties to attempt it. This ostensible contradiction is also why some practitioners have been reluctant to include mediation clauses for EU cross-border commercial disputes. This follows from qualitative research conducted by Howard, who cites one interviewee stating:

> "Our dispute resolution clause has escalation clauses, certain people have to have discussions at certain points. I am not for mandatory mediation. Both parties have to be willing. I am not sure it works if it is required."[60]

perspectief (Burgerlijk Proces & Praktijk no 7), Deventer: Kluwer 2012, para 7.3 (old edition), who, it must be noted, had disagreements with their assessment.

54 CJEU 18 March, ECLI:EU:C:2010:146 (*Alassini*) and CJEU 14 June 2017, ECLI:EU:C:2017:457 (*Menini*), see also para 51; see also e.g. Van Beukering-Rosmuller 2018.

55 Asser/Sieburgh *6-III* 2022/46.

56 E.R. Gathier, 'De afdwingbaarheid van de mediationclausule', in: P.C. van Schelven (ed), *Van Geschil tot oplossing (Recht en Praktijk no 169)*, Deventer: Kluwer 2009, p 167-168.

57 J.M. Bosnak, 'De mediationclausule. Hoe lang nog beperkt houdbaar?', in: C.J.M. Klaassen, G.J. Meijer & C.L. Schleijpen (eds), *Going Dutch. ADR in Nederland, in het bijzonder bij het NAI (Onderneming en recht no 113)*, Deventer: Wolters Kluwer 2019, p 311.

58 See also Asser Procesrecht/Giesen *1* 2015/212.

59 See para 12.2 above.

60 A. Howard, *EU Cross-Border Commercial Mediation. Listening to Disputants – Changing the Frame; Framing the Changes*, Alphen aan den Rijn: Kluwer Law International 2021, p 145.

However, it is far from certain that this is true. Those active in the mediation industry have, in fact, found that even 'forced' mediations are capable of leading to a successful outcome. Experiences show that a good mediator is capable of building rapport with an otherwise recalcitrant participant, thus guiding a seemingly unsalvageable dispute into a fruitful dialogue.[61] Wackie Eysten dismissed the notion that a compelled mediation is pointless, qualifying it as a "fable".[62] His position is supported by other authors as well.[63] A British mediator remarked in an interview: "They came to scoff but stayed to pray!"[64] Bosnak, for his part, writes:

> "In practice (...) there appears to be an unexpectedly high success rate of mediations where initially one of the parties was unwilling. An experience shared by many mediators is the fact that sometimes even parties who were extremely hostile towards each other during the preliminary phase are unexpectedly cooperative towards each other in the initial stage of the actual mediation process."[65]

Not all authors share Bosnak's faith in the mediator's abilities. Titi writes that in cases "where the relationship between the parties is irreparably damaged, imposing mediation would not add a realistic remedy".[66] Empirical research conducted by Jagtenberg & De Roo shows that results differ when parties are compelled to try mediation before being allowed to initiate court proceedings. However, whilst the success rates were deemed to be lower than voluntary mediation, Jagtenberg & De Roo conclude that compulsory mediation can still be effective enough to reduce the judiciary's workload.[67]

Moreover, what does 'voluntary' mediation actually entail? This question is particularly relevant where it concerns mediation clauses. There

61 See also F. Glasl, 'Vrijwilligheid of willigheid van mediation', *Tijdschrift Conflicthantering* 2014, issue 5, p 44, who argues that the assumption that mediation must be based on complete voluntariness is based on ideological and idealistic grounds, and that such a standard would lead to very little disputes being resolved by mediation. Instead, he argues that it is better to focus on 'sufficient willingness'.

62 P.A. Wackie Eysten, 'Mediation en de rechter', *TvA* 2003, p 114.

63 See e.g. Gathier 2009, p 183; E.J.M van Beukering-Rosmuller, 'De juridische afdwingbaarheid van een mediationclausule', *TvA* 2017/2, para 3.2.

64 E.A. Filler, *Commercial Mediation in Europe. An Emprical Study of the User Experience, Global Trends in Dispute Resolution Volume 5*, Alphen aan den Rijn: Kluwer Law International 2012, p 254.

65 Bosnak 2019, p 311 (translated from Dutch).

66 Titi 2019, p 34.

67 R. Jagtenberg & A. de Roo, *De praktijk van mediation in ons omringende landen,* WODC 2003, p 65-66; see also Holas 2021, p 115-116; F. van Zomeren in 'Van 'in gebreke' naar 'in verbinding'. Over de kanteling in het denken over conflictbeslechting en waar de wetgever deze ontwikkeling zou moeten ondersteunen', *NJB* 2018/1298.

are those who take voluntary mediation to mean that, once a dispute has arisen, parties can in no situation be compelled to engage in any way with a mediation process.[68] We would qualify this a classical and/or straightforward understanding of mediation's voluntary nature.

However, in case of an existing mediation clause, one could instead argue that a party's voluntary agreement to try mediation already came into existence the moment it agreed to said clause, and that consequently this clause must be enforceable. In other words, parties voluntarily agree to include a mediation clause, and as such the requirement of voluntary mediation is fulfilled.[69] If considered this way, it seems possible to marry the voluntary nature of mediation with the principle of *pacta sunt servanda*. The documented willingness to agree to mediation translates into an obligation that parties are later expected to fulfil.[70]

12.3.2.2 To what extent would parties be bound to a mediation clause?

Presupposing that mediation clauses can be enforceable, and thus contain a binding obligation, the question is: what exactly are the parties bound to do? In other words, it is necessary to determine what an enforceable obligation to mediate actually entails.

The obligation that follows from a binding mediation clause can be split into two parts. The first part constitutes an obligation of result, and is thus straightforwardly assessed.[71] Parties must cooperate in initiating the mediation and attend at least one session. This part therefore favors the principle of *pacta sunt servanda*.[72] The subsequent second part relates to an obligation of best efforts to negotiate in good faith to reach an agreement through the (now initiated) mediation. However, because mediation is of

68 See e.g. Broekhuijsen-Molenaar 2019, paras 4-5; Coenraad & Ingelse 2017, p 84; De Roo 2007, p 79-80; Holas 2021, p 118.

69 F. Schonewille, 'Interview met Erik Koster, Toine de Bie en Alexander Schild. Een mediationclausule is niet per definitie tandloos', *Tijdschrift Conflicthantering* 2022/76. C.f. also CJEU 14 June 2017, ECLI:EU:C:2017:457 (*Menini*), para 50: "As stated in recital 13 of Directive 2008/52, the voluntary nature of the mediation lies, therefore, not in the freedom of the parties to choose whether or not to use that process but in the fact that 'the parties are themselves in charge of the process and may organise it as they wish and terminate it at any time'."

70 A similar point was made in the Explanatory Memorandum to (one of) the 2013 Bills, see *Parliamentary Papers II* 2012/13, 33 723, p 21.

71 See Bosnak 2019, p 309-310.

72 Bosnak 2019, p 324.

a voluntary nature, parties are therefore free to withdraw from the procedure when they choose to do so.[73]

Of course, requiring parties to attend at least one session may already be enough. As mentioned above, mediators have considered that this initial session could already tip the scales in a party's disposition from uncooperative to more conciliatory. Though, such a practice has also been described and/or criticized as forcing a party to first "get a stamp" before allowing court litigation, in the hopes of persuading it to change its mind.[74] Still, compelling parties to try mediation can, under the appropriate circumstances, be commendable. At the very least, it can be commendable to oblige parties to at least hear out the prospective mediator to explain how mediation works.[75]

The nature of the party's obligations under a mediation clause is one thing. The consequences of not adhering to those obligations is another. There are different types of sanctions or consequences that could be attached to an unfulfilled mediation clause. These range from a party's claim being deemed inadmissible by the court at the most severe end of the spectrum, and to adjournment of the proceedings at the other. As will be explained below, approaches differ across jurisdictions.

12.3.3 Enforceability in different jurisdictions

While this contribution focuses primarily on the Dutch approach to mediation, a broader perspective on the enforceability of mediation clauses is certainly useful to put developments in the Netherlands into context. Particularly, a brief look will be taken at England, Germany, France, Italy, Belgium, Austria, the United States and Singapore. As will be seen below, these jurisdictions generally support the notion that mediation clauses are binding and enforceable.

Starting with England, as seen in Lord Justice Dyson's statements above,[76] there has historically been some skepticism in relation to compelling parties to mediate.[77] However, English courts have accepted that a mediation

73 P. Sanders, 'Het terugkomen op een afspraak tot mediation', *NJB* 2006/673, p 895; Van Beukering-Rosmuller 2017, p 10; Bosnak 2019, p 324.

74 M. Brink, "Verplichtstelling' van mediation?', *NJB* 2011/1998.

75 See e.g. Gathier 2009, p 183; Van Beukering-Rosmuller 2017, para 3.2.

76 *Halsey v Milton Keynes General NHS Trust* [2004] EWCA Civ 576, at [9].

77 *Courtney & Fairbairn Ltd v Tolaini Brothers (Hotels) Ltd* [1975] 1 W.L.R. 297, p 301: "It seems to me that a contract to negotiate, like a contract to enter into a contract, is not a contract known to the law."

clause can be binding in case it contains a sufficiently defined mutual obligation to mediate.[78] More than that, such clauses have also been accepted as establishing a condition precedent to litigation or arbitration if they are expressed clearly as such, meaning that the right to a legal action does not accrue until that condition has been fulfilled. Consequently, a court will have the discretion to stay proceedings commenced in breach of an enforceable mediation clause.[79] In particular, the Justice O'Farrell of the English High Court considered:

> "The following principles can be derived from the above authorities as applicable where a party seeks to enforce an alternative dispute resolution provision by means of an order staying proceedings:
>
> - i) The agreement must create an enforceable obligation requiring the parties to engage in alternative dispute resolution.
> - ii) The obligation must be expressed clearly as a condition precedent to court proceedings or arbitration.
> - iii) The dispute resolution process to be followed does not have to be formal but must be sufficiently clear and certain by reference to objective criteria, including machinery to appoint a mediator or determine any other necessary step in the procedure without the requirement for any further agreement by the parties.
> - iv) The court has a discretion to stay proceedings commenced in breach of an enforceable dispute resolution agreement. In exercising its discretion, the Court will have regard to the public policy interest in upholding the parties' commercial agreement and furthering the overriding objective in assisting the parties to resolve their disputes."[80]

Germany makes use of a more strict regime. In case two commercial entities agree to a mediation clause, this clause is, in principle, binding and enforceable. In case this binding clause is subsequently not adhered to prior to commencing court proceedings, the filed claims are to be deemed inadmissible. The fact that one of the parties is unwilling to mediate is of no influence, nor is the voluntary nature of mediation.[81]

---

78 *Cable & Wireless PLC v IBM United Kingdom Limited* [2002] EWHC 2059 (Comm), at [21]-[34].

79 *Ohpen Operations UK Limited v Invesco Fund Managers Limited* [2019] EWHC 2246 (TCC), at [32], citing *Cable & Wireless PLC v IBM United Kingdom Limited* [2002] EWHC 2059 (Comm), at [21]-[34]; *Holloway v Chancery Mead Ltd* [2008] EWHC 2495 (TCC), at [81]; *Tang v Grant Thornton International Ltd* [2012] EWHC 3198 (Ch), at [59]-[61]; *Emirates Trading Agency LLC v Prime Mineral Exports Pte Ltd* [2014] EWHC 2104 (Comm), at [64]; see also Alexander 2009, p 186.

80 *Ohpen Operations UK Limited v Invesco Fund Managers Limited* [2019] EWHC 2246 (TCC), at [32].

81 Opinion of Advocate General De Bock rendered prior to Supreme Court 12 July 2024, ECLI:NL:PHR:2024:103, para 16.2, citing E. Kajkowska, *Enforceability of Multi-*

France is much the same. The French Supreme Court (*Cour de cassation*) has held that mediation clauses must be deemed to be enforceable.[82] Failure to adhere to them prior to initiating court proceedings results in non-admissibility of the claim.[83] However, in a case where an arbitral tribunal decided a party's claim was admissible despite breach of a mediation clause, the *Cour de cassation* refused to set aside the award in question on the basis of lack of jurisdiction, precisely because of the difference between (in)admissibility and (lack of) jurisdiction.[84]

Italy and Belgium have in common that these countries have enacted statutory provisions on mediation clauses. Under Italian law, particularly under Legislative Decree no 28 of 4 March 2010 (*Decreto Legislativo 4 marzo 2010, nr. 28*), Article 5-sexies, paragraph 1 determines that (translated) "[w]here the contract (…) provide[s] for a mediation clause, mediation is a condition for the admissibility of the legal claim." The consequence of not adhering to the mediation clause is obvious.[85] Article 1725(2) of the Belgian Judicial Code – the Belgian legislator first having enacted laws on mediation to combat judicial backlogs[86] – provides that the court judge or arbitrator faced with a dispute subjected to a mediation clause stays the proceedings at the request of one of the parties, unless he finds that there is no valid clause (anymore). The proceedings are resumed once (one of the) parties notifies the court administrator and other parties that the mediation has ended.

Tiered Dispute Resolution Clauses, Oxford: Hart Publishing 2017, p 65-87; H. Hoffmann, *Mediationsklauseln in Verträgen zwischen Unternehmen* (diss. Keulen), Keulen: Universitäts- und Stadtbibliothek Köln 2019, p 83; see also case law such as OLG Düsseldorf 10 April 2019, 2 U 2/18, para 44; OLG Saarbrücken 29 April 2015, 2 U 31/14, para II.1, LG Dortmund 17 November 2017, 10 O 17/17, para 56.

82 Cour de cassation – Troisième chambre civile – 19 May 2016, n° 15-14.464; Cour de cassation – Chambre mixte 14 February 2003/n° 00-19.423, n° 00-19.424.

83 P.C. Pelletier, 'De la récurrente question de l'exigence de conditions particulières de mise en œuvre du processus conciliatoire necessaires à l'effectivité de la clause de conciliation ou de médiation préalable', *Revue des Contrats* 2 June 2019, p 46; Opinion of Advocate-General De Bock rendered prior to Supreme Court 12 July 2024, ECLI:NL:PHR:2024:103, para 16.3.

84 Cour de cassation – Première chambre civile 1 February 2023/n° 21-25.024.

85 Article 5(2) of the decree provides (translated): "If the judge finds that mediation has not been carried out or has already begun, but has not been concluded, he shall set the next hearing after the expiry of the term referred to in Article 6 [i.e., in principle three months from the initiation of the mediation or expiry of the time limit set by the court for initiating the mediation]. At this hearing, the judge ascertains whether the condition of admissibility has been satisfied and, failing that, declares the inadmissibility of the judicial claim."

86 A. Verbeke & G. Vervaeke, 'Constructief omgaan met conflicten en geschillen', *Nederlands-Vlaams tijdschrift voor mediation en conflictmanagment* 2021, issue 2, p 110.

Austria is one of the European jurisdictions that has not embraced enforceable mediation clauses. As such, these clauses do not prevent the initiation of court proceedings.[87] Instead, it is described as a jurisdiction providing for an "entirely voluntary process" without statutory provisions that compel parties to try mediation before litigation.[88]

Looking outside Europe, other jurisdictions also attach consequences of failing to adhere to mediation clauses. For example, mediation clauses are enforceable in the United States. Formerly described by US courts as involving 'vain orders',[89] parties can now be compelled to honor their mediation clauses. Like in England, mediation clauses can also be seen as establishing a condition precedent to, for example, arbitration. If a party has not fulfilled its obligation to mediate, a judge can decide to dismiss the claims (without prejudice).[90] A judge can also decide to stay the proceedings to allow parties to fulfil their obligations under the mediation clause.[91]

Singapore takes a different approach. In Asia, mediation has obtained a wider cultural significance than may be encountered in Europe, for example. For that reason, mediation clauses form an enforceable precondition to proceedings without requiring the clause to be extensively detailed, as is the case in England. Moreover, if an arbitration agreement provides that parties must mediate first, failure to do so results in an arbitral tribunal not having jurisdiction.[92] The Singapore Court of Appeal ruled:

> "Where the parties have clearly contracted for a specific set of dispute resolution procedures as preconditions for arbitration, those preconditions must be ful-

87 Alexander 2009, p 175.

88 A. Grill, 'Ethical guidelines for mediators. The Austrian status quo', *Nederlands-Vlaams tijdschrift voor Mediation en conflictmanagement* 2019, issue 2/3, p 55.

89 *Lorch Inc. v Bessemer Hall Shopping Center Inc* 294 Ala 17, 310 So 2d 872 (1975) and *Livoti v Elston* 52 AD 2d 444, 384 NYS 2d 484 (App Div 1976), as referred to by Alexander 2009, footnote 7.

90 See e.g. *Bank of Am., N.A. v. SFR Invs. Pool 1, LLC*, No 2:15-CV-0693-GMN-VCF, 2016 WL 389981 (D. Nev. Jan. 31, 2016); *Golden State Foods Corp. v. Columbia/Okura LLC*, No CV 13-8150 RSWL VBKX, 2014 WL 2931127; *Archstone Dev. LLC v. Renval Constr. LLC*, 156 A.D.3d 432, 67 N.Y.S.3d 7 (2017).

91 See e.g. *Getchell v. Suntrust Bank*, No 6:15-CV-1702-ORL-TBS, 2016 WL 740603 (M.D. Fla. Feb. 25, 2016).

92 J. Spigelman, 'The Centrality of Contractual Interpretation. A Comparative Perspective', in: *International Arbitration: Issues, Perspectives and Practice (Liber Amicorum Neil Kaplan)*, Alphen aan den Rijn: Kluwer Law International 2019, p 184, as cited in Opinion of Advocate-General De Bock rendered prior to Supreme Court 12 July 2024, ECLI:NL:PHR:2024:103, para 15.13; see also *Maxx Engineering Works Pte Ltd v PQ Builders Pte Ltd* [2023] SGHC 71.

> filled. (...) Given that the preconditions for arbitration set out in cl 37.2 had not been complied with, and given our view that they were conditions precedent, the agreement to arbitrate in cl 37.3 (even if it were applicable to the Appellant) could not be invoked. The Tribunal therefore did not have jurisdiction over the Appellant and its dispute with the Respondent. (...)."[93]

Approaches across jurisdictions thus differ slightly, but it is clear to see that the majority point in the same direction. Mediation as a compulsory means of dispute resolution has gained widespread acceptance throughout the world. Some jurisdictions, however, have not been so fortunate to have a history of clear treatment of mediation clauses. One of these jurisdictions is the Netherlands, where practitioners had to wait almost two decades to receive much needed clarification from the Supreme Court.

12.3.4 *A new Dutch regime in favour of enforceability*

In the Netherlands, it was unclear in the last decades whether or not mediation clauses are enforceable.[94] In its Lotamblau Judgment, the Supreme Court confirmed the enforceability of mediation clauses, and set out the consequences of failing to adhere to such clauses. By rendering this judgment, the Supreme Court has both corrected a collective misinterpretation of its previous case law by the lower courts, and strengthened the position of mediation in the Netherlands.

12.3.4.1 The 2006 judgment of the Supreme Court

In the early 2000s, Dutch courts had different approaches to mediation and/or other dispute resolution mechanisms meant to be used before initiating court proceedings.[95] For example, in 2002 the The Hague Court of Appeal, faced with an unfulfilled party agreement to conduct a so-called 'minitrial' before initiating proceedings, decided to stay the proceedings indefinitely to allow the parties to undergo that process.[96] In 2004, Arnhem

93 *International Research Corp PLC v Lufthansa Systems Asia Pacific Pte Ltd and another* [2013] SGCA 55, at [62]-[63].

94 As mentioned above, the Netherlands has no statutory legislation governing mediation (clauses).

95 Gathier 2009, p 168 et seq; E.J.M. van Beukering-Rosmuller, *Mediation in juridisch perspectief (Burgerlijk Proces & Praktijk no 7)*, Deventer: Kluwer 2024, para 92.

96 The Hague Court of Appeal 12 December 2002, *NJK* 2003/17, para 5; Gathier 2009, p 170.

District Court even considered a failure to adhere to an agreed upon pre-trial procedure[97] a ground for inadmissibility of the claim.[98]

Other Dutch courts used a different approach. In 2002, the District Court of Amsterdam ruled that a mediation clause cannot be equated with an arbitration clause or binding advice agreement. Although the court did accept, that the parties were in principle obliged to adhere to the clause, the court considered that pre-trial correspondence showed that neither party referred to that clause once a dispute arose. After making reference to the voluntary nature of mediation, the court refused to declare the claim inadmissible.[99] In the same year, the District Court of Haarlem considered compulsory mediation to be contrary to the (voluntary) essence of mediation.[100]

With these different lines of thought, it was clear that practitioners needed guidance from the Supreme Court. On 20 January 2006, the Supreme Court provided just that by rendering a judgment in a family law dispute (specifically: divorce proceedings) between two spouses (the "**2006 Judgment**").[101] During these proceedings, the spouses orally agreed to mediation before the 's Hertogenbosch Court of Appeal. However, shortly after, one of the spouses rescinded the agreement. The other spouse then argued that the Court of Appeal should have still referred them to mediation in light of their agreement. The Supreme Court disagreed, considering as follows (translated):

> "(…) In its currently challenged ruling, the court of appeal expressed deep regret about the woman's stance, but concluded that successful mediation requires the continued consent of both parties, which is currently absent. In its ruling, the court declared the man's appeal inadmissible.
>
> The grounds for the appeal against this ruling argue that the court wrongly, or at least insufficiently motivated, did not refer the parties to mediation, despite their agreement to do so and the case being particularly suitable for mediation. According to the explanation provided for the grounds, the woman is breaching the contract, and her emotions in this context are not legally valid arguments.

97 Specifically, non-binding advice proceedings.
98 Arnhem District Court 14 January 2004, *LJN* AO3003; K. Teuben, 'Gebondenheid aan mediationafspraak', *MvV* 2006, p 93.
99 Amsterdam District Court 16 October 2002, ECLI:NL:RBAMS:2002:AF5797, *NJ* 2003/87, para 5; see also Maastricht District Court 9 November 2005, *LJN* AU6364, which ruled in the same way; Gathier 2009, p 169-170 and 172.
100 Haarlem District Court 4 June 2002, *LJN* AQ2615; Gathier 2009, p 170.
101 Supreme Court 20 January 2006, ECLI:NL:HR:2006:AU3724, *NJ* 2006/75.

> This case involves disputes between two private individuals who, during the course of the proceedings, agreed to attempt an amicable settlement through mediation. Given the nature of mediation, both parties are at liberty at any time to withhold their cooperation or to terminate it for reasons personal to them. Both the legal complaint and the reasoning complaint therefore fail on this ground."[102] (emphasis added)

Thus, the agreement between the two spouses to mediate was, given the nature of mediation, not binding to the parties according to the Supreme Court. This seemingly settled the matter: mediation clauses were considered to be non-enforceable. However, as will be discussed below, the matter was, in fact, far from settled.

12.3.4.2 Discussions among authors contrast with a uniform approach in case law of the lower courts following the 2006 judgment

At first glance, the 2006 Judgment seems straightforward. The agreement to try mediation is not binding on the parties, and thus not enforceable. Closer inspection of the Supreme Court's considerations reveals a critical qualification, however. As shown above, the Supreme Court made a point to mention that the parties involved in the 2006 Judgment were (i) two private individuals, who (ii) agreed to try mediation orally at a court hearing. That raises the question: what if the agreement to try mediation is concluded prior to the proceedings? And would it make a difference if this obligation is laid down in writing and/or between professional rather than private parties? Would such clauses also be unenforceable?

These questions were extensively discussed in scholarly literature following the 2006 Judgment. Advocate General Huydecoper indicated, in his opinion to the Supreme Court prior to the 2006 Judgment, that he could imagine deviating from the voluntary and non-binding nature of mediation in cases in which parties agree *beforehand* that they must try mediation before initiating court proceedings. The Advocate General argued that, in those cases, a party may also be obliged to cooperate at least to some extent in the mediation, even if it is not (or no longer) willing to do so.[103]

Various authors expressed disappointment with the 2006 Judgment. Sanders critiqued the fact that the Supreme Court did not differentiate between

---

102 Supreme Court 20 January 2006, ECLI:NL:HR:2006:AU3724, *NJ* 2006/75.

103 Opinion of Advocate-General Huydecoper rendered prior to Supreme Court 20 January 2006, ECLI:NL:PHR:2006:AU3724, paras. 16 and 18.

withdrawing *before* mediation and withdrawing *after* the mediation had already started.[104] Wackie Eysten found that he was not sure how the Supreme Court would rule on a 'carefully drafted' mediation clause.[105] Wackie Eysten argued that a mediation clause would be binding if it contained an adequately formulated and documented mediation clause.[106]

Bosnak and Schonewille found that the 2006 Judgment was tailored to the unique circumstances of the case and did not contain a general rule.[107] These authors were not alone in this assessment. Teuben remarked that the circumstances of the case – parties agreed to mediation during oral hearings – were quite extraordinary.[108] Also, Schild took the position that the Supreme Court's considerations were not to be understood as generally applicable.[109]

Not only the fact that the agreement to try mediation was concluded orally during a court hearing, but also the fact that the parties were private persons played a role. De Roo pointed out that, the Supreme Court first mentioned that the parties involved were private persons (i.e., "one-shotters with emotions"). According to De Roo, it was this aspect, and not the (lack of) existence of a prior agreement to try mediation, that seemed to be the more important criterion.[110]

Thus, a line of thought came to the forefront entailing that, in case the mediation clause was concluded by professional parties, which included a mediation clause in a commercial contract after (lengthy) negotiations, such parties would (or should) be bound to that clause.[111] Professional parties were considered to be more tightly tethered to the principle of *pacta sunt servanda*, and could thus not escape their obligations.[112]

104 P. Sanders, 'Het terugkomen op een afspraak tot mediation', *NJB* 2006/673, p 895.
105 P.A. Wackie Eysten, 'Redactioneel artikel', *JBPR* 2006/902, paras 7 and 12.
106 P.A. Wackie Eysten, 'Anders dan Sanders?', *TvA* 2012/73, para 5.
107 Bosnak 2019, p 311, referring to F. Schonewille, 'De handhaafbaarheid van de mediationclausule ten behoeve van een echtscheidingsconvenant (II)', *WPNR* 2010, issue 6827, p 43.
108 K. Teuben, 'Gebondenheid aan mediationafspraak', *MvV* 2006/5.3, p 94.
109 F. Schonewille, 'Interview met Erik Koster, Toine de Bie en Alexander Schild. Een mediationclausule is niet per definitie tandloos', *Tijdschrift Conflicthantering* 2022/76.
110 De Roo 2007, p 79.
111 See e.g. K. Teuben, 'Gebondenheid aan mediationafspraak', *MvV* 2006, p 94; Bosnak 2019, p 312.
112 Van Beukering-Rosmuller 2017, p 10.

Not all authors shared in the majority opinion that the 2006 Judgment was a disappointment. De Roo had pleaded in favor of the voluntary nature of mediation, also in light of (case law surrounding) Article 6 ECHR.[113] If mediation clauses would be enforceable, this would harm mediation rather than benefit it.[114] Degenkamp, turning against the concept of mediation as a whole, also praised the 2006 Judgment.[115]

Where academics saw room for debate, courts did not. From the 2006 Judgment onwards, lower courts steadily rejected the notion that a mediation clause could be enforceable, regardless of the parties or circumstances involved, much to the detriment of mediation as a whole. Mediation clauses did not affect the admissibility of a claim submitted to a court or tribunal.[116] Generally speaking, lower courts in some way referred to the voluntary nature of mediation to support their positions. The Gelderland District Court cited the non-binding nature of mediation as (ostensibly) set out in the 2006 Judgment to reject an argument that a bindingly formulated (and unfollowed) mediation clause leads to inadmissibility of a claim.[117] The Rotterdam District Court also rejected the argument that a mediation clause that was passed over leads to a lack of jurisdiction.[118] In various family law cases, Courts of Appeal considered medication agreements non-enforceable.[119]

113 Reference is made to para 12.3.2.1 above, where these considerations are discussed in more detail.

114 De Roo 2007, p 80.

115 J.Th. Degenkamp, 'Mediation R.I.P.? Hoezee? Reactie op Sanders', *NJB* 2006/28, p 1576. In response, Sanders pointed out that both the Court of Appeal and Supreme Court regretted having to make their decisions, P. Sanders, 'Naschrift', *NJB* 2006/28, p 1577. It must be noted that Wackie Eysten did not read such regret in the Supreme Court's considerations, P.A. Wackie Eysten, 'Redactioneel artikel', *JBPR* 2006/902, footnote 8.

116 Van Beukering-Rosmuller 2024, para 92; see also E. Schutte & J. Spierdijk, 'Een mediationclausule als preventiemiddel. Voorkomt het rechtszaken?', *TC* 2022/91; A. Schaberg, 'Mediation en rechtspraak. Vrijwilligheid en vertrouwelijkheid', *Ondernemingsrecht* 2016/4, para 2.

117 Gelderland District Court 5 February 2020, ECLI:NL:RBGEL:2020:1080, *TvA* 2020/37, para 4.2; see also Rotterdam District Court 28 April 2021, ECLI:NL:RBROT:2021:3229, para 4.2.

118 Rotterdam District Court 2 December 2020, ECLI:NL:RBROT:2020:11155, paras 4.7.1-4.7.2.

119 Van Beukering-Rosmuller 2024, para 90, also referring to Supreme Court 8 May 2009, ECLI:NL:HR:2009:BH7132, *RvdW* 2009/614; cf. Opinion of Advocate General De Bock rendered prior to Supreme Court 12 July 2024, ECLI:NL:PHR:2024:103, paras 10.16-10.18, wherein the importance of this judgment is refuted.

Exceptions were exceedingly rare. In 2014, the provisional relief judge of the Gelderland District Court made such an exception. It considered that, whilst compelling parties to participate in mediation is contrary to the essence of mediation (making reference to the 2006 Judgment), there was room to make an exception under the circumstances. The reason for that was that the parties had entered into an agreement that made them dependent on one another, and it was in their best interests to find a structural solution for their dispute. The case was stayed to allow parties to seek mediation.[120] Interestingly, in 2009 an NAI tribunal (with Wackie Eysten as acting arbitrator) faced with (i) a multi-tier arbitration clause (providing for prior mediation which had not been adhered to) (ii) made between two commercial parties, contrasted those circumstances with those in the 2006 Judgment, and considered said judgment not to be leading in that situation. However, the fact that it concerned an arbitral provisional relief procedure meant that, in this case, the claims were still admissible.[121]

In 2017, the Supreme Court rendered the *Hermitage* judgment. In this judgment, the Supreme Court ruled that, under certain circumstances, it is unacceptable under the Dutch law standards of reasonableness and fairness that a party breaks off negotiations. One such circumstance is the presence of a mediation clause.[122] With this, the Supreme Court had finally given mediation practitioners an inch. Mediation clauses could have some kind of (legal) effect in proceedings. Still, it would take seven more years before the Supreme Court would provide further clarity on the question of whether mediation clauses can be enforceable.

12.3.4.3 The Supreme Court accepts enforceable mediation clauses in the lotamblau judgment

In short, in the case that led up to the Lotamblau Judgment Lotamblau Investments[123] and PPSB had entered into an SPA whereby Lotamblau purchased PPSB's shares in Human Connexion B.V. In addition, PPSB extended a loan to Lotamblau. The multi-tier arbitration agreement in the purchase agreement provided that, in case of a dispute, the parties shall

120 Gelderland District Court (provisional relief judge) 19 June 2014, ECLI:NL:RBGEL:2014:3887, paras 4.6-4.11; Van Beukering-Rosmuller 2017, para 3.3.

121 KG NAI 9 February 2007, *TvA* 2008/31. The tribunal considered that the existence of a mediation agreement did not prevent parties from seeking provisional relief.

122 Supreme Court 6 October 2017, ECLI:NL:HR:2017:2566, *NJ* 2017/410 (*Hermitage*), para 3.4.3. See for a more extensive analysis: Bosnak 2019, p 313-314.

123 Called by its former name 'Capabel Solutions Works B.V.' or 'CSW' in the legal proceedings.

first attempt mediation prior to initiating an arbitral procedure. However, once a dispute arose, PPSB bypassed mediation and immediately requested a provisional relief judge to assign an arbitrator to adjudicate said dispute. Lotamblau objected, and argued that the arbitration agreement was conditioned on mediation having been conducted. The provisional relief judge disagreed, and subsequently appointed an arbitrator. During the arbitration, Lotamblau once again argued that the arbitration agreement was conditional on mediation, and that the arbitrator therefore needed to declare that they lacked jurisdiction. Once again, Lotamblau was unsuccessful, and thereafter PPSB's claims were (partially) granted in the subsequent phase.[124]

Lotamblau initiated setting aside proceedings before the The Hague Court of Appeal, arguing that the arbitral tribunal lacked jurisdiction and therefore the award should, *inter alia*, be set aside on the basis of Article 1065(1)(a) DCCP. The The Hague Court of Appeal rejected this argument. In line with the abovementioned case law of lower courts after the 2006 Judgment, it ruled that the mediation clause was not binding, also in light of the voluntary nature of mediation. Thus, Lotamblau's setting aside claim was rejected.[125]

Lotamblau then filed cassation appeal, complaining, in brief, that the Court of Appeal had failed to recognize that mediation clauses can be enforceable. Also, Lotamblau complained that the Court's judgment was incomprehensible, because the clause clearly stated that the parties shall first attempt mediation prior to initiating an arbitral procedure.

Advocate General De Bock agreed with Lotamblau. In an extensive and thoroughly researched opinion, she concluded in favor of an enforceable mediation clause. Though it falls outside the scope of this contribution to address it in its entirety, it is certainly recommended reading. Shortly put, the Advocate General agreed that it does not follow from the 2006 Judgment that parties can never be bound to a mediation clause. In her view, the 2006 Judgment does not exclude that mediation clauses can be

124 These facts are set out in more detail in Opinion of Advocate General De Bock rendered prior to Supreme Court 12 July 2024, ECLI:NL:PHR:2024:103, paras 2-3.

125 The Hague Court of Appeal, ECLI:NL:GHDHA:2022:1851, para 5.11, *TvA* 2023/15.

binding, especially if concluded between professional parties that consciously include mediation clauses in their contracts.[126]

What sanctions would follow in case the mediation clause was bypassed? According to the Advocate General, this depends on the interpretation of the mediation clause. These could range from entirely voluntary or non-binding, to more strict, enforceable provisions.[127] In case of *binding* mediation clauses, the Advocate General rejected the notion that a court or tribunal would have no jurisdiction or that the claim would be inadmissible if a party prematurely initiated court or arbitral proceedings. Instead, the court or tribunal must stay the proceedings so that mediation can be tried.[128] If an arbitral tribunal would render an award without having suspended the proceedings to allow the parties to comply with their obligation to try mediation before initiating arbitral proceedings, the award must be set aside on lack of jurisdiction according to the Advocate General, because a valid arbitration agreement was lacking.[129] In light of the above, she concluded that the Supreme Court should quash the judgment of the Court of Appeal.[130]

The Supreme Court then rendered its judgment. Although the Supreme Court did not fully follow the opinion of the Advocate General, it did confirm that mediation clauses can be binding. Whether or not a mediation clause is binding depends on the interpretation of the mediation clause. If Dutch law applies to the mediation clause, this means that the so-called *Haviltex* standard applies, which entails that the mediation clause has the meaning that the parties could reasonably ascribe to the mediation clause in the given circumstances and what they could reasonably expect from each other in this respect.[131]

A mediation clause may be non-binding. It is also possible that a mediation clause obliges parties to try mediation before initiating legal proceed-

126 Opinion of Advocate General De Bock rendered prior to Supreme Court 12 July 2024, ECLI:NL:PHR:2024:103, paras 11.28-11.30.
127 Opinion of Advocate General De Bock rendered prior to Supreme Court 12 July 2024, ECLI:NL:PHR:2024:103, paras 17.11 and 17.15-17.16.
128 Opinion of Advocate General De Bock rendered prior to Supreme Court 12 July 2024, ECLI:NL:PHR:2024:103, paras 17.21 and 17.25-17.31.
129 Opinion of Advocate General De Bock rendered prior to Supreme Court 12 July 2024, ECLI:NL:PHR:2024:103, para 17.32.
130 Opinion of Advocate General De Bock rendered prior to Supreme Court 12 July 2024, ECLI:NL:PHR:2024:103, para 18.
131 Supreme Court 12 July 2024, ECLI:NL:HR:2024:1078, para 3.2.2 (*Lotamblau*).

ings (or arbitration). The nature of mediation does not preclude such an interpretation. The circumstances in which a mediation clause has been agreed between professional parties, and that the agreement and the resulting dispute are of a commercial nature, may play a role in the interpretation, but do not automatically mean that the mediation clause must be interpreted as requiring the parties to try mediation before initiating proceedings in court (or in arbitration).[132]

If a mediation clause requires mediation to be tested, the scope of that obligation, and thus the question of when a party who wishes to do so may terminate its cooperation in the mediation process, is also a matter of interpretation of the mediation clause. A mediation clause may not be used if its application would have the effect of unacceptably undermining the right of access to justice, which is also guaranteed by Article 6 of the ECHR.[133]

The Lotamblau Judgment also provides guidance on how courts and arbitral tribunals must handle binding mediation clauses. The Supreme Court considers that if a mediation clause stipulates that parties are required to attempt mediation before initiating legal (or arbitral) proceedings and a party starts proceedings without fulfilling that obligation, the judge (or arbitrator) may, at the request of the other party, stay the proceedings to allow the parties to fulfil their obligations under the mediation clause. However, the judge is not obliged to do so. The judge may decide not to suspend the proceedings, for example, because the case is too urgent or because attempting mediation would be futile.[134] A court or tribunal may therefore decline request for suspension of the proceedings, even if it decides that the mediation clause is binding. This is left at the discretion of the court or tribunal.

Despite the foregoing, the Supreme Court did not quash the judgment of the Court of Appeal. The reason is that, according to the Supreme Court, the Court of Appeal had not violated the legal standard formulated by the Supreme Court (for the first time) in the Lotamblau Judgment. Also, the Court of Appeal's interpretation of the mediation clause concluded

132 Supreme Court 12 July 2024, ECLI:NL:HR:2024:1078, para 3.2.2 (*Lotamblau*).

133 Supreme Court 12 July 2024, ECLI:NL:HR:2024:1078, para 3.2.2 (*Lotamblau*), also referring to CJEU 18 March 2010, C-317/08, ECLI:EU:C:2010:146 (*Alassini*) and CJEU 14 June 2017, C-75/16, ECLI:EU:C:2017:457 (*Menini*).

134 Supreme Court 12 July 2024, ECLI:NL:HR:2024:1078, para 3.2.2 (*Lotamblau*).

between Lotamblau and PPSB was not incomprehensible according to the Supreme Court. Therefore, it rejected the cassation appeal.[135]

12.3.5 *What is next for the now-enforceable mediation clause in the Netherlands?*

The Lotamblau Judgment confirms that mediation clauses can be binding, depending on their contents and wording. Below, we will discuss its impact and next steps for parties, courts and arbitral institutions, and the legislator.

12.3.5.1 Drafting of mediation clauses after the Lotamblau Judgment

The Lotamblau Judgment prompts parties to review and revise their dispute resolution clauses in at least three respects, given the importance the Supreme Court attached to how such clauses must be interpreted.

First, if an obligation to try mediation is enforceable or not depends on its interpretation, for which the text is the most important starting point. Therefore, if parties intend a mediation clause to be enforceable, the mediation clause needs to stipulate explicitly that the parties expressly agree that they *shall* or *must* attempt mediation prior to initiating court or arbitral proceedings and that they accept that a court or arbitral tribunal may suspend the proceedings if mediation has not been tried.

Second, the Supreme Court determined that the extent to which parties are obliged to try mediation also depends on the interpretation of the clause. Therefore, in our view, parties would be advised to stipulate as clearly as possible which steps the parties need before they may initiate an arbitration or court proceedings. For example, the mediation clause may prescribe that parties must attend an introductory meeting with a mediator only, that a mediator must be appointed and/or that a mediation agreement must be concluded. Also, the clause may provide that an arbitration or litigation may only be started after mediation has been tried for a fixed amount of time. If the text of the clause is unclear, various other circumstances may come into play under the *Haviltex*-standard and other Dutch law doctrines which can lead to a complicated legal debate.

135 Supreme Court 12 July 2024, ECLI:NL:HR:2024:1078, para 3.3 (*Lotamblau*).

Third, the Supreme Court ruled in the Lotamblau Judgment that a court or tribunal is not obliged to suspend the proceedings if, for example, the case is too urgent or because attempting mediation would be futile. In our view it would make sense to stipulate that the mediation clause does not preclude the parties from requesting relief in summary proceedings (*kort geding*) or emergency arbitration. Also we advise to clarify that the mediation clause does not apply if it is necessary to start (arbitral) proceedings to prevent a lapse of a term for starting proceedings after making a conservatory attachment (*conservatoir beslag*) or to prevent that a statutory limitation period (*verjaringstermijn*) lapses. In the latter case, in our view, parties may still want to determine that the (arbitral) proceedings will be stayed, but only after the proceedings have already been lodged.

Dispute resolution clauses currently in use do not always contain such language and, in our view, deserve a critical review. For example, the Netherlands Arbitration Institute (NAI) provides, on its website, the possibility to generate a draft mediation clause in case NAI-arbitration is used as a safety net.[136] When writing this article, we were informed that the clause will be redrafted following the Lotamblau Judgment. Potential amendments that the NAI rule-makers could consider, are for instance, the following:

Dispute resolution clause: mediation and arbitration

1. All disputes arising in connection with the present agreement, or further agreements resulting therefrom, shall be settled in accordance with the Mediation Rules and Arbitration Rules of the Netherlands Arbitration Institute ('NAI').
2. For the purposes of resolution of each and any dispute that has arisen or might arise further to the present agreement, or any further agreements resulting from the same, the parties hereby expressly commit and fully agree to be bound to the obligation to, prior to initiating an

136 Currently, the model clause reads (in case one opts for (i) NAI arbitration as a safety net, (ii) party appointment and (iii) English proceedings): "For the purposes of resolution of each and any dispute that has arisen or might arise further to the present agreement, or any further agreements resulting from the same, the parties shall – or a party shall – file a request for mediation with the NAI secretariat in accordance with the NAI Mediation Rules. If such request fails to result in a comprehensive resolution of the dispute by conclusion of a contract of settlement as referred to in Article 7(1) (a) of the NAI Mediation Rules, by an arbitral award on agreed terms as referred to in Article 8 of said Rules, or by a combination of both, the dispute – or any part thereof not resolved in any of the aforesaid manners – shall be resolved exclusively in accordance with the NAI Arbitration Rules. The mediator shall be appointed according by the parties. The mediation shall be conducted in the English language."

arbitration, try to resolve the dispute through mediation. For these purposes, a request for mediation must be with the NAI Secretariat in accordance with Article 3 of the NAI Mediation Rules. The mediator shall be appointed in accordance with Article 4 of the NAI Mediation Rules. The mediation shall be conducted in the English language.

3. Parties expressly agree that they shall be entitled to initiate arbitration proceedings in accordance with the NAI Arbitration Rules, but only after:
   (i) a mediation has been initiated as set out in paragraph 2;
   (ii) at least the meeting with the mediator as described in Article 5(1) NAI Mediation Rules has taken place; and
   (iii) no Mediation Agreement as referred to in Article 5(1) NAI Mediation Rules has been concluded or, in the event that a Mediation Agreement has been concluded, the mediation has failed to result in a contract of settlement as referred to in Article 7(1) (a) of the NAI Mediation Rules, an arbitral award on agreed terms as referred to in Article 8 of said Rules, or by a combination of both.

   The place of arbitration shall be [Amsterdam]. The proceedings shall be conducted in the English language.
4. Parties expressly agree that if an arbitration is initiated before a mediation is initiated in accordance with paragraph 2 and before the conditions mentioned in paragraph 3(i)-(iii) have been met, the arbitral tribunal may, at the request of one of the parties, stay the arbitration proceedings until a mediation has been initiated in accordance with paragraph 2 and the conditions of paragraph 3(i)-(iii) have been met.
5. The obligation try mediation before initiating an arbitration as set out above in paragraphs 2 and 3 shall not apply if it is necessary to start arbitration proceedings to prevent a lapse of rights, such as (i) a term for starting proceedings after making a conservatory attachment (*conservatoir beslag*) or (ii) a statutory limitation period (*verjaringstermijn*). Parties expressly agree that, once the arbitration proceedings have been initiated in such scenario, the arbitral tribunal may, at the request of one of the parties, stay the arbitration proceedings until a mediation has been initiated in accordance with paragraph 2 and the conditions of paragraph 3(i)-(iii) have been met.
6. A request to suspend the arbitration proceedings within the meaning of paragraphs 4 and 5 may be made unilaterally by the defendant in the short answer meant in Article 9 of the NAI Arbitration Rules. Thereafter, a request to suspend the arbitration proceedings can only be submitted to the arbitral tribunal jointly by the parties.

7. Paragraphs 2-6 do not preclude the right of a party to start an emergency arbitration within the meaning of Article 41 of the NAI Arbitration Rules. Paragraphs 2-6 shall also apply in case of Expedited Proceedings within the meaning of Article 42 of the NAI Arbitration Rules, unless the parties have agreed otherwise.

In paragraph 12.3 drafted above, the mediation clause does not oblige the parties to conclude a mediation agreement, but only to attend an introductory meeting with the mediator. It is possible to opt for an alternative, in which the parties are obliged to conclude a mediation agreement (and not only to attend an introductory meeting with a mediation). Also, it is possible to include a timeframe in which the mediation should be concluded, which we discuss further below.

12.3.5.2 Potential amendment of procedural rules of court and arbitral institutions

The Lotamblau Judgment may also inspire courts and arbitral institutions to review and revise their procedural rules.[137] In our view, it would at the very least make sense to codify the Lotamblau Judgment in court and arbitral rules, which already contain provisions on when the proceedings may be suspended. It could be added to these rules that, in case of a binding mediation clause, the court or tribunal *may* suspend the proceedings until mediation has been tried (and failed).

Advocate General De Bock suggested that arbitral rules could provide that the tribunal, in principle, *must* stay proceedings if a binding mediation clause has been violated.[138] Given the discretionary power granted to judges and arbitrators in the Lotamblau Judgment, we believe that it would go too far to *oblige* courts and tribunals to suspend the proceedings. However, in our view, it would be possible for courts and arbitral institutions to regulate if and for how long the proceedings should be suspended if a binding mediation clause if violated, when the request for suspension should ultimately be made, and under what conditions the proceedings can be resumed. Courts and arbitral tribunals could try to regulate, among others, the following topics. As long as such provisions do not take away the discretionary nature of the decisions of courts and tribunals, these pro-

137 Opinion of Advocate General De Bock rendered prior to Supreme Court 12 July 2024, ECLI:NL:PHR:2024:103, para 17.33; Bosnak 2019, p 327.

138 Opinion of Advocate General De Bock rendered prior to Supreme Court 12 July 2024, ECLI:NL:PHR:2024:103, para 17.33; Bosnak 2019, p 327.

visions would be in line with the 'system' as set out in the Lotamblau Judgment.

First, how far the obligation to try mediation goes depends on the interpretation of the mediation clause. It would depend on the mediation clause if parties are obliged to conclude a mediation agreement or only to go to an introductory meeting with a mediator (e.g. in Article 5(1) of the NAI Mediation Rules). If a party is obliged to conclude a mediation agreement, the question is how many steps parties should take in the mediation before the arbitration or court proceedings can be continued. Since mediation is voluntary and confidential, in our view, it would simply be possible for a party to report to the court or tribunal that mediation has been unsuccessfully tried, after which the arbitration or court proceedings would have to be resumed. Courts and arbitral rules could be amended to reflect this.

Second, it would not be desirable, in our view, to include a fixed timeframe (e.g. 15 days, 1 month or 3 months) within which parties must try mediation, after which they may start with litigation or arbitration. In our experience, such timeframes can put unnecessary pressure on parties and mediators or provide an unnecessary constraint on the parties to start litigation or arbitration. For this reason, we would advise against including such timeframes in mediation clauses and/or the procedural rules of courts and arbitral institutions. However, for practical purposes it would make sense that if a case is suspended for the parties to try mediation, parties should report within e.g. four weeks (or if necessary: longer) to the court or tribunal on how to continue the proceedings. If the mediation is still pending, this period can be extended as long as both parties agree.

Third, to avoid abuse of mediation clauses, arbitral institutions and courts may include in their rules that a request to suspend the proceedings to try mediation can be made unilaterally only at a very early stage of the proceedings (i.e. in NAI-arbitration: ultimately together with the short answer and in court proceedings, for example, ultimately when the defendant appear in the proceedings). In our view, such provisions are also in line with the notion that mediation must be tried *before* the proceedings are started. Otherwise, a defendant could use the mediation clause at a later stage of the proceedings only to try to derail the proceedings or buy time, which would be against the principle of reasonableness and fairness.

Finally, the Supreme Court determined that judges and arbitrators can decide against staying proceedings in case they deem mediation futile. In our view, this notion can only be applied in so far as it is not contradictory with the language in the mediation clause, which may oblige parties to take certain procedural steps in any event, such as to initiate mediation proceedings and attend an introductory meeting with the mediator, and/or to conclude a mediation agreement (see paragraph 12.3.5.1 above). Moreover, we find that this exception must be applied with reticence. De Groot rightly pointed out that determining whether or not mediation would be futile effectively puts the judge or arbitrator in the mediator's shoes.[139] The judge or arbitrator may lack the mediator's experience(s) and lack of knowledge of the fact that making parties comply with a mediation obligation can be fruitful even if they are skeptical at first.[140] Our recommendation to arbitrators and judges would be to trust in the mediation process, and refer parties to mediation more often than not. This would not only reduce the workload of courts, but also save on both time and money.[141]

12.3.5.3 The next step for the legislator?

For now it is up to legal practitioners, including drafters of dispute resolution clauses and the drafters of the rulesets of courts and arbitral institutions, to respond to the Lotamblau Judgment. It is also conceivable that the legislator takes further action.

First, a next step towards giving (corporate) mediation a more prominent place in Dutch ADR would be to determine that, as Advocate General De Bock suggested, judges and arbitrators *must* in in principle suspend pending proceedings if a binding mediation clause is violated, subject to the exceptions as discussed above. This would take away some of the discretion of judges and arbitrators, which – under the Lotamblau Judgment – may decide not to suspend pending proceedings even if the mediation clause is binding.

Second, another measure that the legislator could take is to provide that courts and tribunals must declare a claim inadmissible if a party initiates court or arbitral proceedings in violation of a binding mediation clause,

139 J.A. de Groot, annotation to Supreme Court 12 July 2024, ECLI:NL:HR:2024:1078, *JAR* 2024/217.

140 See para 12.3.2.1 above.

141 See e.g. the empirical research conducted by Jagtenberg & De Roo mentioned above, showing that compulsory mediation can have beneficial effects on workloads in the judiciary, see Jagtenberg & De Roo 2003, p 65-66.

as is the case in other jurisdictions (e.g. Belgium, Germany and Italy).[142] However, a sanction such as inadmissibility would require a specific basis in the law[143] and would also need to contain exceptions for scenario's in which starting litigation or arbitration is necessary to prevent lapse of rights as discussed above.[144]

It is in our view an open question whether or not such additional measures would be necessary, also given the high degree of discretion that is now passed to judges and arbitrators. It is up to them to deal with mediation clauses in particular cases and to determine whether or not proceedings should be suspended to try mediation. It is too soon in our view to draw any conclusions on the effects of the Lotamblau Judgment on mediation practice. However, in due course, the legislator could evaluate whether or not mediation clauses are sufficiently enforced and whether or not further measures would need to be considered.

12.4 Conclusion

Corporate mediation in the Netherlands provides businesses with a powerful, flexible, and cost-effective means of resolving disputes while maintaining relationships and safeguarding sensitive information. Whether addressing contractual disagreements, internal conflicts, or complex multi-party disputes, mediation offers a collaborative and pragmatic approach to conflict resolution. The growing use of mediation in Dutch corporate practice reflects a broader cultural shift toward consensus-building, efficiency, and sustaining long-term partnerships.

As explored in this article, while mediation is recognized globally as an effective tool for resolving corporate disputes, the Dutch approach distinguishes itself by its emphasis on voluntariness, consensus-building, and maintaining business relationships. The Dutch legal framework, business culture, and the role of mediators provide a unique landscape for corporate mediation that differs from Anglo-American practices, particularly in terms of flexibility and the facilitative nature of the mediation process. However, recent developments, including the Lotamblau Judgment, signal a shift toward enforcing the obligation to try mediation, creating more

142 See para 12.3.3.3 above.
143 See also Opinion of Advocate General De Bock rendered prior to Supreme Court 3 April 2022, ECLI:NL:PHR:2021:1228, para 2.1.
144 See para 12.3.5.1 above.

certainty for businesses that choose mediation as a means of resolving disputes.

The evolution of mediation in the Netherlands, particularly with the rise of proactive mediators and hybrid models like med-arb, provides businesses and their legal counsel with a diverse set of tools for resolving disputes quickly and effectively. This trend reflects the increasing complexity of corporate disputes and the demand for solutions that not only address legal concerns but also protect business interests and preserve long-term relationships.

For legal professionals, a comprehensive understanding of the dynamics of corporate mediation, the evolving role of mediators, and the practical benefits of this approach is crucial in advising clients and navigating the complex landscape of corporate disputes. By embracing these mediation tools, lawyers can better guide their clients toward effective, cost-efficient, and relationship-preserving solutions.

As corporate mediation continues to evolve, both in the Netherlands and globally, the challenge remains to strike the right balance between voluntary participation and enforceability, ensuring that mediation remains a viable alternative to litigation. The Lotamblau Judgment has strengthened the role of mediation in Dutch ADR, offering businesses a more structured pathway for dispute resolution while maintaining the flexibility that makes mediation an attractive option. The Netherlands, with its focus on pragmatism and cooperation, remains a leader in promoting mediation as a cornerstone of corporate dispute resolution, and legal professionals must remain attuned to these developments to effectively leverage mediation for their clients.

In the broader context of ADR, mediation not only provides a means to resolve disputes but also helps businesses safeguard their future, enabling them to focus on sustainable growth while avoiding the disruption and adversarial nature of litigation.

CHAPTER 13

NAI AND NCC(A): COMPETITORS OR PEERS IN RESOLVING INTERNATIONAL COMMERCIAL DISPUTES?

Rieme-Jan Tjittes[1]

13.1 Introduction[2]

In the Netherlands, by amendment of the Dutch Code of Civil Procedure (DCCP)[3] of 1 January 2019, a special chamber was initiated at both the Amsterdam District Court and the Amsterdam Court of Appeal, where international disputes in commercial matters can be litigated entirely in English. The Netherlands Commercial Court (NCC) as a court of first instance, and the Netherlands Commercial Court of Appeal (NCCA) for appeal commenced on that date. This new branch on the tree of government jurisdiction raises the question as to how it relates to international arbitration. When will companies in an international commercial dispute opt for arbitration (under the aegis of the NAI, for example) and when will they opt for the NCC(A)?

Before answering that question, I remark that many commercial disputes are settled amicably at some point, either before the start, during or even after the proceedings in court or in arbitration (see para 13.2). Much research has been done on what may or may not appeal to a company to have

1 Professor dr. R.P.J.L. (Rieme-Jan) Tjittes (LLM) is a lawyer (*advocaat*) and partner Commercial Litigation & Arbitration at BarentsKrans (The Hague, the Netherlands), judge sitting by designation at the NCC, and professor of Private Law at the Vrije Universiteit (Amsterdam). Rieme-Jan frequently acts as an arbitrator in national and international arbitrations under various arbitration rules (i.a. NAI, ICC, AAA/ICDR, UNCITRAL, EDF, SAI, ad hoc).

2 Large parts of this article have been published in Dutch in: R.P.J.L. Tjittes, 'NAI en NCC(A): concurrenten of collega's bij de beslechting van commerciële geschillen?', in: C.J.M. Klaassen et al (eds), *Going Dutch: ADR in Nederland, in het bijzonder bij het NAI (Onderneming en recht no 113)*, Deventer: Wolters Kluwer 2019, p 269-287 and in R.P.J.L. Tjittes, *Commercieel Contractenrecht, deel I, 2e druk*, The Hague: Boom legal 2022, p 43-58.

3 The Netherlands Commercial Court initiated a translation in English of relevant parts of the DCCP: A. Burrough et al, *Code of Civil procedure, Selected Sections and the NCC Rules*, The Hague: Eleven Publishers 2022.

an international dispute adjudicated in arbitration (para 3). When those reasons are contrasted with the features of proceedings at the NCC(A) (as described in para 4), it will become clear in which cases a company would prefer arbitral proceedings and in which cases a company would prefer proceedings before the NCC(A) (para 5).

My conclusion is that for disputes with a high commercial (and financial) interest, in particular if the enforcement of a decision is to take place outside Europe, arbitration will likely remain the most preferable method of dispute resolution. For medium-sized international disputes, where enforcement can take place in Europe, the NCC(A) is an advisable route (para 6).

13.2 Amicable settlement of commercial disputes

When it comes to resolution of disputes related to commercial contracts, it should be borne in mind that the bulk of such disputes do not lead to proceedings in the public courts or to arbitration. International research shows that a commercial dispute is amicably settled in ther majority of cases (57%).[4] Of the disputes that do not get settled amicably, only a minority (32%) lead to court proceedings or arbitration. Apparently, businesspeople just leave it at that in quite some cases. Dutch research showed that, as regards construction contracts, disputes arise in 84% of the cases, but that only 1,6% of these disputes will lead to a legal action (and an even lower percentage will lead to court proceedings or arbitration). In seller-purchaser relations, disputes arise in 67% of the transactions, but legal action is taken in only 0,6% of cases.[5]

An amicable settlement, or a lack of follow-up litigation or arbitration, will be particularly relevant if the parties intend to continue their commercial relationship. If such a commercial interest no longer exists (e.g. because one of the parties is insolvent), there is little reason for an amicable settlement or a waiver of further proceedings.

Research on international arbitration shows that even during arbitral proceedings that are already ongoing, parties regularly attempt to reach

4 Queen Mary University of London, School of International Arbitration, International Arbitration Survey: Corporate choices in International Arbitration – Industry perspectives, 2013 (hereinafter Queen Mary 2013), p 5.

5 See F. van Dijk, *Conflicten in economische ketens*, The Hague: Boom legal 2019, p 27-28.

a settlement: 25% of pending arbitration cases are settled so that no arbitral award needs to be rendered.[6] A large proportion of those settlements (43%) takes place after the arbitration has started, but before the first oral hearing has taken place. In 27% of those cases, the dispute was settled to preserve existing commercial relationships. Settlements after an arbitral award has been made are also quite common: as many as 40% of the companies surveyed reached a settlement that involved negotiating a discount on an order for payment in exchange for immediate payment. Even 19% of the parties that have prevailed in arbitration still agree to a settlement in order to preserve the existing commercial relationship.

13.3 Arbitration

13.3.1 The perceived advantages of arbitration

In international commercial contracts, arbitration is agreed onas the preferred method of dispute resolution in many cases. This is particularly true for larger multinational companies, major commercial contracts (such as Sale Purchase Agreements and Shareholders' Agreements) and large-scale contracts with an important technical aspect (such as large-scale construction, installation, and IT projects). Research and data from arbitral institutions show that disputes over commercial contracts constitute the bulk of arbitrations, followed at a fair distance by construction law disputes and disputes between shareholders in joint ventures.[7]

An international survey of corporate counsel shows that for as many as 90% of counsel, international arbitration is their preferred dispute resolution mechanism (combined with ADR, such as mediation, in a significant 59% of cases).[8]

6 Queen Mary University of London, School of International Arbitration, International arbitration: corporate attitudes and practices, 2008 (hereinafter Queen Mary 2008), p 6 et seq.

7 Queen Mary 2008, p 5.

8 See Queen Mary University of London, School of International Arbitration, International arbitration: Current choices and future adaptations, 2021, p 5 (Queen Mary 2021). This number is in line with earlier research (86%) in 2008, 2013, and 2015 (90%) and 2018 (97%). See (summary) Queen Mary 2008, p 2. See also Queen Mary University of London, School of International Arbitration, Corporate choices in International Arbitration: Industry perspectives', 2013, p 4 (Queen Mary 2013), Queen Mary University of London, School of International Arbitration, International Arbitration Survey: Improvements and Innovations in International Arbitration, 2015 (Queen Mary 2015), p 2 and p 5, and Queen Mary University of London,

They see as the main advantages of arbitration over proceedings in state courts the wide possibility of international enforcement (under the New York Convention 1958) (64%),[9] neutrality, i.e. the avoidance of specific national legal systems and national courts (60%), the flexibility of the arbitral procedure (40%), the possibility that each party may choose its own arbitrator (39%) and confidentiality of the arbitration (36%).[10]

The majority of companies prefer a method of appointing an arbitral tribunal in which each party appoints an arbitrator, who then jointly appoint a Chair (76%).[11] Parties want as much control as possible on the adjudicators of their dispute.

Companies mostly have a policy on whether they intend to have their disputes settled by arbitration or through state court proceedings (81%).[12] If arbitration is chosen, sometimes there are policies regarding the arbitral institution to be chosen (92%), the language of the arbitration (90%), the place of arbitration (85%) and confidentiality (84%). That arbitration must be chosen per se as the dispute resolution mechanism is the policy at only 10% of companies. However, confidentiality (33%) is an absolute requirement.[13] As a general rule, this requirement of confidentiality cannot be realized in public proceedings before the state courts (except where trade secrets or highly sensitive commercial and financial information are to be submitted).

13.3.2 *The perceived disadvantages of arbitration*

The disadvantages of arbitration mentioned by legal counsel are the high cost of arbitral proceedings (67%), the lack of effective sanctions during the proceedings, especially to counteract delaying tactics by lawyers (45%), the lack of applicability of arbitration clauses vis-à-vis third parties (39%), the long duration of arbitral proceedings (34%)(on average, an arbitration

School of International Arbitration, 2018 International Arbitration Survey: The Evolution of International Arbitration (Queen Mary 2018), p 2 and p 5.

9 The 1958 New York Convention, which deals with the recognition and enforcement of foreign arbitral awards, has 172 parties.

10 See Queen Mary 2018, p 7. See earlier and similarly Queen Mary 2015, p 2 and p 6.

11 Queen Mary University of London, 2012. International Arbitration Survey: Current and Preferred Practices in the Arbitral Process, p 2 and p 5.

12 Queen Mary 2010, p 5.

13 Queen Mary 2010, p 6. It is also a 'deal breaker' (27%) when negotiating an arbitration clause (Queen Mary 2010, p 7).

lasts 12-18 months,[14] but outliers upwards are no exception) and lack of efficiency of arbitrators (30%).[15] These disadvantages apparently do not undermine international arbitration being the preferred dispute resolution mechanism in international business.

13.3.3 *The preferred arbitral institutions and seats*

The majority of arbitrations in 2010-2015 were conducted under the banner (and according to the rules) of an arbitral institution (79%). Ad hoc arbitrations are in the minority.[16]

The currently most frequently chosen arbitral institutions are the Court of Arbitration of the International Chamber of Commerce (ICC) (57%), the Singapore International Arbitration Court (SIAC) (49%), the Hong Kong International Arbitration Court (HKIAC) (44%), the London Court of International Arbitration (LCIA) (39%), the China International Economic and Trade Arbitration Commission (CIETAC) (17%), the International Centre for Settlement of Investment Disputes (World Bank) (ICSID) (11%), the Stockholm Chamber of Commerce (SCC) (7%) and the American Arbitration Association/International Centre for Dispute Resolution (AAA/ICDR) (6%).[17] The strong rise of arbitral institutions in Asia to the detriment of institutions like the traditional ones such as ICC and LCIA is remarkable. Ad hoc arbitrations (an arbitration not under the rules of an arbitral institution) are mostly conducted under the regime of the UNCITRAL Arbitration Rules (76%).[18]

The main reasons for choosing a particular arbitral institution are its overall reputation and recognition in the field, a high service level of administration (including efficiency, proactivity, facilities and quality of staff) and previous experience with the institute.[19]

The formal seat of the arbitration most valued is Londen (54%), together with Singapore (54%) and Hong Kong (50%), followed with some distance

14 See International Arbitration, Research-based report on perceived delay in arbitration process, Berwin Leighton Paisner, 2010, p 4.
15 See Queen Mary 2018, p 8. See in similar vein Queen Mary 2015, p 2 and p 7 and Queen Mary 2008.
16 Queen Mary 2015, p 17. See also Queen Mary 2008, p 15 (86%). See also Queen Mary 2010, p 3.
17 Queen Mary 2021, p 10.
18 Queen Mary 2021, p 9.
19 Queen Mary 2018, p 14. This is consistent with previous findings Queen Mary 2015, p 18 and Queen Mary 2010, p 21.

by Paris (35%), Geneva (13%) and New York city (12%).[20] The strong rise of seats in Asia to the detriment of traditional seats like London, Paris and Geneva is noteworthy. The reasons for choosing the 'seat' are mainly the reputation and international recognition of the seat of the arbitration and the neutrality and impartiality of the local law (in aid of arbitration).[21] Where English law is internationally popular, this is true for London as the seat of arbitration as well.

13.4 The Netherlands Commercial Court (of Appeal)

13.4.1 Introduction

As mentioned before: with effect from 1 January 2019, the Netherlands Commercial Court (NCC) and the Netherlands Commercial Court of Appeal (NCCA) commenced. The NCC and the NCCA are special chambers of the Amsterdam District Court and the Amsterdam Court of Appeal respectively, where proceedings can be conducted entirely in English in international cases (Article 32a DCCP). The judgments of the NCC(A) are in principle rendered in English as well.[22]

If the NCC has jurisdiction, the court in summary proceedings (provisional relief judge) of the Amsterdam District Court also has jurisdiction in summary proceedings to hear and decide cases in English (Article 32a(3) DCCP).[23] The same is true for the court in summary proceedings of the NCCA. In practice the NCC will provide a judge to act as the court in summary proceedings.[24]

Appeals in cassation from a judgment in appeal of the NCCA can be filed with the Dutch Supreme Court (DSC). Proceedings before the Supreme Court can in principle only be conducted in Dutch, unless the Supreme Court gives permission to file documents in English. However, the Supreme Court has indicated that it will hear the case based on the docu-

20 Queen Mary 2021, p 6.
21 Queen Mary 2018, p 11. See in a similar vein Queen Mary 2015, p 13.
22 If part of the judgment must be entered in the public registers (for example, a judgment that replaces a notarial deed e.g. for the transfer of property of land, Article 3:300 in conjunction with 3:89 DCC), then those parts are also decided in Dutch (Article 32a(5) DCCP). See Explanatory Note II, *Parliamentary Papers II* 2016/17, 34761, no 3 (hereinafter EN II), p 14.
23 EN II, p 12.
24 See A.I.M. van Mierlo, in: *T&C Rv*, Article 30r, note 7.

ments filed in English in the lower courts and that no translation of these documents in Dutch is required.[25] The Supreme Court's ruling will be in Dutch, but in appropriate cases the Supreme Court will provide a translation in English.[26]

The NCC will hear cases in a panel of three judges (Article 3.5.1 NCC(A) Rules), except in summary proceedings. The NCCA does always sit in a panel of three judges. It is generally considered that decisions by a court that consists of more than a single judge generally have a better quality and are more respected by the parties.[27]

The selection of judges for the NCC(A) is based on criteria such as excellent command of the English language, experience in international commercial practice and the ability to manage complex commercial disputes.[28] In particular, the success of the NCC(A) will depend on the quality of the judges and their decisions. Unlike some other jurisdictions (Abu Dhabi, Dubai, Quatar and Singapore), Dutch law does not allow for non-Dutch nationals to be a judge at the NCC(A).[29]

To date (9 September 2024) there have been 24 cases decided by the NCC (including summary judgments) and two decided by the NCCA. In particular the requirements that it must be explicitly agreed to conduct the procedure before the NCC, and in English (see para 13.4.4 below) are a threshold that is not easily overcome.

---

25 NCC(A) Rules Explanatory Notes, p 40.

26 EN II, p 7. See also Memorandum II, no 6, p 6 as well as MvA I, *Parliamentary Papers I* 2017/18, 34761, B, p 6-7 (hereinafter EN I). The Supreme Court (Supreme Court 15 January 2016, ECLI:NL:HR:2016:65) finds that, in principle, a judge should be presumed to be able to understand productions in English, French and German. See E.J. Numann, 'De NCC – Perspectief van de Hoge Raad', in: E. Bauw, H. Koster & S.A. Kruisinga (eds), *De kansen voor een Netherlands Commercial Court*, The Hague: Boom legal 2018, p 116.

27 J. Hoeben, A.L. Keirse & M.D. Reijneveld, 'Opteren voor de Netherlands Commercial Court', *Contracteren* 2017, issue 2, p 43.

28 See EN I, p 9 (above). See A.E. Dorsman, 'Netherlands Commercial Court', in: M. Holtzer, A.F.J.A. Leijten & D. Oranje (eds), *Geschriften vanwege de Vereniging Corporate Litigation 2015-2016*, Deventer: Wolters Kluwer 2016, p 308-309 en R.A. Boon, 'De Netherlands Commercial Court – Van idee tot oprichting', in: E. Bauw, H. Koster & S.A. Kruisinga (eds), *De kansen voor een Netherlands Commercial Court*, The Hague: Boom legal 2018, p 41-42.

29 See M. Yip & G. Rühl, *Succes and impact of international commercial courts: a first assessment, yearbook of Private International Law 24*, 2022-2023, p 45 et seq para IV under A.

13.4.2 *The reasons for the Dutch legislator to initiate the NCC(A)*

The Dutch legislator has given several reasons for the creation of the NCC(A).[30]

First, that international business is mostly conducted in English. The legislator points out that English is the leading working language in international trade, that contracts are increasingly drafted in English and that advisers more and more correspond with their international clients in English.

Second, that arbitration has become too costly for small and medium enterprises (SMEs).

Third, that the state courts will be relieved of complex international cases, giving them more opportunity to decide other cases.

Fourth, stimulating the investment and trade climate in the Netherlands.[31] In this sense, there is 'regulatory competition' (competition between legal systems), now that 'commercial courts' have been or are being set up in other countries as well.[32]

In the countries surrounding the Netherlands comparable commercial courts exist, although the NCC(A) does have advantages over most of them.[33] I refer to the London Commercial Court (the Commercial Court of the Queen's Bench Division of the High Court of Justice) (disadvantage: wide disclosure obligations, very high lawyer's fees), the 'chambre internationale' of the Tribunal de Commerce Paris and in appeal the Cour d'Appel de Paris (disadvantage: the submissions and the judgment must be in French), and commercial courts set up by various states in Germany such as in Mannheim and Stuttgart and in appeal in Karlsruhe and Stuttgart (disadvantage: the submissions and judgment must be in German).

30 EN II, p 1-3.
31 Further Note II, p 1.
32 See M. Neekilappillai, 'Netherlands Commercial Court. Regelgevingsconcurrentie op de markt voor geschilbeslechting', *NJB* 2017/1231. See for the financial impact of the introduction of the NCC(A) on the Dutch economy: Van Dijk 2019, p 23 et seq.
33 See D.J. Oranje, 'De plussen van de Netherlands Commercial Court', in: B. Bier et al (eds), *Geschriften vanwege de Vereniging Corporate Litigation 2018-2019*, Deventer: Wolters Kluwer 2019, p 303-310.

The parties' choice of forum is usually closely linked to their choice of applicable substantive law.[34] In this context, an important argument put forward by the legislator is that a jurisdiction should encourage freedom of contract and legal certainty in contracts. The legislator noted the following:

> "As an internationally oriented trading country, the Netherlands has a strong interest in ensuring that trade has certainty and clarity on contracts, which can be enforced through the courts if necessary."[35]

Choosing a Dutch court makes particularly sense if Dutch law applies to the parties' legal relationship. As seen in international arbitration, a major reason for choosing a particular seat of arbitration (42%) is that the seat of arbitration is located in the jurisdiction of the applicable law.[36] After all, it is practical to declare a Dutch court to have jurisdiction if Dutch law applies.In that case the court can apply its own, familiar law.

Therefore, in my opinion to make the NCC(A) a success, it will be necessary not only to promote the features of proceedings at the NCC(A), but also to promote Dutch private law (in particular contract law) as the law applicable to an international commercial contract.[37] The place of dispute resolution follows the applicable substantive law in many cases. In my

34 See T. Eisenberg & G.P. Miller, 'The flight to New York: an empirical study of choice of law and choice of forum clauses in publicly-held companies' contracts', *Cardozo Law Review* 2009, p 1504.

35 EN II, p 3. Similarly, Further Note II, p 3.

36 See Zie R.P.J.L. Tjittes, Een Netherlands Commercial Court vereist reclame voor Nederlands recht, *RM Themis* 2014, p 261, E. Bauw, 'Ondernemerschap in de rechtspleging. Over de kansen van een Netherlands Commercial Court', *AA* 2016, p 98, H.N. Schelhaas, 'De markt op met de Nederlandse rechtsorde?', *NTBR* 2017/10, p 74, Neekilappillai 2017, p 1600, J. Hoeben et al, 'De Netherlands Commercial Court tot een succes maken', in: E. Bauw, H. Koster & S.A. Kruisinga (eds), *De kansen voor een Netherlands Commercial Court*, The Hague: Boom legal 2018, p 83 en T. Hartlief, 'Kooplieden in het recht', njb.nl, 26 June 2018. See in international perspective: G. Wagner, 'Dispute resolution as a product: competition between civil justice systems', in: H. Eidenmüller (ed), *Regulatory competition in contract law and dispute resolution*, München: Beck 2013, p 399-400.

37 See P. Kuipers, 'Bedrijf, jurist en de Netherlands Commercial Court', in: E. Bauw, H. Koster & S.A. Kruisinga (eds), *De kansen voor een Netherlands Commercial Court*, The Hague: Boom legal 2018, p 126, Hoeben 2018, p 84-85, P.E. Ernste & F.E. Vermeulen, 'The Netherlands Commercial Court – an attractive venue for international commercial disputes?', *TCR* 2016, p 130, M. van Hooijdonk, 'Internationale uitdagingen voor de Netherlands Commercial Court', in: M. Holtzer, A.F.J.A. Leijten & D. Oranje (eds), *Geschriften vanwege de Vereniging Corporate Litigation 2015-2016*, Deventer: Wolters Kluwer 2016, p 337 en Tjittes 2014, p 261.

firm opinion, Dutch commercial contract law can certainly match (or is even preferred over) the much-chosen English contract law.[38]

Nevertheless, the NCC has shown to be perfectly able to apply foreign law as well, such as English law.[39] In one case decided by the NCC, Professor McKendrick et al said the following about the application of English contract law by the NCC:

> "The decision of the court in Subsea Survey Solution LLC v. South Stream Transport BV demonstrates that the NCC can provide efficient proceedings in the English language for international commercial disputes, even when governed under laws other than Dutch law. The NCC, with the assistance of the party-appointed English law experts, clearly set out how Clause 7 of the Settlement Agreement should be interpreted according to English law and proved to be able to apply English law in a correct manner."[40]

13.4.3 *Tailormade proceedings at the NCC(A)*

Proceedings at the NCC(A) are governed by Dutch civil procedural law (or a relevant international instrument).[41]

The NCC(A) Rules[42] allow for a flexible method of litigation within the boundaries of Dutch civil procedural law. This makes it possible to create a procedural practice similar to international arbitration and/or with elements of a common law procedure.[43] For example, at the beginning of the proceedings (and/or before the oral hearing), a case management conference (CMC) can be organized (often via videoconference) to discuss procedural arrangements and timing, the judges on the case are also the judges that handle the docket[44], the *IBA rules on the taking of evidence in international*

38 See Tjittes 2022, p 38-43.

39 NCC 4 March 2020, ECLI:NL:RBAMS:2020:1388 (*Subsea Survey Solutions LLP v South Stream Transport B.V.*).

40 E. McKendrick, J.M. Luyckx & A.M.M. Hendrikx, 'A NCC Case on Contract Interpretation from an English and Dutch Law Perspective', *European Review of Private Law* 2021, p 88, para 37.

41 Such as the Brussels I Regulation Recast on the recognition and enforcement of judgments within the EU.

42 Rules of Procedure for the International Commercial Chambers of the Amsterdam District Court (NCC District Court) and the Amsterdam Court of Appeal (NCC Court of Appeal), 3rd edition, June 2023, Staatscourant (State Gazette) 2023, 16397, 12 June 2023 (texts in both Dutch and English).

43 See Bauw 2018, p 13-16, who speaks of 'London' elements. I see more similarities with procedural practice in international commercial arbitration.

44 Article 3.5.2 NCC(A) Rules.

arbitration (containing limits on discovery possibilities that lie midway between common law and civil law requirements) can be declared a source of inspiration insofar as they are compatible with the statutory law of evidence (including Article 843a DCCP on the production of documents), the parties may be required to provide the opposing party and the judges with a summary of the substance of the arguments to be presented at the hearing two weeks before the hearing, the court may provide the parties before the hearing with a list of specific topics the court wants to discuss at the hearing[45], and a sound or videorecording of the hearing may be ordered, or a court reporter may be appointed to report on the hearing (in a verbatim report instead of the usual minimal summary in a transcript of the hearing by the court in normal court proceedings).[46] It may also be agreed and ordered at the CMC that parties will submit written witness statements together with their submissions (or at a different moment in time)[47], that the witness hearing will primarily be conducted by counsel (with the focus on cross-examination) and not, as is usual in Dutch proceedings, initially and mainly by the court, and that there will be a confrontation of witnesses amongst each other ('hot tubbing') or with parties[48].

Application of Dutch procedural law also means that there will be a mitigated procedural cost award to be borne by the losing party, consisting of court fees, disbursements for witnesses and experts and the reasonably low fixed attorney's fees.[49] This is in contrast to the so-called 'English rule' (where the losing party has to pay all costs of the winner, including the actual lawyer's fees incurred), which rule usually also applies in arbitration (with a certain margin of reasonableness), and the 'American rule' (under which each party bears its own costs).

The court fee for proceedings at the NCC and the NCCA is approximately four times higher than for normal proceedings[50] but usually far less than the costs in international arbitration (where next to the administration fee of the arbitral institution the arbitrators must be paid as well). The court fee at the NCC(A) is based on the expectation that only complex international commercial disputes will be brought before the NCC(A).[51] In 2024,

45 Article 7.1 NCC(A) Rules.
46 Article 7.7.3 NCC(A) Rules.
47 Article 8.5.2 NCC(A) Rules.
48 Article 8.5.4 NCC(A) Rules.
49 See Ernste & Vermeulen 2016, p 131.
50 Nota II, *Parliamentary Papers II* 2017/18, 34761, no 6 (hereinafter: Further Note II), p 10.
51 Further MoA I, *Parliamentary Papers I* 2018/19, 34761, D (hereinafter: Further Note I), p 4.

for proceedings (on the merits) at the NCC, the court fee is € 18,287 and it is € 24,382 at the NCCA. The court fee for summary proceedings at the NCC in first instance is € 9,143 and it is € 12,191 at the NCCA on appeal. The total cost of an Anglo-American procedure (including lawyers' fees) is generally five times higher than in a Dutch court procedure.[52]

Proceedings before the NCC(A) are as a rule public (Article 27(1) DCCP, Article 4 Judiciary Act (Wet op de Rechterlijke Organisatie), Article 121 Dutch Constitution, Article 6 ECHR and Article 7.5 NCC(A) Rules). Only in the cases exhaustively listed in Article 27(1) DCCP can proceedings fully or partially take place behind closed doors. In disputes about commercial contracts, this is only possible to protect privacy (Article 27(1)(c) DCCP). In the case of corporations, this is the case if confidential business information is at issue.[53] This is not easily accepted. The mere fact that market shares, profit margins or business processes are at issue in a case does not justify a hearing behind closed doors. Public access to justice is considered very important.[54] If there are proceedings concerning an (alleged) trade secret[55] within the meaning of the Trade Secrets Act[56] then the court may, upon request, restrict access to documents or hearings (Article 1019ib(3) DCCP). It can restrict access to the hearing to at least one natural person from each party (if that party is a legal entity such as a company) as well as the lawyers in the proceedings (Article 1019ib(5) DCCP). Article 1019ib DCCP is a lex specialis. The NCC(A) Rules provide for similar instruments to safeguard confidential business information.[57]

52 Raad voor de Rechtspraak, *Plan tot oprichting van de Netherlands Commercial Court. Inclusief kosten-batenanalyse*, 2015, p 17.

53 See Explanatory Note, Parl. Gesch. Wijziging Rv, p 163-164 and compare DSC 29 March 1985, *NJ* 1986, 242 (*Enka/Dupont*).

54 See E. Bauw, 'Een Netherlands Commercial Court vanuit rechtsplegingsperspectief', in: E. Bauw, H. Koster & S.A. Kruisinga (eds), *De kansen voor een Netherlands Commercial Court*, The Hague: Boom legal 2018, p 16.

55 Pursuant to para 1 Trade Secrets Act, a 'trade secret' is, in brief, information that (i) is secret, (ii) therefore possesses commercial value and (iii) is subject to measures to keep it secret (e.g. under a secrecy clause).

56 The Trade Secrets Act aims to implement Directive 2016/943/EU of 8 June 2016 on the protection of undisclosed know-how and business information (trade secrets) from unlawful acquisition, use and disclosure, OJEU 2016, L157, which is due by 9 June 2018.

57 Article 8.4.2 and 8.4.3 NCC(A) Rules.

13.4.4 Requirements for jurisdiction of the NCC(A)

For the NCC(A) to have jurisdiction to decide a dispute, a number of requirements apply. If the NCC(A) lacks jurisdiction, the NCC(A) will refer the case to the competent court.[58] The NCC(A) will consider ex officio whether the jurisdiction requirements have been met.[59]

For the jurisdiction of the NCC it is, firstly, required that the Amsterdam District Court has absolute jurisdiction (subject matter jurisdiction) and territorial jurisdiction (jurisdiction over the parties) in first instance (Article 30r(1) DCCP). Similar requirements are relevant for the jurisdiction of the NCCA in appeal.

I reiterate that the NCC(A) is not a special court, but only a chamber of the Amsterdam District Court and the Amsterdam Court of Appeal respectively. Those judicial bodies must first have international, absolute and relative jurisdiction under the normal international, absolute and relative jurisdiction rules in order for a case to fall within the jurisdiction of the NCC(A), as a chamber of those courts.[60]

International jurisdiction may derive from the normal private international rules of jurisdiction, or a choice of forum clause.[61] Therefore, the NCC(A) cannot hear cases that belong to the exclusive jurisdiction of specialized courts, such as the cantonal sector of the District Court (e.g. in disputes about labor law, and landlord and tenant disputes), the Enterprise Chamber of the Amsterdam Court of Appeal, the Patent Chamber of the District Court of The Hague, or the Maritime Chamber of the Rotterdam District Court.[62]

The fact that Dutch procedural law applies also means that first instance, appeal and/or cassation can be waived, making it possible to limit proceedings to one or two instances (in all kinds of combinations, such as, for example, an agreement that the NCCA will be the first and only instance).

Second, the jurisdiction of the NCC(A) requires that all parties involved have expressly agreed to litigate in English (Article 32a(1) DCCP). The parties' choice for the NCC(A) is a procedural agreement and not a choice of

58 EN II, p 12.
59 See Article 1.3.4 NCC(A) Procedural Rules (NCC) and Article 1.3.5 NCC(A) Rules.
60 EN II, p 4.
61 Further Note II, p 2.
62 EN II, p 11. See also commentary on the NCC(A) Rules, p 25.

forum.[63] A choice for the NCC(A) can only be proven by an instrument in writing (Article 32a(1) DCCP).

The parties must both have 'expressly' agreed to a procedure before the NCC(A). A reference to that effect in the general terms and conditions (GTC), which has been tacitly accepted by the other party, does not meet this requirement, according to the legislator.[64] The same applies to a mere reference in a company's articles of association.[65] However, the parties can subsequently explicitly accept such reference to the jurisdiction of the NCC(A) in general terms and conditions, so that ultimately there is an explicit acceptance (Article 32a(1) DCCP).[66] The NCC ruled that an 'express' agreement only means that the choice of both parties for the NCC has been clearly expressed, has been made intentionally, is not hidden in general terms and conditions of one of the parties, and has been laid down in writing.[67]

It is expected that a small entrepreneur will not agree to English-language proceedings. If he denies the jurisdiction of the NCC(A), the lower ordinary court fee will be due and he will be allowed to litigate in the Dutch language (Article 32a(4) DCCP). He will therefore not be disadvantaged if his opposing party wrongly brings a case before the NCC(A). A party cannot smoke out another party by starting the more expensive NCC proceedings.

For third parties wishing to intervene, joined parties (joining on the side of one of the litigants) are bound by the English language of proceedings agreed by the initial litigants. For an intervening party in indemnity ("vrijwaring") or contribution ("tussenkomst"), the court must determine on the basis of due process whether that party is bound to litigate in English and at an increased court fee.[68]

Third, the jurisdiction of the NCC(A) requires that it must be a "civil or commercial matter" in an "international dispute" that is "within the autonomy of the parties" (Article 32a(1) DCCP, Article 1.3.1 NCC(A) Rules).

63 Further Note I, p 7.
64 EN II, p 11 and Further Note I, p 9.
65 Further Note I, p 9.
66 EN II, p 11. See also Explanatory Memorandum to the NCC(A) Rules of Procedure, p 27. See also NCC 14 April 2020, ECLI:NL:RBAMS:2020:2277 (*X/Tennor Holding*) (para 5.6 under d).
67 NCC 14 April 2020, ECLI:NL:RBAMS:2020:2277 (*X/Tennor Holding*) (para 5.6 under d).
68 EN II, p 14 and Further Note I, p 10. See also Article 2.2 NCC(A) Rules.

A dispute about a "civil or commercial matter" must be understood broadly.[69] The dispute must relate to civil law in the broad sense, such as contractual disputes, claims in tort, property law disputes, and corporate law matters, insurance, finance, intellectual property, public procurement, competition, telecommunication, transportation, government liability, insolvency related matters such as director's liability in bankruptcy, or a trustee's annulment of a legal act and even family and inheritance disputes. The NCCA is also competent to hear cases in first instance about e.g. setting aside of arbitral awards.

The term "international dispute" is an objective concept to be judged by the court; not even by the joint will of the parties can a dispute be made international.[70]

If the circumstances have changed after an NCC clause has been agreed but before a lawsuit is brought before the NCC, the NCC will base its decision on whether the criterion of an 'international dispute' has been met on the circumstances at the time the NCC clause was agreed.[71]

An "international dispute" exists if one of the litigants is domiciled abroad, or if the dispute concerns legal facts or legal acts outside the Netherlands, or if foreign law applies to the dispute.[72] An "international dispute" exists when the dispute has relevant connecting factors to more than one legal system. Relevant connecting factors to assess whether there is an international dispute are, for example, the place where the parties are established and the place where goods are to be delivered, or where the contract needs to be performed. As soon as more than one country is involved, an "international dispute" can be accepted.[73] The Explanatory Memorandum to the NCC(A) Procedural Rules lists a number of situations which, according to the legislator, typically involve an "international dispute":[74]

- If at least one of the parties is domiciled outside the Netherlands, or is a company incorporated abroad, or a legal entity under foreign law, or a subsidiary of such a company;
- If an international treaty (e.g. the Convention on the International Sales of Goods) or foreign law applies to the dispute, or the dis-

69 Explanatory Note NCC(A) Rules, p 25.
70 Further Note I, p 6.
71 NCC(A) Rules, p 26.
72 Further Note I, p 3.
73 Further Note I, p 6.
74 NCC(A) Rules of Procedure, p 25-26.

pute arises from an agreement drawn up in a language other than Dutch[75];

- If at least one of the parties is a company, or belongs to a group of companies, the majority of its globally active employees are employed outside the Netherlands;
- If at least one of the parties is an enterprise, or belongs to a group of enterprises, of which at least half of the consolidated turnover is realized outside the Netherlands;
- If at least one of the parties is a company, or belongs to a group of companies, whose securities are traded on a regulated market (as defined in the Financial Supervision Act) outside the Netherlands;
- If the dispute concerns legal facts or legal acts outside the Netherlands;
- If the dispute otherwise involves a relevant interest outside the Dutch borders.

A dispute between two Dutch parties can therefore also be international, if such as a dispute is governed by foreign law, or if it involves legal facts or legal acts outside the Netherlands.[76] Only if all relevant connecting factors point to one country, an international dispute cannot be accepted.[77] In short: the term "international dispute" must be interpreted very broadly.

The term "a dispute within the autonomy of the parties" is an already existing and familiar legal concept. Cases subject to the exclusive special jurisdiction of other courts as indicated above are therefore not within the jurisdiction of the NCC(A).

The degree of complexity of a dispute is not a jurisdictional or admissibility requirement, but it is expected that the NCC(A) will only handle complex, international commercial disputes involving large monetary interests, such as a dispute over breach of acquisition guarantees, a joint venture or a large real estate project.[78]

75 The latter pointer (that the contract is drafted in a language other than Dutch) seems to allow commercial disputes between Dutch parties to be subject to the NCC(A), such as if an SPA or SHA is drafted in English.

76 Further Note I, p 6.

77 Further Note I, p 3.

78 EN I, p 2 and Further Note I, p 2 and 3.

13.4.5 The NCC(A) jurisdiction clause and other procedural agreements between the parties to be considered

In order to safeguard both the choice of forum for the District Court of Amsterdam (if that court does not already have jurisdiction under the normal rules of jurisdiction) and the express agreement to litigate in English, the NCC(A) recommends including the following jurisdiction clause:

> "All disputes arising out of or in connection with this agreement will be resolved by the Amsterdam District Court following proceedings in English before the Chamber for International Commercial Matters ("Netherlands Commercial Court" or "NCC District Court"), to the exclusion of the jurisdiction of any other courts. An action for interim measures, including protective measures, available under Dutch law may be brought in the NCC's Court in Summary Proceedings (CSP) in proceedings in English. Any appeals against NCC or CSP judgments will be submitted to the Amsterdam Court of Appeal's Chamber for International Commercial Matters ("Netherlands Commercial Court of Appeal" or "NCCA"). The NCC Rules of Procedure apply."

Before or during the proceedings, parties can also provide special arrangements in a customized NCC clause or in another appropriate manner (such as an agreement at the case management conference). Such arrangements may include matters such as the following:

- the law applicable to the substantive dispute (see Article 1.2.1 NCC Rules);
- the appointment of a court reporter for preparing records of hearings and the costs of preparing those records (see Article 7.7.3 NCC Rules);
- an agreement on evidence that departs from the general rules (see Article 8.3 NCC Rules). For example, the *IBA rules on the taking of evidence in international arbitration* can be declared to be a guiding source in document production requests ("DPRs") in addition to the rules on DPRs in the DCCP. Another example of an evidentiary agreement is a confidentiality ring, permitting review of certain materials only by the parties' lawyers;[79]
- the disclosure of confidential documents (see Article 8.4.2 NCC Rules);
- the submission of a written witness statement prior to the witness examination (see Article 8.5.2 NCC Rules);

79 Article 8.4.2 NCC(A) Rules.

- the manner of taking witness testimony (see Article 8.5.4 NCC Rules). For example, that the witness hearing will be conducted by the lawyers and not primarily by the court, that there will be a brief opportunity for direct examination, that the cross-examination will be more extensive,followed by a brief possibility of a brief re-direct examination;
- the costs of the proceedings (see Article 10.2 NCC(A) Rules). For example, the parties may agree that the non-prevailing party in the proceedings has to pay the full amount on legal fees of the prevailing party.

13.5 The preferred choice of international companies: arbitration or NCC(A)?

Arbitration is so far the most preferred method of dispute resolution among international companies (over 90%, see para 13.3). To see whether the NCC(A) is attractive as an alternative to arbitration, it is useful to consider once again why companies choose arbitration. It should be borne in mind that arbitration is mainly an instrument chosen by large companies or in technical sectors as a method of dispute resolution. In small and medium-sized enterprises, arbitration is not the appropriate method of dispute resolution or is less appropriate as a means of dispute resolution. The NCC(A) is therefore in any case a good alternative for medium-sized companies to be able to litigate in English in international cases (for small companies, the costs, including the four times higher court fee, may weigh heavily as a disadvantage).

The main reason why companies choose arbitration is the wide territorial scope of enforcement of an arbitral award (65%). In terms of enforcement, arbitration wins out if the award – roughly speaking – has to be enforced outside the European Union (EU). Within the EU, a judgment of a state court can easily be enforced under the Brussels I Recast Regulation. The 1958 New York Convention, which deals with the recognition and enforcement of arbitral awards, has a very wide territorial scope (there are 172 Contracting States, including the United States, Russia and China). One option that Dutch civil procedure law does not offer, but some foreign legal systems do, is the possibility of converting a judgment into an arbitral award in order to increase the recognition and enforcement of the award through the 1958 New York Convention. However, it must be kept in mind that even if a recognition and enforcement treaty is absent, this does not mean that a judgment of the state court must always be entirely redone before a court in the country where recognition and enforcement of the judgment is sought. It should be borne in mind that in many cases a rather marginal public policy test is sufficient for recognition and enforcement of a foreign court decision (as is the case in the Netherlands).[80]

The second reason for companies to choose arbitration is the neutrality of the forum (64%). A company does not want to be subject to the state judge of its counterparty's country, because that counterparty then may have the advantage of a 'home game' and, moreover, the judge may be a 'home referee', deciding in favour of the 'home company' for reasons of national sympathy, preservation of local employment, or other partisan reasons. An arbitration can be designed to be neutral in this sense, with arbitrators (at least a Chair) who do not have the nationality of either party and with a seat and place of arbitration located outside the countries where the parties are domiciled. For this reason, the NCC(A) may be particularly relevant as a court in international disputes between non-Dutch parties. At the London Commercial Court in 2016-2017, for example, almost 72% of litigants were from outside the UK.[81]

The third reason for choosing arbitration is the flexibility of the procedure (38%). In terms of giving firm guidance in the proceedings, the NCC(A) wins out over arbitration as a rule. Arbitrators are apprehensive about possible setting aside proceedings about their awards, and may therefore be too afraid to act quickly and decisively in procedural disputes ("due process paranoia").[82] Companies find this reluctance of arbitrators to firmly and quickly decide in procedural matters a major drawback of arbitration (46%). Professional judges are also more used to making procedural decisions on a day-to-day basis than arbitrators who act as adjudicators more occasionally. Where arbitration is a service and arbitrators are keen to be reappointed in new cases, there may be a tendency not to make overly intrusive procedural decisions against a party.

80 For the Netherlands, see Article 431(2) DCCP as applied by the Supreme Court in Supreme Court 26 September 2014, ECLI:NL:HR:2014:2838 (*Gazprombank/Bensadon*) and later, for example, Supreme Court 16 July 2021, ECLI:NL:HR:2021:1170 (*Albaniabeg/ENEL*).

81 Further Note II, p 14.

82 See S. Dumoulin, 'Het Netherlands Commercial Court vanuit de onderneming bezien', in: M. Holtzer, A.F.J.A. Leijten & D. Oranje (eds), *Geschriften vanwege de Vereniging Corporate Litigation 2015-2016*, Deventer: Wolters Kluwer 2016, p 327.

Further, proceedings in international arbitration and before the NCC(A) can be modelled similarly. The proposed method of litigation at the NCC(A) as laid down in the NCC(A)'s Rules largely corresponds to the usual procedure in international arbitration and the English courts.

Another reason for companies to choose arbitration, which is on par with the perceived flexibility of the arbitration procedure (38%), is the ability of the parties to choose their own arbitrator. Litigants like to have as much influence as possible on the dispute resolution process. In this respect, arbitration wins out over the NCC(A). In arbitration, the rule is that each party appoints its own arbitrator and those arbitrators jointly appoint a Chair. That procedural course of action, with all the disclosures and conflict checks that have to be done, however does take longer than appointing the chamber of judges in the NCC(A), which judges as a rule have no conflict of interest.

Arbitration also offers the possibility of appointing more specific experts as arbitrators in technical arbitrations. The NCC(A) will have to appoint an expert for technical expertise, which is time-consuming before a final decision can be rendered.

A fourth reason for companies to choose arbitration is the confidentiality of the proceedings (33%). Companies value this highly. In terms of confidentiality, arbitration wins out over the NCC(A). Arbitration is mostly confidential, but government litigation, as a rule, is not. However, it should be borne in mind that if an arbitration is followed by setting aside proceedings part of the arbitral proceedings still becomes public in the court decisions about the setting aside of the award.[83] It should also be noted that arbitration is not automatically confidential; this must be directly or indirectly (via the applicable arbitration rules) agreed, or provided for in arbitration laws.

Companies see the high costs of arbitration as a major disadvantage (68%). Nevertheless, 90% of companies consider arbitration the most appropriate way of resolving an international dispute. From a cost perspective, the NCC(A) wins out over arbitration. The court fees for the NCC(A) may be somewhat hefty by national standards, but from an international perspective the costs are fairly limited. Litigation in England is about five times

83 See, for example, Supreme Court 23 November 2018, ECLI:NL:HR:2018:2162 (*Tiffany/Swatch*) where the necessary facts and circumstances from the NAI arbitration conducted between Swatch and Tiffany are revealed.

more expensive.[84] In arbitration, the administrative costs of the arbitral institution usually also must be paid (which are higher than the court fees of the NCC(A)), and in addition the arbitrators have to be paid as well, whereas in state courts, this is included in the court fees and general public funding.

Both in arbitration and in the NCC(A), parties additionally bear their legal fees. In arbitration, as a rule, the system of a full award of legal costs applies (unless the amount of those costs is unreasonably excessive), which entails a considerable financial risk of having to pay administrative costs, arbitrators' costs and opposing counsel's fees. In Dutch (state) court proceedings, a litigation cost award is a relatively limited risk, as the judges do not need to be paid, the court fees are limited and the legal fees are calculated according to a moderate fixed rate. For the prevailing party, the Dutch system of court litigation is less attractive where he is thus left with the preponderant part of his lawyer's fees. For the non-prevailing party, the Dutch system of moderate court cost orders is pleasant.

What has not been mentioned by companies as an important factor for choosing arbitration, but which I would like to briefly touch upon, is the finality of the arbitral decision. As a rule, arbitration has no appeal option. This is where arbitration wins out over state courts. Arbitration, as a rule, has only one instance, while the state courts in principle have three instances, subject to exceptions. Parties may agree on an arbitral appeal. Moreover, arbitration may be followed by setting aside proceedings in two instances (court of appeal and Supreme Court). Proceedings before the state courts (including the NCC(A)) can be limited by agreement of the parties to one instance (e.g. to the district court, excluding appeal and cassation, or by prorogation directly to the court of appeal excluding cassation).

Finally, I note that not alle disputes are fit for arbitration. Some issues are considered non-arbitrable. For example, in the Netherlands the annulment of a decision of a board of a company is an issue that cannot be arbitrated because of its possible effect on third parties.[85] A dispute on these matters cannot be referred to arbitration but must be decided in state courts.

84 See Bauw 2016, p 94-95.
85 See Supreme Court 10 November 2006, ECLI:NL:HR:2006:AY4033 (*Groenselect*).

13.6 Some brief concluding remarks

International commercial arbitration wins out over state courts when it comes to the possibility of a broad enforcement outside the European Union, confidentiality of proceedings, and the parties' ability to choose the person(s) to decide their dispute (the arbitrators). However, international commercial arbitration is (much) more expensive than governmental jurisdiction (also in the case of proceedings before the NCC(A)) and may well take much longer. Where large (financial) interests of large companies are involved and enforcement must take place outside the EU, it is highly likely that those companies will continue to choose arbitration and not the NCC(A) as the preferred means of resolving their disputes on international commercial contracts. Where the stakes are lower, the costs of proceedings likely play a greater role, and if enforcement of a judgment can take place within the EU, the NCC(A) may be a better alternative than arbitration. Arbitration (e.g. under the arbitration rules of the NAI) and the proceedings at the NCC(A) are therefore not competitors, but peers who complement each other on the table of settling international commercial disputes in the Netherlands.

II – SOME PARTICULAR ASPECTS OF THE ARBITRAL TRIBUNAL & THE ARBITRAL PROCEEDINGS

CHAPTER 14

THE TRIBUNAL SECRETARY REVISITED

Martijn Scheltema[1 2]

14.1 Introduction

The role of tribunal secretaries has been taken for granted for a long time and their position has not aroused a lot of (legal) attention. However, more recently it has been addressed in the setting aside proceedings in the *Yukos*-case, decided by the Dutch Supreme Court.[3] Also, more recent procedural rules of arbitral institutions include some limitations concerning the tasks of the tribunal secretary or include other provisions regarding the tribunal secretary.[4]

Notwithstanding this, use of tribunal secretaries is increasingly popular due to the increase of (international) arbitrations and the rise of full-time arbitrators. The benefit of tribunal secretaries is obvious. The tribunal secretary alleviates the (legal and/or administrative) duties of the arbitrator(s), making the process of arbitration more efficient and potentially reducing cost. Engagement may also include benefits for the tribunal secretary her- or himself as she or he develops expertise in arbitrations as well as in arbitral procedure. Therefore, this role may be performed by more junior lawyers either proposed by one of the arbitrators or the administering institution. The tribunal secretary may also act as a sparring partner for the arbitrator(s) or as his or her (their) legal conscience, especially when the arbitrators are non-lawyers.

---

1 Professor dr M.W. (Martijn) Scheltema (LLM) is Professor of Civil Law at Erasmus University Rotterdam and a lawyer with Pels Rijcken in The Hague.

2 This contribution is based on two pieces I have previously written together with C. Warnink, 'The Tribunal Secretary, A Contractual Maze', in: F. de Ly et al. (ed), *Arbitral Secretaries, Reports from the joint NAI-CEPANI colloquium held on October 5, 2017*, Wolters Kluwer: Deventer 2018, p 55-68 and together with M.A. Rooijakkers, 'De arbitrale secretaris', in: C.J.M. Klaassen et al. (ed), *Going Dutch, ADR in Nederland, in het bijzonder bij het NAI*, Deventer: Wolters Kluwer 2019, p 755-776.

3 Supreme Court 5 November 2021, ECLI:NL:HR:2021:1645, *NJ* 2022/102, annotated by C.M.J. Ryngaert and A.I.M. van Mierlo (*Yukos*).

4 See, e.g., Article 24 para 2 of the arbitration rules of the Netherlands Arbitration Institute (NAI Rules), accessible at https://nai.nl/2024-nai-arbitration-rules/.

However, the role of the tribunal secretary is limited from a legal perspective. For example, it is widely accepted that arbitrators have a personal duty to perform their task. This task is not commensurate with a tribunal secretary acting as an arbitrator.[5] If the tribunal secretary would act as an arbitrator this may even cause the responsible arbitrator(s) to neglect his or her (their) obligations and may give rise to excess of mandate or public policy issues (connected to the breach of due process). Such a role may also trigger issues related to transparency, independency, party autonomy and good administration of justice.[6] However, not many regulatory systems (including the Dutch arbitration law) or procedural rules of administering bodies (like the Netherlands Arbitration Institute, the NAI) address these limitations in a comprehensive manner, although some provisions may be included regarding tribunal secretaries.[7] Usually the challenge of a tribunal secretary and less frequently their appointment are covered in such rules.

14.2 The position of the tribunal secretary

Neither Dutch arbitration law, nor other arbitration laws set forth a comprehensive legal framework regarding the position and role of the tribunal secretary. That being said, some provisions have been adopted. For example, pursuant to Article 1035a of the Dutch Code of Civil Procedure (DCCP) the provisions regarding the challenge of arbitrator(s) and their disclosure obligations equally apply to the tribunal secretary. However, this article (or the supporting legislative documents) do(es) not set forth any requirements regarding the tribunal secretary's qualifications, his or her appointment or his or her tasks and responsibilities (and does not refer

5 C. Partasides, 'The Fourth Arbitrator? The Role of Secretaries to Tribunals in International Arbitration', *Arbitration International* (18) 2002, issue 2, p 147-148, accessible at www.nomodos-ilcantoredelleleggi.it/2018/02/03/fourth-arbitrator-the-controversial-role-of-arbitral-tribunal-secretaries/. A concern growing in the world of arbitration is what is perceived to be the excessive role of some of these assistants – the 'fourth arbitrator'. Partasides – in my opinion rightfully – notes that, regardless of whether or not this concern is justified, such a concern can only damage the legitimacy of an arbitral process.

6 Partasides 2002, p 147-148. Partasides contends that the concern for the 'fourth arbitrator' is not necessarily a problem, but rather that a tribunal secretary is a much needed resource in modern arbitration. Although I concur with this submission to a certain extent, I feel a secretary should not assume the primary obligations of an arbitrator.

7 See, e.g., Article 24 NAI Rules.

to any professional standards to be met in order to perform the function of tribunal secretary).[8]

Considering this rather haphazard legal framework, one may wonder which arguments should support the challenge of a tribunal secretary if his or her functions are unclear and not transparent. As parties may be reluctant to challenge arbitrators (especially if they are appointed (with consent of) by the parties) this may be increasingly so regarding tribunal secretaries.

Since the legislative framework does not offer much clarity on the role of the tribunal secretary, one may turn to the contractual framework. The analysis of this contractual framework may provide some clarity regarding the legal position of the tribunal secretary. The same may be true for the arbitration rules of arbitral institutions.

The abovementioned limitations do not necessarily implicate that a tribunal secretary should not assume any other than a purely administrative role. Tribunal secretaries may assume a role beyond such an administrative one in a manner which is beneficial to the parties. As mentioned, this may reduce the cost of arbitration. However, it should be transparent from the outset which functions and activities this role entails. Therefore, one may consider including some provisions on the requirements for and delineation of the role of a tribunal secretary (as well as on transparency on these issues) in arbitration clauses.[9] This provides more transparency and legal certainty. It may also prevent unnecessary challenges of the tribunal secretary.

In order to prevent a misunderstanding, it should be noted that the tribunal secretary analyzed in this contribution is the person who assists a tribunal in a specific case and not an employee of the administering in-

8 Some questions have been raised in the Dutch Senate regarding the absence of any requirements for the arbitrator or secretary in Dutch arbitration law, *Parliamentary Papers I* 2013/14, 33611, B. The legislator has submitted that these requirements for arbitral secretaries would only be of relevance if none of the arbitrators has a legal background. A tribunal secretary could be added to the tribunal in such cases, according to the legislator. However, if so, this observation does not solve the issue of the absence of qualifications a tribunal secretary has to meet.

9 Obviously, parties themselves may by and large not be aware of this issue so their (external) counsel has to advise on this.

stitution who provides services to all tribunals for which the institution administers arbitrations.[10]

14.3 Assessing contractual relationships

14.3.1 Multi-party relationship

The arbitral clause (or the agreement to arbitrate) is considered a contract for the provision of services according to Dutch arbitration law,[11] aiming at the establishment of a multi-party relationship. It is well settled in Dutch arbitration law that the parties are the commissioning party, who give a mandate to the arbitrator(s). The individual arbitrator(s) is (are) the contracted party (parties). Often, parties agree to appoint their own arbitrator in arbitration agreement and indicate that the arbitrators nominated by the parties will then appoint the Chair of the tribunal. This type of appointment includes grant of power of attorney to the other party to appoint its own arbitrator and grant of power of attorney to these arbitrators to appoint the Chair.[12] The arbitration agreement establishes the most important contractual relationship. It also entails that the arbitrators must live up to the professional standard.[13]

An arbitrator also has a contract with the arbitral institution administering the case, if involved. The parties to the arbitration have a contract with the administering body too (such as the NAI or the ICC), as they agreed to administration of the case by this body in the arbitration agreement. This also implicates that the arbitral institution becomes party to this contract.[14] The relationship with the arbitral institution is usually governed by the arbitration rules of this institution.

10 See for this 'administrator', e.g., F.D. von Hombracht-Brinkman, 'Taken en verantwoordelijkheden van arbitrage-instituten bezien in het licht van de driehoeksverhouding partijen – instituut – arbiters', *TvA* 1994/1.

11 See Article 1029 DCCP It requires the arbitrator to accept his or her mandate in writing. See e.g., H.J. Snijders, *Groene Serie Burgerlijke Rechtsvordering*, Article 1029, note 1.1 and 1.2; B. van Zelst, 'Contracteren met arbiters', *Contracteren* 2014/4, para 2.2. This may be different if a party argues it is not bound by the arbitration agreement and arbitrators decide otherwise. Cf. Supreme Court 4 December 2009, ECLI:NL:HR:2009:BJ7834 (*Greenworld*).

12 See M.W. Scheltema, 'Opdracht en geschil, past dat bij elkaar?', *TvA* 2011/15.

13 See under Dutch law, e.g., Article 7:401 Dutch Civil Code.

14 For a more detailed analysis of this multi-party relationship, see Scheltema 2011.

Therefore, a multi-party relationship is established as depicted in the following figure.

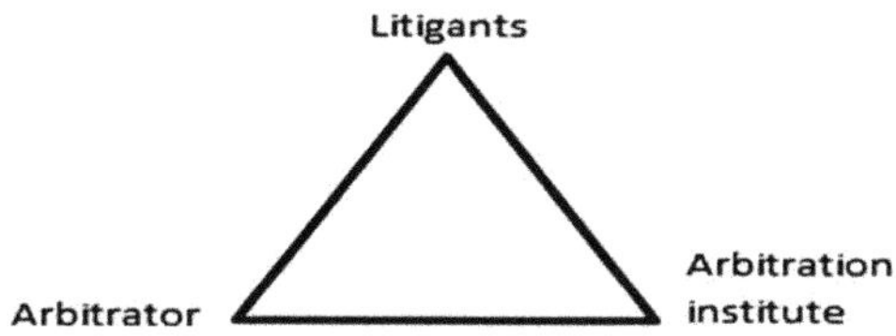

The foregoing does not imply that the different contractual relationships are not separable. For example, if an arbitral award would be set aside because of an invalid arbitration agreement, this does not necessarily imply that the contractual relationships between the arbitrators and the administering arbitral institution as well as the agreement between the arbitral institution and the parties are invalid too.[15]

However, the (contractual) position of the tribunal secretary is not depicted in this figure. The contractual relationships, including the options for appointment of tribunal secretaries, are elaborated on below.[16]

14.3.2 The arbitrator(s) choose(s) the tribunal secretary

The most frequently used option is an appointment of the tribunal secretary as part of the nomination and contracting process between the parties and the arbitrators. Tribunal secretaries at the NAI are appointed in this way. Pursuant to Article 24 paragraph 1 of the NAI Rules the responsible member of the NAI Case Management Committee may appoint a lawyer (a legally qualified person) as a secretary to the arbitral tribunal upon its request. By accepting the NAI Rules, the parties also agree with the appointment procedure regarding the tribunal secretary and are also charged for the cost of such appointment by the NAI.

15 See, e.g. Van Zelst 2014, para 2.2; Scheltema 2011, para 3.

16 The (contractual) position of arbitrators as such will not be discussed in this contribution. See, e.g. Supreme Court 4 December 2009, ECLI:NL:HR:2009:BJ7834 (*Greenworld*); Supreme Court 30 September 2016, ECLI:NL:HR:2016:2215 (*Qnow*). See on this further, e.g., E. Dekker & W. van Boom, 'Arbiters en aansprakelijkheid. Drie aandachtspunten bij herziening aansprakelijkheidsrecht', *NJB* 2013/1543 and more generally Scheltema 2011, para 5; D.A.M.H.W. Strik, 'Aansprakelijkheid(s-beperking) van de arbiter', in: C.J.M. Klaassen et al. (eds), *Going Dutch, ADR in Nederland, in het bijzonder bij het NAI*, Wolters Kluwer: Deventer 2019, p 380-391.

It is not completely clear with whom the tribunal secretary has a contractual relationship in this process. Does a contractual relationship exist between the nominating arbitrator(s) and the tribunal secretary or between the tribunal secretary and the administering body which appoints the tribunal secretary and pays him or her according to the applicable institutional arbitration rules? After all, the cost of the tribunal secretary is usually included in the cost of the administration of the arbitration. Therefore, the question arises whether the secretary is a subcontractor of the arbitrator(s) in the relation to the parties to the arbitration or an auxiliary person of the arbitral institution? The first option may be most feasible as the tribunal secretary is only appointed upon request of the tribunal, and often arbitrators have a say in who will be appointed. Furthermore, the arbitrator(s) who have requested appointment of the tribunal secretary instruct him or her.[17] Beyond this, the existence of a contract (through subcontracting) with arbitrators is not contingent on (payment of) the remuneration of the tribunal secretary by the NAI. That being said, the relationship with the administering institution is not entirely irrelevant. For example, sometimes the institutional rules include a limitation of liability to safeguard the tribunal secretary.[18] Acceptance of these rules by the parties implies the acceptance of the limitation of liability vis-à-vis the tribunal secretary as a subcontractor of the arbitrator(s).

14.3.3 *The parties appoint the tribunal secretary*

Parties may also choose and directly contract with the(ir) desired tribunal secretary through nomination. If the parties follow the recommendation to specify the role (as well as corresponding responsibilities) of the tribunal secretary in their arbitration agreement, a direct contractual relationship between them and the tribunal secretary may be conceivable.

That being said, one may question to what extent contracting parties are able to prevent the tribunal secretary from performing certain tasks or even decline appointment of a tribunal secretary altogether. The choice of the secretary and the role of the secretary are inextricably connected to the role of the arbitrators. For example, if the parties would propose a tribunal secretary the arbitrator(s) would not consider fit to work with, this may cause challenges in the arbitral process. Furthermore, the contractual

17 For example, if the arbitrator is part of a law firm, a (junior) associate of the firm is often engaged for this function. Under such conditions a (new or specific) contract between the arbitrator and the tribunal secretary is not necessary.

18 See, e.g. Article 64 of the NAI Rules.

relationships in the triangle (see above) would become even more complicated. Is the triangle expanded to a square, meaning that the tribunal secretary becomes a contractual counterparty of the parties to the arbitration, just like the arbitrator(s)? In light of this a direct contractual relationship between the parties and the tribunal secretary may not be the preferable option. The tribunal secretary is in a contractual relationship with the arbitrator(s) or, in exceptional cases where the secretary is directly appointed by the administering body, with that body. After all, the secretary assists the arbitrator(s) and parties only in a very indirect way. Beyond this, arbitrator(s) have to agree with the appointment of (a specific) tribunal secretary as they have to work with this secretary and directly instruct him or her. Obviously, this would be less of an issue if parties rule out appointment of a tribunal secretary altogether, but this may raise the question whether arbitrator(s) are willing to perform their tasks without support from a tribunal secretary. Thus, the arbitrator(s) make(s) the final call as to the appointment of the tribunal secretary or the question whether they are willing to arbitrate without a tribunal secretary. The tribunal secretary is an 'auxiliary person' to the arbitral tribunal.

14.3.4 *The administering institution appoints the tribunal secretary*

It is conceivable that the administering institution[19] appoints the tribunal secretary. Thus, the contractual relationship exists between this institution and the tribunal secretary. This model is used by the Dutch Arbitration board for the building disputes ('RvA').[20] Article 7 of the RvA arbitration rules provides that a secretary is added to the arbitral tribunal ex officio.[21] According to the bylaws of the RvA, the RvA maintains a file of lawyers working (temporarily or permanently) at the RvA.[22] The secretary in an RvA-procedure has an 'advisory vote'.[23] The RvA Rules do not elaborate

19 Obviously, this would not be viable in 'ad hoc' arbitrations. Under such conditions only the two previous options remain.

20 See on this e.g., Y.R.R.R. de Mul, 'De rol van de secretaris in bouwarbitrage', *BR* 2004, p 192-195.

21 Article 7 of the RvA Rules states that a secretary is 'added' to the tribunal. These rules are accessible at https://www.raadvanarbitrage.nl/raad-van-arbitrage-voor-de-bouw/_sitefiles/file/arbitragereglement-1-augustus-2021.pdf.

22 This list can be accessed at https://www.raadvanarbitrage.nl/onze-arbiters/.

23 Despite the advisory vote, the RvA Rules do not, unlike the NAI Rules, contain a provision on challenge of arbitrators or secretaries (nor does it contain an article on the impartiality of the independence of the arbitrator). This probably has to do with the fact that the litigants submit their choice of arbitrator for nomination. The nomination is submitted to the board of the RvA. The secretary however, is not nominated, but *added* to the arbitral tribunal. Without any provisions or standards on the

further on what type of role and tasks are included. However, an advisory vote seems to go beyond a purely administrative role. That being said, the appointment process adopted by the RvA seems to be quite exceptional. Thus, a contractual relationship between the administering arbitral institution and the tribunal secretary, established through a direct appointment by the institution, is quite rare. It also raises the question to which extent such a procedure is commensurate with party autonomy, because the parties to the arbitration have no say in this appointment, not even indirectly through their contractual relationships with the arbitrators. On the other hand, one may argue that by accepting the RvA Rules, the parties also accept this appointment procedure.

14.4 Procedural rules in national law and in institutional arbitration rules

14.4.1 Introduction

As has been elaborated on above, the tasks and position of the tribunal secretary are not extensively addressed in national arbitration law, nor in institutional arbitration rules, although some limits regarding the role of the arbitral secretary are included in such rules.

14.4.2 The Netherlands

The tribunal secretary has not received much attention from the Dutch legislator. Pursuant to Article 1035a DCCP, Articles 1033 to 1035 DCCP, regarding challenge and disclosure by arbitrators, shall equally apply to the tribunal secretary.

A little more elaborate are the NAI Arbitration Rules (2024). Article 24 paragraph 1 sets forth that the rules regarding confidentiality (Article 7 para 2), independence and impartiality (Article 13), the appointment (Article 15 para 3), release and replacement (Articles 21 and 22) and challenge of the arbitrator(s) (Article 23), equally apply to the tribunal secretary. It is interesting to note that Article 24 paragraph 2 explicitly limits the role of the tribunal secretary by stating that the work of the tribunal secretary is per-

work of the secretary, it is unclear whether the secretary is functioning accordingly. Therefore – should any of the litigants question the integrity or the professionalism of the secretary – it is unclear what the course of action could or should be or what the consequences would be.

formed for, on behalf of and under the supervision of the arbitral tribunal. According to this paragraph the tribunal secretary has no decision-making power and the arbitral tribunal is not permitted to delegate any decision-making power to a secretary. Furthermore, Article 58 paragraph 2 of the NAI Rules specifies that the costs incurred by the appointment of the tribunal secretary are an element of the advance costs. Finally, Article 64 of the Rules includes the tribunal secretary in the provision concerning limitation of liability.

The RvA Arbitration Rules include Article 7, which provides that the RvA may appoint a tribunal secretary, ex officio, from the list of the institution, to be added to the arbitral tribunal as tribunal secretary in an 'advisory capacity'. Beyond this, Article 23 paragraph 5 sets forth that the same person cannot be appointed as tribunal secretary of the appellate arbitral tribunal that is to rule on the same case.

14.4.3 Foreign institutions and rules

The arbitration rules of the major international arbitral institutions are comparable to those discussed in the previous paragraph. A formal and limited provision on the tribunal secretary is often included. Beyond this, several guidelines and practice notes have been published which address tribunal secretaries and, more specifically, the role and tasks allotted to them.[24]

However, the legal status of these instruments is unclear and, to the extent that they set forth specific standards, it is unclear to whom they apply, whether violations are penalized, and on behalf of whom they are drafted. The answer to the question how litigants, arbitrators and the arbitral institution are responsible for complying with, or may ground claims on, the rules adopted in these instruments diverges and depends on how the instruments in question affect the agreements in the various relationships between those involved in the arbitration. However, it is beyond the scope of this contribution to examine this for each of the arbitral institutions. Nonetheless, these soft law instruments may help to better understand the role and tasks of the tribunal secretary.

24 See, e.g., D. Jones, 'Ethical Implications of Using Paralegals and Tribunal Secretaries', *International Trade/ADR in the South Pacific*, p 251; F. de Ly, 'Rules and Case Law on Tribunal Secretaries', in: F. de Ly et al. (ed), *Arbitral Secretaries. Reports from the joint colloquium held on October 5, 2017*, Wolters Kluwer Belgium 2018, p 23.

Most restrictive are the International Chamber of Commerce (ICC) and London Court of International Arbitration (LCIA). The role of the tribunal secretary is basically limited to arranging case files, marking cited case law, arranging hearing facilities and sending notices on behalf of the arbitral tribunal, keeping time and taking notes, as well as checking spelling and references in arbitral awards.[25] As far as ICC arbitrations are concerned, the tribunal may 'under no conditions' delegate any decision-making power to the arbitral secretary, nor rely on the arbitral secretary to perform any task that is part of the core task assigned to the arbitrators, which is to resolve the dispute. This guidance is comparable with Article 24 paragraph 2 of the NAI Rules.

The 2024 Arbitration Rules of the Hong Kong International Arbitration Centre (HKIAC) only state that the tribunal secretary should conduct his or her tasks impartially and independently and should disclose any circumstances which may raise justifiable doubt as to his or her impartiality.[26] The HKIAC Guidelines on the Use of a Secretary to the Arbitral Tribunal (HKIAC Guidelines) follow the language in the ICC Notes that the arbitral tribunal may not attribute decision-making powers or other tasks that are at the core of its mandate to the tribunal secretary.[27] Nevertheless, the HKIAC Guidelines allow other tasks to be allotted to the tribunal secretary. These include researching case law and literature, drafting memoranda, gathering factual information in the case file, attending and taking notes on the deliberations of the arbitral tribunal, and preparing in draft form non-bearing parts of awards. Of great importance is the so-called unless or opt out clause which, in Article 3.4, precedes the enumeration of the possible tasks of the arbitral secretary: litigants (or arbitrators) who do not wish to leave the aforementioned tasks to the arbitral secretary may make such known. Another safeguard follows from Article 3.6. Arbitrators who have certain tasks, such as the preparation of notes or drafts, performed by the tribunal secretary are obliged to personally analyze all relevant plead-

25 The LCIA Guidance Notes for Arbitrators are accessible at https://www.lcia.org/adr-services/guidance-note.aspx (see especially para 10). The ICC Note to Parties and Arbitral Tribunals on the Conduct of the Arbitration under the ICC Rules of Arbitration can be accessed at https://iccwbo.org/wp-content/uploads/sites/3/2020/12/icc-note-to-parties-and-arbitral-tribunals-on-the-conduct-of-arbitration-english-2021.pdf (see especially para 223).

26 Accessible at https://hkiac.org/sites/default/files/ck_filebrowser/2024%20HKIAC%20ADMINISTERED%20ARBITRATION%20RULES%20-%20English.pdf.

27 These guidelines can be accessed at https://hkiac.org/sites/default/files/ck_filebrowser/PDF/services/HKIAC%20Guidelines%20on%20Use%20of%20Secretary%20to%20Arbitral%20Tribunal_R.pdf.

ings, evidence and other materials at all times. In any case, the drafting of the substantive parts of the orders and awards should be performed by arbitrators themselves according to the guidelines.

A little less restrictive is the Young ICCA Guide on Arbitral Secretaries of the International Court of International Arbitration.[28] Article 3 sets forth – without an opt-out option for parties – that the tribunal secretary, to the extent that he or she is appropriately supervised by the arbitral tribunal and acts at the direction and under the responsibility of the arbitral tribunal, may be assigned duties beyond the provision of administrative support, which may even include drafting certain 'appropriate' parts of the arbitral award. What parts of the award are 'appropriate' within the meaning of this provision is not elaborated on.

Most liberal are the Stockholm Chamber of Commerce Rules (2023 SCC Rules).[29] Article 24 sets forth a general standard which holds that the tribunal may not delegate decision-making powers to the arbitral secretary and must consult the parties on the tribunal secretary's role and tasks. Furthermore, it includes the requirement that the tribunal secretary should be independent and may be challenged, but contains no further limitations to the tasks of the secretary.

The latter approach seems to best reflect the principles of party autonomy and transparency, since it is not the arbitrators but the parties to the arbitration who determine, together with the arbitral tribunal, which role and tasks may or may not be delegated to the tribunal secretary in a specific case. Parties may provide concrete instructions, including restrictions, or, on the contrary, grant a large degree of freedom to the arbitral tribunal in managing the tribunal secretary.

14.5 Addressing excess of the role of the tribunal secretary

14.5.1 Introduction

As discussed above, the tribunal secretary usually has a contractual relationship with the arbitrator(s) and in case he or she is directly appointed

28 Accessible at https://cdn.arbitration-icca.org/s3fs-public/document/media_document/aa_arbitral_sec_guide_composite_10_feb_2015.pdf.

29 Accessible at https://sccarbitrationinstitute.se/sites/default/files/2023-12/scc_arbitration_rules_english_2023.pdf.

by the administering institution, with this institution. Furthermore, the requirements parties have included in the arbitration agreement may be of relevance, although parties are not in a direct contractual relationship with the tribunal secretary. However, such requirements in an arbitration agreement may be seen as a divergence from the applicable arbitration rules by the administering arbitral institution or by the arbitrator(s), who may feel that their freedom to undertake their task is limited too much. Therefore, it is questionable whether parties are always able to implement such requirements.

Even if the parties to the arbitration are able to implement such requirements, but also without such requirements, it will not be easy to assess the tasks and involvement of the tribunal secretary in practice. The way in which the tribunal secretary performs its role in practice is often opaque and parties may have very little information regarding the actual involvement of the tribunal secretary. It is questionable whether and how this lack of information should be addressed. One of the parties may, for example, attempt to get more clarity on this in setting aside proceedings in court, by asking for witness examination of the arbitrators and the tribunal secretary. However, the secrecy of the deliberations of the tribunal (on which parties have agreed by agreeing to arbitration) may be contrary to such an examination. For example, the internal notes and communication between the arbitrator(s) are considered to be confidential.[30] Therefore, it may be challenging for parties to acquire information regarding the actual involvement of the tribunal secretary.

However, if they have this type of information, at least to a certain extent, this raises the question which means parties have to address undesired involvement of the tribunal secretary in the arbitral proceedings.

14.5.2 *Excess of mandate*

A first avenue to address unwarranted involvement of the tribunal secretary may be excess of mandate. Such excess may occur because the parties – who have nominated and/or appointed the tribunal – may (justifiably) expect that their case will be settled by this tribunal and not by others. Therefore, a tribunal secretary cannot de facto act as an arbitrator. Paul di Pietro has eloquently emphasized that parties choose their arbitrators

30 Supreme Court 29 January 2010, ECLI:NL:HR:2010:BK2007 (*Van Wassenaer van Catwijck c.s./Knowsley*).

based on their qualifications, skills and experience and if arbitrators accept this appointment, they are concluding an *intuitu personae* contract with said party.[31] This implies that an arbitrator has to perform his duties on his own. The question is whether tasks may be delegated to arbitral secretary, bearing in mind the duty of arbitrators to perform their tasks personally.[32] This is, for example, explicitly mentioned in Article 24 paragraph 2 of the NAI Rules. In the literature, support can be found for the argument that a tribunal secretary should not assume, de facto, the role of arbitrator and should not decide a case, draft the arbitral award or assume other essential tasks of arbitrators.[33] However, some authors differentiate between a tribunal that consists of (at least) some lawyers and tribunals which do not.[34] Some argue that it is not recommended, but not forbidden either, that arbitral secretaries write parts of the decision,[35] while some argue that preparing drafts of substantial parts of arbitral ward or having decision-making functions is not allowed at all.[36] The Advocate-General in the *Yukos*-case has observed that no general rule on the foregoing can be inferred from this literature.[37]

In the *Yukos*-case the position of the tribunal secretary was part of the grounds decided on by the Supreme Court. Ground 6 of the cassation (appeal) to the Supreme Court held that the arbitral secretary had undertaken substantive tasks and that the tribunal had not been transparent about it. This ground included three sub-grounds. The first related to the inability of the Russian Federation to provide evidence before the court in the setting aside proceedings regarding the role of the arbitral secretary. This shows the relevance of the issue identified before, namely that it may be hard for a party to provide evidence on the tribunal secretary's role. It

31 See also Partasides 2002, p 1.

32 See e.g. G.B. Born, *International Commercial Arbitration, Vol. II: International Arbitral Procedures*, Alphen aan den Rijn: Kluwer Law International 2014, p 1999; M.P.J. Smakman, 'De rol van de secretaris van het scheidsgerecht', *TvA* 2007/2, para 4; Von Hombracht-Brinkman 1994; Scheltema 2011; P. Hirst, 'When does a Tribunal Secretary Overstep the Mark?', *Kluwer Arbitration Blog* 18 April 2017.

33 Born 2014, p 2000; F. De Ly, 'Kroniek Internationale Arbitrage', *TvA* 2012/84; P. Sanders, 'De secretaris van het scheidsgerecht', *TvA* 2007/29, onder 2.

34 F.D. von Hombracht-Brinkman, 'Er zijn secretarissen en secretarissen! Reactie op het artikel van prof. Mr. P. Sanders, 'De secretaris en het scheidsgerecht'', *TvA* 2018/17.

35 Partasides 2002, p 158.

36 M. Polkingborne & Ch. Rosenberg, 'The role of the tribunal secretary in international arbitration: a call for uniform standard', *Dispute Resolution International* (8) 2014, p 127.

37 Opinion of Advocate-General Vlas rendered prior to Supreme Court 5 November 2021, ECLI:NL:HR:2021:1645, *NJ* 2022/102, annotated by C.M.J. Ryngaert & A.I.M. van Mierlo, para 3.185.

may also confirm the position that providing information about this role may be contrary to the secrecy of the tribunal's deliberations. The second sub-ground held that the composition of the arbitral tribunal was contrary to Dutch arbitration law, because the tribunal consisted of an even number of arbitrators, apparently presuming that the arbitral secretary had a substantive role in the decision-making process, and the third that procedural rules relating to the appointment of an arbitral secretary had been violated (which may amount to an excess of mandate or may be contrary to public policy). The Supreme Court dismissed these grounds without further reasoning, which is allowed under Dutch law, pursuant to Article 81 of the Judiciary Organization Act.[38] Apparently, no further clarity was required regarding the tasks of the arbitral secretary. Fortunately, the Advocate-General discussed these grounds more extensively. He concluded that diverging opinions exist regarding the question whether and to which extent a tribunal secretary may perform substantive tasks without violating the presumption that arbitrators perform their tasks personally, but that the prevailing view seems to be that arbitral secretaries may perform substantive tasks, provided that the tribunal oversees these tasks and does not implement the work of the tribunal secretary without any further review. That being said, some authors, according to the Advocate-General, draw a boundary at drafting parts of the award.[39] The Advocate-General does not follow this line of reasoning and observes that there is no general rule which would be contrary to such involvement in principle.[40] However, in cases in which the reasoning of a decision that was prepared by the tribunal secretary is implemented without review, or cases in which the secretary was involved in the decision-making process as an arbitrator, the tribunal would cross a line in his opinion. This has to be proven by the party invoking excess of mandate.[41] This is justified by Article 1065 paragraph 4 DCCP, which provides that only a severe violation of the mandate can give rise to setting aside of an arbitral award.[42] The Advocate-General observed that the Court of Appeal had noticed that no evidence had been provided that relevant substantive decisions were delegated to the tribunal secretary or that he had the final responsibility for parts of the arbitral award.[43] Regarding the ground that the tribunal secretary cannot

38 Supreme Court 5 November 2021, ECLI:NL:HR:2021:1645, *NJ* 2022/102, annotated by C.M.J. Ryngaert & A.I.M. van Mierlo, para 5.6.2.

39 See the Opinion of the Advocate-General (note 34), para 3.184.

40 See the Opinion of the Advocate-General, para 3.185.

41 See the Opinion of the Advocate-General, para 3.185.

42 See also Supreme Court 9 January 2004, ECLI:NL:HR:2004:AK8380 (*Nannini/SFT Bank*); Supreme Court 17 January 2003, ECLI:NL:HR:2003:AE9395 (*IMS/Modsaf I*).

43 See the Opinion of the Advocate-General, para 3.186.

be involved in the decision-making process, the Advocate-General argued that it would indeed be contrary to Dutch arbitration law if the tribunal secretary would de facto act as arbitrator or would assume a role which would result in a de facto participation in the decision-making process as an arbitrator, but that the award was signed by three arbitrators and that the Court of Appeal had not observed such involvement.[44] Building on this, the Advocate-General did not observe that there was a violation of procedural rules connected to the role of the arbitral secretary either.[45] The conclusion one may draw from this case is that the tribunal secretary may perform substantive tasks under Dutch law, but that these are limited to supporting tasks and cannot include a role in the decision-making process as an arbitrator or final responsibility for certain parts of the arbitral award. That being said, even if the tribunal secretary would assume such a role and an excess of mandate would in principle occur, it will often be quite challenging to prove such involvement of the tribunal secretary.

One may consider including a provision on the role of and requirements for the tribunal secretary in an arbitration agreement to prevent the abovementioned issues from occurring, to a certain extent. The parties to the arbitration may have a legitimate interest in doing so. For example, if the parties expect the arbitral tribunal to include only non-lawyers, the parties may have a legitimate interest to require the tribunal secretary to have a legal degree and sufficient expertise in arbitration. This may, for example, be justified to prevent issues in connection with enforcement of the arbitral award. If the arbitration agreement includes such requirements, failure to fulfil these requirements by the arbitrators or the directly appointing administering arbitral institution may amount to excess of mandate. However, if the parties have agreed in an arbitration agreement that the tribunal secretary should conduct no substantive work at all, but only purely administrative tasks, failure to comply with this requirement does not need to result in excess of mandate, especially not if the parties cannot show a legitimate interest in such a requirement. Moreover, it may be questionable whether such a requirement would not contradict the secrecy of deliberations between arbitrators. Obviously, they do not have to disclose who has written which part of the award and who as conducted which (legal) research. As arbitrators do not have to account for this, I feel the same goes for the activities of the tribunal secretary. Disclosing whether and, if so, which part of the award has been drafted by the tribunal secretary will

44 See the Opinion of the Advocate-General, para 3.191.
45 See the Opinion of the Advocate-General, paras 3.193-3.200.

contradict these confidentiality requirements. Therefore, it will hardly be conceivable that the parties are able to assess whether these types of requirements in the arbitration agreement have not been complied with by the arbitral tribunal. Thus, excess of mandate will be hardly conceivable in such cases. Such requirements in arbitration agreements may not be very helpful either. It may also be obvious that the parties to the arbitration are not allowed to instruct the secretary in connection to the *performance* of the tasks by the secretary.

14.5.3 Challenge of the tribunal secretary

As elaborated on above, Article 1035a DCCP entails a provision on the tribunal secretary, providing that the articles on challenge and duties to disclose of arbitrators equally apply to the tribunal secretary. As discussed above in paragraph 3.3, many arbitration rules of arbitral institutions include comparable language.[46] Thus, independency issues in connection to the tribunal secretary have to be disclosed and may give rise to a challenge of this secretary. In practice this will not often raise an issue. As the tribunal secretary usually is a subcontractor of the arbitrator(s), he or she is often a (junior) associate of the law firm of the arbitrator(s) or of an institution the arbitrator works at. If the arbitrator does not have a conflict of interest, the same will generally be true for the secretary. Therefore, disclosure by the arbitrator of any conflict of interest will often be sufficient. That being said, the tribunal secretary has to make his or her own assessment and still has to disclose if any issues arise. Furthermore, arbitrators often also seek consent of the parties regarding a tribunal secretary they envisage to enlist. Obviously, if any issues to disclose in connection to the tribunal secretary should rise, these should be disclosed at this moment. If the parties agree to the appointment, they are not allowed to challenge the secretary on grounds that are or could reasonably have been known to them at the moment of their consent. However, other issues may still amount to a challenge of the tribunal secretary.

Another interesting question may be whether a challenge is feasible if the secretary does not have the qualifications provided for in an arbitration agreement, such as having a legal degree, if parties have implemented our recommendation. I feel this will probably not amount to a ground for a challenge. Even if this degree is required in the arbitration agreement, not

46 See also Article 24 para 1 of the NAI Rules, which set forth that the rules of challenge of an arbitrator equally apply to the tribunal secretary.

having such a degree will not in itself support the conclusion that the tribunal secretary is not independent or not impartial.

14.5.4 *Composition of the tribunal*

Article 1026 paragraph 1 in connection with Article 1065 paragraph 1(b) DCCP set forth that an arbitral tribunal should consist of an odd number of arbitrators and that setting aside of an award may be an option if this provision is not complied with. The question may rise whether setting aside is possible on this ground if a tribunal secretary would de facto assume a role as arbitrator. It has been argued that the rule that the tribunal should consist of an odd number of arbitrators does not function to restrict the role of the tribunal secretary.[47] The decision of the Supreme Court in the Yukos-case, discussed above in paragraph 4.2, also shows that this cannot be a ground for setting aside due to the composition of the tribunal. Therefore, this avenue seems a challenging one for addressing the behavior of a tribunal secretary under Dutch law.

14.5.5 *Liability of the tribunal secretary*

The contractual framework may also be of relevance in connection with potential liability of the secretary. This liability is contingent on the relation and position the tribunal secretary has in the multiple-party contractual framework. As arbitrators and the administering institution, if involved, instruct the tribunal secretary, a (contractual) relationship with the tribunal secretary is deemed to exist with the arbitrators and the administering institution.

Liability of the tribunal secretary vis-à-vis the parties to the arbitration is – under Dutch Law – provided for in Article 6:74 and 6:76 of the Dutch Civil Code (DCC) (vicarious liability), bearing in mind the tribunal secretary has no contractual relationship with the parties, but the arbitrators and the administering tribunal do. Therefore, it is likely that these articles are applicable in both the situation in which the arbitrator(s) appoint(s) the tribunal secretary and the situation in which he or she is appointed by the administering institution. Pursuant to Article 6:76 DCC, the person under

47 Asser Procesrecht/Sanders, Meijer & Ernste *8* 2023/151; P. Sanders, *Het Nederlandse arbitragerecht – Nationaal en internationaal*, Deventer: Kluwer 2001, p 60; A.J. van den Berg, R. van Delden & H.J. Snijders, *Arbitragerecht*, Zwolle: W.E.J. Tjeenk Willink 1988, p 46; H.J. Snijders, *Nederlands arbitragerecht*, Deventer: Wolters Kluwer 2018, paras 4.4.1 and 9.3.3.

whose authority an auxiliary performs his task, is liable for damages to the third party it has contracted with in the same fashion as when it would have performed these tasks itself.

One of the requirements of Articles 6:74 and 76 DCC – in order to impose liability – is a breach of contract by the arbitrators or the administering arbitral institution, because of a non-compliant performance of his or her tasks by the tribunal secretary. In order to meet this requirement, the parties should be aware of the tasks of the tribunal secretary involved. That does not necessarily mean that a list of specific tasks of the tribunal secretary should be prepared in advance. Clarity about the nature of the tasks – whether the tribunal secretary has a purely administrative or also an advisory role – should suffice. It is not relevant whether the arbitrator(s) or the administering institution determinate the nature of these task. The liability Article 6:74 and Article 6:76 DCC impose, will apply to both situations. Consequently, one may wonder whether more substantive involvement of the tribunal secretary would increase liability risks.[48]

However, one may also argue that an administrative role creates a higher liability risk. Some argue that the high threshold for liability of arbitrators in connection to their judicial task does not apply to purely administrative issues, since those tasks do not relate to the judicial task of the arbitration tribunal of which the tribunal secretary is part. For instance, if one of the tasks of the tribunal secretary is to arrange for a room for the hearing and for the necessary equipment, but he fails to arrange this in a timely matter (i.e. before the hearing), the party to the arbitration who ultimately has to pay for these arrangements, should be able to obtain compensation for those costs.

The Dutch Supreme Court has accepted that the liability standard for arbitrators is similar to a judge's. Under Dutch law, the Dutch State is liable for the damage if fundamental principles of due process have been violated to the extent that a fair and independent procedure lacks or if a (regular) judge willfully or consciously recklessly causes by delivering a judgment.[49] Considering that the arbitral agreement is a contract of the provision of services pursuant to Dutch law, the arbitrator's role seems

48 Arguably liability risks may increase in quality arbitrations in which the tribunal secretary is the only lawyer and therefore the person responsible for supervising the arbitral proceedings.

49 Supreme Court 3 December 1971, ECLI:NL:PHR:1971:AB6788, *NJ* 1972/137, annotated by G.J. Scholten (*Hotel Jan Luyken*); Supreme Court 4 December 2009,

to diverge from the role of courts. Theoretically, if the contracted party breaches the contract of assignment, this can result in liability. No willfully or consciously recklessly acts are required. However, the Dutch Supreme Court has ruled that the task of the arbitrator under Dutch arbitration law is similar to that of a regular judge. Therefore, the same standards for liability should apply. In other words, liability for arbitrators will only be accepted in exceptional circumstances.[50]

That being said, where a high threshold is necessary to enable arbitrators to render awards without the threat of being held liable, this may be less compelling in connection to administrative errors. Moreover, these administrative errors may not be susceptible to judicial review in setting aside proceedings. In the *Qnow/B*-case, the Advocate-General argued that a difference should be made between liability due to substantive errors and procedural errors. She concluded that the strict standard for liability should not apply to a procedural error, such as a defect in signing the award.[51] However, the Dutch Supreme Court ruled that no justification exists for such a distinction, because substantive errors can also be qualified as a 'simple' omission or failure.[52] That said, Ernste and Meijer concur with the reasoning of the Advocate-General that the standard for liability should not be the same for liability for administrative and substantive errors.[53] In their view, it is desirable that for procedural errors the regular professional standard rule[54] would be accepted because arbitrators should be prompted to uphold procedural rules in arbitration.[55]

ECLI:NL:HR:2009:BJ7834, *NJ* 2011/131, annotated by J.B.M. Vranken (*Greenworld*). See also Article 42 WRRA.

50 Supreme Court 4 December 2009, ECLI:NL:HR:2009:BJ7834, paras 3.5 and 3.6 (*Greenwolrd/Arbitrators*). The ruling on the strict standard has recently been affirmed by the Dutch Supreme Court, see Supreme Court 30 September 2016, ECLI:NL:HR:2016:2215 (*Qnow/B*). In this case, the arbitral award was set aside, because it was not signed by all of the arbitrators (as Article 1057 lid 2 DCCP requires), but only by the Chair of the tribunal. See on this topic also Strik 2019, p 380-391.

51 Opinion of the Advocate-General, 6 June 2016, ECLI:NL:PHR:2016:472 and Supreme Court 30 September 2016, ECLI:NL:HR:2016:2215 (*Qnow/B*).

52 Supreme Court 30 September 2016, ECLI:NL:HR:2016:2215, para 3.4.3 (*Qnow/B*).

53 P.E. Ernste & G.J. Meijer, 'De rol van de vernietiging van een arbitraal vonnis bij de aansprakelijkheid van arbiters', *AA* 2017, p 684.

54 Under the standard for professional liability it is to be assessed whether a professional has acted in a way to be expected from a reasonably competent and reasonably acting colleague, see also Ernste & Meijer 2017, p 684.

55 Ernste & Meijer 2017, p 684.

Furthermore, administrative errors often are more obvious. That being said, one might argue that liability cannot be accepted for purely administrative tasks, since the functioning of the tribunal secretary under the responsibility of the arbitrator(s) or administering institution does not regard the arbitral award itself. That being said, the position of the tribunal secretary in connection to the thresholds for liability is comparable to that of arbitrators. Therefore, liability of the secretary in his or her advisory role will be conceivable only if a willful or consciously reckless disregard of his or her tasks has occurred. However, the threshold may be lower in connection to administrative tasks. For the performance of those tasks the tribunal secretary could be held liable more easily. That being said, the parties to the arbitration will involve the arbitrators or the administering institution in the liability proceedings because they have a contractual relationship with them in practice. Thus, the error in the performance of his or her tasks by the tribunal secretary will usually be addressed through the contractual framework between the parties and the arbitrators and the administering arbitral institution.

Beyond this, the contractual position of the tribunal secretary is relevant for contractual limitation of his or her liability. The tribunal secretary may benefit from a limitation of liability clause administering institutions usually include in their contractual framework.[56] These limitation clauses may be considered to create a third party beneficiary right ('derdenbeding') on behalf of the tribunal secretary. For example, Article 64 of the NAI Rules includes an explicit waiver of liability on behalf of the tribunal secretary, as already mentioned before.[57]

56 See more elaborately about limitation of liability clauses Strik 2019, p 393.

57 See for other examples Strik 2019, p 393. The LCIA Rules include a waiver of liability in Article 31. However, the tribunal secretary is not explicitly mentioned in this provision. Therefore, it remains questionable whether the limitation also applies to him or her. As the limitation covers the work of arbitrators one may argue the same is true for the arbitral secretary especially if he or she is considered to be a subcontractor of the arbitrator. The ICC has also adopted a limitation of liability clause in article 41 of its 2021 arbitration rules. The arbitrators, any person appointed by the arbitral tribunal, the emergency arbitrator, the Court and its members, the ICC and its employees, and the ICC National Committees and Groups and their employees and representatives shall not be liable to any person for any act or omission in connection with the arbitration, except to the extent such limitation of liability is prohibited by applicable law. The tribunal secretary is not explicitly mentioned.

14.6 Conclusion

I have analyzed the contractual position of the tribunal secretary. The tribunal secretary should by and large be considered as a subcontractor of the arbitrator(s). The only exception to this rule may be when the tribunal secretary is directly appointed by the administering arbitral institution. The tribunal secretary will be a subcontractor of the administering institution in such cases.

The parties to the arbitration may consider including some provisions regarding the position and role of the tribunal secretary in their arbitration agreement. If the parties have made arrangements in the arbitration agreement regarding the tribunal secretary, for example the requirement that he or she has to have a legal degree and expertise in arbitration, this is not irrelevant. Especially those requirements parties have a legitimate interest in would be conceivable if these do not interfere with the secrecy of the deliberations between the arbitrator(s) and secretary.

Setting aside of an arbitral award if the tribunal secretary has assumed a role which is not compatible with the task and responsibilities of arbitrators, such as acting as an arbitrator or rendering unsupervised decisions regarding (important) issues in the arbitration, is challenging. It may oftentimes be quite complicated to prove such excess has taken place because of the secrecy of deliberations between arbitrators (and the arbitral secretary). However, if a party would be able to prove such a role, excess of mandate may be established. A challenge of the tribunal secretary on this ground would be much more complicated, as assuming such a role does not necessarily imply that the tribunal secretary would no longer be impartial or independent. Setting aside based on the composition of the tribunal, alleging that the tribunal secretary acts as 'forth arbitrator', and thus that the tribunal does not consist of an odd number of arbitrators, seems less likely.

Finally, the contractual position of the tribunal secretary is relevant in connection to his or her liability. The position of the tribunal secretary in connection to such liability is comparable to that of the arbitrators. Therefore, liability of the arbitral secretary in his or her advisory role will be conceivable only if a manifest disregard of his or her tasks has occurred. This threshold may be lower in connection to errors in the performance of administrative tasks. In connection to this, the arbitration rules of most arbitral institutions include a limitation of liability, which in some cases explicitly applies to tribunal secretaries.

CHAPTER 15

THE NAI CHALLENGE REGIME

Martine Honée & Camilla Perera-de Wit[1]

15.1 Introduction

The ability to challenge an arbitrator is of fundamental importance to parties. It ensures that a dispute is – at any time – settled by independent and impartial arbitrators. As a replacement of the challenge proceedings before the provisional relief judge of the district court, the NAI makes use of an internal challenge procedure which specifies that challenges are dealt with by the Challenge Committee.[2]

In this contribution, we will first briefly discuss the legal framework of challenges in the Netherlands, followed by the NAI's challenge regime and the procedure before the Challenge Committee. We will also give an insight into the number of cases submitted to the Challenge Committee since 2015, as well as their outcome. Finally, we will broadly outline the Challenge Committee's method of assessment and share some insights that emerge from it.

15.2 The legal framework

A fundamental principle of arbitration is that arbitrators are required to be independent and impartial.[3] The arbitrator's independence and impartiality should be beyond any doubt in the proceedings. Article 1033(1) Dutch Code of Civil Procedure ("DCCP") provides that an arbitrator may be

---

1 M.E. (Martine) Honée LLM, Chair of the NAI's Challenge Committee; senior judge at the Court of Appeal of The Hague & C.M.L. (Camilla) Perera-de Wit LLM, independent arbitrator and mediator; former Secretary General and General Director, Netherlands Arbitration Institute. This article was written in a personal capacity.

2 Article 1(t) 2024 NAI Arbitration Rules.

3 Asser Procesrecht/Sanders, Meijer & Ernste *8* 2023/46-52 and P.L.F. Ribbers, *De bevoor(oor)deelde arbiter. Een onderzoek naar de verplichting tot arbitrale onafhankelijkheid en onpartijdigheid (Burgerlijk Proces & Praktijk no XXI)*, Deventer: Wolters Kluwer 2022, para 128.

challenged if there are justifiable doubts as to that arbitrator's impartiality or independence. The same principle is reflected in the NAI Arbitration Rules.[4] The requirement of justifiable doubts may also be met if an arbitrator *appears* to be partial or dependent.[5] Whether one can speak of such an appearance must be assessed on the basis of the objectified point of view of the challenging party, rather than the view of arbitrator in question. The objectified point of view of the challenging party is shaped around the question what a reasonable third party with knowledge of the relevant facts and circumstances would think.[6] Whether the arbitrator has been nominated by one of the parties is irrelevant in this matter; the requirement of impartiality and independence applies to every arbitrator, regardless of the method of appointment.

Pursuant to Article 1035(1) DCCP, the challenging party must give a reasoned written notice of the challenge to the arbitrator concerned, the counterparty and any co-arbitrators. This notice must be given within four weeks after the reason for the challenge has become known to the challenging party. Subsequently, the arbitrator has two weeks to consider his/her position.[7] The parties may deviate from these time limits by agreement.[8] Moreover, if, following the notice of the challenge, the arbitrator considers it prudent to resign, that does not imply acceptance that the reasons for the challenge had merit (Article 1035(4) DCCP). If the arbitrator does not voluntarily resign as a result of the challenge, any party may, pursuant to Article 1035(2) DCCP, submit a challenge to the provisional relief judge of the district court.

However, the parties can also agree that a challenge will be dealt with by an independent third party, rather than the provisional relief judge of the district court (Article 1035(7) DCCP). This possibility was introduced with the revision of the Dutch Arbitration Act, which entered into force on 1 January 2015. In the Explanatory Memorandum, the legislator indi-

4 Article 23(1) 2024 NAI Arbitration Rules, Article 19(1) 2015 NAI Arbitration Rules.

5 Cf. Supreme Court 18 February 1994, ECLI:NL:HR:1994:ZC1266, *NJ* 1994/765, annotated by H.J. Snijders (*Nordström/Nigoco*) and Supreme Court 29 June 2007, ECLI:NL:HR:2007:AV7405, *NJ* 2008/177, annotated by H.J. Snijders & J. Legemaate.

6 H.J. Snijders, *Nederlands Arbitragerecht. Algemene beschouwingen en artikelsgewijze opmerkingen bij art. 1020-1076 Rv in nationaal en internationaal perspectief*, Deventer: Wolters Kluwer 2018. Article 1033 DCCP, note 2.3. See also IBA Guidelines on Conflicts of Interest in International Arbitration, Part I: General Standards Regarding Impartiality, Independence and Disclosure, under General Standard (2)(b).

7 Article 1035(2) DCCP.

8 Article 1035(1) in conjunction with Article (6) DCCP.

cated that an institutional challenge procedure can also provide for an impartial and independent assessment of a challenge request.[9] By way of example, reference was made to the ICC and PCA's challenge regimes, which, according to the legislator, appear to be covered by sufficient legal safeguards.[10] As of 1 January 2015, the NAI Arbitration Rules provide a specific challenge regime administered by an independent Challenge Committee, operating outside the public courts.[11] This route was chosen to ensure that the confidentiality of arbitration proceedings is safeguarded as much as possible.[12] Hereinafter, the NAI challenge procedure under the 2024 NAI Arbitration Rules will be described further.[13]

15.3 The challenge procedure under the 2024 NAI Arbitration Rules

A challenge request in an NAI arbitration is dealt with by the Challenge Committee pursuant to Article 23 of the 2024 NAI Arbitration Rules. The members of the Challenge Committee are appointed by the NAI Executive Board.[14] Ineligible for appointment to the Challenge Committee are members of the Executive Board, members of the Advisory Board and employees of the NAI.[15] The Challenge Committee consists of at least six members.[16] In practice, more than six members are appointed and currently the Challenge Committee comprises 13 members.[17] The Challenge Committee carries out its work in compliance with the challenge procedure set out in Article 23 and Appendix B of the 2024 NAI Arbitration Rules. In broad terms, this procedure consists of the following.

---

9 *Parliamentary Papers II* 2012/13, 33611, no 3 (Explanatory Memorandum), p 15-16.

10 *Parliamentary Papers II* 2013/14, 33611, no 5 (Note following the report), p 7.

11 Prior to 2010, the NAI also had its own challenge rules, but the option to the provisional relief judge was not closed off at the time. As a result, a challenging party who had been ruled against by the NAI's challenge committee could subsequently submit the challenge to the provisional relief judge. This internal challenge regime was therefore abandoned in 2010.

12 C.J.M. Klaassen, "I have a dream'. Enkele opmerkingen over vertrouwelijkheid en openbaarheid bij arbitrage in 2040', in: R.A.J. van Gestel & J.B.M. Vranken (eds), *Recht en rechtspraak vanaf 2040: Liber amicorum Fred Hammerstein*, The Hague: Boom legal 2021, p 154.

13 The 2024 NAI Arbitration Rules can be found on the NAI's website. The challenge procedure under the 2024 NAI Arbitration Rules differs in parts from the challenge procedure under the 2015 NAI Arbitration Rules, which is set out in a separate addendum, also available on the NAI website.

14 Article B2(2) 2024 NAI Arbitration Rules.

15 Article B2(3) 2024 NAI Arbitration Rules.

16 Article B2(1) 2024 NAI Arbitration Rules.

17 For the composition of the Challenge Committee, please refer to the NAI website.

A challenge begins with a written challenge request (the 'notice of challenge') that must be submitted to the arbitrator(s) concerned, any co-arbitrators, the counterparty and the responsible member of the NAI Case Management Committee. This request must contain the reasons for the challenge.[18] Furthermore, the request must be made within 14 days after the reason for the challenge became known to the challenging party.[19] This is a shorter period than the aforementioned statutory period of four weeks, which is of non-mandatory nature.

If the arbitrator does not subsequently resign within two weeks and the challenging party upholds its challenge, the responsible member of the NAI Case Management Committee sends the challenge request to the Chair of the Challenge Committee.[20] Subsequently, the Chair (or deputy Chair) constitutes a Challenge Chamber as soon as possible, ascertaining that its three members are able to judge independently and impartially the case at hand.[21] The availability of the members of the Challenge Chamber from a time perspective is also important; they should be able to decide on the request within a reasonable period of time. Once the Chair has constituted the Challenge Chamber, it is up to the Challenge Chamber to determine the further conduct of the proceedings. In any case, the procedure will provide for the following:[22]

- the challenging party is given the opportunity to further explain in writing the reasons underlying the challenge;
- the challenged arbitrator, the other party/parties and any co-arbitrators are given the opportunity to respond in writing to the notice of challenge and to any further explanation thereof;
- an oral hearing is held at which the challenged arbitrator, parties and any co-arbitrators are given an opportunity to be heard.

Subsequently, the Challenge Chamber decides as soon as possible on the merits of the challenge. The central issue is whether there are justifiable doubts as to the impartiality or independence of the challenged arbitrator(s).[23] The Challenge Chamber decides by majority vote.[24] The decision and its grounds are given in writing and sent to the parties and the arbitra-

18 Article 1035(1) and (7) DCCP, Article 23(2) and (3) 2024 NAI Arbitration Rules. See also Limburg District Court 20 October 2023, ECLI:NL:RBLIM:2023:7596, para 5.3.
19 Article 23(3) and Article B3(3) 2024 NAI Arbitration Rules.
20 Article B3(1) 2024 NAI Arbitration Rules.
21 Article B3(2) 2024 NAI Arbitration Rules.
22 Article B3(3)(4) 2024 NAI Arbitration Rules.
23 Article 23 2024 NAI Arbitration Rules, Article 19 2015 NAI Arbitration Rules.
24 Article B3(5) 2024 NAI Arbitration Rules.

tor(s).[25] In urgent cases, a decision may be rendered orally, stating the main grounds of the decision. In that case, the full written elaboration must be made available within two weeks of the oral decision.[26]

It should be noted that a challenge does not automatically imply a suspension of the arbitral proceedings. Unlike state courts, arbitral tribunals are not obliged to suspend the proceedings.[27] However, suspension will usually be the obvious course of action, unless the challenging party uses the challenge as a delaying tactic or if continuation of the proceedings is preferable on procedural economic grounds, for example due to the urgency of a case.[28] It should be noted that this possibility to continue the proceedings is not unlimited; the arbitral tribunal may not render a (partial) final award during the challenge, unless the right to challenge is clearly being abused and suspension of the proceedings would be unacceptable in view of the interests of the other party.[29]

The procedure under the 2024 NAI Arbitration Rules described above broadly corresponds to the challenge procedures under the 2015 NAI Arbitration Rules. However, there are some notable differences. For instance, an anti-abuse provision was introduced in 2024.[30] It allows the Challenge Chamber to determine that a subsequent challenge of the challenging party will not be considered in case of abuse. The provision corresponds to Article 39(4) DCCP and is intended to prevent the ability to challenge on improper grounds, such as usage aimed at delaying the proceedings. Another new feature comprises the provision that the decision on the challenge can be published anonymously, unless a party timely objected to it.[31] We will discuss this provision in more detail below. Finally, a dedicated Challenge Committee Secretariat separate from the NAI Secretariat has been added to the Challenge Committee to assist the Challenge Committee and the Challenge Chamber in carrying out the powers conferred upon them.[32] A dedicated Challenge Committee Secretariat underscores

25 Article B3(6) 2024 NAI Arbitration Rules.
26 Article B3(7) 2024 NAI Arbitration Rules.
27 Article 1035(5) DCCP, Article 23(4) 2024 NAI Arbitration Rules.
28 Asser Procesrecht/Sanders, Meijer & Ernste *8* 2023/193.
29 Supreme Court 29 June 2007, ECLI:NL:HR:2007:AV7405, para 3.4.2, *NJ* 2008/177. The Supreme Court referred to the Explanatory Memorandum in which the legislator noted that the arbitral tribunal will usually suspend the proceedings but is not obliged to do so.
30 Article B3(8) 2024 NAI Arbitration Rules.
31 Article B3(6) 2024 NAI Arbitration Rules.
32 Article B1(3) 2024 NAI Arbitration Rules. For the composition of the Challenge Committee Secretariat, please refer to the NAI website.

the independence of the Challenge Committee and the Challenge Chamber, including their independence from the NAI Secretariat and the NAI Case Management Committee. The NAI may have been involved in the appointment of the arbitrator in question and it is therefore important that a challenge procedure is handled outside the scope of the NAI Secretariat and the NAI Case Management Committee.

15.4 Data on NAI Challenges

Since 2015, 24 challenge requests have been submitted to the Challenge Committee. In three cases, the challenge was found to have merit. In 13 cases, the challenge was rejected. In four cases, the challenge request was withdrawn. Once, the challenging party was found inadmissible because the challenge request was submitted too late (i.e. not within the prescribed period of 14 days).[33] The Challenge Chamber also declared itself incompetent on one occasion, because the challenging party also challenged the Challenge Chamber. As a result, the provisional relief judge of the district court had to decide on the matter. Finally, two cases were not considered challenge requests by the Challenge Chamber. All in all, 24 challenges over a period of ten years can be considered as limited. This is even more true considering the fact that seven of the 24 challenge requests related to the same case (or rather: the same arbitral tribunal).

15.5 Method of assessment of a challenge request

To ensure the confidentiality of arbitration proceedings, the decisions of the Challenge Committee have not been published to date. A downside to this approach is that the methods of assessment of the Challenge Committee are also not publicised, which, incidentally, is also the case at other arbitration institutions.[34] Having said this, we are able to share some general comments regarding the method of assessing challenge requests at the NAI.

15.5.1 *Presumption of impartiality and independence*

The first comment concerns a general principle used by the Challenge Committee. Similar to state court case law regarding challenges of state

33 Failure to file on time results in inadmissibility, see *Parliamentary Papers II* 2012/13, 33611, no 3 (Explanatory Memorandum), p 16.

34 Ribbers 2022, para 8.

judges, the Challenge Committee will presume that the challenged arbitrator is impartial and independent, unless facts or circumstances arise that provide substantial indications that he or she has a bias against a party, or at least that there is an objectively justified fear of this being the case.[35] As mentioned earlier, the central question to be answered by the Challenge Committee is what a reasonable third party with knowledge of those facts and circumstances would think.

This presumption of impartiality and independence is based on the declaration of impartiality and independence made by the arbitrator upon accepting his/her appointment. A person who has been asked to act as an arbitrator and who has reason(s) to suspect that there might be justified doubts as to his/her impartiality or independence shall communicate this in writing. To this end, prior to the appointment, any prospective arbitrator shall, inter alia, make a statement confirming his/her independence and impartiality. Any probable reason(s) for justifiable doubts as to the independence or impartiality shall be included in this statement in the form of a *disclosure*.[36] In issuing the disclosure, the prospective arbitrator must consider his/her own position from the parties' point of view.

It should be noted that if the prospective arbitrator fails to comply with his/her disclosure obligation, the possibility exists that the arbitrator may be challenged at a later stage in the proceedings. Challenging an arbitrator merely for nondisclosure, however, does not automatically constitute a well-founded challenge, as will be discussed below.

If the arbitrator does not 'disqualify' himself in light of the disclosure, the responsible member of the NAI Case Management Committee will send a copy of the statement to the parties, and to any co-arbitrators(s) or prospective arbitrators and set a time limit within which any comments may be submitted by the parties. The responsible member of the NAI Case Management Committee, taking into consideration the comments made by the parties, will ultimately decide on the appointment of the arbitrator.[37] The criterion for this decision remains whether, in the opinion of the responsible member of the NAI Case Management Committee, the candidate arbitrator may or may not provide sufficient guarantees for a proper arbitration. This may also pertain to the required availability of the candidate arbitrator and the interest of the parties in expeditious proceed-

35 E.g. Supreme Court 23 December 2022, ECLI:NL:HR:2022:1933.
36 Article 13(3) 2024 NAI Arbitration Rules.
37 Article 15(3) 2024 NAI Arbitration Rules.

ings.[38] Finally, instead of disclosing, the prospective arbitrator may also decide not to accept the appointment and thus not to fill out the aforementioned statement.

15.5.2 *IBA Guidelines on Conflicts of Interest in International Arbitration*

A second observation relates to the IBA Guidelines on Conflicts of Interest in International Arbitration ("IBA Guidelines").[39] The IBA Guidelines were first published in 2004. Very recently, in 2024, the IBA Arbitration Committee further modernised and clarified the subsequent 2014 version, without changing it fundamentally.

The IBA Guidelines are 'soft law', meaning that they are non-binding and must be applied in accordance with applicable laws and regulations. The Guidelines are currently a widely accepted and used instrument in the international arbitration community reflecting (international) standards on the impartiality and independence of arbitrators.

It is relevant to briefly point to the recent publication of the IBA Guidelines 2024 in relation to the aforementioned disclosure. By way of background, Part I of the IBA Guidelines 2024 sets out seven general standards regarding impartiality, independence and disclosure. Part II of the IBA Guidelines 2024 contains lists of situations categorised on an increasing scale of severity divided in (i) green, (ii) orange and (iii) red, with the red category divided into (a) a 'Non-Waivable Red List' and (b) a 'Waivable Red List'.

The Green List is a non-exhaustive list of specific situations where no appearance of a conflict of interest nor an actual conflict of interest can be considered to exist. Thus, the arbitrator has no duty to disclose situations falling within the Green List. The Orange List is a non-exhaustive list of specific situations that, depending on the facts of a given case, may, in the eyes of the parties, give rise to doubts as to the arbitrator's impartiality or independence. The consequence here is that the arbitrator has a duty to disclose such situations. In these situations, the parties are deemed to have accepted the arbitrator if, after disclosure, no timely objection is made. It is in the Orange List where the new IBA Guidelines 2024 have helpfully sought to give further clarity and guidance, leading to the inclusion of additional examples of situations or circumstances which would require

---

38 Explanatory notes 2024 NAI Arbitration Rules, para 9.22.
39 www.ibanet.org.

disclosure by the arbitrators, such as the situation where an arbitrator and their fellow arbitrator(s) currently serve together as arbitrators in another arbitration.[40]

The Non-Waivable Red List includes situations deriving from the overriding principle that no person can be their own judge. Therefore, acceptance of such a situation cannot cure the conflict. The Waivable Red List covers situations that are serious but not as severe. Because of their seriousness, however, these situations should be considered waivable only if and when the parties, being aware of the conflict of interest situation, expressly state their willingness to have such a person act as arbitrator.[41]

Recent challenge cases at the NAI invoked or referred to these guidelines. In one case, the challenge was upheld. The challenged arbitrator had been appointed as arbitrator by the same law firm on several occasions in a short period of time (a situation mentioned in paragraph 3.2.8 of the Orange List). Not only had the challenged arbitrator not disclosed this situation, the arbitrator in question also failed to give full transparency when asked – later on in the proceedings – how many times the arbitrator had been appointed by this law firm.

It should be noted that nondisclosure of a situation on the Orange List does not automatically lead to a successful challenge. As is stated in the explanatory notes to the IBA Guidelines, the fact that an arbitrator did not disclose a situation reflected in the Orange List,

> "should not automatically result in non-appointment, later disqualification, or a successful challenge, as nondisclosure cannot by itself make an arbitrator partial or lacking independence: only the facts or circumstances that the arbitrator failed to disclose can do so".[42]

Disclosure is not an end in and of itself, but rather a means to ensure the integrity of the arbitration. The aforementioned lists provide tools to consider the relevant facts and circumstances, as well as applicable legal standards, to determine whether a conflict of interest could exist. In this context, it is worth noting that, as stated in the notes to the IBA Guidelines, disclosure does not imply the existence of a conflict of interest, nor

40 Article 3.2.13 IBA Guidelines 2024. In the consultation phase of the IBA Guidelines 2024 the NAI has advised to shed clarity on this aspect in the guidelines.
41 IBA Guidelines 2024 Part. II, paras 1-8.
42 IBA Guidelines 2024 Part. II, para 5.

should it by itself result either in a disqualification of the arbitrator or in a presumption regarding disqualification.[43] This aspect was also addressed in a recent decision of the Challenge Committee.[44] During these challenge proceedings, the challenging party had filed a challenge following an additional disclosure made by the arbitrator in question during the course of the arbitration proceedings. The challenge was held to be unfounded; the arbitrator had rightly seen reason to make an additional disclosure, but the situation that was disclosed did not, according to the Challenge Chamber, constitute a substantial indication that the arbitrator was not (or was no longer) impartial or independent, nor were there any objectively justifiable doubts as to the impartiality or independence of the arbitrator.

15.5.3 Assessment of challenge – influence of state court case law

The third observation concerns the assessment of the grounds for challenge. In that assessment, developments seen in state court case law on challenges against court judges can play an important role. One example is case law which holds, in short, that an (interim) decision of the court as such cannot constitute a ground for challenge, because a challenge is not a disguised legal remedy. Pursuant to that case law, the Challenge Chamber is not entitled to rule on whether an (interim) decision was correct or not, or on the failure of the court to decide. In principle, the reasoning of an (interim) decision cannot constitute a ground for challenge either. This is only different if, in light of all circumstances of the case and measured by objective standards, e.g. by the wording used in the reasoning, those reasons cannot be understood in any other way than as evidence of bias on the part of the court.[45] This state court case law has been followed in some decisions of the Challenge Committee; challenges based on an arbitral interlocutory decision that was incorrect in the eyes of the challenging party were held to be unfounded.

15.6 Some final observations

A first observation in this context relates to transparency. Whereas the decisions of the Challenge Committee are currently not published for rea-

43 IBA Guidelines 2024 Part. II, para 4.

44 Strictly speaking, these are decisions of the Challenge Chamber composed of members of the Challenge Committee. This distinction will not be taken into account in the text.

45 See Supreme Court 25 September 2018, ECLI:NL:HR:2018:1770, *NJ* 2019/429.

sons mentioned previously, there is also something to be said in favour of publication, on the understanding that such publication will have to take place on an anonymous basis.[46] Publishing decisions of the Challenge Committee makes the conduct of an NAI challenge procedure transparent. As a result, parties, counsel and arbitrators will get a better understanding of when a challenge request is likely to be successful. Moreover, the Challenge Committee itself may refer to one or more previously published decisions if this seems appropriate. Finally, publication of the decisions of the Challenge Committee will be able to contribute to the confidence of users of NAI arbitrations in the Challenge Committee as an independent third party, as referred to in Article 1035(7) DCCP, which decides after conducting a thorough procedure with proper safeguards. In this respect, transparency will also be able to contribute to confidence in arbitration as a well-functioning dispute resolution mechanism in general. Publication, of course, does not mean that it is necessary to publish the decision in full; it can also be done, for example, by publishing a summary of the Challenge Chamber's decision and not the (anonymised) decision itself.

A second observation relates to the appointment of arbitrators at the NAI. Until 2015, arbitrators were appointed subject to the list procedure, unless otherwise agreed. Under the list procedure, the NAI compiles a list of the names of possible arbitrators. This list contains at least three names if one arbitrator is to be appointed and at least nine names if three arbitrators are to be appointed. The list is sent to both parties. Each party deletes the names of those persons against whom it has strong objections and numbers the remaining names in its order of preference. Based on a comparison of the returned lists, the NAI subsequently appoints the arbitrator or arbitrators. Pursuant to the 2015 NAI Arbitration Rules, this principle was abandoned, and primacy was given to the parties to directly appoint the arbitrators. The 2024 NAI Arbitration Rules retain this structure. If the arbitral tribunal is to consist of one arbitrator, the parties must in principle jointly nominate the arbitrator.[47] If the arbitral tribunal consists of more than one arbitrator, it is in principle up to the parties to each nominate an arbitrator.[48] Nevertheless, the appointment procedure in 2024 also differs from that of 2015 in some respects. For example, where the parties are

46 In this context, see also Article 7(3) in conjunction with Article B3(6) 2024 NAI Arbitration Rules by which the NAI now has a power, under the conditions mentioned in the aforementioned articles, to publish (or have published) the decision on the challenge.

47 Article 16(1) 2024 NAI Arbitration Rules.

48 Article 16(2) 2024 NAI Arbitration Rules.

unable to nominate an arbitrator within the stipulated period, the fallback procedure has changed as now the responsible member of the NAI Case Management Committee will appoint the arbitrator directly. Until 2024, the list procedure still applied as a fallback to come to an appointment in case the parties were unable to appoint. Moreover, under the 2024 Rules, a different appointment mechanism applies to the appointment of the Chair of a tribunal of three or more arbitrators. Under the new arbitration rules, the two appointed co-arbitrators will jointly and in consultation with the responsible member of the NAI Case Management Committee appoint a Chair.[49] This regime is new. The function of this mechanism is to serve as an additional safeguard with regard to promoting diversity and quality in appointments of NAI arbitrators. This may also include a (additional) check for a possible conflict in the appointment of the Chair.

A final comment concerns the independent nature of the Challenge Committee. In its decision of 28 September 2017, the provisional relief judge of the District Court of Rotterdam ruled that the Challenge Committee must be considered an independent third party as referred to in Article 1035(7) DCCP.[50] The provisional relief judge of the District Court of Noord-Holland reached the same conclusion on 15 March 2021.[51] The independent nature of the Challenge Committee was further supported by the addition of its own secretariat in 2024.[52]

15.7 Conclusion

In case a party feels compelled to challenge an arbitrator in an NAI arbitration, the challenge procedure will be conducted under the NAI challenge regime. That procedure is covered by adequate safeguards, as is evidenced by a set of detailed rules as well as decisions of the provisional relief courts. This is important as it serves as a guarantee for impartial and independent dispute resolution. The 2024 NAI Arbitration Rules include new features in relation to the challenge proceedings, namely an anti-abuse provision, a provision on the possibility to publish decisions on challenges anonymously, and a separate and dedicated secretariat to assist the Challenge Committee and the Challenge Chamber in carrying out the powers conferred upon them.

49 Article 16(2) 2024 NAI Arbitration Rules.
50 Rotterdam District Court 28 September 2017, ECLI:NL:RBROT:2017:7456.
51 Noord-Holland District Court 15 March 2021, ECLI:NL:RBNNE:2021:1148.
52 Article 1(p) and Article B1(3) 2024 NAI Arbitration Rules.

In practice, it appears that challenge requests are only submitted to the Challenge Committee on a limited scale. This is a positive observation. Moreover, in view of the practitioners' desire for (more) transparency in arbitration in general and the clarifying and confidence-inspiring effect that publications could have, it would indeed be desirable for the NAI, where possible, to make use of the option of publishing the decisions of the Challenge Committee anonymously, or at least a summary thereof showcasing the most important considerations underlying the decision.

CHAPTER 16

ARBITRATOR'S (LIMITATION OF) LIABILITY

Daniella Strik[1]

16.1 Introduction

When you think of opportunities and possibilities for institutional dispute resolution, arbitrator liability is not the first thing that comes to mind. In my experience, the regime concerning the liability of arbitrators does not play a role in the choice of the place of arbitration by the parties. In some cases, institutional arbitration rules provide that in the absence of a decision on the place of arbitration, the arbitrators will make such a choice.[2] In those cases, it is more likely that the liability regime can be a relevant factor in the decision. More generally, the way in which a particular jurisdiction deals with this issue, as part of a well-functioning national arbitration law, may be important for the overall attractiveness of that country as a potential seat of arbitration. Particularly relevant in this regard are the overall quality and predictability (legal certainty) of the liability regime. It can therefore contribute to the image and thus the attractiveness of a country for arbitration.

This article covers the topic of arbitrators' liability and exoneration under Dutch law. Paragraphs 16.2 and 3 will outline the legal framework and relevant case law. Subsequently, the manner in which various arbitration rules address exoneration of liability for arbitrators is discussed, as well as the way in which such exoneration clauses differ (para 16.4).

1 Prof. Dr. D.A.M.H.W. (Daniella) Strik is a lawyer at Linklaters LLP in Amsterdam and professor International Litigation at Radboud University Nijmegen.

2 See e.g. Article 18 UNCITRAL Arbitration Rules (2021); Article 18(1) ICC Arbitration Rules ("ICC") (2021); Article 17(1) Swiss Arbitration Centre Rules of International Arbitration ("SAC"); Article 25(1) Stockholm Chamber of Commerce Arbitration Rules ("SCC") (2023); Article 21(7) Arbitration Rules of the Netherlands Arbitration Institute ("NAI") (2015). See differently Article 27(1) NAI Rules (2024): "If the place of arbitration has not been determined by the parties by agreement, Amsterdam shall be the place of arbitration."

16.2 No special statutory regime concerning arbitrators' liability and exoneration

Dutch law currently does not have a statutory standard that specifically applies to the liability of arbitrators. The legislation of jurisdictions with significant arbitral institutions that do address arbitrators' liability have different approaches to this issue. For example, paragraph 14a of the United States Uniform Arbitration Act (2000) provides: "*An arbitrator or an arbitration organization acting in that capacity is immune from civil liability to the same extent as a judge of a court of this State acting in a judicial capacity.*" Paragraph 29(1) of the English Arbitration Act 1996 provides: "*an arbitrator is not liable for anything done or omitted in the discharge or purported discharge of his functions as arbitrator unless the act or omission is shown to have been in bad faith*". In other countries, such as Austria, the law only regulates when an arbitrator is liable with regard to specific circumstances. Article 594(4) of the Austrian Code of Civil Procedure provides: "*Ein Schiedsrichter, welcher die durch Annahme der Bestellung übernommene Verpflichtung gar nicht oder nicht rechtzeitig erfüllt, haftet den Parteien für allen durch seine schuldhafte Weigerung oder Verzögerung verursachten Schaden.*" Incidentally, in Austria, liability for other conduct of arbitrators is governed by the general principles of tort and contract law.[3]

In the interest of legal certainty, it would be good if the standard of liability for arbitrators were codified in Dutch legislation.[4] This also increases the accessibility – and therefore knowability – of that standard for foreigners (including (potential) arbitrators). Codification need not stand in the way of further development of the law in this area. After all, this is also not the case for the liability of judges[5] or directors of companies.[6] In liability law, the grounds for some forms of liability have remained unchanged for decades; the development of the law nevertheless has continued in its application to specific cases, from which specific standards of conduct may arise.

3 See S. Riegler, 'Chapter II: The Arbitrator – Arbitrators' Liability', in: Chr. Klausegger et al (eds), *Austrian Arbitration Yearbook 2007*, Bern: Stämpli Verlag AG 2007, para 3b.

4 To this effect, also specifically with regard to codification of the *Greenworld*-criterion, E. Dekker & W.H. van Boom, 'Arbiters en aansprakelijkheid, Drie aandachtspunten bij herziening arbitragerecht', *NJB* 2013/1543, para 6.

5 See Article 42 of the Legal Status of Judicial Officers Act ("*Wet rechtspositie rechterlijke ambtenaren*").

6 See, *inter alia*, Article 2:9 of the Dutch Civil Code.

At present, Dutch law does not provide for a statutory exclusion or limitation of liability specifically for arbitrators either. The inclusion of such a limitation of liability in legislation can contribute to the attractiveness of the Netherlands for (international) arbitration, because it contributes to clarity on this point.

In 2006, a committee led by Van den Berg presented a draft bill for a new arbitration law, which did contain a limitation of liability provision. The first paragraph of Article 1069b of the Dutch Code of Civil Procedure ("DCCP") of the draft bill read as follows:

> "An arbitrator or secretary of the arbitral tribunal shall not be liable for any act or omission in connection with his assignment, except in the case of wilful intent or wilful recklessness."[7]

In the explanatory notes to said draft provision, reference was made to the fact that it was becoming increasingly common in the United States that arbitrators were being held liable in court, that the NAI and ICC had exoneration clauses in their arbitration rules, and that the English Arbitration Act 1996 contained a provision regarding arbitrators' liability as well. It was also put forward that not all arbitrators had professional indemnity insurance and, if they did, this insurance did not (sufficiently) cover liability for acting as arbitrator in all cases.[8]

The Dutch legislator has not adopted this suggestion.[9] It is striking that there has been virtually no discussion about this in Dutch literature.[10] At the time, it seemed as if the chance of successfully being held liable as an

7 In Dutch: "Een arbiter of secretaris van het scheidsgerecht is niet aansprakelijk voor enig handelen of nalaten verband houdende met zijn opdracht behoudens eigen opzet of bewuste roekeloosheid." The second paragraph of that provision concerned the exclusion of liability of third parties appointed by the parties, including the arbitral institution administering the arbitration in question.

8 In his annotation to the Supreme Court case of 4 December 2009, ECLI:NL:HR:2009:BJ7834, *NJ* 2011/131, Vranken (paras 3, 4) criticised this explanatory memorandum as rather short, unenlightening and decidedly thin. More fundamentally, he observes that this proposal is not sufficient in the event of infringement of Community law by arbitrators (para 14).

9 The UNCITRAL Model Law, revised in 2006, also does not contain a limitation of liability provision.

10 The proposal was approvingly received by Tjittes in his annotation to Supreme Court 4 December 2009, ECLI:NL:HR:2009:BJ7834, *JBPr* 2010/6, para 12. Dekker and Van Boom also argued that it was advisable to regulate in the law the extent to which parties can make agreements about the liability of arbitrators and the extent thereof, see Dekker & Van Boom 2013.

arbitrator was estimated to be as big as the chance of being hit by a meteorite.[11]

16.3 Arbitrator's liability in the Netherlands: state of case law

In the Netherlands, some case law on arbitrators' liability has now developed, with mixed outcomes for the arbitrators that were held liable. As will be discussed below, the chances that liability of an arbitrator will be established in court are by no means imaginary.[12]

In the *Greenworld* case, the Supreme Court considered that, with regard to both government-administered justice and arbitration provided for in Book 4 DCCP, an (arbitral) award that has been found to be incorrect after an appeal has been lodged can only lead to liability on the basis of tort in exceptional circumstances.[13] The Supreme Court further considered that arbitrators can only be held personally liable if they have acted intentionally, knowingly recklessly, or with manifest gross disregard for what proper performance of duties entails with regard to the decision that is set aside or annulled.[14] However, the Supreme Court rejected the argument that arbitrators should be subject to the same threshold of liability as other types of service providers or professionals. According to the Supreme Court, the relevant legal test is not whether the arbitrators had discharged their duties as reasonably competent and reasonably acting arbitrators.[15] The Supreme Court considered that "knowingly" – after taking cognisance of the jurisdictional defence put forward – rendering a decision in the arbitral award that forms the basis on which the award is later set

11 In the explanatory memorandum to the draft bill it was stated that in the Netherlands one case was known in case law, namely District Court Breda 11 September 1990, *TvA* 1991, p 28-31, confirmed by the 's-Hertogenbosch Court of Appeal 28 October 1992, ECLI:NL:GHSHE:1992:AD1768, *TvA* 1992, p 231 (*Schetters/Arbiters*). In that case, the arbitrators were not held liable.

12 Asser Procesrecht/Sanders, Meijer & Ernste *8* 2023/200 mention that in practice arbitrators being held liable is exceptional.

13 Supreme Court 4 December 2009, ECLI:NL:HR:2009:BJ7834, para 3.5, *JOR* 2010/175; Asser Procesrecht/Sanders, Meijer & Ernste *8* 2023/203 argued that in this case the claim could also have been based on breach of contract pursuant to Article 6:74 DCC.

14 Supreme Court 4 December 2009, ECLI:NL:HR:2009:BJ7834, para 3.6, *JOR* 2010/175. According to Asser Procesrecht/Sanders, Meijer & Ernste *8* 2023/201 this standard applies both in the event the claim is based on tort as well as on the basis of breach of contract pursuant to Article 6:74 DCC.

15 Supreme Court 4 December 2009, ECLI:NL:HR:2009:BJ7834, para 3.7, *JOR* 2010/175.

aside, is not a sufficient basis for granting the liability claim. The Supreme Court ruled that in this particular case insufficient evidence had been put forward to support the conclusion that the arbitrators had reached their decision intentionally or deliberately recklessly or with manifest gross disregard for what proper performance of duties entails.[16] Apparently, the alleged intent or deliberate recklessness of the arbitrator does not have to be aimed at making a decision with a particular content, but requires that there is awareness of the fact that that decision was "wrong".

Although the Supreme Court made it explicit in the *Greenworld* judgment that arbitrators' liability can only arise in exceptional cases, it follows from this judgment that there can also be liability for a substantively incorrect award – and not only for errors in the context of the process leading to the award or in the event of a violation of fundamental legal principles that prevents a fair and impartial hearing of the case. To that extent, it followed from the *Greenworld* judgment that the threshold for liability of arbitrators is lower than that for the liability of the State for judges according to the criterion for liability for unlawful government jurisdiction as per the 1971 *Hotel Jan Luyken*[17] judgment.[18] After all, even without disregard for fundamental principles of law in which a fair and impartial treatment is at stake, there may be a manifest gross disregard for what proper performance of duties entails. Prior to the *Greenworld* judgment, the *Hotel Jan Luyken* criterion had also been applied to arbitrator's liability by the lower Dutch courts.[19]

The *Greenworld* judgment did not make clear what is meant by intent, deliberate recklessness or manifest gross disregard for what constitutes proper performance of duties in the context of arbitrator's liability. This is unfortunate, because although, for example, the concept of deliberate

16 Supreme Court 4 December 2009, ECLI:NL:HR:2009:BJ7834, para 3.6, *JOR* 2010/175.

17 Supreme Court 3 December 1971, ECLI:NL:HR:1971:AB6788, *NJ* 1972/137 (*Hotel Jan Luyken*) in which it was held that it was only if, in the preparation of a judicial decision, fundamental principles of law had been disregarded to such an extent that it could no longer be said that the case had been dealt with fairly and impartially, and if there was no right of appeal against that decision, that the State could be held liable for the resulting damage in respect of the violation of Article 6 of the ECHR.

18 In this sense also Vranken in his annotation to Supreme Court 4 December 2009, ECLI:NL:HR:2009:BJ7834, *NJ* 2011/131, para 16 and I. Giesen, 'Staatsaansprakelijkheid wegens onrechtmatige rechtspraak', *O&A* 2017/31, para 2.3 and in Asser Procesrecht/Giesen *1* 2015/129; R. Meijer, 'Towards a broader liability of judges and arbitrators?', *MvV* 2010, p 13.

19 Known from 's-Hertogenbosch Court of Appeal 28 October 1992, ECLI:NL:GHSHE:1992:AD1768, *NJ* 1993/339 (*Schetters/Arbiters*) in paras 3.6 and 3.7.

recklessness has traditionally been established in Dutch civil law, it has acquired different meanings in case law in different areas of law over time.[20]

What these concepts mean in the context of arbitrators' liability may develop further in case law. Since the number of cases in which arbitrators are held liable is as yet very small and such claims – for different reasons – to date have not been successful, it may therefore take some time before the contours of these concepts are further fleshed out in the case law. At the moment, we have to make do with a handful of cases in which the criteria developed in the *Greenworld* case have been applied to specific cases, which will be discussed in more detail below.

In 2014, the District Court of Oost-Brabant applied the *Greenworld* standard in a case where it ruled that the arbitrators had acted unlawfully because of the apparent gross disregard of what proper performance of duties entails. The District Court ruled that the arbitrators were at "serious fault" ("*ernstig verwijt*") because they had rendered an award without waiting to see whether a challenge request would be submitted to the provisional relief judge after a notice of challenge was issued to the arbitrators and, if so, to await the decision. Also on appeal, the Court of Appeal of 's-Hertogenbosch ruled that the arbitrators in this case had breached their duties in the execution of the contract for services due to a manifest gross disregard for what a proper performance of duties entails and that they were, in principle, liable for the damage suffered as a result.[21] The Court of Appeal considered that Article 1035 DCCP, which requires a person other than the arbitrator to decide on the merits of a challenge, is such a fundamental principle of procedural law that it should be evident to any (arbitrator) judge that a judicial/arbitral body other than the authority whose award is being challenged needs to decide on the merits of such challenge. In this particular case, in contravention to this fundamental principle, the arbitrators had decided on the request themselves by ruling that the challenge was filed too late and had thus bypassed Article 1035 DCCP. In addition to this, the arbitrators had rendered an award in which almost all of the

20 For employment law, see e.g. Supreme Court 20 September 1996, 6, ECLI:NL:HR:1996:ZC2142, para 3.4, *NJ* 1997/198, Supreme Court 14 October 2005, ECLI:NL:HR:2005:AU2235, para 3.4.2, *NJ* 2005/539, and Supreme Court 1 February 2008, ECLI:NL:HR:2008:BB6175, paras 2.2 and 2.2.1, *RvdW* 2008/176. For transport law see e.g. Article 8:1101(1) DCC. See also J.H. Duyvensz, 'Exoneratie en bewuste roekeloosheid', *WPNR* 2011, issue 6878, p 228-229 and Asser Procesrecht/Sanders, Meijer & Ernste *8* 2023/202.

21 's-Hertogenbosch Court of Appeal 1 December 2015, ECLI:NL:GHSHE:2015:5154, para 3.7, *NJF* 2016/38.

issues in dispute had been decided. Furthermore, the Court of Appeal regarded the fact that according to the bankruptcy report of one of the parties, the content of the draft judgment had already been communicated to the liquidator of that party as a "serious fault".[22]

The claim was nevertheless dismissed by the Court of Appeal because the arbitrators had successfully invoked an exoneration clause in the applicable arbitration rules.[23] This was a provision which excluded the arbitrators' overall liability.[24]

In the subsequent *Qnow* judgment the liability criterion formulated by the Supreme Court in the *Greenworld* case has been extended to apply in situations in which an arbitral award has been set aside on other than substantive grounds.[25] The Supreme Court confirmed that, with regard to arbitrators' liability, there is no ground to distinguish between (certain) procedural errors on the one hand, and errors in the substantive assessment of the case on the other.[26] According to the Supreme Court, in the interest of legal certainty, all errors in the exercise of the judicial task of arbitrators must be assessed according to the same standard; regardless of whether they concern errors or omissions in the substantive assessment that are not a matter of discretion, or compliance with procedural rules, including those in relation to procedural conduct.[27]

The Supreme Court also made it clear in the *Qnow* judgment that the *Greenworld* criterion does not apply to so-called "operational errors" ("*bedrijfsfouten*") as mentioned in the Explanatory Memorandum to the Legal Status of Judicial Officers Act ("*Wet rechtspositie rechterlijke ambtenaren*").[28] These are errors that cannot lead to the setting aside of an (arbitral) award and are also insufficiently related to the judicial task to be understood

22 'S-Hertogenbosch Court of Appeal 1 December 2015, ECLI:NL:GHSHE:2015:5154, para 3.6.1, *NJF* 2016/38.
23 'S-Hertogenbosch Court of Appeal 1 December 2015, ECLI:NL:GHSHE:2015:5154, para 3.14.5, *NJF* 2016/38. See para 4.2.
24 It concerned Article 63 of the Arbitration Rules of the Brabant Chamber of Commerce, on the basis of which an arbitrator could not be held liable "for any act or omission relating to an arbitration to which these Rules apply".
25 Supreme Court 30 September 2016, ECLI:NL:HR:2016:2215, para 3.4.3; Asser Procesrecht/Sanders, Meijer & Ernste *8* 2023/204.
26 Supreme Court 30 September 2016, ECLI:NL:HR:2016:2215, para 3.4.3.
27 Supreme Court 30 September 2016, ECLI:NL:HR:2016:2215, para 3.4.3.
28 Asser Procesrecht/Sanders, Meijer & Ernste *8* 2023/204.

to fall within its scope.[29] Such errors involve, among other things, the search for documents[30] or the abandonment of a file on the train, as a result of which confidential information is made public.[31] Depending on the circumstances of the case, culpable theft of the file under the control of an arbitrator could also be classified as an "operational error". I can imagine that this would also include the arbitrator's refusal to render an award, the omission of the (agreed) filing of an arbitral award,[32] the premature resignation of an arbitrator, the charging of hours not worked and expenses not incurred, and the violation of a duty of confidentiality that the arbitrator is required to observe.[33] Apparently, the ordinary liability standard of a (simple) violation of the law, contract (including the applicable arbitration rules) or a standard of care applies to errors of this category. Hendriksen goes even further and believes that formal errors that lead to nullity should be more likely to (i.e. always) lead to liability than substantive errors of judgment.[34] He cites as examples the erroneous acceptance of the existence of a valid arbitration agreement, failure to comply with the mandate pursuant to the arbitration agreement, conducting an arbitration with an arbitral tribunal that has been constituted in violation of the applicable rules or the arbitral award being contrary to public policy. However, such errors may also have been based on a substantive assessment. I see no reason why the criteria set out in the abovementioned case law of the Supreme Court should not apply in such situations as well.

29 On demarcation problems, see Vranken, annotation to Supreme Court 30 September 2016, ECLI:NL:HR:2016:2215, paras 12-13, *NJ* 2017/141 (*Qnow*) and P.E. Ernste & G.J. Meijer, 'De rol van de vernietiging van een arbitraal vonnis bij de aansprakelijkheid van arbiters', *AA* 2017, p 682-686.

30 *Parliamentary Papers II* 1994/95, 24220, no 3, p 3.

31 J.B.M. Vranken, annotation to Supreme Court 30 September 2016, ECLI:NL:HR:2016:2215, *NJ* 2017/141 (*Qnow*), paras 12 and 13.

32 G.J. Meijer, 'Arbiter en bindend adviseur. De nieuwe strikte (tussen)maatstaf voor de aansprakelijkheid van arbiters…', in: B. Assink, L. Timmerman & J.B. Wezeman (eds), *De vele gezichten van Maarten Kroeze's "bange bestuurders"*, Deventer: Kluwer 2017; Ernste & Meijer 2017, p 682-686; J. van Dunné, 'De aansprakelijkheid van de arbiter', Symposium Studiekring Normatieve Uitleg, 9 November 2018, Rotterdam, http://www.studiekringnormatieveuitleg.nl/wp-content/uploads/2018/11/Jan-van-Dunné-De-aansprakelijkheid-van-de-arbiter-Symposium-9-november-2018.pdf, para 8.

33 See also A. Mourre, 'Chapter 1. Sed Quis Custodite Ipsos Custodes? On Jurisdiction Upon Arbitrators', in: Y. Derains & L. Levy (eds), *Is Arbitration only As Good as the Arbitrator? Status, Powers and Role of the Arbitrator*, International Chamber of Commerce 2011; Ernste & Meijer 2017; Van Dunné 2018, para 8.

34 W. Hendriksen, 'Was getekend', Symposium Studiekring Normatieve Uitleg, 9 November 2018, Rotterdam,http://www.studiekringnormatieveuitleg.nl/wp-content/uploads/2018/11/Walter-Hendriksen-Was-getekend-Symposium-9-november-2018.pdf.

In the *Qnow* judgment, the Supreme Court also clarified that the criterion of "deliberate recklessness" ("*bewuste roekeloosheid*") differs from the criterion of "manifest gross disregard of what constitutes proper performance of duties".[35] According to the Supreme Court, the emphasis on the latter criterion is that the arbitrator in question is at "*serious personal fault*" for his acts or omissions, albeit that culpability is objectified to a certain extent: whether an arbitrator can be blamed for this (objective) fault depends on the circumstances of the case.[36] Meijer refers to this as a "strict" standard of liability.[37] Although that terminology seems to indicate strict liability,[38] the criterion formulated by the Supreme Court – in the words of the Supreme Court – "*that culpability has been objectified to a certain extent*",[39] does not entail pure strict liability. After all, whether an arbitrator can be blamed for that (objectively) depends on the circumstances of the case,[40] which may also include subjective circumstances. Meijer further argues that the origin of this criterion shows that it should actually be regarded as (a species of) "deliberate recklessness", but that it can just as well be said – as Advocate-General Rank-Berenschot put forward in her advisory opinion to the Supreme Court in the *Qnow* case – that this (new) criterion can be regarded as a meaningful addition.[41] The Supreme Court explicitly considered that the criterion of "deliberate recklessness" differs from the criterion of "manifest gross disregard of what constitutes a proper performance of duties"; in my opinion, this cannot be reconciled with being a species thereof.

Since 1997, there has also been a debate in the context of company law about whether the concept of "serious fault" is broader than the concepts of "intent" and "deliberate recklessness".[42] The status quo now seems

35 In his annotation to Supreme Court 4 December 2009, ECLI:NL:HR:2009:BJ7834, *JBPr* 2010/6, Tjittes still wonders whether the gross disregard of proper performance of duties should be mentioned as a separate ground or whether it could not be classified as deliberate recklessness (para 5).

36 Supreme Court 30 September 2016, ECLI:NL:HR:2016:2215, para 3.5.2.

37 See Meijer 2017, p 351 et seq. See Ernste & Meijer 2017.

38 Asser/Bartels & Van Mierlo *3-IV* 2021/187.

39 See Supreme Court 30 September 2016, ECLI:NL:HR:2016:2215, para 3.5.2, *JOR* 2016/324, annotated by S.C.J.J. Kortmann & P.E. Ernste. This has also been pointed out by Meijer 2017, p 356.

40 See Supreme Court 30 September 2016, ECLI:NL:HR:2016:2215, paras 3.5.2 and 3.5.3, *JOR* 2016/324, annotated by S.C.J.J. Kortmann & P.E. Ernste.

41 See Meijer 2017, p 359.

42 For a useful overview of the debate in the literature on the unclear nature of the concept of "serious fault" in the context of directors' liability, see: W.A. Westenbroek, *Bestuurdersaansprakelijkheid in theorie (diss. Rotterdam; Instituut voor ondernemingsrecht no 108)*, Deventer: Wolters Kluwer 2017, p 258-268.

to be that the content of the concept of "serious fault" has broadened beyond the standard of culpability, since it also relates to certain objective elements.[43]

The use of the terminology *"serious personal fault"* in the context of arbitrators' liability also raises questions. Giesen believes that this concept allows (arbitrator) liability to arise at a lower threshold than before.[44] The aforementioned terminology has also been used by the Supreme Court for many years in the context of personal liability of, for example, directors of companies.[45] Although it is generally accepted in that field that this terminology is the core legal standard for the main forms of directors' and officers' liability, there is also criticism of the use of this standard.[46] This criticism relates in particular to the justification for the application of a higher threshold for liability[47] and the lack of clarity about the nature and interpretation of the concept, in particular with regard to (other) degrees of fault.[48]

In this context, it is also relevant that it follows from case law of the Supreme Court that the criterion of *"serious personal fault"* does not apply to the liability of lawyers.[49] For personal liability of lawyers, the criterion *"what may be expected of a reasonably competent and reasonably acting colleague"* applies. The application of this legal standard to arbitrator's liability was rejected by the Supreme Court in the *Greenworld* judgment.[50] The Supreme Court seemed to consider this as an (unacceptable) lower threshold. To that extent, therefore, it cannot be said that a lighter standard

43 See e.g. Westenbroek 2017, p 9, 201.

44 See Giesen 2017, paras 3.4.3 and 5.

45 See, *inter alia*, Supreme Court 8 December 2006, ECLI:NL:HR:2006:AZ0758, *NJ* 2006/659 (*Recipient/Roelofsen*), Supreme Court 5 September 2014, ECLI:NL:HR:2014:2627, *NJ* 2015/22 (*RCI Financial Services*), Supreme Court 5 September 2014, ECLI:NL:HR:2014:2628, *NJ* 2015/21 (*Tulip Air*).

46 See, for example, D.A.M.H.W. Strik, *Grondslagen bestuurdersaansprakelijkheid. Een maatpak voor de board room*, Deventer: Kluwer 2010; F. Verstijlen, 'Van bestuurders, onrecht en verwijtbaarheid', *NJB* 2013/551; Westenbroek 2017.

47 Westenbroek 2017; W.J.M. van Veen, 'Ontwikkelingen jurisprudentie Hoge Raad ondernemingsrecht', *WPNR* 2016, issue 7102, para 3.4.

48 Westenbroek 2017, p 15-21.

49 Supreme Court 18 September 2015, ECLI:NL:HR:2015:2745, paras 3.4.3 and 3.4.4, *NJ* 2016/66 (*Breeweg/Wijnkamp*); Asser Procesrecht/Sanders, Meijer & Ernste *8* 2023/204.

50 Supreme Court 4 December 2009, ECLI:NL:HR:2009:BJ7834, para 3.7, *JOR* 2010/175; Van Dunné 2018 seems to ignore this when he writes that the case law of the Supreme Court on arbitrator's liability does not make a comparison with professional service providers and thus ignores the contractual side of arbitration.

of liability was introduced in the *Qnow* judgment than in the *Greenworld* judgment.

It will be interesting to see how the concept of *"serious personal fault"* will develop in future case law relating to arbitrators' liability. In the *Staleman/ Van der Ven* judgment the Supreme Court set out a catalogue of circumstances in the context of directors' liability that may be relevant when assessing whether there is a "serious fault" in the context of Article 2:9 of the Dutch Civil Code ("DCC").[51] One of the circumstances mentioned in that case was *"the insight and care that may be expected of a director who is equal to his task and performs it conscientiously"*. In the literature, this has been referred to as the criterion of a *"standard director"* (*"maatman"*), against which the actions of the addressed director must be assessed when answering the question of liability.[52] Will such a criterion also be part of the relevant catalogue of circumstances for arbitrators' liability? The logical question that then arises is to what extent the application of that criterion in practice actually deviates from the standard applicable to lawyers' professional liability.[53] In this context, it is worth mentioning that a great deal has been published on (the desirability of) convergence of liability standards of directors and professionals.[54] If the Supreme Court uses the same terminology in different areas of liability, with possibly different content, this would not contribute to legal certainty.

With regard to the *Qnow* case – in which the award was signed only by the Chair and the secretary – the Supreme Court considered that the responsibility of the Chair of an arbitral tribunal to ensure that the provision of Article 1057(2) of the DCCP is complied with must also be regarded as an

51 Supreme Court 10 January 1997, ECLI:NL:HR:1997:ZC2243, para 3.3.1, *NJ* 1997/360.

52 B.F. Assink & W.J. Slagter, *Compendium Ondernemingsrecht* (Deel 1), Deventer: Kluwer 2013, para 51.10; H.G. van den Bunt & J.G. van Erp, 'Het aansprakelijk stellen van bestuurders. Onderzoek naar de overwegingen die spelen bij het al dan niet intern aansprakelijk stellen van bestuurders en interne toezichthouders', *Research and Policy WODC*, Leiden: Boom Lemma Uitgevers 2012, p 40-42.

53 Meijer 2017, p 359 notes that, in his view, the criterion of *"grof plichtsverzuim"* as interpreted by the Supreme Court in the *Qnow* judgment, i.e. as the arbitrator who is supposed to know and also apply the standard, does not seem to differ that much from the standard of the objectified measure. Hendriksen 2018, on the other hand, considers that the rules for arbitrators formulated in the *Greenworld* and *Qnow* case by the Supreme Court are considerably more lenient than the *"maatman"* criterion.

54 See, e.g., A. Hammerstein, 'Inleiding op het symposium Evolutie van het bestuurdersaansprakelijkheidsrecht', in: B.F. Assink et al (eds), *Report of the Symposium held on 27 October 2010, organised by the IVO/EUR (2011)*, p 109; Westenbroek 2017, p 225-228.

essential part of his task and that *"an arbitrator is deemed to be aware of this rule"*.[55] It is striking that the Supreme Court does not consider that an *"arbitrator who is up to his task and performs it conscientiously"* is supposed to be aware of that rule. Should that be read as a confirmation that the Supreme Court deliberately refrained from reviewing the present error against a "standard (*"maatman"*) arbitrator"? The Supreme Court's consideration is very general: apparently the presumed knowledge of the arbitrator does not require the arbitrator to be a lawyer. To that extent, this creates special liability risks for so-called lay arbitrators (non-lawyers) and also underlines the importance of appointing legally trained secretaries. This ruling also raises the question as to which other legal duties are an essential part of the arbitrator's task and which are not.

The Supreme Court ruled that the reasoning of the Court of Appeal of 's-Hertogenbosch in the *Qnow* case with regard to whether the standard of liability was met was insufficient and referred the case to the Arnhem-Leeuwarden Court of Appeal. In the referral proceedings, a factual explanation was given – apparently for the first time – by the sued arbitrator on the course of events surrounding the (non-)signature of the award.[56] It can be deduced from the judgment of the Arnhem-Leeuwarden Court of Appeal that the secretary sent a copy of the final judgment, signed by herself and the Chair, to the parties' lawyers. This method of transmission and signature was in accordance with the arrangements the arbitrators had agreed amongst themselves for practical reasons. In view of the fact that the arbitrators resided in different parts of the Netherlands and in view of the parties' interest in being informed as soon as possible, the awards would be sent to the parties as soon as they were rendered. The awards would be signed by the presiding judge and the secretary on behalf of arbitrators. According to the Chair, it was also agreed that if this were required, the other arbitrators would subsequently sign the agreement. The secretary sent the final award to the District Court of Amsterdam, and the final award signed by the president and the secretary was thus filed at this court. Later, a final award signed by all arbitrators was submitted for filing at the court.

The Arnhem-Leeuwarden Court of Appeal considered that the Chair and his co-arbitrators deliberately chose to have the arbitral award signed only by the Chair and the secretary so that the non-signature was not an

55 Supreme Court 30 September 2016, ECLI:NL:HR:2016:2215, para 3.5.3.

56 Arnhem-Leeuwarden Court of Appeal 16 October 2018, ECLI:NL:GHARL:2018:9111, para 2.8.

"accident".[57] In view of the importance of compliance with the requirement of signature of the award by all arbitrators, the fact that this is an essential part of the task of an arbitrator and the serious consequences of the failure to do so, as the award had been set aside, the Court of Appeal ruled that in these circumstances there had been a gross breach of duty within the meaning of the *Greenworld* standard.[58] According to the Court of Appeal, it did not matter that the arbitrators felt pressure to render a speedy judgment, and chose to do this to serve the interest of the parties in speedy transmission, thereby failing to acknowledge the serious and irreparable consequences that that course of action could have, since an arbitrator is supposed to know this rule and the consequences of non-compliance with that rule. According to the Court of Appeal, the fact that arbitrators did not consider the serious consequences should therefore remain for their account. Whether the arbitrator in the case at hand was aware of the requirement of Article 1057(2) DCCP cannot be determined on the basis of the considerations of the Court of Appeal. The Court of Appeal ruled that the Chair was liable for the damage suffered by Qnow as a result of the setting aside of the final arbitral award.[59]

On 4 June 2019, the Court of Appeal rendered a final judgment, in which Qnow's claims were rejected. The Court of Appeal reached this conclusion on the basis that the operative part of the arbitral award did not contain an enforceable decision, but rather a decision akin to declaratory relief. The arbitrators' decision had not led to an order to pay, because Qnow had not put forward such a claim. Instead, the arbitrators had merely "determined" (and not ordered) that Qnow's counterparties in the arbitral proceedings *"were obliged to each pay an amount of € 3,403,352 without delay"*. This meant that Qnow would in any event have had to initiate civil proceedings in order to obtain an enforceable judgment against their counterparties to obtain a payment order, even if the arbitral award had not been

57 It therefore follows from this factual state of affairs that (the insurer of) the Chair can, in principle, take recourse against his co-arbitrators.

58 Incidentally, the Court of Appeal wrongly considered that the Supreme Court had considered that failure to comply with the provision of Article 1057(2) of the Code of Civil Procedure is a procedural error that is related to the judicial task of arbitrators. After all, the Supreme Court had not ruled on the question whether the conduct in the present case qualified as a procedural error. Court of Appeal Arnhem-Leeuwarden 16 October 2018, ECLI:NL:GHARL:2018:9111, para 2.7. However, this does not appear to be a supporting consideration of the Court.

59 Arnhem-Leeuwarden Court of Appeal 16 October 2018, ECLI:NL:GHARL:2018:9111, para 2.9.

voidable. For this reason, according to the Court of Appeal, there was no causal link between the fault of the arbitrator and the damage.[60]

In a judgment of 30 August 2023, the Amsterdam District Court continued the course set in *Greenworld* and *Qnow*.[61] In this case, the claimant argued that – in addition to the arbitrators – the arbitral institution should also be held liable. The Amsterdam District Court rejected the claims against both the arbitrators and the arbitral institution. The alleged liability related to the costs of the arbitration, which presumably included the arbitrators' fees.[62] The plaintiffs had based their claim primarily on undue payment, because after setting aside of the arbitral award it had been established that no valid arbitration agreement had been concluded between the parties, and, in the alternative, on the unlawful act of the arbitral institution and the (appeal) arbitrators against the plaintiffs. In accordance with the criteria set out in *Greenworld* and *Qnow*, the court considered that "*[a]rbitrators (…) may be held personally liable for the adverse consequences of a decision which has been annulled only if they acted intentionally or knowingly recklessly in that decision or in gross disregard of the proper performance of their duties.*"[63] The court did not distinguish between the alleged liability of the arbitral institution on the one hand and the arbitrators on the other.

According to the plaintiff, the error of the (appeal) arbitrators related to the following: the arbitrators had come to the conclusion that the plaintiff had not sufficiently refuted that the general terms and conditions – which included an arbitration clause – were accessible via the hyperlink made available by its counterparty. On the other hand, the Court of Appeal in the setting aside proceedings had come to the conclusion in the setting aside judgment that the plaintiff had disputed that the hyperlink worked, with sufficient reasons, so that the burden of proof with regard to the provision of the general terms and conditions via the hyperlink had fallen on the other party. The District Court of Amsterdam considered that although the Court of Appeal had come to a different assessment with regard to the reasoning of the positions taken by both parties in the setting aside proceedings, this was insufficient to come to the conclusion (in accordance

60 Arnhem-Leeuwarden Court of Appeal 4 June 2019, ECLI:NL:GHARL:2019:4760, *JOR* 2019/243, annotated by C.L. Schleijpen, p 3041-3047, paras 2.4.-2.5.

61 Amsterdam District Court 30 August 2023, ECLI:NL:RBAMS:2023:5572, *JBPr* 2024/27, annotated by C.L. Schleijpen, p 373-383.

62 See par 3 in the aforementioned note by C.L. Schleijpen to the judgment of the Amsterdam District Court.

63 See para 4.9 of the judgment of the District Court of Amsterdam.

with the *Greenworld* and *Qnow* criteria) that the arbitrators were personally to blame for a serious personal matter.

Peters and Schleijpen have proposed in this regard that the arbitrators' fees could also be recovered by terminating the agreement between the parties and the arbitrator(s) pursuant to Article 6:265 DCC. According to Peters and Schleijpen, in the context of the termination, there could only be a shortcoming in fulfilling the obligation of the arbitrator(s) as referred to in Article 6:265 DCC if the arbitrator(s) were made a serious personal reproach.[64]

Finally, it should be noted that the court made no distinction in the award between the alleged liability of the arbitrators on the one hand and the arbitral institution on the other, nor did it devote any consideration to the nature of the legal relationship between the parties to the arbitration and the arbitral institution, the basis of the liability and/or the criterion that would apply to it. Again, I believe that the criteria for liability of the arbitral institution and the arbitrator(s) do not necessarily coincide. It remains to be seen whether and how these aspects will develop further in case law.

With regard to errors involving the violation of specific legal or other procedural provisions that leave no room for interpretation, the question is whether in practice there is really such a big difference in (the application of) the liability standard for arbitrators and professionals. Both arbitrators and lawyers are presumed to be aware of certain rules that do not allow for an assessment and that violation of them will constitute an "error" ("*fout*"). Examples of these types of errors by lawyers are: summoning too late, failing to submit grievances in time, and not paying court fees (on time).[65] It seems to me that, in practice, there will be hardly any difference between the liability of lawyers and arbitrators in respect of such errors.[66] Incidentally, such errors can also be distinguished from the "operational errors" discussed above.

64 N. Peters & C.L. Schleijpen, 'Fouten van arbiters en de gevolgen daarvan voor hun honorarium', *NTBR* 2021/3.

65 Hendriksen 2018.

66 Hendriksen 2018 notes that the rules for arbitrators, as laid down in the *Greenworld*- and *Qnow* judgments, are considerably more lenient than the *maatman* test, since in the latter case a simple error is sufficient to be able to say that there has been an error, whereas judgments in the *Greenworld* and *Qnow* case nevertheless point strongly in the direction that there must be a serious reproach or even deliberate act contrary to a rule.

I do not read these judgments as meaning that setting aside of the arbitral award is a condition for liability; my interpretation is that the *Greenworld* and *Qnow* judgments just happened to have played out in the context of cases in which the arbitral award was set aside. I think this also follows from the considerations of the Supreme Court:[67] the Supreme Court has not explicitly considered that arbitrators' liability can only arise after the arbitral award has been set aside.[68] Even in cases in which the arbitral award has not been set aside, there may be grounds for arbitrators' liability.[69] If a party has been ordered to pay damages pursuant to an arbitral award and the award cannot be set aside because the alleged error of the arbitrator does not qualify as a ground for setting aside, that party may well have suffered damage if the error has led to the grounds on which the operative part is based. I agree with Ernste & Meijer that such errors should also be assessed in accordance with the standard laid down in the *Greenworld* and *Qnow* judgments.[70] The standard set by the Supreme Court for arbitrator's liability (intent, deliberate recklessness, gross neglect of duty) does not have to coincide with the available grounds for setting aside.

67 Van Dunné 2018 and Hendriksen 2018 seem to have a different opinion.

68 See e.g. Supreme Court 4 December 2009, ECLI:NL:HR:2009:BJ7834, para 3.5, *NJ* 2011/131 (*Greenworld*): "only in exceptional cases an (arbitral) award which was found to be incorrect after an appeal has been lodged can give rise to liability". It does not say that "only in exceptional cases and provided an (arbitral) award that has been found to be incorrect after an appeal has been lodged, may give rise to liability" (emphasis added). It is also clear from para 3.4.3 of the *Qnow* judgment (Supreme Court 30 September 2016, ECLI:NL:HR:2016:2215, *JOR* 2016/324) that the Supreme Court only deals with the different types of errors that may form the basis for setting aside an arbitral award with reference to the *Greenworld* judgment, because that judgment concerned a situation in which an arbitral award had been set aside on substantive grounds and the grounds of the judgment are mainly focused on that. See also Giesen 2017, para 2.3. See differently Asser Procesrecht/Sanders, Meijer & Ernste *8* 2023/205.

69 In this sense also H.J. Snijders, *Nederlands arbitragerecht. Algemene beschouwingen en artikelsgewijze opmerkingen bij de art. 1020-1076 Rv in nationaal en internationaal perspectief*, Deventer: Wolters Kluwer 2018, p 240, N. Peters, *The fundamentals of international commercial arbitration*, Apeldoorn: Maklu 2020, p 216, N. Peters & J.J. Bakker, 'Aansprakelijkheid van arbiters, Enkele gedachten over maatstaf, vernietiging, grondslag, ipr en exoneratie', *MvV* 2020, p 216. See differently: 's-Hertogenbosch Court of Appeal 28 October 1992, ECLI:NL:GHSHE:1992:AD1768, para 4.5.3, *NJ* 1993, 339 (*Schetters/Arbiters*), Ernste & Schleijpen 2019, p 615, Van Dunne 2019, p 122-123.

70 Ernste & Meijer 2017, p 685. See differently: 's-Hertogenbosch Court of Appeal 28 October 1992, ECLI:NL:GHSHE:1992:AD1768, para 4.5.3, *NJ* 1993, 339 (*Schetters/Arbiters*).

16.4 Contractual exoneration clauses

16.4.1 Introduction

It is clear from the aforementioned case law that the liability of arbitrators is not illusory under Dutch law. An arbitrator does not have to be guilty of fraud or corruption to run a liability risk: a procedural accident can happen at any time and the setting aside of an arbitral award can be a prelude to liability.

The case law discussed in the previous paragraph makes the issue of the (im)possibility of exclusion of liability of the arbitrator more topical than at the time of the presentation of the draft bill of the Van den Berg working group (mentioned above). In other countries, too, the development of arbitrators' liability has continued to develop since then.[71] This could be a reason for the Dutch legislator to consider codifying the liability standard and an exoneration in a subsequent revision of Dutch arbitration law.[72] There also seem to be evolving insights in this area in the UNCITRAL working group. Although the UNCITRAL Model Law does not contain an exoneration clause, the UNCITRAL Arbitration Rules, revised in 2010, now contain the following provision (Article 16):

> *"Save for intentional wrongdoing, the parties waive, to the fullest extent permitted under the applicable law, any claim against the arbitrators, the appointing authority and any person appointed by the arbitral tribunal based on any act or omission in connection with the arbitration."*

In particular, the background to that provision is that, in the absence of such a provision, arbitrators do not enjoy the immunity and privileges accorded to judges by law, even though they also exercise quasi-judicial functions. Furthermore, the UNCITRAL Working Group considered it to be an unhealthy situation for arbitrators to have to negotiate with the parties on the exclusion of their liability after the arbitral tribunal had been constituted.[73] A deliberate choice was made for a carve-out in case of "*intentional wrongdoing*" instead of "*negligence*". The latter term was interpreted differently in different countries.[74]

71 Report of the UNCITRAL Working Group on the Work of the 48th Session (New York, 4-8 February 2008), para 39, UN Doc. A/CN.9/646: Australia, England, Japan, etc.

72 Dekker & Van Boom 2013.

73 Report of the UNCITRAL Working Group on the Work of the 48th Session (New York, 4-8 February 2008), paras 39 and 42, UN Doc. A/CN.9/646.

74 Report of the UNCITRAL Working Group on the Work of the 48th Session (New York, 4-8 February 2008), para 43, UN Doc. A/CN.9/646.

Since 1993, the NAI has included an exoneration clause in its arbitration rules.[75] In the current version of the NAI Arbitration Rules of 31 December 2024, this has been included in Article 64, which provides:

> "The NAI, its Executive Board members and employees (including the members of the NAI Case Management Committee), the members of its advisory board, the members of the Challenge Committee, the arbitrator(s), the secretary, the consolidator, any other person that may have been appointed by (one of) these persons or other persons who fulfil a role pursuant to the Rules are not liable either by contract or otherwise for any damage caused by their own or any other person's acts or omissions or caused by the use of any aids in or involving arbitration, all this except where and insofar as mandatory Dutch law precludes this exclusion of liability. To the extent that they are liable at all on the basis of the above, the NAI, its Executive Board members and employees, including the members of the NAI Case Management Committee, are not liable for payment of any amount that is not covered by the advance."

The explanatory notes to the NAI Arbitration Rules do not contain an elaboration on this provision.

It is informative to compare the aforementioned provision with the rules of other arbitral institutions. The first point that stands out is that not all arbitral institutions have included an exoneration clause in their arbitration rules. However, the rules of the most well-known arbitral institutions do contain an exoneration clause.[76] At the time of this book going to press, there was no such provision in the rules of, for example, the Dutch Arbitration Board for the Building Industry ("*Raad van Arbitrage in bouwgeschillen*"), the Beijing Arbitration Commission ("BAC"), and the Vietnam International Arbitration Centre ("VIAC").[77]

16.4.2 *Elements of exoneration clauses in arbitration rules*

The wording of the exoneration clauses in the rules of various institutions differ. A number of elements stand out.

75 Article 66 NAI Arbitration Rules 1993.

76 See in the Netherlands the rules of the Netherlands Arbitration Institute. See in England the rules of the: Chartered Institute of Arbitrators. See in Switzerland the rules of the Swiss Chambers Arbitration Institution.

77 Arbitration Rules of the Arbitration Board for the Building Industry (2021), BAC Rules (2022), VIAC Rules (2017).

16.4.2.1 The group of persons whom the provision is intended to protect

The group of persons or entities for whose protection the exoneration clause is intended varies from the arbitration institution,[78] its (advisory) board members[79] and its employees,[80] members of the challenge committee,[81] and the arbitral tribunal,[82] to the individual arbitrators personally,[83] explicitly *"emergency arbitrators"*,[84] experts,[85] the secretary[86] and others who fulfil a role in the matter or pursuant to the Arbitration Rules.[87]

78 See Article 6.1.1 ADR Institute of Canada ("ADRIC") (2016); Article 37 Arbitration Foundation of Southern Africa ("AFSA") (2021); Article 1.32 CAC (2023); Article 43 Centro de Arbitrage de Mexico ("CAM") (2022); Article 16 Cyprus Arbitration & Mediation Centre ("CAMC") (2022); Article 40 Belgian Centre for Arbitration and Mediation ("CEPANI") (2023); Article 55 Cairo Regional Centre for International Commercial Arbitration ("CRCICA") (2024); Article 41 ICC (2021); Article 31.1 London Court of International Arbitration ("LCIA") (2020); Article 45 Swiss Arbitration Centre Swiss Rules of International Arbitration ("SAC") (2021); Article 52 SCC (2023).

79 Article 64 NAI Arbitration Rules 2024.

80 Article 64 NAI Arbitration Rules 2024.

81 Article 64 NAI Arbitration Rules 2024.

82 See e.g. Article 53 Australian Centre for International Commercial Arbitration ("ACICA") (2021); Article 6.1.1 ADRIC (2016); Article 41.1 Bahrain Chamber for Dispute Resolution ("BCDR") (2022); Article 33 Bangalore International Mediation, Arbitration & Conciliation Centre ("BIMACC") (1996); Article 51 Danish Institute of Arbitration ("DIA") (2021); Article 41.1 Dubai International Arbitration Centre ("DIAC") (2022); Article 41 ICC (2021); Article 46 Hong Kong International Arbitration Centre ("HKIAC") (2024); Article 31.1 LCIA (2020); Article 64 NAI Arbitration Rules (2024).

83 See e.g. Article 37 AFSA (2021); Article 43 CAM (2022); Article 16 CAMC (2022); Article V, para 24, Canadian Commercial Arbitration Centre (CCAC) (2008); Article 40 CEPANI; Article 55 CRCICA; Article 46 HKIAC (2024); Article 41 ICC (2021); Article 13 Japan Commercial Arbitration Association ("JCAA") (2021); In South Korea, Article 56 Korean Commercial Arbitration Board ("KCAB") (2016); Article 31.1 LCIA (2020); Article 45 Resolution Institute Arbitration Rules ("RI") (2023); Article 45 SAC (2021); Article 52 SCC (2023).

84 See, e.g., Article 41.1 BCDR (2022); Article 55 CRCICA (2024); Article 46 HKIAC (2024); Article 31.1 LCIA (2020).

85 See, e.g., Article 41.1 BCDR (2022); Article 16 CAMC (2022); Article 55 CRCICA (2024); Article 51 DIA (2021); Article 41.1 DIAC (2022); Article 46 HKIAC (2024); Article 41 ICC (2021); Article 31.1 LCIA (2020); Article 64 NAI Arbitration Rules (2024); Article 45 SAC (2021); Article 52 SCC (2023).

86 See, e.g., Article 41.1 BCDR (2022); Article 43 CAM (2022); Article 51 DIA (2021); Article 46 HKIAC (2024); Article 41 ICC (2021); Article 56 KCAB (2016); Article 31.1 LCIA (2020); Article 45 SAC (2021); Article 52 SCC (2023).

87 Article 64 NAI Arbitration Rules 2024.

16.4.2.2 Legal basis of the exoneration

The legal basis for the limitation of liability may also differ from one set of rules to another. In most rules, this is formulated as an exclusion of liability: *"shall not be liable for"*. In a few sets of rules, it is, by contrast, framed as an explicit waiver of rights: *"waive their right"*[88] or even *"jointly and severally release, discharge and indemnify"*.[89]

In the event that Dutch law applies to the arbitration agreement, such clauses in arbitration rules are to be regarded as a third-party clause agreed upon for the benefit of the arbitrator within the meaning of Article 6:253 DCC.[90] In any event, at the time of entering into the arbitration agreement, the arbitrators are not a party to it, but a third party. In my view, if this is the case, the arbitrator could, on the basis of Dutch law, accept that third-party clause by relying on it in order to defend him- or herself against a claim for damages. The admissibility of such an exoneration clause must therefore be assessed in accordance with Dutch law. This does not alter the fact that, under Dutch law, it is assumed that the agreement for services ("*overeenkomst van opdracht*") with the arbitrator (also referred to as the arbitrator's contract) must be distinguished from the arbitration agreement.[91] The arbitrator's contract may also include a reference to the arbitration rules (containing this exoneration clause), or even a specific exoneration clause. However, that should not prevent reliance on the third-party clause in the arbitration agreement. It may be the case that the admissibility of the exoneration clause in the arbitrator's contract must be assessed on the basis of the laws of a different jurisdiction than that of the exoneration clause in the arbitration agreement.[92] To that extent, therefore, by choosing in a specific case to invoke (primarily) the exoneration clause in either the arbitration agreement or the one in the arbitrator's contract, an arbitrator could "arbitrate" between the relevant jurisdictions and the regime that determines the admissibility of those clauses. The choice will then be made

88 See e.g. Article 37 The Arbitration and Dispute Resolution Institute of the Oslo Chamber of Commerce ("ADRIOCC") (2017); Article 16 The Chartered Institute of Arbitrators ("CIArb") (2015).

89 See e.g. Article 1.32. Centre of Arbitration and Conciliation Camara de Comercio de Bogotá ('CAC') (2023); Article 15 Hong Kong Mediation Centre ("HKMC") (2014).

90 Pursuant to Article 1020(6) of the DCCP, arbitration rules referred to in an arbitration agreement are deemed to form part of that agreement.

91 See e.g. Snijders 2018, p 231, and B. van Zelst, 'Contracteren met arbiters', *Contracteren* 2014, issue 4, para 2.2.

92 See on the law applicable to the arbitrator's contract, Van Zelst 2014, para 3.

for the provision in respect of which the law applicable to it imposes no or as few restrictions as possible on its admissibility and scope.

An exoneration clause will not be able to protect an arbitrator from liability if he is sued by a party that is not a party to the arbitration agreement.[93] An example of such a situation occurred in the *Greenworld* case where the arbitral tribunal had rendered an arbitral award (ultimately set aside) against a party that was not a party to the arbitration agreement and thus had wrongly assumed to have jurisdiction over that party.[94]

16.4.2.3 Subject matter to which the exclusion relates

Most exoneration clauses in arbitration rules refer to *"acts and omissions[95] in connection with the arbitration under these rules"*.[96] However, in Article 45.1 Deutsche Institution für Schiedsgerichtsbarkeit ("DIS") (2018), the restriction is aimed exclusively at *"such arbitrator's decision-making in the arbitration"*.[97] The exoneration clause in Article 40 CEPANI (2023) draws a distinction between *"any act or omission when carrying out their functions of ruling on a dispute"* – for which liability is excluded except in the case of fraud – and *"any other act or omission in the course of an arbitration proceeding"*, for which liability is also not excluded in the event of gross negligence. In Article 51(1) DIA (2021) *"commencement of an arbitration, the processing of an arbitration or an award made"* are explicitly mentioned.[98]

This can be traced back to the question of what an arbitrator can be held liable for in the first place. In some countries, this is only for the so-called quasi-judicial role (*"adjudicatory function"*), which involves making decisions in the performance of the arbitrator's duty to render an award.[99]

93 In this sense also Tjittes in his annotation to Supreme Court 4 December 2009, ECLI:NL:HR:2009:BJ7834, para 3, *JBPr* 2010/6.
94 Supreme Court 4 December 2009, ECLI:NL:HR:2009:BJ7834, *JOR* 2010/175.
95 Sometimes something is added to this. For example, in Article 46.1 HKIAC: "... save where such act was done or omitted to be done dishonestly".
96 See, for example, Article 37 ADR Services Arbitration ("ADRSA") (2017); Article 37 AFSA (2021); Article 41.1 BCDR (2022); Article 33.01 BIMACC (1996); Article 43 CAM (2009); Article. 55 Cairo Regional Centre for International Commercial Arbitration ("CRCICA") (2024); Article 51 DIA (2021); Article 40.1 DIAC (2022); Article 46 HKIAC (2024) and Article 15 HKMC (2014); Article 13 JCAA (2021); Article 56 KCAB (2016); Article 45 SAC (2021). Occasionally, "negligence" is also explicitly included, see e.g. Article 38 SIAC (2016) and Article 33.01 BIMACC (1996).
97 Article 45.1 DIS (2018).
98 Article 51 DIA (2021).
99 Cf. M. Domke, 'The arbitrator's immunity from liability: a comparative study', *University of Toledo Law Review* (3) 1971, p 100.

In a judgment dated 31 March 2015, the Paris Court of Appeal held that the exoneration clause in the ICC Arbitration Rules[100] only applied to the immunity enjoyed by arbitrators in the exercise of their judicial duties.[101] There is no such restriction in other countries. I assume that this is not the case in the Netherlands either, which means that so-called operational errors do not by their nature fall outside the scope of an exoneration clause governed by Dutch law. The regulations of the ADR Institute of Canada explicitly provide that the arbitral tribunal shall have the same *"protections and immunity as a Judge of the superior courts of Canada"*.[102]

The old regulations of the Portuguese Chamber of Commerce and Industry only included liability for failure to render a judgment in time.[103]

16.4.2.4 Scope of the exoneration

The exoneration clauses in some arbitration rules do not contain restrictive wording. The exoneration clause then simply contains the words *"shall not be liable for any act or omission in connection with any arbitration under the Rules"*.[104] This bears the risk that if the law applicable to the exoneration clause does not allow such a general exclusion of liability, the entire exoneration clause will be null and void.[105] In addition, such a provision may be partially null and void if the law applicable to it does not allow the exclusion of liability on certain grounds.[106] In general, this could only be the case if there is a gap between the bases on which an arbitrator can be successfully held liable and the bases on which no exoneration is allowed.[107]

It is assumed, however, that the words *"any act or omission"* refer not only to the conduct of the arbitrator being held liable, but also to others, such as co-arbitrators, the arbitral institution concerned or third parties for whom they are responsible. Thus, the wording described above also has the effect

100 This exoneration clause related to "any act or omission in connection with the arbitration except to the extent such liability is prohibited by applicable law".
101 Paris Court of Appeal 31 March 2015, No 14/05436 (*Delubac*).
102 Article 6.1.2 ADR Institute of Canada Regulations (2016).
103 Article 33 ACPCAC (2008).
104 See e.g. Article 6.1.1. ADRIC (2016); Article 37 ADRSA (2017); Article 41.1 DIAC (2022).
105 Cf. Y. Derains & E.A. Schwartz, *A Guide to the ICC Rules of Arbitration (2005)*, The Hague: Kluwer Law International 2005; B. van der Bend, M. Leijten & M. Ynzonides, *A Guide to the NAI Arbitration Rules: Including a Commentary on Dutch Arbitration Law*, The Hague: Kluwer Law International 2009, p 386.
106 Cf. Derains & Schwarts 2005; Van der Bend, Leijten & Ynzonides 2009, p 386.
107 Cf. Derains & Schwartz 2005; Van der Bend, Leijten & Ynzonides 2009, p 386.

that the arbitrator can invoke the exoneration for claims based on acts or omissions of third parties.

The most common restrictions in such clauses are *"gross negligence"*,[108] *"fraudulent"*,[109] *"not in good faith"*,[110] *"wilful misconduct"*,[111] *"conscience and deliberate wrongdoing"*,[112] *"intentional wrongdoing"*,[113] *"culpable negligence"*,[114] *"Con culpa grave o de manera dolosa"*,[115] *"deliberate misconduct"*,[116] *"dishonesty"*,[117] and *"recklessness"*.[118] This terminology may be in line with relevant legal criteria in the law of the country where the arbitral institution in question is located. However, that law is not necessarily the law applicable to the question of the admissibility of that exclusion of liability. For that reason, some institutions will have opted for a more general formulation of the exclusion *"to the extent permitted under applicable law"*[119] or *"except to the extent such limitation is prohibited by applicable law"*,[120] without mentioning specific legal qualifications. The latter formulations are intended to allow for the widest possible exclusion of liability as permitted by the applicable law.[121] The law applicable to the exoneration clause will then ultimately determine the scope of said clause in a specific case.

Interesting are the JCAA rules that stipulate that the exclusion of intent and deliberate recklessness only applies with regard to damage suffered in the specific case[122] and the provision of the AFSA (2014) in which a connection is required between intent and deliberate recklessness of the person addressed and the damage/consequence.[123] This is relevant because, for

108 See e.g. Article 37 ADRIOCC (2017); Article 45.2 DIS (2018); Article 13 of the JCAA (2021); Article 45 SAC (2021); Article 52 SCC (2023).

109 See e.g. Article 15 HKMC (2014).

110 See e.g. Article 53 ACICA (2021); Article 40 CEPANI (2023).

111 See e.g. Article 37 ADRIOCC (2017); Article 13 JCAA (2021); Article 56 KCAB (2016); Article 52 SCC (2023).

112 See e.g. Article 41.1 BCDR (2022); Article 31.1 LCIA (2020).

113 See e.g. Article 16 CIArb (2015); Article 16 Cyprus Arbitration & Mediation Centre ("CAMC") (2022); Article 55 CRCICA (2024); Article 45 SAC (2021).

114 See, for example, Article 40 of the Consolat de Mar (2005).

115 See e.g. Article 1.32 CAC (2023).

116 See e.g. Article 56 KCAB (2016).

117 See e.g. Article 46 HKIAC (2024) and Article 15 HKMC (2014).

118 See e.g. Article 56 KCAB (2016).

119 See e.g. Article 41.1 BCDR (2022); Article 16 CAMC (2022); Article 16 CIArb (2015).

120 See e.g. Article 51 DIA (2021); Article 41 ICC Rules (2021).

121 See Derains & Schwartz 2005, p 386.

122 Article 13 JCAA (2021), Article 9.4 TAMARA (2015), Article 9.4 UNUM (2018).

123 Article 21.3 AFSA (2014), Article 9.4 TAMARA (2015) See also the wording of Article 1069b of the draft bill for a new arbitration law of the Van den Berg Committee.

example, it is conceivable that only one of the arbitrators makes a mistake. Think of the presiding judge who finalised the text of the award and sent an unsigned award to the parties without giving his co-arbitrators the opportunity to sign,[124] or one arbitrator being bribed, while the other two arbitrators were not and had no knowledge of the fact that their co-arbitrator had received a bribe. It seems useful to refine the NAI exoneration clause in this respect.

For arbitrators, it is of course important to verify (i) whether any professional indemnity insurance has been taken out for their benefit e.g. by the arbitration institute[125], and (ii) if so, how the applicable exoneration clause sits with such applicable liability insurance policy. Key areas of focus include the jurisdictional enforceability of exoneration clauses, specific exclusions in the insurance policy and the exoneration clause, and the alignment between the two protection mechanisms. With respect to the latter aspect the insurance terms typically define what constitutes a covered claim. If an arbitrator faces a claim that falls outside the exoneration clause, the insurance still may cover such claims. Notably, an exoneration clause in arbitration rules may influence the risk profile for purposes of a professional indemnity insurance and potentially reduce the likelihood of claims. This reduction in risk may indirectly affect the terms set by insurers, including premium payable and deductibles.

16.4.3 *Admissibility of exoneration clauses*

The NAI exoneration clause contains an important exclusion: *"all this except where and insofar as mandatory Dutch law precludes this exclusion of liability"*[126] However, it is not necessarily a given that Dutch law is relevant for determining the validity of this exoneration clause in a specific case. This was particularly an issue under the old NAI Arbitration Rules, which did not contain a choice of law clause (in favour of Dutch law). The law applicable to the question of validity of an exoneration clause will be determined on the basis of the private international law of the country in which the arbitrator will be sued.[127]

124 See H.J. Snijders, 'Aansprakelijkheid van arbiters (QNOW/B), repressie en preventie', *TvA* 2017/1, para 3.

125 See A.F.M. El Shourbagy, *Arbitrator and Arbitral Institutions Liability and Insurance* (diss. Rotterdam) 2021, p 186 et seq describes relevant aspects of professional indemnity insurance for arbitrators. He i.a. describes aspects of the professional indemnity insurance taken out by the NAI at the time, p 223-225.

126 Article 61 NAI Arbitration Rules 2015, Article 64 NAI Arbitration Rules 2024.

127 See also Van der Bend, Leijten & Ynzonides 2009, p 386.

Pursuant to Article 1020 (6) DCCP, the arbitration rules referred to in an arbitration agreement are deemed to form part of that agreement. The same applies to an exoneration clause that is part of it. According to Article 10:166 DCC, an arbitration agreement is materially valid if it is valid (i) under the law chosen by the parties, or (ii) under the law of the place of arbitration, or (iii) if the parties have not made a choice of law, under the law applicable to the legal relationship to which the arbitration agreement relates.[128] According to that provision, Dutch law therefore determines whether an exoneration clause in an arbitration agreement is valid and whether an arbitrator may invoke that third-party clause if the parties have made a choice for Dutch law in respect of the arbitration agreement, the place of arbitration is in the Netherlands or, in the absence of a choice of law in that regard in the arbitration agreement, Dutch law is applicable to the legal relationship to which the arbitration agreement refers. However, this will not necessarily apply to all arbitrations administered by the NAI.

Article 21(7) of the previous version of the NAI Arbitration Rules (2015) stipulated that, if the parties had not chosen a place of arbitration, the arbitrators would make this choice. In the version amended on 1 March 2024, the place of arbitration is governed by a new Article 27(1), which provides that *"Where the place of arbitration is not determined by agreement between the parties, the place of arbitration is Amsterdam."*

In any event, the newly introduced Article 65 of the NAI Arbitration Rules (2024) provides that the legal relationship between the arbitrator(s) and the parties, between the arbitrator(s) and the NAI and between the NAI and the parties, as well as the legal relationship between the arbitrators, the parties or the NAI and other persons playing a role pursuant to the Rules, is governed by Dutch law. As a consequence, the exoneration clause in Article 64 is also governed by Dutch law.

If the exoneration clause is governed by Dutch law, then according to the general rule of Article 6:248(2) DCC it must remain inapplicable insofar as application of the clause would be unacceptable according to the standards of reasonableness and fairness, taking into account all the circumstances

128 The legislative history does not clarify whether and, if so, how these three alternatives are in a hierarchical relationship. See e.g. N. Peters, *IPR, Proces & Arbitrage* (diss. Groningen), no 6.5.3.2, Groningen: University of Groningen 2016; Snijders 2018, Article 1020 DCCP, comment 1.

of the case.[129] This will generally be the case if the damage is caused as a result of intent or deliberate recklessness (*"bewuste roekeloosheid"*) on the part of the debtor.[130] This is partly in line with the criteria developed in the case law on arbitrator liability described above, pursuant to which an arbitrator will only be able to invoke such an exoneration clause in the event his liability would be based on a gross disregard of what the proper performance of duties entails.[131] However, depending on the circumstances of the case, also in such event pursuant to Article 6:248(2) of the DCC reliance on an exoneration may be found to be unacceptable in the light of the standards of reasonableness and fairness.[132]

With regard to the reliance on the exoneration clause, it was held in the judgment of the Court of Appeal of 's-Hertogenbosch referred to above, that it had not been alleged or shown that the arbitrators had intentionally or knowingly made the error in question or had knowingly taken the risk that they acted incorrectly or that there was deliberate recklessness. Thus, the arbitrators could rely on the exoneration clause invoked.[133] In the context of this consideration, the question may also arise whether the statutory challenge provision in Article 1035 DCCP at issue in that case, which the arbitrators had failed to follow, does not constitute such an essential part of the arbitral task that an arbitrator is deemed to be aware of that rule,[134] and if so, what that conclusion would mean for assessing the existence of the degree of fault. Could that not constitute deliberate recklessness (*"bewuste roekeloosheid"*)?

---

129 Cf. Supreme Court 17 February 2012, ECLI:NL:HR:2012:BV6162, para 3.5.2, *NJ* 2012/290 (*Savills Holding Nederland/K.C.M. Pasman Holding*) and Supreme court 15 June 2012, ECLI:NL:HR:2012:BW0727, *NJ* 2015/155 (*PricewaterhouseCoopers/Veldhuyzen van Zanten*); Asser Procesrecht/Sanders, Meijer & Ernste *8* 2023/213.

130 Supreme Court 12 December 1997, ECLI:NL:HR:1997:ZC2524, para 3.6.1, *NJ* 1998/208 (*Stein/Driessen*) (cf. Supreme Court 31 December 1993, ECLI:NL:HR:1993:ZC1210, para 3.2, *NJ* 1995/389 and Supreme Court 5 September 1997, ECLI:NL:HR:1997:ZC2415, para 3.5, *NJ* 1998/63).

131 Peters & Bakker 2020, p 370.

132 According to Meijer 2017, p 359, it must be assumed that an exoneration also has no effect in the event of gross neglect of duty. Asser Procesrecht/Sanders, Meijer & Ernste *8* 2023/213 indicate that it can be argued that gross neglect of duty is a type of intent and conscious recklessness, making any exclusion or limitation of liability ineffective in cases where liability is based on gross neglect of duty.

133 's-Hertogenbosch Court of Appeal 1 December 2015, ECLI:NL:GHSHE:2015:5154, para 3.14.2, *NJF* 2016/38.

134 Also see Supreme Court of 30 September 2016, ECLI:NL:HR:2016:2215, para 3.5.3, in which it was held that overseeing the signing of the arbitral award by all arbitrators (Article 1057 (2) DCCP) is an essential task of the presiding arbitrator of which the presiding arbitrator should be aware.

Another point is that it can be argued that an exoneration clause is presumed to be unreasonably onerous within the meaning of Article 6:233 sub a DCC on the basis of Article 6:237 (f) DCC and therefore voidable in the event that a consumer is a party to the relevant terms and conditions of which it is a part.

16.5 Closing

In the *Greenworld* and *Qnow* judgments, the Supreme Court formulated and refined the standard for arbitrator liability under Dutch law. As a matter of principle, Dutch law provides for a basis for arbitrators' liability. However, codification can be useful in the interest of legal certainty and predictability, in particular for non-Dutch arbitration specialists. Application of this standard to specific case positions, as recently done by the District Court of Amsterdam, will provide more clarity in the future as to whether certain types of arbitral errors will lead to liability. The future (lower) case law will also have to provide guidance on how effective exoneration clauses such as those included in Article 64 of the NAI Arbitration Rules 2024 are when it comes to errors that fall into the category of "*gross disregard of what constitutes a proper performance of duties*".

CHAPTER 17

EMERGENCY AND EXPEDITED ARBITRAL PROCEEDINGS AT THE NETHERLANDS ARBITRATION INSTITUTE

Rogier Schellaars & Fleur Potter[1]

17.1 Introduction

In this contribution, we discuss emergency arbitral proceedings (*arbitraal kort geding*) and expedited arbitral proceedings (*arbitrale spoedbodemprocedures*) at the Netherlands Arbitration Institute ("NAI").

We describe and discuss both proceedings by reference to the 2024 arbitration rules of the NAI (the "NAI Rules 2024")[2] and offer some remarks for potential limited future improvements, in addition to those offered by us in our 'Going Dutch' publication that we made in 2019 in a book compiled to commemorate the NAI's 70th anniversary (the "Going Dutch Publication").[3] In this Going Dutch Publication, we proposed to introduce expedited arbitral proceedings at the NAI. This has, in the meantime been effectuated through the adoption of the NAI Rules 2024, to which one of the authors of this publication contributed.[4]

---

1 R. (Rogier) Schellaars (LLM) and F.M.A. (Fleur) Potter (LLM) work at Van Doorne and OCI N.V. respectively. They make this contribution in a personal capacity. In addition, R. Schellaars has been mandated by the NAI's board to assist in the drafting of parts of the NAI Rules 2024 and is a co-chair to the ICC Arbitration and ADR Commission's Working Group on Expedited Arbitral Proceedings. Of course, no information confidential to the NAI and the ICC is shared in this publication.

2 See extensively, M. Hetterscheidt, 'NAI Arbitragereglement 2024: op weg naar efficientere en snellere beslechting van (internationale) handelsgeschillen', *TCR* 2024, issue 2, p 31-40.

3 R. Schellaars & F.M.A. Potter, 'Een beschouwing over de kansen en mogelijkheden van het arbitraal kort geding en de arbitrale spoedbodemprocedure bij het Nederlands Arbitrage Instituut', in: C.J.M. Klaassen, G.J. Meijer & C.L. Schleijpen (ed), *Going Dutch: ADR in Nederland en in het bijzonder bij het NAI*, Deventer: Kluwer 2019, p 527. This recommendation was also supported by M.L. Verhoeven-de Vries Lentsch & R. Schellaars, 'Arbitral Emergency Proceedings – à la Hollandaise: Twenty Years of Practice', *TvA* 2020/3.

4 See footnote (1).

We also note that, prior to the introduction of the NAI Rules 2024, the emergency arbitral proceedings were referred to as summary arbitral proceedings and have thus been rebranded. No substantive change has been made to this feature of the NAI Rules. In this contribution, we adopt such new terminology.[5]

In this contribution, we also refer to, and rely on, our earlier publication on expedited arbitral proceedings in the so-called 'Geschriften vanwege de Vereniging van Corporate Litigation' (the "VCL publication")[6] and a subsequent modest empirical study that we conducted (in particular) among Dutch lawyers and 'users' of arbitration (the "Study") – which was relative novelty at the time.[7] This empirical study will be repeated under the auspices of ICC Netherlands at the close of 2024 – so we understand.

Conducting empirical research is pertinent, in our opinion. This is so, if only, because, notably, efficiency and speed of (arbitral) proceedings are often held out as universal desirable qualities of dispute resolution and presented as key driver for amendment of arbitration rules and procedural regimes. This applies to the NAI Rules 2024 (in our observation) and also to, for example, the arbitration rules of the International Chamber of Commerce ("ICC") which provide, since the introduction of the 2017 version thereof, for expedited proceedings on the merits.[8] The President of the ICC Court of International Arbitration described the ICC's offering of expedited proceedings and the rationale for the introduction thereof as follows:

> "As to the introduction of our Expedited Rules, effectively providing for an arbitration to be concluded in six months (...) it is an entirely new offer to the business community and an effective answer to the legitimate concerns of the business community as to the time and costs of the arbitration."[9]

---

5 In the NAI Rules of 1 January 2015, emergency arbitral proceedings were referred to as "summary arbitral proceedings" in Article 36. This provision was part of Section 4A of this version of the NAI Rules that provided for "provisional relief".

6 R. Schellaars & F.M.A Potter, 'Expedited Proceedings', in: M. Holtzer, D. Strik & D.J. Oranje (ed), *Writings on behalf of the Association of Corporate Litigation 2015-2016*, Deventer: Wolters Kluwer 2016.

7 We administered a survey in 2019 and did so online by e-mail, via internet forums and otherwise to lawyers, corporate lawyers, academics and lawyers working in government. Those surveyed indicated that they worked mainly in the Dutch jurisdiction and mostly had extensive experience in commercial arbitration at the NAI and the ICC.

8 Article 31 ICC Regulations 2017 in Appendix V.

9 https://https://iccwbo.org/media-wall/news-speeches/new-icc-arbitration-rules-and-note-take-effect/, accessed 21 December 2018.

Although empirical research was limited and the ICC's proposition was not entirely new, as some other institutions had already fielded comparable options to expedited proceedings, it has proven a success (quantitatively and, according to the authors' observations qualitatively). The ICC reported the following statistics on the usage of the ICC's expedited arbitral proceedings in its 2023 statistical report:[10]

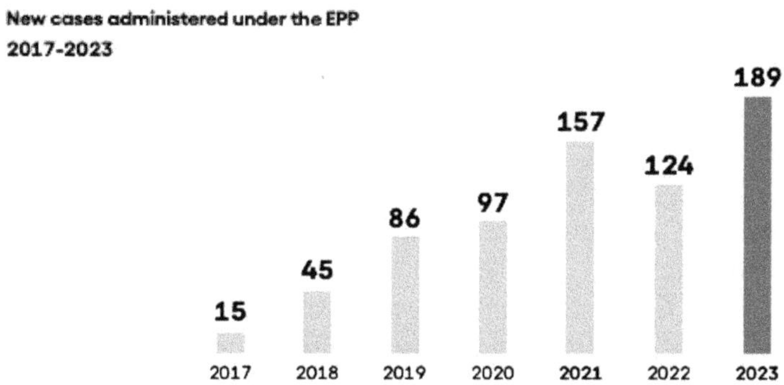

We thus emphasize that empirical research on, for example, speed, costs and market-perceptions on arbitral proceedings and proceedings in the regular courts, remains limited. In so far as arbitral practice is concerned, we observe that, also in current Dutch literature,[11] reference is often made to research conducted by White & Case LLP and Queen Mary College London (the "Queen Mary Research").[12] A key finding in this Queen Mary Research is that:[13]

> *"Arbitration users would be most willing to do without 'unlimited length of written submissions' and 'oral hearings on procedural issues' if this would make their arbitration cheaper or faster."*

In the Netherlands, efficiency and speed are also topical. These concerns also feature, for example, as rationes for the amendment of the evidentiary rules under the Dutch Code of Civil Procedure, which is to take effect per

10 ICC Dispute Resolution 2023 Statistics, reported on: https://iccwbo.org/wp-content/uploads/sites/3/2024/06/2023-Statistics_ICC_Dispute-Resolution_991.pdf.

11 H.J. Snijders, *Nederlands Arbitragerecht*, Deventer: Wolters Kluwer 2018, p 53 and R.J. Tjittes, *Commercieel Contractenrecht*, The Hague: Boom legal 2018, p 28, 29 and 30. Similarly, and by reference to the 2018 Queen Mary Report, R.J. Tjittes, *Commercieel Contractenrecht*, The Hague: Boom legal 2022, p 45-46.

12 The 2021 iteration is the final one, so it seems: https://www.qmul.ac.uk/arbitration/research/2021-international-arbitration-survey/.

13 See: https://www.qmul.ac.uk/arbitration/research/2021-international-arbitration-survey/, at p 2.

1 January 2025.[14] This is further echoed in the recent publication of the new Asser series volume on arbitration and binding advice, with no reference to empirical research.[15]

We already pointed out, in our VCL publication, that – certainly in the Netherlands – only limited research has been done into arbitral practice.[16] In the Final Report on the Fundamental Reconsideration of Dutch Civil Procedure Law, the authors observed that:

> "(...) hardly any [Dutch] research data on what the litigant wants from the civil proceedings."[17]

In recent times, this seems to be changing. We note that the WODC ('Wetenschappelijk Onderzoek en Documentatie Centrum') is, currently, conducting research on the Netherlands Commercial Court. The WODC aims to assess whether or not the NCC is on its way to meet the desired outcome: to offer an institute in which parties can conduct swift and efficient proceedings in the English language.[18] It is remarkable that such research does not seem to have been conducted prior to the constitution of the NCC.

We also note that, under Professor Verkerk's auspices, empirical research was published on the practice in the regular state courts, by reference to research done in judicial databases.[19] This research indicates that it is safe to say that the average duration of proceedings at first instance and in appeal is well over 500 days each.[20] This statistic is relevant, if only with a view to assess or benchmark performance of arbitral tribunals and arbitral institutions; which offer proceedings leading to a final award, with one instance/

14 See extensively on the new instrument, F.J.P. Lock, 'De Wet vereenvoudiging en modernisering bewijsrecht: wat er (niet) gaat veranderen', *TCR* 2024, issue 3, p 67-79. Wet vereenvoudiging en modernisering bewijsrecht (*Stb.* 2024, 62).

15 Asser Procesrecht/Sanders, Meijer & Ernste *8* 2023/236.

16 Schellaars & Potter 2016, p 199-203.

17 See: https://www.qmul.ac.uk/arbitration/research/2021-international-arbitration-survey/, at p 2.

18 The results of this research will be published at www.wodc.nl, so we understand.

19 R. Verkerk, F. van Dijk & D. Pistora, 'De berechting binnen een redelijke termijn. Een empirisch onderzoek naar doorlooptijden in handelszaken', *TCR* 2020, issue 4, p 153-170.

20 Verkerk, Van Dijk & Pistora 2020, para 3.6. In this paragraph, the authors remark that proceedings in commercial disputes last, on average, 692 days for proceedings at first instance and 774 days on appeal.

shot only and aim to do so, for expedited proceedings on the merits at the NAI, within about six months.[21]

In this publication, we focus, in particular, on arbitral proceedings to which the NAI Rules 2024 apply. In doing so, we assume the application of Dutch arbitration law, unless stated otherwise, and refer to provisions of the Dutch Arbitration Act, which has been applicable since 1 January 2015 and is (by and large) set out in Book 4 of the Dutch Code of Civil Procedure. We shall not, however, address the practice at the Arbitration Board for the Construction Industry (*Raad van Arbitrage in bouwgeschillen*), which also provides for emergency arbitration and so-called urgent binding advice proceedings within the specific context of construction disputes and usages at this particular institution.[22]

The structure of this contribution is as follows. In paragraph 17.2 we deal with emergency arbitral proceedings (i.e. the proceedings formerly known as summary arbitral proceedings). In paragraph 17.3 we discuss expedited arbitral proceedings. In paragraph 17.4 we offer limited suggestions for improvement to the NAI Rules 2024. In paragraph 17.5 we provide some final remarks.

17.2 Emergency Arbitration (formerly: summary arbitral proceedings)

The Dutch Arbitration Act provides for a legislative foundation for Emergency Arbitration in Article 1043b DCCP. This provision ties arbitral practice to usages and norms found in similar proceedings in the Dutch state courts, by making reference to Article 254 DCCP which provides for summary proceedings in the state courts (*kort geding*). In respect of this arrangement, we note three points.

First, the connection to practice in the state courts, may be acceptable and understandable to Dutch parties/counsel, but is significantly less so – in our experience and expectation – to non-Dutch parties and/or parties who

21 The time-limit is five months, counting from the case management conference that is held shortly after the commencement of the proceedings (see NAI Rules 2024, Article D11(1)).

22 This institution's official information, on its website, is generally only available in Dutch. See the following pages for its expedited arbitral proceedings: https://www.raadvanarbitrage.nl/onze-procedures/spoedbodemprocedure/.

conduct arbitral proceedings seated outside the Netherlands. The reference to Article 254 DCCP implies that limits imposed on the basis of (*inter alia*) urgency and complexity of summary proceedings before the regular Dutch Courts apply *mutatis mutandis* to Emergency Arbitration. In addition, parties not familiar with Dutch state court practice in this regard need to be alert to, for example, the notion that this practice indicates that no assessment is required with respect to relative chances of parties with respect to the outcome in potential proceedings on the merits.[23]

Second, issues may arise in respect of recognition and enforcement of the outcome of these proceedings outside the Netherlands, the outcome of which is generally considered to be an award and explicitly legislated to be so in Article 1043b(4) of the DCCP.[24]

Third, we consider the introduction of new terminology in the NAI Rules 2024, pursuant to which the English translation of the arbitral summary proceedings (*arbitraal kort geding*) is changed into "Emergency Arbitration" to be of some concern. Non-Dutch lawyers and arbitrators may very well project their non-Dutch norms and usages on the limits applicable to other regimes of emergency arbitration, for example at the ICC, on the application of the literal text of the NAI Rules (as opposed to the Dutch regime under Article 254 DCCP). After all, the concept of emergency arbitration means many things to many people – as also indicated by the ICC Task Force on Emergency Arbitration of 1 April 2019. This Task Force notes as a key conclusion:[25]

> "The Task Force analysis (...) reveals that there is no universal approach to EA proceedings. This variety is apparent with respect to threshold issues, procedural matters, substantive standards and post-emergency arbitration considerations, and is first and foremost the consequence of the choice made in the ICC Rules to leave to the EA a considerable degree of discretion and flexibility."

Indeed, the practice and usage of Emergency Arbitration at the NAI differs fundamentally from the course of affairs at the ICC and the London Court

23 Dutch Supreme Court 15 March 1968, ECLI:NL:HR:1968:AB4858, *NJ* 1968/228.

24 See in this regard: S. Kröll, 'NAI Summary Arbitral Proceedings: Enforceability under the NYC?', *TvA* 2012/19. R. Schellaars, 'NAI arbitraal kort geding – kort, goed en met executabel resultaat', *TvA* 2013/15.

25 See: https://iccwbo.org/wp-content/uploads/sites/3/2019/03/icc-arbitration-adr-commission-report-on-emergency-arbitrator-proceedings.pdf, para 7, p 4. One of the authors of this publication was a member of this Task Force (R. Schellaars).

of International Arbitration ('LCIA').[26] In essence, a key differentiator for the NAI's proceedings when compared to prominent international arbitration rules is that NAI's arrangement entails a more fully-fledged procedure, with low thresholds regarding requisite urgency and that can lead to an arbitral award that lends itself to enforcement (and does not have to be tied to, or be conditional upon, subsequent proceedings on the merits).[27]

17.2.1 Emergency Arbitration at the NAI

Emergency Arbitration is now provided for in Article 40, 41 and Appendix C of the NAI Rules 2024.

Since 1998, the arbitration rules of the NAI have included proceedings which were, as noted earlier, referred to as summary arbitral proceedings until the introduction of the NAI Rules 2024. Prior to the introduction of the NAI Rules 2024, the NAI's Emergency Arbitration variant only applied in proceedings seated in the Netherlands.[28] Extensive empirical research has been carried out into the practice of these proceedings (the Emergency Arbitration Research). The outcome of this research was, but is no longer, accessible via the website of the NAI, and is (at the time of writing) in the process of an update to reflect practice in recent years up to and including 2024. Core parts of this research are published in the Dutch Journal on Arbitration.[29]

17.2.1.1 Emergency Arbitration need not be connected to proceedings on the merits

If arbitral proceedings on the merits are pending, a party seeking interim measures may apply for such measures to either the already appointed arbitral tribunal (Article 40(1)(a) of the NAI Rules 2024); or opt to commence separate emergency arbitral proceedings and appoint a distinct arbitral tribunal (Article 40(1)(b) and 41 of the NAI Rules 2024). If arbitral pro-

26 The 2020 LCIA Rules regulate this in Article 9b (see *TvA* 2014/2). The ICC Rules from 2012 (see *TvA* 2012/2) and (now current) 2021 in Article 29 (see *TvA* 2017/21).

27 A recent summary of the status at the NAI may be found in: Verhoeven-de Vries Lentsch & Schellaars 2020. See footnote (1).

28 The entry requirement with regard to the place of arbitration is contained in Article 35(2) NAI Rules. With some criticism at the introduction of this rule, see G.W. van der Bend & M.A. Leijten, 'The collection of summary proceedings at the Netherlands Arbitration Institute', *AA* 2002, issue 7-8, p 553-558.

29 The Emergency Arbitration Research is reflected in Verhoeven-de Vries Lentsch & Schellaars 2020.

ceedings on the merits are not pending, Article 40(1)(b) and 41 provide the basis for independent emergency arbitral proceedings.

An Emergency Arbitration can therefore be conducted 'independently', in the sense that it can be independent of any subsequent proceedings on the merits. The implications of this proposition are threefold.

In the first place, an arbitral tribunal dealing with Emergency Arbitration under the NAI Rules 2024 is not compelled to assess the chances of success that the parties may or may not have in potential proceedings on the merits.[30]

In the second place, an arbitral tribunal dealing with the case on the merits may assess the merits of the case independently of the outcome of the proceedings in Emergency Arbitration and is not bound by the decision of the emergency arbitrator (Article 40(4) and 41 NAI Rules 2024).

In the third place, it is not necessary for arbitral proceedings on the merits to be conducted following Emergency Arbitration. This is so neither as an entry-requirement to conducting an Emergency Arbitration nor as a requirement for the validity of a decision taken in Emergency Arbitration. This Dutch practice – which is in line with the practice in the Dutch state courts – is not common internationally.[31] For example, the ICC regulates *emergency arbitrations* in accordance with Article 29 and Appendix V of the ICC Arbitration Rules of 2021 ("ICC Rules 2021").[32] Pursuant thereto, within 10 days of receipt by the Secretariat of the ICC of the *Application for Emergency Measures*, a request for arbitration in the main proceedings must be filed.[33] If that requirement is not met, the President of the ICC Court terminates the emergency arbitrator proceedings.[34] Further to the LCIA Arbitration Rules of 2020 ("LCIA Rules 2020"), an 'Emergency Arbitrator' may be appointed *"(...) prior to the formation or expedited formation of the Arbitral Tribunal"*.[35] At that time, substantive proceedings must already have been initiated.[36]

---

30 Dutch Supreme Court 15 March 1968, ECLI:NL:HR:1968:AB4858, *NJ* 1968/228.
31 Asser Procesrecht/Sanders, Meijer & Ernste *8* 2023/231.
32 ICC Rules 2021, Appendix V and LCIA Rules, sub 9B.
33 ICC Rules 2021, Appendix V, Article 1(6).
34 ICC Rules 2021, Appendix V, Article 1(6).
35 LCIA Rules 2020, Article 9.4.
36 LCIA Rules 2020, Article 1 and 9.

17.2.1.2 Requirements – details

Emergency Arbitration may be brought at the NAI if (see Article 40(1)(b) in conjunction with Appendix C, Article C3(2) of the NAI Rules 2024):

(i) the matter is sufficiently urgent; to be decided in Emergency Arbitration;
(ii) the matter is not too complex to be decided in Emergency Arbitration; and
(iii) in view of the interests of the parties, an immediate interim injunction is required.

It is no longer required, further to the NAI Rules 2024, for the seat of the arbitration to be in the Netherlands.[37] That said, this may very well create issues due to the fact that the legislative basis for Emergency Arbitration in the Dutch Arbitration Act does not apply in such instances (because Article 1043b DCCP only applies if the seat of arbitration is in the Netherlands pursuant to the operation of Article 1073 DCCP).

Whether the required criterion urgency, set out in Article C3(2) of the NAI Rules 2024, has been met, is often determined by arbitrators in a manner comparable to the assessment made by the Dutch state courts (by reference to Article 1043b(2) and Article 254 of the DCCP). Article 9.2 of the Explanatory Notes to the NAI Rules 2015 provided some guidance to the effect that a more stringent test applies regarding urgency if the matter is already pending before a tribunal dealing with the case on the merits.[38]

That said, there is no formal reason to apply a test akin to, or even equal to, Article 254 of the DCCP if the arbitration is seated outside the Netherlands, if only because Article 1043b(2) DCCP, which makes reference to Article 254 DCCP, does not apply in such instance.[39] This is novel territory, which will be entered further to the adoption of the NAI Rules 2024 and will be subject to the development of practice over the coming years

37 Compare Article 35(2) of the NAI Rules of 1 January 2015.

38 The Explanatory Notes were attached to the NAI Rules of 1 January 2015 and may be consulted at www.nai-nl.org/downloads/NAI%20Arbitration Rules%20 and%20Annex%20NL.pdf. The Explanatory Notes do not form part of the NAI Rules.

39 Article 254 DCCP is the provision in the Dutch Code of Civil Procedure that provides the basis for a well-developed and nuanced framework for summary arbitral proceedings. It should be noted that this provision is rather succinct and cannot be properly understood and applied by mere reference to the text thereof as it has developed through court practice and decided cases.

(although this may take some time, because proceedings seated outside the Netherlands and conducted on the basis of the NAI Rules are limited in number).

Article C3(2) of the NAI Rules 2024 further provides that the emergency arbitrator may dismiss a claim (in whole or in part) by referring the case to an arbitration on the merits if the case is too complex to be dealt with in the emergency proceedings. The aforementioned Emergency Arbitration Research indicated that arbitrators rarely refer a case to proceedings on the merits.[40] On the basis of our own experience and the Emergency Arbitration Research, we conclude that rather complex cases are dealt with in emergency arbitrations.[41] In respect of this second criterion, we also note that the Dutch perception of acceptable degrees of complexity does not per se need to inform a tribunal if the arbitration is seated outside the Netherlands.[42]

17.2.1.3 Jurisdiction

The Emergency Arbitration Research showed that in 58% of the proceedings no jurisdictional defence was raised.[43] Furthermore, it appears that, in cases where jurisdiction has been contested, that defence was generally unsuccessful.[44]

We have no reason to believe that this statistic will have changed significantly in the past years, but that remains to be verified through upcoming updated Emergency Arbitration Research (which is expected to be published early 2025).

17.2.1.4 Constitution of the Arbitral Tribunal

The rules on appointments of a tribunal in Emergency Arbitration differ from the rules governing arbitral proceedings on the merits, where the use of a party appointed arbitrator is the default position (see Article 16 of the NAI Rules 2024).

---

40 Investigation into Emergency Arbitration, para 3.3.
41 Investigation into Emergency Arbitration, para 3.3.
42 This is so, if only, because Article 1043b(2) DCCP does not apply in such instance.
43 Investigation into Emergency Arbitration, para 3.2.
44 Investigation into Emergency Arbitration, para 3.2.

In Emergency Arbitration, the use of party appointed arbitrators is not common. Upon receipt of the arbitration request, the responsible member of the NAI Case Management Committee directly appoints an emergency arbitrator (Article C2(1) of the NAI Rules 2024). The arbitral tribunal always comprises one arbitrator, regardless of whether the parties have agreed on a different number of arbitrators. Consequently, the agreed method of appointment of arbitrators and/or agreement on a number of arbitrators will not apply, except where parties have expressly agreed otherwise in relation to emergency arbitration (all per Article C2(1)).

The responsible member of the NAI Case Management Committee aims to make the appointment within 24 hours.[45] It is apparent from the Emergency Arbitration Research that the NAI generally meets this timeline and appoints highly experienced arbitrators.

17.2.1.5 Conduct of the proceedings

The NAI Rules 2024 stipulate that the arbitral tribunal shall determine the day, time and place of the hearing date as soon as possible (Article C6). Written pleadings shall be lodged only if the arbitral tribunal so directs (Article C6).

Furthermore, Article C3 of the NAI Rules 2024 provides that various provisions in the NAI Rules 2024 that apply to proceedings on the merits, for example with regard to adversarial proceedings and the taking of evidence, apply equally to Emergency Arbitration. This legislative technique, of cross-referencing and thus providing for equal application of general provisions, is common to Dutch lawyers and should be carefully noted if the NAI Rules 2024 are used and applied by common law trained lawyers.

On the conduct of Emergency Arbitration, we refer to the Emergency Arbitration Research.[46] We note, for now, that these proceedings prove to be highly flexible, allow for limited taking of evidence and deal with cases

45 *'The arbitrator will be appointed by the NAI within one working day of receiving the application for summary proceedings.'* See www.nai-nl.org/nl/nai_arbitrage/procedure/#Arbitral_short_proceedings.

46 Verhoeven-de Vries Lentsch & Schellaars 2020.

of considerable complexity.[47] The authors of the Emergency Arbitration Research observe that:[48]

> "(...) in 65% of the awards rendered, the relief sought by the claimant is granted in whole or in part. The picture with respect to counterclaims is different. Out of the 44 cases in which counterclaims were raised, only 25% were successful. This is quite a finding. We have the impression that claimants generally come well prepared and do not lightly initiate these proceedings."

And also:[49]

> "(...) we observe a very wide variety of relief granted. This includes: claims for specific performance (nakoming); monetary payment; lifting of attachments/ garnishment orders; enforcement of an obligation to conclude an agreement; halting infringement of competition clauses and intellectual property rights; enforcement of a right of inspection of, access to or handing over of documents; an injunction to exercise shareholder rights; and nullification of a decision to terminate an agreement."

17.2.1.6 Award

The Dutch Arbitration Act stipulates that a decision issued in Emergency Arbitration qualifies as an arbitral award (Article 1043b(4) of the DCCP), unless the tribunal determines otherwise. Consequently, an award rendered in a Dutch seated Emergency Arbitration will, at least in the Netherlands, be enforceable in a manner equal to awards issued by tribunals dealing with proceedings on the merits. Enforcement of such an emergency award in the Netherlands is not controversial. Our Study, conducted in 2019 showed that a majority of respondents (80%) are of the opinion that a tribunal should indeed be able to offer relief in Emergency Arbitration, in the form of an enforceable award.[50] This is not likely to be a view held internationally (for which we refer to the already cited work of the ICC's

47 It appears from decided cases, for example in the District Court of Amsterdam on 7 January 2016, that the preliminary relief judge ruled that under the NAI Rules, witnesses can be heard in a timely manner. District Court of Amsterdam 7 January 2016, ECLI:NL:RBAMS:2016:33. This is indicative of known practice where tribunals take liberty in terms of application of Article 1039(1) DCCP.

48 Verhoeven-de Vries Lentsch & Schellaars 2020.

49 Verhoeven-de Vries Lentsch & Schellaars 2020.

50 The question was: *"A tribunal should be able to render preliminary relief in summary arbitral proceedings/emergency proceedings by means of an (enforceable) award and not just an order (i.e. in Dutch: an award and not just an 'order' c.q. assignment)"*. The green bar indicates the percentage of respondents who answered in the affirmative to this question.

Task Force on Emergency Arbitration and our experience gained in partaking in this Task Force's work).[51]

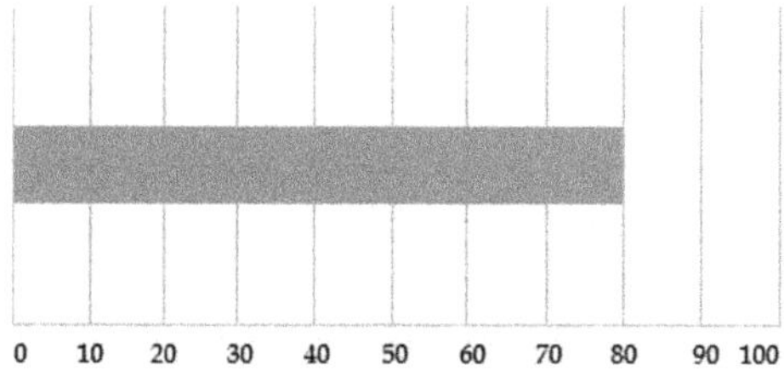

The Dutch Journal on Arbitration includes contributions on international perspectives on enforceability of these Dutch awards rendered in Emergency Arbitration. For example, the German (now) Professor Kröll argued that enforcement abroad on the basis of the New York Convention could be problematic since an arbitral summary judgment would not meet the 'finality' requirement of Article V of the New York Convention.[52] One of the authors to this publication argued the contrary in response.[53] In any event, the body of published cases on this topic outside the Netherlands is limited.[54]

17.2.2 *How do the NAI's Emergency Arbitration relate to the Dutch Arbitration Act – further remarks*

We wish to make the following two additional points in relation to the Dutch Arbitration Act.

First, the Dutch Arbitration Act expressly provides for the possibility of an arbitral tribunal in emergency arbitral proceedings rendering a decision

51 https://iccwbo.org/wp-content/uploads/sites/3/2019/03/icc-arbitration-adr-commission-report-on-emergency-arbitrator-proceedings.pdf.

52 Kröll 2012.

53 Schellaars 2013. This article was partly written in response to Kröll's publication cited above.

54 J.K. van Hezewijk does not refer to new insights in the most recent publication in the Dutch Journal on Arbitration: J.K. van Hezewijk, '"Een gulden regel, waard, dat er voor zijn naleving angstvallig wordt gewaakt"', *TvA* 2024/47; but he does cite the Cygne decision by the Amsterdam District Court of 12 January 2017, ECLI:NL:RBAMS:2017:282, para 4 (*Cygne/Cofco*), in which this court referred to enforceable decisions rendered in emergency arbitration on the basis of the ICC Rules of Arbitration. A recent example was published on Global Arbitration Review's pages: https://globalarbitrationreview.com/article/us-court-enforces-dutch-insurance-award.

on the merits upon unanimous request of the parties (Article 1043b(6) of the DCCP).

Second, the Dutch Arbitration Act prescribes that an arbitral award shall be put in writing (Article 1057(2) DCCP). That does not prevent a tribunal from issuing its decisions in an oral form, initially and subject to the parties not objecting thereto, but does oblige the tribunal to put the award in writing subsequently.[55] The latter ensures compliance with the prescribed contents of arbitral awards (Article 1057(2) and (4) DCCP, in particular).

17.2.3 *The relationship between Emergency Arbitral proceedings and the jurisdiction of the Dutch state courts*

The Dutch Arbitration Act provides, for proceedings seated in the Netherlands, in Article 1022(a)-(c) DCCP, for the interaction between jurisdiction of the Dutch state courts and arbitral tribunals with regard to provisional relief. It provides for the primacy to be with the arbitral tribunal.[56]

Under this regime, the ordinary courts only have jurisdiction if a party (i) does not invoke the existence of an arbitration agreement before submitting a defence; or (ii) if the decision sought cannot or cannot timely be obtained in arbitral proceedings in cases where an arbitration agreement has been invoked.[57] Article 1074(a)-(d) of the DCCP provides for a similar provision for arbitral proceedings with a seat of arbitration outside the Netherlands. With regard to the second requirement (timely), direction can be found in literature and case law.

There is some debate in Dutch literature about the degree to which the parties may deviate, by agreement, from this legislative regime. By and large, we take the view that party-agreement should prevail, to the extent permitted by the mandatory elements of the Dutch Arbitration Act.[58]

In 2016, Messrs. Stouten and Stevens, also with reference to the first edition of the aforementioned Emergency Arbitration Research, concluded that (if the parties have entered into an arbitration agreement with ref-

55 See, with nuance and reference to recent literature, Asser Procesrecht/Sanders, Meijer & Ernste *8* 2023/293.

56 G.J. Meijer et al., *Parliamentary History of the Arbitration Act*, Deventer: Kluwer 2015, p 47.

57 Article 1022c of the Dutch Code of Civil Procedure.

58 Van Hezewijk 2024.

erence to the NAI Rules with a place of arbitration in the Netherlands) a decision on provisional relief can, in general, be obtained in arbitration within the same period of time as a decision can be obtained from the ordinary court as referred to in Article 1022a (conservatory measures and summary proceedings) and 1022b (evidentiary measures) of the DCCP.[59] It emerges from a subsequent update of this Emergency Arbitration Research that, in the majority of emergency arbitral proceedings, an award is rendered within 8 weeks counting from the initial moment in time where the application for Emergency Arbitration was submitted.[60]

In our view, it is safe to conclude that NAI Emergency Arbitration, including a claim for provisional evidentiary measures, meets the "timely requirement" set out in Article 1022c DCCP. This may be different if the Emergency Arbitration under the NAI Rules 2024 is seated outside the Netherlands, although we do not expect that to be the case.

It follows from published case law that Dutch courts regularly declare that they have no jurisdiction in accordance with Article 1022c DCCP. A good example is provided by a judgment of the preliminary relief judge of the District Court Midden-Nederland of 7 June 2017. The court in preliminary relief proceedings confirmed that a provisional injunction could be obtained in good time under the NAI Rules.[61] To that end, the court considered that, on the basis of the NAI Rules, arbitral tribunals aim to render an award in Emergency Arbitration in a short period of time, comparable to the time limit in summary proceedings before the ordinary courts. The court discusses that research and data (there is no specific reference in the judgment to particular sources) indicate that the:

> "(...) average processing times (sic) of summary arbitration proceedings and of summary proceedings before the ordinary courts differ little (...)."[62]

In another case, before the District Court of Amsterdam on 7 January 2016, the preliminary relief judge ruled that under the NAI Rules, witnesses can be heard in a timely manner.[63] In that regard, the court hearing the appli-

59 T. Stouten & L. Stevens, 'The timeliness requirement of Article 1022c and Article 1074d DCCP in summary proceedings', *TvA* 2016/2, para 43.
60 Verhoeven-de Vries Lentsch & Schellaars 2020, para 2, 8th item.
61 District Court of Midden-Nederland 7 June 2017, ECLI:NL:RBMNE:2017:2652, para 4.7.
62 District Court of Midden-Nederland 7 June 2017, ECLI:NL:RBMNE:2017:2652, para 4.7.
63 District Court of Amsterdam 7 January 2016, ECLI:NL:RBAMS:2016:33, para 4.7.

cation for interim measures attaches importance to the degree of discretion which the NAI Rules grant arbitrators with regard to the taking of evidence in general and the hearing of witnesses in particular. It follows from the NAI Rules that parties may apply to arbitrators at any stage of the proceedings with a request to hear witnesses. In view of this and the fact that the NAI Rules provide for provisional relief and hearing witnesses, the court declared that it had no jurisdiction. Furthermore, the preliminary relief judge took the Dutch state courts' workload into account in its judgment: according to the court, it is unlikely that a preliminary witness examination at the court could be held earlier than three months after the request has been granted.[64] In addition, the court also took into account the principle of immediacy (with reference to Article 155 DCCP) and procedural economy, which procedural economy is served by the fact that in the arbitral proceedings there will be more clarity on the points on which witnesses must be heard.[65] Further decided cases have been published on the website of the Dutch judiciary – which by no means contains all decided cases: www.rechtspraak.nl.[66]

We also note that the primacy of the arbitral tribunal, with respect to decision-making on provisional relief, is also recognized by the Dutch judiciary in so far as the application of other arbitration rules is concerned. For example, on 19 June 2018, the District Court in Rotterdam ruled on the arbitration rules of the 'Stichting Transport and Maritime Arbitration Rotterdam Amsterdam' ('TAMARA' – now 'UNUM').[67] The court held that the TAMARA Rules of Arbitration provide for what we now refer to as emergency arbitration, in a manner disconnected from arbitral proceedings on the merits. In this case, the claimant (who wanted the case to be dealt with by the Dutch courts) had not put forward any facts or circumstances from which it could follow that provisional relief could not be (timely) obtained in arbitration. In addition, the District Court also considered that the respondent had indicated that he was only unable to attend on a very few

64 District Court of Amsterdam 7 January 2016, ECLI:NL:RBAMS:2016:33, para 4.10.

65 District Court of Amsterdam 7 January 2016, ECLI:NL:RBAMS:2016:33, para 4.8.

66 See for example: District Court of Noord-Holland 22 February 2023, ECLI:NL:RBNHO:2023:1726; District Court of Rotterdam 12 May 2021, ECLI:NL:RBROT:2021:4372; Court of Appeal The Hague 15 March 2022, ECLI:NL:GHDHA:2022:397; District Court of Rotterdam 26 July 2021, ECLI:NL:RBROT:2021:7210; and Court of Appeal The Hague 20 December 2022, ECLI:NL:GHDHA:2022:2053.

67 District Court of Rotterdam 19 June 2018, ECLI:NL:RBROT:2018:5131, para 4.4.

dates and had promised to appear in the arbitral emergency proceedings.[68] The court thus declared that it has no jurisdiction.

In a case before the District Court of Midden-Nederland, this court ruled on whether the Arbitration Board for the Construction Industry's procedure provides for the possibility of witness examinations in a timely manner.[69] The court held that the arbitrators had already been appointed and that the rules provided for the possibility of hearing witnesses (in this case, at the end of the written procedure).[70] The District Court thus declared that it had no jurisdiction to hear the application and noted (as the District Court in Amsterdam did in a judgment described above[71]) for the sake of completeness that – in view of the workload of a preliminary examination of witnesses before the District Court – it would not be possible to hear witnesses much earlier than three months after the application had been granted. Furthermore, the court considered that the claimants had:

> "(...) indicated that they wished to hear eleven witnesses, which would mean that a preliminary examination of witnesses would take several days."[72] The court also takes into account the "principle of immediacy", which means that "(...) the tribunal will be able to hear the witnesses themselves and to hear first-hand what they testify."[73]

The practice under international arbitration rules is assessed by the Dutch state courts on the basis of the same framework. On 12 June 2015, the District Court of The Hague ruled that an injunction can be obtained in arbitration in good time, since the respondent had argued and substantiated that under the Vienna arbitration rules[74] it is possible to grant provisional relief within a period of a few weeks. The District Court hearing the ap-

68 District Court of Rotterdam 19 June 2018, ECLI:NL:RBROT:2018:5131, para 4.5.

69 District Court of Midden-Nederland 30 September 2015, ECLI:NL:RBMNE:2015:7340, para 4.6.

70 District Court of Midden-Nederland 30 September 2015, ECLI:NL:RBMNE:2015:7340, para 4.3 and 4.4.

71 District Court of Amsterdam 7 January 2016, ECLI:NL:RBAMS:2016:33.

72 District Court of Midden-Nederland 30 September 2015, ECLI:NL:RBMNE:2015:7340, para 4.5.

73 District Court of Midden-Nederland 30 September 2015, ECLI:NL:RBMNE:2015:7340, para 4.6.

74 In view of the timing of the award by the interim relief judge and its reference to Article 33 of the 'Vienna Rules', this is the 2013 VIAC Rules of Arbitration. In this Article 33, however, it concerns an independent arbitral procedure; that is, the interim and conservatory measures must be claimed before an already appointed arbitral tribunal on the merits (see Article 33(1) of these VIAC Rules).

plication for interim measures thus held that it had no jurisdiction on the basis of Article 1074d DCCP.[75]

17.3 Expedited arbitration

In this section, we discuss the newly introduced expedited arbitral proceedings under the NAI Rules 2024 and the relationship between expedited proceedings and the Dutch Arbitration Act. We offered extensive recommendations on this topic in our Going Dutch Publication.[76]

17.3.1 Expedited proceedings on the merits are internationally widely accepted

We refer to expedited arbitral proceedings on the merits as proceedings on the merits in which short timelines are applied for procedural steps and in which the proceedings are generally limited in nature and scope (including with regard to the taking of evidence).[77] Such proceedings will, in principle, result in a final arbitral award. This award is final and thus (save for an unlikely arbitral appeal, which needs to be specifically agreed to) only subject to setting aside (Article 1064a DCCP) or revocation (Article 1068 DCCP).[78]

Substantive elements of our recommendations in the Going Dutch Publication[79] are reflected in the expedited arbitral proceedings introduced through the NAI Rules 2024. Article 42 of the NAI Rules 2024, which provides, notably, for a more detailed arrangement in Appendix D to the NAI Rules 2024, is the core provision.

---

75 District court of The Hague 12 June 2015, ECLI:NL:RBDHA:2015:6959, para 4.2.

76 Schellaars & Potter 2019, para 21.4, p 515-526.

77 Schellaars & Potter 2016, para 3.2. See also the UNCITRAL Working Group II's definition: "*It was generally understood that expedited arbitration was a streamlined and simplified procedure with shortened time frame that made it possible to reach a final resolution of the dispute in a cost- and time-effective manner.*" This wording is contained in the (note) 'Advance Copy' (with serial number A/CN.9/969) of the 'Report of Working Group II (Dispute Settlement) on the work of its sixty-eight session (New York, 5-9 February 2018), para 14. This document can be found at www.uncitral.un.org under 'Working Documents' of 'Working Groups' with submenu 'Working Group II'. This document should be distinguished from a final document with sequence number A/CN/9/934 which can be found on the Working Group II page at www.uncitral.org under '68th session, 5-9 February 2018, New York'.

78 For a detailed description of the general characteristics of emergency procedures, see: Schellaars & Potter 2016, para 3.2.2.

79 Schellaars & Potter 2019.

Arbitration rules of many prominent arbitral institutions have provided special rules for expedited proceedings on the merits, for many years.[80] For example, the Stockholm Chamber of Commerce ('SCC') was an early-mover and has extensive experience with such expedited proceedings.[81] In addition, the ICC adopted a special set of rules for the expedited proceedings on the merits in 2017: the so-called "Expedited Procedure Rules" (appendix VI of the ICC Rules 2017) – which have been slightly updated in the ICC Rules of 2021.

The ICC has opted for a so-called *'opt out'* system, meaning that the ICC's Expedited Procedure applies, unless they are explicitly excluded.[82] The Expedited Procedure applies to matters with a financial interest up to USD 2 million under the ICC Rules 2017 and up to USD 3 million in the ICC Rules 2021.[83]

At the time of writing, the most recent statistics published by the ICC are those of 2023.[84] Figures for the period up to and including 2023 show that since the ICC Rules 2017 came into force, 713 cases have been administered under the ICC Expedited Procedure Rules. In 2023, a record number of 189 new cases were administered under these rules, of which 15 opt-ins (i.e. proceedings on the basis of the Expedited Procedure Rules in matters where it does not automatically apply) were effectuated pursuant to party agreement. In these proceedings (final) awards were, by and large, issued within the 6-month timeframe prescribed in Appendix VI, Article 4(2), counting from the date of the case management conference.[85]

80 See, for example, the Stockholm Chamber of Commerce Rules for Expedited Arbitrations of 2017 ("SCC Expedited Rules 2017"), the Arbitration Rules of the Singapore International Arbitration Centre 2016 ("SIAC Rules 2016"), Rule 5, the Hong Kong International Arbitration Centre 2018 Administered Arbitration Rules ("HKIAC Rules 2018"), section 42 and the Swiss Chambers' Arbitration Institution Swiss Rules of International Arbitration 2012 ("Swiss Rules 2012"), Article 42 and CoA Arbitration Rules 2015, Article 14 and Deutsche Institution für Schiedsgerichtsbarkeit ("DIS") Arbitration Rules 2018 Annex 4 ("DIS Rules 2018").

81 See also the, updated, 2023 arbitration rules for such expedited proceedings at the SCC: https://sccarbitrationinstitute.se/sites/default/files/2022-12/scc_expedited_arbitration_2023_english.pdf.

82 Furthermore, this rule shall apply only if the arbitration agreement was concluded after the entry into force of Appendix VI; i.e. after 1 March 2017, see Article 30(3)(a) ICC Rules 2017.

83 ICC Regulations 2017, Appendix VI, Article 1(2).

84 https://iccwbo.org/wp-content/uploads/sites/3/2024/06/2023-Statistics_ICC_Dispute-Resolution_991.pdf (last visited on 24 September 2024).

85 See www.iccwbo.org/media-wall/news-speeches/icc-court-releases-full-statistical-report-for-2017/.

In our Going Dutch Publication,[86] we also referred to the (then ongoing) work of the UNCITRAL Working Group II. That Working Group had a mandate to examine how the UNCITRAL Arbitration Rules could possibly be amended to provide for an expedited arbitration procedure and/ or to consider whether guidance could be provided to arbitral institutions with respect to providing for an expedited arbitration procedure. This work has been concluded through the adoption of the UNCITRAL Expedited Arbitration Rules and an explanatory note thereto in 2021.[87] These are incorporated in Article 1(5) of the UNCITAL Arbitration Rules and appended thereto.[88] Express consent is required for these expedited rules to apply per this Article 1(5).

We will now turn to review some of the characteristics of expedited arbitral proceedings under the NAI Rules 2024 and the (intended) practice at the NAI. In our Going Dutch Publication, we made reference to the NAI's so-called small claims procedure (known as "TGV") for very small claims below € 100,000. We note this for sake of completeness as it still exists from a formal perspective, but is hardly ever used.[89] Hence, we shall not discuss this arrangement in any further detail in this publication.

17.3.1.1 Gatekeeper function

Not all disputes lend themselves to expedited proceedings. That is why arbitration rules regularly provide for a 'gatekeeper function'. Pursuant thereto, an intervention by an arbitration institute, prior to or after the commencement of Expedited Proceedings, is possible and may cause the case to proceed as a normal arbitral procedure on the merits. See also, for example, the ICC Expedited Procedure, Appendix VI, Article 1(4).

The NAI has also provided for such function, specifically Article D9 of the NAI Rules 2024, through which expedited arbitral proceedings may, in exceptional circumstances, be discontinued and transferred into regular proceedings on the merits. It does not, however, provide for an initial entry-test pertaining to the suitability of the matter for application of its Expedited Arbitration regime.

86 Schellaars & Potter 2019.
87 https://uncitral.un.org/sites/uncitral.un.org/files/media-documents/uncitral/en/21-07996_expedited-arbitration-e-ebook.pdf.
88 https://uncitral.un.org/sites/uncitral.un.org/files/media-documents/uncitral/en/21-07996_expedited-arbitration-e-ebook.pdf.
89 See www.nai.nl/arbitration/small claims procedure.

The transfer of a case from the expedited regime to the regular arrangement for proceedings on the merits may occur at the joint request of the parties or the request of the arbitral tribunal to the responsible member of the NAI Case Management Committee. Subsequent to such a request, it is for the responsible member of the NAI Case Management Committee to decide if the case is (still) suitable to be decided in expedited arbitration (Article D9 2024 Rules). We note that the NAI Case Management Committee is only supposed to act on such requests and not on its own motion. By contrast, under the ICC Rules, the ICC Court may, on its own motion (and subject to certain conditions), decide that the case is no longer subject to its expedited procedure provisions.[90]

We consider such a 'safety valve' necessary, also as part of a set of safeguards that should be in place in the interest of due process. This applies, in particular, because these are proceedings on the merits that do not allow for extensive taking of evidence, which may be required in a given dispute; and do not provide for appeal (absent party agreement to that effect). If expedited proceedings derail (in the sense that fundamental procedural principles are not sufficiently safeguarded)[91] and in the eyes of the arbitral tribunal or the parties should be converted into regular proceedings on the merits, this should be possible.

17.3.1.2 Monetary value of claims

In our Going Dutch Publication, we proposed € 2 million as a monetary threshold, below which expedited arbitral proceedings would apply automatically. This proposal was supported by our Study, to which we made reference in that publication.

The NAI ultimately resolved to apply a threshold of € 1 million, which may be raised by party agreement on an opt-in. The main rationale for this threshold seems to be context-driven: a considerable proportion of the NAI's caseload concerns a monetary value of € 1 million. This is not the case, for example, at the ICC, where the median value in dispute is above $ 5 million. Indeed, for the threshold to be set to € 2 million would imply that, at introduction, these rules would apply to the majority of cases administered at the NAI. Also for that reason, the threshold was set at € 1 million – so we understand.

---

90 ICC Rules 2021, Appendix VI, Article 1(4).

91 Schellaars & Potter 2016, para 3.2.2.

17.3.1.3 Sole arbitrator

The basic principle under the NAI Rules is that the arbitral tribunal in expedited arbitral proceedings comprises one arbitrator to be appointed by the NAI.[92]

Under the NAI Rules 2024, a sole arbitrator is appointed by the responsible member of the NAI Case Management Committee after application of a so-called list procedure (Article D4(2)). This list procedure was common practice for arbitrations in the NAI Rules 2010 and is still a non-mandatory option in the NAI Rules 2024. This makes good sense in the context of expedited proceedings, at it saves time and furthers the appointment of an arbitrator with sufficient experience to handle an expedited arbitration.

The responsible member of the NAI Case Management Committee will transmit an identical list of names to each of the parties. This list will contain three persons eligible for appointment as arbitrators. A party may delete from such list names of persons against whom it holds objections, and may number the remaining names in its order of preference. Subsequently, the completed list must be returned to the responsible member of the NAI Case Management Committee within four days after transmission (Article D4(2) NAI Rules 2024). If this does not result in the appointment of a tribunal (i.e. no match is possible), the responsible member of the NAI Case Management Committee will directly appoint a person not featured on the list issued to the parties (Article D4(4) NAI Rules 2024).

Importantly, the NAI, as opposed to the ICC, does give effect to party agreements which may provide that the number of arbitrators must be more than one. The NAI does so in case either of the parties expresses a wish to stick to a specific number of arbitrators or where an express agreement is in place specifically for the appointment of a tribunal in Expedited Arbitration. This is provided for in Article D4(1) of the NAI Rules 2024. Article D4(1) provides in the relevant part that:

> "The arbitral tribunal will consist of one arbitrator. If the parties have by agreement specified a method of composition of the arbitral tribunal and/or a number of arbitrators, such agreement will be disregarded when appointing an arbitrator in expedited arbitration, unless one of the parties indicates in the request for arbitration or the short answer that it wishes to maintain a (previously) agreed other number of arbitrators, or where the parties have expressly provided for the num-

92 See, with some nuance, in comparison: ICC Rules 2021, Appendix VI, Article 2.

ber of arbitrators and/or method for appointing an arbitral tribunal in expedited arbitration in their agreement for expedited arbitration specifically."

17.3.1.4 Concentrating and accelerating the debate

A common feature in expedited arbitration is that arbitration rules provide for a considerable 'concentration' of the debate through providing only for limited written and oral submissions, all to be made in a short timeframe.[93]

In many cases, it is also possible to dispense with an oral hearing or significantly curtail the scope thereof.[94] The ICC Rules 2021 explicitly provide that a hearing may be dispensed with (Appendix VI, Article 3(5)), if the arbitral tribunal so decides after consulting the parties. The same is permitted and explicitly addressed in Article D8 to the NAI Rules 2024, albeit that a hearing can only be dispensed with in NAI proceedings, if both the parties and the arbitral tribunal agree to do so.

In the case of the Expedited proceedings on the basis of the NAI Rules 2024, only one written exchange of documents takes place (Article D6 2024 NAI Rules 2024). In addition, only one hearing – in addition to the case management conference – will be held (Article D8 NAI Rules 2024), unless otherwise agreed by the parties and the tribunal. The hearing will take place in electronic form (Article D8(2) NAI Rules 2024), subject to contrary agreement by the parties and the tribunal or a decision by the tribunal to provide otherwise. In this regard, we note that party-agreement, including through adoption of the NAI Rules, may be trumped by the need to comply with Article 1036 DCCP (assuming the proceedings are seated in the Netherlands). It is conceivable that Article 1036(2) DCCP warrants additional oral or written submissions in addition to those provided for in Article D6 and D8 of the NAI Rules 2024.

17.3.1.5 Limited possibility of providing evidence

Arbitration rules often provide for potential limitations to or even exclusion of the possibility of exhibiting documents in Expedited proceedings.[95]

93 See, for example, ICC Rules 2021, Appendix VI, Article 3 and the DIS Rules 2018, Annex 4, Article 3.

94 See, for example, ICC Rules 2017, Appendix VI, Article 3 (5) and Swiss Rules 2012, Article 42 (1)(c) and SCC Expedited Rules 2017, Article 33 and DIS Rules 2018, Annex 4, Article 4.

95 See, for example, ICC Rules 2021, Appendix VI, Article 3 (4). See also the UNCITRAL Working Group II's Explanatory Note to the UNCITRAL Expedited Arbitration Rules, para 82.

The same applies to examination of witnesses and/or hearings of experts.[96] This is not explicitly done in Appendix D to the NAI Rules 2024. That said, the general provision on taking of evidence of Article 34 of the NAI Rules 2024 applies by reference (see in Article D6(2)). Consequently, a tribunal may curtail the taking of evidence in expedited arbitral proceedings and should be expected to do so given the nature of these proceedings. Again, compliance with Article 1036 DCCP may trump such limitations.

17.3.1.6 Short (and hard) deadline for issuing an award

Arbitration rules further, typically, provide for short and hard time limits for the arbitral tribunal to issue a final award in expedited proceedings.[97] The NAI Rules 2024 now provide for a five-month time limit for the issuance of an award, counting from the case management conference (see Article D11(1)). This is a challenging deadline: it entails that the tribunal has only limited time available to complete the drafting process for the award after the hearing. The tribunal is ultimately empowered to make use of Article 5(3) NAI Rules 2024 to, in exceptional circumstances, extend this time limit.

Parties may also, in some circumstances, waive the right to receive a reasoned award.[98] This is not expressly provided for in the NAI Rules 2024; but may be done through application of Article 1057(5) DCCP, pursuant to which the parties need to agree thereto in writing after the commencement of the arbitral proceedings.

We advocated the application of 'scrutiny light' to an award in expedited arbitral proceedings at the NAI when we published our contribution to the Going Dutch publication of 2019.[99] This position was premised on the fact that such an award may have far-reaching consequences due to the fact that it is, in principle, final and not appealable (bearing in mind also that the award will be drafted by, in principle, a sole arbitrator and after relatively short proceedings). The NAI did indeed introduce a form of scrutiny light in Article 50 of the NAI Rules 2024, but did not express its scrutiny process to also cover (limited review of) reasoning of the award.

96 See, for example, ICC Rules 2017, Appendix VI, Article 3 (4).
97 See, for example, ICC Rules 2017, Appendix VI, Article 4 (1) and SIAC Rules 2016 Rule 5.2 (d), SCC Expedited Rules 2017, Article 43 and DIS Rules 2018, Annex 4, Article 1.
98 See, for example, Article 34(3) of the UNCITRAL Expedited Arbitration Rules.
99 Schellaars & Potter 2019.

The NAI might reconsider this position, at the occasion of future revisions of the NAI Rules 2024.

In our opinion, the instruction in the ICC Note to the Parties and Tribunals, in its version of 1 January 2021, also expresses the need for reasoning of awards correctly and further, correctly, makes the point that the award may be more succinct in certain areas (when compared to regular proceedings on the merits that is and which could also apply to NAI proceedings):[100]

> "Any award under the Expedited Procedure Provisions must be reasoned. In such arbitrations, it is particularly appropriate to keep the factual and/or procedural sections of the award to what the arbitral tribunal considers necessary for the understanding of the award, and state the reasons of the award in as concise a fashion as possible."

In the 1 January 2019 version of this ICC Note, the wording was still a bit different and less prescriptive:[101]

> "Any award under the Expedited Procedure Provisions shall be reasoned. Arbitral tribunals may limit the factual and/or procedural sections of the award to what they consider to be necessary to the understanding of the award, and state the reasons of the award in as concise a fashion as possible."

17.3.2 How does the expedited proceedings relate to the Dutch Arbitration Act?

As noted, if Dutch arbitration law applies, Article 1036 DCCP offers fundamental guidance, with regard to the conduct of arbitral proceedings. It does so in the following terms, which we consider important to repeat at this juncture:[102]

> "Without prejudice to the mandatory provisions of this Title, arbitration proceedings shall be conducted in the manner agreed by the parties. To the extent that the parties have not provided for the arrangement of interim arbitration, it shall,

100 For more than 25 years, the ICC has published a 'Note to Parties and Arbitral Tribunals on the Conduct of the Arbitration under the ICC Rules of Arbitration' on its website (see https://iccwbo.org/news-publications/arbitration-adr-rules-and-tools/note-parties-arbitral-tribunals-conduct-arbitration, para 151).

101 https://www.iccwbo.be/wp-content/uploads/2018/12/20190101-icc-note-to-parties-and-arbitral-tribunals-on-the-conduct-of-arbitration.pdf, para 117.

102 We use the translation offered by the NAI on its website: https://nai.nl/dutch-arbitration-act/.

> without prejudice to the provisions of this Title, be conducted in the manner determined by the arbitral tribunal."

Consequently, agreements made on, for example, the exchange of pleadings and the provision of evidence should in principle be complied with.[103] Limitations that may arise from mandatory rules must, however, also be adhered to: this includes the fundamental procedural principles of, notably, adversarial proceedings and equal hearing laid down in Article 1036(2) DCCP.[104] Compliance with mandatory rules of applicable law may trump party agreement, including to the extent that such party agreement follows from agreed upon arbitration rules – such as the NAI Rules 2024.

The review of arbitral proceedings by reference to the applicable legal requirements is (ultimately) up to the competent state courts – and this is no different in so far as expedited arbitral proceedings are concerned. In the Netherlands, this review is carried out, in particular, in the context of the decision to grant an exequatur pursuant to Article 1062 and 1063 DCCP and also if a party claims annulment of an arbitral award on the grounds that it is contrary to public order pursuant to Article 1065(1)(e) DCCP and/or breach of mandate pursuant to Article 1065(1)(c) DCCP. The same applies to revocation of an award, which may be sought on limited grounds (Article 1068 DCCP).

We note, as a final remark, that the regime applicable to enforcement, annulment and/or revocation of arbitral awards will apply, without limitation and/or variation, to awards rendered in Expedited Arbitration under the NAI Rules 2024. This may be different if the parties refrain from an oral hearing (which is permitted under Article 1038b DCCP) in view of the provisions of the New York Convention 1958; and/or applicable arbitration law at a place of arbitration, if such place is located outside the Netherlands.[105]

As noted, in our Going Dutch Publication, we included various further proposed provisions for a new set of expedited arbitration rules to be included in the NAI Rules. These have been implemented in whole or in part in the NAI Rules 2024. We offer the following remaining remarks.

103 Article 1036 to 1042 of the Dutch Code of Civil Procedure.
104 Asser Procesrecht/Sanders, Meijer & Ernste *8* 2023/236.
105 Schellaars & Potter 2016, para 3.2.1.

17.3.3 Expedited Proceedings: further remarks on the structure

In the first place, we recommend that the parties and tribunals take the case management hearing seriously and have a meaningful exchange of views with a view to the necessary procedural efficiency and speed and with a view to maintaining due process.[106] At this occasion, agreements should ideally be reached on the taking of evidence, procedural documents, a hearing and time limits. This applies, *a fortiori*, because these proceedings are one-shot only and will lead to a final award on the merits.

In the second place, we did, in our Going Dutch Publication, not consider it to be wise and necessary to stipulate that the request for arbitration and the short answer constitute a statement of claim and statement of defence respectively (an arrangement to this effect exists at the SCC).[107] We maintain this position.

Thirdly as a rule, an oral (virtual) hearing must take place, unless the parties and the tribunal agree not to conduct an oral hearing. The NAI Rules 2024 explicitly provide that the arbitral tribunal shall also need to concur that no hearing is required: it may, after all, consider a hearing to be required (Article D8(1) NAI Rules 2024). We consider this to be the right approach.

Fourthly, we were, and are, not in favour of a hard deadline for the delivery of an award. Our position has, however, not been adopted in the NAI Rules 2024. These provide for a five-month time limit counting from the date of the case management conference. We highlight that this timeline entails a very serious commitment of all involved (the parties, tribunal and NAI Case Management Committee) and suggest to explicitly verify, prior to its appointment, if the tribunal indeed has the time to deliver on this timeline and commitment.

Fifthly, we made some remarks on the ambit of the scrutiny-light procedure under the NAI Rules 2024, above, which we suggest to also pertain

106 The SCC, in its Rules for Expedited Arbitrations 2017, provides in Rule 29(3) a provision urging the arbitrator and the parties in such a way with regard to the "*case management conference and timetable*': '*Having regard to the circumstances of the case, the Arbitrator and the parties shall seek to adopt procedures enhancing the efficiency and expeditiousness of the proceedings.*"

107 SCC Rules for Expedited Arbitrations 2023 and, earlier 2017, Article 6 and Article 9 (introductory phrase).

to non-binding remarks on the reasoning of awards. To this, we now add some further perspective under a separate heading directly below.

17.3.3.1 Assurance of the quality of arbitral awards: introduction of 'scrutiny light'

The NAI Rules 2015 did not provide for a formal basis for the NAI to carry out checks on the quality of arbitral awards by (part of) the NAI. This was, and is, different, especially at the ICC, where the *'scrutiny'* procedure is applied. We advocated the application of a scrutiny light regime to the expedited proceeding under the proposed NAI Rules. This has been implemented through Article D11(2) and Article 50(4) of the NAI Rules 2024.

The NAI's regime is comparable to the 2018 DIS Arbitration Rules, the DIS had introduced a procedure that provides for such a *'scrutiny light'*. The DIS describes its approach as follows:

> "The arbitral tribunal shall send a draft of the award to the DIS for review. The DIS may make observations with regard to form and may suggest other non-mandatory modifications to the arbitral tribunal. The arbitral tribunal shall remain exclusively responsible for the content of the award."[108]

We made reference in our Going Dutch Publication to our Study indicating strong support for such scrutiny light in the Netherlands.[109] This view surprised us and strengthened our opinion that this scrutiny mechanism is appropriate with respect expedited arbitration. The NAI completes this scrutiny light process within 5 days, in respect of expedited proceedings.[110] Our research indicated the following on the question whether or not "arbitral awards should be checked/scrutinized by the arbitration institute for manifest errors prior to the issuance thereof (if only because an appeal is generally not possible and with a view to annulment (nullification) and enforcement)?":[111]

---

108 2018 DIS Arbitration Rules, Article 39.3.

109 Schellaars & Potter 2019.

110 https://nai.nl/nl/arbitrage/.

111 Our research question was: The question was: *"Arbitral awards should be checked/scrutinised by the arbitration institute for manifest errors prior to the issuance thereof (if only because an appeal is generally not possible and with a view to annulment (nullification) and enforcement)?"*

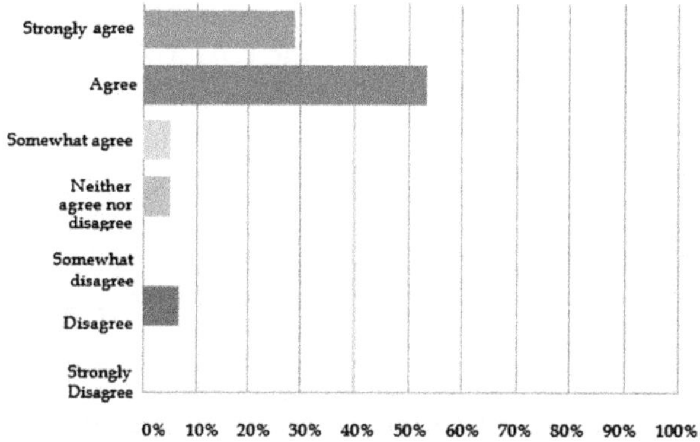

17.3.3.2 Appeal: show the parties the way, but don't impose it

We pointed out in our Going Dutch Publication that expedited arbitral proceedings, with their limited room for debate and taking of evidence, can indeed lead to a non-appealable final arbitral award that in principle qualifies for recognition and enforcement in and outside the Netherlands. Hence, procedural safeguards should be in place, in our view, in addition to those afforded by, notably, Article 1036 DCCP.[112]

We were – and are – not in favour of the introduction of an arbitral appeal as a 'standard' or default proviso at the NAI. That said, we can well imagine – and we also observed support for this on the basis of results of our Study – that the NAI offers or draws more attention to an appeal as a choice. As far as we are concerned, this is more about 'showing the way' than imposing appeal. In any case, the model clauses for an arbitration agreement may indicate that and how the parties can arrange an arbitral appeal.

Our Study showed that 34% of the respondents prefer to have the option of a full appeal after the conclusion of expedited arbitral proceedings.[113] Just under 30% of respondents were neutral on this point. Furthermore, 38% of the respondents indicated that they would like an appeal limited to '*manifest errors of law*' (a term that also appears in English arbitration prac-

112 Schellaars & Potter 2019.

113 The question was: "*If I would be/represent a party in expedited proceedings on the merits, I do wish to have the option for a full appeal (i.e. in Dutch: arbitraal hoger beroep ten gronde):*".

tice). 26% of the respondents were neutral about this.[114] Hence, this may be considered, again, in a next iteration of the NAI Rules and/or be covered in the to-be-published set of Explanatory Notes to the NAI Rules 2024.

17.3.4 Emergency Arbitration

In our Going Dutch Publication, we made some limited suggestions to improve the NAI's provisions for emergency arbitral proceedings.[115] One pertinent point remains.

We advocated that, in order to meet the criticism regarding the 'finality' of an arbitral emergency award in the light of Article V of the New York Convention 1958,[116] the Explanatory Notes to the NAI Rules 2024 (which have not been published yet) may include wording to made clearer that such an arbitral award is final and binding between the parties, unless a different outcome is reached in *any* subsequent proceedings on the merits.

In addition, and as a result of the rebranding from summary proceedings to emergency arbitration, we advocate a clear explanation, in the NAI's envisaged Explanatory Notes to the NAI Rules 2024, to the effect that the NAI's version of emergency arbitration should not be equated with proceedings that go by the same name at, for example, the ICC and LCIA. It is, in our view, pertinent to make clear that the NAI's emergency arbitral proceedings are premised on the Dutch concept of emergency arbitration (*kort geding*) and thus provide for different forms relief and conditions for availability thereof, than one may expect under other international arbitration rules.

17.4 Concluding Remarks

We are pleased to be able to reflect, in this contribution, on the newly introduced Expedited Arbitration arrangement in the NAI Rules 2024. This new arrangement no doubt strengthens the NAI's position in the Dutch and international markets. For international parties, this presents yet another basis to justify "Going Dutch".

114 The question was: "*If I would be/represent a party in expedited proceedings on the merits, I do wish to have the ability for an appeal (arbitraal hoger beroep) limited to (just) manifest errors of law:*".

115 Schellaars & Potter 2019.

116 Kröll 2012.

CHAPTER 18

ARBITRATION AND CONFIDENTIALITY: EXISTENCE AND RAMIFICATIONS OF A PRINCIPLE

Filip De Ly[1]

18.1 Introduction

Until recently, it was generally accepted and hardly controversial that arbitration was confidential and that such confidentiality was both a feature and an important advantage of arbitration. This contribution will discuss recent developments relating to the principle of confidentiality in arbitration which show that the principle – especially in a number of foreign countries and in a number of special cases – is under pressure, and that therefore further regulation seems desirable.[2] This assessment will not only address the question of whether arbitration should be confidential, but will also be aimed at clarifying the ramifications of the principle.

18.2 Assumption of confidentiality in arbitration and its foundations

For decades – including in the Netherlands – it was assumed that arbitration was confidential[3]. This did not cause or hardly caused any problems, which meant that the confidentiality principle enjoyed an uncontroversial and dormant existence. Moreover, there was scarcely any reflection in relation to the dogmatic foundation of the principle.

1 F. (Filip) De Ly (LLM) is professor of Private International Law and Private Comparative Law at the Erasmus School of Law, Erasmus University Rotterdam.

2 For recent literature, see, inter alia, J. Sawang, *Geheimhaltung und rechtliches Gehör im Schiedsverfahren nach deutschem Recht*, Tübingen: Mohr Siebeck 2010, p 368 et seq.; M. Stojcevski & B. Zeller, 'Confidentiality and Privacy Revisited', *Arbitration*, 78 (4), p 332; A. Malatesta & R. Sali (ed), *The Rise of Transparency in International Arbitration, The Case for the Anonymous Publication of Arbitral Awards*, Huntington, New York: Iuris 2013, p 228 et seq.; P. Callens et al, *Arbitrage en Vertrouwelijkheid*, Brussels: Bruylant 2014, p 352 et seq.; C.J.M. Klaassen,'"I have a dream". Enkele opmerkingen over vertrouwelijkheid en arbitrage in 2040', in: R.A.J. van Gestel & J.B.M. Vranken (ed), *Recht en rechtspraak vanaf 2040. Liber amicorum Fred Hammerstein*, The Hague: Boom legal 2021, p 142-156; Asser Procesrecht/Sanders, Meijer & Ernste *8* 2023/58-62.

3 H.J. Snijders, *Nederlands Arbitragerecht*, Deventer: Wolters Kluwer 2018, p 290-291.

From a pragmatic point of view, it can be argued that it was a feature of arbitration that practitioners needed to resolve disputes not only in private, but also on a non-disclosure basis. Confidentiality thus developed from a feature to an inherent principle of arbitration. From a principled point of view, however, one can identify other foundations for confidentiality.

If one compares arbitration with court litigation, it could be argued that the constitutional principles of public hearings and adjudication (Article 121 of the Dutch Constitution) are not applicable to arbitration, which itself is constitutionally sanctioned by Article 17 of the Dutch Constitution. In light of this, one could infer *a contrario* that the requirements of Article 121 of the Dutch Constitution do not apply in arbitration. However, as The Netherlands does not have a statutory confidentiality provision (more on this later), the question remains whether such an *a contrario* reasoning can really be followed.

The existence of a confidentiality principle is therefore to be found elsewhere. Here, particular attention can be paid to the contractual basis of (most) arbitrations. The arbitration agreement could then be interpreted or applied in such a way that the parties have implicitly agreed to confidentiality, and that their agreement can thus be interpreted to that effect or at the least that the additional effect of the principle of reasonableness and fairness must lead to confidentiality or that an implied confidentiality term can be read into the arbitration agreement.[4] A similar contract law-based reasoning can also be followed on the basis of the principle of privity of the agreement. Privity implies that arbitration is private and that only the parties and persons authorised by them can participate in both the proceedings and the hearing, and that third parties can – without permission of the parties – be excluded therefrom. From this principle of *privacy*, that is to say the private nature of arbitration, one can then infer the confidentiality of arbitration: third parties are not entitled to information on whether an arbitration is pending, on procedural documents, or on the arbitral award.

Finally, one could also assign a more procedural basis to the confidentiality of arbitration, but as of yet this has not yet occurred. In that respect, one might think of the lack of third party-effect of an arbitration agreement where, in principle – aside from consolidation – third parties cannot join,

4 Cf. G.J. Meijer, *Overeenkomst tot arbitrage*, Deventer: Kluwer 2011, p 86, which highlights this discussion in the light of waiver of Article 6 ECHR rights.

intervene or be impleaded without consent of the parties to the arbitral proceedings. Moreover, confidentiality orders may be sought from an arbitral tribunal by virtue of the inherent power of the arbitral tribunal to take appropriate measures to ensure due process.

The foregoing mainly concerns the confidentiality of arbitration between the parties to the proceedings. However, the aforementioned bases – with the exception of the pragmatic variant – do not answer the question whether and why other parties involved in an arbitration, such as arbitrators and arbitral institutions in particular, are bound by confidentiality.

All in all, then, confidentiality in arbitration seems to rest on both tradition and pragmatic considerations. Comparative law research shows, however, that since 1995 this situation has come to an end.

18.3 Australian and Swedish unrest

On 7 April 1995, the High Court of Australia rendered a judgment in *Esso Australia Resources Ltd v Plowman* ("*Esso v Plowman*")[5] and rejected a request that documents produced in an arbitration be kept confidential on the grounds that confidentiality is not an essential feature of private arbitration, nor part of the essence of the arbitration agreement or the contractual relationship between the parties. It must be said that the general public interest played a role in this case as the supervisory body on the energy sector requested production of the documents at stake as part of its supervisory task concerning prices passed on to consumers. Nevertheless, concerns arose that this judgment had broader ramifications and that confidentiality in Australian arbitrations might have had its day.

Five years after *Esso v Plowman*, the Swedish Supreme Court rendered a judgment in *Bulgarian Foreign Trade Bank Ltd v A.I. Trade Finance Inc* ("*Bulbank*").[6] In setting aside and revocation proceedings against a final arbitral award, Bulbank argued that the arbitration agreement had been terminated due to a breach of contract, because the other party, A.I. Trade Finance, had published an interim arbitral award without Bulbank's con-

5 Australian High Court 7 April 1995, [1995] HCA 19, XXI Y.B. Comm. Arb., 1996, p 137.

6 Swedish Supreme Court 27 October 2000, *Bulgarian Foreign Trade Bank Ltd v AI Trade Finance Inc*, (2001) XXVI Y.B. Comm. Arb. 291; see further on this subject F. De Ly, 'Kroniek Internationale Arbitrage', *TvA* 2002, p 37-40.

sent. According to Bulbank, this constituted a breach of the confidentiality obligation inherent to the arbitration agreement. Setting aside of the final arbitral award was also sought on the basis of the partiality and lack of independence of the chair of the arbitral tribunal, a member of the Swedish Supreme Court, who had discussed the arbitral award with another member of the Supreme Court and had given the latter a copy of the award. This argument must be understood to mean that passing on the arbitral award to a colleague at the Supreme Court in a situation in which that Court was to decide on a similar case was detrimental to Bulbank because it prejudged Bulbank's possible later setting aside action that could also eventually be decided by that same court. Thus, the chair had discredited himself and doubts could be raised as to his impartiality and independence. When Bulbank's case came before the Supreme Court, the court only granted leave to hear the question of breach of confidentiality; on the question of independence and impartiality of the chair of the arbitral tribunal, such leave was denied. Subsequently, the Supreme Court held in relation to the former question that there was no implicit duty of confidentiality arising from Swedish arbitration law. While it is true that parties usually observe confidentiality, the Court held that this is not in itself normative in the sense that an obligation arises therefrom. The Supreme Court also indicated that comparative law views on confidentiality in arbitration differ and that Swedish arbitration law is procedural in nature and does not regulate the contractual aspects of the arbitration agreement, so that confidentiality could not be derived from the Swedish Arbitration Act either.

18.4 Attention for confidentiality: legislation and Arbitration Rules

Esso v Plowman and *Bulbank* broke with the traditional paradigm of confidentiality in arbitration and set the arbitration world abuzz. At the very least, there was great interest regarding what, if anything at all, should be done to restore the paradigm to its former glory. This led to a number of legislative initiatives or amendments to arbitration rules or to reconsiderations that did not lead to changes.[7] These developments can be divided into three categories.

7 For a more comprehensive overview, see F. De Ly, L. Radicati di Brosolo & M. Friedman, *Confidentiality in International Commercial Arbitration, Report and Recommendations of the Committee on International Commercial Arbitration of the International Law Association* (Hague Conference 2010, Report of the seventy-fourth conference), The Hague, London: International Law Association 2010, p 186-221, *Arb. Int.* (28) 2012, p 355-396.

A first category of cases concerns countries or rules that began to protect and regulate confidentiality as a result of the departure from the traditional paradigm described above. A striking example is the 2010 amendment to the Australian International Arbitration Act, which regulates confidentiality in Sections 23C-G, albeit on an "opt in" basis, i.e. the parties must expressly choose a confidentiality regime. However, in 2015, the "opt in" regime was replaced by an "opt out" regime.[8] New Zealand (2007) and Hong Kong (2010) went further and opted for a system where confidentiality in arbitration was regulated by law and did not depend on party choice. A reform of French arbitration law codified confidentiality with respect to domestic arbitrations (but not for international arbitrations).[9]

In practice, a regulation on confidentiality was also felt to be necessary, leading to most arbitral institutions adopting a provision on this matter in their arbitration rules.[10] To this can be added the ICC which, since the revision of its Arbitration Rules in 2012, has a provision leaving the ramifications of confidentiality to the arbitral tribunal at the request of a party (Article 22(3)); this provision remained unchanged in the 2017 and 2021 ICC Arbitration Rules.

A second category concerns countries or rules that accepted the reversal of the traditional paradigm, but refrained from enacting provisions dealing with such reversal. Sweden decided not to overrule *Bulbank*, nor did it do so in the amended Arbitration Act 2019 that came into force on 1 March 2019. However, the Stockholm Chamber of Commerce did amend its arbitration rules in this regard, which since 2007 have provided that the Chamber and the arbitral tribunal – though not the parties – will safeguard the confidentiality of both the arbitration and the arbitral award. This rule has been extended in 2017 to the cover the tribunal's secretary as well (Article 3). Another striking example is UNCITRAL, which did not address the question of confidentiality of arbitral procedures conducted under the new Arbitration Rules, with the exception of the hearing and the award, when it revised its arbitration rules in 2010. An underlying consideration for that decision was in any event that investment arbitrations, in which confidentiality is seen from perspectives other than in commercial arbitration, are often conducted under the UNCITRAL Arbitration Rules and that UNCITRAL wanted to avoid disturbing the trend towards more transparency in investment arbitrations with a provision on confidentiality.

8 Civil Law and Justice (Omnibus Amendments) Act 2015, Schedule 1, Section 66.
9 F. De Ly, 'Kroniek Internationale Arbitrage', *TvA* 2011, p 159.
10 See De Ly, Radicati di Brosolo & Friedman 2010, p 366-367 and Appendix 1, B.

The same reasoning underpinned the French choice not to include a confidentiality provision in relation to international arbitrations.

A third category of countries or rules also saw no need to respond to the paradigmatic shift, because confidentiality was sufficiently entrenched in case law and was thus not threatened by said shift. This is particularly the case in England, where case law has embraced confidentiality and has allowed only very limited exceptions to a generally formulated duty of confidentiality.[11] The current process of revision of the English Arbitration Act confirms this position and no statutory provision is envisaged as to confidentiality.[12]

The interim conclusion drawn from the above is that there is no global consensus on whether to accept a principle of confidentiality in arbitration, nor is there global consensus on the scope of this principle and the extent of the protection of confidentiality. On the other hand, the importance of confidentiality and the desire to regulate it properly is recognised by arbitral institutions. This led the International Commercial Arbitration Committee of the International Law Association to the pragmatic conclusion that the parties themselves are most suited to regulate confidentiality by means of a suitable confidentiality clause, to be included in either the arbitration agreement or elsewhere (e.g. in the *Terms of Reference* or in a *procedural order*) and to drafting a model provision for that purpose.[13]

18.5 The Netherlands and confidentiality

The aforementioned developments largely went by without attention in the Netherlands, mainly because few, if any, problems arose in relation to confidentiality issues. However, in 2010, on my initiative, and following the revision of the Arbitration Rules of the Netherlands Arbitration Institute ("NAI"), an Article 55(1) was included in the NAI Arbitration Rules (2010), which provided that arbitration is confidential and that all individuals involved either directly or indirectly are bound to secrecy, save for cases in which and insofar as disclosure ensues from the law or the agreement of the parties.

---

11 *Dolling-Baker v Merrett & Another* (CA 1990) [1991] 2 All ER 890; *Ali Shipping Corporation v Shipyard 'Trogir'* (CA) [1998] 2 All ER 136; *Emmott v Michael Wilson & Partners* [2008] EWCA Civ 184.

12 Arbitration Bill HL 59 (27 March 2024).

13 De Ly, Radicati di Brosolo & Friedman 2010, p 382-384.

Following the long preliminary process towards the new Dutch Arbitration Act,[14] the Van den Berg Commission that prepared the Act briefly discussed confidentiality and was fairly unanimous in its decision – modelled after Article 55(1) of the NAI 2010 Arbitration Rules – to propose a short statutory confidentiality provision. After years of inactivity, Van den Berg's Preliminary Draft ("Preliminary Draft") was taken up by the Ministry of Security and Justice which led to consultation rounds in which confidentiality was proposed in line with the Preliminary Draft. However, the Bill subsequently did not include a statutory confidentiality provision following the advice of the Dutch Association for the Judiciary which feared that such a provision would be abused.[15] The Bill led to the Arbitration Law Modernisation Act which followed this advice. This means that the Netherlands has to live without a statutory confidentiality provision. However, the Minister of Security and Justice did expressly state in the Memorandum of Reply to the Bill that arbitration, even without a statutory provision, is in principle confidential except in arbitrations with a public law character such as investment arbitrations. The Minister therefore did not consider it necessary to regulate confidentiality by law because it would not be easy to formulate this principle in a legal text.[16]

Notwithstanding the absence of a statutory confidentiality provision in the new Arbitration Act and despite the reassurances of the Minister of Security and Justice, arbitral practice in the Netherlands continues to benefit from a confidentiality provision in arbitration rules. Thus, Article 55(1) of the NAI Arbitration Rules 2010 has been reproduced verbatim and placed in a more prominent position under the general section of the NAI Arbitration Rules 2015, i.e., in Article 6, and has been incorporated in Article 7(1) of the 2024 NAI Arbitration Rules.

The absence of a statutory provision is regrettable. From a perspective of transparent legislation, a statutory provision is obviously preferable to a statement of the responsible minister in the parliamentary history to the Dutch Arbitration Act, even in a memorandum of reply. In addition, a statutory codification of unwritten law is necessary not only with regard to affirming the principle of confidentiality in itself but also with regard to

14 Act of 2 June 2014 amending Book 3, Book 6 and Book 10 of the Dutch Civil Code and the Fourth Book of the Dutch Code of Civil Procedure in connection with the modernisation of arbitration law (*Stb.* 2014, 200).

15 *Parliamentary Papers II* 2013/14, 33611, no 5, p 8.

16 *Parliamentary Papers I* 2013/14, 33611, C, p 2-4 (*MoA*).

defining the ramifications of such a principle.[17] This is not impossible or difficult as inspiration can be drawn from provisions of foreign laws and from (institutional) arbitration rules.

18.6 Ramifications of the principle of confidentiality

18.6.1 Definition of the principle of confidentiality

A summary definition of the confidentiality principle seems necessary to clarify what it entails. From there, an assessment can follow as to which categories of arbitrations need confidentiality and which categories could or should be excluded from it. Also, a definition is relevant for characterization purposes, from both a national and private international law perspective.

Prior to that, it can be said that confidentiality does not primarily refer to external information in relation to the arbitral proceedings. Whether, for example, documents must be produced if it is argued that they are covered by an obligation of confidentiality of any kind is a question of evidentiary law to be resolved in arbitration, but it does not fall within what is commonly understood as confidentiality in arbitration. After all, the latter refers to the internal information of the arbitration itself and not what is brought into it from the outside. However, the two overlap as soon as external information is brought into the arbitration, and that information is then protected by confidentiality.[18]

Most arbitration laws and rules regulating confidentiality hardly contain any provisions pertaining to the aforementioned questions[19] and focus mainly on the ramifications discussed below (see para 18.6.2 to 18.6.6). The exceptions are New Zealand, which provides that arbitral proceedings must be conducted in private and that the agreement to arbitrate implies that neither the parties nor the arbitral tribunal shall disclose confidential information to third parties (Sections 14A and 14B of the Arbitration Act 1996, as amended in 2007). Scotland also has a provision in this regard in Rule 26 of Schedule 1 to the Arbitration Act 2010, which provides that

17 See already F. De Ly, 'Het Wetsvoorstel modernisering van het arbitragerecht en de internationale arbitrage', *TvA* 2013/38, p 147-149; N. Peters, 'Drie jaar nieuwe arbitragewet: tien suggesties voor verbetering', *TCR* 2018, issue 4, p 103-105.

18 See for example, in applying the 2010 or the 2020 IBA Rules on the Taking of Evidence in International Arbitration, Rule 3(13) (confidentiality of documents produced in arbitration), available at www.ibanet.org.

19 For an overview, see De Ly, Radicati di Brosolo & Friedman 2010, p 360ff.

disclosure by the tribunal, any arbitrator or a party of confidential information can give rise to a claim on the basis of breach of an obligation of confidentiality. Australia has a statutory provision which provides that neither the arbitral tribunal nor the parties are to disclose confidential information to third parties (Section 23C International Arbitration Act 1974, as amended in 2010 and 2015). As discussed earlier, the initial intention in the Netherlands was simply to provide that arbitration is confidential.

The aforementioned overview shows that – with the exception of New Zealand which opted for a contractual basis – other countries favour more of a procedural approach by including confidentiality in their arbitration act and thus qualifying confidentiality issues as procedural. This is particularly important for the question of enforcement for breach of confidentiality agreements and – in international arbitrations – for the application of the confidentiality regime based on the connecting factor of the place of arbitration. If confidentiality had been introduced in the Netherlands in the Arbitration At as envisaged by the Van den Berg Preliminary Draft, it would have been applicable pursuant to Article 1073(1) of the Dutch Code of Civil Procedure if the place of arbitration is in the Netherlands. This would avoid difficult problems of private international law such as characterization and applicable law which have not clearly been solved in absence of an express statutory provision, as confidentiality is based on a statement in the parliamentary history.[20]

Without a statutory confidentiality provision, party agreements can provide relief. One could think, in particular, of confidentiality clauses in (institutional) arbitration rules. Enforcement is then conducted via the contractual route; breach of a confidentiality obligation can then be dealt with via a broadly worded arbitration clause in a pending arbitration or in a new arbitration. In terms of conflict of laws, it is then advisable to include in the confidentiality clause that it is governed by the law of the place of arbitration to avoid discussion on the applicable law.

At this point, it is appropriate to reflect briefly on the increase of investment arbitrations over the past twenty-five years, which has influenced ideas and approaches on respectively confidentiality in and transparency of arbitration.[21] These are not arbitrations conducted under the World

20 On this, see De Ly, Radicati di Brosolo & Friedman 2010, p 368-370.

21 This does not alter the fact that these arbitrations with regard to investments within the European Union or with countries with which the European Union has concluded trade agreements (Canada, Singapore, Japan, South Korea) are on their

Bank Convention of 1965 (ICSID arbitrations), which are governed by the provisions of this Convention and have essentially been disconnected from national arbitration law, including in relation to enforcement of the arbitral award rendered. The New York Convention is not applicable to enforcement of such awards, but instead a treaty obligation implies that these arbitral awards are to be enforced as if they were a judgment of a court of the state where enforcement is sought. On the other hand, an area of overlap between private law arbitration and investment arbitration does exist where a dispute between a foreign investor and the host country becomes subject to arbitration in a third country under both the arbitration law of that third country and the arbitration rules of UNCITRAL, the (Arbitration Institute of the) Stockholm Chamber of Commerce or another arbitral institution. Such disputes are not of a private law nature, but involve the question of State liability towards foreign investors for alleged violation of investor protection provisions found in bilateral or multilateral investment treaties. Given the specific nature of these disputes, a call and desire has arisen for these disputes not to be private and confidential, thus challenging the traditional paradigm of confidentiality in arbitration with respect to such investment arbitrations.

In this context, particular mention should be made of the activities of UNCITRAL which, in 2014, adopted the *UNCITRAL Rules on Transparency in Treaty-based Investor-State Arbitration*[22] which are applicable to investment treaties that provide for arbitration under the UNCITRAL Arbitration Rules and have been concluded from 1 April 2014 onward. These rules also apply to investment treaties concluded before that date if the parties to such a treaty or to a dispute arising from such a treaty agree to it. The latter is also applicable in cases in which parties agree to application of the rules even though the treaty does not refer to the UNCITRAL Arbitration Rules. The rules include provisions under which the initiation of arbitration, most procedural documents and the hearing are public and provide for publication of documents in a public register. Given the recent entry into force and non-retroactive application of the rules, few documents are currently public under these transparency rules.

The transparency envisaged by the aforementioned UNCITRAL rules will therefore, for the time being, have to be sought elsewhere. To this end, on 10 December 2014, UNCITRAL adopted the *Mauritius Convention on Trans-*

---

way out and will be resolved by arbitrations of a public international law nature whether through an investment court or otherwise.

22 Available at www.uncitral.org.

parency[23] which aims to introduce the UNCITRAL rules in all investment arbitrations in relation to new arbitrations initiated against a State that becomes a party to the Mauritius Convention from the date of entry into force for such a State. The Mauritius Convention entered into force on 18 October 2017 but currently has only nine State parties for which the Convention has entered into force (Australia, Benin, Bolivia, Cameroon, Canada, Gambia, Iraq, Mauritius and Switzerland). Incidentally, to date, only the European Union and twenty-three states have signed the convention including the Netherlands that signed on 18 May 2016.[24]

Despite the modest success of the UNCITRAL initiatives there is a clear trend towards more transparency for investment arbitrations. For this reason, I have previously suggested that a statutory regulation on confidentiality in arbitration should take this development into account.[25] Unfortunately, neither a statutory regulation nor a special place for investment arbitrations has been included in the 2014 Dutch Arbitration Act.

A final aspect concerns the question of how confidentiality relates to the European Convention on Human Rights ("ECHR") particularly whether a qualified requirement of confidentiality is compatible with the ECHR. Until quite recently, this did not seem to pose a problem and – partly on the basis of a consideration in the *Nordström*-case[26] – it could legitimately be argued that a clear and unequivocal choice for arbitration implied a waiver of the ECHR right to a public hearing and judgment.[27] However, the decision of the European Court of Human Rights of 2 October 2018 in the joined cases *Mutu and Pechstein v Switzerland*[28] places this in a different light. In this case, Pechstein complained, among other things, that she had been denied a public hearing in all instances (the International

23 Available at www.uncitral.org.

24 Also available at www.uncitral.org.

25 De Ly 2013, p 147-149. That proposal read as follows:
"An arbitration shall be confidential and all persons directly and indirectly involved shall be bound to secrecy, except and to the extent that disclosure arises from international or community regulations, the law, the parties' agreement or, to the extent not provided for by the parties, an order of the arbitral tribunal."

26 ECtHR 27 November 1996, Application no 28101/95 (*Nordström-Janzon and Nordström-Lehtinen v. The Netherlands*), available at https://hudoc.echr.coe.int.

27 See F. De Ly, 'Arbitration and the European Convention on Human Rights', in: L. Levy & Y. Derains (ed), *Liber Amicorum en l'honneur de Serge Lazareff*, Paris: Pedone 2011, p 194-198; Meijer 2011, p 86.

28 ECtHR 2 October 2018, cases 40575/10 and 67474/10, available at https://hudoc.echr.coe.int. The judgment has since become final as no leave to review the judgment was granted by the Grand Chamber of the Court.

Skating Union's Disciplinary Commission, during the arbitration before the Court of Arbitration for Sport ("CAS") and during the setting aside proceedings against the CAS' arbitral award before the Swiss Federal Supreme Court) throughout the proceedings concerning her alleged doping, and that, thus, her rights under Article 6 ECHR had been violated. The ECtHR held that Switzerland had to vouch for arbitration proceedings before the CAS as the setting aside proceedings under the applicable Swiss international arbitration law implied oversight by Switzerland over the arbitral proceedings. Moreover, the Court found that there was no voluntary and unequivocal choice by Pechstein to arbitrate before the CAS, but a mandatory choice, because a professional skater must enter into the arbitration agreement and has no alternative to skate professionally without doing so. For this reason, the court concluded that Pechstein had not waived her Article 6 ECHR rights. Although the right to a public hearing – given the exceptions to it provided for in Article 6 ECHR – is not absolute, the Court nevertheless unanimously ruled that the CAS should have granted her a public hearing given the disciplinary nature of the case, the complexity of the evidence of her alleged doping, the importance of the case to Pechstein's career and reputation, and the fact that Pechstein had expressly requested a public hearing. In contrast, according to the Court the setting aside proceedings before the Swiss Supreme Court did comply with Article 6 ECHR in light of the limited scope of the scrutiny in the setting aside proceedings, in which no taking of evidence is allowed. As a result of this ruling, the CAS has since changed its practice and moved to public hearing of its cases.

Mutu and Pechstein v Switzerland has potentially far-reaching, but currently unclear implications. The essential question is when arbitrations are considered mandatory. However, at present it seems limited to monopoly-like situations where the other party has no alternative but to accept the arbitration agreement. Nor is it clear whether this ruling is limited to disciplinary proceedings, for example in relation to doping usage, or whether it also covers civil proceedings. The latter point relates to the parallel *Mutu*-case in which Romanian footballer Mutu had been dismissed by football club Chelsea for alleged cocaine use. In a first procedure, the dismissal by Chelsea was upheld, following which Chelsea claimed damages in a second procedure. These damages were granted on appeal at the CAS. Mutu unsuccessfully challenged this decision at the Swiss Supreme Court in setting aside proceedings, and then argued before the ECtHR that there was a violation of Article 6 ECHR on the grounds of lack of independence and impartiality of two of the three CAS arbitrators. The Court held that although Mutu – unlike Pechstein – had voluntarily entered into arbitration with Chelsea, he had not unequivocally waived his ECHR right to an independent and impartial judge as he had unsuccessfully challenged one of the CAS arbitrators during the proceedings. It goes beyond the scope of this contribution to discuss this aspect further. However, it is important to mention that the *Mutu*-case may also be relevant in relation to the principle of confidentiality. Mutu – unlike Pechstein – had not requested a public hearing during the many proceedings, so this aspect of a possible violation of Article 6 ECHR was not addressed in the Court's judgment. However, taking into account the Court's analysis on the challenge of one of the arbitrators, one could argue that it is sufficient to complain about a lack of public hearing during a civil law arbitration to infer that one has not unequivocally waived the Article 6 ECHR right to a public hearing. In other words, the question arises whether the Court intended to rule that one cannot waive Article 6 ECHR guarantees in advance in an arbitration agreement except in an unambiguous manner, so that the right to public hearing in arbitration also falls within the scope of Article 6 ECHR and that only an assessment remains against the exceptions of Article 6 ECHR, which – in view of the considerations in Pechstein – would not readily be accepted given the parties' interests in a dispute and the characteristic that arbitrators act as fact-finders.

Mutu and Pechstein v Switzerland thus raises more questions than it answers. With regard to confidentiality and arbitration this, in my view, does not mean the end of confidentiality, but rather the need to build an ECHR safety valve into legislation and arbitration rules to ensure *ECHR compliance.*[29]

18.6.2 Confidentiality principle and party autonomy

Given the important role of party autonomy in private law arbitration, it seems to me that the principle of confidentiality is part of non-mandatory law so that parties can deviate from it and build in broader or narrower protections subject to the mandatory law of the applicable rules or any potential priority rules such as on mandatory provisions containing exceptions to confidentiality.

29 In my view, the provision mentioned in footnote 25 is sufficient as the reference to international and community regulations and to the law ensures ECHR conformity.

18.6.3 *Object of the principle of confidentiality*

One of the key questions surrounding confidentiality and arbitration concerns the objective scope of the confidentiality obligation, *i.e.*, what is covered by confidentiality[30]. A distinction must be made between arbitral proceedings themselves and proceedings relating to arbitration before the state court.

With regard to arbitral proceedings, confidentiality starts from the moment the proceedings commence, usually from the request for arbitration up to and including the arbitral award, and thus covers the fact that an arbitration is in progress between the parties[31], all procedural and documentary evidence, including witness and expert statements, correspondence, hearing reports, hearing transcripts and decisions and awards of the arbitral tribunal, including the outcome of the arbitration. It is unclear how long confidentiality lasts; it may be assumed that it continues even after the end of the arbitration, for a reasonable period as determined by the circumstances of the case and the interests to be protected.[32]

Many arbitration laws and regulations that contain a confidentiality provision generally define the objective scope of the confidentiality commitment as all information obtained during or as a result of the arbitration.[33] In this regard, the Van den Berg Preliminary Draft limited itself to wording the principle as such that arbitration is confidential without explicitly specifying what information the principle refers to.

Particular questions arise in this context with regard to the identification of the parties' counsel, arbitrators or witnesses or experts. For marketing reasons, one regularly sees counsel, arbitrators or experts indicating in a general sense which arbitrations they are or were involved in without further identification of the parties. In a number of scenarios, however, with further detective work or with the help of industry insiders, one will be able to find out which parties and disputes are involved. Great caution is therefore required from the perspective of confidentiality when

30 See Snijders 2018, p 294-295.
31 See De Ly, Radicati di Brosolo & Friedman 2010, p 370-371.
32 De Ly, Radicati di Brosolo & Friedman 2010, p 377-378.
33 See De Ly, Radicati di Brosolo & Friedman 2010, p 361-363 and p 371-372. By contrast, Section 15 of the Australian International Arbitration Act does list in detail which procedural documents or acts are covered by confidentiality (p 362).

compiling such marketing information on, for example, websites or CVs. A recent development here is that the ICC – on an opt-out basis – recently started publishing information on the appointment of arbitrators on its website without naming the parties. The information includes the arbitrator's name, nationality, role in the arbitration (sitting only, co-arbitrator or chair), method of appointment (by the ICC Court, by a party or by the co-arbitrators) and whether the case is still active or closed. This is intended to provide more insight into how arbitrators in ICC cases are appointed and how many cases they have in their portfolio. If no further information is provided, this will enhance transparency with regard to future arbitrator appointments in relation to their experience in ICC arbitrations as well as their availability to handle cases with time and care. A similar publication system exists on the NAI website but is limited to the identification of arbitrators, their residence and date and way of appointment.

Although the arbitral award should be confidential par excellence, exceptions exist in practice for the purposes of publication of awards or extracts thereof in anonymised form, usually in the practice of arbitral institutions or, as is the case with the NAI Arbitration Rules (2024), on the basis of the rules, which stipulate in Article 7(3) that the NAI is authorised to have the award published without stating the names of the parties and leaving out all other information that might reveal the parties' identities, unless a party objects to such publication within two months of the date of the award. On that basis, NAI awards are regularly and routinely published in the Dutch Journal of Arbitration (*Tijdschrift voor Arbitrage*), unless a party has exercised its opt-out right. Moreover, the awards that are thus susceptible to publication are additionally screened in advance by the NAI, more specifically on the basis of potential problems with publication, including scenarios in which a case contains features or specifications that allow for the identification of the dispute or the parties. Incidentally, not all awards submitted to the Journal's editors are published; only awards that are relevant to the industry from a substantive or arbitration law perspective are published. This exception to the objective scope of confidentiality contributes to the dissemination of substantively relevant information that provides a picture of arbitral practice and that may be relevant for development of the law with regard to, in particular, questions of arbitral procedures or substantive matters that are rarely litigated in state courts (e.g. construction law or disputes concerning share transfers). The latest development regarding publication of arbitral awards concerns the ICC, which has developed a new policy whereby awards will be published unless a party objects to publication in a timely manner.[34]

With regard to proceedings before a state court, one can think mainly of proceedings during the arbitration such as challenge proceedings before a state court and, after the end of the arbitral proceedings, in particular setting aside and enforcement proceedings, as well as proceedings before a state court to gather evidence, even against arbitrators or arbitral institutions. Given the public nature of hearings before a state court and of the judgment, unless the law provides otherwise (Article 27 and 29 of the Dutch Code of Civil Procedure), and in the absence of an exception with regard to arbitration, parts of the arbitration's confidentiality risk falling away as soon as proceedings are instituted before the state court, which is contradictory in cases in which confidentiality aims to keep information about the dispute secret even after an arbitral award has been rendered. If the parties have a common interest in keeping such arbitral proceedings confidential after the arbitration, this will usually remain so, but if no such interest is present, a party may leak information so that the existence and outcome of the arbitration becomes public knowledge in addition to what information emerges about the arbitration in any judgment of a state court. This is at the least cause for concern if it pertains to proceedings before a state court that are initiated during the arbitration, partly because it is unclear whether closed-door proceedings under Article 27(1)(d) of the Dutch Code of Civil Proceedings can take place in those cases. Furthermore, it is not clear whether the parties can agree on this in advance.

In common law where there are no or fewer constitutional restrictions on *in camera* hearings, this poses fewer problems. Sections 22 and 23 of the Singapore International Arbitration Act and Sections 14G-I of the New Zealand Arbitration Act, for example, allow *in camera* hearings at the request of a party.[35] This is also possible in England, where the award either is not published or is only published in highly anonymised form.[36]

---

34 See Note to Parties and Arbitral Tribunals on the Conduct of the Arbitration under the ICC Rules of Arbitration (https://iccwbo.org/news-publications/arbitration-adr-rules-and-tools/note-parties-arbitral-tribunals-conduct-arbitration) dated 29 December 2020 with effect from 1 January 2021.

35 De Ly, Radicati di Brosolo & Friedman 2010, p 360-362.

36 On that, see especially the English Court of Appeal in its judgment of 25 March 2004 in *Department of Economic Policy and Development of the City of Moscow and Government of Moscow v. Bankers Trust Company and International Industrial Bank* (available at www.courtservice.gov.uk) and on that subject F. De Ly, 'Kroniek Internationale Arbitrage', *TvA* 2008, p 119-120.

18.6.4 Persons subject to confidentiality[37]

A second key element concerns the question of who is bound by confidentiality, or the passive side of the obligation. This mainly includes the parties, their counsel and the arbitral tribunal but also secretaries of arbitral tribunals[38], arbitral institutions[39], witnesses, experts, court reporters and interpreters and translators. In many cases, arbitration acts are concerned with the parties and arbitral tribunal and occasionally also the secretary of the arbitral tribunal, witnesses and experts.[40]

On the other hand, there is also an active side of the obligation, namely in relation to whom the debtor is held to the obligation.[41]

The first aspect poses few problems as it is fairly clearly determinable who is involved in an arbitration. The Van den Berg Preliminary Draft had also rightly defined this broadly as anyone directly or indirectly[42] involved in an arbitration.

The second aspect has been less discussed or examined and mainly concerns the relationship between the actors within the arbitral proceedings and, more specifically, arbitrators and arbitral institutions. For arbitrators, this concerns not only the commitment not to disclose information about the arbitration to third parties, but also the secrecy of deliberations, i.e., not to disclose information that is shared only between arbitrators to other actors in the arbitral proceedings.[43] The first examples are dissenting, concurring or separate opinions in which – to the extent permitted under applicable rules – an arbitrator indicates why he disagrees with procedural

37 See also Asser Procesrecht/Sanders, Meijer & Ernste *8* 2023/63.

38 On confidentiality and secretaries, see F. De Ly, 'Rules and Case law on Tribunal Secretaries', in: F. de Ly & L. Demeyere (ed), *Arbitral Secretaries*, Mechelen: Wolters Kluwer Belgium 2018, p 29-30.

39 De Ly, Radicati di Brosolo & Friedman 2010, p 374.

40 De Ly, Radicati di Brosolo & Friedman 2010, p 361.

41 Snijders 2018, p 295.

42 A particular problem with regard to indirect stakeholders arises with regard to insurance companies and parties funding the arbitration. With regard to third-party funders, see I. Dimitrova, 'Third-Party Funding and Confidentiality in International Commercial Arbitration: A Recipe for Uncertainty?', *TDM* (15) 2018, issue 4, p 1-36. See also UNCITRAL's recent work on third-party funding, *Possible Reform of Investor-State Dispute Settlement (ISDS), Third-Party Funding*, Note by the Secretariat, A/CN.9/WG.III/WP.157 (24 January 2019) containing a brief discussion on confidentiality.

43 For legislation and arbitration rules that expressly include this commitment, see De Ly, Radicati di Brosolo & Friedman 2010, p 373.

but especially substantive aspects of the case that have been decided by a majority of the arbitral tribunal. To the extent that these opinions do not disclose anything about the manner in which the arbitral tribunal reached its decision, but merely indicate why an arbitrator reached a different decision from the majority, this does not constitute a violation of the secrecy of deliberations. However, if these opinions do address elements, especially if they may lead to setting aside of the arbitral award, they may be in breach of confidentiality obligations. This is even more true if an arbitrator starts leaking information to a party (usually the party that appointed him) or communicates confidential documents exchanged between arbitrators to a party or all parties. These are clear breaches of confidentiality obligations that are, however, difficult to prove and enforce. During the proceedings, they may give rise to a challenge. Also, a liability claim can be brought against the arbitrator but will often run up against any exemption clauses and the need to prove deliberate recklessness or intent to circumvent them.

A barely explored issue concerns the question whether and to what extent arbitrators may disclose information to arbitral institutions beyond the normal exchange of information between the arbitral tribunal and an institution concerning the progress or finances of the proceedings or concerning the review of the draft award. In matters in which the institution has no role to play, such as situations where questions of procedural or substantive law the arbitral tribunal is having trouble with arise, the review of *procedural orders* or a possible breakdown in relations between arbitrators, the exchange of information or requests for advice should be avoided or surrounded with safeguards. One such safeguard may be that the institution should always confirm the communication in writing, indicate on what basis in the arbitration rules or otherwise intervention by the institution is possible, what the object of the institution's intervention is and how the institution has intervened. In particular, it should be avoided that the institution becomes a *seventh arbitrator*[44] that intervenes on specific points outside its remit only to give general advice on mainly procedural aspects. The same care obviously applies with regard to interventions by institutions vis-à-vis the parties prior to, during or after the arbitration.

44 On secretaries as a possible fourth arbitrator, see F. De Ly & L. Demeyere (ed), *Arbitral Secretaries*, Mechelen: Wolters Kluwer Belgium 2018, p 120 and especially C. Partasides, 'The Fourth Arbitrator? The Role of Secretaries to Tribunals in International Arbitration', *Arb.Int.* (18) 2002, p 147-163. The fifth and sixth arbitrator then refers to the assistance of associates of the co-arbitrators who sometimes also play a relevant role.

Finally, similar considerations apply in the relationship between witnesses or experts and third parties, the parties, the arbitrators and arbitral institutions. In the external relationship, confidentiality is evident; in the internal relationship with arbitrators and institutions, what was argued above with regard to the relationship between arbitrators and institutions applies *mutatis mutandis*. With regard to the relationship with parties and counsel, a distinction should be made between party witnesses and party-appointed experts on the one hand, and witnesses and experts appointed by the arbitral tribunal on the other. The latter category is not substantially different from that of arbitrators and institutions with respect to internal confidentiality. The tricky point is the confidentiality of information exchanged between a party and a party-witness or party-appointed expert, which raises the essential question whether an adversarial or inquisitorial system applies in arbitration. In the former system, party witnesses and experts are primarily seen as instruments of proof by a party with little judicial review whereas in an inquisitorial system, the delivery of evidence is more dependent on judicial direction and control. An example of the tension between the two systems can be found in the *2020 IBA Rules on the Taking of Evidence in International Arbitration*, which allows for witness preparation in Article 4(3) and, under the 2010 version of these Rules but no longer under the 2020 Rules, required independence only in relation to an expert appointed by the arbitral tribunal (Article 6(1) and (2)). The sharing of confidential information can be made transparent by including the documents and other information communicated in a witness or expert report. Nevertheless, secret exchanges between parties and party witnesses and party experts remain problematic. However, this disadvantage can be offset by an adversarial examination at the hearing and by the evaluation of evidence by the arbitral tribunal in the award.

18.6.5 Exceptions to confidentiality

What preceded concerned the objective and subjective ramifications of the principle of confidentiality. However, this principle is not absolute, and it is generally accepted that the principle is qualified by exceptions. These might include disclosures to third parties required by or pursuant to law, such as with regard to listed companies.

From a comparative law perspective, a number of categories can be distinguished which are mainly drawn from English jurisprudence which was inspired by case law in the field of banking secrecy.[45]

45 See in particular the case law cited in footnote 11.

A first exception relates to consent of the other party; confidential information obtained in or in connection with an arbitration may be disclosed to a third party if the other party consents.[46]

A second exception relates to compliance with a statutory disclosure requirement or a disclosure order issued by a supervisory body or other administrative authority.

A third exception is judicial authorisation. Under common law, it is generally assumed by statute or under court rules or on the basis of the inherent jurisdiction of the court that state courts have the power to order disclosure of information obtained in arbitration[47] as a correlate of the powers to prohibit disclosure of information. In the Netherlands and other civil law countries – in the absence of a statutory or contractual arrangement and ambiguity regarding the basis of the confidentiality commitment – this matter has not crystallised. It is conceivable, however that, for example, summary proceedings are initiated to obtain a remedy – in the absence of the involved party's consent – where the court order equals consent.

A fourth exception concerns cases in which it is necessary to disclose information to third parties, even without the consent of the other party or leave of a state court. This is first and foremost the case in proceedings before a state judge in connection with the arbitration such as parallel proceedings between the same parties before state judges and arbitrators, proceedings on interim and conservatory measures before a state court, other proceedings during the arbitration and, of course, setting aside and (recognition and) enforcement proceedings. For the Netherlands, this does not involve actual exceptions to confidentiality insofar as it concerns the earlier discussed constitutional and statutory requirements on public hearings and judgments. Another area of application is one where confidential information from the arbitration must be communicated in other proceedings to substantiate rights or defences in such other proceedings.[48]

A fifth exception is the open standard of the general public interest in cases where the private interests of the party opposing disclosure must clearly give way to the general public interest in disclosure.[49]

---

46 De Ly, Radicati di Brosolo & Friedman 2010, p 375.

47 De Ly, Radicati di Brosolo & Friedman 2010, p 361-362 (New Zealand) and p 362-363 (Australia).

48 De Ly, Radicati di Brosolo & Friedman 2010, p 376.

49 *Emmott v Michael Wilson & Partners* [2008] EWCA Civ 184 and most recently *Chartered Institute of Arbitrators v B, C and D* [2019] EWHC 460 (Comm) concerning dis-

18.6.6 Procedural aspects

The Achilles' heel of confidentiality obligations is the enforcement of such obligations[50]. For this reason, care must, first of all, be taken to ensure that the necessary procedures are built in to prevent breaches or plug leaks as soon as they arise.

In the unfortunate event that confidential information is nevertheless disclosed to persons not entitled to it, a breach of the confidentiality obligation could turn out to be harmless. The other extreme scenario is that the breach involves material information and could lead to significant consequences. In that case, damages are suffered by the creditor of the confidentiality obligation which, however, are often difficult to prove or quantify.

The issue of enforcement of confidentiality obligations in arbitration has received little attention.[51] A first question concerns the question of jurisdiction. If a breach of a confidentiality obligation falls within the scope of the arbitration agreement, then a party's breach may give rise to a change of claim or a counterclaim within an ongoing arbitration (depending on the applicable provisions on new claims) or to a new arbitration. In other cases (i.e. breach of confidentiality by an arbitrator, an institution, a witness, an expert or another involved party), then a liability claim will have to be pursued before a state court. Relevant in such proceedings are the existence of any exemption clauses, as well as the aforementioned problem of proving the damage suffered.

Another issue concerns the issue whether breach of a confidentiality obligation can be invoked to challenge the arbitration agreement or arbitral award.

The former came up in the aforementioned Bulbank case, in which it was argued, *inter alia*, that the other party's breach of a confidentiality obligation constituted an attributable breach under the arbitration agreement so that, after a partial award, Bulbank was no longer bound by the arbitral agreement and, therefore, by the final award rendered thereafter. This del-

ciplinary proceedings against an arbitrator who had concealed a conflict of interest and where it was held that some documents from the challenge proceedings before the state court should be disclosed in the public interest for the purpose of the disciplinary proceedings.

50 See also Asser Procesrecht/Sanders, Meijer & Ernste *8* 2023/64.

51 De Ly, Radicati di Brosolo & Friedman 2010, p 376-377.

icate issue was avoided by the Swedish Supreme Court by accepting that there was no implied confidentiality obligation. If a confidentiality obligation does exist and is breached, then it will have to be assessed under the applicable law whether all the requirements for attributable breach are met and whether this can lead to the termination of the arbitration agreement, in connection to which the question also arises whether in this respect the arbitration agreement can be characterized as a separate agreement if it is an arbitration clause in a main contract. It seems to me that this is not the case as the arbitral clause is part of the main contract so that a party cannot escape the arbitration agreement in case of breach of a confidentiality obligation.

A second aspect of the aforementioned issue raises the question of whether and on what ground breach of a confidentiality obligation by itself – that is, without other elements such as violation of right to a fair hearing – can lead to setting aside of the arbitral award or refusal of leave for enforcement. This question arose in a 2016 judgment of the Swiss Federal Supreme Court.[52] In a dispute between professional football clubs regarding the transfer of a football player, the acquiring club lost the arbitration on appeal to CAS. The latter then sought the setting aside of the arbitral award before the Tribunal fédéral on, *inter alia,* the grounds that the arbitral award had been leaked to the press prior to the communication of the award to the parties. The claim to set the award aside was rejected because it was not proven that the CAS or an arbitrator had leaked the award to the press. However, the Swiss Federal Supreme Court ruled in general terms that breach of a confidentiality obligation is not in itself a ground for setting aside of an arbitral award, but did not rule out the possibility of unequal treatment of parties if the leaking of information by an arbitrator to one of the parties could affect the other party's evidentiary position. Nor did it rule out that breach of a duty of confidentiality could, under circumstances, violate procedural public policy.

Breach of confidentiality obligations also came up in English setting aside proceedings, in which the setting aside claim was dismissed on other grounds, but where, in *obiter dicta,* the Court addressed the hypothetical question whether remission to the arbitral tribunal would have taken place in the event of an setting aside of the award.[53] In the setting aside proceedings, Symbion had submitted an e-mail from its appointed arbitra-

52 Tribunal fédéral 8 March 2016, 4A_510/2015 available at www.bger.ch.
53 *Symbion Power LLC v Venco Imtiaz Construction Company* [2017] EWHC 348 (TCC), available at www.bailii.org.

tor to Symbion's counsel to the following effect, as contained in the court judgment:

> "In mid-2014, Symbion's party-appointed arbitrator (whom I shall call Arbitrator A) sent an e-mail to Symbion's arbitration counsel. It was not copied to any other member of the Tribunal or to any representative of Venco. He put in the subject line: 'HIGHLY CONFIDENTIAL: NOT TO BE USED IN THE ARBITRATION'. He expressed the view that he could send such an e-mail to arbitration counsel because it was about the "selection" of the chairman but said that it was sent on the explicit condition that it could not be referred to in the arbitration or afterwards. The e-mail then went on to say that both party-appointed arbitrators were upset by the conduct of the chairman; it expressed highly negative views about him; and Arbitrator A said that he was meeting the chairman and would encourage him to resign."

In no uncertain terms, the English judge condemned this unilateral communication between an arbitrator and counsel for one of the parties, but found that this would not have been a reason for him not to remit the case to the arbitral tribunal, because two years had passed after the e-mail, during which time the arbitral tribunal had cooperated and reached a final award. It is notable that Symbion had not raised breach of the duty of confidentiality by its appointed arbitrator as a ground for setting aside in its request for setting aside of the award.

Once again, therefore, it appears that breaches of confidentiality obligations are difficult to enforce, even in setting aside proceedings directed against the arbitral award.

18.7 Conclusion

Confidentiality in arbitration was one of the traditional paradigms of arbitration law, but has been questioned over the past thirty years, mainly in light of the uncertainties of its dogmatic basis. From a comparative law perspective, it is also no longer universally accepted. Legislation and (institutional) arbitration rules have pragmatically attempted to solve some issues with different ramifications, while also leaving ambiguities. This contribution mainly aimed to highlight the aforementioned ramifications with a view of identifying problem areas, solutions and possible regulatory improvements.

III – THE ARBITRAL AWARD

CHAPTER 19

THE AWARD ON COSTS IN ARBITRATION: SUGGESTIONS TO PROMOTE PREDICTABILITY, TRANSPARENCY AND UNIFORMITY

Mirjam van de Hel-Koedoot & Pieter Fritschy[1]

19.1 Introduction

There is no doubt that the costs of arbitration are usually identified as an important viewpoint when weighing the advantages and disadvantages of arbitration vis-à-vis state court litigation. Remarkably, unlike most other viewpoints that play a role in this comparison, it is by no means always clear whether the costs of arbitration should be considered an advantage, or rather a disadvantage of this method of dispute resolution.[2]

It is in any event a fact that the costs of arbitration are generally high – in most cases considerably higher than the costs of proceedings before a (Dutch) state court.[3] One reason for this is that, whereas a state court judge is paid by the state, the arbitrators' fees and disbursements will have to be borne by the parties themselves. In the case of institutional arbitration, the administrative costs of the relevant arbitration institute also play a role in this regard. However, in practice, the most important element of costs in arbitration is often the legal assistance of the parties (cf. Articles 56(2) and 59(3) NAI Rules). As Born puts it with respect to international arbitration, *"arbitration can be expensive, in large part because of the fees of the parties' legal representatives"*.[4]

---

1 M. (Mirjam) van de Hel-Koedoot (LLM) & P.B. (Pieter) Fritschy (LLM) are both lawyers at NautaDutilh N.V. in Amsterdam.

2 Cf. P. Sanders, *Het Nederlandse arbitragerecht*, Kluwer: Deventer 2001, p XIII: "Whether those costs always turn out in favor of arbitration remains to be seen. Arbitration pro bono does not exist and, unlike judges, arbitrators must be paid by the parties."

3 See M. van de Hel-Koedoot, 'The costs (award) in arbitration. An overview using the NAI Arbitration Rules', *TvA* 2009/13 (citing G.J. Meijer, *Agreement to Arbitrate* (diss. Erasmus University Rotterdam), 2008, para 10.4.5.2).

4 G.B. Born, *International Commercial Arbitration* (vol. II), Deventer: Wolters Kluwer 2009, p 2488. See also Decisions on Costs in International Arbitration – ICC Arbitration and ADR Commission Report (*ICC Dispute Resolution Bulletin* 2015, issue 2, p 3), which shows that 83% of the costs of arbitration (at the ICC) are legal fees.

It is of course true that the parties will ordinarily have to obtain legal assistance in proceedings before the state courts as well, so that at first sight this element of costs does not lend itself well as a point of view when comparing arbitration and state court proceedings. However, at least from a Dutch law perspective, the costs of legal assistance can lead to a relevant difference between arbitration and state court proceedings in light of the differences in *cost awards*. After all, in proceedings before the (Dutch) state court, it is clear in advance that, regardless of the outcome of the proceedings, the parties will for the most part bear their own costs of legal assistance.[5] Indeed, in practice, the costs of legal assistance awarded to the successful party in such proceedings are very marginal compared to the actual costs incurred in this respect. Importantly, parties are aware of that fact in advance, so that they already know prior to the proceedings that they will not be ordered to pay the real costs of legal assistance incurred by the opposing party or, conversely, that they will not be fully reimbursed for their costs of legal assistance by the opposing party.

As will be discussed in this article, this is different for arbitration. This means that the risk of loss (expressed in monetary terms) is potentially higher in an NAI arbitration than in proceedings before the state court. Conversely, for a party which expects to prevail, NAI arbitration may be a more attractive option than state court litigation, as the NAI Rules at least offer the *possibility* that this party will be able to recover a large part or even all of its legal fees from the other party.

However, it is unclear to which extent it is realistic for a party to assume that in NAI arbitrations the prevailing party will have most or even all of its costs for legal assistance compensated by the other party. In this contribution, these and other cost-related *uncertainties* associated with the choice for NAI arbitration in the Netherlands will be discussed in detail.[6] The main idea behind this contribution is to prevent situations where uncertainties about the costs of arbitration and – especially – about which party bears these costs at the end of the proceedings can constitute a reason for parties to choose state court proceedings over arbitration in the Nether-

5 The estimation of the costs of legal assistance of the prevailing party in state court proceedings is done by using the so-called liquidation rate.

6 The premise here, of course, is that the parties have failed to reach an *agreement* on costs and the award on costs (such as an agreement that full litigation costs will be awarded). Thus, this article discusses the general rules on which the arbitral tribunal is dependent absent such an agreement.

lands. This is all the more a real threat given the aforementioned relatively high costs of arbitration.[7]

This article will therefore offer several suggestions to eliminate those potential uncertainties of prospective parties to NAI arbitrations as much as possible. First, in paragraph 19.2, a brief description of the general principles regarding costs in the NAI Rules will be provided. Then, in paragraph 19.3, the viewpoints laid down in the new Article 59(4) NAI Rules will be discussed in some detail. Paragraph 19.4 will then deal with the tension between discretion and the values of predictability, transparency and uniformity. After that, in paragraph 19.5, a proposal will be formulated regarding the possibility of a brief party debate regarding costs and the award on costs. Paragraph 19.6 argues that such a party debate will have to be reflected in an obligation for the arbitral tribunal to properly reason its award on costs. It is hoped that these suggestions, either individually or collectively, can contribute to the removal of the abovementioned uncertainties concerning costs and cost awards in Dutch institutional arbitrations.

19.2 Costs in the current NAI Rules: general principles

This paragraph will discuss the current provisions in the (2024) NAI Rules as they relate to arbitration costs.

The Sixth Paragraph of the NAI Rules, covering Articles 56 to 59, is devoted entirely to the subject of costs. Article 56(1) NAI Rules contains a definition of "the costs of the arbitration", which are defined there as (i) the administration fees (Article 56(1)(a) and Article 57 NAI Rules), (ii) the fees and disbursements of the arbitrator(s) (Article 56(1)(b) and Article 58 NAI Rules) and (iii) the other costs which, in the opinion of the arbitral tribunal, were necessarily incurred in the arbitration (Article 56(1)(c) NAI Rules). In Article 56(2) NAI Rules, it is explicitly provided that the costs of legal assistance do not form part of the costs of the arbitration in the sense of the definition in Article 56(1) NAI Rules. This explicit distinction between the costs of the arbitration and the costs of legal assistance sets

7 O.E. Browne & R. Price, 'Saving Time and Money by Sanctioning Bad Behaviour', *Transnational Dispute Management* (4) 2018, p 13: "In many cases, the costs of the arbitration together with each party's legal costs can be very significant, sometimes representing a high percentage of the value of the claim on the merits."

the stage for a differentiated treatment of those two categories of costs in the NAI Rules, as will be discussed below.

The prior NAI Rules (i.e. the 2015 NAI Rules) gave rise to some confusion with respect to the distinction between the costs of the arbitration and the costs of legal assistance. In those 2015 NAI Rules, the definition of the costs of the arbitration seemingly included the costs of legal assistance. The fact that those 2015 NAI Rules contained a regime for the award of the costs of the arbitration as well as a separate regime for the costs of legal assistance thereby seemingly gave rise to a paradox, as the costs for legal assistance seemed to fall within both of the different regimes. It is therefore to be welcomed that the new NAI Rules explicitly provide that the costs of legal assistance are conceptually distinct from the costs of the arbitration and that they are treated differently in the context of the award on costs.

In the current NAI Rules, Article 59 NAI Rules relates to the award on costs. Both Article 59(2) and Article 59(3) NAI Rules are to some extent based on the general principle – laid down in many other arbitration rules[8] – that an award on costs should reflect the relative success or failure of the parties to the arbitration. As a general rule, Article 59(2) NAI Rules provides that the unsuccessful party *"is ordered to pay the costs of the arbitration, except in exceptional circumstances at the arbitral tribunal's discretion"*. Furthermore, if the parties are each partially unsuccessful, then *"the arbitral tribunal may order the parties to each pay part of the costs of the arbitration"*. Thus, inversely, under Article 59(2) NAI Rules the arbitral tribunal only has discretion *not* to order a fully unsuccessful party to pay all of the costs of the arbitration to the extent it is willing to find that "exceptional circumstances" exist.

As said, the costs of legal assistance fall under a different regime. On the basis of Article 59(3) NAI Rules, *"[t]he arbitral tribunal may order the unsuccessful party to pay reasonable compensation for the successful party's legal assistance, if and insofar as these costs were necessarily incurred in the arbitration in the arbitral tribunal's opinion."* It is clear that Article 59(3) NAI Rules gives the arbitral tribunal considerable discretion to allocate the costs of legal assistance among the parties in a manner which is – in the arbitral tribunal's view – reasonable. After all, Article 59(3) NAI Rules explicitly uses discretionary language (*"the arbitral tribunal may (...)"*). Furthermore, that

8 This principle is explicitly enshrined in Rule 28.4 of the LCIA Rules, which provides that "[t]he Arbitral Tribunal shall make its decisions on both Arbitration Costs and Legal Costs on the general principle that costs should reflect the parties' relative success and failure in the award or arbitration or under different issues." See also SCC Rules, Rule 44; UNCITRAL Rules, Rule 42(1).

provision contains a reasonableness criterion, which seemingly gives the arbitral tribunal even more discretionary powers in this regard.

An interesting question, however, is how the criterion of *"reasonable compensation"* relates to the proviso *"if and insofar as these costs were necessarily incurred in the arbitration in the arbitral tribunal's opinion"*. If "reasonable compensation" should be understood as being simply equivalent to *"costs [which] were necessarily incurred in the arbitration in the arbitral tribunal's opinion"*, then it is clear that the question of the necessity of the relevant costs is central to the arbitral tribunal's determination in this regard. If, on the other hand, the necessity of the costs is understood as a threshold criterion, then the required reasonableness constitutes a *further* condition to be decided upon by the arbitral tribunal. Either way, it should be clear that Article 59(3) NAI Rules gives the arbitral tribunal significant discretion in deciding to which extent the unsuccessful party should bear the successful party's costs of legal assistance.

19.3 Costs in the current NAI Rules: the viewpoints of the new Article 59(4)

In a prior publication, the authors of this article pointed out that the freedom arbitral tribunals had with respect to costs under the 2015 NAI Rules posed a serious risk to the values of predictability, transparency and uniformity in the context of cost awards.[9] One of the recommendations of the authors was to explicitly include certain viewpoints in the NAI Rules which could be deemed relevant in awarding costs, such as the procedural conduct of the respective parties.[10] The authors therefore welcome the inclusion of Article 59(4) in the new NAI Rules, which provides:

> "When deciding on the division of the costs of the arbitration and the costs of legal assistance, the arbitral tribunal may take into account the manner in which parties conducted the proceedings as well as whether each of the parties promoted the speedy and efficient conduct of the proceedings. If, in the opinion of the arbitral tribunal, a party has unreasonably delayed the arbitral proceedings, the arbitral tribunal may take this into account in its decision on the division of the costs of the arbitration and the costs of legal assistance."

9 M. van de Hel-Koedoot & P.B. Fritschy, 'De kostenveroordeling in arbitrage: suggesties ter bevordering van voorspelbaarheid, transparantie en uniformiteit', in: C.J.M. Klaassen, G.J. Meijer & C.L. Schleijpen (eds), *Going Dutch: ADR in Nederland, in het bijzonder bij het NAI (Onderneming en recht no 113)*, Deventer: Wolters Kluwer 2019, p 575-592.

10 Van de Hel-Koedoot & Fritschy 2019, p 580-585.

The objection could be raised, of course, that this provision in fact changes little, since an arbitral tribunal already had the discretion to take such circumstances into account if it so desired. To this objection it may be conceded that Article 59(4) NAI Rules indeed does not seem to alter the powers already possessed by an arbitral tribunal in the context of the award on costs. Its purpose, however, is of a different nature. Indeed, the purpose is to emphasize the importance of a cooperative procedural attitude and to bring this – as well as the possible consequences of not having such a cooperative attitude – explicitly to the attention of parties, their counsel and the arbitral tribunal.

This new provision does, however, raise a number of questions. Firstly, it is unclear whether the powers granted to an arbitral tribunal under Article 59(4) NAI Rules allow it to deviate from the rules laid down in Article 59(2) and 59(3) NAI Rules. For example, is an arbitral tribunal, in deviation from the text of Article 59(3) NAI Rules, allowed to order a *prevailing* party to pay any legal fees incurred by the other party if that prevailing party has unreasonably delayed the proceedings? In all likelihood, that question should be answered negatively.

Moreover, it is not entirely clear whether the circumstances mentioned in Article 59(4) NAI Rules have a special status vis-à-vis other potentially relevant circumstances or whether they merely constitute non-exhaustive examples of circumstances which may be deemed relevant in the context of Article 59(2) NAI Rules (as "exceptional circumstances at the arbitral tribunal's discretion") and Article 59(3) NAI Rules (as reasons to use the arbitral tribunal's discretion laid down in that provision). If Article 59(4) NAI Rules is intended to provide an exhaustive list of relevant viewpoints, then that certainly does not do justice to the fact that many considerations seem to be potentially relevant in this respect, such as the broader background of the case and the professionalism and respective financial resources of the parties. If, on the other hand, Article 59(4) NAI Rules is to be understood as formulating a non-exhaustive list of relevant considerations, then the inclusion of these particular circumstances seems somewhat random. It is for this reason that the authors of this article suggested in the past to make clear that an arbitral tribunal should *in any event* take into account the respective parties' procedural conduct when deciding on costs.[11]

11 Van de Hel-Koedoot & Fritschy 2019, p 585.

As to what procedural conduct could be relevant under Article 59(4) NAI Rules, one could for example think about unnecessarily delaying or holding up the proceedings by raising irrelevant or hopeless issues.[12] Another example might be an unnecessarily voluminous document production request. In this way, a party that insists on such a form of document production can foresee that, especially if it is (to some extent) a fishing expedition, it runs the risk of being presented with the bill for it later when the award on costs is made.

Moreover, Article 59(4) NAI Rules also seems to allow the arbitral tribunal to take into account the potentially improper motives behind certain procedural conduct. Unfortunately, as is generally known, intentional delay and/or obstruction sometimes occur in arbitration proceedings. Legal literature sometimes refers to this as "*bad faith litigation*" or even "*guerrilla tactics*".[13] Although no ready-made definitions are available in this connection[14], a broad definition of these notions should in any case also include intentional delay and disruption of the procedural order. Examples are the intentional late submission of exhibits or even procedural documents[15] and the raising of frivolous objections and/or procedural issues.

19.4 The tension between discretion and the values of predictability, transparency and uniformity

As is clear from the foregoing, arbitral tribunals have significant discretion in arriving at a particular cost award under the NAI Rules. Although it can be argued that such discretion enables the arbitral tribunal to arrive at a fair award on costs in each individual case, unhindered by too strict general rules, it also means that the values of predictability, transparency and uniformity in the determination of cost awards are at risk of being compromised. This fear is confirmed by the fact that in practice there are indeed large differences in how costs are handled and awarded. These differences concern both the way in which the costs of the arbitration are divided between the parties as well as the amount of costs that are awarded

12 For a comprehensive overview, see P. Sluijter, *Sturen met proceskosten: Wie betaalt de prijs van verstorend procesgedrag?* (diss. Tilburg), Kluwer: Deventer 2011, chapter 3.

13 G.J. Horvath et al, 'Chapter 1, para 1.02: Categories of Guerrilla Tactics', in: G.J. Horvath & S. Wilske (eds), *Guerrilla Tactics in International Arbitration (International Arbitration Law Library no 28)*, Alphen aan den Rijn: Kluwer Law International 2013, p 3-16.

14 Horvath et al 2013, p 5.

15 Cf. Browne & Price 2018, p 3.

(sometimes only a fraction of the actual costs incurred, sometimes significant amounts).

The differences described above entail a form of unpredictability that, precisely in view of the high amounts at stake in this context (both in absolute terms and relative to the principal sum), may pose a significant risk to parties considering arbitration. As mentioned above, some suggestions will therefore be formulated to promote the predictability, transparency and uniformity of cost awards in NAI arbitrations.

19.5 Possibility of brief party debate regarding costs and the award on costs

In this paragraph, it will be argued that the NAI Rules should explicitly include that the parties are free to briefly state in their cost submission whether, in their opinion, there is reason for the arbitral tribunal to take into account certain procedural conduct of the parties in its decision on costs. The idea behind this proposal is that the quality of the cost award – to be understood as: the extent to which it does justice to the role that the parties actually played in the way the proceedings were conducted – will significantly increase if the parties can briefly comment on both their own and the other party's procedural conduct.

This proposal means that parties can for example bring to the attention of the arbitral tribunal the fact that the other party in their opinion has unnecessarily delayed or complicated the proceedings. What is crucial here is that the parties must give reasons in this respect. In other words, this proposal invites parties to indicate specifically what procedural conduct they believe has led to an increase in the costs of the proceedings as a whole. Such contentions can be called "cost contentions": contentions that specifically address the cost-increasing effect of certain aspects[16] or even phases[17] of the proceedings provoked by the opposing party. In addition, the parties may, if they wish, raise "division contentions", with which they make explicit and justify the manner in which they believe the costs of the arbitration should reasonably be divided between the parties.

16 For example, extensive correspondence provoked by either party on a minor issue.

17 One can think, for example, of a jurisdictional defense that is bound to fail, which nevertheless led to a "bifurcation" of the proceedings. The opposing party, which has unnecessarily incurred costs due to this defense, can explicitly bring this to the attention of the arbitral tribunal under the proposal formulated here.

Several objections can be raised to this proposal. The first objection concerns the adversarial principle: will parties not be surprised by cost contentions and division contentions to which they cannot subsequently respond? To overcome this objection, the proposal assumes a system of simultaneity, with this simultaneity extending over two rounds. The parties are first invited to submit to the arbitral tribunal on the same date their cost submission as well as their reasoned cost and division contentions (the "first round"). Thereafter, the parties are once again given the opportunity to respond briefly – again at the same time – to the other party's cost submission (the "second round"), during which the reasonableness and necessity of the costs of legal assistance incurred by the other party can also be addressed. This prevents one of the parties from enjoying a procedural advantage over the other party by not having to submit its own contentions until after the other party has submitted its cost submissions. At the same time, this two-round system protects both parties from being surprised by the opposing party's contentions: after all, the contentions submitted with the cost statements can still be responded to in the second round.

This means, however, that the contentions in the second round should be strictly limited to a response to the other party's cost submission, including of course the contentions formulated therein. As in state court proceedings in which a limitation of the party debate takes place after a certain written round[18], it also applies here that the arbitral tribunal will ultimately have to determine whether the contentions in the second round are sufficiently in line with the party debate conducted up to that point. If not, the arbitral tribunal may disregard those contentions due to a violation of due process.

A second objection is that the proposal leads in a sense to an infinite regress. After all, the party cost debate will in itself involve costs, while *these* costs will not be covered by the parties' contentions in this cost debate: those contentions will logically extend only to procedural behavior exhibited *up to the cost phase*. Therefore, should there not be room for a *second* cost debate in which the parties' processual behavior during the first cost phase can be addressed? The infinite regression is obvious.

As is true of many philosophical problems, their practical weight should not be overestimated. The "party debate" proposed here on the costs

18 Cf. R.H. de Bock, *Tussen waarheid en onzekerheid: Over het vaststellen van feiten in de civiele procedure* (diss. Tilburg), Kluwer: Deventer 2011, p 146.

incurred during the arbitration should be limited in scope; this applies to the contentions submitted with the cost submission in the first round and even more so to the responses the parties may formulate to them in the second round. It is ultimately up to the arbitral tribunal to make sure this debate remains focused. This role of the arbitral tribunal, aimed at limiting the debate, includes not only supervising the *scope* of the arguments put forward in the "costs debate" but also their *nature*. After all, it must be prevented that the cost debate is used by one of the parties to continue the dispute on the merits. It is the responsibility of the arbitral tribunal to be aware of this and not to allow the costs debate to derail in such a way.

If the arbitral tribunal does indeed keep a tight rein on the costs debate, the additional costs incurred as a result will be relatively low. Moreover, the benefits of such a short debate on costs can potentially be great, as it offers the parties the opportunity to specifically inform the arbitral tribunal about nearly all of the costs incurred during the proceedings (i.e. all costs minus the costs of the costs debate) and about the asserted role played by both parties in that regard. In addition, the arbitral tribunal may, of course, of its own accord take note of any uncooperative and disruptive behavior displayed by either party during the costs debate.

Implementation of the proposal formulated in this paragraph in the NAI Rules could be done via a newly added article, which would read as follows:

> "The arbitral tribunal shall give the parties an opportunity to submit simultaneously, at a time to be determined by the arbitral tribunal, a statement of costs incurred and evidence thereof. The parties may thereby indicate to the arbitral tribunal, giving reasons, how in their opinion the costs of the arbitration should be divided between the parties. The arbitral tribunal shall then grant the parties the opportunity to briefly respond, again simultaneously, to the other party's statement of costs.?"

19.6 Arbitral tribunal's obligation to provide reasons

One of the starting points of the suggestions formulated in this article is that it is often difficult to understand on what basis the arbitral tribunal has arrived at a certain award on costs. One could argue that this is partly due to the fact that in most cases the arbitral tribunal has not received specific cost-oriented arguments from the parties. If that were the case, it would be reasonable to assume a related obligation to provide reasons on the part of the arbitral tribunal. But even without such specific cost-oriented arguments, Article 59 NAI Rules offers room to recognize, at least in certain situations, an increased obligation of the arbitral tribunal to provide reasons in this regard. These suggestions will be explained in more detail below.

For purposes of overview, it is advisable to distinguish a number of situations. A first scenario assumes that – in line with what has been argued in favor of in Paragraph 19.5 – the arbitral tribunal has received contentions from both parties regarding the parties' procedural conduct and the consequences that, according to the parties, should be attached to it in the context of the award on costs. In such a situation, the arbitral tribunal must in any case give reasons why it does or does not go along with the arguments put forward by the parties. This will in any event improve the transparency of the way in which the arbitral tribunal arrived at its cost award, regardless of the content of the cost award that is ultimately made.

In addition, regardless of whether or not the parties have submitted cost-oriented contentions to the arbitral tribunal, it is reasonable to assume an increased obligation to provide reasons if the arbitral tribunal decides to deviate from the general rule laid down in Article 59(2) NAI Rules that the unsuccessful party shall be ordered to pay the costs of the arbitration. This means that, if the arbitral tribunal indeed decides to deviate from this principle, the arbitral tribunal must explicitly motivate why it considers that *"exceptional circumstances"* within the meaning of that provision exist. Conversely, this increased obligation to provide reasons does not apply if no exceptional circumstances have been demonstrated and no contentions to that effect have been made by the parties – the arbitral tribunal may suffice with noting that fact and applying the main rule of Article 59(2) NAI Rules.

In addition, the arbitral tribunal must also motivate its allocation of costs if the parties are each partially (un)successful (Article 57(2), second sentence, NAI Rules). There is all the more reason for this if the relative success of the parties does not clearly correspond to the allocation chosen by the arbitral tribunal in this respect.

With respect to Article 59(3) NAI Rules, matters are more complicated. After all, Article 59(3) NAI Rules does not contain a clear main rule, but rather a (broad) discretionary power[19] of the arbitral tribunal to order or

19 Cf. M. van de Hel-Koedoot, 'Postscript', *TvA* 2009/44.

not to order the unsuccessful party to pay *"reasonable compensation"* for the necessarily incurred costs of legal assistance of the prevailing party. Precisely in view of the fact that the text of Article 59(3) NAI Rules in itself offers little direction (and, at least prima facie, merely lays down a discretionary *power*), it is desirable to adopt, in any event, a regular obligation for the arbitral tribunal to provide reasons with respect to the question of whether any costs of legal assistance should be awarded to the prevailing party at all. Thus, *in any event,* the arbitral tribunal will have to provide reasons as to why it does or does not use its discretionary power under Article 59(3) NAI Rules to award the costs of legal assistance to the successful party.

If the arbitral tribunal decides to award costs of legal assistance on the basis of Article 59(3) NAI Rules, there should be an obligation to provide *additional* reasons if the arbitral tribunal nevertheless decides *not* to award certain of such costs for being unreasonable and/or unnecessary. In other words: the starting point is that an award on costs of legal assistance is, by its nature, in principle complete, unless the arbitral tribunal provides a reasoned explanation as to why, all things considered, it is *not* justified to award complete costs of legal assistance.

The above leads, schematically, to the following overview:

	Contentions regarding costs and division of costs raised by (either) party	Article 59(3): whether or not to award costs of legal assistance	Article 59(3): incomplete allocation of costs of legal assistance	Article 59(2): allocation of costs of arbitration to the successful party	Article 59(2): no order to pay costs of arbitration as unsuccessful party	Article 59(2): division of costs of arbitration if parties are each partially successful
Obligation to provide reasons	X	X	X			X
Increased obligation to provide reasons					X	

It is obviously undesirable to include these various obligations to state reasons in the NAI Rules. For this reason, the alternative of a "Reasoning Handbook for Arbitrators", which includes the above rules regarding the obligation to provide reasons, could be considered.

19.7 Conclusion

In this article, several suggestions have been made to eliminate potential uncertainties about the costs of arbitration and about which party bears these costs at the end of the proceedings as much as possible. To this end, it has been suggested that parties to NAI arbitrations be more actively involved in a more comprehensive discussion regarding costs. It has also been suggested that the arbitral tribunal can play a role in increasing the clarity and predictability of cost awards in NAI arbitrations. In this way, this article hopes to contribute to the removal of possible uncertainties regarding costs and cost awards in Dutch institutional arbitrations, as a result of which the NAI may become an even more attractive alternative to state court proceedings.

CHAPTER 20

THE ORAL ARBITRAL AWARD

Toon van Mierlo[1]

20.1 Introduction

Under Dutch law, a state court has the option of deciding on the case orally (i.e. pronounce the ruling from the bench) during or immediately after the oral hearing. The Dutch Code of Civil Procedure ('DCCP') has an explicit provision to that effect. This provision was introduced on 1 September 2017 as Article 30p DCCP and supplemented,[2] amended and renumbered to Article 29a DCCP on 1 May 2023.[3] Article 30p DCCP, for its part, no longer exists today. Nevertheless, I pay detailed attention to this provision because the Dutch Supreme Court case law on Article 30p DCCP to be discussed in 20.2.3 led to Article 29a DCCP.

Pursuant to Article 1057(2) DCCP, an arbitral award must be made in writing. The question whether an arbitral award can also be made orally has so far received little attention in literature.[4] In this contribution, I will answer this question in the affirmative. I do this against the background of the NAI Arbitration Rules 2024 that have recently come into force, in which the possibility of an oral award has been opened for a few special cases in Article B3(7) and Article C8 of the said Rules. These provisions are discussed in more detail in 20.4.4 below.

---

1 Professor A.I.M. (Toon) van Mierlo is lawyer at HabrakenRutten in Amsterdam, arbitrator, member of the Challenge Committee of the NAI and emeritus professor at the Erasmus School of Law in Rotterdam and at the University of Groningen.

2 Act amending the Code of Civil Procedure and the General Administrative Law Act in connection with the simplification and digitalization of procedural law. Act of 13 July 2016, *Stb.* 2016, 288. See for the Parliamentary History of this act – and two other accompanying acts – A.I.M. van Mierlo & K.J. Krzemiński (eds), *Parliamentary History of Civil Procedure Legislation simplifying and digitising procedural law ('KEI')*, Deventer: Wolters Kluwer 2016 ("*Parl. Gesch. Rv ('KEI')* 2016").

3 Act of 25 January 2023, *Stb.* 2023, 41. See also A.I.M. van Mierlo, *WPNR* 2023, issue 7412, p 413-414. For the sake of completeness, it should be noted that Article 29a DCCP is excluded in cassation proceedings. See Article 418(2) DCCP. See further F.J.P. Lock, in: *T&C Rv*, Article 29a DCCP, note 1.

4 See, positively, H.J. Snijders, *Nederlands arbitragerecht*, Deventer: Wolters Kluwer 2018, Article 1057, note 2.

In particular, the questions that will be discussed below relate to (i) what an oral arbitral award should entail, and (ii) how the arbitral tribunal should record its oral award.

By way of introduction, I will first set out the background and genesis of Article 30p DCCP (para 20.2). In that context, I will also discuss an important decision of the Dutch Supreme Court of 20 April 2018 (i.e. shortly after the introduction of Article 30p DCCP). I will then briefly discuss the amendments to Article 30p DCCP, primarily as a consequence of the Supreme Court's decision and the renumbering to Article 29a DCPP as of 1 May 2023 (para 20.3). Subsequently, I will pay attention to Dutch arbitration law and discuss, more specifically, the way in which arbitral awards are made, the substantive requirements prescribed by law and the oral arbitral award in practice (para 20.4). The two questions raised above relating to the contents and written record of an oral arbitral award will be addressed as well. The final paragraph contains a short conclusion.

20.2 Ruling by the court

20.2.1 Main rule: in writing

The Dutch Code of Civil Procedure adopts the principle that a court judgment (*vonnis*) and a court decision or order (*beschikking*) are rendered in written form.

In proceedings initiated by a writ of summons (*dagvaardingsprocedure*), the judge's ruling is called a judgment. A judgment must meet the requirements listed in Article 230(1) DCCP, which reads as follows (unofficially translated):

> "The judgment states:
> a. the names and residence of the parties, and the names of their authorised representatives or lawyers;
> b. the course of the proceedings;
> c. the conclusion of the summons and the parties' claims;
> d. the conclusion of the prosecution's conclusion in cases where it has been heard;
> e. the grounds for the decision, including the facts on which the decision is based;
> f. the decision;

g. the name of the judge or, in the case of a plurality of judges, the names of the judges by whom the judgment was delivered;
h. the day of the verdict."

These provisions entail that the judgment – apart from what I call for convenience: the 'administrative data' (see (1), under a, g and h) – must show the course of the proceedings and also state the claim made in the writ of the summons and the positions taken by the claimant and the defendant respectively. Finally, the judgment must also contain the grounds for the decision, including the facts on which the decision is based. In short: the judgment must contain the reasoning for the decision. Regarding the latter, "every court decision must at least be reasoned in such a way that it provides sufficient insight into the reasoning behind it to make the decision verifiable and acceptable both to the parties and to third parties, including, in the case of an appellate proceeding, the higher court".[5] Under Dutch law, the judicial duty to give a reasoned decision is not only laid down in Article 230(1), under e., DCCP, but also in Article 5 of the Act Judicial Organization ('RO') ("and shall contain the grounds on which these decisions are based") and in Article 121 of the Dutch Constitution ("grounds on which they are based").

If a judgment does not meet one or more of the requirements laid down in Article 230 DCCP, it is nevertheless binding. The nullity of a judgment can only be effectuated by making use of a legal remedy, such as appeal.[6] This applies equally if the judgment was rendered by a judge or justice who was disbarred or not yet sworn in before the judgment was rendered.[7] Even in such a scenario, the closed system of legal remedies implies that nullity of the judgment can only be effectuated by filing an appeal or an appeal in cassation. I wonder whether this is not unnecessarily cumbersome in cases where a judgment has been rendered by a judge that is not (or no longer) competent to do so. For cases like this, the law mentions nullity as a sanction in Article 5(2) RO. In my opinion, it would be much simpler if nullity could be invoked before and determined in and by the

5 See Supreme Court 4 June 1993, ECLI:NL:HR:1993:ZC0986, para 3.4, *NJ* 1993/659, annotated by D.W.F. Verkade (*Vredo/Veenhuis*).

6 Supreme Court 13 September 1991, ECLI:NL:HR:1991:ZC0329, *NJ* 1991/767 (*Dreesmann/Vede*).

7 Supreme Court 18 November 2016, ECLI:NL:HR:2016:2607, *NJ* 2017/202, annotated by H.B. Krans & P. van Schilfgaarde (*Meavita*); Supreme Court 13 April 2018, ECLI:NL:HR:2018:604, *NJ* 2019/108, annotated by H.B. Krans (*Cadenza c.s./ Fairstar Dockwise*) and Supreme Court 6 October 2017, ECLI:NL:HR:2017:2561, *NJ* 2018/373, annotated by A.I.M. van Mierlo (*T./Raad voor de Kinderbescherming*).

court that delivered the judgment in question in the first place. However, this would require a statutory provision. Consideration could be given to introducing a new Article 32a DCCP, immediately following the provisions on correcting and supplementing judgments, decisions and orders (Articles 31 and 32 DCCP).[8]

Regarding the content of a judgment, a 'lightened regime' applies when the court issues a default judgment in the event that the defendant has not appeared in court despite having been duly summoned (the so-called judgment *in absentia*). In such a case, in order to save time and costs, an abridged form of judgment may suffice on the basis of Article 230(2) DCCP, in which, with regard to the requirements mentioned in Article 230(1), under a., c., e. and f., DCCP reference may be made to a certified copy of the writ of summons, which is to be attached to the default judgment. In the event the claim is granted, the reasoning in such cases is particularly short in practice and in line with the standard the law prescribes in Article 139 DCCP: 'the claim does not appear to be unlawful or without merit and will therefore be awarded'. A more detailed reasoning than this is not required and, in general, not possible because the claim has not been contested.

Finally, Article 230(3) DCCP provides that the judgment must be signed by the judge or, in the case the chamber consists of multiple judges, by the president of the chamber and the clerk (*griffier*). The judgment is rendered in public. Article 6 ECHR determines that 'the judgment shall be pronounced publicly'. That said, it is sufficient if the judgment is available at the registry and both parties and any other interested party can obtain a copy thereof. Nowadays, the judgment is often sent by the registry to the parties' counsel via a protected internet environment.

In addition to proceedings that are initiated by a writ of summons, we also have proceedings in the Netherlands that begin with a petition (*verzoekschriftprocedure*). Such proceedings lead to a decision. According to Article 287(1) DCCP, the provisions of Article 230 para (1) and (3) DCCP also apply mutatis mutandis to decisions.

Furthermore, the provisions of Article 230(2) apply to decisions of the preliminary relief judge on petitions that has been handed to him directly, the so called *stempelbeschikkingen*. In that case, a certified copy of the original

8 See also in this respect para 7 of my note under Supreme Court 6 October 2017, ECLI:NL:HR:2017:2561, *NJ* 2018/373 (*T./Raad voor de Kinderbescherming*).

petition is attached to the decision or the decision is made on that petition, so that – in the same way as explained above in the context of a judgment in default – the requirements mentioned in Article 230(1), under a., c., e. and f., DCCP can be derived therefrom. This is, for example, the case if a creditor is granted permission by the preliminary relief judge to impose a prejudgment attachment on one or more assets of the debtor (article 700 DCCP). In such a case, the decision is often given on the original petition and reads no more than 'permitted as requested, for an amount of EUR [X], under the condition…'.

Hereafter, where possible, for the sake of brevity, I use the term 'judgment' for all types of judicial decisions (including a judgment, a decision, a *stempelbeschikking* or an order).

20.2.2 Oral ruling; Article 30p DCCP (old) as predecessor of Article 29a DCCP

The written form is not a constitutive requirement; a judgment may also be given orally at or immediately after a hearing (hereinafter in brief: the 'oral ruling').

For a long time, oral rulings were only permitted by law in the case of an interim judgment.[9] In practice, however, it also occurred in final judgments and in decisions in petition proceedings. With regard to the latter, reference can be made to, for example, family law practice.[10] In civil juvenile cases, oral rulings are often made at or immediately after the hearing. The same happens when dealing with urgent requests such as emergency out-of-home placements, provisional custodial orders and provisional guardianship measures that are given outside office hours, in which the juvenile court issues rulings by telephone without an oral hearing. Interim oral rulings are also made in family cases. An example is the ruling, after consultation with the parties at the hearing, that these parties will turn to a counselling agency for parental guidance. Finally, in alimony and divorce cases, an interim oral ruling could include an order to a party to provide

9 See Article 232(2), opening words and under a, DCCP (old): "Articles 230 and 231(1) DCCP may be derogated from to the extent necessary: a. if an interim judgment is rendered at an appearance of the parties at a hearing as referred to in Articles 87 and 88 DCCP and if all parties have appeared there (...)."

10 The following examples are all taken from J.C.E. Ackermans-Wijn, 'De mondelinge uitspraak volgens artikel 30p Rv in familiezaken', *EB* 2017/76, p 177.

evidence, the appointment of an expert or the decision on a request for inspection, copy or extract of certain data pursuant to Article 843a DCCP.[11]

In general terms, it can be noted that the possibility of an oral ruling is used in cases where there is such an urgent interest in a ruling by the judge that a (full) written elaboration thereof cannot be awaited, and the ruling is therefore initially given in oral form only for this reason.[12] Should this be necessary for the purpose of enforcement, an abridged ('heads-up') ruling will also be issued on paper, followed a few days later by the provision of a copy of the fully reasoned ruling.

On 1 September 2017, the oral judgment was first given a more general legal basis in Article 30p DCCP (old), which is supplemented, amended and renumbered to Article 29a DCCP as per 1 May 2023. The old provision already applied to *all* courts (with the exception of the Supreme Court) and in *all* proceedings (i.e. proceedings that lead to either a judgment or a decision). As far as currently relevant, Article 30p DCCP stipulated the following (unofficially translated):

> "1. The court may, if all the parties have appeared at the oral hearing, give an oral ruling at or after the oral hearing.
> 2. Notwithstanding Articles 230 and 287, the oral ruling shall consist of the ruling and the grounds for the ruling.
> 3. A court record (*process-verbaal*) is made of the oral ruling by the judge.
> 4. The court record shall be signed by the judge. If the judge is unable to sign, this shall be noted in the court record.
> 5. The court shall make a copy of the court record available to the parties within two weeks of the oral hearing. The copy provided to a party who may proceed to enforcement shall be in executory form."

Pursuant to Article 30p(1) DCCP, the possibility of an oral ruling only existed if all parties have appeared at the oral hearing. The oral ruling itself consists – in deviation from Article 230 DCCP – of the ruling and the grounds for the ruling, i.e. the reasoning (Article 30p(2) DCCP). Therefore, the other requirements of Article 230 DCCP[13] do not have to be adhered to in the oral ruling. However, I doubt whether the latter also applies to the

11 On 1 January 2025, Article 843a DCCP will be replaced on the basis of the *Wet vereenvoudiging en modernisering bewijsrecht* (Act of 6 March 2024, *Stb.* 2024, 62) by Articles 194-195a DCCP.

12 See also in this respect Supreme Court 20 April 2018, ECLI:NL:HR:2018:650, para 3.3.3, *NJ* 2020/337.

13 See for these requirements the text of Article 230 DCCP, as quoted in para 20.2.1 above.

facts, as is assumed in literature by some authors.[14] This seems to me to apply only to (simple) cases in which there is no dispute between the parties about the facts. Where this is not the case, the court was, in my view, not be able to give an oral ruling under Article 30p DCCP nor will be able under Article 29a DCCP without including an overview of the relevant facts. However, this does not affect the fact that even then – as will be discussed in below – an oral ruling is possible if, for example, this is required for reasons of urgency. In that case, shortly afterwards, the ruling, including the facts on which it is based, should still be made available in written form to the parties.

In cases where an oral ruling is given, a *proces-verbaal* of that ruling (the 'court record') must be made and signed by the judge (Article 30p(3) and (4) DCCP); signature by the clerk is not required. This court record only contains the ruling and the grounds therefor. There is no room for a further written ruling. A copy of the court record must be available to the parties as soon as possible but no later than two weeks after the oral ruling is rendered (Article 30p(4) DCCP). Failure to meet this deadline shall not invalidate the oral ruling or otherwise deprive it of legal effect.[15]

A course of action in which the judge renders an oral ruling a few days after the hearing and elaborates this ruling in writing is not in line with Article 30p DCCP.[16]

20.2.3 No exclusivity Article 30p DCCP; Supreme Court 20 April 2018

Shortly after the introduction of Article 30p DCCP, Ackermans-Wijn pointed out in her contribution already mentioned in footnote 10 that, compared to current practice, Article 30p DCCP led to a limitation of the possibilities of oral adjudication in family cases.

Less than six months later, the Supreme Court was given the opportunity to comment on the matter and to give an interpretation of the provision of Article 30p DCCP in its decision of 20 April 2018.[17] The case concerned a

14 See R.H. de Bock, in: *GS Burgerlijke Rechtsvordering*, Article 30p DCCP, note 5 (with further bibliographical references, online).

15 See Supreme Court 21 February 2020, ECLI:NL:HR:2020:320, *NJ* 2020/339, annotated by H.B. Krans (*Moeder/Stichting Jeugdbescherming Brabant*).

16 See Supreme Court 21 January 2022, ECLI:NL:HR:2022:58, *NJ* 2022/39. This is also the case under the regime of Article 29a DCCP.

17 Supreme Court 20 April 2018, ECLI:NL:HR:2018:650, *NJ* 2020/337, annotated by H.B. Krans.

mental healthcare case in which the public prosecutor requested the court to issue a provisional authorization to continue a person's stay in a psychiatric hospital.[18] Article 30p DCCP applied to these proceedings. The oral hearing took place on 19 October 2017. At the hearing, the public prosecutor was not present. This is not unusual in these types of cases. At the end of the oral hearing, the court ruled orally and granted the requested authorization by stating on the prosecutor's request: "Granted this day a provisional authorization for the duration of six (6) months", bearing the date 19-10-'17, the judge's name and his signature. A few days later, the clerk issues a copy of a fully written out judgment signed by the judge and clerk, bearing the date of judgment: 19 October 2017. A copy of the court record is provided by the clerk only after the party that it concerned filed an appeal in cassation. In cassation, this party complained that the court did not give an oral ruling in accordance with the procedure of Article 30p DCCP. For instance, not all parties were present at the hearing (the public prosecutor was absent) and the court did not comply with the provisions of Article 30p(3)-(5) DCCP with regard to the court record.

The Supreme Court considers that the restrictions on the possibility of oral judgments laid down in Article 30p DCCP are new compared to existing practice. Regarding this existing practice, the Supreme Court considers (para 3.3.4) (unofficially translated):

> "In the (...) practice – hereafter: the existing practice – the oral ruling is usually elaborated in this way that the court orally communicates its ruling and (main) grounds for it to the parties present, and in the following days elaborates the ruling in writing. That written elaboration usually mentions the date on which the ruling was given orally. If the ruling must be enforced immediately after orally given, it is first recorded in writing in a (much) abbreviated form, in a form that can be enforced. The latter is done, inter alia, in the form of an abbreviated ruling (sometimes referred to as a heads-up ruling) or in the form chosen by the court in this case, of a note on the application (sometimes referred to as an 'emergency order'). In either case, the ruling is then followed by the full written elaboration referred to above."

With regard to the legal restrictions mentioned above in para 20.2.2, the Supreme Court considers (para 3.3.5):

---

18 Until 1 January 2020, this type of case was governed by the *Wet bijzondere opneming in psychiatrische ziekenhuizen*. Since then it has been regulated in the *Wet verplichte geestelijke gezondheidszorg* (Act of 24 January 2018, *Stb.* 2018, 37) and the *Wet zorg en dwang* (Act of 29 September 2021, *Stb.* 2021, 468).

> "The objections to these restrictions are considerable. After all, the interest in an immediate ruling may, under circumstances, outweigh the interest of a party not appearing at the hearing not to be confronted with an oral ruling delivered outside its presence, especially if that ruling is available to it in written form shortly afterwards (...)."

> "Moreover, the (...) rule that oral rulings can only be elaborated on by recording the orally communicated ruling and the grounds for it in a court record restricts the possibility of oral rulings in principle to simple cases. In more complex cases, it is not usually possible to communicate all the grounds for the ruling orally in detail immediately. Thus, such cases, even where there are compelling reasons for an immediate ruling, are in principle excluded from the possibility of an oral ruling. After all, if the way of Article 30p DCCP were to be chosen in such cases, the reasons for the judgment would soon fail, in connection with the complexity of the case, which would be to the detriment of both the acceptability of the ruling to the parties and the controllability in a subsequent instance, neither of which is acceptable (cf. inter alia Supreme Court 4 June 1993, ECLI:NL:HR:1993:ZC0986, *NJ* 1993/659 (*Vredo/Veenhuis*))."

In the Supreme Court's view, the parliamentary history[19] shows that the existing practice, which relates to cases where an urgent interest exists, can be continued according to the legislator's intention for those cases. The Supreme Court then continues (para 3.3.7):

> "The provision of Article 30p DCCP, also according to the explanatory notes given to it, apparently applies in particular to simple cases, in which there need not be an urgent interest in the ruling and in which the (...) rules [of Article 30p DCCP; AvM] are practically applicable."

The Supreme Court then concludes that the court can thus give oral rul ings in two ways (para 3.3.8):

> "The court may therefore give oral rulings both in accordance with existing practice and under Article 30p DCCP, in the former case if there is an urgent interest (...), in the latter case if the ruling is one that lends itself to it."

The Supreme Court then dismissed the cassation appeal, because the court that issued the provisional care authorisation had chosen the path of existing practice and not the application of Article 30p DCCP.[20]

19 In this connection, the Supreme Court refers in para 3.3.6 to comments in the Explanatory Memorandum and the Memorandum of Reply to the Report. See *Parl. Gesch. Rv ('KEI')* 2016/II.1.1 (p 608) and II.1.3 (p 639), respectively.

20 See for the implications of this decision for family cases: J.C.E. Ackermans-Wijn, 'Mondelinge uitspraak in familiezaken na de uitspraak van de Hoge Raad van 20 april 2018', *EB* 2018/67, p 131 et seq.

20.2.4 *Five further rules applicable to oral rulings*

In its decision of 20 April 2018 discussed above in 20.2.3, the Supreme Court formulated in paras 3.4.2 to 3.4.6 five further rules applicable to oral judgments based on existing practice (with subsequent written elaboration) and Article 30p DCCP (with subsequent a written court record), respectively. These rules – in brief – boil down to the following:
(i) an oral ruling is an exception to the main rule that a ruling is in writing;
(ii) the date of ruling is the day of the oral ruling;
(iii) the written elaboration (existing practice) or the court report (Article 30p DCCP) should be available as soon as possible;
(iv) in case of filing an appeal, a party should have at least two weeks to present the grounds for the appeal;
(v) the written elaboration is from the judge(s) who gave the oral ruling.

On each of these rules, I note the following.

(i) Oral ruling is the exception
The legal principle is that a ruling by a judge is made in writing before it is pronounced. This can only be deviated from if there is a sufficiently compelling reason to do so. According to the Supreme Court, this is the case if:
- such an urgent interest exists that a (full) written elaboration of the ruling cannot be awaited (and is therefore followed – which the Supreme Court refers to in para 3.3.4 as the 'existing practice'); or
- the ruling lends itself to this (and thus an oral ruling as referred to in Article 30p DCCP is chosen).

(ii) Date of ruling is day of oral hearing
If the ruling is given orally – either in accordance with the existing practice or pursuant to Article 30p DCCP – the day on which it is given is deemed to be the day of the ruling. This day is also decisive for the commencement of the appeal period with regard to the ruling.[21]

(iii) Provision of written elaboration
If the existing practice is followed, the fully written elaboration of the oral ruling should be made available as soon as possible, preferably within a few days.

21 Cf. also the Explanatory Memorandum to Article 230 DCCP, A.I.M. van Mierlo & F.M. Bart (eds), *Parl. Gesch. Burgerlijk Procesrecht*, Deventer: Kluwer 2002, p 403.

Here, according to the Supreme Court, in accordance with the provisions of Article 30p(5) DCCP, a deadline of no later than two weeks after the oral ruling can be assumed.

The date of the written elaboration shall be the date of the oral ruling, with an express indication that it concerns the written elaboration of the ruling already given orally. Mention must also be made of the date on which the written elaboration was adopted, so that it is verifiable by the parties and the court in a subsequent instance.[22]

Although the Supreme Court does not expressly comment on this, failure to meet the deadline for making the written elaboration available to the parties does not affect the validity of the oral ruling in question and does not in itself constitute grounds for setting it aside by a higher court.[23] In my opinion, this also follows from the rule formulated by the Supreme Court in the subsequent consideration entailing that a party must always have a certain minimum period of time available for submitting grounds for the appeal. This rule removes any objections to late availability of the written elaboration or the court record, respectively. This – fourth – rule boils down to the following.

(iv) Appeal against oral ruling; minimum time limit for raising grounds

Conceivably, a party may wish to lodge an appeal against the oral ruling. In that case, there is sometimes an obligation to state the grounds for the appeal when lodging it. For example, in cassation, the notice of appeal must contain the grounds on which the appeal in cassation is based.[24] Similarly, in the case of an appeal against a decision on a petition, the notice of appeal must contain the grounds of appeal.[25]

Specifically for these cases, the Supreme Court formulated a more detailed rule which boils down to a sort of guaranteed minimum period: parties must always have at least two weeks available for submitting the grounds for the appeal. It could be that the time limit for appeal is shorter than two weeks (e.g. in bankruptcy cases). In such a case, a party must at least

22 See para 3.4.4.

23 The Supreme Court has ruled along those lines in Supreme Court 21 February 2020, ECLI:NL:HR:2020:320, *NJ* 2020/339, annotated by H.B. Krans (*Moeder/Stichting Jeugdbescherming Brabant*).

24 See Article 407(2)(d) DCCP and Article 426a(2) DCCP respectively.

25 See Article 359 DCCP in conjunction with Article 278 DCCP. However, in the case of an appeal against a judgment rendered at first instance, this is not the case. See Article 343 DCCP.

have that shorter time limit for submitting the grounds of appeal.[26] If the written elaboration of the ruling has become available and a party has less than the aforementioned minimum period at its disposal, an extension will take place up to the required minimum period, counting from the day following the day on which the written elaboration of the oral judgment is available. The appeal itself should, according to the Supreme Court, always be lodged within the appeal period. If the written elaboration is not yet available then the appeal should be lodged on grounds to be further specified (*nader aan te voeren gronden*).[27]

The two-week period is in line with other case law of the Supreme Court. For example, it also applies if, as a result of an error or omission committed by (the registry of) the district court or court of appeal, the person lodging an appeal or an appeal in cassation did not know in time and could not reasonably have known that the court had rendered a decision and, as a result of an error or omission not attributable to him, the decision was not sent or provided to him until after the expiry of the period for lodging an appeal or an appeal in cassation. In such a case, the Supreme Court adopts an extension of the period for appeal by a period of (also) 14 days – or such shorter period as corresponds to the statutory period for appeal in a given procedure – after the day on which the judgment or decision was issued or sent. The Supreme Court equates such a scenario with the scenario where the registry has sent or provided the judgment or decision within the appeal period, but so late that it is not even reasonable to, within that period, to lodge an appeal by submitting a notice of appeal that does not contain the grounds of appeal.[28]

With regard to the two-week period, attention should also be drawn to the case in which the application in cassation contains a reservation to supplement or amend the formulated grounds of appeal in cassation as a result of not having the court record of the hearing in due time. In that case, the applicant may also supplement and amend the appeal in cassation after the expiry of the cassation period, provided that this relates to grounds that could not have been raised in an application filed within the appeal period. According to the Supreme Court, such a so-called supplementary application must be submitted expeditiously, whereby a period of four-

26 See para 3.4.5.

27 One speaks of a 'blank appeal' in such a case. See H.J. Snijders & A. Wendels, *Civiel Appel (Burgerlijk Proces & Praktijk no 2)*, Deventer: Kluwer 2009, no 253.

28 See Supreme Court 28 November 2003, ECLI:NL:HR:2003:AN8489, *NJ* 2005/465, annotated by W.D.H. Asser (*X/Raad voor de Kinderbescherming*).

teen days – or so much shorter a period as corresponds to the statutory appeal period in a given procedure – after the day of delivery or sending of the court record applies.[29]

The rule formulated by the Supreme Court refers to cases in which oral rulings has been given in accordance with the existing practice. It is obvious to assume that this rule applies equally if an oral ruling has been given under Article 30p DCCP and the court subsequently makes the court record available to the parties in accordance with Article 30p(5) DCCP.

(v) The written elaboration is from judge(s) who gave the oral judgment
The judge(s) who renders the oral ruling according to the existing practice should also determine the written elaboration thereof. This should therefore be taken into account when deciding whether to give an oral ruling. Should a judge resign before the written elaboration has been provided, it will – necessarily – be sufficient to record the oral ruling in a court record, since the further written elaboration of the oral ruling (the "pointing out" of the ruling or the establishment of its text) is no longer possible by the judges who rendered the oral ruling. According to the Supreme Court,[30] the fact that the judge already resigned from office does not prevent the ruling from being recorded in a court record (which, after all, only concerns the ruling orally given at the hearing and its grounds).

In written judicial rulings (judgments, decisions or orders), the *rendering* of that ruling must be distinguished from its *pronouncement*. The rendering of the ruling refers to the adoption of the ruling, while pronouncing it involves making the ruling public. Pronouncing always takes place after adoption of the ruling.[31] As a rule, a ruling by three judges is adopted after these judges have discussed the case internally (in chambers). After this, one of the judges draws up a first draft ruling in accordance with the outcome of these deliberations. This draft is then circulated among the other judges concerned, each of whom has the opportunity to provide his or her input, after which the judges – possibly after circulating one or more further drafts – jointly adopt the final ruling. Judges are bound to maintain confidentiality 'of what is expressed in chambers on pending cases'.[32] In

29 See Supreme Court 23 December 2006, ECLI:NL:HR:2005:AU3720, *NJ* 2006/31.
30 See para 3.4.6.
31 See also H.B. Krans in his note (paras 4 et seq.) to Supreme Court 18 November 2016, ECLI:NL:HR:2016:2607, *NJ* 2017/202 (*Meavita*).
32 See Article 7 Judicial Organisation Act.

court proceedings in the Netherlands, we do not have the system of *dissenting opinions*. Fortunately!

The procedure for oral rulings judgments is not much different from that for written rulings; before the ruling is pronounced, the ruling is adopted. In the existing practice, the pronounced ruling is then worked out in the written elaborations. However, this written elaboration is not 'adopting' in the (aforementioned) sense of determination of the judicial ruling.

A written ruling must be set aside, after an appeal has been lodged, if there is a judge at the foot of this ruling who has already been resigned from office before the written ruling was issued.[33]

In the case of an oral ruling, the ruling is first delivered (as a rule: after a short adjournment of the hearing) and then pronounced at the hearing. The subsequent resignation of one or more of the judges involved has then no consequences for the validity of the ruling concerned. However, the further written elaboration by the judges can no longer take place after the resignation of one or more of them.

For this, the Supreme Court offers a practical *escape*.[34] In such a case, the resignation does not preclude preparing and issuing a court record (which, after all, concerns only the ruling communicated at the hearing and the grounds for it).[35]

If the choice is made to apply Article 30p DCCP – and thus to insert in a court record only the ruling and the grounds for it communicated at the hearing – the subsequent resignation of a judge who gave the oral ruling is meaningless. The written court record will then indicate the judge's inability to attend.

20.3 Article 29a DCCP instead of Article 30p DCCP (old)

As already noted above, Article 30p DCCP has been renumbered as Article 29a DCCP with effect from 1 May 2023. The original text has also under-

33 See Supreme Court 18 November 2016, ECLI:NL:HR:2016:2607, *NJ* 2017/202, annotated by H.B. Krans & P. van Schilfgaarde (*Meavita*); Supreme Court 13 April 2018, ECLI:NL:HR:2018:604, *NJ* 2019/108, annotated by H.B. Krans (*Cadenza c.s./Fairstar Dockwise*).

34 See para 3.4.6.

35 This escape route has not been received with equal enthusiasm by everyone. See rather critically: Ackermans-Wijn 2018, p 134.

gone various amendments. Now, the text also includes (see e.g. Article 29a(5) and (6) DCCP) the Supreme Court decision of 20 April 2018, as discussed above. The entire Article 29a DCCP reads as follows (unofficially translated):

> "1 The court may, if all the parties have appeared at the oral hearing, give an oral ruling at or after the oral hearing.
> 2. Notwithstanding Articles 230 and 287, the oral ruling shall consist of the ruling and the grounds for the ruling.
> 3. A court record of the oral ruling shall be drawn up by the court and signed by the judge. If the judge is unable to sign, this shall be noted in the court record.
> 4. The court shall make a copy of the court record available to the parties as soon as possible, but in any event within two weeks of the oral ruling. The copy provided to the party who is entitled to enforce the ruling shall be in executory form.
> 5. If, due to an urgent interest, the written ruling cannot be awaited, the court may, notwithstanding(1) above, whether or not all parties have appeared at the oral hearing, give an oral ruling at or after the oral hearing. Contrary to(2) above, this oral ruling shall include the ruling and the main grounds of the ruling.(3) and (4) shall not apply to this oral ruling.
> 6. If an oral ruling is given pursuant to(5) above, the court shall, if necessary, prepare an abridged ruling in executory form. In any event, a full written elaboration of the oral ruing shall be made available to the parties as soon as possible, but in any event within two weeks after the oral ruling, subject to the requirements contained in Articles 230 and 287 DCCP. The written elaboration shall mention the date of the oral ruling as well as the date of adoption of the written elaboration of that ruling. If an abridged ruling has not been drawn up in executory form, the full written elaboration of the oral ruling has been drawn up in executory form."

20.4 Arbitral awards

20.4.1 The adoption of the judgment; majority decision-making

The process of making an arbitral award is not significantly different from that of a judgment, decision or order by a state court. Here too, the making of the arbitral award precedes its pronouncement. If the arbitral tribunal consists of more arbitrators, then, as a rule, after internal deliberations among the arbitrators, one or more drafts circulate among the arbitrators before the final award is made. In that context, arbitral decisions are generally made unanimously, sometimes by majority vote, unless the parties have agreed otherwise.[36] With regard to the latter, one can think of the cases – rare or never occurring in practice – where it has been agreed that unanimity is required or that the chair of the arbitral tribunal has a deciding vote if a majority decision cannot be taken spontaneously.[37] In daily practice, in my experience, arbitral awards are mostly unanimous. *Dissenting opinions* are in – at least – Dutch legal practice an almost unknown phenomenon. If a *dissent* is given, it does not imply that the *dissenting* arbitrator does not agree with the arbitral award as a result of the joint deliberation between arbitrators.[38] Incidentally, the law does not prohibit such opinions. Article 49(6) NAI Arbitration Rules 2024 provides in this regard:

> "The award will not state a minority opinion. A minority may express its opinion to the other arbitrators and the parties in a separate written document. This document is not considered to be part of the award."

Personally, I am not in favour of dissenting opinions.[39] This is made no different by the fact that – as the Supreme Court already ruled in 2008 – the opinion does not form part of the arbitral award.[40] A dissenting opinion undermines collegial decision-making in the arbitral tribunal, can easily lead to a breach of the principle of secrecy of the internal deliberations among the judges (*geheim van de raadkamer*) that also applies in arbitrations and can quickly be seen as a painful form of narcissism, complacency and arrogance on the part of the dissenting arbitrator, not to mention that a dissenting opinion – especially if given by the arbitrator appointed by the (partially) unsuccessful party – may cast reasonable doubt on the neutrality of the arbitrator in question and possibly constitute an undesirable invitation to setting aside proceedings.[41]

---

36 See the first sentence of Article 1057(1) DCCP, as well as Article 49(1) NAI Arbitration Rules 2024. Unlike e.g. Article 31(1) ICC Arbitration Rules, the NAI Arbitration Rules 2024 do not have a rule that in the absence of a majority of votes, the award is made by the Chair of the arbitral tribunal alone.

37 See the Explanatory Memorandum to Article 1057 DCCP, *Parliamentary Papers II* 1983/84, 18464, no 3, p 24.

38 In the same sense, Amsterdam Court of Appeal 25 April 2017, ECLI:NL:GHAMS:2017:1496, *TvA* 2017/48 (*The Swatch/Tiffany*).

39 In another sense (and setting out some principles for the creation, form and content of a dissenting opinion) B. van Zelst, 'Dissenting opinions in arbitrage', *TvA* 2015/21.

40 See Supreme Court 8 December 2008, ECLI:NL:HR:2008:BF3799, para 3.3, *NJ* 2009/6 (*Bursa/Güris*).

41 The latter has previously been pointed out by R. van Delden, *International commercial arbitration*, Deventer: Kluwer 1996, no 163.

20.4.2 *The arbitral award shall be in writing*

Once the arbitral tribunal has decided what the decision will be, it must, by law, entrust this decision to paper. The award shall be in writing (Article 1057(2) DCCP). This requirement also applied under the Arbitration Act 1986 and in arbitration law that preceded it, section 637 DCCP (old). Sanders believes that 'in writing' is a *must*; only when the award is in writing does it constitute an award.[42]

Article 1057(4) DCCP lists exactly what (minimum) requirements the contents of a written arbitral award must meet (unofficially translated):

> "The award, in addition to the decision, shall in any case include:
> a. the names and residences of the arbitrators or arbitrators;
> b. the names and residences of the parties;
> c. the date of the award;
> d. place of arbitration;
> e. the grounds for the decision given in the award."

while Article 1057(5) DCCP provides (unofficially translated):

> "Notwithstanding(4) under e., the award shall not contain grounds for the decision given if:
> a. the award concerns only the mere determination of the capacity or condition of things as referred to in Article 1020(4), under a, DCCP;
> b. the establishment of a settlement referred to in Article 1069 DCCP; o
> c. in all other cases, after the arbitration has been initiated, the parties agree in writing that no grounds for the decision will be given."

The key is not only to make a good decision, but also to put that decision down in a good judgment. Nolen notes in this regard:[43]

> "This work too requires the greatest care, for a good decision laid down in a bad award may leave parties unsatisfied and may even bring upon them the misery of years of court proceedings, ending in the setting aside of the award. The parties are then, at the expense of a lot of time, money and effort, even further away from the end point than before the commencement of arbitration."

Under current law – the above comment by Nolen dates from 1957 – there are limited possibilities for setting aside an arbitral award. The grounds

42 P. Sanders, *Het Nederlandse arbitragerecht*, Deventer: Kluwer 2001, p 134.
43 W. Nolen, *Handbook for arbitrators*, Zwolle: W.E.J. Tjeenk Willink 1957, p 163.

for this are listed in Article 1065(1), opening words and under a.-e., DCCP. It follows from the word 'only' in the opening words of Article 1065(1) DCCP that this enumeration is exhaustive; an arbitral award cannot therefore be set aside on grounds other than those listed in Article 1065(1) DCCP. The grounds for setting aside should be applied with restraint, according to settled case law of the Dutch Supreme Court.[44] Looking at the specific grounds listed in Article 1065(1) DCCP against the background of the requirements to be met by an arbitral award pursuant to Article 1057(4) DCCP, the following picture emerges.

If an arbitral award does not meet one or more of the substantive requirements set out in Article 1057(4) DCCP, setting aside the award is only an issue if the award is not supported by reasons. This refers to the requirement in Article 1057(4), under e., DCCP that the arbitral award contains 'the grounds for the decision given in the award'. In the event of an incorrect statement or complete or partial absence of the information mentioned in Article 1057(4), under a.-d., DCCP, setting aside is not a relevant issue at all. In such a case, a party may request the arbitral tribunal to correct its award on the basis of Article 1060(2) DCCP.

Of the requirements mentioned in Article 1057 para (4) DCCP, by far the most important part of an arbitral award are the 'grounds for the decision' and the decision itself. The latter is contained in the operative part. It seems to me that the grounds for the decision refer not only to the reasoning but also – as is expressly stated in the context of court judgments in Article 230(1), under d., DCCP – to the facts on which the decision is based. Nolen describes a 'good judgment' as:

> "an award, which, firstly, meets the legal requirements (...) and, secondly, fully and clearly reflects: 1° the contentions, arguments and claims of the parties; 2° the arbitrators' reasoning, the grounds on which their award is based; 3° the decision on what the parties sought".[45]

44 See, inter alia, Supreme Court 17 January 2003, ECLI:NL:HR:2003:AE9395, *NJ* 2004/384, annotated by H.J. Snijders (*International Military Services/Modsaf-IR*) and Supreme Court 9 January 2004, ECLI:NL:HR:2004:AK8380, *NJ* 2005/190, annotated by H.J. Snijders (*Nannini/SFT Bank*). This is an exception when it comes to the application of the adversarial principle (see Supreme Court 25 May 2007, ECLI:NL:HR:2007:BA2495, *NJ* 2007/294 (*Spaanderman/Anova Food*)). The same can be assumed when relying on the ground that there is no valid agreement to arbitrate.

45 Nolen 1957, p 163.

This description – over 60 years later – still applies unreservedly, with the emphasis on "the arbitrators' reasoning, the grounds on which their award is based". A good reasoning of the decision increases the acceptance rate of the award. When drafting an (arbitral) award, in my experience, most of the time goes into this, leaving aside the time involved in establishing the facts relevant to the decision.

Under Article 1065(1), under d., DCCP, an arbitral award may be set aside on the ground that it fails to state reasons.[46] Initially, it was assumed in case law that setting aside on this ground was only possible in the event of a lack of reasoning and therefore not in the event of defective reasoning. The leading thought was that the court does not have the power to review the substance of an arbitral award on this ground for setting aside.[47] This jurisprudence was later clarified – in the Supreme Court's Nannini-judgment[48] – in the sense that the absence of a statement of reasons should be put on a par with the case where, although a statement of reasons was given, no cogent explanation for the decision in question could be discerned therein. In practice, regular attempts were made – mostly fruitless – to have arbitral awards set aside on the basis of the Nannini-standard. In 2006, the Supreme Court made a further clarification by ruling that the court must apply the Nannini-standard with restraint, in the sense that it should intervene in arbitral decisions only in telling cases; only if a statement of reasons is lacking, or if an arbitral award is so poorly reasoned that it must be put on a par with a wholly unreasoned award, may the court set aside this award on the ground that the arbitral award is not reasoned.[49] Since then, it must be assumed that setting aside is possible only if the arbitral award is manifestly unsoundly motivated.[50] Certainly in cases involving institutional arbitration (such as ICC, NAI and UNUM (Transport Arbitration & Mediation), formerly TAMARA, among others), this will not quickly be the case.

46 On the following, see previously G.J. Meijer & A.I.M. van Mierlo, 'Aantasting van arbitrale vonnissen', *WPNR* 2014, issue 7003, p 64 (at (d)).

47 See Supreme Court 25 February 2000, ECLI:NL:HR:2000:AA4947, *NJ* 2000/508, annotated by H.J. Snijders (*Benetton International/Eco Swiss China Time*).

48 Supreme Court 9 January 2004, ECLI:NL:HR:2004:AK8380, *NJ* 2005/190, annotated by H.J. Snijders (*Nannini/SFT Bank*).

49 Supreme Court 22 December 2006, ECLI:NL:HR:2006:AZ1593, *NJ* 2008/4, annotated by H.J. Snijders (*Kers/Rijpma*).

50 See also Snijders 2018, Article 1057, para 5.2 (p 462).

20.4.3 *The oral arbitral award*

The question arises whether, in view of the provision in Article 1057(2) DCCP, an arbitral tribunal can also render an oral award. Following Van Rossem and Cleveringa's statements on the matter, Sanders answers this question in the negative.[51] Although in practice arbitrators sometimes announce immediately after the final hearing what the operative part of the award will be, Sanders is of the opinion that the consequences of an arbitral decision remain attached to the mandatory rule of a written award.[52]

Sanders' view is not convincing. It must be admitted that a written elaboration is necessary to bring an action for setting aside. However, this in itself cannot, in my view, serve as an argument for the proposition that an oral award has no arbitral effect. I would therefore consider that arbitrators – like the courts – can indeed make an oral award, but – also like the courts – have the obligation to record this oral award in writing.[53] As to the time limit within which this written record should be made, it seems obvious to follow the Supreme Court's decision of 20 April 2018, discussed above, and to assume that this record should be made as soon as possible, preferably within a few days, but no later than two weeks after the oral award. Should this period – unexpectedly – be exceeded, this does not affect the validity of the oral award. In such a case the person seeking to bring an action for setting aside does have at least two weeks available for raising the relevant grounds.

An action for setting aside must be instituted within three months. This period can – leaving aside special periods in the event of correction and addition of an award or arbitral appeal[54] – start at two moments. The 'first term' starts after the day the award was dispatched to the parties (Article 1064a(2), first sentence, DCCP). Because the day of dispatch cannot always be ascertained accurately, the 'backstop' under Article 1058(2) DCCP is that the award is deemed to have been dispatched four weeks after the date of the award. In the case of an oral award, the first term starts in my view 'after the day of the oral award'. In my opinion, there is no need for the 'backstop'

51 P. Sanders, *Aantasting van arbitrale vonnissen* (diss. Leiden), Zwolle: W.E.J. Tjeenk Willink 1940, p 134. See also R.P. Cleveringa, *Mr. W. van Rossem's verklaring van het Nederlands Wetboek van Burgerlijke Rechtsvordering*, Zwolle: W.E.J. Tjeenk Willink 1972, Article 637, note 2 (p 1385).

52 Sanders 2001, p 134 (under B sub 1).

53 See also G.J. Meijer, in: *T&C Rv*, Article 1057 DCCP, note 3, under a, as well as Snijders 2018, Article 1057, note 2 (p 449).

54 On this, see G.J. Meijer, in: *T&C Rv*, Article 1064a DCCP, note 3, under d and e.

from Article 1058(2) DCCP, because the parties are familiar with the contents of the award immediately after it is orally pronounced. The written elaboration thereof is not important in this respect.

If the parties have agreed to make use of the provision of Article 1058(1), under b., DCCP (i.e. deposit of the award with the registry of the district court) this possibility of setting aside shall expire three months after the deposit of the award.

The second time limit applies in case there is a so called condemnatory arbitral award. This period starts to run when this award, provided with the leave for enforcement as referred to in Article 1062 DCCP, is served on the other party. In the case of an oral award, it seems to me that the interim relief judge of the district court of the district in which the place of arbitration is located will grant such leave only after the written elaboration of the oral award has been submitted to him together with the application for leave to enforce.

The fact that arbitrators can make oral decisions – with a subsequent determination in a written elaboration – is already evident from a 2010 Supreme Court ruling:[55]

> "However, to the extent that the arbitrators have made decisions at the hearing, or the parties have reached agreements or recognized the opposing party's contentions as correct, it follows from the nature of the mandate accepted by the arbitrators that they are indeed bound, at the request of the parties or one of them, to still record those decisions, agreements or recognitions in a written report. This applies even if not expressly agreed between the litigants and the arbitrators."

It cannot be inferred from this legal consideration of the Supreme Court that a decision on the main claim could not be made orally. In my opinion, the consideration is formulated in such a general way that it includes the possibility of an oral award in arbitration. This does not alter the fact that certainly in case of a condemnatory award a written award is generally preferable, precisely with a view to its enforcement.

55 Supreme Court 29 January 2010, ECLI:NL:HR:2010:BK2007, para 3.5.2, *NJ* 2011/270, annotated by H.J. Snijders (*Van Wassenaer c.s./Knowsley*). This paragraph of law is also expressly referred to by G.J. Meijer, in: *T&C Rv*, Article 1057 DCCP, note 3, under a.

The recognition of the possibility of giving an oral arbitral award does not mean that the 'fence is down' in arbitration law. Here too an oral award is an exception, which should only be used if there is a sufficiently compelling reason for it, such as an urgent interest in obtaining a decision.

20.4.4 Daily practice?

The oral arbitral award appeared in various arbitration schemes in earlier times. For instance, Sanders refers to an apparent regulation at the Arbitration Tribunal for the Flower Bulb Trade, as well as Article 20(13) of the Statutes of the Arbitration Council for Construction Companies.[56] If I am not mistaken, both these regulations now no longer exist. The 2015 Arbitration Regulations of the Arbitration Tribunal for the Flower Bulb Trade, in Article 21, only recognizes the possibility of the written award, while the 2016 Arbitration Regulations for the Council of Arbitration for the Construction Industry, in Article 14(12), still recognizes the possibility of an oral award for urgent disputes (whereby the reference to Article 12 of these Rules sees to, as I understand it, a written record of the oral award):

> "If possible and expedient, at the sole discretion of the Arbitral Tribunal, the Arbitral Tribunal shall make an oral award as early as the day of the oral hearing or at a time to be determined by the Arbitral Tribunal, without prejudice to the provisions of Article 12 of these Rules."

Since the beginning of 2018, Article 78(5) of the KNVB Arbitration Regulations has expressly provided for the possibility of rendering an oral award.[57] The text of this is largely based on the provisions of the former Article 30p DCCP. With effect from 1 January 2019, based on the experience gained by the College of Arbitrators of the KNVB in 2018 and in response to the Supreme Court decision of 20 April 2018 discussed above, this provision has been somewhat amended in parts and reads, as far as currently relevant:

> "In the event that there is such an urgent interest in a ruling that a (full) written elaboration thereof cannot be awaited, the Arbitration Board may issue an oral award at or after the hearing. Contrary to paragraph 3 of this Article, the oral award shall consist of the decision and the (main) grounds for it. The Arbitration Board shall prepare a written elaboration of the oral award in accordance with(3)

56 Sanders 2001, p 134 (under B sub. 1). See also A.J. van den Berg, R. van Delden & H.J. Snijders, *Arbitration Law*, Zwolle: W.E.J. Tjeenk Willink 1992, no 7.11.

57 For the record, I mention that I was closely involved in the adaptation of these arbitration rules.

of this Article, which shall also contain the measure for decision-making. The written elaboration shall mention as the date of pronouncement of the award the day on which the oral award was rendered and the explicit note that it concerns the written elaboration of the award already rendered orally, stating the date on which this written elaboration was established. It shall be signed by the arbitrators and a copy made available to the parties within two weeks after the oral award in the manner provided for in Article 14 of these Rules. (...)."

The provision in Article 78(5) of the KNVB Arbitration Regulations was included at the time for, for example, cases playing towards the end of the transfer period (the so-called *transfer window*). In making the oral award, the measure for decision-making – *'amiable compositeurs'* – is also mentioned. This decision criterion, set out in Article 71 of the KNVB Arbitration Regulations, is then reflected in the written elaboration. After all, this elaboration is done in accordance with the provisions of Article 78 (3) of the KNVB Arbitration Rules, and in this, under d., the decision criterion is mentioned explicitly. As far as I can tell, the KNVB Arbitration Committee has made only a few oral awards.

Meanwhile, the NAI has also 'moved on' somewhat and opened in its Arbitration Rules 2024 the possibility of an oral award in Emergency arbitration. Although not entirely comparable, a similar possibility of an oral decision exists on the basis of Article B3(7) of the Arbitration Rules 2024 for the so-called Challenge Chamber of the challenge Committee handling challenge requests as referred to in Article 23 of the Arbitration Rules 2024 and Appendix B.[58]

For 'regular' proceedings, the requirement of a written award still applies. As regards to emergency arbitration, Article C8(2)-(5) of the NAI Arbitration Rules 2024 provides, more or less in the same way as in the KNVB Arbitration Regulations and (now) Article 29a DCCP, the following:

58 Article B3(7) reads as follows: "Without prejudice to any provision of applicable mandatory arbitration law, the Challenge Chamber may issue an oral decision during or following the oral hearing if there is such urgency that a full written elaboration of the decision cannot be awaited. The oral decision must state both the decision and the main reasons of the decision. With due observance of the provisions of(6), a full written elaboration of the oral decision will be made available to the parties as soon as possible and in any event within two weeks of the oral decision. The written elaboration must state the date of the oral decision as well as the date on which the written elaboration of that decision is set."

"2. Without prejudice to any provision of applicable mandatory law, the arbitral tribunal may make an oral award during or following the hearing if there is such urgency that a full written elaboration of the award cannot be awaited.
3. The award referred to in paragraph 2, constitutes an award, to which the provisions of Section Five and Section Six of the Rules apply, it being understood that, in derogation of the provisions of Article 50 of the Rules, the award only needs to contain the requirements referred to in (e), (g), (h) and (i).
4. As soon as possible, but in any case within two weeks of the oral award, as referred to in paragraph 2, with due observance of the requirements set forth in Article 49 (3) and Article 50 (1) (a) to (i) inclusive of the Rules, a complete written elaboration of the oral award is to be made available to the parties in the manner provided for in Article 49 and Article 52 of the Rules.
5. The written elaboration must state the date of the oral award as well as the date on which the written elaboration of that award is set."

20.5 Closing remarks

Arbitral dispute resolution at the Netherlands Arbitration Institute ('NAI') manifests itself in high quality arbitral awards, with the support the arbitrators receive from the NAI staff being of great value. The NAI kindly sees to it that the arbitral tribunal renders an arbitral award with diligence. One of the arguments in favor of arbitration is that of speed; an arbitral decision generally comes more quickly than a judgment.[59]

In 2019, in a contribution to the volume "*Going Dutch: ADR in Nederland, in het bijzonder bij het NAI*" on the occasion of the 70th anniversary of the Netherlands Arbitration Institute NAI, I advocated a prudent introduction of the possibility of oral arbitral awards also within the NAI Rules of Arbitration.[60] Back then I wrote, as far as currently relevant:

It would, especially in cases where – in terms of the KNVB's Arbitration Regulations – 'there is such an urgent interest in a ruling that a (full) written elaboration of it cannot be awaited', be an asset if the NAI Arbitration Rules also contain a provision stating in so many words that arbitrators may also render an award orally, without prejudice to the obligation to

59 See: A.I.M. van Mierlo, 'Het mondelinge arbitraal vonnis', in: C.J.M. Klaassen, G.J. Meijer & C.L. Schleijpen (eds), *Going Dutch: ADR in Nederland, in het bijzonder bij het NAI (Onderneming & Recht no 113)*, Deventer: Wolters Kluwer 2019, p 595-620.

60 Along the same lines Snijders 2018, General Introduction, note 1.8.2 (p 54).

lay down the award in writing in – depending on the circumstances of the case – an official report or a written elaboration.

> "As long as the NAI Arbitration Rules do not contain an express provision as advocated above, I expect that in NAI context the written award will remain standard practice. Whether this is desirable in every case is doubtful; the possibility of making an oral award offers a solution precisely in those cases where waiting for a written award takes too much time. *Time for a change!*"

It is with some joy to note that the NAI has picked up on the signal and included the possibility of oral awards in its 2024-Rules in the context of emergency arbitration (and in challenge proceedings). Now it is up to the legislator to act, for example in the form of a provision similar to Article 29a DCCP in a new Article 1057a DCCP. Let's keep our fingers crossed!

CHAPTER 21

FROM SETTLEMENT TO AWARD: CHALLENGES AND OPPORTUNITIES OF CONSENT AWARDS

Pietro Ortolani[1]

21.1 Introduction

Pursuant to Article 51(1) of the 2024 NAI Arbitration Rules, if the parties to an NAI arbitration reach a settlement during the course of the proceedings, they may jointly request the arbitral tribunal to record the terms of such a settlement in an award, which is commonly referred to as 'consent award', 'award by consent' or 'award on agreed terms'. This practice of recording a settlement agreement in an arbitral award is far from new: already the Greek rhetorician Isocrates mentions it twice, in *Trapeziticus*[2] and in *Against Callimachus*.[3] Isocrates explains how the parties to a legal dispute found a settlement and decide to appoint an arbitrator, not to resolve the case, but simply to record their agreement. According to Isocrates, the purpose of this practice is to ensure that the parties will 'fulfil their obligations'[4] and to avoid being exposed to future disputes.[5]

Despite its long tradition, the consent award is still a subject of debate. On the one hand, transforming a settlement agreement into an enforceable title can be beneficial, especially in situations where the parties' future compliance with the agreement is doubtful.[6] On the other hand, it is some-

1 P. (Pietro) Ortolani is a full Professor of digital conflict resolution at the Radboud University, Nijmegen (the Netherlands).

2 Isocrates, 'Trapeziticus', 19, in: L. van Hook (ed), *Isocrates Volume 3*, Harvard: Loeb Classical Library 1945, p 210-251 (hereafter Isocrates 1945a).

3 Isocrates, 'Tegen Callimachus', 10, in: L. van Hook (ed), *Isocrates Volume 3*, Harvard: Loeb Classical Library 1945, p 252-297 (hereafter Isocrates 1945b); see also Y. Kryvoi & D. Davydenko, 'Consent Awards in International Arbitration: From Settlement to Enforcement', *Brooklyn Journal of International Law* (40) 2015, p 827-868, 829; D. Roebuck, 'Best to Reconcile: Mediation and Arbitration in the Ancient Greek World', *Arbitration: The Journal of the Chartered Institute of Arbitrators* (66) 2000, p 275-287.

4 Isocrates 1945a, p 19.

5 Isocrates 1945b, p 10.

6 H.J. Snijders, in: *GS Burgerlijke Rechtsvordering*, Article 1069 Rv (online, updated 1 May 2018); E. Sussman, 'The New York Convention Through a Mediation Prism',

times unclear to what extent the mechanisms that domestic and international law create for the enforcement of an arbitral award can be used for a consent award.[7] This chapter will investigate the topic from a comparative law perspective, but with a specific focus on the NAI arbitration and mediation rules and on the Netherlands.

The remainder of this contribution consists of six paragraphs. Paragraph 21.2 describes the reasons why the parties may want to record their settlement agreement into an arbitral award. Paragraph 21.3 addresses the scenario where the parties reach a settlement after an arbitration has been initiated between them. Paragraph 21.4, in turn, considers the different hypothetical situation where the settlement is reached before the beginning of the arbitration, and arbitral proceedings are therefore initiated for the sole purpose of obtaining a consent award. Subsequently, paragraph 21.5 describes some of the obstacles that may exist for consent awards at the setting aside and at the recognition and enforcement stage. Paragraph 21.6 reflects on the interplay between the practice of consent awards and the enforcement of mediated settlement agreements under the Singapore Convention. Finally, paragraph 21.7 concludes.

21.2 Why go from settlement to award?

Generally speaking, resolving a dispute through a settlement can offer certain advantages, compared to an adjudicative decision (such as an arbitral award, or a court judgment). First of all, with a settlement, the parties can save time and costs;[8] especially in international commercial relations, both litigation and arbitration require significant resources, which could be partially spared if a settlement is found. A settlement also enhances predictability: with an

Dispute Resolution Magazine (15) 2009, p 10-13; E. Sussman, 'Final Step: Issues In Enforcing The Mediation Settlement Agreement', in: A.W. Rovine (ed), *Contemporary Issues in International Arbitration and Mediation: The Fordham Papers*, Leiden: Brill 2008, p 343-359; B.L. Steele, 'Enforcing International Commercial Mediation Agreements Under the New York Convention', *U.C.L.A. Law Review* (34) 2007, p 1385-1412.

7 For this reason, the consent award is dubbed a "legal dogmatic *monstrum*" by H.J. Snijders, in: *GS Burgerlijke Rechtsvordering*, Article 1069 Rv (online, updated 1 May 2018).

8 The growing costs of arbitration for the parties are demonstrated by the popularity of third-party funding: L. Bench Nieuwveld & V.S. Sahani, *Third-Party Funding in International Arbitration*, Deventer: Wolters Kluwer 2017; J. von Goeler, *Third-Party Funding in International Arbitration and its Impact on Procedure*, Deventer: Wolters Kluwer 2016.

agreement, the parties end their dispute without being exposed to protracted uncertainty, and the risk of a potentially negative decision is eliminated. Furthermore, settlement protects the reputation of the parties and avoids the risk of exposure of delicate information to external observers.[9] Additionally, if the parties reach a settlement, they may be able to restore their commercial relationship and resume business in the future; conversely, the same outcome may be less likely after years of adversarial arbitral proceedings.[10]

Despite these many advantages, settlement has a significant potential drawback: it typically cannot be enforced directly the way an arbitral award can. Hence, if one of the parties fails to comply with the terms of the settlement agreement, the other party must initiate court or arbitration proceedings in order to obtain a title and gain access to enforcement. There are numerous possible reasons why the possibility of a swift enforcement is crucial. For instance, the settlement agreement may impose obligations that the parties must perform over a certain (potentially long) period of time. In this case, it is possible that the financial situation of the parties or the general conditions of the market will change over time; for these reasons, a settlement that the parties had initially accepted may later be deemed undesirable by one of them. In other situations, a party may agree to a settlement in bad faith, without ever having a real intention to comply with its terms. Obviously, the possibility of enforcement is a strong incentive against this type of bad faith behavior. Even when it is not used in practice, thus, enforceability of settlement agreements via an award can play a key role as a 'nudge', discouraging abuses of the system.[11]

In specific situations, there may also be additional reasons why the possibility of direct enforcement of a settlement agreement is desirable. For instance, whenever one of the parties to a dispute is a State or an entity of a State,[12] the signature of an arbitrator can have a 'political' value. More spe-

9 In principle, arbitration may be conducted confidentially. However, the possibility of divulgation of delicate information cannot be entirely ruled out, especially in the context of setting aside or recognition and enforcement proceedings.

10 According to some authors, arbitration is becoming increasingly adversarial: V.K. Rajah, 'W(h)ither adversarial commercial dispute resolution?', *Arbitration International* (33) 2017, p 17-34.

11 For a comparative analysis on the role of nudging in inducing party compliance see P. Ortolani & D. Shestowsky, 'Disputant Psychology in International Arbitration: What Can a Comparison with Domestic Arbitration Teach Us?', in: T. Cole (ed), *The Roles of Psychology in International Arbitration*, Deventer: Deventer Kluwer 2017, p 113-142.

12 This situation occurs frequently in international arbitration. In 2023, for instance, 16% of new ICC arbitrations involved a state or a state entity: International Chamber of Commerce, 'ICC Dispute Resolution 2023 Statistics', p 6.

cifically, public criticisms concerning the decision to settle a dispute can be easier to deflect if the agreement is confirmed by an arbitral award.[13]

Given the numerous advantages that enforceability of settlement agreements brings about, it is not surprising that the parties try to achieve this result through consent awards, i.e. arbitral awards that incorporate the terms of the settlement agreement. The following paragraph discusses the feasibility of this technique in the situation where the parties have already commenced an arbitration, but have subsequently managed to resolve their dispute consensually.

21.3 Settlement reached after the commencement of arbitration

In some cases, the law of the seat expressly authorizes the parties and the arbitrator(s) to record the settlement agreement in an arbitral award. When the *lex arbitri* expressly acknowledges the possibility of a consent award, it typically clarifies that the tribunal has the possibility to issue the award if the parties request it, but is not under an obligation to do so. It is also commonly provided that, unlike what happens with a 'ordinary' awards, consent awards must not contain a reasoning. A good example is found in Articles 30 and 31 of the UNCITRAL Model Law on International Commercial Arbitration: these provisions empower the tribunal to issue a consent award on the parties' request, and excludes the need to state the reasons on which the award is based. In the Netherlands, Article 1069 of the Dutch Code of Civil Procedure (DCCP) is essentially similar, and it also specifies that a consent award can only be set aside if it is incompatible with public policy. The same approach is followed by many other arbitration statutes, such as the English Arbitration Act 1996.[14]

Similar provisions are contained in many arbitration rules, such as the aforementioned Article 51(1) of the 2024 NAI Arbitration Rules, Article 36(1) of the 2021 UNCITRAL Arbitration Rules or Article 33 of the 2021 ICC Rules. Typically, these rules rest on two main cornerstones. First, a consent award can only be made if the parties request it unanimously; in the absence of such a request, the tribunal should simply close the proceedings, without rendering any award on the merits. Second, the issuance of a

13 N. Blackaby, C. Partasides & A. Redfern, *Redfern and Hunter on International Arbitration*, Oxford: Oxford University Press 2023, para 9.36.

14 Arbitration Act 1996, para 51.

consent award for the tribunal is a possibility, but never an obligation: the arbitrators remain free to deny the issuance of a consent award, normally without the need to state reasons.[15] Interestingly, this has not always been the case: in the past, some arbitration rules obliged the tribunal to make a consent award, if requested by the parties. For instance, Article 17 of the 1988 ICC Rules required the tribunal to issue a consent award upon the parties' request.[16]

Although the tendency to regulate consent awards is now widespread, not all national laws follow it. In the United States, for instance, the Federal Arbitration Act (FAA) does not regulate the case where the parties ask the tribunal to make a consent award. Nevertheless, even if the *lex arbitri* is silent on this point, the possibility to record the parties' agreement in an award should not necessarily be always excluded. For instance, in the United States, courts tend to qualify a consent award as a valid arbitral award, despite the lack of guidance in the FAA.[17]

In practice, the possibility that the parties will find a settlement and that their agreement will be recorded in an award is not rare. Only in 2023, consent awards were issued in 32 arbitrations administered by the ICC, out of

15 Article 1069(1) DCCP.

16 Marchisio's historical investigation on the regulation of the consent award in the ICC Rules demonstrates that, in the 1927 and 1933 versions of the Rules, the tribunal was asked to review the parties' settlement agreement mainly for the purpose of ensuring accuracy and correcting ambiguous wordings, rather than to review the legality of the settlement and its compatibility with public policy. See Giacomo Marchisio, 'A comparative analysis of consent awards: accepting their reality', *Arbitration International* (32) 2016, p 334 with reference to ICC Document No 5747, Arbitration Committee, 19 December 1935.

17 See e.g. *McGuire v. Safeguard Metals, LLC*, No 23-CV-05874-SVW-MRW, 2023 WL 6386497 (C.D. Cal. Sept. 28, 2023); *Actors' Equity Ass'n v. Paradise Square Prod. Servs. Inc.*, No 22 CIV. 7325 (PAE), 2023 WL 3293577 (S.D.N.Y. May 5, 2023); *Teamsters Loc. 630 v. W. Cent. Produce*, No 221CV09294MWFJPRX, 2022 WL 3636167 (C.D. Cal. May 26, 2022); *New York City & Vicinity Dist. Council of Carpenters v. J.M.R. Concrete Corp.*, No 16-CV-711 (ENV) (ST), 2018 WL 2078476 (E.D.N.Y. Feb. 26, 2018); *Trustees for Mason Tenders Dist. Council Welfare Fund v. Golden Dev. & Constr. Corp., No 15 CIV. 769 (GBD)*, 2018 L 2316632 (S.D.N.Y. May 7, 2018*); S.C. Johnson & Son, Inc. v. Ghersy Grp. Integrated Commc'ns, LLC*, No 17-22380-CIV, 2017 WL 7796162 (S.D. Fla. Sept. 25, 2017), report and recommendation adopted, No 17-CV-22380, 2017 WL 7798660 (S.D. Fla. Nov. 13, 2017); *Country-Wide Ins. Co. v. Montero*, 153 A.D.3d 816, 817, 61 N.Y.S.3d 109 (N.Y. App. Div. 2017); *LVGV, LLC v. Nat'l Cash Servs., Inc.*, No SACV1700012CJCDFMX, 2017 WL 8186770 (C.D. Cal. Apr. 7, 2017); *Trustees of the New York City Dist. Council of Carpenters Pension Fund v. NYC Constr. Serv. Inc.*, No 1:15-CV-3813-GHW, 2016 WL 894551 (S.D.N.Y. Mar. 8, 2016); *New Jersey Bldg. Laborers Statewide Ben. Funds & Trustees Thereof v. Demco Inc.*, No CIV. 2:15-2919 KM, 2015 WL 4640642 (D.N.J. Aug. 3, 2015).

a total of 520 awards approved by the ICC Court in that year.[18] The same is also true for investor-State disputes: according to the latest statistics of the International Centre for the Settlement of Investment Disputes (ICSID), 35% of all cases under the ICSID Convention or the ICSID Additional Facility Rules are settled or otherwise discontinued, and 11% of those settled or discontinued cases result in settlements recorded in arbitral awards at the request of the parties.[19]

Of course, the fact that arbitration rules and national arbitration statutes allow the arbitral tribunal to make a consent award does not say much about how the arbitrators will make use of their power, and more generally interpret their role with regard to settlement. In practice, different approaches are likely to exist, depending on an arbitrators' background and legal culture. For instance, arbitrators with a continental European background may be more proactive in encouraging and facilitating the settlement, while arbitrators coming from common law systems may be less willing to do so, in order to avoid an appearance of partiality or bias.[20] Some arbitration rules try to harmonize these different approaches, giving specific guidance to tribunals as to how the settlement may (or may not)

---

18 International Chamber of Commerce, 'ICC Dispute Resolution 2023 Statistics', p 15.

19 International Centre for Settlement of Investment Disputes, 'The ICSID Caseload – Statistics (Issue 2024-2)', p 12-14.

20 The 2024 IBA Guidelines on Conflicts of Interest in International Arbitration expressly acknowledge this problem: in the explanation to General Standard 4, it is observed that 'the concept of the Arbitral Tribunal assisting the parties in reaching a settlement of their dispute in the course of the arbitration proceedings is well-established in some jurisdictions, but not in others'. The Guidelines also try to devise a solution, requiring the agreement of the parties. More specifically, pursuant to General Standard 4(d) of the Guidelines, 'An arbitrator may assist the parties in reaching a settlement of the dispute, through conciliation, mediation, or otherwise, at any stage of the proceedings. However, before doing so, the arbitrator should receive an express agreement by the parties that acting in such a manner shall not disqualify the arbitrator from continuing to serve as arbitrator. Such express agreement shall be considered to be an effective waiver of any potential conflict of interest that may arise from the arbitrator's participation in such a process, or from information that the arbitrator may learn in the process. If the assistance by the arbitrator does not lead to the final settlement of the case, the parties remain bound by their waiver. However, consistent with General Standard 2(a) and notwithstanding such agreement, the arbitrator shall resign if, as a consequence of the arbitrator's involvement in the settlement process, the arbitrator develops doubts as to the arbitrator's ability to remain impartial or independent in the future course of the arbitration.' Thus, even if the Guidelines point to the parties' consent as a way to pre-empt future arbitrator challenges, they do acknowledge the risk that being exposed to information during the settlement attempt will prevent the arbitrator from remaining impartial or independent.

be facilitated. In particular, according to the ICC Case Management Techniques,[21] the arbitrators may encourage the parties to consider settlement of all or part of the dispute either by negotiation or through any form of amicable dispute resolution methods such as, for example, mediation under the ICC Mediation Rules; however, the arbitrators can only take the initiative to facilitate settlement if all of the parties and members of the tribunal agree to it.

The formal structure of a consent award is different from the one of an 'ordinary' award. Commonly, a consent award describes the facts of the case, the positions of the parties, and the procedural history. The award typically acknowledges that the parties have reached a settlement and, therefore, closes the proceedings. In the same award, the tribunal can also rule on the costs of the arbitration. The settlement agreement itself is normally enclosed as an attachment to the award, and the terms of the settlement are incorporated by reference into the award. In other words, by referring to the settlement agreement that the parties have reached and drafted, the arbitrators transform that agreement into a part of the award.[22]

A tribunal must, first and foremost, ensure the validity and enforceability of any awards it renders.[23] This is the main reason why, under most national laws and arbitration rules, a tribunal can refuse to issue a consent award. As paragraph 21.5 will analyze in further detail, there may be different reasons why the arbitrator(s) may think that a consent award would

21 Appendix IV to the 2021 ICC Rules.

22 See ICC Final Award No 16426/2011, cited in Marchisio 2016, p 335. However, another method is also possible: in some cases, the tribunal only decides on the costs and closes the proceedings, without specifying that the settlement is incorporated in the award. If this is the case, it is probably impossible to obtain recognition and enforcement of the settlement under the New York Convention; sometimes, however, the parties have no interest in this sense, if they have already complied with the terms of the settlement before the issuance of the award. In this case, the main added value of having an award is not enforceability, but the possibility of having a dismissal with prejudice, precluding future lawsuits concerning the same subject-matter: this happened, for instance, in ICC Final Award No 12656/2006, cited by Marchisio 2016, p 336. This, however, is only possible if the award has *res judicata* effects. In the Netherlands, these effects seem to only derive from an arbitral award where the tribunal has actually adjudicated the dispute, and not from consent awards: Amsterdam Court of Appeal 8 April 2014, ECLI:NL:GHAMS:2014:4228, r.o. 3.4; Supreme Court 16 October 2015, ECLI:NL:HR:2015:3092, r.o. 3.5.1-3.5.3. Similar doubts have existed for a long time on other legal systems, such as Italy: see G. Fabbrini, 'L'accertamento privato', *Rivista Trimestrale di Diritto e Procedura Civile* (13) 1960, p 631-662. This, however, does not mean that the settlement agreement is not binding between the parties.

23 ICC Case Management Techniques, Appendix IV to the 2021 ICC Rules, point (h)(2).

not be enforceable. If, for instance, the settlement agreement includes an anticompetitive clause (such as a market sharing agreement), the courts of EU Member States would probably refuse recognition and enforcement on public policy grounds, as required by the Court of Justice of the European Union since *Eco Swiss*.[24]

On the basis of the fact that national laws and arbitration rules give tribunals a wide discretion in deciding whether to issue a consent award or not, it would apparently seem reasonable to assume that the arbitrators will check the contents of the parties' agreement thoroughly, to determine whether some element of the settlement may be regarded as incompatible with public policy or mandatory provisions of the applicable law. However, a 'reality check' is in order: in the practice of arbitration, the arbitrators may not always have all the information necessary to make such assessment.[25] The problem is particularly evident in the case of a 'sham' arbitration, i.e. a dispute simulated between the parties. In other words, sometimes the parties may have no actual dispute, but only use arbitration to obtain an enforceable title to use for other (sometimes illicit) purposes. For example, in an arbitration seated in London, a sole arbitrator issued a consent award, ordering one of the parties to make a payment in favour of the other one. However, at the recognition and enforcement stage, evidence surfaced that no real dispute had ever existed between the parties. The debtor, in fact, was a company approaching insolvency, and the award had been used to reduce the assets of the company before the declaration of insolvency.[26] In these cases, of course, the tribunal should refuse to issue a consent award. More generally, the issuance of a consent award should be denied, if the facts of the case suggest that the parties do not genuinely want to resolve a dispute, but are trying to use arbitration for fraudulent purposes. However, depending on the behavior of the parties and the contents of the file, it might be difficult for the arbitrator(s) to understand upfront that the parties are simulating the dispute.

---

24 CJEU, C-126/97, *Eco Swiss China Time Ltd v Benetton International NV*, ECLI:EU:C:1999:269.

25 W.W. Park, 'Arbitrator Integrity', in: M. Waibel et al (eds), The Backlash against Investment Arbitration, Deventer: Kluwer 2010, p 189-251, 246 with reference to *Gulf Petro Trading Co., Inc. v. Nigerian National Petroleum Corp.*, 512 F.3d 742 (5th Cir. 2008).

26 *Société Viva Chemical (Europe) NV v APTD*, Paris Court of Appeal, 9 April 2009, 07/17769, cited in Marchisio 2016, p 342. See also *Yukos Capital S.A.R.L. (Luxembourg) v. OAO Tomskneft VNK (Russian Federation)*, Federal Arbitrazh Court, District of Tomsk, A67-1438/2010, 7 July 2010, in: A.J. van den Berg (ed), *Yearbook Commercial Arbitration XXXV*, Deventer: Kluwer 2010, p 435.

21.4 Settlement reached after mediation and recorded in an arbitral award

Interesting questions arise when the parties have reached an agreement in the context of mediation, and wish to have the terms of their settlement recorded into an arbitral award, even if they never agreed to use arbitration for the genuine purpose of resolving their dispute.

Arbitration and mediation are two distinct procedures with different (and even, to a certain extent, irreconcilable) characteristics.[27] Arbitration is a form of private adjudication governed by due process and adversariality; mediation, by contrast, aims at facilitating the agreement of the parties. The mediator, unlike the arbitrator, is allowed to communicate with one of the parties without involving the other one, and can use techniques such as 'caucusing', which would generally not be acceptable in arbitration. Furthermore, in the case of 'rule-based mediation', the mediator may reveal his/her opinion about the merits of the case during the procedure; arbitrators, instead, should never state their opinions on the merits of the dispute whilst the arbitral proceedings are still pending. Furthermore, arbitrators should base their assessment of the facts of the case on the evidence that the parties submit; a mediator, instead, should help the parties find a settlement, which may well not hinge on an objective assessment of the facts on the basis of evidence. The behaviour of the parties is also significantly different in the two procedures. In mediation, a party participating in good faith may wish not to present all possible legal arguments in their favour, e.g. because doing so would only exacerbate the conflict by enumerating the different ways in which the other party allegedly disregarded their obligations. In arbitration, instead, the parties are expected to present all legal arguments that are relevant for their case, and may face consequences such as estoppel/preclusion if they fail to promptly do so.

Despite doubts concerning the use of consent awards in mediation, many sets of mediation rules expressly acknowledge the possibility to appoint the mediator as an arbitrator, if the parties have found a settlement during the mediation, for the sole purpose of making a consent award. For instance, this is the case of the NAI Mediation Rules: under Article 8, "(t) he parties and the mediator may agree that the settlement agreement (...) will be laid down in an arbitral settlement award within the meaning of

27 C. Bühring-Uhle, L. Kirchhoff & G. Scherer, *Arbitration and Mediation in International Business* (Second Edition), Deventer: Kluwer 2006.

Article 1069 of the Dutch Code of Civil Procedure (…) and with due observance of Article 50 of the NAI Arbitration Rules. The agreement concluded for that purpose will also apply as an arbitration agreement, pursuant to which the mediator or an odd number of members of a panel of mediators will be appointed as the arbitrator(s) and Rotterdam, the Netherlands, will be the place of arbitration." A similar provision is included in the 2023 SCC Mediation Rules: according to Article 13, "(i)n case of settlement, the parties may, subject to the consent of the Mediator, agree to appoint the Mediator as an arbitrator and request him or her to confirm the settlement agreement in an arbitral award."

Despite the fact that some mediation rules foresee the issuance of a consent award, the arbitration law of many States is not well-suited for this purpose. In the Netherlands, Article 1069 DCCP requires that the settlement be reached during arbitral proceedings,[28] rather than before them. The UNCITRAL Model Law adopts a similar approach: according to Article 30, a consent award can be made if the parties find a settlement 'during arbitral proceedings'. In addition, doubts could be cast as to the validity of a submission agreement concluded after the settlement, at a time when the dispute no longer exists between the parties.[29] If the parties resolve the dispute through mediation before the commencement of any arbitral proceedings, provisions such as Article 1069 DCCP of Article 30 of the UNCITRAL Model Law are not directly applicable. This, in turn, raises the question of whether such a use of consent awards is allowed at all.[30]

In order to enable the use of consent awards in mediation, a less strict interpretation of the aforementioned 'during arbitral proceedings' requirement has been suggested: as Snijders argues, it could be imagined that the settlement reached during mediation is subject to a condition precedent, namely that it be subsequently recorded in an arbitral award.[31] According to this line of reasoning, the settlement is not definitive until a consent award has been made; the parties, therefore, start reaching a settlement during the mediation, but the settlement only becomes final with the consent award (and, therefore, during arbitral proceedings). This reading faces at least two objections. First, the parties who reach a settlement agreement during a mediation typically do not specify that the

28 H.J. Snijders, in: *GS Burgerlijke Rechtsvordering*, Article 1069 DCCP.

29 See Article 1020(1) DCCP and Article II(1) of the New York Convention.

30 Asser Procesrecht/Sanders, Meijer & Ernste *8* 2023/441; G.J. Meijer, in: *T&C Rv*, Article 1069 DCCP.

31 H.J. Snijders, in: *GS Burgerlijke Rechtsvordering*, Article 1069 DCCP.

issuance of a consent award is a condition precedent. In fact, a consent award is normally only an added value, but not a condition in the absence of which no settlement agreement exists. If the settlement agreement does not expressly indicate the issuance of a consent award as a condition precedent, it should generally be concluded that the agreement is subject to no condition precedent at all. Second, even if the parties have specifically indicated that their agreement is subject to the condition precedent of the issuance of a consent award, this condition is not fulfilled 'during arbitral proceedings', but only after the conclusion of the arbitration.[32]

Apart from the chronological requirements imposed by provisions such as Article 1069 DCCP or Article 30 of the UNCITRAL Model Law, the use of consent awards in the context of mediation also creates an additional problem. The fact that the parties have already found a settlement when they conclude the arbitration agreement has important consequences on the architecture of the contracts which make arbitration possible. When two or more parties agree to use arbitration, they normally wish to give a third party (the arbitrator) the power to adjudicate certain disputes between them. In this case, instead, the parties have already determined what the resolution of the dispute should be. Therefore, if the arbitration agreement is concluded after the parties have already found a settlement, the nature of the arbitration agreement itself is out of the ordinary. In turn, this special characteristic of the agreement to arbitrate has important consequences for the nature of the arbitrator's mandate. More specifically, the arbitrator receives a mandate not to adjudicate a dispute (similarly to what a judge would do), but merely to perform a notarial function, recording the settlement into an award. These unique features may raise questions at the setting aside and/or the recognition and enforcement stage, as the next paragraph will illustrate.

32 According to Ernste, Meijer and Snijders, the arbitral proceedings should be deemed to be pending until the award has become final: P.E. Ernste, *Bindend advies*, Deventer: Kluwer 2012, p 99; H.J. Snijders, *Nederlands Arbitragerecht. Algemene beschouwingen en artikelsgewijze opmerkingen bij de art. 1020-1076 RV in nationaal en internationaal perspectief*, Deventer: Wolters Kluwer 2018, p 597; Asser Procesrecht/Sanders, Meijer & Ernste *8* 2023/441. Here, the parties subject their settlement agreement to the condition precedent of the issuance of a consent award precisely because they wish to ensure that their settlement will produce the same effects as an arbitral award. Therefore, the condition precedent can only be fulfilled once the award has become binding between the parties.

21.5 Challenges at the setting aside and recognition and enforcement stages

Assuming that a consent award has been made, the most relevant practical question is whether it is valid and enforceable. In principle, there are several objections that could be raised. If one of the parties seeks recognition and enforcement outside of the seat of arbitration, these objections will typically relate to one of the grounds for refusal listed in Article V of the New York Convention, or in other treaties or national laws governing the recognition and enforcement of foreign awards. At the seat, instead, these objections may be invoked to obtain setting aside, or to resist domestic enforcement.[33] This paragraph will examine different possible objections and assess whether and how they are relevant for different types of consent awards.

a. Nature of the consent award

The first question that arises is whether the consent award is, in fact, an arbitral award at all. In principle, it could be argued that a decision issued by an arbitrator only qualifies as an award if it has the genuine purpose of adjudicating a dispute, determining whether the parties' claims should be upheld or rejected. Conversely, if the dispute is already resolved and the sole purpose of the decision is to transform a pre-existing settlement agreement into an enforceable title, the debtor could object by arguing that no dispute has been adjudicated by the tribunal, and thus no arbitral award exists *stricto sensu*.[34] In other words, the question is whether the substance of the award should prevail over its form.[35]

As mentioned above,[36] many national laws (such as Dutch law, and legislations based on the UNCITRAL Model Law) expressly allow arbitral tribunals to issue consent awards if the parties find a settlement during the arbitral proceedings. If the law expressly acknowledges this possibility, there is no doubt that a consent award qualifies as an award from the point of view of the law of the seat, despite the theoretical conundrums that this

33 See e.g. Article 1065 DCCP and Articles 34 and 36 UNCITRAL Model Law.

34 For instance, this line of reasoning has been followed in France by Cass Civ 1e 14 November 2012, *M A c Société B-C, Revue de l'Arbitrage* (2013) p 138; Cass Civ 2e, 7 October 1981.

35 *Resort Condominiums International Inc. v. Ray Bolwell and Resort Condominiums, Pty. Ltd.*, Supreme Court of Queensland, 389, 29 October 1993', in: A.J. van den Berg (ed*), Yearbook Commercial Arbitration 1995 – Volume XX, Yearbook Commercial Arbitration, Volume 20,* Alphen aan den Rijn: Kluwer Law International 1995, p 628.

36 See para 21.3 above.

type of award may raise. This, however, does not mean that courts in other states will adopt the same approach: national courts are not bound by the fact that a tribunal characterized a certain document as an award,[37] or by the fact that foreign law extends the concept of "award" to include consent awards. In light of this, even if the seat is in a state (like the Netherlands) whose law expressly states that a consent award has the same legal status and effects as any other arbitral award, the tribunal should be particularly cautious when making a consent award in cases where it is foreseeable that the enforcement may at least partially take place abroad. In such a case, it is difficult to exclude the risk that, although the consent award is an award at the seat, it will not be granted recognition and enforcement in the state where the debtor has assets because the courts of that state will consider that the consent award is not an award in the sense of e.g. Article I(2) of the New York Convention or other instruments governing the recognition and enforcement of foreign awards. Fortunately, however, even in states where the national law does not contain such a friendly regulation of consent awards, courts have recently dismissed this type of objection, holding that a consent award is an arbitral award for the purposes of the New York Convention, as long as the parties' intention to crystallize their agreement in the form of an award is clear;[38] this is, for example, the case in the United States.[39]

More complex problems arise in the different case where the settlement agreement is reached before the arbitration is pending. In this case, as illustrated above, the provisions of law governing the making of a consent award may not be directly applicable, since the settlement is not reached "during arbitral proceedings". Therefore, there is a double risk: apart from the risk that foreign courts will not regard the consent award as a real

37 Supreme Court 15 June 2018, ECLI:NL:HR:2018:918, *TvA* 2018/77: the enforcement authorities of the requested state are free to perform a *de novo* assessment of the legal nature of the document that the tribunal defined as "arbitral award".

38 See e.g. *Nuovopignone International Srl v. Cargo Motors Private Limited & Anr.*, High Court of Delhi, O.M.P.(EFA)(COMM.) 11/2021, 30 May 2023', in: S.W. Schill (ed), *ICCA Yearbook Commercial Arbitration 2024 – Volume XLIX, Yearbook Commercial Arbitration, Volume 49*, Alphen aan den Rijn: Kluwer Law International 2024.

39 *Albtelecom SH.A v. UNIFI Communications, Inc.*, United States District Court, Southern District of New York, 16 Civ. 9001 (PAE), 22 March 2021, in: S.W. Schill (ed), *ICCA Yearbook Commercial Arbitration 2021 – Volume XLVI, Yearbook Commercial Arbitration, Volume 46*, Alpen aan den Rijn: Kluwer Law International 2021, p 513-517; *Transocean Offshore Gulf of Guinea VII Limited et al. v. Erin Energy Corporation (f/k/a CAMAC Energy Inc.)*, United States District Court, Southern District of Texas, Houston Division, Civil Action No H-17-2623, 12 March 2018, in: S.W. Schill (ed), *ICCA Yearbook Commercial Arbitration 2018 – Volume XLIII, Yearbook Commercial Arbitration, Volume 43*, Alphen aan den Rijn: Kluwer Law International 2018, p 722-724.

award, there is also the risk that the courts at the seat of arbitration will decline enforcement as well.[40]

b. Invalidity of the agreement to arbitrate

Depending on the circumstances, the award debtor could potentially argue that no valid agreement to arbitrate exists. More specifically, this ground for refusal may be relevant in cases where the parties reached a settlement before agreeing to arbitrate (e.g. in mediation), and subsequently entered into a submission agreement for the sole purpose of obtaining a consent award, as discussed in paragraph 21.4 above. Similar issues may arise if the parties find an agreement during the course of an arbitration (and thus, already in the presence of a hypothetically valid agreement to arbitrate), but the settlement deals with subject matters that were not covered by the original agreement to arbitrate.[41] This, in turn, would require an expansion of the agreement to arbitrate *ratione materiae*, in order to allow the tribunal to issue a consent award concerning matters that were not originally subject to the tribunal's jurisdiction. In these circumstances, it could be argued that the conclusion of the submission agreement, or the enlargement of the original arbitration agreement, take place at a moment when the dispute no longer exists between the parties, thus leading to the invalidity of the agreement. In order to prevent this type of problem at the recognition and enforcement stage, the parties can specify in their settlement agreement that the settlement does not become final, until it is recorded in a consent award. In this case, the award creditor could argue that the dispute still existed, when the parties entered into or modified their arbitration agreement for the purpose of obtaining a consent award.

c. Absence of reasoning

A significant obstacle for a consent award is the fact that, normally, it does not contain any statement of the reasons on which it is based. In some states, this problem is resolved by providing that a consent award, unlike other awards, does not need to contain any reasoning: this is the case of the Netherlands, as clarified in Article 1069(2)(b) DCCP. As already explained, however, this does not guarantee that the same approach will be taken in other jurisdictions.

40 *Michael D. Castro v. Tri Marine Fish Company LLC et al.*, United States Court of Appeals, Ninth Circuit, No 17-35703, 27 February 2019, in: S.W. Schill (ed), *ICCA Yearbook Commercial Arbitration 2019 – Volume XLIV, Yearbook Commercial Arbitration, Volume 44*, Alphen aan den Rijn: Kluwer Law International 2019, p 800-804.

41 See also sub-paragraph d below.

As for the New York Convention, it is unclear whether any of the grounds for refusal of Article V may be invoked to resist the recognition and enforcement of a consent award, on the basis of the fact that it does not contain any reasoning. None of the grounds of Article V mention reasoning expressly; for this reason, many national courts allow the enforcement of unreasoned award, even if their national law requires that awards made in the territory of that state contain reasons.[42] By contrast, other courts have occasionally denied enforcement due to lack of reasoning, typically on grounds of public policy.[43]

d. Ultra Petita

Another possible objection against a consent award is that the tribunal exceeded its mandate. This can happen, in particular, if the settlement concerns rights that were not the subject-matter of the dispute that initially arose between the parties. In practice, this is far from rare: in order to find a settlement and resolve a dispute, two parties may make concessions to each other regarding rights that have nothing to do with the original dispute. Let us suppose, for instance, that S (a steel company) and B (a construction company) enter into a contract for the construction of a new steel factory. The contract contains an arbitration clause. Once the construction is completed, S refuses to pay a part of the price. B, then, commences arbitration against S. S objects to B's claim, arguing that the factory has not been built in accordance with the project. However, during the arbitral proceedings, the parties reach a settlement. B waives the right to receive the remaining payment. S, in turn, agrees to supply B with steel, to be used in other construction projects in the next two years. It is undeniable that, if the parties had not found a settlement agreement, the tribunal could have never devised such a solution for the dispute. More specifically, the tribunal could only have determined whether S should have paid the rest of the price to B; the arbitration agreement, however, would not have allowed the tribunal to force the parties to enter into a new contract for the supply of steel. Hence, it is clear that the settlement agreement goes beyond the limits of the original agreement to arbitrate. The question arises,

---

42 Cour d'Appel, Nancy, 29 January 1958, *Revue de l'Arbitrage* (1958), p 123; Oberlandesgericht. Düsseldorf, 15 December 2009, <https://newyorkconvention1958.org/index.php?lvl=notice_display&id=306>; Cour d'Appel, Brussels, 24 January 1997 and Tribunal de Première Instance, Brussels, 25 January 1996, in: A.J. van den Berg (ed), *ICCA Yearbook Commercial Arbitration 2021 – Volume XXII*, Deventer: Kluwer 1997, p 643.

43 *Mut. Shipping Corp. v. Bayshore Shipping Co., The Montan* [1985] 1 Lloyd's Rep. 189 (English Ct. App.) (unreasoned award contrary to English public policy); *Domotique Secant Inc. v. Smart Sys. Tech. Inc.*, [2005] Can. LII 36874 (Québec S.Ct.).

then, whether the tribunal acts *ultra petita*, if it records the settlement in an arbitral award.

At first sight it could be argued that, if the tribunal makes a consent award, it does not act *ultra petita*, because the unanimous request of the parties to record the terms of the settlement into an award amounts to an enlargement of the original *ratione materiae* boundaries of the agreement to arbitrate.[44] Kryvoi and Davydenko[45] and Marchisio,[46] however, argue that this cannot be the case. According to Marchisio, in particular, if the settlement agreement deals with aspects that were never discussed during the arbitral proceedings, the tribunal would be unable to properly assess whether some elements of the settlement may be contrary to public policy or mandatory law. This is an important concern: if the tribunal knows nothing about the new elements that the parties introduce in the settlement agreement, which were never discussed in the arbitration, there is a practical risk that the problematic aspects of the settlement will not be detected. However such a risk of party autonomy abuse is, in itself, no reason to conclude that the parties are prevented from enlarging the scope of the agreement to arbitrate, when they reach a settlement. Rather, the solution to this problem is to be found in the discretionary power of the tribunal to reject the request of a consent award. In other words, the tribunal should be particularly cautious when the settlement contains clauses on aspects that have never been discussed in the arbitration, and retains the right to refuse the issuance of a consent award if suspicions arise as to the reason why certain subject-matters (which were not covered by the original agreement to arbitrate nor discussed during the arbitration) form part of the settlement.

e. Violation of the rules of procedure chosen by the parties

Making a consent award is particularly delicate in cases where the law of the seat and the rules chosen by the parties do not mention this possibility expressly. In this case, the debtor could in theory object that the arbitral procedure was not in accordance with the agreement of the parties. However, such an objection must normally be rejected. A tribunal may only

44 N. Alexander, *International and Comparative Mediation, Global Trends in Dispute Resolution*, Deventer: Kluwer 2009, p 312. See also Article 7(5) van de UNCITRAL Model Law, concerning the possibility for the parties to extend the original boundaries *ratione materiae* of the agreement to arbitrate by means of their procedural behaviour.

45 Kryvoi and Davydenko 2015, p 854.

46 Marchisio 2016, p 337.

issue a consent award if the parties unanimously request it. With this request, the parties implicitly reach an agreement on the arbitral procedure, empowering the tribunal to make a consent award, even if the rules of procedure say nothing in this respect. The parties, therefore, are prevented from raising with type of objection at a later stage: case law concerning the New York Convention consistently confirms that the parties can only complain that the arbitral procedure was not in accordance with their agreement if no express or implicit procedural agreement has been reached during the arbitral proceedings.[47]

f. Inability to present the case

It is apparently paradoxical that a party may argue that they were unable to present the case, after having not only reached a settlement agreement, but having also requested that such agreement be recorded in an award. As already mentioned above with reference to the rules of procedure chosen by the parties, the request to obtain a consent award should be seen as a waiver of the right to make objections based on procedural irregularities.[48] There is, however, a problem: it is not clear to what extent the parties are free to waive their right to obtain a fair arbitral procedure. In certain jurisdictions, courts may consider that the parties maintain their right to resist recognition and enforcement or challenge the validity of the award on grounds of serious procedural irregularity, even if they explicitly waived this right before the making of the award. If that is the case, it could be possible to invoke both Article V(1)(b) and Article V(2)(b) of the New York Convention at the recognition and enforcement stage. In other

47 The same rationale underlies Article 1065(4) DCCP. See also Amsterdam District Court 10 May 2012, ECLI:NL:RBAMS:2012:BW7066; *Michael D. Castro v. Tri Marine Fish Company, LLC, et al.*, United States District Court, Western District of Washington, Case No C17-8RSL, 31 July 2017, in: A.J. van den Berg (ed.), *Yearbook Commercial Arbitration XLIII*, Alphen aan den Rijn: Kluwer International 2018. A similar estoppel effect, preventing the losing party from raising an objection after the end of the arbitration if they failed to raise the same issue during the arbitral proceedings (where it was possible for them to do so), exists in many legal systems: see e.g. Australia (*Armada (Singapore) Pte Ltd (Under Judicial Management) v. Gujarat NRE Coke Limited*), Federal Court of Australia, New South Wales District Registry, NSD 644 of 2012, 17 June 2014, in: A.J. van den Berg (ed), *Yearbook Commercial Arbitration XXXIX*, Alphen aan den Rijn: Kluwer International 2014, p 344; Germany (OLG Cologne, 26 February 2014, in: A.J. van den Berg (ed), *Yearbook Commercial Arbitration XLI*, Alphen aan den Rijn: Kluwer International 2016, p 484; China (*Alstom Technology Ltd v. Insigma Technology Co Ltd*), Hangzhou Intermediate People's Court, Zhejiang, 6 February 2013, in: A.J. van den Berg (ed), *Yearbook Commercial Arbitration XXXIX*, Alphen aan den Rijn: Kluwer International 2014, p 380.

48 It is for this reason that, in some legal systems, consent awards cannot be set aside on grounds of violation of the right to be heard.

cases, instead, the parties are prevented from arguing that the way the arbitral procedure was conducted infringed upon their right to present their case, if they previously agreed that the procedure be conducted in that particular way.[49]

The need to respect certain fundamental procedural guarantees is one of the main reasons why, as explained above, many national laws only provide for the possibility of a consent award if the settlement is reached during the course of an arbitration. For this reason, the use of a consent award after a successful mediation can be problematic: as also explained above,[50] mediation rarely offers the same procedural guarantees as arbitration. Therefore, if the parties find an agreement through mediation and then request a consent award, they must often also waive the right to present their case in a procedure governed by the type of due process that arbitration affords. However, as already mentioned, depending on the applicable law, the parties may not be allowed to waive their right to present their case, even if they expressly request a consent award. This risk is taken into account by Ernste and Meijer, when discussing the possibility of making a binding advice enforceable through a consent award.[51] In this context, it is correctly observed that a binding advice procedure is more informal than an arbitration; it is therefore possible that the principles of due process that would be followed in an arbitration are not upheld in a binding advice. For this reason, Ernste argues that before issuing a consent award, it is necessary to assess whether the binding advice procedure offered suffi-

49 On the waiver of fundamental procedural rights in arbitration see European Court of Human Rights, *Beg SpA vs. Italy*, 20 May 2021, Application No 5312/11. An indication that the parties are allowed, under certain conditions, to waive certain fundamental procedural rights can also be found in *U.S. Steel Mining co., L.L.C. v Wilson Downhole Serv.*, 2006 WL 2869535 (W.D. Pa. Oct. 5, 2006). In that case, the same person acted first as a mediator and then as an arbitrator. In the mediation and arbitration agreement, the parties expressly provided as follows: "The Parties anticipate that ex parte communications with the Arbitrator will occur during the course of the mediation. The Parties agree that the Arbitrator, in evaluating each Party's best and final offer, may rely on information he deems relevant, whether obtained in an ex parte communication or otherwise, in making the final Award." The parties did not find a settlement agreement in the mediation and the arbitrator issued an award. The award was indeed partially based on confidential information that one of the parties had disclosed to the arbitrator during the mediation. The losing party challenged the award, arguing that due process had been violated, as the decision was based on information that had not openly discussed in the arbitration. The court, however, concluded that the parties had allowed this to happen in their agreement.

50 See para 21.4 above.

51 Ernste 2012, p 98-100; Asser Procesrecht/Sanders, Meijer & Ernste *8* 2023/441.

cient due process guarantees.[52] Applying the same line of reasoning, *mutatis mutandis*, to mediation, the use of a consent award when the settlement agreement is found during a prior mediation (and not during the arbitral procedure) would often not be possible, for instance in cases where the mediator engaged in *ex parte* communications with the disputants.[53]

g. Incompatibility with substantive public policy
Finally, a consent award can be incompatible with substantive public policy. This assessment must be conducted on a case-by-case basis, depending on the contents of the award. In principle, most states interpret the concept of substantive public policy strictly; there are, however, cases where the settlement reached by the parties may not be compatible with the applicable substantive public policy principles. As already mentioned,[54] this can often be the case when the parties reach an agreement that is incompatible with EU competition law. For this reason, as illustrated, the tribunal can refuse the issuance of a consent award.

It must be highlighted once again that, in practice, the tribunal may not be aware of important circumstances, in light of which the request for a consent award should be declined; this could for example occur in a sham arbitration, where the dispute is simulated by the parties for reasons such as tax avoidance or money laundering.[55] If the tribunal perceives the existence of such a problematic situation, then the consent award should not be issued. If a consent award is issued in such circumstances, it may be set aside at the seat of arbitration,[56] or declined recognition and enforcement on the same grounds.

52 Ernste 2012, p 100.
53 Interestingly, in a recent Mexican case, a consent award has been used to give enforceability to the outcome of a blockchain-based dispute resolution procedure which does not afford many of the due process guarantees commonly associated with arbitration. Despite this, the competent Mexican court granted leave to enforce the consent award: on the use of this technique see C. Sharma, 'Blockchain arbitral award: potential challenges in recognition and enforcement under the New York Convention', *Romanian Arbitration* (16) 2022, p 85-110.
54 See para 21.3 above.
55 See para 21.3 above.
56 See Article 1069(2)(a) DCCP; see also, outside of the Netherlands, *State of Libya v. SA Société Orléanaise d'Electricité et de Chauffage Electrique – SORELEC*, Cour d'appel, Paris, Pole 1, Chamber 1, RG No 18/02568, 17 November 2020', in: S.W. Schill (ed), *ICCA Yearbook Commercial Arbitration 2023 – Volume XLVIII, Yearbook Commercial Arbitration, Volume 48*, Alphen aan den Rijn: Kluwer International 2023, p 217-218.

21.6 Relationship between the consent award and the United Nations Convention on International Settlement Agreements Resulting from Mediation

In 2018 UNCITRAL adopted the Convention on International Settlement Agreements Resulting from Mediation,[57] also known as Singapore Convention, which entered into force on 12 September 2020. At the time of writing, the Convention is in force in 14 States and has been signed by 44 other States, including the United States and the United Kingdom. The main purpose of the Singapore Convention is to create a regime parallel to the one of the New York Convention, ensuring the enforceability[58] of settlement agreements reached in the context of mediation.

In cases where the Singapore Convention allows for the enforcement of settlements reached during mediation, it may become superfluous to use a consent award for the same purpose. In other words, the parties would possibly have no interest to appoint the mediator or another person as an arbitrator entrusted with the task of issuing a consent award, if the same result (enforceability) can already be obtained through the Singapore Convention, without attempting to 'convert' the settlement agreement into an arbitral award. Nevertheless, the possibility that a settlement reached through mediation will be recorded in a consent award cannot be entirely excluded. If this indeed happens, it is important to understand the potential interaction between the New York and the Singapore Conventions.

In principle, the Singapore Convention wants to avoid that the creditor has two mechanisms to enforce the same settlement agreement. To this end, Article 1(3)(b) specifies that the Singapore Convention does not apply to 'settlement agreements that have been recorded and are enforceable as an arbitral award'. Thus, if the parties request a consent award, they will

57 United Nations, Treaty Series, vol. 3369C.N.154.2019.TREATIES-XXII.4 of 8 May 2019 (Issuance of Certified True Copies) and C.N.155.2019.TREATIES-XXII.4 of 8 May 2019 (Opening for signature).

58 It must be acknowledged that the text of the Convention raises some doubts: rather than referring to recognition and enforcement, as the New York Convention does, the Singapore Convention refers to "enforcement", without any further specification. It is unclear, therefore, whether a settlement agreement can automatically become an enforceable title pursuant to Article 2, or whether the settlement can only be used in court proceedings. On this issue see T. Schnabel, 'The Singapore Convention on Mediation: A Framework for the Cross-Border Recognition and Enforcement of Mediated Settlements', *Pepp. Disp. Resol. L.J.* (19) 2019, p 1.

maybe gain the possibility to have enforcement under the New York Convention (subject to the possible objections analysed in paragraph 21.5 of this chapter), but they also automatically lose the ability to obtain enforcement pursuant to the Singapore Convention. There is, however, a further complication that must be taken into account here. It is possible that, at the seat of arbitration where the consent award was made, the *lex arbitri* regards this type of award as perfectly enforceable. At the same time, however, it is possible that, in the different State where the debtor has their assets, a consent award is not regarded as an award, and courts refuse to apply the New York Convention (or any other instrument governing the enforcement of foreign awards) to it. The question, hence, is whether there is a risk that the enforcement of a consent award will 'slip through the cracks' and be declined under both the Singapore and the New York Convention.

This question should be answered negatively. An important argument, in this sense, can be found in the comparison of the aforementioned Article 1(3)(b) of the Singapore Convention with Article 1(3)(a). Article 1(3)(a) provides that the Singapore Convention is not applicable if the settlement agreement has been reached in the court of a state and is 'enforceable as a judgment in the State of that court'. Article 1(3)(b), instead, does not contain any territorial specification, but only says that the Convention is not applicable if the settlement agreement is 'recorded and (...) enforceable as an arbitral award', without any reference to the seat of arbitration. In other words, the Singapore Convention does not specify the law that must be applied to determine whether a settlement is 'enforceable as an arbitral award', and therefore whether the carve-out of Article 1(3)(b) is triggered. Hence, if the creditor cannot use the New York Convention in the state where the debtor has their assets, it would be wrong to consider the settlement as 'enforceable as an arbitral award' in the sense of Article 1(3)(b), for the mere fact that it is considered enforceable at the seat of arbitration. Instead, it is necessary to interpret the concept of 'enforceable as an arbitral award' in a broad sense, consistently with the wording of the Singapore Convention. Therefore, the Singapore Convention should be understood as a safety net for settlements that have been recorded into an arbitral award, to be used whenever the courts of the state of enforcement conclude that such a consent award is not enforceable under the New York Convention or any other international or domestic legal instrument regulating the recognition and enforcement of foreign awards.

21.7 Conclusions

This contribution has analysed the use of the consent award as a technique to transform a settlement agreement into an enforceable title. The consent award was originally meant to be used when the parties reach a settlement during arbitral proceedings. In practice, however, there is a tendency to use it in mediation as well: the parties conclude an agreement to arbitrate after then have reached a settlement, for the sole purpose of obtaining an enforceable title.

Despite the practical utility of the consent award (both for parties engaging in arbitral proceedings and for parties that have successfully mediated their dispute), there can be legal obstacles against it, both at the seat of arbitration and outside of it. This chapter has provided a comparative overview of these obstacles, differentiating where necessary between different settings (e.g. on the basis of whether the parties were already arbitrating when they reached a settlement). First of all, there is a risk that a consent award will not be considered an award at all. Furthermore, some of the grounds for setting aside or denial of recognition and enforcement may potentially be invoked, depending on the setting and the facts of the case. Therefore, despite the practical efforts to equate a consent award to any other type of arbitral award, the peculiarity of this type of award cannot entirely be suppressed. In some cases, an alternative avenue to obtain enforcement of settlement agreements reached through mediation may be provided by the Singapore Convention, where applicable.

CHAPTER 22

TIME LIMITS FOR CORRECTION AND SUPPLEMENTATION, AS WELL AS RECOMMENDATIONS TO AVOID CLERICAL ERRORS AND FAILURES TO DECIDE

Isabelle van den Nieuwendijk[1]

22.1 Introduction[2]

In principle, an arbitration ends with a final and binding arbitral award between the parties (cf. Article 1059 DCCP). After receiving the arbitral award, however, the parties and their lawyers would do well – in addition to considering possible legal remedies – to study the arbitral award promptly and carefully for 'irregularities'. In practice – certainly in larger arbitration proceedings – it is not uncommon for the arbitral tribunal to have made clerical errors in the arbitral award or to have failed to decide on one or more claims or counterclaims presented by the parties. To address this issue – as early as in the Dutch Arbitration Act (*Arbitragewet*) of 1986 – the means of correction and supplementation of the arbitral award on the basis of Article 1060 DCCP and Article 1061 DCCP, respectively, were created.[3] Many arbitration rules also provide for correction and supplementation[4], such as the Netherlands Arbitration Institute (NAI) Arbi-

---

1 I.P.M. (Isabelle) van den Nieuwendijk (LLM) is partner at 4DArbitration.

2 This contribution is a translation and updated version of my contribution 'De termijnen voor verbetering en aanvulling, mede in het licht van het NAI Arbitragereglement, alsmede aanbevelingen ter voorkoming van kennelijke fouten en nalaten te beslissen', in: C.J.M. Klaassen, G.J. Meijer & C.L. Schleijpen (eds), *Going Dutch: ADR in Nederland, in het bijzonder bij het NAI,* Deventer: Wolters Kluwer 2019, p 621-650.

3 See Act of 2 July 1986, *Stb.* 1986/372.

4 See e.g. Article 38 and 39 United Nations Commission on International Trade Law (Uncitral) Arbitration Rules (2021), Article 36 International Chamber of Commerce (ICC) Arbitration Rules (2021) and Article 27 London Court of International Arbitration (LCIA) Arbitration Rules (2020). Many arbitration laws and arbitration rules also provide for the possibility of interpretation of the arbitral award if there is an ambiguity that requires explanation or clarification. Cf. e.g. Article 33(1)(b) Uncitral Model Law (2006) and Article 37 Uncitral Arbitration Rules (2021). The possibility of interpretation of the arbitral award is still lacking in the Dutch Arbitration Act and the parties cannot – strictly speaking – agree to this on the basis of the law either, in my view, at least not beyond the limits of the arbitral tribunal's mandate. However, it can be argued that interpretation is possible until the end of the arbitral

tration Rules (2024) (hereinafter also: "NAI") (see Article 54 and Article 55 NAI). Correction serves to ensure that the parties obtain the award as the arbitral tribunal intended by correcting the clerical error(s)[5], while supplementation[6] serves to ensure that all claims presented by the parties are decided upon by the arbitral tribunal.[7]

Correction and supplementation are not legal remedies. Correction and supplementation are exceptions to the principle that an arbitral award can only be contested by a legal remedy and are therefore also exceptions to the finality of the arbitral award. Together with the remedy of an arbitral appeal (Article 1061a et seq DCCP), correction and supplementation are also the only means by which the arbitral award can be 'challenged' before an *arbitral tribunal*.[8] The request for correction and/or supplementation extends the mandate of the arbitral tribunal, or at least the mandate is deemed not to have ended (see Article 1058(3) DCCP and Article 46(2) NAI).[9]

---

tribunal's mandate, i.e. until four weeks after the date of the arbitral award (Article 1058(2) and (3) DCCP). See on this subject I.P.M. van den Nieuwendijk, 'Interpretatie van arbitrale vonnissen', *TvA* 2020/2, p 47-55.

5 For the sake of simplicity, I use 'clerical error' as an umbrella term for the errors mentioned in Article 1060 (1) and (2) DCCP, although the errors in Article 1060 (2) DCCP need not be clerical. The law refers to the correction of a "manifest computing error, clerical error or other manifest error which lends itself to simple correction" (Article 1060*(1)* DCCP*)* and the correction of "the particulars referred to in Article 1057(4)(a) to (d) inclusive" if these particulars are stated incorrectly or are partially or wholly absent from the award (Article 1060*(2)* DCCP*)*. These particulars include (a) the names and domiciles of the arbitrator or arbitrators, (b) the names and domiciles of the parties, (c) the date of the award, and (d) the place of the award. Cf. Article 54(1) and (2) NAI (in conjunction with Article 50(1) under (a), (b), (i) and (j) NAI).

6 On supplementation in general, see my article 'Aanvulling van arbitrale vonnissen (Article 1061 Rv)', *TvA* 2002, p 3-10 and on supplementation of the grounds of the arbitral award, see my contribution 'Aanvulling van de motivering; het meerdere dus ook het mindere!', in: G.J. Meijer, P. Storm & L. Timmerman (eds), *Piet Sanders: Een honderdjarige vernieuwer*, The Hague: Boom legal 2012, p 233-242.

7 Cf. Article 24 DCCP. On the distinction between correction and supplementation, see my annotation under Supreme Court 13 July 2007, ECLI:NL:HR:2007:BA5199, para 3, *JBPr* 2007/76.

8 Arbitral appeal, however, is brought before an arbitral *appellate* court, while correction and supplementation must in principle be requested from the *same* arbitral tribunal. Setting aside and revocation are instituted before the ordinary court (Article 1064a(1) DCCP and Article 1068(2) DCCP, respectively). And the referral back (*remission*) by the ordinary court during setting aside proceedings may also come back to the *same* arbitral tribunal, but not directly (Article 1065a DCCP).

9 Article 1058(3) DCCP states: "Without prejudice to the provisions of Articles 1060, 1061, and 1065a, the mandate of the arbitral tribunal shall terminate when the last final award is sent to the parties or, in the event referred to in the first paragraph

This contribution will deal comprehensively with the time limits regarding correction and supplementation under Dutch law. First, the time limit within which a request for correction and/or supplementation must be made will be discussed (see para 22.2). Next, I consider the duration of the procedure for correction and supplementation and whether a time limit exists for the arbitral tribunal to decide on a request for correction and/or supplementation (see para 22.3). In addition, I examine the alternatives that are available if the time limit for correction and supplementation has expired (see para 22.4). I also discuss the effect of a request for correction and/or supplementation on the time limit for a claim for setting aside the arbitral award (see para 22.5). I go on to make four recommendations for arbitrators and/or arbitration institutes, to reduce clerical errors and failures to decide on claims and to further guarantee the quality and uniformity of arbitral awards, namely: (i) a checklist for the arbitral award (ii) a checklist for correction and supplementation, (iii) additional administrative fees in the event of a request for correction and/or supplementation, and (iv) 'scrutiny' of the arbitral award (see para 22.6). The conclusion follows in paragraph 22.7.

22.2 Time limit for request for correction and/or supplementation

22.2.1 General

With the entry into force of the current Arbitration Act (2015)[10], the time limit for the request for correction and/or supplementation has become regulatory law.[11] The Arbitration Act includes three possible time limits for

under (b), upon the deposit of the last final award with the registry of the district court." Article 46(2) NAI provides: "Without prejudice to the provisions of Article 54 and Article 55, the mandate of the arbitral tribunal is terminated by the transmission of the final award to the parties."

10 See *Stb.* 2014, 200 and 2014, 254. The Dutch Arbitration Act is included in the Dutch Code of Civil Procedure, book 4.

11 Regarding the change to the effect that parties can now agree on a different time limit, see G.J. Meijer & A.I.M. van Mierlo, *Parl. Gesch. Arbitragewet 2015*, Memorandum of Understanding (2015), Article 1060 DCCP, para I.58.3, p 124. With the addition "within a time limit as agreed by the parties", the Arbitration Act (2015) is more in line with foreign arbitration laws in this regard (see, e.g. Article 33(1) Uncitral Model Law, Article 1715(1) Belgian Arbitration Act, Article 1058(2) German Arbitration Act and Section 57(4) English Arbitration Act) and an agreed arbitration agreement with a time limit other than the statutory time limit will no longer cause problems.

the request for correction and ex officio correction[12] and four possible time limits for the request for supplementation, namely:[13]

1. within a time limit agreed between the parties (Article 1060(1), (2) and (4) DCCP and Article 1061(1) DCCP) (see para 22.2.2);
2. in the absence of an agreed time limit, until three months after the day the arbitral award was sent (Article 1060(1), (2) and (4) DCCP and Article 1061(1) DCCP in conjunction with Article 1058(2) DCCP) (see para 22.2.3);
3. in the absence of an agreed time limit and if the parties have agreed to deposit, three months after the day of deposit of the arbitral award at the registry of the court (Article 1058(5) DCCP) (see para 22.2.4).

The fourth time limit applies to supplementation only if the parties have agreed on arbitral appeal (Article 1061a et seq. DCCP):

4. the arbitral award rendered at first instance can then only be supplemented in arbitral appeal in accordance with Article 1061 DCCP. The request to that effect must be made within the time limit applicable to the arbitral appeal (i.e. within a time limit agreed between the parties or within three months after the day the arbitral award was sent; see Article 1061c DCCP). The parties may deviate from this provision of Article 1061h DCCP by agreement (see Article 1061h DCCP).

I will discuss the first three mentioned time limits for a request for correction and/or supplementation in sequence (para 22.2.2-2.4). The time limit for supplementation if an arbitral appeal has been agreed upon will not be considered, since arbitral appeal is the exception rather than the rule. The NAI Arbitration Rules do not provide for the possibility of arbitral appeal either.[14] For the sake of completeness, I note that the General Time Limits Act (*Algemene termijnenwet*) also applies to requests for correction and/or supplementation, as Article 1077 DCCP does not exclude Articles 1060 and 1061 DCCP. The General Time Limits Act regulates how statutory dead-

12 In the following, I will not specifically name the ex officio correction. What applies to the request for correction also applies to the ex officio correction, unless otherwise stated.

13 Unlike correction, supplementation is *not* possible ex officio.

14 However, the parties could possibly agree to arbitral appeal separately. It is then up to the Netherlands Arbitration Institute (or another institute) to decide whether it wants to administer the arbitral appeal. If it does not, the parties will be able to agree to ad hoc arbitral appeal. On this point, see G.J. Meijer, *Overeenkomst tot arbitrage (Serie Burgerlijk Proces & Praktijk no 13)*, Deventer: Kluwer 2011, para 4.7.3.6, p 911. If the NAI wishes to administer the arbitral appeal, the time limit for supplementation as set out in Article 55(1) NAI does not apply but the time limit in Article 1061h DCCP applies instead, since the request for supplementation will then only be allowed in an arbitral appeal.

lines should be handled when they expire on a Saturday, Sunday, or public holiday.

Finally, I would like to note that, in practice, the request for correction and/or supplementation of the arbitral award may in turn give rise to a request for correction and/or supplementation by the opposing party.[15] This request will then in principle have to be made within the (agreed) time limit, and will not – in the context of hearing the parties – be permitted to be made as a response to the first request only after the ordinary time limit has already expired. A case could be made, however, that just as with the claim for setting aside, a request can be made in counterclaim, i.e. outside the regular time limit for a request for correction and/or supplementation.[16]

22.2.2 *Starting point is the agreed time limit*

22.2.2.1 General

The basic principle is that, for the request for correction and/or supplementation, the parties can opt to agree on a time limit themselves (Article 1060(1), (2) and (4) DCCP and Article 1061(1) DCCP[17]).[18]

15 Under the Hong Kong International Arbitration Centre (HKIAC) Rules (2024), the arbitral tribunal even has the power to make further corrections to the arbitral award necessitated by or consequential on (a) the interpretation of any point or part of the arbitral award or (b) the issue of any additional award. The same applies to supplementation and interpretation (see Arts. 38.4, 39.3, 40.3 HKIAC).

16 Cf. G.J. Meijer & I.P.M. van den Nieuwendijk, 'Termijnen voor de vordering tot vernietiging', in: R.S. Meijer et al (eds), *Accompli (Liber Amicorum Professor M.E. Koppenol-Laforce)*, The Hague: Boom legal 2021, p 189 et seq.

17 Pursuant to Article 33(1) and (3) Uncitral Model Law, the parties may, according to the wording "unless another period of time has been agreed upon by the parties" (para 1) and "Unless otherwise agreed by the parties" (para 3), also agree on another time limit for the request for correction and/or supplementation. However, for the *ex officio* correction, the parties cannot agree on a different time limit and a time limit of "within thirty days of the date of the award" applies (Article 33(2) Uncitral Model Law).

18 Thus, although not advisable, it could also be agreed "at any time" (cf. the regulation of correction and supplementation of a court decision: Article 31(1) DCCP and Article 32(1) DCCP). However, unlike the ordinary court, the arbitral tribunal is not a 'fixed tribunal'. Thus, the possibility exists that the arbitral tribunal will no longer be able to meet for various reasons. In such cases, an arbitrator will then have to be replaced (Article 1030 DCCP; Article 22 NAI) or an entirely new arbitral tribunal may even have to be constituted (Article 1027 DCCP; Article 15 NAI).

It can be questioned whether the possibility of making different agreements regarding the time limit for correction and supplementation pertains only to the *duration* of the time limit or also to its *commencement*. The Explanatory Memorandum of the DCCP does not provide a definite answer to this question.[19] It may be derived from the legislative text of Article 1060(1) DCCP itself, which states, "A party may, within a time-limit as agreed by the parties *or* within three months after the day the award was sent." [emphasis added: IvdN]. Because of the use of the word "or" – by which the agreed time limit is set off against the statutory time limit of three months after the day the award was sent – it may be assumed, in my opinion, that it also pertains to the commencement of the time limit. After all, if this were otherwise, many arbitration rules that assume a different commencement of the time limit would also be ineligible for application. Moreover, with the option to agree on the deposit of the arbitral award, the law also provides for a different commencement of the time limit (Article 1058(5) DCCP).

The agreed time limit will usually be a time limit as included in the arbitration rules declared applicable by the parties, such as the NAI Arbitration Rules (see para 22.2.2.2), but may also be a further agreement between the parties. I note here that the further agreed time limit between the parties always takes precedence over the time limit agreed upon by the parties in arbitration rules, even if the agreed rules do not allow for a further agreement, provided the arbitration institute agrees.[20] The parties may deviate from the agreed applicable arbitration rules insofar as they are not mandatory law (cf. Article 1036(1) DCCP). For example, the fiction of sending the arbitral award in Article 1058(2) DCCP[21] is a provision of mandatory law, which cannot be deviated from. If the agreed arbitration rules agreement assume a time limit linked to the sending of the arbitral award, then Article 1058(2) DCCP will also apply to it. In my opinion, if both parties wish to correct and/or supplement the arbitral award, in principle the possibility is also not excluded that a different time limit may be agreed upon after the arbitral award has been rendered, but before the expiry of the statutory time limit, as the parties are permitted to deviate from the time limit by

19 See footnote 11.

20 If the institute proceeds to administer the arbitration, I believe that can be seen as implied consent.

21 Article 1058(2) DCCP reads: "The award shall be deemed to have been sent if four weeks have elapsed after the date of the award".

agreement.[22] For the sake of completeness, I also note that, if the parties themselves have agreed on a time limit for correction and supplementation, this time limit also applies to the ex officio correction.[23]

22.2.2.2 Arbitration Rules

Most arbitration rules contain a time limit for the request for correction and/or supplementation. Compare, for example, Article 38(1) Uncitral Arbitration Rules (2021): "1. Within thirty days after the receipt of the award (...)", Article 36(2) and (3) ICC Arbitration Rules (2021): "(...) within thirty days from receipt of the award (...)" and Article 27.1 LCIA Arbitration Rules (2020): "27.1 Within 28 days of receipt of any award (...)". Most of these time limits are *shorter* than the statutory three-month time limit of Article 1060 and 1061 DCCP (see para 22.2.3) and provide for the commencement of the time limit the *receipt* of the arbitral award. Thus, this also differs from the commencement of the statutory time limit for correction and supplementation, which is based on the *sending* of the arbitral award. Therefore, these time limits, too, are not subject to the fiction of Article 1058(2) DCCP regarding the sending of the arbitral award.[24] The old NAI Arbitration Rules (2015) in Article 47(1), (2) and (4) and Article 48(1) NAI still provided "within *two* months after the *date* of the award" for the time limit for a request for correction and/or supplementation and consequently also deviated from the statutory time limit on two points. Some years ago, I proposed including the statutory time limit in the NAI Arbitration Rules, so that parties would not accidentally overlook the shorter time limit in the NAI Arbitration Rules and then submit a request for correction and/or supplementation too late, as has sometimes occurred in practice.[25] In Article 54(1) and 55(1) of the current NAI Arbitration Rules (2024), this proposal has been followed and the statutory time limit has been adhered to: "within three months after the date of transmission of the award". The fiction of Article 1058(2) DCCP does apply to this time limit.

22 Incidentally, it may be questioned whether in this case the further agreement of the time limit does not also require the consent of the arbitral tribunal. After all, the mandate of the arbitral tribunal has – strictly speaking – already been terminated (cf. Article 1058(3) DCCP).

23 Unlike Article 33(2) Uncitral Model Law, where the parties cannot agree on a different time limit for the *ex officio* correction (see also footnote 17). There is a time limit of "within thirty days of the date of the award" for the ex officio correction

24 See footnote 21.

25 In Van den Nieuwendijk 2019, para 26.2.2.2.

As mentioned above (see para 22.2.2.1), the parties may deviate from the time limit in the arbitration rules by further agreement, provided that the institute can agree to this. It must be said that in practice this does not happen very often.

22.2.3 *No agreed time limit: within three months after the day the arbitral award was sent*

In the absence of an agreed time limit, the time limit for a request for correction and/or supplementation is within three months after the day the arbitral award was sent (Article 1060(1), (2) and (4) DCCP and Article 1061(1) DCCP[26]).[27] The time limit is linked to the sending of the arbitral award. Pursuant to Article 1058(1)(a) DCCP, the arbitral tribunal shall ensure that it sends the original of the arbitral award, or a copy thereof certified by an arbitrator or the third party designated by the parties, to the parties as soon as possible. This is also where the aforementioned fiction of Article 1058(2) DCCP comes into play: "The award shall be deemed to have been sent if four weeks have elapsed after the date of the award".[28] Once the arbitral award is received by the parties, the request for correction and/or supplementation can be made. For example, if the arbitral award is dated 7 March 2024 and sent on the same day, the time limit for the request for correction and/or supplementation will be 4 July 2024 (7 March 2024 + four weeks = 4 April 2024 + three months = 4 July 2024).

In the event of an agreed time limit for the request for correction and/or supplementation, this *statutory* three-month time limit will in principle not apply, unless the parties have agreed otherwise by further agreement. However, provisions of mandatory law simply apply in those cases, such

26 In the absence of an agreed time limit, pursuant to Article 33 (1) and (3) Uncitral Model Law, a time limit of "within thirty days of receipt of the award" applies to the request for correction and/or supplementation.

27 With the entry into force of the current Arbitration Act, while the starting point is a time limit as agreed between the parties, in the absence of this agreement the time limit for correction and supplementation has been extended from 30 days to three months. This extension was included in connection with the harmonisation of time limits in ordinary courts. Cf. e.g. the time limit for appeal (Article 339(1) DCCP) and cassation (Article 402(1) DCCP), which is also three months.

28 Based on the contents and purpose of, as well as the terminology in, Article 1058(2) DCCP, it must be assumed that we are dealing here with an irrefutable presumption. See Meijer & Van den Nieuwendijk 2021, p 175 et seq. See also Meijer & Van den Nieuwendijk 2021 for the case where the arbitral award was not sent to (the known address of) a party or was sent to that address after the time limit for correction and/or supplementation had expired.

as Article 1058(2) DCCP (which qualifies for application if the time limit in the agreed arbitration rules is linked to the sending of the arbitral award).

22.2.4 *No agreed time limit but deposit: three months from the day of deposit of the arbitral award*

Although the deposit of the arbitral award is no longer standard under the Arbitration Act, the parties may still agree to do so (Article 1058(1)(b) DCCP). In such cases, and only in the absence of an agreed time limit, the starting time for the request for correction and/or supplementation is the date of the deposit, as follows from Article 1058(5) DCCP: "Unless the parties have agreed other time limits as referred to in Articles 1060, 1061, 1061c, a time limit of three months from the date of the deposit of the award with the registry of the court shall apply, if the parties have agreed such deposit." For example, if an arbitral award dated 7 March 2024 was deposited immediately on that same day, the last day for a request for correction and/or supplementation would be 7 June 2024. Moreover, the deposit of the arbitral award is not a prerequisite for the request for correction and/or supplementation. The parties may submit a request for correction and/or supplementation from the moment of receipt of the arbitral award – thus even before the deposit if it occurs later – until three months after the day of deposit.[29] Upon discovery of a clerical error or failure to decide on a claim, parties would do well to inquire when the arbitral award was deposited to see if the time limit has already expired. If the parties have agreed NAI arbitration *and* deposit of the arbitral award (cf. Article 45(1)(b) NAI), then – as follows from the above – the agreed time limit will simply apply. This applies unless the parties indicate by further agreement that they still want the time limits to start with the deposit, and the NAI agrees (see para 22.2.2.1 and para 22.2.2.2).

22.3 Length of procedure and decision period

On average, a procedure for correction and/or supplementation need not take a long time. After a request for correction and/or supplementation[30] or an intended ex officio correction, the arbitral tribunal will first have to

29 Cf. G.J. Meijer & A.I.M. van Mierlo, *Parl. Gesch. Arbitragewet 2015*, Memorandum of Understanding to Article 1060 DCCP, para III.42.5, p 748.

30 The request for correction and/or supplementation must be submitted to the NAI Secretariat, which will send a copy of the request to the arbitral tribunal and the opposing party "as soon as possible" (see Article 54(3) NAI and Article 55(2) NAI).

give the parties the opportunity to comment on the matter (Article 1060(5) DCCP and Article 1061(3) DCCP and Article 54(5) NAI and Article 55(3) NAI). A time limit for this is not prescribed by law and the NAI Arbitration Rules do not have a time limit for this either.[31] An arbitral tribunal will itself determine a suitable time limit – partly depending on the size of the request (i.e. correction of one or more clerical errors and/or supplementation of one or more claims or counterclaims) – at its own discretion (in accordance with Article 1036 DCCP and, in the case of NAI arbitration, in accordance with Article 25(1) NAI: "(...) the arbitral tribunal (...) determines the time limits within which the proceedings will be conducted (...)"[32]). In practice, the request for correction and/or supplementation can potentially in turn give rise to a request for correction and/or supplementation for the other party (see also para 22.2.1 *in fine*).

A time limit within which the arbitral tribunal should then decide on the request for correction and/or supplementation is also lacking in the Arbitration Act and in the NAI Arbitration Rules.[33] Even in the case of an *ex*

31 Unlike, for example, the ICC Arbitration Rules (2021), where Article 36(4) provides: "After transmission of an application pursuant to Article 36(2) or 36(3) to the arbitral tribunal, the latter shall grant the other party or parties a short time limit, normally not exceeding 30 days, from receipt of the application by that party or parties, to submit any comments thereon."

32 On the relationship Article 21(1) (old) NAI (now: Article 25(1) NAI) and Article 1036 DCCP, see G.J. Meijer & H.J. van der Baan, 'NAI Arbitragereglement 2015', *TvA* 2015/37, para 1.

33 This is in contrast to, for example, the Uncitral Model Law where Article 33(1) *in fine* expressly provides that "If the arbitral tribunal considers the request to be justified, it shall *make the correction* (...) *within thirty days* of receipt of the request." [emphasis added: IvdN]. The same applies to the ex officio correction of Article 33(2) Uncitral Model Law. And for supplementation, Article 33(3) Uncitral Model Law provides: "(...) If the arbitral tribunal considers the request to be justified, it shall *make the additional award within sixty days*." [emphasis added: IvdN]. Article 33(4) Uncitral Model Law does allow the arbitral tribunal, if necessary, to extend the time within which it shall make the correction or supplementation. However, this does not apply to the ex officio correction of Article 33(2) Uncitral Model Law. See also the Uncitral Arbitration Rules (2021) where the correction must be made within 45 days after receipt of the request (Article 38(1)) and the ex officio correction even within 30 days (Article 38(1)), and the supplementation must be made within 60 days after the request to that effect, with the possibility of extension of the latter time limit (Article 39(2)). See also Article 36 of the ICC Arbitration Rules (2021) where the ex officio correction by the Arbitral Tribunal must be submitted for approval to the Court within 30 days from notification of the award (Article 36(1)). For the correction, interpretation or supplementation on request the following applies: the arbitral tribunal shall submit its decision on the application in draft form to the Court not later than 30 days from expiry of the time limit for the receipt of any comments from the other party or parties or within such other period as the Court may decide (Article 36(4)).

officio correction by the arbitral tribunal, the time limit for its decision is not immediately fixed. Although Article 1060(4) DCCP stipulates for an ex officio correction that the arbitral tribunal may "proceed" with the correction "within a time limit as agreed by the parties or within three months after the day the award was sent" (cf. also Article 54(4) NAI), in my opinion this should be interpreted as meaning that the arbitral tribunal only communicates a proposal for correction to the parties within the agreed time limit (or in the absence thereof the statutory time limit) and at the same time gives the parties a time limit within which they may comment on the proposed correction.[34] The correction itself based on the proposal may take place later.[35] This ensures that the arbitral tribunal has sufficient time to hear the parties.[36] The determination of when the arbitral tribunal will render a decision on the request for correction and/or supplementation and the ex officio correction is thus reserved to the arbitral tribunal. This is consistent with Article 1048 DCCP, which provides that the determination of the date on which the award will be made shall be at the exclusive discretion of the arbitral tribunal. See in this connection also Article 46(1) NAI, which stipulates that, in all cases, the award will be made expeditiously. The parties may, however, terminate the mandate of the arbitral tribunal in the event of unacceptable slowness (Article 1029(5) DCCP and Article 21(5) NAI).

The decision period will sometimes be somewhat longer for supplementation than for correction. In the case of supplementation, it entails not only the decision on the request for supplementation but also, after the granting of the request, the decision on the claim that was not decided on.[37] Therefore, after the request for supplementation is granted, a 'procedure' will follow regarding the claim that was not decided on, which will eventually result in the granting or rejection of that claim in an additional award (Article 1061(4) DCCP and Article 55(4) NAI).[38] The Arbitration Act provides

34 As an aside, I note that now that the time limit has been extended to three months (instead of 30 days) with the enactment of the current Arbitration Act (2015), hearing the parties on the proposed correction, and the correction itself, should very well be possible within three months.

35 This is in contrast to, for example, the Uncitral Model Law (2006); see footnote 33.

36 G.J. Meijer & A.I.M. van Mierlo, *Parl. Gesch. Arbitragewet 2015*, Memorandum of Understanding (2015), Article 1060 DCCP, para I.58.3, p 124.

37 Therefore, the Uncitral Model Law (2006) and the Uncitral Arbitration Rules (2013) also have a longer decision period for supplementation (60 days) than for correction (30 days).

38 Cf. Van den Nieuwendijk 2002, p 7, para 6.3.3 and Van den Nieuwendijk 2012, p 234, para 2. See also G.J. Meijer, in: *T&C Rv*, Article 1061 DCCP, note 3b (online, updated 1 January 2024).

nothing about this procedure for supplementation, except that it results in an additional award. Insofar as the parties have not agreed on this themselves, the arbitral tribunal itself will determine how to conduct this procedure, in accordance with Article 1036 DCCP or, in case of NAI arbitration, in accordance with Article 25(1) NAI. Depending on when during the procedure the claim or counter claim was overlooked, this procedure for supplementation may take a shorter or longer period.

If – after granting the request for correction and/or supplementation – a corrected award[39] or an additional award follows, the arbitral tribunal (and in case of NAI arbitration: the responsible member of the NAI Case Management Committee) will in any event send this award "as soon as possible" to the parties (Article 1060(6) DCCP and Article 1061(4) DCCP in conjunction with Article 1058(1) DCCP; cf. Article 54(7) NAI and Article 55(4) NAI in conjunction with Article 52(1) NAI). The rejection of a request for correction and/or supplementation shall be communicated to the parties in writing by the arbitral tribunal (and in case of NAI arbitration: through the intervention of the responsible member of the NAI Case Management Committee) (Article 1060(7) DCCP and Article 1061(5) DCCP; cf. Article 54(8) NAI and Article 55(5) NAI). In the case of a rejection, the Arbitration Act does not state that the rejection must be communicated "as soon as possible", but in practice this will likely be necessary.

The 'extended' mandate of the arbitral tribunal ends (i) with the sending of the corrected or additional award or (ii) with the sending of the notice of rejection of the request for such an award.[40] And if deposit of the arbitral award has been agreed upon, the 'extended' mandate ends (i) with the deposit of the corrected or additional award or (ii) with the deposit of

---

39 Pursuant to Article 1060(6) DCCP, the correction may be made and signed on the original and the copies of the award, or it may be mentioned in a separate document signed by the arbitral tribunal, which document is deemed to be part of the award. In NAI arbitration, the correction will always take place on a separate signed document, which document is deemed to be part of the award (Article 54(6) NAI).

40 Again, the fiction regarding the sending of the arbitral award of Article 1058(2) DCCP applies. Although a correction or a rejection of a request for correction or supplementation is not an arbitral award, the starting time for the claim for setting aside after a correction and/or supplementation is also linked to the sending of the arbitral award (see Article 1065(7) DCCP). See G.J. Meijer & A.I.M. van Mierlo, *Parl. Gesch. Arbitration Act 2015*, Memorandum of Amendment (2015), Article 1058 DCCP, para I.56.5, p 119-120.

the rejection of the request for such an award (Article 1058(3) DCCP and Article 46(2) NAI).[41]

22.4 Time limit has expired; alternatives?

22.4.1 General

The question is what possibilities remain if the parties have allowed the time limit for correction and supplementation to expire unused or only discover the clerical error after the time limit has expired, e.g. during enforcement of the arbitral award. If the time limit is exceeded, the request for correction and/or supplementation will, in principle, be declared inadmissible.[42] However, the time limit for a request for correction and/or supplementation is not mandatory law, as the parties may agree otherwise. A case could therefore be made that the arbitral tribunal will not declare a late request for correction and/or supplementation inadmissible ex officio if the request was not made within the time limit, but only if the other party invokes the exceeding of the time limit.[43] I can also imagine that, in the case of a slightly late request, the arbitral tribunal will hear both parties first anyway instead of immediately declaring the request inadmissible. After all, it is possible that both parties would like a correction and/or supplementation, whether or not of the same errors or claims respectively. However, the arbitral tribunal itself will also have to agree to deal with the late request – especially if the time limit is exceeded for a relatively long period of time – because, strictly speaking, the arbitral tribunal's mandate already ended with the expiration of the time limit (Article 1058(3) DCCP).[44] The possibility even exists that the arbitral tribunal will no longer be able to 'meet' for various reasons. In such cases, an arbitrator will be replaced (Article 1030 DCCP; Article 22 NAI) or – if necessary – a new ar-

41 This will be different only in the case of correction and/or supplementation of an interim or partial final award before the final award is rendered.

42 For an example – under the old Arbitration Act (1986) – where a request for correction was rejected for being out of time, see: NAI 29 September 2003, *TvA* 2006/3. Moreover, there was also no place for ex officio correction (within the time limit) since the claimant itself had made the mistake in its claim, namely an incorrect euro conversion. See also RvA Metaalnijverheid en -Handel 13 September 2010, *TvA* 2011/62, para 14.

43 Cf. for corresponding reasoning with respect to arbitral appeal G.J. Meijer, in: *T&C Rv*, Article 1061c DCCP (online, updated 1 January 2024), with reference to W.D.H. Asser & G.J. Meijer in their note to Amsterdam District Court 25 September 1996, *TvA* 1998/2, p 68-69.

44 See also Asser Procesrecht/Sanders, Meijer & Ernste *8* 2023/346 and 352.

bitral tribunal will even have to be constituted (Article 1027 DCCP; Article 15 NAI). This, of course, is not preferable. If a declaration of inadmissibility does follow, a distinction will have to be made between correction (see para 22.4.2) and supplementation (see para 22.4.3) with respect to the possibilities after the expiration of the time limit.

22.4.2 *Time limit has expired for request for correction*

As for the expiration of the time limit for correction of a clerical error, the following applies. The obvious thing to do is to read the arbitral award as it was intended by the arbitral tribunal.[45] Of course, this will only be possible if there is a *clerical* error.[46] If one of the parties does not want to cooperate with the reading of the award as it was intended by the arbitral tribunal, an enforcement dispute[47] before the interim relief judge on the basis

45 Cf. also H.J. Snijders, *Nederlands Arbitragerecht*, Deventer: Wolters Kluwer 2018, Article 1060 DCCP, note 3, who advocates reading the arbitral award including or with correction of the clerical error. Similarly, Stein/Rueb, *Compendium Burgerlijk Procesrecht*, Deventer: Wolters Kluwer 2021, para 14.1.15, p 9382 (and P.A. Stein, *De nieuwe arbitragewet*, Deventer: Kluwer 1986, p 20), who advocates reading the arbitral award in accordance with the intention of the arbitral tribunal, provided that this intention is known to third parties.

46 There is a clerical error if what the arbitral tribunal intended to decide can be determined with sufficient certainty. Cf. Supreme Court 26 November 2021, ECLI:NL:HR:2021:1769, r.o. 3.1.3, *NJ* 2021/389 (*De vrouw/De man*).

47 See also G.J. Meijer, in: *T&C Rv*, Article 1060 DCCP, note 3b (online, updated 1 January 2024); P. Sanders, *Het Nederlandse arbitragerecht*, Deventer: Kluwer 2001, V-K under Introduction (a), p 158; Snijders 2018, Article 1060 DCCP, note 3. For examples of an enforcement dispute involving an arbitral award, see Supreme Court 3 January 1997, ECLI:NL:HR:1997:ZC2240, *NJ* 1998/127, annotated by H.J. Snijders, *TvA* 1998, p 125-127, annotated by W.D.H. Asser (*PBS/Diepgrond*); Pres. Amsterdam District Court 3 July 1997, ECLI:NL:RBAMS:1997:AH7225, *KG* 1997/225; Pres. The Hague District Court 10 April 1997, ECLI:NL:RBSGR:1997:AH7163, *KG* 1997/159, *TvA* 1998, p 75-76, annotated by A.J. van den Berg. In an enforcement dispute, however, there is no place for a reassessment of the dispute in arbitration, see Supreme Court 23 March 2007, ECLI:NL:HR:2007:AZ5441, *NJ* 2007/177 (*De Bruin/AM Wonen*). Cf. in this connection, however, also – albeit in setting aside proceedings – De Vries Lentsch-Kostense in her opinion for Supreme Court 12 July 2013, ECLI:NL:HR:2013:CA0259 (*Eiser/Slotervaart Hospital*), *RvdW* 2013/884, ECLI:NL:PHR:2013:CA0259, para 14: "Furthermore, if there is no agreement between the parties on the interpretation of the arbitral award and the interpretation thereby constitutes a point of dispute (...), the Court of Appeal must independently render a judgment on the matter, in which it is not bound by the positions of the parties" (with reference to *PBS/Diepgrond*). Idem B.J. Drijber in his opinion for Supreme Court 23 November 2018, ECLI:NL:HR:2018:2162 (*Tiffany/Swatch*), *RvdW* 2018/1302, ECLI:NL:PHR:2018:1060, paras 53-54.

of Article 438(2) DCCP could offer a solution.[48] However, purely declaratory and constitutive awards do not lend themselves to enforcement, as a result of which these awards do not lend themselves to an enforcement dispute. The only other alternative is a claim for setting aside the arbitral award.[49] Since no concurrence rule applies to correction and setting aside as is provided for in Article 1065(6) DCCP for supplementation and setting aside (see para 22.5),[50] it can be deduced *a contrario* that setting aside is also possible,[51] provided that the time limit for this has not yet expired and the clerical error can be categorised under one of the grounds for setting aside as included in Article 1065(1)(a-e) DCCP.[52] Examples would include a situation where an arbitral tribunal did not comply with its mandate (Article 1065(1)(c) DCCP), as a clerical error caused it to award something different or more than claimed.[53] Or a situation where a clerical error gives rise to a

48 I am assuming here that leave for enforcement has already been obtained. An enforcement procedure of a Dutch arbitral award is in principle also *ex parte*, i.e. without the other party being summoned. If the other party is summoned, it could possibly – if it has an interest in doing so – plead for rejection of the leave for enforcement. This is possible if the clerical error can be categorised under one of the grounds for setting aside (Article 1063(1) DCCP) (see also *infra*), assuming the time limit for doing so has not yet expired (see Article 1063(2) DCCP). An enforcement procedure of a foreign arbitral award is *inter partes* (Article 1075 DCCP and Article 1076 DCCP). Whether a clerical error could fall under one of the grounds for refusal is open to debate, but this issue is beyond the scope of this contribution.

49 In the exceptional case where the parties have agreed on arbitral appeal (Article 1061b DCCP) and the deadline for it has not yet expired, arbitral appeal is also among the possibilities.

50 I note that, with the entry into force of the current Arbitration Act, a different commencement of the time limit for the claim for setting aside – as already applied after a request for supplementation – now also applies after a request for correction (Article 1065(7) DCCP) (see on this subject para 5).

51 Cf. also Snijders 2018, Article 1060 DCCP, no 6. Furthermore, the Supreme Court ruled in its judgment of 23 April 2010, ECLI:NL:HR:2010:BK8097, *NJ* 2011/475, annotated by H.J. Snijders (*Areb/Ameg*), that Article 1060 DCCP does not allow correction of a decision by which the arbitral tribunal went beyond the limits of its mandate. Failure to rely on the latter in a request to the arbitral tribunal to correct a manifest computing error or clerical error in the award pursuant to Article 1060(1) DCCP cannot, therefore, be regarded as participating in the proceedings without making an objection as referred to in Article 1065(4) DCCP. Thus, a party cannot forfeit the right to subsequently bring a claim for setting aside.

52 Although the Supreme Court ruled in its judgment of 23 April 2010, ECLI:NL:HR:2010:BK8097, *NJ* 2011/475 (*Areb/Ameg*), that Article 1060 DCCP does not allow for the correction of a decision by which the arbitral tribunal exceeded the limits of its mandate, in my opinion this does not refer to the case in which the arbitral tribunal exceeded its mandate as a result of a clerical error (this was not the case in that judgment either). See also H.J. Snijders in his note to the aforementioned judgment in *NJ* 2011/475, para 5.

53 Take the example where the arbitral tribunal accidentally included one zero too many in the award in the dispositive section, while the correct amount could be

violation of the duty to state reasons (Article 1065(1)(d) DCCP).[54] The question of whether the arbitral award can actually set aside in the case of a clerical error, or whether, for instance, the court should read the arbitral award in a corrected manner or refer the case back to the arbitral tribunal, falls outside the scope of this contribution.

22.4.3 *Time limit has expired for request for supplementation*

When the time limit for a request for supplementation expires, the parties have fewer options than when the time limit for a request for correction expires. The option of reading the arbitral award as the arbitral tribunal intended, as in the case of a clerical error, is excluded. After all, the arbitral tribunal failed to decide on one of the claims, and that is not a clerical error, unless what the decision in the operative section should have been can be deduced from the grounds of the arbitral award. In that case, however, there is a clerical error[55] and correction rather than supplementation should have been requested (and what was discussed in the previous paragraph applies). The parties have also forfeited the right to claim for setting aside the arbitral award, in view of the concurrence rule in Article 1065(6) DCCP in conjunction with Article 1065(1)(c) DCCP (see on this

---

deduced from the grounds. Cf. H.J. Snijders in his annotation under Supreme Court 23 April 2010, ECLI:NL:HR:2010:BK8097 (*Areb/Ameg*), *NJ* 2011/475: "(...) the case where the violation of the mandate precisely consists of a manifest computing error or clerical error, as in the case where 10 times as much is awarded – one zero too many – as claimed and substantiated earlier in the arbitral award."

54 See, for example: Amsterdam District Court 9 April 2014, ECLI:RBAMS:2014:2290, where the arbitral award was partially set aside because the arbitral tribunal applied a correction twice for the same intra-group sale of goods without giving reasons; Utrecht District Court 28 December 2011, ECLI:RBUTR:2011:BV2887, where the arbitral award was also partially set aside because the arbitrator made several manifest computing errors in the context of an exit agreement due to a wrong starting point, and double-counted, without giving reasons for these decisions.

55 Supreme Court 10 July 2009, ECLI:NL:HR:2009:BI4193, para 4, *RvdW* 2009/860 (*De man/De vrouw*), in conjunction with opinion A-G L. Strikwerda 10 July 2009, ECLI:NL:PHR:2009:BI4193, para 15; Supreme Court 19 November 2010, ECLI:NL:HR:2010:BN7084, para 4.2.2, *RvdW* 2010/1373 (*Nieuwe Dam c.s./VVE c.s.*); Supreme Court 28 June 2013, ECLI:NL:HR:2013:38, para 5.3, *NJ* 2013/521, annotated by L.C.A. Verstappen; Den Bosch Court of Appeal 28 February 2023, ECLI:NL:GHSHE:2023:668, para 3.6.1. Cf. also Th.B. ten Kate & M.M. Korsten-Krijnen, *Herroeping, verbetering en aanvulling van burgerrechterlijke uitspraken (Serie Burgerlijk Proces & Praktijk no 5)*, Deventer: Kluwer 2013, para III.4.1, p 237-238. T.F.E. Tjong Tjin Tai, in: *GS Burgerlijke Rechtsvordering*, Article 32 DCCP, note 1, with reference to Ten Kate & Wesseling-van Gent 2013. See also A-G M.L.C.C. Lückers in the opinion before Supreme Court 10 May 2019, ECLI:NL:HR:2019:699 (*De man/De vrouw*), *RvdW* 2019/611, *JBPr* 2019/34, annotated by G.C.C. Lewin, ECLI:NL:PHR:2019:171, para 2.3.

subject also para 22.5). Article 1065(6) DCCP stipulates that if and to the extent that the arbitral tribunal has failed to decide on one or more claims or counterclaims that were subject to its judgment, a claim for setting aside under Article 1065(1)(c) DCCP (violation of the mandate of the arbitral tribunal) can only be instituted if an additional award has been rendered or a request for supplementation has been wholly or partially rejected. Thus, a claim for setting aside based on the violation of the mandate because the arbitral tribunal has failed to decide is also excluded (Article 1065(1)(c) DCCP).[56] However, the parties do have the option, in principle, to initiate entirely new arbitral proceedings to consider the claim(s) on which the arbitral tribunal failed to give a decision.[57] The authority of res judicata will in principle not prevent this (Article 1059 DCCP). To this end, a new arbitral tribunal will have to be appointed (whether or not consisting of the same arbitrators), since the mandate of the previous arbitral tribunal will have ended with the expiry of the time limits (cf. Article 1058(3) DCCP and Article 46(2) NAI). And finally, under special circumstances, an enforcement dispute at the ordinary court could perhaps still offer a solution.[58]

22.5 Time limit for application for setting aside after request for correction and/or supplementation

For the claim for setting aside after a correction and/or supplementation, or after a full or partial rejection of the request thereto, a different com-

56 In the exceptional case where the parties have agreed on an arbitral appeal, supplementation may only be requested in an arbitral appeal (Article 1061h DCCP; formerly Article 1061(6) (old) DCCP). In that case, the time limit for supplementation is the time limit for arbitral appeal: within a time limit as agreed between the parties or within three months after the day the arbitral award was sent (Article 1061c DCCP).

57 Cf. Van den Nieuwendijk 2002, p 3 et seq, para 5 and para 7.2 and Snijders 2018, Article 1061 DCCP, note 6. Supplementation may also be possible if the standard phrase "Dismisses all additional or other claims" (or similar expressions) has been used, provided that the rejection does not relate to the claim on which the arbitral tribunal failed to decide. See on this subject Supreme Court 10 April 2004, ECLI:NL:HR:2009:BH2465, *JBPr* 2009/25 (*Teeuwe/Trijber*), and also my annotation thereon.

58 See Supreme Court 3 January 1997, ECLI:NL:HR:1997:ZC2240, *NJ* 1998/127, annotated by H.J. Snijders, *TvA* 1998, p 125-127, annotated by W.D.H. Asser (*PBS/Diepgrond*) and its continuation: Amsterdam District Court 3 July 1997, ECLI:NL:RBAMS:1997:AH7225, *KG* 1997/225. The Supreme Court ruled that the court of appeal was allowed to make a decision on the area that the arbitrators had not addressed and were not reasonably expected to address. Cf. Van den Nieuwendijk 2002, p 3 et seq, para 5 and para 7.2 and Snijders 2018, Article 1061 DCCP, note 6; see also footnote 47.

mencement of the time limit applies compared to the regular time limits of Article 1064a(2) DCCP.[59] Pursuant to Article 1065(7) DCCP[60], the claim for setting aside expires three months after the day a corrected or additional award was sent or written communication was sent of the rejection of the request to render such an award. And to the extent that the parties have agreed to deposit the award, the claim for setting aside shall expire three months after the deposit of a corrected or additional award or of the written communication of the rejection of the request for such an award. This different commencement of the time limit for the claim for setting aside is due to the concurrence rule for supplementation and setting aside contained in Article 1065(6) DCCP. This concurrence rule implies that a claim for setting aside pursuant to Article 1065(1)(c) DCCP, i.e. violation of the arbitral tribunal's mandate on the ground of failure to decide on one or more claims or counterclaims, can only be instituted if an additional award has been rendered or a request to that effect has been wholly or partially rejected. For all other grounds for setting aside (according to the parliamentary history[61]) – even if an additional award is requested – the time limits of Article 1064a(2) DCCP apply, so also for the claim for setting aside based on the violation of the arbitral tribunal's mandate on a ground other than the failure to decide on one or more claims or counterclaims.[62] It must be assumed that, for correction – despite the absence of a similar concurrence rule – the same has to apply as regards the time limit for setting aside. The different commencement of the time limit for the claim for setting aside thus applies only to those grounds for which the arbitral tribunal has been asked to render a corrected award and/or additional award. It is also important that the fiction of Article 1058(2) DCCP also applies to this different time limit for the claim for setting aside. That is, for the application of Article 1065(7) DCCP, the arbitral award is deemed

59 For a detailed description of the time limits for setting aside, in particular also on the fiction of the sending of the arbitral award as contained in Article 1058(2) DCCP, see Meijer & Van den Nieuwendijk 2021.

60 With the entry into force of the Arbitration Act 2015, the final sentence of Article 1065(7) DCCP declared this different setting aside time limit to apply mutatis mutandis to the correction of the arbitral award referred to in Article 1060 DCCP (Article 1065(7), third sentence, DCCP). Cf. Article 34(3) Uncitral Model Law (2006): "An application for setting aside may not be made after three months have elapsed from the date on which the party making that application had received the award or, if a request had been made under Article 33 [correction, interpretation of supplementation; IvdN], from the date on which that request had been disposed of by the arbitral tribunal".

61 G.J. Meijer & A.I.M. van Mierlo, *Parl. Gesch. Arbitragewet 2015*, Explanatory Memorandum to Article 1065 DCCP, para III.48.3, p 777.

62 See also in this regard my annotation to Amsterdam District Court 21 December 2012, *JBPr* 2012/73.

to have been sent four weeks after the date of the corrected or additional award or the rejection of a request to that effect.[63] Furthermore, I note that this different time limit for the claim for setting aside does not apply to the second time limit (as provided in Article 1064a(2), third sentence, DCCP) after service on the other party of the corrected or additional award and/or the arbitral award provided with leave for enforcement. However, it can be argued that this is an error on the part of the legislator.[64]

22.6 Recommendations

22.6.1 General

Finally, I would like to make four recommendations for arbitrators and/or arbitration institutes (in particular, the NAI Arbitration Rules), which could possibly reduce the number of clerical errors, failures to decide on claims and counterclaims and the number of setting asides, and further guarantee the quality and uniformity of arbitral awards: (i) a checklist for the arbitral award (ii) a checklist for correction and supplementation, (iii) a request for additional administration fees in the event of a request for correction and/or supplementation, and (iv) a 'scrutiny' provision.

22.6.2 Checklist for the arbitral award

First, I recommend a checklist for arbitrators to use when preparing the arbitral award (similar to the ICC Award Checklist[65]). This list should set out elements (in terms of form and content) that the arbitral award should ideally meet. It would include elements prescribed by law and/or the

63 A correction or a denial of a request for correction are not arbitral awards. An additional award is a separate arbitral award but a rejection of a request to supplement is not. The point is that the fiction also applies to the commencement of the time limit for the claim for setting aside. The parliamentary history explicitly mentions Article 1065(7) DCCP in this connection. See G.J. Meijer & A.I.M. van Mierlo, *Parl. Gesch. Arbitragewet 2015*, Memorandum of Amendment (2015), Article 1058 DCCP, para I.56.5, p 119-120.

64 Cf. I.P.M. van den Nieuwendijk, 'De nieuwe arbitragewet bezien vanuit het perspectief van de gewone rechter', *TCR* 2014, p 109; G.J. Meijer, in: *T&C Rv*, Article 1064a DCCP, note 3c and Article 1065 DCCP, note 10b (online, updated 1 January 2024); Meijer & Van den Nieuwendijk 2021, para 4, p 189; Snijders 2018, Article 1064a DCCP, note 2; otherwise: M. Raas, 'De tweede vernietigingstermijn', *TvA* 2019/47, para 3.1.

65 See <https://iccwbo.org/wp-content/uploads/sites/3/2016/04/ICC-Award-Checklist-English.pdf>.

NAI Arbitration Rules (such as the names and domiciles of the parties and arbitrators, the grounds of the decision, the place of the award and the date and signature of the award (cf. Article 1057(4) DCCP and Article 50(1) NAI)), but also additional items such as page numbering, table of contents, indication of the type of award, mention of case number, and description of the parties' claims. Preferably, for uniformity, a model NAI arbitral award could also be used, which could be completed by the arbitral tribunal. I refer to Appendix 1 to this contribution for a suggested checklist for arbitrators for preparing an arbitral award. I hereby expressly note that this checklist is not exhaustive and not binding, as the list also includes elements not required by law and/or the NAI Arbitration Rules.

22.6.3 *Checklist for correction and supplementation*

Second, I suggest a checklist for arbitrators for correction and supplementation similar to the ICC Checklist on Correction and Interpretation of Awards.[66] Preferably, for uniformity, a model decision for correction and supplementation could also be used here, which could be completed by the arbitral tribunal. When sending a copy of the request for correction and/or supplementation to the arbitral tribunal, the NAI Secretariat should also send the checklist and the model decision for correction and supplementation.[67] I refer to Appendix 2 to this contribution for a suggested checklist for arbitrators for correction and supplementation. Again, I expressly note that this checklist is not exhaustive and not binding, as the list also includes elements not required by law and/or the NAI Arbitration Rules. Furthermore, I point out that, under the NAI Arbitration Rules, the correction is made in a separate document that is deemed to be part of the arbitral award (Article 54(6) NAI; cf. Article 1060(6) DCCP) and that an additional award counts as an arbitral award (to which the provisions applicable to an arbitral award also apply) (Article 55(4) NAI; Article 1061(4) DCCP). A rejection of a request for correction and/or supplementation is not an arbitral award but may possibly include an order for costs. The request for additional administration fees as suggested in paragraph 22.6.4 may avoid enforcement problems regarding this order for costs.[68] Strictly

66 See <https://iccwbo.org/wp-content/uploads/sites/3/2016/11/ICC-Checklist-on-Correction-and-Interpretation-of-Awards-ENGLISH.pdf>.

67 Article 54(3) NAI and Article 55(2) NAI.

68 The ICC Note on Correction and Interpretation of Arbitral Awards and ICC Checklist on Correction and Interpretation of Awards designate a rejection with an award of costs as a "Decision and *Addendum on Costs*" [emphasis added: IvdN]. The Addendum is considered part of the arbitral award for which correction was sought. Strictly speaking, there is no basis for this in the Dutch Arbitration Act. Therefore,

speaking, a decision to correct and a rejection of a request for correction and/or supplementation need not meet the requirements for an arbitral award, but a reasoning for the correction or rejection of a request for correction and/or supplementation is, in my opinion, desirable.

22.6.4 *Request for additional administration fees*

My third recommendation is that, upon receipt of the request for correction and/or supplementation, the responsible member of the NAI Case Management Committee requests additional administration fees[69] from the applicant(s) (in accordance with Article 58(3) NAI).[70] Indeed, a request for correction and/or supplementation may entail additional costs, including additional fees for arbitrators, administration costs and legal assistance costs claimed by the other party.

In my opinion, if the arbitral tribunal proceeds to correct the arbitral award, the costs this entails will, in principle, have to be borne by the arbitral tribunal, or at least it must be assumed that the costs of the procedure to correct the award are, in principle, already included in the (already awarded) arbitrators' fees. After all, it is the arbitrators who made the mistake. The additional administration fees will then be refundable.[71] A different approach may be justified for the making of an additional award. Although the failure to decide is attributable to the arbitral tribunal, the work has not yet been completed. After all, a decision still needs to be made on one or more claims that were initially overlooked. For this additional work, depending on its scope, a case could be made that a reasonable fee is due.

I propose a request for additional administration fees to avoid enforcement problems regarding this cost award.

69 Pursuant to the "Note to parties and arbitral tribunals on the conduct of the arbitration under the ICC rules of arbitration", the Secretariat may first submit the request for correction to the ICC Court for consideration of whether – based on the circumstances of the case – additional administration fees are necessary: <https://iccwbo.org/wp-content/uploads/sites/3/2020/12/icc-note-to-parties-and-arbitral-tribunals-on-the-conduct-of-arbitration-english-2021.pdf>.

70 If the other party also makes a request for correction and/or supplementation, additional administration fees will also be requested from that party (cf. Article 58(4) NAI).

71 I consider it desirable, however, not to require additional administration fees if it is *prima facie* evident that there is a clerical error. See also N. Peters & C.L. Schleijpen 2021, 'Fouten van arbiters en de gevolgen daarvan voor hun honorarium', *NTBR* 2021/3, para 5.1, p 24.

If the request for correction and/or supplementation is rejected, the costs will, in my opinion, in principle have to be borne by the party that made the request (cf. Article 59 NAI). These might also include the costs of legal assistance claimed by the other party (cf. Article 59(3) NAI). Requiring additional administration fees with a request for correction and/or supplementation may also discourage parties from making a request frivolously and will reduce problems in enforcing an order for costs in a decision rejecting the request (see also para 22.6.3).

22.6.5 A 'scrutiny' provision

Some years ago, I recommended the inclusion of a 'scrutiny' provision in the NAI Arbitration Rules[72], similar to Article 34 ICC Arbitration Rules[73] and Article 32.3 of the Singapore International Arbitration Centre (SIAC) Rules.[74] My proposal was that the arbitral tribunal would first submit its draft arbitral award to the Administrator (now: responsible member of the NAI Case Management Committee) before rendering the arbitral award.[75] The administrator would be allowed, if necessary, to require modifications on form from the arbitral tribunal and – if necessary after adjustment by the arbitral tribunal – to approve the arbitral award on form before the arbitral tribunal could render the arbitral award. In the new NAI Arbitration Rules, my proposal of a 'scrutiny' provision has been adopted in watered-down form. The provision at Article 50(4) NAI reads as follows:

> "4. The arbitral tribunal is to transmit a draft of the award to the responsible member of the NAI Case Management Committee. The responsible member of

72 In Van den Nieuwendijk 2019, para 26.6.5.

73 Article 34 ICC Arbitration Rules (2021): "Before signing any award, the arbitral tribunal shall submit it in draft form to the Court. The Court may lay down modifications as to the form of the award and, without affecting the arbitral tribunal's liberty of decision, may also draw its attention to points of substance. No award shall be rendered by the arbitral tribunal until it has been approved by the Court as to its form."

74 Article 32.3 SIAC Rules (2016): "Before making any Award, the Tribunal shall submit such Award in draft form to the Registrar. Unless the Registrar extends the period of time or unless otherwise agreed by the parties, the Tribunal shall submit the draft Award to the Registrar not later than 45 days from the date on which the Tribunal declares the proceedings closed. The Registrar may, as soon as practicable, suggest modifications as to the form of the Award and, without affecting the Tribunal's liberty to decide the dispute, draw the Tribunal's attention to points of substance. No Award shall be made by the Tribunal until it has been approved by the Registrar as to its form."

75 Cf. also Article 54 China International Economic and Trade Arbitration Commission (CIETAC) Arbitration Rules (2024).

> the NAI Case Management Committee may make recommendations with respect to the provisions of paragraph 1(a), (b), (c), (d), (f), (g), (i) and (j), without prejudice to the discretion of the arbitral tribunal. Additionally, the responsible member of the NAI Case Management Committee may point out to the arbitral tribunal manifest computational or clerical errors in the draft of the award or any other manifest errors contained therein that lend themselves to simple rectification and any omission to decide on one or more claims or counterclaims that have been subjected to the arbitral tribunal's discretion. The arbitral tribunal remains responsible for both the content and form of the award."

On two essential points, the NAI provision differs from Article 34 ICC Arbitration Rules and Article 32.3 SIAC Rules. First, both articles also contain the possibility of suggestions on *substance*, without affecting the arbitrators' freedom to decide: "The Court (...) without affecting the arbitral tribunal's liberty of decision, may also draw its attention to points of substance (...)".[76] Secondly, both articles contain the condition of approval on form before the arbitral tribunal can render the arbitral award: "No award shall be rendered by the arbitral tribunal until it has been approved by the Court as to its form", as I had also proposed for the NAI. For the NAI, however, both of these points were still a bridge too far. In essence, the scrutiny provision lays down existing NAI practice. Thus, the responsible member of the NAI Case Management Committee may *not* make recommendations regarding the *reasons* and *decision* in the arbitral award (Article 50(1)(e) and (h) NAI), which are excluded in the enumeration of Article 50(4) NAI. Also, *no* approval on form is required before the arbitral tribunal can render an arbitral award. Thus, the responsible member of the NAI Case Management Committee will not be able to enforce their recommendations. It should also be noted that it is commendable that the responsible member of the NAI Case Management Committee is explicitly allowed to point out clerical errors and failures to decide on a claim to the arbitral tribunal.

When 'checking' the arbitral award, the responsible member of the NAI Case Management Committee will also have to go through the checklist

76 This is the wording from Article 34 ICC Arbitration Rules, but Article 32.3 SIAC Rules contains similar wording: see footnote 74. Article 32.3 SIAC Rules further provides only for the administrator to make *suggestions* on form ("The Registrar may (...) suggest modifications as to the form of the Award (...)") rather than actual modification as to form requirements by the ICC Court ("The Court may lay down modifications as to the form of the award (...)" (Article 34 ICC Arbitration Rules). The SIAC Rules do go on to require the administrator to approve the award on form before the arbitral tribunal can make its award.

for arbitrators (see Appendix 1)[77] and will thus also be able to pick out, among other things, the clerical errors (including the omissions that are subject to correction as mentioned in Article 1060(2) DCCP and Article 54(2) NAI[78]), check whether all claims and counter claims have been decided on and also check whether the arbitral award contains reasoning on each of the parts of or on each of the decisions in the dispositive section.[79]

22.7 In conclusion

In this contribution, I have taken a comprehensive look at the time limits for correction and supplementation of an arbitral award. The starting point for the time limit for the request for correction and/or supplementation is the time limit *agreed* between the parties. In the absence thereof, the statutory time limit of within three months after the date the arbitral award was sent applies (Article 1060(1), (2) and (4) DCCP and Article 1061(1) DCCP). Thus, the statutory three-month time limit is non mandatory in nature. For the statutory time limit or a time limit in agreed arbitration rules that is linked to the *sending* of the arbitral award, the fiction regarding the sending in Article 1058(2) DCCP will apply. The arbitral award is deemed to have been sent if four weeks have elapsed after the date of the arbitral award. If the parties have agreed on the deposit of the arbitral award, only in the absence of an agreed time limit does a time limit of three months after the day of deposit of the arbitral award apply (Article 1058(5) DCCP). The same time limits apply to the ex officio correction (Article 1060(4) DCCP).

The agreed time limit will usually be found in the arbitration rules agreed between the parties. In practice, one should be aware that most arbitration rules provide for a shorter time limit than the statutory three-month time limit of Articles 1060 and 1061 DCCP. These rules usually also assume the starting time of *receipt* of the arbitral award instead of the *sending* of the arbitral award. Thus, the fiction of Article 1058(2) DCCP does not apply to these rules. Meanwhile, the NAI Arbitration Rules (2024) do assume a three-month time limit after the day the arbitral award was sent. Thus, in an NAI arbitration, the fiction of Article 1058(2) DCCP does apply. A time limit within which the arbitral tribunal should decide on the request for

77 The checklist ticked off by arbitrators should also preferably be sent with the draft award to the responsible member of the NAI Case Management Committee.

78 See footnote 5.

79 On supplementing the reasoning of the arbitral award, see Van den Nieuwendijk 2012, p 233-242.

correction and/or supplementation is lacking in the Arbitration Act and is thus left to the discretion of the arbitral tribunal, unless the parties have agreed otherwise. Often arbitration rules do contain a provision for this.

If the time limit for a request for correction and/or supplementation has expired, in principle – at the other party's request, I would argue – a declaration of inadmissibility will follow. If a declaration of inadmissibility is made, the parties have only a limited number of alternatives, including an enforcement dispute in the event of a clerical error and, in the event of a failure to decide on a claim, initiating entirely new arbitral proceedings for the claim(s) on which a decision has been omitted.

A different commencement of the time limit than the regular time limits of Article 1064a(2) DCCP (Article 1065(7) DCCP) applies to the claim for setting aside after a corrected and/or additional award or after a full or partial rejection of the request to that effect. Pursuant to Article 1065(7) DCCP, the claim for setting aside expires three months after the day a corrected or additional award was sent, or written communication was sent of the rejection of the request for such an award. It should be borne in mind that this other time limit applies only to the claim for setting aside that relates to the clerical error and/or the claim on which a decision has been omitted.

With the use of the checklists (for the arbitral award and for correction and supplementation) as proposed, the request for additional administration fees and the 'scrutiny' of the arbitral award, I expect that the number of clerical errors and/or failures to decide on claims in arbitral awards will be reduced and that, as a result, the number of requests for correction and/or supplementation, refusals of leave to enforce and claims for setting aside can also be further reduced. This will also further guarantee the quality and uniformity of arbitral awards.

APPENDIX 1 CHAPTER 22

NAI AWARD CHECKLIST (2024)[1]

1. General

☐ **A.** NAI case reference number on front page.
☐ **B.** Award clearly identified in its title as interim, partial, final or award by consent.[2]
☐ **C.** Designation of party names with claimant(s) or defendant(s) on front page.
☐ **D.** Enumeration of the members of the arbitral tribunal on front page.
☐ **E.** Date of the award on front page.
☐ **F.** Table of contents.
☐ **G.** Page numbering.
☐ **H.** Paragraph numbering.
☐ **I.** Abbreviations defined and used consistently.
☐ **J.** Translations of quotations in languages other than the language of the arbitration.
☐ **K.** Indication of the applicable version of the NAI Arbitration Rules (*eg*, 2015, 2024).

2. Identification of Parties, their Representatives and Arbitrator(s).

☐ **A.** Names and addresses of the parties.[3] Clarify the identity of any parties to the arbitration that are different from the parties to the contract.
☐ **B.** Names and addresses of the parties' representatives.
☐ **C.** Names and addresses of the arbitrator(s).[4]

---

1 This Checklist was inspired by the ICC Award Checklist. With the permission of the ICC, I was allowed to include this edited Checklist. See the ICC website for the (latest version of the) ICC Award Checklist: <https://iccwbo.org/news-publications/arbitration-adr-rules-and-tools/icc-award-checklist-english-version/>.
2 Article 47 NAI.
3 Article 50(1)(b) NAI.
4 Article 50(1)(a) NAI.

3. Arbitration agreement and Choice of law

☐ **A.** Quotation of the entire arbitration agreement(s).
☐ **B.** Record of any agreed amendments to the arbitration agreement(s).
☐ **C.** The parties to the arbitration agreement.
☐ **D.** Quotation of relevant choice of law clause.[5]

4. Procedural history

☐ **A.** Summary of procedural steps to date[6] (*eg*, request for arbitration, short answer, case management conference, procedural orders, communications made, parties' submissions, hearing, etc).
☐ **B.** Indication of the decisions of the responsible member of the NAI Case Management Committee (*eg*, confirmation of appointment and, if applicable, number of arbitrators, etc).
☐ **C.** Description of method of constitution of the arbitral tribunal and appointment of arbitrators.[7]
☐ **D.** The time limit for making the award communicated to the parties by the arbitral tribunal[8], including any extensions that have occurred.
☐ **E.** The date on which the draft award was submitted to the responsible member of the NAI Case Management Committee in accordance with the scrutiny provision of Article 50(4) NAI.
☐ **F.** If a prior award has already been rendered: a brief summary of the proceedings from the time the prior award was rendered and a reference to the prior award, what was decided therein and the date of its dispatch to the parties.

5. Jurisdiction

☐ **A.** If the jurisdiction of the arbitral tribunal[9] is contested, or if one of the parties fails to appear in the arbitration, the award will have to include the arbitral tribunal's decision on jurisdiction or state why it is not necessary.

6. Claims of the Parties and Grounds of the Arbitral Tribunal

☐ **A.** A description of the parties' claim(s) and (if applicable) counterclaim(s) (quotation of the parties' request for relief), including amendments to the claim.[10]
☐ **B.** A description of the parties' positions.

---

5 Article 48(2) NAI.
6 Article 50(1)(c) NAI.
7 Article 16-18 NAI.
8 In accordance with Article 46 NAI.
9 Article 12 NAI.
10 Article 50(1)(d) NAI.

☐ **C.** The grounds of the decision[11] with a reasoning on each of the decisions in the dispositive section and a reasoning on all essential defenses.

7. Cost of the Arbitration (Final Award only)

☐ **A.** Determination of arbitration costs:[12]

- i. administration fees;[13]
- ii. arbitrators' fees and disbursements;[14]
- iii. what is on deposit;[15]
- iv. other costs;[16]
- v. costs of legal assistance.[17]

8. Dispositive Section, Place of Arbitration, Date and Signature

☐ **A.** The measure for decision making used[18]: "The arbitral tribunal deciding according to the rules of law" or "The arbitral tribunal deciding as amiable compositeur".

☐ **B.** If applicable, the decision on jurisdiction.
A decision[19] on all of the parties' claim(s) and counterclaim(s), including amendment(s) to the claim(s) and counterclaim(s), as formulated by the parties in the most recent requests for relief and as listed earlier in the award in the description of the parties' claims.
If it is not a final award, notice that the decision on the remaining claims are reserved for one or more future awards.

☐ **C.** An order to pay the costs of the arbitration.[20]

☐ **D.** An order to pay legal fees, to the extent that it is a final award.[21]

☐ **E.** At the conclusion of the dispositive section of a final award: "Dismisses any other or further claims", unless it follows from the nature of the award that this is unnecessary.

---

11 Article 50(1)(e) NAI. This is subject to exception if, after the arbitration is commenced, the parties have agreed in writing that no grounds will be given for the decision (Article 50(3) NAI).

12 Article 50(1)(f) NAI in conjunction with Article 59 NAI. If the award is an order for injunctive relief, a partial final award or an interim award, these costs may be stayed until a later date in the proceedings (Article 50(2) NAI).

13 Article 57 NAI and Article F2 NAI.

14 Article 58 NAI and Article F3 NAI.

15 Article 58 NAI.

16 Article 56(1)(c) NAI.

17 Article 56(2) NAI in conjunction with Article 59 NAI.

18 Article 50(1)(g) NAI in conjunction with Article 48 NAI.

19 Article 50(1)(h) NAI.

20 Article 50(1)(f) NAI in conjunction with Article 59 NAI in conjunction with Article 56 NAI. See also footnote 12.

21 Article 56(2) NAI in conjunction with Article 59 NAI.

☐ **F.** After the dispositive section: the place of arbitration,[22] the date[23] of the award and the signature(s)[24] of arbitrator(s) (as indicated below):

Place of Arbitration: ________________________________ (city, country)

Date: ________________________________

Signature(s): ________________________________

[name of arbitrator]

22 Article 50(1)(i) NAI.

23 Article 50(1)(j) NAI. The date must be after the date of sending the arbitral award to the responsible member of the NAI Case Management Committee (in accordance with the scrutiny provision of Art 50(4) NAI) and may not be before the last arbitrator has signed.

24 Article 49 NAI. If a minority of the arbitrators refuses to sign or is unable to sign (and it cannot be expected that this impediment will cease to exist shortly), the other arbitrators shall make mention of this in the signed award (Article 49(5) NAI).

APPENDIX 2

NAI CHECKLIST ON CORRECTION AND SUPPLEMENTATION (2024)[1]

1. General

☐ **A.** NAI case reference number on front page.

☐ **B.** Decision clearly identified on front page as:
- i. "Decision to correct".[2]
- ii. "Decision rejecting request for correction".
- iii. "Additional Award".[3]
- iv. "Decision rejecting request for supplementation".

☐ **C.** Indication of the case reference number and date of the award to which the request for correction and/or supplementation relates.[4]

☐ **D.** Designation of party names with claimant(s) or defendant(s) on the cover sheet.

☐ **E.** Enumeration of the members of the arbitral tribunal on front page.

☐ **F.** Date of decision on front page.

☐ **G.** Table of contents (if necessary).

☐ **H.** Page numbering.

☐ **I.** Paragraph numbering.

☐ **J.** Abbreviations defined and used consistently.

☐ **K.** Translations of quotations in languages other than the language of the arbitration.

☐ **L.** Indication of the applicable version of the NAI Arbitration Rules.

☐ **M.** Check – if the place of arbitration is not in the Netherlands – whether the applicable arbitration law allows for correction and supplementation.

---

1 This checklist was inspired by the ICC Checklist on Correction and Interpretation of Awards. With the permission of the ICC, I was allowed to include this edited Checklist. See the ICC website for the (latest version of the) Checklist on Correction and Interpretation of Awards: <https://iccwbo.org/publication/icc-checklist-correction-interpretation-awards-1998-2012-icc-arbitration-rules/>.

2 If there are also rejections also "Decision rejecting request for correction".

3 If there are also rejections also "Decision rejecting request for supplementation". Pursuant to Article 55(4) NAI (and Article 1061(4) DCCP) an additional award constitutes an arbitral award to which the provisions of the fifth section of the NAI Arbitration Rules ("The Award") also apply. In the following, this 'mutatis mutandis provision' for the reference to the articles on the award is no longer separately named (as opposed to the provision for correction, Article 54(6) NAI, because the correction is only a separate document, which is deemed to be part of the arbitral award).

Article 54(6)(b) NAI.

2. Identification of Parties, their Representatives and Arbitrator(s).

☐ **A.** Names and addresses of parties.[5]

☐ **B.** Names and addresses of the parties' representatives.

☐ **C.** Names and addresses of arbitrator(s).[6]

3. Contents

☐ **A.** Summary of all procedural steps from the date that the award was sent to the parties to date[7] (when the award for which correction and/or supplementation was requested was sent, date of receipt of the request for correction and/or supplementation and whether the request was made in a timely manner, date on which the request was sent in copy by the responsible member of the NAI Case Management Committee to the other parties and the arbitral tribunal, etc).

☐ **B.** A reference to the award to which the correction[8] and/or supplementation relates (including date and case reference number).

☐ **C.** A description of the parties' request for correction and/or supplementation.[9]

☐ **D.** Indication that the arbitral tribunal has given the parties an opportunity to comment on the request for correction and/or supplementation or the ex officio correction[10] (and the time limit given to them to do so).

☐ **E.** A description of the parties' positions.

☐ **F.** The grounds of the decision[11] to grant or deny the request for correction and/or supplementation, including whether the request falls within the scope of Article 54 NAI (correction) or Article 55 NAI (supplementation).

☐ **G.** If a request for correction is granted or an ex officio correction follows: what the correction consists of and the correction itself.[12]

---

5 Article 50(1)(b) NAI (for correction, see also Article 54(6)(a) NAI).

6 Article 50(1)(a) NAI (for correction, see also Article 54(6)(a) NAI).

7 Article 50(1)(c) NAI.

8 Article 54(6)(b) NAI.

9 Cf. Article 50(1)(d) NAI.

10 Article 54(5) NAI and Article 55(3) NAI.

11 Article 50(1)(e) NAI. This is subject to exception if, after the arbitration is commenced, the parties have agreed in writing that no grounds will be given for the decision (Article 50(3) NAI).

12 Article 54(6)(c) NAI.

- ☐ **H.** If a request for supplementation is granted: a decision on the 'undecided claim(s)' (granted or denied in the dispositive section) and the grounds therefor.[13]
- ☐ **I.** The date on which the draft additional award was submitted to the responsible member of the NAI Case Management Committee in accordance with the scrutiny provision of Article 50(4) NAI.

4. Costs

- ☐ **A.** Determination of arbitration costs, to the extent applicable in the event the request is denied:[14]
  - i. administrative fees;[15]
  - ii. arbitrators' fees and disbursements;[16]
  - iii. what is on deposit;[17]
  - iv. other costs;[18]
  - v. costs of legal assistance.[19]

5. Dispositive Section, Place of Arbitration, Date and Signature

- ☐ **A.** The measure for decision making used[20]: "The arbitral tribunal, deciding according to the rules of law" or "The arbitral tribunal, deciding as amiable compositeur".
- ☐ **B.** A decision[21] on the request for correction and/or supplementation:
  - Rejection of request for correction.
  - Granting the request for correction and correction of the award as stated above.
  - Rejection of request for supplementation.
  - Granting the request for supplementation, and either granting or rejecting the 'undecided claim'.
- ☐ **C.** An order to pay the costs of the arbitration[22], to the extent applicable in the event of a dismissal.

13 Article 50(1)(e) NAI. This is subject to exception if, after the arbitration is commenced, the parties have agreed in writing that no grounds will be given for the decision (Article 50(3) NAI).

14 Article 50(1)(f) NAI in conjunction with Article 59 NAI.

15 Article 57 NAI and Article F2 NAI.

16 Article 58 NAI and Article F3 NAI.

17 Article 58 NAI.

18 Article 56(1)(c) NAI.

19 Article 56(2) NAI in conjunction with Article 59 NAI.

20 Article 50(1)(g) NAI in conjunction with Article 48 NAI.

21 Article 50(1)(h) NAI.

22 Article 50(1)(f) NAI in conjunction with Article 59 NAI in conjunction with Article 56 NAI.

☐ **D.** An order to pay legal fees[23], to the extent applicable in the event of a rejection.

☐ **E.** After the dispositive section: the place of arbitration[24], the date[25] of the decision and the signature(s)[26] of arbitrator(s) (as indicated below):

Place of Arbitration: ________________________________ (city, country)

Date: ________________________________

Signature(s): ________________________________

[name of arbitrator]

23 Article 56(2) NAI in conjunction with Article 59 NAI.

24 Article 50(1)(i) NAI.

25 Article 50(1)(j) NAI (for correction Article 54(6)(d) NAI, it being understood that the date of the award to which the correction relates remains decisive). The date must be after the date of sending the decision on the request for correction and/or supplementation to the responsible member of the NAI Case Management Committee (in accordance with the scrutiny provision) and may not be before the last arbitrator has signed.

26 Article 49 NAI (and for correction, see also Article 54(6)(e) NAI). If a minority of the arbitrators refuse to sign or are unable to sign (and it cannot be expected that this impediment will cease to exist shortly), the other arbitrators shall make mention thereof in the signed award (Article 49(5) NAI).

CHAPTER 23

SETTING ASIDE OF ARBITRAL AWARDS: LESSONS FOR (NAI) ARBITRATORS?

Pauline Ernste & Carmen Schleijpen[1]

23.1 Introduction

Arbitrators should be careful that their award is not subject to setting aside.[2] The judgments in the cases *Greenworld v. Arbitrators* and *Qnow v. B.* illustrate that setting aside of an arbitral award plays an important role in connection to liability of arbitrators, in addition to the fact that it must be established that the arbitrator acted with intent or deliberate recklessness or that the error constitutes a serious breach of duty.[3] Case law shows that

1 P.E. (Pauline) Ernste is professor of Dispute Resolution in the (inter)national legal practice at the Radboud Business Law Institute (OO&R) of Radboud University Nijmegen. C.L. (Carmen) Schleijpen (LLM) is a lecturer in civil law at the Faculty of Law of Radboud University Nijmegen and a PhD candidate in the field of arbitration at the Radboud Business Law Institute (OO&R). This contribution is an updated and edited version of an article published in 2019 in Dutch: P.E. Ernste & C.L. Schleijpen, 'De vernietiging van arbitrale vonnissen: lessen voor (NAI-)arbiters?', in: C.J.M. Klaassen, G.J. Meijer & C.L. Schleijpen (eds), *Going Dutch: ADR in Nederland, in het bijzonder bij het NAI (Onderneming en Recht nr. 113)*, Deventer: Wolters Kluwer 2019, p 651-700.

2 See H.J. Snijders, 'Aansprakelijkheid van arbiters (QNOW/B), repressie en preventie', *TvA* 2017/1, p 1; H.J. Snijders, 'Aansprakelijkheid van arbiters, repressie en preventie. Ontwikkelingen in Nederland en beschouwingen mede in Belgisch perspectief', in: N. Carette & B. Weyts (eds), *Verantwoord aansprakelijkheidsrecht (liber amicorum Aloïs van Oevelen)*, Antwerpen/Cambridge: Intersentia 2017, p 541. Already in 1940, Piet Sanders' dissertation on setting aside of arbitral awards was published, see P. Sanders, *Aantasting van arbitrale vonnissen*, Zwolle: W.E.J. Tjeenk Willink 1940. The subject is still topical more than eighty years later.

3 See Supreme Court 30 September 2016, ECLI:NL:HR:2016:2215, *NJ* 2017/141, annotated by J.B.M. Vranken (*Qnow/B*); Supreme Court 4 December 2009, ECLI:NL:HR:2009:BJ7834, *NJ* 2011/131, annotated by J.B.M. Vranken (*Greenworld/Arbiters*). That liability is not imaginary is illustrated by the referral judgments in the *Qnow*-case: Arnhem-Leeuwarden Court of Appeal 16 October 2018, ECLI:NL:GHARL:2018:9111 and Arnhem-Leeuwarden Court of Appeal 4 June 2019, ECLI:NL:GHARL:2019:4760, *JOR* 2019/243, annotated by C.L. Schleijpen. See also 's-Hertogenbosch Court of Appeal 8 December 2015, ECLI:NL:GHSHE:2015:5154 and Oost-Brabant District Court 15 October 2014, ECLI:NL:RBOBR:2014:6276. The liability claims in these cases were ultimately dismissed, but the threshold for liability was met.

setting aside proceedings are initiated several times a year. Although this does not always lead to the setting aside of the arbitral award, the setting aside claim succeeds in a non-negligible number of cases.[4] In some cases, there is clearly an error of the arbitrator that provides a ground for setting aside the arbitral award, for example if a signature of one or more arbitrators is missing.[5] This omission makes the award subject to setting aside under Article 1065(1)(d) of the Dutch Code of Civil Procedure (hereinafter DCCP) and is relatively easy to establish. However, this does not apply to all of the grounds for setting aside. For example, when is a breach of the mandate serious enough to merit setting aside of an arbitral award? Or when has the equal right to be heard been violated or has an arbitral award not been sufficiently reasoned?

The case law of the lower courts shows that an arbitral award will only be set aside if there is something seriously wrong with the award, but also that the dividing line between what leads to setting aside and what does not cannot always be drawn sharply. As a result, it is not always clear to an arbitrator under which circumstances an arbitral award is subject to setting aside, nor how he[6] is expected to act. In this contribution, we attempt to provide more clarity on this point and give arbitrators tools to prevent their arbitral awards from being set aside. We do so by analysing case law and literature on setting aside of arbitral awards. It is also important for (NAI) arbitrators to take note of the case law on the setting aside of arbitral awards, so that they can learn from it and apply these lessons to their own conduct in arbitral proceedings. We will first discuss the grounds for setting aside of an arbitral award laid down in Article 1065 DCCP and the manner in which these grounds are interpreted and applied in case law (para 23.2). With respect to setting aside proceedings, we note that since 2015, after the current Dutch Arbitration Act came into force,[7] the claim to set aside an arbitral award must be brought before the Court of Appeal as a judge in first instance. This entails that the setting aside claim will only be reviewed in proceedings in one fact-finding instance and in cassation

4 See also M. Boevink, 'Successfully setting aside arbitral awards in the Netherlands, What are the odds?', *TvA* 2024/2.

5 See Amsterdam District Court 28 September 2005, ECLI:NL:RBAMS:2005:AU4950 (*Qnow*) and Supreme Court 5 December 2008, ECLI:NL:HR:2008:BF3799, *JBPr* 2009/2, annotated by H.W. Wiersma (*Bursa/Güris I*). The latter case concerned a defect in the signing of the notice as referred to in Article 1057(3) DCCP.

6 Throughout this contribution, he shall also be read as she and as they.

7 See *Stb.* 2014, 200 (Dutch Arbitration Act 2015) and *Stb.* 2014, 254 (Decree concerning the date of entry into force of the Dutch Arbitration Act). The (new) Arbitration Act entered into force on the 1st of January 2015.

proceedings. Before 2015, setting aside proceedings could be conducted in two fact-finding instances (i.e. the District Court and the Court of Appeal) and in cassation proceedings before the Dutch Supreme Court. In paragraph 23.3 we discuss remission of arbitral awards as laid down in Article 1065a DCCP and the meaning thereof for setting aside of arbitral awards. We conclude with some points for (NAI) arbitrators to consider (para 23.4).

23.2 Grounds for setting aside

23.2.1 In general

The remedy of setting aside an arbitral award is considered an *ultimum remedium*.[8] The Supreme Court has explicitly ruled on several occasions that the grounds for setting aside of an arbitral award must be applied with restraint by state courts.[9] The Supreme Court bases this finding on the fact that setting aside proceedings may not be used as a form of disguised appeal and that the public interest in an effectively functioning means of dispute resolution through arbitration means that state courts should only intervene in arbitral awards in *striking cases*.[10] However, as will be shown below, this restraint does not apply to all grounds for setting aside. Article 1065(1) DCCP exhaustively lists the grounds for setting aside of an arbitral award. Setting aside may take place if there is no arbitration agreement or no valid arbitration agreement (ground a), the arbitral tribunal was not composed in accordance with the applicable rules (ground b), the arbitral tribunal has not complied with its mandate (ground c), the arbitral

8 See Asser Procesrecht/Sanders, Meijer & Ernste *8* 2023/521; G.J. Meijer & A.I.M. van Mierlo, *Parlementaire Geschiedenis Arbitragewet*, Deventer: Wolters Kluwer 2015, p 161, cf. p 158-159; P. Sanders, *Het Nederlandse arbitragerecht. Nationaal en Internationaal*, Deventer: Kluwer 2001, p 186.

9 See for example Supreme Court 9 January 2004, ECLI:NL:HR:2004:AK8380, para 3.5.2, *NJ* 2005/190, annotated by H.J. Snijders (*Nannini/SFT*); Supreme Court 17 January 2003, ECLI:NL:HR:2003:AE9395, para 3.3, *NJ* 2004/384, annotated by H.J. Snijders (*IMS/Modsaf*); Supreme Court 4 December 2020, ECLI:NL:HR:2020:1952, para 3.3.1 (*Russische Federatie/HVY*); Supreme Court 5 November 2021, ECLI:NL:HR:2021:1645, para 5.4.9, *NJ* 2022/102, annotated by C.M.J. Ryngaert & A.I.M. van Mierlo (*Russische Federatie/HVY*).

10 See for example Supreme Court 17 January 2003, ECLI:NL:HR:2003:AE9395, para 3.3, *NJ* 2004/384 (*IMS/Modsaf*), annotated by H.J. Snijders; Supreme Court 5 November 2021, ECLI:NL:HR:2021:1645, paras 5.4.9 and 5.5.4, *NJ* 2022/102, annotated by C.M.J. Ryngaert & A.I.M. van Mierlo (*Russische Federatie/HVY*); Supreme Court 17 March 2023, ECLI:NL:HR:2023:422, para 3.3, *NJ* 2023/115 (*Attero/Gemeenten & Gewesten*).

award has not been signed in accordance with Article 1057 DCCP or has not been sufficiently reasoned (ground d), or if the award is contrary to public policy in its content or in the manner of its formation (ground e). The restrained review does not apply in case of the (alleged) absence of an arbitration agreement (ground a) or in case of a(n) (alleged) violation of the equal right to be heard (ground e).[11]

Whether an arbitral award is ultimately subject to setting aside depends on a large number of circumstances, including forfeiture of rights (Article 1065(2)-(4) DCCP)[12] and failure to request an additional award, if (part of) the claim has not been decided on (Article 1061 in conjunction with Article 1065(6) DCCP). The ground for setting aside can be taken away in advance if an additional arbitral award has been rendered (Article 1061 DCCP). Finally, the party invoking setting aside may have insufficient interest in doing so (Article 3:303 of the Dutch Civil Code, hereinafter DCC)[13] and, since the introduction of the Arbitration Act in 2015, it is conceivable that the error in the arbitral award may be remedied via remission pursuant to Article 1065a DCCP, so that setting aside need not follow (see para 23.3).

Despite the restrained review, setting aside of an arbitral award regularly occurs. Our analysis of the case law on setting aside of arbitral awards was not limited to a specific time period. We analysed the case law published up to September 2024.[14] Cases decided before the introduction of the Arbi-

11 See, *inter alia*, Supreme Court 25 May 2007, ECLI:NL:HR:2007:BA2495, para 3.5, *TvA* 2008/10, annotated by J.J. van Haersolte-van Hof (*Spaanderman/Anova Food*); Supreme Court 24 April 2009, ECLI:NL:HR:2009:BH3137, para 4.3.1, *NJ* 2010/171, annotated by H.J. Snijders (*IMS/Modsaf II*); Supreme Court 26 September 2014, ECLI:NL:HR:2014:2837, para 4.2, *NJ* 2015/318, annotated by H.J. Snijders (*Ecuador/Chevron*); Supreme Court 5 November 2021, ECLI:NL:HR:2021:1645, *NJ* 2022/102, annotated by A.I.M. van Mierlo & C.M.J. Ryngaert (*Russische Federatie/HVY*).

12 For Article 1065(4) DCCP it follows from Supreme Court 23 April 2010, ECLI:NL:HR:2010:BK8097, *NJ* 2011/475, annotated by H.J. Snijders (*AREB/AMEG*) that it relates to a form of forfeiture of rights (para 3.4.2). For Article 1065(2) and (3) DCCP, it is not clear whether it refers to loss of rights or forfeiture of rights. See G.J. Meijer, *T&C Rv*, Article 1065, note 1c and 8a (online, updated 1 January 2024); H.J. Snijders, note to Supreme Court 23 April 2010, ECLI:NL:HR:2010:BK8097, *NJ* 2011/475, para 2b; Sanders 2001, p 191-192.

13 See H.J. Snijders, in: *GS Burgerlijke Rechtsvordering*, Article 1065 DCCP, note 1.2 (online, updated 1 May 2018).

14 Searches for case law were conducted via <www.rechtspraak.nl>, <www.rechtsorde.nl> and <www.legalintelligence.nl>. On <www.rechtspraak.nl>, the following search terms were used: 1065 Rv, vernietiging EN arbitraal vonnis and vernietiging arbitraal vonnis. The following filters were applied: Burgerlijk procesrecht, Europees civiel recht, verbintenissenrecht, geen subrechtsgebied, Uitspraak. On <www.rechtsorde.nl>, the search term 1065 DCCP was used, together with the

tration Act 2015 were also included in the analysis as they are also relevant for the application of the Arbitration Act 2015. A total of 272 cases heard by lower courts and the Supreme Court were studied,[15] of which 55 cases involved setting aside of an arbitral award. It follows that although setting aside is not common, the risk of setting aside is real. For this contribution, we assessed on what ground(s) the setting aside claim was based, the circumstances put forward in order to achieve setting aside, the ground(s) upon which the claim was granted and the reason for setting aside or granting it. In this contribution, we focus on the arbitrator's *conduct*: when does the conduct of the arbitrator(s) lead to setting aside of the arbitral award? In the following paragraphs, we highlight some interesting cases and try to indicate where the dividing line lies for the arbitrator. In answering this research question, we focus on commercial arbitration and only discuss cases concerning setting aside of an arbitral award rendered in an investment arbitration if the ground(s) for setting aside of the award invoked in the case does (do) not specifically involve investment arbitration.

23.2.2 *Absence of a valid arbitration agreement (Article 1065(1)(a) DCCP)*

The first ground for setting aside of an arbitral award mentioned in Article 1065(1) DCCP is the absence of a valid arbitration agreement (ground a). This ground was raised in 56 of the cases examined and led to setting aside of the award in 13 cases. If there is no valid arbitration agreement, the arbitral tribunal should decline jurisdiction. It should be noted that it follows from the case law of the Supreme Court that a declaration by the arbitral tribunal that it lacks jurisdiction is not eligible for setting aside. The Supreme Court referred to Article 1052(5) DCCP and the parliamentary history of the provision, from which it follows that a declaration of lack of jurisdiction based on the absence of a valid arbitration agreement means that the state courts have jurisdiction to hear the case. According to

---

filter jurisprudentie (case law). On <www.legalintelligence.nl>, the following search terms were used: 1065 Rv, vernietiging EN arbitraal vonnis and vernietiging arbitraal vonnis. For the first search term, the filter Rechtspraak was used. For the other two search terms, two additional filters were used, namely: Burgerlijk recht and Burgerlijke rechtsvordering. Further case law was found via literature studied for this contribution. Those cases were also included in the analysis. The list of cases examined for this contribution can be accessed via <https://doi.org/10.34973/qkr3-8s55>.

15 This concerns cases against which no appeal is available or appeal is no longer available. Thus, if the case was litigated in two or three judicial instances, this counts as one case.

the Supreme Court, this excludes a claim for setting aside.[16] This case law is criticized in academic literature and there are several reasons to argue that a declaration by the arbitral tribunal that it lacks jurisdiction should be eligible for setting aside.[17]

An arbitrator is competent to rule on his own jurisdiction (Article 1052(1) DCCP).[18] A party that has appeared in the arbitral proceedings must raise a plea that the arbitral tribunal does not have jurisdiction on the ground of non-existence of a valid arbitration agreement before submitting a defence, on pain of forfeiting the right to rely on this later in the arbitral proceedings or before the court in setting aside proceedings (Article 1065(2) in conjunction with Article 1052(2) DCCP, see also Article 12(1)-(3) NAI Arbitration Rules 2024).[19] An arbitrator is generally not allowed to decide *ex officio* whether or not he has jurisdiction over the dispute if a party did

16 See Supreme Court 21 April 2023, ECLI:NL:HR:2023:636, paras 3.1-3.3, *JBPr* 2023/57, annotated by B. van Zelst & B.A. Keizers (*X c.s./Venezuela*); Supreme Court 5 July 2024, ECLI:NL:HR:2024:1024 (*Güris/Bursa*). Earlier case law of lower courts did however consider that a declaration of lack of jurisdiction could be set aside, albeit on the basis of Article 1065(1)(b)-(e) DCCP. It was held that these grounds did not call into question the declaration of lack of jurisdiction as such. See The Hague District Court 15 August 2012, ECLI:NL:RBSGR:2012:BX6825, para 4.7; The Hague Court of Appeal 29 January 2021, ECLI:NL:GHDHA:2021:14, paras 15-20. See also A-G Drijber in his non-binding opinion rendered prior to Supreme Court 21 April 2023, ECLI:NL:HR:2023:636, paras 6.63-6.99, *JBPr* 2023/57 (*X c.s./Venezuela*).

17 Asser Procesrecht/Sanders, Meijer & Ernste *8* 2023/477; B. van Zelst & B.A. Keizers, note to Supreme Court 21 April 2023, ECLI:NL:HR:2023:636, para 9, *JBPr* 2023/57 (*X c.s./Venezuela*).

18 Since such a decision of an arbitrator in that respect also says something about the jurisdiction of the state court, the latter has the last word on the arbitral award on jurisdiction in the context of enforcement or setting aside proceedings (Article 1062-1063 DCCP and Article 1065(1)(a) DCCP, respectively). See in detail: H.J. Snijders, in: *GS Burgerlijke Rechtsvordering*, Article 1052 DCCP, note 1 (online, updated 1 May 2018); G.J. Meijer, *Overeenkomst tot arbitrage. Bezien in het licht van het bewijsvoorschrift van artikel 1021 Rv (diss. Rotterdam; Burgerlijk Proces & Praktijk nr. 13)*, Deventer: Kluwer 2011, p 862-867.

19 In The Hague Court of Appeal 19 June 2022, ECLI:NL:GHDHA:2022:1295, paras 5.3.6-5.3.7; The Hague Court of Appeal 19 June 2022, ECLI:NL:GHDHA:2022:1296, paras 5.3.6-5.3.7; The Hague Court of Appeal 19 June 2022, ECLI:NL:GHDHA:2022:1297, paras 5.2.7-5.2.8 the Russian Federation stated that it had not appeared in the arbitral proceedings and thus had not forfeited the right to rely on Article 1065(1)(a) DCCP in the setting aside proceedings. The Court of Appeal followed this submission and considered that the Russian Federation had not forfeited its right to invoke Article 1065(1)(a) DCCP.

not raise a defence on jurisdiction.[20] It is assumed in academic literature that an arbitral tribunal is obliged to test *ex officio* whether the case is arbitrable (Article 1020(3) DCCP)[21] and (in business-to-consumer arbitrations) whether an arbitration clause is (not) an unfair term within the meaning of Directive 93/13/EEC on unfair terms in consumer contracts[22] or unreasonably onerous (Article 6:236(n) DCC[23]).[24] In addition, it is argued that the arbitral tribunal may assess, of its own motion, whether it has jurisdiction if the defendant does not appear in the arbitral proceedings.[25] If arbitrators erroneously declare that they have jurisdiction over the dispute submitted to arbitration, the state court may set aside the arbitral award due to lack of a valid arbitration agreement.

---

20 See G.J. Meijer, in: *T&C Rv*, Article 1065 DCCP, note 2c (online, updated 1 January 2024).

21 See G.J. Meijer, in: *T&C Rv*, Article 1052 DCCP, note 2c (online, updated 1 January 2024); Asser Procesrecht/Sanders, Meijer & Ernste *8* 2023/119; H.J. Snijders, in: *GS Burgerlijke Rechtsvordering*, Article 1052 DCCP, note 2.1 (online, updated 1 May 2018); Meijer & Van Mierlo 2015, p 722; Meijer 2011, p 863-866.

22 OJ EU L 95/29.

23 Article 6:236(n) reads as follows: "In an agreement between a user and a counterparty, who is an individual not acting in the conduct of a business or profession, the following provisions contained in general terms and conditions are deemed to be unreasonably onerous: (…) that provides for dispute resolution by a person other than the court having jurisdiction under the law, unless it allows the counterparty a period of at least one month from the date when the user has invoked the provision in writing against the counterparty, to opt for dispute resolution by the court having jurisdiction under the law; (…)". See H. Warendorf et al (eds), *Warendorf Dutch Civil and Commercial Law Legislation*, Deventer: Wolters Kluwer, Article 236 CC Bk 6.

24 See for example G.J. Meijer, in: *T&C Rv*, Article 1052 DCCP, note 2c (online, updated 1 January 2024); Asser Procesrecht/Sanders, Meijer & Ernste *8* 2023/114, 119, 335; H.J. Snijders, in: *GS Burgerlijke Rechtsvordering*, Article 1052 DCCP, note 2.1 (online, updated 1 May 2018); Meijer & Van Mierlo 2015, p 194. This can be argued on the basis of (an extension of) the case law of the Court of Justice of the European Union (hereinafter CJEU/CJEC) and of the Dutch Supreme Court concerning *ex officio* review in setting aside and *exequatur* proceedings. See in particular CJEC 26 October 2006, C-168/05, ECLI:EU:C:2006:675, *NJ* 2007/201, annotated by M.R. Mok (*Mostaza Claro v Centro Móvil Milenium SL*); CJEC 6 October 2009, C-40/08, ECLI:EU:C:2009:615, *NJ* 2010/11, annotated by M.R. Mok (*Asturcom*); CJEU 16 November 2010, C-76/10, ECLI:EU:C:2010:685 (*Pohotovost*); Supreme Court 8 November 2019, ECLI:NL:HR:2019:1731, *NJ* 2020/305, annotated by H.J. Snijders (*Intermaris*).

25 See for example G.J. Meijer, in: *T&C Rv*, Article 1052 DCCP, note 2c, 3d and 4c (online, updated 1 January 2024); Asser Procesrecht/Sanders, Meijer & Ernste *8* 2023/119, 239; H.J. Snijders, in: *GS Burgerlijke Rechtsvordering*, Article 1052 DCCP, note 2.1 (online, updated 1 May 2018).

It should be noted that the test by the state court in this context is, by way of exception, not restrictive.[26] The Supreme Court ruled in the *Russian Federation v. HVY*-case that this assessment is not limited to whether the arbitral tribunal assumed jurisdiction on the proper grounds. The public interest in an effectively functioning means of dispute resolution through arbitration entails that the court should not set aside an arbitral award on the sole ground that the arbitral tribunal incorrectly reasoned its decision that it had jurisdiction to hear the dispute. The court in setting aside proceedings is therefore free to rule, on grounds other than those used by the arbitral tribunal, that the arbitral tribunal was right to consider that it had jurisdiction. According to the Supreme Court, a different view would result in situations in which the court would rule that the grounds used by the arbitral tribunal are insufficient for the jurisdiction assumed by the tribunal, that the arbitral tribunal did have jurisdiction on other grounds, but that the arbitral award must nevertheless be set aside. The consequence would be that, although a valid arbitration agreement exists, the dispute must be decided by the state court unless the parties agree otherwise (Article 1067 DCCP[27]). This is inconsistent, the Supreme Court concluded, with the parties' demonstrated intention to submit their dispute not to a state court but to an arbitral tribunal.[28] Below, we outline some cases that have arisen in practice that illustrate some of the issues that could arise in determining whether a valid arbitration agreement exists between the parties.

The validity of an arbitration agreement should be assessed on the basis of the general rules on formation of agreements. Insofar as Dutch law applies, Article 3:33 *et seq*. DCC and Article 6:217 *et seq*. DCC, and in case of formation of an electronic contract Article 6:227a DCC, apply.[29] The rules on interpretation of contracts also apply.[30] In cases in which the jurisdic-

26 See Supreme Court 26 September 2014, ECLI:NL:HR:2014:2837, para 4.2, *NJ* 2015/318, annotated by H.J. Snijders (*Ecuador/Chevron*).

27 We note that this case was rendered under the Arbitration Act 1986, but the principles laid down in the case are also relevant under the current Arbitration Act (2015).

28 See Supreme Court 5 November 2021, ECLI:NL:HR:2021:1645, para 5.2.7, *NJ* 2022/102, annotated by A.I.M. van Mierlo & C.M.J. Ryngaert (*Russische Federatie/HVY*). See also The Hague Court of Appeal 19 June 2022, ECLI:NL:GHDHA:2022:1295, para 5.3.11; The Hague Court of Appeal 19 June 2022, ECLI:NL:GHDHA:2022:1296, para 5.3.11; The Hague Court of Appeal 19 June 2022, ECLI:NL:GHDHA:2022:1297, para 5.2.11.

29 See Asser Procesrecht/Sanders, Meijer & Ernste *8* 2023/73. See also The Hague Court of Appeal 5 April 2022, ECLI:NL:GHDHA:2022:576, paras 5.6-5.7.

30 See for an illustration of this Court of Appeal 20 June 2023, ECLI:NL:GHAMS:2023:1441. The claim to set the arbitral award aside for lack of a valid arbitration agreement was dismissed.

tion of the arbitral tribunal is based on an arbitration clause in general terms and conditions, several (particular) issues may arise regarding the validity of the arbitration clause. For example, it is conceivable that a party takes the position that the general terms and conditions were not validly agreed upon in the arbitral proceedings. The arbitral tribunal must assess whether an arbitration clause is valid on the basis of the general rules on formation of contracts already referred to above, as well as the provisions laid down in Article 6:231 *et seq*. DCC, concerning general terms and conditions.[31] If the arbitral tribunal wrongly assumes that the general terms and conditions including an arbitration clause have been validly agreed upon, this may constitute a ground for setting aside of the arbitral award, according to case law.[32]

We have come across several cases in which the question in the setting aside proceedings was whether the arbitration clause was unreasonably onerous and thus whether a valid arbitration agreement existed between the parties.[33] An arbitration clause in general terms and conditions is voidable if it is unreasonably onerous (Article 6:233(a) DCC) or because the user of the general terms and conditions has not given the counterparty a reasonable opportunity to take note of the terms and conditions (Article 6:233(b) in conjunction with Article 6:234 DCC).[34] In several of the cases analysed for this contribution, the arbitral award was set aside on the basis of Article 1065(1)(a) DCCP, because it was found in the setting aside proceedings that the arbitration clause was unreasonably onerous[35] or that the

31 See Meijer 2011, p 459-461.

32 See 's-Hertogenbosch Court of Appeal 17 March 2015, ECLI:NL:GHSHE:2015:929, para 3.3.2 and 3.3.8; Supreme Court 27 March 2009, ECLI:NL:HR:2009:BG6443, *NJ* 2010/170, annotated by H.J. Snijders (*Ruwa Bulbs*).

33 See Rotterdam District Court 8 November 2017, ECLI:NL:RBROT:2017:8850, paras 4.5.8-4.5.9; 's-Gravenhage District Court 29 May 2013, ECLI:NL:RBDHA:2013:6325, paras 4.4-4.8, *NJF* 2013/332 (claim to nullify the arbitration clause time-barred under Article 3:52(1)(b) in conjunction with Article 6:235(4) DCC); 's-Hertogenbosch Court of Appeal 17 March 2009, ECLI:NL:GHSHE:2009:BH6958, paras 4.4-4.7; Supreme Court 23 March 1990, ECLI:NL:HR:1990:AD1068, *NJ* 1991/214, annotated by H.J. Snijders (*Botman/Van Haaster*).

34 Article 6:233 DCC reads as follows: "A provision in general terms and conditions may be nullified: a. if it is unreasonably onerous to the counterparty, taking into consideration the nature and the further content of the agreement, the manner in which the terms and conditions were established, the mutually apparent interests of the parties and the other circumstances of the case; or b. if the user has not given the counterparty a reasonable opportunity to take note of the general terms and conditions". See Warendorf et al, Article 233 CC Bk 6.

35 Supreme Court 23 March 1990, ECLI:NL:HR:1990:AD1068, *RvdW* 1990/71 (*Botman/Van Haaster*). In this case, the Supreme Court uses the phrase 'unreasonably

counterparty had not been provided with a reasonable opportunity to take note of general terms and conditions including the arbitration clause.[36] As regards the latter point, an arbitration clause has been nullified (pursuant to Article 6:233(b) DCC) because the user of the general terms and conditions had not sufficiently proven that the general terms and conditions were (actually) accessible through a hyperlink on the quotation sent to the counterparty. The counterparty had argued that the general terms and conditions were not accessible via the hyperlink and relied on a print screen of an error notification in that respect. The Amsterdam Court of Appeal ruled that the user of the general terms and conditions had not shown that the hyperlink worked, nor that the general terms and conditions were visible once the hyperlink had been clicked on.[37] In the liability proceedings that followed, the claim against the arbitration institute (the *Raad voor Arbitrage in Bouwgeschillen)* and the arbitrators was dismissed.[38] With respect to the foregoing we note that the Court of Justice of the European Union has held that *choice-of-court* clauses are validly concluded within the meaning of Article 23(1) and (2) of the Lugano II Convention[39] if such a clause is laid down in general terms and conditions to which the written contract refers by including a hyperlink to a website and, by following that link, the general terms and conditions can be viewed, downloaded and printed prior to the written contract being signed. It is not required that the party against whom the choice-of-court clause operates was asked to accept the general terms and conditions by ticking a box on the website.[40] It is necessary that the hyperlink functions and that it can be activated by a party exercising ordinary diligence.[41] It should be noted that Article 6:233 and Article 6:234

onerous', even though the judgment was rendered before the current Civil Code was introduced.

36 See Amsterdam Court of Appeal 23 February 2021, ECLI:NL:GHAMS:2021:521; Leeuwarden Court of Appeal 24 August 2005, ECLI:NL:GHLEE:2005:AU1555.

37 Amsterdam Court of Appeal 23 February 2021, ECLI:NL:GHAMS:2021:521, paras 3.14-3.19.

38 See Amsterdam District Court 30 August 2023, ECLI:NL:RBAMS:2023:5572, *JBPr* 2024/27, annotated by C.L. Schleijpen.

39 Convention on jurisdiction and the recognition and enforcement of judgments in civil and commercial matters, OJ L 339, 21 December 2007, p 3-41.

40 CJEU 24 November 2022, C-358/21, ECLI:EU:C:2022:923 (*Tilman SA/Unilever Supply Chain Company AG*), in particular para 59.

41 Cf. CJEU 24 November 2022, C-358/21, ECLI:EU:C:2022:923, paras 51-52 (*Tilman SA/Unilever Supply Chain Company AG*).

DCC[42] cannot be invoked by so-called large counterparties meant in Article 6:235(1) DCC.[43,44]

In business-to-consumer relations, as stated above, the arbitrator should consider *ex officio* whether an arbitration clause in general terms and conditions is unreasonably onerous within the meaning of Article 6:236(n)

42 Article 6:234 DCC reads as follows: "1. A user shall have given the counterparty an opportunity referred to in Article 233 (b), if he has given the general terms and conditions to the counterparty before or at the time the agreement was entered into, or has provided the terms and conditions in accordance with the procedure set out in Article 230c or, if this is not reasonably possible, he has given the counterparty notice before the agreement is entered into that the terms and conditions are available with him or have been lodged at the chamber of commerce indicated by him or with the office of the clerk of a court and that they will be sent on request. If the terms and conditions were not handed to the counterparty prior to or at the entry into the agreement, the provisions may also be nullified if the user did not send him the terms and conditions, without delay and at his own expense, at the request of the counterparty. The provisions in respect of the obligation to send the terms and conditions shall not apply to the extent that the user cannot reasonably be required to send them.
2. The user shall also have given the counterparty an opportunity referred to in Article 233(b), if, prior to or at the agreement being entered into, he has made the general terms and conditions available to the counterparty by electronic means in such a manner that these can be stored by him and will be accessible so that he may review them later or, where this is not reasonably possible, if, prior to the agreement being entered into, he has notified the counterparty where he may review the terms and conditions by electronic means and that they will be sent on request by electronic means or in any other manner.
If the terms and conditions were not made available to the counterparty prior to or at the agreement by electronic means being entered into, the provisions shall also be subject to nullification if the user did not send the terms and conditions, without delay and at his own expense, at the request of the counterparty by electronic means or in any other way.
3. The express consent of the counterparty shall be required in respect of the provision of reasonable means to read the general terms and conditions as referred to in paragraph (2), if the agreement is not entered into by electronic means.". See Warendorf et al, Article 234 CC Bk 6.

43 Article 6:235 DCC reads as follows: "1. The grounds for nullification referred to in Articles 233 and 234 may not be invoked by: a. a legal person referred to in Article 360 of Book 2 which, at the time of entry into the agreement, has recently published its annual accounts or a legal person in respect of which, at that time, Article 403(1) of Book 2 has recently been applied; b. a party to which the provision in subparagraph (a) does not apply, if, at the aforementioned time, fifty or more persons work for it or if, at that time, a statement pursuant to the <Handelsregisterwet 2007> (Commercial Registry Act 2007) shows that fifty or more persons work for it. (...)". See Warendorf et al, Article 235 CC Bk 6.

44 Such a counterparty could invoke the restrictive effect of reasonableness and fairness though (Article 6:248(2) DCC).

DCC (and an unfair term within the meaning of Directive 93/13/EEC).[45] It follows from Article 6:236(n) DCC that a clause that provides for resolution of a dispute by someone other than the competent state court is unreasonably onerous if it does not give the consumer (at least) one month of reflection time after invoking the clause to opt for proceedings before the state courts. A natural person not acting in the exercise of a profession or business is considered a consumer according to Article 6:236 DCC.[46] It follows from the Supreme Court judgment in the *Intermaris*-case that a state court in enforcement proceedings and (arguably also) in setting aside proceedings is obliged to assess *ex officio* whether an arbitration clause is unfair withing the meaning of European consumer law.[47] In this case one of the preliminary questions submitted to the Supreme Court was whether the state court hearing an application for leave to enforce an arbitral award made against a consumer pursuant to Article 1062 in conjunction with Article 1063 DCCP is obliged to consider *ex officio* whether the arbitration clause is unfair or unreasonably onerous according to the criteria in Directive 93/13/EEC and Article 6:236(n) DCC. The Supreme Court answered this question in the affirmative. In the judgment, the Supreme Court also referred to Article 1065(1)(a) DCCP. This seems to entail that even in setting aside proceedings, state courts are obliged to assess *ex officio* whether an arbitration clause is unfair within the meaning of European consumer law and thus is valid or not. It is argued that the fact that an arbitral award based on an unfair arbitration clause is exposed to setting aside or that such a clause cannot be enforced, combined with the fact that the state court even has to review this *ex officio*, entails that the arbitrator should also apply Article 6:236(n) DCC and Directive 93/13/EEC *ex officio*.[48]

There are also cases in which an arbitrator has to assess whether the dispute submitted to him is 'covered' by a valid arbitration agreement fol-

45 In principle, Article 6:236(n) DCC applies only to consumers, according to the beginning of the provision. However, it is assumed in the literature that Article 6:236 and Article 6:237 DCC have some consequential effect with respect to other (small) counterparties. See for example Asser/Sieburgh *6-III* 2022/502; M.H. Wissink, 'De lijsten met 'verboden' en 'verdachte' bedingen', in: B. Wessels & R.H.C. Jongeneel (eds), *Algemene voorwaarden*, Deventer: Wolters Kluwer 2017, p 247-248; J. Hijma, *Algemene voorwaarden (Mon. BW no. B55)*, Deventer: Wolters Kluwer 2016, paras 31-32.

46 See also, for example, Asser/Sieburgh *6-III* 2022/499; Wissink 2017, p 243-246; Hijma 2016, para 29.

47 See Supreme Court 8 November 2019, ECLI:NL:HR:2019:1731, para 2.3, *NJ* 2020/305, annotated by H.J. Snijders (*Intermaris*).

48 See Asser Procesrecht/Sanders, Meijer & Ernste *8* 2023/335.

lowing invocation of a lack of jurisdiction by one of the parties to the arbitration. This occurs in practice when parties conclude several agreements with each other, but only one of those agreements contains an arbitration clause. In such a case, a dispute pertaining to the other agreement, which does not provide for arbitration, cannot be settled via arbitration. If an arbitrator nevertheless considers himself competent to rule on the dispute, this may lead to setting aside of the arbitral award.[49]

Invocation of a lack of jurisdiction may furthermore result in an arbitrator having to test whether the parties involved in the arbitration are parties to the arbitration agreement[50] and whether the choice for arbitration was *voluntary* and *unambiguous*.[51] In practice, an arbitrator may have to rule on the question as to whether a party involved in the arbitration was acting as a representative in his (its) own name or on behalf of someone else with respect to the (conclusion of the) arbitration agreement.[52] If the arbitral tribunal wrongly assumes that a party involved in the arbitration as a representative was acting in its own name and was itself bound by the arbitration agreement, setting aside may follow.[53]

With respect to the foregoing, we note that a director of a company who signs the arbitration agreement is not automatically personally bound to that agreement. The Amsterdam District Court set aside an arbitral award in a case in which the arbitral tribunal nevertheless considered itself competent to rule on a dispute concerning liability of the director of a company for payment of a sum of money under the agreement including the arbitration clause.[54] An arbitral award was also set aside in a case in which a representative had not acted on behalf of the alleged counterparty to the arbitration agreement, which meant that the latter was not bound to that agreement and was therefore wrongly involved in the arbitration.[55]

49 See Utrecht District Court 8 August 2007, ECLI:NL:RBUTR:2007:BB1410, paras 4.7-4.9, *NJF* 2007/501.

50 See for an example of this The Hague Court of Appeal 5 April 2022, ECLI:NL:GHDHA:2022:576, paras 5.15-5.23.

51 More nuanced: the choice to *waive the right* of access to state courts (Article 17 of the Constitution and Article 6 ECHR). On this, see Meijer 2011, p 51-59.

52 Cf., concerning representation in general, Supreme Court 11 March 1977, ECLI:NL:HR:1977:AC1877, *NJ* 1977/521, annotated by G.J. Scholten (*Kribbebijter*).

53 See Supreme Court 4 May 2012, ECLI:NL:HR:2012:BW1271, Amsterdam Court of Appeal 15 June 2010, ECLI:NL:GHAMS:2010:BN6930 and Amsterdam District Court 14 January 2009, ECLI:NL:RBAMS:2009:BH5578.

54 See Amsterdam District Court 10 September 1997, ECLI:NL:RBAMS:1997:AG3247, paras 4.1-4.4, *JOR* 1998/2.

55 See Rotterdam District Court 16 May 2018, ECLI:NL:RBROT:2018:3826.

Importantly, third parties are in principle not bound by an arbitration agreement unless there is an (accepted) ground upon which binding force can be based, such as subrogation or acceptance (by the third party) of a third-party clause[56] (cf. Article 6:253 *et seq*. DCC).[57] Joint and several liability for payment obligations is insufficient to accept that a third party is bound to the arbitration agreement, as illustrated by the judgment in the case *Grünland & Greenworld v. Sagro*.[58] It also follows from case law that the fact that the parties to the arbitration are bound to the main contract containing an arbitration clause does not automatically entail that they are also bound to the arbitration clause, as that agreement is considered to be a separate agreement (cf. Article 1053 DCCP).[59] In the case of *Geosolutions c.s. v. Sina HK*, the Amsterdam Court of Appeal (partially) set aside an arbitral award in which the tribunal had accepted jurisdiction towards a legal entity (Sina HK) that had placed its signature underneath a license agreement between its subsidiary and Geosolutions B.V. The Amsterdam Court of Appeal ruled that the circumstances of the case, including the text of the license agreement and of the arbitration agreement, could not support the conclusion that Sina HK was a party to the arbitration agreement, also taking into account the reasoned challenge to the jurisdiction of the tribunal by Sina HK.[60]

In practice, so-called multi-tiered dispute resolution clauses are used. For example, the parties may include a dispute resolution clause in their con-

56 See for an example of this The Hague Court of Appeal 29 March 2022, ECLI:NL:GHDHA:2022:570, paras 2.1-2.5. The appeal in cassation was dismissed on the basis of Article 81 Judiciary Organization Act, see Supreme Court 1 September 2023, ECLI:NL:HR:2023:1145.

57 See Meijer 2011, p 615 et seq on third parties and the arbitration agreement.

58 See Supreme Court 20 January 2006, ECLI:NL:HR:2006:AU4523, *NJ* 2006/77 (*Grünland & Greenworld/Sagro*). In this case, the arbitral awards were partially set aside (insofar as they were rendered against Greenworld). The NAI was the administering institution in the arbitration.

59 See Arnhem-Leeuwarden Court of Appeal 24 September 2013, ECLI:NL:GHARL:2013:7057, paras 4.6-4.12; Arnhem District Court 7 September 2011, ECLI:NL:RBARN:2011:BS8667, paras 4.6-4.10. See, *inter alia*, N. Blackaby et al, *Redfern and Hunter on International Arbitration (Seventh Edition)*, Oxford: Oxford University Press 2023/2.107/2.119; G.B. Born, *International Commercial Arbitration (Third Edition)*, Alphen aan den Rijn: Kluwer Law International 2021, para 3.01 (online, updated March 2024); H.J. Snijders, in: *GS Burgerlijke Rechtsvordering*, Article 1053 DCCP, note 1 (online, updated 1 May 2018); Meijer 2011, p 223-224.

60 Amsterdam Court of Appel 30 August 2022, ECLI:NL:GHAMS:2022:2493, paras 4.5-4.33 and Supreme Court 15 March 2024, ECLI:NL:HR:2024:403 (appeal in cassation rejected on the basis of Article 81 of the Judiciary Organization Act). This concerned an arbitral award rendered in an NAI arbitration. The award was set aside insofar as it concerned Sina HK.

tract which provides for resolution of the dispute through mediation, and, if this is unsuccessful, through arbitration. Such clauses may give rise to the question as to the consequences of not first trying to resolve the dispute through mediation. The Supreme Court has ruled that the answer to the question whether a party is obligated to first try mediation depends on the content of the mediation clause. According to the Supreme Court the content of a mediation clause must be determined through interpretation. Under Dutch law, this comes down to the meaning that the parties could reasonably attach to the mediation clause in light of the circumstances of the case and to what the parties could reasonably expect of each other in that respect. This is a well-known standard under Dutch law, referred to as the 'Haviltex-standard' (*Haviltex*-maatstaf).[61] A mediation clause may have a non-obligatory character, but such a clause may also entail an obligation for the parties to first try to resolve the dispute via mediation. The character of mediation does not preclude this. The fact that the clause was concluded by professional parties and that the contract and the dispute are of a business nature play a role in interpreting the mediation clause, but those factors do not automatically entail that the parties are obligated to first attempt to resolve their dispute through mediation. The scope of the duty to try to resolve the dispute through mediation and the question as to when a party wishing to end her cooperation in the mediation may do so must also be determined through interpretation of the mediation clause. The mediation clause may not be applied if such application would infringe upon the right of access to court in an unacceptable manner.[62] In the event there is an obligation to first attempt to resolve the dispute through mediation, but a party to the dispute first initiates arbitral proceedings, the arbitrator may stay the arbitral proceedings upon the request of the other party, to provide the parties with the opportunity to first attempt resolution of the dispute through mediation. According to the Supreme Court, this is not mandatory though. A request for a stay of the proceedings can be declined, for example in light of the urgent nature of the dispute or because it would be fruitless to attempt mediation.[63] This is something

61 Formulated in the *Haviltex*-case, Supreme Court 13 March 1981, ECLI:NL:HR:1981:AG4158, *NJ* 1981/635, annotated by C.J.H. Brunner.

62 See for the foregoing Supreme Court 12 July 2024, ECLI:NL:HR:2024:1078, para 3.2.2.

63 See Supreme Court 12 July 2024, ECLI:NL:HR:2024:1078, para 3.2.3. Prior to this judgment, the Court of Appeal had dismissed a setting aside claim based on (*inter alia*) Article 1065(1)(a) DCCP, ruling that the dispute resolution clause at hand did not obligate the parties to first attempt to resolve the dispute through mediation. See The Hague Court of Appeal 13 September 2022, ECLI:NL:GHDHA:2022:1851, pa-

arbitrators should look out for in practice, with a view to how to react as regards the course of the arbitral proceedings.

A case that we did not come across in setting aside proceedings that arose in connection to commercial arbitration, but which can indeed lead to setting aside of an arbitral award due to lack of a valid arbitration agreement, is the situation in which the dispute is non-arbitrable (not capable of settlement through arbitration). It is assumed that in such a situation the arbitral award can be set aside on the basis of Article 1065(1)(a) or Article 1065(1)(e) DCCP.[64]

23.2.3 *Composition of the arbitral tribunal (Article 1065(1)(b) DCCP)*

Usually, an arbitrator is appointed and thus has no influence on the composition of the arbitral tribunal. Nevertheless, we recommend arbitrators to consider whether the tribunal has been composed in accordance with the applicable rules in the event one of the parties to the arbitration argues that the arbitral tribunal has not been composed in accordance with those rules. The rules on the composition of an arbitral tribunal include both statutory rules (i.e. Articles 1023, 1026, 1027 and 1028 DCCP) and the rules agreed upon by the parties to the arbitration in this regard. If the arbitral tribunal is not composed in accordance with these rules, it lacks jurisdiction.[65] If the arbitrators nevertheless declare that they have jurisdiction, this may constitute a ground for setting aside of the arbitral award pursuant to Article 1065(1)(b) DCCP.[66] A party who participated in the composition of the arbitral tribunal cannot invoke the arbitrators' lack of jurisdiction in setting aside proceedings. The same applies to a party who *did not* cooperate in the composition of the tribunal but *did* appear in the arbitral proceedings and failed to invoke the arbitral tribunal's lack of jurisdiction before all defences (Article 1065(3) in conjunction with Article 1052(3) DCCP).[67]

---

ras 5.7-5.13. The objections against this finding were dismissed in the cassation proceedings on the basis of Article 81 Judiciary Organization Act.

64 See Meijer & Van Mierlo 2015, p 20; *Parliamentary Papers II* 1983/84, 18464, no 3, p 29. See also G.J. Meijer, in: *T&C Rv*, Article 1065 DCCP, note 2c and Article 1020 DCCP, note 6k (online, updated 1 January 2024); G.J. Meijer & A.I.M. van Mierlo, 'Aantasting van arbitrale vonnissen', *WPNR* 2014, issue 7003, p 62; Sanders 2001, p 24-25.

65 See Asser Procesrecht/Sanders, Meijer & Ernste *8* 2023/496.

66 See G.J. Meijer, in: *T&C Rv*, Article 1052 DCCP, note 1 and Article 1065 DCCP, note 3 (online, updated 1 January 2024).

67 Asser Procesrecht/Sanders, Meijer & Ernste *8* 2023/497. See for example The Hague Court of Appeal 5 April 2022, ECLI:NL:GHDHA:2022:489, para 5.7; The Hague Court of Appeal 29 March 2022, ECLI:NL:GHDHA:2022:570, para 3.3.

Case law provides several examples of successful setting aside claims based on Article 1065(1)(b) DCCP. The ground was raised in 16 of the cases examined and led to setting aside in four cases. An arbitral tribunal is not composed in accordance with the applicable rules as meant in Article 1065(1)(b) DCCP if it does not consist of the number of arbitrators prescribed in statute or as agreed upon by the parties to the arbitration, for example in the applicable institutional arbitration rules. In that respect, it follows from case law that an arbitral award is subject to setting aside if, contrary to Article 1026 DCCP (see also Article 12 NAI Arbitration Rules 2015 and Article 14 NAI Arbitration Rules 2024), it was rendered by an even number of arbitrators.[68] Case law furthermore shows that involvement of an arbitral secretary or assistant to the arbitral tribunal does not (automatically) entail that the arbitral tribunal was composed in an incorrect manner. In that regard, we mention the following two cases. Firstly, in the case of *the Russian Federation v. HVY*, one of the grounds upon which the Russian Federation based its claim to set aside the arbitral award was the (alleged) irregular composition of the arbitral tribunal. In that respect, the Russian Federation argued that the arbitral award had been made by four rather than three arbitrators, because the assistant to the arbitral tribunal had allegedly been involved in the tribunal's decision-making process as a fourth arbitrator. According to the The Hague Court of Appeal, however, the fact that the assistant had played a role in the formation of the arbitral awards did not mean that he had acted as a fourth arbitrator. The Court of Appeal considered that an assistant or arbitral secretary may perform (even substantive) tasks and even fulfil a role in drafting the arbitral award, as long as the arbitral tribunal ultimately decides whether to adopt the draft texts or not. What is important is that the arbitral tribunal remains ultimately responsible for the decision(s) in the arbitral award and that the arbitral tribunal does not delegate any decision-making power to the secretary.[69] The Supreme Court rejected the objections against this point in the appeal in cassation on the basis of Article 81 of the Judiciary Organization Act.[70] Secondly, in a case heard by the Amsterdam Court of Appeal the Court had to answer the question as to whether an arbitral award had

68 See Utrecht District Court 8 August 2007, ECLI:NL:RBUTR:2007:BB1410, paras 4.10-4.14, *NJF* 2007/501.

69 The Hague Court of Appeal 18 February 2020, ECLI:NL:GHDHA:2020:234, paras 6.6.1-6.6.13, *JOR* 2020/164, annotated by N. Peters. The Russian Federation also argued (unsuccessfully) that the tribunal had breached its mandate with respect to the work carried out by the assistant. In that regard, it was argued that the arbitrators had breached their obligation to personally fulfil their mandate.

70 See Supreme Court 5 November 2021, ECLI:NL:HR:2021:1645, *NJ* 2022/102, annotated by A.I.M. van Mierlo & C.M.J. Ryngaert (*Russische Federatie/HVY*). See for

been rendered by an even number of arbitrators because, according to the parties, the secretary had in fact also acted as a second arbitrator in the arbitration. The arbitrator had reported that the secretary was much more than a clerk or secretary and that the secretary had participated in the deliberations on the case. In addition, the secretary had asked questions during the hearing. The Amsterdam Court of Appeal ruled that this did not mean that the decision of the arbitrator was not exclusively his own and that there were insufficient grounds to assume that the award had been rendered by two arbitrators (instead of one arbitrator).[71]

An improper method of appointment (e.g. in violation of Article 1027 and Article 1028 DCCP or Article 15-19 NAI Arbitration Rules 2024) could theoretically lead to setting aside of the arbitral award. However, we are not aware of any successful examples of this from published case law.[72] Furthermore, arbitrators should have the appropriate qualifications, as prescribed in the applicable (institutional) arbitration rules. For example, case law shows that an arbitral award has been set aside because it was rendered by an arbitral tribunal that did not include arbitrators who were members of a particular association, as required in the applicable arbitration rules[73] and, in a different case, because the chair of the arbitral tribunal was not the (vice) chair of the administering arbitration institute, as was required in the applicable arbitration rules.[74] If one of the parties to the arbitration argues that an arbitrator or the arbitral tribunal does not have the qualifications agreed upon by the parties, the arbitral tribunal should assess whether the arbitrator(s) meets (meet) these qualifications. The rules agreed upon can be interpreted broadly in certain cases. If the arbitration rules prescribe that (at least) one of the arbitrators must belong to a certain professional group, this requirement may also be met under

similar considerations on the role of an arbitral secretary '-Hertogenbosch Court of Appeal 21 January 2020, ECLI:NL:GHSHE:2020:172, paras 4.4.1-4.4.2.

71 Amsterdam Court of Appeal 17 April 2018, ECLI:NL:GHAMS:2018:1305, paras 2.3-2.5. See also G.J. Meijer, in: *T&C Rv*, Article 1065, note 3 (online, updated 1 January 2024).

72 See H.J. Snijders, in: *GS Burgerlijke Rechtsvordering*, Article 1065 DCCP, note 3 (online, updated 1 May 2018); Meijer & Van Mierlo 2014, p 62. See for several examples of cases in which in which the setting aside claim was unsuccessful: Amsterdam Court of Appeal ECLI:NL:GHDHA:2022:1851, paras 5.14-5.22; Amsterdam Court of Appeal 8 November 2016, ECLI:NL:GHAMS:2016:4433, para 3.13; Rotterdam District Court 25 November 2009, ECLI:NL:RBROT:2009:BK4498, paras 5.2-5.5.

73 See Amsterdam Court of Appeal 28 June 1939, ECLI:NL:GHAMS:1939:34, *NJ* 1940/103. See also Sanders 2001, p 192.

74 See 's-Hertogenbosch Court of Appeal 17 March 2015, ECLI:NL:GHSHE:2015:929, para 3.4.3.

certain circumstances if someone from a comparable professional group is appointed as arbitrator. For example, the Arnhem District Court accepted that a jaw surgeon belongs to a professional group similar to a dermatologist.[75]

Finally, an arbitral award can be set aside because it was made by (successfully) challenged arbitrators.[76] In the case cited, the arbitrators had not resigned after the notice of challenge had been given and had not suspended the arbitral proceedings.[77] This lead to a situation in which the arbitral award had been rendered before the (final) decision on the challenge – namely that it was well-founded – had been taken. The award was subsequently found to have been rendered by a tribunal that was not composed in accordance with the applicable rules. It follows from this judgment that arbitrators are well advised to suspend the proceedings and wait to render the arbitral award until a decision on a challenge request is taken (Article 1035(5) DCCP, see also Article 23(4) NAI Arbitration Rules 2024), or to resign (Article 1035(2) DCCP, see also Article 23(5) NAI Arbitration Rules 2024).

23.2.4 *Breach of mandate (Article 1065(1)(c) DCCP)*

23.2.4.1 In general

Arbitrators should comply with their mandate. If they do not, the arbitral award may be set aside under Article 1065(1)(c) DCCP if the breach is serious in nature (Article 1065(4) DCCP). A breach of mandate is of a serious nature if the outcome would have been different in the event the arbitra-

75 See Arnhem District Court 3 December 2008, ECLI:NL:RBARN:2008:BG6981, paras 4.37-4.38.

76 See Oost-Brabant District Court 16 November 2011 (unpublished). The relevant considerations of the judgment can be found in the judgments concerning the liability of the arbitrators. See for the liability proceedings (in which the arbitrators were ultimately not held liable) 's-Hertogenbosch Court of Appeal 8 December 2015, ECLI:NL:GHSHE:2015:5154 and Oost-Brabant District Court 15 October 2014, ECLI:NL:RBOBR:2014:6276.

77 An obligation to stay the proceedings pending the challenge does not exist, see *Parliamentary Papers II* 1983/84, 18464, no 3, p 13. However, arbitrators are not permitted to render a partial or final award before the challenge request has been assessed, except in 'urgent cases' and in cases in which the request for challenge was (in short) submitted with obvious abuse of right. See Supreme Court 19 June 2007, ECLI:NL:HR:2007:AV7405, para 3.4.2, *NJ* 2008/177, annotated by H.J. Snijders & J. Legemaate (*Aegon/N.*).

tors had remained within the limits of their mandate.[78] The tribunal's mandate has a formal and a substantive part. The formal part of the mandate is determined by the statutory procedural rules, the rules agreed upon by the parties and the rules determined by the arbitral tribunal with respect to the proceedings.[79] The substantive part of the mandate concerns that which an arbitrator must rule on and the decision-making standard that is to be applied.[80] The substantive part of the mandate is evidenced by the claims, defences and facts presented by the parties.[81] A breach of mandate can take several forms, which are discussed in the following paragraphs. It follows from our study of the case law that parties regularly seek to set aside an arbitral award on this ground. Breach of mandate was invoked in 173 of the cases examined. However, this only led to setting aside of the arbitral award in nine of those cases.

23.2.4.2 Essential defences

The scope of the legal dispute in the arbitration is limited by the (counter) claims and defences.[82] Arbitrators should address all claims submitted. They must also address all affirmative, essential defences of the other party.[83] If the arbitral tribunal fails to do so, it is not possible to request and render an additional arbitral award, but, according to case law, it is possible to claim setting aside of the arbitral award for breach of the arbitrators'

78 See Meijer & Van Mierlo 2015, p 157; I.P.M. van den Nieuwendijk, 'De nieuwe arbitragewet bezien vanuit het perspectief van de gewone rechter', *TCR* 2014, p 110. See for an application of this principle, for example: Noord-Nederland District Court 14 September 2016, ECLI:NL:RBNNE:2016:4063, para 4.13; Rotterdam District Court 14 October 2009, ECLI:NL:RBROT:2009:BK3449.

79 See Asser Procesrecht/Sanders, Meijer & Ernste *8* 2023/500; Meijer & Van Mierlo 2015, p 776; Meijer & Van Mierlo 2014, p 62-63. See also Supreme Court 28 September 1990, ECLI:NL:HR:1990:AD1240, *NJ* 1991/230, annotated by J.B.M. Vranken (*Huybregts/Van Tuyl*); Supreme Court 17 January 2003, ECLI:NL:HR:2003:AE9395, *NJ* 2004/384, annotated by H.J. Snijders (*IMS/Modsaf-IR I*).

80 See G.J. Meijer, in: *T&C Rv*, Article 1065 DCCP, note 4d (online, updated 1 January 2024); *Parliamentary Papers II* 1983/84, 18464, no 3, p 29.

81 See Sanders 2001, p 193.

82 See G.J. Meijer, in: *T&C Rv*, Article 1065 DCCP, note 4e (online, updated 1 January 2024).

83 See Supreme Court 30 March 1973, ECLI:NL:HR:1973:AB6417, *NJ* 1973/226, annotated by P.A. Stein (*Kaaphoeve/Swinkels*). See also H.J. Snijders, in: *GS Burgerlijke Rechtsvordering*, Article 1065 DCCP, note 4.2.6 (online, updated 1 May 2018); G.J. Meijer, in: *T&C Rv,* Article 1065 DCCP, note 4h (online, updated 1 January 2024). See also The Hague Court of Appeal 7 January 2020, ECLI:NLGHDHA:2021:1, para 5.

mandate.[84] If the defence in question cannot be regarded as essential, the setting aside claim will not succeed.[85] It follows from case law that a defence is not essential if it relates to assertions that (only) serve to support the defence[86] or are not relevant to the final decision.[87] This is also in line with Article 1065(4) DCCP, from which it follows that an arbitral award can only be set aside in case a breach of mandate is of a serious nature. A point that was not essential to the decision will not have led to a different outcome, which in turn entails that the breach is not of a serious nature. This requirement is related to the principle that the state court in setting aside proceedings must apply a restrictive review in its examination of whether the arbitral tribunal violated its mandate under Article 1065(1)(c) DCCP.[88] The claimant in the setting aside proceedings should assert and prove that the arbitral tribunal did not respond to an essential defence and therefore breached its mandate.[89]

84 See Leeuwarden Court of Appeal 26 April 2011, ECLI:NL:GHLEE:2011:BQ5698. See also: Arnhem District Court 20 April 2011, ECLI:NL:RBARN:2011:BQ3150, in which the arbitrators had awarded a monetary claim in accordance with the claim without giving reasons and while the amount of the claim had been disputed. The setting aside claim can be brought without first requesting an additional arbitral award, see: Supreme Court 14 February 1997, ECLI:NL:HR:1997:ZC2276, *NJ* 1998/109, annotated by H.J. Snijders (*Mannaerts q.q./Van Rhienen*). See also G.J. Meijer, in: *T&C Rv*, Article 1061 DCCP, note 1a (online, updated 1 January 2024). The argument is sometimes advanced in the context of both Article 1065(1)(c) and Article 1065(1)(d) DCCP. See for an example of this, in which the argument was *dismissed*, The Hague Court of Appeal 23 June 2020, ECLI:NL:GHDHA:2020:1095.

85 See Rotterdam District Court 28 January 2009, ECLI:NL:RBROT:2009:BH3378, paras 3.7-3.17; The Hague Court of Appeal 7 January 2020, ECLI:NL:GHDHA:2020:1, para 9; Amsterdam Court of Appeal 28 May 2024, ECLI:NL:GHAMS:2024:1426, para 5.9.

86 See Rotterdam District Court 2 July 2008, ECLI:NL:RBROT:2008:BD6977.

87 See Amsterdam Court of Appeal 27 November 2018, ECLI:NL:GHAMS:4323, para 4.10; Haarlem District Court 5 March 2008, ECLI:NL:RBHAA:2008:BC6686, paras 5.8-5.9.

88 See Supreme Court 5 November 2021, ECLI:NL:HR:2021:1645, para 5.5.4, *NJ* 2022/102, annotated by C.M.J. Ryngaert & A.I.M. van Mierlo (*Russische Federatie/HVY*); See also Advocate General Drijber in his non-binding opinion rendered prior to Supreme Court 23 November 2018, ECLI:NL:HR:2018:2162 (*Tiffany/Swatch*), para 31; The Hague District Court 16 September 2020, ECLI:NL:RBDHA:2020:8929, para 4.7. See also Asser Procesrecht/Sanders, Meijer & Ernste *8* 2023/498.

89 See 's-Hertogenbosch Court of Appeal 19 September 2023, ECLI:NL:GHSHE:2023:2979, paras 4.9-4.10; Arnhem-Leeuwarden Court of Appeal 15 February 2022, ECLI:NL:GHARL:2022:1138, para 4.5. See also Arnhem-Leeuwarden Court of Appeal 19 March 2019, ECLI:NL:GHARL:2450, para 4.3, in which the Court of Appeal considers that the claimant in the setting aside proceedings should prove that claimant raised the defence in the arbitral proceedings.

It also follows from case law that an arbitral tribunal does not always need to explicitly decide on an essential defence, but may also do so implicitly without running the risk of setting aside of the arbitral award. In general, the answer to the question to what extent an arbitral tribunal should explicitly respond to an essential defence depends on the nature of the point in question in light of the legal dispute presented to them.[90] Therefore, an arbitral tribunal will not need to respond to a statement that is less substantiated in (as) much detail.[91] Case law (of the lower courts) shows the following in this regard. An arbitral tribunal can implicitly decide on the (essential) defence by rejecting it in the context of another argument or defence[92] or an implicit decision on the (essential) defence may follow from the considerations of the arbitral award read in conjunction with each other.[93] As an extension of this, not all assertions or arguments raised by a party need to be addressed in the arbitral award, if it is clear from the award and from the conduct of the arbitral proceedings that those assertions and arguments were indeed considered in the decision-making process.[94] Furthermore, an implied decision may be accepted in situations in which multiple arguments are raised and the arbitral tribunal decides on the essence of the defence in question, even though the tribunal has not decided on each individual argument advanced in the context of that

90 See Supreme Court 30 December 1977, ECLI:NL:HR:1977:AC6162, *NJ* 1978/449, annotated by P.A. Stein (*De Ploeg/Kruse*).

91 See 's-Gravenhage District Court 7 September 2012, ECLI:NL:RBSGR:2012:BX6825, paras 4.16-4.19.

92 See Amsterdam Court of Appeal 27 November 2018, ECLI:NL:GHAMS:2018:4323, para 4.9; Amsterdam District Court 12 March 2014, ECLI:NL:RBAMS:2014:2399, paras 4.20-4.22.

93 See The Hague Court of Appeal 28 June 2022, ECLI:NL:GHDHA:2022:1122, paras 8.43-8.44; The Hague Court of Appeal 23 June 2020, ECLI:NL:GHDHA:2020:1095, para 4.5; 's-Gravenhage District Court 14 May 2014, ECLI:NL:RBDHA:2014:6150, para 4.10. See also Amsterdam District Court 1 May 2013, ECLI:NL:RBAMS:2013:CA3727, paras 4.4-4.7, in which the court considered that by treating a letter as an explanation, the arbitrators had implicitly ruled that the letter did not contain an additional, unauthorised ground for termination.

94 See for example The Hague Court of Appeal 23 June 2020, ECLI:NL:GHDHA:2020:1095, para 5.5; Amsterdam District Court 9 April 2014, ECLI:NL:RBAMS:2014:2290, paras 4.3-4.6, which overruled the objection that the arbitrators had not explicitly mentioned various amounts in the context of the settlement of a cooperation relating to the mining, processing and trading of diamonds, in their award, with reference to the extensive exchange of financial records and lengthy debates with the parties' accountants about those amounts during the hearing days; Amsterdam District Court 17 December 2008, ECLI:NL:RBAMS:2008:BH2280, paras 5.4-5.5, which referred to earlier considerations in the judgment, where the relevant contention had been implicitly addressed.

defence.[95] It is clear from the above that there must have been some concrete indication that the arbitrators included the defence in their decision. If such an indication is missing, setting aside of the arbitral award may follow.[96]

According to case law, arbitrators do not breach their mandate if they take a decision on the law that they deem to be legally sound, but which differs from the parties' submissions with regard to the law.[97] The fact that one of the parties disagrees with the decision or reasoning behind the decision does not mean that the arbitral award can be set aside on the basis of breach of mandate.[98] There is no room in setting aside proceedings for a review of the arbitral award on the merits.[99] Furthermore, merely leaving a statement of a party in the arbitral award unaddressed is not sufficient ground for setting aside of the arbitral award.[100] The arbitral tribunal may, of course, ignore points that fall outside the scope of the dispute (and of their mandate).[101]

Finally, it follows from case law that an arbitral tribunal did not breach its mandate by deciding on a set-off defence, even if the claim to be set off was not subject to arbitration.[102] In principle, an arbitrator may not rule on a (counter)claim that is not covered by the arbitration agreement and therefore not subject to his judgment.[103] However, in the case of a set-off

95 See The Hague Court of Appeal 10 May 2016, ECLI:NL:GHDHA:2016:3324, para 35.

96 See Leeuwarden Court of Appeal 26 April 2011, ECLI:NL:GHLEE:2011:BQ5698, paras 3.14, 3.20, in which the fact that claim for damages had been granted did not, in and of itself, indicate that the arbitral tribunal had included the asserted set-off defence in their decision.

97 See Amsterdam District Court 21 August 2013, ECLI:NL:RBAMS:2013:6253, para 4.8.9.

98 See Rotterdam District Court 14 December 2011, ECLI:NL:RBROT:2011:BU9663, para 4.6; Rotterdam District Court 2 July 2009, ECLI:NL:RBROT:2009:BJ1300, para 3.6.

99 See Amsterdam Court of Appeal 25 June 2019, ECLI:NL:GHAMS:2019:2136, para 3.11.

100 See Amsterdam District Court 9 April 2014, ECLI:NL:RBAMS:2014:2290, para 4.2.

101 See Rotterdam District Court 10 July 2007, *TvA* 2007/59; Rotterdam District Court 8 March 2006, ECLI:NL:RBROT:2006:AV5278.

102 See Supreme Court 23 March 2018, ECLI:NL:HR:2018:428 (*AA Accountants*) and Advocate General Valk's non-binding opinion rendered prior to the case, paras 2.33 et seq. See also Meijer 2011, p 761-764, referring to Supreme Court 28 September 1990, ECLI:NL:HR:1990:AD1240, *NJ* 1991/230, annotated by J.B.M. Vranken (*Huybregts/Van Tuyl*).

103 If the arbitration agreement also extends to the claim to be set off, no problems arise since the arbitrators will have decided on a claim that is also subject to arbitration. See Meijer 2011, p 760.

defence, the success of that defence affects whether the claim that *is* subject to arbitration should be granted. This makes it an essential defence, upon which the arbitral tribunal must decide, even though the claim itself, strictly speaking, falls outside the scope of the arbitration agreement. It is assumed in this respect that the arbitrator may examine whether the counterclaim exists[104] and, if that is evidently the case, he may grant the set-off defence.[105] In doing so, the arbitrator is only saying that the principal claim does not have to be paid (in full).[106] If the counterclaim is not established and cannot be easily determined, the arbitrator is well advised to reject the set-off defence on the basis of Article 6:136 DCC.[107] If, however, the arbitrator conducts an investigation in that regard to determine the (scope of the) counterclaim, he goes beyond the confines of his mandate and, according to case law, setting aside may follow.[108]

23.2.4.3 The arbitral tribunal failed to decide on one or more claims

A breach of mandate also occurs when the arbitral tribunal has failed to decide on one or more (counter)claims. In arbitral proceedings in which a large number of claims are submitted, it happens in practice that the arbitral tribunal overlooks one or more claims and does not include a decision on them in the arbitral award. In light of this, Snijders has rightly noted that this is not an academic risk.[109] Examples of claims an arbitral tribunal has failed to decide on are an interest claim,[110] a VAT claim,[111] a claim for an order for costs of the proceedings,[112] and a claim for imposition of a penalty.[113]

---

104 See Meijer 2011, p 764-765.

105 See H.J. Snijders, 'Rond de arbitrage met name in bouwzaken', in: H.J. Snijders & S.L. Buruma (eds), *Bouwarbitrage en civiele rechter (preadvies 1995-23)*, Deventer: Kluwer 1995, p 30-31.

106 It is also sometimes argued in the literature that that decision has no *res judicata* effect. See Advocate General Valk in his non-binding opinion rendered prior to Supreme Court 23 March 2018, ECLI:NL:PHR:2018:21 (*AA Accountants*), paras 2.33-2.42 and references there; Snijders 1995, p 31.

107 See Snijders 1995, p 31.

108 See Oost-Brabant District Court 31 August 2016, ECLI:NL:RBOBR:2016:4862, paras 4.4-4.9.

109 See H.J. Snijders, in: *GS Burgerlijke Rechtsvordering*, Article 1061 DCCP, note 2 (online, updated 1 May 2018). See also NAI 26 May 2009, *TvA* 2010/31.

110 See NAI 30 November 2010, *TvA* 2011/37.

111 See NAI 30 November 2010, *TvA* 2011/37.

112 See SGI 20 June 1991.

113 See H.J. Snijders, in: *GS Burgerlijke Rechtsvordering*, Article 1061, note 1 (online, updated 1 May 2018).

Case law shows that, on several occasions, parties have argued, in support of a claim for setting aside on the basis of Article 1065(1)(c) DCCP, that the arbitral tribunal had failed to rule on one or more (counter) claims, but that this did not result in setting aside of the arbitral award.[114] In some cases, the reason for this was that under Article 1065(6) DCCP it is obligatory to first request an additional award on the basis of Article 1061 DCCP, in which the omission could be remedied.[115] On the basis of Article 1061(1) DCCP the most diligent party may request the arbitral tribunal to render an additional award concerning one or more claims or counterclaims submitted to arbitration, but not decided on by the arbitral tribunal. Article 55 NAI Arbitration Rules 2024 also provides for the possibility to request an additional award that largely corresponds to Article 1061 DCCP. Such a request can be granted if a decision on a claim is not reflected in the arbitral award, neither in the recitals nor in the operative part, or if the claim is included in the reasoning of the award, but the arbitral tribunal has failed to include the final decision on the claim in the operative part.[116] It follows from the judgment of the Supreme Court in the case *Mannaerts q.q v. Van Rhienen*[117] that an arbitral award cannot be supplemented under Article 1061 DCCP if an essential defence was not addressed. In this case, Van Rhienen successfully sought setting aside of an arbitral award in which he had been ordered to comply with a non-compete clause. The arbitrator had disregarded his expressly submitted defence that Jardin, the original counterparty in the proceedings, had forfeited its rights in that respect. In the

---

114 In the following cases, the failure to decide one or more (counter)claims did not lead to setting aside of the arbitral award: Supreme Court 22 March 2013, ECLI:NL:HR:2013:BY8099, para 3.4.1 (*Bursa/Güris*); The Hague Court of Appeal 12 March 2013, ECLI:NL:GHDHA:2013:BZ6559, paras 2.6-2.9; Rotterdam District Court 14 December 2011, ECLI:NL:RBROT:2011:BU9663, para 4.7; Arnhem District Court 20 April 2011, ECLI:NL:RBARN:2011:BQ3150, para 4.5; Rotterdam District Court 14 October 2009, ECLI:NL:RBROT:2009:BK3449, para 5.7; Amsterdam District Court 27 August 2008, ECLI:NL:RBAMS:2008:BF3726, paras 4.6-4.7; Rotterdam District Court 5 October 2005, *TvA* 2007/24, para 5.8; Utrecht District Court 21 February 2001, ECLI:NL:RBUTR:2001:ZL1120, *NJ* 2002/527, paras 4.3 and 4.6.

115 This occurred in the following cases: Arnhem District Court 20 April 2011, ECLI:NL:RBARN:2011:BQ3150, para 4.5; Rotterdam District Court 14 October 2009, ECLI:NL:RBROT:2009:BK3449, para 5.7.

116 See G.J. Meijer, in: *T&C Rv*, Article 1061, note 3b (online, updated 1 January 2024). To illustrate the first point, in particular, see Arnhem District Court 20 April 2011, ECLI:NL:RBARN:2011:BQ3150, para 4.5; Rotterdam District Court 14 October 2009, ECLI:NL:RBROT:2009:BK3449, para 5.7; Amsterdam District Court 27 August 2008, ECLI:NL:RBAMS:2008:BF3726, paras 4.6-4.7, in which all parts of the original claim were ultimately decided on in the additional arbitral award by including the phrase 'rejects that which was more or otherwise claimed'.

117 Supreme Court 14 February 1997, ECLI:NL:HR:1997:ZC2276, para 3.3, *NJ* 1998/109, annotated by H.J. Snijders (*Mannaerts q.q./Van Rhienen*).

proceedings before the Supreme Court, Jardin's trustee (Mannaerts) took the position that Van Rhienen should first have requested an additional award on the basis of Article 1061 DCCP before bringing a setting aside claim and that Van Rhienen's setting aside claim was therefore inadmissible. The Supreme Court rejected this appeal in cassation and held that an additional award can only be requested if a decision on one or more parts of the claim is lacking in the arbitral award.[118] It must be inferred from this that a request for an additional award should be rejected on the basis of Article 1061 DCCP in the event an expressly submitted defence has not been included in the assessment of the tribunal.[119] The arbitral award will, however, be at risk of setting aside on the basis of Article 1065(1)(c) DCCP (see para 23.2.4.2).

As stated above, any interested party may request the arbitral tribunal to render an additional award (Article 1061(1) DCCP). In most cases the interested party will be the claimant. However, it may also be the respondent. This will occur when the arbitral tribunal has not decided on the costs claimed by the respondent or on the counterclaims filed by the respondent.[120] A party's request must be made in writing and the arbitral tribunal will send a copy of the request to the other party (Article 1061(2) DCCP). Article 55(2) of the NAI Arbitration Rules 2024 provides that the request should be made to the NAI Secretariat, which will send it to the arbitral tribunal and the other party as soon as possible. The arbitral tribunal is not allowed to render an additional arbitral award *ex officio* pursuant to Article 1061 Rv.

The decision on the request for an additional award may entail a rejection or a grant of the request. The rejection of a request for an additional award is communicated to the parties by the arbitral tribunal (Article 1061(5) DCCP). It does not have the status of an arbitral award, but according to Article 1061(5) DCCP, the tribunal shall notify the parties in writing of the rejection and a copy of this notice must be signed by an arbitrator or by the secretary to the arbitral tribunal. In arbitrations according to the NAI Arbitration Rules 2024, it is clear from Article 55(5) of those Rules that

118 See I.P.M. van den Nieuwendijk, 'Aanvulling van arbitrale vonnissen', *TvA* 2002, p 3.

119 See Leeuwarden Court of Appeal 26 April 2011, ECLI:NL:GHLEE:2011:BQ5698, paras 3.13, 3.19 and 3.26; Arnhem District Court 20 April 2011, ECLI:NL:RBARN:2011:BQ3150, para 4.4; Amsterdam District Court 17 December 2008, ECLI:NL:RBAMS:2008:BH2280, para 5.2.

120 See G.J. Meijer, in: *T&C Rv*, Article 1061 DCCP, note 2a (online, updated 1 January 2024).

this written communication is made through the intervention of the NAI Case Management Committee. Furthermore, a copy of the communication may be deposited at the registry of the court in whose district the place of arbitration is situated pursuant to Article 1058(1)(b) DCCP (Article 1061(5) DCCP), provided there is an agreement between the parties regarding the deposit of arbitral awards. Article 55(5) NAI Arbitration Rules 2024 shows that the NAI Case Management Committee shall ensure this. No legal remedies are available against rejection of a request for an additional arbitral award. However, it is possible to subsequently bring an action to set aside the original arbitral award pursuant to Article 1065(1)(c) DCCP.[121] If the arbitral tribunal is of the opinion that it has indeed failed to decide on part of the claim and that this part of the claim should still be considered, the tribunal will grant the request for an additional arbitral award. No appeal is available against such a decision. However, grant of a request for an additional award will result in an additional award containing the rejection or grant of the claim upon which the arbitral tribunal failed to decide in the first place. This award is an arbitral award, against which the remedy of setting aside is available.[122] The law does not specify the conduct of the proceedings with respect to the part of the claim that has not yet been decided on. The 2024 NAI Arbitration Rules do not regulate this either. To the extent that the parties have not reached an agreement on this matter, the arbitral tribunal may determine the proceedings in an informal manner, in compliance with the procedural rules for the arbitration. In that regard, the equal right to be heard is decisive. It will depend on the circumstances of the case what the scope of the proceedings will be after granting the request for an additional award. For example, the arbitral tribunal will usually be able to render an additional award immediately upon granting the request for such an award, in the event the tribunal has included the part of the claim not dealt with in the reasoning of the arbitral award but has erroneously failed to decide on it in the operative part of the award. If the arbitral tribunal did not consider the claim at all and did not address the unaddressed part of the claim in the reasoning either, the tribunal will need some time to study the documents addressing the parties' submission concerning the part of the claim that was not decided on, before it renders an additional award. In that case, the arbitral tribunal may wait to provide the decision on the request for an additional award and may give said decision at the same time the additional award is rendered. The tribunal may also decide on the request for an additional award first

121 See Van den Nieuwendijk 2002, p 8.
122 See Van den Nieuwendijk 2002, p 9.

(in advance) and render the additional award later. In exceptional cases, it may be necessary for the parties to be heard further on the point in question. In that case, the decision to grant the request for an additional arbitral award and the additional arbitral award will not coincide.[123]

Grant of the request for an additional award does not provide any indication as to whether the tribunal will grant or reject the claim(s) that have not (yet) been decided. It will result in a separate arbitral award containing the grant or dismissal of the claim that was not decided on in the original award. As alluded to above, an additional arbitral award is an arbitral award to which Articles 1049-1068 DCCP apply (see Article 1061(4) DCCP).

23.2.4.4 Supplementation of facts

The scope and boundaries of the legal dispute in arbitration are determined by the parties to the arbitration, in particular by the claims, counterclaims (if submitted) and the defences. In practice it is regularly argued that the arbitrators have breached their mandate by exceeding the boundaries of the legal dispute. In that respect, it is advanced that the arbitrators have based their decision on facts that have not been asserted by the parties. However, courts often dismiss this argument, ruling that the point in question was in fact part of the legal dispute and part of the debate between the parties.[124]

It is unanimously accepted in academic literature that supplementation of the facts or of the factual basis of the case constitutes a breach of mandate.[125] Unlike in proceedings before state courts, the impermissibility of the supplementation does not (directly) follow from Article 24 and Article

123 See Van den Nieuwendijk 2002, p 8; G.J. Meijer, in: *T&C Rv*, Article 1061 DCCP, note 3b (online, updated 1 January 2024); H.J. Snijders, in: *GS Burgerlijke Rechtsvordering*, Article 1061, note 5 (online, updated 1 May 2018).

124 See for example Arnhem-Leeuwarden Court of Appeal 15 February 2022, ECLI:NL:GHARL:2022:1138, paras 4.4-4.5; The Hague Court of Appeal 18 February 2020, ECLI:NL:GHDHA:2020:234, paras 6.5.1-6.5.15; Arnhem-Leeuwarden Court of Appeal 8 October 2019, ECLI:NL:GHARL:2019:8203, paras 4.3-4.5.

125 See Asser Procesrecht/Sanders, Meijer & Ernste *8* 2023/506; G.J. Meijer, in: *T&C Rv*, Article 1065 DCCP, note 4j (online, updated 1 January 2024); H.J. Snijders, in: *GS Burgerlijke Rechtsvordering*, Article 1065 DCCP, note 4.2.5 (online, updated 1 May 2018).

149(1) DCCP,[126] but seems to find its basis in the principle of party autonomy.[127] It also follows from case law that the supplementation of facts or of the factual basis may constitute a ground for setting aside of an arbitral award.[128] According to the Amsterdam District Court and the Amsterdam Court of Appeal, the arbitral tribunal should, in determining the parties' rights and obligations, only rely on facts of which the parties were able to verify and question the accuracy and completeness.[129] In that regard, we emphasize that the arbitrators may not take a surprise decision.[130] In a different case, the Amsterdam District Court further considered that (alleged) supplementation of facts could only lead to setting aside of the arbitral award if it was evident to the state court that the arbitral tribunal had

---

126 Article 24 DCCP reads as follows: "The court examines and decides the case only on the basis of what the parties have brought forward in support of their claim or request or defence, except where the law provides otherwise", See A. Burrough et al, *Code of Civil Procedure. Selected Sections and the NCC Rules,* Eleven: The Hague 2022, p 28. Article 149(1) DCCP reads as follows: "Except where the law provides otherwise, the court basis its judgment only on facts and rights which have been alleged or imparted to the court in the proceedings and which have been established in accordance with the rules this paragraph. The court must accept facts or rights alleged by a party and not disputed or not adequately disputed by the counterparty. The court may, however order evidence to be taken where acceptance of such allegation would entail legal consequences that are beyond the autonomy of the parties to agree". See Burrough et al 2022, p 90.

127 See G.J. Meijer, in: *T&C Rv*, Article 1065 DCCP, note 4j (online, updated 1 January 2024).

128 See (successfully) Amsterdam Court of Appeal 28 July 2005, ECLI:NL:GHAMS:2005:AU7487, paras 4.8-4.9, *NJF* 2005/427 and Amsterdam District Court 27 November 2002, ECLI:NL:RBAMS:2002:AS3630, para 7, *BR* 2004/46, in which the arbitral tribunal had based its decision on information that had not been submitted by the parties; Supreme Court 1 March 1957, ECLI:NL:HR:1957:AG2019, *NJ* 1957/210, in which the arbitral tribunal had based its decision on an agreement of a different nature (an agreement to convert a natural obligation into a civil obligation) than the agreement that had actually been concluded between the parties (a settlement). In doing so, the arbitral tribunal had also used an incorrect standard for their decision. See also (unsuccessfully) Amsterdam Court of Appeal 4 October 2022, ECLI:NL:GHAMS:2022:2819, para 3.2, in which, according to the Court of Appeal, the arbitral tribunal based its decision on a substantive assessment of the value alleged by the respondent and contested by the claimant.

129 See Amsterdam Court of Appeal 28 July 2005, ECLI:NL:GHAMS:2005:AU7487, paras 4.8-4.9, *NJF* 2005/427 and Amsterdam District Court 27 November 2002, ECLI:NL:RBAMS:2002:AS3630, para 7, *BR* 2004/46.

130 See in this respect (in combination with breach of public policy) The Hague District Court 16 June 2021, ECLI:NL:RBDHA:2021:6069, paras 6.40-6.49; Arnhem-Leeuwarden Court of Appeal 25 May 2021, ECLI:NL:GHARL:2021:5021, paras 4.7-4.9, paras 4.13-4.14; Amsterdam Court of Appeal 11 December 2018, ECLI:NL:GHAMS:2018:4547, paras 3.1-3.5. In all of these cases, the setting aside claim was dismissed.

relied on facts contrary to those put forward by the parties. This was not the case in the case at hand, according to the Amsterdam District Court.[131]

A state court will not set aside an arbitral award if an arbitral tribunal also based its decision on facts that were indeed submitted by the parties and those facts provide sufficient support for the final decision.[132] Errors in the establishment of the facts do not constitute a ground for setting aside of an arbitral award, according to case law.[133] The same is true as regards failure to include the facts under a separate heading in the award.[134] Also according to case law, the arbitral tribunal may interpret the agreements, rules and regulations, and the documents underlying the dispute. The arbitrators do not breach their mandate if, in doing so, they arrive at an interpretation the parties had to take into account.[135]

23.2.4.5 Addition to the grounds

An arbitrator is allowed to add to the (legal) grounds *ex officio* (cf. Article 25 DCCP).[136] This does not lead to a breach of mandate. It is assumed that arbitrators should apply 'super' mandatory law (law that is of public policy) *ex officio*.[137] As for 'ordinary' mandatory law (that is not of public policy) and non-mandatory law, the asserted facts must give rise to the addition in question. In both cases, the addition in and of itself is in principle not a ground for setting aside of the arbitral award. It follows from literature and from case law that the limit of what is permissible is to be determined on the basis of the question as to whether the final de-

131 See Amsterdam District Court 12 March 2014, ECLI:NL:RBAMS:2014:2399, paras 4.7-4.13.

132 See The Hague Court of Appeal 27 June 2017, ECLI:NL:GHDHA:2017:1711, para 19; Noord-Nederland District Court 14 September 2016, ECLI:NL:RBNNE:2016:4063, para 4.5.

133 See Arnhem District Court 19 November 2003, ECLI:NL:RBARN:2003:AN9171, para 4.7. The argument made here was in fact that the arbitrators had ignored essential assertions due to misinterpretation.

134 See Oost-Nederland District Court 27 March 2013, ECLI:NL:RBONE:2013:BZ8089, para 4.19.

135 See Amsterdam Court of Appeal 3 August 2006, *TvA* 2007/56.

136 Article 25 DCCP reads as follows: "The court supplies alternative legal basis on its own initiative". See Burrough et al 2022, p 28.

137 See H.J. Snijders, in: *GS Burgerlijke Rechtsvordering*, Article 1065, note 4.2.3 (online, updated 1 May 2018); G.J. Meijer & P.E. Ernste, 'De Arbitragewet 2015, bezien in het licht van dwingend recht en regelend recht', *RMThemis* 2015, p 102. Cf. for state courts: W. Hugenholtz & W.H. Heemskerk (continued by W. Heemskerk, M.E.A. Möhring, K. Teuben & A.F. Veldhuis), *Hoofdlijnen van Nederlands burgerlijk procesrecht*, Dordrecht: Convoy Uitgevers 2024, p 184.

cision based on the addition of the grounds was reasonably foreseeable for the unsuccessful party, in light of the debate between the parties and the facts asserted by the parties.[138] If the decision is reasonably foreseeable for the unsuccessful party, an arbitral tribunal may proceed to add to the grounds. If the decision based on the addition of the grounds is not to be expected, an arbitral tribunal should hear the parties on the matter. If the arbitral tribunal fails to do so and proceeds to add to the grounds, this will constitute a surprise decision and the arbitral award may be set aside for breach of mandate (Article 1065(1)(c) DCCP) and/or the right to be heard (Article 1065(1)(e) DCCP). In our opinion, it is therefore advisable that an arbitral tribunal explicitly discusses an addition to the grounds with the parties, if it concerns 'ordinary' mandatory law or non-mandatory law, so that the parties can comment on it. Obviously, this only concerns exceptional cases. The arbitral tribunal may indeed take a decision with which one of the parties disagrees.[139]

23.2.4.6 To grant more or something other than claimed

The arbitral tribunal may not award more or something different than that which was claimed by the parties (the so-called *ultra petita* decisions).[140] The assessment by the state court of whether more has been granted than claimed is made on the basis of a comparison between what was claimed and what was granted by the arbitral tribunal.[141] In that respect, it seems that the arbitrators can take both the claim(s) and that which can be deduced from the statement of claim and other statements of the case into account.[142]

138 Thus, the arbitral tribunal may not apply 'ordinary' mandatory law and directory law outside the ambit of the legal dispute. See Meijer & Ernste 2015, p 102-103. For an application of this, see: Oost-Nederland District Court 27 March 2013, ECLI:NL:RBONE:2013:BZ8089, paras 4.13-4.16. Cf. for the state courts: Supreme Court 26 September 2003, ECLI:NL:HR:2003:AF9414, paras 5.2-5.3, *NJ* 2004/460 (*Regiopolitie Gelderland Zuid/Hovax*); Supreme Court 21 December 2001, ECLI:NL:HR:2001:AD3997, *NJ* 2004/34, annotated by W.D.H. Asser (*Panama Caribic/Town House Development*).

139 See Amsterdam Court of Appeal 4 March 2014, ECLI:NL:GHAMS:2014:644; Amsterdam District Court 7 December 2011, ECLI:NL:RBAMS:2011:BV3821, paras 4.1-4.2.

140 See H.J. Snijders, in: *GS Burgerlijke Rechtsvordering*, Article 1065 DCCP, notes 4.1.1-4.1.2 (online, updated 1 May 2018); Meijer & Van Mierlo 2014, p 63; Sanders 2001, p 195.

141 The same test suffices to determine whether something other than claimed was granted. See The Hague Court of Appeal 17 February 2015, ECLI:NL:GHDHA:2015:222, para 24 and Rotterdam District Court 27 March 2013, ECLI:NL:RBROT:2013:BZ6030, paras 5.6.1-5.6.2. See for an application of this principle Amsterdam District Court 9 April 2014, ECLI:NL:RBAMS:2014:2290, paras 4.5-4.6; Rotterdam District Court 4 July 2010, ECLI:NL:RBROT:2010:BN7876, para 4.6.6.

142 See The Hague District Court 20 October 2021, ECLI:NL:RBDHA:2021:12258, para 5.71.

If the arbitral tribunal has decided *ultra petita*, the arbitral award may be set aside for breach of mandate.[143] For example, granting a claim unconditionally, while it was submitted as a conditional claim, is not allowed.[144] Neither is extending the term of a contract when this was neither claimed nor argued by either party to the arbitration.[145] The arbitrator may, however, grant more if the parties agreed during the arbitral proceedings that the arbitral tribunal should rule on further points in dispute.[146] In that case, the parties have extended the arbitrator's mandate. The arbitral award may, furthermore, not be set aside if that which was added to the claim was not granted[147] and in the event the tribunal has only clarified a point of which the parties were aware and which was debated in the operative part of the award.[148] It follows from the case law that non-compliance with the limitations concerning the scope of the dispute as laid down in the arbitration agreement may also constitute a ground for setting aside of an arbitral award.[149] Finally, if the arbitrators grant less than that which was claimed and therefore fail to rule on (part of) the claims (*infra petita*), a request for an additional award is the appropriate course of action (Article 1061 DCCP, see para 23.2.4.3).[150]

143 See Oost-Brabant District Court 22 October 2014, ECLI:NL:RBOBR:2014:6279, para 4.4.

144 See Leeuwarden Court of Appeal 26 April 2011, ECLI:NL:GHLEE:2011:BQ5698, paras 3.5-3.7.

145 See 's-Hertogenbosch Court of Appeal 22 November 2016, ECLI:NL:GHSHE:2016:5201, para 4.6. Cf. the decision of the court ruling in first instance: Oost-Brabant District Court 22 October 2014, ECLI:NL:RBOBR:2014:6279, para 4.4, which assesses the issue in the context of the surprise decision. Both courts acknowledged that the arbitrator had acted from a pragmatic point of view: by extending the term of the contract, the arbitrator intended to compensate the damages resulting from the breach of contract by one of the parties, due to early termination of the contract, and to avoid a possible second arbitration. Although the arbitrator had been given the (broad) mandate to "render such decision as [...][the arbitrator] in the proper administration of justice", this did not allow the arbitrator to also extend the contract. Cf. with regard to state courts: Supreme Court 17 December 2004, ECLI:NL:HR:2004:AR2390.

146 See Amsterdam Court of Appeal 17 April 2018, ECLI:NL:GHAMS:2018:1305, paras 2.6-2.7.

147 See Amsterdam Court of Appeal 1 November 2011, ECLI:NL:GHAMS:2011:BU7752, paras 2.9-2.10.

148 See Amsterdam Court of Appeal 28 May 2024, ECLI:NL:GHAMS:2024:1426, para 5.4.

149 See Amsterdam Court of Appeal 25 April 2017, ECLI:NL:GHAMS:2017:1496, in which the court held that the tribunal was allowed to assume that there were 'implied obligations'. Cf. the judgment rendered by the court ruling in first instance: Amsterdam District Court 4 March 2015, ECLI:NL:RBAMS:2015:1181. The appeal in cassation was rejected on the basis of Article 81 Judiciary Organization Act, see Supreme Court 23 November 2018, ECLI:NL:HR:2018:2162 (*Tiffany/Swatch*).

150 See Meijer & Van Mierlo 2014, p 63; Sanders 2001, p 195. See also The Hague Court of Appeal 25 February 2020, ECLI:NL:GHDHA:2020:254, para 6.3; The Hague Court of Appeal 19 May 2020, ECLI:NL:GHDHA:2020:1031, para 4.3.

There are also several examples of cases in which a party has argued that the arbitrators have breached their mandate, because they have granted something different than claimed. Such claims have, thus far, been unsuccessful.[151] In one case, the The Hague Court of Appeal found that something different than claimed had been granted by the arbitrators. The arbitrators had ordered a party in the arbitration to perform repair works while the other party had claimed alternative compensation. The Court of Appeal referred the case back to the arbitral tribunal pursuant to Article 1065a DCCP (see further para 23.3).[152] The arbitrators proceeded to render new awards containing an order to pay alternative compensation. After the suspension of the setting aside proceedings, the Court of Appeal held that the ground for setting aside had been removed and the claim to set the arbitral awards aside was dismissed.[153]

23.2.4.7 Wrong decision-making standard

The parties themselves can largely influence the standard according to which the arbitral tribunal should decide. The parties can agree that the tribunal shall decide as *amiable compositeur* (Article 1054(3) DCCP).[154] If the parties did not reach an agreement regarding the decision-making standard, the arbitral tribunal shall decide according to the rules of law (Article 1054(1) DCCP).[155] The NAI Arbitration Rules 2024 adopt the same approach (see Article 48). If the arbitral tribunal does not subsequently decide in accordance with the standard agreed upon, the arbitral award can be set aside for breach of mandate.[156] It follows from the case law that the state court applies a marginal test: if the award states that the arbitrators decided as *amiable compositeur*, but they should have decided in accordance with the rules of law, the award can already be set aside on

151 See for example The Hague Court of Appeal 16 October 2018, ECLI:NL:GHDHA:2018:2639 (interim judgment) and The Hague Court of Appeal 21 May 2019, ECLI:NL:GHDHA:2019:1132 (judgment after remission); The Hague Court of Appeal 1 October 2019, ECLI:NL:GHDHA:2019:2500, paras 5.1-5.6; 's-Hertogenbosch Court of Appeal 17 May 2022, ECLI:NL:GHSHE:2022:1550, paras 3.25-3.29.

152 The Hague Court of Appeal 16 October 2018, ECLI:NL:GHDHA:2018:2639.

153 The Hague Court of Appeal 21 May 2019, ECLI:NL:GHDHA:2019:1132.

154 That may also be the instruction to decide on the basis of reasonableness and fairness. See Oost-Nederland District Court 27 March 2013, ECLI:NL:RBONE:2013:BZ8089, paras 4.9-4.10.

155 Again, the parties can exercise influence through a choice of law (Article 1054(2) DCCP).

156 See H.J. Snijders, in: *GS Burgerlijke Rechtsvordering*, Article 1065 DCCP, note 4.2.2 (online, updated 1 May 2018); Meijer & Van Mierlo 2014, p 63-64.

that ground.[157] An arbitral award may not be set aside if it is clear from the (text of the) reasoning of the award that the arbitral tribunal applied the correct decision-making standard and that the fact that the wrong standard is mentioned in the arbitral award is a manifest error.[158] We have not encountered an example of this exact situation. However, in a similar situation, the 's-Hertogenbosch Court of Appeal decided that a failure to explicitly state the decision-making standard in the award was not sufficient to set aside the arbitral award as it was stated in the award that the arbitral tribunal rendered its decision in accordance with the mandate given to the tribunal and it was clear from the (letter providing the) mandate which standard had to be applied.[159] In light of the foregoing the arbitrator is advised to adhere to the applicable decision-making standard, but also to include the correct standard in the award. By contrast, an incorrect application of the *correct* decision-making standard cannot lead to setting aside of the award, as this would require a substantive review of the award, which is not allowed in setting aside proceedings.[160] In light of this, courts in setting aside proceedings do not assess whether the law was correctly applied.[161]

23.2.4.8 Breach of the formal side of the mandate

The elements described above concern the material side of the arbitrator's mandate. However, an arbitrator should also take the formal side of his

157 See Supreme Court 27 March 2009, ECLI:NL:HR:2009:BG4003, paras 4.4.2-4.4.3, *NJ* 2010/169, annotated by H.J. Snijders (*Hendrix Poultry/Burshan*); Supreme Court 22 December 1978, ECLI:NL:HR:1978:AC6449, *NJ* 1979/521 (*Zaunbrecher/Muyzert*); Supreme Court 23 December 1943, ECLI:NL:HR:1943:201, *NJ* 1944/164 (*Drost/Schippers*); Amsterdam District Court 18 April 2007, ECLI:NL:RBAMS:2007:BB1857, paras 4.3.1-4.3.3. Sometimes this still goes wrong. See Amsterdam District Court 4 March 2015, ECLI:NL:RBAMS:2015:1181; 's-Hertogenbosch Court of Appeal 20 February 2007, ECLI:NL:GHSHE:2007:AZ9780. In the first case, the judgment of the district court was reversed on appeal because the district court had conducted a substantive assessment based on the reasoning. See Amsterdam Court of Appeal 25 April 2017, ECLI:NL:GHAMS:2017:1496.

158 See Supreme Court 27 March 2009, ECLI:NL:HR:2009:BG4003, para 4.4.2, *NJ* 2010/169, annotated by H.J. Snijders (*Hendrix Poultry/Burshan*).

159 See 's-Hertogenbosch Court of Appeal 19 September 2023, ECLI:NL:GHSHE:2023:2979, para 4.7.

160 See for example Middelburg District Court 30 July 2008, ECLI:NL:RBMID:2008:BE0035; 's-Hertogenbosch Court of Appeal 17 May 2022, ECLI:NL:GHSHE:2022:1550, para 3.24; The Hague Court of Appeal 23 January 2024, ECLI:NL:GHDHA:2024:32, para 5.7.

161 See The Hague Court of Appeal 10 October 2017, ECLI:NL:GHDHA:2017:2813, paras 4.3.1-4.3.2.

mandate into account.[162] The procedural side of an arbitrator's mandate is determined by the applicable procedural statutory rules and the agreed upon arbitration rules. The state court in setting aside proceedings can interpret the applicable arbitration rules in order to assess whether the arbitral tribunal has complied with them.[163] In doing so, however, the state court must exercise restraint, so that violation of the applicable procedural rules is only accepted in striking cases.[164] In a case before the Arnhem-Leeuwarden Court of Appeal the question arose whether the arbitral tribunal applied the (institutional) arbitration rules agreed upon by the parties. The Court of Appeal concluded that the tribunal had applied the correct set of arbitration rules and dismissed the setting aside claim. The mere fact that the rules agreed upon by the parties had been replaced by a new set of rules did not mean that the new rules applied to the arbitration. In addition, it had not been shown that the parties (had) agreed to apply the new arbitration rules.[165]

The applicable procedural rules include Article 1059 DCCP, concerning *res judicata* force of arbitral awards. The Supreme Court has confirmed that an arbitral award can be set aside in the event an arbitral tribunal fails to resolve the dispute submitted to arbitration in accordance with Article 1059 DCCP. However, the court in setting aside proceedings must exercise restraint in that regard.[166] In the case at hand, the The Hague Court of Appeal had misjudged that principle, as it has essentially assessed whether

162 See H.J. Snijders, in: *GS Burgerlijke Rechtsvordering*, Article 1065 DCCP, notes 4.2.4 and 4.2.7 (online, updated 1 May 2018); Meijer & Van Mierlo 2014, p 63.

163 See Supreme Court 17 January 2003, ECLI:NL:HR:2003:AE9395, para 3.3, *NJ* 2004/384, annotated by H.J. Snijders (*IMS/Modsaf-IR*); Supreme Court 28 September 1990, ECLI:NL:HR:1990:AD1240, para 3.6, *NJ* 1991/230, annotated by J.B.M. Vranken (*Huybregts/Van Tuyl*); Amsterdam District Court 29 December 2021, ECLI:NL:RBAMS:2021:7648, para 5.21. Obviously unless such an explanation is contractually excluded by the parties. It is assumed that such an agreement *de facto* also excludes the possibility of setting aside the arbitral award for breach of the formal part of the mandate. See G.J. Meijer, 'International Military Services ...', in: P.J.M. von Schmidt auf Altenstadt, F.E. Vermeulen & B.T.M. van der Wiel (eds), *Middelen voor Meijer*, The Hague: Boom legal 2013, p 226-229.

164 See G.J. Meijer, in: *T&C Rv*, Article 1065 DCCP, note 4b (online, updated 1 January 2024); Amsterdam Court of Appeal 1 November 2011, ECLI:NL:GHAMS:2011:BU7752, para 2.13; Arnhem District Court 20 October 2010, ECLI:NL:RBARN:2010:BO2585, para 4.1.

165 See Arnhem-Leeuwarden Court of Appeal 22 April 2022, ECLI:NL:GHARL:2022:1340.

166 See Supreme Court 17 March 2023, ECLI:NL:HR:2023:422, paras 3.2-3.3, *NJ* 2023/115 (*Attero/Gemeenten & Gewesten*). See also Advocate General Vlas in his non-binding opinion rendered prior to Supreme Court 2 December 2022, ECLI:NL:PHR:2022:808, para 3.12.

the arbitral tribunal had applied Article 1059 DCCP correctly.[167] According to the Supreme Court, the Court of Appeal should only have assessed whether the arbitrators has applied the standard laid down in Article 1059 DCCP. It was clear that the arbitrators had indeed applied that standard, which meant that there was no ground to set aside the arbitral award.[168]

According to the case law of the lower courts, a breach of the procedural side of the mandate occurs, for example, if an arbitrator takes a decision in the final arbitral award that deviates from a binding final decision given in an interim arbitral award.[169] An arbitrator may only go back on his earlier decision if there is a so-called *novum*.[170] While the fact that a binding final decision is later shown to be incorrect may be a reason to revise an earlier (decision in an) award, it is not a ground for setting aside of an arbitral award, because the binding final decision is a substantive decision.[171]

In theory, an arbitrator will also breach his mandate if he conducts the arbitration as an *ad hoc* arbitration, while arbitration according to the arbitration rules of a specific arbitration institute was intended.[172]

The formal side of the mandate also includes procedural agreements made between the parties and arbitrators, such as the agreement to settle the dispute in two stages (bifurcation) and time periods agreed upon. As to the former, one could think of an agreement to separate the proceedings in a jurisdiction phase and a merits phase, or the agreement to separate the proceedings into a phase on liability and a phase on damages. In principle,

---

167 The Court of Appeal set aside the arbitral award for breach of Article 1059 DCCP, see The Hague Court of Appeal 29 June 2021, ECLI:NL:GHDHA:2021:1119.

168 See Supreme Court 17 March 2023, ECLI:NL:HR:2023:422, paras 3.4 and 3.7, *NJ* 2023/115 (*Attero/Gemeenten & Gewesten*).

169 See Supreme Court 24 April 2009, ECLI:NL:HR:2009:BH3137, paras 4.6.1-4.6.2, *NJ* 2010/171, annotated by H.J. Snijders (*IMS/Modsaf-IR*) and The Hague Court of Appeal 21 December 2006, ECLI:NL:GHSGR:2006:479, paras 2.1-3.40, 6.1-6.10. After all, a final decision given in an interim award has *res judicata* effect (Article 1049 in conjunction with Article 1059 DCCP). See also (unsuccessfully): Amsterdam District Court 7 December 2011, ECLI:NL:RBAMS:2011:BV3821, para 4.3.

170 See The Hague District Court 7 September 2012, ECLI:NL:RBSGR:2012:BX6825, paras 4.8-4.15, in which the applicable arbitration rules (the UNCITRAL Arbitration Rules 1976) provided for this possibility. See for an application of this, in the context of Article 1065(1)(e) DCCP, Court of Appeal 's-Gravenhage 22 August 2011, ECLI:NL:GHSGR:2011:4513, paras 2.3-2.8.

171 See The Hague Court of Appeal 3 September 2013, ECLI:NL:GHDHA:2013:3403, paras 14-16, upheld in cassation, see Supreme Court 22 May 2015, ECLI:NL:HR:2015:1272.

172 See 's-Hertogenbosch Court of Appeal 20 February 2007, ECLI:NL:GHSHE:2007:AZ9780 (unsuccessful).

an arbitrator should adhere to those agreements, unless the parties deviate from them during the course of the proceedings.[173] However, a breach of internal procedural rules applicable between the arbitrators only does not constitute a breach of mandate according to the judgment in the *Benetton v. Eco Swiss*-case.[174]

23.2.5 Defects in the signing of the arbitral award (Article 1065(1)(d) DCCP)

The arbitral tribunal must ensure that the award it renders is signed by all of the arbitrators (cf. Article 1057(2) DCCP). If a minority of the arbitrators refuses to sign the award or if the minority is unable to do so, the other arbitrators must state this in the award signed by them (Article 1057(3) DCCP; see also Article 49(5) NAI Arbitration Rules 2024). Signing of the arbitral award, which also includes the notice referred to in Article 1057(3) DCCP,[175] is an essential part of the award and is a guarantee of the collegiality of the decision-making within the tribunal.[176] This ground was put forward in 13 of the published cases studied by us. This led to setting aside of the award in five of those cases.

173 See in this respect Amsterdam District Court 12 March 2014, ECLI:NL:RBAMS:2014:2399, paras 4.14-4.15. Here, it was agreed that the proceedings would be conducted in two phases: one phase on the interpretation of an indemnity and then a phase on the scope of the (damages) claim under the indemnity, including the extent of contributory negligence. During the proceedings, one of the parties raised the issue of contributory negligence. In light of the extensive discussion that followed in that regard, the arbitrators were permitted to provide a decision concerning contributory negligence. See also The Hague Court of Appeal 28 February 2023, ECLI:NL:GHDHA:2023:318, parsa 6.13-6.17, concerning a time limit to submit a damages claim and the consequences of a failure to comply with that time limit.

174 See Supreme Court 25 February 2000, ECLI:NL:HR:2000:AA4947, paras 3.2.2-3.2.3, *NJ* 2000/508, annotated by H.J. Snijders (*Benetton/Eco Swiss*).

175 The notification forms part of the award. Under the old arbitration law, there was no requirement for the notification to be made *in* the award. Failure to sign the notification could therefore lead to setting aside of the award. See Supreme Court 21 January 1966, ECLI:NL:HR:1966:AB5441, *NJ* 1966/214 (*Scheeuwe/James Smith and Sons*).

176 See H.J. Snijders, in: *GS Burgerlijke Rechtsvordering*, Article 1057, note 3 (online, updated 1 May 2018). See also: Supreme Court 5 December 2008, ECLI:NL:HR:2008:BF3799, para 3.4.2, *JBPr* 2009/2, annotated by H.W. Wiersma (*Bursa/Güris*). Signing the award should therefore be considered an essential part of the arbitrator's task. See also Opinion of A-G Rank-Berenschot rendered prior to Supreme Court 30 September 2016, ECLI:NL:2016:PHR:472, para 2.26; Supreme Court 30 September 2016, ECLI:NL:HR:2016:2215, para 3.5.1, *NJ* 2017/141, annotated by J.B.M. Vranken (*Qnow/B.*); Arnhem-Leeuwarden Court of Appeal 16 October 2018, ECLI:NL:GHARL:2018:9111, para 2.9.

It follows from case law[177] and literature[178] that an arbitral award will be set aside if it is not signed. It is, however, also argued in academic literature that the arbitral award does not exist if it is not signed at all, as an essential part of the award is missing. There is only an arbitral award the moment it is signed (later on). On this basis, it is argued that Article 1065(1)(d) DCCP only comes into play in situations where there is a defect in signing the award and not also in cases where the award is not signed by any of the arbitrators.[179] In such cases (in which the signature is (partly) present but defective), setting aside may follow, as the following cases show. An arbitral award signed by a secretary and a chair of an arbitral tribunal on behalf of the other two arbitrators provides a ground for setting aside, according to the *Qnow*-judgment. The arbitral award was signed by the other two arbitrators two months after it was filed, but that could not cure the defect in the original arbitral award. This was because the fact that the award was signed by all of the arbitrators at a later stage did not ensure that all arbitrators had been involved in making the arbitral award, nor that they had been able to influence the decision reached, nor that they could agree with the content of the award at the time it was made.[180] In ensuing liability proceedings, it was held that the conduct of the chair of the tribunal met the high threshold for liability of an arbitrator.[181] However, the liability claim was ultimately dismissed due to lack of causation between the error and the (purported) loss.[182]

A less stringent system applies to signing an order of the arbitral tribunal. Arbitral awards and orders both contain decisions of the arbitral tribunal, but orders generally contain informal decisions, which usually do not per-

177 See Amsterdam Court of Appeal 3 November 2020, ECLI:NL:GHAMS:2020:2936, para 4.5; Utrecht District Court 8 August 2007, ECLI:NL:RBUTR:2007:BB1410, paras 4.15 and 4.23, *NJF* 2007/501.

178 See G.J. Meijer, in: *T&C Rv*, Article 1057 DCCP, note 3b and Article 1065 DCCP, note 5 (online, updated 1 January 2024); Meijer & Van Mierlo 2014, p 64.

179 See H.J. Snijders, in: *GS Burgerlijke Rechtsvordering*, Article 1057 DCCP, note 3 (online, updated 1 May 2018); Sanders 2001, p 197; A.J. van den Berg, R. van Delden & H.J. Snijders, *Arbitragerecht*, Zwolle: W.E.J. Tjeenk Willink 1992, p 112. See also: Arnhem-Leeuwarden Court of Appeal 27 September 2000, ECLI:NL:GHLEE:2000:AD3236, *NJ* 2001/225.

180 See Amsterdam Court of Appeal 29 March 2007, *TvA* 2008/53 and Amsterdam District Court 28 September 2005, ECLI:NL:RBAMS:2005:AU4950, paras 5.4-5.10. See also Amsterdam Court of Appeal 3 November 2020, ECLI:NL:GHAMS:2020:2936, para 4.5.

181 See Arnhem-Leeuwarden Court of Appeal 16 October 2018, ECLI:NL:GHARL:2018:9111 (in particular para 2.9).

182 See Arnhem-Leeuwarden Court of Appeal 4 June 2019, ECLI:NL:GHARL:2019:4760, *JOR* 2019/243, annotated by C.L. Schleijpen.

tain to the merits of the case at hand.[183] The District Court and Court of Appeal in The Hague have held that a 'Tribunal's Order' that determined the end of the tribunal's mandate was materially an arbitral award that could be subject to setting aside.[184] However, both courts held that *formally* the Tribunal's Order was in fact an order, which meant that the requirements for signing an arbitral award, as laid down in Article 1057(2) DCCP and in the applicable arbitration rules, did not apply. In light of this, the fact that the order was signed (only) by the chair of the tribunal, did not constitute a ground for setting aside of the order.[185] It seems to follow from this that less stringent signature requirements apply in case of an order that is materially an arbitral award. In our view, this decision can be questioned. If substance is decisive and the order is materially deemed to be an arbitral award that could be subject to setting aside, then the 'order' should, in our view, meet the statutory requirements for an arbitral award. Depending on the perspective followed, remission (Article 1065a DCCP) could provide a means to prevent setting aside of an order that is deemed to be an arbitral award in the event it is not signed in accordance with Article 1057 DCCP. We discuss remission in paragraph 23.3.

According to case law, a dissenting opinion of an arbitrator who refuses to sign the award cannot remedy a failure to sign the notice as referred to in Article 1057(3) DCCP. After all, a dissenting opinion is separate to the arbitral award[186] and cannot be equated with the aforementioned notice.[187] However, an arbitrator is allowed to sign the arbitral award *'subject*

183 Asser Procesrecht/Sanders, Meijer & Ernste *8* 2023/290-291; H.J. Snijders, in: *GS Burgerlijke Rechtsvordering*, Article 1049, note 2 (online, updated 1 May 2018).

184 The Hague District Court 17 March 2021, ECLI:NL:RBDHA:2021:2055, para 4.17 and The Hague Court of Appeal 28 February 2023, ECLI:NL:GHDHA:2023:318, para 6.8. The Court of Appeal *assumes* that the order is an arbitral award (according to its substance).

185 The Hague District Court 17 March 2021, ECLI:NL:RBDHA:2021:2055, para 4.46 and The Hague Court of Appeal 28 February 2023, ECLI:NL:GHDHA:2023:318, paras 6.26-6.27.

186 See J.D.M. Lew, L.A. Mistelis & S. Kröll, *Comparative International Commercial Arbitration*, The Hague: Kluwer Law International 2003, paras 24-46; E. Gaillard & J. Savage, *Fouchard, Gaillard, Goldman on International Commercial Arbitration*, The Hague: Kluwer Law International 1999, para 1402.

187 See Supreme Court 5 December 2008, ECLI:NL:HR:2008:BF3799, *JBPr* 2009/2, annotated by H.W. Wiersma (*Bursa/Güris*) and (at length) the non-binding opinion of Advocate General Wesseling-Van Gent rendered prior to this judgment, ECLI:NL:PHR:2008:BF3799, paras 2.22-2.34. See further on (the role of) dissenting opinions in arbitration: B. van Zelst, 'Dissenting opinions in arbitrage', *TvA* 2015/21, p 33-38 and P.E. Ernste & G.J. Meijer, 'Dissenting opinions in arbitrage: wenselijk?', in: P. Koerts & E.F. Verheul (eds) *Toonaangevend,* Deventer: Wolters Kluwer 2024, p 15-24.

to dissenting opinion'. The dissenting opinion indicates that although an arbitrator has a different opinion, he acquiesces in the majority opinion by signing the award. To that extent, therefore, the dissenting opinion is not in conflict with the rationale behind signing an arbitral award.[188]

Nowadays, it is also possible to prepare an arbitral award in electronic form by providing an award with a qualified electronic signature (Article 1072b DCCP), as referred to in Article 3(12) of Regulation 910/2014/EU ("EIDAS Regulation").[189] In that case, (a copy of) the digital arbitral award is equated with an original and certified copy of an arbitral award (Article 1072b in conjunction with Article 1057(2) DCCP).[190] The question is whether setting aside of the arbitral award should follow if the signature does not meet the technical requirements of the EIDAS Regulation. This question has not (yet) been addressed by the courts. In this situation, the electronic award cannot be considered equivalent to a written arbitral award on the basis of the law and is not signed in accordance with Article 1057(2) DCCP. In our opinion, this could, in principle, constitute a ground for setting aside of the arbitral award. By opting for a qualified electronic signature, the Dutch legislator has implicitly indicated that this is the only way to achieve a level of reliability equal to that of a signature 'in ink', and that any other form of signature does not qualify as a signature within the meaning of Article 1057(2) DCCP. The question is, however, whether Article 1065(1)(d) DCCP should be interpreted so strictly in the event the arbitrators are identifiable by means of the electronic signature and it is clear that all arbitrators were involved in the making of the arbitral award and

188 See Amsterdam Court of Appeal 25 April 2017, ECLI:NL:GHAMS:2017:1496, paras 3.39-3.43; Amsterdam District Court 4 March 2015, ECLI:NL:RBAMS:2015:1181, paras 4.9-4.11.

189 See OJ EU L 257/73. It should concern "[...] an advanced electronic signature that is created by a qualified electronic signature creation device, and which is based on a qualified certificate for electronic signatures". A qualified certificate for electronic signatures shall, according to Article 28 of the Regulation, meet the requirements set out in Annex 1 of the Regulation. See on the different types of signatures under the Regulation, *inter alia*, T.F.E. Tjong Tjin Tai, in: *GS Vermogensrecht*, Article 3:15a DCC, note 6 (online, updated 24 January 2019); E.D.C. Neppelenbroek, in: *T&C Rv*, Article 3:15a DCC, notes 1-2 (online, updated 1 March 2024); *Parliamentary Papers II* 2015/16, 34413, no 3, p 62-64.

190 See Meijer & Van Mierlo 2015, p 171; G.J. Meijer, in: *T&C Rv*, Article 1072b DCCP, note 5 (online, updated 1 April 2024). Article 1072b DCCP was amended by Act of 21 December 2016, *Stb.* 2017, 13, in connection to the implementation of Regulation 910/2014/EU. Article 1072b(3) DCCP now explicitly refers to Article 3(12) of the Regulation (see *Parliamentary Papers II* 2015/16, 34413, no 3, p 67).

intended to sign it.[191] We believe it should not. This is in line with the principle that the grounds for setting aside should be applied with restraint.[192] Such an approach is also in line with a decision of the Amsterdam District Court, in which a *written* award was set aside because it contained a scan of the signature of one of the arbitrators, rather than a handwritten signature. Here, the Amsterdam District Court attached importance to the fact that it could not be shown that the arbitrator in question had been involved in the formation of the arbitral award.[193] *A contrario* and focusing on electronic signatures, it could be inferred from this that if such involvement can be demonstrated, inclusion of a signature that does not meet the requirements of the EIDAS Regulation should also not necessarily lead to setting aside of the arbitral award. Potential problems with enforcement of the award abroad is a reason why arbitration institutes do not make use of the possibility of digitally signing the arbitral award for the time being.[194] At present, the NAI also does not make use of this possibility.[195]

Finally, according to case law, addenda or arbitration reports to which the arbitrators explicitly refer in their award need not be signed separately.[196] If arbitrators include the wrong place where the award was rendered in the award and fail to include the places of residence of the arbitrators, setting aside is not possible.[197] An application for rectification (Article 1060(2)

---

191 Indeed, the signature serves as a safeguard for collegial decision-making. See H.J. Snijders, in: *GS Burgerlijke Rechtsvordering*, Article 1057 DCCP, note 3 (online, updated 1 May 2018). Cf. with regard to the enforcement of an electronic arbitral award under the New York Convention: P.E. Ernste & G.J. Meijer, 'Instemming met de overeenkomst to arbitrage en e-arbitrage: het Nederlandse perspectief', in: D. de Meulemeester et al (eds), *Liber Amicorum. 50 jaar oplossingen*, Mechelen: Wolters Kluwer 2019. p 249-251.

192 Cf. also Sanders 2001, p 160 and p 197, who wants to get rid of errors in signing the award as a ground for setting aside altogether.

193 See Amsterdam District Court 29 January 2014, ECLI:NL:RBAMS:2014:793, paras 4.4-4.6.

194 See H.J. Snijders, in: *GS Burgerlijke Rechtsvordering*, Article 1072b DCCP, note 2.5 (online, updated 1 May 2018); R. Jacobsz, 'Een verslag van de expertmeeting over E-arbitration (en breder)', *TvA* 2016/66.

195 See P.E. Ernste, F. Petillion & T. Vaal, 'Greener arbitrations: the role of arbitration institutions', in: *The CEPANI & NAI approach towards Topical Trends in Arbitration. Reports form the Fourth joint CEPANI – NAI Colloquium held on 22 April 2022*, Mechelen: Wolters Kluwer 2022, p 93-94.

196 See Roermond District Court 22 August 2012, ECLI:NL:RBROE:2012:BX5101, para 4.8.3.

197 See Haarlem District Court 5 March 2008, ECLI:NL:RBHAA:2008:BC6686, para 5.10; Utrecht District Court 8 August 2007, ECLI:NL:RBUTR:2007:BB1410, para 4.15, *NJF* 2007/501.

in conjunction with Article 1057(4)(a-d) DCCP) is the appropriate route in that case.[198]

23.2.6 *Failure to state reasons (Article 1065(1)(d) DCCP)*[199]

Article 1057(4)(e) DCCP states that an arbitral award should contain the reasons for the decision given in the arbitral award. If an arbitral tribunal fails to state reasons for its decision, the award may be set aside pursuant to Article 1065(1)(d) DCCP.[200] It is also sometimes argued in the literature that the setting aside claim can be based on Article 1065(1)(e)DCCP.[201] The parties can exclude the requirement to provide the grounds for the decision in the arbitral award (Article 1057(5)(c) DCCP). In that case, the parties cannot base a subsequent setting aside claim on a defective reasoning of the award.[202]

A defect in the reasoning of an arbitral award is often invoked as a ground for setting aside of the arbitral award, but the argument rarely succeeds. In 180 of the analyzed cases the setting aside claim was based on a defect in the reasoning of an arbitral award. The claim succeeded in only eight cases. The reason why such claims are unsuccessful in the majority of cases is that the state court should exercise restraint in assessing whether the ground for setting aside mentioned in Article 1065(1)(d) DCCP arises. Setting aside proceedings may under no circumstances function as a disguised appeal and a substantive review of the arbitral award is therefore,

198 See *Parliamentary Papers II* 1983/84, 18464, no 3, p 24, p 29.

199 The topics touched upon in para 23.2.6 and para 23.2.7 of this contribution are reflected in several judgments examined. In the interest of clarity, we have limited ourselves to three judgments per footnote. The selection was made on the basis of geographical spread, judicial authority and clarity of the relevant consideration(s) in the judgment.

200 See Amsterdam District Court 9 April 2014, ECLI:NL:RBAMS:2014:2290, paras 4.7-4.8; Utrecht District Court 28 December 2011, ECLI:NL:RBUTR:2011:BV2887, paras 4.5-4.11.

201 See H.J. Snijders, in: *GS Burgerlijke Rechtsvordering*, Article 1065 DCCP, note 6 (online, updated 1 May 2018); Sanders 2001, p 197. Sanders has proposed to remove Article 1065(1)(d) DCCP in its entirety. See also *inter alia* (unsuccessfully) The Hague Court of Appeal 18 July 2017, ECLI:NL:GHDHA:2017:2009, paras 14.1-14.3; Utrecht District Court 4 November 2009, ECLI:NL:RBUTR:2009:BK4955; Amsterdam Court of Appeal 3 August 2006, *BR* 2007/254.

202 It is assumed that the possibility of exclusion will entail that fewer cases are eligible for setting aside. See M.W. Knigge, 'Ongemotiveerd en onaantastbaar? Over de gevolgen van een uitsluiting van het motiveringsvereiste voor de controle op arbitrale vonnissen door de overheidsrechter', in: W.H. van Boom et al (eds), *Een kwart eeuw: Privaatrechtelijke opstellen, aangeboden aan prof. mr. H.J. Snijders*, Deventer: Wolters Kluwer 2016, p 253-270.

in light of this, out of the question.[203] According to the case law of the Supreme Court, the state court may only intervene in *striking* cases, i.e. if the award lacks any reasoning whatsoever or if the statement of reasons for the decision is so unsound that it is impossible to discover any valid explanation for the decisions in the arbitral award. In such cases, the reasoning must be equated to a total lack of reasoning.[204] This criterion is often reiterated as a point of departure for the assessment in case law of the lower courts.[205] Subsequently, several courts conduct only a marginal review of the reasoning of the award, holding that the reasoning is logical, (sufficiently) clear or sound (or a comparable phrasing), or that the award contains sufficient grounds for the decision.[206] In our view, this is an illustration of the restrictive review courts in setting aside proceedings should apply in this context. However, there are also courts that meticulously review the reasoning of the arbitral award to determine whether the reasoning is completely lacking or is defective.[207] In our view, this is contrary to the case law of the Supreme Court discussed above.

It also follows from case law that an arbitral award may be set aside if the arbitral tribunal has provided only a general reasoning for its decision that does not cover the specific defences put forward by the parties.[208] The same applies if the arbitral tribunal did not give reasons for its decision on an essential defence, although setting aside on this basis is not com-

203 See Supreme Court 22 December 2006, ECLI:NL:HR:2006:AZ1593, para 3.3, *NJ* 2008/4, annotated by H.J. Snijders (*Kers/Rijpma*); Supreme Court 9 January 2004, ECLI:NL:HR:2004:AK8380, para 3.5.2, *NJ* 2005/190, annotated by H.J. Snijders (*Nannini/SFT*); Supreme Court 25 February 2000, ECLI:NL:HR:2000:AA4947, para 3.3, *NJ* 2000/508, annotated by H.J. Snijders (*Benetton/Eco Swiss*).

204 See Supreme Court 22 December 2006, ECLI:NL:HR:2006:AZ1593, *NJ* 2008/4, annotated by H.J. Snijders (*Kers/Rijpma*); Supreme Court 9 January 2004, ECLI:NL:HR:2004:AK8380, *NJ* 2005/190, annotated by H.J. Snijders (*Nannini/SFT*).

205 See for example Arnhem-Leeuwarden Court of Appeal 19 March 2019, ECLI:NL:GHARL:2019:2450, para 4.1; The Hague Court of Appeal 19 May 2020, ECLI:NL:GHDHA:2020:1031, para 4.5; 's-Hertogenbosch Court of Appeal 17 May 2022, ECLI:NL:GHSHE:2022:1550, para 3.21.

206 See for example Court of Appeal Amsterdam 11 February 2020, ECLI:NL:GHAMS:2020:465, paras 4.7-4.8; The Hague Court of Appeal 25 February 2020, ECLI:NL:GHDHA:2020:254, para 7.4; Arnhem-Leeuwarden Court of Appeal 25 May 2021, ECLI:NL:GHARL:2021:5021, para 4.12.

207 See for example Arnhem-Leeuwarden Court of Appeal 8 October 2019, ECLI:NL:GHARL:2019:8203, paras 4.6-4.13; Amsterdam Court of Appeal 25 May 2021, ECLI:NL:GHAMS:2021:1464, paras 3.4-3.12; The Hague Court of Appeal 21 June 2022, ECLI:NL:GHDHA:2022:1320, paras 5.6-5.7.

208 See Arnhem-Leeuwarden Court of Appeal 18 April 2017, ECLI:NL:GHARL:2017:3283, paras 3.3-3.8.

mon in practice.[209] An example of a case in which an arbitral award was set aside on this ground is the *Nannini/SFT*-case. In this case, the arbitral tribunal had assumed that the causal link between the breach of a contractual guarantee by SFT and the loss suffered by Nannini had already been determined in proceedings prior to the arbitration. However, it had only been decided in those proceedings that SFT had breached the contractual guarantee. The causal link had to be established in the arbitration. In light of this, the reasoning of the decision not to address the causal link, as provided by the arbitral tribunal, was considered so flawed that it did not provide a valid explanation for the decision.[210]

It furthermore follows from case law that arbitrators are not required to explicitly address all the parties' assertions and defences.[211] What is most important is that they provide a reasoned decision on the essential main points.[212] According to case law, the extent of the reasoning will depend on the parties' submissions and the debate conducted.[213] The reasoning

209 This argument only led to setting aside of the arbitral award in the *Nannini/SFT*-case, already cited. See for several examples of cases in which the argument was not successful: Supreme Court 22 December 2006, ECLI:NL:HR:2006:AZ1593, paras 3.4-3.5, *NJ* 2008/4, annotated by H.J. Snijders (*Kers/Rijpma*); The Hague Court of Appeal 17 February 2015, ECLI:NL:GHDHA:2015:222, paras 21-23, 25-30; Arnhem-Leeuwarden Court of Appeal 15 February 2022, ECLI:NL:GHARL:2022:1138, paras 4.4-4.5. In some cases, the argument is advanced under both Article 1065(1)(c) and Article 1065(1)(d) DCCP. See for example 's-Hertogenbosch Court of Appeal 21 January 2020, ECLI:NL:GHSHE:2020:172, paras 3.5.1-3.5.2.

210 See Supreme Court 9 January 2004, ECLI:NL:HR:2004:AK8380, *NJ* 2005/190, annotated by H.J. Snijders (*Nannini/SFT*).

211 See, *inter alia,* The Hague Court of Appeal 28 February 2023, ECLI:NL:GHDHA:2023:318, para 6.25; 's-Hertogenbosch Court of Appeal 21 January 2021, ECLI:NL:GHSHE:2020:172, para 3.5.2; Amsterdam Court of Appeal 17 January 2017, ECLI:NL:GHAMS:2017:140, paras 2.7, 2.11. Similarly Arnhem-Leeuwarden Court of Appeal 23 July 2024, ECLI:NL:GHAMS:2024:2078, para 3.6. In Rotterdam District Court 27 March 2013, ECLI:NL:RBROT:2013:BZ6030, para 5.8, the large number of documents and submissions during the proceedings contributed to the conclusion that the arbitrators did not have to address all the points raised.

212 See G.J. Meijer, in: *T&C Rv*, Article 1065 DCCP, note 6c (online, updated 1 January 2024). See also, for example, Arnhem-Leeuwarden Court of Appeal 18 April 2017, ECLI:NL:GHARL:2017:3283; Amsterdam District Court 7 December 2011, ECLI:NL:RBAMS:2011:BV3821; Supreme Court 9 January 2004, ECLI:NL:HR:2004:AK8380, *NJ* 2005/190, annotated by H.J. Snijders (*Nannini/SFT*). It is not always necessary to provide reasons for a decision on non-essential points. See, *inter alia*, Arnhem District Court 20 April 2011, ECLI:NL:RBARN:2011:BQ3150, para 4.3; Haarlem District Court 5 March 2008, ECLI:NL:RBHAA:2008:BC6686, paras 5.8-5.9; Rotterdam District Court 5 October 2005, *TvA* 2007/24, para 5.6.

213 See, *inter alia,* Arnhem-Leeuwarden Court of Appeal 11 September 2017, ECLI:NL:GHARL:2017:144, paras 5.8-5.10; Amsterdam District Court 21 Au-

of a decision may be implicit,[214] i.e. it may follow from several considerations of the arbitral award read in conjunction with each other,[215] from the rejection of another point advanced or from the reasoning pertaining to another point,[216] or from the arbitral award as a whole.[217]

It follows from case law that no ground for setting aside is present if the reasoning concerning rejection of one claim also explains why the other claim or 'that which was additionally or otherwise claimed' was rejected.[218] However, setting aside may follow if the reasons for the decision on one claim totally fail to provide any insight into the decision on the other claim[219] or if the arbitrators provide reasons to reject an assertion or claim that do not preclude such a decision.[220] Finally, a NAI award was set aside

gust 2013, ECLI:NL:RBAMS:2013:6253. The arbitrator may interpret the assertions to some extent. See District Court 's-Gravenhage 14 May 2014, ECLI:NL:RBDHA:2014:6150, paras 4.2-4.8. A misrepresented assertion that is addressed later on cannot, in and of itself, lead to setting aside of the arbitral award. See 's-Gravenhage District Court 7 October 2015, ECLI:NL:RBDHA:2015:11637, para 4.29.

214 See, *inter alia*, Supreme Court 30 December 1977, ECLI:NL:HR:1977:AC6162, *NJ* 1978/449, annotated by P.A. Stein (*De Ploeg/Kruse*); Arnhem-Leeuwarden Court of Appeal 8 November 2016, ECLI:NL:GHARL:2016:8942, paras 5.9-5.10; Amsterdam Court of Appeal 4 March 2014, ECLI:NL:GHAMS:2014:644, paras 3.6-3.8; The Hague Court of Appeal 20 October 2009, ECLI:NL:GHSGR:2009:BK0923, para 4-6.

215 See for example Amsterdam Court of Appeal 25 May 2021, ECLI:NL:GHAMS:2021:1464, para 3.10; The Hague Court of Appeal 10 October 2017, ECLI:NL:GHDHA:2017:2813, paras 4.4.4-4.4.13; Rotterdam District Court 8 March 2006, ECLI:NL:RBROT:2006:AV5278, paras 4.8-4.11.

216 See Arnhem-Leeuwarden Court of Appeal 4 June 2024, ECLI:NL:GHARL:2024:3753, para 3.18; The Hague Court of Appeal 24 November 2020, ECLI:NL:GHDHA:2020:2833, para 4.7, The Hague Court of Appeal 1 October 2019, ECLI:NL:GHDHA:2019:2500, para 6.1.

217 See, among other examples, Amsterdam District Court 12 March 2014, ECLI:NL:RBAMS:2014:2399, para 4.19; The Hague District Court 7 September 2012, ECLI:NL:RBSGR:2012:BX6825, paras 4.20-4.23; Rotterdam District Court 14 October 2009, ECLI:NL:RBROT:2009:BK3449, para 5.10.

218 See for example The Hague District Court 14 May 2014, ECLI:NL:RBDHA:2014:6150, para 4.15; Oost-Brabant District Court 20 November 2013, ECLI:NL:RBOBR:2013:6515, para 4.6; Arnhem District Court 7 May 2008, ECLI:NL:RBARN:2008:BD2370, paras 4.5-4.7.

219 See Haarlem District Court 13 January 2010, ECLI:NL:RBHAA:2010:BL1528, paras 7.1-7.5.

220 See Utrecht District Court 21 November 2001, *TvA* 2002/2, p 82-83, paras 4.4-4.6. In this case, the arbitrators had dismissed the allegation that mismanagement, breach of contract and fraud had been committed by one of the parties in the arbitration, thereby observing that both parties were assisted by experts and had thus been sufficiently able to inform themselves. However, this did not necessarily preclude the allegations made. The arbitrators had further failed to provide insight into the method of calculation applied, see paras 4.7-4.10.

pursuant to Article 1065(1)(d) and (e) DCCP in a case in which the arbitrators rejected a request of the non-prevailing party in the arbitral proceedings to provide witness testimony in favour of the declaratory judgment claimed by that party, while that party carried the burden of proof in this regard. The arbitrators had justified this decision by stating that the party in question could not provide evidence through witnesses that could outweigh what could have been demonstrated by evidence that the same party had not been able to produce at an earlier stage of the proceedings and that was thus not known to the arbitrators. With this reasoning, the arbitrators did not explain why further witness testimony could never outweigh documents of which the content was unknown to the arbitrators. Moreover, the arbitrators had prejudged the evidence before it could be given.[221]

It follows from case law that the presence of 'a' statement of reasons is usually sufficient.[222] There is, in principle, no place for setting aside of an arbitral award on account of an *inadequate* reasoning.[223] The (in)correctness of the reasons given, both in fact and in law, cannot be questioned in setting aside proceedings.[224] Incomprehensibility, lack of clarity or incompleteness of the reasoning does not expose the arbitral award to setting aside either.[225] Furthermore, the fact that a party does not agree with the

221 See The Hague Court of Appeal 14 October 2004, ECLI:NL:GHSGR:2004:AS6294, *Prg.* 2005/14, para 9.

222 See for example Amsterdam Court of Appeal 1 August 2017, ECLI:NL:GHAMS:2017:3133, para 3.16; Amsterdam Court of Appeal 25 April 2017, ECLI:NL:GHAMS:2017:1496, para 3.49; Arnhem-Leeuwarden Court of Appeal 3 March 2009, ECLI:NL:GHLEE:2009:BH5276.

223 See H.J. Snijders, in: *GS Burgerlijke Rechtsvordering*, Article 1065 DCCP, note 6 (online, updated 1 May 2018). See also, *inter alia*, 's-Gravenhage District Court 12 February 2014, ECLI:NL:RBDHA:2014:1752, para 4.14; Rotterdam District Court 22 May 2013, ECLI:NL:RBROT:2013:CA1243, para 4.7; Rotterdam District Court 4 July 2012, ECLI:NL:RBROT:2012:BX1286, para 4.17.

224 See, *inter alia*, Arnhem-Leeuwarden Court of Appeal 30 October 2018, ECLI:NL:GHARL:2018:9499, paras 5.7-5.12; Rotterdam District Court 22 May 2013, ECLI:NL:RBROT:2013:CA1243, para 4.7; Amsterdam District Court 17 April 2013, ECLI:NL:RBAMS:2013:CA1397, para 4.4. Similarly, The Hague Court of Appeal 7 January 2020, ECLI:NL:GHDHA:2020:1, para 7. Cf. Amsterdam Court of Appeal 1 November 2016, ECLI:NL:GHAMS:2016:4315, para 3.11; Amsterdam District Court 15 April 2015, ECLI:NL:RBAMS:2015:2442, paras 4.21-4.22. We note that an arbitral award containing reasons and/or a decision that is contrary to mandatory law that is of public policy cannot be set aside on the basis of Article 1065(1)(d) DCCP, but *does* qualify for setting aside on the basis of Article 1065(1)(e) DCCP.

225 See for example, The Hague Court of Appeal 28 January 2014, ECLI:NL:GHDHA:2014:71, para 20; Utrecht District Court 24 October 2012, ECLI:NL:RBUTR:2012:BY1976, para 4.8; Rotterdam District Court 14 October 2009, ECLI:NL:RBROT:2009:BK3449, para 5.10. However, an arbitral award

decision taken by the arbitrator(s) cannot lead to setting aside of the arbitral award.[226] In addition, the reasoning may be brief, also considering the nature and scope of the dispute submitted to arbitration.[227] Finally, an arbitrator may refer to expert opinions to provide grounds for the decision taken in the arbitral award.[228] The choice as to which opinions or submissions to refer to is up to the arbitrator and does not constitute a ground for setting aside of the award.[229]

In general, it can be inferred from case law on setting aside of arbitral awards for failure to state reasons that the threshold for setting aside on that ground is high. The arbitrator must take a reasoned decision on all *essential* points. The reasoning must, in essence, support and provide an explanation for the decision.

---

that does not reach the level of comprehensibility and readability that can be expected does not go unnoticed, see: Amsterdam District Court 27 August 2008, ECLI:NL:RBAMS:2008:BF3726, paras 4.1-4.2. Cf. also The Hague Court of Appeal 2 April 2019, ECLI:NL:GHDHA:2019:629, para 3.8; Arnhem-Leeuwarden Court of Appeal 29 September 2020, ECLI:NL:GHARL:2020:7803, para 3.9. In the first case, it was stated that while there was no ground for setting aside of the award, the reasoning was far from ideal. In the second case, the court ruled that the reasoning could be questioned, but that this was not a ground for setting aside of the award.

226 See, *inter alia*, The Hague Court of Appeal 25 February 2020, ECLI:NL:GHDHA:2020:254, para 7.4; Arnhem-Leeuwarden Court of Appeal 8 November 2016, ECLI:NL:GHARL:2016:8942, paras 5.9-5.10; Amsterdam Court of Appeal 4 March 2014, ECLI:NL:GHAMS:2014:644, paras 3.6-3.8.

227 See for example Rotterdam District Court 8 November 2017, ECLI:NL:RBROT:2017:8850, para 4.11; Amsterdam Court of Appeal 1 August 2017, ECLI:NL:GHAMS:2017:3133, para 3.17.3; Amsterdam Court of Appeal 19 April 2016, ECLI:NL:GHAMS:2016:1552, para 3.5.3.

228 The Hague Court of Appeal 18 December 2012, ECLI:NL:GHSGR:2012:BZ0888, para 8.2, provided due regard is given to the equal right to be heard with respect to the expert; Rotterdam District Court 8 November 2017, ECLI:NL:RBROT:2017:8850, paras 4.8-4.11, even if the arbitrator's own reasoning is brief.

229 See, *inter alia*, 's-Gravenhage District Court 10 September 2014, ECLI:NL:RBDHA:2014:16345, para 4.13; The Hague Court of Appeal 3 September 2013, ECLI:NL:GHDHA:2013:3403, paras 20-22; Rotterdam District Court 28 January 2009, ECLI:NL:RBROT:2009:BH3378, para 3.35. What does seem to be important is that the arbitrator explains why he follows a particular opinion. Incidentally, the arbitrator may provide a reason for the decision that deviates from a statement submitted by the parties. See Amsterdam District Court 1 May 2013, ECLI:NL:RBAMS:2013:CA3727, paras 4.13-4.14.

23.2.7 *Breach of public policy (Article 1065(1)(e) DCCP)*

23.2.7.1 In general

The last ground upon which an arbitral award can be set aside is breach of public policy (Article 1065(1)(e) DCCP).[230] This ground was invoked in 175 of the cases analyzed and led to setting aside of the arbitral award in 15 of those cases. An arbitral award may be in breach of public policy due to the way it came into being in the event of a violation of the equal right to be heard, the principle of independence and impartiality or the principle to provide reasons for the decision. The arbitral award may also be contrary to public policy in regard to its content, for example if the dispute is not capable of settlement via arbitration (arguably)[231] or if it violates law that is of public policy.

23.2.7.2 Breach of mandatory (EU) law of a fundamental nature

Not every breach of a statutory provision means that an arbitral award is subject to setting aside due to a breach of public policy. An arbitral award is only subject to setting aside pursuant to Article 1065(1)(e) DCCP if the content or enforcement of the award breaches mandatory law of such a fundamental character that compliance with it may not be prevented by procedural restrictions.[232] This is true in case of breach of national law that is of public policy and in case of breach of fundamental EU law. To our knowledge, only non-application of Article 101 of the Treaty on the Functioning of the European Union (hereinafter TFEU) can lead (and has led) to

230 See H.J. Snijders, in: *GS Burgerlijke Rechtsvordering*, Article 1065 DCCP, note 7 (online, updated 1 May 2018); G.J. Meijer, in: *T&C Rv*, Article 1065 DCCP, note 7 (online, updated 1 January 2024).

231 See Asser Procesrecht/Sanders, Meijer & Ernste *8* 2023/515; Meijer & Van Mierlo 2014, p 62, p 65; A.J. van den Berg, 'Voorontwerp Nieuwe Arbitragewet', *TvA* 1984, p 216, referring to *Parliamentary Papers II* 1983/84, 18464, no 3, p 29. It is however also argued that the arbitral award is contrary to public policy due to the way it came into being in this case, see N. Peters, *Openbare orde en arbitrage* (inaugural lecture Groningen), Deventer: Wolters Kluwer 2023, p 8. See in that respect also Asser Procesrecht/Sanders, Meijer & Ernste *8* 2023/515.

232 See for this criterion Supreme Court 21 March 1997, ECLI:NL:HR:1997:AA4945, *NJ* 1998/207, annotated by H.J. Snijders (*Eco Swiss/Benetton*). This is different in the event of breach of a provision of directory or 'ordinary' mandatory law. In that case it can, at most, be argued that the arbitrators breached the formal side of their mandate (see Meijer & Ernste 2015, p 104-105). In that case, the breach will have to be of a *serious nature* in order for the award to be set aside (Article 1065(4) DCCP).

setting aside of an arbitral award on this ground.[233] Article 6 of the (Dutch) Competition Act, for example, is not a public policy provision.[234] Breach of that provision can therefore not lead to setting aside of an arbitral award on the basis of Article 1065(1)(e) DCCP.[235] There are several examples of cases in which it was argued that the arbitral award should be set aside because of breach of a provision of public policy. In most cases, those claims were dismissed because there was no breach of a provision of public policy or the provision advanced was not a provision of public policy.[236]

23.2.7.3 Fraud and corruption

It follows from case law that parties invoke Article 1065(1)(e) DCCP on the ground that a legal act was entered into under the influence of fraud or corruption and was wrongly not declared invalid by the arbitral tribunal[237] and/or on the ground that fraud was committed during the arbitral proceedings.[238] In the *Bariven v. Wells*-case, for example, Bariven argued

233 See CJEC 1 June 1999, C-126/97, ECLI:EU:C:1999:269, paras 36-41, *NJ* 2000/339, annotated by H.J. Snijders (*Eco Swiss/Benetton*); Supreme Court 1 February 2000, ECLI:NL:HR:2000:ZC2315, para 2.1, Supreme Court 25 February 2000, ECLI:NL:HR:2000:AA4947, *NJ* 2000/508, annotated by H.J. Snijders; Supreme Court 21 March 1997, ECLI:NL:HR:1997:AA4945, *NJ* 1998/207, annotated by H.J. Snijders; Amsterdam Court of Appeal 12 October 2000, ECLI:NL:GHAMS:2000:AE0833, paras 2.7-2.28, *NJ* 2002/111. The *Eco Swiss v. Benetton*-case shows that Article 101 TFEU must be equated to law that is of public policy for the purpose of Article 1065(1)(e) DCCP. See further Asser Procesrecht/Sanders, Meijer & Ernste *8* 2023/515.

234 See Supreme Court 16 January 2009, ECLI:NL:HR:2009:BG3582, *NJ* 2009/54, para 3.3 (*Gemeente Heerlen/Whizz Croissanterie*).

235 See Haarlem District Court 13 January 2010, ECLI:NL:RBHAA:2010:BL1528, paras 6.13-6.15. See also H.J. Snijders, in: *GS Burgerlijke Rechtsvordering*, Article 1065 DCCP, note 7 (online, updated 1 May 2018).

236 See for example The Hague Court of Appeal 24 November 2020, ECLI:NL:GHDHA:2020:2833 (provisions of mandatory insolvency law); Amsterdam Court of Appeal 7 February 2023, ECLI:NL:GHAMS:2023:310 (rules concerning CE markings); Arnhem-Leeuwarden Court of Appeal 16 January 2024, ECLI:NL:GHARL:2024:381 (certain rules of company law).

237 See for example The Hague Court of Appeal 22 October 2019, ECLI:NL:GHDHA:2019:2677, *JBPr* 2020/48, annotated by G.J. Meijer & P.E. Ernste (*Bariven/Wells*) and Supreme Court 16 July 2021, ECLI:NL:HR:2021:1171, *JBPr* 2022/5, annotated by M. van Hel-Koedoot & R.H. Hansen (*Wells/Bariven*); The Hague Court of Appeal 16 February 2021, ECLI:NL:GHDHA:2021:180, para 5.39; Supreme Court 5 November 2021, ECLI:NL:HR:2021:1645, *NJ* 2022/102, annotated by A.I.M. van Mierlo & C.M.J. Ryngaert (*Russian Federation/HVY*).

238 See for example The Hague Court of Appeal 19 July 2022, ECLI:NL:GHDHA:2022:1294, *JBPr* 2023/66, annotated by J.K. van Hezewijk (unsuccessful); Supreme Court 5 November 2021, ECLI:NL:HR:2021:1645, *NJ* 2022/102, annotated by A.I.M. van Mierlo & C.M.J. Ryngaert (*Russian Federation/HVY*) (unsuccessful). These cases all concern investment arbitration. It is, however,

in the setting aside proceedings before the The Hague Court of Appeal that the arbitral award should be set aside on the basis of Article 1065(1)(e) DCCP, because the tribunal had not attached any legal consequences to alleged corruption. In that respect, Bariven stated that the purchase agreement which was at issue in the arbitral proceedings was obtained under the influence of corruption. Employees of Bariven had been paid bribes so that Wells would obtain lucrative contracts from Bariven. It follows from case law that there can only be a violation of public policy if the content or the enforcement of the arbitral award violates mandatory law which is of such a fundamental nature that compliance with that law should not be prevented by procedural restrictions. In the *Bariven v. Wells*-case, the The Hague Court of Appeal was of the opinion that an arbitral award that attaches legal effects to an agreement that was obtained through corruption should be equated with an award that violates fundamental mandatory law. According to the Court of Appeal, the requirements of the rule of law preclude attaching legal effects to an agreement obtained through corruption. This is a fundamental principle of the Dutch legal order that should be equated with mandatory law of such a fundamental character that its observance may not be prevented by procedural restrictions. An arbitral award that attaches legal effects to an agreement obtained through corruption should be set aside because it is contrary to public policy, according to the The Hague Court of Appeal. The Court of Appeal then formulated a standard to determine whether there is a violation of the prohibition of corruption. According to the Court of Appeal, the decisive factor is whether the agreement would not have come into being (at all) or would not have come into being under the same conditions if the corruption had not occurred. In that case, the agreement cannot be separated from the corruption. An order to enforce such an agreement means that corruption is facilitated and this is contrary to public policy. The The Hague Court of Appeal did not apply a restrictive review in this case. It assessed the question whether the disputed purchase agreement was indeed concluded under the influence of corruption, not only on the basis of the facts established by the arbitral tribunal, but also on the basis of established facts that had occurred after the arbitral tribunal's decision. The Court of Appeal set aside the arbitral award as it was of the opinion that there was strong evidence that the purchase agreement was concluded under the influence of corruption.[239] As a result of procedural rules in cassation proceedings, the

also possible that parties commit fraud or deliberately withhold information during the arbitration in commercial arbitration.

239 See The Hague Court of Appeal 22 October 2019, ECLI:NL:GHDHA:2019:2677, *JBPr* 2020/48, annotated by G.J. Meijer & P.E. Ernste (*Bariven/Wells*), paras 5.5-5.7 and 5.13.

Supreme Court did not answer the question whether the standard of review (i.e., an unrestrictive approach in case of alleged fraud or corruption) applied by the The Hague Court of Appeal was correct.[240] However, the standard applied by the Court of Appeal is contrary to the later judgment of the Supreme Court in the case of *Russian Federation v. HVY*. In that case, the Supreme Court explicitly considered that the court in setting aside proceedings should also apply a restrictive review in situations in which one of the parties argues that the arbitral tribunal wrongly did not declare an agreement that was obtained under the influence of fraud or corruption invalid and/or in situations in which it is argued that fraud was committed during the arbitral proceedings.[241] In the setting aside proceedings, the Russian Federation stated that illegal conduct was committed prior to the arbitration regarding a transaction that was subject of the arbitral proceedings. The The Hague Court of Appeal held, however, that the arbitral tribunal had rightly decided that the alleged conduct had a tenuous link to the relevant transaction.[242] In cassation, the Supreme Court held that this consideration was well reasoned and was not incomprehensible. The appeal in cassation thus failed on this point.[243] According to Meijer & Ernste a setting aside claim based on Article 1065(1)(e) DCCP on the ground that a legal act was entered into under the influence of fraud or corruption and consequently wrongly not declared invalid by the arbitral tribunal should be based on facts and evidence that was submitted to the arbitral tribunal.[244] In light of this, we recommend arbitrators to provide the parties ample opportunity to substantiate allegations of fraud and corruption as a full review of the alleged fraud or corruption can only take place in these proceedings. If the arbitral tribunal disregards the contentions and evidence because a party should have submitted these at an earlier stage of the proceedings, the arbitral award may be set aside pursuant to Article 1065(1)(e) DCCP due to breach of the equal right to be heard.[245]

240 See Supreme Court 16 July 2021, ECLI:NL:HR:2021:1171, *JBPr* 2022/5, annotated by M. van Hel-Koedoot & R.H. Hansen (*Wells/Bariven*).

241 See Supreme Court 5 November 2021, ECLI:NL:HR:2021:1645, para 5.4.9, *NJ* 2022/102, annotated by A.I.M. van Mierlo & C.M.J. Ryngaert (*Russian Federation/HVY*).

242 See The Hague Court of Appeal 18 February 2020, ECLI:NL:GHDHA:2020:234, para 5.1.11.7, *JOR* 2020/164, annotated by N. Peters (*HVY/Russian Federation*).

243 See Supreme Court 5 November 2021, ECLI:NL:HR:2021:1645, paras. 5.4.10-5.4.11, *NJ* 2022/102, annotated by A.I.M. van Mierlo & C.M.J. Ryngaert (*Russian Federation/HVY*).

244 See Asser Procesrecht/Sanders, Meijer & Ernste *8* 2023/516.

245 See G.J. Meijer & P.E. Ernste, annotation to The Hague Court of Appeal 22 October 2019, ECLI:NL:GHDHA:2019:2677, *JBPr* 2020/48 (*Bariven/Wells*), para 9.

In the case of *Russian Federation v. HVY*, the Russian Federation stated that the arbitral awards should also be set aside on the basis of Article 1065(1)(e) DCCP because these awards were contrary to public policy due to fraud committed by HVY *during* the arbitral proceedings. The fraud was argued to consist of submitting false statements, withholding documents and failing to produce various documents and correspondence in the arbitral proceedings.[246] The The Hague Court of Appeal decided that such fraud committed during the arbitral proceedings can only be addressed in revocation proceedings (Article 1068 DCCP) and cannot be assessed in setting aside proceedings on the basis of Article 1065(1)(e) DCCP. The Court of Appeal therefore dismissed the claim as the Russian Federation had based its claim on Article 1065(1)(e) DCCP. The Russian Federation filed an appeal in cassation and complained, *inter alia*, that the The Hague Court of Appeal erred in ruling that factual contentions that could have justified an appeal for revocation within the meaning of Article 1068 DCCP cannot also lead to the setting aside of an arbitral award on the basis Article 1065(1)(e) DCCP. The Russian Federation argued that it had a free choice between Article 1068 DCCP and Article 1065(1)(e) DCCP. This complaint succeeded. The Supreme Court ruled that in such a case, in addition to the route of revocation (Article 1068 DCCP), the route of setting aside under Article 1065 DCCP is also open, since the legislative history does not provide indications to the contrary and the legal effect of both articles is the same.[247] However, in the referral proceedings the Amsterdam Court of Appeal did not set aside the arbitral awards. The Court of Appeal held that the Russian Federation did not invoke the procedural fraud in time in the setting aside proceedings and could have submitted the relevant documents regarding the procedural fraud at an earlier stage of the setting aside proceedings. The Amsterdam Court of Appeal superfluously considered that it was unlikely that the arbitral tribunal would have reached a different decision on the basis of the relevant documents.[248]

246 See Supreme Court 5 November 2021, ECLI:NL:HR:2021:1645, para 5.1.1, *NJ* 2022/102, annotated by A.I.M. van Mierlo & C.M.J. Ryngaert (*Russian Federation/HVY*).

247 See Supreme Court 5 November 2021, ECLI:NL:HR:2021:1645, paras. 5.1.8-5.1.12, *NJ* 2022/102, annotated by A.I.M. van Mierlo & C.M.J. Ryngaert (*Russian Federation/HVY*).

248 See Amsterdam Court of Appeal 20 February 2024, ECLI:NL:GHAMS:2024:351, *JBPr* 2024/37, annotated by W.J.L. de Clerck.

23.2.7.4 Breach of the equal right to heard

The equal right to be heard means that the parties should be given an equal opportunity to present their case in writing and orally and to take note of all the evidence and assertions made and/or submitted during the arbitral proceedings and which may influence an arbitrator's final decision on the dispute submitted to arbitration.[249] It thus includes a right to bring the matter before an arbitrator, a right to contradict and a right to equal treatment.[250] For arbitration, this follows from Article 1036(2) DCCP.[251] Violation of this principle may lead to setting aside of the arbitral award[252] on the basis of breach of mandate and breach of public policy (Article 1065(1) (c) and (e) DCCP). Importantly, it is established case law that the usual restraint regarding the review and application of the grounds for setting aside does not apply in the event of a violation of the equal right to be heard.[253] All (relevant) circumstances of the case tend to be included in the assessment by the court in setting aside proceedings. Breach of the equal right to be heard in and of itself seems to be sufficient for setting aside. The Supreme Court has not expressly ruled on the question as to whether it is a condition for setting aside of the arbitral award on this ground that the violation was *detrimental* to the aggrieved party. It is debated in the literature whether such a 'detriment criterion' should be accepted.[254]

---

249 See Hugenholtz/Heemskerk 2024, p 10; Snijders et al, *Nederlands burgerlijk procesrecht*, Deventer: Wolters Kluwer 2022, p 38-40. See also ECtHR 7 June 2001, no 39594/98, para 74 (*Kress v. France*); ECtHR 23 June 1993, no 12952/87, para 63 (*Ruiz-Mateos v. Spain*).

250 Following Snijders et al 2022, p 39-40 (general procedural law) and C.S.K. Fung Fen Chung, *Bewijsmiddelen in het arbitraal geding* (diss. Rotterdam), The Hague: Sdu 2004, p 56-57.

251 See on this (at length) Fung Fen Chung 2004, p 55-66.

252 See G.J. Meijer, in: *T&C Rv*, Article 1065 DCCP, note 7b (online, updated 1 January 2024); Meijer & Van Mierlo 2014, p 65; H.J. Snijders, in: *GS Burgerlijke Rechtsvordering*, Article 1065 DCCP, note 7 (online, updated 1 May 2018); Sanders 2001, p 198.

253 See Supreme Court 24 April 2009, ECLI:NL:HR:2009:BH3137, para 4.3.1, *NJ* 2010/171, annotated by H.J. Snijders (*IMS/Modsaf II*); Supreme Court 25 May 2007, ECLI:NL:HR:2007:BA2495, para 3.5, *NJ* 2007/294 (*Spaanderman/Anova*).

254 Sanders believes that this requirement should not be imposed (see for example P. Sanders, annotation to Supreme Court 18 June 1993, ECLI:NL:HR:1993:ZC1003, *TvA* 1993/3, p 164-169 (*Van der Lely/VDH*)). See differently for example H.J. Snijders, note to Supreme Court 18 June 1993, *NJ* 1994/449 (Van der *Lely/VDH*), para 4. It has been held in the case law of the lower courts that an arbitral award cannot be set aside on this ground if the outcome of the case would have been the same without the breach or if the interests of the party in question were not harmed. See Arnhem District Court 28 July 2004, ECLI:NL:RBARN:2004:AQ6834; Utrecht District Court 26 June 2002, ECLI:NL:RBUTR:2002:1620, para 4.4. See differently 's-Hertogenbosch Court of Appeal 5 October 2021, ECLI:NL:GHSHE:2021:3015, para 6.12.

In practice, violation of the equal right to be heard is regularly invoked in support of a claim to set aside an arbitral award. The argument was successful in only twelve cases. According to case law, the equal right to be heard is breached if a party is not given the opportunity to respond (whether or not by means of counter-evidence) to witness testimony[255] or to the other party's comments on a draft award sent to the parties, while the comments touched upon points that had not yet formed part of the debate during the arbitration.[256] The same applies if the arbitral tribunal (partly) bases its award on a report, which is in turn based on several documents that were unknown to one of the parties in the arbitration, and on witness examinations, the precise content of which was also unknown to the parties.[257] In the event the decision in an arbitral award that is to the detriment of a party is based on documents that party has not received and has not been able to respond to, the award is subject to setting aside.[258] Setting aside may furthermore follow due to breach of the equal right to be heard if the arbitrators (largely) base their award on an informal conversation with the accountants of the parties to the arbitration,[259] an expert report or a statement of defence with which not all of the parties were familiar.[260] An award may furthermore be set aside if one of the parties to the arbitration is not heard by the expert appointed by the arbitrators – neither before the report was drafted, nor after the report had been prepared and the party in question had requested to be heard – while the expert did converse with the representatives of the other party to the arbitration and the claim submitted by that other party was granted on the basis of the conclu-

255 See Supreme Court 25 May 2007, ECLI:NL:HR:2007:BA2495, para 3.6, *NJ* 2007/294 (*Spaanderman/Anova*). The arbitrators had allowed testimony from a party witness brought to the hearing, even though the witness was not impartial and independent and, moreover, worked for one of the parties. The mere circumstance that Anova did have the opportunity to cross-examine the witness at the hearing did not change the conclusion. See in the same sense Arnhem District Court 28 July 2004, ECLI:NL:RBARN:2004:AQ6834.

256 See Arnhem District Court 28 July 2004, ECLI:NL:RBARN:2004:AQ6834.

257 See 's-Gravenhage Court of Appeal 31 March 2015, ECLI:NL:GHDHA:2015:713, paras 16-17; Supreme Court 12 July 2013, ECLI:NL:HR:2013:CA0259, *TvA* 2014/61, annotated by R. Schellaars (reference judgment).

258 's-Hertogenbosch Court of Appeal 5 October 2021, ECLI:NL:GHSHE:2021:3015, paras 6.4-6.17.

259 See Supreme Court 18 June 1993, ECLI:NL:HR:1993:ZC1003, paras 3.2-3.3, *NJ* 1994/449, annotated by H.J. Snijders (*Van der Lely/VDH*). The fact that the parties could have been aware of the content of the conversation (through their accountants) and could have approached the arbitral tribunal on their own initiative with a request to comment on the statements (and possibly provide further evidence) did not alter this conclusion.

260 See The Hague Court of Appeal 28 December 2010, ECLI:NL:GHSGR:2010:BP7374, para 4-9.

sions in the report of the expert.[261] In addition, an arbitral tribunal should give the parties the opportunity to submit a procedural document and should inform the parties of the starting date of the arbitral proceedings,[262] the content of the mandate and the substantiation of the claim. After all, a party should know what it has to defend itself against.[263] If this does not happen, it follows from case law that the equal right to be heard has been breached, which can constitute a ground for setting aside of the arbitral award. Furthermore, it seems setting aside can occur in case of a surprise decision (see also breach of mandate,[264] para 23.2.4 above).[265] There is no surprise decision if the decision in question follows logically from another decision[266] or from the debate held at the hearing,[267] or if the party seeking

261 Utrecht District Court 26 June 2002, ECLI:NL:RBUTR:2002:1620, paras 4.1-4.5.

262 See Utrecht District Court 8 August 2007, ECLI:NL:RBUTR:2007:BB1410, para 4.17. The respondent had only received an e-mail from the chair of the arbitral tribunal in which the chair requested respondent to propose a date for consultation. The respondent only became aware of the exact content of the dispute when he received the arbitral award.

263 See Zutphen District Court 29 February 2012, ECLI:NL:RBZUT:2012:BW3693, paras 7.16-7.22. This was a case that had already been before the subdistrict court. The respondent had not been informed of the precise mandate of the arbitral tribunal. Assuming that the case was the same in substance as the case before the subdistrict court, the party in question did not appear. The district court set aside the award insofar as the claim exceeded the amount awarded in preliminary relief proceedings.

264 Sometimes this argument is invoked in connection to both Article 1065(1)(c) DCCP and Article 1065(1)(e) DCCP. See for example Amsterdam Court of Appeal 11 December 2018, ECLI:NL:GHAMS:2018:4547.

265 See Amsterdam District Court 15 March 2006, ECLI:NL:RBAMS:2006:AV7057, in which the District Court found that the arbitrators had made an adjustment to the obligation to pay damages on the basis of contributory negligence, while the parties had not debated this and had not had an opportunity to comment on it. This judgment was overturned upon appeal, however, see Amsterdam Court of Appeal 6 December 2007, ECLI:NL:GHAMS:2007:BC4592, *TvA* 2009/20. The Court of Appeal held that there had been no surprise decision because the arbitrators had evidently and not incomprehensibly held that the point had also been advanced in support of the defences in question. This argument has been advanced in the case law several times, be it unsuccessfully. See, for example: The Hague District Court 16 September 2020, ECLI:NL:RBDHA:2020:8929, paras 5.28, 5.32 and 5.36-5.37, The Hague Court of Appeal 28 June 2022, ECLI:NL:GHDHA:2022:1122, paras 8.38-8.41 and Supreme Court 17 November 2023, ECLI:NL:HR:2023:1592; The Hague District Court 20 October ECLI:NL:RBDHA:2021:12258, paras 5.30-5.34; Arnhem-Leeuwarden Court of Appeal 30 October 2018, ECLI:NL:GHARL:2018:9499, para 5.14.

266 See Oost-Nederland District Court 27 March 2013, ECLI:NL:RBONE:2013:BZ8089, para 4.22.

267 See Dordrecht District Court 2 December 2009, ECLI:NL:RBDOR:2009:BK4879, paras 4.2-4.9; Arnhem District Court 7 May 2008, ECLI:NL:RBARN:2008:BD2370, para 4.10; 's-Gravenhage District Court 20 June 2007, ECLI:NL:RBSGR:2007:BB0455, para 4.8

setting aside could (reasonably) expect the interpretation of the claim(s) upon which the tribunal decided.[268] As an extension of the foregoing, arbitrators breach the equal right to be heard if they supplement the claim *ex officio* in a way not envisaged by the parties.[269] Furthermore, the arbitrators must hear the parties with respect to a request for an additional award and must send a copy of the request to the other party in the arbitration (Article 1061(2) and (3) DCCP). Failure to do so exposes the additional award (but not also the final, original award) to setting aside for breach of the equal right to be heard.[270] Finally, an arbitral award may be set aside for breach of the equal right to be heard in the event an arbitral tribunal grants a request for correction of the interest percentage included in the arbitral award after that award is rendered, in breach of the applicable procedural rules concerning amendments to claim and in breach of a procedural agreement made with the parties on the (non-)admissibility of new submissions at the final stage of the proceedings, and without hearing the other party on the correction before rendering the award on correction.[271]

The fact that the parties to the arbitration had the *opportunity* to take note of documents or submissions and respond to them is usually sufficient for the award not to be subject to setting aside. It is not required that the parties made use of this possibility.[272] It follows from case law that the course

---

268 See Arnhem-Leeuwarden Court of Appeal 8 October 2019, ECLI:NL:GHARL:2019:8203, paras 4.14-4.15.

269 See Oost-Brabant District Court 22 October 2014, ECLI:NL:RBOBR:2014:6279, paras 4.3-4.6 and 's-Hertogenbosch Court of Appeal 22 November 2016, ECLI:NL:GHSHE:2016:5201, paras 4.4-4.9, in which the arbitrators had extended the duration of a contract. In this case, the argument was also dealt with in the context of breach of mandate, Article 1065(1)(c) DCCP.

270 See Amsterdam District Court 27 August 2008, ECLI:NL:RBAMS:2008:BF3726, para 4.8.

271 Amsterdam District Court 19 December 2018, ECLI:NL:RBAMS:2018:8247, paras 4.4-4.8. The award was partially set aside insofar as the interest rate exceeded the rate originally granted. Upon appeal, the Amsterdam Court of Appeal held that the arbitral award should indeed be (partially) set aside, be it insofar as interest was granted. See Amsterdam Court of Appeal 26 October 2021, ECLI:NL:GHAMS:2021:3237, paras 3.4-3.5.1. In that regard, the Court of Appeal ruled that the course of events was also a ground for setting aside on the basis of Article 1065(1)(c) DCCP (para 3.4.1). In cassation, however, the Supreme Court overturned the judgment of the Amsterdam Court of Appeal and confirmed the judgment of the Amsterdam District Court. See Supreme Court 24 March 2023, ECLI:NL:HR:2023:438 (*HCCEEH/Alpha*). The arbitration was administered by the NAI.

272 See Court of Appeal 's-Gravenhage 10 May 2016, ECLI:NL:GHDHA:2016:3324, paras 11, 18-19; Court of Appeal 's-Gravenhage 28 January 2014, ECLI:NL:GHDHA:2014:71, para 8; Rotterdam District Court 9 November 2005, *TvA* 2007/25, para 3.4. Similarly Arnhem-Leeuwarden Court of Appeal 4 June 2024, ECLI:NL:GHARL:2024:3753, paras 3.19-3.20, in which it was ruled that the

of the proceedings is also important in this respect. A favourable attitude of the arbitrators and the length of the oral hearing carry weight in the assessment as to whether the equal right to be heard has been breached.[273] It is not always necessary – with a view to the equal right to be heard – to hold a further written or oral round,[274] unless new arguments come to light, to which the parties have not yet had sufficient opportunity to respond. If the (essential) point in question has been dealt with extensively in the proceedings and the point was debated or could have been debated, setting aside of the arbitral award will not follow.[275] Moreover, the arbitrators do not need to give the parties the opportunity to comment on each decision, or on the final decision on the dispute.[276]

Case law shows that an arbitral award is not subject to setting aside if the point with respect to which the parties were insufficiently heard was not the sole ground for the decision and the other grounds can sufficiently support the decision.[277] The same applies if the decision was not based on the argument or evidence on which the parties were insufficiently heard.[278] Finally, case law shows that certain circumstances are deemed to be at the risk of a party bringing the setting aside claim. A party's own oversight or

party had been given the chance to take note of documents relevant to the dispute, but had not made use of this opportunity.

273 See Court of Appeal 's-Gravenhage 10 May 2016, ECLI:NL:GHDHA:2016:3324, in which the arbitrators had clearly done their best to accommodate the party in question with respect to a number of documents submitted at a fairly late stage of the proceedings, including by showing willingness to stay the proceedings.

274 See Amsterdam Court of Appeal 19 April 2016, ECLI:NL:GHAMS:2016:1552, paras 3.6.4-3.6.6; Amsterdam Court of Appeal 4 March 2014, ECLI:NL:GHAMS:2014:644, para 3.10.

275 See for example Arnhem-Leeuwarden Court of Appeal 30 October 2018, ECLI:NL:GHARL:2018:9499, para 5.14; Amsterdam Court of Appeal 26 June 2018, ECLI:NL:GHAMS:2018:2112, para 4.12; Court of Appeal 's-Gravenhage 10 May 2016, ECLI:NL:GHDHA:2016:3324. This also applies to points with respect to which the arbitrators have already taken a preliminary decision in the interim award, but which could still be debated afterwards (see Amsterdam District Court 21 August 2013, ECLI:NL:RBAMS:2013:6253, paras 4.4.6, 4.7.1).

276 See Arnhem-Leeuwarden Court of Appeal 30 October 2018, ECLI:NL:GHARL:2018:9499, para 5.14; District Court Dordrecht 2 December 2009, ECLI:NL:RBDOR:2009:BK4879, para 4.13.

277 See Amsterdam Court of Appeal 17 January 2017, ECLI:NL:GHAMS:2017:140, para 2.15; Rotterdam District Court 2 March 2011, ECLI:NL:RBROT:2011:BP9334. See similarly Arnhem-Leeuwarden Court of Appeal 25 May 2021, ECLI:NL:GHARL:2021:5021, para 4.6.

278 See, *inter alia*, Amsterdam Court of Appeal 25 April 2017, ECLI:NL:GHAMS:2017:1496, paras 3.37-3.38; Arnhem District Court 20 October 2010, ECLI:NL:RBARN:2010:BO2585, para 4.19; Rotterdam District Court 9 November 2005, *TvA* 2007/25, paras 3.3-3.4.

vagueness in communication comes at his risk.[279] Furthermore, if a party has agreed to a certain situation or course of events, then a subsequent invocation by that party of breach of equal right to be heard will not be successful.[280]

23.2.7.5 Evidence

The conduct of an arbitrator with respect to the taking of evidence in arbitral proceedings may also constitute a ground for setting aside of an arbitral award pursuant to Article 1065(1)(e) DCCP. Pursuant to Article 1039(1) DCCP, the arbitral tribunal shall be free to determine the rules of evidence, the admissibility of evidence, the allocation of the burden of proof and the evaluation of evidence (see also Article 34(1) NAI Arbitration Rules 2024).[281] According to case law, the arbitrator determines the rules for the taking of evidence[282] and is not bound by the rules of evidence applicable to the state courts (in particular Article 166(1) DCCP).[283] The arbitrator

---

279 See Court of Appeal 's-Gravenhage 28 January 2014, ECLI:NL:GHDHA:2014:71, para 8; Amsterdam District Court 27 November 2013, ECLI:NL:RBAMS:2013:8644, para 4.7, in which a party was aware of a conversation between the secretary and the opposing party, but had not objected against it; Groningen District Court 12 March 2003, *TvA* 2004/33, in which a party communicated by telephone that he could not attend the hearing because of 'an urgent reason'. The District Court held that the arbitrator did not have to infer a request to stay the proceedings from this.

280 See 's-Gravenhage District Court 14 March 2007, ECLI:NL:RBSGR:2007:BA2946, para 2.5, in which a party who was given a list of questions about the case at the end of the morning session (of the hearing) indicated that he had been sufficiently heard at the end of the afternoon session; Arnhem District Court 20 October 2010, ECLI:NL:RBARN:2010:BO2585, paras 4.11-4.14, in which the statement of response had been submitted at the hearing and the claimant was given a half-hour break to read it. The claimant agreed to this and did not show that he had not had enough preparation time during the remainder of the hearing. See also The Hague Court of Appeal 25 October 2022, ECLI:NL:GHDHA:2022:2047, paras 5.11-5.12. Due to COVID-19 restrictions, no oral hearings could be scheduled and the arbitrators had proposed to decide the case on the basis of written submissions. The arbitrators had given the parties the opportunity to ask for an oral hearing within a certain time period though. The party seeking setting aside of the arbitral award had not made use of that opportunity and had not objected once the time period to respond had elapsed.

281 See Hugenholtz/Heemskerk 2024, p 370. See also: Court of Appeal 's-Gravenhage 27 June 2017, ECLI:NL:GHDHA:2017:1711, para 11; 's-Gravenhage District Court 7 October 2015, ECLI:NL:RBDHA:2015:11637, para 4.16; Rotterdam District Court 31 July 2013, ECLI:NL:RBROT:2013:6619, para 4.10.

282 See Supreme Court 24 April 2009, ECLI:NL:HR:2009:BH3137, *NJ* 2010/171, annotated by H.J. Snijders (*IMS/Modsaf II*).

283 Article 166(1) DCCP reads as follow: "The court directs, at a party's request that an evidentiary hearing be held for the purpose of giving testimony where the law permits testimony by witnesses and the facts that the party has offered to prove are

must, however, adhere to the fundamental principles of procedural law, in particular the equal right to be heard and the duty to provide reasons for the decision. Whether such a principle has been violated depends on the circumstances of the case.[284]

Case law shows that, in principle, an arbitrator may reject an offer of proof,[285] considering, for example the (late) time of submission and the size of the documents.[286] However, courts do impose requirements on the reasoning of such a decision. If the arbitrator rejects a specifically formulated offer of proof, he will have to provide sufficiently sound reasons for doing so.[287] In case of a general (or generally phrased) offer of proof, a statement of reasons concerning the decision on the offer does not always seem necessary, but it is advisable to still include such a statement.[288] The reason to reject an offer of proof may be that the arbitrators see no point in further evidence, in light of the fact that there was ample opportunity (for the party in question) to elaborate on the case,[289] or that the arbitrators

---

in dispute and may be material in the disposition of the case. The court may give such directions on its own initiative". See Burrough et al 2022, p 96.

284 See Supreme Court 24 April 2009, ECLI:NL:HR:2009:BH3137, paras 4.3.1-4.4.1, *NJ* 2010/171, annotated by H.J. Snijders (*IMS/Modsaf II*). These principles are often repeated in the case law of the lower courts. See for example Amsterdam Court of Appeal 29 January 2019, ECLI:NL:GHAMS:2019:224, para 3.9; 's-Hertogenbosch Court of Appeal 21 January 2020, ECLI:NL:GHSHE:2020:172, para 3.4.2; 's-Hertogenbosch Court of Appeal 19 September 2023, ECLI:NL:GHSHE:2023:2979, para 4.8.

285 See for example Amsterdam Court of Appeal 29 January 2019, ECLI:NL:GHAMS:2019:224, paras 3.10-3.11; Arnhem District Court 3 December 2008, ECLI:NL:RBARN:2008:BG6981, para 4.8; Court of Appeal 's-Gravenhage 14 October 2004, ECLI:NL:GHSGR:2004:AS6294, *Prg.* 2005/14, para 8.

286 See The Hague Court of Appeal 27 June 2017, ECLI:NL:GHDHA:2017:1711, para 11; The Hague Court of Appeal 15 February 2011, ECLI:NL:GHSGR:2011:BP8229, para 9.

287 If this is not the case, setting aside follows, see The Hague Court of Appeal 14 October 2004, ECLI:NL:GHSGR:2004:AS6294, *Prg.* 2005/14, para 9, cited above (para 23.2.6). See also (unsuccessfully): Supreme Court 24 April 2009, ECLI:NL:HR:2009:BH3137, para 4.4.1, *NJ* 2010/171, annotated by H.J. Snijders (*IMS/Modsaf II*); Limburg District Court 9 August 2017, ECLI:NL:RBLIM:2017:7710, paras 4.7-4.9; Amsterdam Court of Appeal 23 November 2010, ECLI:NL:GHAMS:2010:BP0825, para 3.7. Cf. for the state courts: Hugenholtz/Heemskerk 2024, p 113, which requires a 'justification in law'. Of course, that may not be tested in the proceedings to set aside the arbitral award.

288 See, for example, 's-Gravenhage District Court 10 February 2010, *TvA* 2010/60, para 4.16; Haarlem District Court 13 January 2010, ECLI:NL:RBHAA:2010:BL1528, paras 6.10-6.12; Rotterdam District Court 25 March 2009, ECLI:NL:RBROT:2009:BI2235, para 4.3-4.4.

289 See Limburg District Court 9 August 2017, ECLI:NL:RBLIM:2017:7710, paras 4.7-4.9; 's-Gravenhage District Court 10 February 2010, *TvA* 2010/60, para 4.16; Haarlem District Court 13 January 2010, ECLI:NL:RBHAA:2010:BL1528, paras 6.10-6.12.

consider the evidence irrelevant to their decision and therefore reject the offer of proof.[290]

The arbitral award is *not* subject to setting aside if the decision to reject the offer of proof is based on several grounds and only one ground contains an 'irregularity'.[291] If a party had sufficient opportunity to submit evidence, but failed to do so without a good reason, that comes at his own risk.[292] Furthermore, some courts have held that there is no (fundamental) right to an expert examination.[293]

In case law, the question has arisen whether an arbitral award should be set aside because the arbitrators (allegedly) formed a prognosis as to the evidence to be furnished. For state judges, there is a prohibition on anticipation of the outcome of witness testimony (*prognoseverbod*). In a nutshell, this entails that a judge may not disregard an offer of proof on the basis of the expected outcome of the taking of evidence.[294] In light of Article 1039(1) DCCP, we believe the arbitrator is not automatically bound to this prohibition. In fact, case law on setting aside of arbitral awards suggests that the prohibition on anticipation of witness testimony does not apply to arbitrators (if the parties have not agreed otherwise).[295] That being said, it is also argued that

290 See, *inter alia*, Rotterdam District Court 31 July 2013, ECLI:NL:RBROT:2013:6619, paras 4.11-4.12; Amsterdam Court of Appeal 23 November 2010, ECLI:NL:GHAMS:2010:BP0825, para 3.7; Amsterdam Court of Appeal 10 March 2005, ECLI:NL:GHAMS:2005:AU1909, para 4.5. The same applies to an offer of proof in proceedings before the state courts, see: Hugenholtz/Heemskerk 2024, p 113.

291 See Limburg District Court 9 August 2017, ECLI:NL:RBLIM:2017:7710, para 4.7; 's-Gravenhage District Court 14 March 2007, ECLI:NL:RBSGR:2007:BA2946, paras 2.10-2.12.

292 See Amsterdam Court of Appeal 29 January 2019, ECLI:NL:GHAMS:2019:224, paras 3.10-3.11; Limburg District Court 9 August 2017, ECLI:NL:RBLIM:2017:7710, para 4.8; Rotterdam District Court 25 March 2009, ECLI:NL:RBROT:2009:BI2235, paras 4.3-4.4.

293 See The Hague Court of Appeal 25 October 2022, ECLI:NL:GHDHA:2022:2047, para 5.13; 's-Gravenhage Court of Appeal 22 August 2011, ECLI:NL:GHSGR:2011:4513, para 3.2. Cf., with regard to the ICC Arbitration Rules 2017 and in the context of Article 1065(1)(d) DCCP, Amsterdam Court of Appeal 7 February 2023, ECLI:NL:GHAMS:2023:310, para 4.5.

294 See See Asser Procesrecht/Asser 3 2022/225; Hugenholtz/Heemskerk 2024, p 113; Supreme Court 1 April 2005, ECLI:NL:HR:2005:AR7925, *NJ* 2006/5; Supreme Court 9 July 2004, ECLI:NL:HR:2004:AO7817, para 3.6, *NJ* 2005/270, annotated by W.D.H. Asser.

295 's-Hertogenbosch Court of Appeal 21 January 2020, ECLI:NL:GHSHE:2020:172, para 3.4.3. See also Limburg District Court 9 August 2017, ECLI:NL:RBLIM:2017:7710, para 4.7.

arbitrators should not include a prognosis concerning the result of the taking of evidence in their assessment of an offer of proof.[296]

In 2007, the Supreme Court ruled that arbitrators are allowed to collect evidence and conduct their own investigation as part of their *assessment of* evidence, especially if arbitrators have been appointed with a view to their specific expertise. However, the parties must agree (unequivocally) that the arbitrators also rely on the results of their investigation to form their opinion. Furthermore, according to the Supreme Court, arbitrators are obliged to observe the principles of due process in conducting their investigation. That investigation must furthermore comply with the fundamental principles of procedural law: the manner of conducting the investigation and the results of the investigation must, for example, be verifiable for the parties and the evidence must be carefully collected.[297] Despite the fact that the Supreme Court has not considered this in the context of setting aside proceedings, a failure to observe the requirements for conducting one's own investigation will, in our opinion, constitute a ground for setting aside of the arbitral award under Article 1065(1)(e) DCCP.

23.2.7.6 Breach of the principle of impartiality and independence

The arbitrator must be independent and impartial during the arbitration. However, there is a high threshold for setting aside of an arbitral award for breach of the principle of impartiality and independence. The appearance of partiality is insufficient for setting aside.[298] It follows from the *Nordström v. Van Nievelt*-judgment[299] that setting aside is only possible in this regard in the event it must be assumed, in light of the circumstances of the case,

---

296 Fung Fen Chung 2004, p 170. See also 's-Gravenhage Court of Appeal 14 October 2004, ECLI:NL:GHSGR:2004:AS6294, para 9, *Prg.* 2005/14. In this case, the arbitral award was set aside for breach of the equal right to be heard. The arbitrators had disregarded an offer of proof (witness testimony). It was held that the arbitrators had formed a prognosis on the outcome of the taking of evidence and that the reason provided for the rejection of the offer of proof gave no explanation as to the decision. The tribunal had stated that the party in question could not provide evidence that would outweigh what could have followed from documents that were not submitted.

297 See Supreme Court 29 June 2007, ECLI:NL:HR:2007:AV7405, *NJ* 2008/177, annotated by H.J. Snijders & J. Legemaate (*Aegon/N.*).

298 See H.J. Snijders, in: *GS Burgerlijke Rechtsvordering*, Article 1065 DCCP, note 7 (online, updated 1 May 2018); G.J. Meijer, in: *T&C Rv*, Article 1065 DCCP, note 7b (online, updated 1 January 2024); Meijer 2011, p 85; Sanders 2001, p 81-82.

299 Supreme Court 18 February 1994, ECLI:NL:HR:1994:ZC1266, *NJ* 1994/765, annotated by H.J. Snijders and *TvA* 1994, p 187-189, annotated by P. Sanders (*Nordström/Van Nievelt*). See also ECRM 27 November 1996, *NJ* 1997/505, annotated by P.J.

that the arbitrator was not impartial or independent, or that it would be unacceptable to hold the party who did not prevail in the arbitration to the award, because of the seriousness of the doubts as to the arbitrator's impartiality or independence. Moreover, a person who argues that an arbitrator was not impartial cannot set aside the arbitral award on this ground if that person was aware of the lack of impartiality during the arbitral proceedings or if the fact that that person was not aware of it during the arbitration can be attributed to him.[300] Indeed, if the person invoking lack of impartiality was or (in short) should have been aware of the circumstances, the appropriate course of action is to challenge the arbitrator. By leaving that option unused, the person in question has essentially forfeited the right to invoke the circumstances in question.[301] A review of case law shows that in many cases a claim to set aside the arbitral award for breach of the principle of independence and impartiality fails on this ground.[302]

Examples of cases in which an arbitral award was set aside for breach of the principle of independence and impartiality include cases in which there is a dispute between the arbitrators and a party to the arbitration regarding payment of their fees in related arbitral proceedings that were already concluded,[303] situations in which an arbitrator has a demonstrable, significant financial interest in the outcome of the case[304] or cases in which

Boon and *TvA* 1997/26, annotated by R.A. Lawson & H.J. Snijders (*Nordström/Netherlands*); Fung Fen Chung 2004, p 53-55.

300 Supreme Court 18 February 1994, ECLI:NL:HR:1994:ZC1266, para 3.8, *NJ* 1994/765, annotated by H.J. Snijders (*Nordström/Van Nievelt*). This threshold was not met in the following cases: 's-Hertogenbosch Court of Appeal 17 May 2022, ECLI:NL:GHSHE:2022:1550, paras 3.10-3.15; Arnhem-Leeuwarden Court of Appeal 8 October 2019, ECLI:NL:GHARL:2019:8203, paras 4.16-4.18.

301 This entails that the threshold for setting aside of an award on this ground is higher than for a challenge. See also: H.J. Snijders, in: *GS Burgerlijke Rechtsvordering*, Article 1065 DCCP, note 7 (online, updated 1 May 2018); G.J. Meijer, in: *T&C Rv*, Article 1065 DCCP, note 7b (online, updated 1 January 2024); Fung Fen Chung 2004, p 53. An arbitrator can be challenged in case of justifiable doubts as to the arbitrator's impartiality or independence (Article 1033(1) DCCP).

302 See, for example, Amsterdam District Court 27 November 2013, ECLI:NL:RBAMS:2013:8644, paras 4.5-4.6; Amsterdam Court of Appeal 22 September 2009, *TvA* 2010/39, para 3.3; 's-Gravenhage District Court 25 February 2009, ECLI:NL:RBSGR:2009:BJ3581, paras 4.5-4.6.

303 See District Court Overijssel 14 October 2015, ECLI:NL:RBOVE:2015:4600, paras 4.1-4.3. Cf. para 3.1.5, Orange List of the IBA Guidelines on Conflicts of Interest in International Arbitration (2024, hereinafter the IBA Guidelines).

304 See Breda District Court 27 February 2001, ECLI:NL:RBBRE:2001:AE0837, *NJ* 2002/135, in which the arbitrator had several claims against party B in the arbitration through two companies of which he was the (sole) director. The claims had been assigned by party A in the arbitration. Moreover, the arbitrator had provided substantial amounts as loans to party A. Because of the seriousness of the error

the arbitrator has a business relationship with one of the parties, which evidently influenced his assessment of the case.[305] Furthermore, the principle of impartiality and independence may be at issue if the arbitral award is based on a report of a committee that later turns out to be unbalanced in its composition (i.e. in favour of the prevailing party in the arbitration), so that the impartiality of the committee could reasonably be questioned. By extension, the arbitral award is tainted.[306]

An arbitral award can also be set aside, in theory, in the event of an unbalanced arbitral tribunal, (evidently) composed in favour of one of the parties,[307] in case of deliberate concealment by an arbitrator of a personal or business relationship with a party, combined with objective facts or circumstances that give rise to serious doubts as to the arbitrator's independence and impartiality,[308] in the event one party is evidently favoured, for example because it comes to light after the arbitration (upon reading the arbitral award) that an arbitrator deliberately ignored assertions, docu-

and in light of the successful challenge of the arbitrator, the *interim* award was, by way of exception, set aside. Cf. as regards the circumstances that led to setting aside of the arbitral award para 1.3, Non-Waivable Red List of the IBA Guidelines. Pursuant to Article 1064a(3) in conjunction with Article 1064 DCCP, a claim to set an interim award aside can only be submitted together with the claim to set aside the final award or partial (final) award. See for an example of a case in which no exception to this principle was made: The Hague District Court 25 January 2023, ECLI:NL:RBDHA:2023:5704. The setting aside claim against the interim award was inadmissible.

305 Utrecht District Court 8 August 2007, ECLI:NL:RBUTR:2007:BB1410, paras 4.18-4.22, in which the relationship alone was insufficient for the conclusion that the arbitrator was biased. Decisive weight was attached to the fact that the arbitrator had also made statements to the detriment of the other party; Amsterdam Court of Appeal 22 September 2009, *TvA* 2010/39, para 3.3, in which the party in question could already have been aware of the business relationship during the arbitration and therefore could not invoke the relationship in the setting aside proceedings. See regarding the circumstances also para 2.3.4, Waivable Red List and 3.4.4, Orange List of the IBA Guidelines, depending on whether the entity to which the arbitrator is affiliated is directly or indirectly involved in the dispute.

306 See 's-Gravenhage Court of Appeal 31 March 2015, ECLI:NL:GHDHA:2015:713, paras 10-19. See also Supreme Court 12 July 2013, ECLI:NL:HR:2013:CA0259 (reference judgment). Prior to the judgment in cassation, this stance was adopted by the District Court (Utrecht District Court 4 August 2010, ECLI:NL:RBUTR:2010:BN3804), but *not* by the Court of Appeal (Amsterdam Court of Appeal 8 November 2011, ECLI:NL:GHAMS:2011:BU3265).

307 See Amsterdam Court of Appeal 26 March 2013, ECLI:NL:GHAMS:2013:3429, para 3.9.

308 See, *inter alia,* Noord-Nederland District Court 26 November 2014, ECLI:NL:RBNNE:2014:6076, paras 4.5.3.1-4.5.3.2; 's-Gravenhage Court of Appeal 28 January 2014, ECLI:NL:GHDHA:2014:71, para 14; Rotterdam District Court 11 May 2011, ECLI:NL:RBROT:2011:BQ6204, paras 4.8-4.17.

ments (submitted as evidence) and objections of the other party[309] and in case of bribery of an informant.[310] In the cases cited, the claim to set aside the arbitral award did not succeed because the circumstances had already come to light during the arbitration and the option to challenge the arbitrator(s) had not been used. However, examples of circumstances that could lead to setting aside of the arbitral award if discovered after the arbitration has ended can still be derived from these cases.

The mere impression (in retrospect) that the arbitrators were biased,[311] the mere presence of a connection or tie between the arbitrator(s) and a party to the arbitration[312] or the fact that the decision taken by the arbitrator(s) differs from the view of the party invoking setting aside of the arbitral award is insufficient for setting aside on this ground, according to case law.[313] Thus, the argument that an arbitrator is partial must be sufficiently substantiated.[314] According to several judgments, the mere breach of a disclosure obligation (by an arbitrator) is also insufficient ground for setting aside of the arbitral award for breach of the principle of impartiality and

309 See Rotterdam District Court 8 November 2017, ECLI:NL:RBROT:2017:8850, para 4.14.

310 See The Hague Court of Appeal 17 February 2015, ECLI:NL:GHDHA:2015:222, paras 33-37.

311 See Amsterdam Court of Appeal 4 October 2022, ECLI:NL:GHAMS:2022:2819, paras 3.4.2-3.4.4, para 3.6, in which it was also held that the fact that the arbitrator attached procedural consequences to the procedural conduct of the party in question does not automatically entail that there are doubts as to the arbitrator's impartiality, even if the decision in that respect is strict (para 3.4.3); 's-Gravenhage Court of Appeal 23 January 2018, ECLI:NL:GHDHA:2018:62, para 7; Arnhem District Court 20 April 2011, ECLI:NL:RBARN:2011:BQ3150, para 4.12. Even if there is some substantiation of the argument, the impression will not lead to setting aside if the circumstances put forward do not clearly indicate bias or dependence of the arbitrator. See The Hague Court of Appeal 17 February 2015, ECLI:NL:GHDHA:2015:222, paras 38-40. See further: Amsterdam Court of Appeal 17 January 2017, ECLI:NL:GHAMS:2017:140, paras 2.16-2.19 (appearance of partiality raised by a recovered memory).

312 See Supreme Court 18 February 1994, ECLI:NL:HR:1994:ZC1266, *NJ* 1994/765, annotated by H.J. Snijders (*Nordström/Van Nievelt*). See also District Court Noord-Nederland 26 November 2014, ECLI:NL:RBNNE:2014:6076, para 4.5.3.2; The Hague Court of Appeal 28 January 2014, ECLI:NL:GHDHA:2014:71, para 14; Haarlem District Court 13 January 2010, ECLI:NL:RBHAA:2010:BL1528, paras 6.5-6.9.

313 See The Hague Court of Appeal 28 January 2014, ECLI:NL:GHDHA:2014:71, para 13; Amsterdam District Court 1 May 2013, ECLI:NL:RBAMS:2013:CA3727, para 4.24. See also, similarly, Amsterdam Court of Appeal 4 October 2022, ECLI:NL:GHAMS:2022:2819, paras 3.4.2 and 3.6.

314 See Zutphen District Court 29 February 2012, ECLI:NL:RBZUT:2012:BW3693, para 7.15; Amsterdam Court of Appeal 1 November 2011, ECLI:NL:GHAMS:2011:BU7752, para 2.16.

independence.[315] This applies equally to the fact that an arbitrator was successfully challenged in another, unrelated arbitration.[316] Worth mentioning is the argument that the arbitral award should be set aside because large companies often arbitrate through an arbitration institute, such as the NAI, which means that the arbitrators in question have an interest in the outcome of the arbitration. The Amsterdam District Court did not accept this argument and dismissed the claim to set aside the arbitral award based on breach of the principle of independence and impartiality.[317]

The foregoing shows that a conflict of interest can lead to setting aside of an arbitral award. If an arbitrator foresees a conflict of interest, it is recommended that an arbitrator does not accept his appointment.[318] If the arbitrator does not foresee that he will be guided in his assessment by a circumstance outside the case at hand, but suspects that the parties might get the impression that he is biased because of that circumstance, it is advisable to inform the parties accordingly (see also Article 13(3) and (4) NAI Arbitration Rules 2024). Here, the IBA Guidelines on Conflicts of Interest in International Arbitration (2024) can serve as a guideline, as the lists contained in the Guidelines generally reflect circumstances present in the case law discussed.

23.3 Remission (Article 1065a DCCP)

With the introduction of the Arbitration Act 2015, remission was included in Article 1065a DCCP.[319] This provision allows the court to stay the setting aside proceedings in order to remit the case back to the arbitral tribunal. Remission is an efficient alternative to setting aside and helps ensure that setting aside of an arbitral award is an *ultimum remedium* by enabling the arbitral tribunal to repair the ground for setting aside.[320] Remission is expected to result in fewer arbitral awards being set aside. An arbitrator

315 See Noord-Nederland District Court 26 November 2014, ECLI:NL:RBNNE:2014:6076, paras 4.5.3.1-4.5.3.2; 's-Gravenhage District Court 12 February 2014, ECLI:NL:RBDHA:2014:1752, para 4.7; Rotterdam District Court 11 May 2011, ECLI:NL:RBROT:2011:BQ6204, paras 4.8-4.17.

316 See 's-Gravenhage District Court 12 February 2014, ECLI:NL:RBDHA:2014:1752, paras 4.7-4.8.

317 See Amsterdam District Court 17 December 2008, ECLI:NL:RBAMS:2008:BH2280, para 5.6.

318 Cf. in this respect General Standard 2, under (a), of the IBA Guidelines.

319 See Meijer & Van Mierlo 2015, p 160-161 and p 527.

320 See Meijer & Van Mierlo 2015, p 527.

should therefore bear in mind that his task may not be over after rendering the arbitral award.

Article 1065a(1) DCCP states that the (competent) court of appeal may, both at the request of any of the parties to the arbitration and on its own initiative, suspend the setting aside proceedings and refer the case back to the arbitral tribunal. The court of appeal may remit the case back to the tribunal but is not obligated to do so. In other words, the court of appeal has a discretionary power. It follows from the text of Article 1065a(1) DCCP that the court of appeal can only remit the case to the arbitral tribunal if there is a ground for setting aside of the arbitral award in the case at hand. The ground for setting aside may also concern (only) part of the arbitral award.[321] The court of appeal can only remit the case back to the arbitral tribunal in the event certain, specific grounds for setting aside are present. According to the legislator, an arbitral award cannot be remitted to the arbitral tribunal if there is no valid arbitration agreement (Article 1065(1)(a) DCCP) or if the arbitral award is contrary to public policy (Article 1065(1)(e) DCCP).[322] In the literature, the exclusion of remission in case of 'ground e' has been questioned. After all, it is not inconceivable that an arbitral tribunal could undo this ground for setting aside after remission. In that respect, one could think of a breach of European (Union) law, but also of breach of equal right to be heard.[323] That said, as regards the possibility of remission in Article 1065a(1) DCCP, the legislator mainly envisioned situations in which the arbitrator(s) failed to provide reasons in an arbitral award (Article 1065(1)(d) DCCP), more specifically by failing to discuss a ground to grant or reject the claim.[324] As to breach of mandate (Article 1065(1)(c) DCCP), it is assumed in the literature that remission is possible. This has also been confirmed in case law. Remission has taken place in a situation in which something different was awarded than claimed, and in a case in which an incorrect decision-making standard was applied by the arbitrators.[325] There is a debate in the literature as to whether remission

321 See Meijer & Van Mierlo 2015, p 157.

322 See Meijer & Van Mierlo 2015, p 160-161.

323 See Sanders 2001, p 212; G.J. Meijer, in: *T&C Rv*, Article 1065a, note 2 (online, updated 1 January 2024); H.J. Snijders, in: *GS Burgerlijke Rechtsvordering*, Article 1065a DCCP, note 1 (online, updated 1 May 2018); N. Peters & B. van Zelst, '*Remission* in de nieuwe Arbitragewet', *TCR* 2013, p 122-123 (only with regard to breach of equal right to be heard).

324 See Meijer & Van Mierlo 2015, p 162.

325 See The Hague Court of Appeal 16 October 2018, ECLI:NL:GHDHA:2018:2639 (interim judgment) and The Hague Court of Appeal 21 May 2019, ECLI:NL:2019:GHDHA:2639 (final judgment in which the Court of Appeal decided that the ground for setting aside had been undone); Amsterdam Court of

is possible in case of a failure to comply with the signature requirement under Article 1057(2) DCCP (ground d). Kortmann & Ernste have argued that this is not possible. According to Kortmann & Ernste, the legislator cannot have intended to disallow repair of such an error through rectification (Article 1060 DCCP), but to allow repair at a later stage via remission pursuant to Article 1065a DCCP.[326] Article 1060 DCCP provides the possibility of (simple) rectification of an arbitral award, which is done by the arbitral tribunal that made the arbitral award. Errors in signing the arbitral award cannot be rectified via this route.[327] Peters & Van Zelst and Snijders, on the other hand, assume that an error in signing the award can indeed be remedied via remission.[328] Meijer takes an intermediate position. According to Meijer, the fact that an assessment is made by a court in case of remission, unlike in the case of rectification under Article 1060 DCCP, justifies that an error in signing the award can be remedied through remission in exceptional cases. According to Meijer, such an exceptional case occurs if the two arbitrators who did not sign the arbitral award were willing to sign, but were not given the opportunity to do so by the chair. According to Meijer, the state court can then test whether the arbitrators were willing to sign the arbitral award.[329] The Amsterdam Court of Appeal has remitted a case in which only the chair and the arbitral secretary had signed the award back to the tribunal. In that case, the ground for setting aside was reversed by the arbitral tribunal and the award remained intact.[330] The Court of Appeal noted that it was the intention of the arbitrators for all of them to sign the award.[331] It is also debated in the literature whether remission is possible if the arbitral tribunal has not been composed in

Appeal 27 November 2018, ECLI:NL:GHAMS:2018:4323 (interim judgment) and Amsterdam Court of Appeal 10 December 2019, ECLI:NL:GHAMS:2019:4407 (final judgment in which the Court of Appeal decided that the ground for setting aside had been repaired).

326 See S.C.J.J. Kortmann & P.E. Ernste, note to Supreme Court 30 September 2016, ECLI:NL:HR:2016:2215, para 8, *JOR* 2016/324 (*Qnow/B.*).

327 See G.J. Meijer, in: *T&C Rv*, Article 1060 DCCP, note 1c (online, updated 1 January 2018).

328 See Peters & Van Zelst 2013, p 124; Snijders 2017, para 3.

329 See G.J. Meijer, 'De strikte (tussen)maatstaf voor de aansprakelijkheid van arbiters…', in: B.F. Assink et al (eds), *De vele gezichten van Maarten Kroeze's bange bestuurders (Instituut voor Ondernemingsrecht no 104)*, Deventer: Wolters Kluwer 2017, p 360.

330 See Amsterdam Court of Appeal 3 November 2020, ECLI:NL:GHAMS:2020:2936 (interim judgment) and Amsterdam Court of Appeal 28 September 2021, ECLI:NL:GHAMS:2021:3133 (final judgment).

331 Amsterdam Court of Appeal 3 November 2020, ECLI:NL:GHAMS:2020:2936, paras 4.5-4.7.

accordance with the applicable rules (Article 1065(1)(b) DCCP). Sanders,[332] unlike Peters & Van Zelst,[333] is of the opinion that this is not possible.

The setting aside proceedings shall be suspended by the state court pending the remission. The court may attach a time limit to the suspension.[334] State courts have, to date, suspended setting aside proceedings for three or six months.[335] The court of appeal will state in its judgment the ground or grounds upon which the arbitral award will be set aside (if not remedied) so that the arbitral tribunal can remove those grounds.[336] Remission entails that the mandate of the arbitral tribunal is revived. The arbitral tribunal must determine a further procedural order for the proceedings after remission, after hearing the parties. This should take into account the period during which the setting aside proceedings are suspended. Remission gives an arbitral tribunal the opportunity to remove the ground for setting aside.[337] In light of this, we recommend that arbitrators take a serious look at the judgment of the court of appeal. Article 1065a(2) DCCP provides that the parties should be given the opportunity to be heard before the arbitral tribunal decides. If the arbitral tribunal is of the opinion that a ground for setting aside can be removed, it must render an arbitral award accordingly (Article 1065a(3) DCCP). According to the legislator, the arbitral tribunal may reach a decision in that award that differs from the decision in the earlier award.[338] The award rendered by the tribunal replaces the award with respect to which setting aside is claimed. The new arbitral award is submitted to the court of appeal. The court of appeal then lifts the suspension or allows the time period for remission to expire. Article 1065a(4) DCCP provides that the court of appeal then decides in accordance with what it considers appropriate, taking into account the circumstances. In any event, the court of appeal must assess whether the grounds for setting aside have been removed. If the answer is 'no', a (second) referral to the arbitral tribunal is not an obvious choice, though the law does not, strictly speaking, prevent this.[339]

332 See Sanders 2001, p 213.
333 See Peters & Van Zelst 2013, p 123.
334 See Sanders 2001, p 213; Peters & Van Zelst 2013, p 123-124.
335 See The Hague Court of Appeal 16 October 2018, ECLI:NL:GHDHA:2018:2639; Amsterdam Court of Appeal 27 November 2018, ECLI:NL:GHAMS:2018:4323; Amsterdam Court of Appeal 3 November 2020, ECLI:NL:GHAMS:2020:2936.
336 See Meijer & Van Mierlo 2015, p 161.
337 See Meijer & Van Mierlo 2015, p 161.
338 See Meijer & Van Mierlo 2015, p 120. At the time of the Proposal to amend the Arbitration Act 1986, there was still a lack of clarity on this issue (see Peters & Van Zelst 2013, p 121-122).
339 See Meijer & Van Mierlo 2015, p 161.

23.4 Conclusion

An arbitrator will, at all times, want to avoid setting aside of his arbitral award. In this contribution, we have given an insight into the circumstances under which an arbitral award will or will not be set aside under Dutch law, on the basis of an analysis of the literature and case law. By doing so, we wish to give (NAI) arbitrators guidance on the manner in which they should conduct themselves in arbitral proceedings to prevent setting aside of the arbitral award and possible subsequent liability proceedings.

As part of the assessment of his jurisdiction, an arbitrator should be wary of the fact that he has to check, *ex officio*, whether the dispute is arbitrable (Article 1020(3) DCCP) and, in case of a business-to-consumer arbitration, whether or not the arbitration clause in the general terms and conditions is unreasonably onerous (Article 6:236(n) in conjunction with 6:233(a) DCC). In determining whether a valid arbitration agreement exists between the parties, an arbitrator may, following a defence by a party to the arbitration in that regard, be confronted with the questions whether a representative of a company was acting on behalf of someone else or in his own name when concluding the arbitration agreement, whether third parties are bound by the arbitration agreement and whether the dispute submitted to arbitration falls within the scope of the arbitration agreement. Furthermore, arbitrators may have to assess whether an arbitration clause in general terms and conditions is valid, in particular whether the counterparty had a reasonable opportunity to take note of the general terms and conditions. According to case law, an incorrect assessment of these questions by the arbitrator can lead to setting aside of the arbitral award for lack of a valid arbitration agreement. Arbitrators should also pay attention in case of a multi-tiered dispute resolution clause which provides for mediation and, if the dispute cannot be resolved in that manner, for arbitration (see para 23.2.2). It is also conceivable that one or more parties to the arbitral proceedings take the view that the arbitral tribunal was not composed in accordance with the applicable rules. If this is indeed the case, the arbitral tribunal should decline jurisdiction. In this regard, the arbitral tribunal should pay particular attention to the number of arbitrators and the prescribed qualifications of the arbitrators (see para 23.2.3).

With regard to breach of mandate, we can conclude from the case law examined that, in practice, this ground is often invoked in setting aside proceedings, but that the ground has rarely led to setting aside. From the cases in which breach of mandate was invoked as a ground for setting aside, we can infer that an arbitrator can avoid setting aside of the arbitral award by deciding on all parts of the claim(s) and counterclaim(s) and addressing all essential defences in the award (see para 23.2.4.2 and para 23.2.4.3). It is therefore advisable to pay attention to the determination of the claims and the essential defences before drafting the arbitral award. In addition, it follows from case law that it is important that arbitrators do not award more or something different than claimed (para 23.2.4.6) and that they include the correct decision making-standard in the arbitral award (para 23.2.4.7). The latter entails that arbitrators are required to examine the arbitration agreement on this point. Furthermore, it follows from case law that supplementation of the facts or of the factual basis by arbitrators is a ground for setting aside of the arbitral award. An arbitrator will therefore have to refrain from doing so. An arbitrator should only base his decision on facts that the parties have asserted, the accuracy and completeness of which they have been able to verify and challenge during the arbitral proceedings (para 23.2.4.4). An arbitrator may supplement the legal grounds *ex officio* (cf. Article 25 DCCP). As regards the supplementation of 'ordinary' mandatory law and directory law, however, the supplementation of the legal grounds must be in line with the debate between the parties and with the facts asserted by the parties. Supplementation of legal grounds should not lead to a surprise decision (see para 23.2.4.5). Finally, an arbitrator must also take into account the formal side of the mandate. This requires arbitrators to act in accordance with the Dutch Arbitration Act, the applicable arbitration rules and the procedural agreements between the parties and arbitrators. Breach of mandate has also been accepted in case law in a situation in which an arbitral tribunal deviated from a final binding decision taken in an interim award in the final award. Such deviation is only allowed in case of a *novum* (para 23.2.4.8).

It goes without saying that arbitrators are required to reason their award on the essential points of the case and that absence of a reasoning can lead to setting aside of an arbitral award. This is the ground for setting aside that is most often invoked in practice. The reasoning does not need to be explicit, as long as it can be deduced from the award. If the reasoning of the award provides no explanation for the decision whatsoever, the arbitral award can be set aside on the basis of Article 1065(1)(d) DCCP because of a manifestly defective reasoning. We therefore recommend that an arbitral tribunal pays due attention to the reasoning and checks whether it responds to the parties' essential defences (see para 23.2.6). As regards signing the award, arbitrators should ensure that *all* arbitrators on the tribunal sign the award *themselves* and in the prescribed manner *before* it is rendered, in order to safeguard the collegiality of the decision (see para 23.2.5).

It follows from case law that setting aside of an arbitral award is also regularly sought on the basis of breach of public policy. An arbitral award is only subject to setting aside if the content or enforcement of the award breaches mandatory law of such a fundamental character that compliance with it may not be prevented by procedural restrictions. This is true in case of breach national law that is of public policy and in case of breach of fundamental EU law (para 23.2.7.2). The notion of public policy includes the equal right to be heard. Under this principle, an arbitral tribunal must give the parties an (equal) opportunity to express their views on the essential points of the dispute. The parties should also have this opportunity in the context of an expert report upon which the decision of the arbitrators is based. Case law on setting aside of arbitral awards also shows that an arbitral tribunal should consistently take care to provide the parties an (equal) opportunity to respond to new submissions, documents and statements of witnesses, experts and the parties themselves. Furthermore, a tribunal that takes a surprise decision breaches the right to be heard, according to the case law. Finally, in the event the parties have agreed that no new submissions can be made from a certain point in the arbitral proceedings, arbitrators should not accept new submissions without hearing both parties. Moreover, the arbitrators should not correct the arbitral award in light of a new submission (on which the parties were not heard) (para 23.2.7.4). As regards the use of witness testimony in arbitration, case law clarifies that the answer to the question as to whether such evidence is allowed is determined against the background of the equal right to be heard. In addition, rejection of an offer of proof must be supported by reasons. Failure to observe these principles in the context of an offer of proof may lead to a breach of public policy (para 23.2.7.5). Furthermore, the IBA Guidelines can play an important role in setting aside proceedings when determining whether the principle of impartiality and independence has been breached. In the event of a conflict of interest, an arbitrator (or a prospective arbitrator) should either not accept his appointment or inform the parties, depending on the seriousness of the conflict of interest (para 23.2.7.6). Finally, it follows from case law that parties also invoke Article 1065(1)(e) DCCP on the ground that a legal act was entered into under the influence of fraud or corruption and was wrongly not declared invalid by the arbitral tribunal and/or on the ground that fraud was committed during the arbitral proceedings. The Supreme Court explicitly considered that a restrictive review should also be applied in such cases (para 23.2.7.3).

Certain grounds for setting aside can be removed by the arbitral tribunal if the court of appeal before which the setting aside claim is heard remits the case back to the arbitral tribunal once it is established that there is a ground for setting aside. According to the parliamentary history to the Dutch Arbitration Act and to case law, remission is possible under Article 1065a DCCP if the ground for setting aside is a breach of mandate or a failure to state reasons for the decision. According to the legislator, remission is not possible in case of absence of a valid arbitration agreement and in the event of a breach of public policy. Regarding the grounds for setting aside under Article 1065(1)(b) DCCP (the arbitral tribunal has not been composed in accordance with the applicable rules) and Article 1065(1)(d) DCCP (a failure to comply with the signature requirement under Article 1057(2) DCCP), there is a debate in the literature whether remission is possible. Since the introduction of Article 1065a DCCP in 2015 three cases have been remitted back to the arbitral tribunal during setting aside proceedings. The question is whether remission results in a large decrease in the number of cases in which arbitral awards are set aside. It is conceivable that remission has only a limited significance in that regard in case the possibility of remission is only limited to the grounds breach of mandate, lack of reasoning and (certain) defects in signing the award (see on the possibility of remission in case of defects in signing the award para 23.3). Indeed, our analysis shows that there were 22 cases in which an arbitral award was set aside for breach of mandate, lack of reasoning or defects in the signing of the award. In the majority of cases (33 cases), the arbitral award was set aside on other grounds, namely lack of a valid arbitration agreement, a composition of the arbitral tribunal that was not in accordance with the applicable rules or a violation of equal right to be heard. That being said, if an arbitral tribunal is given the opportunity to remove the ground for setting aside of the award through remission, we recommend that arbitrators take a serious look at the judgment of the court of appeal.

Based on the case law we examined, we conclude that NAI arbitrators are doing well. Out of 272 cases, 48 involved an arbitral award rendered by an arbitrator or arbitral tribunal in an NAI arbitration. There were only eight cases in which such an arbitral award was actually set aside by the state court. The limited number of arbitral awards that are submitted to a court of appeal in setting aside proceedings and the even more limited number of awards that are actually set aside confirms the high quality of the NAI. This is a nice selling point for the NAI that could be marketed even more both nationally and internationally.

IV – CLOSING REMARKS

CHAPTER 24

ARBITRATION IN THE NETHERLANDS, IN PARTICULAR NAI ARBITRATION

Conclusion and closing remarks

Carla Klaassen & Gerard Meijer[1]

24.1 Introduction

The decision to create this volume was made in response to "market demand" for an English version of the earlier volume published in 2019 by the Netherlands Arbitration Institute ("NAI") in cooperation with the Radboud Business Law Institute ("OO&R"), titled: "Going Dutch: ADR in Nederland, in het bijzonder bij het NAI".[2] However, it cannot be said that this volume merely functions as a "simple" translation of that 2019 publication. Instead, it further focuses its attention on arbitration (rather than Alternative Dispute Resolution ("ADR") in a broader sense). That said, due consideration is provided to corporate mediation, though especially in light of its relationship to arbitration. Moreover, this volume consists in part of contributions also present in the earlier volume – updated to account for the relevant developments – and in part of entirely new contributions. One of its aims is to provide guidance for non-Dutch readers seeking to learn about arbitration in the Netherlands, in particular arbitration under the 2024 NAI Arbitration Rules. In this respect, the editors

---

1 Professor C.J.M. (Carla) Klaassen is Professor of Civil Law and Civil Procedure at Radboud University Nijmegen (Onderzoekcentrum Onderneming & Recht), Extraordinary Professor of Private Law at the University of Curacao and Vice-Chair of the Board of the Netherlands Arbitration Institute, Professor G.J. (Gerard) Meijer is a partner at Linklaters LLP in Amsterdam, Professor of Arbitration & Dispute Resolution at the Erasmus School of Law, Erasmus University Rotterdam, and Chair of the Board of the NAI. The authors would like to thank C.L. (Carmen) Schleijpen and T. (Thomas) de Boer for their support in writing this conclusion and for their efforts as co-editors of this volume. Carmen Schleijpen (LLM) is a lecturer at Radboud University Nijmegen and a PhD Candidate at the Radboud Business Law Institute of Radboud University Nijmegen. Her doctoral research concerns the civil liability of arbitrators. Thomas de Boer (LLM) is an associate at Linklaters LLP in Amsterdam.

2 C.J.M. Klaassen, G.J. Meijer & C.L. Schleijpen (eds), *Going Dutch: ADR in Nederland, in het bijzonder bij het NAI*, Deventer: Wolters Kluwer 2019.

also refer to the comprehensive overview of the *new* 2024 NAI Arbitration Rules and the corresponding Explanatory Notes, to be found in the Appendix of this volume. Finally, this volume aims to provide a contribution to scholarly debates in this respect and also celebrates the 75th anniversary of the NAI (in 2024). Below, we outline some of the thoughts expressed in the volume, to which we respond at times.

24.2 What (types of) disputes lend themselves to (NAI) arbitration?

It is well known that arbitration is a most flexible form of dispute resolution. As such, arbitration can provide a more than appropriate dispute resolution mechanism for all sorts of disputes. There are certain cases, however, where a dispute may require more expertise or is not always easily capable of settlement via arbitration for various reasons. Moreover, arbitration as a whole can be placed in different contexts, such as when compared to other forms of ADR, like mediation, or state court proceedings. Below, we provide a brief overview of the authors' contributions in respect of all these aspects.

24.2.1 Specialised arbitration institutes under the auspices of the NAI

Verduyn presents the Court of Arbitration for Art ("CAfA"), an arbitration institute founded in 2018 under the auspices of the foundation of Authentication in Art and the NAI. The CAfA has its own set of arbitration rules, the CAfA Rules, supplemented and modified to meet the wishes of the international art community (see para 2.2.2). One interesting aspect of the CAfA is that it features both an Arbitrator Pool and an Expert Pool. The former consists of those with both an expertise in law, and significant experience in relevant art related fields. The latter consists of a carefully selected group of experts in the field of forensic science, material analysis or provenance of art objects, in particular for authentication purposes (see paras 2.2.3-2.2.4). A fitting mechanism to ensure that art related disputes, which can become exceedingly niche in nature, are expertly dealt with by those most equipped to deal with them. One other unique feature is that CAfA awards can be published in an anonymised form, whilst the name or identity of the art object may be revealed to ensure that fake pieces or forgeries cannot recirculate in the art market (Article 51 CAfA Rules) (see para 2.2.5). Verduyn also examines which types of art-related disputes are suitable for arbitration by the CAfA, paying particular attention to (i) ownership: cultural heritage and looted art, (ii) copyright to works of (applied) art and (iii) contracts related to artworks (para 2.3). Verduyn finally sums up the advantages of arbitration under the CAfA, listing considerations such as the aforementioned expertise of those involved, the confidentiality of the proceedings and the award, the costs, and the enforceability of the award (para 2.4). She concludes by stating, *inter alia*, that CAfA arbitration is a suitable means of resolving various kinds of art-related disputes, and that it is worthwhile drawing attention to the opportunities that it has to offer (para 2.5).

The world of aviation is another field that requires specific expertise. Schäfer and Morbach present the newly formed Hague Court of Arbitration for Aviation ("Hague CAA"), a new arbitration institute launched in 2022 that operates under the auspices of the NAI. They consider the strengths of this new institute in light of the increasingly complex aspects of aviation disputes. Such disputes can take many shapes, and will often require specific expertise, which the Hague CAA can offer. To illustrate, Schäfer and Morbach examine the mechanisms found in the 2023 Hague CAA Rules through which arbitrators can quickly, and properly, resolve aviation disputes. These include a default choice for expedited proceedings, an early determination mechanism and emergency arbitration. They conclude that, with its rules, the Hague CAA is a good choice for any sort of aviation dispute, and a great addition to the already strong arbitration market in the Netherlands.

24.2.2 *The various types of disputes and the (potential) role of NAI arbitration*

Verschuur examines whether the field of IP lends itself well to arbitration (chapter 4), with a focus on Dutch law and NAI arbitration. She indicates that various differing IP related laws can present an obstacle to choosing arbitration by assigning exclusive jurisdiction to the courts of The Hague, and that the expertise that has been built at those courts can also attract IP related cases that are not exclusively adjudicated by those courts (para 4.2.1). The assignment of exclusive jurisdiction to the courts of The Hague compared to other courts does not answer the question whether arbitration is excluded. The limited court and arbitral case law is inconclusive on this matter. However, Verschuur states that the existence of a specific designation of a court does not exclude arbitration, and that one must rather examine whether the arbitration agreement will serve to determine legal consequences that may not be freely determined by the parties (see Article 1020(3) DCCP). Such a situation may present itself when the sought decision affects third parties, for example. This could be the case where the nullity of an IP right is sought (para 4.2.2.4). Verschuur concludes that arbitration is excluded only in specific circumstances (see para 4.2.5). If an IP dispute *can* be submitted to arbitration, however, the next question is whether this is desirable. Verschuur examines the benefits of arbitration (para 4.3.1) and court litigation (para 4.3.2) and concludes that arbitration is particularly appropriate for (i) complex technical disputes, (ii) disputes in which confidentiality, for whatever reason, is of great importance, and (iii) disputes in which a significant budget is available and in which the parties want clarity on the matter in one instance, in a (relatively) manageable period of time and (iv) disputes in which enforcement issues are at stake (para 4.4).

Ten Brink asks the question what arbitration can do for the field of IT disputes (chapter 5). Contrary to what one may expect given the great amount of failed IT projects in both public and private spheres, Ten Brink explains that the number of proceedings over IT disputes in the public courts and in arbitration is limited. A potential reason is that (failed) IT projects are a "legal minefield", with many uncertainties and thus litigation risks on both sides, thus meaning that there is an incentive for parties to resolve their matters out of court (para 5.1). In light of this complexity of IT disputes, Ten Brink raises the possibility to compose multidisciplinary arbitral tribunals, consisting of both legal and IT experts, as one important advantage of arbitration over court litigation. She wonders, however, whether the market also sees and appreciates the advantages of arbitration. Ten Brink points to the fact that "NLdigital", the trade association for IT companies, refers to the so-called Foundation for the Settlement of Automation Disputes ("SGOA"), for example. A clear picture emerges that there is no uniform approach to speak of, and that many other standard terms and conditions or standard contracts do not refer to the SGOA, let alone contain a choice for arbitration, at all (see para 5.4.2). Ten Brink seems to consider the NAI, along with the SGOA, to be an obvious choice when parties do opt for arbitration. Still, she closes by stating that there is still a world to win for the NAI in this field. Thus, the NAI must put in "relentless energy" to make sure that it makes itself known to suppliers and buyers in the IT industry (see para 5.5).

Conway and Goedhart take stock of various developments in the international arbitration practice and construction practice which have been implemented in the NAI's arbitral proceedings, those that are gradually being implemented, and those which are yet to be implemented (chapter 6). For example, they examine the ways of gathering evidence used by the NAI, and consider that the midstream conference adopted under the 2024 NAI Rules may be an outcome for the construction industry (see para 6.3.2). When it comes to the practices that are yet to be implemented, Conway and Goedhart provide an extensive overview of the way in which delay and disruption claims are dealt with on an international level and/or in other jurisdictions. In particular, they consider the described methods to be suitable for a more widespread application, also in the Dutch market (see para 6.4). The NAI still has a role to play in increasing awareness on the benefits offered by arbitration in construction disputes, for example the parties' ability to appoint an arbitrator in accordance with their own preference. Moreover, the NAI can also better position itself in the construction market by setting frameworks for construction claim-related analyses that may need to be conducted during construction disputes. Conway and Goedhart close by stating that, in light of the amount of opportunities available to the NAI, the "future is looking bright" (para 6.5). Within this context, we would like to make mention of the fact that the NAI Rules are now structured in a way that places general provisions first, followed by several appendices for various specific topics. This structure allows the NAI to add additional appendices, for example for construction arbitration, also on the basis of the suggestions of Conway and Goedhart.

In chapter 7 Kemp and Menasalvas Garrones discuss the possibilities of arbitration in Dutch corporate disputes. They define – for the purpose of their contribution – the term corporate disputes as disputes involving matters traditionally viewed as issues belonging to the field of corporate law, including disputes about the division of power between and behaviour of corporate bodies of the company and minority shareholder protection (para 7.2). Kemp and Menasalvas provide a broad overview of the possibilities to resolve corporate disputes through arbitration and how to facilitate these possibilities. They make various concrete recommendations to solve the challenges that may be encountered when resolving corporate disputes through arbitration (para 7.5). They conclude that the Netherlands as a progressive arbitration and corporate law jurisdiction, and the NAI as the perfectly placed arbitration institute, could help push the cart towards these steps and can ensure that the possibilities for settling corporate disputes through arbitration are increased (para 7.5).

In chapter 8, Vloemans gives her view on the role that arbitration, specifically NAI arbitration, can play in insurance disputes. In this context, she defines insurance disputes as disputes in relation to coverage under an insurance contract (para 8.1). Vloemans answers the question whether insurance disputes lend themselves to arbitration with a resounding "yes", also indicating that institutional arbitration is preferable to *ad hoc* arbitration in this respect. Nevertheless, she does point out some (procedural) hurdles that must be overcome to be able to arbitrate in insurance disputes. This includes the circumstance that these disputes often involve a third party who is not a party to the insurance contract and an arbitration clause included therein (para 8.2.1). Reference is also made in this context to the direct claim that a third, injured party with personal injury has against the liability insurer under Article 7:954 of the DCC (para 8.2.4). Vloemans enters into a debate with Meijer in relation to the possible ways in which such third parties can still be held to an arbitration clause not agreed to by them.

In case of arbitration the NAI can be of good service, as far as Vloemans is concerned. In her opinion, there is no need in the Netherlands for an arbitration institute that specifically focuses on administering insurance disputes (which she concludes after comparing the situation in some other countries). Vloemans also praises the NAI for providing assistance in appointing arbitrators in *ad hoc* arbitration (the same is true for the appointment of binding advisors). As far as points of attention go, Vloemans recommends that NAI is mindful that there be a sufficient amount of arbitrators who specialise in insurance law (para 8.3.1).

Tzankova and Meinen then address the meaning of arbitration in the context of mass claim dispute resolution in the so-called "Global Village". Within this context, they speak of "Global Disputes" (defined in para 9.2). They first discuss the ways in which mass claims can be brought before the Dutch public courts, particularly the procedure in force since 2020 (and amended in 2023) under the Settlement of Mass Claims in Collective Action Act ("WAMCA"). Thereafter, they make a comparison with arbitration and its typical features. Their comparison continues by taking the possibilities of court litigation on the one hand and arbitration on the other in relation to specific areas (of law), specifically: consumer law, financial law and competition law. For several reasons, they conclude that court adjudication is more advantageous for claimants and access to justice than arbitration. They state: "Ironically, when it comes to mass claims arbitration has evolved into a strategic tool, a dispute resolution mechanism that no longer facilitates, but 'hampers' the access to justice. That is a somewhat disappointing conclusion that does not do justice to the potential that arbitration could have for the resolution of mass claims."

Croisant and Wiliński write about the "ESG megatrend", entailing a wave of new regulations and landmark court cases, as well as new litigation and liability risks. These developments also have an effect on arbitration, its practitioners and the NAI. Croisant and Wiliński first set out the relevant guidelines, codes and legislation. While ESG-related obligations were first considered soft law, these have increasingly become sources of inspiration for mandatory requirements over time (para 10.1). Activist non-profit organisations and other types of claimants have taken up a litigious stance in relation to these requirements, and now often seek enforcement thereof vis-à-vis other companies at the state courts, and it seems that the end point of these developments is not yet in sight. Furthermore, so-called parent company litigation is also on the rise, wherein parent companies are held to account for harms caused by other entities within their group (para 10.2). Though it may appear to some that these ESG-related disputes are firmly entrenched in the realm of state court litigation, Croisant and Wiliński make clear that arbitration has a role to play as well. For example, such disputes can become the subject of commercial arbitrations where contracts also impose certain ESG covenants on the parties, such as the imposition of an obligation to reduce the carbon footprint of industrial projects. Post-M&A disputes, too, could lead to ESG-related arbitrations where certain environmental representations and warranties were made in a share purchase agreement (para 10.3) The NAI, being home to an expert group of independent adjudicators, can certainly administer such arbitral proceedings. Croisant and Wiliński recommend that the arbitration community, including the NAI and its users, continue to adapt its rules and practices to suit ESG-related disputes (para 10.5).

24.2.3 *Arbitration in the Dutch Caribbean*

In chapter 11, Barten discusses the possibilities of dispute resolution by way of arbitration in the Caribbean parts of the Kingdom of the Netherlands: the countries Aruba, Curaçao and Sint Maarten and the BES islands (the public entities Bonaire, Sint Eustatius and Saba). Each of these constituent countries and the BES islands has its distinct civil law system but these legal systems are closely related to each other and especially to the legal system of the Netherlands. However, even though the procedural laws of the Dutch Caribbean are also closely related to Dutch law, there are important differences. Arbitration is an area in which major differences have also emerged between Dutch and Dutch Caribbean laws. Barten explores several aspects of arbitration law in the Caribbean parts of the Kingdom, highlighting notable differences compared to Dutch law. One of the most remarkable points is that the Caribbean part of the Kingdom of the Netherlands chose to fully implement the latest adopted version of the UNCITRAL Model Law on International Commercial Arbitration (the "Model Law"), hoping that this would make the jurisdictions more attractive for international arbitral proceedings. In contrast, the European Netherlands has not fully implemented the Model Law. Barten discusses what the resulting differences are. Barten also identifies a big difference regarding the extent to which arbitration is used in the Caribbean compared to the European Netherlands: it is (still) rather limited in the Caribbean. Partly in light of the enforcement possibilities under the New York Convention, which after all applies to the Kingdom of the Netherlands and therefore also to the Caribbean parts of it, arbitration deserves more attention and consideration in the Netherlands. With their well-established legal systems and reliable judiciaries, the Dutch Caribbean jurisdictions still have a significant opportunity to attract more international arbitration, Barten argues. Arbitration through the NAI could be a good choice, even if the parties wish to arbitrate according to the arbitration law of the islands. After all, choosing arbitration at the NAI does not affect the place of arbitration – and thus the applicable arbitration law – which may be located outside the Netherlands. Parties should nevertheless consider carefully whether they wish to designate a Dutch Caribbean territory as the place of arbitration. Another option for parties doing business in the Dutch Caribbean would be to designate Amsterdam as the place of arbitration, for example. This does not prevent oral pleadings from taking place within the Dutch Caribbean of course, nor does it prevent the arbitral tribunal from applying the laws of the Caribbean territories. A potential advantage may be that setting aside proceedings may be conducted in English before the NCC[3] and that any setting aside proceedings will be limited to two court instances. In addition, Dutch courts issue exequaturs on an *ex parte* basis in respect of arbitral awards rendered in the Netherlands potentially expediting the enforcement process if such enforcement is expected to take place in the European Netherlands, Barten concludes.

24.2.4 *Corporate mediation*

Kamminga and Fleuren reflect on corporate mediation (chapter 12). This form of mediation is (also) on the rise in the Netherlands. Corporate mediation lends itself well to being used in combination with arbitration. To begin with, Kamminga and Fleuren examine the distinctive characteris-

3 Hereinafter to be understood as the Netherlands Commercial Court of First Instance and the Netherlands Commercial Court for Appeal together.

tics of corporate mediation in the Netherlands, drawing comparisons with Anglo-American approaches. They also pay attention to the role of the NAI in providing mediation services. Subsequently, the authors discuss the enforceability of mediation clauses in the Dutch legal system, also referring to the recent Lotamblau Judgment of the Dutch Supreme Court. The evolution of mediation in the Netherlands, particularly with the rise of proactive mediators and hybrid models like med-arb, provides businesses and their legal counsel with a diverse set of tools for resolving disputes quickly and effectively. This trend reflects the increasing complexity of corporate disputes and the demand for solutions that not only address legal concerns but also protect business interests and preserve long-term relationships, Kamminga and Fleuren rightly note.

24.2.5 The NAI alongside the NCC

Part I of this volume concludes with a discussion by Tjittes on the relative positions of the NCC and the NAI: competitors or peers in resolving international commercial disputes? In relation to adjudication in the English language – though not in relation to other languages – the emergence of the NCC has meant that the NAI has lost one argument in favour of choosing (its) arbitration, as the NCC also provides for proceedings to take place in English. Other arguments that carry weight in favour of arbitration (at the NAI) over court litigation remain unchanged, such as the parties' influence on the arbitrator(s) to be appointed and the confidentiality of arbitration. Tjittes believes that for medium-sized international disputes between medium-sized companies the NCC offers a good alternative to arbitration if enforcement can take place in Europe. However, for disputes with high commercial (and financial) stakes, especially where enforcement of an award is to take place outside Europe, arbitration (including arbitration at the NAI), will remain the preferred method of dispute resolution. Tjittes cites the wide range of possibilities for enforcement under the New York Convention, the possibility of appointing one's own arbitrator and the secrecy of the arbitral proceedings as arguments that outweigh the higher costs of arbitration in such cases compared to state court proceedings (para 13.6; see further also para 13.5). Furthermore, to put this into perspective, Tjittes points to international research showing that commercial disputes are settled in the majority of cases (57%), and that even where parties do not settle, court or arbitration proceedings are initiated only in a minority of cases (32%) (para 13.2). Tjittes also recalls international research showing that of 97% of the corporate lawyers of large companies questioned, arbitration is their preferred dispute resolution mechanism, in 49% of cases combined with other forms of ADR, such as mediation (para 13.3). Tjittes concludes, however, that the NCC and the NAI are no competitors, but peers, who complement each other on the table of international commercial disputes in the Netherlands.

24.3 Some particular topics regarding the arbitral tribunal & the arbitral proceedings

In 2024, the NAI Arbitration Rules as have been in place since 2015 have been updated, partially amended and supplemented. This volume contains a number of contributions that pay special attention to particular topics relating to the arbitral tribunal and the arbitral proceedings under these (updated) Rules. In addition, as mentioned before, you will find the Rules and the corresponding Explanatory Notes in the Appendix of this volume, which also cover topics not addressed elsewhere in this volume.

24.3.1 The position of the arbitral secretary

Scheltema discusses the position of the arbitral secretary (chapter 14). According to Scheltema the use of tribunal secretaries is increasingly popular due to the increase of (international) arbitrations and the rise of full-time arbitrators. However he notes that the role of tribunal secretaries has been taken for granted for a long time and their position has not aroused a lot of (legal) attention, but this has changed a little bit recently. More recent arbitration rules of arbitration institutes include some provisions and/or limitations concerning the tasks of the tribunal secretary. See for instance Article 24(2) of the 2024 NAI Arbitration Rules, which provides that the work of a secretary is performed for, on behalf of and under the supervision of the arbitral tribunal: "A secretary has no decision-making authority. The arbitral tribunal is not permitted to delegate any decision-making power to a secretary." Scheltema analyses the position of the secretary in more detail. Among other things, he discusses the (contractual) position of the secretary and the ways in which a secretary can be appointed and challenged, as well as the liability of the secretary. He also compares the 2024 NAI Arbitration Rules concerning the secretary with the rules of some other foreign institutes.

Scheltema concludes that the tribunal secretary should be considered as a subcontractor of the arbitrator(s). The only exception to this rule may be when the tribunal secretary is directly appointed by the administering arbitration institute. The tribunal secretary will be a subcontractor of the administering institute in such cases. Setting aside of an arbitral award if the tribunal secretary has assumed a role which is not compatible with the task and responsibilities of arbitrators, such as acting as an arbitrator or rendering unsupervised decisions regarding (important) issues in the arbitration, seems unlikely, Scheltema notes. The position of the tribunal secretary in connection to his liability is comparable to that of the arbitrators, according to Scheltema. Therefore, liability of the arbitral secretary in his or her advisory role will be conceivable only if a manifest disregard of his or her tasks has occurred. This threshold may be lower in connection with errors in the performance of administrative tasks. In connection to this, the arbitration rules of most arbitration institutes include a limitation of liability, which in some cases explicitly applies to tribunal secretaries: see for example Article 64 2024 NAI Arbitration Rules.

24.3.2 Challenges

Honée and Perera-de Wit discuss the new features of the NAI challenge regime (chapter 15). The NAI's challenge regime is set out in Article 23 and Appendix B of the 2024 NAI Rules. One notable addition in the new Rules is an anti-abuse provision (Article B3(8) 2024 NAI Rules) that allows the Challenge Chamber to determine that a subsequent challenge of the challenging party will not be considered in case of abuse. Moreover, anonymised challenge decisions can now be published (see para 15.3). Though, historically speaking, such publication has not occurred, Honée and Perera-de Wit were still able to provide valuable insights on the amount of challenges (para 15.4) and the general application of the methods of assessment involved. They discuss the meaning of the presumption of impartiality and independence of arbitrators, the IBA Guidelines on Conflicts of Interest in International Arbitration, and the assessment of the grounds for challenge (see para 15.5). In light of the increasing demand of transparency, however, Honée and Perera-de Wit do indeed encourage publication of (anonymised) challenge decisions. This would, *inter alia*, boost confidence of users of NAI arbitrations in the quality of the decisions of the Challenge Committee as an independent third party (para 15.6). Still, Honée and Perera-de Wit close with the encouraging observation that challenge requests are only submitted to the Challenge Committee on a limited scale (para 15.7), which surely already speaks to the quality of arbitrators and the mechanisms of their selection.

24.3.3 *Liability risks*

You can't make an omelette without breaking a few eggs. This saying (of course) also applies to arbitration. Sometimes mistakes lead to damage, or at least the perception of damage, resulting in (a) liability (claim). What risks do arbitrators run in their work? Viewed through another lens: what options are open to parties to arbitration if they believe that an arbitrator has caused damages by not properly fulfilling his role, particularly in the context of liability therefor? Strik discusses this issue in this volume (chapter 16).[4] The way that national courts handle liability matters and especially the qualities and predictability of the applicable liability regime may influence the parties' choice of the place of arbitration due to their contribution to a country's image in relation to, and thus attractiveness for, arbitration. Dutch law does not have a liability standard specifically focused on (only) arbitrators. Strik advocates for change in this regard (para 16.2). Such change would be to the benefit of legal certainty and provide (increased) opportunity for both Dutch and non-Dutch practitioners, including arbitrators, to make themselves familiar with the applicable standards. She also advocates for the inclusion of a statutory limitation of liability, as already proposed by the Van den Berg Committee in 2006 (paras 16.2 and 16.1). The NAI's arbitration rules – unlike the rules of some other Dutch or non-Dutch institutes – do contain a limitation of liability. Strik discusses several issues that may arise in connection to (the applicability of) a limitation of liability clause in a specific case.

24.3.4 *Emergency and expedited arbitration*

Schellaars and Potter focus their attentions on the emergency and expedited arbitral proceedings at the NAI (chapter 17). In doing so, they also rely on empirical research and figures relating to (the experiences with) the speed of arbitration. Moreover, they specifically assess arbitral proceedings on the basis of the 2024 and 2015 NAI Rules, conducted under Dutch arbitration law (para 17.1). When it comes to emergency arbitration, Schellaars and Potter note that the Dutch legislator has provided for a legislative foundation for emergency arbitration in Article 1043b DCCP, which itself makes reference to Article 254 DCCP, governing summary proceedings before the Dutch state courts. As a result, Schellaars and Potter are concerned that the connection between arbitral proceedings and

4 Also see Scheltema's contribution (chapter 14.4), which discusses the liability of the secretary of the arbitral tribunal (para 14.4.5).

Dutch state court practice may result in confusion for non-Dutch parties, which could also extend to confusion regarding the norms and limits of the NAI's emergency arbitration. Though we understand the concern, we believe that emergency arbitration has become a commonly known and used mechanism throughout various arbitration institutes, and note that this mechanism is not homogenously regulated across those institutes (or their rulesets), let alone jurisdictions. Consequently, we believe that 'our' emergency arbitration, due to its many similarities (and only few differences) with those other proceedings, will not necessarily be considered the 'odd one out', or necessarily an easily misunderstood figure. In any event, Schellaars and Potter's extensive examination of the NAI's emergency arbitration will certainly take away many of the questions potential users may have (para 17.2). For example, their observation that NAI emergency arbitration is not conditioned on later initiation or current existence of arbitral proceedings on the merits is one that may pique the interest of prospective users. Schellaars and Potter also describe the expedited arbitration, newly introduced in the 2024 NAI Rules. Again, they extensively describe the criteria and features that characterise such proceedings (para 17.3). One criterion relates to the monetary threshold of € 1 million which the claimant's claim must not exceed – a choice that Schellaars and Potter understand. One such feature is the necessary "safety valve", allowing the transfer of expedited proceedings to 'regular' proceedings. Safeguards such as these ensure that, where a dispute demands it, the parties' interests in due process can be effectively protected by 'slowing the proceedings down', as it were, and allowing for more extensive proceedings. Schellaars and Potter close by stating that the new arrangement of the expedited arbitration has no doubt strengthened the NAI's position in the Dutch and international markets. Quite fittingly, they remark that this development has given international parties yet another reason to justify "Going Dutch" (para 17.4).

24.3.5 *Confidentiality*

De Ly addresses a characteristic that has, at least traditionally, been attributed to arbitration and is frequently cited as an advantage of arbitration over state court litigation: confidentiality. Confidentiality is even considered a principle inherent to arbitration. De Ly first raises the question of what this is actually based on and questions the bases that could be put forward for this point of view. He concludes that confidentiality in arbitration seems to rest mainly on tradition and pragmatic considerations. He points out that confidentiality in arbitration has been under pressure for some time. In this regard, De Ly also points to the influence of the development of investment arbitration on the views on confidentiality and transparency in the context of arbitration in para 18.6.1. Admittedly, investment arbitration, unlike "ordinary" arbitration, does not involve disputes of a private law nature, but the calls against private and confidential investment arbitrations has had a wider effect on opinions about confidentiality of arbitration in a general sense, according to De Ly.

The circumvention or, if one wishes, breach of the (alleged) confidentiality of arbitration by various foreign courts has led to divergent reactions from legislators and arbitration institutes (see paras 18.3 and 18.4). Regardless of the contents of these responses, it is safe to at least conclude that there is no global consensus as to whether arbitration is, or should be, confidential in nature. The current 2024 NAI Arbitration Rules contain a provision on confidentiality (Article 6), corresponding with an initiative by De Ly added in the 2010 NAI Arbitration Rules. However, the Arbitration Act in force in the Netherlands since 2015 does not contain a regulation on confidentiality, which De Ly regrets. Such a statutory provision on the confidentiality principle as well as a statutory definition of its contours would, in his opinion, have provided more guidance, both from a national law perspective and from a private international law perspective. In the context of the question of the scope and viability of confidentiality in arbitration, De Ly also draws some fascinating lines to recent case law of the ECtHR on Article 6 ECHR (para 18.6.1). It is true that (again) this does not concern civil proceedings, but disciplinary proceedings (in the sports world), but according to De Ly it is not inconceivable that these proceedings may also have consequences for the permissibility of non-public civil arbitral proceedings. All the more reason, as far as he is concerned, to regulate confidentiality via legislation, as well as to build an "ECHR safety valve" into arbitration rules.

De Ly discusses several other aspects surrounding the (desirable) scope of confidentiality in arbitration and its consequences. For example, he is critical of counsel, arbitrators and experts mentioning their involvement in arbitrations on websites and in other contexts for marketing purposes. That being said, he apparently finds publication of arbitrator appointments on the website (also) introduced by the NAI acceptable, provided – as we understand it – that this does not include information about the substance of the case (para 18.6.3). Nor does De Ly have any objections to the anonymous publication of NAI awards, unless a party objects in a timely manner in advance. He seems to acknowledge the useful function that this can fulfil for the benefit of, among other things, the development of law, not only in the field of arbitral procedural law, but also in relation to substantive matters in cases that are subjected more commonly to arbitration than state court litigation (see also para 18.6.3).

A point of attention that De Ly raises in the context of the scope of confidentiality is the communication between arbitrators (and others involved in the proceedings) and the administering arbitration institute. It is necessary to avoid situations in which the institute acts as a "seventh arbitrator" (in addition to the secretary and associates of (co-)arbitrators, who are referred to as fourth, fifth or sixth arbitrators, respectively). Another concern De Ly raises relates to the exchange of confidential information between the parties and party witnesses and experts (see para 18.6.4 for both issues). Finally, De Ly points out that, leaving aside the fact that the principle of confidentiality has several exceptions, enforcement of this principle – to whatever extent one wishes to adhere to it today – is a challenging endeavour.

24.4 The arbitral award

In the end, it is a simple truth that arbitral proceedings are initiated with a view to obtaining an enforceable award. These awards do come with their own considerations and challenges, however. A number of these are set out in the contributions to this volume, of which we provide a brief overview below.

24.4.1 Costs

An unmistakable aspect of the decision to choose between court litigation or arbitration is the costs that are involved. In their contribution, Van de Hel-Koedoot and Fritschy take on the task of examining the award on costs in NAI arbitration (chapter 19). They state that the costs of arbitration are generally high – and in most cases considerably higher than the costs of proceedings before a (Dutch) state court. The most important element of these costs is often related to the legal assistance of the parties. More specifically, parties may risk having to pay the costs of legal assistance of the opposing parties, or (inversely) they may in fact be able to get those costs reimbursed entirely. This cannot be said for certain, however, and for that reason Van de Hel-Koedoot and Fritschy offer several suggestions to eliminate those uncertainties as much as possible. Particularly, they examine the NAI's current regime of the cost award, found in Article 59 of the 2024 NAI Rules and now supplemented by the rule that the arbitral tribunal may take into account the manner in which parties have conducted the proceedings (Article 59(4) 2024 NAI Rules), and consider that arbitral tribunals have significant discretion in arriving at a particular cost order under the Rules. They raise the possibility that the concomitant uncertainties may pose a risk to parties considering arbitration (paras 19.2-19.4). For that reason, they argue that the NAI Rules should explicitly include that the parties are free to briefly state in their cost submission whether, in their opinion, there is reason for the arbitral tribunal to take into account certain procedural conduct of the parties in its decision on costs. Specifically, parties can make it known that, in their opinion, the other party has unnecessarily delayed or complicated the proceedings. In accordance with their proposal, such "cost contentions" can then be debated in two rounds, where in both instances parties simultaneously submit their contentions (para 19.5). In addition, Van de Hel-Koedoot and Fritschy find that it is often difficult to understand on what basis the arbitral tribunal has arrived at a certain award on costs. They take the position that, regardless of whether cost-oriented arguments have been made, Article 59 2024 NAI Rules leaves room to recognise an (increased) obligation of the arbitral tribunal to offer reasons in this regard. Essentially, Van de Hel-Koedoot and Fritschy argue that the arbitral tribunal must, in principle, always provide reasons for their cost order. There are two exceptions to (or deviations from) this premise. First, in case there are no (argued) "exceptional circumstances" as meant in Article 59(2) 2024 NAI Rules, which provides that the unsuccessful party is ordered to pay the costs of the arbitration except in exceptional circumstances, the arbitral tribunal may suffice by (simply) applying the main rule of 59(2) NAI Rules after taking note of the lack of such circumstances. Second, an *increased* obligation to provide reasons may be assumed if the tribunal deviates from that main rule – the arbitral tribunal must explicitly motivate why exceptional circumstances exist (para 19.6). Also with these suggestions, Van de Hel-Koedoot and Fritschy hope to come to a result where the NAI may become an even more attractive alternative to state court proceedings (para 19.7).

24.4.2 The possibility of an oral award

On the basis of Article 1057(2) DCCP, an arbitral award must be made in writing. The Dutch Arbitration Act does not provide for the possibility of an oral arbitral award. This differs from the new Article 29a DCCP, which was added on 1 May 2023 (and which replaced Article 30p DCCP, which itself was introduced on 1 September 2017). Whereas Sanders believes that the award being written is a *must*, Van Mierlo finds that his views are unconvincing (chapter 20). He considers that arbitrators – like the courts – can indeed make an oral award, but – also like the courts – have the obligation to record this oral award in writing. He may count on support from both Snijders and Meijer on this point. As to the time limit within which the written record of the oral award must be made, Van Mierlo seeks guidance from the Supreme Court's decision of 20 April 2018, and assumes that this record should be made as soon as possible, preferably within a few days, but no later than two weeks after the oral award. Should this period – unexpectedly – be exceeded, this does not affect the validity of the oral award. However, it can have consequences for the determination of which date the person seeking to bring an action for setting aside the (oral) award must ultimately raise the relevant grounds (see para 20.4.3, where Van Mierlo also discusses other relevant aspects of the oral arbitral award). The oral award, like an oral court judgment, remains the exception, justified only when there is a sufficiently compelling reason for it such as an urgent interest in obtaining a decision. That said, Van Mierlo applauds the NAI's decision to include the possibility of an oral award in its new 2024 Rules. Aside from a (similar) possibility to issue an oral decision in challenge proceedings (Article B3(7) 2024 NAI Rules), NAI arbitrators can now render an oral award in emergency arbitration on the basis of Article C8 2024 NAI Rules. Van Mierlo takes joy from this amendment, and encourages the legislator to supplement the Dutch Arbitration Act with its own version of Article 29a DCCP (para 20.4.4-20.5).

24.4.3 *Consent awards*

Ortolani pays attention to various aspects of the so-called arbitral consent award, both from a national and international perspective (chapter 21). An arbitral consent award is understood as an award in which an arbitral tribunal records a settlement reached by the parties, upon their request (see Article 1069 DCCP). This can occur during the course of the arbitral proceedings. It can also occur after parties have, for example, concluded a settlement agreement in the context of mediation and wish to have the terms of their settlement recorded into an arbitral award. Both the 2024 NAI Rules (Article 51) and the 2017 NAI Mediation Rules (Article 8) explicitly provide for this possibility (as do the rules of various other ADR institutes). Parties usually request that their settlement be recorded in a consent award for the purposes of enforcement, but other considerations may also play a role in this choice (see para 21.2). Consent awards can be subject to complications, or at least raise various questions, however, particularly (though not limited to) where it concerns the ability to seek recognition and enforcement thereof. This applies in particular to an arbitral consent award based on the outcome of a mediation. Ortolani points out that Dutch law does not provide a basis for such a consent award, as Article 1069 DCCP requires that settlement be reached during arbitral proceedings, rather than before them (similarly Article 30 of the UNCITRAL Model Law). Ortolani also raises the issue that a submission agreement concluded after the settlement, and thus when there is no longer a dispute between the parties, may be considered invalid. The "trick" proposed by Snijders, namely to determine that it could be imagined that the settlement reached during mediation is subject to a condition precedent, namely that it be subsequently recorded in an arbitral award, does not convince Ortolani (see further para 21.4). In para 21.5, Ortolani points out various grounds for refusal and setting aside that could play a role in the (international) recognition and enforcement of an arbitral consent award. An arbitral tribunal that is being requested to render a consent award must be aware of these potential issues. It is clear, however, that it is not possible to always mitigate the associated risks. Ortolani further points out that the "Convention on International Settlement Agreements Resulting from Mediation", established within the framework of UNCITRAL and also known as the Singapore Convention, might result in solving a number of the (enforcement) issues Ortolani set out, but there are still some lingering questions and potential complications (para 21.6). Regardless of the exclusion of liability of arbitrators and the institutes itself, as applied by most ADR institutes including the NAI, Ortolani's contribution illustrates the desirability of alerting parties to the potential risks of an arbitral consent award, at least for the time being.

24.4.4 *Flawed awards*

On the rare occasion that an award does not stand up to scrutiny, there are a few options that are open to the parties, the arbitrators, and the courts. Correction and supplementation of the award is one option, for example, provided that the circumstances allow for such a measure. Another option is to set aside the award. Such setting aside may be prevented, however, if the court instead decides to remit the award to the arbitral tribunal. Van den Nieuwendijk, and Ernste and Schleijpen discuss these topics in detail.

Van den Nieuwendijk elaborates on the possibility to correct (manifest) clerical errors in an award (by party request or on an *ex officio* basis) and the possibility to supplement an award if the tribunal has failed to decide on all claims presented by the parties (chapter 22). She then extensively assesses the various time limits that can apply to correction and/or supplementation (see para 22.2), and warns that these time limits are often *shorter* than the statutory time limit of three months. The same was the case in the old 2015 NAI Rules, which provided that requests for correction and/or supplementation had to be made two months after the date of the award. However, in Article 54(1) and 55(1) the new 2024 NAI Rules provide that such a request must be made within three months after the date of transmission of the award, also meaning that parties will have an additional four weeks as Dutch statutory law provides for a fiction that entails that awards shall be deemed to have been sent if four weeks have elapsed after the date of the award (Article 1058(2) DCCP) (see para 22.2.1-22.2.2). She also discusses the length of the proceedings for correction and/or supplementation (para 22.3), and the options that are open to parties if the aforementioned time limits have already expired, such as an interpretation of the arbitral award as it was intended by the arbitral tribunal in case of a clerical error (para 22.4).

Moreover, Van den Nieuwendijk makes four different recommendations for arbitrators and/or arbitration institutes (and the NAI in particular) (para 22.6). This includes a checklist for arbitrators, which they may use when preparing the arbitral award (similar to the ICC Award Checklist), and a checklist for arbitrators regarding correction and supplementation (similar to the ICC Checklist on Correction and Interpretation of Awards). She includes her suggested checklists as appendices to her contribution. Moreover, she recommends that the NAI (or rather the responsible person of the Case Management Committee) request additional administration fees from applicants seeking correction and/or supplementation. This would also be done to discourage parties from making a request frivolously. If the request for correction is valid, and a correction follows, the additional administration fees will then be refundable. This approach may not be suitable when an additional award is made, however. Finally, Van den Nieuwendijk examines the NAI's new scrutiny provision (Article 50(4) 2024 NAI Rules). Van den Nieuwendijk argues that, aside from the additional award, this scrutiny should also apply to the decision to correct and a rejection of a request for correction and/or supplementation. She expects that, by usage and implementation of her suggestions, the number of clerical errors and/or failures to decide certain claims in arbitral awards will be reduced and that, as a result, the number of requests for correction and/or supplementation, refusals of leave to enforce and claims for setting aside can also be further reduced. This would also further guarantee the quality and uniformity of arbitral awards (para 22.7).

Ernste and Schleijpen demonstrate in their contribution that case law of the lower courts shows that an arbitral award will not quickly be set aside. This is the correct approach (in our opinion): the effectiveness of arbitration requires that the action to set aside an award must qualify as an ultimum remedium, rather than a means to effectuate an (disguised) appeal. That said, the setting aside of an award still occurs on a regular basis. In their updated study of case law up to September 2024, Ernste and Schleijpen found that of the 272 cases studied, 55 led to the setting aside of the arbitral award. Thus, while it is not a common occurrence, the risk of setting aside is real. The dividing line between what leads to setting aside and what does not cannot always be drawn sharply, however, and arbitrators cannot always know what circumstances expose an award to setting aside and how they are supposed to act to avoid setting aside. Though it is likely impossible to draw a clear dividing line between the permissible and impermissible, as specific (relevant) circumstances will always differ from case to case, it is imperative that the setting aside courts maintain their restrictive approach – also in light of the aforementioned number of cases wherein an award was set aside. In an extensive examination, Ernste and Schleijpen aptly take on the task of investigating available case law and literature on the setting aside of arbitral awards, as well as the role that the option of remission (pursuant to Article 1065a DCCP) plays within this context, to formulate a number of points, subdivided between the different setting aside grounds of Article 1065(1) DCCP, that the (NAI) arbitrator must pay attention to during the proceedings and when drafting the award. One example is the necessary (and proper) determination of which parties are actually bound to the arbitration agreement in question. Another is the adherence to the relevant requirements when signing the award. Still, while caution is always prudent, not every purported mistake must lead to setting aside. This already follows quite clearly from the aforementioned restrictive approach the setting aside courts must use. The subsequent question is whether the mechanism of remission could play a bigger part in this. Sadly, it appears that, at present, arbitrators would do well not to count on a potential remission. There are some encouraging signs of its usage by the courts, however,[5] and it must also be said that Er-

5 The Hague Court of Appeal 16 October 2018, ECLI:NL:GHDHA:2018:2639, *TvA* 2019/10; Amsterdam Court of Appeal 27 November 2018, ECLI:NL:GHAMS:2018:4323, *TvA* 2019/14; Arnhem-Leeuwarden Court of Appeal 7 May 2024, ECLI:NL:GHARL:2024:3159, *TvA* 2024/60.

nste and Schleijpen conclude that NAI arbitrators are already doing well, regardless of court practice. Out of 48 cases involving an award rendered by NAI arbitrators, only eight were set aside. Of course, in this context we would also like to make mention of the NAI and its supporting role, especially with the new provision on scrutiny in the NAI Rules.

24.5 Other topics

These past years, the NAI has undertaken multiple initiatives and made a number of changes – also to its Rules – to update and to enhance the quality of its proceedings and services. Many of these have been discussed by the authors in their contributions, and some of these are found and addressed in the 2024 NAI Arbitration Rules and the Explanatory Notes (to be found in the Appendix of this volume). Below, we will highlight three of these initiatives and/or amendments based on the importance thereof.

24.5.1 Quality assurance

As NAI founder Piet Sanders once remarked, the quality of arbitration is determined by those who act as arbitrators.[6] The basic principle in arbitration is that the parties have the lead in appointing the arbitral tribunal. Although, in an arbitral tribunal consisting of multiple arbitrators, both co-arbitrators will usually appoint the chair (along with the NAI Case Management Committee), they will usually take the parties' wishes or at least objections to a particular chair into account. Appointment as arbitrator or appointment as chairman by the co-arbitrators are not in themselves subject to any (quality) requirements, even if the arbitration is under the purview of an institute such as the NAI. In the course of the proceedings, the NAI Arbitration Rules provide for the possibility of releasing an arbitrator or arbitral tribunal from their mandate in the event of dysfunction.[7] With the paradigm shift introduced by the 2024 NAI Arbitration Rules where it is now the NAI (Case Management Committee) that appoints the arbitrator, albeit mostly on the basis of preceding nominations of the parties,[8] the NAI has increased opportunity to monitor the quality of the arbitrators to be appointed. By way of example, it should also be noted that, in principle, the NAI requires that arbitrators who are on its arbitrator

6 P. Sanders, *Het Nederlands arbitragerecht. Nationaal en internationaal*, Deventer: Kluwer 2001, p 58.
7 Article 21(5) and (6) 2024 NAI Arbitration Rules.
8 Article 15(3) 2024 NAI Arbitration Rules.

list (and thus eligible for appointment) attend the arbitration course offered by the NAI as well as the course on drafting awards within a certain period of time.

24.5.2 Diversity and inclusion

The NAI has greatly increased its efforts in advocating for diversity and inclusion in the arbitral process. Starting in 2020, the NAI began publishing statistics in relation to this topic. Where the statistics first showed that a great majority of the arbitrators who were appointed (by the parties and co-arbitrators, via the list procedure, or directly by the NAI) were male, the ratio has markedly improved in the following years.[9] Moreover, the 2024 NAI Arbitration Rules now contain an explicit provision meant to promote the added value of diversity in arbitration. Article 15(5) provides that, when nominating and appointing arbitrators, the parties (or their counsel), the co-arbitrator(s) and the responsible member of the NAI Case Management Committee will take account of the benefits of diversity and inclusivity. The new Rules benefit the cause of diversity in one more way, however. Article 16(2) provides that, in case an arbitral tribunal consisting of three or more members is to be composed, the two appointed co-arbitrators will, within fourteen days of a request to that effect by the responsible member of the NAI Case Management Committee, jointly with the latter on the basis of unanimity appoint a chair, stating the name, address, place of residence, telephone number and email address of the chair. During the deliberations, the responsible member can clarify and point to certain persons that have a certain profile or that are suited to take on the role of arbitrator and/or chair. The NAI has worked diligently the past years to ensure that its pool of arbitrators has become more diverse, especially in relation to age and gender. This new process is aimed at preventing a perception that only a small group of persons gets appointed as arbitrators, who subsequently only appoint themselves.

Indeed, the benefits of diversity and inclusion are evident. Diverse viewpoints, provided the opportunity to be shared, are a definite benefit to the decision-making process, also (and perhaps especially) in relation to the discussions amongst the members of the arbitral tribunal. The image of arbitration will also benefit from a more diverse cast. A diverse group of

9 In 2023, arbitrators appointed by the parties and co-arbitrators were 32 % female and 68 % male, arbitrators appointed via the list procedure were 39 % female and 61 % male, and arbitrators appointed directly by the NAI were 54 % female and 46 % male.

(potential) arbitrators will allow arbitration as a form of dispute resolution to stay in touch with the needs of its users.

24.5.3 E-arbitration and sustainability

Spurred on by the COVID-pandemic, the NAI has taken steps to promote a more sustainable way of conducting arbitral proceedings, which are now also enshrined in the 2024 NAI Arbitration Rules. Particularly, the usage of electronic means of communications has been given a more prominent place. Article 4(2) of the Rules provides that (in principle) requests, communications and other documents will only be transmitted electronically, either by email or by submitting or posting them on the NAI arbitration platform. In expedited proceedings, both the case management conference and the hearing will also (in principle) be held electronically (Article D5 and D8(2)). This is not a requirement as such in regular proceedings, however Article 26(2)(c) provides that during the case management conference the arbitral tribunal will address the use of electronic means, in particular the NAI arbitration platform, as well as the need for specific data security measures when electronic means are used. By adding this provision, the NAI seeks to ensure that also in these proceedings the arbitral tribunal actively checks what the parties' wishes are in relation to electronic hearings. Finally, Article 25(5) provides that the parties, the person or persons representing them, the arbitral tribunal, the responsible member of the NAI Case Management Committee and the NAI Secretariat will take aspects of sustainability into account when conducting the proceedings. Aside from electronic means of conducting the proceedings, this provision also refers to the usage of suppliers and service providers that make use of sustainable business practices, as well as the limitation of CO_2 emissions when travelling on the basis of the arbitration.

On a more general note, the NAI has also signed the Green Pledge in 2022. Also in that light, it is determined to promote increasingly green and sustainable arbitrations.

24.6 Conclusion

Arbitration and the NAI are thriving. Users of (NAI) arbitration describe it as a good, efficient and high-quality method of dispute resolution, as several reflections in the volume also make clear. Admittedly, the cost of arbitration is quite often perceived as high compared to the cost of state court proceedings, but ultimately this turns out to be somewhat misleading.[10] This is mainly because arbitral proceedings generally have a shorter turnaround time than proceedings at the state courts, and appeal (and cassation) are, in principle, not an issue (unless the parties agree otherwise). Positive reviews of arbitration and arbitration at the NAI does not mean that the NAI has reason to rest on its laurels, however. It is important to maintain and further strengthen this reputation, both at a national and international level. The NAI Board, together with the director, the other NAI staff and the Advisory Board, is happy to take on this challenge. In doing so, it feels partly inspired by the contributions in this volume. Aside from the positive, the NAI Board can take cognisance of the challenges and areas for improvement identified by the authors, such as the necessity to further develop corporate mediation.

On behalf of the NAI Board, we once again thank the authors for their contributions!

10 See Tomas Vaal: https://www.generalcounsel.nl/diamondbox/bespaar-tijd-en-kosten-met-arbitrage/.

APPENDIX

NAI RULES (31 December 2024)

Article 1	–	Definitions	670
Article 2	–	Netherlands Arbitration Institute	671
Article 3	–	Scope and amendments of the Rules	672
Article 4	–	Communications	672
Article 5	–	Time limits	673
Article 6	–	Language	673
Article 7	–	Confidentiality of the arbitration and publication of awards, orders and decisions	674
Article 8	–	Request for arbitration	674
Article 9	–	Short answer	676
Article 10	–	Purport of the request for arbitration and the short answer	677
Article 11	–	Multi-contract	678
Article 12	–	Contesting the jurisdiction of the arbitral tribunal	678
Article 13	–	The arbitrator	679
Article 14	–	Number of arbitrators	679
Article 15	–	Composition of the arbitral tribunal	680
Article 16	–	Nomination of prospective arbitrators by a party	681
Article 17	–	List procedure	682
Article 18	–	Another method of composition of the arbitral tribunal agreed upon by the parties	683
Article 19	–	Composition of the arbitral tribunal where there are multiple claimants and/or respondents	684
Article 20	–	Making available of the arbitration file	684
Article 21	–	Release from mandate	684
Article 22	–	Replacement of an arbitrator	685
Article 23	–	Challenge of an arbitrator	685
Article 24	–	Secretary	686
Article 25	–	Manner of proceedings	687
Article 26	–	Case management conference and determining the order of the proceedings	687
Article 27	–	Place of the arbitration	688

Article 28	–	Appearance in person or by legal representative	688
Article 29	–	Exchange of written statements	689
Article 30	–	Midstream conference	689
Article 31	–	Counterclaim	689
Article 32	–	Hearing	689
Article 33	–	Amendment of the claim	690
Article 34	–	Evidence in general	690
Article 35	–	Production of documents	690
Article 36	–	Witnesses and experts	691
Article 37	–	Appointment of an expert by the arbitral tribunal	691
Article 38	–	On-site inspection	692
Article 39	–	Default of a party	692
Article 40	–	Interim measures	693
Article 41	–	Emergency arbitration	693
Article 42	–	Expedited arbitration	694
Article 43	–	Joinder or intervention and impleader	694
Article 44	–	Consolidation of arbitral proceedings	695
Article 45	–	Early determination	696
Article 46	–	Time limit	696
Article 47	–	Types of awards	696
Article 48	–	Measure for decision-making	696
Article 49	–	Decision and signing	697
Article 50	–	Contents of the award	697
Article 51	–	Award on agreed terms	698
Article 52	–	Transmission and deposit of the award	699
Article 53	–	Binding effect of the award	699
Article 54	–	Rectification of the award	699
Article 55	–	Additional award	700
Article 56	–	Costs of the arbitration and costs of legal assistance	700
Article 57	–	Administration fees	701
Article 58	–	Advance on costs, fees and disbursements of the arbitrator(s)	701
Article 59	–	Award on costs	703
Article 60	–	Timely objection	704
Article 61	–	Competent provisional relief judge	704
Article 62	–	Contingencies	704
Article 63	–	Processing of personal data and data protection	704
Article 64	–	Limitation of liability	704
Article 65	–	Choice of forum	705

Article A1 –	Tasks and composition	705
Article A2 –	Conduct	706
Article A3 –	Decision-making by the members of the NAI Case Management Committee	706
Article B1 –	Duties of Challenge Committee, Challenge Chamber and the Challenge Committee Secretariat	706
Article B2 –	Composition of Challenge Committee, Challenge Chamber and the Challenge Committee Secretariat	707
Article B3 –	Conduct of Challenge Committee and Challenge Chamber	708
Article C1 –	Request for arbitration	709
Article C2 –	Composition of the arbitral tribunal	710
Article C3 –	Conduct of the proceedings	710
Article C4 –	Contesting the jurisdiction of the arbitral tribunal	710
Article C5 –	Counterclaim	711
Article C6 –	Hearing	711
Article C7 –	Costs	711
Article C8 –	Award	711
Article D1 –	Applicability	712
Article D2 –	Request for arbitration	712
Article D3 –	Short answer	713
Article D4 –	Composition of the arbitral tribunal	713
Article D5 –	Case management conference and determining the order of the proceedings	714
Article D6 –	Procedure	714
Article D7 –	Counterclaim	715
Article D8 –	Hearing	715
Article D9 –	Decision on expedited arbitration	716
Article D10 –	Costs	716
Article D11 –	Award	716
Article E1 –	Request for consolidation	717
Article E2 –	Designation of consolidator	717
Article E3 –	Requirements	717
Article E4 –	Decision	717
Article E5 –	Arbitral tribunal after consolidation	718
Article F1 –	The monetary interest of the claims	718
Article F2 –	Administration fees	719
Article F3 –	The arbitrator(s) fees, disbursements and the advance	720

SECTION ONE – GENERAL

Article 1 – Definitions

In these Rules, the following terms have the following meaning:

(a) "appointment": the appointment of an arbitrator pursuant to these Rules;
(b) "Executive Board": the executive board of the NAI;
(c) "day": a calendar day;
(d) "third person": one or, insofar as applicable, more legal or natural persons making a request for joinder or intervention in accordance with Article 43 or one or, insofar as applicable, more legal or natural persons impleaded in accordance with Article 43;
(e) "claimant": one or, insofar as applicable, more claimants;
(f) "prospective arbitrator": a natural person of legal capacity who has been nominated for appointment as an arbitrator in accordance with Section Three and Section Four;
(g) "NAI": the Netherlands Arbitration Institute (*Stichting Nederlands Arbitrage Instituut*);
(h) "NAI Case Management Committee": the committee established by the Executive Board whose members are entrusted with the administration of arbitrations as defined in the Rules. The composition of the NAI Case Management Committee and the duties of its members are detailed in Appendix A;
(i) "NAI arbitration platform": a digital data processing system of the NAI which participants can use to exchange documents electronically;
(j) "NAI Secretariat": the members of the NAI who are entrusted with supporting the administration of arbitrations by the members of the NAI Case Management Committee as defined in the Rules and Appendix A;
(k) "arbitration agreement": an agreement by which the parties bind themselves to submit to arbitration any disputes that have arisen or may arise between them from a defined legal relationship, whether contractual or not, and/or an agreement by which the parties bind themselves to submit to arbitration the determination only of the quality or condition of goods, and/or the determination only of the quantum of damages or monetary amount owed, and/or the filling of gaps or modification of the legal relationship as referred to in the first part of this sentence;
(l) "party" or "parties": the claimant and/or the respondent, and/ or a third person;

(m) "Rules": these NAI Arbitration Rules, including Appendices A, B, C, D, E and F, which Appendices form an integral part of these Rules;
(n) "consolidator": the person charged with deciding on requests for consolidation as referred to in Article 44 and Appendix E;
(o) "arbitral tribunal": an arbitral tribunal consisting of one or more arbitrators that has been composed in accordance with the provisions of the Rules or according to the applicable rules of arbitration law in an arbitration under the Rules;
(p) "Challenge Committee Secretariat": the persons designated by the Executive Board who are entrusted with supporting the processing of challenge requests as referred to in Article 23 and in Appendix B;
(q) "documents": procedural and other documents, including data on a data carrier as well as procedural and other documents submitted by electronic means;
(r) "respondent": one or, insofar as applicable, more respondents;
(s) "chair": the chair of the arbitral tribunal appointed in accordance with Article 15(7), Article 16, Article 17, Article 18, Article 41, Article 42 or Article 44, in conjuction with Article 15(3), or Article 15(2)(d), and in the case of an arbitral tribunal composed of a single arbitrator, that arbitrator;
(t) "Challenge Committee": the committee entrusted with handling challenge requests as referred to in Article 23 and Appendix B; and
(u) "Challenge Chamber": the chamber composed by the chair of the Challenge Committee to decide on the merits of a challenge pursuant to Article 23 and Appendix B.

Article 2 – Netherlands Arbitration Institute

1. The NAI is a foundation (stichting) incorporated under Dutch law.
2. The NAI itself does not resolve disputes that are submitted or to be submitted to an arbitral tribunal.
3. Decisions and/or actions by members of the NAI Case Management Committee, the NAI Secretariat, the Challenge Committee, the Challenge Chamber, the Challenge Committee Secretariat and/or the consolidator are binding on the parties and the arbitral tribunal, except where the Rules provide otherwise.
4. Without prejudice to any provision of applicable mandatory arbitration law, the parties and the arbitral tribunal (and the members of the arbitral tribunal) are deemed to have waived any right of appeal, revision or review with respect to decisions as referred to in paragraph 3.

Article 3 – Scope and amendments of the Rules

1. The Rules apply where the parties have referred to arbitration by or before the NAI or in accordance with the Rules.
2. The Rules apply in the form they have at the time at which the arbitration is commenced. Amendments to the Rules have no effect on arbitrations that have already been commenced at the time of amendment of the Rules.
3. In derogation of paragraph 2, Article 44 and Article 48(1) and (3) only apply to arbitration agreements concluded on or after 1 January 2015 in which the parties have referred to arbitration by or before the NAI or in accordance with the Rules, unless the parties have agreed otherwise. Arbitration agreements concluded before 1 January 2015 continue to be subject to Article 45 and, in connection therewith Article 1(g), of the NAI 2010 Arbitration Rules. In derogation of paragraph 2, Article 42(1) applies only to arbitration agreements concluded on or after 1 March 2024.

Article 4 – Communications

1. All communications must be made in writing in the manner provided for in this article.
2. Subject to the provisions of Article 8(3), Article 9(1) and (4), Article 52 and Article 54(7), requests, communications or other documents will only be transmitted electronically, either by email or by submitting or posting them on the NAI arbitration platform.
3. The time at which a request, communication or other document is transmitted electronically is:
   (a) when transmitted by email: the time at which the request, communication or other document reaches a data processing system for which the sender has no responsibility; or
   (b) when using the NAI arbitration platform: the time at which the request, communication or other document is placed on the NAI arbitration platform.
4. The time at which a request, communication or other document is received electronically is:
   (a) when transmitted by email: the time at which the request, communication or other document reaches a data processing system for which the recipient is responsible; or

(b) when using the NAI arbitration platform: the time at which the request, communication or other document is placed on the NAI arbitration platform.

Article 5 – Time limits

1. For the purposes of the Rules, a time limit commences on the day a request, communication or other document is transmitted and, if not transmitted in electronic form as provided for in Article 4, on the day of receipt of a request, communication or other document except where the Rules or the arbitral tribunal explicitly provide otherwise.
2. The responsible member of the NAI Case Management Committee is authorised, at the request of a party, the arbitral tribunal, or of its own motion, to extend or shorten the time limits as referred to in Article 6(2) and (3), Article 9(4), Article 13(3), Article 15(4) and (7), Article 16(1) and (2), Article 17(2), Article 18, Article 26(1) and (3), Article 45(2), Article 46(1), Article 57(4) and Article 58(4). The same applies to the time limits in Article C7(2), Article C8(1), Article D3, Article D4(2) and (5), Article D5, Article D7(2), Article D9, Article D10(2), Article D11(1), Article E2(1) and Article E5(1).
3. In exceptional circumstances, the arbitral tribunal is authorised, at the request of a party or of its own motion, to extend a time limit set by the arbitral tribunal or agreed by the parties.

Article 6 – Language

1. The proceedings are conducted in the language or languages agreed by the parties or, in the absence of such agreement, in the language or languages determined by the arbitral tribunal. Until such time as the arbitral tribunal has determined the language or languages, the responsible member of the NAI Case Management Committee may provisionally determine the language or languages.
2. Until such time as the arbitral tribunal has determined the language or languages referred to in paragraph 1, the responsible member of the NAI Case Management Committee may, at the request of the counterparty or of its own motion, require a party to submit, within a time limit as determined by the responsible member of the NAI Case Management Committee, a translation of the requests, communications and/or other documents it has submitted in a language in which the counterparty is proficient.
3. Without prejudice to the provisions of paragraphs 1 and 2, if any request, communication or other document is made in a language in

which the responsible member of the NAI Case Management Committee or the arbitral tribunal is not proficient, the responsible member of the NAI Case Management Committee and the arbitral tribunal may require the party making the request or communication or submitting the document to arrange for a translation into a language determined by the responsible member of the NAI Case Management Committee or the arbitral tribunal, within a time limit determined by the responsible member of the NAI Case Management Committee or the arbitral tribunal.

4. The arbitral tribunal may make arrangements for the presence of an interpreter at a hearing.

Article 7 – Confidentiality of the arbitration and publication of awards, orders and decisions

1. An arbitration is confidential and all persons involved either directly or indirectly in an arbitration are bound to secrecy, except and insofar as disclosure ensues from the law or the parties' agreement.
2. The responsible member of the NAI Case Management Committee will send a confidentiality statement to the prospective arbitrator. The responsible member of the NAI Case Management Committee will send the statement referred to in Article 13(3), the request for arbitration, the short answer and other procedural agreements between the parties to the prospective arbitrator only after receiving the confirmation of confidentiality.
3. The NAI may publish, or have published, an award, order or a decision on a challenge, omitting the names of the parties and leaving out all other information that might reveal the parties' identities, except where a party objects to such publication with the NAI Secretariat within two months of the date of the award, order or decision on a challenge.

SECTION TWO – COMMENCEMENT OF THE ARBITRATION

Article 8 – Request for arbitration

1. An arbitration is commenced by submitting a request for arbitration to the NAI Secretariat. The arbitration is deemed to have been commenced on the day of receipt of the request for arbitration by the NAI Secretariat.
2. The request for arbitration must contain the following information:

(a) the name, the address, the postal code, the place of residence, the telephone number, the email address and, as applicable, the VAT number of each of the parties;
(b) the name, the address, the postal code, the place of residence, the telephone number and the email address of the person or persons representing the claimant in the arbitration;
(c) the email address at which and by which the claimant can be reached for electronic communications for the duration of the arbitration, and for the purposes referred to in Article 52, Article 54 and Article 55;
(d) a brief description of the dispute;
(e) a clear statement of the relief sought with a specification of the monetary interest of each of the claims, including interest, as well as an estimate of the monetary interest of each of the non-monetary claims;
(f) a reference to the arbitration agreement(s) and any other agreement(s) to which the arbitration relates, along with copies of the agreements concerned;
(g) insofar as applicable, the parties' agreement regarding an expedited arbitration as referred to in Article 42(2) or, in the absence of an agreement as referred to in Article 42(2), the claimant's preference on this matter;
(h) insofar as applicable, the name, the address, the postal code, the place of residence, the telephone number and the email address of the prospective arbitrator(s) nominated by the claimant or by the parties;
(i) where the parties have agreed on a method of composition of the arbitral tribunal that differs from Article 16, the method of composition of the arbitral tribunal;
(j) the agreement between the parties concerning the number of arbitrators, the qualifications of the arbitrator(s), the place of arbitration and the language of the arbitration or, in the absence of an agreement between the parties in this regard, the claimant's preferences on these matters;
(k) the name of any party other than the parties to the arbitration that has made an arrangement with a party to the arbitration for the financing of claims or counterclaims on the basis of which the financing party has a beneficial interest in the outcome of the arbitration. If such an arrangement is made with a party to the arbitration only after submission of the request for arbitration, this party must share this information with all other parties to

the arbitration, the prospective arbitrator(s) or the arbitrator(s) and the responsible member of the NAI Case Management Committee as soon as possible; and

(l) insofar as applicable, other details of the arbitral proceedings, including whether the arbitration is being commenced pursuant to Article 11(1).

3. The request for arbitration is to be submitted in one of the manners provided for in Article 4(2). If the claimant is unable to do so, the request for arbitration may be submitted in another manner. The NAI Secretariat will confirm receipt of the request for arbitration to the claimant, stating the date of receipt.
4. The responsible member of the NAI Case Management Committee may suspend the handling of the request for arbitration where the request does not yet satisfy the requirements mentioned in paragraph 2. This suspension does not prejudice the provisions of paragraph 1.
5. The request for arbitration may be withdrawn as long as the composition of the arbitral tribunal has not been completed. Afterwards, the request for arbitration may only be withdrawn with the permission of the arbitral tribunal, which will give the parties an opportunity to be heard. Article F2(5) applies in full.

Article 9 – Short answer

1. The NAI Secretariat will transmit a copy of the request for arbitration to the respondent, stating the date of receipt, and will invite the respondent to submit a short written answer in response. A copy of the invitation will simultaneously be transmitted to the claimant.
2. The short answer must contain the following information:
   (a) the name, the address, the postal code, the place of residence, the telephone number, the email address and, as applicable, the VAT number of the respondent;
   (b) the name, the address, the postal code, the place of residence, the telephone number and the email address of the person or persons representing the respondent in the arbitration;
   (c) the email address at which and by which the respondent can be reached for electronic communications for the duration of the arbitration, and for the purposes referred to in Article 52, Article 54 and Article 55;
   (d) a response to the information referred to in Article 8(2)(e), (f), (g), and (j) and, to the extent that it concerns the parties' nomination of one or more prospective arbitrators, the information referred to in Article 8(2)(h), (i), and also (j);

(e) insofar as applicable, the name, the address, the postal code, the place of residence, the telephone number and the email address of the prospective arbitrator(s) nominated by the parties;
(f) the name of any party other than the parties to the arbitration that has made an arrangement with a party to the arbitration for the financing of claims or counterclaims on the basis of which the financing party has a beneficial interest in the outcome of the arbitration. If such an arrangement is made with a party to the arbitration only after submission of the short answer, this party must share this information with all other parties to the arbitration, the prospective arbitrator(s) or the arbitrator(s) and the responsible member of the NAI Case Management Committee as soon as possible; and
(g) insofar as applicable, any other particulars concerning the arbitral procedure, including a response to the particulars specified by the claimant as referred to in Article 8(2)(l).

3. In the short answer, the respondent may file a counterclaim against the claimant with due observance of the provisions of Article 31(2). The requirements mentioned in Article 8(2)(d),(e), (f) and (l) apply *mutatis mutandis* to the filing of a counterclaim.
4. The respondent must submit the short answer to the NAI Secretariat within fourteen days of the transmission of the invitation referred to in paragraph 1 in one of the manners provided for in Article 4(2) and transmit a copy of the short answer to the claimant at the same time. If the respondent is unable to transmit the short answer electronically, the short answer may be submitted to the NAI Secretariat by other means within this time limit, with a copy transmitted to the claimant at the same time. The NAI Secretariat will confirm to the parties the receipt of the short answer.

Article 10 – Purport of the request for arbitration and the short answer

1. The request for arbitration and the short answer do not prejudice the parties' right to present a statement of claim or a statement of defence, respectively, with due observance of the provisions in Article 29.
2. Insofar the responsible member of the NAI Case Management Committee is involved in the determination of an estimate of the monetary interest of the claims or counterclaims, the determination of the number of arbitrators and/or the direct appointment of the arbitrator(s), the responsible member of the NAI Case Management Committee

may rely on the request for arbitration and the short answer to derive the necessary information.

Article 11 – Multi-contract

1. Without prejudice to any other provision of the Rules, claims relating to disputes arising from more than one contract may also be dealt with in a single arbitration, to the extent that such disputes between the same parties are subject to arbitration by or before the NAI or in accordance with the Rules.
2. If, prior to the completion of the composition of the arbitral tribunal, a party disputes that the conditions of paragraph 1 have been met, the responsible member of the NAI Case Management Committee will decide whether the arbitration will be administered in accordance with the provisions of paragraph 1, where applicable in anticipation of a possible decision of the arbitral tribunal on the basis of paragraph 3.
3. Once the composition of the arbitral tribunal has been completed, a party may submit to the arbitral tribunal that the conditions of paragraph 1 have not been met. The arbitral tribunal will decide in accordance with the provisions of paragraph 1.

Article 12 – Contesting the jurisdiction of the arbitral tribunal

1. A party that has appeared in the arbitration and that wishes to contest the jurisdiction of the arbitral tribunal must do so before submitting any defence, i.e. in the statement of defence or, where no statement of defence is filed, no later than in the first written or oral defence after the arbitral tribunal has been constituted.
2. Cooperating in the appointment of the arbitrator(s) in the manner provided for in Section Three and Section Four does not cause the parties to forfeit the right to contest the jurisdiction of the arbitral tribunal on the ground of the non-existence of a valid arbitration agreement.
3. If a party that has appeared in the arbitration has omitted to contest the jurisdiction of the arbitral tribunal in accordance with the provisions of paragraph 1, its right to rely on this later, in the arbitration or before the court, is forfeited, except where jurisdiction is contested on the ground that the dispute is not capable of settlement by arbitration.
4. The arbitral tribunal decides on pleas contesting its jurisdiction.
5. If the arbitral tribunal decides it has no jurisdiction, the declaration of lack of jurisdiction qualifies as an award. The provisions of Section Five, Section Six, and Section Seven apply in full.

6. An arbitration agreement is to be considered and decided upon as a separate agreement. The arbitral tribunal has the power to decide on the existence and the validity of the main contract of which the arbitration agreement forms part or to which it is related.
7. A plea contesting the jurisdiction of the arbitral tribunal does not prevent the responsible member of the NAI Case Management Committee from administering the arbitration. This is subject to the Rules.

SECTION THREE – THE ARBITRAL TRIBUNAL

Article 13 – The arbitrator

1. Any natural person of legal capacity may be appointed as an arbitrator. Subject to the provisions of Article 16(3) and Article 17(4), no person is precluded from appointment by reason of his or her nationality.
2. An arbitrator must perform his or her mandate independently, impartially and to the best of his or her knowledge.
3. A prospective arbitrator intending to accept an assignment as an arbitrator must make a statement prior to appointment by the responsible member of the NAI Case Management Committee confirming his or her independence and impartiality, availability, electronic means of contact in accordance with the Rules and acceptance of the mandate, subject to appointment by the responsible member of the NAI Case Management Committee. In the statement, a prospective arbitrator who has reason to suspect that there might be justifiable doubts as to his or her impartiality or independence must communicate this in writing, stating the suspected reason(s). Prior to the appointment, the responsible member of the NAI Case Management Committee will transmit copies of the statement to the parties and, where the arbitral tribunal consists of more than one arbitrator, to the other arbitrator(s) or to the other prospective arbitrator(s) and set a time limit for the parties to submit any comments.
4. An arbitrator who, during the arbitration, suspects that justifiable doubts as to his or her impartiality or independence might arise must without delay communicate this in writing to the responsible member of the NAI Case Management Committee, the parties and, where the arbitral tribunal consists of multiple arbitrators, to the other arbitrators in writing, stating the suspected reason(s).

Article 14 – Number of arbitrators

1. The proceedings are conducted before a single arbitrator or another odd number of arbitrators.
2. Where the parties have not agreed on the number of arbitrators, or where the agreed method of determining that number of arbitrators is not carried out and the parties cannot reach agreement on the number, the responsible member of the NAI Case Management Committee will set the number at one or three, taking account of the parties' preferences, the scope of the dispute, the monetary interest of the claims, the complexity of the dispute and the parties' interest in efficient proceedings.
3. If the parties have agreed on an even number of arbitrators, an additional arbitrator will be appointed as the chair in accordance with the provisions of Article 16(2).

Article 15 – Composition of the arbitral tribunal

1. The arbitral tribunal is composed once the arbitrator(s) has (have) been appointed.
2. The arbitral tribunal is composed on the basis of the methods mentioned in this provision as well as in Article 16, Article 17, and Article 18.
3. Following the nomination of a prospective arbitrator, the responsible member of the NAI Case Management Committee will appoint the prospective arbitrator as arbitrator, subject to the provisions of paragraphs 6 and 7. Paragraph 6 applies *mutatis mutandis* to a direct appointment pursuant to paragraph 2(d).
4. Subject to the provisions of Article 18, Article C2(3) and Article D4(5), the appointment by the responsible member of the NAI Case Management Committee of the prospective arbitrator(s) is made within three months of the arbitration being commenced.
5. The parties, the person or persons representing them, the arbitrator(s) and the responsible member of the NAI Case Management Committee will take account of the benefits of diversity and inclusivity when nominating prospective arbitrator(s) and when appointing arbitrator(s) under the Rules.
6. A person will not be appointed as an arbitrator by the responsible member of the NAI Case Management Committee under the provisions of this Section Three and Article C2, Article D4 and Article E5 if, in the opinion of the responsible member of the NAI Case Management Committee, the appointment is not in accordance with the

Rules or if the person in question offers insufficient safeguards for sound arbitration.

7. If, pursuant to paragraph 6, the nomination of the prospective arbitrator is not followed, the responsible member of the NAI Case Management Committee will, within fourteen days after the responsible member of the NAI Case Management Committee has communicated this to the prospective arbitrator, the parties, and the arbitrator(s) already appointed, request the party or parties that was or were entitled to nominate the prospective arbitrator in question or the consolidator entitled to nominate the prospective arbitrator(s) in question based on Article E5(1), to nominate another prospective arbitrator. If the parties have agreed on appointment under the list procedure referred to in Article 17, the responsible member of the NAI Case Management Committee will, in accordance with that procedure, invite the parties to express their preferences and/or objections with respect to any persons not featured on the initial list. On the basis of the foregoing, the responsible member of the NAI Case Management Committee will appoint an arbitrator, co-arbitrator or chair, with due observance of the provisions of paragraph 6. If this does not result in the appointment of an arbitrator, the responsible member of the NAI Case Management Committee will directly appoint the relevant arbitrator.

Article 16 – Nomination of prospective arbitrators by a party

1. Where an arbitral tribunal consisting of one arbitrator is to be composed, the parties must notify the responsible member of the NAI Case Management Committee, no later than fourteen days after the date on which the short answer must be submitted, of the name, address, postal code, place of residence, telephone number and email address of the prospective arbitrator nominated by them jointly. The responsible member of the NAI Case Management Committee will appoint this prospective arbitrator pursuant to Article 15(3). If such notification is not received by the responsible member of the NAI Case Management Committee within this period, this member will directly appoint the arbitrator.
2. Where an arbitral tribunal consisting of three or more arbitrators is to be composed, the claimant and the respondent must, in the request for arbitration and short answer, respectively, each nominate a prospective arbitrator to be appointed as a co-arbitrator by the responsible member of the NAI Case Management Committee pursuant to

Article 15(3). If the request for arbitration or the short answer does not contain a nomination for the appointment of an arbitrator, the responsible member of the NAI Case Management Committee will directly appoint the arbitrator. The two appointed co-arbitrators will, within fourteen days of a request to that effect by the responsible member of the NAI Case Management Committee, jointly with the latter on the basis of unanimity appoint a chair, stating the name, address place of residence, telephone number and email address of the chair. If the chair has not been appointed within the aforementioned fourteen-day time period, the responsible member of the NAI Case Management Committee will directly appoint the arbitrator.

3. Where an arbitral tribunal consisting of three or more arbitrators needs to be composed in an arbitration between parties that do not have the same nationality, each of the parties may, in the request for arbitration or the short answer, require that the chair does not have the same nationality as any of the parties.

Article 17 – List procedure

1. In derogation of the method of composition provided for in Article 16, the parties may agree that the arbitrator(s) be nominated in accordance with the list procedure provided for in this Article 17. In the event of nomination of the prospective arbitrator(s) in accordance with the list procedure, the responsible member of the NAI Case Management Committee will transmit to the parties the list referred to in paragraph 2 as soon as possible after receipt of the short answer or, where a short answer is not submitted, after expiry of the time limit for submitting the short answer.
2. The responsible member of the NAI Case Management Committee will transmit an identical list of names of persons to each party. This list must contain at least three names in the event that one arbitrator is to be appointed and at least nine names, three of which being potential chairs, in the event that three or more arbitrators are to be appointed. A party may delete from the list the names of persons against whom this party has strong objections, and may number the remaining names in its order of preference. A party is not required to send a copy of the list to the counterparty. If the responsible member of the NAI Case Management Committee has not received a list back from a party within fourteen days after transmitting it, it is assumed

that all of the persons named on the list are equally acceptable to that party.

3. With due observance of any preferences and/or objections expressed by the parties, the responsible member of the NAI Case Management Committee will invite persons named on the list to serve as arbitrators. The responsible member of the NAI Case Management Committee will then appoint the arbitrator(s) based on the preferences and/or objections expressed by the parties. If the lists returned by the parties show that there is an insufficient number of persons who are acceptable as arbitrators to each of the parties, or a person will not or cannot accept the responsible member of the NAI Case Management Committee's invitation to serve as arbitrator or proves unable to serve as arbitrator for any other reasons and an insufficient number of persons remain that are acceptable as arbitrators to each of the parties, the responsible member of the NAI Case Management Committee will proceed to directly appoint a person who was not featured on the list issued to the parties.
4. Where an arbitral tribunal needs to be composed in accordance with this Article 17 in an arbitration between parties that do not have the same nationality, each of the parties may submit a notice to the responsible member of the NAI Case Management Committee stating the requirement that the chair does not have the same nationality as any of the parties.

Article 18 – Another method of composition of the arbitral tribunal agreed upon by the parties

If the parties have agreed upon a method of composition of the arbitral tribunal that deviates from Article 16 or Article 17, the nomination of (a) prospective arbitrator(s) to be appointed as arbitrator(s) will take place in the manner agreed upon by the parties. If all or part of the agreed method of composition of the arbitral tribunal has not been carried out within the period agreed upon by the parties or, failing that, within four weeks after the arbitration has been commenced, the responsible member of the NAI Case Management Committee will directly appoint the relevant arbitrator(s).

Article 19 – Composition of the arbitral tribunal where there are multiple claimants and/or respondents

1. If there are multiple claimants and/or respondents and the composition of the arbitral tribunal takes place in the manner provided in Article 16, in case of an arbitral tribunal consisting of three or more arbi-

trators, claimants will jointly nominate an arbitrator and respondents will jointly nominate an arbitrator.

2. If either the claimants fail to jointly nominate an arbitrator or the respondents jointly fail to nominate a prospective arbitrator within the time limit set in Article 16(2), all members of the arbitral tribunal will be appointed in the manner provided in Article 17.

Article 20 – Making available of the arbitration file

1. Once all the members of the arbitral tribunal have been appointed, the NAI Secretariat will immediately make the arbitration file available to the arbitral tribunal. The NAI Secretariat will promptly notify the parties of this.
2. After the NAI Secretariat has made the arbitration file available to the arbitral tribunal in accordance with paragraph 1, the parties must send their requests, communications and other documents directly to the arbitral tribunal, simultaneously transmitting these to all other parties. Every request, communication or other document must be sent simultaneously to the NAI Secretariat. The preceding sentence also applies to other requests, communications or documents from the arbitral tribunal to the parties.

Article 21 – Release from mandate

1. An arbitrator may be released from his or her mandate at his or her own request, either by consent of the parties or by consent of the responsible member of NAI Case Management Committee.
2. An arbitrator may be released from his or her mandate by the parties jointly. The parties must immediately communicate the release of mandate to the arbitrator in question and, where the arbitral tribunal consists of more than one arbitrator, the other arbitrators, as well as to the responsible member of the NAI Case Management Committee.
3. An arbitrator who has become de jure or de facto unable to perform his or her mandate may, at the request of any party, be released from his or her mandate by the responsible member of the NAI Case Management Committee.
4. The responsible member of the NAI Case Management Committee may, of its own motion, release an arbitrator from his or her mandate if he or she (i) has de jure or de facto become unable to perform his or her mandate, or (ii) is not performing his or her mandate in accordance with the Rules.

5. An arbitral tribunal may, at the request of any party, be released from its mandate by the responsible member of the NAI Case Management Committee, if, taking account of all the circumstances, it fails to perform its mandate without undue delay even after repeated demands for action have been made.
6. In the events mentioned in paragraphs 1, 3, 4 and 5, the responsible member of the NAI Case Management Committee will not proceed to release the arbitrator or the arbitral tribunal from the mandate until the parties have been given the opportunity to make their positions known to the responsible member of the NAI Case Management Committee.

Article 22 – Replacement of an arbitrator

1. Unless the parties have agreed on another manner of replacement, an arbitrator who has been released from his or her mandate or an arbitral tribunal that has been released from its mandate for any reason whatsoever will be replaced in accordance with the rules applicable to the original manner of appointment. The same applies in the event of the death of an arbitrator.
2. The proceedings become suspended by operation of law for the duration of the replacement of an arbitrator or an arbitral tribunal. After replacement, the proceedings will move forward from the stage they had reached prior to the replacement, except where the arbitral tribunal wishes to handle the case again in full or in part.

Article 23 – Challenge of an arbitrator

1. An arbitrator may be challenged by a party in accordance with the provisions of this Article 23 if there are justifiable doubts as to his or her impartiality or independence. A party may not challenge an arbitrator if it has acquiesced in his or her appointment, except where that party only became aware of the ground for the challenge afterwards.
2. A party that has reasons to challenge an arbitrator must base its challenge request on these reasons, on pain of forfeiture of the right to invoke them later in the arbitral proceedings or in court.
3. The challenging party must give written notice of the challenge, stating reasons, to the arbitrator concerned, the counterparty, the responsible member of the NAI Case Management Committee and, if the arbitral tribunal consists of multiple arbitrators, the other arbitrators. The notice of the challenge must be given within fourteen days after the reason for the challenge becomes known to the challenging party.

4. The arbitral tribunal may suspend the arbitral proceedings at any time from the day of receipt of the notice referred to in paragraph 3.
5. If a challenged arbitrator resigns, this does not imply acceptance that the reasons for the challenge are well-founded. If a challenged arbitrator resigns, the NAI Secretariat will notify the parties and, if the arbitral tribunal consists of more than one arbitrator, the other arbitrators, of this in writing.
6. If the challenged arbitrator resigns or if the Challenge Chamber decides that the challenge is well-founded, the arbitrator will be released from his or her mandate and will be replaced in accordance with the provisions of Article 22(1).
7. If a challenged arbitrator does not resign within fourteen days after the day of receipt of a notice that is within the time limit as referred to in paragraph 3, a Challenge Chamber will, if the challenge is upheld within the time limit pursuant to Article B3(2), at the request of the challenging party, decide whether the challenge is well-founded.
8. The challenge procedure referred to in this Article 23 is governed by Appendix B.

Article 24 – Secretary

1. At the request of the arbitral tribunal, the responsible member of the NAI Case Management Committee may appoint a legally qualified person as the arbitral tribunal's secretary. The provisions of Article 7(2), Article 13, Article 15(3), Article 21, Article 22 and Article 23 apply *mutatis mutandis* to a secretary.
2. The work of a secretary is performed for, on behalf of and under the supervision of the arbitral tribunal. A secretary has no decision-making authority. The arbitral tribunal is not permitted to delegate any decision-making power to a secretary.

SECTION FOUR – PROCEDURE

Article 25 – Manner of proceedings

1. Without prejudice to any provision of applicable mandatory arbitration law, the arbitral tribunal determines the manner in which and the time limits within which the proceedings will be conducted, with due observance of any arrangements between the parties in that regard, the provisions of the Rules and the circumstances of the arbitration.

2. The arbitral tribunal treats the parties equally. The arbitral tribunal must give the parties the opportunity mutually to set out and explain their positions and to comment on each other's positions and on all documents and other information brought to the attention of the arbitral tribunal during the proceedings. The arbitral tribunal may not base its decision, where it is unfavourable for one party, upon documents and other information on which that party was not sufficiently able to comment.
3. The arbitral tribunal must guard against unreasonable delay of the proceedings and, if necessary, at the request of a party or of its own motion, take measures to effectuate a just, efficient and final settlement of the dispute.
4. If a party fails to wholly or partially satisfy any provision mentioned in Section Four or any order, decision or measure of the arbitral tribunal under the provisions of Section Four, the arbitral tribunal may draw any conclusions from such failure that it considers appropriate.
5. The parties, the person or persons representing them, the arbitral tribunal, the responsible member of the NAI Case Management Committee and the NAI Secretariat will take aspects of sustainability into account when conducting the proceedings.

Article 26 – Case management conference and determining the order of the proceedings

1. A case management conference is to be held as soon as possible, but no later than three weeks after the NAI Secretariat has made the arbitration file available to the arbitral tribunal in accordance with Article 20(1). The arbitral tribunal determines the time, the place and the manner in which the case management conference is held.
2. The arbitral tribunal will in any event address the following topics at the case management conference:
   (a) also having regard to the provisions of Article 8(2)(e), the monetary interest of the claim or each of the claims, including interest, as well as the monetary interest of the non-monetary claims;
   (b) the question whether, also in view of the nature of the case, expedited arbitration as referred to in Article 42 must or may be followed;
   (c) the use of electronic means, in particular the NAI arbitration platform, as well as the need for specific data security measures when electronic means are used;

(d) the preference or need for the exchange of further written statements after the exchange of the statement of claim and the statement of defence as referred to in Article 29;
(e) preferences regarding the midstream conference as referred to in Article 30;
(f) the rules of evidence as referred to in Article 34;
(g) the preference or need for the production of documents as referred to in Article 35;
(h) the preference or need for the taking of evidence through the hearing of witnesses and/or experts as referred to in Article 36 and Article 37 and the manner in which such evidence will be taken;
(i) directions or measures concerning the protection of personal data as referred to in Article 63.

3. As soon as possible, but no later than two weeks after the case management conference, the arbitral tribunal, after consultation with the parties, will determine the order of proceedings, including a (provisional) timetable for the further course of the arbitration, including a provisional date for the award with due observance of the provisions of Article 46(1).

Article 27 – Place of the arbitration

1. Where the place of arbitration is not determined by agreement between the parties, the place of arbitration is Amsterdam.
2. Regardless of the place of arbitration, the arbitral tribunal may hold hearings, deliberate and hear witnesses and experts at any place, within or outside the Netherlands, it considers appropriate.

Article 28 – Appearance in person or by legal representative

Each party may appear in the proceedings in person, or be represented by a practising lawyer or by a representative authorised in writing for this purpose. Each party may be assisted by any persons of its choice.

Article 29 – Exchange of written statements

1. Unless the parties have agreed otherwise, the arbitral tribunal gives the claimant and the respondent the opportunity to present a statement of claim and a statement of defence, respectively.
2. Unless parties have agreed otherwise, the arbitral tribunal is free to determine whether any further written statements may be presented.

Article 30 – Midstream conference

The arbitral tribunal may at any stage of the proceedings, and will in any case after the submission of the statement of defence, order a midstream conference, taking place electronically or otherwise, for the purpose of providing information, consultation on the further course of the arbitration or for exploring the possibility of a settlement. The arbitral tribunal may also re-address the points of Article 26(2). Having heard the parties, the arbitral tribunal may designate its chair to conduct the midstream conference, unless the parties have agreed otherwise.

Article 31 – Counterclaim

1. A counterclaim is admissible if it is subject to the same arbitration agreement as the one on which the claim is based or if that same arbitration agreement has been expressly or tacitly declared applicable by the parties.
2. A counterclaim that is not filed at the latest with the statement of defence or, in the absence thereof, no later than with the first written or oral defence conducted after the NAI Secretariat has made the arbitration file available to the arbitral tribunal based on Article 20(1), cannot be filed afterwards in the same arbitration, except in exceptional circumstances at the arbitral tribunal's discretion.
3. Article 11, Article 12, Article 29, Article 33, Article 39, Article 57, Article 58 and Appendix F apply *mutatis mutandis* to the counterclaim.

Article 32 – Hearing

1. The arbitral tribunal gives the parties the opportunity to explain their case at an oral hearing, except where the parties waive that opportunity. The arbitral tribunal determines the time and place of the hearing and the manner of the hearing.
2. In addition to the parties and persons mentioned in Article 24, Article 28, Article 36 and Article 37, the arbitral tribunal, after consulting with the parties, may admit other persons to the hearing.
3. Except as provided for in Article 30 and Article 34(2), hearings are held in the presence of the full arbitral tribunal.
4. If a party, although properly having been called, fails to appear at a hearing without asserting well-founded reasons, the arbitral tribunal may move the arbitral proceedings forward and make an award.

Article 33 – Amendment of the claim

1. A party may amend or increase its claim or the grounds thereof until the beginning of the last hearing or, if no hearing is held, in the last admissible written statement. After that time, this is no longer allowed, except in exceptional circumstances at the arbitral tribunal's discretion. A party may reduce its claim(s) at any time. Article F2(5) applies in full.
2. The counterparty is authorised to object to an amendment or increase of the claim if it will be unreasonably hindered in its defence or if the proceedings will be unreasonably delayed as a result. The arbitral tribunal, after giving the parties an opportunity to be heard, will decide on the counterparty's objection as soon as possible.
3. The arbitral tribunal must give a party that has not appeared as referred to in Article 39 the opportunity to comment on an amendment or increase.

Article 34 – Evidence in general

1. Unless the parties have agreed otherwise, the arbitral tribunal is free to determine the rules of evidence, the admissibility of evidence, the allocation of the burden of proof and the evaluation of evidence.
2. Unless the parties have agreed otherwise, the arbitral tribunal, after giving the parties an opportunity to be heard, may designate its chair to hear witnesses or experts or to conduct an on-site inspection or viewing.

Article 35 – Production of documents

1. Unless the parties have agreed otherwise, the written statements referred to in Article 29 are, in as much as possible, to be accompanied by the documents relied upon by the parties.
2. Unless the parties have agreed otherwise, the arbitral tribunal may, at any party's request or of its own motion, order the inspection of, a copy of, or an extract from, specific documents related to the dispute from the party which has these documents at its disposal. The arbitral tribunal determines the conditions under which and the manner in which inspection of a copy of or an extract from documents are provided.

Article 36 – Witnesses and experts

1. The arbitral tribunal may allow the parties to furnish evidence by means of hearing witnesses and experts or, at any party's request or of its own motion, order the parties to furnish evidence by means of hearing witnesses and experts.
2. The arbitral tribunal may determine the form in which statements of witnesses and experts are given. A party may submit written witness statements or expert advice it has obtained along with the statements as referred to in Article 29. If a party so requests or if the arbitral tribunal so determines, the party submitting the advice is to call the expert to provide a further explanation at the hearing.
3. If an oral examination of witnesses or experts is to take place, the arbitral tribunal will determine the time, place and order for the oral examination and the manner in which the examination will be conducted.
4. The names of the witnesses or experts that a party wishes to have heard must be communicated to the arbitral tribunal and the counterparty in a timely manner.
5. Where the arbitral tribunal considers it necessary, it will hear the witnesses after they have sworn or affirmed that they will tell the whole truth and nothing but the truth.
6. The arbitral tribunal decides whether and in what form a report of the examination will be drawn up. A report of the examination must in any event be drawn up where the chair hears the witnesses or experts in accordance with Article 34(2).

Article 37 – Appointment of an expert by the arbitral tribunal

1. The arbitral tribunal may appoint one or more experts to give written advice. The arbitral tribunal must consult the parties regarding the terms of reference to be issued to the expert. The arbitral tribunal must transmit to the parties a copy of the decision to appoint an expert and the terms of reference given to the expert as soon as possible.
2. If a party does not provide the expert with the information he or she requires or render the cooperation he or she needs, the expert may ask the arbitral tribunal to order the relevant party to do so.
3. After receipt of the expert's report, the arbitral tribunal sends a copy thereof to the parties as soon as possible.
4. At the request of any of the parties, the experts will be heard at a hearing of the arbitral tribunal. If a party wishes to make such a request, it

must notify the arbitral tribunal and the counterparty of this as soon as possible. At the hearing, the arbitral tribunal must give the parties the opportunity to ask the expert questions.

5. Without prejudice to the provisions in paragraph 4, the arbitral tribunal must give the parties the opportunity to be heard regarding the advice of the experts appointed by the arbitral tribunal.

Article 38 – On-site inspection

The arbitral tribunal may, at the request of any of the parties or of its own motion, inspect a site or conduct a viewing, within or outside the Netherlands. The arbitral tribunal must give the parties the opportunity to be present at the on-site inspection or viewing and to subsequently express their views on the on-site inspection or viewing.

Article 39 – Default of a party

1. If the claimant fails to present a statement of claim as referred to in Article 29 within the time limit determined by the arbitral tribunal or to reasonably explain its claim within a time limit determined by the arbitral tribunal in accordance with an order of the arbitral tribunal, without asserting well-founded reasons, the arbitral tribunal may, by award, or in another manner it considers appropriate, bring an end to the arbitral proceedings.
2. If the respondent fails to present a statement of defence as referred to in Article 29 within the time limit determined by the arbitral tribunal, despite having been granted due opportunity to do so and without asserting well-founded reasons, the arbitral tribunal may immediately make an award.
3. The award referred to in paragraph 2 will wholly or partially award the claim, except where the claim appears to the arbitral tribunal to be unlawful or unfounded. The arbitral tribunal may, before making its award, require proof from the claimant of one or more of its assertions.

Article 40 – Interim measures

1. An arbitral tribunal may grant the following interim measures:
   (a) during pending arbitral proceedings on the merits, the arbitral tribunal may, at the request of any of the parties and with due observance of the provisions of this Article 40, grant interim measures related to the claim or counterclaim as filed;

(b) regardless of whether arbitral proceedings on the merits are pending, in all urgent cases that require immediately enforceable interim measures in view of the parties' interests, an arbitral tribunal specifically composed to that end may, at the request of any of the parties, grant interim measures in emergency arbitration with due observance of the provisions of Article 41. If the place of arbitration has not been determined for the arbitral proceedings on the merits, the place of arbitration of the emergency arbitration is Amsterdam.

2. The arbitral tribunal referred to in paragraph 1 may, in conjunction with the interim measures, require each party to provide sufficient security, including the provision of security for the claim or counterclaim in the main action and the costs of the arbitral proceedings on the merits, the latter including the costs of legal assistance.
3. Without prejudice to any provision of applicable mandatory arbitration law, the decision on the interim measures may be taken in the form of an order by the arbitral tribunal or in the form of an award, to which the provisions of Section Five and Section Six and Article 7(3) are applicable. At the request of a party, the arbitral tribunal, having heard the other party or parties, may convert an order by the arbitral tribunal into an award, in which it must state the request.
4. The decision on the interim measures does not in any way prejudice the arbitral tribunal's ultimate decision in the arbitral proceedings on the merits.

Article 41 – Emergency arbitration

Emergency arbitration as referred to in Article 40(1)(b) is commenced in accordance with the provisions contained in Appendix C. Furthermore, Article 40(2), (3) and (4) as well as Section One and Section Seven apply to emergency arbitration. The provisions of Section Two to Section Six inclusive only apply to the extent referred to in Appendix C.

Article 42 – Expedited arbitration

1. The rules on expedited arbitration as contained in the Rules and Appendix D apply when:
   (a) the arbitration agreement(s) providing for arbitration by or before the NAI or in accordance with the Rules was or were entered into on or after 1 March 2024;
   (b) the total amount claimed by the claimant in the request for arbitration does not exceed € 1,000,000; and

(c) the parties have not ruled out the application of the rules on expedited arbitration.

2. The parties may, even if the provisions of paragraph 1 are not met, agree in writing to apply the expedited arbitration rules set forth in the Rules and Appendix D.
3. Expedited arbitration is commenced in accordance with Appendix D.
4. Without prejudice to any provision of applicable mandatory arbitration law, the provisions of Section One and Section Seven apply *mutatis mutandis* to expedited arbitration. The provisions of Section Two to Section Six inclusive only apply to expedited arbitration to the extent referred to in this Article 42 and Appendix D.
5. If, pursuant to what is provided in Article D9, the responsible member of the NAI Case Management Committee decides that the case is not suitable to be decided on in expedited arbitration, the case will be taken forward as an arbitration on the merits.

Article 43 – Joinder or intervention and impleader

1. At the written request of a third person who has an interest in arbitral proceedings to which the Rules apply, the arbitral tribunal may allow that person to join or intervene in the proceedings, provided that the same arbitration agreement as between the original parties applies or enters into force between the original parties to the arbitration and the third person. By allowing the joinder or intervention, the third person becomes a party to the proceedings.
2. The request must be submitted to the NAI Secretariat. The NAI Secretariat will transmit a copy of the request to the parties and to the arbitral tribunal as soon as possible.
3. Regardless of whether the same arbitration agreement as between the original parties applies or enters into force between the parties and the third person, by submitting the request for joinder or intervention, the third person agrees that the provisions of Section Six and Section Seven, except for Article 61, apply *mutatis mutandis*.
4. At the written request of a party, the arbitral tribunal may allow that party to implead a third person, provided that the same arbitration agreement as between the original parties in the arbitration applies or enters into force between the requesting party and the third person.
5. After receiving a request referred to in paragraphs 1 and 4, the arbitral tribunal must give the parties and the third person the opportunity to make their opinions on the request known. The arbitral tribunal will not allow the admission of a party by way of joinder, intervention or impleader if the arbitral tribunal considers that its admission

would cause unreasonable delay to the arbitral proceedings. Nor will the arbitral tribunal allow an impleader if the arbitral tribunal sees no plausible case in advance that the third party will be required to bear the adverse consequences of any order against the requesting party.

6. The arbitral tribunal may suspend the proceedings after receipt of a request as referred to in paragraph 1 and paragraph 4. After lifting the suspension or allowing the joinder or intervention, or an impleader, the arbitral tribunal will decide on the further course of the proceedings, except where the parties have made provisions for this by agreement.

Article 44 – Consolidation of arbitral proceedings

1. Unless the parties have agreed otherwise, in respect of pending arbitral proceedings governed by the Rules, a party may, in accordance with Appendix E, request a consolidator to be designated to order that these proceedings are consolidated with other pending arbitral proceedings governed by the Rules.
2. Consolidation may be ordered insofar as:
   (a) it does not cause unreasonable delay in the pending proceedings, also in view of the stage they have reached; and
   (b) the arbitral proceedings are so closely connected that the good administration of justice renders it expedient to hear and determine them together to avoid the risk of irreconcilable decisions resulting from separate proceedings.
3. Without prejudice to any provision of applicable mandatory arbitration law, Appendix E and the provisions of Section Six and Section Seven, except for Article 61, apply *mutatis mutandis* to the request for consolidation and/or any subsequent appointment of the arbitrator(s) and determination of the remuneration of the arbitrator(s).

Article 45 – Early determination

1. At the request of a party, the arbitral tribunal may, with respect to one or more issues of law and/or fact, decide by way of an early determination procedure that a claim, counterclaim or defence is:
   (a) manifestly inadmissible;
   (b) manifestly outside the jurisdiction of the arbitral tribunal; or
   (c) manifestly legally unfounded.
2. The arbitral tribunal, after hearing the counterparty, decides whether the request for an early determination referred to in paragraph 1 can be considered. If the arbitral tribunal considers the request, the par-

ties must be given the opportunity to present their views before the arbitral tribunal decides on the request. The early determination may be given in the form of an order by the arbitral tribunal or in the form of an award, to which the provisions of Section Five and Section Six and Article 7(3) apply. The arbitral tribunal must render its decision within 30 days after the arbitral tribunal has notified the parties that the request for an early determination will be considered.

SECTION FIVE – AWARD

Article 46 – Time limit

1. The arbitral tribunal must make its award within eight weeks after the last hearing as referred to in Article 32 or after the last admissible written statement of one of the parties in the arbitration. In all cases, the award will be made expeditiously.
2. Without prejudice to the provisions of Article 54 and Article 55, the mandate of the arbitral tribunal is terminated by the transmission of the final award to the parties.

Article 47 – Types of awards

The arbitral tribunal may make a final award, a partial final award or an interim award. In accordance with Article 51, the arbitral tribunal may record the agreed terms of a settlement in an award.

Article 48 – Measure for decision-making

1. Subject to the provisions of Article 3(3), the arbitral tribunal decides according to the rules of law.
2. If a choice of law has been made by the parties, the arbitral tribunal decides in accordance with the rules of law designated by the parties. Failing such designation of law, the arbitral tribunal decides in accordance with the rules of law which it considers appropriate.
3. The arbitral tribunal decides as *amiable compositeur* if the parties, by agreement, have instructed it to do so.
4. In any event, in its decision the arbitral tribunal will take into account any applicable trade usages.

Article 49 – Decision and signing

1. If the arbitral tribunal consists of three or more arbitrators, it decides by a majority of votes.
2. If the arbitral tribunal consists of three or more arbitrators, procedural matters of minor importance may be decided by the chair if he or she has been so authorised by the co-arbitrators, unless the parties have agreed otherwise.
3. The award containing the decision must be drawn up in writing in at least three copies and signed by the arbitrator, where an arbitral tribunal consists of one arbitrator, or by all the arbitrators, where the arbitral tribunal consists of multiple persons.
4. Without prejudice to any provision of the applicable mandatory arbitration law, the award may also be made in electronic form by affixing it with a qualified electronic signature or qualified electronic signatures as referred to in Article 3(12) of Regulation (EU) No. 910/2014 of the European Parliament and of the Council of 23 July 2014 on electronic identification and trust services for electronic transactions in the internal market and repealing Directive 1999/93/EC (OJEU 2014, L 257).
5. If a minority of the arbitrators refuses to sign, this must be stated by the other arbitrators in the award signed by them. A similar statement must be made if a minority is incapable of signing and it is unlikely that the impediment will cease to exist shortly.
6. The award will not state a minority opinion. A minority may express its opinion to the other arbitrators and the parties in a separate written document. This document is not considered to be a part of the award.

Article 50 – Contents of the award

1. The award must in any event contain:
   (a) the name and place of residence of the arbitrator, where an arbitral tribunal consists of one arbitrator, or the names and places of residence of all the arbitrators, where an arbitral tribunal consists of multiple arbitrators;
   (b) the name and place of residence of each of the parties;
   (c) a brief summary of the proceedings;
   (d) a description of the claim(s) and any counterclaim(s);
   (e) the reasons for the decision given in the award;
   (f) the determination and order to pay the arbitration costs as referred to in Article 59;

(g) the statement whether in accordance with the provisions of Article 48 the arbitral tribunal is deciding according to the rules of law or as *amiable compositeur*;
(h) the decision;
(i) the place where the award is made as determined in accordance with the provisions of Article 27(1); and
(j) the date on which the award is made.

2. If the arbitral tribunal's award is an order for interim measures, an interim award or a partial final award, the determination of the arbitration costs and the order to pay these as referred to in paragraph 1(f) may be stayed until a later time in the proceedings.
3. In derogation of the provisions of paragraph 1(e), the award may contain no grounds for the decision given if, after the arbitration has been commenced, the parties agree in writing that no grounds will be given for the decision.
4. The arbitral tribunal is to transmit a draft of the award to the responsible member of the NAI Case Management Committee. The responsible member of the NAI Case Management Committee may make recommendations with respect to the provisions of paragraph 1(a), (b), (c), (d), (f), (g), (i) and (j), without prejudice to the discretion of the arbitral tribunal. Additionally, the responsible member of the NAI Case Management Committee may point out to the arbitral tribunal manifest computational or clerical errors in the draft of the award or any other manifest errors contained therein that lend themselves to simple rectification and any omission to decide on one or more claims or counterclaims that have been subjected to the arbitral tribunal's discretion. The arbitral tribunal remains responsible for both the content and form of the award.

Article 51 – Award on agreed terms

1. If a settlement is reached between the parties during the course of the proceedings, the parties may jointly request the arbitral tribunal to record the terms of such a settlement in an award.
2. The award on agreed terms referred to in paragraph 1 is regarded as an award to which the provisions of this Section Five and Section Six and Article 7(3) apply, it being understood that the award, in derogation of the provisions of Article 50(1)(e), need not contain any grounds for the decision rendered.

Article 52 – Transmission and deposit of the award

1. On behalf of the arbitral tribunal, the responsible member of the NAI Case Management Committee ensures that an original of the award is transmitted to the parties as soon as possible.
2. An original of the award will be kept in the NAI archives for a period of ten years. Any party may, during that period, request that the responsible member of the NAI Case Management Committee provides a copy of an original of the award certified by the responsible member of the NAI Case Management Committee.

Article 53 – Binding effect of the award

An award is binding upon the parties with effect from the day on which it is made. The parties undertake to comply with the award as soon as possible.

Article 54 – Rectification of the award

1. A party may, within three months after the date of transmission of the award, request in writing that the arbitral tribunal correct a manifest computing error, a manifest clerical error or another manifest error that lends itself to simple rectification in the award.
2. If the particulars referred to in Article 50(1)(a), (b), (i) and (j) are stated incorrectly or are partially or wholly absent from the award, a party may, within three months after the date of transmission of the award, request in writing that the arbitral tribunal correct such particulars.
3. The request must be submitted to the NAI Secretariat. The NAI Secretariat will transmit a copy of the request to the arbitral tribunal and the counterparty as soon as possible.
4. Within three months after the date of the transmission of the award, the arbitral tribunal may also of its own motion proceed to the correction as referred to in paragraph 1 and paragraph 2.
5. Before the arbitral tribunal decides on the request referred to in paragraph 1 or paragraph 2, or decides of its own motion to proceed to the correction as referred to in paragraph 4, it must give the parties the opportunity to comment on the matter.
6. If the arbitral tribunal proceeds to make a correction, it will be mentioned by the arbitral tribunal in a separate document, which document is considered to be a part of the award. The document will be drawn up in at least triplicate and must contain:

(a) the particulars stated in Article 50(1)(a) and (b);
(b) a reference to the award to which the correction relates;
(c) the correction;
(d) the date of the correction, it being understood that the date of the award to which the correction relates remains decisive; and
(e) a signature to which the provisions of Article 49 apply.

7. The responsible member of the NAI Case Management Committee ensures that the document referred to in paragraph 6 is sent to the parties as soon as possible. The provisions of Article 52 apply *mutatis mutandis*.
8. If the arbitral tribunal denies the request for the correction, it must so notify the parties by intervention of the responsible member of the NAI Case Management Committee.

Article 55 – Additional award

1. Within three months after the date of transmission of the award, a party may request the arbitral tribunal to make an additional award on any claims or counterclaims that were presented to the arbitral tribunal but on which the arbitral tribunal did not decide.
2. The request must be submitted to the NAI Secretariat. The NAI Secretariat will transmit a copy of the request to the arbitral tribunal and the counterparty as soon as possible.
3. The arbitral tribunal must give the parties the opportunity to comment on the request before deciding on it.
4. An additional award constitutes an award to which the provisions of this section apply.
5. If the arbitral tribunal denies a request for an additional award, it must so notify the parties by intervention of the responsible member of the NAI Case Management Committee.

SECTION SIX – COSTS

Article 56 – Costs of the arbitration and costs of legal assistance

1. Costs of the arbitration include:
   (a) the administration fees;
   (b) the fees and disbursements of the arbitrator(s); and
   (c) the other costs which, in the opinion of the arbitral tribunal, were necessarily incurred in the arbitration.

2. The costs of legal assistance do not form part of the costs of the arbitration.

Article 57 – Administration fees

1. Upon submission of the request for arbitration, the claimant will owe, within the time limit set by the responsible member of the NAI Case Management Committee, administration fees as determined by the responsible member of the NAI Case Management Committee in accordance with Appendix F.
2. If the respondent files a counterclaim, the respondent will also owe, within the time limit set by the responsible member of the NAI Case Management Committee, administration fees as determined by the responsible member of the NAI Case Management Committee in accordance with Appendix F.
3. With due observance of Article F1(3) and Article F2(4), the responsible member of the NAI Case Management Committee may increase the administration fees during the proceedings if it appears that the total monetary interest of the claim(s) or counterclaim(s) is higher than initially assumed when determining the administration fees as referred to in paragraph 1 and paragraph 2. In case of an increase in the administration fees, the claimant and the respondent, respectively, will owe a supplement to the administration fees according to the provisions of Article F2.
4. If after a second reminder by the responsible member of the NAI Case Management Committee, the administration fees owed by a party are not received by the NAI within fourteen days, that party is deemed to have withdrawn its claim(s) or counterclaim(s). This party is not, on the mere basis of this withdrawal, prevented from bringing the same claim(s) or counterclaim(s) again at a later date in other proceedings.

Article 58 – Advance on costs, fees and disbursements of the arbitrator(s)

1. As soon as possible after the composition of the arbitral tribunal, the arbitral tribunal will consult with the responsible member of the NAI Case Management Committee as to the amount of an advance for the fees and disbursements of the arbitrator(s) payable by the claimant or the respondent pursuant to paragraph 2, which advance will be held in deposit by the NAI upon receipt. The amount of the advance is determined by the responsible member of the NAI Case Management Committee in accordance with the provisions of Article F3.

2. The responsible member of the NAI Case Management Committee will require an advance payment from the claimant. If the respondent has filed a counterclaim, the responsible member of the NAI Case Management Committee may also require the respondent to make an advance payment. The costs as referred to in Article 56(1)(b) will be paid from this advance. The costs and disbursements of the secretary as appointed by the responsible member of the NAI Case Management Committee and of the expert, technical assistance or interpreter appointed by the arbitral tribunal are also to be paid from the advance, if and insofar as these costs were incurred by the arbitral tribunal. If the parties have agreed to deposit the award with the court registry, the advance is also to be used to pay the associated costs.
3. The responsible member of the NAI Case Management Committee may redetermine the amount of the advance in accordance with Article F3 and require the claimant and/or respondent to supplement the advance to be kept in deposit until no later than fourteen days after the last hearing or until no later than fourteen days after the arbitral tribunal's receipt of the last admissible written statement.
4. The arbitral tribunal may suspend the arbitration in respect of the claim or the counterclaim as long as the relevant party has not made the advance required. If the NAI does not receive the advance required from a party within fourteen days after a second reminder from the responsible member of the NAI Case Management Committee, that party will be deemed to have withdrawn its claim(s) or counterclaim(s). This party is not, on the mere basis of this withdrawal, prevented from bringing the same claim(s) or counterclaim(s) again at a later date in other proceedings.
5. The responsible member of the NAI Case Management Committee notifies the arbitral tribunal and the parties of the advance held in deposit.
6. In consultation with the arbitral tribunal, the responsible member of the NAI Case Management Committee reasonably determines the fees and disbursements for (each of) the arbitrator(s) in accordance with the provisions of Article F3.
7. If an arbitrator has been released of his or her mandate prior to the last final award or the mandate of the arbitral tribunal has been terminated prior to the last final award, the responsible member of the NAI Case Management Committee may, at the request of the arbitrator in question or of the arbitral tribunal and in accordance with

Article F3(7), determine a fee and disbursement allowance for (each of) the arbitrator(s). In connection with this, the responsible member of the NAI Case Management Committee may, in derogation of the provisions of paragraph 3, require the claimant and/or respondent to supplement the advance.

Article 59 – Award on costs

1. Subject to the provisions of Article 56, Article 57 and Article 58 as well as the provisions of Appendix F, the arbitral tribunal determines the costs of the arbitration.
2. The arbitral tribunal orders a party to pay the costs of the arbitration. The unsuccessful party is ordered to pay the costs of the arbitration, except in exceptional circumstances at the arbitral tribunal's discretion. If the parties are each partially unsuccessful, the arbitral tribunal may order the parties to each pay part of the costs of the arbitration.
3. The arbitral tribunal may order the unsuccessful party to pay reasonable compensation for the successful party's legal assistance, if and insofar as these costs were necessarily incurred in the arbitration in the arbitral tribunal's opinion.
4. When deciding on the division of the costs of the arbitration and the costs of legal assistance, the arbitral tribunal may take into account the manner in which parties conducted the proceedings as well as whether each of the parties promoted the speedy and efficient conduct of the proceedings. If, in the opinion of the arbitral tribunal, a party has unreasonably delayed the arbitral proceedings, the arbitral tribunal may take this into account in its decision on the division of the costs of the arbitration and the costs of legal assistance.
5. The arbitral tribunal takes the advance made under Article 58 into account when ordering a party to pay the costs. Insofar as the advance made by a party is used to pay the costs of the arbitration that the other party is ordered to pay in accordance with the previous paragraph 2, the latter party will be ordered to reimburse the former party for such amount.
6. Payment of the costs of the arbitration and/or the costs of legal assistance may also be ordered if a party did not expressly seek such payment.

SECTION SEVEN – FINAL PROVISIONS

Article 60 – Timely objection

A party that has appeared in the proceedings must file an objection with the arbitral tribunal without unreasonable delay, sending a copy to the counterparty and the NAI Secretariat, as soon as it knows or reasonably should know of any act contrary to or failure to act in accordance with any provision of these Rules, the arbitration agreement or any order, decision or measure of the arbitral tribunal. If a party fails to do so, the right to rely on this later, in the arbitral proceedings or before the courts, is forfeited.

Article 61 – Competent provisional relief judge

If the place of arbitration is located in the Netherlands, the provisional relief judge of the Amsterdam District Court has jurisdiction for the circumstances as referred to in Article 1027(3) (appointment of the arbitrator(s)), Article 1028 (privileged position of a party with regard to the appointment of the arbitrator(s)) and Article 1041a (hearing an unwilling witness) of the Dutch Code of Civil Procedure.

Article 62 – Contingencies

Without prejudice to the provisions of Article 25(1), in all events not provided for in the Rules, action is to be taken in accordance with the spirit of the Rules.

Article 63 – Processing of personal data and data protection

1. The processing of personal data by the NAI is subject to the applicable regulations on the protection of personal data as well as to NAI's privacy notice, which can be consulted on the NAI website.
2. The NAI and the arbitral tribunal may, with due observance of the applicable provisions of mandatory law, issue instructions regarding the security of information and/or protection of (personal) data that are binding on the parties, and, in the case of instructions from the NAI, also on the arbitral tribunal.

Article 64 – Limitation of liability

The NAI, its Executive Board members and employees (including the members of the NAI Case Management Committee), the members of its advisory board, the members of the Challenge Committee, the arbitrator(s), the secretary, the consolidator, any other person that may have been appointed by (one of) these persons or other persons who fulfil a role pursuant to the Rules are not liable either by contract or otherwise for any damage caused by their own or any other person's acts or omissions or caused by the use of any aids in or involving arbitration, all this except where and insofar as mandatory Dutch law precludes this exclusion of liability. To the extent that they are liable at all on the basis of the above, the NAI, its Executive Board members and employees, including the members of the NAI Case Management Committee, are not liable for payment of any amount that is not covered by the advance.

Article 65 – Choice of forum

The legal relationship between the arbitrator(s) and the parties, between the arbitrator(s) and the NAI and between the NAI and the parties, as well as the legal relationship between the arbitrators, the parties or the NAI and other persons playing a role pursuant to the Rules, is governed by Dutch law. The Amsterdam District Court has jurisdiction over all disputes arising out of or in connection with the aforementioned legal relationships.

APPENDIX A – THE NAI CASE MANAGEMENT COMMITTEE AND THE NAI SECRETARIAT

Article A1 – Tasks and composition

1. The members of the NAI Case Management Committee are entrusted with the administration of arbitrations as defined in the Rules and Appendix A. The NAI Case Management Committee consists of the NAI employees designated as such by the Executive Board. The Executive Board has no access to or influence over the administration of individual cases. The NAI Case Management Committee has at least two members.
2. The NAI Secretariat supports the members of the NAI Case Management Committee in carrying out the members of the NAI Case Management Committee's duties and powers as referred to in the Rules. The NAI Secretariat is also entrusted with receiving and transmitting documents as provided for in the Rules. The NAI Secretariat is made up of Counsel, Legal Counsel, and Case Managers.

Article A2 – Conduct

1. The members of the NAI Case Management Committee distribute among themselves the required work relating to the administration of arbitrations pending under the auspices of the NAI. Members of the NAI Case Management Committee may, for purposes of absence or otherwise, assign work to each other temporarily or permanently. Parties and arbitrators will be able to ascertain which member of the NAI Case Management Committee is responsible for the administration of a specific arbitration.
2. The members of the NAI Case Management Committee may confer with one another on their work relating to the arbitrations they administer, also where this concerns matters in individual arbitrations.
3. The members of the NAI Case Management Committee are supported in their work by one or more members of the NAI Secretariat. Parties and arbitrators will be able to ascertain which member of the NAI Secretariat is supporting a member of the NAI Case Management Committee in his or her work.

Article A3 – Decision-making by the members of the NAI Case Management Committee

Each member of the NAI Case Management Committee has independent decision-making authority with respect to the administration of a specific arbitration for which that member is responsible in accordance with Article A2(1).

APPENDIX B – CHALLENGE PROCEDURE

Article B1 – Duties of Challenge Committee, Challenge Chamber and the Challenge Committee Secretariat

1. The Challenge Committee is the committee constituted by the Executive Board that is charged with handling challenge requests as referred to in Article 23 of the Rules and Appendix B.
2. The Challenge Chamber is the chamber constituted by the chair of the Challenge Committee to decide on the merits of a challenge pursuant to Article 23 of the Rules and Appendix B.
3. The Challenge Committee Secretariat assists the Challenge Committee and the Challenge Chamber in carrying out the powers conferred upon them.

Article B2 – Composition of Challenge Committee, Challenge Chamber and the Challenge Committee Secretariat

1. The Challenge Committee consists of at least six members, including, in any event, one chair and one deputy chair.
2. Members of the Challenge Committee are appointed and removed by the Executive Board. The Executive Board appoints one chair and one deputy chair from among the members of the Challenge Committee.
3. Members of the Executive Board, the NAI advisory board and NAI employees are not eligible for appointment as a member of the Challenge Committee.
4. The deputy chair of the Challenge Committee performs the duties of the chair of the Challenge Committee when the chair is absent or unable to do so.
5. A member of the Challenge Committee is appointed for a term of up to four years and may be reappointed no more than once for a term of up to four years. The Challenge Committee establishes a schedule of retirement.
6. A member of the Challenge Committee leaves office:
    1. by his or her death;
    2. by his or her bankruptcy, receivership or by becoming subject to debt restructuring;
    3. upon the loss of the free disposition of his or her assets;
    4. by retiring according to the schedule;
    5. by written notice of resignation;
    6. by his or her removal by the Executive Board; or
    7. by acceptance of an appointment as a member of the Executive Board or the NAI advisory board as well as by employment with the NAI.
7. A Challenge Chamber is constituted by the chair of the Challenge Committee and consists of three members of the Challenge Committee.
8. The Challenge Committee has a secretariat as referred to in Article B1(3). The Executive Board designates persons to serve on the Challenge Committee Secretariat.
9. Members of a Challenge Chamber and the members of the Challenge Committee Secretariat receive compensation for each challenge request as determined by the Executive Board.

Article B3 – Conduct of Challenge Committee and Challenge Chamber

1. If in the event of a challenge as referred to in Article 23 of the Rules, the challenged arbitrator does not resign, the responsible member of the NAI Case Management Committee, to the extent that the challenging party, when asked by the responsible member of the NAI Case Management Committee, expressly upholds the challenge, sends the notification of the challenge as referred to in Article 23(3) of the Rules to the chair of the Challenge Committee. If the challenging party does not expressly uphold the challenge within fourteen days after being asked by the responsible member of the NAI Case Management Committee, the challenge is deemed to have been withdrawn.
2. If the challenge is maintained, the chair of the Challenge Committee will as soon as possible put together a Challenge Chamber consisting of three members of the Challenge Committee, who will decide impartially and independently whether the challenge is well-founded. The Challenge Chamber appoints one chair from among its members.
3. The Challenge Chamber is to give the challenging party, within a period of time to be determined by the Challenge Chamber, the opportunity to further explain in writing the reasons underlying the notice of the challenge as referred to in Article 23(3) of the Rules. The challenged arbitrator, the parties and the other arbitrators of the tribunal are to be given the opportunity to respond in writing to the notice of the challenge and to the further explanation of the challenging party within a short time limit to be determined by the Challenge Chamber.
4. Before the Challenge Chamber decides on the merits of the challenge, an oral hearing is to be held at which the challenged arbitrator, parties and the other arbitrators are given the opportunity to be heard orally.
5. For the remainder, the challenge proceedings are conducted before the Challenge Chamber in the manner determined by the Challenge Chamber for the challenge in question. The Challenge Chamber must decide on the merits of the challenge as soon as possible. The Challenge Chamber decides by majority vote. The decision and its grounds are given in writing.
6. The written decision of the Challenge Chamber, stating the reasons for the decision, must be signed by the chair of the Challenge Chamber and in his or her absence by one of the other members of the Challenge Chamber, and is sent as soon as possible by the Challenge Committee Secretariat to the parties to the arbitration, the challenged

arbitrator, the responsible member of the NAI Case Management Committee and, where the arbitral tribunal consists of several arbitrators, to the other arbitrators. The Challenge Chamber's decision may be published pursuant to the provisions of Article 7(3) of the Rules.

7. Without prejudice to any provision of applicable mandatory arbitration law, the Challenge Chamber may issue an oral decision during or following the oral hearing if there is such urgency that a full written elaboration of the decision cannot be awaited. The oral decision must state both the decision and the main reasons of the decision. With due observance of the provisions of paragraph 6, a full written elaboration of the oral decision will be made available to the parties as soon as possible and in any event within two weeks of the oral decision. The written elaboration must state the date of the oral decision as well as the date on which the written elaboration of that decision is set.
8. Where the Challenge Chamber finds that the challenging party has abused its right to raise a challenge, the Challenge Chamber may determine that a subsequent challenge will not be considered. This will be noted in the decision of a Challenge Chamber.

APPENDIX C – EMERGENCY ARBITRATION

Article C1 – Request for arbitration

1. Emergency arbitration, as referred to in Article 41 of the Rules, is commenced by submitting a request for emergency arbitration to the NAI Secretariat.
2. An emergency arbitration is deemed to have been commenced on the day of receipt of the request for emergency arbitration by the NAI Secretariat.
3. The request must contain the information as referred to in Article 8(2) (a), (b), (c), (d), (e), (f), (k) and (l) of the Rules, the agreed place of arbitration, the agreed language of the arbitration and a description of the grounds of the claim and of the grounds on which the urgent interest is based as required by Article 40(1)(b) of the Rules. Article 8(3) and (4) of the Rules apply *mutatis mutandis*.
4. The claimant must immediately and properly bring a copy of the request, along with any documents, to the attention of every respondent. Proof that notice has been given to every respondent must be submitted before the start of the hearing mentioned in Article C6.

Article C2 – Composition of the arbitral tribunal

1. As soon as possible after receipt of the request, the responsible member of the NAI Case Management Committee directly appoints an emergency arbitrator to decide in the emergency arbitration. If the parties have by agreement specified a method of appointing the arbitral tribunal and/or a number of arbitrators, such agreement will be disregarded when appointing the emergency arbitrator as referred to in the first sentence of this paragraph, unless the parties have expressly provided for a method for appointing an arbitral tribunal in emergency arbitration.
2. Any natural person of legal capacity may be appointed as an arbitrator in emergency arbitration. No person shall be precluded from appointment as arbitrator in emergency arbitration by reason of his or her nationality. Article 13(2), (3), (4), Article 15(2)(d), (6), Article 20, Article 21, Article 22(2), Article 23, Article 24 of the Rules apply in full. In the events as referred to in Article 22(1) of the Rules, a new emergency arbitrator will be appointed in the manner provided for in paragraph 1.
3. The appointment of the arbitral tribunal in accordance with the procedure provided for in this Article C2 is to be made as soon as possible after the emergency arbitration is commenced.

Article C3 – Conduct of the proceedings

1. The provisions of Article 25, Article 27, Article 28, Article 33 to Article 39 inclusive, and Article 43 of the Rules apply *mutatis mutandis* to the conduct of the proceedings in emergency arbitration.
2. If the arbitral tribunal finds that the case is insufficiently urgent or too complex to be decided in emergency arbitration, it may deny all or part of the claim for that reason while referring the parties to arbitration on the merits. If arbitral proceedings on the merits are not yet pending, they may be commenced pursuant to Article 8 of the Rules, with due observance of the provisions of Section Six of the Rules.

Article C4 – Contesting the jurisdiction of the arbitral tribunal

If the respondent wishes to contest the jurisdiction of the arbitral tribunal, it must raise such a plea before submitting a defence, *i.e.* before the start of the hearing referred to in Article C6 or, if a written statement is presented prior to that hearing, in that statement at the latest. Article 12 of the Rules applies *mutatis mutandis*.

Article C5 – Counterclaim

The respondent may present a counterclaim in the emergency arbitration. A counterclaim must be filed by means of a written statement to be presented to the arbitral tribunal ultimately at the hearing referred to in Article C6, with copies simultaneously being transmitted or handed to the claimant and transmitted to the NAI Secretariat.

Article C6 – Hearing

The arbitral tribunal determines as soon as possible the date, time and place of the hearing as well as the manner in which the hearing in the emergency arbitration is to be conducted and immediately communicates this information to the parties. Parties may only submit written statements if the arbitral tribunal so determines, without prejudice to the provisions of Article C4 and Article C5. Article 32(2) of the Rules applies *mutatis mutandis.*

Article C7 – Costs

1. The provisions of Section Six of the Rules apply to the emergency arbitration, it being understood that the administration fees must have been paid and the advance must have been deposited prior to the hearing as referred to in Article C6. Where a counterclaim is filed at the hearing, this must be effected as soon as possible after the end of that hearing.
2. The arbitral tribunal may suspend the hearing or stay its decision if any of the parties have failed to satisfy their payment obligations pursuant to paragraph 1. If, after a single reminder from the responsible member of the NAI Case Management Committee, a party fails to satisfy its payment obligation pursuant to paragraph 1 within the time limit specified by this member, it is deemed to have withdrawn its claim(s) or counterclaim(s). The party concerned is not, on the mere basis of this withdrawal, prevented from bringing the same claim(s) or counterclaim(s) again at a later date in other proceedings.

Article C8 – Award

1. The arbitral tribunal will render its award within two weeks after the last hearing referred to in Article C6. In all cases, the award will be rendered expeditiously. Subject to this provision, Section Five of the Rules applies *mutatis mutandis.*

2. Without prejudice to any provision of applicable mandatory arbitration law, the arbitral tribunal may make an oral award during or following the hearing if there is such urgency that a full written elaboration of the award cannot be awaited.
3. The award referred to in paragraph 2, constitutes an award, to which the provisions of Section Five and Section Six of the Rules apply, it being understood that, in derogation of the provisions of Article 50 of the Rules, the award only needs to contain the requirements referred to in (e), (g), (h) and (i).
4. As soon as possible, but in any case within two weeks of the oral award, as referred to in paragraph 2, with due observance of the requirements set forth in Article 49(3) and Article 50(1)(a) to (i) inclusive of the Rules, a complete written elaboration of the oral award is to be made available to the parties in the manner provided for in Article 49 and Article 52 of the Rules.
5. The written elaboration must state the date of the oral award as well as the date on which the written elaboration of that award is set.

APPENDIX D – EXPEDITED ARBITRATION

Article D1 – Applicability

1. The rules on expedited arbitration as contained in the Rules and Appendix D apply when:
   (a) the arbitration agreement(s) providing for arbitration by or before the NAI or in accordance with the Rules was or were entered into on or after 1 March 2024;
   (b) the total amount claimed by the claimant in the request for arbitration does not exceed € 1,000,000; and
   (c) the parties have not ruled out the application of the rules on expedited arbitration.
2. The parties may, even if the provisions of paragraph 1 are not met, agree in writing to apply the expedited arbitration rules set forth in the Rules and Appendix D.

Article D2 – Request for arbitration

Expedited arbitration is commenced by submitting a request for arbitration to the NAI Secretariat to which Section Two of the Rules applies.

Article D3 – Short answer

The NAI Secretariat will invite the Respondent to submit, within fourteen days of the transmission of the invitation to do so, the short answer to which the Section Two of the Rules applies. The NAI Secretariat's invitation will give notice that the rules in expedited arbitration will be followed. The claimant is notified that the rules on expedited arbitration will apply concurrently with the invitation referred to in Article 9(1) of the Rules.

Article D4 – Composition of the arbitral tribunal

1. The arbitral tribunal will consist of one arbitrator. If the parties have by agreement specified a method of composition of the arbitral tribunal and/or a number of arbitrators, such agreement will be disregarded when appointing an arbitrator in expedited arbitration, unless one of the parties indicates in the request for arbitration or the short answer that it wishes to maintain a (previously) agreed other number of arbitrators, or where the parties have expressly provided for the number of arbitrators and/ or method for appointing an arbitral tribunal in expedited arbitration in their agreement for expedited arbitration specifically.
2. For the purpose of the composition of the arbitral tribunal in the expedited arbitration, the responsible member of the NAI Case Management Committee will transmit to each of the parties an identical list of names of three persons who are eligible for appointment as arbitrators. A party may delete from the list the names of persons against whom this party has strong objections, and may number the remaining names in its order of preference and must return this list to the responsible member of the NAI Case Management Committee within four days after transmission. A party is not required to send a copy of the list to the counterparty. If the responsible member of the NAI Case Management Committee has not received a list back from a party within four days, it is assumed that all of the persons named on the list are equally acceptable to that party.
3. With due observance of any preferences and/or objections expressed by the parties, the responsible member of the NAI Case Management Committee will invite persons named on the list to serve as arbitrators. The responsible member of the NAI Case Management Committee will then appoint an arbitrator based on the preferences and/or objections expressed by the parties.

4. If the lists returned by the parties show that there is an insufficient number of persons who are acceptable as arbitrators to each of the parties, or a person will not or cannot accept the responsible member of the NAI Case Management Committee's invitation to serve as arbitrator or proves unable to serve as arbitrator for any other reasons and an insufficient number of persons remain that are acceptable as arbitrators to each of the parties, the responsible member of the NAI Case Management Committee will proceed to directly appoint a person who was not featured on the list issued to the parties.
5. The composition of the arbitral tribunal in accordance with the procedure set forth in this Article D5 is to take place within one month after the expedited arbitration is commenced.
6. Article 13, Article 15(3), (5), (6) and (7), Article 20, Article 21, Article 22(2), Article 23 and Article 24 of the Rules apply *mutatis mutandis* to expedited arbitration. In the case referred to in Article 22(1) of the Rules, a new arbitrator will be appointed in the manner provided for in paragraph 1, paragraph 2, paragraph 3, paragraph 4 and paragraph 5.

Article D5 – Case management conference and determining the order of the proceedings

The arbitral tribunal determines, in consultation with the parties, the time, the manner and the format for a case management conference within four days after it has been composed. The case management conference is held to enable the arbitral tribunal to establish a timetable and a procedural order. The case management conference will be held in electronic format and is to take place as soon as possible, but no later than fourteen days from the date of composition of the arbitral tribunal, unless the parties have agreed otherwise. For the remainder Article 26 of the Rules applies to the extent that the nature of expedited arbitration does not preclude its application.

Article D6 – Procedure

1. Unless the parties and the arbitral tribunal agree otherwise, the parties may submit one written document each: a statement of claim by the claimant and a statement of defence by the respondent. The claimant has the right to raise a defence against a counterclaim by means of a statement of defence on the counterclaim.
2. Section One, Article 11, Article 12, Article 20 to Article 25 inclusive, Article 27, Article 28, Article 33 to Article 39 inclusive, Article 40(1),

Article 43, Article 44 and Article 45 and Section Seven of the Rules apply *mutatis mutandis* to the expedited arbitration.

3. Where a claim is increased pursuant to Article 33 of the Rules and this causes the total monetary interest of the claim(s) and the counterclaim(s) combined to exceed € 1,000,000, the arbitral tribunal retains its jurisdiction, except where one of the parties then insists on the other number of arbitrators originally agreed. The responsible member of the NAI Case Management Committee will then invite the parties to each nominate one or more arbitrators within a specified time limit. The arbitrator appointed pursuant to Article D4 and Article 15(3), or Article 15(2)(d), of the Rules will then be designated as the chair.

Article D7 – Counterclaim

1. The respondent is entitled to present a counterclaim in the expedited arbitration. The counterclaim must be filed no later than in the statement of defence.
2. Where a counterclaim is filed and causes the total monetary interest of the claim(s) and the counterclaim(s) combined to exceed € 1,000,000, the arbitral tribunal retains its jurisdiction, except where one of the parties then insists on the other number of arbitrators originally agreed. The responsible member of the NAI Case Management Committee will then invite the parties to each nominate one or more arbitrators within a specified time limit. The arbitrator appointed pursuant to Article D4 and Article 15(3), or Article 15(2)(d), of the Rules will then be designated as the chair.
3. Where a counterclaim is increased pursuant to Article 33 and this causes the total monetary interest of the claim(s) and the counterclaim(s) combined to exceed € 1,000,000, the arbitral tribunal retains its jurisdiction, except where one of the parties then insists on the other number of arbitrators originally agreed. The responsible member of the NAI Case Management Committee will then invite the parties to each nominate one or more arbitrators within a specified time limit. The arbitrator appointed pursuant to Article D4 and Article 15(3), or Article 15(2)(d), of the Rules will then be designated as the chair.

Article D8 – Hearing

1. Only one hearing will be held in the expedited arbitration as referred to in Article 32 of the Rules, unless the parties and the arbitral tribunal agree otherwise.

2. The hearing will take place in electronic form, unless the parties and the arbitral tribunal agree otherwise or the arbitral tribunal decides otherwise.

Article D9 – Decision on expedited arbitration

Exceptional circumstances may merit that the parties jointly and/or the arbitral tribunal make or makes a request to the responsible member of the NAI Case Management Committee to decide that the case is not suitable to be decided in an expedited arbitration. If the responsible member of the NAI Case Management Committee decides that the case is not suitable to be decided in expedited arbitration, the case will be moved forward as an arbitration on the merits. In that event, the arbitral tribunal retains its jurisdiction, unless one of the parties insists on the other number of arbitrators originally agreed. If required, the responsible member of the NAI Case Management Committee will then invite the parties to each nominate one or more arbitrators within a specified time limit. The arbitrator appointed pursuant to Article D4 and Article 15(3), or Article 15(2)(d), of the Rules will then be designated as the chair.

Article D10 – Costs

1. The provisions of the Section Six of the Rules apply to an expedited arbitration, it being understood that the administration fees must be paid and the advance must be deposited prior to the case management conference as referred to in Article D5.
2. The arbitral tribunal may suspend the hearing or stay its decision if any of the parties have failed to satisfy their obligations pursuant to paragraph 1. If, after a single reminder from the responsible member of the NAI Case Management Committee, a party fails to satisfy its payment obligation pursuant to paragraph 1 within the time limit specified by this member, it is deemed to have withdrawn its claim(s) or counterclaim(s). This party is not, on the mere basis of this withdrawal, prevented from bringing the same claim(s) or counterclaim(s) again at a later date in other proceedings.

Article D11 – Award

1. The arbitral tribunal must issue its award within five months after the case management conference. In all cases, the award will be made expeditiously.
2. Section Five and Article 7(3) of the Rules apply *mutatis mutandis* to expedited arbitration.

APPENDIX E – CONSOLIDATION OF ARBITRAL PROCEEDINGS

Article E1 – Request for consolidation

A request for consolidation as referred to in Article 44 of the Rules must be submitted in writing to the NAI Secretariat. The NAI Secretariat will transmit a copy of the request to all parties and, if appointed, the arbitrators. Each of the pending arbitral proceedings may be suspended by the arbitral tribunal from the day of receipt of the request.

Article E2 – Designation of consolidator

1. The consolidator is designated as follows. The responsible member of the NAI Case Management Committee invites the parties to jointly nominate a consolidator within fourteen days, which nomination shall be followed by a designation by the responsible member of the NAI Case Management Committee. If the parties have not nominated a consolidator within this time limit, the responsible member of the NAI Case Management Committee will directly designate a consolidator.
2. Unless all parties have agreed otherwise, none of the arbitrators appointed in the arbitral proceedings of which the consolidation is being requested may be designated as a consolidator.
3. Article 13, Article 15(5), (6) and Article 20 to Article 24 inclusive of the Rules apply *mutatis mutandis* to the nomination by the parties or direct designation by the responsible member of the NAI Case Management Committee of the consolidator.

Article E3 – Requirements

Consolidation may be ordered insofar as:
(a) it does not cause unreasonable delay in the pending proceedings, also in view of the stage they have reached; and
(b) the arbitral proceedings are so closely connected that the good administration of justice renders it expedient to hear and determine them together to avoid the risk of irreconcilable decisions resulting from separate proceedings.

Article E4 – Decision

The consolidator may grant or refuse the request, after having given all parties and, if appointed, the arbitrators the opportunity to make their opinions known. The decision is communicated by the responsible member of the NAI Case Management Committee to all parties and the arbitral tribunals concerned.

Article E5 – Arbitral tribunal after consolidation

1. If the consolidator orders that the proceedings are to be consolidated, the parties will in mutual consultation nominate the prospective arbitrator(s) for the consolidated proceedings, which nomination is followed by appointment by the responsible member of the NAI Council pursuant to Article 15(3) of the Rules. If the parties have not reached an agreement on the nomination of the arbitral tribunal within the time limit set by the responsible member of the NAI Case Management Committee, the consolidator will nominate the prospective arbitrator(s) for the consolidated arbitration, which nomination pursuant to Article 15(3) will be followed by appointment as arbitrator(s) by the responsible member of the NAI Case Management Committee. Article 13, Article 14 and Article 15 of the Rules apply *mutatis mutandis* to this appointment. The Rules continue to apply in full to the consolidated arbitral proceedings.
2. The appointment of the arbitrator(s) in the consolidated proceedings causes the mandate of the arbitrator(s) who are not reappointed in the consolidated proceedings to terminate. The consolidator, in consultation with the responsible member of the NAI Case Management Committee, will, if necessary and with due observance of the provisions of Article 58 of the Rules, determine the remuneration for the work performed by such arbitrator(s).

APPENDIX F – COSTS OF THE ARBITRATION

Article F1 – The monetary interest of the claims

1. Based on the information in the request for arbitration and/or the short answer, the responsible member of the NAI Case Management Committee makes a preliminary estimate of the monetary interest of the claim(s) and any counterclaim(s), including any contingent claims or counterclaims, in order to determine the administration fees and the amount of the advance. This preliminary estimate will also include an estimation of the monetary interest of claims of undetermined value.
2. If the information on the monetary interest of the claims or counterclaims is lacking in the request for arbitration and/or in the short

answer or if, in the opinion of the responsible member of the NAI Case Management Committee, the estimate made by a party is manifestly too low, the responsible member of the NAI Case Management Committee has the discretion to determine the monetary interest of the claims and/or counterclaims.

3. If during the course of the proceedings it is shown that the total monetary interest of the claims or counterclaims is higher than initially assumed, the responsible member of the NAI Case Management Committee may redetermine the monetary interest.

Article F2 – Administration fees

1. The administration fees are calculated based on the monetary interest of the claims or counterclaims and Table A below, as adopted by the Executive Board.

*Table A – Administration fees excluding VAT**

up to				€	25,000.- :	€	660.-
from	€	25,000.-	to	€	50,000.- :		0.60%
from	€	50,000.-	to	€	75,000.- :		0.96%
from	€	75,000.-	to	€	100,000.- :		0.85%
from	€	100,000.-	to	€	150,000.- :		0.45%
from	€	150,000.-	to	€	200,000.- :		0.025%
from	€	200,000.-	to	€	500,000.- :		0.167%
from	€	500,000.-	to	€	1,000,000.- :		2.40%
from	€	1,000,000.-	to	€	2,000,000.- :		0.50%
from	€	2,000,000.-	to	€	5,000,000.- :		0.167%
from	€	5,000,000.-	to	€	10,000,000.- :		0.13%
from	€	10,000,000.-	to	€	20,000,000.- :		0.085%
from	€	20,000,000.-	to	€	30,000,000.- :		0.04%
from	€	30,000,000.-	to	€	40,000,000.- :		0.07%
from	€	40,000,000.-	to	€	50,000,000.- :		0.065%
from	€	50,000,000.-	to	€	75,000,000.- :		0.034%
from	€	75,000,000.-	to	€	100,000,000.- :		0.01%
from	€	100,000,000.-	to	€	250,000,000.- :		0.005%
from	€	250,000,000.-				€	75,000

2. Upon receipt of the request for arbitration, the responsible member of the NAI Case Management Committee will determine the administration fees as soon as possible and send the claimant an invoice for these fees.

3. If the respondent files a counterclaim it will owe administration fees. The responsible member of the NAI Case Management Committee will determine the administration fees as soon as possible and will invoice the respondent for these fees.
4. The responsible member of the NAI Case Management Committee may increase the administration fees referred to in Article 57(3) of the Rules in the event of an increase of a claim or counterclaim, in the event of new claims or counterclaims or in the event of an adjustment of the monetary interest in accordance with Article F1(3). The responsible member of the NAI Case Management Committee will then re-determine the administration fees and send an additional invoice.
5. The administration fees will remain payable and will not be refunded if a request for arbitration is withdrawn or if one or more claim(s) or counterclaim(s) are withdrawn or if the total monetary interest of the claim(s) and counterclaim(s) is reduced.

Article F3 – The arbitrator(s) fees, disbursements and the advance

1. The hourly rate of the arbitrators is determined based on the total monetary interest of the claim(s) and counterclaim(s) in accordance with Table B below, as adopted by the Executive Board.

*Table B – Hourly arbitrator rates excluding VAT**

Total monetary interest (€)	Hourly rate of arbitrator (€)	
	Expedited/on the merits	Emergency arbitration
0 – 50,000	175	225
50,001 – 100,000	200	250
100,001 – 200,000	225	275
200,001 – 500,000	225	275
500,001 – 1,000,000	300	350
1,000,001 – 2,000,000	325	375
2,000,001 – 5,000,000	375	425
5,000,001 – 10,000,000	400	450
10,000,001 – 20,000,000	425	475
20,000,001 – 30,000,000	475	525
30,000,001 – 40,000,000	525	575
40,000,001 – 50,000,000	550	575
50,000,001 – 75,000,000	550	575
75,000,001 – 100,000,000	550	575
100,000,001 – 250,000,000	550	575
250,000,001 – 500,000,000	550	575
more than 500,000,000	550	575

2. The amount of the advance is determined by the responsible member of the NAI Case Management Committee based on the total monetary interest of the claim(s) and counterclaim(s), the applicable hourly rates and the expected work and disbursements of the arbitral tribunal.
3. In making the determination as referred to in paragraph 2, the responsible member of the NAI Case Management Committee uses Table C below as adopted by the Executive Board. The responsible member of the NAI Case Management Committee may deviate from the standard advances listed below where this is merited by the complexity of the proceedings.

*Table C – Benchmarks for advances including any VAT**

Total monetary interest (€)	Benchmark for 1 arbitrator (€)	Benchmark for 3 arbitrators (€)
0 – 50,000	8,750	22,000
50,001 – 100,000	11,500	25,000
100,001 – 200,000	13,500	28,000
200,001 – 500,000	14,500	33,750
500,001 – 1,000,000	20,000	50,000
1,000,001 – 2,000,000	23,000	58,500
2,000,001 – 5,000,000	30,000	75,000
5,000,001 – 10,000,000	43,000	98,500
10,000,001 – 30,000,000	48,000	120,000
30,000,001 – 50,000,000	62,000	153,000
50,000,001 – 100,000,000	67,000	168,000
100,000,001 – 250,000,000	70,500	173,000
250,000,001 – 500,000,000	79,000	185,500
more than 500,000,000	90,000	225,000

4. For the hourly rates of secretaries appointed by the responsible member of the NAI Case Management Committee, the responsible member of the NAI Case Management Committee uses Table D below as adopted by the Executive Board.

*Table D – Hourly rates secretary excluding VAT**

Total monetary interest (€)		Hourly rate of secretary (€)
0 – 50,000		100
50,001	– 100,000	100
100,001	– 200,000	100
200,001	– 500,000	100
500,001	– 1,000,000	150
1,000,001	– 2,000,000	150
2,000,001	– 5,000,000	150
5,000,001	– 10,000,000	175
10,000,001	– 20,000,000	175
20,000,001	– 30,000,000	175
30,000,001	– 40,000,000	175
40,000,001	– 50,000,000	190
50,000,001	– 75,000,000	190
75,000,001	– 100,000,000	225
100,000,001	– 250,000,000	225
250,000,001	– 500,000,000	225
more than 500,000,000		300

5. The NAI has no obligation to pay any costs that are not covered by an advance kept in deposit. The costs of the secretary appointed by the responsible member of the NAI Case Management Committee, the expert, technical assistance or interpreter appointed by the arbitral tribunal, as referred to in Article 58(2) of the Rules, are paid from the advance with priority.
6. No interest is paid on the amount of the advance placed in deposit. Any negative interest may be charged to the advance by the NAI.
7. If an arbitrator has been released from his or her mandate based on Article 21(1), (2), (3) and (4), Article 23(6) of the Rules or Article E5(2) prior to the last final award, or if the mandate of the arbitral tribunal has been terminated prior to the last final award, with the exception of cases as referred to in Article 21(5) of the Rules, the responsible member of the NAI Case Management Committee has discretionary authority to determine, at the request of the arbitrator(s) concerned, an amount to be paid by parties in compensation for the fees and disbursements of the arbitrator(s).
8. The fees set, or to be set, by the responsible member of the NAI Case Management Committee will remain payable upon the withdrawal of an arbitration application or claim(s) or counterclaim(s) or a reduction in the total monetary interest of the claim(s) or counterclaim(s).

* The Executive Board may amend the Rules, including the tables in this Appendix. The most recent version of the Rules can be accessed at www.nai.nl.

EXPLANATORY NOTES TO THE 2024 NAI ARBITRATION RULES

Introduction

These explanatory notes contain a commentary to the 2024 NAI Arbitration Rules, which are in force as of 31 December 2024, being the clerical brush-up of the new Rules first introduced on 1 March 2024.[1] The notes are structured thematically. The topics are dealt with in chronological order, in the sense that the order of the topics reflects the stages at which such topics may be relevant during an arbitration.

1. The Netherlands Arbitration Institute (Appendix A)

1.1 The Netherlands Arbitration Institute (hereinafter: NAI) was established in 1949. It is a foundation established under Dutch law, the most important task of which being the administration of arbitration proceedings.

1.2 The NAI's mission is to promote arbitration, binding advice and other legal means for the prevention, limitation and resolution of disputes. Since its inception, the NAI has pursued this goal by, among other things, providing actors involved in trade and industry with a soundly regulated arbitral procedure. These Arbitration Rules form the basis of that procedure.

1.3 In addition, the NAI may be designated by the parties as the appointing authority for the appointment of arbitrators, even if the parties have not agreed to the applicability of these Arbitration Rules. In addition to arbitration, the NAI also offers binding advice and mediation as forms of alternative dispute resolution, for which it has drawn up separate rules.

---

1 The NAI Board wishes to express its gratitude to Ms. W.M.A. Malcontent (LLM), Administrator and member of the NAI Case Management Committee at the NAI in Rotterdam, the Netherlands, to Ms. S.I. Paoletta (LLM), former Senior Legal Counsel at the NAI in Rotterdam, the Netherlands and, as of August 2024, associate at Avizor in Amsterdam, and to Mr. T. de Boer, (LLM), associate at Linklaters LLP in Amsterdam, for their invaluable work on these explanatory notes.

1.4 With regard to arbitration, the NAI offers five different types of proceedings: (i) arbitration proceedings on the merits, (ii) emergency arbitration, (iii) expedited arbitration, (iv) small claims proceedings and (v) appointment of arbitrators in ad hoc proceedings.

1.5 The governance of the NAI is structured as follows. First, reference is made to the Executive Board, which consists of individuals from the academic, business, and legal communities. The Executive Board is responsible for the management of the foundation, particularly in relation to determining and approving the strategy and policy thereof. The Executive Board has no insight into or influence on the outcome of individual cases.

1.6 The Executive Board is overseen by the advisory board of the NAI. The advisory board provides both solicited and unsolicited advice to the Executive Board. The advisory board also has no insight into or any influence on the outcome of individual cases.

1.7 Second, the NAI Secretariat administers the arbitration proceedings under the direction of the NAI Case Management Committee.

1.8 Finally, the NAI has an independent Challenge Committee consisting of judges and lawyers who decide on challenges through the ad hoc composition of Challenge Chambers. The Challenge Committee, its Challenge Committee Secretariat and its members may have no involvement in the proceedings in which the challenge was first raised.

2. The NAI Arbitration Rules (Article 1 and Article 2)

2.1 The NAI most recently revised its Arbitration Rules on 31 December 2024 (hereinafter: Rules). These Rules are based on the Dutch Arbitration Act (Articles 1020-1076 of the Dutch Code of Civil Procedure), which entered into force on 1 January 2015.

2.2 The Rules govern the procedure for the following arbitration services of the NAI: (i) arbitration on the merits, (ii) emergency arbitration, and (iii) expedited arbitration.

2.3 The Rules are structured in such a way that the appendices form an integral part of the Rules. The appendices concern: (i) the functioning of the NAI Case Management Committee (Appendix A), (ii) the challenge procedure (Appendix B), (iii) emergency arbitration (Appendix C), (iv) expedited arbitration (Appendix D), (v) the consolidation of arbitral proceedings (Appendix E), and (vi) the costs of the arbitration (Appendix F). The appendices set out in detail the additional (Appendices B and E) and alternative (Appendices C and D) procedures provided for in the Rules. Appendices A and F provide for further explanation, substantiation and transparency regarding the governance and functioning of the NAI Case Management Committee and the NAI Secretariat and the regulation on the provisions regarding the costs of the arbitration. These appendices are to be read in combination with the respective relevant provision provided for in the main body of the Rules. For ease of reading and user-friendliness, Appendices B to E are written in such a way as to provide a complete overview of the specific proceedings in question. For this reason, the key standards and provisions are included both in the Rules as well as in the appendices.

2.4 Article 3(2) provides that the Rules shall apply in the version in force at the time at which the arbitration is commenced, irrespective of the date on which the arbitration agreement was concluded. The only exceptions are the provisions relating to the consolidation of arbitral proceedings (Article 44 and Appendix E), the decision-making measure to be applied by the arbitrators (Articles 48(1) and 48(3)) and expedited arbitration (Article 42 and Appendix D). Articles 44 and 48(1) and (3) apply only if (i) the arbitration agreement was concluded on or after 1 January 2015 or (ii) the parties have agreed otherwise (Article 3(3)). Article 42(1) applies only if the arbitration agreement was concluded on or after 1 March 2024.

3. Format and contents of an agreement for NAI arbitration (Article 3 and Article 27)

3.1 Arbitration requires an agreement. Such an agreement may take the form of a clause in a contract requiring future disputes to be submitted to arbitration (the arbitration clause). For existing disputes, an arbitration agreement takes the form of a submission agreement.

3.2 Arbitration in accordance with the NAI Arbitration Rules requires that the parties have agreed on the applicability of these Rules. The parties must have referred the dispute to arbitration by or before the NAI or in accordance with the Rules (Article 3(1)). The NAI recommends that the following arbitration clause be included in the contract.

"All disputes arising in connection with the present agreement, or further agreements resulting therefrom, shall be settled in accordance with the Arbitration Rules of the Netherlands Arbitration Institute"

3.3 On the NAI website, www.nai.nl, one will find the model clause generator, which can assist in drafting a tailored arbitration clause or submission agreement.

3.4 The NAI also recommends the inclusion of the place of arbitration in the arbitration clause. The 'place of arbitration' determines the applicable arbitration law. It is merely a legal concept: hearings may be held anywhere in the world (Article 27(2)). The Rules provide that, if the parties have not agreed on the place of arbitration, the place of arbitration shall be Amsterdam (Article 27(1)). The place of arbitration being Amsterdam leaves open the possibility of conferring exclusive jurisdiction to the Netherlands Commercial Court for proceedings related to the arbitration. For this, the NAI website contains a model clause, which was drafted together with the Netherlands Commercial Court. See https://nai.nl/draft-a-model-clause and www.rechtspraak.nl/English/NCC/Pages/default.aspx.

3.5 In their arbitration agreement, the parties may decide to already determine, inter alia, the number of arbitrators, the method of appointment of the arbitral tribunal, and the language of the proceedings. They may also exclude the consolidation of arbitral proceedings.

3.6 If the parties have not agreed to arbitration through an arbitration clause, they can still submit any disputes that have arisen between them to NAI arbitration by entering into a submission agreement. For this purpose, a written document will suffice if it contains: (a) the names of the parties, (b) an indication of the disputes that the parties wish to submit to arbitration (preferably broadly worded), and (c) the provision that these disputes are to be resolved in accordance with the NAI Arbitration Rules.

4. Communications and time limits (Article 4 and Article 5)

4.1 From the outset, the Rules provide only for electronic communication (Article 4(2)). One exception is the inability of a party to do so (Article 8(3) and Article 9(1) in conjunction with (4)). Another exception to this is the transmission of an original award. The parties will always receive an electronic courtesy copy of the award and will also receive a copy of the original award by post (Article 52).

4.2 According to the Rules, electronic communication can take place in two ways, namely either by e-mail or by using the NAI arbitration platform.

4.3 From 1 March 2024, the NAI provides its users with a secure digital environment, the NAI arbitration platform, for their exchanges in NAI arbitrations. Thus, those involved in the arbitration will always have a complete overview of all aspects of the proceedings in a digitally secure environment. In principle, the procedural documents (including exhibits) are uploaded to the NAI arbitration platform. The arbitral tribunal will also upload documents relating to the procedural order and decisions to the NAI arbitration platform. More information on the NAI arbitration platform can be found on the website of the NAI (www.nai.nl/nai-arbitration-platform-manual).

4.4 Article 4(3) and (4) of the NAI Rules provides when a request, communication or other document is transmitted and/or received.

4.5 Except where the Rules or the arbitral tribunal expressly provide otherwise, a time limit commences on the day on which a request, communication or other document is transmitted (e.g., Article 9(4), Article 17(2), Article 54(1) and Article 55(1)) and, if not transmitted in electronic form as provided for in Article 4, the time limit commences on the date of receipt of the request, communication or other document (Article 5(1)). See for an exception under the Rules e.g.: Article 23(7) and Article 58(3).

4.6 The responsible member of the NAI Case Management Committee is authorised to extend or shorten the time limits listed in Article 5(2) at the request of a party, at the request of the arbitral tribunal, or of its own motion.

4.7 In some places, the Rules specify the time limit in days. A day is defined as "a calendar day" (Article 1(c)). The Rules do not regulate holidays or time zones. The NAI will provide clarity on the deadline in cases where public holidays or time zones play a role. The arbitral tribunal and the parties are encouraged to discuss this topic at the first case management conference if appropriate, and to include it in the first procedural order.

4.8 It goes without saying that, in the event of a defaulting party, the NAI will take the necessary steps to ensure that the defaulting party is notified of all steps leading up to the appointment of the arbitral tribunal. The NAI will also take measures to deliver the award to a defaulting party. If necessary, this may be done by registered letter or by courier. These circumstances may result in the time limits being adjusted accordingly, taking into account the principles of reasonableness and due process.

5. Confidentiality (Article 7)

5.1 Article 7 provides that NAI arbitration is confidential and that all persons directly or indirectly involved are bound to secrecy, except and insofar as disclosure is required by law or by agreement between the parties.

5.2 To guarantee this confidentiality, any prospective arbitrator will be required to sign a confidentiality statement when first contacted by the NAI Secretariat (Article 7(2)). No documents or confidential information will be shared until the prospective arbitrator has returned this statement.

5.3 The NAI is authorised to publish, or have published, an award, an order or a decision on a challenge in anonymous form. The responsible member of the NAI Case Management Committee shall ensure that the award, order or decision on a challenge is anonymised and/or summarised in order to maintain the confidentiality of the arbitration. However, if a party objects to the publication of the award, order or decision on a challenge with the NAI Secretariat within two months of the date thereof, it will not be published (Article 7(3)).

6. Commencement of arbitration (Articles 4, 8, 9 and 10)

6.1 Both in case of an arbitration clause and in case of a submission agreement, NAI arbitration is commenced by submitting a request for arbitration to the NAI Secretariat, either by using the online form on the NAI website (www.nai.nl/arbitration), as recommended by the NAI, or via e-mail (secretariaat@nai.nl) (Article 4(2) and Article 8(3)). If the claimant is unable to do so, the request for arbitration must be submitted in another manner (Article 8(3)).

6.2 The request must contain the particulars set out in Article 8(2)(a) through (l). Article 8(2) is structured in such a way that the requirements that do not begin with "insofar as applicable" are mandatory and must therefore be addressed in the request for arbitration. The responsible member of the NAI Case Management Committee is authorised to suspend the processing of the request as long as it does not satisfy the requirements set out in Article 8(2) (Article 8(4)). Also, the request for arbitration may be withdrawn as long as the composition of the arbitral tribunal has not been completed or only with permission of the arbitral tribunal if the composition of the arbitral tribunal has been completed (Article 8(5)).

6.3 The NAI Secretariat will send a copy of the request for arbitration to the respondent. The respondent then has fourteen days to submit a short answer in response (Article 9). At the same time, the respondent may submit a (conditional or unconditional) counterclaim (Article 9(3)). Although it is preferable that any counterclaim be known at the earliest possible stage of the proceedings (in particular with a view to the arbitrator or arbitrators to be appointed), the respondent may submit a counterclaim at a later stage. It must do so at the latest with the statement of defence or, if no statement of defence is submitted, at the latest with the first written or oral defence after the arbitration file has been made available to the arbitral tribunal by the NAI Secretariat pursuant to Article 20(1) (Article 31(2)).

6.4 The request for arbitration and the short answer may not be exhaustive. Their primarily purpose is to (i) provide the NAI Secretariat with the information necessary for the administration of the arbitration and (ii) provide insight into the nature and circumstances of the dispute with an eye to determining the number of arbitrators and the appointment of the arbitrator(s). Once the arbitrators have been appointed, the parties will be given full opportunity to present their arguments. The short answer is not considered to be a 'first defence' within the meaning of, for example, Article 10. Nor do the request for arbitration and the short answer constitute a statement of claim and statement of defence. Unless otherwise agreed, these statements will only be submitted after the arbitrators have been appointed (Articles 10, 29, and 31).

6.5 The claimant and respondent must, in the request for arbitration and the short answer respectively or – if it arises later – thereafter, each share the name of any party other than the parties to the arbitration that has made an arrangement with a party to the arbitration for the financing of claims or counterclaims on the basis of which the party the name of which will be shared has a beneficial interest in the outcome of the arbitration (Article 8(2)(k) and Article 9(2)(f)).

6.6 The commencement of emergency arbitration is governed by Article 40 in conjunction with Article 41 and Appendix C. Please see Section 14 for an explanation of emergency arbitration proceedings in general and the manner in which the Rules provide for such proceedings.

6.7 The commencement of expedited arbitration is provided in Article 42 and Appendix D. Please see Section 15 for the explanatory notes regarding expedited arbitration.

7. Multi-contract arbitration (Article 11)

7.1 Multi-contract arbitration allows claims arising from disputes under more than one contract to be dealt with in a single arbitration. This is possible if the following two conditions are met: (i) the relevant disputes arise between the same parties, and (ii) the relevant disputes are independently subject to arbitration by or before the NAI or in accordance with the Rules (Article 11(1)).

7.2 If, prior to the completion of the composition of the arbitral tribunal, a party disputes that the conditions of Article 11(1) have been met, the responsible member of the NAI Case Management Committee will decide whether the arbitration will be administered in accordance with the provisions of Article 11(1), where applicable in anticipation of a possible decision of the arbitral tribunal on the basis of Article 11(3). Once the composition of the arbitral tribunal has been completed, a party may submit to the arbitral tribunal that the conditions of Article 11(1) have not been met. The arbitral tribunal will decide in accordance with the provisions of Article 11(1).

8. The jurisdiction of the arbitral tribunal (Article 12)

8.1 It is not the responsibility of the NAI Case Management Committee to assess whether the parties have agreed to (NAI) arbitration and have declared the Arbitration Rules applicable. Instead, it is left to the arbitral tribunal to decide on pleas contesting its jurisdiction (Article 12(4)).

8.2 A respondent who wishes to contest the jurisdiction of the arbitral tribunal on the basis of the absence of a valid (NAI) arbitration agreement must do so in a timely manner. This can be done at the latest in the statement of defence or, in the absence thereof, in the first written or oral defence after the arbitral tribunal has been constituted (Article 12(1)). If the respondent has failed to raise such a plea in a timely manner, it will not be possible to raise the non-existence of an (NAI) arbitration agreement later in the arbitral proceedings or before the court (unless it raises the plea on the ground that the dispute is not capable of being settled by arbitration). Similar rules apply to emergency and expedited arbitration (Article C4 and Article D3).

9. Appointment of arbitrators

a. Impartiality and independence (Article 13)

9.1 The fundamental principle of impartiality and independence of arbitrators is set forth in Article 13(2).

i. Prior to the appointment

9.2 Each prospective arbitrator must, prior to the appointment, inter alia, make a statement confirming his or her independence and impartiality. If the prospective arbitrator has reason to suspect that there might be justifiable doubts as to his or her impartiality or independence he or she must communicate this in writing, stating the suspected reason(s) (Article 13(3)). The arbitrator may seek guidance from the lists in the IBA Guidelines when considering whether or not to make a disclosure.

9.3 The responsible member of the NAI Case Management Committee sends the abovementioned statement to the parties and, where the arbitral tribunal consists of more than one arbitrator, to the other arbitrator(s) or to the other prospective arbitrator(s) and sets a time limit for the parties to submit any comments. All statements made by the prospective arbitrator will be distributed by the NAI Case Management Committee to the addressees mentioned in the preceding sentence. This applies both to a statement in which the prospective arbitrator confirms his or her independence and impartiality *with* a disclosure of reasons to suspect that there might be justifiable doubts as to his or her impartiality and a statement in which the prospective arbitrator confirms his or her independence and impartiality *without* a disclosure of reasons to suspect that there might be justifiable doubts as to his or her impartiality. Of course, a statement in which a prospective arbitrator does not confirm his or her independence and impartiality will also be distributed.

ii. **During the proceedings**

9.4 If, during the course of the arbitral proceedings, an arbitrator suspects that there might be justifiable doubts as to his or her impartiality and independence, he or she shall so inform the responsible member of the NAI Case Management Committee, the parties and, if the arbitral tribunal consists of multiple arbitrators, to the co-arbitrators, in writing. The suspected reason(s) for these justifiable doubts will also be stated (Article 13(4)).

b. **Number of arbitrators (Article 14)**

9.5 Arbitral proceedings are conducted before an arbitral tribunal composed of an odd number of arbitrators (Article 14(1)). In most cases the arbitral tribunal will consist of one or three arbitrators. If the parties have agreed on an even number of arbitrators, an additional arbitrator will be appointed as chair of the arbitral tribunal to make the number of arbitrators an odd number (Article 14(3)).

9.6 If the parties have not agreed on the number of arbitrators, or if they cannot reach an agreement on this, the responsible member of the NAI Case Management Committee will set the number of arbitrators at one or three. In doing so, the responsible member of the

NAI Case Management Committee will take account of the parties' preferences, the scope of the dispute, the monetary interest of the claims, the complexity of the dispute and the parties' interest in efficient proceedings (Article 14(2)). As a rule, the number of arbitrators will be set at one for an arbitration involving a monetary interest of less than € 1,000,000, and three if the monetary interest exceeds that amount.

c. Composition of the arbitral tribunal (Article 15)

9.7 Article 15(1) states that the arbitral tribunal is composed once the arbitrator(s) has (have) been appointed. Thus, according to the Rules, the composition of an arbitral tribunal requires appointment of its arbitrators, most often preceded by their nomination. The arbitral tribunal is composed on the basis of the methods mentioned in Article 15 as well as in Article 16, Article 17 and Article 18 (Article 15(2)). Nominations may be made in a number of ways. Appointments are made by the responsible member of the NAI Case Management Committee (see also Article 15(3)).

9.8 This section outlines the composition of the arbitral tribunal in arbitration on the merits. See Section 14 for more on the composition of the arbitral tribunal in emergency arbitrations and Section 15 for expedited arbitrations.

i. Party nomination and appointment of the chair of the arbitral tribunal (Article 16)

9.9 Unless the parties have agreed otherwise, the arbitral tribunal will in principle be composed on the basis of a nomination by the parties of one or more prospective arbitrators, followed by the appointment by the responsible member of the NAI Case Management Committee (Article 16 and Article 15(3)).

9.10 If the arbitral tribunal consists of one arbitrator, the parties will jointly nominate a prospective arbitrator when submitting the request for arbitration or the short answer (or at the latest within the time limit as stated in Article 16(1)). If they fail to do so within this time limit, the arbitrator will be directly appointed by the responsible member of the NAI Case Management Committee.

9.11 If the arbitral tribunal consists of three arbitrators, Articles 16(2) provides that the claimant and the respondent will each nominate a prospective co-arbitrator in the request for arbitration and the short answer, respectively. If one of the parties fails to do so within the time limit, the responsible member of the NAI Case Management

Committee will directly appoint the related co-arbitrator. Subsequently, within fourteen days after the responsible member of the NAI Case Management Committee has requested them to do so, the two appointed arbitrators will, jointly with the responsible member of the NAI Case Management Committee on the basis of unanimity appoint a chair of the arbitral tribunal, stating the name, address, place of residence, telephone number and email address of the chair. The clause "jointly (...) on the basis of unanimity" refers to the appointment process through which the co-arbitrators and the responsible member of the NAI Case Management Committee will jointly appoint the chair of the arbitral tribunal on the basis of unanimity after having consulted one another. If the joint appointment does not occur within the given time limit, the responsible member of the NAI Case Management Committee will directly appoint the arbitrator. In the appointment process under Article 16(2), the responsible member of the NAI Management Committee will act in accordance with the duties provided for under Article 15(5) and (6) (see Sections 9.22-9.23).

ii. List procedure (Article 17)

9.12 In derogation of Article 16, parties may agree that the arbitrator(s) will be appointed in accordance with the list procedure set out in Article 17 in conjunction with Article 15(3). Under the list procedure, the responsible member of the NAI Case Management Committee will, upon receipt of the short answer, draw up a list of the names of possible arbitrators and transmit this list to the parties.

9.13 This list contains at least three names if one arbitrator is to be appointed and at least nine names if three arbitrators are to be appointed. Once the list is transmitted, each party has fourteen days to delete from the list the names of persons against whom it has strong objections and to rank the remaining names in its order of preference. A party is not required to send a copy of the list with its preferences to the counterparty. On the basis of a comparison of the returned lists, the responsible member of the NAI Case Management Committee will then appoint the arbitrator(s). The responsible member of the NAI Case Management Committee is not required to provide the parties with new lists if the returned lists contains an insufficient number of persons who are acceptable as arbitrator(s) to each of the parties. The same applies if there is a sufficient number of persons on the returned lists who are unable or unwilling to accept their appointment. Then, the responsible member of the

NAI Case Management Committee may proceed to directly appoint a person who was not featured on the list issued to the parties.

9.14 The list procedure is the standard method of appointing arbitral tribunal, consisting of one arbitrator, in expedited arbitration. See Section 15 below.

iii. A method of nomination agreed upon by the parties which deviates from Article 16 or Article 17 (Article 18)

9.15 If the parties have agreed on a method of composition of the arbitral tribunal which deviates from Article 16 or Article 17, the nomination of (a) prospective arbitrator(s) to be appointed as arbitrator(s) will take place in the manner agreed upon by the parties.

9.16 If the agreed method of composition of the arbitral tribunal has not been carried out in whole or in part within the period agreed upon by the parties or, failing that, within four weeks of the commencement of the arbitration, the responsible member of the NAI Case Management Committee will directly appoint the relevant arbitrator(s).

iv. Nomination of the arbitral tribunal where there are multiple claimants and/or respondents (Article 19)

9.17 If there are multiple claimants and/or respondents and the composition of the arbitral tribunal takes place in the manner provided in Article 16, in case of an arbitral tribunal consisting of three or more arbitrators, claimants will jointly nominate an arbitrator and respondents will jointly nominate an arbitrator (Article 19(1)).

9.18 If either the claimants fail to jointly nominate an arbitrator or the respondents jointly fail to nominate a prospective arbitrator within the time limit set in Article 16(2), all members of the arbitral tribunal will be appointed via the list procedure (Article 19(2)).

v. Nomination of arbitral tribunal after consolidation of arbitral proceedings by consolidator

9.19 Article E5(1) provides for the nomination of the arbitrator(s) for the arbitral tribunal after consolidation. See Section 17 below.

vi. Direct appointment by the responsible member of the NAI Case Management Committee

9.20 Direct appointments by the responsible member of the NAI Case Management Committee are made if the parties fail to nominate the arbitrator(s) within the time limits provided for in the Rules or as agreed upon by the parties. In this way, direct appointments constitute the fallback method of appointing of the arbitral tribunal.

9.21 In emergency arbitration, the direct appointment is the standard method of appointing the emergency arbitrator. See Section 14 below.

vii. Appointment of arbitrator(s) by the NAI Case Management Committee after nomination

9.22 The responsible member of the NAI Case Management Committee will not appoint a prospective arbitrator if, in the opinion of the responsible member of the NAI Case Management Committee, the prospective arbitrator offers insufficient safeguards for sound arbitration (Article 15(3) in conjunction with Article 15(6)). As and when necessary, the responsible member of the NAI Case Management Committee may also, with a view to a proper application of Article 25(3), take into account the required availability of the arbitrator and the parties' interest in preventing any unnecessary delays of the proceedings. The appointment by the responsible member of the NAI Case Management Committee does not affect the possibility of challenging an arbitrator; the final decision on a challenge request is reserved to the Challenge Committee (see Section 18 below).

9.23 The parties, the person or persons representing them, the arbitrator(s) and the responsible member of the NAI Case Management Committee shall consider the benefits of diversity and inclusivity when nominating prospective arbitrator(s) and when appointing arbitrator(s) under the Rules (Article 15(5)).

d. Termination of mandate (Article 21 and Article 22)

9.24 The mandate of the arbitrator shall, in principle, terminate upon the transmission of the final award to the parties (Article 46(2)). The mandate can also be terminated at an earlier stage of the arbitration. Article 21 gives the parties or the responsible member of the NAI Case Management Committee the authority to release an arbitrator from his or her mandate. The termination of an arbitrator's mandate does not automatically terminate the mandates of the other arbitrators (except as provided in Article 21(5)).

9.25 In the event that an arbitrator has been released from his or her mandate and the arbitration has not been withdrawn, the released arbitrator shall be replaced. Article 22 regulates such replacements and the continuation of the proceedings.

9.26 In addition to the termination of an arbitrator's mandate pursuant to Article 21, an arbitrator's mandate will also be terminated if the arbitrator is challenged (Article 23 and Appendix B) and the grounds for that challenge are found to be well-founded by the Challenge Chamber (see Section 18 below).

9.27 Moreover, Article 58(7) and Article F3(7) provide that, in the event the mandate of the arbitrator has been terminated prior to the final award, the responsible member of the NAI Case Management Committee may, at the request of the arbitrator concerned, determine a fee and disbursement allowance for the arbitrator.

9.28 In the case of (i) a rectification of the award (Article 54), (ii) an additional award (Article 55), or (iii) a remission during setting aside and/or revocation proceedings, the arbitrator's mandate terminates at a later date than the date of the transmission of the final award.

10. Appointment of the secretary of the arbitral tribunal (Article 24)

10.1 The arbitral tribunal can request the responsible member of the NAI Case Management Committee to appoint a secretary to the arbitral tribunal. The secretary has to be legally qualified. Where the qualification was obtained is irrelevant.

10.2 Like the arbitrator(s), to be appointed the secretary must be independent, impartial and preserve confidentiality. In this respect, the secretary is held to the same standards as the arbitrators. The secretary is required to make the statements on confidentiality and independence and impartiality as mentioned in Article 7(2) and Article 13(3) respectively. See Section 9(a).

10.3 The mandate and scope of work of the secretary is determined by the arbitral tribunal. The work of the secretary is performed for, on behalf of and under the supervision of the arbitral tribunal.

10.4 The secretary has no decision-making power, and the arbitral tribunal is not permitted to delegate any decision-making power to a secretary (Article 24(2)).

11. Conduct of the arbitration

11.1 Without prejudice to any provision of applicable mandatory arbitration law, the arbitral tribunal determines the manner in which and the time limits within which the proceedings will be conducted, with due observance of any arrangements between the parties in that regard, the provisions of the Rules and the circumstances of the arbitration (Article 25(1)).

11.2 The arbitral tribunal must treat the parties equally (Article 25(2)). The Rules also provide that the arbitral tribunal must guard against unreasonable delay of the proceedings and, if necessary, take measures to effectuate a just, efficient and final settlement of the dispute (Article 25(3)).

11.3 Furthermore, all parties to the arbitration must take into account sustainability aspects in the conduct of the arbitration (Article 25(4)).

11.4 Regarding the conduct of the arbitration, the Rules provide as follows. First, after the appointment of the arbitrator(s), a case management conference must be held within three weeks after the NAI Secretariat has made the arbitration file available to the arbitral tribunal (Article 20(1) and Article 26(1)).

11.5 Article 26(2) sets out a non-exhaustive but mandatory list of nine topics that should be addressed at the case management conference. The topic of expedited arbitration (Article 26(2)(b)) should only be addressed to the extent that it is relevant given the nature of the dispute.

11.6 Subsequently, no later than two weeks after the case management conference, the arbitral tribunal will determine the order of proceedings, including a (provisional) timetable for the further conduct of the arbitration, which should include a provisional date for the award with due observance of the provisions of Article 46(1) (Article 26(3)).

11.7 In most cases, the arbitration shall proceed in the following order. The claimant and the respondent are given the opportunity to submit a statement of claim and a statement of defence, respectively (Article 29(1)). Then, the arbitral tribunal will order a midstream conference (Article 30). This may be followed by a second exchange of statements (a statement of reply and a statement of rejoinder) (Article 29(2)). Pursuant to Article 35(1), the aforementioned written statements are, as much as possible, accompanied by the documents relied upon by the parties, unless the parties have agreed otherwise. On the basis of Article 35(2), the arbitral tribunal may order the inspection of, a copy of, or an extract from, specific documents related to the dispute from the party which has these documents at its disposal. After the exchange(s) of written submissions, a hearing will be held (Article 32), during which each of the parties may orally explain its case. Witnesses and/or experts may also be heard at this hearing, or at a separate hearing (Article 36). After the hearing and any cost submissions made, the arbitral tribunal will deliberate and render its award. See para 11.8 for the time limit within which the award must be rendered. A draft of the award is transmitted to the NAI Case Management Committee for a formal review (Article 50(4)). The award shall be made in three copies and signed by each member of the arbitral tribunal (Article 49(3)). The NAI Secretariat, on behalf of the arbitral tribunal, will send an original of the award to the parties (Article 52).

11.8 At the end of the hearing, the arbitral tribunal may communicate with the parties regarding the date on which it will make its award, taking into account the provisional date already communicated to the parties in the procedural order and Article 46(1), which provides that the arbitral award must be made within eight weeks after the last hearing. If the parties have waived a hearing as referred to in Article 32(1), the arbitral tribunal may so inform the parties after the last statement has been submitted. The time limit communicated to the parties may, in exceptional circumstances, be extended on the basis of Article 5(3) (i.e., by the arbitral tribunal). The maximum time limit of eight weeks may be extended on the basis of Article 5(2) (i.e., by the responsible member of the NAI Case Management Committee).

12. Costs (Article 56, Article 57, Article 58, Article 59 and Appendix F)

12.1 Section Six of the Rules and Appendix F provide the framework for the (determination of the) costs of arbitration. Article 56(1) makes clear that the costs of the arbitration consist of (i) the administration fees, (ii) the fees and disbursements of the arbitrator(s), and (iii) the other costs which, in the opinion of the arbitral tribunal, were necessarily incurred in the arbitration. The costs under (i) and (ii) are determined by the responsible member of the NAI Case Management Committee (Article F2 and F3).

12.2 The administration fees are due at the time the request for arbitration or a counterclaim is submitted (Article 57(1) and Article 57(2)). The amount of administration fees payable depends on the monetary interest of the claim(s) or counterclaim(s) (see Table A under Article F2(1)). This entails that the responsible member of the NAI Case Management Committee must provisionally determine the monetary interest upon the receipt of the request for arbitration. In order to assist the responsible member of the NAI Case Management Committee, the claimant must include, in its request for arbitration, a specification of the monetary interest of each of the claims, including interest, as well as an estimate of the monetary interest of each of the non-monetary claims (Article 8(2)(e)). The (underlying) monetary interest of claims for declaratory relief and contingent claims or counterclaims must also be specified (Article F1(1)). If, in the opinion of the responsible member of the NAI Case Management Committee, a party's estimate is manifestly too low, the responsible member of the NAI Case Management Committee has the discretion to determine a (higher) monetary interest (Article 57(3) and F1(2)).

12.3 The monetary interest is not only relevant for the determination of the administration fees to be paid, but also for the determination of the hourly rate of the arbitrator(s) and of the possible secretary (see Table B under Article F3(1) and Table D under Article F3(4), respectively) and, thus, also for the amount of the advance on costs due (see Table C under Article F3(3)).

12.4 The responsible member of the NAI Case Management Committee may increase the administration fees in the event of an increase of a claim or counterclaim, in the event of new claims or counterclaims or in the event of an adjustment of the monetary interest. (Article F2(4) in conjunction with Article 57(3) and Article F1(3)). See for the arbitrator fees para 12.7.

12.5 Where it concerns the fees and disbursements of the arbitrator(s), the following should be taken into account. When the prospective arbitrator is invited by the NAI Secretariat to act as arbitrator in a specific arbitration, the applicable hourly rate is communicated to him or to her. Once the arbitral tribunal has been composed, the arbitral tribunal is requested to consult with responsible member of the NAI Case Management Committee so that the latter may determine the amount of the advance that a party or the parties need to deposit so as to cover the fees and disbursements of the arbitrator(s) (Article 58(1)). The amount of the advance is determined by the responsible member of the NAI Case Management Committee on the basis of Table C and the substantiation of the expected work to be performed by the arbitrator(s) (Article F3(2)).

12.6 The advance paid by a party or by the parties will be used to pay the arbitrators' fees and disbursements at the end of the proceedings (Article 58(2)). The NAI has no obligation to pay any costs that are not covered by an advance kept in deposit (Article F3(5)).

12.7 Similarly to the administration fees (see para 12.4), the responsible member of the NAI Case Management Committee may redetermine the amount of the advance in accordance with Article F3 and require the claimant and/or the respondent to supplement the advance to be kept in deposit until no later than fourteen days after the last hearing or until no later than fourteen days after receipt of the last admissible written statement by the arbitral tribunal (Article 58(3)).

12.8 If, after the second reminder from the responsible member of the NAI Case Management Committee to pay the administration fee and/or the advance on costs, fees and disbursements of the arbitrator(s), no payment is made within fourteen days thereafter, the defaulting party will be deemed to have withdrawn its claim(s) or counterclaim(s). This party is not, on the mere basis of this withdrawal, prevented from bringing the same claim(s) or counterclaim(s) again at a later date in other proceedings (Article 57(4) and Article 58(4)). The administration fees and reasonable compensation determined by the responsible member of the NAI Case Management Committee remain payable (Article F2(5) and F3(8)).

12.9 To make the (total) costs more transparent, the NAI provides a cost calculator on its website for users who wish to quickly obtain an estimate of the total costs of the arbitration (www.nai.nl/arbitration, under 10).

12.10 The arbitrator's fees and disbursements are determined by the responsible member of the NAI Case Management Committee on the basis of the time that the arbitrator(s) spent on the proceedings, the monetary interest of the claims and counterclaims, the complexity of the proceedings and the amount of the advance (Article 58(6) and F3).

12.11 Arbitration may also involve other costs, such as the costs of witnesses, experts and the secretary of the arbitral tribunal. The costs of the secretary of the arbitral tribunal are considered to be disbursements of the arbitrator, while the other costs mentioned are 'other costs' within the meaning of Article 56(1)(c) (i.e., costs which, in the opinion of the arbitral tribunal, were necessarily incurred in the arbitration).

12.12 In principle, the arbitral tribunal will order the unsuccessful party to pay the costs of the arbitration. If both parties are partially successful, the arbitral tribunal may apportion the costs of the arbitration in whole or in part (Article 59(2)). The foregoing standard also applies to the costs of legal assistance (Article 59(3)).

12.13 Any fees set or to be set by the responsible member of the Case Management Committee on the basis of the Rules will remain payable and will not be refunded if a request for arbitration is withdrawn or if one or more claim(s) or counterclaim(s) are withdrawn or if the total monetary interest of the claim(s) and counterclaim(s) is reduced (Article F2(5) and F3(8)).

12.14 If, at the end of the arbitration, there is a positive balance of the deposit, the surplus will be returned to the party who made the deposit or to the party entitled to it pursuant to the cost order in the arbitral award.

13. The award (Article 46 and Article 50)

13.1 The arbitral tribunal must make its award within eight weeks after the last hearing (Article 46(1)).

13.2 Article 50(1)(a) to (j) provides what must be included in the award. Exceptions to these requirements apply only to the award on agreed terms (Article 51(2)).

13.3 Pursuant to Article 50(1)(f), the final award must also contain the determination and order to pay the arbitration costs as referred to in Article 59. When deciding on the division of the costs of the arbitration and the costs of legal assistance, the arbitral tribunal may take into account the manner in which the parties conducted the proceedings as well as whether each of the parties promoted the speedy and efficient conduct of the proceedings. If, in the opinion of the arbitral tribunal, a party has unreasonably delayed the arbitral proceedings, the arbitral tribunal may take this into account in its decision on the division of the costs of the arbitration and the costs of legal assistance (Article 59(4)). Thus, party conduct may play a role in the arbitrator's cost order.

13.4 The scrutiny of the draft award by the NAI Case Management Committee referred to in Article 50(4) must also have taken place within the eight weeks referred to in para 13.1. This will normally not take more than five working days, depending on the complexity of the dispute, and the length and type of the award (see para 11.7 above). In order to perform the scrutiny, the arbitral tribunal is to transmit a draft of the award to the responsible member of the NAI Case Management Committee. The responsible member of the NAI Case Management Committee may then make recommendations with respect to the provisions of paragraph 1(a), (b), (c), (d), (f), (g), (i) and (j), without prejudice to the discretion of the arbitral tribunal. Additionally, the responsible member of the NAI Case Management Committee may point out to the arbitral tribunal manifest computational or clerical errors in the draft of the award or any other manifest errors contained therein that lend themselves to simple rectification and any omission to decide on one or more claims or counterclaims that have been subjected to the arbitral tribunal's discretion. The arbitral tribunal remains responsible for both the content and form of the award, however.

14. Interim measures and emergency arbitration (Article 40, Article 41 and Appendix C)

14.1 Article 40(1) provides for the possibility of seeking interim measures in two instances:
(a) during pending arbitral proceedings on the merits, the arbitral tribunal may, at the request of any of the parties and with due observance of the provisions of Article 40, grant interim measures related to the claim or counterclaim as filed;
(b) regardless of whether arbitral proceedings on the merits are pending, in all urgent cases that require immediately enforceable interim measures in view of the parties' interests, an arbitral tribunal specifically composed to that end may, at the request of any of the parties, grant interim measures in emergency arbitration with due observance of the provisions of Article 41. If the place of arbitration has not been determined for the arbitral proceedings on the merits, the place of arbitration of the emergency arbitration is Amsterdam.

14.2 In the case of emergency arbitration, the arbitral tribunal consists of one arbitrator, who will be appointed by the responsible member of the NAI Case Management Committee. If the parties have agreed on a method of appointment of the arbitral tribunal and/or a multiple number of arbitrators, this will not apply to the appointment of the arbitral tribunal in emergency arbitration, unless the parties have provided otherwise (Article C2(1)). The further course of the emergency arbitration is governed by the provisions of Article 41 and Appendix C. Unlike arbitration on the merits, emergency arbitration is subject to shorter time limits. This also applies to the costs provisions. For example, only a single reminder will be sent to the parties before to the claim(s) and/or counterclaim(s) are deemed to have withdrawn (Article C7(2)) (see also para 12.8).

14.3 The arbitral tribunal may, in conjunction with the interim measures sought by each party, require that sufficient security is provided, including the provision of security for the claim or counterclaim in the main action and the costs of the arbitral proceedings on the merits (Article 40(2)). This power is not only given to the arbitral tribunal in emergency arbitration referred to in Article 41, but also to the arbitral tribunal on the merits when deciding a claim for interim measures as referred to in Article 40(1)(a). Article 40(2) also corresponds with the rule provided for in Article 1043b(2) of the Dutch

Code of Civil Procedure, which applies in any event in arbitral proceedings with a place of arbitration located in the Netherlands.

14.4 The decision on the interim measures shall in no way prejudice the final decision in the arbitral proceedings on the merits (Article 40(4)). The decision may take the form of an order of the arbitral tribunal or the form of an award (Article 40(3)).

14.5 The arbitral tribunal will render its award within two weeks after the last hearing. Within these two weeks, the scrutiny of the draft award by the NAI Case Management Committee referred to Article 50(4) must also have taken place. In principle, the scrutiny takes up to three working days in emergency arbitration (for more on the scrutiny of the draft award, see Section 13).

14.6 The arbitral tribunal may make an oral award during or following the hearing if there is such urgency that a full written elaboration of the award cannot be awaited (Article C8(2)-(4)).

14.7 Emergency arbitration can also be used in international arbitration proceedings, regardless of whether the place of arbitration is located in the Netherlands or not. If the place of arbitration is located in the Netherlands, it is not required to conduct subsequent proceedings on the merits. If the place of arbitration is located outside the Netherlands, this needs to be determined on the basis of the applicable arbitration act.

15. Expedited arbitration (Article 42 and Appendix D)

15.1 Article 42 and Appendix D contain the rules for expedited arbitration. Expedited arbitration offers an expedited procedure for the conduct of the arbitration.

15.2 In order for the rules on expedited arbitration to apply automatically, three conditions must be met. First, the arbitration agreement(s) providing for arbitration by or before the NAI or in accordance with the Rules must have been concluded on or after 1 March 2024. Second, the total amount claimed by the claimant in the request for arbitration does not exceed € 1,000,000. Third, the parties must not have excluded the application of the rules on expedited arbitration. Alternatively, the rules for expedited arbitration will apply if the parties agree in writing to the application of such rules (Article 42(1) and (2)).

15.3 The parties will be informed of the applicability of the expedited arbitration rules at the same time as respondent is invited to submit a short answer (Article D3 and Article 9(1)).

15.4 In expedited arbitration as referred to in Article 42 and Appendix D, the arbitral tribunal consists of one arbitrator. The rules provide for two exceptions to this rule: (i) where one of the parties states in the request for arbitration or the short answer that it wishes to retain a different (previously) agreed number of arbitrators and, (ii) where the parties have expressly and specifically provided for the number of arbitrators and/or the method of appointment of an arbitral tribunal in an expedited arbitration in their agreement for expedited arbitration (Article D4(1)).

15.5 In the absence of a specific agreement between the parties to expedited arbitration, the Rules provide that the arbitrator shall be appointed by the list procedure (Article D4(2), Article D4(3), Article D4(4)).

15.6 The further conduct of the proceedings is governed by the provisions of Article 42 and Appendix D. Noteworthy is the provision regarding the case management conference, which is to be held in electronic format no later than fourteen days from the date of composition of the arbitral tribunal (Article D5), the provision regarding the limited exchanges of written statements (Article D6), and the provision entailing that only one hearing will be held, which will take place in electronic form (Article D8). Reference is also made to the provision entailing that the award is to be rendered within five months after the case management conference (Article D11). Within this time limit, the scrutiny of the draft award by the NAI Case Management Committee as referred to in Article 50(4) must also have taken place. Normally, the scrutiny will take place within three working days. The time limit for a party's payment obligations are shorter. Only a single reminder is sent to parties before the claim(s) and/or counterclaim(s) are deemed to have been withdrawn (Article D10(2)) (see also para 12.8).

15.7 The interrelationship between the arbitration proceedings on the merits and the expedited proceedings is governed by Article D6(3), Article D7(2), Article D7(3) and Article D9.

15.8 Articles D6 and D7 provide that, where the total monetary interest of the claim(s) exceeds the amount of € 1,000,000 as a result of an increase of the claim or the filing of a counterclaim, the arbitral tribunal, consisting of one arbitrator, retains its jurisdiction except where one of the parties insists on the other number of arbitrators originally agreed. The responsible member of the NAI Case Management Committee will then invite the parties to each nominate one or more arbitrators within a specified time limit. The arbitrator already appointed pursuant to Article D4 and Article 15(3), or Article 15(2)(d), of the Rules will then be designated as the chair.

15.9 Article D9 provides that exceptional circumstances may merit that the parties jointly and/or the arbitral tribunal make or makes a request to the responsible member of the NAI Case Management Committee to decide that the case is not suitable to be decided in an expedited arbitration. If the responsible member of the NAI Case Management Committee decides that the case is not suitable, the case will be moved forward as an arbitration on the merits. The arbitral tribunal will then retain its jurisdiction, unless one of the parties insists on the other number of arbitrators originally agreed. If required, the responsible member of the NAI Case Management Committee will then invite the parties to each nominate one or more arbitrators within a specified time limit. The arbitrator appointed pursuant to Article D4 and Article 15(3), or Article 15(2)(d), of the Rules will then be designated as the chair.

16. Early determination (Article 45)

16.1 On basis of Article 45, the arbitral tribunal may, at the request of a party, dismiss a claim, counterclaim or defence that is manifestly inadmissible, manifestly outside the jurisdiction of the arbitral tribunal, or manifestly legally unfounded.

16.2 The arbitral tribunal will hear the counterparty in order to decide whether the request for an early determination procedure can be considered. If the arbitral tribunal decides that the request for an early determination can be considered, the arbitral tribunal must render its decision within 30 days after the arbitral tribunal has notified the parties that the request for an early determination will be considered. The decision to dismiss a claim, counterclaim or defence by way of early determination may take the form of an order of the arbitral tribunal or an award (Article 45(2)). Specifically, the dismissal of a claim will take the form of an award. The refusal to dismiss a claim may take the form of an order.

17. Consolidation (Article 44 and Appendix E)

17.1 A party may submit a request to NAI Secretariat for the consolidation of arbitral proceedings with other arbitral proceedings that are governed by the Rules (Article 44(1)). Such consolidation may be ordered insofar as it does not cause unreasonable delay in the pending proceedings (Article 44(2) and Article E3).

17.2 The NAI Secretariat will send a copy of the request for consolidation to all parties and to the arbitrators, if already appointed, and will invite the parties to jointly appoint within fourteen days a consolidator who will decide on the request for consolidation (Articles 44(1) and Article E2). The arbitral tribunal may stay the pending arbitral proceedings from the date of receipt of the request for consolidation (Article E1). If the parties fail to agree, the responsible member of the NAI Case Management Committee will directly designate a consolidator (Article E2(1)). In principle, none of the arbitrators appointed in the arbitral proceedings of which the consolidation is being requested may be designated as a consolidator (Article E2(2)).

17.3 Before deciding on the request for consolidation, the consolidator will give the parties and, insofar as already appointed, the arbitrators the opportunity to make their opinions known (Article E4).

17.4 If the consolidator orders consolidation, the parties will nominate, in consultation with each other, the prospective arbitrator(s) for the consolidated proceedings. If the parties are unable to reach agreement in this regard within the time limit specified by the responsible member of the NAI Case Management Committee, the consolidator will, at the request of the most diligent party, nominate the prospective arbitrator(s) (Article E5(1)).

17.5 The mandate of the arbitrator(s) appointed to the proceedings that were separately commenced will terminate if they are not re-appointed in the consolidated proceedings. To the extent necessary, the consolidator, in consultation with the NAI Case Management Committee, will determine the remuneration for the work carried out by such arbitrator(s) (Article E5(2)).

18. Challenge (Article 23 and Appendix B)

18.1 If, after the appointment of an arbitrator, there are justifiable doubts as to the independence or impartiality of an arbitrator, that arbitrator may be challenged by a party. A party may not challenge an arbitrator if it has acquiesced in his or her appointment, except where that party only became aware of the ground for the challenge afterwards (Article 23(1)).

18.2 A party that wishes to challenge an arbitrator must, within fourteen days after the party wishing to challenge an arbitrator has become aware of the grounds for the challenge, give written notice of the challenge to the arbitrator concerned, to the other party and, if the arbitral tribunal consists of multiple arbitrators, to the other arbitrators and to the responsible member of the NAI Case Management Committee (Article 23(3)).

18.3 The challenged arbitrator may resign within fourteen days after the receipt of a timely notice of challenge (Article 23(6) and (7)). If a challenged arbitrator resigns, this does not imply acceptance that the reasons for the challenge are well-founded (Article 23(5)). If the challenged arbitrator does not resign, the responsible member of the NAI Case Management Committee will forward the notice of the challenge to the chair of the Challenge Committee only if the challenge is expressly upheld at that stage by the challenging party (Article 23(7) and Article B3(1)). If the challenging party does not expressly uphold the challenge within fourteen days of being requested to do so by the responsible member of the NAI Case Management Committee, the challenge shall be deemed to have been withdrawn.

18.4 If the challenge is maintained, the chair of the Challenge Committee will, as soon as possible, put together a Challenge Chamber consisting of three members of the Challenge Committee, who will decide impartially and independently whether the challenge is well-founded. The Challenge Chamber appoints a chair from among its members (Article B3(2)).

18.5 The Challenge Committee is constituted by the Executive Board and is charged with handling challenge requests as referred to in Article 23 of the Rules and Appendix B. The Challenge Committee is independent and completely separate from the NAI Secretariat and the NAI Case Management Committee. To this end, the Challenge Committee also has its own secretariat (Article B1). Article B2 regulates the composition of Challenge Committee, Challenge Chamber and the Challenge Committee Secretariat.

18.6 The manner in which the challenge procedure is to be conducted is further set out in Appendix B. Before deciding on the merits of the challenge, the Challenge Chamber shall (i) give the challenging party the opportunity to further explain in writing the reasons underlying the notice of challenge, (ii) to give the challenged arbitrator, the parties and the other arbitrators of the tribunal the opportunity to respond and (iii) to hold an oral hearing (Article B3(3) and Article B3(4)).

18.7 If an arbitrator resigns in response to a challenge request or if the Committee finds the challenge request to be well-founded, the arbitrator concerned will be replaced in accordance with the rules applicable to the original appointment, unless the parties have agreed otherwise (Article 23(6) and Article 22(1)). Article F3(7) gives the responsible member of the NAI Case Management Committee the discretionary authority to determine at the request of the arbitrator(s) concerned the renumeration of said former arbitrator(s). Under circumstances no compensation may be granted.

18.8 Without prejudice to any provision of applicable mandatory arbitration law, the Challenge Chamber may issue an oral decision during or following the oral hearing if there is such urgency that a full written elaboration of the decision cannot be awaited. The oral decision must state both the decision and the main reasons of the decision. With due observance of the provisions of Article B3(6), which governs the written decision of the Challenge Chamber, a full written elaboration of the oral decision will be made available to the parties as soon as possible and in any event within two weeks of the oral decision. The written elaboration must state the date of the oral decision as well as the date on which the written elaboration of that decision is set (Article B3(7)).

18.9 The costs of the challenge, including the remuneration of the members of the Challenge Chamber is determined in advance by the Executive Board and paid by the NAI (Article B2(9)).

18.10 If the Challenge Chamber finds that the challenging party has abused its right to raise a challenge, the Challenge Chamber may decide that a subsequent challenge will not be considered. This will be noted in the decision of a Challenge Chamber (Article B3(8)).

18.11 The Challenge Chamber's decision may be published pursuant to Article 7(3) of the Rules (see para 5.3).

19. Processing of personal data (Article 63)

19.1 The processing of personal data by the NAI is subject to the applicable regulations on the protection of personal data as well as to NAI's privacy statement as published on the website (www.nai.nl/privacy-statement).

19.2 The NAI and the arbitral tribunal may, in compliance with the applicable provisions of mandatory law, issue instructions regarding the security of information and/or the protection of (personal) data which are binding on the parties, and, in the case of instructions from the NAI, also on the arbitral tribunal (Article 63(2)). To this end, the NAI uses the NAI arbitration platform to carry out its case administration and management (see para 4.3).

20. Exclusion of liability (Article 64)

20.1 The NAI, its Executive Board members and employees (including the members of the NAI Case Management Committee), the members of its advisory board, the members of the Challenge Committee, the arbitrator(s), the secretary, the consolidator, any other person that may have been appointed by (one of) these persons or other persons who fulfil a role pursuant to the Rules are not liable either by contract or otherwise for any damage caused by their own or any other person's acts or omissions or caused by the use of any aids in or involving arbitration, all this except where and insofar as mandatory Dutch law precludes this exclusion of liability.

20.2 To the extent that they are liable at all on the basis of the above, the NAI, its Executive Board members and employees, including the members of the NAI Case Management Committee, are not liable for payment of any amount that is not covered by the advance.

The NAI Secretariat will be pleased to provide additional information regarding NAI arbitration (P.O. Box 21075, 3001 AB Rotterdam, 'Delftse Poort', Weena 505, 3013 AL Rotterdam, telephone: +31-10-2816969; email: secretariaat@nai.nl; website: www.nai.nl.

SERIE ONDERNEMING EN RECHT

In de Serie Onderneming en Recht zijn de volgende delen verschenen:

0. W.C.L. van der Grinten, S.C.J.J. Kortmann, A.J.M. Nuytinck, H. Wammes *(red.)*,
Onderneming en Nieuw Burgerlijk Recht, Zwolle 1991.

1. S.C.J.J. Kortmann, P.J. Dortmond, A.W. Kist, N.E.D. Faber, A. van Hees, F.J.P. van den Ingh, A.J.M. Nuytinck *(red.)*,
Financiering en Aansprakelijkheid, Zwolle 1994.

2. S.C.J.J. Kortmann, N.E.D. Faber *(red.)*,
Geschiedenis van de Faillissementswet,
Deel 2-I Heruitgave Van der Feltz, I, Zwolle 1994.
Deel 2-II Heruitgave Van der Feltz, II, Zwolle 1994.
Deel 2-III Wetswijzigingen, Zwolle 1995.
Deel 2-IV Voorontwerp Insolventiewet, Deventer 2007.

3. A.G. van Solinge,
Leeuwe- en andere delen, Enkele gedachten over winstverdeling bij personen- en kapitaalvennootschappen, Zwolle 1995.

4. J. Beuving,
Factoring, Zwolle 1996.

5. D.J. Hayton, S.C.J.J. Kortmann, A.J.M. Nuytinck, A.V.M. Struycken, N.E.D. Faber *(red.)*,
Vertrouwd met de Trust, Trust and Trust-like Arrangements, Deventer 1996.

6. S.C.J.J. Kortmann, N.E.D. Faber, J.J. van Hees, S.H. de Ranitz *(red.)*,
De curator, een octopus, Deventer 1996.

7. S.C.J.J. Kortmann, N.E.D. Faber, A.A. van Rossum, H.L.E. Verhagen *(red.)*,
Onderneming en 5 jaar nieuw Burgerlijk Recht, Deventer 1997.

8. J.J. van Hees,
Leasing, Deventer 1997.

9. G.A.J. Boekraad,
Afwikkeling van de faillissementsboedel, Deventer 1997.

10. S.C.J.J. Kortmann, F.J. Oranje, A.A. van Rossum, J.W.H. van Wijk *(red.)*,
Overheid en onderneming, Deventer 1998.

11. S.C.J.J. Kortmann, N.E.D. Faber, E. Loesberg *(red.)*,
Corporate Governance *in perspectief*, Deventer 1998.

12. W.A.K. Rank,
De (on)hanteerbaarheid van het Nederlandse recht voor de moderne financiële praktijk, Deventer 1998.

13. S.C.J.J. Kortmann, W.A.K. Rank, M.H.E. Rongen, G. van Solinge, H.L.E. Verhagen *(red.)*,
Onderneming en Effecten, Deventer 1998.

14. R.E. van Esch,
Electronic Data Interchange (EDI) en het vermogensrecht, Deventer 1999.

15. C.M. Hilverda,
Faillissementsfraude, Deventer 1999.

16. Gerard van Solinge, M.P. Nieuwe Weme,
Gedragsregels inzake een openbaar bod op aandelen, Deventer 1999.

17. S.C.J.J. Kortmann, N.E.D. Faber, J.A.M. Strens-Meulemeester *(red.)*,
Vertegenwoordiging en Tussenpersonen, Deventer 1999.

18. J. Stuyck, M. Waelbroeck, B.L.P. van Reeken, S.B. Noë, F.O.W. Vogelaar *(red.)*,
Competition law in the EU and the Netherlands. A practical guide, Deventer 2000.

19. S.O.H. Bakkerus,
Bancaire aansprakelijkheid, Deventer 2000.

20. C.J.M. Klaassen,
Schadeveroorzakend handelen in functie, Deventer 2000.

21. J.M.A. Berkvens, N.E.D. Faber, S.C.J.J. Kortmann, A. Oskamp *(red.)*,
Onderneming en ICT, Deventer 2000.

22. I.P. Asscher-Vonk, N.E.D. Faber, S.C.J.J. Kortmann, E. Loesberg *(red.)*,
Onderneming en Werknemer, Deventer 2001.

23. J.J. Dammingh,
Bemiddeling door de makelaar bij de koop en verkoop van onroerende zaken, Deventer 2002.

24. S.C.J.J. Kortmann, C.J.H. Jansen, G. van Solinge, N.E.D. Faber *(red.)*,
Onderneming en 10 jaar nieuw Burgerlijk Recht, Deventer 2002.

25. C.J.M. Klaassen, R.J.N. Schlössels, G. van Solinge, L. Timmerman (*red.*),
Aansprakelijkheid in beroep, bedrijf of ambt, Deventer 2003.

26. Th.C.J.A. van Engelen,
Onverkoopbare vermogensrechten. Artikel 3:83(3) BW nader beschouwd, Deventer 2003.

27. R.H. Maatman,
Het pensioenfonds als vermogensbeheerder, Deventer 2004.

28. Ewan McKendrick,
The Creation of a European Law of Contract, Deventer 2004.

29. D.W. Aertsen,
De Trust. Beschouwingen over invoering van de trust in het Nederlandse recht, Deventer 2004.

30. C.G. van der Plas,
De taak van de rechter en het IPR, Deventer 2005.

31. A. Steneker,
Kwaliteitsrekening en afgescheiden vermogen, Deventer 2005.

32. B.P.M. van Ravels,
Grenzen van voorzienbaarheid, Deventer 2005.

33. N.E.D. Faber,
Verrekening, Deventer 2005.

34. D.R. Doorenbos, S.C.J.J. Kortmann, M.P. Nieuwe Weme (*red.*),
Marktmisbruik, Deventer 2006.
Handboek Marktmisbruik, Deventer 2008 (*tweede druk*).

35. R.H. Maatman,
"Het belangrijkste financiële product", Deventer 2006.

36. B.F.L.M. Schim,
Giraal effectenverkeer en goederenrecht, Deventer 2006.

37. T.H.D. Struycken,
De numerus clausus in het goederenrecht, Deventer 2007.

38. D.R. Doorenbos,
Naming & Shaming, Deventer 2007.

39. I.P. Asscher-Vonk, A. van Hees, R.H. Maatman, B.J. Schoordijk (*red.*),
Onderneming en integriteit, Deventer 2007.

40. D. Busch, D.R. Doorenbos, N. Lemmers, R.H. Maatman, M.P. Nieuwe Weme, W.A.K. Rank (*red.*),
Onderneming en financieel toezicht, Deventer 2007.

41. N.E.D. Faber, C.J.H. Jansen, N.S.G.J. Vermunt (*red.*),
Fiduciaire verhoudingen "Libellus amicorum prof. mr. S.C.J.J. Kortmann", Deventer 2007.

42. A.S. Hartkamp, C.H. Sieburgh, L.A.D. Keus (*red.*),
De invloed van het Europese recht op het Nederlandse privaatrecht, Deventer 2007.
Deel 42-I Algemeen deel
Deel 42-II Bijzonder deel

43. A.J. Verdaas,
Stil pandrecht op vorderingen op naam, Deventer 2008.

44. N.E.D. Faber, J.J. van Hees, S.C.J.J. Kortmann, N.S.G.J. Vermunt, Ch.A.M. Domingus-Schwencke (*red.*),
De bewindvoerder, een octopus, Deventer 2008.

45. L.G. Verburg,
De Koers van de bestuurder, Deventer 2008.

46. M.P. Nieuwe Weme, G. van Solinge (*red.*),
Handboek Openbaar Bod, Deventer 2008.

47. J.W.P.M. van der Velden,
Beleggingsfondsen naar burgerlijk recht, Deventer 2008.

48. H. Verschueren, M.S. Houwerzijl (*red.*),
Arbeidsrecht over de grenzen heen: België, Nederland, Europa, de wereld, Deventer 2009.

49. N.E.D. Faber, H.W. Heyman, C.J.M. Klaassen, Ch.A.M. Domingus-Schwencke, C. Rijckenberg (*red.*),
Knelpunten bij beslag en executie, Deventer 2009.

50. M.S. Houwerzijl, S.S.M. Peters (*red.*),
Exit. Onderneming, werknemer en het einde van de dienstbetrekking, Deventer 2009.

51. D. Busch, C.M. Grundmann-van de Krol (*red.*),
Handboek Beleggingsondernemingen, Deventer 2009.

52. J.C.A. Houdijk,
Publieke belangen in het mededingingsrecht: een onderzoek in vijf domeinen, Deventer 2009.

53. C.M. Hilverda,
Faillissementsfraude (*derde druk*), Deventer 2009.

54. N.E.D. Faber, C.M. Grundmann-van de Krol, F.E.J. Beekhoven van den Boezem, N.S.G.J. Vermunt *(red.)*,
De Kredietcrisis, Deventer 2010.

55. J.B. Spath,
Zaaksvervanging, Deventer 2010.

56. F.E.J. Beekhoven van den Boezem,
Credit Claims, Deventer 2010.

57. D. Busch, D.R. Doorenbos, C.M. Grundmann-van de Krol, R.H. Maatman, M.P. Nieuwe Weme, W.A.K. Rank (*red.*),
Onderneming en financieel toezicht, Deventer 2010.

58. N.E.D. Faber, H.J. Damkot, N.S.G.J. Vermunt, Ch.A.M. Domingus (*red.*),
Bancaire zekerheid, Liber amicorum mr. J.H.S.G.K. Timmermans, Deventer 2010.

59. L.G. Verburg,
Het Nederlands ontslagrecht en het BBA-Carcinoom, Deventer 2010.

60. A.D.W. Soedira,
Het akkoord, Deventer 2011.

61. D. Busch,
Naar een beperkte aansprakelijkheid van financiële toezichthouders?, Deventer 2011.

62. A.J. Tekstra,
Verrekening door de fiscus, Deventer 2011.

63. S.E. Bartels, A.J. Verdaas, R.J. van der Weijden (*red.*),
Effecten en vermogensrecht, Deventer 2011.

64. R.H. Maatman, R.M.M.J. Bauer, D. Busch, L.G. Verburg (*red.*),
Onderneming en pensioen, Deventer 2011.

65. J.W.A. Biemans,
Rechtsgevolgen van stille Cessie, Deventer 2011.

66. C.J.M. Klaassen, G. van Solinge, H.M. de Mol van Otterloo, P.E. Ernste (*red.*),
Onderneming en ADR, Deventer 2011.

67. N. van Tiggele-van der Velde, R.G.L. Gerrits, P. Soeteman, J.H. Wansink (*red.*),
"Verzekering ter beurze". Coassurantie in theorie en praktijk, Deventer 2011.

68. B. Bierens, C.M. Grundmann-van de Krol, D.J.R. Lemstra en T.M. Stevens (*red.*),
Handboek Beursgang, Deventer 2011.

69. P.J. van der Korst, R. Abma, G.T.M.J. Raaijmakers (*red.*),
Handboek onderneming en aandeelhouder, Deventer 2012.

70. M.H.E. Rongen,
Cessie, Deventer 2012.

71. V.P.G. de Serière,
Als de (stille?) noodklok luidt... Overheidsingrijpen in privaatrechtelijke verhoudingen ten behoeve van stabiliteit in de financiële sector, Deventer 2012.

72. N.E.D. Faber, J.J. van Hees, N.S.G.J. Vermunt (*red.*),
Overeenkomsten en insolventie, Deventer 2012.

73. C.M. Hilverda,
De bestrijding van faillissementsfraude: waar een wil is .. .., Deventer 2012.

74. P.E. Ernste,
Bindend advies, Deventer 2012.

75. R.J. van der Weijden,
De faillissementspauliana, Deventer 2012.

76. D.R. Doorenbos, M.J.C. Somsen, G.V. Naber (*red.*),
Onderneming en sanctierecht, Deventer 2013.

77. P.T.J. Wolters,
Alle omstandigheden van het geval, Deventer 2013.

78. D. Busch, C.J.M. Klaassen, T.M.C. Arons (red.),
Aansprakelijkheid in de financiële sector, Deventer 2013.

79. D. Busch, M.P. Nieuwe Weme (*red.*),
Christels koers, Liber amicorum prof. mr. drs. C.M. Grundmann-van de Krol, Deventer 2013.

80. S.R. Damminga,
Ongerechtvaardigde verrijking en onverschuldigde betaling als bronnen van verbintenissen, Deventer 2013.

81. A.S. Hartkamp, C.H. Sieburgh, L.A.D. Keus, J.S. Kortmann (*red.*),
The Influence of EU Law on National Private Law, Deventer 2014.
Volume 81-I General Part
De invloed van het Europese recht op het Nederlandse privaatrecht, Deventer 2014.
Deel 81-II Bijzonder deel

82. C.J.H. Jansen, L.G. Verburg (*red.*),
Onderneming en beloning, Deventer 2014.

83. C.J.M. Klaassen, N. van Tiggele-van der Velde, P.E. Ernste, A.Ch.H. Franken (*red.*), Verzekering en ADR, Deventer 2014.

84. G.J.L. Bergervoet, Borgtocht, Deventer 2014.

85. R.W.E. van Leuken, Rechtsverhoudingen tussen particulieren en de verdragsrechtelijke verkeersvrijheden, Deventer 2015.

86. V.J.M. van Hoof, Generale zekerheidsrechten in rechtshistorisch perspectief, Deventer 2015.

87. C.J.H. Jansen, De wetenschappelijke beoefening van het burgerlijke recht in de lange 19e eeuw, Deventer 2015.

88. P. Laaper, Uitbesteding in de financiële sector, Deventer 2015.

89. C. Spierings, De eenzijdige rechtshandeling, Deventer 2016.

90. B.A. Schuijling, Levering en verpanding van toekomstige goederen, Deventer 2016.

91. C. van Ewijk, M. Heemskerk, R.H. Maatman en E. Nijman (*red.*), Pensioen 2020, Deventer 2016.

92. V. Tweehuysen, Het uniciteitsbeginsel in het goederenrecht, Deventer 2016.

93. C.J.H. Jansen, De wetenschappelijke beoefening van het burgerlijke recht tussen 1940 en 1992, Deventer 2016.

94. P.J. van der Plank, Natrekking door onroerende zaken, Deventer 2016.

95. S. van Dongen, Groepen van Contracten, Deventer 2016.

96. I.P.M. Ligteringen, Privaatrechtelijke gevolgen van een schending van het mededingingsrecht, Deventer 2016.

97. M. Huizingh, Contractsoverneming, Deventer 2016.

98. B.M. Katan,
Toerekening van kennis aan rechtspersonen, Deventer 2017.

99. S.E. Bartels, J.B. Spath, K. Everaars (*red.*),
Tenietgaan van beperkte rechten, Deventer 2017.

100. S.E. Bartels, C.J.H. Jansen, B.A. Schuijling, N.S.G.J. Vermunt (*red.*),
Vertrouwen in het Burgerlijke recht, Liber Amicorum Prof. mr. S.C.J.J. Kortmann, Deventer 2017.

101. I.P.M.J. Janssen,
De civielrechtelijke zorgplicht van de beleggingsdienstverlener jegens de niet-particuliere cliënt, Deventer 2017.

102. C.J.H. Jansen, M.M.C. van de Moosdijk, R.W.E. van Leuken (*red.*),
Nijmeegs Europees Privaatrecht, Deventer 2018.

103. G.J.C. Rensen, J.J. van den Broek (*red.*),
Grensoverschrijdende omzetting, Deventer 2018.

104. D.R. Doorenbos, M.P. Nieuwe Weme, J.B.S. Hijink, T.M. Stevens (*red.*),
Handboek Marktmisbruik, Deventer 2018 (*derde druk*).

105. T.M.C. Arons, J. de Bie Leuveling Tjeenk, D. Busch, C.J.M. Klaassen (*red.*),
Collectief schadeverhaal: ondernemingen, belangenorganisaties en hun achterban, Deventer 2018.

106. G.J.L. Bergervoet, T. Hutten, B.A. Schuijling, N.S.G.J. Vermunt (*red.*),
Financiering van de productieketen, Deventer 2018.

107. S.W. van den Berg,
Waarderingsvragen in het ondernemings- en insolventierecht, Deventer 2019.

108. E.M. Hoogervorst, C.J.H. Jansen, M.M.C. van de Moosdijk, A. Knigge (*red.*),
Kartelschade, Deventer 2019.

109. T.E. Booms,
Aanvullen van subjectieve rechten, Deventer 2019.

110. M.A. Heilbron,
Retentierecht en uitwinning, Deventer 2019.

111. B. Snijder-Kuipers, A.T.A. Tilleman (*red.*),
Handboek WWFT, Deventer 2019.

112. D. Busch, C.W.M. Lieverse (*red.*),
Handboek beleggingsondernemingen, Deventer 2019 (*tweede druk*).

113. C.J.M. Klaassen, G.J. Meijer, C.L. Schleijpen (*red.*),
Going Dutch: ADR in Nederland, in het bijzonder bij het NAI, Deventer 2019.

114. N.B. Pannevis,
Achtergestelde vorderingen, Deventer 2019.

115. C.M. Harmsen,
Administratieplicht en aansprakelijkheid voor het boedeltekort, Deventer 2019.

116. C.J.H. Jansen, B.A. Schuijling, I. Aronstein (*red.*),
Onderneming en digitalisering, Deventer 2019.

117. K.W.C. Geurts,
Zekerheid voor leverancierskrediet, Deventer 2019.

118. A.M. Mennens,
Het dwangakkoord buiten surceance en faillissement, Deventer 2020.

119. J.E. de Klerk,
Instellingen voor collectieve belegging in effecten, Deventer 2020.

120. S.E. Bartels, D.F.H. Stein, V. Tweehuysen,
Verjaring, Deventer 2020.

121. J.W.A. Dousi,
De uitleg van Anglo-Amerikaanse boilerplate-bedingen in Nederlandse contracten, Deventer 2020.

122. D. Busch, V.P.G. de Serière, C.W.M. Lieverse, F.E.J. Beekhoven van den Boezem, R.H. Maatman, B. Bierens (*red.*), Zorgplicht in de financiële sector, *Bundel ter gelegenheid van het tienjarig bestaan van het Instituut voor Financieel Recht*, Deventer 2020.

123. K. Everaars,
Wijziging van beperkte rechten, Deventer 2021.

124. F.G. Laagland (*red.*),
Verburg: geciteerd en besproken, *Liber Amicorium prof. mr. L.G. Verburg*, Deventer 2021.

125. R. Bobbink,
Antichresis en pandgebruik. De bevoegdheid van de zekerheidsgerechtigde tot gebruik, beheer en vruchttrekking in rechtshistorisch en rechtsvergelijkend perspectief, Deventer 2021.

126. T.F. Walree,
Schadevergoeding bij de onrechtmatige verwerking van persoonsgegevens, Deventer 2021.

127. I. Palm-Steijenberg,
Personentoetsingen in de financiële sector, Deventer 2021.

128. P.A. Fruytier,
De civielrechtelijke inbedding van het besluitenaansprakelijkheidsrecht, Deventer 2021.

129. N.M. Brouwer,
De cyberverzekering vanuit civielrechtelijk perspectief, Deventer 2021.

130. P.T.J. Wolters, A.U. Janssen & P. Ortolani (*red.*),
Digitalisering en conflictoplossing, Deventer 2021.

131. F.E.J. Beekhoven van den Boezem & B. Bierens (*red.*),
Geld en betalingsverkeer, Deventer 2022.

132. R.J. ter Rele,
Beperkte rechten op eigen goederen, Deventer 2022.

133. R.H. Maatman, M. Heemskerk, M.G. Knoef & Th.E. Nijman (*red.*),
Pensioen 2025, Deventer 2022.

134. J.C.T.F. Lokin,
Afscheiding van bestanddelen, Deventer 2022.

135. J.A. Hofman,
De beveiliging van persoonsgegevens, Deventer 2022.

136. M.D. Reijneveld,
Gegevensbescherming in faillissement, Deventer 2022.

137. F.G. Laagland & J. Kloostra (*red.*),
Driehoeksverhoudingen in het arbeidsrecht, Deventer 2023.

138. A. Sikkema-Lenaerts,
Particuliere beleggingsgeschillen bij Kifid, Deventer 2023.

139. E.A.L. van Emden,
Toerekening van externe kennis bij onrechtmatige daad, Deventer 2023.

140. T. Hutten,
Pandrecht op aandelen, Deventer 2023.

141. B.A. Schuijling, M. van Wingerden & Frenken (*red.*),
Het bancaire belang, *Opstellen aangeboden aan mr. H.J. Damkot*, Deventer 2023.

142. T.E. De Wijkerslooth-van der Linden,
Voor risico van de ondernemer, Deventer 2023.

143. F.P.C. Strijbos, B.A. Schuijling B. Bierens & P. Cent (*red.*),
Duurzaam bankieren, Deventer 2023.

144. D.F.H. Stein,
Hoofdelijke aansprakelijkheid, Deventer 2024.

145. F.F.L. van der Linden van Sprankhuizen, C.J.H. Jansen & B.A. Schuijling (*red.*),
Ondernemingsgericht privaatrecht en ESG, Deventer 2024.

146. N.M. Hoek, C.J.H. Jansen, A.U. Janssen & P.H.L.M. Kuypers (*red.*),
Spanningen tussen duurzaamheid en Europees recht, Deventer 2024.

147. A.U. Janssen & T.F. Walree (*red.*),
Winstafdracht in het privaatrecht, Deventer 2024.

148. A.M.M. Menken,
Rechten van polishouders bij portefeuilleoverdracht, juridische fusie en juridische splitsing door verzekeraars, Deventer 2024.

149. R. Leuyerink, S.E. Bartels & W.H. van Boom (*red.*),
Prijs en privaatrecht, Deventer 2024.

150. P. Teunissen,
Verbod en evenredigheid in het intellectuele-eigendomsrecht, Deventer 2024.

151. J. Kloostra,
De positie van de werker bij platformwerk, Deventer 2024.

152. L.G. Verburg,
De bestuurder van de NV of BV, Deventer 2024.

153. T.J. Vennmanns,
Access to justice in times of technological acceleration: The possible impact of digitalization on judicial debt collection procedures of one-shotters, Deventer 2024.

154. S.C. Pepels,
Restructuring groups of companies under the European Insolvency Regulation (recast), Deventer 2024.

155. W. Rijnenberg,
Zekerheid en faillissement, een grondslagenonderzoek naar de faillissementsrechtelijke positie van schuldeisers met pand- en hypotheekrechten, Deventer 2025.

156. R.J. Versteeg,
Kwalitatieve aansprakelijkheid voor opstallen in het publieke domein, in het bijzonder bij het beheer en bezit van opstallen door de overheid, Deventer 2025.

157. M. Heemskerk, C.J.H. Jansen, S.C.J.J. Kortmann & R.H. Maatman,
Houdbaar pensioen, Deventer 2025.

158. C.J.M. Klaassen, G.J. Meijer, T. de Boer & C.L. Schleijpen,
Arbitration in the Netherlands, in particular NAI Arbitration, Deventer 2025.

www.ingramcontent.com/pod-product-compliance
Ingram Content Group UK Ltd.
Pitfield, Milton Keynes, MK11 3LW, UK
UKHW020223290926
15470UKWH00001B/353

9 789403 528496